R. Gupta's®

POPULAR MASTER GUIDE

Guru Gobind Singh Indraprastha University (GGSIPU)

B.Com (Hons)

Common Entrance Test (CET)

by

RPH Editorial Board

2026 EDITION

RAMESH PUBLISHING HOUSE, NEW DELHI

Published by
O.P. Gupta *for* Ramesh Publishing House

Admin. Office
12-H, New Daryaganj Road, Opp. Officer's Mess,
New Delhi-110002 ✆ 23275224, 23245124

E-mail: info@rameshpublishinghouse.com
For Online Shopping: www.rameshpublishinghouse.com

Showroom
- Balaji Market, Nai Sarak, Delhi-6 ✆ 23253720, 23282525
- 4457, Nai Sarak, Delhi-6, ✆ 23918938

Book Code: R-1583

ISBN: 978-93-5012-360-7

Price: ₹ 490

Printed at: Deepak Offset, Delhi

CONTENTS

SCHEME OF THE EXAMINATION

ELIGIBILITY:

To apply for the B.Com (Hons.) entrance test, aspirants need 50% marks in aggregate in Class 12 or equivalent with a pass in five subjects (one language and four elective subjective subjects).

SUBJECTS OF ENTRANCE TEST:

	Subject	Weightage
(*i*)	General English	25%
(*ii*)	Logical Reasoning	25%
(*iii*)	Data Interpretation	35%
(*iv*)	General Awareness	15%

Sample Paper

Guru Gobind Singh Indraprastha University (GGSIPU)

B.Com (Hons) Common Entrance Test (CET)

GENERAL ENGLISH

1. Choose the option which when filled in the blank makes the sentence below meaningful and grammatically correct.

Sumit ________ to the wedding. He has an important engagement that day.

A. could go
B. needed to go
C. can't go
D. haven't to go

2. Choose the option which when filled in the blank makes the sentence below meaningful and grammatically correct.

________ I have your permission to leave the office early?

A. Would
B. Would not
C. Can't
D. May

3. Spot the error part in the sentence below, if any. Your option would be (D) if there is no error.

Do you think you/should come over at/6 pm tomorrow?

A. Do you think you
B. 6 pm tomorrow?
C. should come over at
D. no error

4. Identify the part of the sentence with an error, if any?

Bismillah would play *(a)*/ the shehnai when *(b)*/ he was very young. *(c)*/ No error *(d)*

A. *(b)*
B. *(d)*
C. *(c)*
D. *(a)*

5. Identify the part of the sentence with an error, if any?

You can't borrow *(a)*/ my car if *(b)*/ you like to go for a drive. *(c)*/ No error *(d)*

A. *(d)*
B. *(b)*
C. *(c)*
D. *(a)*

6. Spot the error part of the sentence below, if any.

You can listen to /what the doctor says/ if you want to/ get cured.

A. You can listen to
B. what the doctor says
C. if you want to
D. get cured.

7. Identify the part of the sentence with an error if any. If there is no error, mark 'No error' as the answer.

I'm not sure./ Kiran should/ be in Delhi.

A. I'm not sure.
B. Kiran should
C. be in Delhi
D. No error

8. Fill in the blank with appropriate question tags.

Now you can make question tags, ________?

A. can you
B. won't you
C. can't you
D. will you

9. Fill in the blank with appropriate question tags.

Let us start now, ________?

A. shall we
B. should we
C. could be
D. would be

1. C	2. D	3. C	4. D	5. D	6. A	7. B	8. C	9. A

10. Fill in the blank with appropriate word/phrase to make the sentence below grammatically correct and meaningful.

He believed that he _____ turn out to be a cheat.

A. will B. would
C. should D. must

11. Fill in the blank with appropriate word/phrase to make the sentence below grammatically correct and meaningful.

Tell me the reason _______ they could not marry.

A. that B. so
C. why D. because

12. Fill in the blank with appropriate word/phrase to make the sentence below grammatically correct and meaningful.

He would have believed if he_______ with his own eyes last week.

A. saw B. have seen
C. had seen D. could see

13. Fill in the blank with appropriate word/phrase to make the sentence below grammatically correct and meaningful.

As he is obstinate ______ not obey the instructions.

A. so he will B. that he would
C. he will D. he must

14. Spot the error part of the sentence below

Everybody was/watching/the TV,/won't they?

A. won't they B. everybody was
C. watching D. the TV

15. Fill in the blank with appropriate word/phrase to make the sentence below grammatically correct and meaningful.

Your business is likely to fall _______ for want of sufficient investment.

A. off B. through
C. down D. at

16. Robert was cut ____ because he had been deceived by the shopkeeper.

A. off B. down
C. up D. out

17. What is the synonym of the word 'dainty'?

A. insipid B. exquisite
C. deformed D. spiritual

18. The police officer has become <u>implacable</u> for criminals.

What is the meaning of the underlined word?

A. considerate B. friendly
C. relentless D. empathetic

19. Choose the word which is the opposite in meaning of the word 'niggardly'.

A. extravagant B. shameful
C. ruthless D. pompous

20. A person who enjoys eating and eats large amounts of food is called _______.

A. Gourmand B. Hedonist
C. Cuisines D. Bohemian

Directions (Qs. No. 21-25): *Read the passage and answer the questions*

The political endorsement that was recently given to a party by the Rajasthan Governor has reignited the debate on the independence and neutrality of the constitutional post. The governor's office has often courted controversy for the incumbent's political views. However, there is a marked difference between seemingly routine deviations from strict constitutional norms and the recent case, in which the alleged impropriety is neither subtle nor cloaked in specious constitutional justifications.

The Sarkaria Commission described the Governor as a "Constitutional sentinel and a vital link between the Union and the State." In S.R. Bommai (1994), the Supreme Court said, "The office of the governor... is intended to ensure the protection and sustenance of the constitutional

10. B	**11.** C	**12.** C	**13.** C	**14.** A	**15.** B
16. C	**17.** B	**18.** C	**19.** A	**20.** A	

process of the working of the constitution by the elected executive." M.K. Gandhi said about the Governor's office: "He would be an arbiter when there was a constitutional deadlock in the State and he would be able to play an impartial role." In the contemporary constitutional landscape, the Governor is expected to advance the cause of 'federalism' and 'democracy' which form a part of the basic structure of the Constitution.

21. Which of the following is the synonym of specious?
A. refined B. superficial
C. possible D. correct

22. What can be concluded from the paragraph 1?
I. The post of the governor is controversial yet unimportant.
II. The current case is typical example of a routine departure from norms.
III. The Governors are often abused.
A. Only II B. Only III
C. II and III D. None of the above

23. What is the tone of the author in the second paragraph?
A. Factual B. Understanding
C. Worried D. Pensive

24. What was the opinion of the Sarkaria Commission about the role of a Governor?
I. He would serve as an important link between the Union and State.
II. He would be the custodian of the constitution.
III. He is to be an arbiter in case of a deadlock in the state.
A. Only I B. Only III
C. Only I and II D. None of the above

25. Which of the following issues does the office of the governor is lacking currently?
I. Redundancy.
II. Autonomy.
III. Impartiality
A. Only I B. Only III
C. Only II and III D. None of the above

LOGICAL REASONING

26. Which number will replace the question mark (?) in the following series?
17, 51, 58, 116, 123, 123, ?
A. 150 B. 120
C. 130 D. 140

27. Select the figure that will replace the question mark (?) in the following figure series.

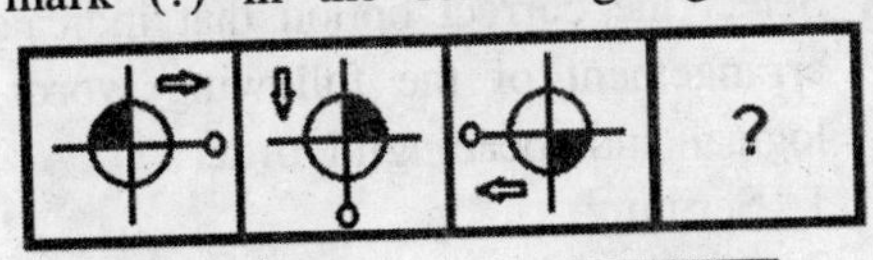

A. 
B. 
C. 
D. 

28. Study the given pattern carefully and select the number that can replace the question mark (?) in it.

?	8	11
7	6	5
48	63	72

A. 4 B. 6
C. 5 D. 7

29. In a code language, if '265' is written as 'PNH', '187' is written as 'OXB', and '248' is written as 'NUB', then which of the following letters represents the number '4'?
A. U B. B
C. N D. P

21. B 22. D 23. A 24. C 25. C 26. C 27. C 28. C 29. A

30. Two different positions of the same dice are shown, the six faces of which are numbered from 1 to 6. Select the number that will be on the face opposite to the face showing '5'.

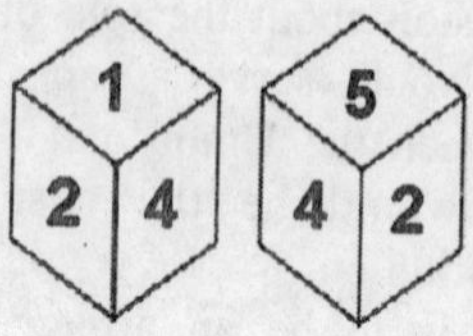

A. 3 B. 1
C. 6 D. 4

31. Select the letter-cluster that can replace the question mark (?) in the given letter-cluster series.

AE, KQ, EI, LR, IO, ?, OU, NT

A. MR B. NR
C. MS D. NS

32. In a code language, 'TORCH' is written as 'UNPSDI' and 'BEST' is written as 'CDFTU'. How will 'MARKS' be written in that language?

A. NABSLU B. NZCSLT
C. OZBSMT D. NZBSLT

33. Which number will replace the question mark (?) in the following series?

2430, ? , 270, 90, 30, 10

A. 800 B. 805
C. 810 D. 540

34. Which two signs should be interchanged to make the given equation correct?

$25 - 5 \times 50 \div 10 + 35 = 155$

A. × and – B. × and +
C. + and – D. × and ÷

35. A cube is made by folding the given sheet. In the cube so formed, which of the following pairs of symbols will NOT be on the opposite faces?

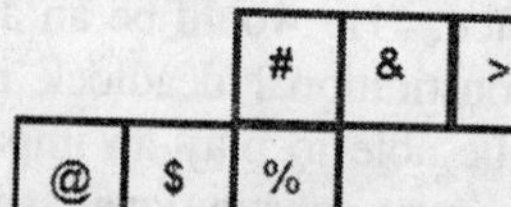

A. & and $ B. $ and #
C. @ and % D. # and >

36. Select the figure that will replace the question mark (?) in the following figure series.

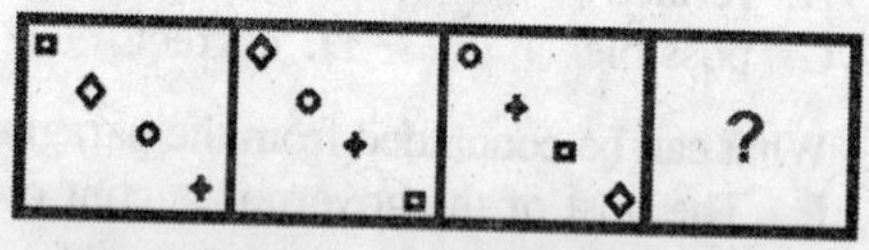

A. 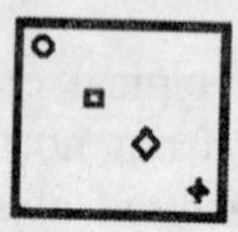 B. 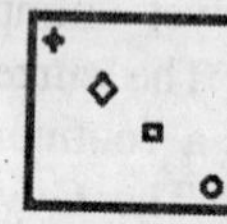

C. 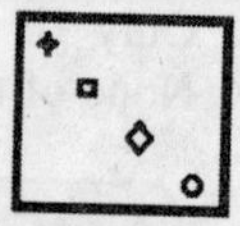 D. 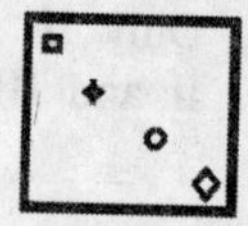

37. Four friends are playing carrom and sitting on the four sides of the carrom board. B is to the right of C. D is to the left of A. Who is sitting to the left of C?

A. Data is inadequate
B. D
C. B
D. A

38. Select the correct option that indicates the arrangement of the following words in a logical and meaningful order.

1. Scrutiny
2. Applications
3. Interview
4. Job offer
5. Joining

A. 1, 3, 2, 4, 5 B. 2, 4, 1, 5, 3
C. 3, 1, 5, 4, 2 D. 2, 1, 3, 4, 5

30. B **31.** C **32.** D **33.** C **34.** A **35.** B **36.** C **37.** D **38.** D

39. If 18 October 2006 was Wednesday, then what was the day of the week on 17 October 2000?

A. Tuesday B. Wednesday
C. Monday D. Sunday

40. The given Venn diagram best represents the relationship between which set of classes given in the options?

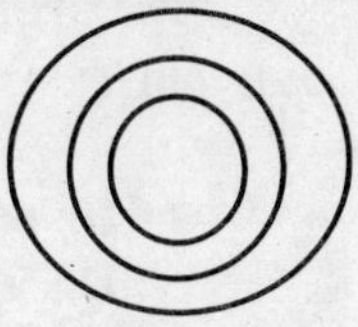

A. Males, Fathers, Sons
B. Sisters, Females, Mothers
C. Fathers, Males, Doctors
D. Engineers, Brothers, Males

41. One day, 90 students were travelling in a bus and the ratio of the number of boys to that of girls was 2 : 1. The next day, the number of students remained the same, but the ratio of the number of boys to that of girls became 3 : 2. What was the difference between the numbers of boys travelling in the bus on both the days?

A. 6 B. 30
C. 14 D. 18

42. In a code language, if 'you are there' is written as 'ter der jer', 'we stay here' is written as 'yer mer ner', 'we are late' is written as 'ser ner der', and 'I stay there' is written as 'yer fer jer', then how would 'you stay late' be written in this language?

A. ter yer ser
B. ter yer mer
C. der yer ser
D. ter mer ser

43. Three of the following four letter-clusters are alike in a certain way and one is different. Pick the odd one out.

A. CFILO B. UXADG
C. OMSVY D. ORUXA

44. Select the option that is related to the third letter-cluster in the same way as the second letter-cluster is related to the first letter-cluster.

ABSORPTION : ROSBANOITP :: VISUALIZER : ?

A. AUSIVREILZ B. VUAISREZIL
C. AUSIVREZIL D. UASIVERZIL

45. Ronita's only brother Vikram is the husband of Kritika's mother Sejal. How is Ronita's mother Chandni related to Kritika?

A. Mother-in-law
B. Maternal grandmother
C. Paternal aunt
D. Paternal grandmother

46. In a code language, 'DENT' is written as '51' and 'LOAD' is written as '40'. How will 'COST' be written in that language?

A. 65 B. 62
C. 75 D. 57

47. Two statements are given, followed by three conclusions numbered I, II and III. Assuming the statements to be true, even if they seem to be at variance with commonly known facts, decide which of the conclusions logically follow(s) from the statements.

Statements:

All photographs are newspapers.
Some photographs are computers.

Conclusions:

I. Some computers are photographs.
II. Some computers are newspapers.
III. Some newspapers are photographs.

A. All of the conclusions follow
B. Only conclusions I and II follow
C. Only conclusions II and III follow
D. Only conclusions I and III follow

39. A **40.** A **41.** A **42.** A **43.** C **44.** C **45.** D **46.** A **47.** A

48. Two numbers are named as Number A and Number B. The sum of Number A, its square and its cube is 399. The sum of Number B, its square and its cube is 819. What would be the square of the number obtained by adding Number A and Number B?

A. 324 B. 225
C. 289 D. 256

49. Select the correct combination of mathematical signs that can sequentially replace the * signs from left to right to balance the following equation.

31 * 2 * 60 * 30 * 15 * 49

A. ×, +, ÷, −, =
B. −, ÷, +, ×, =
C. ×, ÷, +, −, =
D. ×, −, +, ÷, =

50. If 'A' denotes 'addition', 'B' denotes 'multiplication', 'C' denotes 'subtraction', and 'D' denotes 'division', then what will be the value of the following expression?

35 B 2 A 5 B (40 C 37) A (8 B 4) D 16 C 14 = ?

A. 54 B. 66
C. 73 D. 56

DATA INTERPRETATION

Directions (Qs. No. 51-54): *Read the following directions carefully and answer the following question.*

Line graph represents the total number of population visited in Museum A, B and C on Sunday.

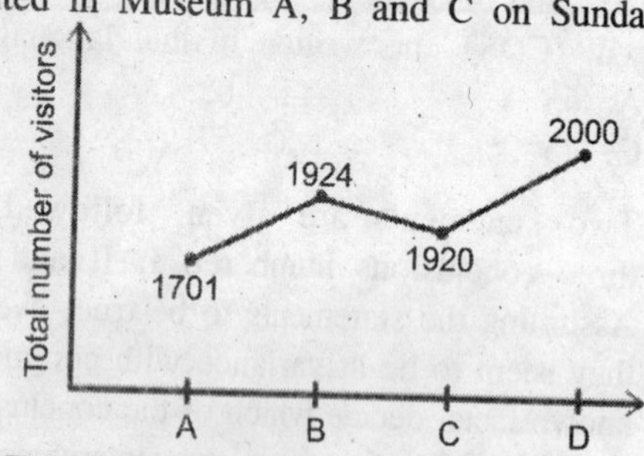

Table represent the number of male visited in Museum out of total population.

Museum	Number of Male out of total people who visited in Museum
A	2/9
B	11/13
C	13/16
D	19/50

51. If the number of male and number in Museum E are 7.69% more than the number of male who visited in Museum C and the number of female are 300 less than the number of Male visited in Museum B. Then find the difference between the number of male and female who visited Museum E?

A. 600 B. 560
C. 628 D. 678

52. Museum A is in village Rampur where the number of population was 1,24,000 and the ratio of male and female 15 : 16. Then, find the percentage of total female on Sunday in Rampur village to the total number of male in Museum B?

A. More than 4043%
B. Between 3508% to 4040%
C. Less than 3886%
D. Both option (A) and (C)

53. What are the difference between male who visited museum B and C together to the average of female who visited museum A, B and C together? (approx. value)

A. 1962 B. 1700
C. 1882 D. 1688

48. D **49.** A **50.** C **51.** C **52.** B **53.** D

54. If the cost price of male ticket and the female ticket is ₹ X and ₹ (X-5). And the museum B get the revenue ₹ 94720. Find the total revenue getting from male ticket from museum A?

A. 18900 B. 20800
C. 20600 D. 18700

Directions (Qs. No. 55-58): *Read the following instruction and answer the following question.*

Tabular graph shows the number of article sold by shop Pesto.

Months	Average of article sold by (A, B & C)	% of article sold by A out of total	Article sold by C
April	100	20%	160
May	120	25%	70
June	72	50%	65

55. Find the difference between the number of article sold by C sold by pesto in June and April months?

A. 86 B. 55
C. 95 D. 42

56. The price of article sold by B is ₹ 180 and in the month of June they offer discount of $p\%$ and the company will get ₹ 12420. Find the p?

A. 40 B. 50
C. 75 D. 60

57. If out of the total number of products sold by A in June, 25% were returned due to defects, then find the ratio of non defective products sold by A in June and the number of products sold by C in April?

A. 25 : 31 B. 27 : 32
C. 21 : 32 D. 8 : 5

58. In April, if person B sold two types of products *i.e.* TV and Refrigerator in the ratio of 7 : 5, then find the difference between the total number of TVs sold by B in April and total number of products sold by B in June.

A. 50 B. 70
C. 80 D. 55

Directions (Qs. No. 59-62): *Answer the questions based on the information given below.*

The table given below illustrates the number of bikes sold by four distinct companies in two different consecutive years 2021 and 2022.

Company	Number of bikes sold in 2021	Number of bikes sold in 2022
A	240	160
B	1120	800
C	960	480
D	640	160

59. If the number of bikes sold by company 'X' in 2022 is 50% of that by company 'B' in the same year then what is the respective ratio between the number of bikes sold by company 'X' and company 'B' together in 2022 and that by company 'C' and company 'D' together in the same year?

A. 5 : 4 B. 13 : 16
C. 15 : 8 D. 21 : 16

60. If the respective ratio of the number of bikes sold by company 'Y' in 2021 to that by company 'D' in the same year is 7:8 then what is the average number of bikes sold by companies 'Y', 'A', 'B', and 'C' together in 2021?

A. 720 B. 760
C. 780 D. 800

61. The total number of bikes sold by company 'B' in 2021 and 2022 together is what percent more/less than the total number of bikes sold by company 'C' in 2021 and 2022 together?

A. 25% B. 33.33%
C. 50% D. 66.66%

54. A 55. C 56. A 57. B 58. B 59. C 60. A 61. B

62. What is the average number of bikes sold by company 'C' and company 'D' together in the year 2023, if the number of bikes sold by in 2023 is 75% less for company 'C' and 60% less for company 'D' compared to their respective sales in 2021?

A. 238
B. 240
C. 244
D. 248

63. The following pie charts show the number of students studying in different departments of an institute during the academic years 2019 and 2020. The total number of students was 2000 and 2400, respectively, in academic years 2019 and 2020.

What is the ratio of Commerce and Computer Science students taken together in 2019 to Engineering and Medical students taken together in 2020?

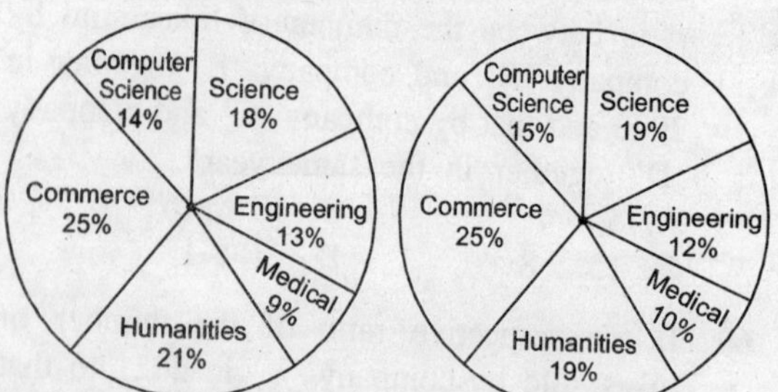

Academic year 2019 Academic year 2020

A. 22 : 39
B. 65 : 44
C. 44 : 65
D. 39 : 22

64. The following bar graph shows exports of cars of type A and B (in ₹ millions) from 2014 to 2018. Study the graph and answer the question that follows.

Exports of Cars of Type A and B (in ₹ millions) during 2014 to 2018.

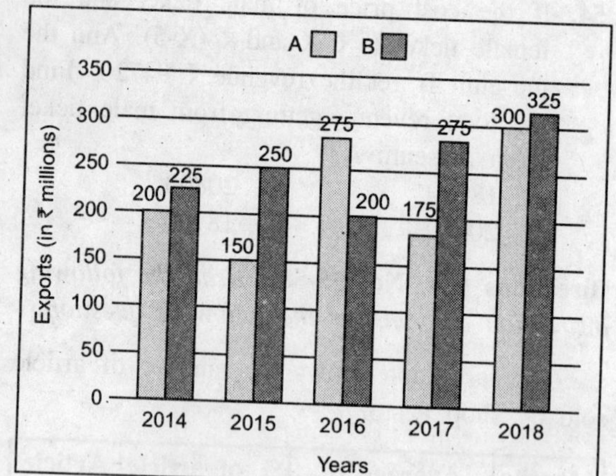

The total exports of cars of type A in 2014 to 2018 is what per cent more than the total exports of cars of type B in 2015 to 2017? (Correct to one decimal place)

A. 44.3%
B. 41.3%
C. 50.4%
D. 51.7%

65. Study the histogram and answer the question given below.

The graph represents the number of students obtaining a percentage of marks in class X Board examination in 2018 in a school.

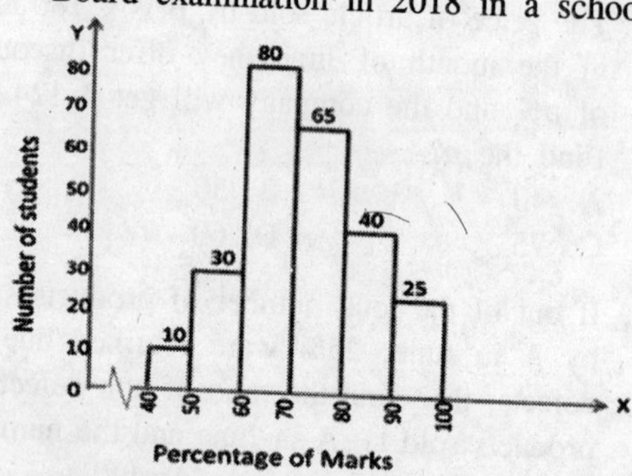

The number of students who have secured less than 60% marks is what per cent less than the number of students who have secured 80% marks and above?

A. 33.5%
B. 29.7%
C. 38.5%
D. 37.4%

62. D 63. B 64. D 65. C

66. Monthly expenditure of a family on different heads is shown in the following pie chart. The family earns ₹ 1,08,000 every month. What is the amount spent on Rent every month (in ₹)?

Expenditure on different Heads

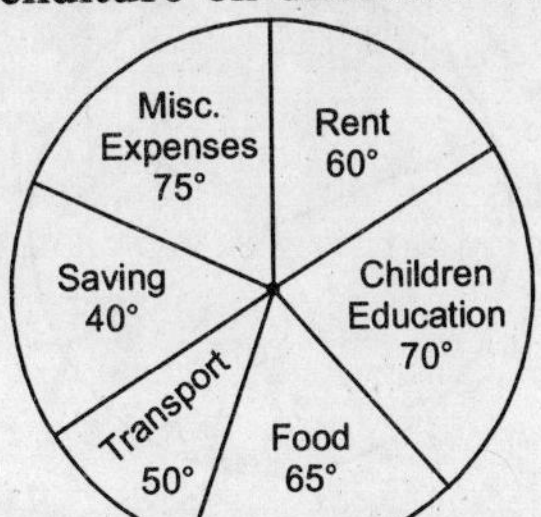

A. 17,500 B. 21,000
C. 15,000 D. 18,000

67. The following pie chart shows the distribution of percentage of a certain corporate office employees in various age groups.

Total number of employees of the corporate office = 2500

Study the chart carefully and answer the question that follows.

Pie-Chart presenting the information about the percentage distribution of a certain corporate office employees by their ages.

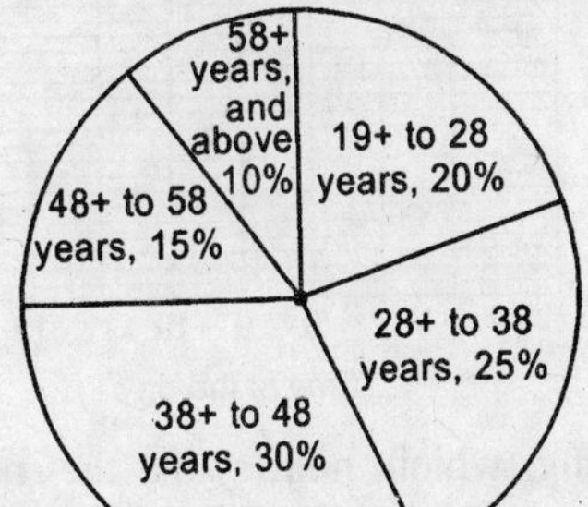

The number of the corporate office employees of age group of 38+ years and above is how much percentage more than that of 28+ to 38 years?

A. 120% B. 20%
C. 150% D. 80%

68. Study the given bar graph and answer the question that follows.

The bar graph shows the exports of cars of type A and B (in ₹ millions) from 2014 to 2018.

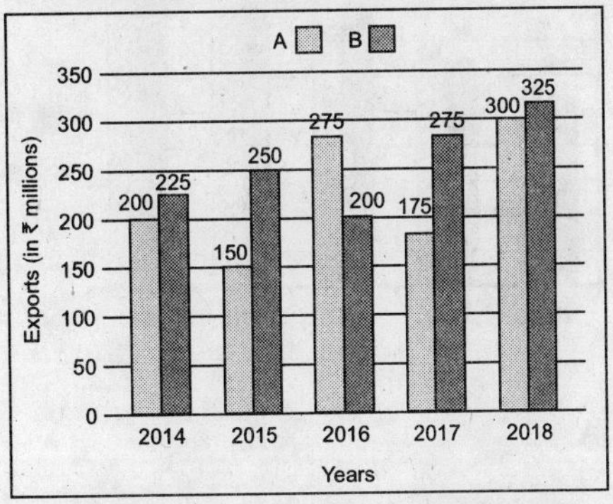

The total exports of cars of type A from 2014 to 2016 is approximately what percentage less than the total exports of cars of type B from 2015 to 2017 (correct to one decimal place)?

A. 10.4% B. 11.7%
C. 11.3% D. 13.8%

69. The number of cars passing the road near a colony from 6 am to 12 noon has been shown in the following histogram.

What is the minimum change percentage in the number of cars in comparison to the previous hour? (correct to 2 decimal places)

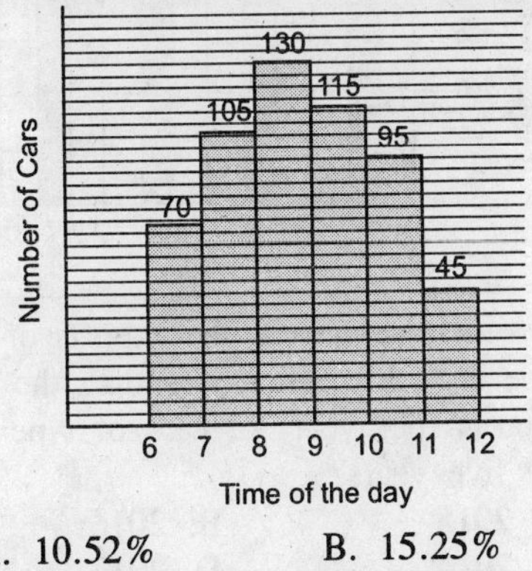

A. 10.52% B. 15.25%
C. 11.54% D. 23.81%

66. D	67. A	68. D	69. C

70. The following bar graph shows receipts and expenditure of a business firm over 5 years.
Gain = Receipts - Expenditure.
What is the percentage of increase in expenditure from 2018 to 2019 as compared to 2018?

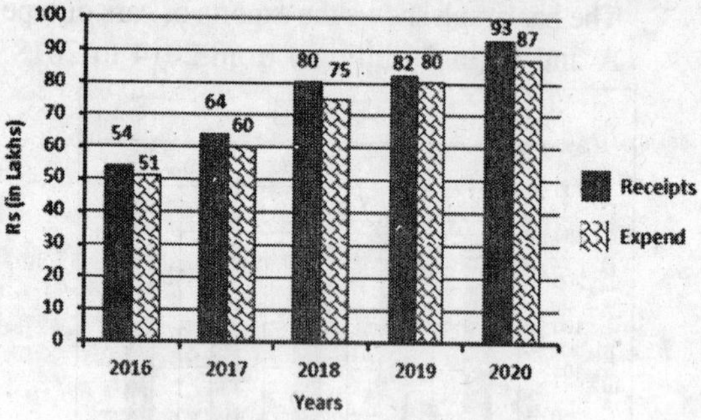

A. $2\frac{1}{2}$ B. $6\frac{2}{3}$

C. $8\frac{3}{4}$ D. $6\frac{1}{4}$

71. Study the given bar graph and answer the question that follows.

The bar graph shows the exports of cars of type A and B (in ₹ millions) from 2014 to 2018.

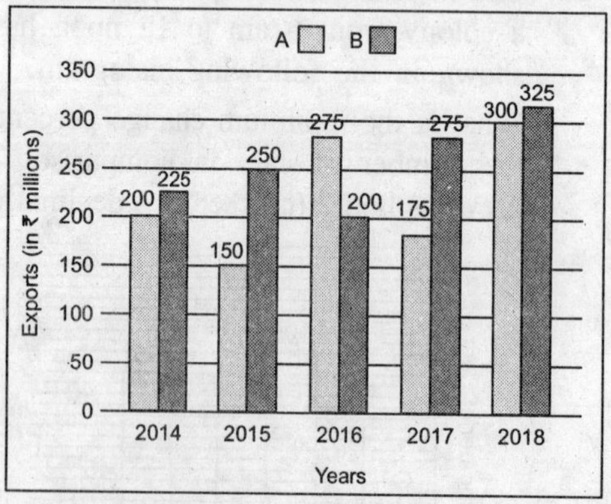

In which year were the exports of cars of type B ₹ 20 million less than the average exports (per year) of cars of type A over the five years?

A. 2015 B. 2016
C. 2014 D. 2017

72. Study the given pie chart and answer the question that follows.

The pie chart shows the breakup of the total number of employees of a company working in different offices (A to E), in degrees.

The total number of employees = 3600.

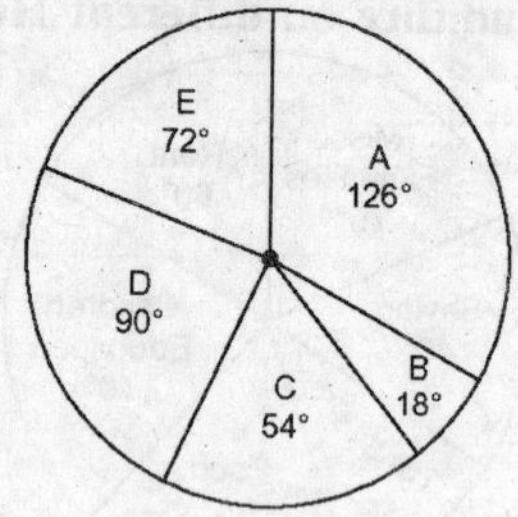

If the percentage of male employees in office C is 20% and that of female employees in office D is 40%, then what is the ratio of the number of female employees in office D to that of female employees in office C?

A. 3 : 2 B. 2 : 3
C. 3 : 8 D. 5 : 6

73. The number of cars passing the road near a colony from 6 am to 12 noon has been shown in the following histogram.

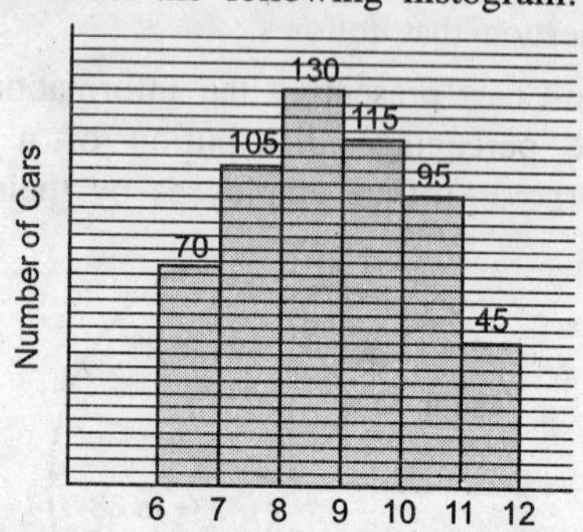

During which hour(s) is the number of cars passed less than the average number of cars passed from 7 am to 12 noon?

A. 6-7, 10-11, 11-12
B. 10-11, 11-12
C. 7-8, 8-9, 9-10
D. 6-7, 11-12

70. B **71.** B **72.** D **73.** A

74. The given bar graph shows the income and expenditure (in crore ₹) of a company over 5 years, from 2014 to 2018. Study the bar graph and answer the question that follows.

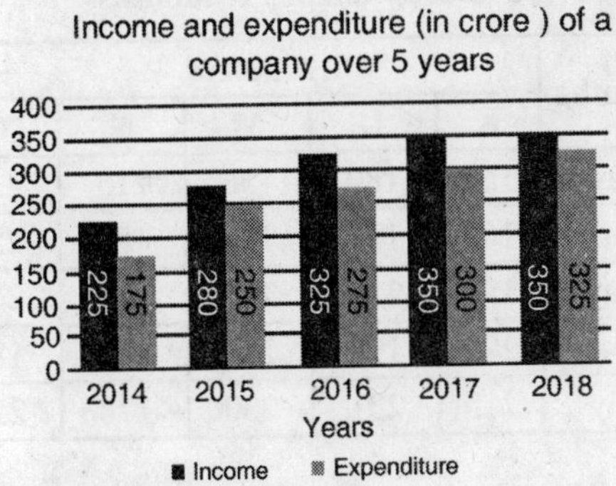

What is the difference (in crore ₹) between the expenditure for the years 2017 and 2018 taken together and the income for the years 2015 and 2016 taken together?

A. 15 B. 20
C. 18 D. 16

75. Performance of 1800 students in grades has been shown in the following pie chart.

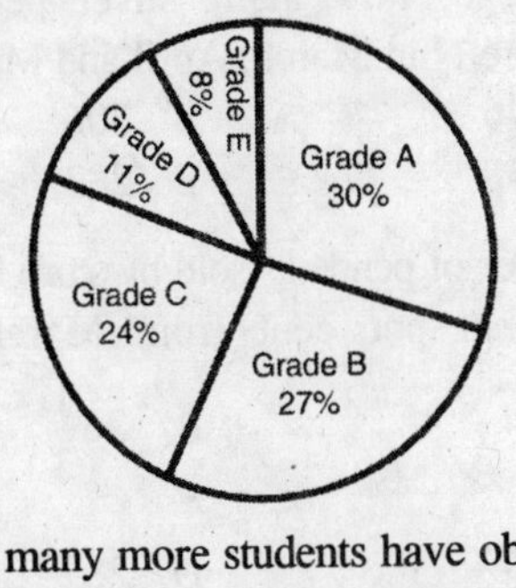

How many more students have obtained grade B than those who have obtained grade C?

A. 50 B. 60
C. 54 D. 3

Directions (Qs. No. 76 and 77): *Table given below shows the number of male and female participated in an event from five different schools (A, B, C, D & E). Study the table carefully and answer the following questions.*

Schools	Male	Female
A	650	450
B	540	420
C	720	500
D	560	450
E	680	320

76. Find average number of female participated from school – A, B & D.

A. 400 B. 380
C. 350 D. 440

77. Total male participated from school – B & D together are how much more or less than total female participated from school – A & C together?

A. 150 B. 110
C. 170 D. 120

Directions (Qs. No. 78 and 79): *Study the bar chart given below and answer the following questions.*

Bar chart shows the number of books read by 4 different persons (A, B, C & D) in 2005 and 2006.

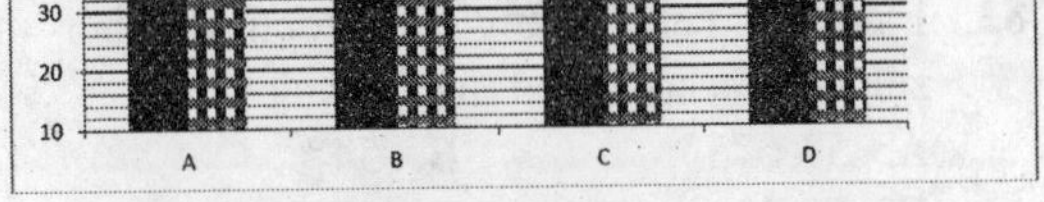

78. Find average number of books read by A, C & D in 2005.

A. 64 B. 70
C. 75 D. 60

79. Find ratio of books read by B & C together in 2005 to books read by A & D together in 2006.

A. 15 : 16 B. 5 : 6
C. 1 : 5 D. 4 : 7

74. B **75.** C **76.** D **77.** A **78.** B **79.** A

Directions (Qs. No. 80-82): *Pie chart given below shows total number of students who opted different subjects for exam in July 2017. Study the data carefully and answer the following questions.*

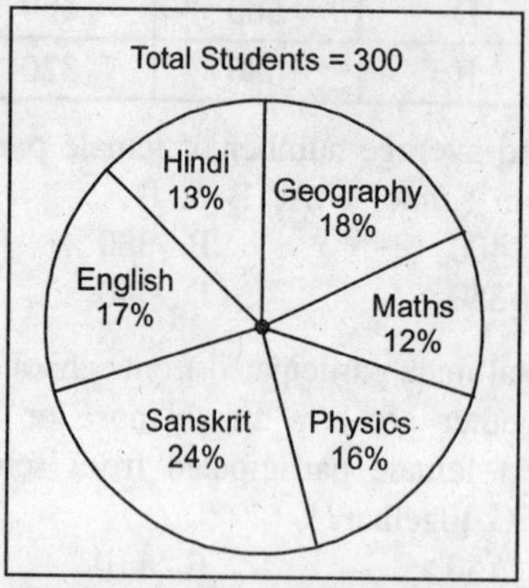

80. Total number of students who opted for Geography and Maths together is how much less than total number of students who opted for Sanskrit and Physics together?

A. 24 B. 27
C. 30 D. 33

81. Find the total number of students who gave exams in August, 2017 if total number of students is increased by 20% in August, 2017 as compared to July, 2017.

A. 450 B. 420
C. 390 D. 360

82. Find the central angle of total number of students who opted for Physics?

A. 57.6° B. 54°
C. 50.4° D. 43.2°

Directions (Qs. No. 83-85): *Read the data and answer the given questions.*

Number of pendants sold by 5 stores during 5 months

Months	Stores				
	K	L	M	N	O
March	154	180	156	215	237
April	167	199	179	181	254
May	191	219	211	163	263
June	205	198	259	165	181
July	215	231	230	178	250

83. What is the average number of pendants sold by store M in all the given months together?

A. 207 B. 213
C. 215 D. 211

84. All the given stores sell only two types of pendants—Gold and Silver. If the respective ratio of Gold and silver pendants sold by store N in March, April and May together is 7 : 6, how many silver pendants sold by store N in March, April and May together?

A. 246 B. 306
C. 258 D. 282

85. Number of pendants sold by store L, increased by what per cent from March to July?

A. $24\frac{1}{3}$ B. $26\frac{1}{3}$
C. $30\frac{2}{3}$ D. $28\frac{1}{3}$

GENERAL AWARENESS

86. Who among the following won the Major Dhyan Chand Khel Ratna Award in 2024?

A. D. Gukesh B. Manu Bhaker
C. Praveen Kumar D. All of the above

87. Which athlete won the Arjuna Award for Athletics in 2024?

A. Jyothi Yarraji B. Sucha Singh
C. Sandeep Sangwan D. Harmanpreet Singh

80. C **81.** D **82.** A **83.** A **84.** C **85.** D **86.** D **87.** A

88. Where was the 29th session of the Conference of the Parties (CoP29) to the UNFCCC held from November 11 to November 22, 2024?

A. Paris, France
B. Madrid, Spain
C. Baku, Azerbaijan
D. New York, USA

89. In which type of economy, all activities are organised by market?

A. Mixed economy
B. Liberal economy
C. Market economy
D. Centrally planned economy

90. The first Nuclear test was under-taken in India in the year:

A. 1975　B. 1974
C. 1973　D. 1977

91. Which Commission replaced the Planning Commission in 2015?

A. NITI Aayog
B. NIYAM Aayog
C. NAGRIK Aayog
D. Jan Aayog

92. ________ is the science and art of cultivating fruits, vegetables, flowers and ornamental plants.

A. Sericulture　B. Floriculture
C. Viniculture　D. Horticulture

93. Which Article of the Indian Constitution mentions that 'No person shall be prosecuted and punished for the same offence more than once'?

A. Article 20(1)
B. Article 20(4)
C. Article 20(3)
D. Article 20(2)

94. Which physicist is best known for his experiments on generating and confirming the existence of electromagnetic waves?

A. Heinrich Rudolf Hertz
B. Isaac Newton
C. JJ Thomson
D. Albert Einstein

95. The Great Bath was found in:

A. Ropar　B. Mohenjo-daro
C. Rakhigarhi　D. Alamgirpur

96. Which sport does Rhythm Sangwan, who was recently in the news, plays?

A. Wrestling　B. Cricket
C. Shooting　D. Hockey

97. Who is the author of the book "Yug Purush, Bharat Ratna, Atal Ji"?

A. Ramesh Pokhriyal
B. Praveen Kumar Pandey
C. Ramesh Datt Dikshit
D. Neeraj Srivastava

98. Which festival is celebrated in north India when Pongal is celebrated in Tamil Nadu?

A. Holi
B. Makar Sankranti
C. Diwali
D. Baishaki

99. Lucknow Gharana and Jaipur Gharana are related to which dance?

A. Jatra　B. Ghumar
C. Kathak　D. Ottan Thullal

100. Which of the following was India's First Biosphere Reserves?

A. Sunderbans
B. Nanda Devi
C. Nilgiri
D. Pachmarhi

88. C	**89.** C	**90.** B	**91.** A	**92.** D	**93.** D	**94.** A	**95.** B
96. C	**97.** A	**98.** B	**99.** C	**100.** C			

EXPLANATORY ANSWERS

1. **(C):** The sentence "Sumit ________ to the wedding. He has an important engagement that day." is correctly completed by "can't go." This is because "can't go" correctly conveys that Sumit is unable to attend due to a prior engagement. The other options are incorrect: "could go" suggests possibility, not impossibility; "needed to go" implies obligation, not inability; and "haven't to go" is grammatically incorrect as it should be "don't have to go."

2. **(D):** The correct option is "May." The sentence "_______ I have your permission to leave the office early?" requires a formal and polite request, and "May" is the appropriate word for this context. "Would" and "Would not" are more about hypothetical situations or willingness, while "Can't" is negative and inappropriate for a polite request.

3. **(C):** The error in the sentence "Do you think you/should come over at/6 pm tomorrow?" is in part (C) "should come over at." The correct phrase should be "should come over by". The preposition "at" is incorrectly placed before the time, disrupting the sentence flow.

4. **(D):** The error in the sentence "Bismillah would play/the shehnai when/he was very young./No error" is in part (A) "Bismillah would play." It should be "Bismillah played" or "Bismillah used to play" to correctly convey past habitual action. "Would play" is incorrect in this context as it is generally used for future not the past.

5. **(D):** The error in the sentence "You can't borrow/my car if/you like to go for a drive./No error" is in part (*a*) "You can't borrow." The correct sentence should be "You can borrow my car if you like to go for a drive."

6. **(A):** The error in the sentence "You can listen to/what the doctor says/if you want to/get cured" is in part (*a*) "You can listen to." It should be "You should listen to" to imply recommendation or necessity rather than permission.

7. **(B):** The error in the sentence "I'm not sure./Kiran should/be in Delhi." is in part (*b*) "Kiran should." It should be "Kiran might" or "Kiran could" to indicate uncertainty. "Should" implies a sense of obligation or expectation, which doesn't fit the context of uncertainty.

8. **(C):** The correct option is "can't you." The sentence "Now you can make question tags, ___________?" requires a positive statement followed by a negative question tag. Therefore, "can't you" correctly follows the positive statement "Now you can make question tags."

9. **(A):** The correct option is "shall we." The sentence "Let us start now, _________?" requires the question tag "shall we" to seek agreement or confirmation in a polite manner. The other options are grammatically incorrect or inappropriate for this context.

10. **(B):** The correct option is "would." The sentence "He believed that he _____ turn out to be a cheat." uses "would" to indicate a belief about a future event in a past context. "Will" is incorrect because it suggests certainty in the future without the past context. "Should" and "must" imply obligation or necessity, which don't fit here.

11. **(C):** The correct option is "why." The sentence "Tell me the reason ______ they

could not marry." requires "why" to explain the cause or reason. "That" would be used to introduce a clause, "so" implies a result, and "because" would make the sentence redundant. "Why" properly introduces the reason in this context.

12. **(C):** The correct option is "had seen." The sentence "He would have believed if he______ with his own eyes last week." requires "had seen" to correctly form a third conditional sentence, which expresses a hypothetical situation in the past. "Saw" and "have seen" do not fit the past perfect requirement, and "could see" is not appropriate here.

13. **(C):** The correct option is "he will." The sentence "As he is obstinate _____ not obey the instructions." requires "he will" to indicate the consequence of his obstinacy. "So he will" is redundant, "that he would" and "he must" imply a different meaning than intended. "He will not obey" correctly completes the sentence.

14. **(A):** The error in the sentence "Everybody was/ watching/ the TV,/ won't they?" is in part (A) "won't they." The correct question tag should be "weren't they" to match the past continuous tense "was watching." "Won't they" is incorrect as it does not match the tense and form of the main clause.

15. **(B):** The correct option is "through." The sentence "Your business is likely to fall _______ for want of sufficient investment." requires "through" to mean that the business is likely to fail due to insufficient investment. "Off," "down," and "at" do not convey the intended meaning of failure due to lack of investment.

16. **(C):** The correct option is "up." The sentence "Robert was cut ____ because he had been deceived by the shopkeeper." uses "up" to mean that Robert was very upset or emotionally disturbed. "Off," "down," and "out" do not accurately convey the emotional impact of being deceived.

17. **(B):** The synonym for "dainty" is "exquisite." "Dainty" refers to something that is delicately beautiful or fine. "Exquisite" similarly means beautifully made or designed. "Insipid" means lacking flavor, "deformed" means misshapen, and "spiritual" relates to the spirit, none of which are synonymous with "dainty."

18. **(C):** The meaning of "implacable" is "relentless." "Implacable" describes someone who cannot be appeased or pacified and is unyielding in their stance. "Considerate" and "empathetic" suggest understanding and kindness, while "friendly" indicates amiability, none of which are synonymous with "implacable."

19. **(A):** The word opposite in meaning to "niggardly" is "extravagant." "Niggardly" means miserly or stingy, while "extravagant" means spending much more than is necessary or lavish. "Shameful" means deserving or bringing shame, "ruthless" means having no pity, and "pompous" means self-important, none of which are antonyms for "niggardly."

20. **(A):** A person who enjoys eating and eats large amounts of food is called a "Gourmand." A "Gourmand" refers to someone who has a great love for food and eats in large quantities. A "Hedonist" seeks pleasure, "Cuisines" refers to styles of cooking, and a "Bohemian" is an unconventional lifestyle, none of which specifically relate to eating large amounts of food.

21. **(B):** The correct option is "superficial." The word "specious" means something that appears to be true or correct, but is actually false or deceptive. In the context of the

passage, "specious" describes justifications that seem plausible on the surface but lack real validity. "Refined" means elegant, "possible" means feasible, and "correct" means accurate, none of which convey the deceptive quality implied by "specious."

22. (D): The correct option is "None of the above." The passage indicates that the post of the governor is significant and often subject to controversy. It explicitly states that the recent case is not a routine departure from norms and does not suggest that governors are often abused. Therefore, none of the provided statements correctly summarize the passage.

23. (A): The correct option is "Factual." The tone of the second paragraph is factual as the author presents historical references and legal opinions about the role of the governor. The author cites the Sarkaria Commission and the Supreme Court ruling to provide an objective explanation of the governor's constitutional responsibilities, without displaying emotion or personal bias.

24. (C): The correct option is "Only I and II." The passage states that the Sarkaria Commission described the Governor as a "Constitutional sentinel and a vital link between the Union and the State," indicating that the Governor serves as an important link between the Union and State (I) and as a custodian of the constitution (II). The statement about the Governor being an arbiter in case of a deadlock is attributed to M.K. Gandhi, not the Sarkaria Commission, so option III is not correct in this context. Therefore, the correct conclusion includes both statements I and II.

25. (C): The correct option is "Only II and III." The passage discusses the lack of autonomy and impartiality in the governor's office, particularly highlighting the political endorsements that compromise neutrality. It does not suggest that the governor's office is redundant; instead, it underscores the importance of the governor's constitutional role. Therefore, the issues of autonomy and impartiality are the ones currently lacking.

26. (C): 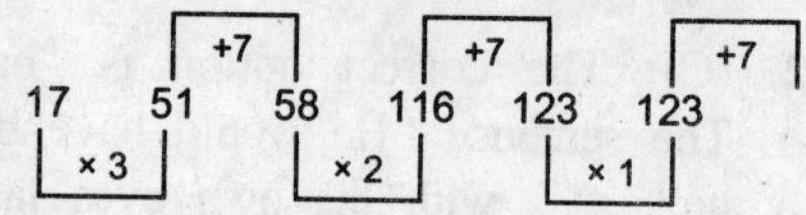

Here, ? = Missing number

$= 123 + 7$

$= 130.$

28. (C):

?	8	11
7	6	5
48	63	72

From 3rd column

$72 - 11 \times 5 = 72 - 55 = 17$

From 2nd column

$63 - 8 \times 6 = 63 - 48 = 15$

Similarly, the 1st column should be

$48 - x \times 7 = 13$

$\Rightarrow \quad 7x = 48 - 13 = 35$

$\Rightarrow \quad x = 5$

Hence, ? = x = 5.

29. (A): Given,

$$\begin{array}{ccc} 2 & 6 & 5 \\ \downarrow & \downarrow & \downarrow \\ P & N & H \end{array}$$

$$\begin{array}{ccc} 1 & 8 & 7 \\ \downarrow & \downarrow & \downarrow \\ O & X & B \end{array} \quad \text{and} \quad \begin{array}{ccc} 2 & 4 & 8 \\ \downarrow & \downarrow & \downarrow \\ N & U & B \end{array}$$

Here, U represents the number 4.

31. (C):

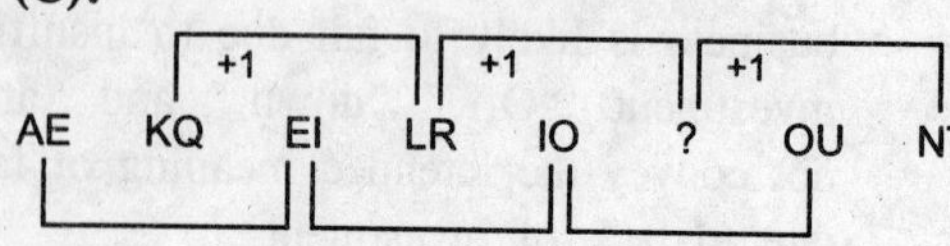

Here, ? = letter-cluster

= LR + 1

= MS [MS + 1 = NT]

32. (D):

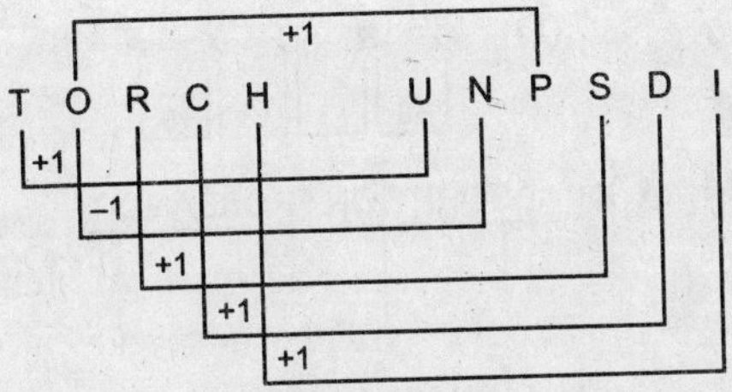

and

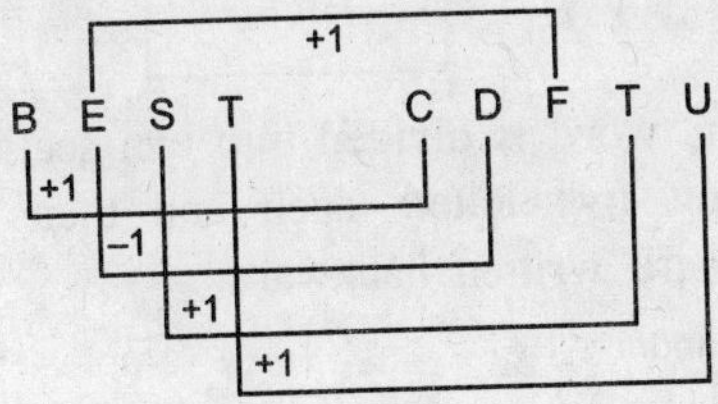

Similarly,

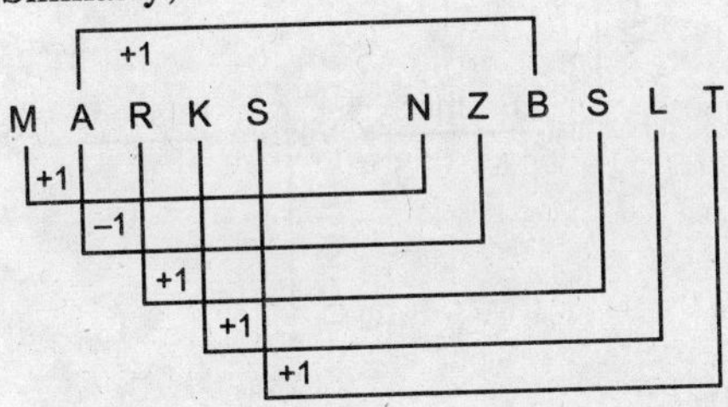

33. (C):

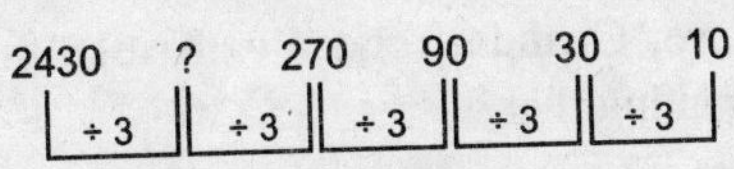

Here, $2430 \div 3 = 810$

and $810 \div 3 = 270$

$\therefore$? = Missing number = 810.

34. (A): $25 - 5 \times 50 \div 10 + 35 = 155$

(A) $\times$ and $-$

$\therefore 25 \times 5 - 50 \div 10 + 35$

$= 25 \times 5 - 5 + 35$

$= 125 - 5 + 35$

$= 160 - 5 = 155$

(B) $\times$ and $+$

$25 - 5 + 50 \div 10 \times 35$

$= 25 - 5 + 5 \times 35$

$= 25 - 5 + 175$

$= 200 - 5$

$= 195$

(C) $+$ and $-$

$25 + 5 \times 50 \div 10 - 35$

$= 25 + 5 \times 5 - 35$

$= 25 + 25 - 35$

$= 50 - 35 = 15$

(D) $\times$ and $\div$

$25 - 5 \div 50 \times 10 + 35$

$= 25 - \frac{1}{10} \times 10 + 35$

$= 25 - 1 + 35$

$= 60 - 1 = 59.$

37. (D): Four friends are playing carrom and sitting on the four sides of the carrom board.

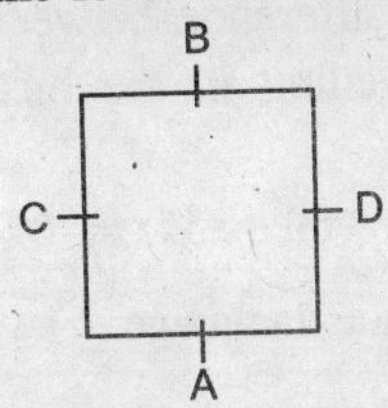

Here, A is sitting to the left of C.

38. (D): Applications → Scrutiny → Interview → Job offer → Joining

39. (A): Period from 17 October 2000 to 18 October 2006 = 17 October 2000-2001 + 17 October 2001-2002 + 17 October 2002-2003 + 17 October 2003-2004 + 17 October 2004-2005 + 17 October 2005-2006 + 18 October 2006

$\therefore$ Total number of odd day

$= 1 + 1 + 1 + 2 + 1 + 1 + 1 = 8$

$= 7 + 1$ (odd day)

$\because$ 18 October 2006 was Wednesday.

$\therefore$ 17 October 2000 will be 1 day before Wednesday = Tuesday.

41. (A): One day,

The number of boys students

$= 90 \times \frac{2}{2+1}$

$= 90 \times \frac{2}{3} = 30 \times 2 = 60$

and the number of girls students

$= 90 - 60 = 30$

The next day,

The number of boys students

$$= 90 \times \frac{3}{3+2}$$

$$= 90 \times \frac{3}{5}$$

$$= 18 \times 3$$

$$= 54$$

and the number of girls students

$$= 90 - 54 = 36$$

Hence, the difference between the number of boys travelling in the bus on both the days

$$= 60 - 54 = 6.$$

42. (A): In a code language

Given,

'you are there'→ 'ter der jer' (*i*)

'we stay here'→ 'yer mer ner' (*ii*)

'we are late'→ 'ser ner der' (*iii*)

'I stay there'→ 'yer fer jer' (*iv*)

From (*i*) and (*iii*)

are → der

From (*i*) and (*iv*)

there → jer ∴ you → ter

From (*ii*) and (*iii*)

we → ner

From (*ii*) and (*iv*)

stay → yer ∴ I → fer

we → ner, are → der

∴ late → ser

Therefore, 'you stay late' is written as 'ter yer ser'.

43. (C): (A) C F I L O (+3, +3, +3, +3)

(B) U X A D G (+3, +3, +3, +3)

(C) O M S V Y (–2, +6, +3, +3)

(D) O R U X A (+3, +3, +3, +3)

44. (C): ABSORPTION : ROSBANOITP

Similarly, VISUA LIZER AUSIV REZIL

Here, the word is divided into two sections containing five letters each and then the sections are written backwards.

45. (D):

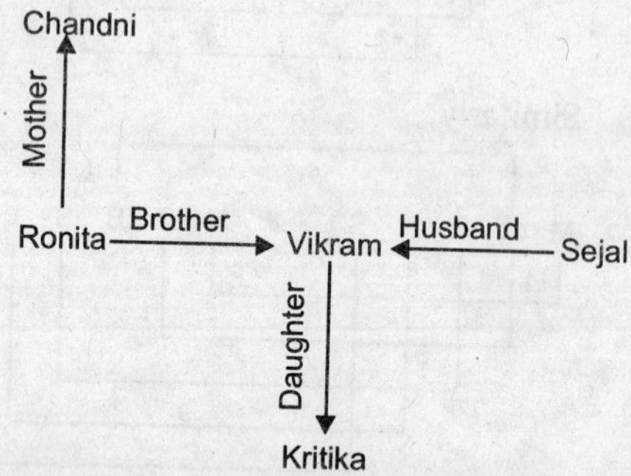

Here, Chandni related to Kritika as paternal grandmother.

46. (A): In a code language

'DENT' is written as '51'

DENT = 4 + 5 + 14 + 20 = 43

and 43 + 8 = 51

and 'LOAD' is written as '40'

LOAD = 12 + 15 + 1 + 4 = 32

and 32 + 8 = 40

Similarly,

COST = 3 + 15 + 19 + 20 = 57

and 57 + 8 = 65

Hence, 'COST' is written as '65'.

50. (C): Given, A = +, B = ×,

C = –, D = ÷

35 B 2 A 5 B (40 C 37) A (8 B 4) D 16 C 14

$= 35 \times 2 + 5 \times (40 - 37) + (8 \times 4) \div 16 - 14$

$= 35 \times 2 + 5 \times 3 + 32 \div 16 - 14$
$= 35 \times 2 + 5 \times 3 + 2 - 14$
$= 70 + 15 + 2 - 14$
$= 87 - 14$
$= 73.$

52. (B): Number of female was in Rampur before Sunday

$$= \frac{16}{31} \times 124000$$
$$= 64000$$

Total no. of female population in village Rampur on Sunday

$$= 64000 + 1323$$
$$= 65323$$

$$\text{Required \%} = \frac{65323}{1628} \times 100$$
$$= 4012.46\%.$$

54. (A): $\because$ Revenue generating by male in museum B

$$= 1628 \times x$$

Revenue generating by female in museum B

$$= 296(x - 5)$$

$$\text{Total revenue} = 1628x + 296(x - 5)$$
$$= 94720$$

$$\Rightarrow 1628x + 296x - 1480 = 94720$$
$$\Rightarrow 1924x = 94720 + 1480$$
$$= 96200$$
$$\Rightarrow x = \frac{96200}{1924} = 50$$

$\therefore$ Total revenue getting from male ticket from museum A = 378 × 50 = ₹ 18900.

59. (C): From the given table,

The number of bikes sold by X in 2022

$$= 800 \times \frac{50}{100} = 400$$

$\therefore$ The number of bikes sold by X and B together in 2022

$$= 400 + 800$$
$$= 1200$$

and the number of bikes sold by C and D together in the same year

$$= 480 + 160$$
$$= 640$$

Hence, required ratio = 1200 : 640 = 15 : 8.

60. (A): From given table:

$$Y : 640 = 7 : 8$$
$$\Rightarrow Y = \frac{640 \times 7}{8}$$
$$= 80 \times 7$$
$$= 560$$

$\therefore$ The average number of bikes sold by companies

$$= \frac{Y + A + B + C}{4}$$
$$= \frac{560 + 240 + 1120 + 960}{4}$$
$$= \frac{2880}{4}$$
$$= 720.$$

62. (D): From given table,

The number of bikes sold by C and D together in 2023

$$= 960 \times \frac{100 - 75}{100} + 640 \times \frac{100 - 60}{100}$$
$$= 960 \times \frac{1}{4} + 640 \times \frac{2}{5}$$
$$= 240 + 256$$
$$= 496$$

Hence, the average number of bikes sold

$$= \frac{496}{2}$$
$$= 248.$$

63. (B): From given pie-chart

Academic year : 2019

Total number of students = 2000

Commerce and Computer Science

$= 25\% + 14\%$

$= 39\%$

$\therefore$ Number of Commerce and Computer Science students

$= 2000 \times \frac{39}{100} = 780$

And Academic year : 2020,

Total number of students = 2400

Engineering and Medical students

$= 12\% + 10\% = 22\%$

$\therefore$ Number of Engineering and Medical students

$= 2400 \times \frac{22}{100}$

$= 24 \times 22$

$= 528$

Hence, Required ratio $= 780 : 528 = 390 : 264$

$= 65 : 44.$

64. (D): From given graph:

The total exports of cars of type A in 2014 to 2018

$= 200 + 150 + 275 + 175 + 300 = 1100$ ...(*i*)

and the total exports of cars of type B in 2015 to 2017

$= 250 + 200 + 275 = 725$ ...(*ii*)

$\therefore$ Type A was sold more than type B

$= 1100 - 725 = 375$

$\therefore$ Percentage of more sell $= \frac{375}{725} \times 100$

$= \frac{37500}{725} = \frac{1500}{29}$

$= 51.7241\%$

$= 51.7\%.$

65. (C): From the given histogram

The number of students who have secured less than 60% marks $= 10 + 30 = 40$

and the number of students who have secured 80% marks and above $= 40 + 25 = 65$

$\therefore$ Difference % $= \frac{65-40}{65} \times 100$

$= \frac{2500}{65} = 38.4615$

$= 38.5\%.$

66. (D): From, the given pie-chart

Family earning every month = ₹ 108000

$\therefore$ The amount spent on rent every month

$= 108000 \times \frac{60°}{360°} = 108000 \times \frac{1}{6}$

$= 18000 \times 1$

= ₹ 18000.

67. (A): Number of employees of age 28+ to 38 years

$= \frac{25}{100} \times 2500 = 625$

Number of employees of age 38 + to 38 years and above

$= \frac{55}{100} \times 2500$

$= 1375$

Difference $= 1375 - 625$

$= 750$

$\therefore$ Much more % $= \frac{750}{625} \times 100$

$= 120\%.$

68. (D): Total exports of cars of type A from 2014 to 2016

$= 200 + 150 + 275$

$= 625$

Total exports of cars of type B from 2015 to 2017

$= 250 + 200 + 275$

$= 725$

Less $= 725 - 625$

$= 100$

Less % $= \frac{100}{725} \times 100 = 13.79\%$

$= 13.8\%$

(correct to one decimal place).

69. (C): $130 - 115 = 15$

Required % $= \frac{15}{130} \times 100$

$= \frac{300}{26} = 11.538$

$= 11.54\%$

(Correct to 2 decimal places).

70. (B): From given bar graph,

Expenditure in 2018 = 75

Expenditure in 2019 = 80

∴ Required % of increase in expenditure

$= \frac{80-75}{75} \times 100$

$= \frac{500}{75} = \frac{20}{3} = 6\frac{2}{3}\%.$

71. (B): From the given bar-graph

The average exports (per year) of cars of type A over the 5 years

$= \frac{200+150+275+175+300}{5} = \frac{1100}{5}$

= ₹ 220 million

As, 220 − 20 = ₹ 200 million

Hence, the exports of cars of type B were ₹ 20 million less than the average exports in 2016.

72. (D): From the given pie-chart

The total number of employees = 3600

∴ $360° = 3600$

⇒ $1° = \frac{3600}{360}$

⇒ $1° = 10$

Office A = 126°

Office B = 18°

Office C = 54°

Office D = 90°

Office E = 72°

∴ The number of employees in Office C

$= 54 \times 10$

$= 540$

∴ Male employees $= 540 \times \frac{20}{100} = 108$

∴ Female employees $= 540 - 108$

$= 432$

The number of employees in office D

$= 90 \times 10$

$= 900$

∴ Male employees $= 900 \times \frac{60}{100} = 540$

∴ Female employees $= 900 - 540$

$= 360$

Hence, Required ratio = female in D : female in C

= 360 : 432

= 90 : 108

= 10 : 12

= 5 : 6.

73. (A): Total no. of cars passed from 7 am to 12 noon

= 105 + 130 + 115 + 95 + 45 = 490

Average $= \frac{490}{5} = 98$

The no. of cars passed less than the average

= 6 – 7, 10 – 11 and 11 – 12

Hence, the correct option is (A).

74. (B): Income for the year 2015 and 2016

= 325 + 280

= 605 crores

Expenditure for the year 2017 and 2018

= 300 + 325

= 625 crores

Required difference = 625 – 605

= 20 crores.

75. (C): Required no. of students

$= (27\% - 24\%)$ of 1800

$= 3\%$ of 1800

$= \frac{3}{100} \times 1800 = 54.$

76. (D): Required average

$= \frac{450+420+450}{3} = 440$

77. (A): Total male participated from school - B & D together

$= 540 + 560$

$= 1100$

Total female participated from school - A & C together

$= 450 + 500$

$= 950$

Required difference $= 1100 - 950$

$= 150.$

78. (B): Required average

$= \frac{72+90+48}{3} = 70.$

79. (A): Required ratio $= \frac{60+90}{90+70}$

$= \frac{150}{160} = 15 : 16.$

80. (C): Required difference

$= \frac{(24+16)-(18+12)}{100} \times 300$

$= (40 - 30) \times 3 = 30.$

81. (D): Total number of students who gave exam in August, 2017

$= 300 \times \frac{120}{100} = 360.$

82. (A): Required central angle

$= 16 \times 3.6 = 57.6°.$

83. (A): Required average

$= \frac{156+179+211+259+230}{5}$

$= \frac{1035}{5} = 207.$

84. (C): Total amount of gold and silver in N

$= 215 + 181 + 163 = 559$

Amount of silver $= \frac{6}{13} \times 559$

$= 6 \times 43 = 258.$

85. (D): Required % increase

$= \frac{(231-180)}{180} \times 100$

$= \frac{51}{180} \times 100 = \frac{85}{3} = 28\frac{1}{3}\%.$

90. (B): On May 18, 1974, India conducted its first nuclear test in Pokhran, code-named Operation Smiling Buddha.

91. (A): The NITI Aayog (National Institution for Transforming India) was established on January 1, 2015, to replace the Planning Commission.

92. (D): Horticulture is the branch of agriculture focused on the cultivation of fruits, vegetables, flowers, and ornamental plants.

93. (D): Article 20(2) of the Indian Constitution states that "No person shall be prosecuted and punished for the same offence more than once." This principle is known as double jeopardy, which protects individuals from being tried and punished multiple times for the same offence.

94. (A): Heinrich Rudolf Hertz was a pioneering German physicist who is best known for his experiments that confirmed the existence of electromagnetic waves, as predicted by James Clerk Maxwell's equations.

95. (B): The Great Bath is one of the most famous structures of the ancient Indus Valley

Civilization, located in Mohenjo-daro (in present-day Pakistan). It is believed to have been used for ritual bathing, indicating the significance of cleanliness and water in the culture.

96. (C): Rhythm Sangwan is a prominent figure in the sport of shooting. Recently, she has been in the news for her remarkable performances in national and international shooting competitions. Her achievements have garnered significant attention, highlighting her as a rising star in the field of shooting. This categorically sets her apart from other sports such as wrestling, cricket, and hockey.

97. (A): The book "Yug Purush, Bharat Ratna, Atal Ji" was authored by Ramesh Pokhriyal. The book is a tribute to the former Indian Prime Minister Atal Bihari Vajpayee, capturing his life, political journey, and contributions to the nation. Ramesh Pokhriyal, a seasoned politician and writer, provides an insightful look into Atal Ji's legacy, making this work a notable literary piece.

98. (B): Makar Sankranti is the festival celebrated in North India around the same time as Pongal in Tamil Nadu. Both festivals mark the harvest season and are celebrated in January. Makar Sankranti signifies the transition of the sun into the zodiac sign of Capricorn. It is a major harvest festival celebrated with various regional customs and traditions, such as flying kites, preparing sweets made of sesame and jaggery, and taking holy dips in rivers.

99. (C): Kathak is the dance form associated with Lucknow Gharana and Jaipur Gharana. These gharanas or schools of Kathak have distinct styles and techniques. The Lucknow Gharana is known for its expressive, graceful, and intricate movements, while the Jaipur Gharana emphasizes complex footwork and spins. Kathak is one of the eight classical dance forms of India and has a rich tradition of storytelling through dance and music.

100. (C): The Nilgiri Biosphere Reserve was India's first biosphere reserve, established in 1986. It is located in the Western Ghats and Nilgiri Hills in South India. The reserve encompasses parts of Tamil Nadu, Kerala, and Karnataka. It is recognized for its rich biodiversity and is home to numerous endemic species of flora and fauna. The Nilgiri Biosphere Reserve plays a crucial role in conservation efforts and sustainable development in the region.

YOUR SPACE

Previous Paper (Solved)

Guru Gobind Singh Indraprastha University (GGSIPU)

B.Com (Hons) Common Entrance Test (CET), 2022*

GENERAL ENGLISH

1. Choose the correct meaning of the idiomatic expression "at an arm's length".
   A. To be very close.
   B. Avoid to be very close.
   C. To be at 3 feet distance.
   D. None of the above.

2. Chose the correct option to complete the sentence given below:
   I never have ______ on my friends.
   A. depended nor will depend
   B. depended or will depend
   C. nor will depend
   D. or will depend

3. Choose the correct sentence from the options below:
   A. I said to her that to give me that notebook.
   B. I asked her to give me that notebook.
   C. I said her to give me this notebook.
   D. I told to her to give me that notebook.

4. Many a man (A)/ have (B)/ been arrested (C)/ by the police. (D)
   A. A B. B
   C. C D. D

5. I had told him yesterday (A) / that I did not (B)/ find him(C)/ at home. (D)
   A. A B. B
   C. C D. D

6. Ram and Rishab performed their ______ duties.
   A. respected B. respectful
   C. respective D. respect of

7. Select the sentence which is grammatically correct from the following:
   A. The youngster will benefit from the experience.
   B. The youngster will benefit by the experience.
   C. The youngster will benefit of the experience.
   D. The youngster will benefit out of the experience.

8. Identify the word which is similar in meaning to "ABODE":
   A. Sanctuary B. Residence
   C. Reformatory D. Dwelling

9. Rudra is ______ his boss.
   A. angry at B. angry with
   C. angry against D. angry for

10. I look forward to ______ you.
    A. meet B. meeting
    C. have meet D. met

11. Radha as well as Charu (A)/ are playing (B)/ in the room. (C)/ No error (D)
    A. A B. B
    C. C D. D

12. Choose the correct sentence from the options below:
    A. As I was leaving home, it began to rain.
    B. When leaving home, it began to rain.
    C. Since I was leaving home, it began to rain.
    D. Before leaving home, it began to rain.

13. Identify the word which is similar in meaning to "RENOUNCE":
    A. Relinquish B. Withdraw
    C. Forgive D. Repeat

* *Exam held on 24-06-2022.*

14. Choose the correct sentence from the options below:
A. She is either right nor wrong
B. She is both right or wrong
C. She is neither right or wrong
D. She is neither right nor wrong

15. Choose the correct choice that can be substituted for the following.
"Extreme old age when a man behaves in an irrational manner".
A. Imbecility B. Senility
C. Dotage D. Superannuation

16. Employees are not satisfied with the revised pay structure but they have ______ .
A. reconciled to it
B. reconciled with it
C. reconciled at it
D. reconciled for it

17. Choose the correct option to complete the sentence given below.
It is difficult to say that ______ .
A. they shall agree
B. they should agree
C. they will agree
D. they would agree or not

18. Choose the correct meaning of the idiomatic expression "in a melting pot".
A. to take an important decision
B. to be prone to bad influences
C. in a helpless situation
D. in the process of changing

19. Find the odd word out of the options given below:
A. Blue B. Crimson
C. Ruby D. Scarlet

20. The day he received his degree was a ______ for him.
A. historical day B. historic day
C. history day D. hysteric day

21. Find the odd word out of the options given below.
A. Expert B. Professional
C. Civilized D. Maestro

22. Identify the word which is opposite in meaning to "SQUANDER".
A. Waste B. Conserve
C. Presume D. Donate

23. I ______ on these lines before I realized my mistake.
A. was worked B. am working
C. worked D. had been working

24. Identify the part with grammatical error in the sentence given below.
My sister (A)/ like painting, (B)/ dancing and cooking. (C)/ No error (D)
A. A B. B
C. C D. D

25. Choose the correct option to complete the sentence given below:
She told me that ______
A. earth revolving B. earth revolves
C. the earth revolves D. earth revolved

LOGICAL REASONING

26. Complete the series:
E – 5, G – 7, I – 9, K – 11, ?, ?
A. L – 13, N – 14 B. M – 13, O – 15
C. L – 12, M – 14 D. K – 12, M – 14

27. A tree always has which of the following:
A. Branches B. Leaves
C. Fruits D. Roots

28. Which interchange of signs will correct the following equation?
$35 + 7 \times 5 \div 5 - 6 = 24$
A. × & – B. + & ×
C. ÷ & + D. – & +

29. First bunch of bananas has $\frac{1}{4}$ again as many bananas as a second bunch. If the second bunch has 3 bananas less than the first bunch, then the number of bananas in the first bunch is:
A. 9 B. 10
C. 12 D. 15

30. Arrange the words given below in a meaningful sequence:
1. Presentation 2. Recommendation
3. Arrival 4. Discussion
5. Introduction
A. 5, 3, 4, 1, 2 B. 3, 5, 4, 2, 1
C. 3, 5, 1, 4, 2 D. 5, 3, 1, 2, 4

31. Marathon is to race as hibernation is to:
A. Winter B. Bear
C. Dream D. Sleep

32. A man sells a file cover at a profit of 25%. Had he bought it at 25% less and sold for 25 less, he would still have gained 25%. Find the cost of the article.
A. 100 B. 40
C. 60 D. 50

33. If the second Sunday of a month falls on the 8th, what is the date of the fourth day after the third Saturday of that month?
A. 26 B. 15
C. 25 D. 24

34. Complete the series:
BZ, HT, NN, ??, ZB
A. LF B. SX
C. TH D. TI

35. Choose the best option:
A car always has
A. Driver B. Bonnet
C. Bumper D. Wheels

36. A man climbs 30 feet at the beginning of each hour and rests for a while when he slips back 20 feet before he again starts climbing in the beginning of the next hour. If he begins his ascent at 8.00 a.m., at what time will he first touch a flag at 120 feet from the ground?
A. 5 PM B. 6 PM
C. 7 PM D. 6.30 PM

37. Find the odd number out.
A. 11 B. 21
C. 31 D. 41

38. A farmer built a fence around his square plot. He used 27 fence poles on each side of the square. How many poles did he need altogether?
A. 100 B. 102
C. 104 D. 108

39. Safe : Secure :: Protect : ?
A. Lock B. Guard
C. Sure D. Conserve

40. In a certain code MAIN is written as '9364' and DEAR is written as '8532'. How is MEND written in that code?
A. 9548 B. 9458
C. 9538 D. 9528

41. Which word does NOT belong with the others?
A. index B. glossary
C. chapter D. book

42. Choose the missing character from the given options:

5	6	7
3	4	5
9	10	11
345	460	?

A. 535 B. 577
C. 755 D. 775

43. In a group of cows and hens, the number of legs are 14 more than twice the number of heads. The number of cows is:
A. 5 B. 7
C. 10 D. 11

44. Choose the missing character from the given options:

5	5	2
2	4	1
8	3	10
40	30	?

A. 10 B. 12
C. 13 D. 20

45. A Tiebreaker is an additional contest carried out to establish a winner among tied contestants. Choose one situation from the options below that best represents a Tiebreaker.
A. At halftime, the score is tied at 2-2 in a hockey match.
B. Serena and Maria have each secured 1 set in their match at Wimbledon.

C. The umpire tosses a coin to decide which team will have bat first.
D. SRH and RCB each finished at 140 all out.

46. Complete the series:
240, ?, 120, 40, 10,
A. 180 B. 240
C. 420 D. 480

47. At the end of a business conference the 11 people present all shake hands with each other once. How many handshakes will there be altogether?
A. 55 B. 66
C. 54 D. 65

48. A family has one cake. The father took 1/4 of the cake and he had 3 times as much as each of the other members had. The total number of family members is:
A. 3 B. 7
C. 10 D. 12

49. Read the following statement and identify the correct choice:
"Anger is energy in a more proactive way and how to channelize it is itself a skill."
Assumptions-I : Anger needs to be channelized.
Assumption-II : Only skilful people can channelize anger to energy.
A. only assumption I is implicit.
B. only assumption II is implicit.
C. either I or II is implicit.
D. if neither I nor II is implicit.

50. Sachin walks a certain distance and comes back on a scooter, taking a total time of 40 minutes. He could walk both ways in 60 minutes. How long would it take for him to ride scooter both ways? Scooter speed is assumed as constant.
A. 15 minutes B. 20 minutes
C. 25 minutes D. 30 minutes

DATA INTERPRETATION

Directions (Qs. No. 51-55): *Read the given information carefully and answer these questions.*

The speed of a train over a 3-hour period was as follows (the time count does not begin from the starting of train)

Time (in minutes)	Speed at the given time (in km/hour)
0	35
30	41
45	44
60	47
90	53
120	59
150	65
180	71

51. If the same formula for the speed of the train was valid even before the data given in the table, at what time (before the start of the train as per given table) would the train have started?
A. 35/12 hours B. 12/35 hours
C. 7/2 hours D. 2/7 hours

52. During the three-hour period shown in the table, the speed of the train increased by ______%.
A. 119.42 B. 65.68
C. 97.22 D. 102.85

53. At time *t*, measured in minutes after the beginning of the time period, which of the following gives the speed of the train in accordance with the table?
A. $35 + t/5$ B. $t/2 + t/3 + t/4$
C. $t/5 + t/7$ D. None of these

54. How fast was the train travelling 2 hours after the beginning of the time period (in km/hour)
A. 65 B. 67
C. 59 D. None of these

55. What is the total distance travelled by the train over this 3-hour period?
A. 459 km B. 159 km
C. 385 km D. None of these

Directions (Qs. No. 56-60): *Read the given information carefully and answer these questions.*

A survey of movie goers from five cities A, B, C, D and E is given below. The first column gives the percentage of viewers in each city who watch less than one movie a week. The second column gives the total number of viewers who view one or more movies per week.

City	I	II
A	60	2400
B	20	3000
C	85	2400
D	55	2700
E	75	8000

56. The highest number of movie watchers in any given city is:
A. 36000 B. 32000
C. 16000 D. 6000

57. How many viewers in city C watch less than one movie a week?
A. 2040 B. 13600
C. 16000 D. 3600

58. A city with the second lowest number of movie watchers is:
A. City E B. City D
C. City B D. City C

59. The total number of all movie goers in the five cities who watch less than one movie per week is:
A. 50000 B. 36000
C. 18500 D. 45250

60. Which city has the highest number of viewers who watch less than one movie a week?
A. City E B. City D
C. City B D. City C

Directions (Qs. No. 61-65): *Read the given information carefully and answer these questions.*

Two products P and Q can be made on either of the two extrusion machines M1 and M2. The time in minutes, taken by these products according to the machines used are given as below. Assume 8 working hours per day.

Product	M1	M2
P	8	10
Q	6	6

61. If P and Q are produced in the ratio 3 : 1, what is maximum of total of P and Q that can be produced in a day?
A. 120 B. 160
C. 116 D. 166

62. If P is produced only on machine M1 and Q is produced only on machine M2. What is the unutilised time on M2 in a day, if P and Q are produced in 1 : 1 ratio?
A. 20 minutes B. 60 minutes
C. 120 minutes D. 150 minutes

63. If each product requires working on both the machines and the time required on each machine is as indicated in the table, what is the maximum production possible in a day, assuming only P is produced?
A. 80 B. 180
C. 60 D. 48

64. The cost of working of machine M1 is ₹ 1000/hour and that of machine M2 is ₹ 800/hour. What is the minimum cost of producing 100 units of P and 100 units of Q?
A. ₹ 23333 B. ₹ 21333
C. ₹ 213.33 D. ₹ 26666

65. What is the unutilised time for machine M1?
A. 86 minutes B. 96 minutes
C. 90 minutes D. 108 minutes

Directions (Qs. No. 66-70): *Read the given information carefully and answer these questions.*

In a school of 2500 students, the students are taught four different languages, viz. English, Hindi, Punjabi and Sanskrit. The ratio of girls to boys in the school is 3 : 2. 16% of the boys learn only Punjabi. 23% of the girls learn only Punjabi and Hindi. 14% of the total number of students learn only English. Boys learning only Punjabi and Hindi are 120% of the girls learning the same. One-tenth of the boys learn only Sanskrit. Girls learning only Punjabi are 130% of the boys learning the same. 19% of the boys learn only English. Remaining boys learn only Sanskrit, Hindi and English.

32% of the girls learn only Hindi and Sanskrit. Remaining girls learn only Hindi, English and Sanskrit.

66. How many girls do not learn Hindi?
A. 368 B. 416
C. 346 D. 428

67. What is the total number of students learning Punjabi?
A. 1017 B. 1464
C. 1024 D. 1127

68. What is the total number of girls learning English and Sanskrit?
A. 787 B. 867
C. 947 D. 897

69. How many students study at least two languages at a time?
A. 1582 B. 1462
C. 1670 D. 1682

70. What is the total number of boys learning Hindi?
A. 480 B. 550
C. 620 D. 650

Directions (Qs. No. 71-75): *Answer the questions on the basis of the two figures given below:*

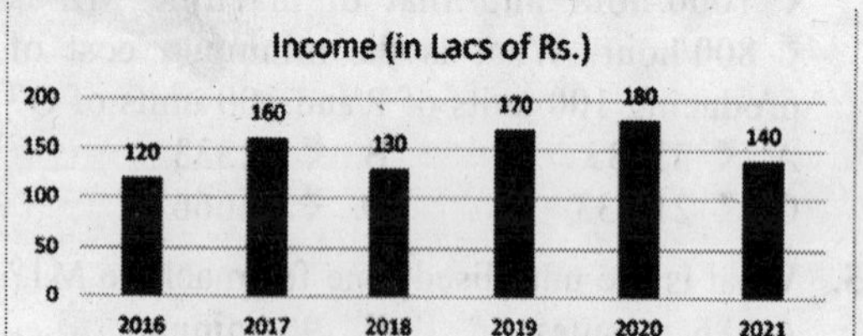

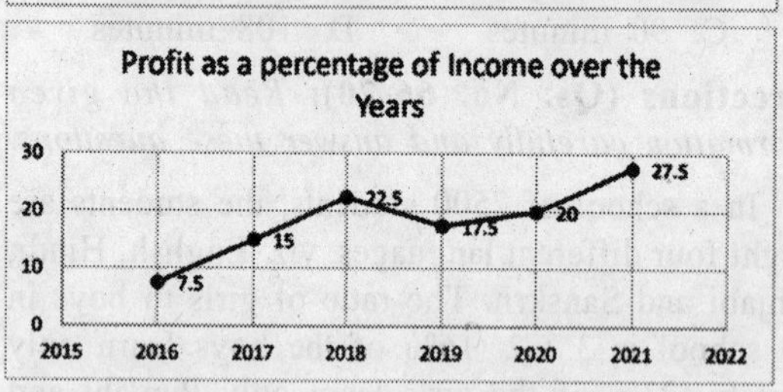

71. For which year expenditure was minimum?
A. 2016 B. 2018
C. 2020 D. 2021

72. In which of the following years the amount of profit was maximum?
A. 2018 B. 2019
C. 2020 D. 2021

73. What was the expenditure for the year 2020?
A. 136 B. 140.25
C. 144 D. 142

74. In which of the following years the amount of profit was maximum?
A. 2018 B. 2019
C. 2020 D. 2021

75. In which year maximum amount of rise or fall was observed in profit (in ₹) in comparison to previous year?
A. 2016 B. 2017
C. 2020 D. 2021

Directions (Qs. No. 76-80): *Study the following graph carefully and answer the questions that follow.*

Number of players (in hundred) participated in a sports event in three different sports in six different years

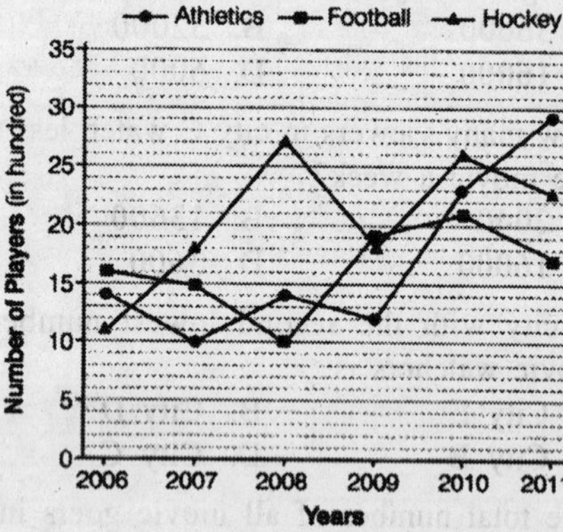

76. What was the difference between the number of players participated in athletics in the year 2010 and the number of players participated in hockey in the year 2009?
A. 660 B. 500
C. 580 D. 700

77. What was the approximate per cent decrease in the number of players participated in football in the year 2008 as compared to previous year?
A. 30% B. 34%
C. 44% D. 48%

78. What was the approximate average number of players participated in hockey over all the years together?

A. 2034 B. 2104
C. 2046 D. 2146

79. If 23% of the players participated in athletics in the year 2006 found positive in doping test, what was the number of players participated in athletics in the year 2006 found negative in doping test?
A. 1048 B. 1026
C. 1064 D. 1078

80. Total number of players participated in all the sports together in the year 2007 was approximately, what per cent of the total number of players participated in football over all the years together?
A. 35% B. 44%
C. 49% D. 51%

Directions (Qs. No. 81-85): *Study the following table and answer the question given below it.*

Classification of 100 students based on the marks obtained by them in Physics and Chemistry in an examination

Subjects	Marks out of 50				
	40 and above	30 and above	20 and above	10 and above	0 and above
Physics	9	32	80	92	100
Chemistry	4	21	66	81	100
Average (aggregate)	7	27	73	87	100

81. If at least 60% marks in Physics are required for pursuing higher studies in Physics, how many students will be eligible for pursuing higher studies in it?
A. 27 B. 32
C. 34 D. 41

82. If it is known that at least 23 students were eligible for a symposium on Chemistry, then the minimum qualifying marks in Chemistry for eligibility to symposium would lie in the range:
A. 40-45 B. 30-40
C. 20-30 D. below 20

83. What is the number of students scoring less than 40% marks in aggregate?
A. 13 B. 19
C. 20 D. 27

84. What is the difference between the number of students passed with 30 as cut-off marks in Chemistry and those passed with 30 as cut-off marks in the aggregate?
A. 3 B. 4
C. 5 D. 6

85. The percentage of number of students getting at least 60% marks in Chemistry over those at least 40% marks in aggregate, is approximately?
A. 26% B. 27%
C. 29% D. 31%

GENERAL AWARENESS

86. Ukraine's currency is called ______ .
A. Forint B. Lempira
C. Hryvnia D. Kina

87. India's first Human Space Mission is known as ________ .
A. Vyom Mitra B. Mangalyaan
C. Shukrayaan D. None of the above

88. Which of the following are the components of Digital Economy?
A. e-business
B. e-business infrastructure
C. e-commerce
D. all the above

89. The State that was ranked at 1st position as per Ease of Doing Business Index of States and Union Territories 2021 is:
A. Andhra Pradesh
B. Uttar Pradesh
C. Maharashtra
D. Telangana

90. Pulitzer Prize is awarded for outstanding work in the field of:
A. Science and Technology
B. Environmental Studies
C. International Understanding
D. Literature and Journalism

91. The type of US Visa issued to intra company managers or executives is:
A. H1B B. R1
C. O D. LI

92. Who among the following is the sitting Chief Justice of Supreme Court of India?
A. Justice D.Y. Chandrachud
B. Justice L. Nageswara Rao
C. Justice Vipin Sanghi
D. None of the above

93. Which country among the following is ranked lowest in the Environmental Performance Index 2022?
A. Pakistan B. Bangladesh
C. Nigeria D. India

94. Nobel prize in Chemistry for the year 2021 was awarded to ______
A. Benjamin List B. David MacMillan
C. Both A & B D. Neither A nor B

95. The second largest Public Sector Bank in India as on January 2022 is:
A. State Bank of India
B. Bank of Baroda
C. Punjab National Bank
D. Canara Bank

96. David Card has received Nobel Prize for his ______.
A. methodological contributions to analysis of causal relationships
B. empirical contributions to labour economics
C. contribution to the improvements in auction theory
D. experimental approach to alleviating global poverty

97. According to the UN World Happiness Report 2022, India is ranked at ______ position.
A. 136th B. 143rd
C. 141st D. 112th

98. Which of the following are conferred with the power to prepare and maintain SEBCs list under the 105th Constitutional Amendment Act?
A. Union of India
B. Concerned States
C. Concerned Union Territories
D. All the above

99. An Era of Darkness: The British Empire in India was written by:
A. Geetanjali Shree
B. Shashi Tharoor
C. Amitav Ghosh
D. Vikram Seth

100. Wassenar Arrangement is related to:
A. Nuclear Fuel Supply Control
B. Commercial Aircrafts Supply Control
C. Missile Technology Transfer Control
D. Arms Export Control

ANSWERS

1. (B)	2. (A)	3. (B)
4. (B)	5. (A)	6. (C)
7. (A)	8. (B)	9. (B)
10. (B)	11. (B)	12. (A)
13. (A)	14. (D)	15. (B)
16. (A)	17. (D)	18. (C)
19. (A)	20. (B)	21. (C)
22. (B)	23. (D)	24. (B)
25. (C)		

26. (B): E-5, G-7, I-9, K-11, ?, ?

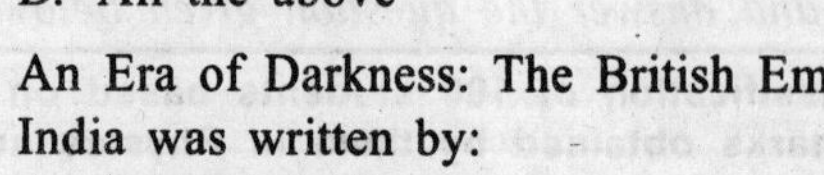

Hence, the missing terms
= M-13, O-15.

27. (D)

28. (C): $35 + 7 \times 5 \div 5 - 6 = 24$

A. × & −

$\therefore \quad 35 + 7 - 5 \div 5 \times 6 = 24$

$\Rightarrow \quad 35 + 7 - 1 \times 6 = 24$

$\Rightarrow \quad 35 + 7 - 6 = 24$

$\Rightarrow \quad 42 - 6 = 24$

$\Rightarrow \quad 36 = 24$ (Incorrect)

B. + & ×

$\therefore \quad 35 \times 7 + 5 \div 5 - 6 = 24$

$\Rightarrow \quad 35 \times 7 + 1 - 6 = 24$

$\Rightarrow \quad 245 + 1 - 6 = 24$

$\Rightarrow \quad 246 - 6 = 24$

$\Rightarrow \quad 240 = 24$ (Incorrect)

C. ÷ & +

$\therefore \quad 35 \div 7 \times 5 + 5 - 6 = 24$

$\Rightarrow \quad 5 \times 5 + 5 - 6 = 24$

$\Rightarrow \quad 25 + 5 - 6 = 24$

$\Rightarrow \quad 30 - 6 = 24$

$\Rightarrow \quad 24 = 24$ (Correct)

D. – & +

$\therefore \quad 35 - 7 \times 5 \div 5 + 6 = 24$

$\Rightarrow \quad 35 - 7 \times 1 + 6 = 24$

$\Rightarrow \quad 35 - 7 + 6 = 24$

$\Rightarrow \quad 41 - 7 = 24$

$\Rightarrow \quad 34 = 24$ (Incorrect)

Hence, option (C) is the right answer.

29. (D)

30. (C): Meaningful sequence:
Arrival → Introduction → Presentation → Discussion → Recommendation.

31. (D)

32. (A): Let the C.P. of the article = ₹ x
then, the S.P. of the article

$$= x \times \frac{125}{100} = ₹\ \frac{5}{4}x$$

Again, $\quad \text{C.P.} = x \times \frac{100-25}{100} = \frac{3}{4}x$

and $\text{S.P.} = \frac{5}{4}x - 25$

$\therefore \quad \text{Profit} = \text{S.P.} - \text{C.P.} = \frac{5}{4}x - 25 - \frac{3}{4}x$

$$= \frac{2}{4}x - 25 = \frac{1}{2}x - 25$$

$$\text{Profit }\% = \frac{\text{Profit} \times 100}{\text{C.P.}}$$

$$\Rightarrow \quad 25 = \frac{\left(\frac{1}{2}x - 25\right) \times 100}{\frac{3}{4}x}$$

$$\Rightarrow \quad 25 \times \frac{3}{4}x = 50x - 2500$$

$$\Rightarrow \quad 50x - \frac{75}{4}x = 2500$$

$$\Rightarrow \quad \frac{125}{4}x = 2500$$

$$\Rightarrow \quad x = \frac{2500 \times 4}{125} = \frac{100 \times 4}{5} = 80$$

Hence, the cost of the article
= S.P. of the article

$$= \frac{5}{4}x = \frac{5}{4} \times 80 = ₹\ 100.$$

33. (C): Given, the second Sunday = 8th
∴ The first Sunday = 1st day
⇒ The first Saturday = 7
⇒ The second Saturday = 14
⇒ The third Saturday = 21
Hence, the date of the fourth day after the third Saturday of the month = 21 + 4 = 25.

34. (C):

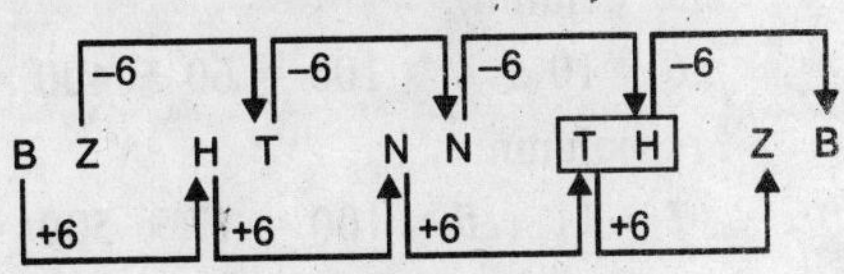

Hence, the missing term = TH.

35. (D)

36. (B): Given, the height of the flag = 120 feet
beginning time = 8.00 AM
∵ He climbs every hour
= 30 – 20 = 10 feet
∴ 120 feet = 90 feet + 30 feet
= 9 hours + 1 hour
= 10 hours

He will touch the flag after 10 hours from his beginning *i.e.,* at 6 PM.

37. (B): A. 11

B. $21 = 3 \times 7$

C. 31

D. 41

Hence, 21 is the odd number.

38. (C): Here, the number of poles on each side of the square = 27

$\therefore$ The total number of poles on 4 sides of the square

$= 4 \times 27 - 4$ [Four corners = 4 poles]

$= 108 - 4$

$= 104.$

39. (B)

40. (A): Given, M A I N → 9 3 6 4 and D E A R → 8 5 3 2

Similarly, M E N D → 9 5 4 8

Hence, MEND is written as 9548.

41. (D)

42. (B): From the given options:

Ist column:

$5 \times 9 + 3 \times 100 = 45 + 300 = 345$

2nd column:

$6 \times 10 + 4 \times 100 = 60 + 400 = 460$

3rd column:

$7 \times 11 + 5 \times 100 = 77 + 500 = 577.$

43. (B): Let the number of cows and hens in a group are x and y

Then, the number of heads = $x + y$

and the number of legs = $4x + 2y$

According to question,

$$4x + 2y = 2(x + y) + 14$$

$$\Rightarrow \quad 4x + 2y = 2x + 2y + 14$$

$$\Rightarrow \quad 4x - 2x = 14$$

$$\Rightarrow \quad 2x = 14$$

$$\Rightarrow \quad x = 7$$

Hence, the number of cows are 7.

44. (A):

5	5	2
2	4	1
8	3	10
40	30	?

$$5 \times 8 \times 2 = \frac{80}{2} = 40$$

$$5 \times 4 \times 3 = \frac{60}{2} = 30$$

$$2 \times 1 \times 10 = \frac{20}{2} = 10$$

Hence, 10 will come at the place of question mark.

45. (D)

46. (B): 240 → (÷ 1) → **240** → (÷ 2) → 120 → (÷ 3) → 40 → (÷ 4) → 10

Hence, 240 will come at the place of question mark.

47. (A): Required number $= {}^{11}C_2$

$$= \frac{11!}{2!\,9!} \qquad \left[\because {}^nC_r = \frac{n!}{r!(n-r)!}\right]$$

$$= \frac{11 \times 10 \times 9!}{2 \times 9!} = 55$$

Hence, 55 handshakes will there be altogether.

48. (C): Required number of family member = 10

Because $\frac{10}{4} + 3\left(\frac{10}{4}\right) = \frac{10}{4} + \frac{30}{4} = \frac{40}{4} = 10.$

49. (B): Only skilful people can channelize anger to energy. Hence assumption II is implicit.

50. (B): Let a certain distance = d km

Walking speed = x km/h

and Scooter's speed = y km/h

Then, $\frac{d}{x} + \frac{d}{y} = 40$ ...(*i*)

When walking both sides, then,

$$\frac{d}{x} + \frac{d}{x} = 60 \Rightarrow \frac{2d}{x} = 60$$

$$\Rightarrow \quad \frac{d}{x} = 30 \quad ...(ii)$$

From (*i*) and (*ii*),

$$30 + \frac{d}{y} = 40 \Rightarrow \frac{d}{y} = 10$$

$$\because \quad \frac{d}{y} + \frac{d}{y} = 2\frac{d}{y} \left[\frac{d}{y} = 10 \text{ minutes}\right]$$

$$= 2 \times 10 = 20 \text{ minutes}$$

Hence, he would take 20 minutes to ride scooter both ways.

51. (A): Required time $= \frac{35}{12}$ hours.

52. (D): 3-hour period = 180 minutes

Speed of the train increased

$= 71 - 35 = 36$

$$\% \text{ increase} = \frac{36}{35} \times 100 = \frac{3600}{35}$$

$= 102.85\%$.

53. (A): $35 + \frac{t}{5} = 35 + \frac{30}{5} = 35 + 6 = 41$

$$35 + \frac{45}{5} = 35 + 9 = 44$$

$$35 + \frac{60}{5} = 35 + 12 = 47$$

....

$$35 + \frac{180}{5} = 35 + 36 = 71$$

Hence, $35 + \frac{t}{5}$ gives the speed of the train in accordance with the table.

54. (C): $35 + \frac{120}{5} = 35 + 24 = 59$ km/hr

Hence, speed of the train travelling 2 hours after the beginning of the time period

= 59 km/hr.

55. (B): Average speed $= \frac{415}{8} = 51.875$ km/hr

= 52 km/hr

Total distance travelled

= Average speed × time

= 52 × 3 = 156 km ≅ 159 km.

For Qs. No. 56-60:

City	I	II	I + II	I
A	60	2400	6000	3600
B	20	3000	3750	750
C	85	2400	16000	13600
D	55	2700	6000	3300
E	75	8000	32000	24000

56. (B): The highest number of movie watchers in city E = 32000.

57. (B): The number of viewers in city C watch less than one movie a week = 13600.

58. (B): City D with the second lowest number of movie watchers = 6000.

59. (D): The total number of all movies goers in the five cities who watch less than one movie per week

= 3600 + 750 + 13600 + 3300 + 24000

= 45250.

60. (A): City E has highest number (24000) of viewer who watch less than one movie a week.

61. (A)	**62. (C)**	**63. (D)**
64. (B)	**65. (B)**	**66. (A)**
67. (D)	**68. (C)**	**69. (D)**
70. (B)	**71. (D)**	**72. (D)**
73. (C)	**74. (A)**	**75. (B)**

76. (B): From the given graph,

The number of players participated in athletics in the year 2010 = 2300

and the number of players participated in hockey in the year 2009 = 1800

∴ Required difference = 2300 – 1800 = 500.

77. (B): From the given graph,

The number of players participated in football in the year 2008 = 1000

and in the previous year (2007) = 1500

Required % decrease

$$= \frac{1500-1000}{1500} \times 100 = \frac{500}{1500} \times 100 = \frac{1}{3} \times 100$$

= 33.33333 = 34% (approximate).

78. (A): From the given graph

The average number of players participated in hockey over all the years together

$$= \frac{1100+1800+2700+1800+2600+2200}{6}$$

$$= \frac{12200}{6} = 2033.33333 = 2034.$$

79. (D): Given, 23% of the players partcipated in athletics in the year 2006 found positive in doping test.

∴ The number of participated players found negative in doping test

$$= 1400 \times \frac{100-23}{100} = 14 \times 77 = 1078.$$

80. (B): From the given graph,

Total number of players participated in all the sports together in the year 2007

= 1000 + 1500 + 1800 = 4300

and the total number of players participated in football over all the years together

= 1600 + 1500 + 1000 + 1900 + 2100 + 1700

= 9800

Hence, the required %

$$= \frac{4300}{9800} \times 100 = \frac{4300}{98}$$

= 43.8775 = 44%. (approximate)

81. (B): From the given table,

Percentage marks required in Physics = 60%

$$= 50 \times \frac{60}{100} = 30 \text{ marks in Physics}$$

∴ Number of students eligible for pursuing higher study in Physics will be 32.

82. (C): From the given table:

In Chemistry,

Number of students obtained 40 marks and above = 4 students

Number of students obtained 30 marks and above = 21 − 4 = 17 students

Number of students obtained 20 marks and above = 66 − 21 = 45 students

Since at least 23 students were eligible

Hence, their required range of marks

= 20 − 30.

83. (D): $\because$ 40% marks out of 50 = $50 \times \frac{40}{100} = 20$

Now, scoring less than 40% marks in aggregate

= scoring less than 20 marks

= 10 and above + 0 and above

= (87 − 73) + (100 − 87) = 14 + 13 = 27.

84. (D): From the given table,

The difference between the number of students passed with 30 as cut-off marks in Chemistry and those passed with 30 as cut-off marks in the aggregate = 27 − 21 = 6.

85. (C): From the given table,

$\because$ 60% marks in Chemistry = $50 \times \frac{60}{100} = 30$

$\because$ At least 60 marks in Chemistry

= At least 30 marks in Chemistry

= 4 + (21 − 4) = 4 + 17 = 21

and 40% marks in aggregate = $50 \times \frac{40}{100} = 20$

$\because$ Atleast 20 marks in aggregate

= 7 + (27 − 7) + (73 − 27)

= 7 + 20 + 46 = 73

Hence, the required percentage

$$= \frac{21}{73} \times 100 = 28.7671\% = 29\% \text{ (approx.)}$$

86. (C)	**87. (D)**	**88. (D)**
89. (A)	**90. (D)**	**91. (D)**
92. (D)	**93. (D)**	**94. (C)**
95. (C)	**96. (B)**	**97. (A)**
98. (D)	**99. (B)**	**100. (D)**

Previous Year Paper

GGSIPU – B.Com (H) Entrance Exam 2021*

GENERAL ENGLISH

1. There are ________ views on the issue of giving bonus to employees (choose the most suitable word)

A. independent B. modest
C. aggressive D. divergent

2. What is the synonym of 'Articulate'?

A. Intelligible B. Interesting
C. Promote D. Presumption

3. Change the word 'gold' into a verb:

A. Guilt B. Gild
C. Gilt D. Gilded

4. The Christmas tree was ________ with stars and other beautiful trinkets (fill in the most suitable word).

A. enticed B. endowed
C. adorned D. cast

5. What is the antonym of 'Culminate'?

A. Begin B. Downfall
C. Lead up to D. Destruction

6. What is the synonym of 'Morbid'?

A. Gigantic B. Gruesome
C. Gagged D. Dim

7. ______ refers to a person who has a great admiration for himself/herself.

A. Narcissist B. Iconoclast
C. Numismatist D. Misanthrope

8. The cricket match proved to be a big draw implies:

A. A nail biting contest
B. A game without result
C. A spoilt match
D. A big source of attraction

9. What does the idiom 'to make clean breast of' mean?

A. To gain prominence
B. To praise oneself
C. To destroy something
D. To speak openly about something

10. Change the word 'Book' into an adjective by selecting the appropriate option:

A. Booklet B. Bookish
C. Booking D. Booker

11. Her brother is so ______ that he could not ______ the fork during the salad part of the dinner.

A. uncouth, finish
B. uncouth, use
C. disciplined, ignore
D. well dressed, touch

12. Give one word for 'A building where birds are kept':

A. Apiary B. Aviary
C. Menagerie D. Cache

13. Swati said, 'I bought a dress for my birthday. It costs me an arm and leg.'

A. It is very expensive
B. It is very cheap
C. It is not worth it
D. It is worth it

14. An epilogue is a section at the ______ of a book that suggests a conclusion.

A. Beginning B. Middle
C. Cover page D. End

15. Choose the option which gives the correct meaning for the given idiom
Burn the candle at both ends

A. Perform an act with the utmost inelegance
B. Waste a precious resource through negligence and carelessness

* *Held on 29-08-2021.*

C. To work with diligence and consistency
D. To do more than one ought to and overextend oneself

16. A ______ is a mix of discordant sounds.
A. Cacophony B. Cape
C. Cadence D. Cantankerous

17. Fill in a suitable preposition in the following sentence.
Please don't laugh _____ those beggars
A. In B. To
C. At D. On

18. Out of the three sentences given as A, B and C find out which two or three sentences convey the same meaning:
(*a*) There are only a few good programmes on television that I like watching.
(*b*) There aren't many good programmes on television worth watching.
(*c*) There are several programmes on television that are not worth watching.
A. (*a*)(*b*) B. (*b*)(*c*)
C. (*a*)(*b*)(*c*) D. (*a*)(*c*)

19. As this country has become more ______, industrial and internationalized, it has, like all Western democracies, experienced a necessary increase in the ______ of the executive.
A. urbanized, role
B. objective, wealth
C. synthesized, efficiency
D. civilized, convenience

20. Which of the following pair of words have the same relationship between each other as the given pair of words?
Tree : Sapling
A. Rock : Mountain B. Hut : Building
C. Horse : Foal D. Large : Tiny

21. Choose the correct antonym for the given word.
Ancestor
A. Kin B. Descendant
C. Forefather D. Predecessor

22. Select the word which exhibits the same relationship with each other as the given pair of words:
Pilfer : steal :: ______ : equip
A. return B. damage
C. exercise D. furnish

23. Fill the blank with the correct option '_____ looking for the lost book.'
A. They B. They are
C. Their D. There

24. Give one word for 'A geometrical figure with eight sides'.
A. Parallelogram B. Pentagon
C. Hexagon D. Octagon

25. Choose the option which gives the correct meaning for the given idiom.
Bend over backwards
A. To show unusual talent
B. To go out of the way, especially to please
C. To twist rules according to convenience
D. To join another camp for benefits

LOGICAL REASONING

26. 'WORK' is coded as '4-12-9-16', then how will you code 'WOMAN'?
A. 4-12-14-26-13 B. 4-26-14-13-12
C. 23-12-26-14-13 D. 23-15-13-1-14

27. Find the alternative which will replace the question mark?
DIG : CFB : : JOT : ?
A. KRY B. ILM
C. ILO D. KLO

28. The cricket ball is lighter than the hockey ball and volleyball is lighter than the football. Hockey ball is lighter than the football but heavier than the tennis ball. Which of the following is the heaviest?
A. Hockey ball B. Cricket ball
C. Volley ball D. Football

29. How many M are there in the following letter series which are preceded by D or N?

FDMLKDMNMFTTLOPODMTMLF

A. 1 B. 2

C. 3 D. 4

30. What should come in the place of question mark (?)

A C F J ?

A. Q B. O

C. T D. U

31. Six persons A, B, C, D, E and F are standing in a circle. B is between F and C, A is between E and D, F is to the left of D. Who is between A and F?

A. B B. C

C. D D. E

32. The next term in the series ABD, DGK, HMS, MTB .... is:

A. RUH B. PSK

C. SBL D. NSA

33. Shyam travels 7 km North, then he turns his right and walks 3 km, he again turns to his right and moves 7 km forward. Now in which direction is he from his starting point?

A. North B. South

C. East D. West

34. In the following alphabetical series, how many times L, M, N come in such a way that M is not middle of N and L?

N Z L X M N L M Y N M L Y M L N L M B Z A M X L N Y

A. 4 B. 3

C. 2 D. 1

35. If a rectangle were called a circle, a circle a point, a point a triangle and a triangle a square, the shape of a wheel is:

A. Rectangle B. Circle

C. Point D. Triangle

36. In a row of 40 girls, when Komal was shifted to her left by 4 places, her rank form the left end of the row became 10th. What was the rank of Swati from the end of the row if Swati was 3 places to the right of Komal's original position?

A. 22 B. 23

C. 25 D. 24

37. Sumit writes all the numbers from 0 to 99. The number of times digit 3 will be written is:

A. 18 B. 19

C. 20 D. 21

38. In certain code, 'COVALENT' is code as BWPDUOFM. The code of 'ELEPHANT' will be:

A. QMUBIADH B. MFUIQRTW

C. EPHNTEAS D. QFMFUOBI

39. Among five friends, Ahmed is in the middle by age. Kamal is youngest. Salim is older than Nayan who is younger than Alka and Ahmed. Who is the oldest among them?

A. Kamal B. Salim

C. Alka D. Data inadequate

40. As 'Furniture' is related to 'Table'. In the same way 'Stationary' is related to:

A. Chair B. Office

C. Room D. Pencils

41. The missing term in the series 2, 7, 24, 77, ?, 723 is:

A. 238 B. 432

C. 542 D. 320

42. Identify wrong number in the given series:

864, 420, 200, 96, 40, 16, 6

A. 420 B. 96

C. 400 D. 40

43. Rohan ranks seventh from the top and twenty-sixth from the bottom in a class. How many students are there in the class?

A. 31 B. 32

C. 33 D. 34

44. Dinesh walks 6 km in the West then he turns to his right and moves 8 km, then he turns to his left and moves 9 km then he turns to right and moves 12 km. Now in which direction is he from his starting point and how far?

A. 15 NE B. 35 NE

C. 25 NW D. 45 SE

45. If the following words are arranged in the dictionary order, then which will be the last word?

Dream, Dredge, Dread, Drench, Dreary

A. Drench B. Dread
C. Dreary D. Dream

46. A is sister of B. F is daughter of G. C is mother of B. D is father of C. E is mother of D. A is related to D as:
A. Grand daughter B. Daughter
C. Daughter-in-law D. Sister

47. A person walks 30 m in front and 30 m to the right. Then every time turning to his left, he walks 10, 30 and 30 m respectively. How far is he from his starting point?
A. 40 m B. 30 m
C. 10 m D. 20 m

48. If in a certain code Language ADVENTURE is written as BFYISZBAN then how will COUNTRY be coded in the same language?
A. DPVOUSZ B. DQXRYXF
C. EQWPVTA D. BNTMSQX

49. In a certain code language 'GIVE' is written as 'VIEG' and 'OVER' is written as 'EVRO' How will 'DISK' be written in that same code?
A. SIDK B. KISD
C. KDSI D. SIKD

50. All the six member of a family A, B, C, D, E and F are travelling together. B is the son of C but C is not the mother of B. A and C are a married couple. E is the brother of C. D is the daughter of A. F is the brother of B. How many children does C have?
A. 2
B. 1
C. 3
D. Can't be determined

DATA INTERPRETATION

51. Study the table carefully and answer the question given below. In six years, the number of students taking admissions and leaving from the five different colleges which were founded in 2010 is given below.

	A		B		C		D		E	
College Years	Δ	L	Δ	L	Δ	L	Δ	L	Δ	L
2010	1125	-	1050	-	1200	-	1600	-	1550	-
2011	330	220	450	250	420	230	440	250	350	225
2012	290	210	325	215	400	250	400	260	380	230
2013	345	200	285	210	360	225	395	220	410	220
2014	380	250	300	190	340	240	420	225	440	210
2015	350	230	340	220	410	280	460	240	425	215

Note: Δ - admitted, L - Leaving

What is the average number of students studying in all the five colleges in 2012?
A. Other than the given options
B. 1594
C. 1694
D. 1574

52. Study the following table and answer the question.

Number of candidates appeared and qualified in a competitive examination from different states over the years.

	Year									
State	1997		1998		1999		2000		2001	
	A	Q	A	Q	A	Q	A	Q	A	Q
M	5200	720	8500	980	7400	850	6800	775	9500	1125
N	7500	840	9200	1050	8450	920	9200	980	8800	1020
P	6400	780	8800	1020	7800	890	8750	1010	9750	1250
Q	8100	950	9500	1240	8700	980	9700	1200	8950	995
R	7800	870	7600	940	9800	1350	7600	945	7990	885

Note: A - Appeared, Q - Qualified

In which of the given years the number of candidates appearing from State P have maximum percentage of qualified candidates?
A. 1997 B. 1999
C. 2000 D. 2001

53. The following Pie-chart represents the percentage wise distribution of lecturers in 6 different subjects in a total number of 1600 lecturers and Table represents the ratio of male to female lecturers in various courses.

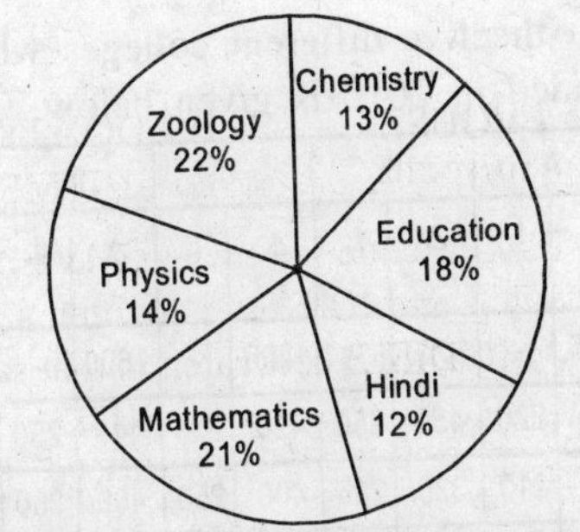

Lectures	Males : Females
Mathematics	3 : 4
Education	5 : 3
Hindi	1 : 3
Chemistry	1 : 7
Physics	9 : 5
Zoology	7 : 9

What is the total number of Male lecturers in the university?

A. 696 B. 702

C. 712 D. 668

54. The following bar graph shows the number of deaths due to fire accidents in the summer of 1992. The figure legend given in the block represents the bar from left to write, e.g., 30th March to 11th April bar on the extreme left shows 140 deaths.

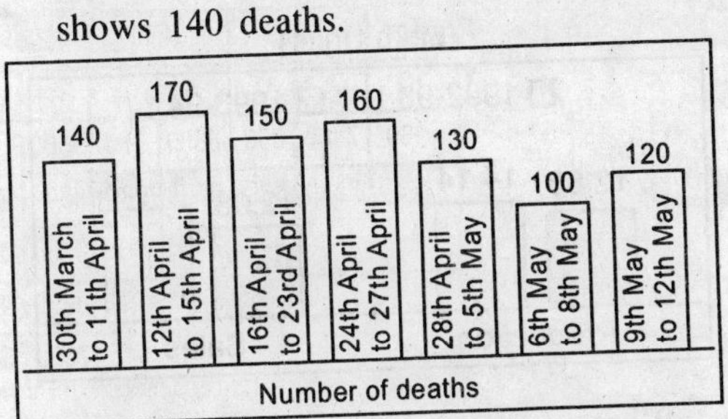

Use this graph to find out average number of deaths per day during the given period.

A. 22.04 B. 22.5

C. 23.09 D. 21.08

55. Study the following table and answer the question.

Number of candidates appeared and qualified in a competitive examination from different states over the years.

State	1997		1998		1999		2000		2001	
	A	Q	A	Q	A	Q	A	Q	A	Q
M	5200	720	8500	980	7400	850	6800	775	9500	1125
N	7500	840	9200	1050	8450	920	9200	980	8800	1020
P	6400	780	8800	1020	7800	890	8750	1010	9750	1250
Q	8100	950	9500	1240	8700	980	9700	1200	8950	995
R	7800	870	7600	940	9800	1350	7600	945	7990	885

Note: A - Appeared, Q - Qualified

Combining the states P and Q together in 1998, what is the percentage of the candidates qualified to that of the candidate appeared?

A. 10.87% B. 11.49%

C. 12.35% D. 12.54%

56. In the following graph describes the distance travelled by a car from City A to City B. which are 425 km apart. Study the graph and the answer the following question.

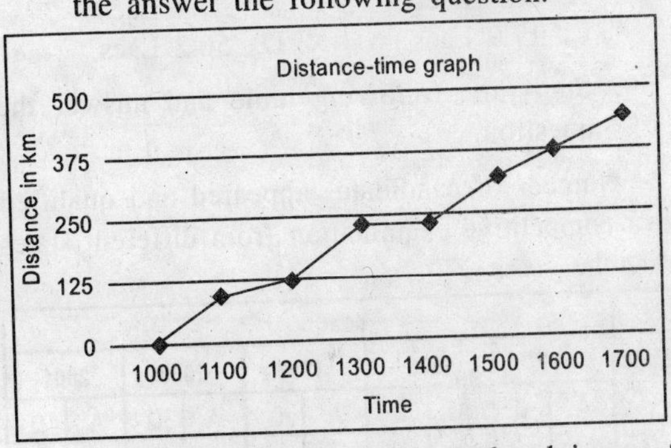

During which hour did the car break journey?

A. 1100 - 1200 hours

B. 1600 - 1700 hours

C. 1400 - 1600 hours

D. 1300 - 1400 hours

57. The result of an exam is given below:

Out of 2000 students who appeared

(*i*) 1300 failed in Telugu

(*ii*) 330 failed in Telugu and Punjabi

(*iii*) 740 failed in Punjabi, 848 failed in Telugu and Bengali

(*iv*) 1160 failed in Bengali, 250 failed in Bengali and Punjabi

The number of students who failed in Telugu or Bengali but not in Punjabi is:

A. 1254
B. 1438
C. 1260
D. 1352

58. The following graph shows the population of four metro cities i.e., Mumbai, Delhi, Chennai, Kolkata in the beginning of the year 2010. If the most populous city has 40% female population, and the least has 35% of female population, then the difference between the male population of these two cities is closest to:

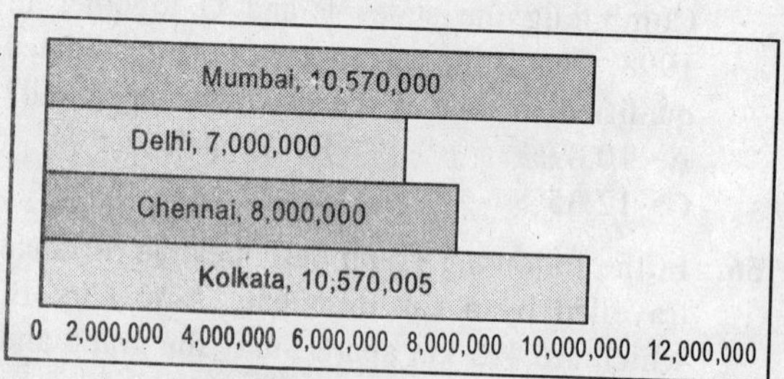

A. 60.5 Lacs
B. 57.4 Lacs
C. 17.9 Lacs
D. 56.2 Lacs

59. Study the following table and answer the question.

Number of candidates appeared and qualified in a competitive examination from different states over the years.

State	Year 1997		1998		1999		2000		2001	
	A	Q	A	Q	A	Q	A	Q	A	Q
M	5200	720	8500	980	7400	850	6800	775	9500	1125
N	7500	840	9200	1050	8450	920	9200	980	8800	1020
P	6400	780	8800	1020	7800	890	8750	1010	9750	1250
Q	8100	950	9500	1240	8700	980	9700	1200	8950	995
R	7800	870	7600	940	9800	1350	7600	945	7990	885

Note: A - Appeared, Q - Qualified

The percentage of total number of qualified candidates to the total number of appeared candidates among the five states in 1999 is?

A. 11.49%
B. 11.84%
C. 12.21%
D. 12.57%

60. Study the table carefully and answer the question given below. In six years, the number of students taking admissions and leaving from the five different colleges which were founded in 2010 is given below.

College Years	A Δ	A L	B Δ	B L	C Δ	C L	D Δ	D L	E Δ	E L
2010	1125	-	1050	-	1200	-	1600	-	1550	-
2011	330	220	450	250	420	230	440	250	350	225
2012	290	210	325	215	400	250	400	260	380	230
2013	345	200	285	210	360	225	395	220	410	220
2014	380	250	300	190	340	240	420	225	440	210
2015	350	230	340	220	410	280	460	240	425	215

Note: Δ - admitted, L - Leaving

What is the difference behaviour the number of students taking admission between 2011 and 2015 in college D and B?

A. 415
B. 395
C. 435
D. Other than the given options

61. The following graph shows the commercial vehicles in Lakh units that includes Ashok Leyland, Telco, Bajaj Tempo and DCM-Toyota.

(Lakh Units)

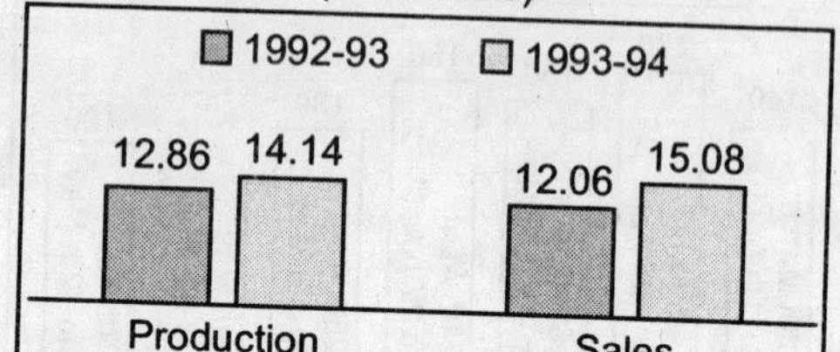

What was the percentage increases in the production of commercial vehicles over the period mentioned?

A. 9%
B. 9.8%
C. 11%
D. 10.5%

62. Observe the pie chart given below and answer the question based on it.

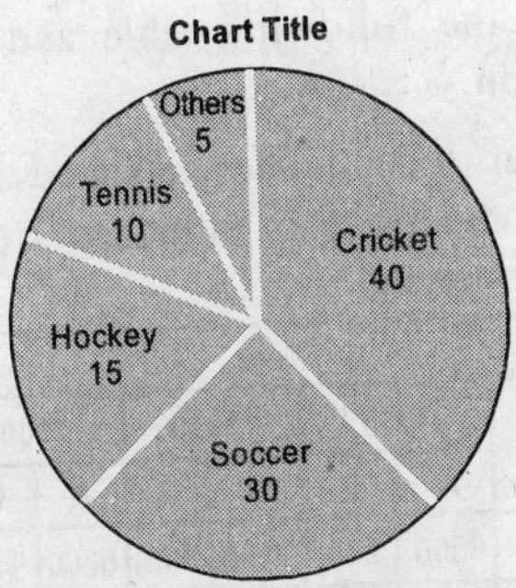

Which of the following is a reasonable conclusion for the given data?

A. 1/30th student voted for soccer

B. Hockey is the least popular sport

C. The number of students who voted for soccer is two times the number of students who voted for tennis

D. Number of students who like tennis is ¼th as those for cricket

63. In the following graph describes the distance travelled by a car from City A to City B, which are 425 km apart. Study the graph and the answer the following question.

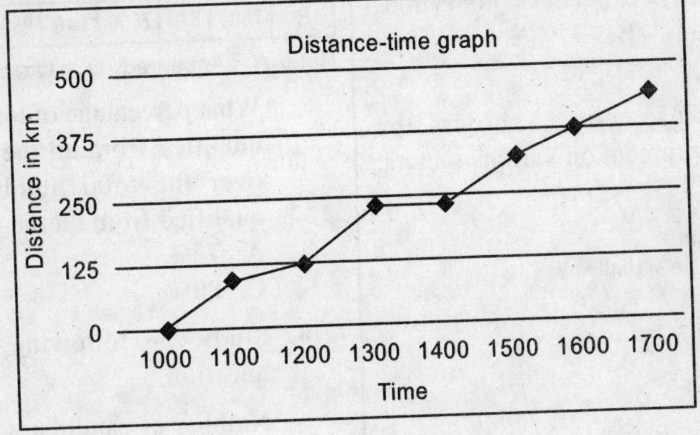

How far did the car go in the 3rd hour?

A. 75 km
B. 100 km
C. 225 km
D. 50 km

64. Observe the pie chart given below and answer the question based on it.

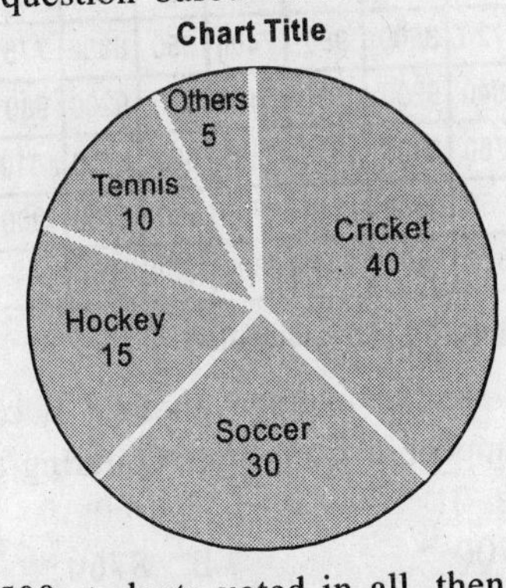

If 500 students voted in all, then how many voted for 'Others' as their favourite sport?

A. 10
B. 20
C. 5
D. 25

65. The following table shows the bank rates for 100 units of various foreign currencies converted to Indian rupees. If Rohit buys 100 Pounds Sterling and 200 UAE Dirham, how much money in Rupees does he need to give to the seller of the foreign currency?

S.No.	Currencies	Selling (₹)	Buying (₹)
1.	Pound Sterling	4759	4723
2.	US Dollar S	3152	3120
3.	Deutsche Mark	1880	1833
4.	Swiss Franc	2123	2060
5.	French Franc	558	543
6.	Swedish Kroner	414	397
7.	Japanese Yen	29.70	29.00
8.	Australian Dollar	2133	2080
9.	U.A.E. Dirham	858	849

A. ₹ 3,382
B. ₹ 6,421
C. ₹ 4,621
D. ₹ 6,382

66. The following pie chart shows the expenditure of government on various sectors.

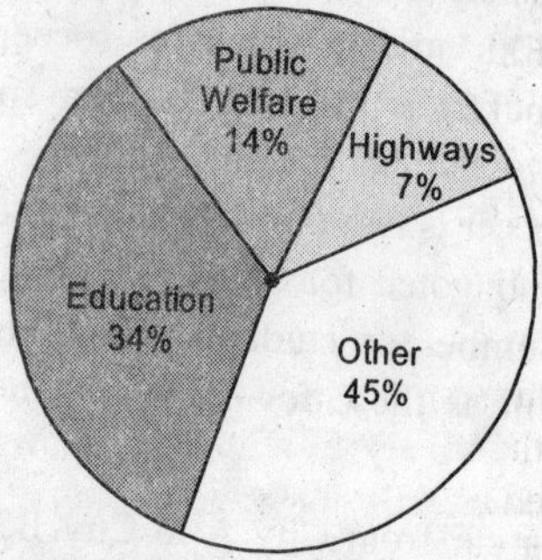

Approximately how many times the amount spending on highways is spent on education?

A. 10 B. 3
C. 5 D. 15

67. The following pie chart shows the expenditure of government on various sectors.

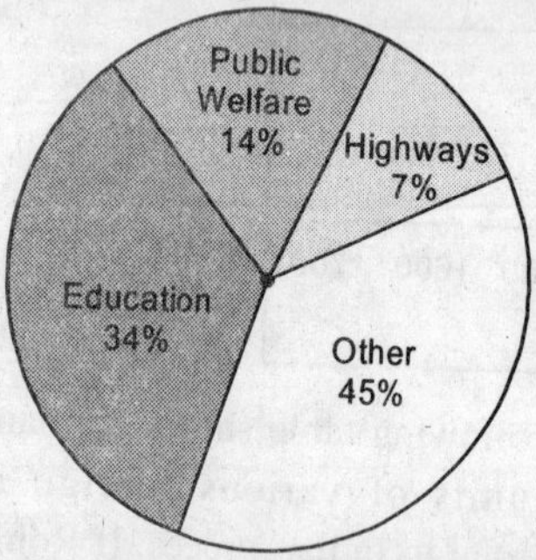

Approximately what fraction of the total expenditures are spent on highways and public welfare combined?

A. 2/5 B. 1/5
C. 1/2 D. 2/3

68. The result of an exam is given below:
Out of 2000 students who appeared
(*i*) 1300 failed in Telugu
(*ii*) 330 failed in Telugu and Punjabi
(*iii*) 740 failed in Punjabi, 848 failed in Telugu and Bengali
(*iv*) 1160 failed in Bengali, 250 failed in Bengali and Punjabi

The number of students who failed in all the three subjects is:

A. 346 B. 140
C. 210 D. 228

69. Study the following table and answer the question.

Number of candidates appeared and qualified in a competitive examination from different states over the years.

State	Year									
	1997		1998		1999		2000		2001	
	A	Q	A	Q	A	Q	A	Q	A	Q
M	5200	720	8500	980	7400	850	6800	775	9500	1125
N	7500	840	9200	1050	8450	920	9200	980	8800	1020
P	6400	780	8800	1020	7800	890	8750	1010	9750	1250
Q	8100	950	9500	1240	8700	980	9700	1200	8950	995
R	7800	870	7600	940	9800	1350	7600	945	7990	885

Note: A - Appeared, Q - Qualified

What percentage of total number of candidates qualified from all the states together in 1997 over the total number of candidates that qualified from all the states together in 1998?

A. 72% B. 77%
C. 80% D. 83%

70. Study the following table and answer the question.

Number of candidates appeared and qualified in a competitive examination from different states over the years.

State	Year									
	1997		1998		1999		2000		2001	
	A	Q	A	Q	A	Q	A	Q	A	Q
M	5200	720	8500	980	7400	850	6800	775	9500	1125
N	7500	840	9200	1050	8450	920	9200	980	8800	1020
P	6400	780	8800	1020	7800	890	8750	1010	9750	1250
Q	8100	950	9500	1240	8700	980	9700	1200	8950	995
R	7800	870	7600	940	9800	1350	7600	945	7990	885

Note: A - Appeared, Q - Qualified

What are the average number of candidates who appeared from State Q during the given years?

A. 8700 B. 8760
C. 8990 D. 8920

71. Observe the pie chart given below and answer the question based on it.

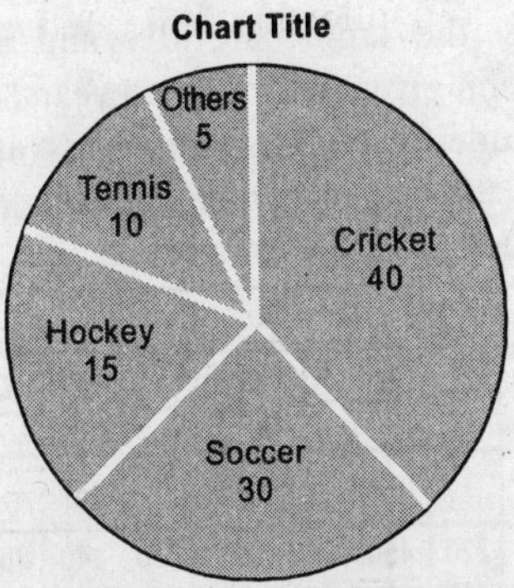

Which sport received 2/5 of the votes?

A. Cricket B. Soccer

C. Hockey D. Tennis

72. In the following question, study the two pie-charts and answer the following question:

April Month's Salary = ₹ 24,000

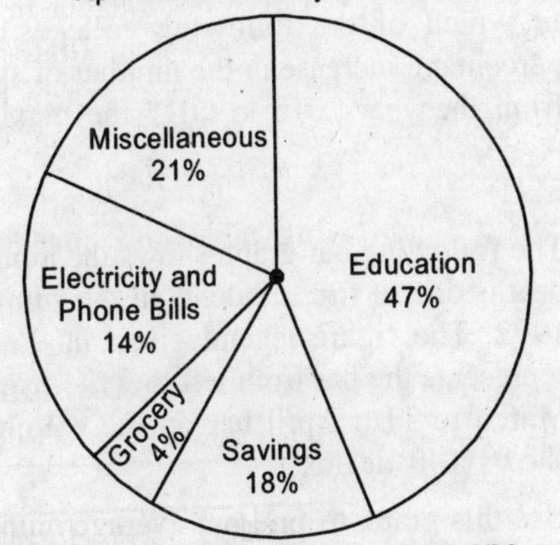

May Month's Salary = ₹ 25,000

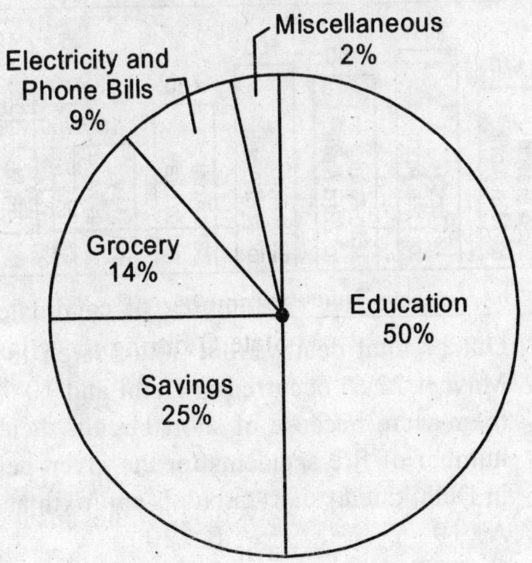

From the salary of May, the amount spent on grocery and electricity are:

A. ₹ 6250, ₹ 3360

B. ₹ 3500, ₹ 5040

C. ₹ 3500, ₹ 2250

D. ₹ 2160, ₹ 480

73. Study the table carefully and answer the question given below. In six years, the number of students taking admissions and leaving from the five different colleges which were founded in 2010 is given below.

	A		B		C		D		E	
College Years	Δ	L	Δ	L	Δ	L	Δ	L	Δ	L
2010	1125	-	1050	-	1200	-	1600	-	1550	-
2011	330	220	450	250	420	230	440	250	350	225
2012	290	210	325	215	400	250	400	260	380	230
2013	345	200	285	210	360	225	395	220	410	220
2014	380	250	300	190	340	240	420	225	440	210
2015	350	230	340	220	410	280	460	240	425	215

Note: Δ - admitted, L - Leaving

The number of students leaving college from the year 2010 to 2015 is approximately what per cent of the number of students taking admission in the same college and during the same year?

A. 37% B. 43%

C. 39% D. 41%

74. The result of an exam is given below: Out of 2000 students who appeared

(*i*) 1300 failed in Telugu

(*ii*) 330 failed in Telugu and Punjabi

(*iii*) 740 failed in Punjabi, 848 failed in Telugu and Bengali

(*iv*) 1160 failed in Bengali, 250 failed in Bengali and Punjabi

The number of students who failed in Telugu but not in Bengali is:

A. 452 B. 898

C. 1502 D. 948

75. The result of an exam is given below: Out of 2000 students who appeared

(*i*) 1300 failed in Telugu

(*ii*) 330 failed in Telugu and Punjabi

(*iii*) 740 failed in Punjabi, 848 failed in Telugu and Bengali
(*iv*) 1160 failed in Bengali, 250 failed in Bengali and Punjabi

The number of students who failed in Bengali but not in Punjabi is:

A. 910 B. 764
C. 772 D. 904

76. The table shows the distribution of weekly income of 49 workers in a company.

Weekly Income (₹)	58	59	60	61	62	63	64	65	66
No. of Workers	2	3	6	15	10	5	4	3	1

First Quartile $(Q_1) = \left(\frac{N+1}{4}\right)$ th item

Coefficient of Quartile deviation (Q.D.)

$$= \left(\frac{Q_3 - Q_1}{Q_2 + Q_1}\right)$$

Calculate the collective income during the first and third quartile.

A. 120 B. 122
C. 124 D. 126

77. Study the following table and answer the question.

Number of candidates appeared and qualified in a competitive examination from different states over the years.

State	Year									
	1997		1998		1999		2000		2001	
	A	Q	A	Q	A	Q	A	Q	A	Q
M	5200	720	8500	980	7400	850	6800	775	9500	1125
N	7500	840	9200	1050	8450	920	9200	980	8800	1020
P	6400	780	8800	1020	7800	890	8750	1010	9750	1250
Q	8100	950	9500	1240	8700	980	9700	1200	8950	995
R	7800	870	7600	940	9800	1350	7600	945	7990	885

Note: A - Appeared, Q - Qualified

What is the percentage of candidates qualifying from State N for all the years together, over the candidates appearing from State N during all the years together?

A. 11.15% B. 11.47%
C. 12.16% D. 12.36%

78. Study the table carefully and answer the question given below. In six years, the number of students taking admissions and leaving from the five different colleges which were founded in 2010 is given below.

	A		B		C		D		E	
College Years	Δ	L	Δ	L	Δ	L	Δ	L	Δ	L
2010	1125	-	1050	-	1200	-	1600	-	1550	-
2011	330	220	450	250	420	230	440	250	350	225
2012	290	210	325	215	400	250	400	260	380	230
2013	345	200	285	210	360	225	395	220	410	220
2014	380	250	300	190	340	240	420	225	440	210
2015	350	230	340	220	410	280	460	240	425	215

Note: Δ - admitted, L - Leaving

In which of the following colleges, is the percentage increase in the number of students from the year 2010 to 2015 the maximum?

A. D B. A
C. B D. C

79. The following bar graph shows the number of deaths due to fire accidents in the summer of 1992. The figure legend given in the block represents the bar from left to write, e.g., 30th March to 11th April bar on the extreme left shows 140 deaths.

Use this graph to find out average number of deaths per day during the given period.

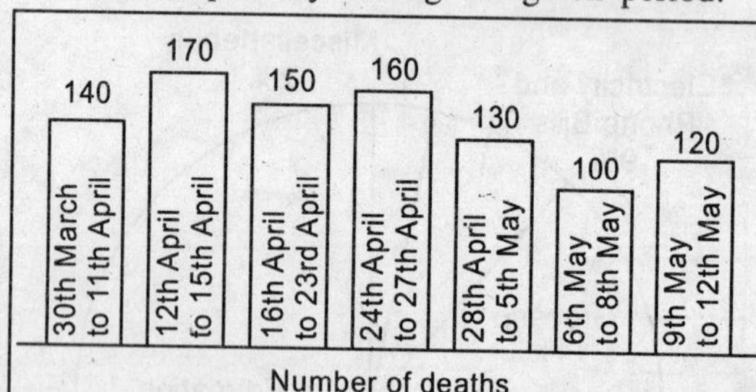

Out of total deaths from 30th March to 8th May, if 22 % occurred in Delhi and 10 % of them were because of short circuit, then the number of fire accidents for the given period in Delhi due to short circuit is approximately?

A. 19 B. 20
C. 22 D. 23

80. In the following graph describes the distance travelled by a car from City A to City B. which are 425 km apart. Study the graph and the answer the following question.

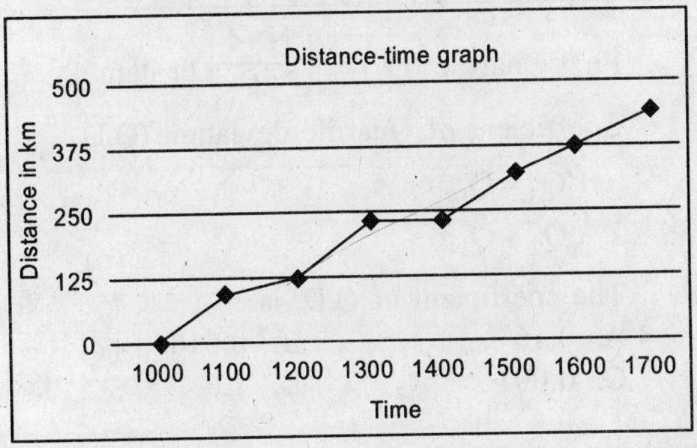

During which hour(s) the speed of the car was maximum?

A. 1100 - 1200 hours
B. 1400 - 1600 hours
C. 1200 - 1300 hours
D. 1600 - 1700 hours

81. Study the table carefully and answer the question given below. In six years, the number of students taking admissions and leaving from the five different colleges which were founded in 2010 is given below.

College Years	A		B		C		D		E	
	Δ	L	Δ	L	Δ	L	Δ	L	Δ	L
2010	1125	-	1050	-	1200	-	1600	-	1550	-
2011	330	220	450	250	420	230	440	250	350	225
2012	290	210	325	215	400	250	400	260	380	230
2013	345	200	285	210	360	225	395	220	410	220
2014	380	250	300	190	340	240	420	225	440	210
2015	350	230	340	220	410	280	460	240	425	215

Note: Δ - admitted, L - Leaving

What was the number of students studying in college B in 2014?

A. 1555
B. Other than the given options
C. 1445
D. 1545

82. The result of an exam is given below:
Out of 2000 students who appeared

(*i*) 1300 failed in Telugu
(*ii*) 330 failed in Telugu and Punjabi
(*iii*) 740 failed in Punjabi, 848 failed in Telugu and Bengali
(*iv*) 1160 failed in Bengali, 250 failed in Bengali and Punjabi

The number of students who failed in Punjabi but not in Telugu is:

A. 320 B. 178
C. 212 D. 410

83. The following graph shows the commercial vehicles in Lakh units that includes Ashok Leyland, Telco, Bajaj Tempo and DCM-Toyota.

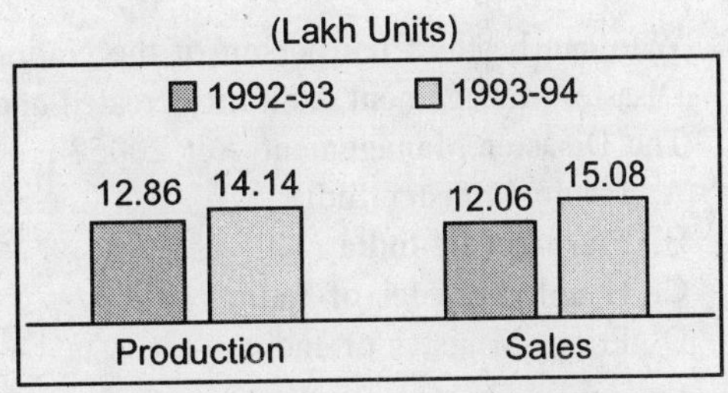

What was the percentage increase in the sales of commercial vehicles over the period mentioned?

A. 33.33% B. 16%
C. 25% D. 22.85%

84. The following Pie-chart represents the percentage wise distribution of lecturers in 6 different subjects in a total number of 1600 lecturers and Table represents the ratio of male to female lecturers in various courses.

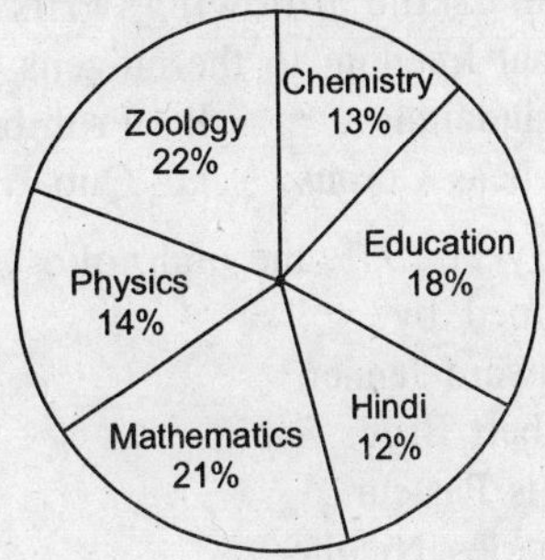

Lectures	Males : Females
Mathematics	3 : 4
Education	5 : 3
Hindi	1 : 3
Chemistry	1 : 7
Physics	9 : 5
Zoology	7 : 9

What is the ratio of the number of female lecturers in Physics to the number of male lecturers in Mathematics?

A. 3 : 7 B. 2 : 9
C. 5 : 9 D. 5 : 3

85. The table shows the distribution of weekly income of 49 workers in a company.

Weekly Income (₹)	58	59	60	61	62	63	64	65	66
No. of Workers	2	3	6	15	10	5	4	3	1

First Quartile $(Q_1) = \left(\frac{N+1}{4}\right)$ th item

Coefficient of Quartile deviation (Q.D.)

$= \left(\frac{Q_3 - Q_1}{Q_2 + Q_1}\right)$

The coefficient of Q.D. is?

A. 0.16 B. 0.016
C. 0.0016 D. 1.6

GENERAL AWARENESS

86. Who can be the Chairperson of the National Disaster Management Authority created under The Disaster Management Act 2005?

A. Home Minister India
B. President of India
C. Health Minister of India
D. Prime Minister of India

87. Identify the 5 states of India that shares their boundaries with Nepal?

A. Uttar Pradesh, Bihar, Jharkhand, West Bengal & Sikkim
B. Uttarakhand, Uttar Pradesh, Bihar, West Bengal & Sikkim
C. Uttar Pradesh, Uttarakhand, Bihar, Jharkhand & West Bengal
D. Uttarakhand, Bihar, Jharkhand, West Bengal & Sikkim

88. Which of the following writs guarantee personal freedom to the citizens of India?

A. Mandamus B. Prohibition
C. Habeas Corpus D. Quo-Warranto

89. In the year 1955, the oral polio vaccine was developed by?

A. Edward Jenner
B. Albert Bruce Sabin
C. Lois Pasteur
D. Charles Nicolle

90. Who among the following was the immediate successor of Guru Nanak?

A. Guru Angad B. Guru Arjun
C. Guru Amardas D. Guru Ramdas

91. Which one of the following is not correct for Prokaryotic cells?

A. Prokaryotic cells contain a nucleus and many organelles
B. Prokaryotic cells are morphologically most primitive
C. Prokaryotic cells are devoid of membrane bound organelles
D. Prokaryotic cells are represented by bacteria

92. A revolution in wireless communication began in the first decade of the 20th century with the pioneering developments in radio communications by?

A. William O'Shaughnessy
B. Guglielmo Marconi
C. Charles Wheatstone
D. Vladimir Zworykin

93. Which couple won the Nobel Prize for Physics in 1903 for their joint research on radiation. The lady was the first woman to get a Nobel Prize?

A. Mark Waugh & Steve Waugh
B. Wilbur Wright & Orville Wright

C. Pierre Curie & Marie Curie
D. Stan Laurel & Bony Laurel

94. _______ is a mystical form of Islam, which believes in a philosophy of love and universal oneness.

A. Judaism B. Bahai
C. Sufism D. Atheism

95. Full form of SAARC is:

A. The South Asian Association for Regional Cooperation
B. The South American Association for Regional Cooperation
C. The Seoul and American for Regional Cooperation
D. The South Argentina Association for Regional Cooperation

96. Which among the following constitutional amendment act, reduced the voting age from 21 years to 18 years for the Lok Sabha and state legislative assembly elections?

A. 59th Amendment Act
B. 60th Amendment Act
C. 61st Amendment Act
D. 62nd Amendment Act

97. Radio Broadcasting was renamed as ALL INDIA RADIO in the year:

A. 1936 B. 1962
C. 1947 D. 1957

98. Study of reptiles and amphibians is known as:

A. Horology B. Edaphology
C. Emetology D. Herpetology

99. Consider the following pairs [Caves-location]

1. Bhimbetka Caves – Madhya Pradesh
2. Bagh Caves – Uttarakhand
3. Udayagiri Caves – Odisha
4. Elephanta Caves – Maharashtra
5. Barabar Caves – Bihar

Which of the following is/are correctly matched?

A. 1, 2, 3 & 4 only B. 2, 3, 4 & 5 only
C. 1, 3, 4 & 5 only D. 1, 2, 4 & 5 only

100. Namdhapa National Park is the largest National park in North East India and it is home to the common Indian leopard, snow leopard, clouded leopard and tiger is located in the State of?

A. Meghalaya B. Mizoram
C. Arunachal Pradesh D. Nagaland

ANSWERS

1	2	3	4	5	6	7	8	9	10
C	A	C	C	A	B	A	D	D	B
11	**12**	**13**	**14**	**15**	**16**	**17**	**18**	**19**	**20**
B	B	A	D	D	A	C	C	A	D
21	**22**	**23**	**24**	**25**	**26**	**27**	**28**	**29**	**30**
B	D	B	D	B	A	C	D	D	B
31	**32**	**33**	**34**	**35**	**36**	**37**	**38**	**39**	**40**
C	C	C	A	C	D	C	D	B	D
41	**42**	**43**	**44**	**45**	**46**	**47**	**48**	**49**	**50**
A	B	B	C	A	A	C	B	D	C
51	**52**	**53**	**54**	**55**	**56**	**57**	**58**	**59**	**60**
B	D	A	A	C	D	D	C	B	D
61	**62**	**63**	**64**	**65**	**66**	**67**	**68**	**69**	**70**
B	D	C	D	B	C	C	D	C	C
71	**72**	**73**	**74**	**75**	**76**	**77**	**78**	**79**	**80**
A	C	A	A	A	C	A	B	A	C

81	82	83	84	85	86	87	88	89	90
D	D	C	C	B	D	B	C	B	A
91	**92**	**93**	**94**	**95**	**96**	**97**	**98**	**99**	**100**
A	B	C	C	A	C	A	D	C	C

EXPLANATORY ANSWERS

26. W O R K is coded as

W → 4, O → 12, R → 9, K → 16

W O M A N will be coded as

W → 4, O → 12, M → 14, A → 26, N → 13

27.

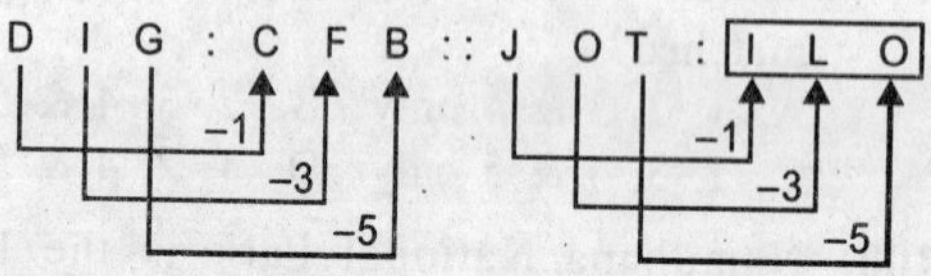

Hence, ILO will be written at the place of question mark.

28. Clearly, Football is the heaviest.

29.

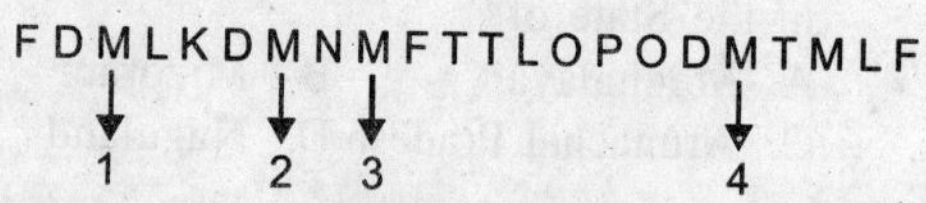

There are 4 times M has come in the given letter series preceded by D or N.

30.

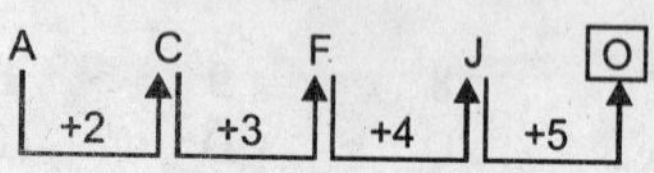

Hence, O should come at the place of question mark.

31.

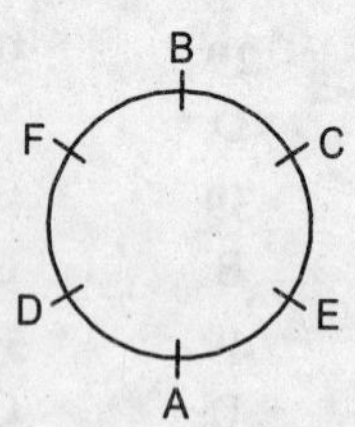

Clearly, D is standing between A and F.

32.

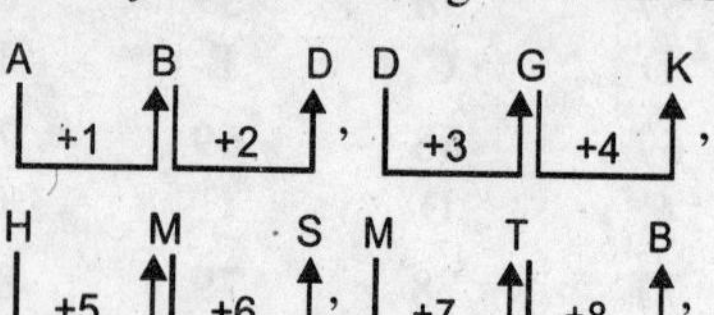

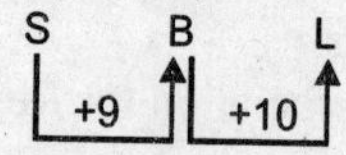

Hence, the next term in the given series will come SBL.

33.

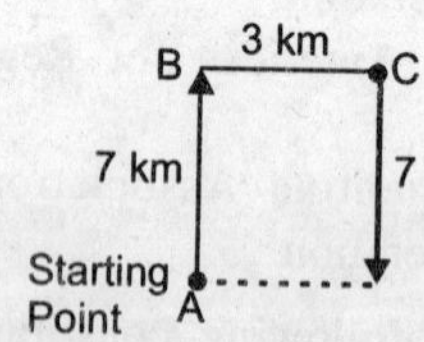

Shyam in the East direction from his starting point.

34.

Hence, L, M, N have come 4 times.

35. Wheel like a circle and circle denoted by a point.

Hence, Option (C) is correct

36.

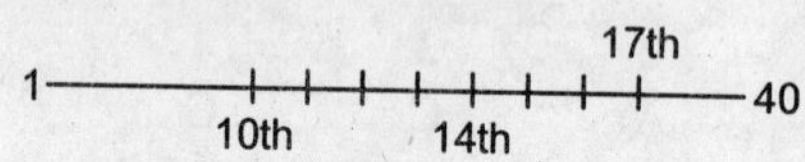

Komal's rank from left be 10th

Komal's original rank from left be 14th

Swati's rank from left be 17th

∴ Swati's rank from right be 40 – 16 = 24th

Hence, Option (D) is correct.

37. Sumit writes 0 to 99 numbers.

1 to 10	3	one time
11 to 20	13	one time
21 to 30	23, 30	two times
31 to 40		10 times
41 to 50	43	one time
51 to 60	53	one time
61 to 70	63	one time
71 to 80	73	one time

81 to 90   83   one time
91 to 99   93   one time
The number of 20 times digit 3 will be written from 0 to 99.
Hence, Option (C) is correct.

38.
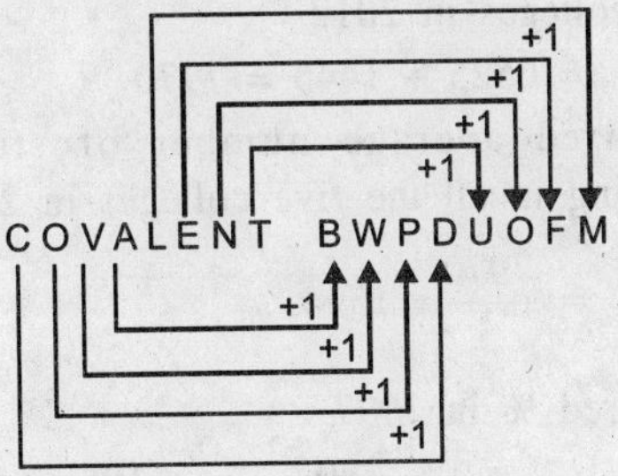

Similarly,
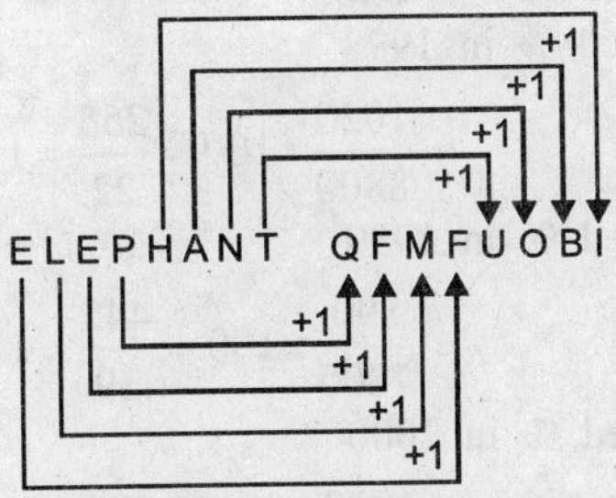

Hence, Option (D) is correct.

39.
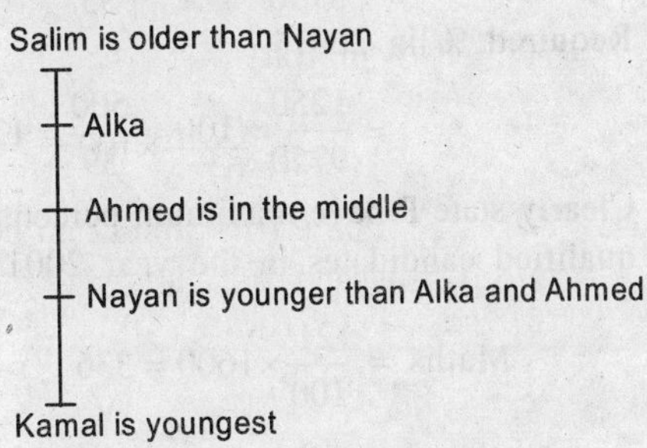

∴ Salim is the oldest among them
Hence, Option (B) is correct

40. Furniture is related to Table, in the same way stationary is related to pencils.
Hence, Option (D) is correct.

41.
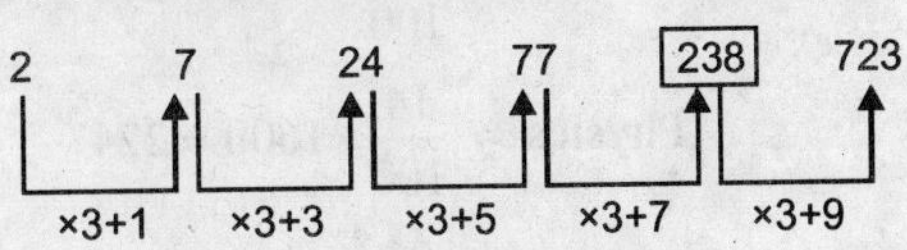

Hence, 238 will come at the place of question mark.

42.
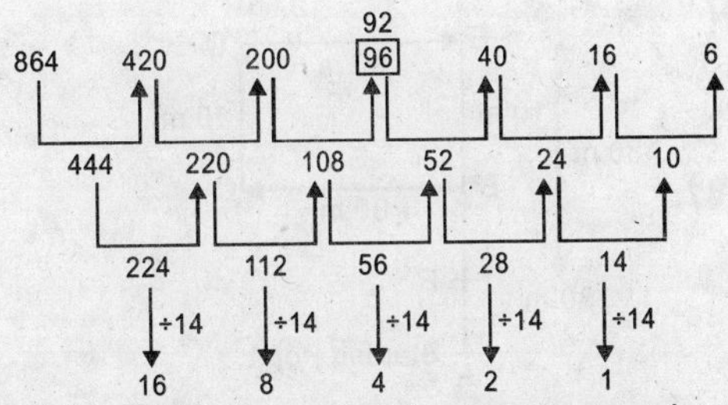

Hence, Wrong number in the given series is 96.

43.
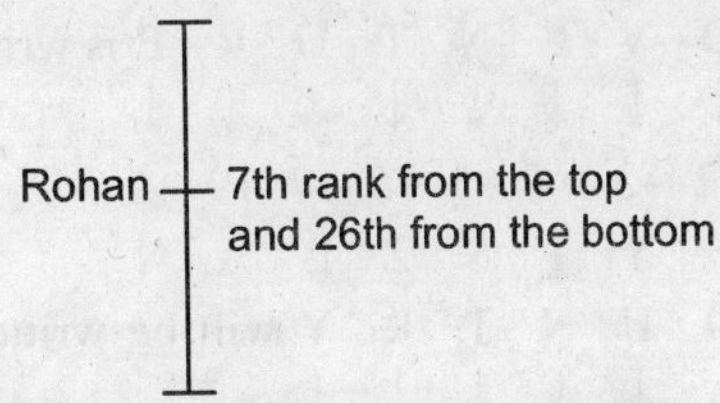

Total = 26 + 6 = 32
Hence, there are 32 students in the class
Hence, Option (B) is correct.

44.
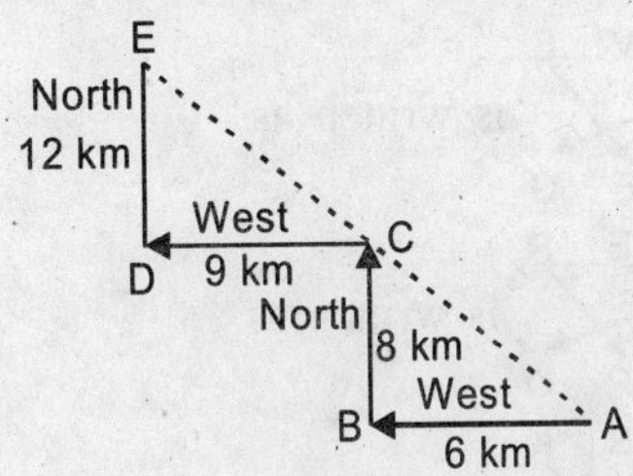

Dinesh is in North-West direction from his starting point.
Distance from the starting point
= EC + AC
= 15 + 10
= 25 km.

45. Dream, Dredge, Dread, Drench, Dreary
The last word will be Drench.
Hence, Option (A) is correct.

46.
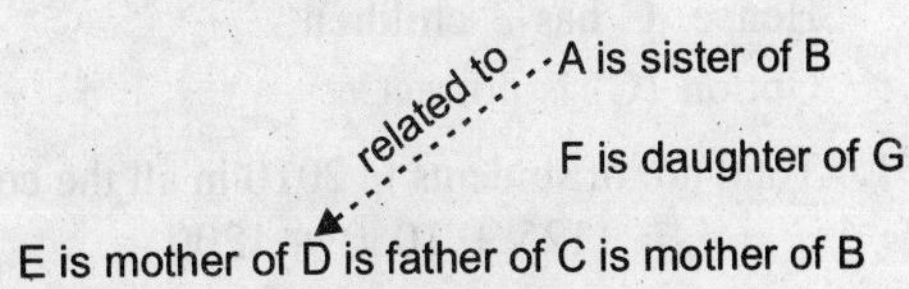

Clearly, A is grand daughter of D
Hence, Option (A) is correct.

47. 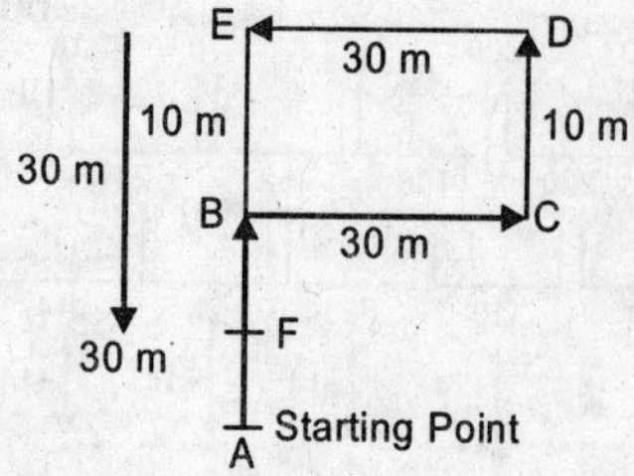

Distance from starting point = AE – EF

= 40 – 30 = 10 m.

48. A D V E N T U R E is written as

↓ ↓ ↓ ↓ ↓ ↓ ↓ ↓ ↓

+1 +2 +3 +4 +5 +6 +7 +9 +9

B F Y I S Z B A N

C O U N T R Y will be written as

↓ ↓ ↓ ↓ ↓ ↓ ↓

+1 +2 +3 +4 +5 +6 +7

D Q X R Y X F

Hence, Option (B) is correct.

49. 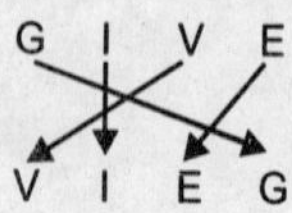

is written as

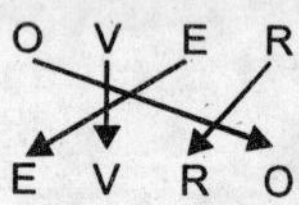

is written as

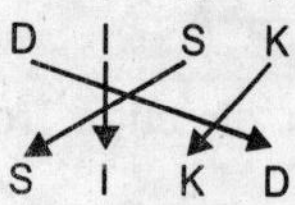

will be written as

50. 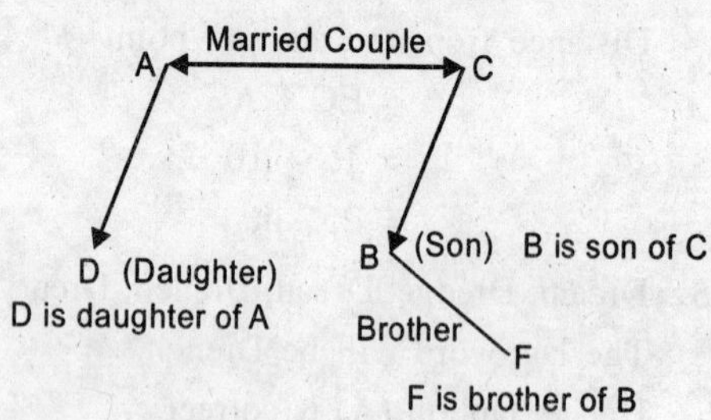

Hence, C has 3 children.

Option (C) is correct.

51. Total no. of students in 2010 in all the colleges

= 1125 + 1050 + 1200 + 1600 + 1550 = 6525

Total no. of students in 2011 and 2012 in all colleges

= 620 – 430 + 775 – 465 + 820 – 480 + 840 – 510 + 730 – 455

= 190 + 310 + 340 + 330 + 275

= 1445

Total number of students studying in all the five colleges in 2012

= 6525 + 1445 = 7970

Required average number of students studying in all the five colleges in 2012

$$= \frac{7970}{5} = 1594.$$

52. Required % in 1997

$$= \frac{780}{6400} \times 100 = \frac{195}{16} = 12.18\%$$

Required % in 1998

$$= \frac{1020}{8800} \times 100 = \frac{255}{22} = 11.59\%$$

Required % in 1999

$$= \frac{890}{7800} \times 100 = \frac{445}{39} = 11.41\%$$

Required % in 2000

$$= \frac{1010}{8750} \times 100 = \frac{404}{35} = 11.54\%$$

Required % in 2001

$$= \frac{1250}{9750} \times 100 = \frac{500}{39} = 12.82\%$$

Clearly state P have maximum percentage of qualified candidates in the year 2001.

53.

$$\text{Maths} = \frac{21}{100} \times 1600 = 336$$

$$\text{Education} = \frac{18}{100} \times 1600 = 288$$

$$\text{Hindi} = \frac{12}{100} \times 1600 = 192$$

$$\text{Chemistry} = \frac{13}{100} \times 1600 = 208$$

$$\text{Physics} = \frac{14}{100} \times 1600 = 224$$

$$\text{Zoology} = \frac{22}{100} \times 1600 = 352$$

Number of male lecturers in Maths

$$= \frac{3}{7} \times 336 = 3 \times 48 = 144$$

Number of male lecturers in Education

$$= \frac{5}{8} \times 288 = 5 \times 36 = 180$$

Number of male lecturers in Hindi

$$= \frac{1}{4} \times 192 = 48$$

Number of male lecturers in Chemistry

$$= \frac{1}{8} \times 208 = 26$$

Number of male lecturers in Physics

$$= \frac{9}{14} \times 224 = 144$$

Number of male lecturers in Zoology

$$= \frac{7}{16} \times 352 = 154$$

Total number of male lecturers in the university

= 144 + 180 + 48 + 26 + 144 + 154 = 696.

54.

	No. of death	No. of days
30th March to 11th April:	140	13
12th April to 15th April:	120	4
16th April to 23rd April:	150	8
24th April to 27th April:	160	4
28th April to 5th May:	130	8
6th May to 8th May:	100	3
9th May to 12th May:	120	4

Total no. of death

= 140 + 120 + 150 + 160 + 130 + 100 + 120 = 970

Total no. of days

= 13 + 4 + 8 + 4 + 8 + 3 + 4

= 44 days

∴ Average no. of death per day during the given period

$$= \frac{970}{44} = 22.04.$$

55. In 1998, total no. of appeared candidates in state P and Q = 8800 + 9500 = 18300

Total no. of qualified candidates in state P and Q = 1020 + 1240 = 2260

$$\text{Required\%} = \frac{2260}{18300} \times 100 = \frac{2260}{183}$$

= 12.349%

= 12.35%

56. Clearly, 1300 to 1400 hours the car had broken journey.

58. No. of female in Kolkata

$$= \frac{40}{100} \times 10570005 = 4228002$$

No. of female in Delhi

$$= \frac{35}{100} \times 7000000 = 2450000$$

No. of male in Kolkata

= 10570005 − 4228002

= 6342003

No. of male in Delhi

= 7000000 − 2450000

= 4550000

Required difference

= 6342003 − 4550000

= 1792003 = 17.9 lacs.

59. In 1999 Total no. of appeared candidates

= 42150

Total no. of qualified candidates = 4990

$$\text{Required\%} = \frac{4990}{42150} \times 100$$

$$= \frac{49900}{4215}$$

$$= \frac{9980}{843} = 11.838\%$$

= 11.84%.

63. Car travelled in 3rd hour = 225 km.

64. $5\% \text{ of } 500 = \frac{5}{100} \times 500 = 25.$

65. Rohit buys 100 ponds = ₹ 4723

Rohit buys 200 U.A.E. = ₹ 849 × 2 = ₹ 1698

∴ Rohit has paid to the seller of the foreign currency

= ₹ 4723 + ₹ 1698 = ₹ 6421.

66. Let x times more amount spend on Education.

7% highways × x = 34% of education

$$\therefore \quad x = \frac{34}{7} = 4.857 = 5$$

Hence, 5 times money spend on education.

67. $\frac{7}{14} = \frac{1}{2}$.

68. $n(A \cup B \cup C) = n(A) + n(B) + n(C) - n(A \cap B) - n(B \cap C) - n(C \cap A) + n(A \cap B \cap C)$

$2000 = 1300 + 740 + 1160 - 330 - 848 - 250 + n(A \cap B \cap C)$

$\Rightarrow 2000 = 3200 - 1428 + n(A \cap B \cap C)$

$\Rightarrow 2000 + 1428 - 3200 = n(A \cap B \cap C)$

$\Rightarrow 3428 - 3200 = n(A \cap B \cap C)$

$\Rightarrow n(A \cap B \cap C) = 228.$

69. Total candidates qualified in all the states in 1997

= 720 + 840 + 780 + 950 + 872 = 4160

Total candidates qualified in all the states in 1998

= 980 + 1050 + 1020 + 1240 + 940 = 5230

$$\text{Required\%} = \frac{4160 \times 100}{5230}$$

$$= \frac{41600}{523} = 79.54\% = 80\%$$

Hence, Option (C) is correct.

70. Total numer of candidates appeared from state Q during the given years

= 8100 + 9500 + 8700 + 9700 + 8950 = 44950

$$\text{Average} = \frac{44950}{5} = 8990$$

Hence, Option (C) is correct.

71.

$$\text{Cricket} = \frac{40}{100} = \frac{2}{5}.$$

$$\text{Soccer} = \frac{30}{100} = \frac{3}{10}$$

$$\text{Hockey} = \frac{15}{100} = \frac{3}{20}$$

$$\text{Tennis} = \frac{10}{100} = \frac{1}{10}$$

Hence, Option (A) is correct.

72. From the salary of May the amount spent on grocery

$$= \frac{14}{100} \times 25000$$

= ₹ 3500

Amount spent on electricity

$$= \frac{9}{100} \times 25000$$

= ₹ 2250

Hence, Option (C) is correct.

73. Total no. of students who leaved from all the colleges

= 1110 + 1085 + 1225 + 1195 + 1100 = 5715

Total no. of students who taking admission in all the colleges

= 2820 + 2750 + 3130 + 3715 + 3555 = 15970

$$\text{Required\%} = \frac{5715}{15970} \times 100$$

$$= \frac{57150}{1597} = 35.785\%$$

= 36% which is the not in the given option

= 37% (nearest to 36%).

74. The number of students who failed in Telugu but not in Bengali

= 1300 − 848 = 452.

75. The number of students who failed in Bengali but not in Punjabi

= 1160 − 250 = 910.

76.

X	f	cf
58	2	2
59	3	5
60	6	11
61	15	26
62	10	36
63	5	41
64	4	45
65	3	48
66	1	49

$$Q_1 = \left(\frac{n+1}{4}\right) = \frac{49+1}{4} = \frac{50}{4}$$

$= 12.5$ Just greater than in

$Cf = 26$ corresponding in $x = 61$

$\therefore$ $Q_1 = 61$

$Q_2 = 62$

$Q_3 = 63$

$$\text{Co-efficient of (Q.D.)} = \frac{Q_3 - Q_1}{Q_3 + Q_1} = \frac{2}{124}$$

$\therefore$ Collective income $= Q_3 + Q_1$

$= 63 + 61 = 124.$

77. Number of qualifying candidates from state N during all the years

$= 840 + 1050 + 920 + 980 + 1020 = 4810$

Number of appearing candidates from state N during all the years

$= 7500 + 9200 + 8450 + 9200 + 8800 = 43150$

$$\text{Required\%} = \frac{4810}{43150} \times 100 = \frac{9620}{863}$$

$= 11.147\% = 11.15\%.$

78. Percentage increase in college A

$$= \frac{785}{1125} \times 100 = \frac{628}{9}\% = 69.77\%$$

Percentage increase in college B

$$= \frac{615}{1050} \times 100 = \frac{410}{7} = 58.57\%$$

Percentage increase in college C

$$= \frac{705}{1200} \times 100 = \frac{235}{4} = 58.75\%$$

Percentage increase in college D

$$= \frac{920}{1600} \times 100 = \frac{230}{4} = 57.5\%$$

Percentage increase in college E

$$= \frac{905}{1550} \times 100 = \frac{1810}{31} = 58.38\%$$

Clearly, percentage increase in college A is maximum.

79. Total no. of death from 30th March to 8th May

$= 140 + 170 + 150 + 160 + 130 + 100 = 850$

$$22\% \text{ of } 850 = \frac{22}{100} \times 850 = 11 \times 17 = 187$$

$$10\% \text{ of } 187 = \frac{10}{100} \times 187 = 18.7 \cong 19$$

Hence, the number of fire accidents in Delhi due to short circuit = 19.

80. Speed of the car was maximum during 1200 – 1300 hrs because in this period the distance covered 225 – 125 = 100 km which is maxi-mum distance given interval of time.

81. The number of students taking admissions in college B from 2010 to 2014

$= 1050 + 450 + 325 + 285 + 300 = 2410$

The number of students leaving college B from 2010 to 2014

$= 250 + 215 + 210 + 190 = 865$

$\therefore$ The number of students studying in college B in 2014

$= 2410 - 865 = 1545.$

82. The number of students who failed in Punjabi but not in Telugu

$= 740 - 330 = 410.$

83. Increase in the sales of commercial vehicles

$= 15.08 - 12.06 = 3.02$

$$\text{Required\% increase} = \frac{3.02}{12.06} \times 100$$

$$= \frac{30200}{1206} = 25\%.$$

84. No. of lecturers in Physics

$$= \frac{14}{100} \times 1600$$
$$= 224$$

No. of female lecturers in Physics

$$= \frac{5}{14} \times 224$$
$$= 80$$

No. of lecturers in Mathematics

$$= \frac{21}{100} \times 1600$$
$$= 336$$

No. of male lecturers in Mathematics

$$= \frac{3}{7} \times 336$$
$$= 144$$

Required ratio $= \frac{80}{144} = \frac{5}{9} = 5:9.$

85.

X	*f*	*cf*
58	2	2
59	3	5
60	6	11
61	15	26
62	10	36
63	5	41
64	4	45
65	3	48
66	1	49

First quartile $Q_1 = \frac{(N+1)}{4}$th term

$= \frac{50}{4}$th term $= 12.5$

Clearly, $Q_1 = 61, Q_2 = 62, Q_3 = 63$

$\therefore$ Co-efficient of Q.D. $= \frac{Q_3 - Q_1}{Q_3 + Q_1} = \frac{63-61}{63+61}$

$$= \frac{2}{124} = \frac{1}{62} = 0.016.$$

Previous Year Paper

GGSIPU – B.Com (H) Entrance Exam 2020*

1. D introduces C saying. He is the husband of the granddaughter of the father of my father. How is C related to D?

A. Uncle B. Brother-in-law
C. Brother D. Cousin

2. Find the missing term in the following series:

1, 2, 9, 28, ____, 126, 217

A. 65 B. 56
C. 271 D. 172

3. If a heavy-load trailer travels 7 miles in 1 hour and 10 minutes. What is its speed in miles per hour?

A. 6 B. 8
C. 6.5 D. 8.5

4. Aditi travels 10 km towards North. From there, she travels 4 km towards South. Then she travels 2.5 km towards East. How far is she from the starting point?

A. 6.5 km B. 6 km
C. 8.5 km D. 12.5 km

5. Salman starts from his house, travels a distance of 6 meters westwards, then travels a distance of 5 meters northwards, then a distance of 5 meter eastwards, and then a distance of 5 meter southwards. What is his distance from his house presently?

A. 1 meter B. 2 meter
C. 3 meter D. 4 meter

6. Choose the word which is not a similar in meaning of the given word.

Baffle

A. Enlighten B. Puzzle
C. Mystify D. Confuse

7. If X % Y = X + Y + XY – 10, then 10 % 12 is equal to:

A. 130 B. 132
C. 134 D. 142

8. Choose the correct order of the sentences marked (*a*), (*b*), (*c*) and (*d*) to form a logical paragraph.

(*a*) On the other hand, in Gita, he is the guru, the fountainhead of knowledge

(*b*) Lord Krishna is a multifaceted personality.

(*c*) He is a friend to the Pandavas and Draupadi: a spouse to Rukmini, with an equal reciprocation of love and respect; a lover-most pure and intense-to Radha.

(*d*) On the one hand, in Mahabharata, he is the portrayed as a politician and diplomat.

(*e*) He is a friend, a spouse and a lover - all in one.

A. *adbce* B. *dabce*
C. *bdaec* D. *bedcb*

9. Identify a relationship between the given words and choose the word having similar relationship from the given choices:

Explicit : Implied, ____ :: ____

A. Vicious : Violent
B. Vibrant : Spirited
C. Vicarious : Indirect
D. Extempore : Rehearsed

10. In a certain language. PEN is written as QDM, then how BOOK will be written in that code?

A. CMJN B. CNNJ
C. CNLS D. NMJP

11. Fan is related to Wings in the same way as Wheel is related to ____.

A. Round B. Spokes
C. Cars D. Moves

12. Identify the **odd** one from the following:

A. Jahangir
B. Akbar
C. Vikramaditya
D. Shah Jahan

13. Choose the word which is not a similar in meaning of the given word.

* *Held on 11-09-2020.*

Fascinating
A. Fastidious B. Enchanting
C. Engrossing D. Enthralling

14. Choose the option that completes the sentence most meaningfully and appropriately:

A minor ____ on the road sometimes culminates into bloody bloodbath.
A. alteration B. friendship
C. altercation D. relationship

15. Choose the correct order of the sentences marked (*a*), (*b*), (*c*) and (*d*) to form a logical paragraph.
(*a*) "Sugar is the largest industry in my part of the country", he said.
(*b*) Otherwise, it had been reserved for the cooperatives earlier.
(*c*) At the same time, it was decontrolled and therefore you could set up a new sugar mill in the private sector.
(*d*) Now sugar may seem a strange choice but for him it was a fairly natural one.
A. *dabc* B. *dacb*
C. *adbc* D. *abcd*

16. Given interchanges: 'signs + and –, numbers 10 and 6', identify the correct response from the following:
A. 6 – 10 + 4 = 20 B. 6 + 10 – 8 = 26
C. 6 – 10 – 4 = 6 D. 6 + 10 – 12 = 16

17. There are two pairs, the first pair follows some relationship. Use the same relationship to find the second analogy of the second pair.
9 : 16 :: 49 : ?
A. 63 B. 64
C. 46 D. 36

18. There are two pairs, the first pair follows some relationship. Use the same relationship to find the second analogy of the second pair.
2500 : 2450 :: 3600 : ?
A. 3500 B. 3560
C. 3460 D. 3540

19. Choose the word which is not a similar in meaning of the given word.
Conquer
A. Triumph B. Victorious
C. Lose D. Overpower

20. Choose the correct order of the sentences marked (*a*), (*b*), (*c*) and (*d*) to form a logical paragraph.
(*a*) Only the next day, when it made its first attempt to free itself, did we realize how strong and dangerous it was.
(*b*) It thrust its head into a chink between two boards and began to prose them apart with unexpected ease.
(*c*) At first it was absolutely quiet.
(*d*) I gave an order for enormous box of stout cedar boards to be made at one, and we placed the Anaconda into it.
A. *abcd* B. *cdab*
C. *dabc* D. *dcab*

21. Bank is relatd to Money in the same way as Transport is related to ____.
A. Goods B. Movement
C. Road D. Traffic

22. Choose the word which is not a similar in meaning of the given word.
Scintillating
A. Shining B. Exciting
C. Boring D. Lively

23. A clock shows 8:30. If the minute hand points to West, in what direction will the hour hand points?
A. North B. South-West
C. South D. North-West

24. Guess the meaning of the underlined words in the context and choose the similar in meaning for the same.
Beneficiary: Who is the legitimate <u>beneficiary</u> of Princess Gayatri Devi's huge wealth?
A. proprietor B. caretaker
C. inheritor D. bungler

25. If 'pink' means 'blue', 'blue' means 'white', 'white' means 'black', 'black' means 'red' and 'red' means 'green', then what is the colour of the 'blood'?
A. red B. green
C. blue D. black

26. Choose the word which is not a similar in meaning of the given word.

Deplorable

A. Admirable B. Dishonorable

C. Disgraceful D. Unforgiveable

27. Guess the meaning of the underlined words in the context and choose the similar in meaning for the same.

Collateral: In lack of collateral of guarantor many bona fide citizens are unable to secure loan from a bank.

A. documents B. money

C. security D. support

28. Guess the meaning of the underlined words in the context and choose the similar in meaning for the same.

Equitable: Marxism believes in equitable distribution of wealth.

A. just B. unjust

C. equal D. improper

29. Guess the meaning of the underlined words in the context and choose the similar in meaning for the same.

Arbitrate: The judge was known for his impartiality; and he arbitrated the case with full judiciousness.

A. judged

B. meddled

C. fabricated

D. favored

30. Identify a relationship between the given words and choose the word having similar relationship from the given choices:

Fission : Fusion :: Flamboyant : ____.

A. Exuberant B. Excited

C. Extinguished D. Sad

31. Identify a relationship between the given words and choose the word having similar relationship from the given choices:

Defunct : Working ::

A. Obsequious : Sycophantic

B. Obsolescent : Declining

C. Obsessed : Preoccupied

D. Deify : Demonize

32. One morning after sunrise, Sita and Gita were standing in a chowk in Mumbai with their back towards each other. Sita's shadow fell exactly towards right hand side. Which direction was Gita facing?

A. East B. West

C. North D. South

33. Identify a relationship between the given words and choose the word having similar relationship from the given choices:

Dated : Modern, ____ :: ____

A. Avarice : Greed

B. Authentic : True

C. Dawn : Dusk

D. Augment : Increase

34. A woman wants to go to a restaurant. If she coves 2 km towards East and after taking turn to South, she covers 1.5 km more to reach the restaurant. How much distance she travels to reach restaurant?

A. 3 km B. 3.5 km

C. 4 km D. 4.5 km

35. Choose the correct order of the sentences marked (*a*), (*b*), (*c*) and (*d*) to form a logical paragraph.

(*a*) Peace is a natural state of being

(*b*) When agitations end, peace is naturally experienced.

(*c*) In other words, peace already exists until someone makes noise.

(*d*) Therefore, peace underlines all out agitations.

A. *bcda* B. *adcb*

C. *abcd* D. *acdb*

36. Identify the **odd** one from the following:

A. Crow B. Pigeon

C. Tiger D. Parrot

37. Find the missing term in the following series:

2, 6, 12, 20, 30, ____, 56

A. 32 B. 42

C. 34 D. 24

38. If $(16)(3^2) = X(2)^3$, then X =

A. 81 B. 18

C. 72 D. 16

39. Last year, an appliance store sold an average (arithmetic mean) of 42 microwaves per month. In the first 10 months of this year, the store sold an average of only 20 microwaves per month. What is the average number of microwaves sold per month for the entire 22-month period?

A. 21 B. 32
C. 30 D. 44

40. Choose the option that completes the sentence most meaningfully and appropriately:

The army vehicles, weapons and uniform are the colour of leaves of plants in order to ____ them so that the enemy cannot spot them easily.

A. decorate B. camouflage
C. adorn D. beautify

41. There are two pairs, the first pair follows some relationship. Use the same relationship to find the second analogy of the second pair.

16 : 2 :: 256 : ?

A. 4 B. 5
C. 6 D. 7

42. Guess the meaning of the underlined words in the context and choose the similar in meaning for the same.

Banish: The hardcore criminals in Britain of the past years were banished and they had to spend the remaining days of their life in distant colonies like Australia.

A. introduced B. confined
C. awarded D. exiled

43. Find the missing term in the following series:

5, 30, 6, 42, 7, 56, ____, 72, 9

A. 4 B. 6
C. 5 D. 8

44. In a certain code language, 432 means 'grass is green', 31 means 'green tree' and 162 means 'tree is long'. Which digit in that language means 'long'?

A. 6 B. 3
C. 8 D. 4

45. Choose the option that completes the sentence most meaningfully and appropriately:

Education polished her to become civilized, ____ and impressive.

A. eloquent B. hyperactive
C. ambiguous D. insensitive

46. In a certain code language, 'Ja, Li, Su' means 'They are beautiful' 'Ha, Do, Ja, To' means 'You seem very beautiful', ''Do, Su, Re' means 'They can do' and Yun, Sun, Pun ra' means 'How beautiful he is'. In what language which of the following means 'are'?

A. Ja B. Li
C. Re D. Su

47. Identify a relationship between the given words and choose the word having similar relationship from the given choices:

Myriad : Numbered : Nebulous : ____

A. Numerous B. Nimble
C. Indistinct D. Distinct

48. Choose the option that completes the sentence most meaningfully and appropriately:

When depression ensues, logically the prices should fall for lack of buyers; but actually prices were ____ in the months following depression.

A. reduced B. depreciated
C. fell D. escalated

49. Choose the correct order of the sentences marked (*a*), (*b*), (*c*) and (*d*) to form a logical paragraph.

(*a*) The sky was clear with hardly any clouds.
(*b*) Then finally descended the dawn.
(*c*) Then, I started feeling tired.
(*d*) Therefore, first I tried to find constellations in the sky.

A. *acdb* B. *bdca*
C. *adcb* D. *cabd*

50. Choose the option that completes the sentence most meaningfully and appropriately:

People gathered in hope of listening to a fine oratory. Quite the opposite, they left the venue ____.

A. satisfied B. confused
C. surprised D. disappointed

Directions (Qs. Nos. 51 to 60): *Answer the next TEN questions on the basis of the information given below on the profitability of sample business entities (in ₹ Crore) in a given year:*

Business Entities	Profits	Sales	Dividend	Term Borrowings	Capital
Alpha	200	2000	50	200	800
Beta	100	500	100	100	1000
Gamma	50	500	20	50	200

51. Which of the three business entities enjoyed the highest profitability?
A. Alpha B. Gamma
C. Beta D. Can't say

52. Based on given information, which company is better placed as to its debt repayment competence?
A. Alpha B. Beta
C. Gamma D. Can't say

53. What is the dividend payout of sample companies during given time frame?
A. 46.52% B. 48.57%
C. 57.42% D. 52.18%

54. The information furnished on the business profitability points which kind of market conditions in an emerging economy like India?
A. Recovery B. Recession
C. Expansion D. Decline

55. Which business enjoyed superior debt servicing competence during the given time perspective?
A. Alpha B. Beta
C. Gamma D. Its equal to All

56. What is the profitability of sample business entities?
A. 11.16% B. 13.67%
C. 11.67% D. 13.16%

57. In order to break the inertia indicated in information furnished on business profitability, which policy intervention do you call for a large size emerging economy?
A. Fiscal intervention
B. Monetary intervention
C. Pump printing
D. All of these

58. In which of the following business entity, the return on investment was lower than the other entities?
A. Alpha B. Beta
C. Gamma D. Can't say

59. Based on the said information, in your opinion, which entity is expected to command higher premium on listing on exchanges?
A. Alpha B. Beta
C. Can't say D. Gamma

60. In your opinion, what could be the reason(s) that warranted Beta entity dole out equal sum as dividend as it borrowed?
A. Maintain stock price
B. Tax management
C. Both (A) and (B)
D. Neither (A) nor (B)

61. In a family, each daughter has the same number of brothers as she has sisters and each son has twice as many sisters as he has brothers. How many sons are there in the family?
A. 4 B. 2
C. 3 D. 5

62. A, B and C started a business in which A has invested 2 times of B and B has invested 5 times of C. What is the profit share of B in a total profit of ₹ 25600?
A. ₹ 12000 B. ₹ 8000
C. ₹ 16000 D. ₹ 4000

63. A vendor earns a profit of 20% on selling a book at a 16% discount on the printed price. The ratio of the cost price and the printed price is ____.
A. 5 : 6 B. 7 : 10
C. 5 : 7 D. 6 : 12

64. What is the number whose twenty fifth part multiplied by its fifth part yield 1125?
A. 375 B. 365
C. 350 D. 485

65. A fruit seller mixes three varieties of grapes costing ₹ 80, ₹ 45 and ₹ 30 per kg, in the ratio of 1 : 4 : 6 in terms of weight and sells the mixture at ₹ 50 per kg. What percentage of profit does he make?

A. 25%
B. 24%
C. 30%
D. 32%

66. A and B invest in a business in a ratio of 2 : 3. If 10% of the total profit goes for donations and if A's share is ₹ 1080, then find the total profit.
A. ₹ 3000
B. ₹ 2800
C. ₹ 2400
D. ₹ 3200

Directions (Qs. Nos. 67 to 71): *Answer the next FIVE questions on the basis of the information given below.*

Classification of 100 students based on the marks obtained (out of 50) by them in Physics and Chemistry in an examination is given below:

	40 and above	30 and above	20 and above	10 and above	zero and above
Physics	9	32	80	92	100
Chemistry	4	21	66	81	100
Average	7	27	73	87	100

67. The number of students scoring less than 40 per cent marks in aggregate is:
A. 13
B. 19
C. 20
D. 27

68. What is the difference between the number of students passed with 30 as cut-off in Chemistry and those passed with 30 as cutoff marks in aggregate?
A. 3
B. 4
C. 5
D. 6

69. The percentage of number of students getting at least 60 per cent mark in Chemisty over those getting at least 40 per cent marks in aggregate, is approximately:
A. 21%
B. 27%
C. 29%
D. 31%

70. If at least 60 per cent marks in Physics are required for pursuing higher studies in Physics, how many students will be eligible to pursue higher studies in Physics?
A. 27
B. 32
C. 34
D. 41

71. If it is known that at least 23 students were eligible for a Symposium on Chemisty, then the minimum qualifying marks in Chemistry for eligible to Symposium would lie in the range:
A. 40-45
B. 30-40
C. 20-30
D. Below 20

Directions (Qs. Nos. 72 to 75): *Solve the next FOUR questions based on the data given below on the Production, Exports and Per Capita Consumption of rice in country for five years from 2012 to 2016:*

Year	Production (in million Kg)	Exports (in million Kg	Per Capita Consumption (in Kg)
2012	186.5	114	36.25
2013	202	114	35.2
2014	238	130	38.7
2015	221	116	40.5
2016	215	88	42

Where, Per Capita Consumption = (Consumption in million Kg)/(population in million) and Consumption (in million Kg) = Production – Exports.

72. What is population of the country in the year 2014 (in million)?
A. 2.79
B. 2.85
C. 2.64
D. 2.72

73. In which year, the population of country was the highest?
A. 2015
B. 2016
C. 2013
D. 2014

74. The ratio of Exports to Consumption in the given period was the highest in the year:
A. 2014
B. 2015
C. 2012
D. 2013

75. The percentage increase in the consumption of rice over the previous year was the highest in which year?
A. 2015
B. 2016
C. 2013
D. 2014

Directions (Qs. Nos. 76 to 80): *Answer the next FIVE questions from the information given below:*

Year	Production (Lakh Tonnes)	Import (Lakh Tonnes)	Consumption (Lakh Tonnes)	Cost of Import (₹ Crore)
2000 – 01	90	20	110	645
2001 – 02	85	31	116	1540
2002 – 03	90	35	125	1336
2003 – 04	98	28	126	1935
2004 – 05	97	25	122	2220

76. During which of the following years did import register the largest increase in the quantity over the previous year?
A. 2000-01 B. 2002-03
C. 2001-02 D. 2003-04

77. The total production during the year 2002-03 was what percentage of that of consumption?
A. 54 per cent B. 82 per cent
C. 72 per cent D. 80 per cent

78. What was the ratio of production to imports in the year 2003-04?
A. 7 : 9 B. 9 : 7
C. 9 : 2 D. 7 : 2

79. What was the cost of imports per ton during year 2004-05?
A. ₹ 8080 B. ₹ 28,880
C. ₹ 8,880 D. ₹ 80,080

80. During which of the following years did the production contribute the highest percentage to meet the consumption?
A. 2000-01 B. 2002-03
C. 2001-02 D. 2003-04

Directions (Qs. Nos. 81 to 85): *Answer the next FIVE questions from the information given below on the production (in Tonnes) of four crops during the period 1997-2000.*

Year	Wheat	Rice	Sugarcane	Pulses
1997	100	91	15	71
1998	120	88	18	75
1999	125	97	21	79
2000	131	107	25	88

81. Which crop witnessed the highest growth rate in production during the given period?
A. Sugarcane B. Wheat
C. Pulses D. Rice

82. What would be the actual production of wheat in 2001, if the growth rate in the year 2001 is the same the average annual growth rate for the given period?
A. 171.61 B. 143.65
C. 110.33 D. None of these

83. The average annual growth rate of wheat production during the given period is:
A. 31 B. 43.67
C. 9.66 D. 93

84. By what per cent is the average wheat production more than the average sugarcane production in the given period?
A. 19.90 B. 502.53
C. 167.67 D. 83.40

85. The production of pulses in 1998 is what per cent of total production of rice during the given period?
A. 19.58 B. 85.23
C. 81.72 D. 28.12

86. Which of the following mobile apps has been launched by the 'Google' to help children in primary schools to learn and read in Hindi and English?
A. Kaho B. Bolo
C. Chalo D. Padho

87. Mission Indradhanush is designed to:
A. Vaccinate all children against seven common disease
B. Ensure timely supply of water for farm operations
C. Opening public health centers in rural areas
D. Ensure equal rights for the LGBTQ community

88. 'Higher than Hopes' is a biography of:
A. Mother Teresa B. Bishop Tutu
C. Nelson Mandela D. Mahatma Gandhi

89. Which of the following is a large blood vessel that carries blood away from the heart?
A. Vein B. Artery
C. Capillary D. Nerve

90. Mahatma Gandhi launched Kheda Satyagrah in Gujarat in 1918 to support the cause of:
A. Mill owners B. Land lords
C. The peasants D. Textile workers

91. Kaziranga national park is located in which state?
A. Gujarat B. Kerala
C. Rajasthan D. Assam

92. Which of the following is greenhouse gas?
A. Carbon monoxide B. Sulphur dioxide
C. Carbon dioxide D. Oxygen

93. 'Natya-Shastra' the main source of India's classical dances was written by:
A. Nara Muni B. Abhinav Gupta
C. Bharat Muni D. Tandu Muni

94. Which of the following mountain passes from the 'tri-junction' of India, China and Myanmar?
A. Nathu La B. Jelep La
C. Bomdi La D. Diphu

95. Who is the author of the book 'A Brief History of Time'?
A. Michael Green B. Stephen Hawking
C. Noamha Hirari D. Carl Sagan

96. Which of the following was most probably the first metal to be used in India?
A. Iron B. Gold
C. Copper D. Silver

97. The famous 'Hornbill festival' is celebrated in which of the following states of India?
A. Nagaland
B. Assam
C. Mizoram
D. Meghalaya

98. The five-nation group BRICS has established its own developmental bank called?
A. BRICS Development Bank
B. The Bank
C. BRICS Bank
D. New Development Bank

99. Which organ of the body produces the fluid known as bile?
A. Liver B. Gall bladder
C. Pancreas D. Kidney

100. The ratio of width of our national Flag to its length is:
A. 3 : 5 B. 2 : 3
C. 2 : 4 D. 3 : 4

ANSWERS

1	2	3	4	5	6	7	8	9	10
B	A	A	A	A	A	B	C	D	B
11	**12**	**13**	**14**	**15**	**16**	**17**	**18**	**19**	**20**
B	C	A	C	B	D	B	D	C	D
21	**22**	**23**	**24**	**25**	**26**	**27**	**28**	**29**	**30**
A	C	D	C	D	A	C	A	A	C
31	**32**	**33**	**34**	**35**	**36**	**37**	**38**	**39**	**40**
C	C	C	B	D	C	B	B	B	B
41	**42**	**43**	**44**	**45**	**46**	**47**	**48**	**49**	**50**
A	D	D	A	A	B	A	D	C	D
51	**52**	**53**	**54**	**55**	**56**	**57**	**58**	**59**	**60**
C	A	B	A	D	C	D	B	D	C
61	**62**	**63**	**64**	**65**	**66**	**67**	**68**	**69**	**70**
C	B	B	A	A	A	D	D	C	B
71	**72**	**73**	**74**	**75**	**76**	**77**	**78**	**79**	**80**
C	A	B	C	D	B	C	D	C	A
81	**82**	**83**	**84**	**85**	**86**	**87**	**88**	**89**	**90**
A	B	C	B	B	B	A	C	B	C
91	**92**	**93**	**94**	**95**	**96**	**97**	**98**	**99**	**100**
D	C	C	D	B	C	A	D	A	B

Previous Year Paper

GGSIPU – B.Com (H) Entrance Exam 2019*

DATA INTERPRETATION

Directions (Qs. Nos. 1 to 5): *Study the following table carefully and answer the questions given below it:*

Crimes Registered in 2009 in the Various States (Incidence and Rate per 100000 Population)

Crimes/States		UP	MP	Delhi	Bihar
Dacoity	Incidence	8800	2650	500	7800
	Rate	6.2	4.0	4	5.6
Murder	Incidence	9200	892	480	8200
	Rate	7.0	2.0	4.5	6.2
Rape	Incidence	7800	582	138	2850
	Rate	6.2	3.2	0.4	2.8

1. What is the average rate per hundred population of murder for all the given states?

A. 0.00492 B. 4.92
C. 0.492 D. 49.2

2. What is the difference between the number of murder for UP and the number of rape for Delhi?

A. 1562 B. 9262
C. 9062 D. 962

3. What is the maximum number of the incidence of crimes per lac population for a which state?

A. 24700 B. 25800
C. 27500 D. 26800

4. What is the percentage difference of incidence of dacoity in UP as compared with Bihar?

A. 13% B. 11%
C. 14% D. 15%

5. Which state has the minimum rate of incidence for the crime of rape?

A. MP B. UP
C. Bihar D. Delhi

Directions (Qs. Nos. 6 to 10): *Study the following table and answer the questions that follow:*

Yearly Production (in thousand) of Scooters in Different Factories

Factory	1985	1986	1987	1988	1989
P	20	15	24	13	17
Q	16	23	41	20	15
R	14	21	30	16	12
S	25	17	15	12	22
T	40	32	39	41	35
Total	**115**	**108**	**149**	**102**	**101**

6. In which year, the production of scooters of all factories was equal to the yearly average number of scooters produced during 1985-1989?

A. 1985 B. 1986
C. 1987 D. 1988

7. Which factory/factories showed a decreases of 25% in the production of scooter 1989 as compared to 1988?

A. P B. S
C. Q and R D. P and T

8. The ratio of the production of scooters by factory P to that by factory T in 1985 is:

A. 2 : 3 B. 1 : 2
C. 3 : 2 D. 2 : 1

9. In which year was the total production of scooters the maximum?

A. 1989 B. 1986
C. 1987 D. 1985

10. In which year was the total production of scooters of all factories 20% of the total production of scooters during 1985-1989?

A. 1988 B. 1985
C. 1986 D. 1989

* *Held on 29-05-2019.*

Directions (Qs. Nos. 11 to 15): *Study the following table carefully to answer the questions that follow:*

Populations (in thousands) of Six States Over the Years

Years	States					
	A	B	C	D	E	F
1992	125	210	85	150	98	138
1995	135	225	89	170	110	152
1998	142	240	93	180	130	160
2001	148	250	99	215	140	175
2004	155	270	105	230	145	190
2007	160	290	110	240	160	198

11. What was the average population of all the states together in 1998?

A. 157500 B. 175000
C. 157200 D. 172500

12. Population of the state C in 2001 is approximately what per cent of the total population of all states together in the year?

A. 12 B. 11
C. 10 D. 8

13. Approximately, what is the per cent rise in population of state C in 2007 from 1995?

A. 29 B. 30
C. 28 D. 24

14. Which state had the highest per cent rise in population from 2001 to 2004?

A. C B. B
C. D D. F

15. What is the average population of state D for all the years together?

A. 195700 B. 197500
C. 175900 D. 179500

Directions (Qs. Nos. 16 to 20): *Study the following graph carefully and answer the questions that follow:*

Birth Rates of Different States

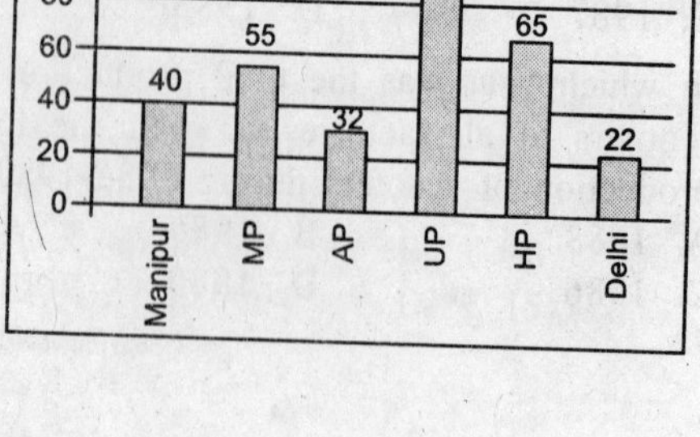

16. Which of the following state has 20% less the rate of birth than that of HP?

A. AP B. Manipur
C. MP D. None of these

17. The ratio of the state having highest birth rate to the state having lowest birth rate is:

A. 95 : 22 B. 22 : 95
C. 5 : 7 D. 7 : 5

18. What is the average Birth rates of all the states excepting UP?

A. 40 B. 43 (App.)
C. 45 D. 44

19. The average birth rate is by what per cent greater or lower than the birth rate of UP?

A. 43 B. 50
C. 46 D. 48

20. The pair of the birth rates of which of the following states is equal?

A. Manipur and MP; UP
B. MP and AP; HP
C. HP and Delhi; MP
D. MP and Delhi; UP

Directions (Qs. Nos. 21 to 25): *Study the following graph carefully and answer the questions that follow:*

Trade Deficit of a Country

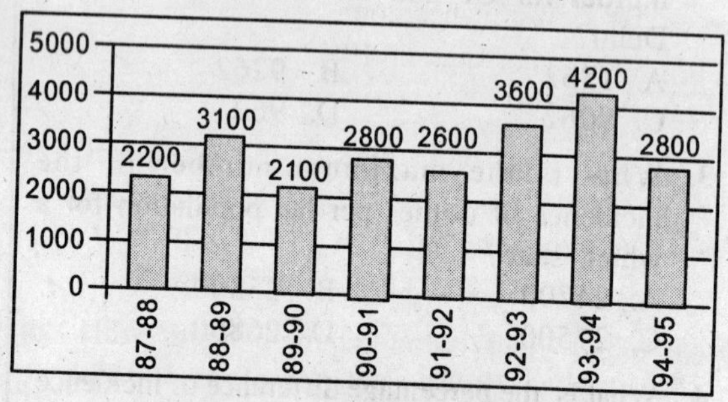

21. The deficit in 93-94 was roughly how many times the deficit in 90-91?

A. 1.4 B. 1.5
C. 2.5 D. 0.4

22. The increase in deficit in 93-94 was how much per cent of the deficit in 89-90?

A. 200 B. 150
C. 100 D. 210

23. In which of the following years, the per cent increase of deficit was highest over its preceding year?
A. 92-93 B. 90-91
C. 93-94 D. 88-89

24. The ratio of the number of years, in which the trade deficit is above the average deficit, to those in which the trade deficit is below the average deficit is:
A. 3 : 5 B. 5 : 3
C. 4 : 4 D. 3 : 4

25. The deficit in 92-93 was approximately how much per cent of the average deficit?
A. 150 B. 140
C. 125 D. 90

Directions (Qs. Nos. 26 to 30): *Study the following graph carefully and answer the questions that follow:*

Sales in ₹ (Thousands)

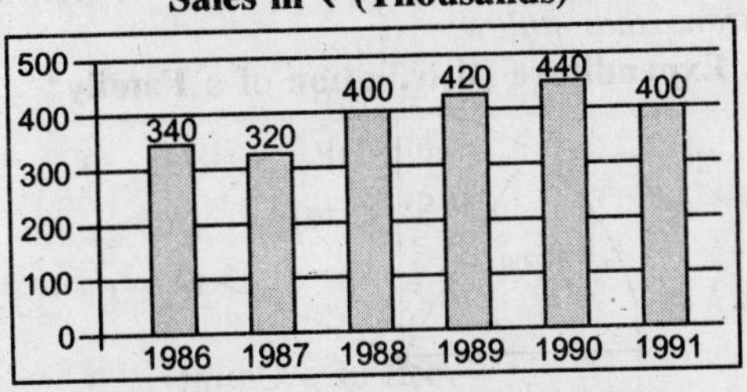

26. By how much amount are the sales in 1989 more than that in 1987?
A. ₹ 100 B. ₹ 10,000
C. ₹ 1,00,000 D. ₹ 10,00,000

27. The sales in 1987 are how many times to that in 1988?
A. 0.8 B. 1.25
C. 8 D. 0.25

28. In which year do the sales show the least per cent increase over those in the previous year?
A. 1986 B. 1988
C. 1989 D. 1990

29. The ratio of the number of years for which the sales were above average to the number of years for which the sales were below average is:
A. 2 : 1 B. 3 : 2
C. 4 : 3 D. 1 : 2

30. What are the approximate average sales (in thousands) for the years 1988 to 1991?
A. 420 B. 425
C. 430 D. None of these

Directions (Qs. Nos. 31 to 35): *Study the following graph carefully and answer the questions that follow:*

Number of Students Studying in Various Colleges from Various Faculty (Number in Thousands)

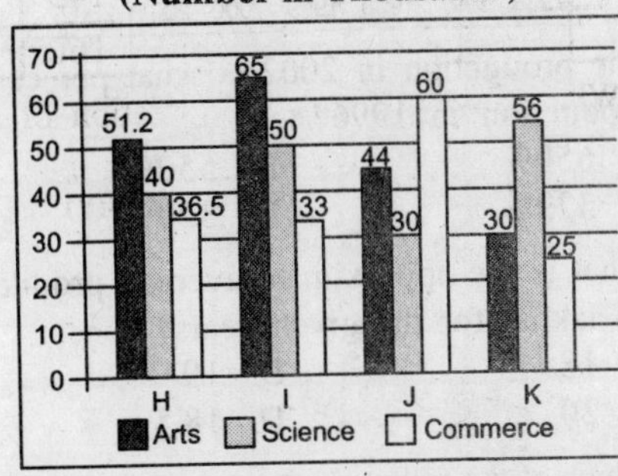

31. What is the difference between the total number of students studying in college H and those studying in college K?
A. 16100 B. 15800
C. 16300 D. 16700

32. What is the total number of students studying in all the colleges together?
A. 520900 B. 520700
C. 610200 D. 510800

33. What is the respective ratio of the students from the faculty of Science from colleges H and I together to the students from the same faculty from colleges J and K together?
A. 43 : 45 B. 41 : 43
C. 45 : 43 D. 43 : 41

34. The number of students from the faculty of Science from college 1 are approximately what per cent of the total number of students studying in that college?
A. 34% B. 36%
C. 80% D. 40%

35. What is the average number of students from the faculty of Commerce from all the colleges together?
A. 36825 B. 38655
C. 35625 D. None of these

Directions (Qs. Nos. 36 to 39): *Study the following graph carefully and answer the questions that follow:*

Production of a Company (in Lakh Units) over the years

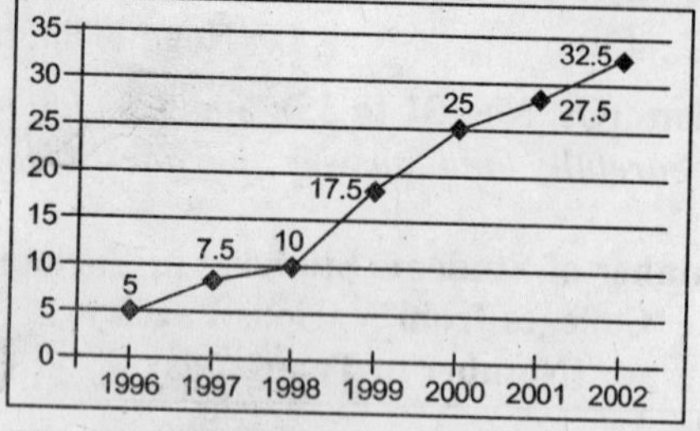

36. The production in 2002 is what per cent of production in 1996?
A. 650% B. 550%
C. 329% D. 320%

37. What is the approximate average production (in lakhs) for the given years?
A. 18 B. 19
C. 20 D. 18.5

38. Which of the following is the highest difference in production between two adjacent years?
A. 5 lakhs B. 10 lakhs
C. 9 lakhs D. 7.5 lakhs

39. Which year had the highest per cent increase in production over the previous year?
A. 2000 B. 1999
C. 2002 D. 1997

Directions (Qs. Nos. 40 to 44): *Study the following diagram of Pie Chart carefully and answer the questions that follow:*

Percentage of Amount Spent by a Country on Various Sports for One year

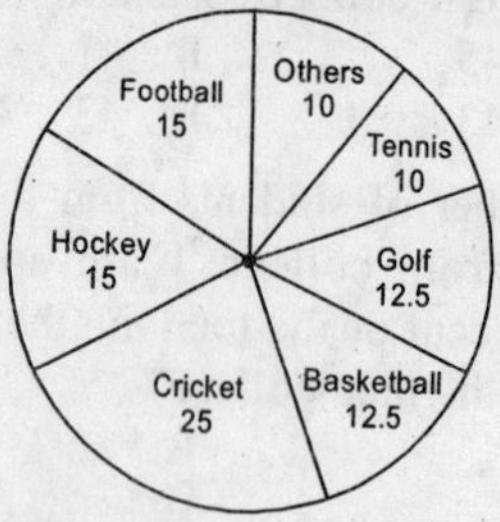

40. If the total amount spent on sports during the year was ₹ 1,50,00,000, then the amount spent on Cricket and Hockey together was:
A. ₹ 60,00,000 B. ₹ 50,00,000
C. ₹ 37,50,000 D. ₹ 15,00,000

41. If the total amount spent during the year was ₹ 1,20,00,000, how much was spent on Basketball?
A. ₹ 12,50,000 B. ₹ 10,00,000
C. ₹ 12,00,000 D. ₹ 15,00,000

42. The ratio of the total amount spent on Football to that spent on Hockey was:
A. 1 : 15 B. 1 : 1
C. 15 : 1 D. 3 : 2

43. The graph shows that the most popular game is:
A. Hockey B. Football
C. Cricket D. Basketball

44. The country spent the same amount of money on:
A. Hockey and Tennis
B. Golf and Tennis
C. Golf and Basketball
D. Cricket and Football

Directions (Qs. Nos. 45 to 47): *Study the following diagraph of Pie Chart carefully and answer the questions that follow:*

Expenditure Distribution of a Family

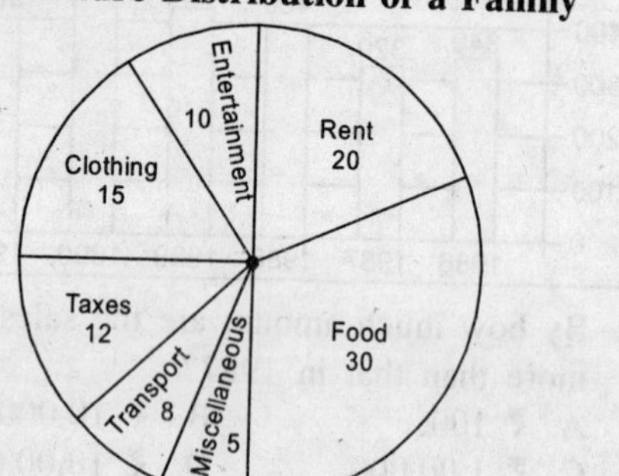

45. If the family spends ₹ 6,500 per month, how much are its taxes?
A. ₹ 780 B. ₹ 9,360
C. ₹ 9,800 D. ₹ 10,080

46. How much degrees should there be in the central angle showing clothing, taxes and transportation combined?
A. 100 B. 110
C. 120 D. 126

47. How much more money per month is spent by the family on food as compared to the rent, if the family spends ₹ 6,500 per month?
A. ₹ 650 B. ₹ 700
C. ₹ 750 D. ₹ 800

Directions (Qs. Nos. 48 to 52): *Study the following diagram of Pie Chart carefully and answer the questions that follow:*

The Gross Investments of Life Insurance Corporation of India (In Crores of Rupees) in Different Sectors are Shown

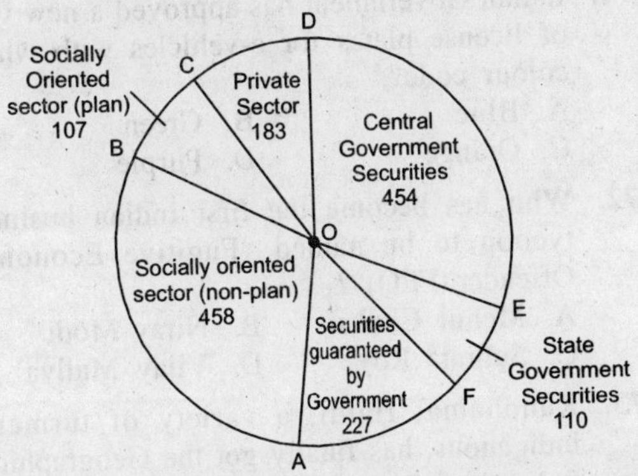

48. The percentage of gross investments in State Government securities is nearly:

A. 7.1% B. 7.8%
C. 8.6% D. 9.2%

49. The magnitude of ∠AOC is nearly:

A. 123° B. 132°
C. 126° D. 115°

50. The investment in socially oriented sector (Plan and Non-plan) is ______ than the investment in Government securities (central and state) by ______ .

A. more, 4 crore B. more, 1 crore
C. more, 111 crore D. less, 106 crore

51. The investment in private sectors is nearly ______ per cent higher than the investments in State Government Securities.

A. 66 B. 54
C. 46 D. 40

52. The ratio of the area of the circle above COF to the area of the circle below it is nearly:

A. 1 : 2 B. 35 : 37
C. 83 : 88 D. 88 : 83

GENERAL AWARENESS

Directions (Qs. Nos. 53 to 88): *Choose the most appropriate option.*

53. Satpura National Park is located in which state?

A. Andhra Pradesh B. Chhattisgarh
C. Madhya Pradesh D. Jharkhand

54. Which of the following is the main Standing Committee of Lok Sabha?

A. Committee on Public Undertaking
B. Estimates Committee
C. Committee on Public Accounts
D. All of the above

55. Who is empowered to declare National Emergency in India?

A. Parliament of India
B. President of India
C. Prime Minister of India
D. Supreme Court of India

56. What disease among the following arise out of Vitamin B_1 deficiency?

A. Pellagra B. Gingivitis
C. Beriberi D. Scurvy

57. Why Indian team was not allowed to participate in Soccer World Cup in 1950 despite qualifying for it?

A. They didn't have coach
B. They were unable to pay participation fees in USD
C. The players didn't opted for dope test
D. The players wanted to play bare feet

58. Vanessa Ponce de Leon won the Miss World 2018 crown belongs to which country?

A. Venezuela B. Mexico
C. Argentina D. Brazil

59. For the celebration of International Women's Day (IWD-2019), which Indian sportsperson has been selected as Barbie role model?

A. Saina Nehwal B. Mary Kom
C. Dipa Karmakar D. Geeta Phogat

60. Greta Thunberg, who has been nominated for 2019 Nobel Peace Prize, is an environmental Activist of which country?

A. South Africa B. Sweden
C. Australia D. Canada

61. Irfan Kolothum Thodi, who recently qualified for 2020 Tokyo Olympics, is associated with which sports?
A. Athletics B. Rowing
C. Swimming D. Fencing

62. What is "poly-Oxime", that was developed recently by Indian researchers and was making news?
A. Hardest nano-material
B. Skin Gel
C. AC coolant
D. A pesticide

63. Which neighbouring country of India has recently declared sugarcane juice as 'national drink'?
A. Pakistan B. Bangladesh
C. Nepal D. Bhutan

64. The researchers at which IIT have developed smartphone-based sensor to detect adulteration in milk?
A. IIT Bombay B. IIT Hyderabad
C. IIT Madras D. IIT Delhi

65. India signed a MoU for the establishment of the Joint Task Force on Blue Economy with which country?
A. Denmark B. Norway
C. Sweden D. Poland

66. Who became the first Indian mountaineer and youngest man to climb the 7 highest peaks and volcanic summits across all continents?
A. Satyarup Siddhanta B. Mingma Sherpa
C. Krushnaa Patil D. Kuntal Joisher

67. 'Ideate for India' is the joint collaboration between National e-governance Division and which technological giant?
A. IBM B. INTEL
C. MICROSOFT D. GOOGLE

68. The International Day for Mine Awareness and Assistance in Mine Action is observed every year on:
A. April 4 B. April 11
C. April 14 D. April 18

69. The NuGen Mobility Summit 2019 will be held in India is related to:
A. Automotive technologies
B. Mobile technologies
C. Construction technologies
D. Robot technologies

70. Phayeng Village of Manipur has been tagged as the India's first ______ settlement.
A. Organic B. Carbon-positive
C. Solar driven D. Literate

71. Indian Government has approved a new type of license plates for e-vehicles with which colour code?
A. Blue B. Green
C. Orange D. Purple

72. Who has become the first Indian business tycoon to be named "Fugitive Economic Offender (FEO)"?
A. Mehul Choksi B. Nirav Modi
C. Subrata Roy D. Vijay Mallya

73. Kandhamal Haldi, a variety of turmeric indigenous, has finally got the Geographical Indication (GI) tag from Intellectual Property of India is produced in which state of India?
A. Uttarakhand B. Odisha
C. Telangana D. Jharkhand

74. Which Institute has developed next generation lighter bullet proof jackets, christened 'Bhabha Kavach'?
A. DRDO
B. BARC
C. IIT Bombay
D. Indian Ordnance Factory

75. Dalveer Bhandari is an Indian member of the:
A. ILO B. ICJ
C. IMF D. WHO

76. "The Girl in Room 105" is a fictional novel written by:
A. Kiran Desai B. Chetan Bhagat
C. Aravind Adiga D. Vikram Seth

77. Panini was an ancient:
A. Sanskrit philologist and grammarian
B. Poet and physician
C. Poet and mathematician
D. Mathematician and astrologer

78. The Treaty of Versailles was the most important of the peace treaties that brought ______ to an end.
A. World War II B. World War I
C. French Revolution D. Battle of Waterloo

79. What is the number of Schedules in the Constitution of India?
A. 11 B. 12
C. 16 D. 14

80. World Bank Headquarters located at:
A. Washington DC B. Zurich
C. Beijing D. Prague

81. The constellation in Indian Mythology called "Sapta Rishi" is coterminous with which among the following?
A. Ursa Minor B. Orion
C. Ursa Major D. Scorpio

82. Which among the following fishes does not have Central Nervous System?
A. Star Fish B. Cuttle Fish
C. Cat Fish D. Jelly Fish

83. Which among the following country is known as "Land of White Elephant"?
A. Indonesia B. Thailand
C. Sri Lanka D. India

84. Which among the following is the National Sports of USA?
A. Rugby B. Bowling
C. Baseball D. Basketball

85. Which among the following freedom fighter is known to have written "Gita Rahasya"?
A. B.C. Roy B. B.G. Tilak
C. G.K. Gokhale D. K.M. Munshi

86. "Rajatarangini" was written by:
A. Kalidas B. Kalhana
C. Banabhatta D. Bhushanabhatta

87. The term "Grand Slam" is associated with which of the following games?
A. Lawn Tennis B. Basketball
C. Badminton D. Golf

88. The Battle of Buxar was fought in ______.
A. 1764 B. 1780
C. 1775 D. 1790

GENERAL ENGLISH

Directions (Q. No. 89-96): *The questions are based on the passage below. Choose the most appropriate option.*

1. "Photography" is derived from the Greek words photos ("light") and graphein ("to draw"). The word was first used by the scientist Sir John F.W. Herschel in 1839. It is a method of recording images by the action of light, or related radiation, on a sensitive material.
2. Alhazen (Ibn Al-Haytham), a great authority on optics in the Middle Ages who lived around 1000 AD, invented the first pinhole camera, (also called the Camera Obscura) and was able to explain why the images were upside down. The first casual reference to the optic laws that made pinhole cameras possible, was observed and noted by Aristotle around 330 BC, who questioned why the sun could make a circular image when it shined through a square hole.
3. On a summer day in 1827, Joseph Nicephore Niepce made the first photographic image with a camera obscura. Prior to Niepce people just used the camera obscura for viewing or drawing purposes not for making photographs. Joseph Nicephore Niepce's heliographs or sun prints as they were called were the prototype for the modern photograph, by letting light draw the picture.
4. Niepce placed an engraving onto a metal plate coated in bitumen, and then exposed it to light. The shadowy areas of the engraving blocked light, but the whiter areas permitted light to react with the chemicals on the plate. When Niepce placed the metal plate in a solvent, gradually an image, until then invisible, appeared. However, Niepce's photograph required eight hours of light exposure to create and after appearing would soon fade away.
5. Fellow Frenchman, Louis Daguerre was also experimenting to find a way to capture an image, but it would take him another dozen years before Daguerre was able to reduce exposure time to less than 30 minutes and keep the image from disappearing afterwards.
6. Louis Daguerre was the inventor of the first practical process of photography. In 1829, he formed a partnership with Joseph Nicephore Niepce to improve the process Niepce had developed. In 1839 after several years of

experimentation and Niepce's death, Daguerre developed a more convenient and effective method of photography, naming it after himself —the daguerreotype. Daguerre's process 'fixed' the images onto a sheet of silver-plated copper. He polished the silver and coated it in iodine, creating a surface that was sensitive to light. Then, he put the plate in a camera and exposed it for a few minutes. After the image was painted by light, Daguerre bathed the plate in a solution of silver chloride. This process created a lasting image, one that would not change if exposed to light.

7. In 1839, Daguerre and Niepce's son sold the rights for the daguerreotype to the French government and published a booklet describing the process. The daguerreotype gained popularity quickly; by 1850, there were over seventy daguerreotype studios in New York City alone.

89. Who was the first one to observe the optic laws whose knowledge was needed in order to design a pinhole camera?
A. Daguerre B. Niece
C. Alhazen D. Aristotle

90. Who made the qualitative leap necessary to invent the camera in the modern sense of the word?
A. Aristotle B. Niepce
C. Daguerre D. Both B and C

91. Which word in the passage also means "revelation"?
A. Image B. Obscura
C. Exposure D. Coated

92. Which of the following is the right chronological order of appearance for these figures important in the history of the camera?
A. Niepce, Aristotle, Daguerre, Alhazen
B. Alhazen, Daguerre, Niepce, Aristotle
C. Alhazen, Aristotle, Niepce, Daguerre
D. Aristotle, Alhazen, Niepce, Daguerre

93. Which word in the passage also means "the first or preliminary model of something"?
A. Daguerreotype B. Prototype
C. Image D. Camera obscura

94. Which word in the passage means the same as "taking place or progressing slowly or by degrees"?
A. Solvent B. Shadowy
C. Casual D. Gradually

95. Which word in the passage means the opposite of "unorthodox"?
A. Gradually B. Casual
C. Conventional D. Fixed

96. Which word in the passage means the opposite of "concerned"?
A. Conventional B. Casual
C. Solvent D. Gradually

Directions (Q. No. 97-103): *Choose the most appropriate option to fill in the blanks.*

97. Money ________ to a political campaign should be used for political purposes and nothing else.
A. attracted B. forwarded
C. contributed D. ascribed

98. Most candidates spend ________ they can raise on their campaigns, but others wind up on election day with a ________ .
A. all; debt B. whatever; liability
C. everything; surplus D. every cent; deficit

99. Can public opinion be influenced so that it ________ rather than encourages the proliferation of the sale of firearms?
A. redoubles B. advances
C. inverts D. impedes

100. The critic praised the scenery of the film enthusiastically, but ______ her enthusiasm when she discussed its plot and characterizations.
A. expanded B. established
C. augmented D. tempered

101. The tools found in the New Mexico excavation are ________ as a single implement might have several edges, each with a different use.
A. ancient B. primitive
C. ferrous D. versatile

102. This treatise is concerned only with the process unique to the period in question; therefore, no attempt has been made to ________ phenomena ________ to that era.
A. include; unrelated B. omit; irrelevant
C. re-create; germane D. discuss; essential

103. A virtuous person will not shout ________ in public; he or she will respect the ________ of other people.

The first blank is obviously a negative word, something that a good person would not shout; the second blank is a positive word, something that a good person would respect. Here are the choices:

A. obscenities; feelings
B. loudly; comfort
C. anywhere; presence
D. blessings; cynicism

Directions (Q. No. 104-107): *Choose the option that is most similar to the word given.*

104. kin
A. exult B. twist
C. friend D. relative

105. pensive
A. oppressed B. caged
C. thoughtful D. happy

106. banish
A. exile B. hate
C. fade D. clean

107. fraud
A. malcontent B. argument
C. imposter D. clown

Directions (Q. No. 108-111): *Choose the option that is most dissimilar to the given word.*

108. access
A. ingress B. entrance
C. entry D. outlet

109. anxiety
A. worry B. concern
C. certitude D. solicitude

110. baneful
A. noxious B. beneficial
C. injurious D. malign

111. churl
A. aristocrat B. lout
C. clodhopper D. bumpkin

LOGICAL REASONING

Directions (Q. No. 112-116): *Complete the equation on the analogy of the letters preceded by sign "::" by providing relevant letters in question mark (?) on right side of the sign ::*

112. ABC : DEF : : GHI : (?)
A. AFC B. JKL
C. IJK D. FIG

113. BCd : Def : : FGh : (?)
A. FGH B. fgH
C. HIJ D. Hij

114. BDf : FHj : : JLn : (?)
A. CDf B. NPQ
C. NPr D. JLN

115. ONM : JIH : : TSR : (?)
A. TSU B. OMN
C. VWX D. XYZ

116. Abc : KLM : : PqR : (?)
A. StU B. PQR
C. STU D. stu

Directions (Q. No. 117-120): *Choose the most appropriate option.*

117. As Provocation is to Appeasement, ______ is to Soil.
A. Stain B. Purify
C. Clarify D. Filter

118. As Partial is to Fair, ______ is to Particular.
A. Individual B. Careful
C. Precise D. General

119. As Stiff is to Flexible, ______ is to Follow.
A. Lead B. Precede
C. Walk D. Similar

120. As Feast is to Fast, ______ is to Slow.
A. Quick B. Speed
C. Late D. Early

Directions (Q. No. 121-124): *Find out the correct letter pair from the alternative given in answer choice below:*

121. Vitamin C : Scurvy
A. Vitamin A : Goiter
B. Vitamin B : Beriberi
C. Iodine : Anemia
D. Iron : Sickness

122. Duck : Waddles
A. Dog : Moves
B. Mouse : Scampers
C. Swims : Fish
D. Fly : Birds

123. Book : Author
A. Song : Musician
B. Poem : Poet
C. Movie : Writer
D. Dish : Cook

124. Army : Major
A. Army : Colonel
B. Army : Commander
C. Captain : Navy
D. General : Army

Directions (Q. No. 125-129): *In this type of question, a series of single, pairs or groups of letters or combinations of letters and numerals are given. The terms of the series form a certain pattern as regards the position of the letters in the English alphabet. You are required to decipher this pattern and accordingly find the missing term or the wrong term in the series.*

125. 5E, 10I, 15M, 20Q, ?
A. 22N
B. 23P
C. 25U
D. 29V

126. 6A, 9D, 12G, 15J, ?
A. 20E
B. 19P
C. 21Q
D. 18M

127. 3, C, 5, D, 7, E, 9, F, 11, ?
A. J
B. G
C. I
D. K

128. 7, E, 10, J, 13, O, 16, T, 19, ?
A. V
B. T
C. Z
D. Y

129. 4B2, 8F3, 16J5, 32M9, ?
A. P62J5
B. 39C2
C. 39M9
D. 64P17

Directions (Q. No. 130-146): *Choose the most appropriate option.*

130. If 20 books are placed in row on book shelf, librarian who is facing North shifted Dictionary to her left by fourth place, now dictionary is at tenth place from left corner. What will be the place of Panchatantra from the right end if it was three places to the right to dictionaries original place.
A. 2nd position
B. 3rd position
C. 4th position
D. 5th position

131. Amita finds that she is ninth from the right and sixth from the left. How many girls should be added so that there will be 20 girls in a line?
A. 10 girls
B. 4 girls
C. 8 girls
D. 6 girls

132. If there are 21 chapters in Micro economics book and chapter on Demand is Eighth from starting and chapter on supply is fifteenth from last and chapter on equilibrium is next to that of demand chapter, then how many chapters are then between supply and equilibrium chapter?
A. 1
B. 3
C. 2
D. 4

133. In Mango festival, if Alphonso is fifteenth from the left end. These are thrice as many on the right of Alphonso as they were in left Mangoes. How many types of mangoes are there between Alphonso and Sindoori *i.e.,* seventh from the right end in a row facing North?
A. 35
B. 36
C. 37
D. 38

134. If a caterer has displayed his dishes in a row facing North, Paneer is tenth to the left of chicken, that is twenty first from the right end. If noodles are fifteenth from the left end, is sixth to the right of Paneer. How many dishes are there in the row?
A. 39 dishes
B. 36 dishes
C. 34 dishes
D. 43 dishes

135. On a staircase, Javid is sixth from the bottom and Shabana is fifth from the top and Rehana is standing between the two. What could be the minimum number of staircase?
A. 14 Stairs
B. 16 Stairs
C. 12 Stairs
D. 8 Stairs

136. Rahul was painting beads with white colour. By mistake he painted fifth bead with red colour, while counting in reverse order beads that was in a mistakenly coloured red was found to be fifty third, then beads painted by Rahul in white colour are:
A. 58 beads
B. 57 beads
C. 55 beads
D. 56 beads

137. Rupali has to answer certain questions in a test. She did not know the answer of eighth question from starting and fifth question from the last and there were four in middle of these two questions. If rest of all the questions answered by Rupali were correct, then correct answers given by her are:

A. 12 B. 16
C. 17 D. 15

138. In a class of 29 students, if Pankaj ranked eight from the top then his rank from bottom is:

A. 21 B. 20
C. 19 D. 18

139. Student standing on 2nd stair from top called the teacher who is standing at 4th stair from bottom and there are seven stairs between them, then total stairs are:

A. 12 B. 13
C. 14 D. 15

140. Find total members in a family if four members in family are younger than Sham and he is ninth from the top.

A. 11 B. 15
C. 14 D. 13

141. Students were standing in a queue for viva. Misha finds that she is tenth from starting and seventh from last. How many girls are there in a class if five girls have skipped the viva?

A. 21 B. 20
C. 19 D. 18

142. A student is standing for auditions in a queue. One student is eight in order from the both ends. How many students are there in the queue?

A. 12 B. 13
C. 14 D. 15

143. Persons are standing in queue for filling form to apply smart cards. One person is fourth from the both ends. How many persons are there in the queue?

A. 5 B. 7
C. 9 D. 11

144. In a company, employees are sitting in a row. Anushka finds that she is fourth from the left end and seventh from the right end. How many employees should be added to the row such that there are 9 employees in a row?

A. 7 B. 9
C. 11 D. 13

145. In a meeting, employees are sitting in a row to discuss the new project with employer. Priya is fifth from the left and Seerat is fourth from right end in a row. If there are two employees between Priya and Seerat. How many persons are there in a meeting?

A. 5 B. 11
C. 15 D. 20

146. Traffic is jammed due to strike and vehicles are in a queue. Audi is at fifth place from front. Local bus is at seventh place from back. Bike is standing exactly between two. What is Audi's position from Bike? If total number of vehicle are 21.

A. 4 B. 5
C. 6 D. 7

Directions (Q. No. 147-150): *The following question are based on the data given below regarding candidates appeared in an entrance test consists of five qualifying sections.*

Candidates appeared	52,500
Failed in Quantitative aptitude only	390
Failed in Reasoning only	1,375
Failed in English only	745
Failed in GK only	735
Failed in Computers only	1,105
Passed in all five sections	28,425
Passed in 3 sections only	7,490
Passed in 2 sections only	6,250
Passed in 1 section only	4,175

147. If candidate failed in a single section implies candidate disqualified. Then how many candidates have been disqualified from the test?

A. 22,265 B. 21,387
C. 24,075 D. 21,195

148. How many candidates passed in at least four sections?

A. 24,986 B. 4,350
C. 32,775 D. 26,535

149. Total number of candidates who have failed in all five sections are:

A. 24,075 B. 2,185
C. 4,815 D. 1,810

150. What per cent of candidates passed in exactly four sections?

A. 6.3% B. 8.3%
C. 7.8% D. 9%

ANSWERS

1 A	2 C	3 B	4 *	5 D	6 A	7 C	8 B	9 C	10 B
11 A	12 C	13 D	14 D	15 B	16 D	17 A	18 B	19 C	20 A
21 B	22 C	23 D	24 A	25 C	26 C	27 A	28 D	29 A	30 D
31 D	32 B	33 C	34 A	35 D	36 A	37 A	38 D	39 B	40 A
41 D	42 B	43 C	44 C	45 A	46 D	47 A	48 A	49 B	50 B
51 A	52 C	53 C	54 B	55 B	56 C	57 D	58 B	59 C	60 B
61 A	62 B	63 A	64 B	65 B	66 A	67 B	68 A	69 A	70 B
71 B	72 D	73 B	74 D	75 B	76 B	77 A	78 B	79 B	80 A
81 C	82 D	83 B	84 C	85 B	86 B	87 A	88 A	89 D	90 C
91 C	92 D	93 B	94 D	95 C	96 B	97 D	98 C	99 D	100 D
101 D	102 A	103 A	104 D	105 C	106 A	107 C	108 D	109 C	110 B
111 A	112 B	113 D	114 C	115 B	116 A	117 A	118 D	119 A	120 A
121 B	122 B	123 B	124 A	125 C	126 D	127 B	128 D	129 D	130 C
131 D	132 A	133 A	134 A	135 D	136 D	137 D	138 A	139 B	140 D
141 A	142 D	143 B	144 B	145 B	146 B	147 A	148 C	149 D	150 B

EXPLANATORY ANSWERS

1. Average rate per 100000 population of murder for all the given State

$$= \frac{7+2+4.5+6.2}{4} = \frac{19.7}{4} = 4.925$$

Average rate per 100 population of murder for all the given State

$$= \frac{4.925}{100000} \times 100 = 0.004925.$$

2. Required number of difference

$$= 9200 - 138 = 9062.$$

3. Number of Incidence of crime per lac population for UP

$$= 8800 + 9200 + 7800 = 25800$$

Number of Incidence of crime per lac population for MP

$$= 2650 + 892 + 582 = 4124$$

Number of Incidence of crime per lac population for Delhi

$$= 500 + 480 + 138 = 1118$$

Number of Incidence of crime per lac population for Bihar

= 7800 + 8200 + 2850 = 18850

So, Maximum number of incidence of crimes is 25800.

5. Rate of Incidence for the crime of rape of State Delhi is Minimum.

6. Yearly average number of scooters produced during 1985-1989

$$= \frac{115+108+149+102+101}{5} = \frac{575}{5} = 115$$

Which is equal to the production of scooters in 1985.

7. In Factory 'P' $= \frac{17-13}{13} \times 100$

= 30.77% increase

In Factory 'Q' $= \frac{20-15}{20} \times 100$

= 25% decrease

In Factory 'R' $= \frac{16-12}{16} \times 100$

= 25% decrease

In Factory 'S' $= \frac{22-12}{12} \times 100$

= 83.33% increase

In Factory 'T' $= \frac{41-35}{41} \times 100$

= 14.63% decrease

So, In Q and R factories showed a decreases of 25% production of scooter 1989 as compared to 1988.

8. Required Ratio = 20 : 40 = 1 : 2.

9. In 1987, the total production of scooters was maximum.

10. Total production of scooters during 1985-1989

= 115 + 108 + 149 + 102 + 101 = 575

20% of the total production

$= 575 \times 20\% = 575 \times \frac{20}{100} = 115$

Which is equal to the production of scooters in 1985.

11. Required Average

$$= \frac{142+240+93+180+130+160}{6}$$

$$= \frac{945}{6} = 157.5$$

= 157.5 × 1000 = 157500.

12. Required percentage

$$= \frac{99}{148+250+99+215+140+175} \times 100$$

$$= \frac{9900}{1027} = 9.64\% \sim 10\%.$$

13. Population of State 'C' in 1995 = 89000

Population of State 'C' in 2007 = 110000

$$\% \text{ increase} = \frac{110000-89000}{89000} \times 100$$

$$= \frac{21000}{89000} \times 100 = \frac{2100}{89}$$

= 23.59% ~ 24%.

14. % rise in population of State A from 2001 to 2004

$$= \frac{155-148}{148} \times 100 = 4.73\%$$

% rise in population of State B from 2001 to 2004

$$= \frac{270-250}{250} \times 100 = \frac{2000}{250} = 8\%$$

% rise in population of State C from 2001 to 2004

$$= \frac{105-99}{99} \times 100 = \frac{600}{99} = 6.06\%$$

% rise in population of State D from 2001 to 2004

$$= \frac{230-215}{215} \times 100 = \frac{1500}{215} = 6.98\%$$

% rise in population of State E from 2001 to

$$2004 = \frac{145-140}{140} \times 100 = \frac{500}{140} = 3.57\%$$

% rise in population of State F from 2001 to

$$2004 = \frac{190-175}{175} \times 100 = \frac{1500}{175} = 8.57\%$$

∴ Highest per cent rise in population from 2001 to 2004 in State 'F'.

15. Required Average of State 'D' for all the years together

$$= \frac{150+170+180+215+230+240}{6}$$

$$= \frac{1185}{6} = 197.5$$

$= 197.5 \times 1000 = 197500.$

16. 20% Birth rate of HP = 65 × 20%

$$= \frac{65 \times 20}{100} = 13$$

∴ Required birth rate = 65 − 13 = 52

52, Birth rate none of the State

Hence, option (D) is the correct.

17. Required Ratio = 95 : 22.

18. Required Average Birth Rate

$$= \frac{40+55+32+65+22}{5} = \frac{214}{5}$$

= 42.8 ~ 43 (App.)

19. Average birth rate of all the State

$$= \frac{40+55+32+95+65+22}{6} = \frac{309}{6} = 51.5$$

Required per cent $= \frac{95-51.5}{95} \times 100$

= 45.79% ~ 46% (Lower)

20. Birth rate of Manipur and MP

= 40 + 55 = 95

Birth rate of UP = 95

Hence, birth rate of Manipur and MP, UP is equal.

21. Trade deficit in 93-94 = 4200

Trade deficit in 90-91 = 2800

Required Ratio $= \frac{4200}{2800} = 1.5$

Hence, Trade deficit in 93-94 is 1.5 times of trade deficit in 90-91.

22. Trade deficit in 93-94 = 4200

Trade deficit in 89-90 = 2100

∴ Increase in deficit $= \frac{4200-2100}{2100} \times 100$

$$= \frac{2100}{2100} \times 100 = 100\%.$$

23. In 88-89,

$$\frac{3100-2200}{2200} \times 100 = \frac{90000}{2200} = 40.91\%$$

In 89-90,

$$\frac{2100-3100}{3100} \times 100 = \frac{-100000}{3100} = -32.25\%$$

In 90-91,

$$\frac{2800-2100}{2100} \times 100 = \frac{70000}{2100} = 33.33\%$$

In 91-92,

$$\frac{2600-2800}{2800} \times 100 = \frac{-20000}{2800} = -7.14\%$$

In 92-93,

$$\frac{3600-2600}{2600} \times 100 = \frac{100000}{2600} = 38.46\%$$

In 93-94,

$$\frac{4200-3600}{3600} \times 100 = \frac{90000}{3600} = 25\%$$

In 94-95,

$$\frac{2800-4200}{4200} \times 100 = \frac{-140000}{4200} = -33.33\%$$

∴ Highest increase in 88-89 over its preceding year 87-88.

24. Average deficit of all the years

$$= \frac{2200+3100+2100+2800+2600+3600+4200+2800}{8}$$

$$= \frac{23400}{8} = 2925$$

Number of years, in which trade deficit is above the average deficit = 3

Number of years, in which trade deficit is below the average deficit = 5

Required Ratio = 3 : 5.

25. From Previous question,

Average Trade deficit = 2925

Required percentage $= \frac{3600}{2925} \times 100$

= 123.08% ~ 125%.

26. Sales in 1987 = 320000

Sales in 1989 = 420000

Required Amount = 420000 − 320000

= 1,00,000.

27. Sales in 1987 = 320000
Sales in 1988 = 400000

$$\text{Required Ratio} = \frac{320000}{400000} = 0.8$$

∴ Sales in 1987 is 0.8 times of the sales in 1988.

28. Per cent increase over the previous year

$$\text{In 1987} = \frac{320-340}{320} \times 100 = \frac{-2000}{320}$$
= –6.25% (decrease)

$$\text{In 1988} = \frac{400-320}{320} \times 100 = \frac{8000}{320}$$
= 25% (increase)

$$\text{In 1989} = \frac{420-400}{400} \times 100 = \frac{20}{4}$$
= 5% (increase)

$$\text{In 1990} = \frac{440-420}{420} \times 100 = \frac{2000}{420}$$
= 4.76% (increase)

$$\text{In 1991} = \frac{400-440}{440} \times 100 = \frac{-4000}{440}$$
= –9.09% (decrease)

∴ Least per cent increase is in 1990.

29. Average Sales

$$= \frac{340+320+400+420+440+400}{6} = \frac{2320}{6}$$
= 386.66 thousands

Number of years for which the sales above average = 4

Number of years for which the sales below average = 2

Required Ratio = 4 : 2 = 2 : 1.

30. Required Average Sales for the years

$$\text{1988 to 1991} = \frac{400+420+440+400}{4}$$
$$= \frac{1660}{4} = 415 \text{ thousands.}$$

31. Total students studying in college H
= 51.2 + 40 + 36.5 = 127700

Total students studying in college K
= 30 + 56 + 25 = 111000

∴ Required difference
= 127700 – 111000 = 16700.

32. Total number of students studying in all the colleges together
= (51.2 + 40 + 36.5) + (65 + 50 + 33) + (44 + 30 + 60) + (30 + 56 + 25)
= 127.7 + 148 + 134 + 111
= 520.7 × 1000 = 520700.

33. Number of students from the faculty of Science from Colleges H and I together
= 40 + 50 = 90 × 1000 = 90000

Number of students from the faculty of Science from Colleges J and K together
= 30 + 56 = 86 × 1000 = 86000

Required Ratio = 90000 : 86000
= 90 : 86 = 45 : 43.

34. Number of students from the faculty of Science from college I
= 50 × 1000 = 50000

Total number of students studying in college I
= 65 + 50 + 33
= 148 × 1000 = 148000

Required percentage

$$= \frac{50000}{148000} \times 100 = 33.78\% \sim 34\%.$$

35. Required Average of faculty of Commerce from all the college

$$= \frac{36.5+33+60+25}{4} = \frac{154.5}{4} = 38.625$$
= 38.625 × 1000 = 38625.

37. Required Average

$$= \frac{5+7.5+10+17.5+25+27.5+32.5}{7}$$
$$= \frac{125}{7} = 17.85 \text{ lakhs} \sim 18 \text{ lakhs.}$$

38. Difference in production in 1995-1997
= 7.5 – 5 = 2.5 lakh

Difference in production in 1997-1998
= 10 – 7.5 = 2.5 lakh

Difference in production in 1999-1998
= 17.5 – 10 = 7.5 lakh

Difference in production in 2000-1999
= 25 – 17.5 = 7.5 lakh

Difference in production in 2001-2000
= 27.5 – 25 = 2.5 lakh

Difference in production in 2002-2001
$= 32.5 - 32 = 0.5$ lakh

$\therefore$ Highest difference in production is 7.5 lakh.

39. Per cent increase in production in year 1997 over previous year 1996

$$= \frac{7.5-5}{5} \times 100 = 50\%$$

Per cent increase in production in year 1998 over previous year 1997

$$= \frac{10-7.5}{7.5} \times 100 = 33.33\%$$

Per cent increase in production in year 1999 over previous year 1998

$$= \frac{17.5-10}{10} \times 100 = 75\%$$

Per cent increase in production in year 2000 over previous year 1999

$$= \frac{25-17.5}{17.5} \times 100 = 42.86\%$$

Per cent increase in production in year 2001 over previous year 2000

$$= \frac{27.5-25}{25} \times 100 = 10\%$$

Per cent increase in production in year 2002 over previous year 2001

$$= \frac{32.5-27.5}{27.5} \times 100 = 18.18\%$$

Highest per cent increase in the year 1999.

40. Percentage of amount spent on Cricket and Hockey together = 25 + 15 = 40%
Required Amount = 1,50,00,000 × 40%
= 60,00,000.

41. Percentage of amount spent on Basketball = 12.5%
$\therefore$ Required amount spent on Basketball = 1,20,00,000 × 12.5% = 15,00,000.

42. Required Ratio $= \frac{\text{Total} \times 15\%}{\text{Total} \times 15\%} = 1:1.$

43. $\because$ Highest percentage of amount is spent on cricket.
So, Cricket is the most popular game.

44. $\because$ Percentage of amount spent on Golf and Basketball is same *i.e.*, 12.5%.

45. $\because$ Expenditure on Taxes = 12%
$\therefore$ Required amount = 6500 × 12%
= ₹ 780.

46. % Expenditure on clothing, taxes and transportation combined
= 15 + 12 + 8 = 35%
$\therefore$ Required Central Angle

$$= \frac{360°}{100} \times 35 = 126°.$$

47. Required Amount = 6500 × (30 – 20)%
= 6500 × 10% = 650.

48. Required percentage

$$= \frac{110 \text{ Crore}}{(110+227+458+107+183+454)\text{Crore}} \times 100$$

$$= \frac{11000}{1539} = 7.1\%.$$

49. Magnitude of $\angle AOC$

$$= \frac{(107+458)}{(110+227+458+107+183+454)} \times 360°$$

$$= \frac{565 \times 360°}{1539} = \frac{203400}{1539}$$

$= 132.16° \sim 132°.$

50. Total investment in socially oriented sector (plan and non-plan)
= 107 + 458 = 565 crore
Total Investment in Govt. Securities (Central and State) = 454 + 110 = 564 crore.
Required difference = (565 – 564) crore
= 1 crore more.

51. Required percentage

$$= \frac{183-110}{110} \times 100 = \frac{7300}{110} = 66.36\% \sim 66\%.$$

52. Required Ratio of Area

$$= \frac{(183+454+110) \times \frac{\pi r^2}{\text{Total}}}{(107+458+227) \times \frac{\pi r^2}{\text{Total}}} = \frac{747}{792} = \frac{83}{88}.$$

Previous Year Paper

GGSIPU – B.Com (H) Entrance Exam 2018*

ENGLISH LANGUAGE AND COMPREHENSION

Directions (Qs. Nos. 1 to 8) : *Read the following passage carefully and choose the most appropriate option.*

1. There have been plenty of flashpoints in cricket in the more than 75 years since an England team led by Douglas Jardine and under the auspices of Marylebone Cricket Club (MCC), arrived in Australia. Even so, few have been as controversial as the 1932/33 Bodyline series where Jardine's despised tactics not only threatened the future of Test cricket but undermined the bonds of the British Empire. Jardine, a cold, calculating product of Winchester and Oxford, devised a strategy of dangerously short-pitched bowling using his two fast bowlers, Harold Larwood and Bill Voce, to combat Don Bradman, Australia's sporting hero of the Depression-ravaged times.

2. "The Don" had been rewriting cricket's record books since his Test debut in 1928 and when the Australians won the five-Test series 2-1 in England in 1930, Bradman amassed 974 runs at a batting average of 139.14, an aggregate record that stands to this day. Jardine's theory of directing his bowlers to bowl at leg stump and make the ball rear into the batsman's body became known as "Bodyline." When Jardine was appointed England captain for the Australian tour, one of his former Winchester schoolmasters, Rockley Wilson, is said to have warned he might win the Ashes but he would lose a dominion in the process.

3. Passions became so inflamed that during the third Test at the Adelaide Oval in January 1933, seething spectators threatened to jump the fence as anti-English feelings soared. Bill Woodfull, Australia's gentlemanly captain, was twice struck by bumpers and wicket-keeper Bert Oldfield edged a ferocious delivery from Larwood on to his temple, collapsed beside the pitch and was carried from the field unconscious. It produced one of the immortal quotes in Test cricket when Woodfull told the English management: "There are two teams out there, and only one of them is playing cricket." Behind the scenes there were frantic political negotiations to save the tour and restore frayed diplomatic relations between Britain and Australia.

4. The British coalition government's Dominion Secretary JH Thomas later described Bodyline as the most troublesome affair of his ministerial career. England's emphatic 4-1 series victory brought both opprobrium and praise for Jardine. The campaign curbed Bradman's batting average to 56.57. He scored just one century in his four Tests with a series aggregate of 396 runs. Without the Bodyline series, Bradman would have finished his career with a Test average of 104.76 instead of 99.94.

5. Larwood, the former Nottinghamshire coalminer, claimed a series-high 33 wickets at 19.51 but events soured him. The 28-year-old paceman never played for England again. Larwood later migrated to Australia with his wife Lois, and his five daughters and lived in Sydney until his death in 1995, at the age of 90. Jack Fingleton, who played in three of the Bodyline Tests, echoed the feelings of others in the Australian team when he later

* *Held on 05-05-2018.*

wrote: "I do not think there was one single batsman who played in most of those Bodyline games who ever afterwards recaptured his love for cricket."

6. It says much for the series that Bodyline remains the only chapter in cricket's history that film-makers have thought worth dramatising, with a television mini-series first broadcast in Australia in 1984. Jardine resigned as England captain before Australia's 1934 Ashes tour and retired from first-class cricket aged 33. That same year MCC outlawed systematic bowling of fast and short-pitched balls at batsmen standing clear of their wicket. Bradman, once lauded as the greatest living Australian, died in Adelaide on February 25, 2001 aged 92, while Jardine died from lung cancer aged 57, in Montreux, Switzerland, in June 1958.

1. Why is the only television mini-series on cricket ever made based on the Bodyline series?
A. Because it included a lot of drama, off-field and on-field
B. Because people died during the series
C. Because England won the series
D. Because Jardine wanted to become filmstar

2. Why did anti-English feelings soar during the series?
A. Because the Australians did not want English colonization
B. Because they hated all English
C. Because the game was not being played in the right spirit
D. Because Australia were winning

3. What word in the passage means "harsh criticism or censure"?
A. Emphatic B. Jardine
C. Ferocious D. Opprobrium

4. What word in the passage means "definite and clear"?
A. Emphatic B. Opprobrium
C. Troublesome D. Diplomatic

5. What word in the passage means the same as "threadbare"?
A. Frantic B. Frayed
C. Unconscious D. Resigned

6. What word in the passage means the opposite of "gentle"?
A. Ferocious B. Ravaged
C. Ministerial D. Frayed

7. What word in the passage means "gave way"?
A. Ravaged B. Collapsed
C. Frantic D. Opprobrium

8. Who was responsible for masterminding the Bodyline strategy?
A. Bradman B. Jardine
C. Larwood D. Woodfull

Directions (Qs. Nos. 9 to 14) : *Which of the phrases given as options means the same as the phrase underlined in the sentence.*

9. <u>I have always disliked cleaning but I've finished it all now.</u>
A. I have always disliked cleaning but I've finished it all now.
B. I haven't been liking cleaning but I've finished it all now.
C. I have always disliked cleaning but I'd finished it all now.
D. I have always dislike cleaning but I have finished it all now.

10. You went to the Caribbean for Christmas didn't you? <u>How was the journey like?</u>
A. How was the journey like?
B. In whose was the journey?
C. Which was the journey like?
D. What was the journey like?

11. <u>The countries corporation tax rate was very high so the managing director decided to relocate the company to one more.</u>
A. The countries corporation tax rate was very high so the managing director decided to relocate the company to one more.
B. The country's corporation tax rate was very high so the managing director

decided to relocate the company to another.

C. The country's corporation tax rate was very high so the managing director decided to relocate the company to one more.

D. The countries corporation tax rate was very high so the managing director decided to relocate the company to another.

12. The Bank of Ausralia raised its principal interest rate by a half percentage point to 5.25%, which is expected to cool demand and make future increases less likely.

A. The Bank of Ausralia raised its principal interest rate

B. The Bank of Ausralia's principal interest rate raised

C. The Bank of Ausralia raised its principal interest rates

D. The Bank of Ausralia raised it principal interest rate

13. The current exchange rate of 115.1 make many Americans less well off than they were a year ago.

A. The current exchange rate of 115.1 make

B. The current exchange rate of 115.1 makes

C. The current exchange rate of 115.1 were to make Answer

D. The current exchange rate of 115.1 is making for

14. I do not think employers should expect people to stay late to get a job finished.

A. employers should expect people

B. employers ought expect people

C. employers had better expect people

D. employers should not expect people

Directions (Qs. Nos. 15 to 24): *Complete the sentence by choosing the most appropriate option.*

15. Juan's friends found him in a ____ mood after he learned he would be homecoming king.

A. jovial B. stealthy
C. paltry D. gullible

16. His suit of armour made the knight _____ to his enemy's attack, and he was able to escape safely to his castle.

A. vulnerable
B. churlish
C. invulnerable
D. static

17. Choosing a small, fuel-efficient car is a _____ purchase for a recent college graduate.

A. corrupt B. tedious
C. unhallowed D. judicious

18. Such a _____ violation of school policy should be punished by nothing less than expulsion.

A. copious B. flagrant
C. raucous D. nominal

19. With all of the recent negative events in her life, she felt _____ forces must be at work.

A. resurgent B. premature
C. malignant D. punctilious

20. The ____ rumours did a great deal of damage even though they turned out to be false.

A. bemused B. prosaic
C. apocryphal D. ebullient

21. When her schoolwork got to be too much, Pam had a tendency to _____, which always put her further behind.

A. dedicate B. rejuvenate
C. ponder D. procrastinate

22. Richa's glance was a ______ invitation to speak later in private about events of the meeting.

A. treacherous B. scintillating
C. tactful D. tacit

23. She reached the _____ of her career with her fourth novel, which won't the Pulitzer Prize.

A. harbinger B. apogee
C. metamorphosis D. dictum

24. The ______ townspeople celebrated the soldier's return to his home by adorning trees with yellow ribbons and ballons.

A. somber B. jubilant
C. pitiless D. cunning

Directions (Qs. Nos. 25 to 32): *Choose the option that is most dissimilar to the given word.*

25. Jocund
A. Sad B. Funny
C. Sly D. Dangerous

26. Surreptitious
A. Rigorous B. Blatant
C. Spectacular D. Suspicious

27. Immaculate
A. Immature B. Imaginable
C. Defiled D. Desperate

28. Equivocal
A. Equal B. Equivalent
C. Separate D. Unambiguous

29. Foolhardy
A. Tough B. Distrustful
C. Rash D. Prudent

30. Glamorous
A. Chic B. Drab
C. Shiny D. Stylish

31. Counterfeit
A. Real B. Illiterate
C. Prescription D. Strike

32. Juvenile
A. Childish B. Rejuvenate
C. Fast D. Mature

Directions (Qs. Nos. 33 to 38): *Choose the option that is most similar to the given word.*

33. Ineffable
A. Unpleasant B. Inscribable
C. Indescribable D. Irrepressible

34. Pedantic
A. Pedagogic B. Pedestrian
C. Over-concerned D. Over-scrupulous

35. Peripheral
A. Sentimental B. Fleeting
C. Circumstantial D. Marginal

36. Perception
A. Estimation B. Duty
C. Obligation D. Precedence

37. Decadent
A. Subtle B. Degenerating
C. Aristocratic D. Strange

38. Garrulous
A. Grand B. Loud
C. Cogent D. Talkative

LOGICAL REASONING

Directions (Qs. Nos. 39 to 43): *Read the below information carefully and answer the questions that follow:*

In a family of three generations, there are eight members. A and B are sisters.

F is the grand-daughter of E. H is the only nephew of A. D is the brother-in-law of B.

C is the father-in-law of G. There are three married couples in the family. Each couple has atleast one child.

39. How is F related to H?
A. cousin B. uncle
C. brother D. father

40. How is E related to G?
A. grandmother B. aunt
C. mother-in-law D. mother

41. How is D related to E?
A. uncle B. son
C. son-in-law D. grandmother

42. How is C related to F?
A. father B. grandfather
C. uncle D. grandmother

43. In the family, the ratio of male members to female members is:
A. 3 : 5 B. 5 : 3
C. 1 : 1 D. 2 : 3

Directions (Qs. Nos. 44 to 48): *Study the following information carefully and answer the questions given below.*

A, B, C, D, E, F, G, H and K are sitting around a circle facing the centre. F is fourth to the right of A, who is third to the right of B. K is fourth to the left of B and third to the right of D. C is third to the right of H. E is second to the left of G.

44. Who is fourth to the left of G?
A. G B. A
C. D D. C

45. What is E's position with respect to B?
A. second to the left B. third to the right
C. fourth to the right D. third to the left

46. Who is third to the right of K?
A. F B. E
C. G D. A

47. Who is on the immediate right of F?
A. B B. G
C. E D. A

48. In which of the following combinations is the third person sitting between the first and the second person?
A. EGF B. BGH
C. GFB D. ADC

Directions (Qs. Nos. 49 to 53): *These questions are based on the following information:*

Seven actors P, Q, R, S, T, V, W are selected to perform in three soaps to be telecasted in morning matinee and evening.

There are atleast two actors in each soap and only one of them is male. There are three categories of actors; two child artists, two comedians, and three cinema stars among them.

(*i*) R is a female comedian and she does not act with the pair of sisters P and V.
(*ii*) Q, a male child artist, acts with only W, a cinema star who acts in morning soap.
(*iii*) S is a male comedian.
(*iv*) No two persons of a particular category act together.
(*v*) P is not a comedian and acts in the matinee soap.

49. To which category does V belong?
A. Child artist B. Comedian
C. Cinema star D. Either (A) or (C)

50. In which soap does R act?
A. Morning B. Matinee
C. Evening D. Either (B) or (C)

51. Which of the following represents the three cinema starts?
A. WTV B. WTP
C. WTV or TWP D. None of these

52. Which of the following is not correct?
A. T – male – cinemastar
B. Q – female – child artist
C. P – female – cinema star
D. W – female – cinema star

53. How many male cinema stars are there among them?
A. One B. Two
C. Three D. Data inadequate

Directions (Qs. Nos. 54 to 58): *Each of the following question is based on the following three-digit numbers.*

524, 923, 488, 843, 252

54. If all digits of each of the numbers are arranged in a descending order (within the number itself) and then the numbers are arranged in an ascending order, which will be the middle digit of the third number?
A. 3 B. 4
C. 2 D. 6

55. If one is subtracted from the middle digit of each of the numbers and then the positions of the first and third digits are interchanged, which of the following will be the first digit of the second highest number after they are arranged in descending order?
A. 9 B. 2
C. 7 D. 4

56. What will be the difference between the last digits of the highest number and the lowest number after the positions of the first two digits in each number are interchanged?
A. 4 B. 7
C. 2 D. 1

57. Which of the following is the sum of the middle digit of the lowest number and the last digit of the highest number?
A. 4 B. 7
C. 8 D. 2

58. If the first digit of each number is replaced with its predecessor and then the numbers are arranged in a descending order, which of the following will be the second digit of the second number from the top?

A. 4 B. 2
C. 7 D. 8

Directions (Qs. Nos. 59 to 68): *Choose the most appropriate option.*

59. JW, LR, ON, SK, ?

A. XI B. XK
C. VJ D. VI

60. XC, UF, QJ, LO, ?

A. EU B. FU
C. EV D. FV

61. 4, 484, 49284, ?, 493817284

A. 49337384 B. 49338284
C. 49373294 D. 4937284

62. B C D H I J N O P T U V ?

A. Z B. X
C. Y D. W

63. 425, 417, 390, 326, ?, –15, –358

A. 193 B. 201
C. 187 D. 311

64. 8, 13, 23, 43, 83, 163, ?

A. 289 B. 297
C. 323 D. 317

65. If each vowel in the word 'MOTIVATE' is replaced with the next letter as well as each consonant is replaced with the previous letter according to the English alphabet order and the new group of letters are arranged in the order. Then which of the following letter will be fifth from the right end?

A. P B. O
C. K D. L

66. Select the pair which resembles the given set of numbers:
16, 36, 64

A. 4, 9, 144 B. 16, 100, 256
C. 25, 49, 121 D. 9, 81, 169

67. Mirage : Desert : : ?

A. sky : illusion B. rain : rainbow
C. rainbow : sky D. image : mirror

68. Given set : (10, 12, 15)

A. (21, 23, 27) B. (30, 32, 36)
C. (60, 62, 66) D. (68, 70, 73)

Directions (Qs. Nos. 69 to 73): *In each of the following questions, four words have been given out of which three are alike in some manner while the fourth one is different. Choose the odd one out.*

69. A. 676 B. 529
C. 841 D. 852

70. A. Atal Behari Vajpayee
B. P.V. Narasimha Rao
C. Manmohan Singh
D. Rajiv Gandhi

71. A. Binocular B. Mirror
C. Magnifier D. Telescope

72. A. Helium B. Nitrogen
C. Carbon dioxide D. Aluminium

73. A. Beetle B. Owl
C. Butterfly D. Mosquito

Directions (Qs. Nos. 74 to 77): *Choose the most appropriate option.*

74. If number of chickens is double the number of hens, then which of the following could not be the total number of birds?

A. 324 B. 1023
C. 792 D. 256

75. A man uses gloves of two colours white and grey. If he has 20 pairs of each colour in a drawer, suppose he take out gloves at random without looking, how many must he take out to be sure that he has a matching pair?

A. 3 B. 13
C. 2 D. 5

76. If one eighth of a half of the cake is eaten by father and rest of the cake is divided among three children. Approximately, what per cent of a cake did each child get?

A. 31.25% B. 24.6%
C. 35% D. 37%

77. If '×' denotes '+', '+' denotes '÷', '÷' denotes '–', '–' denotes '×' then the value of the expression 6 – 9 × 8 + 2 ÷ 5 will be:

A. 54 B. 53
C. 72 D. 73

DATA INTERPRETATION

Directions (Qs. Nos. 78 to 82): *The table below represents the production of cars of different companies.*

	Cars production (in lakhs)			
Years	Maruti	Hyundai	GM	BMW
2000-01	450	159	452	482
2001-02	452	1523	152	154
2002-03	459	123	228	420
2003-04	456	455	380	460
2004-05	962	260	340	500

78. During the period 2000-01 to 2004-05, what was the percentage of total production of Maruti?

A. 30.8%
B. 31.3%
C. 32.6%
D. 33.1%

79. During the year 2004-05, the percentage increase in the production of Maruti cars over the previous year was:

A. 117%
B. 265%
C. 111%
D. 109%

80. The average production of all the cars for a company in 2003-04 was:

A. 435
B. 466
C. 425
D. 438

81. The increase in the production of GM cars in 2003-04 over the previous year was:

A. 67%
B. 66.6%
C. 68%
D. 65%

82. The total number of Hyundai cars produced in 2001-02 to 2003-04 was:

A. 2100
B. 2170
C. 2101
D. 2120

Directions (Qs. Nos. 83 to 87): *Answer the questions based on the graph, which shows the number of family members in a family who are graduates, postgraduates and illiterates across 4 generations.*

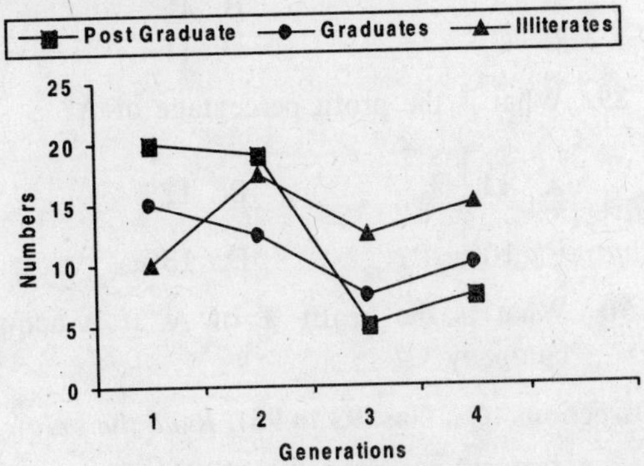

83. In which generation is the ratio of postgraduates and illiterates in the family the least?

A. 1
B. 2
C. 3
D. 4

84. For any generation, what is the greatest and the least difference between the number of graduates and illiterates?

A. 6, 4
B. 5, 4
C. 5, 2
D. 6, 1

85. Find the number of illiterates in the generation in which number of graduates is the least.

A. 7
B. 5
C. 9
D. 15

86. If the study expenses of each graduate are ₹ 50,000 and those of each postgraduate are ₹ 80,000, what are the study expenses for generation 3?

A. ₹ 12,30,000
B. ₹ 16,80,000
C. ₹ 11,66,000
D. ₹ 7,60,000

87. What was the difference between the numbers of graduates and post graduates in generation of 2?

A. 1
B. 0
C. 2
D. 5

Directions (Qs. Nos. 88 to 92): *Answer the questions based on the following table which shows the sales, costs and profits of 4 companies (in ₹).*

Values	A	B	C	D
Sales	50,000	1,70,000	50,000	1,10,000
Costs	45,000	1,43,000	40,000	80,000
Profits	5,000	27,000	10,000	30,000

88. Which company has the highest amount of profit?

A. A
B. B
C. C
D. D

89. What is the profit percentage of A?

A. $11\frac{1}{9}\%$
B. 12%
C. 10%
D. 13%

90. What is the profit % of A, if it acquires company C?

A. 17.64%
B. 18%
C. 17%
D. 19%

91. Which company shows the highest profit per cent?

A. A
B. B
C. C
D. D

92. If the cost for D becomes the cost for B and vice-versa, what will be the profit percentage of B?

A. 112.5%
B. 117.63%
C. 109%
D. 107.10%

Directions (Qs. Nos. 93 to 95): *Read the below information carefully and answer the following questions:*

A factory was opened in 1994 with certain initial strengths in different unit as shown in the table. In the beginning of the subsequent years some of the workers left and some new workers were deployed Number of workers left or Joined in between Details are given in the table given below. Study it carefully and answer the questions that follow:

Year 1994 / Initial Strength	UNIT									
	A 156		B 132		C 98		D 76		E 125	
	Left	Joined	Left	Joined	Left	Joined	Left	Joined	Left	Joined
1995	12	15	23	32	12	36	06	26	11	13
1996	17	18	16	14	08	19	17	28	11	15
1997	09	20	12	12	17	14	09	16	19	16
1998	32	40	14	17	23	35	12	23	23	14
1999	22	35	11	15	18	25	14	24	32	38
2000	26	32	17	21	13	18	11	19	21	36

93. The strength of workers in Unit C in 1996 is approximately what per cent of the strength in Unit E in 1997?

A. 98
B. 102
C. 104
D. 110

94. What was the total strength of workers in all the five units in 1996?

A. 570
B. 607
C. 690
D. 670

95. What was the approximate increase/decrease in the strength of the workers in Unit D in 1998 with respect to its initial strength?

A. 57.37% increase
B. 64.47% increase
C. 64.47% decrease
D. 57.37% decrease

Directions (Qs. Nos. 96 and 97): *The below graph and table show prices of three commodities and the population consuming the same during four years.*

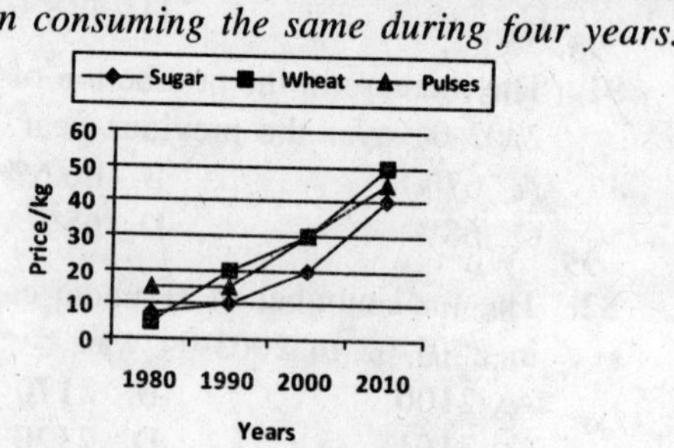

Year	Population
1980	1,55,000
1990	3,85,000
2000	7,95,000
2010	17,98,000

96. If the consumption of sugar per person was 171 kg in 1980 and 105 kg in 2010, then what is the % change in income spent on sugar?

A. 3518.7% B. 3436.7%
C. 3461.4% D. 3568.3%

97. If in 2015, the price of sugar increased by 18% over that of sugar in 2010 and the number of persons increased by 3% with the consumption per person having decreased by 48% in the same period, what was the % change in total expenditure over the same period?

A. 518% B. 37.5%
C. 36.8% D. 36.9%

Directions (Qs. Nos. 98 to 102): *Answer the questions based on the following bar graph:*

Number of Arts, Science and Commerce students in different colleges

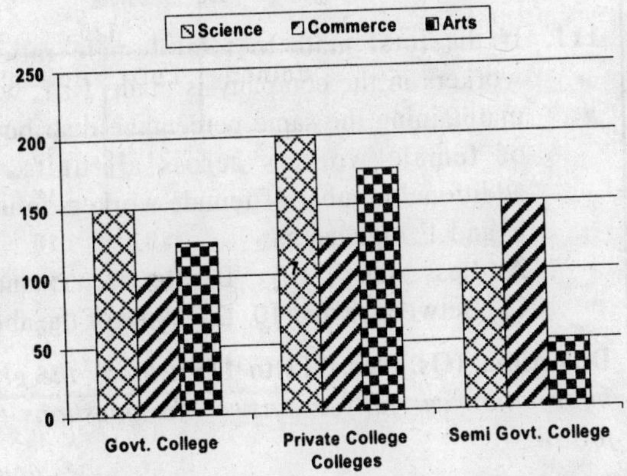

98. What was the total number of students in Govt. College?

A. 380 B. 375
C. 500 D. 400

99. What was the total number of students in Semi Govt. College after one year, assuming an increase of 10%?

A. 300 B. 330
C. 350 D. 325

100. What per cent of commerce students are studying in Semi Govt. College?

A. 40% B. 50%
C. 60% D. 45%

101. What per cent more students of commerce background are there in Semi Govt. College as compared to a Private college?

A. 20% B. 25%
C. 15% D. 28%

102. Total number of science students in Private College is what per cent of the total number of science students?

A. 44.44% B. 45%
C. 43.33% D. 44.5%

Directions (Qs. Nos. 103 and 104): *Study the following pie chart and table carefully to answer the questions that follow:*

Total cars = 700 Distribution of cars

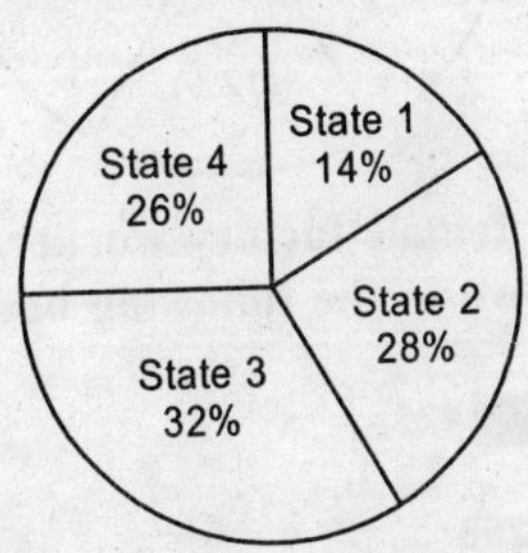

Table showing the ratio of diesel to petrol engine cars, which are distributed among four different states:

State	Diesel Engine Cars	Petrol Engine Cars
State-1	3	4
State-2	5	9
State-3	5	3
State-4	1	1

103. What is the difference between the number of diesel engine cars in State-2 and the number of petrol engine cars in State-4?

A. 159 B. 21
C. 28 D. 34

104. The number of petrol engine cars in State-3 is what per cent more than the number of diesel engine cars in State-1?

A. 100 B. 200
C. 125 D. 225

Directions (Qs. Nos. 105 to 111): *Answer the questions based on the given data.*

The Industrial Relations (IR) personnel of six spinning units—A, B, C, D, E and F—submitted the following data of the workers on roll to the HR Head of a textiles company.

Total number of factory workers = 10500
percentage of Factory Workers

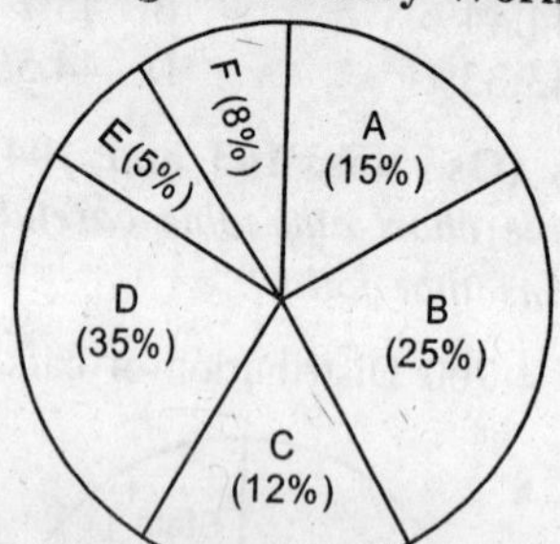

Number of female factory workers in each unit is shown in the following bar graph:

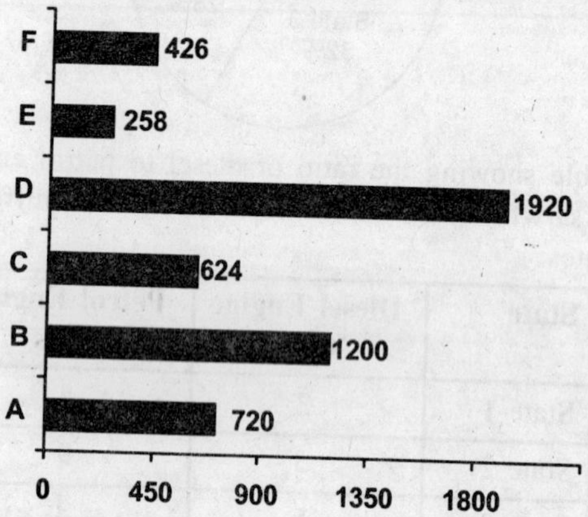

105. What is the total number of male workers in spinning units A, B and C together?

A. 2478 B. 2800
C. 2540 D. 2920

106. Which of the following units has the highest number of male workers?

A. B B. A
C. D D. F

107. Which of the following units has the least male to female worker ratio?

A. A B. D
C. F D. C

108. What is the ratio of the total number of male workers in spinning units A and B to the total number of female workers in spinning units C and E?

A. 400 : 150 B. 1140 : 880
C. 380 : 147 D. 48 : 11

109. What is the difference between the number of male workers and the number of female workers in the spinning unit E?

A. 7 B. 8
C. 10 D. None of these

110. If equal numbers of male and female workers opt to shift from Factory D to Factory C, such that the latter's strength does not exceed 1500 workers, what is the maximum percentage of females out of the total strength that opted for the shift?

A. 6.25% B. 5.75%
C. 3.56% D. 3.27%

111. If the total male to total female ratio of workers in the company is made 1 : 1, while maintaining the same percentage distribution of female workers across all units, the additional number of female workers in units E and F together is:

A. Less than 5 B. Between 5 and 8
C. Between 8 and 10 D. None of the above

Directions (Qs. Nos. 112 to 115): *Study the given information carefully to answer the questions that follow:*

An organization consists of 2400 employees working in different departments *viz,* HR, Marketing, IT, Production and Accounts. The ratio of male to female employees in the organization is 5 : 3. Twelve per cent of the males work in the HR department. Twenty-four per cent of the females work in the Accounts department. The ratio of males to females working in the HR department is 6 : 11. One-ninth of the females work in the IT department. Forty-two per cent of the males work in the production department. The number ten per cent of females working in the Production department is of that of the males working in the same. The remaining females work in the Marketing department.

The total number of employees working in the IT department is 285. 22% of the males work in the Marketing department and the remaining work in the Accounts department.

112. The number of males working in the IT department forms approximately what per cent of the total number of males in the organization?
A. 5 B. 12
C. 21 D. 8

113. What is the total number of females working in the HR and Marketing departments together?
A. 363 B. 433
C. 545 D. 521

114. The total number of employees working in the Accounts department forms what per cent of the total number of employees in the organization? (Rounded off to two digits after decimal)
A. 19.34 B. 16.29
C. 11.47 D. 23.15

115. The number of females working in the Production department forms what per cent of the total number of females in the organization?
A. 7 B. 2
C. 4 D. 15

Directions (Qs. Nos. 116 and 117): *Read the below information carefully and answer the questions that follow.*

Kanwar saves every next day double the amount of money he saves every day in order to buy a premium leather jacket. After a week, when he visits the outlet, the shop owner tells him that the season's discount has got over and he would now not be able to avail the 16.67% discount.

116. If Ramesh had only ₹ 500 more than the amount of money that was enough to buy the jacket at the said discount, by what amount was he short if he had started his saving with ₹ 100 the first day?
A. ₹ 12700 B. ₹ 14640
C. ₹ 2000 D. ₹ 1940

117. Ramesh was able to purchase the jacket the next day and was left with 20% of his savings. If Ramesh paid ₹ 20,400 for the jacket, with what amount did he start his saving?
A. ₹ 50 B. ₹ 75
C. ₹ 100 D. ₹ 125

Directions (Qs. Nos. 118 to 122): *Answer the questions based on the given data.*

A total of 1150 candidates contested the Assembly Elections in Bihar. They belong either to the RJD or JD(U). 60 male candidates of the RJD lost the elections. 700 candidates belong to the JD(U). 200 RJD candidates lost the elections. 100 male candidates lost the elections. 300 candidates of the JD(U) are either male candidates who have lost or female candidates who have won. 400 female candidates are either the RJD candidates who won or the JD(U) candidates who lost. 150 male candidates who belong to the JD(U) won the elections.

118. What is the number of JD(U) party male candidates who lost the election?
A. 40 B. 50
C. 100 D. 150

119. By what number is the number of female candidates contesting the elections more than the number of male candidates contesting the elections?
A. 200 B. 250
C. 350 D. 450

120. How many female candidates of the RJD won the elections?
A. 100 B. 150
C. 200 D. 250

121. What is the number of female candidates of RJD who lost the elections?
A. 120 B. 130
C. 140 D. 150

122. What is the number of JD(U) female candidates who lost the elections?
A. 150 B. 200
C. 230 D. 250

Directions (Qs. Nos. 123 and 124): *Answer the questions based on the given data.*

Given pie chart shows the percentage distribution of students that applied for different

MBA entrance exams in 2008 and the table gives the application fee (in ₹) of each exam.

Total number of students = 1137600

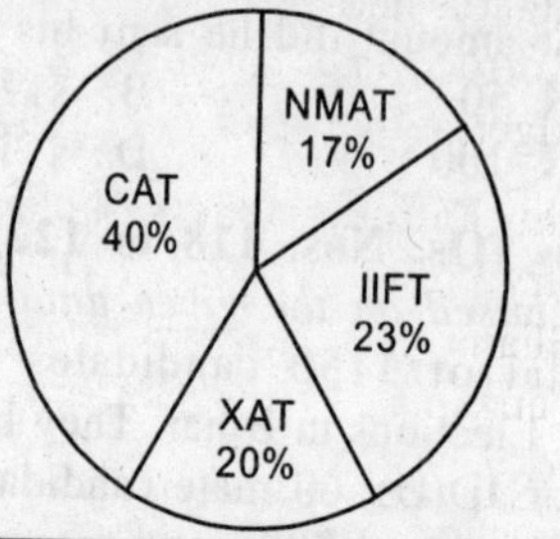

MBA Exam	Application Fee (in ₹)
CAT	1715
IIFT	1895
XAT	2315
NMAT	2945

123. What is the total fee given by all the 1137600 students for applying to all entrance exams?

A. ₹ 2,37,34,64,800 B. ₹ 2,31,24,64,800
C. ₹ 2,37,24,64,800 D. ₹ 2,31,84,64,900

124. In 2009, the number of students who applied for CAT increased by 18% and application fee of the Exam was also hiked by 39%. What % of the total fee given by all the students was the fee paid by students who applied for CAT if the number of applications of other exams as well as their application fee remained the same as in 2008?

A. 43.3% B. 44.56%
C. 47.3% D. 42.5%

Directions (Qs. Nos. 125 to 127): *Choose the most appropriate option.*

125. Arun decides to refurbish his study. He decides to change the old wallpaper of the four walls. He also decides to buy a rectangular Turkish carpet to be placed in the centre of the floor, leaving 2 feet from each edge. The room is 12 feet long, 8 feet broad and 3 m high. It has two windows measuring 0.75 m × 1 m and a door measuring 1.5 m × 1 m. He decides to use a wood panelled false ceiling to give a modern look to the roof. He also wants to get rid of his study table too large for his small room and wants a sleek 1.5 mm thick tiled shelf constructed instead, with the base not more than 2.5 feet by 3 feet. The cost of a Turkish carpet is ₹ 50/sq.m and that of the wallpaper is 32 paise/sq.m.

A sleek 0.75 mm thick tile of 10 cm × 5 cm costs ₹ 10 per piece.

The cost of the wooden paneling is ₹ 20/sq.m. Arun earmarked an expenditure of ₹ 3000 for the complete refurbishing job. What percentage (approx.) is the actual expense more/less than the earmarked?

A. 2% B. 3%
C. 4% D. 5%

126. Kapil had a debt of ₹ 20,000 to be paid off. To discharge the same, he first invested a sum of money at 4% p.a. for the first two years, 6% p.a. for the next five years and 8% p.a. for the period beyond seven years. The simple interest accrued by the sum for a total period of nine years was ₹ 1512. He deposited the amount so obtained in equal proportion in two banks, one at 8% p.a. and another at 10% p.a. for 3.5 years and 5 years. At the end of the tenure of each, he lent out the lesser amount accrued at 18% simple interest for 8 years and the greater one for a period of 10 years at 15% simple interest. The amount received early was then locked at 10% compounded half yearly for a period of two years. What proportion (approx.) of the debt got serviced by Kapil if the final amount accrued after above investments was used solely to pay off his debt?

A. 40% B. 50%
C. 60% D. 81%

127. 400 tourists visited New York for the first time. Each visited at least one place among Statue of Liberty, Wall Street and Empire State Building. 200 tourists visited the Statue of Liberty and 240 tourists visited Wall Street. If the number of visitors who visited Empire State Building is 160, then what is the maximum possible number of tourists who visited only Wall Street?

A. 133 B. 200
C. 160 D. 80

GENERAL AWARENESS

128. Which of the following mountain ranges form a dividing line between the Ganges Plain and the Deccan Plateau?
A. Aravalli B. Vindhya
C. Satpura D. Ajanta

129. The famous hill-station 'Kodaikanal' lies in:
A. Nilgiri hills B. Palani hills
C. Cardamom hills D. Javadi hills

130. Asia's largest tulip garden is located in which state?
A. Jammu & Kashmir B. Assam
C. Sikkim D. Uttarakhand

131. Barak valley in Assam is famous for which among the following?
A. Petroleum Production
B. Tea Cultivation
C. Bamboo Industry
D. Cottage Industries

132. Garo Hills is a part of which among the following states of India?
A. Nagaland B. Meghalaya
C. Manipur D. Mizoram

133. Majuli, the largest river island in the world is located in which among the following states of India?
A. Assam B. Manipur
C. Nagaland D. Tripura

134. Which among the following was steel plant of India is sometimes called India's First Swadeshi Steel Plant?
A. Bengal Iron Works Company
B. TISCO
C. IISCO
D. Bokaro Steel Plant

135. The K2 Peak is located in which among the following ranges?
A. Central Himalayas B. Trans-Himalayas
C. Karakoran range D. Kumaun Himalayas

136. Which of the following countries are separated by the Strait of Gibraltar?
A. Portugal and Morocco
B. Algeria and Spain
C. Morroco and Spain
D. Algeria and Portugal

137. Mount Kilimanjaro is located in which country?
A. Ghana B. Kenya
C. Tanzania D. Namibia

138. The 'Saptanga Theory of State' (Theory of Seven Limbs of the State) was propounded by:
A. Kautilya in Arthashastra
B. Manu in Manusmriti
C. Kalhana in Rajatarangini
D. Banabhatta in Harshacharita

139. Who were Manu, Yajnavalkya, Narada and Brihaspati?
A. Law givers of ancient India
B. Gods of Vedic religion
C. Buddhist scholars and logicians
D. Celebrated mathematicians and astronomers of ancient India

140. Which of the following dynasty was ruling in India, when Alexander invaded India?
A. Nanda Dynasty
B. Shunga Dynasty
C. Maurya Dynasty
D. Shishunaga Dynasty

141. The Golden age of the "Gupta Literary Renaissance" is said to be the reign of whom among the following?
A. Chandragupta I B. Chandragupta II
C. Kumaragupta D. Skandgupta

142. Who founded the Ramakrishna Mission in 1896 to carry on humanitarian relief and social work?
A. Ramakrishna Paramahansa
B. Swami Dayananda Saraswati
C. Swami Vivekananda
D. Blavatsky and Olcott

143. Whic among the following Viceroys was associated with the "Ilbert Bill Controversy"?
A. Lord Curzon B. Lord Lytton
C. Lord Ripon D. Lord Hardinge

144. Which among the following great revolutionaries was the brain behind the 'Chittagong Armoury Raid'?

A. Ganesh Ghosh
B. Chandrashekhar Azad
C. Surya Sen
D. Lala Hardayal

145. Under which among the following acts, Civil Services started in India?

A. Charter Act 1813 B. Charter Act 1833
C. Charter Act 1853 D. Charter Act 1793

146. Who among the following was the first Non-Congress chief minister of India?

A. Indulal Yagnik
B. NG Ranga
C. EMS Naboodiripad
D. Shankar Dayal Sharma

147. Who among the following was the President of Indian National Congress at the time of Independence?

A. Dr. Rajendra Prasad
B. J.B. Kriplani
C. Dr. Bhimrao Ambedkar
D. Jawahar Lal Nahru

148. The name of which of the following women is known for working in close association with Chandra Shekhar Aazad in the famous Kakori train dacoity?

A. Raj Kumari Gupta
B. Kusum Agraval
C. Prakashvati Yakshapal
D. Basanti Devi

149. Ahalyabai, the saintly queen of Maheshwar (Central India) belonged to which dynasty?

A. Scindhya dynasty B. Peshwa dynasty
C. Holkar dynasty D. Rajput dynasty

150. The ONLY active volcano of South Asia is located in which of the following countries?

A. India B. Sri Lanka
C. Maldives D. Mauritius

ANSWERS

1	2	3	4	5	6	7	8	9	10
A	C	D	A	B	A	B	B	A	D
11	**12**	**13**	**14**	**15**	**16**	**17**	**18**	**19**	**20**
B	A	B	A	A	C	D	B	C	C
21	**22**	**23**	**24**	**25**	**26**	**27**	**28**	**29**	**30**
D	D	B	B	A	B	C	D	D	B
31	**32**	**33**	**34**	**35**	**36**	**37**	**38**	**39**	**40**
A	D	C	A	D	A	B	D	C	A
41	**42**	**43**	**44**	**45**	**46**	**47**	**48**	**49**	**50**
B	C	A	D	D	C	B	A	D	C
51	**52**	**53**	**54**	**55**	**56**	**57**	**58**	**59**	**60**
C	B	C	B	D	A	C	A	A	B
61	**62**	**63**	**64**	**65**	**66**	**67**	**68**	**69**	**70**
B	A	B	C	D	B	C	D	D	A
71	**72**	**73**	**74**	**75**	**76**	**77**	**78**	**79**	**80**
B	D	B	D	C	A	B	B	C	D
81	**82**	**83**	**84**	**85**	**86**	**87**	**88**	**89**	**90**
B	C	C	A	D	D	D	D	A	A
91	**92**	**93**	**94**	**95**	**96**	**97**	**98**	**99**	**100**
D	A	C	D	B	C	C	B	B	B
101	**102**	**103**	**104**	**105**	**106**	**107**	**108**	**109**	**110**
A	A	B	A	D	C	A	C	D	A
111	**112**	**113**	**114**	**115**	**116**	**117**	**118**	**119**	**120**
A	B	D	B	A	D	C	A	D	B

121	122	123	124	125	126	127	128	129	130
C	D	C	B	C	B	B	B	B	A
131	**132**	**133**	**134**	**135**	**136**	**137**	**138**	**139**	**140**
B	B	A	D	C	C	C	A	A	A
141	**142**	**143**	**144**	**145**	**146**	**147**	**148**	**149**	**150**
B	C	C	C	B	C	B	A	C	A

EXPLANATORY ANSWERS

For Qs. No. 39 to 43.

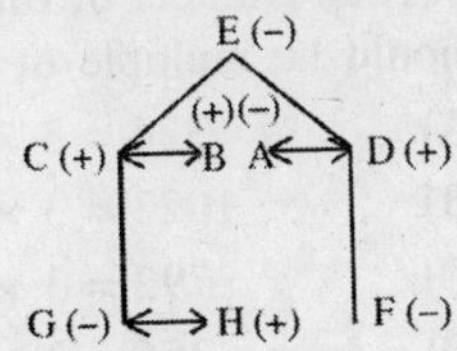

F is the grand-daughter of E; A and B are sister; C and D are brothers; C is the father-in-law of G.

39. F related to H as brother.

40. Grand mother (E is the grand-mother of G)

41. D related to E as Son.

42. C related to F as Uncle.

43. Male D, C, H; Female A, B, E, G, G required ratio = 3 : 5.

For Qs. Nos. 44 to 48.

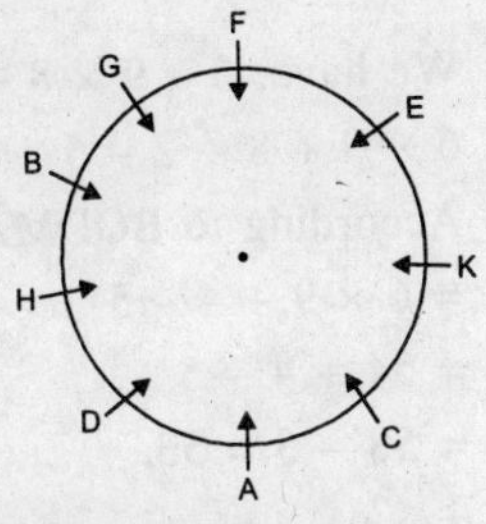

44. C is fourth to the left of G.

45. Third to the left.

For Qs. Nos. 49 to 53.

Evening	Matinee	Morning	Artist	Child artist	Comedian	Cinema star
✗	✓	✗	P(−)	✓	✗	✓
✗	✗	✓	Q(+)	✓	✗	✗
✓	✗	✗	R(−)	✗	✓	✗
✗	✓	✗	S(+)	✗	✓	✗
✓	✗	✗	T(+)	✓	✗	✓
✗	✓	✗	V(−)	✓	✗	✓
✗	✗	✓	W(−)	✗	✗	✓

49. Either (A) or (C).

50. Evening.

51. WTV or TWP.

52. Q–Female–Child artist

53. Three.

54. 542, 932, 884, 843, 522
(Digit in Descending order)
522, 542, 843, 884, 932
(Number in Ascending order)
Third Number = 843, Middle digit = 4.

55. 514, 913, 478, 833, 242
[1 substract from middle digit]
415, 319, 874, 338, 242
[First and Third digit interchange]
874, 415, 338, 319, 242 [Descending order]
Second Highest Number = 415
First digit = 4.

56. 254, 293, 848, 483, 522
[First two digit interchanged]
Highest Number = 848
Last digit = 8
Lowest Number = 254
Last digit = 4
Required difference = 8 − 4 = 4.

57. Lowest Number = 252
Middle digit = 5
Highest Number = 923
Last digit = 3
Required Sum = 5 + 3 = 8.

58. 424, 823, 388, 743, 152
(First digit replace by its predecessor)

823, 743, 424, 388, 152
(Arrange in descending order)
Second Number from the Top = 743
Second digit = 4.

59. J W L R Q N S K [X I]

(+2, +3, +4, +5 ; −5, −4, −3, −2)

∴ XI will come at the place of question mark.

60. X C U F Q J L O [F U]

(−3, −4, −5, −6 ; +3, +4, +5, +6)

∴ FU will come at the place of question mark.

62. B C D H I J N O P T U V [Z]

(+4, +4, +4, +4)

∴ Z will come at the place of question mark.

63. 425 417 390 326 [201] −15 −358

−8 $(-2)^3$, −27 $(-3)^3$, −64 $(-4)^3$, −125 $(-5)^3$, −216 $(-6)^3$, −343 $(-7)^3$

∴ 201 will come at the place of question mark.

64. 8 13 23 43 83 163 [323]

+5, +10, +20, +40, +80, +160

×2, ×2, ×2, ×2, ×2

∴ 323 will come at the place of question mark.

65. M O T I V A T E

−1↓ +1↓ −1↓ +1↓ −1↓ +1↓ −1↓ +1↓

L P S J U B S F

B F J L P S S U (Arrange in Order).

↑

5th from right

66. Given Set (16, 36, 64) = $4^2, 6^2, 8^2$
In the given set all Number is the square of even number. Therefore only option (B) Set (16, 100, 256) = $4^2, 10^2, 16^2$ follow this rule.

68. In the given set the difference between First number and Second nuber is −2, and the difference between second number and third number is −3.
So, Set (68, 70, 73) follow the same rule.

69. Except (D) 852, all other numbers are the Square of a Number.

72. Except (D) Aluminium, all others are Gas.

73. Except (B) Owl, all others are Insect.

74. Let total Hen is x,
So, total Chicken will be $2x$
∵ Total Birds = $2x + x = 3x$
∴ Total Number of Birds given in the option should be multiple of 3.

(A) $324 = 3 \times 108$
(B) $1023 = 3 \times 341$
(C) $792 = 3 \times 264$
(D) $256 = 3 \times 85 + 1$

So, 256 is not the multiple of 3, 256 could not be the total number of birds.

76. $$\text{Rest Part} = 1 - \frac{1}{8} \times \frac{1}{2} = \frac{15}{16}$$

$$\text{Part get by each child} = \frac{1}{3} \times \frac{15}{16} = \frac{5}{16}$$

$$\text{Percentage} = \frac{5}{16} \times 100 = 31.25\%.$$

77. We have, 6 − 9 × 8 + 2 ÷ 5
6 × 9 + 8 ÷ 2 − 5
According to BODMAS Rule,
= 6 × 9 + 4 − 5
= 54 + 4 − 5
= 58 − 5 = 53.

78. Total production of Maruti (Period 2000-01 to 2004-05) = 450 + 452 + 459 + 456 + 962
= 2779 lakh

Total production of Hyundai Cars
= 159 + 1523 + 123 + 455 + 280
= 2540 lakh

Total production of GM Cars
= 452 + 152 + 228 + 380 + 340
= 1552 lakh

Total production of BMW Cars
= 482 + 154 + 420 + 460 + 500
= 2016 lakh

Total Cars = 2779 + 2540 + 1552 + 2016

= 8887 lakh

Required Percentage

$$= \frac{2779}{8887} \times 100$$

= 31.27% ≃ 31.3%.

79. In 2003-05, Maruti car production

= 456 lakh.

In 2004-05 Maruti car production

= 962 lakh

$$\% \text{ increase} = \frac{962 \times 456}{456} \times 100$$

= 110.96% ≃ 111.

80. Required Average

$$= \frac{456 + 455 + 380 + 460}{4} = \frac{1751}{4}$$

= 437.75 ≃ 438 lakh

81. In 2002-03, GM car production = 228 lakh

In 2003-04 GM car production = 380 lakh

$$\% \text{ increase} = \frac{380 - 228}{228} \times 100$$

$$= \frac{15200}{228} = 66.6\%.$$

82. Total Hyundai car produced from 2001-02 to 2003-04 = 1523 + 123 + 455 = 2101 lakh.

88. Company D has the highest profit.

89. $\% \text{ Profit of A} = \frac{5000}{45000} \times 100 = 11\frac{1}{9}\%.$

90. Total cost (A + C) = 45000 + 40000

= 85000

Total profit (A + C) = 5000 + 10000

= 15000

$$\% \text{ Profit} = \frac{15000}{85000} \times 100$$

= 17.64%.

91. % Profit of Company A

$$= \frac{5,000}{45,000} \times 100 = 11\frac{1}{9}\%$$

= 11.11%

% Profit of Company B

$$= \frac{27,000}{1,43,000} \times 100 = 18.88\%$$

% Profit of Company C

$$= \frac{10,000}{40,000} \times 100 = 25\%$$

% Profit of Company D

$$= \frac{30,000}{80,000} \times 100 = 37.5\%$$

∴ Company 'D' shows the highest profit.

92. Cost of B = 80,000

Profit of B = 1,70,000 − 80,000 = 90,000

$$\% \text{ Profit} = \frac{90,000}{80,000} \times 100 = 112.5\%.$$

96. In 1980 Total Income spent on Sugar

= 8 × 171 × 1,55,000 = ₹ 21,20,40,000

In 2010 total Income spent on Sugar

= 40 × 105 × 17,98,000 = ₹ 7,55,16,00,000

% Change

$$= \frac{7,55,16,00,000 - 21,20,40,000}{21,20,40,000} \times 100$$

= 3461.4%.

97. Let the Sugar consumption in 2010

= 100 kg/person

Then, the Sugar consumption in 2015

= 52 kg/person (48% decrease)

Sugar price in 2010 = ₹ 40/kg

Sugar price in 2015 = 40 × 118%

= ₹ 47.2/kg (18% increase)

Number of person in 2010 = 17,98,000

Number of person in 2015

= 17,98,000 × 103% (3% increase)

= 18,51,940

% change in total expenditure

$$= \frac{52 \times 47.2 \times 1851940 - 100 \times 40 \times 17,98,000}{100 \times 40 \times 17,98,000} \times 100$$

$$= \frac{4,54,54,01,536 - 7,19,20,00,000}{7,19,20,000}$$

$$= \frac{-2,64,65,98,464}{7,19,20,000} = -36.79 = -36.8\%.$$

98. Total Student in Govt. College
$= 150 + 100 + 125 = 375.$

99. Total students in Semi-Govt. College
$= 100 + 150 + 50 = 300$
After one year total student
$= 300 \times 110\% = 330.$

100. Required percentage $= \frac{150}{300} \times 100 = 50\%.$

101. Commerce students in private collge = 125
Commerce students in Semi-govt. collge = 150
$= \frac{150-125}{125} \times 100 = \frac{25}{125} \times 100 = 20\%.$

102. Total Science students in all college
$= 150 + 200 + 100$
$= 450$
Science students in private collge = 200
Required percentage $= \frac{200}{450} \times 100 = 44.44\%.$

103. Total Car in State-2 $= 700 \times 28\% = 196$
In State-2;
Diesel Engine Cars $= 196 \times \frac{5}{14} = 70$
Total car in State-4 $= 700 \times 26\% = 182$
In State-4:
Petrol Engine cars $= 182 \times \frac{1}{2} = 91$
Required difference $= 91 - 70 = 21.$

104. In State-3 Petrol engine cars
$= 700 \times 32\% \times \frac{3}{8} = 84$
In State-1 Diesel engine cars
$= 700 \times 14\% \times \frac{3}{7} = 42$
$= \frac{84-42}{42} \times 100 = \frac{4200}{42} = 100\%.$

105. Total male worker in spinning units A, B and C
= Total worker in A, B and C – Female worker in A, B and C
$= 10{,}500(15\% + 25\% + 12\%) - (720 + 1200 + 624)$
$= 5460 - 2544 = 2916 \simeq 2920$

106. Male worker in A unit
$= 10500 \times 15\% - 720 = 855$
Male worker in B unit
$= 10500 \times 25\% - 1200$
$= 2625 - 1200 = 1425$
Male worker in C unit
$= 10500 \times 12\% - 624$
$= 1260 - 624 = 636$
Male worker in D unit
$= 10500 \times 35\% - 1920$
$= 3675 - 1920 = 1755$
Male worker in E unit
$= 10500 \times 5\% - 258 = 267$
Male worker in F unit
$= 10500 \times 8\% - 426$
$= 840 - 426 = 414$
∴ Highest Male workers are in D unit.

107. Required ratio are
A unit $= \frac{855}{720} = 1.19$
B unit $= \frac{1425}{1200} = 1.19$
C unit $= \frac{636}{624} = 1.02$
D unit $= \frac{1755}{1920} = 0.91$
E unit $= \frac{267}{258} = 1.03$
F unit $= \frac{414}{428} = 0.97.$

108. Total male worker in unit A and B
$= 855 + 1425 = 2280$
Total female worker in unit C and E
$= 624 + 258 = 882$
Required ratio $= 2280 : 882 = 380 : 147.$

109. Required difference $= 267 - 258 = 9.$

110. $(636 + x) + (624 + x) = 1500$
$2x = 240$
Number of Shift Male = Female $= x = 120$
[∵ Total Female of D = 1920]
Required % $= \frac{120}{1920} \times 100 = 6.25\%.$

For Qs. Nos. 112 to 115.

Department Name	Male	Female
HR	180	330
Production	630	63
Marketing	330	191
IT	185	100
Accounts	175	216

112. Required percentage

$= \frac{185}{1500} \times 100 = 12.33\% \simeq 12\%.$

113. Total Female in HR Department and Marketing Department = 330 + 191 = 521.

114. Required percentage $= \frac{(175+216)}{2400} \times 100$

$= 16.29\%.$

115. Required percentage of female in production department $= \frac{63}{900} \times 100 = 7\%.$

116. Total Saving

= 100 +200 + 400 + 800 + 1600 + 3200

= 12700

Money to Buy at said discount

= 12700 − 500 = 12200

$\because$ (100 − 16.67%) = 83.33%

$\therefore$ 83.33% unit value = 12,200

100% unit value $= \frac{12,200}{83.33} \times 100$

$= 14640.58 \simeq 14640$

Short Amount = 14640 − 12700

= 1940.

117. Let Starting Saving amount = ₹ x

Total Saving of Ramesh till next day

$x + 2x + 4x + 8x + 16x + 32x + 64x + 128x$

$= 255x$

Paid amount = 80% of saving

$255x \times 80\% = 20,400$

$x = \frac{20,400 \times 100}{255 \times 80}$

$x = 100.$

For Qs. Nos. 118 to 121.

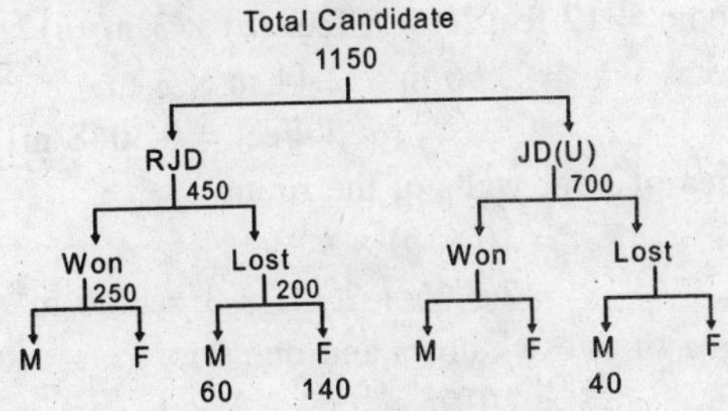

118. Male Candidate of JD(U) party who lost the election

= Total male candidate who lost the election − RJD male candidate who lost the election

= 100 − 60 = 40.

121. Number of Female candidate of RJD Who lost the election

= Total lost − male candidate lost

= 200 − 60 = 140.

123. Total students applied for CAT

= 1137600 × 40% = 455040

Total students applied for IIFT

= 1137600 × 23% = 261648

Total students applied for XAT

= 1137600 × 20% = 227520

Total students applied for NMAT

= 1137600 × 17% = 193392

Total fee

= 455040 × 1715 + 261648 × 1895 + 227520 × 2315 + 193392 × 2945

= 780393600 + 495822960 + 526708800 + 569539440 = 2372464800.

124. In 2009, Number of students applied for CAT

= 455040 × 118% [18% increase]

= 536947.2 ~ 536947

Fee = 1715 × 139% [39% hike] = ₹ 2383.85

Fee paid by CAT students

= 536947 × 2383.85 = 1280001105.95

Total fee = 1280001105.95 + 495822960 + 526708800 + 569539440

Total fee = 2872072305.95

$\therefore$ Required percentage

$= \frac{1280001105.95}{2872072305.95} \times 100 = 44.56\%.$

125. We have,

Room = 12 feet (l) × 8 feet (b) × 3 m (h)

= 3.66 m × 2.44 m × 3 m

[∵ 1 Feet = 0.3048 m]

Area of Four walls of the room

$= 2(l + b) \times h$

$= 2(3.66 + 2.44) \times 3 = 36.6\ m^2$

Area of two windows and one door

$= 2(0.75 \times 1) + 1.5 \times 1$

$= 1.5 + 1.5 = 3\ m^2$

Rest Area of the wall for wall paper

$= 36.6 - 3 = 33.6\ m^2$

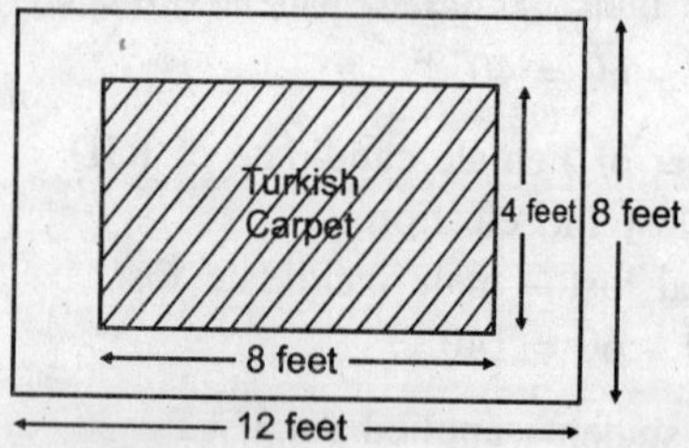

Area of Turkish Carpet

$= 8 \times 4 = 32\ Feet^2 = 2.97\ m^2$

[∵ $1\ Feet^2 = 0.0929\ m^2$]

Area of Wooden Paneling roof $= l \times b$

$= 12 \times 8 = 96\ Feet^2 = 8.92\ m^2$

Sleek = 2.5 Feet × 3 Feet × 1.5 mm

= 76.2 cm × 91.44 cm × 1.5 mm

[1 Feet = 30.48 cm]

Cost for Refurnish

Turkish Carpet = 2.97 × 50 = ₹ 148.5

Wall paper = 33.6 × 32

= 1075.2 paise = ₹ 10.75

$$\text{Sleek} = \frac{76.2 \times 91.44 \times 1.5}{10 \times 5 \times 0.75} \times 10$$

= ₹ 2787.09

Wooden Paneling Roof = 8.92 × 20 = ₹ 178.4

Total Expense to Refurnish the room

= ₹ 148.5 + ₹ 10.75 + ₹ 2787.09 + ₹ 178.4

= ₹ 3124.74 ≃ ₹ 3125

Arun earmarked expense = ₹ 3000

So, Actual Expense more than the earmarked is

$$= \frac{3125 - 3000}{3000} \times 100 = \frac{125}{30} = 4.17\% \simeq 4\%.$$

126. We have Debt = 20,000

Let ₹ x invest by Kapil

$$\frac{x \times 4 \times 2}{100} + \frac{x \times 6 \times 5}{100} + \frac{x \times 8 \times 2}{100} = 1512$$

$$\frac{8x}{100} + \frac{30x}{100} + \frac{16x}{100} = 1512$$

$$\frac{54x}{100} = 1512$$

$$x = \frac{151200}{54} = ₹\ 2800$$

Now Deposit in each Bank = ₹ 1400

$$\text{Bank-1:}\quad I = \frac{1400 \times 35 \times 8}{100} = 392$$

A = 1400 + 392 = ₹ 1792

(lesser amount)

$$I = \frac{1792 \times 18 \times 8}{100} = 2580.48$$

A = 1792 + 2580.48 = ₹ 4372.48

(Amount received early)

$$\text{Bank-2:}\quad I = \frac{1400 \times 10 \times 5}{100} = 700$$

A = 1400 + 700 = ₹ 2100

(greater amount)

$$I = \frac{2100 \times 15 \times 10}{100} = 3150$$

A = 2100 + 3150 = ₹ 5250

For Half early,

$$r' = \frac{r}{2} = \frac{10\%}{2} = 5\%$$

$t' = 2 \times t = 4$ years

∴ Amount Received after lacker

$$= 4372.48\left(1 + \frac{5}{100}\right)^4$$

$$= \frac{4372.48 \times 21 \times 21 \times 21 \times 21}{20 \times 20 \times 20 \times 20}$$

= 5314.78

Total Amount got by Kapil

= 5314.78 + 5250 = 10564.78

∴ Required percentage

$$= \frac{10564.78}{20,000} \times 100 = 52.82\% \simeq 50\%.$$

Previous Paper (Solved)

GGSIPU—B.Com(H) Entrance Exam-2013*

GENERAL ENGLISH

Directions (Qs. 1-8): *Read each sentence to find out whether there is any error in it. The error, if any, will be in one part of the sentence. The number of that part is the answer. If there is no error, the answer is '(D)'. (Ignore the errors of punctuation, if any).*

1. Mahendra was reading (A)/the magazine (B)/ that Shashi give him. (C)/No error (D)

2. I will encourage each one (A)/of my friends to follow (B)/the teachings of Gandhiji in their lives. (C)/No error (D)

3. Raju never know (A)/how much money (B)/ Devi had sent for him. (C)/No error (D)

4. Without question (A)/Mohan is (B)/good singer than anyone else present here. (C)/No error (D)

5. Jagan said that he was (A)/very sorry for (B)/ having keep me waiting for sometime. (C)/ No error (D)

6. He is looking for (A)/ an opportunity (B)/ to come out of the meeting room. (C)/No error (D)

7. The conference was (A)/ attended by (B)/ more than one hundred delegates. (C)/ No error (D)

8. The police (A)/must have based (B)/the accusation at the evidence. (C)/No error (D)

Directions (Qs. 9-10): *Pick out the word/group of words that is most Opposite in meaning of the word/group of words given.*

9. Blended

A. mixed B. derived
C. separated D. inserted

10. Admit

A. avoid B. dislike
C. deny D. observe

Directions (Qs. 11-13): *The sentences given in each question, when properly sequenced, form a coherent paragraph. Each sentence is labelled with a letter. Choose the most logical order of sentences from among the given choices to construct a coherent paragraph.*

11. 1. People who start up their own business typically come from two extreme backgrounds: One is the business family background and the other is a steady professional family background.

2. Typically, people from different backgrounds face and different kinds of basic problems.

3. The people from both the backgrounds find it very difficult to establish and manage an enterprise.

4. Starting up and managing a small business is not a joke.

A. 4231 B. 2134
C. 4132 D. 3412

12. 1. Venture capital is recommended as the ideal source of financing for a successfully small business.

2. Several companies including start ups have been funded by dedicated venture funds during this decade.

3. Despite this, an average Indian entrepreneur understands and appreciation of venture capital concept has been woefully inadequated.

4. In the Indian context, though venture capital has been a relatively late entrant, it has already made a reasonable impact.

A. 1234 B. 1423
C. 1324 D. 1432

13. 1. Progress in diagnosis, in preventive medicine and in treatment, both medicinal and surgical, has been rapid and breathe taking.

2. Much in medicine which is not taken for granted was undreamt of even as recently as 20 years ago.

Note: GGSIPU has introduced B.Com(H) Course for the first time in year 2013. And for admission the First Common Entrance Test was conducted by the University on 8 June, 2013.

3. Presently small pox has been eradicated, poliomyelitis practically banished, tuberculosis has become curable and coronary artery disease surgically relievable.
4. The dramatic surge in the field of molecular biology and research by immunologists and geneticists has succeeded in controlling parasitic diseases like malaria and river blindness that affect millions of people round the world.

A. 2431 B. 2134
C. 2314 D. 2413

Directions (Qs. 14-18): *Read the given passage carefully and attempt the questions that follow.*

It is an old saying that knowledge is power. Education is an instrument, which imparts knowledge and therefore, indirectly controls power. Therefore, ever since the dawn of our civilisation, persons in power have always tried to supervise or control education. It has been handmaid of the ruling class. During the Christian Era, the ecclesiastics controlled the institution of education and diffused among the people, the gospel of the Bible and religious teachings. These gospels and teachings were no other than a philosophy for the maintenance of the existing society.

It taught the poor man to be meek and to earn his bread with the sweat of his brow, while the priests and the landlords lived in luxury and fought duels for the slightest offence. During the Renaissance, education passed more from the clutches of the priest into the hands of the prince. In other words, it became more secular. Under the control of the monarch, education began to devise and preach the infallibility of its masters, the monarch or king. It also invented and supported fantastic theories like 'The Divine Right Theory' and that the king can do no wrong etc. With the advent of the industrial revolution, education took, a different turn and had to please the new masters.

It now no longer remained the privilege of the baron class, but was thrown open to the new rich merchant class of the society. The philosophy, which was in vogue during this period was that of 'Laissez Faire' restricting the function of the state to a mere keeping of laws and non-interference in the workings of the free market.

14. What does the theory 'Divine Right of King' stipulate?
A. The kings are God
B. That the right of governing is conferred upon the kings by God
C. They have the right to be worshipped like Gods by their subjects
D. That the right of kings are divine and therefore sacred

15. Who controlled education during the Renaissance?
A. The common people
B. The prince
C. The church and the priests
D. None of the above

16. What did the ruling class in the Christian Era think of the poor man?
A. That he is the beloved of God
B. That he deserves all sympathy of the rich
C. That he should be strong and lord over others
D. That he is meant for serving the rich

17. Who controlled the institution of education during the Christian Era?
A. The secular leaders of society
B. The church and the priests
C. The monarchs
D. The common people

18. What does the word 'fallibility' mean?
A. That every man is open to error
B. Sensitivity
C. The virtue of not making mistake
D. That some divine power is responsible for determining the fate of the man

Directions (Qs. 19-21): *Select the most suitable word from the four choices given to each sentence to complete it meaningfully.*

19. I take interest .... film making.
A. to B. for
C. on D. in

20. The Indian economy badly needs to .... an export oriented economic structure.
A. prepare B. develop
C. achieve D. gain

21. This violence has succeeded in .... our attention to the demands of employees.

A. taking B. inviting
C. dividing D. drawing

Directions (Qs. 22-26): *Select the word that is spelt correctly.*

22. A. Paraphernalia B. Paraphrenalia
C. Parapherenalia D. Paraphrennalia

23. A. Enterprenuer B. Entrepreneur
C. Entrepenur D. Enteruepeur

24. A. Onomaetopoeia B. Onomoatopoeia
C. Onomatopoeia D. Onomatapoeia

25. A. Hemorhage B. Haemorhhage
C. Haemorrhage D. Hemoorhage

26. A. Dylexsia B. Dyslexia
C. Dislexia D. Dislecsia

Directions (Qs. 27-31): *Choose the explanation that catches the spirit of the idiom given in each question.*

27. El-Dorado
A. An imaginary place
B. High altitude
C. A literary man
D. A country full of gold and precious stones

28. Quantum ramifactus
A. the amount of damage suffered
B. the amount of damage caused
C. the amount of damage paid
D. the amount of damage received

29. To blaze a trail
A. To set on fire
B. To blow the trumpet
C. To initiate work in a movement
D. To be hopeful

30. A snake in the grass
A. A secret or hidden enemy
B. An unreliable person
C. Unforeseen happening
D. A dangerous enemy

31. Have too many irons in the fire
A. Engaged in too many enterprises at the same time
B. Facing too many problems at the same time
C. Said or done too many things at the same time
D. To incite the feeling amongst the people

Directions (Qs. 32-36): *Select the best option from the four alternatives given below.*

32. Unless he ...... this office, I will not say anything.
A. left B. did not leave
C. leaves D. had left

33. .... I would help all the poor people.
A. If I am rich B. If I was rich
C. If I were rich D. In case I am rich

34. I .... the news an hour ago.
A. have heared B. heared
C. was hearing D. have been hearing

35. He spoke .... about his prospects.
A. consciously B. conscientiously
C. confidentially D. confidently

36. The boy is not interested in playing, ...?
A. doesn't he B. isn't he
C. didn't he D. is he

Directions (Qs. 37-38): *Pick out the word/group of words that is most nearly the same in meaning of the word/group of words given.*

37. Found
A. saw B. establish
C. realise D. started

38. Poor
A. weak B. worried
C. unfortunate D. scared

LOGICAL REASONING

39. *a* is the mother of *b* and *c*. If *d* is the husband of *c*. What is *a* to *d*?
A. Mother B. Sister
C. Aunt D. Mother-in-law

40. In a certain code "TRIPPLE" is written as 'SQHOOKD'. How is 'DISPOSE' written in that code?
A. CHRORDN B. ESOPSID
C. CHRONRD D. ESJTPTF

Directions (Qs. 41-43): *In each of the following questions, a set of five alternative figures 1, 2, 3, 4 and 5 followed by a set of four alternatives A, B, C and D is provided. It is required to select the alternative which represents three out of the five alternative figures which when fitted into each other would form a complete square.*

41. 

(1) (2) (3) (4) (5)

A. 145 B. 245
C. 123 D. 234

42. 

(1) (2) (3) (4) (5)

A. 124 B. 125
C. 234 D. 245

43. 

(1) (2) (3) (4) (5)

A. 124 B. 345
C. 123 D. 135

Directions (Qs. 44 and 45): *In each question below are given two statements numbered I and II. You have to take the two given statements as true even, if they seem to be at variance with commonly known facts. Read all the conclusions and then decide which of the given conclusions logically follow from the given statements, disregarding commonly known facts.*

44. Statements

I. All vegetables have gravy.
II. All lunch has vegetable.

A. All lunch has gravy
B. All gravy has lunch
C. Both (A) and (B)
D. None of the above

45. Statements

I. Karan Johar is a good director.
II. Directors are intelligent.

A. All intelligent are directors
B. Karan Johar is intelligent
C. Both (A) and (B)
D. None of the above

46. Which word *does not* belong the others?

A. Guitar B. Flute
C. Violin D. Cello

47. Which word *does not* belong the others?

A. Street B. Freeway
C. Interstate D. Expressway

Directions (Qs. 48-52): *Read the information given below to answer the questions.*

(*i*) Kareena's dieting schedule consists of having only one fruit on a given day of the week.
(*ii*) Dietician has prescribed banana, papaya, pomegranate, apple and grape from Sunday to Friday, one day being a fasting day. Kareena cannot eat any fruit on Saturday.
(*iii*) Pomegranate day is neither on the first day nor on the last day but earlier than the papaya day.
(*iv*) Apple day is on the immediate next day of papaya day.
(*v*) Banana day is on the immediate previous day of the fasting day.
(*vi*) Apple day and grape day must have a gap of two days between them.
(*vii*) Grape day is the day immediately following the fasting day.

48. Which of the following is the fasting day?

A. Monday B. Tuesday
C. Wednesday D. Thursday

49. Banana day and apple day have a gap of how many days between them?

A. One B. Two
C. Three D. Four

50. Which day is grape day?

A. Monday B. Tuesday
C. Thursday D. Wednesday

51. Which day is pomegranate day?

A. Sunday B. Monday
C. Thursday D. Wednesday

52. Which of the following is the correct statement?

A. Apple day is after papaya day
B. Banana day is on Wednesday
C. Fasting day is on Tuesday
D. Papaya day is earlier than banana day

Directions (Qs. 53-56): *Each question given below consists of a statement, followed by two arguments numbered I and II. You have to decide which of the arguments is a 'strong' argument and which is a 'weak' argument.*

Give answer

A. if only Argument I is strong
B. if only Argument II is strong
C. if neither I nor II is strong
D. if both I and II are strong

53. Statement: Should India encourage exports, when most things are insufficient for internal use itself?

Arguments

I. Yes, we have to earn foreign exchange to pay for our imports.

II. No, even selective encouragement would lead to shortages.

54. Statement: Should all the drugs patented and manufactured in Western countries be first tried out on sample basis before giving licence for sale to general public in India?

Arguments

I. Yes, many such drugs require different doses and duration for Indian population and hence it is necessary.

II. No, this is just not feasible and hence cannot be implemented.

55. Statement: Should there be students union in college/university?

Arguments

I. No, this will create a political atmosphere in the campus.

II. Yes, it is very necessary for students who are future political leaders.

56. Statement: Should India make efforts to harness solar energy to fulfil its energy requirements?

Arguments

I. Yes, most of the energy sources used at present is exhaustible.

II. No, harnessing solar energy requires a lot of capital, which India lacks in.

Directions (Qs. 57-61): *Complete the series by choosing the correct option.*

57. 0, 1, 1, 2, 3, 5, 8, 13, 21, ?

A. 34 B. 35
C. 33 D. 36

58. A-10, E-15, I-20, M-25, ...

A. Q-5 B. Q-30
C. P-30 D. R-30

59. 17, 30, 74, 150, ?, 606

A. 250 B. 303
C. 300 D. 302

60. 2, 1, 4, 3, 6, 5, 8, ?

A. 9 B. 10
C. 7 D. 8

61. 1, 4, 27, 256, ?

A. 625 B. 3125
C. 3025 D. 1225

Directions (Qs. 62-64): *In the following questions, group the given figures into three classes using (a) figure only once.*

62. Group the given figures into three classes using each figure only once.

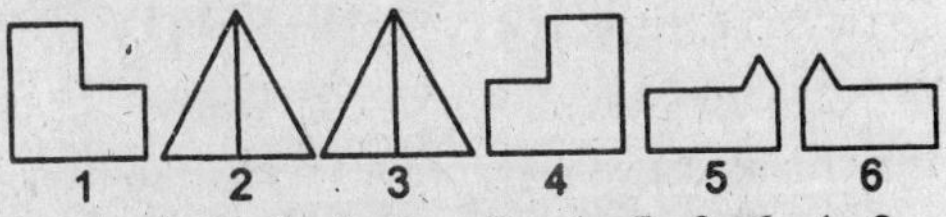

A. 1, 4; 2, 3; 5, 6 B. 1, 5; 2, 6; 4, 3
C. 1, 6; 2, 3; 4, 5 D. 1, 2; 3, 6; 4, 5

63. Group the given figures into three classes using each figure only once.

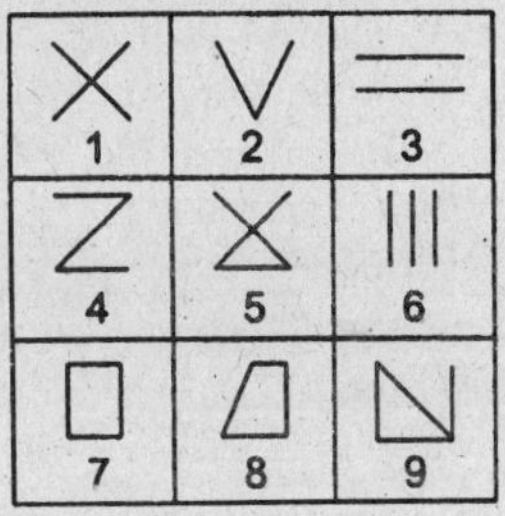

A. 1, 2, 3; 4, 5, 6; 7, 8, 9
B. 1, 3, 5; 2, 4, 6; 7, 8, 9
C. 1, 5, 9; 3, 6, 2; 4, 7, 8
D. 1, 9, 7; 2, 8, 5; 3, 4, 6

64. Group the given figures into three classes using each figure only once.

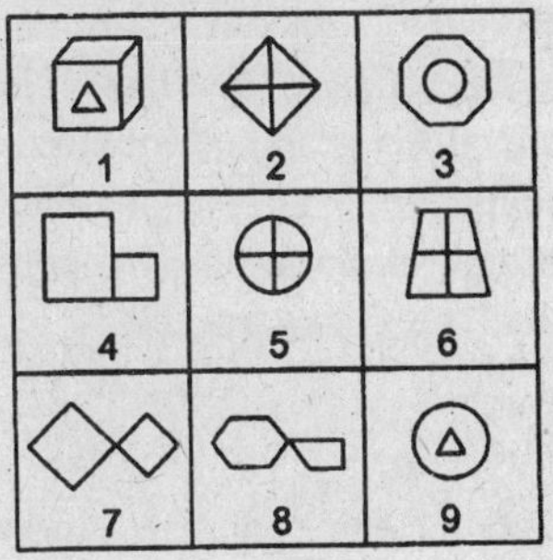

A. 1, 3, 9; 2, 5, 6; 4, 7, 8
B. 1, 3, 9; 2, 7, 8; 4, 5, 6
C. 1, 2, 4; 3, 5, 7; 6, 8, 9
D. None of the above

Directions (Qs. 65 and 66): *In each of the following questions, arrange the words in a meaningful, logical order and then select the appropriate sequence from the alternatives given below each of the groups of words.*

65. I. Curd II. Grass
III. Butter IV. Milk
V. Cow
A. V, II, IV, I, III B. V, II, III, IV, I
C. IV, II, V, III, I D. II, V, IV, III, I

66. I. Windows II. Walls
III. Floor IV. Foundation
V. Foof VI. Room
A. IV, V, III, II, I, VI B. IV, III, V, VI, II, I
C. IV, II, I, V, III, VI D. IV, I, V, VI, II, III

Directions (Qs. 67 and 68): *In each of the following questions, four words have been given out of which three are alike in same manner, while the fourth-one is different. Choose out the odd one.*

67. A. Mustard B. Seasame
C. Corn D. Onion

68. A. Manure B. Nitrogen
C. Ammonia D. Urea

69. In the following number series, only one number is wrong. Find out the wrong number.

1, 3, 12, 25, 48

A. 3 B. 12
C. 25 D. 48

70. Raju decided to marry 3 yr after he gets a job. He was 17 yr, old when he passed class 12th. After passing class 12th, he had completed his graduation course in 3 yr and PG course in 2 yr. He got the job exactly 1 yr after completing his PG course. At what age, will he get married?
A. 27 yr B. 26 yr
C. 28 yr D. 23 yr

Directions (Qs. 71 and 72): *Find the statement that must be true according to the given information.*

71. The pacific yew is an evergreen tree that grows in the pacific North-West. The pacific yew has a fleshy, poisonous fruit. Recently taxol, a substance found in the bark of the pacific yew, was discovered to be a promising new anticancer drug.
A. Taxol is poisonous when taken by healthy people
B. Taxol has cured people from various diseases
C. People should not eat the fruit of the pacific yew
D. The pacific yew was considered worthless util taxol was discovered

72. Vincent has a paper route. Each morning, he delivers 37 newspapers to customers in his neighbourhood. It take Vincent 50 min to deliver all the paper.

If Vincent is sick or has other plans, his friend Thomas, who lives on the same street, will sometimes deliver the papers for him.
A. Vincent and Thomas live in the same neighbourhood
B. It takes Thomas more than 50 min deliver the papers
C. It is dark outside when Vincent begins his deliveries
D. Thomas would like to have his own paper route

73. *a* told *b*, 'yesterday I met the only brother of the daughter of my grandmother'. Whom did A meet?
A. Cousin B. Brother
C. Nephew D. Father

74. If '+' means multiplication '–' means division '×' means minus, '÷' means plus, then (280 – 10 × 20) – 8 ÷ 6 is equal to
A. 7 B. 112
C. –392 D. 58

75. If '*a*' means '×', *b* means '÷', *c* means '+' and *d* means '–', then what is the value of 180 *b* 15 *d* 11 *c* 8 *a* 10?
A. 80 B. 81
C. 83 D. 92

QUANTITATIVE APTITUDE & DATA INTERPRETATION

Directions (Qs. 76-80): *Study the graph carefully to answer the questions that follow.*

Number of players participating in three different games in five different schools

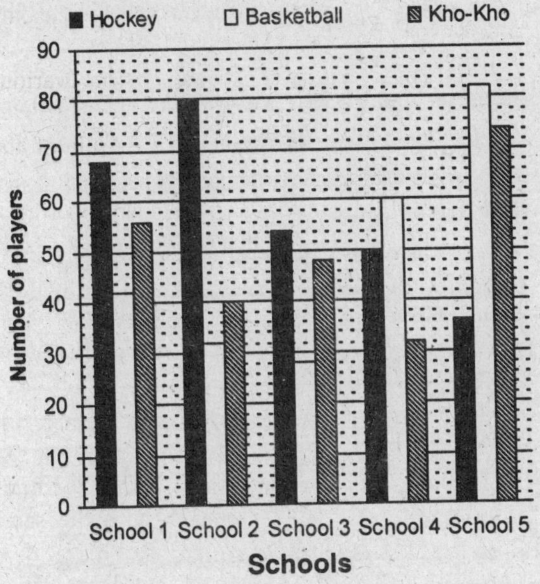

76. What is the total number of players participating in hockey from all the five schools together?

A. 324 B. 288
C. 342 D. 284

77. What is the respective ratio between number of players participating in basketball from school 1 and the number of players participating in Kho-Kho from school 3?

A. 5 : 7 B. 7 : 9
C. 7 : 8 D. 9 : 7

78. In which school is the number of players participating in hockey and basketball together second highest?

A. School 1 B. School 2
C. School 3 D. School 4

79. Number of players participating in Kho-Kho from school 4 is what per cent of number of players participating in hockey from school 2?

A. 42 B. 48
C. 36 D. 40

80. 25% of the number of the players participating in hockey from school 5 are females. What is the number of the hockey players who are males in school 5?

A. 15 B. 18
C. 30 D. 27

Directions (Qs. 81-85): *Study the following pie chart and answer the following questions.*

Percentage-wise distribution of employees in six different professions

Total number of employees = 26800

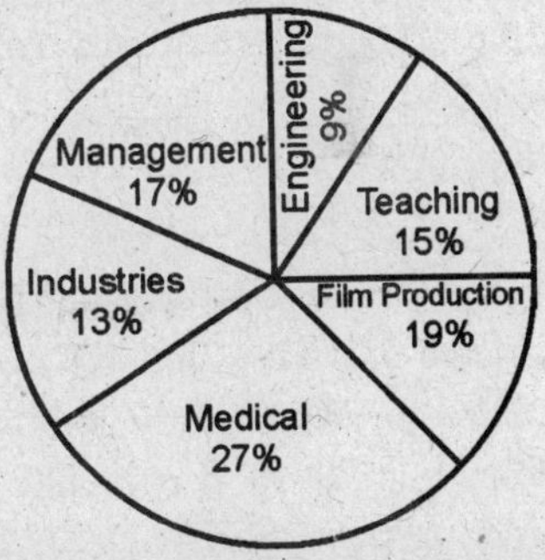

81. What is the difference between the total number of employees in teaching and medical profession together and the number of employees in management profession?

A. 6770 B. 7700
C. 6700 D. 7770

82. In management profession three-fourth of the number of employees are female. What is the number of male employees in management profession?

A. 1239 B. 1143
C. 1156 D. 1139

83. 25% of employees from film production profession went on a strike. What is the number of employees from film production who have not participated in the strike?

A. 3271 B. 3819
C. 3948 D. 1273

84. What is the total number of employees in engineering profession and industries together?

A. 5698 B. 5884
C. 5687 D. 5896

85. In teaching profession if three-fifth of the teachers are not permanent, what is the number of permanent teachers in the teaching profession?

A. 1608 B. 1640
C. 1764 D. 1704

86. There are four calculators and it is known that exactly two of them are defective. They are tested one by one in a random order, till both the defective calculators are identified. Then, the probability that only two test are required is

A. 5/6 B. 1/2
C. 1/6 D. 1/3

87. In a survey among 80 people, 50 people like arrange marriage and 70 people like love marriage. What is the minimum and maximum number of people like both the marriages, respectively?

A. 40, 45
B. 40, 50
C. 30, 40
D. Cannot be determined

88. A shopkeeper buys a number of books for ₹ 80. If he had bought 4 more for the same amount, each book would have cost ₹ 1 less. How many books did he buy?

A. 8 B. 16
C. 2 D. 28

89. In a certain colony of cancerous cells, each cell divides into two every minute. How many cells will be produced from the single cell, if the rate of division continues for 12 min?

A. 9180 B. 8190
C. 8910 D. None of these

90. A car crosses a man walking at 6 km/h. The man can see the things upto 450 m only in one direction due to fog. He sees the car which was going in the same direction for 4.5 min. What is the speed of the car?

A. 9 km/h
B. 12 km/h
C. 12.5 km/h
D. 15 km/h

Directions (Qs. 91-95): *Study the following graph carefully to answer the questions that follow.*

Cost of three different fruits (In rupees per kg) in five different cities

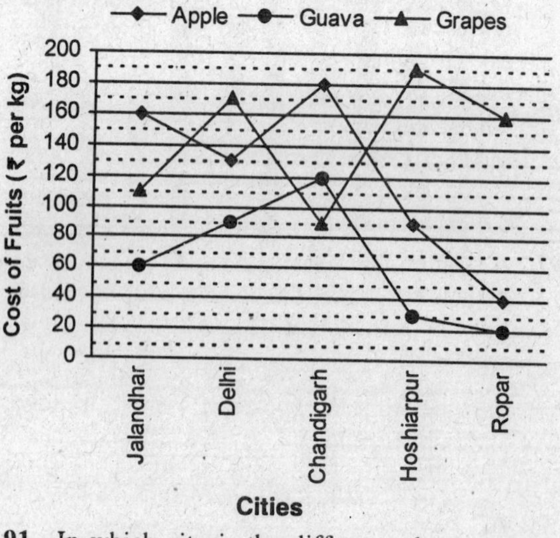

91. In which city is the difference between the cost of 1 kg of apple and cost of 1 kg of guava second lowest?

A. Jalandhar B. Delhi
C. Chandigarh D. Hoshiarpur

92. Cost of 1 kg of guava in Jalandhar is approximately what per cent of the cost of 2 kg of grapes in Chandigarh?

A. 66 B. 24
C. 28 D. 34

93. What total amount will Ram pay to the shopkeeper for purchasing 3 kg, of apples and 2 kg of guavas in Delhi?

A. ₹ 530 B. ₹ 450
C. ₹ 570 D. ₹ 620

94. Ravinder had to purchase 45 kg of grapes from Hoshiarpur. Shopkeeper gave him discount of 4% per kg. What amount did he pay to the shopkeeper after the discount?

A. ₹ 8208 B. ₹ 8104
C. ₹ 8340 D. ₹ 8550

95. What is the respective ratio between the cost of 1 kg of apples from Ropar and the cost of 1 kg of grapes from Chandigarh?

A. 3 : 2 B. 2 : 3
C. $2^2 : 3^2$ D. $4^2 : 9^2$

96. A club has raised 75% of the amount it needs for a new building by receiving an average donation of ₹ 600 from the people already solicited. The people already solicited represents 60% of the people the club will ask for donations. If the club is to raised exactly the amount needed for new building, what should be the average donation from remaining people to be solicited?

A. 250 B. 300
C. 400 D. 600

97. A retailer cheats both to his wholeseller and his customer by 10% by his faulty balance *i.e.*, he actually weighs 10% more while purchasing from wholeseller and weighs 10% less while selling to his customer. What is the net profit percentage, when he sells at CP?

A. $22\frac{2}{11}\%$ B. $22\frac{2}{9}\%$
C. 20% D. 21%

98. The compound interest on a certain sum for 2 yr is ₹ 756 and simple interest is ₹ 720. If the sum is invested such that the SI is ₹ 900 and the number of years is equal to the rate per cent per annum, find the rate per cent.

A. 4 B. 5
C. 6 D. 1

99. Two pipes A and B can fill a cistern in 15 h and 10 h, respectively. A tap C can empty the full cistern in 30 h. All the three taps were open for 2 h, when it was remembered that emptying tap had been left open. It was then closed. How many hours more would it take for the cistern to be filled?

A. 8 h 30 min B. 1.2 h
C. 6 h 24 min D. 5 h 35 min

100. Two horses start trotting towards each other, one from a to b and another from b to a. They cross each other after one hour and the first horse reaches b, 5/6 h before the second horse reaches b, distance between a and b is 50 km. What is the speed of the slower horse?

A. 30 km/h B. 15 km/h
C. 25 km/h D. 20 km/h

Directions (Qs. 101-105): *Study the radar graph carefully and answer the questions that follow.*

Number of students (in thousands) in two different universities in six different years. Number of students

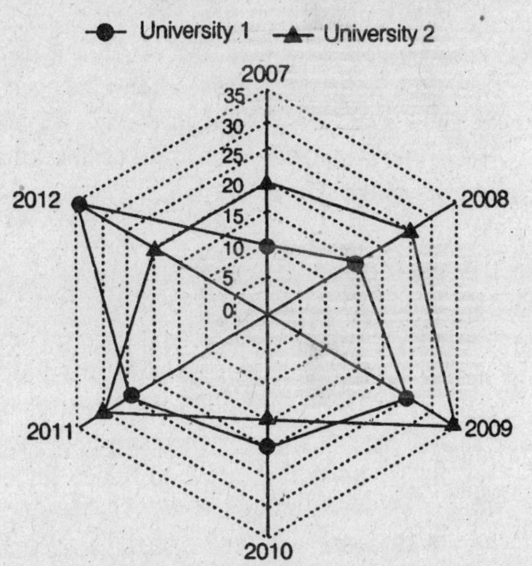

101. What was the difference between the number of students in university 1 in the year 2010 and the number of students in university 2 in the year 2012?

A. 0 B. 5000
C. 15000 D. 10000

102. What is the sum of the number of students in university 1 in the year 2007 and the number of students in university 2 in the year 2011 together?

A. 50000
B. 55000
C. 45000
D. 57000

103. If 25% of the students in university 2 in the year 2010 were females, what was the number of male students in the university 2 in the same year?

A. 11250
B. 12350
C. 12500
D. 11500

104. What was the per cent increase in the number of students in university 1 in the year 2011 as compared to the previous year?

A. 135
B. 15
C. 115
D. 25

105. In which year was the difference between the number of students in university 1 and the number of students in university 2 highest?

A. 2008
B. 2009
C. 2010
D. 2012

106. *a* and *b* can do a piece of work in 8 days, *b* and *c* can do the same work in 12 days and *a* and *c* can complete it in 8 days. In how many days *a*, *b* and *c* can complete the whole work, working together?

A. 4
B. 6
C. 1
D. 9

107. Mr Mittal purchased two steel factories, one in India and other one in Malaysia for total ₹ 72 crore. Later on, he sold the Indian factory at 16% profit and Malaysian factory at 24% profit. Thus, he gained a total profit of 19%. The selling price of Indian factory is

A. ₹ 45 crore
B. ₹ 52.2 crore
C. ₹ 8.55 crore
D. Cannot be determined

108. The unit digit of the expression

$$\frac{1\times2\times3\times4\times5\times6\times7\times8\times9\times10}{100} \text{ is}$$

A. 7
B. 9
C. 8
D. None of these

109. The least number which when divided by 2, 3, 4, 5 and 6 leaves the remainder 1 in each case. If the same number is divided by 7, it leaves no remainder. The number is

A. 231
B. 301
C. 371
D. 441

110. The ages of Vinay, Varsha, Veera and Vikram are in the arithmetic progression but not in the same order. The ratio of ages of Vinay and Varsha is 6 : 5 and Veera is to Vikram is 7 : 8. Two years later, the age of Varsha and Vikram will be 2 : 3. Find the ratio of ages of Vinay and Veera.

A. 7 : 6
B. 5 : 8
C. 6 : 7
D. 8 : 9

111. A dealer buys an article for ₹ 380.00. What price should he mark so that after allowing a discount of 5% he still makes a profit of 25% on the article?

A. ₹ 500
B. ₹ 475
C. ₹ 95
D. ₹ 465

112. In a factory, the production of scooters rose to 48400 from 40000 in 2 yr. The rate of growth per annum is

A. 20%
B. 10%
C. 30%
D. 8%

113. If $x + \frac{1}{x} = 3$, then $x^2 + \frac{1}{x^2}$ will be

A. 9
B. 10
C. 27
D. 7

114. When $16x^4 + 12x^3 - 10x^2 + 8x + 20$ is divided by $4x - 3$, the quotient and the remainder are respectively

A. $4x^3 + 6x^2 + 2x$ and $\frac{61}{2}$

B. $4x^3 + 6x^2 + \frac{7}{2}$ and $\frac{51}{2}$

C. $6x^2 + 2x + \frac{2}{7}$ and $\frac{61}{2}$

D. $4x^3 + 6x^2 + 2x + \frac{7}{2}$ and $\frac{61}{2}$

115. The sum of two numbers is 2490. If 6.5% of one number is equal to 8.5% of the other, the numbers are

A. 1411 and 1079 B. 1412 and 1080
C. 1141 and 1709 D. 1214 and 1800

116. If the quantity of soft drink left is pour into a conical flask whose height and base radius are same as that of cylinder so as to fill the conical flask completely, the quantity of the soft drink left in the cylinder as a reaction of its total capacity is

A. 1/3 B. 1/9
C. 1/6 D. 1/10

117. Two buses start from the opposite points of a main road, 150 km apart. The first bus runs for 25 km and takes a right turn and then runs for 15 km. It then turns left and runs for another 25 km and takes the direction back to reach the main road. In the mean time, due to the minor break down the other bus has run only 35 km along the main road. What would be the distance between the two buses at this point?

A. 65 km B. 80 km
C. 75 km D. 85 km

118. In the number series 4, 10, 23, 50, 104, 216 and 439 the wrong number is

A. 10 B. 23
C. 104 D. 50

119. The price of 2 trousers and 4 shirts is ₹ 1600 with the same amount one can buy 1 trouser and 6 shirts. If one wants to buy 12 shirts he has to pay

A. ₹ 2400 B. ₹ 4800
C. ₹ 1200 D. ₹ 3700

120. If $x = \left(\frac{3}{2}\right)^2 \left(\frac{2}{3}\right)^{-4}$, the value of x^{-2} is

A. $\left(\frac{2}{3}\right)^{12}$ B. $\left(\frac{3}{2}\right)^{12}$

C. $\left(\frac{6}{5}\right)^{-12}$ D. $\left(\frac{5}{6}\right)^{-12}$

Directions (Qs. 121-125): *Study the following bar graph carefully and answer the following questions.*

Earnings (in ₹) of three different persons on four different days

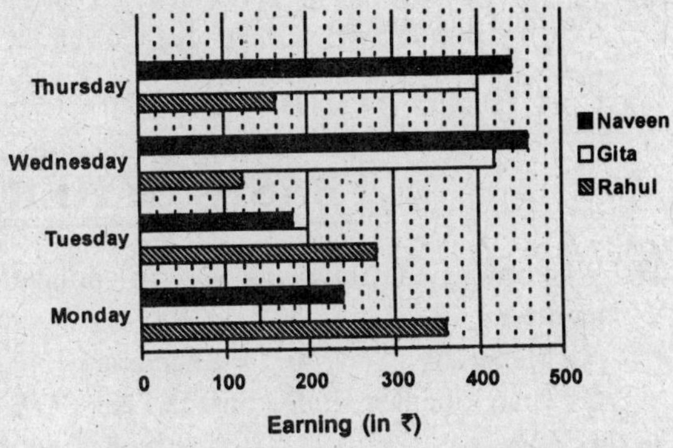

121. Gita donated her earnings of Wednesday to Naveen. What was Naveen's total earnings on Wednesday after Gita's donation?

A. ₹ 520 B. ₹ 550
C. ₹ 540 D. ₹ 560

122. What is the difference between Rahul's earnings on Monday and Gita's earnings on Tuesday?

A. ₹ 40 B. ₹ 20
C. ₹ 50 D. ₹ 30

123. What is the respective ratio between Naveen's earnings on Monday, Wednesday and Thursday?

A. 7 : 3 : 5 B. 8 : 6 : 5
C. 8 : 7 : 4 D. 9 : 3 : 4

124. What is Gita's average earnings over all the days together?

A. ₹ 285 B. ₹ 290
C. ₹ 320 D. ₹ 310

125. What is the total amount earned by Rahul and Naveen together on Tuesday and Thursday together?

A. ₹ 1040 B. ₹ 1020
C. ₹ 980 D. ₹ 940

126. 120 men had food provision for 200 days. After 5 days, 30 men died of an epidemic. The food will last for further

A. 280 days B. 260 days
C. 290 days D. 252 days

127. Out of the total income, X spends 20% on house rent and 70% of the remaining amount on household expenditure. If X saves ₹ 1800, the total income is

A. ₹ 8000 B. ₹ 9500
C. ₹ 7500 D. ₹ 8500

128. P sells a table to Q at a profit of 10% and Q sells it to R at a profit of 12%. If R pays ₹ 246.40 for it, then how much had P paid for it?

A. 200.00 B. 300.00
C. 248.00 D. 346.00

BASIC GENERAL AWARENESS

129. Who among the following was an eminent painter?

A. Meherally B. V Shantaram
C. Uday Shankar D. Sarada Ukil

130. The Chairmanship/Presidency of the UN Security Council rotates among the council members in

A. every month
B. every 3 months
C. every 6 months
D. every year

131. Which one of the following natural regions is best known for the production of grapes?

A. Mediterranean B. Monsoon
C. Hot desert D. Equatorial

132. Which is the first state in India to come out with an exclusive 'Budget for Agriculture'?

A. Tamil Nadu B. Maharashtra
C. Karnataka D. Andhra Pradesh

133. The energy derived from the Sum is

A. insolation B. insulation
C. isolation D. radiation

134. Special Economic Zone (SEZ) Act became effective in

A. 2004 B. 2005
C. 2006 D. 2007

135. Arakan and Pegu Yomas are located in

A. Nepal B. Bhutan
C. China D. Myanmar

136. Who is the author of the poetry collection, '*These Errors are Correct*' in English?

A. Jeet Thayil B. Robin Mehta
C. Peter Hawk D. V S Naipaul

137. The seven pagodas of Mahabalipuram are witness to the art patronised by the

A. Pallavas B. Pandyas
C. Cholas D. Cheras

138. Who among the following Peshwas was popularly known as Nana Saheb?

A. Balaji Vishwanath B. Baji Rao
C. Madhav Rao I D. Balaji Baji Rao

139. Which one of the following was the first fort constructed by the British in India?

A. Fort St Angelo B. Fort St David
C. Fort St George D. Fort St William

140. Devaluation of rupee in India was first introduced in the year

A. 1949 B. 1966
C. 1972 D. 1990

141. Where is the headquarters of Survival International located?

A. Geneva B. London
C. Hague D. Ottawa

142. Find out the odd one

A. Nobel Prize
B. Magsaysay Award
C. Jnanpith Award
D. Commonwealth Writers' Prize

143. Golf player Vijay Singh belongs to which country?

A. Fiji
B. Mauritius
C. Trinidad and Tobago
D. India

144. Treasury Bills are sold in India by

A. SEBI B. State Governments
C. Commercial Banks D. RBI

145. Which continent has the highest number of countries?
A. Africa B. Europe
C. Asia D. South America

146. The famous book '*Anna Karenina*' written by
A. Boris Pasternak B. Victor Hugo
C. Lewis Carroll D. Leo Tolstoy

147. Which of the following is not a chief organ of the United Nations Organisations?
A. International Labour Organisation
B. Security Council
C. International Court of Justice
D. General Assembly

148. The Megatons to Megawatts Programme was launched with the agreement between which countries?
A. Russia and USA B. USA and Mexico
C. USA and Canada D. Mexico and Brazil

149. The Battle of Plassey was fought in
A. 1757 B. 1784
C. 1748 D. 1795

150. Tripitaka are sacred books of
A. Buddhists B. Hindus
C. Jains D. None of these

ANSWERS

1	**2**	**3**	**4**	**5**	**6**	**7**	**8**	**9**	**10**
C	C	A	C	C	A	B	D	D	C
11	**12**	**13**	**14**	**15**	**16**	**17**	**18**	**19**	**20**
A	A	C	D	B	D	B	C	D	B
21	**22**	**23**	**24**	**25**	**26**	**27**	**28**	**29**	**30**
D	A	A	C	A	B	D	D	D	A
31	**32**	**33**	**34**	**35**	**36**	**37**	**38**	**39**	**40**
C	C	D	A	D	D	A	C	D	C
41	**42**	**43**	**44**	**45**	**46**	**47**	**48**	**49**	**50**
B	B	D	A	B	B	A	A	D	B
51	**52**	**53**	**54**	**55**	**56**	**57**	**58**	**59**	**60**
D	A	A	A	D	A	A	B	D	C
61	**62**	**63**	**64**	**65**	**66**	**67**	**68**	**69**	**70**
B	A	A	A	A	C	D	B	C	B
71	**72**	**73**	**74**	**75**	**76**	**77**	**78**	**79**	**80**
C	A	D	A	B	B	C	A	D	D
81	**82**	**83**	**84**	**85**	**86**	**87**	**88**	**89**	**90**
C	D	B	D	A	C	B	B	B	B
91	**92**	**93**	**94**	**95**	**96**	**97**	**98**	**99**	**100**
B	D	C	A	C	B	D	B	C	D
101	**102**	**103**	**104**	**105**	**106**	**107**	**108**	**109**	**110**
A	C	A	D	D	B	B	C	B	C
111	**112**	**113**	**114**	**115**	**116**	**117**	**118**	**119**	**120**
A	B	D	D	A	C	A	C	A	A
121	**122**	**123**	**124**	**125**	**126**	**127**	**128**	**129**	**130**
C	A	D	B	D	B	C	A	D	A
131	**132**	**133**	**134**	**135**	**136**	**137**	**138**	**139**	**140**
A	C	A	A	D	A	A	D	C	B
141	**142**	**143**	**144**	**145**	**146**	**147**	**148**	**149**	**150**
B	C	A	D	A	D	A	A	A	A

SOME SELECTED EXPLANATORY ANSWERS

39. Here, c is daughter of a and d is the husband of c. So, a is mother-in-law of d.

40. 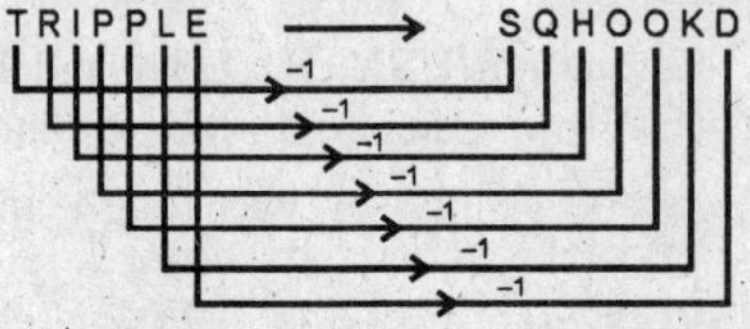

Similarly,

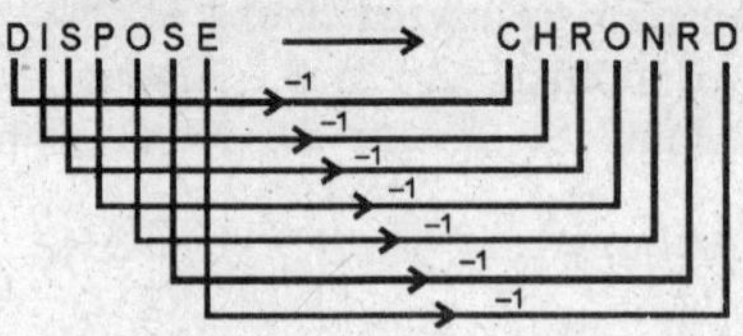

44. 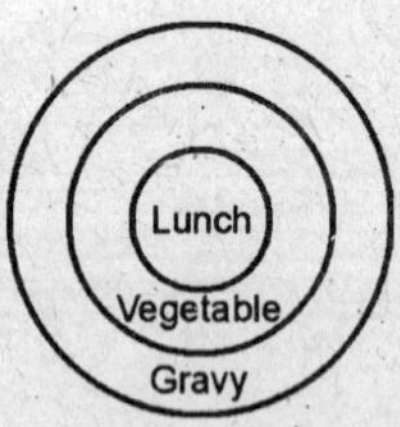

As all vegetable are gravy and all lunch are vegetable So, all lunch are gravy.

45. 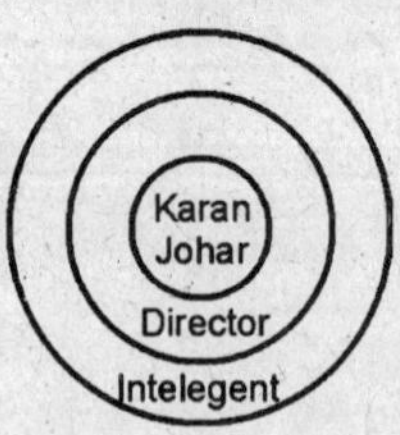

46. Guitar, Violin and Cello like instruments uses string in its design, whereas flute is a wind instrument.

47. Freeway, Interstate and Expressway are roadway where speed limit set very high.

48-52. Kareena's dieting Schedule is as follows:

Day	**Fruit**
Sunday	Banana
Monday	Fasting
Tuesday	Grapes
Wednesday	Pomegranate
Thursday	Papaya
Friday	Apple
Saturday	No fruit day

57. 0, 1, 1, 2, 3, 5, 8, 13, 21, **34**

0 + 1 = 1, 1 + 1 = 2, 2 + 1 = 3, 3 + 2 = 5, 5 + 3 = 8, 8 + 5 = 13, 13 + 8 = 21, 21 + 13 = **34**

58. Here, with place difference in +4, numerical values difference arises as +5.

Hence, Numerical value of Q = 25 + 5 = 30.

59. 17, 36, 74, 150, 302, 606

17 × 2 + 2, 36 × 2 + 2, 74 × 2 + 2, 150 × 2 + 2, 302 × 2 + 2

60. 2, 1, 4, 3, 6, 5, 8, 7,

+2 +2 +2 (alternate terms 2 → 4 → 6 → 8)

+2 +2 +2 (alternate terms 1 → 3 → 5 → 7)

61.

1,	4,	27,	256,	3125
↓	↓	↓	↓	↓
$(1)^1$	$(2)^2$	$(3)^3$	$(4)^4$	$(5)^5$

63. Number of lines in figure 1, 2, 3 = 2
Number of lines in figure 4, 5, 6 = 3
Number of lines in figure 7, 8, 9 = 4.

65. Cow grazes grass. She gives us milk from milk we can butter and curd.

69. $(1)^2 - \left(\frac{1}{2}\right)^2$, $(2)^2 - (1)^2$, $(4)^2 - (2)^2$, $(6)^2 - (3)^2$, $(8)^2 - (4)^2$.

70. Raju age when he passed class 12th = 17yrs.
Raju age when he passed graduation
= 17 + 3 = 20 yrs.
Raju age when he passed PG
= 20 + 2 = 22 yrs.
Raju age when he got the job
= 22 + 1 = 23 yrs.
Raju age when he get married = 26 yrs.

73. Only brother of the daughter of her grand mother is meet to his father.

74. In code language (280 – 10 × 20) – 8 ÷ 6 can be written as (280 ÷ 10 – 20) ÷ 8 + 6
= (28 – 20) ÷ 8 + 6
= 8 ÷ 8 + 6 = 1 + 6 = 7.

75. 180 b 15 d 11 c 8 a 10
= 180 ÷ 15 – 11 + 8 × 10
= 12 – 11 + 80 = 1 + 80 = 81.

77. Required ratio = 42 : 48 = 7 : 8.

80. Percentage of male player from school 5
$= 100 - 25 = 75\%$

$\therefore$ Required Number = $36 \times \frac{75}{100} = 27$.

81. Number of employees in (teaching + medical) – Management

$= 26800\left\{\frac{(15+27)-17}{100}\right\} = 6700$.

82. Number of male employees in management profession

$= 26800 \times \frac{17}{100} \times \left(1-\frac{3}{4}\right) = 1139$.

85. Number of teachers in permanent profession

$= 26800 \times \frac{15}{100} \times \left(1-\frac{3}{5}\right) = 1608$.

86. Number of ways of selecting two defective out of two defective calculators

$= {}^2C_2 = 1$

Number of ways of selecting two calculator out of four calculator = ${}^4C_2 = 6$.

Hence, required probability

$= \frac{{}^2C_2}{{}^4C_2} = \frac{1}{6}$.

87. Minimum number of people like both the marriage (arrange and love)
$= 50 + 70 - 80 = 40$.
and, maximum number of people like both the marriage can be
= Min. {arrange marriage and love marriage}
= 50.

88. Let Shopkeeper bought x number of books in ₹ 80.

Cost of one book = $\frac{80}{x}$

According to the question,

$\frac{80}{x} - \frac{80}{x+4} = 1$

or, $x(x + 4) = 80(x + 4) - 80x$

or, $x^2 + 4x - 320 = 0$

$(x + 20)(x - 16) = 0$

$\therefore$ $x = 16$.

90. Let speed of Car = x km/h.
Then relative speed of the Car w.r.t. man
$= (x - 6)$ km/h
$= (x - 6)\frac{5}{18}$ m/sec.

Speed = $\frac{\text{Distance}}{\text{Time}}$

$(x-6)\frac{5}{18} = \frac{450}{4.5\times60} = \frac{5}{3}$.

$\therefore$ $x = 12$ km/h.

92. Cost of 1 kg of guava in Jalandhar = ₹ 60
Cost of 2 kg of grapes in Chandigarh
$= 2 \times 90 =$ ₹ 180

$\therefore$ Required percent = $\frac{60}{180} \times 100 = 34\%$.

94. Cost price of 45 kg of grapes
$= 190 \times 45 = 8550$

Discount 4% = $8550 \times \frac{96}{100}$ = ₹ 8208.

96. Let amount needs for a new building is x and number of member in the club who solicited is y.

According to the question,

$\frac{75y}{100} = \frac{60}{100} x \times 600$

or, $\frac{3}{4}y = \frac{3}{5}x \times 600 \Rightarrow y = 480x$

again, remaining amount needed for the building = $y - \frac{3y}{4} = \frac{y}{4}$

when $\frac{y}{4}$ amount is collected from

$x - \frac{3x}{5} = \frac{2x}{5}$

People, its average = $\frac{\frac{y}{4}}{\frac{2x}{5}}$

or, $\frac{480x \times 5}{8x} = 300$.

100. Let speed of horse a and b are x km/h and y km/h respectively.
According to the question,
$x + y = 50 \Rightarrow x = (50 - y)$

and $\frac{50}{y} - \frac{50}{x} = \frac{5}{6}$

or, $\frac{50}{y} - \frac{50}{50-y} = \frac{5}{6}$

$\Rightarrow$ $60(50 - y) - 60y = y(50 - y)$

or, $y^2 - 170y + 3000 = 0$

$\therefore$ $y = 20$ km/h

Hence, speed of slower horse = 20 km/h.

101. Number of students in university-1 in 2010
= 20,000

Number of students in university-2 in 2012
= 20,000

Hence, Difference in Number = 0

103. 25% of the student are female

So, 75% of the student are male in university-2

Hence, Required Number

$= 15{,}000 \times \frac{75}{100} = 11{,}250.$

104. Increase in number of student from university-1
= 25,000 – 20,000 = 5,000

Hence, Percentage increase in number

$= \frac{5{,}000}{20{,}000} \times 100 = 25\%.$

106. a and b one day work $= \frac{1}{8}$

b and c one day work $= \frac{1}{12}$

a and c one day work $= \frac{1}{8}$

a, b and c one day work $= \frac{1}{2}\left[\frac{1}{8} + \frac{1}{12} + \frac{1}{8}\right]$

$= \frac{1}{2} \times \frac{1}{3} = \frac{1}{6}$

$\therefore$ While working together, they can finish whole work in 6 days only.

109. L.C.M. of 2, 3, 4, 5, and 6 = 60

Now, (k. 60 + 1), where k = Natural Number is divisible by 7.

For least values of k = 5.

5 × 60 + 1 = 301 is divisible by 7.

111. C.P. = ₹ 380.00, Let S.P. = x

From question,

$\frac{x \times 95}{100} = \frac{380 \times 125}{100} \Rightarrow \frac{19x}{20} = 475$

$\therefore$ x = ₹ 500.

114.

$$
\begin{array}{r|l}
 & 4x^3 + 6x^2 + 2x + 7/2 \\
4x-3 & 16x^4 + 12x^3 - 10x^2 + 8x + 20 \\
 & 16x^4 - 12x^3 \\
 & - \quad + \\
\hline
 & 24x^3 - 10x^2 \\
 & 24x^3 - 18x^2 \\
 & - \quad + \\
\hline
 & 8x^2 + 8x \\
 & 8x^2 - 6x \\
 & - \quad + \\
\hline
 & 14x + 20 \\
 & 14x - \frac{21}{2} \\
 & - \quad + \\
\hline
 & \frac{61}{2}
\end{array}
$$

$\therefore$ Quotient $= 4x^3 + 6x^2 + 2x + \frac{7}{2}$

Remainder $= \frac{61}{2}$

118. 4, 10, 23, 50, 105, 216, 439

4 × 2 + 2, 10 × 2 + 3, 23 × 2 + 4, 50 × 2 + 5, 105 × 2 + 6, 216 × 2 + 7

124. Gita's average earning

$= \frac{400 + 420 + 200 + 140}{4}$ = ₹ 290.

126. $M_1 = 120$, $D_1 = 200 - 5 = 195$

$M_2 = 120 - 30 = 90$, $D_2 = ?$

From, $M_1D_1 = M_2D_2$

$120 \times 195 = 90 \times D_2$

$D_2 = \frac{120 \times 195}{90} = 260$

128. Let P C.P. is x,

Then, $x \times \frac{110}{100} \times \frac{112}{100} = 246.40$

$\therefore$ $x = \frac{246.4 \times 100 \times 100}{110 \times 112}$

$= 200$

Hence, P paid for it = ₹ 200.

*Based on memory

ENGLISH

1. Spelling Test

The most common errors in English are of spellings of words. Even the most learned men are sometimes confused about the correct spellings of some words. One must keep and use a dictionary religiously. Never ignore and let pass a new word casually.

A number of question to test your knowledge of spellings are compiled here. Try to solve as many as you can.

MULTIPLE CHOICE QUESTIONS

Directions (Qs. 1 to 200): *Find the correctly spelt word.*

1. A. Discriminate B. Discremineta C. Discrimenate D. Discriminat

2. A. Juddicious B. Judiceous C. Judicious D. Judiceus

3. A. Accompalish B. Ackmplesh C. Acomplush D. Accomplish

4. A. Damage B. Dammage C. Damaige D. Dammege

5. A. Lackdaisical B. Lackadaisical C. Lckadaisicle D. Lackadisical

6. A. Efficiant B. Effecient C. Efficient D. Eficient

7. A. Survellance B. Surveilance C. Surveillance D. Survaillance

8. A. Schedule B. Schdule C. Schedale D. Schedeule

9. A. Occurad B. Occurred C. Ocurred D. Occured

10. A. Licentious B. Licontious C. Licenttious D. Licientious

11. A. Chancelery B. Chancellery C. Chancellary D. Chancelary

12. A. Itenerary B. Itinarery C. Itinarary D. Itinerary

13. A. Grieff B. Grief C. Grieef D. Grrief

14. A. Indipenseble B. Indispansible C. Indispensable D. Indipensable

15. A. Guarantee B. Garuntee C. Guaruntee D. Gaurantee

16. A. Meddicine B. Medicine C. Medicene D. Medicinne

17. A. Benefeted B. Benefitted C. Benifited D. Benefited

18. A. Kleptomonia B. Kleptemonia C. Kleptomania D. Klaptomania

19. A. Sepalchrle B. Sepalchral C. Sepulchrle D. Sepulchral

20. A. Acommodation B. Acomodation C. Accomodation D. Accommodation

21. A. Teracherous B. Treacherous C. Treacheraus D. Treachereans

22. A. Querrelsome B. Quarrelsame
C. Quarrelsome D. Querralsome

23. A. Farmament B. Farmement
C. Fermament D. Fremament

24. A. Sympathetic B. Smypathetic
C. Sympothetic D. Sympethetic

25. A. Pecification B. Pacification
C. Pecifacation D. Pecefication

26. A. Meritricious B. Merefrecious
C. Meretricious D. Merritricious

27. A. Hypocritical B. Hypocretical
C. Hypocriticel D. Hypocirticel

28. A. Vaingloriaus B. Vaniglorious
C. Vaniglerious D. Vaingloreus

29. A. Imprecticability B. Impracticebility
C. Impracticibility D. Impracticability

30. A. Prograssive B. Progressive
C. Progresive D. Prograsive

31. A. Incradulous B. Incredulous
C. Incridulous D. Incredalous

32. A. Uncivilized B. Uncevilized
C. Uncivillized D. Uncevelized

33. A. Osttentatious B. Ostentetious
C. Ostentatious D. Ostenttatious

34. A. Extravagant B. Extreragent
C. Extreregant D. Extravegent

35. A. Missunderstood B. Miesunderstood
C. Misunderstood D. Misunderstod

36. A. Belligerent B. Beligirent
C. Belligarant D. Belligerrent

37. A. Pasiveness B. Passiveness
C. Passeveniss D. Passivines

38. A. Astonished B. Astronished
C. Astoneshed D. Asstonished

39. A. Obnosious B. Obnoxeous
C. Obnoxious D. Obnoseous

40. A. Polyendry B. Poliendry
C. Pollyendry D. Polyandry

41. A. Sincerely B. Sencerely
C. Sincerelly D. Sincerrely

42. A. Efflorascence B. Eflorescene
C. Effllorescence D. Efflorescence

43. A. Vulnarable B. Valnerable
C. Velnerable D. Vulnerable

44. A. Rigourous B. Rigerous
C. Rigorous D. Regerous

45. A. Omenous B. Ominous
C. Ommineous D. Omineous

46. A. Puerille B. Puerrile
C. Puerile D. Purrile

47. A. Satellite B. Sattellite
C. Satelite D. Sattelite

48. A. Pesanger B. Passenger
C. Pessenger D. Pasanger

49. A. Humurous B. Humorous
C. Humoreus D. Humorrous

50. A. Equinimity B. Equanimmity
C. Equannimity D. Equanimity

51. A. Exeggerate B. Exaggerate
C. Exadgerate D. Exagerate

52. A. Fariegn B. Forein
C. Foriegn D. Foreign

53. A. Rennaissance B. Rennaisance
C. Renaisance D. Renaissance

54. A. Excesive B. Excessive
C. Exccessive D. Exccesive

55. A. Forcaust B. Forcast
C. Forecast D. Forecaste

56. A. Valuptuous B. Volluptous
C. Voluptuous D. Volupttuous

57. A. Entrepraneur B. Entreprenuer
C. Entrapreneur D. Entrepreneur

58. A. Paralleted B. Paralelled
C. Parralleled D. Parallelled

59. A. Ocasion B. Occassion
C. Occasion D. Ocassion

60. A. Boquet B. Bouquet
C. Bouquete D. Bouquette

61. A. Loquacieous B. Lequacious
C. Loquacious D. Lequocious

62. A. Cataclysm B. Cataclism
C. Catacilysm D. Cataclesm

63. A. Chettering B. Chaterring
C. Chattering D. Chatering

64. A. Fulfilment B. Fulffilment
C. Fulfilmient D. Fullfilment

65. A. Conjectore B. Conjecture
C. Cenjecture D. Cenjectire

66. A. Endication B. Endicaltion
C. Indication D. Indicetion

67. A. Splendour B. Spllendour
C. Splandour D. Splendeur

68. A. Excllusion B. Exclussion
C. Exclusion D. Exclosion

69. A. Discourage B. Disscourage
C. Discourege D. Discaurage

70. A. Curageous B. Courageous
C. Courrageous D. Couregeous

71. A. Abandon B. Abanddon
C. Abendon D. Abbandon

72. A. Embarassment B. Emberrassement
C. Embarrassment D. Embbaresment

73. A. Veneration B. Venration
C. Venneration D. Venerration

74. A. Tacciturnity B. Taciturnity
C. Taciturrnity D. Tacitturnity

75. A. Despponding B. Despending
C. Desponding D. Dessponding

76. A. Bueyant B. Buoyant
C. Bueeyant D. Buoyent

77. A. Eccintric B. Eccentrie
C. Eccentric D. Eccintrie

78. A. Corrigible B. Corigible
C. Corregible D. Corrigiblle

79. A. Amandable B. Amendable
C. Amenddable D. Amendablle

80. A. Occasional B. Occassional
C. Occesional D. Occessional

81. A. Exttirpate B. Extirpete
C. Extirpate D. Exterpate

82. A. Vorecious B. Varacious
C. Voarcious D. Voracious

83. A. Insolvent B. Insolvant
C. Insollvent D. Insolvvent

84. A. Querrel B. Querral
C. Quarrel D. Quarel

85. A. Contrebution B. Contribution
C. Contributtion D. Conterbution

86. A. Desgrace B. Disgrece
C. Disgrice D. Disgrace

87. A. Harassment B. Herassment
C. Harasment D. Harassmient

88. A. Tranquilitty B. Tranquility
C. Trenquility D. Tranquillity

89. A. Imaginative B. Imeginative
C. Imagenative D. Imaginetive

90. A. Suficient B. Suficiant
C. Sufficient D. Sufficiant

91. A. Adequate B. Edequate
C. Adaquete D. Edaquete

92. A. Expairienced B. Experianced
C. Experienced D. Experrienced

93. A. Flatering B. Fletering
C. Flattering D. Fletaring

94. A. Cuttiveted B. Culltrivated
C. Cultivated D. Caltivated

95. A. Materialistic B. Materielistic
C. Meterialistic D. Matterialistic

96. A. Praiceworthy B. Peiseworthy
C. Praiseworthy D. Praisaworthy

97. A. Tranquil B. Trenquil
C. Tranquel D. Trinquil

98. A. Neggardly B. Nigardly
C. Niggerdly D. Niggardly

99. A. Magnanimity B. Megnanimity
C. Magnenimity D. Magnanimety

100. A. Darogate B. Derogate
C. Derogeta D. Deragate

101. A. Philanthropist B. Philenthropist
C. Phelanthropist D. Philanthropest

102. A. Ephameral B. Ephimeral
C. Ephemeral D. Ephemerel

103. A. Fanaticism B. Fenaticism
C. Faneticism D. Fanatecism

104. A. Profesional B. Professionel
C. Professional D. Profissional

105. A. Ameteur B. Amateur
C. Amataur D. Amateor

106. A. Philenderer B. Philandarer
C. Philanderer D. Philonderer

107. A. Honorary B. Henorary
C. Honerary D. Honorery

108. A. Darmatologist B. Dermatologist
C. Dermetologist D. Dermatologest

109. A. Compansation B. Compensetion
C. Compensotion D. Compensation

110. A. Quadruplets B. Quedruplets
C. Quadroplets D. Quadruplats

111. A. Econemist B. Economest
C. Economist D. Econimist

112. A. Catholic B. Cetholic
C. Cathelic D. Cathilic

113. A. Unfevourable B. Unfevaurable
C. Unfavourable D. Unfivourable

114. A. Bombastic B. Bombestic
C. Bombostic D. Bombastie

115. A. Posthumaus B. Posthomous
C. Posthumous D. Pasthumous

116. A. Epitaph B. Epetaph
C. Epiteph D. Epitoph

117. A. Falicitate B. Felicitate
C. Falecitate D. Falecetate

118. A. Schezophrenia B. Schizaphrenia
C. Schizophrenia D. Schizophrania

119. A. Claustrophobia B. Cloustrophobia
C. Claustraphobia D. Claustrophabia

120. A. Connoiseur B. Connaisseur
C. Connaissour D. Connoisseur

121. A. Transperency B. Transparency
C. Transpirency D. Tranporency

122. A. Superanuation B. Superennuation
C. Superannuation D. Superannuetion

123. A. Antiquated B. Antiqueted
C. Antequated D. Antiquatted

124. A. Adalescent B. Addescant
C. Adolescent D. Adolascent

125. A. Newrologist B. Neurologist
C. Neurologest D. Newrologest

126. A. Obstatricion B. Obstitricion
C. Obstetricion D. Obstetracion

127. A. Illiterate B. Iliterate
C. Illitarate D. Illiterete

128. A. Thioretical B. Theoretical
C. Theoratical D. Theoritical

129. A. Mersenary B. Marcenary
C. Marcenery D. Mercenary

130. A. Archeic B. Arcaic
C. Archeic D. Archaic

131. A. Dormetory B. Durmitory
C. Dormitori D. Dormitory

132. A. Aristocracy B. Arestocracy
C. Arestocracy D. Aristocrecy

133. A. Lagislature B. Legislature
C. Lageslature D. Legesleture

134. A. Dormetory B. Dormitery
C. Dormitory D. Dermitory

135. A. Garulous B. Garrulaus
C. Gorrulous D. Garrulous

136. A. Regecide B. Regicide
C. Rigecide D. Ragicide

137. A. Epicurean B. Epecurean
C. Epicurian D. Epicorean

138. A. Commetti B. Commitee
C. Committee D. Comitte

139. A. Inemitable B. Inimitable
C. Inimetable D. Inimitabli

140. A. Pletocray B. Plitocracy
C. Plotocracy D. Plutocracy

141. A. Immortal B. Emortal
C. Immortel D. Immortol

142. A. Perrhic B. Pyrrhic
C. Pyrrhec D. Porrhec

143. A. Chauvinism B. Chouvinism
C. Chevinism D. Cauvinism

144. A. Rumenate B. Ruminote
C. Rimunote D. Ruminate

145. A. Teciturn B. Tociturn
C. Tecitorn D. Taciturn

146. A. Verteran B. Viteran
C. Veterain D. Veteran

147. A. Antitode B. Antedote
C. Antidote D. Autitote

148. A. Audeble B. Audible
C. Audcble D. Audebli

149. A. Bellicose B. Billicose
C. Bellecose D. Belicose

150. A. Pilferage B. Peliferage
C. Pilfarege D. Poliferage

151. A. Ribut B. Rebit
C. Rebut D. Rebute

152. A. Sychologist B. Psycologist
C. Psychologist D. Psychogist

153. A. Neucteus B. Neucleus
C. Nucleus D. Neocleus

154. A. Negotcate B. Negociate
C. Negotiate D. Nagotiate

155. A. Skelled B. Skilled
C. Skiled D. Skillid

156. A. Logecal B. Logical
C. Lagical D. Logicle

157. A. Effeciency B. Efficiency
C. Eficiency D. Efficency

158. A. Cumpartment B. Compartment
C. Compartant D. Comportent

159. A. Continuous B. Cuntinuous
C. Continus D. Contineuous

160. A. Valuable B. Valueable
C. Valuabel D. Valoble

161. A. Courteous B. Curteous
C. Corteous D. Courtus

162. A. Prophecy B. Phropecy
C. Propecy D. Propheci

163. A. Lonesome B. Lonsome
C. Lonesum D. Lonsum

164. A. Formedable B. Formidable
C. Formidabul D. Formdable

165. A. Inibriated B. Enibrited
C. Inebriated D. Inubrited

166. A. Guellible B. Guiellible
C. Guillibel D. Guillible

167. A. Subsequent B. Subsiquent
C. Subsequint D. Subquent

168. A. Alein B. Alien
C. Abein D. Abien

169. A. Misogynesm B. Mesogynism
C. Misogynism D. Misosogesim

170. A. Sanguini B. Sangune
C. Sangiune D. Sanguine

171. A. Exemplary B. Eximplary
C. Exemplari D. Examplary

172. A. Sycophants B. Sicophants
C. Sycopants D. Sycophints

173. A. Petchy B. Patchy
C. Patchi D. Patche

174. A. Impassi B. Impasse
C. Impase D. Inpassi

175. A. Aceelerate B. Accilerate
C. Accelerate D. Accelerati

176. A. Vendictive B. Vindective
C. Vindictive D. Vindictivi

177. A. Prudint B. Prudient
C. Prudente D. Prudent

178. A. Superfluons B. Superfleos
C. Superflous D. Superfluous

179. A. Expidite B. Expedeti
C. Expedite D. Expedit

180. A. Livity B. Levity
C. Levety D. Levite

181. A. Reluctant B. Riluctant
C. Reluctent D. Relictunt

182. A. Desparge B. Disparage
C. Disperage D. Disparege

183. A. Maegre B. Meager
C. Meagre D. Megre

184. A. Accedental B. Aceedent
C. Accidantle D. Accidental

185. A. Cheapiness B. Chaepness
C. Chepness D. Cheapness

186. A. Febulous B. Fabulus
C. Fabulous D. Fibulous

187. A. Colusion B. Collision
C. Colision D. Collison

188. A. Eradicated B. Erradicated
C. Eradecated D. Eradiceted

189. A. Ageonise B. Agonise
C. Agonice D. Agonisee

190. A. Comit B. Commiet
C. Commit D. Commite

191. A. Tasiturn B. Taciturn
C. Taceturn D. Tacitorn

192. A. Omnevorous B. Omnivorous
C. Omniverous D. Omnivarous

193. A. Feud B. Fued
C. Fiud D. Feued

194. A. Pselm B. Slam
C. Psalm D. Salm

195. A. Haphazard B. Hapahazard
C. Haphzard D. Haphazrd

196. A. Peevishness B. Pievishness
C. Peivishness D. Peeveshness

197. A. Gelactic B. Galectic
C. Galactic D. Galactec

198. A. Imbibision B. Imbision
C. Embibition D. Imbibition

199. A. Zoparasite B. Zooparaset
C. Zooparasite D. Zoprasite

200. A. Neuralgia B. Nuraliga
C. Neurolgia D. Neuraltia

ANSWERS

1	2	3	4	5	6	7	8	9	10
A	C	D	A	B	C	C	A	B	A
11	**12**	**13**	**14**	**15**	**16**	**17**	**18**	**19**	**20**
C	D	B	C	A	B	B	C	D	D
21	**22**	**23**	**24**	**25**	**26**	**27**	**28**	**29**	**30**
B	C	C	A	B	C	A	B	D	B
31	**32**	**33**	**34**	**35**	**36**	**37**	**38**	**39**	**40**
B	A	C	A	C	A	B	A	C	D
41	**42**	**43**	**44**	**45**	**46**	**47**	**48**	**49**	**50**
A	D	D	C	B	C	A	B	B	D
51	**52**	**53**	**54**	**55**	**56**	**57**	**58**	**59**	**60**
B	D	D	B	C	C	D	A	C	B
61	**62**	**63**	**64**	**65**	**66**	**67**	**68**	**69**	**70**
C	A	C	A	B	C	A	C	A	B
71	**72**	**73**	**74**	**75**	**76**	**77**	**78**	**79**	**80**
A	C	A	B	C	B	C	A	B	A

81	**82**	**83**	**84**	**85**	**86**	**87**	**88**	**89**	**90**
C	D	A	C	B	D	A	B	A	C
91	**92**	**93**	**94**	**95**	**96**	**97**	**98**	**99**	**100**
A	C	C	C	A	C	A	D	A	B
101	**102**	**103**	**104**	**105**	**106**	**107**	**108**	**109**	**110**
A	C	A	C	B	C	A	B	D	A
111	**112**	**113**	**114**	**115**	**116**	**117**	**118**	**119**	**120**
C	A	C	A	C	A	B	C	A	D
121	**122**	**123**	**124**	**125**	**126**	**127**	**128**	**129**	**130**
B	C	A	C	B	C	A	B	D	D
131	**132**	**133**	**134**	**135**	**136**	**137**	**138**	**139**	**140**
D	A	B	C	D	B	A	C	B	D
141	**142**	**143**	**144**	**145**	**146**	**147**	**148**	**149**	**150**
A	B	A	D	D	D	C	B	A	A
151	**152**	**153**	**154**	**155**	**156**	**157**	**158**	**159**	**160**
C	C	C	C	B	B	B	B	A	A
161	**162**	**163**	**164**	**165**	**166**	**167**	**168**	**169**	**170**
A	A	A	B	C	D	A	B	C	D
171	**172**	**173**	**174**	**175**	**176**	**177**	**178**	**179**	**180**
A	A	B	B	C	C	D	D	C	B
181	**182**	**183**	**184**	**185**	**186**	**187**	**188**	**189**	**190**
A	B	C	D	D	C	B	A	B	C
191	**192**	**193**	**194**	**195**	**196**	**197**	**198**	**199**	**200**
B	B	A	C	A	A	D	D	C	A

2. Synonyms and Antonyms

There are thousands of words in English language. No one can remember their meanings easily but with regular practice one can memorise most of them. A number of words with their Synonyms and Antonyms are compiled here. Try to learn as many as you can and answer the questions thereafter.

Words	Synonyms	Antonyms
Abandon	Cease, Forsake	Continue
Abhor	Hate, Loathe, Detest	Like, Love
Abiding	Enduring, Durable	Fleeting
Able	Proficient, Competent	Incompetent, Unfit
Ability	Skill, Power	Disability, Inability
Abortive	Fruitless, Futile	Fruitful, Successful
Abolish	Destroy, Undo	Restore, Revive
Abridge	Shorten, Curtail	Lengthen, Expand
Absolve	Forgive, Pardon, Excuse	Condemn
Accelerate	Hasten	Retard
Accord	Agreement, Harmony	Discord, Disagreement
Accumulate	Collect, Store, Amass	Distribute, Scatter
Adamant	Hard, Inflexible	Flexible
Adversity	Misfortune, Distress	Prosperity
Adept	Expert, Skilful	Inexpert, Unskillful
Aggravate	Heighten, Intensify	Quell, Suppress
Agile	Nimble	Clumsy, Undeft
Alert	Vigilant	Heedless
Allay	Calm, Soothe, Assuage	Arouse
Ameliorate	Improve, Advance, Amend	Worsen, Deteriorate
Ambiguous	Vague, Unclear	Clear
Amiable	Lovable, Agreeable	Disagreeable
Annihilate	Destroy	Create
Arduous	Hard, Strenuous	Easy

Words	Synonyms	Antonyms
Attack	Assault	Defend
Audacity	Boldness	Cowardice
Auspicious	Favourable, Propitious, Lucky	Ominous, Inauspicious, Unlucky
Austre	Harsh, Severe, Rigorous	Easy-going
Authentic	True, Genuine	Spurious, False
Avarice	Greed	Generosity
Averse	Unwilling, Loth, Disindined	Willing, Inclined
Aversion	Hostility, Hatred	Affinity, Liking
Base	Low, Mean, Ignoble	Noble, Exalted
Boisterous	Noisy, Stormy	Calm, Quiet
Brave	Courageous, Daring, Bold, Plucky	Cowardly, Dastardly, Timid
Brief	Short, Concise, Laconic	Lengthy, Diffuse
Bright	Vivid, Radiant	Dull, Dark
Brutal	Savage, Cruel	Humane, Kindly
Callous	Hard, Cruel, Indifferent	Soft, Tender, Concerned
Cautious	Careful, Wary	Rash, Reckless, Foolhardy
Censure (*n*)	Blame, Condemnation	Praise,
(*vb*)	Blame, Condemn	Praise, Commend
Circumscribed	Restricted, Confined, Limited	Unconfined, Unrestricted
Civil	Polite, Courteous, Gracious, Urbane	Rude, Uncivil, Impolite, Ungracious
Compassionate	Pitiful, Sympathetic, Merciful	Unsympathetic, Merciless, Cruel
Compress	Condense, Abbreviate	Expand, Lengthen
Conspicuous	Noticeable, Manifest	Inconspicuous
Constant	Steady, Steadfast, Uniform	Inconstant, Variable
Cordial	Friendly, Warm, Hearty	Cold, Unfriendly
Covert	Hidden, Secret	Overt, Open
Cruel	Savage, Ruthless, Vicious	Kind, Gentle, Benevolent
Cursory	Rapid, Superficial	Thorough, Exhaustive, Intensive
Credible	Believable, Probable, Plausible	Incredible, Unbelievable, Fantastic
Crafty	Cunning, Sly	Artless, Simple, Ingenuous
Costly	Expensive, Dear	Cheap, Inexpensive
Confidence	Trust, Reliance	Distrust, Doubt
Death	Decease, Demise	Existence, Life
Dearth	Scarcity, Lack, Want, Paucity, Shortage	Plenty, Abundance
Decay	Dissolution, Decline, Decomposition, Disintegration	Regeneration
Deference	Respect, Reverence	Disrespect, Irreverence
Deficient	Lacking, Inadequate	Complete, Sufficient

Words	Synonyms	Antonyms
Desolate	Lonely, Deserted	Crowded, Occupied
Destitute	Wanting, Needy	Rich, Affluent
Diligence	Industry, Perseverance	Idleness
Disgrace	Dishonour, Discredit	Honour, Credit
Dwindle	Decrease, Shrink	Grow, Increase
Earthly	Terrestrial, Mundane	Celestial, Heavenly, Unearthly
Eligible	Qualified, Suitable	Ineligible, Unsuitable
Emancipate	Liberate, Free	Enslave
Excited	Impassioned, Stimulated	Composed, Cool, Impassive
Extraordinary	Uncommon, Remarkable, Marvellous	Commonplace, Ordinary
Extravagant	Lavish, Prodigal, Wastrel, Spendthrift	Thrifty, Economical, Frugal
Fabricate	Construct, Make	Destroy
Fabulous	Fictitious, Mythical	Actual, Real
False	Untrue, Mendacious	True, Genuine
Famous	Well-known, Renowned	Obscure, Unknown
Fantastic	Fanciful, Imaginative, Visionary	Practical, Down to earth
Fearful	Nervous, Anxious, Afraid, Scared	Fearless, Dauntless
Felicity	Happiness	Sorrow
Gaiety	Joyousness, Hilarity	Mourning, Dullness
Garrulous	Talkative, Loquacious	Taciturn, Silent, Reserved
Generous	Liberal, Magnanimous	Stingy, Miserly
Gigantic	Huge, Colossal	Minute, Small
Graphic	Vivid, Pictorial, Meaningful	Vague
Guest	Visitor	Host
Guile	Fraud, Trickery	Artlessness, Ingenuousness
Gratitude	Gratefulness	Ingratitude, Ungratefulness
Gratuitous	Voluntary, Spontaneous, Unwarranted	Involuntary, Forced
Hamper	Hinder, Obstruct	Facilitate, Ease
Haughty	Arrogant, Proud	Humble, Modest
Hazardous	Dangerous, Perilous	Safe, Secure Protected
Headstrong	Obstinate, Stubborn	Weak-willed, Flexible
Hope	Belief, Conviction, Expectation	Despair, Hopelessness
Improvident	Prodigal, Carelessness	Provident, Economical

Words	Synonyms	Antonyms
Incessant	Unceasing, Continuous	Discontinuous
Indolent	Slothful, Lethargic	Active, Energetic
Joy	Delight, Pleasure	Sadness, Gloom
Jolly	Jovial, Merry	Gloomy, Sad
Judicious	Discreet, Prudent	Indiscreet, Injudicious
Knowledge	Enlightenment, Learning	Ignorance, Stupidity
Laborious	Industrious, Assiduous	Slothful, Lazy
Laxity	Slackness, Looseness	Firmness
Lenient	Mild, Forbearing	Strict, Stern
Lethal	Deadly, Fatal, Mortal	Life-giving, Vital, Vivifying
Liberal	Generous, Tolerant	Intolerant, Illiberal
Liberty	Freedom, Independence	Slavery, Bondage
Lively	Animated, Active	Dull, Listless
Loyal	Faithful, Devoted	Treacherous, Disloyal, Unfaithful
Lucky	Fortunate	Unlucky, Unfortunate
Lucrative	Profitable	Unprofitable
Magnanimous	Generous, Largehearted	Ungenerous, Stingy
Malady	Illness, Ailment	Health
Manifest	Noticeable, Obvious	Obscure, Puzzling
Meagre	Small	Plentiful, Large
Mean	Low, Abject	Noble, Exalted
Mendacious	False, Untruthful	Truthful
Misery	Sorrow, Distress	Happiness, Joy
Morbid	Sick, Diseased	Healthy
Mournful	Sorrowful, Sad	Joyful, Happy
Negligent	Careless, Heedless	Careful
Notorious	Infamous, Disreputable	Reputable
Obedient	Submissive, Compliant, Docile	Disobedient, Recalcitrant, Wayward
Obsolete	Antiquated, Out-of-Date	Current, Modern
Opportune	Timely, Seasonable	Inopportune
Opulence	Wealth, Riches	Penury, Poverty
Onerous	Heavy, Burdensome	Light, Easy
Palatable	Tasty, Delicious	Unpalatable
Pathetic	Touching	Joyous, Cheery
Persuade	Urge, Induce	Dissuade
Praise (*vb*)	Applaud, Eulogise	Condemn
(*n*)	Applause, Eulogy	Condemnation

Words	Synonyms	Antonyms
Precarious	Risky, Uncertain	Safe, Certain
Quaint	Odd, Singular	Usual, Ordinary
Quell	Suppress, Subdue	Agitate, Arouse
Rare	Uncommon, Scarce	Common, Ordinary
Refined	Polished, Elegant	Crude, Coarse
Remote	Distant	Near, Close
Renown	Fame, Reputation	Infamy, Notoriety
Rigid	Stiff, Unyielding	Flexible, Yeilding
Remorseful	Regretful, Repentant	Unrepentant
Rebellion	Revolt, Mutiny, Insurgency	Loyalty
Scared	Holy, Consecrated	Profane, Unholy
Sane	Sensible, Sound	Insane
Scold	Chide, Rebuke	Praise
Serious	Grave, Earnest	Frivolous
Shy	Bashful	Bold, Impudent
Simple	Plain, Artless	Complex, Cunning, Shrewd
Solitary	Single, Lonely, Secluded	Numerous, Multitude
Shallow	Superficial	Deep
Spurious	Sham, False	Genuine, Authentic
Stagnant	Still, Motionless	Moving
Surplus	Excess	Deficit, Shortage
Tame	Gentle, Mild, Domesticated	Savage, Wild
Teacher	Instructor, Educator	Student, Pupil
Tedious	Wearisome, Monotonous	Agreeable, Lively
Temporal	Worldly, Secular	Spiritual
Temperate	moderate	Immoderate, Intemperate
Tortuous	Winding, Circuitous	Straight, Direct
Tough	Hard, Strong	Tender, Soft, Flexible
Transient	Temporary, Fleeting	Lasting, Durable, Permanent
Trustworthy	Reliable	Unreliable, Untrustworthy
Tranquil	Calm	Agitated
Ugly	Unsightly, Repulsive	Beautiful, Attractive
Useful	Advantageous, Serviceable	Useless
Vehemence	Passion, Force	Apathy, Indifference
Vindictive	Revengeful	Forgiving
Wholesome	Healthy	Unwholesome, Morbid, Unhealthy, Diseased

Words	Synonyms	Antonyms
Wicked	Evil, Impious	Pious, Good
Wise	Sagacious, Erudite	Foolish, Stupid
Wreck	Ruin, Destroy	Create, Construct
Yield	Surrender, Submit	Resist, Revolt
Yielding	Submissive, Supple	Inflexible, Intractable
Yoke	Oppression, Bondage	Freedom
Zeal	Passion, Fervour	Apathy, Indifference
Zest	Relish, Enthusiasm	Distaste, Disrelish

MULTIPLE CHOICE QUESTIONS

Directions (Qs. 1 to 100): *In the following questions choose the word which best expresses the meaning of the given word.*

1. INDICT
A. Condemn B. Reprimand
C. Accuse D. Allege

2. SCINTILLATING
A. Smouldering B. Gilittering
C. Touching D. Warming

3. REFECTORY
A. Restaurant B. Parlour
C. Living Room D. Dining Room

4. DISTINCTION
A. Diffusion B. Disagreement
C. Different D. Degree

5. IMPROVEMENT
A. Advancement B. Betterment
C. Promotion D. Preference

6. ADVERSITY
A. Failure B. Helplessness
C. Misfortune D. Crisis

7. TURN UP
A. Land up B. Show up
C. Crop up D. Come up

8. DEIFY
A. Flatter B. Challenge
C. Worship D. Face

9. ERROR
A. Misadventure B. Misgiving
C. Ambiguity D. Blunder

10. SHALLOW
A. Artificial B. Superficial
C. Foolish D. Worthless

11. MASSACRE
A. Murder B. Stab
C. Assissinate D. Slaughter

12. COMBAT
A. Conflict B. Quarrel
C. Feud D. Fight

13. VORACIOUS
A. Wild B. Hungry
C. Angry D. Quick

14. IMPROMPTU
A. Offhand B. Unimportant
C. Unreal D. Effective

15. RABBLE
A. Mob B. Noise
C. Roar D. Rubbish

16. TEPID
A. Hot B. Warm
C. Cold D. Boiling

17. MAYHEM
A. Jubilation B. Havoc
C. Excitement D. Defeat

18. TIMID
A. Fast B. Slow
C. Medium D. Shy

19. CANTANKEROUS
A. Quarrelsome B. Rash
C. Disrespectful D. Noisy

20. PRECARIOUS
A. Cautious B. Critical
C. Perilous D. Brittle

21. TACITURNITY
A. Dumbness B. Changeableness
C. Hesitation D. Reserve

22. INEBRIATE
A. Dreamy B. Stupefied
C. Unsteady D. Drunken

23. HARBINGER
A. Massenger B. Steward
C. Forerunner D. Pilot

24. INTIMIDATE
A. To hint B. Frighten
C. Bluff D. Harass

25. IRONIC
A. Inflexible
B. Bitter
C. Good-natured
D. Disguisedly sarcastic

26. STRINGENT
A. Tense B. Stringy
C. Strict D. Causing to shrink

27. ECSTATIC
A. Animated B. Bewildered
C. Enraptured D. Illful

28. COMMENSURATE
A. Measurable B. Proportionate
C. Beginning D. Appropriate

29. DESTITUTION
A. Humility B. Moderation
C. Poverty D. Beggary

30. ASCEND
A. Leap B. Grow
C. Deviate D. Mount

31. UNCOUTH
A. Ungraceful B. Rough
C. Slovenly D. Dirty

32. LYNCH
A. Hang B. Madden
C. Killed D. Shoot

33. LAUD
A. Lord B. Eulogy
C. Praise D. Extolled

34. CORRESPONDENCE
A. Agreements B. Contracts
C. Documents D. Letters

35. VENUE
A. Place B. Agenda
C. Time D. Duration

36. STERILE
A. Barren B. Arid
C. Childless D. Dry

37. SYNOPSIS
A. Index B. Mixture
C. Summary D. Puzzle

38. GERMANE
A. Responsible B. Logical
C. Possible D. Relevant

39. PONDER
A. Think B. Evaluate
C. Anticipate D. Increase

40. CANNY
A. Obstinate B. Handsome
C. Clever D. Stout

41. ABUNDANT
A. Ripe B. Cheap
C. Plenty D. Absent

42. CONSEQUENCES
A. Results B. Conclusions
C. Difficulties D. Applications

43. SHIVER
A. Shake B. Rock
C. Tremble D. Move

44. DILIGENT
A. Progressive B. Brilliant
C. Inventive D. Hard-working

45. DISTANT
A. Far B. Removed
C. Reserved D. Separate

46. FORAY
A. Excursion B. Contest
C. Ranger D. Intuition

47. FRUGALITY
A. Foolishness B. Extremity
C. Enthusiasm D. Economy

48. GARNISH
A. Paint B. Garner
C. Adorn D. Abuse

49. VIGOUR
A. Strength B. Boldness
C. Warmth D. Enthusiasm

50. CANDID
A. Apparent B. Explicit
C. Frank D. Bright

51. BRIEF
A. Limited B. Small
C. Little D. Short

52. GARRULITY
A. Credulity B. Senility
C. Loquaciousness D. Speciousness

53. FURORE
A. Excitement B. Worry
C. Flux D. Anteroom

54. NEUTRAL
A. Unbiased B. Non-aligned
C. Undecided D. Indifferent

55. LAMENT
A. Complain B. Comment
C. Condone D. Console

56. MASTERLY
A. Crafty B. Skilful
C. Meaningful D. Cruel

57. MOROSE
A. Annoyed B. Gloomy
C. Moody D. Displeased

58. BARE
A. Uncovered B. Tolerate
C. Clear D. Neat

59. FEEBLE
A. Weak B. Vain
C. Arrogant D. Sick

60. PRESTIGE
A. Influence B. Quality
C. Name D. Wealth

61. WARRIOR
A. Soldier B. Sailor
C. Pirate D. Spy

62. ENTIRE
A. Part B. Quarter
C. Whole D. Half

63. RESCUE
A. Command B. Help
C. Defence D. Safety

64. INFREQUENT
A. Never B. Usual
C. Rare D. Sometimes

65. WRETCHED
A. Poor B. Foolish
C. Insane D. Strained

66. DIVERSION
A. Amusement B. Distortion
C. Deviation D. Bylane

67. AWAKENED
A. Enlightened B. Realised
C. Shook D. Waken

68. HASITATED
A. Stopped B. Paused
C. Slowed D. Postponed

69. PIOUS
A. Pure B. Pretentious
C. Clean D. Devout

70. TORTURE
A. Torment B. Chastisement
C. Harassment D. Terror

71. ATTEMPT
A. Serve B. Explore
C. Try D. Explain

72. RESTRAINT
A. Hindrance B. Repression
C. Obstacle D. Restriction

73. CHASTE
A. Honest B. Dignified
C. Virtuous D. Noble

74. INSOMNIA
A. Lethargy B. Sleeplessness
C. Drunkenness D. Unconsciousness

75. TRANSIENT
A. Transparent B. Fleeting
C. Feeble D. Fanciful

76. MANDACIOUS
A. Full of confidence
B. False
C. Encouraging
D. Provocative

77. VORACIOUS
A. Truthful B. Gluttonous
C. Funny D. Venturous

78. CONNOISSEUR
A. Ignorant B. Lover of art
C. Interpreter D. Delinquent

79. REPERCUSSION
A. Clever reply B. Recollection
C. Remuneration D. Reaction

80. REPEAL
A. Sanction B. Perpetuate
C. Pass D. Cancel

81. INFAMY
A. Dishonour B. Glory
C. Integrity D. Reputation

82. FAKE
A. Original B. Imitation
C. Trustworthy D. Loyal

83. DEBACLE
A. Collapse B. Decline
C. Defeat D. Disgrace

84. ADMONISH
A. Punish B. Curse
C. Dismiss D. Reprimand

85. EMBEZZLE
A. Misappropriate B. Balance
C. Remunerate D. Clear

86. CORPULENT
A. Lean B. Gaunt
C. Emaciated D. Obese

87. AUGUST
A. Common B. Ridiculous
C. Dignified D. Petty

88. STRINGENT
A. Dry B. Strained
C. Rigorous D. Shrill

89. INSOLVENT
A. Poor B. Bankrupt
C. Penniless D. Broke

90. EXTRICATE
A. Pull B. Free
C. Tie D. Complicate

91. INEXPLICABLE
A. Confusing B. Unaccountable
C. Chaotic D. Unconnected

92. GRATIFY
A. Appreciate B. Frank
C. Indulge D. Pacify

93. ALERT
A. Energetic B. Observant
C. Intelligent D. Watchful

94. UNTIE
A. Unfold B. Unchain
C. Undo D. Unhinge

95. OBJECT
A. Challenge B. Disapprove
C. Deny D. Disobey

96. BROWSE
A. Heal B. Deceive
C. Examine D. Strike

97. SALACITY
A. Bliss B. Depression
C. Indecency D. Recession

98. ZANY
A. Clown B. Pet
C. Thief D. Magician

99. WARY
A. Sad B. Vigilant
C. Distorted D. Tired

100. RECKLESS
A. Courageous B. Rash
C. Bold D. Daring

Directions (Qs. 101 to 200): *In the following questions choose the word which is the exact opposite of the given words.*

101. DEAR
A. Priceless B. Free
C. Worthless D. Cheap

102. FLAGITIOUS
A. Innocent B. Vapid
C. Ignorant D. Frivolous

103. LIABILITY
A. Property B. Assets
C. Debt D. Teasure

104. VIRTUOUS
A. Wicked B. Corrupt
C. Vicious D. Scandalous

105. ENCOURAGE
A. Dampen B. Disapprove
C. Discourage D. Warn

106. MORTAL
A. Divine B. Immortal
C. Spiritual D. Eternal

107. LEND
A. Borrow B. Cheat
C. Pawn D. Hire

108. COMIC
A. Emotional B. Tragic
C. Fearful D. Painful

109. ADDITION
A. Division B. Enumeration
C. Subtraction D. Multiplication

110. MINOR
A. Big B. Major
C. Tall D. Heavy

111. REPEL
A. Attend B. Concentrate
C. Continue D. Attract

112. ARTIFICIAL
A. Red B. Natural
C. Truthful D. Solid

113. CAPACIOUS
A. Limited B. Caring
C. Foolish D. Changeable

114. PROVOCATION
A. Vocation B. Pacification
C. Peace D. Destruction

115. METICULOUS
A. Mutual B. Shaggy
C. Meretricious D. Slovenly

116. ABLE
A. Disable B. Inable
C. Unable D. Misable

117. COMFORT
A. Uncomfort B. Miscomfort
C. Discomfort D. None of these

118. GAIN
A. Loose B. Fall
C. Lost D. Lose

119. SYNTHETIC
A. Affable B. Natural
C. Plastic D. Cosmetic

120. ACQUITTED
A. Freed B. Burdened
C. Convicted D. Entrusted

121. STRINGENT
A. General B. Vehement
C. Lenient D. Magnanimous

122. FLIMSY
A. Frail B. Filthy
C. Firm D. Flippant

123. BUSY
A. Occupied B. Engrossed
C. Relaxed D. Engaged

124. ADAPTABLE
A. Adoptable B. Flexible
C. Yielding D. Rigid

125. LOVE
A. Villainy B. Hatred
C. Compulsion D. Force

126. BALANCE
A. Disbalance B. Misbalance
C. Debalance D. Imbalance

127. RELINQUISH
A. Abdicate B. Renounce
C. Possess D. Deny

128. MOUNTAIN
A. Plain B. Plateau
C. Precipice D. Valley

129. FICKLE
A. Courageous B. Sincere
C. Steadfast D. Humble

130. PERENNIAL
A. Frequent B. Regular
C. Lasting D. Rare

131. RARELY
A. Hardly B. Definitely
C. Frequently D. Periodically

132. STARTLED
A. Amused B. Relaxed
C. Endless D. Astonished

133. ADHERENT
A. Detractor B. Enemy
C. Alien D. Rival

134. QUIESCENT
A. Indifferent B. Troublesome
C. Weak D. Unconcerned

135. CONDENSE
A. Expand B. Distribute
C. Interpret D. Lengthen

136. BENIGN
A. Malevolent B. Soft
C. Friendly D. Unwise

137. OBSCURE
A. Implicit B. Obnoxious
C. Explicit D. Pedantic

138. HYPOCRITICAL
A. Gentle B. Sincere
C. Amiable D. Dependable

139. EVASIVE
A. Free B. Honest
C. Liberal D. Frank

140. INDUSTRIOUS
A. Indifferent B. Indolent
C. Casual D. Passive

141. EXTRICATE
A. Manifest B. Palpable
C. Release D. Entangle

142. LUCID
A. Glory B. Noisy
C. Obscure D. Distinct

143. INSIPID
A. Tasty B. Stupid
C. Discreet D. Feast

144. OBEYING
A. Ordering B. Following
C. Refusing D. Contradicting

145. VICTORIOUS
A. Defeated B. Annexed
C. Destroyed D. Vanquished

146. COMMISSIONED
A. Started B. Closed
C. Finished D. Terminated

147. VANITY
A. Pride B. Humility
C. Conceit D. Ostentious

148. ZENITH
A. Acme B. Top
C. Nadir D. Pinnacle

149. TANGIBLE
A. Ethereal B. Concrete
C. Actual D. Solid

150. REPRESS
A. Inhibit B. Liberate
C. Curb D. Quell

151. EPILOGUE
A. Dialogue B. Prelude
C. Post script D. Epigram

152. FRAUDULENT
A. Candid B. Direct
C. Forthright D. Genuine

153. LOQUACIOUS
A. Reticent B. Talkative
C. Garrulous D. Verbose

154. NIGGARDLY
A. Frugal B. Thrifty
C. Stingy D. Generous

155. PERTINENT
A. Irrational B. Irregular
C. Insistent D. Irrelevant

156. FAINT-HEARTED
A. Warm-hearted B. Full-blooded
C. Hot-blooded D. Stout-hearted

157. VIOLENT
A. Humble B. Harmless
C. Gentle D. Tame

158. STATIONARY
A. Active B. Mobile
C. Rapid D. Busy

159. HONORARY
A. Dishonourable B. Reputed
C. Paid D. Official

160. COMMON
A. Rare B. Small
C. Petty D. Poor

161. FRUGAL
A. Copious B. Extravagant
C. Generous D. Ostentatious

162. MALICIOUS
A. Kind B. Boastful
C. Generous D. Indifferent

163. FAMILIAR
A. Unpleasant B. Dangerous
C. Friendly D. Strange

164. PRELIMINARY
A. Final B. First
C. Secondary D. Initial

165. DOUBTFUL
A. Famous B. Certain
C. Fixed D. Important

166. REMISS
A. Forgetful B. Watchful
C. Dutiful D. Harmful

167. INDISCREET
A. Reliable B. Honest
C. Prudent D. Stupid

168. FRESH
A. Faulty B. Sluggish
C. Disgraceful D. Stale

169. ANNOY
A. Praise B. Rejoice
C. Please D. Reward

170. TRANSPARENT
A. Semi-transparent B. Muddy
C. Opaque D. Dark

171. REVEALED
A. Denied B. Concealed
C. Ignored D. Overlooked

172. EXTRAVAGANCE
A. Luxury B. Poverty
C. Economy D. Cheapness

173. CROWDED
A. Busy B. Congested
C. Quiet D. Deserted

174. SHRINK
A. Contract B. Spoil
C. Expand D. Stretch

175. ENMITY
A. Important B. Unnecessary
C. Friendship D. Likeness

176. EXODUS
A. Influx B. Home-coming
C. Return D. Restoration

177. CULPABLE
A. Defendable B. Blameless
C. Careless D. Irresponsible

178. SUBSERVIENT
A. Aggressive B. Straightforward
C. Dignified D. Supercilious

179. AWARE
A. Uncertain B. Ignorant
C. Sure D. Doubtful

180. GRACEFUL
A. Rough B. Expert
C. Miserable D. Awkward

181. AUTONOMY
A. Slavery B. Subordination
C. Dependence D. Submissiveness

182. NADIR
A. Modernity B. Zenith
C. Liberty D. Progress

183. CONCEDE
A. Object B. Refuse
C. Grant D. Accede

184. SUPPRESS
A. Encourage B. Grow
C. Praise D. Permit

185. FAMOUS
A. Disgraced B. Notorious
C. Evil D. Popular

186. EXPAND
A. Contract B. Condense
C. Congest D. Conclude

187. ARROGANT
A. Polite B. Cowardly
C. Meek D. Gentlemanly

188. ENORMOUS
A. Soft B. Average
C. Tiny D. Weak

189. URBANE
A. Illiterate B. Backward
C. Discourteous D. Orthodox

190. HOSTILITY
A. Courtesy B. Hospitality
C. Relationship D. Friendliness

191. BELITTLE
A. Praise B. Flatter
C. Exaggerate D. Adore

192. HAPLESS
A. Cheerful B. Consistent
C. Fortunate D. Shapely

193. HAPHAZARD
A. Fortuitous B. Indifferent
C. Deliberate D. Accidental

194. GREGARIOUS
A. Antisocial B. Glorious
C. Horrendous D. Similar

195. VALUABLE
A. Invaluable B. Worthless
C. Inferior D. Lowly

196. ABSOLUTE
A. Deficient B. Faulty
C. Limited D. Scarce

197. CONFESS
A. Deny B. Refuse
C. Contest D. Contend

198. GULLIBLE
A. Incredulous B. Fickle
C. Easy D. Stylish

199. HIRSUTE
A. Scaly B. Bald
C. Erudite D. Quiet

200. HINDRANCE
A. Aid B. Persuasion
C. Cooperation D. Agreement

ANSWERS

1	**2**	**3**	**4**	**5**	**6**	**7**	**8**	**9**	**10**
C	B	D	C	B	C	B	C	D	B
11	**12**	**13**	**14**	**15**	**16**	**17**	**18**	**19**	**20**
D	D	B	A	A	B	B	D	A	B
21	**22**	**23**	**24**	**25**	**26**	**27**	**28**	**29**	**30**
D	D	C	B	D	C	C	B	C	D
31	**32**	**33**	**34**	**35**	**36**	**37**	**38**	**39**	**40**
A	C	C	D	A	A	C	D	A	C
41	**42**	**43**	**44**	**45**	**46**	**47**	**48**	**49**	**50**
C	A	C	D	A	A	D	C	A	C
51	**52**	**53**	**54**	**55**	**56**	**57**	**58**	**59**	**60**
D	C	A	A	A	B	B	A	A	C
61	**62**	**63**	**64**	**65**	**66**	**67**	**68**	**69**	**70**
A	C	B	D	A	A	D	B	A	A
71	**72**	**73**	**74**	**75**	**76**	**77**	**78**	**79**	**80**
C	D	C	B	B	B	B	B	D	D
81	**82**	**83**	**84**	**85**	**86**	**87**	**88**	**89**	**90**
A	B	A	D	A	D	C	C	B	B
91	**92**	**93**	**94**	**95**	**96**	**97**	**98**	**99**	**100**
B	D	D	C	B	C	C	A	B	B
101	**102**	**103**	**104**	**105**	**106**	**107**	**108**	**109**	**110**
D	A	B	C	C	B	A	B	C	B
111	**112**	**113**	**114**	**115**	**116**	**117**	**118**	**119**	**120**
D	B	A	B	D	C	C	D	B	C
121	**122**	**123**	**124**	**125**	**126**	**127**	**128**	**129**	**130**
C	C	C	D	B	D	C	D	C	D
131	**132**	**133**	**134**	**135**	**136**	**137**	**138**	**139**	**140**
D	B	B	A	C	A	C	B	B	B
141	**142**	**143**	**144**	**145**	**146**	**147**	**148**	**149**	**150**
D	C	A	A	A	D	B	C	A	B
151	**152**	**153**	**154**	**155**	**156**	**157**	**158**	**159**	**160**
B	D	B	D	D	D	C	B	C	A
161	**162**	**163**	**164**	**165**	**166**	**167**	**168**	**169**	**170**
B	C	D	A	B	C	C	D	C	C
171	**172**	**173**	**174**	**175**	**176**	**177**	**178**	**179**	**180**
B	C	D	D	C	A	A	C	B	A
181	**182**	**183**	**184**	**185**	**186**	**187**	**188**	**189**	**190**
C	B	B	B	B	B	A	C	C	D
191	**192**	**193**	**194**	**195**	**196**	**197**	**198**	**199**	**200**
C	C	C	A	B	C	A	A	B	A

3. One Word Substitution

There are many words in English language which can be perfectly used for a number of words. These words help in expressing ideas in a short and correct manner for the right occasion. Such words not only enhance the vocabulary but also enable you to economise in the use of words to a great extent.

Ambiguous : (of a statement) having more than one meaning.

Amphibian : an animal that can live both on earth and water.

Anaemia : deficiency of red blood cells or haemoglobin.

Anonymous : (of a person) of unknown name.

Anorexia : loss of appetite for food.

Anthology : a published collection of poems (from different poets).

Aquarium : a transparent bank of water in which the fish are kept.

Atheist : (of a person) who does not believe in the existence of God.

Archaeology : the study of science of historical relics or monuments.

Auditorium : a big hall, built for the gathering of people (audience).

Autograph : synatuses of an important person written as a memento for an admirer.

Bibliography : a list of books representing some scholarly work for reference.

Bibliophile : a great lover of books.

Biography : life history of a person written by someone else.

Biology : the study of living organisms.

Botany : the science that deals with the study of plant life.

Bureaucracy : a government run by officials.

Cannibal : (a person) who eats human flesh.

Carnivorous : (of an animal) feeding on other animals.

Catalogue : a systematic complete list of items.

Catastrophe : an event that occurs suddenly causing a great damage or suffering.

Congenital : (of a physical abnormality) present from birth.

Contagious : (of a disease) spread from one person or organism to the other directly or in an indirect way.

Credulous : (of a person) easily ready to believe something.

Incredulous : (of a person) not ready to believe something or somebody.

Cruciform : having the shape of a cross.

Cryptology : art of writing and solving codes.

Cryptogram : a text written in codes.

Cacophony : a great discordant noise.

Cacography : bad handwriting.

Cosmology : the science of origin and development of universe.

Democracy : a government of people.

Dendrology : the scientific study of trees.

Diabolism : worship of the devil.

Effulgent : shining brightly.

Egocentric : thinking only of oneself.

Endogamy : the practice or custom of marrying only within a local community.

Endomorph : a person with soft round body.

Epigraphy : the study and interpretation of ancient inscriptions.

Epilogue : a section or speech at the end of a book especially for giving the conclusion to what has been written.

Equinox : the time or date, when the day and night are of the same length.

Effervescent : giving off bubbles.

Fermentation : the chemical breakdown of a substance by yeasts or some bacteria, etc.

Fictitious : not real.

Folicide : the killing of one's son or daughter.

Floriferous : producing many flowers.

Fratricide : the killing of one's brother.

Fatal : a disease which ends in death.

Garrulous : excessively talkative.

Gigantic : of very big size.

Gluttonous : one who eats too much.

Gregarious : living in flocks or being fond of company.

Germicide : of something that kills germs.

Haemolysis : destruction of red blood cells.

Haemostasis : the stopping of flow of blood.

Homicide : the killing of human beings.

Horticulture : the art of garden cultivation.

Homogeneous : a combination of different elements.

Herbivorous : (of an animals) feeding on herbs.

Hypertension : pressure of blood more than normal.

Hypotension : pressure of blood less than normal.

Immiscible : (of a liquid) not forming a homogenous mixture with other liquids.

Immortal : never dying.

Incorrigible : one which cannot be corrected.

Indolent : lazy; less active.

Loquacious : (a person) who talks excessively.

Lithography : the art of printing or drawing on stones.

Luxurious : extremely comfortable.

Matricide : killing of one's mother.

Misogynist : a person who hates women.

Misogamist : a person who hates marriage.

Monogamy : the practice of marrying only one wife or husband.

Meticulous : a person who is very particular about every minute details.

Nepotism : the practice of providing opportunities to their friends or relatives by those who are in power.

Narcotic : a drug which is illegally sold and which causes addiction to the regular taker.

Nascent : new and lacking in maturity.

Optimist : a person who looks at the bright side of things.

Omniscient : having unlimited knowledge.

Omnipotent : all powerful.

Omnipresent : present everywhere at the same time.

Opaque : a thing that cannot be seen through.

Polygamy : the practice of having more than one wife at the same time.

Pessimist : a person who always looks at the dark side of things.

Panacea : a remedy for all diseases.

Patricide : killing of one's father.

Regicide : killing of the king.

Remuneration : money paid for a work.

Simultaneous : an incident happening at the same time.

Scrupulous : (of a person or process) diligent and extremely attentive to details.

Sequacious : (of a person) lacking originality of thoughts.

Soliloqy : the act of speaking to oneself.

Teetotaller : a person who does not drink.

Theist : a person who believes in the existence of God.

Tenant : a person who stays in a house and pays rent for it.

Vociferous : (of a person) speaking loudly and vehemently.

Vivacious : (of a woman) attractive and sprightly.

Xenophobia : extreme fear from strangers.

MULTIPLE CHOICE QUESTIONS

Directions (Qs. 1 to 200): *In questions given below out of four options choose the one which can be substituted for the given words/sentences.*

1. An assembly of listeners
A. Audience B. Nostrum
C. Ostracise D. Obituary

2. That which cannot be heard
A. Audible B. Pregnant
C. Inaudible D. Bobemian

3. A person who hates mankind
A. Philanthropist B. Misanthropist
C. Nihilist D. Theist

4. Animals that suckle their young ones
A. Mammals B. Pisces
C. Amphibian D. Birds

5. Murder of infants
A. Regicide B. Suicide
C. Homicide D. Infancide

6. Short lived or fleeting
A. Permanent B. Ephemeral
C. Effeminate D. Optimist

7. A person whose thoughts are turned inward and who never opens his heart to others
A. Extrovert B. Introvert
C. Sceptic D. Ambivert

8. Word for word
A. Verbatim B. Compound
C. Synonym D. Oral

9. A truth which is often repeated
A. Aesthetics B. Truism
C. Verbose D. Truant

10. Belief in the role of a strong dictator is
A. Fanaticism B. Fascism
C. Nepotism D. Dogmatism

11. A person who does things only for pleasure
A. Professional B. Radical
C. Amateur D. Empiric

12. A person who practices celibacy
A. Celibate B. Mature
C. Married D. Widower

13. That which can be easily carried
A. Portable B. Impregnable
C. Invisible D. Apostate

14. One who flirts with ladies
A. Solvent B. Gentleman
C. Philanderer D. Popular

15. An office for which no salary is paid
A. Hospitable B. Free
C. Honorary D. Gratis

16. One who firmly believes in fate or destiny
A. Honorary B. Gratis
C. Dermatologist D. Fatalist

17. A word which has the same meaning as another
A. Contemporary B. Substitute
C. Synonym D. Antonym

18. Allowance due to a wife from her husband on legal separation
A. Wage B. Compensation
C. Debt D. Alimony

19. Four children born at the same time
A. Alibi B. Twins
C. Allergy D. Quadruplets

20. An insect with many legs
A. Biped B. Butterfly
C. Centipede D. Quadruped

21. Birds moving from one place to another
A. Migratory B. Respiratory
C. Obituary D. Transitory

22. To change hostility into friendship
A. Surrogate B. Castigate
C. Placate D. Complicate

23. The study of the art of printing is
A. Typography B. Phenology
C. Astrology D. Graphology

24. One who studies the history of development of mankind is
A. Anthropologist B. Botanist
C. Economist D. Historian

25. A handwriting which cannot be easily read
A. Lucid B. Edible
C. Illegible D. Legible

26. Government in which all religions are honoured is called
A. Fanatic B. Ascetic
C. Secular D. Catholic

27. One who does not show favour to anyone is called
A. Impartial B. Unfavourable
C. Prejudiced D. Rude

28. To throw light on something difficult
A. Amplify B. Expand
C. Explain D. Elucidate

29. A style that is full of words is known as
A. Elegant B. Complicated
C. Verbose D. Bombastic

30. A book or paper written by hand is known as
A. Script B. Manuscript
C. Draft D. Hand-written

31. A disease which ends in death is known as
A. Life-suck B. Cancer
C. Fatal D. Deadly

32. Those are practised by statesmen is called
A. Diplomacy B. Viewpoint
C. Statesmanship D. Politics

33. What we say about a man after his death is called
A. Epitome B. Elegy
C. Posthumous D. Epitaph

34. One who looks at the dark side of things is known as
A. A pessimist B. An inconoclast
C. An optimist D. A fatalist

35. The act of speaking through one's thoughts when alone
A. Bilocation B. Dialogue
C. Monologue D. Soliloquey

36. To congratulate someone in a formal manner
A. Solemnise B. Celebrate
C. Facilitate D. Felicitate

37. A disease of the mind causing an uncontrollable desire to steal
A. Kleptomania B. Schizophrenia
C. Claustrophobia D. Megalomania

38. A person pretending to be somebody he is not
A. Liar B. Magician
C. Imposter D. Rogue

39. One who dabbles in fine arts for the love of it and not for monetary gains
A. Dilettante B. Professional
C. Connoisseur D. Amateur

40. A prima facie case is such
A. As it turns out to be at the end
B. As it seems at first sight
C. As it seems to the court after a number of hearings
D. As it is made to seem at first sight

41. Tending to move away from the centre or axis
A. Centripetal B. Awry
C. Centrifugal D. Axiomatic

42. A drawing on transparent paper
A. Transparency B. Blue print
C. Red print D. Negative

43. Somethings that relates to everyone in the world
A. Usual B. General
C. Universal D. Common

44. Continuing fight between parties, families, clans, etc.
A. Quarrel B. Skirmish
C. Feud D. Enmity

45. Extreme old age when a man behaves like a fool
A. Senility B. Superannuation
C. Imbecility D. Dotage

46. One who does not believe in existence of God
A. Stoic B. Egoist
C. Atheist D. Naive

47. That which is preceptible by touch is
A. Tenacious B. Contagious
C. Tangible D. Contingent

48. Words used in ancient times but no longer in general use now
A. Ancient B. Extinct
C. Archaic D. Antiquated

49. Incapable of being seen through
A. Potable B. Ductile
C. Opaque D. Obsolete

50. A fixed orbit in space in relation to earth
A. Geo-centric B. Geological
C. Geo-stationary D. Geo-synchronous

51. A long vehement speech
A. Abuse B. Abhor
C. Tirade D. Vulgar

52. The body at the state of growth between boyhood and youth, is
A. Youth B. Adolescent
C. Mature D. Adult

53. The doctor who specializes in the treatment of nervous system
A. Neurologist B. Oculist
C. Opticum D. Obstetrician

54. A person who has an extensive knowledge
A. Illiterate B. Innocent
C. Erudite D. Scholar

55. The science or art of conducting negotiations between nations
A. Erratic B. Wandering
C. Diplomacy D. Epicure

56. One who relies on experiment not on theory
A. Theoretical B. Empiric
C. Practical D. Scientist

57. One incredulous of human goodness
A. Naxalite B. Hedonist
C. Cynic D. Stoic

58. That which cannot be explained
A. Ennui B. Interesting
C. Emancipate D. Inexplicable

59. Animals which like to live in flocks
A. Isolate B. Gregarious
C. Voracious D. Precarious

60. A person blindly attached to any opinion, system or party
A. Fatalist B. Bourgeois
C. Bigot D. Fallible

61. One who is well versed in the knowledge of plants and vegetables
A. Botanist B. Vegetarian
C. Scientist D. Non-vegetarian

62. A place where one lives permanently
A. Bourgeois B. Refugee
C. Domicile D. Confiscate

63. A battle or a match which neither party wins
A. Detergent B. Caucus
C. Equal D. Draw

64. A piece of writing full of words or using more words than required
A. Vociferous B. Verbose
C. Sadist D. Voracity

65. The violation or profaning sacred things
A. Pantheism B. Sceptic
C. Sacrilege D. Opportunist

66. One who eats only vegetables and abstains from meat of animals
A. Gentle B. Mercenary
C. Non-vegetarian D. Vegetarian

67. One who cannot be easily pleased
A. Sycophant B. Reserved
C. Flatterer D. Fastidious

68. A supporter of the cause of women
A. Feminist B. Effiminate
C. Loquacious D. Sophist

69. A person who hates women
A. Monogamy B. Misogamist
C. Misogynist D. Gynaecologist

70. Without payment or free of cost
A. Hedonist B. Stoic
C. Precious D. Gratis

71. A person who changes sides
A. Ductile B. Anarchist
C. Communist D. Turncoat

72. A letter or a document which do s not bear the name of its writer
A. Acknowledge B. Pseudonym
C. Elite D. Anonymous

73. Incapable of being effaced, or cancelled or obliterated
A. Obviously B. Delegate
C. Indelible D. Delible

74. An associate in an office or institution
A. Accomplice B. Crew
C. Colleague D. Tyro

75. A person's first public speech
A. Maiden speech B. Inaugural
C. Libertine D. Final speech

76. That which is endless
A. Irrefutable B. Underscore
C. Refutable D. Interminable

77. One skilled in the disease of the eyes
A. Neurologist B. Dentist
C. Oculist D. Obstetrician

78. The study of energy is
A. Geography B. Biology
C. Physics D. Chemistry

79. Words inscribed on a tomb
A. Alibi B. Epitaph
C. Writ D. Monument

80. One who manages funerals
A. Undertaker B. Anarchist
C. Agnosite D. Belligerent

81. A style in which a writer seeks to display his knowledge is known as
A. Superficial B. Pedantic
C. Showy D. Extravagant

82. One who keeps guard is known as a
A. Soldier B. Policeman
C. Gate-keeper D. Watchman

83. One who is insensible to kind thought is known as
A. Unsympathetic B. Unkind
C. Callous D. Inconsiderate

84. An address poem is called
A. Elegy B. Sonnet
C. Ode D. Epic

85. One who does a job for monetary consideration is known as
A. Materialist B. Trader
C. Mercenary D. Businessman

86. That which cannot be changed
A. Unchanged B. Revocable
C. Changeless D. Irrevocable

87. Money paid to employees on retirement is called
A. Advance B. Deposit
C. Gratuity D. Pension

88. To make the facts known is called
A. Message B. Information
C. Intimation D. News

89. Property inherited from one's father is called
A. Ancestry B. Patrimony
C. Legacy D. Matrimony

90. Ordinary and common-place remarks
A. Satire B. Humour
C. Examples D. Platitude

91. One who is not easily pleased by anything
A. Precarious B. Maiden
C. Mediaeval D. Fastidious

92. Malafide case is one
A. Which is undertaken after a long delay
B. Which is not undertaken at all
C. Which is undertaken in bad faith
D. Which is undertaken in good faith

93. The absence of Law and order
A. Revolt B. Rebellion
C. Anarchy D. Mutiny

94. To slap with a flat object
A. Gnaw B. Chop
C. Swat D. Hew

95. A person who tries to deceive people by claiming to be able to do wonderful things
A. Magician B. Trickster
C. Impostor D. Mountebank

96. A government by the nobles
A. Bureaucracy B. Autocracy
C. Aristocracy D. Democracy

97. The custom or practice of having more than one husband at the same time
A. Polyphony B. Polychromy
C. Polygyny D. Polyandry

98. To issue a thunderous verbal attack
A. Animate B. Invigorate
C. Fulminate D. Languish

99. Present opposing arguments or evidence
A. Reprimand B. Criticise
C. Rebut D. Rebuff

100. Deriving pleasure from inflicting pain on others
A. Sadism B. Malevolence
C. Bigotry D. Masochism

101. The policy of extending a country's empire and influence
A. Imperialism B. Communism
C. Internationalism D. Capitalism

102. One who knows everythings
A. Omnipotent B. Scholar
C. Omniscient D. Literate

103. One who eats everything
A. Irresistible B. Insolvent
C. Omnivorous D. Omniscient

104. The act of violating the sanctity of the church is
A. Sacrilege B. Desecration
C. Heresy D. Blasphemy

105. A school boy who cuts classes frequently is a
A. Sycophant B. Defeatist
C. Truant D. Martinet

106. The part of a government which is concerned with making of rules
A. Bar B. Court
C. Legislature D. Tribunal

107. That which cannot be corrected
A. Indelible B. Illegible
C. Incorrigible D. Unintelligible

108. That which cannot be believed
A. Implausible B. Unreliable
C. Incredible D. Incredulous

109. A small shop that sells fashionable clothes, cosmetics etc.
A. Booth B. Store
C. Stall D. Boutique

110. A large sleeping-room with many beds
A. Hostel B. Bedroom
C. Basement D. Dormitory

111. One who talks too much
A. Pregnable B. Quite
C. Illogical D. Garrulous

112. One that lives on another
A. Parasite B. Eligible
C. Independent D. Rudimentary

113. A material through which water cannot pass
A. Fragile B. Fireproof
C. Pillion D. Waterproof

114. The murderer of a King
A. Regicide B. Fanatic
C. Suicide D. Fratricide

115. Talking to one's self
A. Egotism B. Soliloquy
C. Egoism D. Ennui

116. One who is given to sensual enjoyments
A. Cynic B. Epicurean
C. Fanatic D. Eccentric

117. A lover of books
A. Brittle B. Bibliophile
C. Biographer D. Philosopher

118. That which is bound to happen
A. Wavering B. Inevitable
C. Opaque D. Doubtful

119. A place where birds are kept
A. House B. Zoo
C. Stable D. Aviary

120. One who walks on foot
A. Rider B. Omnipotent
C. Pedestrian D. Traveller

121. The crime of literary theft
A. Panacea B. Partiality
C. Plagiarism D. Pluralism

122. A medicine that induces sleep is known as
A. Poppy B. Opium
C. Poison D. Narcotic

123. A word no longer in use is called
A. Non-existent B. Ancient
C. Obsolete D. Out-dated

124. Nations engaged in war are known as
A. Enemies B. Belligerents
C. Mongers D. Neutrals

125. A line of persons waiting
A. Queue B. Masses
C. Passengers D. Gathering

126. A dramatic performance
A. Mascot B. Mosque
C. Mask D. Masses

127. A person who speaks many languages
A. Polyglot B. Bilingual
C. Linguist D. Monolingual

128. The raison d'etre of a controversy is
A. The finesse with which participants handle it
B. The unending hostility the parties concerned have towards each other
C. The enthusiasm with which it is kept alive
D. The reason or justification of its existence

129. To walk with slow or regular steps is to
A. Stride B. Pace
C. Advance D. Limp

130. A person of good understanding, knowledge and reasoning power
A. Literate B. Expert
C. Intellectual D. Snob

131. Teetotaller means
A. One who abstains from taking wine
B. One who abstains from theft
C. One who abstains from malice
D. One who abstains from meat

132. Very pleasing to eat
A. Sumptuous B. Tantalising
C. Palatable D. Appetising

133. Parts of a country behind the coast or a river's banks
A. Archipelago B. Swamps
C. Isthmus D. Hinterland

134. Giving undue favours to one's own kith and kin
A. Worldliness B. Corruption
C. Nepotism D. Favouritism

135. One who sacrifices his life for a cause
A. Soldier B. Revolutionary
C. Martyr D. Patriot

136. A person who eats human beings
A. Cannibal B. Nostrum
C. Cynosure D. Animal

137. A thing fit to be eaten
A. Farrier B. Edible
C. Eradicate D. Audible

138. That which cannot be limited
A. Optimist B. Mimicry
C. Inimitable D. Genealogy

139. A territory ruled by a monarch
A. Aristocracy B. Monarchy
C. Democracy D. Plutocracy

140. That which is not subject to death
A. Mortal B. Earthy
C. Immature D. Immortal

141. A victory gained at too great an expense
A. Bloody B. Pyrrhic
C. Decisive D. Celibacy

142. The doctor who specializes in the treatment of corns
A. Oculist B. Podiatrist
C. Cardiologist D. Optician

143. A person who feels sorry for a wrong he has done
A. Compunctious B. Overt
C. Illiterate D. Literate

144. A person who advocates extreme Patriotism
A. Atheism B. Chauvinism
C. Socialism D. Democracy

145. To ponder over to meditate
A. Alleviate B. Expedite
C. Ruminate D. Ascetic

146. One who is habitually silent
A. Chalter box B. Taciturn
C. Indifferent D. Verbose

147. A letter which is not claimed by anyone
A. Wasted letter B. Epigram
C. Dead letter D. Epicure

148. A well experienced person
A. Veteran B. Tyro
C. Outlandish D. Novice

149. Medical examination of a dead body
A. Psychologist B. Post-mortem
C. Dissection D. Caesarian

150. One who is all powerful
A. Wait B. Embezzle
C. Omnipotent D. Effigy

151. The killing of one man by another man
A. Insecticide B. Suicide
C. Homicide D. Fillicide

152. A drug which produces sleep or stupor, torpor, etc.
A. Amulet B. Narcotic
C. Yawning D. Insomnia

153. Science of the study of old age is called
A. Exbiology B. Anthropology
C. Genetics D. Gerontology

154. That which cannot be understood
A. Infallible B. Unintelligible
C. Incorrigible D. Intelligible

155. Anything that destroys the effect of poison
A. Poison-free B. Preserver
C. Antidote D. Saver

156. One who is at home in all countries
A. Universal B. International
C. Cosmopolitan D. Metropolitan

157. A person who has no regard for others' feeling is known as
A. Boastful B. Haughty
C. Inconsiderate D. Unkind

158. A place where bees are kept is called
A. A-hive B. A sanctuary
C. An apiary D. A mole

159. An expression of mild disapproval
A. Denigration B. Reproof
C. Warning D. Denigration

160. A voice load enough to be heard
A. Laudable B. Oral
C. Audible D. Applaudable

161. A style in which a writer makes a display of his knowledge
A. Ornate B. Pompous
C. Pedantic D. Verbose

162. One who is fond of fighting
A. Militant B. Belligerent
C. Bellicose D. Aggressive

163. To take secretly in small quantities
A. Theft B. Defalcation
C. Pilferage D. Robbery

164. One who is honourably discharged from service
A. Relieved B. Emancipated
C. Emeritus D. Retired

165. An actor who plays humorous parts
A. Fool B. Joker
C. Clown D. Comedian

166. A building for storing threshed grain
A. Store B. Granary
C. Hangar D. Dockyard

167. To cause troops, etc., to spread out in readiness for battle
A. Align B. Disperse
C. Deploy D. Collocate

168. One who is determined to exactfull vengeance for wrongs done to him
A. Vindictive B. Vsurer
C. Vindicator D. Virulent

169. List of the business or subjects to be considered at a meeting
A. Plan B. Agenda
C. Schedule D. Time-table

170. A person who brings goods illegally into the country
A. Smuggler B. Importer
C. Exporter D. Fraud

171. To talk without respect for something sacred or holy
A. Vulgarity B. Rudeness
C. Obscenity D. Blasphemy

172. Communication between mind and mind
A. Tell-tale B. Telephone
C. Telepathy D. Amistice

173. A player, who acts, not by speaking, but wholly by gesticulations
A. Pantomine B. Patent
C. Paronyms D. Patricide

174. To set free from restraint or bondage
A. Detest B. Manipulate
C. Emancipate D. Conjecture

175. An elderly unmarried woman
A. Spinster B. Vandal
C. Adult D. Bachelor

176. One who makes or compiles a dictionary
A. Lexicographer B. Photographer
C. Publisher D. Manuscript

177. One who is deprived of the protection of law
A. Iconoclast B. Citizen
C. Belligerent D. Outlaw

178. A vain boasting fellow
A. Gallant B. Fool
C. Braggart D. Chivalrous

179. A general pardon of political offenders
A. Arson B. Amnesty
C. Emergency D. Arsenal

180. A woman of very fair complexion with light hair and light blue eyes
A. Pretty B. Blonde
C. Beauty D. Braggart

181. The principle of living and acting for the welfare of others
A. Egoism B. Misogynism
C. Asceticism D. Altruism

182. The study of earthquakes is
A. Zoology B. Physiology
C. Seismology D. Etymology

183. The study of religion is
A. Philology B. Astrology
C. Philosophy D. Theology

184. An object which has no life
A. Animate B. Living
C. Movable D. Inanimate

185. A round about way of speaking
A. Circumlocution B. Gourmet
C. Flamboyant D. Eccentric

186. A person who cannot pay his debts
A. Arsonist B. Agnostic
C. Solvent D. Bankrupt

187. One who is irreverent towards God
A. Fatalist B. Bigot
C. Blasphemers D. Fanatic

188. One who is incapable of being tired
A. Indefatigable B. Extempore
C. Opportunist D. Fatigable

189. A list of books
A. Epilogue B. Epigram
C. Catalogue D. Phrase

190. Animals living on plants
A. Cliche B. Celibate
C. Herbivorous D. Carnivorous

191. That which cannot be passed through
A. Present B. Passage
C. Impassable D. Passable

192. A thing through which rays of light cannot pass
A. Transparent B. Species
C. Waif D. Opaque

193. A thing which is not fresh
A. Old B. New
C. Juicy D. Stale

194. A place for invalids and convalescents
A. Irony B. Hospitable
C. Dipsomania D. Sanatorium

195. A child born after the death of his father
A. Posthumous B. Consort
C. Censer D. Premature

196. A person interested in reading books and nothing else
A. Student B. Book-worm
C. Book-keeper D. Scholar

197. A man of odd habits
A. Introvert B. Moody
C. Eccentric D. Cynical

198. A tank for fishes or water plants
A. Pyrrhic B. Expiate
C. Aviary D. Aquarium

199. Person anxious for or trying to provoke war:
A. warhead B. wary
C. warmonger D. extremist

200. Young and ambitious professional-person, working in a city:
A. yokel B. yankee
C. zippy D. yuppie

ANSWERS

1	2	3	4	5	6	7	8	9	10
A	C	B	A	D	B	B	A	B	B
11	12	13	14	15	16	17	18	19	20
C	A	A	C	C	D	C	D	D	C
21	22	23	24	25	26	27	28	29	30
A	C	A	D	C	C	A	D	C	B
31	32	33	34	35	36	37	38	39	40
C	A	D	A	D	D	A	C	D	B
41	42	43	44	45	46	47	48	49	50
C	A	C	C	D	C	C	C	C	C
51	52	53	54	55	56	57	58	59	60
C	B	A	C	C	B	C	D	B	C
61	62	63	64	65	66	67	68	69	70
A	C	D	B	C	D	D	A	C	D
71	72	73	74	75	76	77	78	79	80
D	D	C	C	A	D	C	C	B	A
81	82	83	84	85	86	87	88	89	90
B	D	C	C	C	D	C	C	B	A
91	92	93	94	95	96	97	98	99	100
D	C	C	C	B	C	D	C	C	A
101	102	103	104	105	106	107	108	109	110
A	C	C	A	C	C	C	C	D	D
111	112	113	114	115	116	117	118	119	120
D	A	D	A	B	B	B	B	D	C
121	122	123	124	125	126	127	128	129	130
C	D	D	B	A	B	C	D	B	C
131	132	133	134	135	136	137	138	139	140
A	C	D	C	C	A	B	C	B	D
141	142	143	144	145	146	147	148	149	150
B	B	A	B	C	B	C	A	B	C
151	152	153	154	155	156	157	158	159	160
C	B	D	B	C	C	C	C	B	C
161	162	163	164	165	166	167	168	169	170
C	C	C	D	C	B	C	A	B	A
171	172	173	174	175	176	177	178	179	180
D	C	A	C	A	A	D	C	B	B
181	182	183	184	185	186	187	188	189	190
D	C	D	D	A	D	C	A	C	C
191	192	193	194	195	196	197	198	199	200
C	D	D	D	A	B	C	D	C	D

4. Idioms & Phrases

An idiom is a group of words established by usage as having a meaning different from the individual words.

A phrase is a small group of words standing together as an idiomatic expression. The use of idioms and phrases makes your expression more effective and powerful.

Learn and practise as many as you can.

IDIOMS AND IDIOMATIC PHRASES

1. **ABC** (basic principles)
   She does not know the ABC of photography.
2. **To cut a sorry figure** (present oneself in a bad way)
   She cut a sorry figure on the stage.
3. **Cut loose** (Keep away)
   India should cut loose from bad politics.
4. **To give a red carpet reception** (to give a warm welcome)
   The PM was given a red carpet reception in America.
5. **To dance one's tune** (to follow someone submissively)
   He always dances to his brother's tune.
6. **To turn a deaf ear to** (to disregard)
   She turned a deaf ear to her parents' advice.
7. **To call a spade a spade** (to speak the truth)
   Gandhiji always called a spade a spade.
8. **To bring to book** (to scold)
   The naughty boy was brought to book by the teacher.
9. **From hand to mouth** (without any saving)
   The poor factory worker is living from hand to mouth.
10. **Once in a blue moon** (seldom)
    She visits her brother once in a blue moon.
11. **To cut short** (to reduce)
    Smoking will cut short your life.
12. **By hook or by crook** (by any means fair or foul)
    He wants to get money by hook or by crook.
13. **In the good books of** (be good in one's mind)
    Jack is in the good books of his teachers.
14. **At sixes and sevens** (in disorder)
    The drawing room articles were lying at sixes and sevens on the floor.
15. **To grease the palm of** (to bribe)
    Rohit greased the palm of the clerk and got the file moved.
16. **Through thick and thin.** (under all circumstances)
    We'll stand by you through thick and thin.
17. **At one's beck and call** (ready to obey)
    He had a dozen men at his beck and call.
18. **To die by inches** (to die a painful death)
    The old man died by inches.
19. **To eat one's words** (to retract one's statement)
    You'll have to eat your words because you have spoken without thinking.
20. **To burn the midnight oil** (to work hard)
    You'll have to burn the midnight oil if you want to get good marks.

21. **Fair and square** (clean)
One must be fair and square in one's dealing.

22. **To poke one's nose into** (to meddle with)
It is bad to poke your nose into others' affair.

23. **To fall flat** (to have no effect)
His father's advice fell flat on him.

24. **To make a clean breast of** (to confess)
He made a clean breast of his involvement in the bomb blast.

25. **To get the better of** (overcome)
Anger got the better of him.

26. **A wet blanket** (a discouraging person)
Don't allow Rakesh to accompany you to the hunting trip because he is a wet blanket.

27. **A big gun** (an important person)
Mr Smith is a big gun in our city.

28. **In black and white** (in written)
Don't give him anything in black and white.

29. **Neck and neck** (even)
There is a neck and neck fight between the two boxers.

30. **At a stone's throw** (at a short distance from)
My school is at a stone's throw from my house.

31. **Cut-throat competition** (a stiff competition)
There is a cut-throat competition among the publishers in the market.

32. **Black sheep** (a traitor)
Later on Mr XYZ proved a black sheep.

33. **By dint of** (by means of)
By dint of hard work, she earned a lot of money.

34. **A man of word** (a person who keeps his promise)
Mr Sharma is a man of word.

35. **A man of a few words** (a remarkable person)
Gandhiji was a man of a few words.

36. **In cold blood** (mercilessly)
The old woman was murdered in cold blood.

37. **At arm's length** (to keep away)
We should always keep bad boys at arm's length.

38. **Keep the ball rolling** (to maintain the progress of some activity)
After the death of his father he had to take the charge of his office to keep the ball rolling.

39. **A bolt from the blue** (a sudden and unexpected event)
The news of my friend's death came to me like a bolt from the blue.

40. (*i*) **Break ones back** (to work hard to get something)
He broke his back to earn his livelihood.

(*ii*) **To break somebody's back** (to give too much work to him to do)
She broke his back by giving him so much hard work to do.

41. **Break the back of** (accomplish the hardest part of a certain job)
There is nothing to be worried about as we've already broken the back of the problem.

42. **Beat about the bush** (to go on talking on some worthless topic)
Stop this beating about the bush, come to the main task.

43. **Throw cold water on** (to discourage)
She tried to throw cold water on his plan but he was well-determined.

44. **Hard of hearing** (somewhat deaf)
She is a bit hard of hearing.

45. **Come what may** (no matter what happens)
I'll do it come what may.

46. **Beyond one's means** (beyond one's budget)
He is living beyond his means, therefore, he is sure to get ruined.

47. **A man of letters** (a scholar)
Radha Krishnan was a man of letters.

48. **Chips of the same block** (having the same taste)
They are the chips of the same block.

49. **The long and short of** (in brief)
The long and short of his lecture is that we should live like brothers.

50. **In full swing** (in full force)
The studies of the students are going on in full swing.

VERBAL PHRASES

Back

Back up (to make a queue)
The vehicles began to back up.
Back down (withdraw claim in the presence of opposition)
The leader backed down from his previous statement.
Back off (draw back some plan or action)
They backed off from building a flyover.
Back out (withdraw from a promise, etc.)
The government backed out of its promise.

Break

Break down (stop working) My car broke down on the highway.
Break into (enter in certain premises by breaking the door, etc.)
Last night a thief broke into my neighbour's.
Break off (stop all of a sudden)
She broke off and began to think over about her/his hand.
Break out (spread)
Cholera has broken out in the town.
Break out of (escape from)
A prisoner broke out of the prison last night.
Break up (disperse)
The cloud of fog began to break up as the sun rose.
Break something up (Cause something to break into small pieces)
She broke up the chewing gum to distribute it among the girls.
Break with (Cut off connection after quarrelling with someone)
He has broken with his brother.

Call

Call on (pay a visit to somebody)
I'll call on Mohan's today.
Call out (to start)
The workers have called out a strike.
Call off (to stop the strike etc.)
The workers have called off the strike.
Call at (to visit someone's house)
I called at his house yesterday.
Call in (send for)
Please call in the doctor.

Carry

Carry on (continue)
Please carry on your work.
Carry something out (perform a task)
Our company is carrying out a big deal with a foreign company.
Carry something over (postpone)
The fancy dress competition had to be carried over till Monday)
Carry someone off (kill somebody)
Cancer carried her off on the day of her 20th birthday.

Come

Come of age (get established)
As our company has come of age, so, there is no problem in selling our goods.
Come of (belong to)
She comes of a royal family.
Come over (surmount)
We at last came over all our problems.
Come off (to take place)
The marriage of my brother comes off in the next month.
Come round (agree)
At last he came round to my views.
Come under (fall in the category of)
All these animals come under the same species.
Come down with (suffer from)
She came down with whopping cough.
Come from (be the nature of)
She came from London.
Come about (happen)
The explosion came about when the worker struck the match to light a cigarette.

Cut

Cut off (die)

The princess was cut off in the prime of her life.

Cut down (reduce)

The prices of consumer goods should be cut down.

Cut someone out (exclude someone)

His father cut him out of his will.

Fall

Fall in

She fell in love with the prince.

Fall down (fail)

The deal fell down for lack of transparency.

Fall out (quarrel)

She fell out with his elder brother.

Fall through (fail)

The project fell through for lack of funds.

Get

Get away (escape)

She got away with her life.

Get by (to accomplish something with great difficulty)

She is not rich. She has just enough to get by.

Get on (perform)

How are you getting on with your studies?

Get out (become known)

The news got out that the PM was paying a visit to Russia.

Get over (overcome)

At last I got over all obstacles.

Get up (rise)

When do you get up in the morning?

Give

Give up (stop)

He gave up smoking.

Give out (emit)

Garlic gives out a pungent smell.

Give in (collapse)

The bridge gave in under the heavy load.

Give away (distribute)

The Principal gave away the prizes.

Give out (announce)

It was given out that the President of India would visit the place soon.

Go

Go off (explode)

The gun went off suddenly.

Go on (continue)

She went on about how she flew the aeroplane.

Go through (examine)

I'll go through this book later on.

Go up (be built)

The construction of the house is going up.

Grind

Grind on (continue for a long time in a tedious way)

The discussion over political issues ground on.

Grind something out (produce something a tedious way)

She will grind some more short stories.

Look

Look out (be careful)

Look out! there is a snake.

Look down upon (hate)

We should not look down upon the poor.

Look at (watch)

Look at the blackboard.

Look after (take care of)

We ought to look after our old parents.

Look into (investigate)

The new police inspector will look into the matter.

Look up (rise)

The prices of consumer goods are looking up.

Look back (think of the past)

It made her feel disolate when she looked back on things of the past.

Make

Make up (to fulfil)

I'll make up my deficiency in Mathematics.

Make out (understand)

I could not make out what she said.

Make up one' mind (to resolve)

I have made up my mind to settle in the USA.

Make off (leave hurriedly)

She made off without informing anybody.

Make something over (transfer)

She should make her property over to her sons.

Make over (hand over)

He made over the charge of the file to Mr Robert.

Pull

Pull back (retreat)

The government has pulled back from its previous policy.

Pull something down (demolish)

The authorities concerned pulled down a few building which were illegally built on government land.

Pull out (pluck)

The child pulled out a few petals of the flower.

Pull through (recover)

The patient will pull through.

Push

Push on (continue a journey)

It was getting darker but we pushed on.

Push at (exert force)

He pushed at the bell, but it did not ring.

Push for (demand persistently)

The workers have been pushing for the installation of new machines since 2003.

Put

Put out (extinguish)

She put out the light.

Put on (wear)

He put on an overcoat.

Put off (postpone)

The plan had to be put off.

Put by (spare something for future)

We must put by some money for future.

Put up with (stay)

Your aunt is out of town for a couple of days, you may put up with us till she comes.

Put something down (record something)

She put a new idea down on the paper.

Take

Take after (resemble)

He takes after his father.

Take off (remove)

He took off his shoes.

Take something out (obtain)

You may take out some money from Rohit if you want to purchase this car.

Take to (fall into the habit of)

He took to gambling.

Turn

Turn something down (reject something)

The judge turned down his appeal.

Turn on (attack)

The thief turned on him with a knife.

MULTIPLE CHOICE QUESTIONS

Directions (Qs. 1 to 150): *Pick out from the alternatives the one that gives the correct meaning of the given phrase or idiom.*

1. Above board

A. A voyage
B. Beyond doubt
C. Uncertianty
D. Honest and frank

2. A bed of roses

A. always successful
B. a comfortable situation
C. very easy
D. transient pleasure

3. Add fuel to the fire

A. to activate the flames of an existing controversy
B. to spread a summour
C. to increase the differences
D. to speed up the work

4. A sleeping partner
A. one who does not work
B. unenthusiast
C. lethargic
D. exuberant

5. Apple of discord
A. the cause of separation
B. the basis of differentiation
C. the cause of friction
D. the state of confusion

6. A man of straw
A. a characterless person
B. worthless person
C. an indecisive person
D. unreliable person

7. Apple of one's eye
A. a very loving person
B. recalcitrant
C. a person full of male volence
D. a person who is very dear to one

8. A hard nut to crack
A. a difficult problem
B. a difficult situation
C. an intolerable person
D. a skinflint

9. Apple-pie order
A. handling two work simultaneously
B. extremely neat and tidy
C. two persons handling the same work
D. in a haphzard way

10. To pin one's faith
A. to be sure of somebody's favour
B. to be unsure of favour
C. to be insincere to others
D. to deceive a close friend

11. At arm's length
A. one arm distance
B. to keep one at distance
C. to be indifferent
D. an intimate relationship

12. A fish out of water
A. a dangerous situation
B. death
C. being in a position which is disagreeable
D. a lonely person

13. At one's wits end
A. to be in an embarrassing situation
B. to be in a state of utter perplexity
C. to satisfy one's own desire
D. to abrogate

14. A black sheep
A. scoundrel
B. ruthless
C. vagabond
D. a traitorous person

15. At sixes and sevens
A. in a state of confusion or disorder
B. returning to an earlier on primitive form or state
C. in a state of retrospection
D. in the days of childhood

16. A labour of love
A. a hard-working staff
B. work done only for love
C. to believe in work and not in reward
D. an unpaid servent

17. A Herculean task
A. unmanageable assignment
B. confusing and tiring procedure
C. work requiring extra ordinary strength to be done
D. almost impossible to acheive something

18. A bolt from the blue
A. an unexpected and calamitous blow
B. a retaliating attack
C. tumult
D. a sudden pleasant surprise

19. At the mercy of
A. totally in the power of
B. to leave everything on God
C. to surrender
D. the supremacy of God's will

20. At the eleventh hour
A. at the time of death
B. moment just after the work is completed
C. moment just after the work is assigned
D. at the last moment

21. A hornet's nest
A. a dangerous situation
B. a house built after great difficulty
C. an unpleasant situation
D. a difficult task

22. At the bottom of
A. secret cause of
B. at another's support
C. to find a base
D. a heavy loss

23. At daggers drawn
A. a dual
B. at enmity
C. a hot debate
D. one confronted with his rival

24. A man of parts
A. a man of superior ability
B. a highly responsible man
C. a workaholic person
D. a man of pretension

25. A man of words
A. a garrulous person
B. a trustworthy person
C. a gregarious person
D. a boastful person

26. An out and outer
A. a traitor
B. a man living in the border area
C. a first rate person
D. at an extreme point

27. To make an ass of oneself
A. to behave foolishly
B. to laugh at oneself
C. to make someone fool
D. a ridiculous person

28. The Augustan Age
A. an age of Great kings
B. the period of highest purity and refinement in any national literature.
C. a golden age in music
D. a period of prudent writers

29. In open arms
A. to welcome cordially
B. to be brave
C. fighting openly
D. ambitions to have all sorts of worldly pleasures

30. All the sundry
A. all except one
B. only intellectuals
C. the whole elite class
D. everyone without distinction

31. Backstairs influence
A. improper influence
B. the ultimate outcome
C. retarded development
D. indirect influence

32. Bad blood
A. active hostility
B. retribution
C. very ill
D. retaliation

33. Beat a retreat
A. grand and pompous
B. to withdraw
C. to warn
D. not to come straight to the point

34. To have a bee in one's bonnet
A. to be obsessed with one idea
B. prejudiced
C. to have a single penny
D. None of the above

35. Behind the scenes
A. the hidden cause
B. self-contained
C. influencing events secretly
D. one's contribution which is yet to be considered

36. To bell the cat
A. to bring others to one's own opinion
B. to harm an enemy
C. try to render a common enemy harmless
D. to come to a common conclusion

37. Between the devil and the deep sea
A. about to die
B. to be on a wrong path
C. to be in a dilemma
D. between two dangers

38. To blow hot and cold in the same breath
A. to condemn and criticize
B. a hot discussion
C. to consider all the aspects
D. to be imperious and amiable by terms

39. Blow one's own trumpet
A. to be self-centered
B. to indulge in self praise
C. self-contained
D. to neglect other's opinion

40. To go to all lengths
A. to take all necessary steps
B. try to achieve something by all possible means

C. to visit all places
D. to consider details minutely

41. To burn the candle at both ends
A. to expend ones energy without regard to health
B. to live lavishly
C. to get exhausted
D. to torture

42. To bury the hatchet
A. to forgive someone
B. to forget past quarrels and animosity
C. to keep the intention secret
D. to defeat utterly

43. By the sweat of one's brow
A. very furious B. hard labour
C. short-tempered D. to feel insulting

44. Bear the palm
A. to help voluntarily
B. to form a team
C. to be victorious
D. a joint venture

45. Blow over
A. pass off
B. to propagate
C. to spread a rumour
D. to ditch or deceive someone

46. Blood is thicker than water
A. to favour the near ones
B. thought of approaching death is more severe than the actual death.
C. kinship is stronger than friendship
D. Blood and water are equally important

47. By word of mouth
A. loquacious B. verbosity
C. orally D. theoritically

48. By leaps and bounds
A. very quickly B. by any means
C. by illegal means D. vicariously

49. To back out
A. a narrow-escape from a danger
B. to attack from behind
C. to support someone indirectly
D. to retreat cautiously from a difficult position

50. To bear down upon
A. to humiliate
B. to take a responsibility
C. to interfere deliberately
D. to approach deliberately

51. Between two fires
A. subject to a double attack
B. between two rivals
C. between two extreme difficulties
D. a difference of opinions

52. To make no bones
A. to make no excuse
B. not to hesitate
C. to make no commitments
D. to make no monetary gains

53. To carry coals to Newcastle
A. to bestow a gift which is not really necessary
B. to place a thing to a wrong place
C. to transfer something from one place to another
D. to recognise the value of a person

54. Cats' paw
A. a person who is used as a tool by another person
B. very slowly and quietly
C. very cleverly
D. to share a responsibility

55. To catch a tartar
A. to overcome a serious problem
B. to attack one who turns out to be stronger than is expected
C. to achieve the goal
D. to struggle hard

56. Cheek of jowl
A. very soft
B. close together
C. intimate relationship
D. low in status

57. A chip of the old block
A. a symptom of a serious disease
B. a child of a parent
C. a part of a whole
D. offsprings who display characteristics of their parents

58. To cool one's heels
A. to be kept waiting
B. to give a cold response to somebody
C. to follow somebody
D. to answer all the queries of somebody

59. To cleanse the Augean stables
A. to clean something which has not been cleaned for a long time
B. to wind up a joint business
C. to remove the stains of blood
D. to remove the traces of murder

60. A cry in wilderness
A. the cry of the poors
B. a warning that goes unheeded
C. a speech made by a less important leader
D. a cry out of deep sorrow

61. To cut one's coat according to one's cloth
A. to work according to one's capacity
B. to allot portfolio according to one's capability
C. to live within one's means
D. to live as one desires

62. Chicken hearted
A. coward B. brave
C. kind D. mortal

63. Cut the Gordian knot
A. to solve a difficulty
B. to escape a hurdle
C. to perform the inaugural ceremony
D. to break the silence

64. To clip one's wings
A. to lessen one's power
B. to defame
C. to dismiss
D. to punish

65. To come round
A. to agree with another's point of view
B. to come back to the point of origin
C. a circular movement
D. to wander

66. To call to order
A. a command
B. to rebuke for improper or incorrect behaviour
C. to obey an order
D. to show superiority

67. To cover one's tracks
A. to maintain the secrecy
B. to hide one's weaknesses
C. to carefully hide all traces of one's actions
D. to conceal the falsity

68. To eat the calf in the cows belly
A. infanticide
B. to leave the work unfinished
C. to reject a plan of an important project
D. to be too ready to anticipate

69. To cap the globe
A. to surpass everything
B. to acheive great success
C. to discover something new
D. to travel around the world

70. To throw up one's cards
A. to make a last effort
B. to cease to struggle
C. to end up the game
D. to come out victorious

71. To let the cat out of the bag
A. to disclose a secret
B. to set free
C. a person without a shelter
D. to permit the thief to run away

72. To cave in
A. to interfere B. to prohibit
C. to find a way D. to give way

73. To chuck up
A. to abandon B. to decorate
C. to summarize D. to cut into pieces

74. A dead letter
A. a delayed report
B. a false report
C. something exaggerated
D. something which is null and void

75. To die in harness
A. to die in office
B. to die with great pain
C. a premature death
D. a cruel murder

76. At the drop of a hat
A. without fail
B. without delay
C. against the self-respect
D. against the will

77. Day in and day out
A. always
B. forever
C. to break a promise done earlier
D. to remain busy always

78. Ducks and drakes
A. various hindrances
B. to spend lavishly
C. by all efforts
D. to spend miserly

79. Champ at
A. to pounce at
B. be impassioned
C. be composed
D. be eager or impatient

80. Burn one's fingers
A. to get oneself into trouble
B. to commit a blunder
C. a heavy monetory loss
D. to be in great rage

81. Down in the dumps
A. in a solitary mood
B. in a bad mood
C. to be in an unfavourable situation
D. to decline

82. To beg the question
A. to beg the pardon
B. to request for some extra-time to finish the work
C. unanswerable
D. to assume in the premises something which is to be proved

83. To do a thing on the sly
A. to do a thing stealthily, without drawing attention to it
B. a good work went unnoticed
C. work done under pressure
D. a highly risky job

84. To have had one's day
A. to be past one's prime
B. to have visited only once
C. poverty
D. the childhood days

85. To carry the day
A. to be victorious
B. an ongoing discussion
C. a memorable day
D. a miserable phase of life

86. A day after the fair
A. a delayed decision
B. too late to see anything
C. just after the occurence of the event
D. the passing of good days

87. At death's door
A. on the point of expiring
B. on the point of gun
C. to show bravery
D. a gradual deterior

88. To pay the debt of nature
A. to die
B. to give birth
C. to safeguard the natural things
D. to avoid environmental pollution

89. To do up
A. to finish off   B. to mend
C. to improve   D. to make tidy

90. To do away with
A. to break   B. to destroy
C. to get rid of   D. to forget

91. To have to do with
A. to be interested in
B. to do something under compulsion
C. work done unenthusiastically
D. to complete

92. To egg on
A. just a beginning
B. to urge on
C. to develop something
D. an initial stage

93. To face the music
A. to face the consequences
B. to get filled with ecstasy
C. to be lucky
D. to lead a happy life

94. To end in smoke
A. all efforts in vain
B. the end of life
C. to come to nothing
D. to end the enmity

95. Eye to eye with
A. agree completely
B. a confrontation
C. full of anger
D. a quarrel between the two persons

96. To eat humble pie
A. to harass a humble person
B. a celebration or a treat without any cause
C. to confess that one is in the wrong
D. food provided to the needy or poor

97. Easy come easy go

A. what is gained without difficulty is spent without much thought
B. anything which is surplus
C. without any difficulty
D. to achieve something without any struggle

98. To eat out one's heart

A. to break one's heart
B. to deceive someone
C. to get deceived
D. to suffer intensely

99. To see with half an eye

A. to see with great ease
B. to dislike
C. to see stealthily
D. to feel jealous

100. A fair-weathered friend

A. A friend always eager to help
B. A friend who deserts one in times of adversity
C. a selfish friend
D. a true friend

101. A far cry

A. an unfulfilled desire
B. a very low voice
C. remote from
D. a distant place

102. To feather one's nest

A. to provide for one's own comfort
B. to be proud
C. to succeed again
D. to decorate one's house

103. To fish in troubled waters

A. to be in trouble
B. to make capital out of other's troubles
C. to be in trouble because of other's fault
D. to laugh at other's trouble

104. To follow suit

A. to follow the command
B. to obey the rules
C. to work in accordance with
D. to behave in the same manner

105. To get the hang of a thing

A. to understand the implications of something
B. to get a trace of theft
C. to find a new resource
D. to have some indications

106. To get wind of

A. to get news about something much before the event actually takes place
B. to forget the event that had taken place
C. to spread a rumour
D. to have some idea of a conspiration

107. French leave

A. a long leave
B. a small leave
C. absence from one's place of work without prior information
D. to leave the place forever

108. To steal a march upon

A. to outshine somebody
B. to rob
C. to move forward
D. to crush the enemy

109. A fly in the ointment

A. to poison one's ear
B. one that causes a massive loss
C. something that decreases the value or quality of a person or thing
D. a deterioration in quality

110. A long face

A. a sad or mournful countenance
B. a very shameful defeat
C. a shameful act
D. an ugly face

111. To set one's face against

A. to criticise openly
B. to oppose with determination
C. a biased disapproval
D. to show disappointment

112. To fall away from

A. to decline
B. to desert
C. to avoid
D. to leave

113. To fall flat

A. to cause no amusement or interest
B. to lie down
C. to defeat the opponent
D. to plead

114. To live on the fat of the land

A. to depend solely on agriculture
B. to live in a posh locality
C. to live in outskirt of the city
D. to have every luxury

115. To fight for one's own hand
A. to fight for one's own right
B. to struggle for livelihood
C. to struggle for one's pesonal interests
D. to fight for compensation against physical injury

116. To have a finger in the pie
A. to be mixed up in any affair
B. to interfere in other's work
C. to have a share in the profit
D. to be a member of an organisation

117. Neither fish, flesh nor good red herring
A. an unsuccessful person
B. having no pronounced character
C. a person of unpleasing personality
D. a person living in poverty

118. To fly in the face of
A. to be superfluous
B. to support directly
C. to oppose directly and in a reckless fashion
D. to show superiority upon others

119. To put one's foot on another's neck
A. to crush or stample upon him
B. to crush one's progress
C. to put the blame of one on another person
D. to retalitate

120. In full cry
A. in full volume
B. in hot pursuit
C. a verbosity
D. manifestation of grief

121. To give a piece of one's mind
A. to rebuke
B. to give an idea
C. to present one's view
D. to judge one's intelligence on the basis of his work or contributions

122. Gift of the gab
A. the ability of verbosity
B. the ability of writing creatively
C. the ability to speak in an impressive manner
D. a man of versatile genius

123. To give the cold shoulder
A. to give support
B. to be indifferent
C. to express anger silently
D. to behave in a cold manner with someone

124. To give devil his due
A. to give an evil person credit for whatever good he has done
B. to punish one who has committed sin
C. an evil person meeting a tragic end
D. to give devil his share

125. To give up the ghost
A. to die
B. to sacrifice
C. to murder
D. to convert from vicious to virtuous

126. To give wide berth to
A. to give more space
B. to keep far away from
C. to appreciate more than what one deserves
D. to maintain a distance

127. To go to pieces
A. to tear
B. to feel disheartened
C. to be wrecked completely
D. to dismantle

128. To have too many irons in the fire
A. to be engaged in too many things
B. to handle more than one work at the same time
C. to have lot of energy
D. to have various plans in the mind

129. To put a spoke in one's wheel
A. to obstruct one in his work
B. to assist one in his work
C. to interfere one in his work
D. to increase the strength of a team

130. On the rack
A. in a dilemma
B. tortured by anxiety
C. highly curious
D. to be in a disadvantageous position

131. To get into hot water
A. an acute pain
B. to be in trouble
C. to face a short-tempered person
D. to be in hypertension

132. Fish and blood
A. by extreme means
B. by unlawful ways
C. human nature
D. life-like

133. From hand to mouth
A. to harm and humiliate
B. to be a bankrupt
C. to spend all that is earned
D. to feed someone

134. Go through fire and water
A. Joy and sorrow come together
B. to overcome all difficulties
C. to face the misfortune
D. to be prepared to face any difficulty

135. Hit the nail on the head
A. to take revenge openly
B. to insult on the face
C. to do a wrong thing
D. to do exactly the right thing

136. Put the cart before the horse
A. to reverse the natural order
B. to put obstruction
C. to cause problem for others
D. to stop one's advancement

137. Pay back in one's own coin
A. to save money
B. to treat in the same way as one has been treated
C. to get the return of the investment
D. to give a befitting reply

138. Rest one's oars
A. to be satisfied with what one has already achieved
B. to be in a pleasant mood
C. to feel exhausted
D. to live lavishly

139. Spick and Span
A. Brand new B. throughout
C. a short duration D. transient

140. To stand on ceremony
A. to stick to order
B. to attend a ceremony
C. to stand at-ease
D. To behave in a stiff, strictly correct way

141. To worm out
A. to detect a germ
B. to discover the cause
C. to remove the fault
D. to discover by persistent questioning

142. Red letter day
A. a day of great importance
B. an Independence day
C. the day on which bloodshed had taken place
D. a memorable day

143. To be all the rage
A. to be vigorous
B. to be very popular
C. a man of bad reputation
D. to be furious

144. To take time by the forelock
A. to act immediately
B. to take time to act
C. a mental exercise
D. delay in taking decisions

145. To rub the wrong way
A. to go on wrong path
B. to annoy
C. to wander
D. to go stray

146. To make up to
A. to amend
B. try to rectify a wrong
C. to modify
D. to substitute

147. To bring home the bacon
A. to come to a common conclusion
B. to invent
C. to be successful in an undertaking
D. to discover

148. To be in a brown study
A. to spend the leisure
B. to brood
C. to be absent minded because of deep thought
D. to introspect

149. To go on a wild goose chase
A. try to achieve something unknown
B. to have faith in a general belief
C. to say the same which is said by the majority
D. to follow blindly

150. To bite one's lips
A. to feel shameful
B. to feel shy
C. to be furious
D. to be in doubt

ANSWERS

1	2	3	4	5	6	7	8	9	10
D	B	A	A	C	B	D	A	B	A
11	**12**	**13**	**14**	**15**	**16**	**17**	**18**	**19**	**20**
B	C	B	A	A	B	C	A	A	D
21	**22**	**23**	**24**	**25**	**26**	**27**	**28**	**29**	**30**
C	A	B	A	B	C	A	B	C	D
31	**32**	**33**	**34**	**35**	**36**	**37**	**38**	**39**	**40**
A	A	B	A	C	C	D	D	B	B
41	**42**	**43**	**44**	**45**	**46**	**47**	**48**	**49**	**50**
A	B	B	C	A	C	C	A	D	D
51	**52**	**53**	**54**	**55**	**56**	**57**	**58**	**59**	**60**
A	B	A	A	B	B	D	A	A	B
61	**62**	**63**	**64**	**65**	**66**	**67**	**68**	**69**	**70**
C	A	A	A	A	B	C	D	A	B
71	**72**	**73**	**74**	**75**	**76**	**77**	**78**	**79**	**80**
A	D	A	D	A	B	A	B	D	A
81	**82**	**83**	**84**	**85**	**86**	**87**	**88**	**89**	**90**
B	D	A	A	A	B	A	A	D	C
91	**92**	**93**	**94**	**95**	**96**	**97**	**98**	**99**	**100**
A	B	A	C	A	C	A	D	A	B
101	**102**	**103**	**104**	**105**	**106**	**107**	**108**	**109**	**110**
C	A	B	D	A	A	C	A	C	A
111	**112**	**113**	**114**	**115**	**116**	**117**	**118**	**119**	**120**
B	B	A	D	C	A	B	C	A	B
121	**122**	**123**	**124**	**125**	**126**	**127**	**128**	**129**	**130**
A	C	D	A	A	B	C	A	A	B
131	**132**	**133**	**134**	**135**	**136**	**137**	**138**	**139**	**140**
B	C	C	D	D	A	B	A	A	D
141	**142**	**143**	**144**	**145**	**146**	**147**	**148**	**149**	**150**
D	A	B	A	B	B	C	C	A	C

5. FILL IN THE BLANKS

Fill in the blanks is such an exercise that begins from the primary schooling and continues till the highest competitive examinations. With regular practice one can master it easily.

MULTIPLE CHOICE QUESTIONS

Directions (Qs. 1 to 150): *Pick out the most effective word(s) from the given words to fill in the blank to make the sentence meaningfully complete.*

1. While the contest in Kashmir has international ....., the outcome in Gujarat will be of enormous significance at the national level.
A. ravening B. ramifications
C. reconnaissance D. renunciation

2. No amount of post facto sophistry can conceal the ..... and inflammable crudity of this exhortation.
A. cruel B. shameful
C. horrible D. horrendous

3. There were ..... voices coming out from the amalgam.
A. discordant B. sneering
C. impalpable D. disquisite

4. Online learning can also offer a ..... of exciting and technology driven courses.
A. spectrum B. spume
C. spate D. stolidity

5. Work experience does carry some weight, the extent of which is a matter of ..... .
A. erudition B. decision
C. determination D. conjecture

6. The curricula of education has to respond and reshape with ..... modification according to the needs and aspirations of the dynamic society.
A. ambient B. alliterate
C. allotropic D. ample

7. It may look ..... to pronounce but this is the reality that the situation is that of the largest concentration illiterate population is an existence.
A. surprising B. contradictory
C. paradoxical D. contrary

8. If we take the global, developmental ....., education is not only a master key but also acts as a catalyst in the positive direction.
A. context B. pretext
C. progress D. continuum

9. It is mainly the utmost utilization of knowledge which emanates from the deep-delved ..... in every human being.
A. acquisition B. core
C. mind D. self

10. The book is a rare ..... of facts and figures illustrating every aspect of education.
A. chronicle B. compendium
C. combination D. presentation

11. The ..... reason behind the terrorist attack on the temple is obvious.
A. devious B. diabolical
C. factual D. original

12. He had the ..... to reject plans.
A. disquisition B. gibe
C. gumption D. grudge

13. Unable to ..... the election process in Kashmir, the terrorists have spread out all over India.
A. serounge B. scruff
C. scuttle D. scuffle

14. Their hopes of a communal ..... is not going to come true.

A. conflagration B. plenipotentiary
C. podium D. coterie

15. Fundamentalism refers to an ideology which takes certain articles of faith to be ....., beyond question.

A. inviolable B. invulnerable
C. irrefragable D. ineverent

16. The separation of Church and State has its origins in the vicious and ..... 16th century sectarian wars within European Christanity.

A. debacle B. debilitating
C. debase D. dastard

17. It's time to look beyond the simplistic ..... between secularism and fundamentalism.

A. dichotomy B. disarray
C. diabolical D. fetid

18. When unemployment is rampant, the future is ..... and fraught with worry, depression and frustration.

A. fluster B. foible
C. occlude D. ominous

19. We are worried by the ..... tendencies prevailing in our social and political life.

A. flotsam B. fissiparous
C. perfidy D. aphoristic

20. The intellectual experience had culminated new methodology in ..... .

A. assuage B. value
C. pedagogy D. pedantic

21. Human rights awareness is ignited to propagate in conflagration which could ..... down to the masses.

A. perfidy B. Kindle
C. percolate D. exude

22. It is no use living a wretched life, where human dignity is an ..... .

A. abyss B. abhor
C. abnegation D. chastise

23. Upheavals and ..... de-humanisation are the paralytic traumas which degrade and nullify glamorisation of the human values.

A. profilgate B. entropic
C. obdurate D. intransigence

24. The driver tried to ..... the fears of the passenger by announcing that the accident has been prevented.

A. overcome B. remove
C. eradicate D. allay

25. ..... should be removed among the people and equal chances should be given to those who have been denied equality so long.

A. Distinction B. Diaphanous
C. Differences D. Disparities

26. It is uncertainty and ..... of purpose which create defects in our present system of education.

A. confusion B. ambivalence
C. vaguness D. doubt

27. The golden jubilee of the Independence of India is being celebrated in an ..... and jubilant manner.

A. joyful B. pleasant
C. ecstatic D. eclat

28. Education has become capable of meeting all the changes of the ..... society by broadening the new paths of learning.

A. dynamic B. growing
C. developing D. modern

29. The world and inevitably India, are in the ..... of major economic and technological changes.

A. gulf B. tendentious
C. insularity D. thores

30. ..... officer finally surrendered before the court yesterday, after being on the run for two months.

A. Crustacean B. Complacent
C. Fugitive D. Beguile

31. Gujrat riots have attracted national and international ..... .

A. opprobrium B. oposum
C. repugnance D. reconnoitre

32. The political and administrative leadership may have been determined to prevent any mischief makers from running ..... .

A. gauche B. amok
C. catharic D. berserk

33. After her long illness she is suffering from general ..... .

A. fawning B. debility
C. lethargic D. inchoate

34. They are so poor that they have to .....
A. slack B. slander
C. skir ıp D. bicker

35. ..... about in the corridors.
A. fecund B. droll
C. carp D. skulk

36. The Queen's request was .... to a command.
A. tantamount B. tenet
C. nexus D. nascent

37. We cannot ..... base metals into gold.
A. transmute B. trek
C. sodden D. impede

38. ..... an official tour to Switzerland.
A. Warble B. Wane
C. Wangle D. Warren

39. His inattention in the classroom is a clear ..... of failure.
A. pristine B. propriety
C. prognosis D. prognostic

40. I find singing ..... challenging.
A. intrinsically B. incredibly
C. extrinsically D. preposterously

41. Educating people to think your way is ....
A. prodigious B. presumptuous
C. sagacious D. unpretentious

42. The birth of United Nations Organisation in 1945 was a ..... device to achieve specific objectives in the realm of world order.
A. subjugate B. precarious
C. pragmatic D. unabated

43. Inefficiency and delaying habits are the ..... of Indian offices.
A. averse B. assuagement
C. banal D. bane

44. It is a most ..... situation for a young person to find a place under the sun and lead a comfortable though har-working life.
A. exhilarating B. barberous
C. bucolic D. cantankerous

45. The hot weather created a feeling of ..... and encouraged drowsiness.
A. uninterested B. lethargic
C. lassitude D. exhaustion

46. One prefers to be alone than to be in his company because of his ..... temper.
A. stoic B. smattering
C. sleight D. irascible

47. The boss scolded him in a ..... voice.
A. preposturous B. loud
C. suave D. strident

48. The ..... provided by the government to those affected by the flood were not sufficient.
A. ensconce B. victuals
C. baroque D. accrue

49. Zakir Hussain is a tabla .....
A. abettor B. adroit
C. virago D. virtuouso

50. He took ..... at his remarks and resigned immediately.
A. umbrage B. surly
C. unseemly D. valour

51. The more your action and thought are allied and ..... the happier you grow.
A. diverget B. unravelled
C. integrated D. invincible

52. Many of the advances of civilisation have been conceived by young people just on the ..... of adulthood.
A. boundary B. threshold
C. peak D. horizon

53. Wheat ..... carbohydrates, vitamins, proteins and dietary fibre in our daily diet.
A. has B. gives
C. yields D. provides

54. The cinema ..... a welcome escape from cramped and dull city life and the Indians are avid movie-goers.
A. depicts B. highlights
C. follows D. offers

55. This machine is difficult to build ..... easy to maintain.
A. but B. and
C. for D. if

56. Farida sings very well and ..... does Salim.
A. even B. too
C. also D. so

57. Government buildings are .... on the Republic Day.
A. enlightened B. lightened
C. illuminated D. glowed

58. Sonika is quite intelligent but rather ..... .
A. idealistic B. generous
C. lazy D. optimistic

59. You've only three months more to complete the course. Don't give ..... now.
A. out B. away
C. up D. off

60. About twenty clerks were made ..... when the bank introduced computers.
A. dispensable B. redundant
C. expendable D. obsolete

61. To err is ..... to forgive divine.
A. beastly B. human
C. inhuman D. natural

62. God is .....
A. graceful B. gracious
C. grateful D. greatful

63. The king ..... the rebel.
A. excused B. forgave
C. pardoned D. none of these

64. The boy was cured ..... typhoid.
A. from B. of
C. for D. through

65. Jawaharlal spent his childhood ..... Anand Bhawan.
A. at B. in
C. on D. across

66. The boy fell ..... the bicycle.
A. of B. off
C. from D. under

67. Affix a revenue stamp and put your signature ..... it.
A. on B. upon
C. above D. over

68. The answer was written ..... blue ink.
A. with B. by
C. in D. on

69. The park ..... as far as the river.
A. extends B. advances
C. enlarges D. emerges

70. My father ..... down for a nap.
A. lay B. laid
C. lain D. lie

71. I put ..... the light and slept.
A. up B. down
C. in D. out

72. I shall call ..... you tomorrow.
A. at B. on
C. with D. by

73. West Bengal ..... plentiful rainfall and is consequently a very green part of the country.
A. misses B. receives
C. expects D. regrets

74. If you work beyond your capacity, you will naturally feel .....
A. drowsy B. tired
C. confident D. giddy

75. I have read one novel by Premchand. I want to read ..... novel by him.
A. other B. another
C. all D. few

76. Fate smiles ..... those who untiringly grapple with stark realities of life.
A. with B. over
C. on D. round

77. Those who persist in their endeavour at long last triumph ..... the odds of life.
A. over B. on
C. upon D. about

78. The parliament invested the new organisation ..... judicial authority.
A. by B. with
C. from D. through

79. She has an aversion ..... taking even onion and garlic.
A. with B. at
C. against D. to

80. Brothers must live in harmony. They must never fall .....
A. off B. out
C. apart D. away

81. The man came in a van to ..... the television set.
A. mend B. reform
C. correct D. alter

82. He was accused .... stealing his aunt's necklace.
A. for B. with
C. of D. on

83. Indeed, all over the world, more and more people are ..... coffee.
A. wanting B. drinking
C. liking D. partaking

84. He felt no ..... as he plunged the knife into her back.
A. qualms B. scruple
C. conscience D. morals

85. A sanguine outlook is associated with the .....
A. rationalist B. socialist
C. philanthropist D. optimist

86. True brevity ..... in saying only what needs to be said.
A. consists B. depicts
C. portrays D. resides

87. He became enamoured ..... her grace when he first saw her dance.
A. with B. of
C. buy D. in

88. We shall not be able to use your alibi in court unless we can find someone to ..... your statements.
A. corroborate B. avouch
C. verify D. approve

89. In a little-publicised deal, Pepsi, Cola has ..... the entire soft drink market in Afghanistan.
A. occupied B. conquered
C. swallowed D. captured

90. If negotiations are to prove fruitful, there must not only be sincerity on each side, but there must also be ..... in the sincerity of the other side.
A. faith B. belief
C. substance D. certainty

91. My first lesson ..... forgiveness came from my father
A. upon B. about
C. in D. on

92. He knew everything better than anybody else, and it was an affront to his ..... vanity that you should disagree with him.
A. overstrung B. overweening
C. overwhelming D. overwrought

93. He passed the examination in the first class because he .....
A. was hard working for it
B. worked hardly for it
C. had worked hard for it
D. was working hard for it

94. The American ..... presented his credentials to the President of India.
A. adviser B. ambassador
C. delegate D. representative

95. Man does not live by ..... alone.
A. food B. bread
C. meals D. diet

96. You cannot devise a method which ..... all possibility of error.
A. excludes B. includes
C. avoids D. ignores

97. When the morning ..... the murder was discovered.
A. occurred B. arrived
C. came D. happened

98. My uncle decided to take ..... and my sister to the market.
A. I B. mine
C. me D. myself

99. Hardly had he arrived ..... it started raining.
A. before B. when
C. than D. after

100. It is fourteen years since I ..... him.
A. have seen B. had seen
C. saw D. see

101. The criminal seems to have acted in ..... with three others.
A. collusion B. coalition
C. collision D. cohesion

102. I think they allow their children too much .....
A. liberality B. latitude
C. lassitude D. levity

103. This book is quite similar ..... .
A. with the 'Treasure Island'
B. of that film we saw at school
C. to the one I read last week
D. than a story told by our teacher

104. If you persist in telling lies to me I shall sue you ..... slander.
A. to B. on
C. for D. with

105. The traveller slept under the ..... shade of the banyan tree.
A. cold B. cool
C. cooling D. dark

106. The waiter hasn't brought the coffee ..... I've been here an hour already.
A. till B. up
C. yet D. still

107. This brand of TV is quite inferior ..... that one.
A. than B. to
C. with D. over

108. Her parents will never give their ..... to such an unsuitable match.
A. acquiescene B. consent
C. agreement D. willingness

109. He is so ..... that he immediately believed my story of ghosts.
A. innocent B. credulous
C. vociferous D. credible

110. He is a very careful person, he never takes sides but remains ..... .
A. impartial B. unbiased
C. neutral D. prejudiced

111. The stenographer is very efficient. He is ..... to his firm.
A. a boon B. a credit
C. a blessing D. an asset

112. His conduct is bad, and his honesty is not ..... suspicion.
A. above B. beyond
C. under D. in

113. I hate sitting ..... him as he always smells of garlic.
A. besides B. along
C. at D. beside

114. A man remains narrow-minded, self complacent and ignorant unless he visits other people and ..... from them.
A. earns B. borrows
C. learns D. hears

115. The English schemed to continue their rule in India by playing off one community ..... the other.
A. before B. upon
C. against D. with

116. When their examinations are over, the children gleefully ..... the books they had been reading.
A. shelve B. sidetrack
C. overthrow D. abandon

117. If you smuggle goods into the country, they may be ..... by the customs authority.
A. possessed B. punished
C. confiscated D. fined

118. That the poor in our country, are happy is.....
A. a dream B. a vision
C. an ideal D. an illusion

119. ..... of any kind of demoralising.
A. Addiction B. Habit
C. Custom D. Tradition

120. The sun is shining brightly, please ..... the light.
A. put off B. put out
C. take off D. put on

121. Health is too important to be ..... .
A. discarded B. despised
C. detested D. neglected

122. In the modern materialistic society, the only aim of the people appears to be to ..... money by fair means or foul.
A. print B. produce
C. acquire D. extort

123. However, the group's long-term strategy is to ..... on core sector businesses connected with infrastructure and energy.
A. breed B. develop
C. concentrate D. depend

124. But the introductory fee does not stop after the initial handshake; brokers have to ..... it up after each transaction.
A. bring B. cough
C. boost D. give

125. Colgate has also set an ambitious aim of ..... on eight per cent value shared of tooth paste market by the end of the first years.
A. cornering B. soliciting
C. distributing D. keeping

126. A stone that goes on rolling ..... no moss.
A. collects B. gets
C. gathers D. accumulates

127. The river overflowed its ..... and flooded the area.
A. edges B. fronts
C. limits D. banks

128. In hot weather I like lying in the ..... of a tree.
A. shade B. shelter
C. protection D. shadow

129. She ...... ₹ 80 out of the bank every Friday.
A. obtains B. draws
C. pulls D. extracts

130. He is too dull ..... this problem.
A. solving B. to solving
C. to solve D. solves

131. At one point, it looked as if an area of agreement would ....., specially over the issue of productivity linked wages.
A. develop B. come out
C. emerge D. grow

132. I listened, but I had no idea what he was ..... about.
A. saying B. talking
C. telling D. discussing

133. The lovers were meeting each other secretly, but their ..... affair was soon known to everyone.
A. clandestine B. covert
C. unknown D. candid

134. When I was a child, I ..... to school every day instead of going by cycle.
A. had walked
B. walked
C. have walked
D. have been walking

135. She ..... from the crowd because of her height and flaming red hair.
A. stood out B. stood off
C. stood up D. stood by

136. He lives near a lovely ...... of countryside.
A. length B. piece
C. section D. stretch

137. We had a ..... of warm weather in February.
A. time B. spell
C. length D. phase

138. The grapes are now ..... enough to be picked.
A. ready B. mature
C. ripe D. advanced

139. The robbers were arrested and ..... prison yesterday.
A. brought into B. brought to
C. taken into D. taken to

140. His father-in-law ..... him up in business.
A. put B. made
C. set D. built

141. People who ..... on horses usually lose in the end.
A. gamble B. play
C. risk D. place

142. He is the person who is ..... to blame.
A. mostly B. sure
C. most D. bound

143. The Hubble Space Telescope will search for planets around other stars, a key to the ..... for extraterrestrial life, and examine interstellar dust and gases out of which stars are born.
A. perception B. discovery
C. enquiry D. quest

144. Soft minded individuals are ..... to embrace all kinds of superstitions
A. disposed B. eager
C. reluctant D. prone

145. He is a person of sound character and ..... disposition.
A. beneficent B. morous
C. amiable D. amicable

146. It being an ..... issue, it is not correct to introduce questions of morality into the debate.
A. moral B. immoral
C. amoral D. irrelevant

147. The communalist represents the ..... of everything noble that we have inherited from our culture and history.
A. antithesis B. antidote
C. immorality D. antagonism

148. In a large cities people are cut ..... from nature.
A. away B. off
C. out D. down

149. Man must ..... now to stop pollution.
A. act B. perform
C. operate D. behave

150. There is a keen ..... in each trade.
A. contest B. comparison
C. competition D. cooperation

ANSWERS

1	2	3	4	5	6	7	8	9	10
B	D	A	A	D	C	C	D	A	B
11	**12**	**13**	**14**	**15**	**16**	**17**	**18**	**19**	**20**
B	C	C	A	A	B	A	D	B	C
21	**22**	**23**	**24**	**25**	**26**	**27**	**28**	**29**	**30**
C	A	B	D	D	B	C	A	D	C
31	**32**	**33**	**34**	**35**	**36**	**37**	**38**	**39**	**40**
A	B	B	C	D	A	A	C	D	B
41	**42**	**43**	**44**	**45**	**46**	**47**	**48**	**49**	**50**
B	C	D	A	C	D	D	B	B	A
51	**52**	**53**	**54**	**55**	**56**	**57**	**58**	**59**	**60**
C	B	D	D	A	D	C	C	C	B
61	**62**	**63**	**64**	**65**	**66**	**67**	**68**	**69**	**70**
B	B	C	B	A	B	A	C	A	A
71	**72**	**73**	**74**	**75**	**76**	**77**	**78**	**79**	**80**
D	C	B	B	B	C	A	B	D	B
81	**82**	**83**	**84**	**85**	**86**	**87**	**88**	**89**	**90**
A	C	B	A	D	A	B	A	D	A
91	**92**	**93**	**94**	**95**	**96**	**97**	**98**	**99**	**100**
D	A	C	B	B	A	C	C	B	C
101	**102**	**103**	**104**	**105**	**106**	**107**	**108**	**109**	**110**
A	B	C	C	B	C	B	B	B	A
111	**112**	**113**	**114**	**115**	**116**	**117**	**118**	**119**	**120**
D	A	D	C	C	D	C	D	A	B
121	**122**	**123**	**124**	**125**	**126**	**127**	**128**	**129**	**130**
D	C	C	A	A	C	D	A	B	C
131	**132**	**133**	**134**	**135**	**136**	**137**	**138**	**139**	**140**
C	B	A	B	A	D	B	C	D	C
141	**142**	**143**	**144**	**145**	**146**	**147**	**148**	**149**	**150**
A	C	D	D	C	D	A	A	A	C

6. SENTENCE IMPROVEMENT

One may use the same words in many ways but the best way is only one that makes the perfect usage of the words and conveys the proper meaning of the expression. Try it yourself in the following questions.

MULTIPLE CHOICE QUESTIONS

Directions (Qs. 1 to 100): *In these questions, a part of the sentence is bold. Below are given alternatives to the bold part at A, B and C which may improve the sentence. Choose the correct alternative. In case no improvement is needed, your answer is D.*

1. For most people who exercise **at the** morning, there is no getting around the question: Eat and run? Or run and eat later?
A. in the B. in
C. at the time of D. No Improvement

2. Are ad agencies even attempting to peer into the keyhole of this indulgence sanctum to garner consumer insights **ahead of** the curve?
A. above B. over
C. within D. No Improvement

3. Too many people rush into the world of credit and don't stop to think about how **their actions could affect their** credit score and ability to qualify for credit in the future.
A. their actions may affect their
B. their actions might affect their
C. their actions will affect their
D. No Improvement

4. According to the report, **number of deal with** vaccines were energized by concerns around avian flu, SARS, and biodefense products, while looming patent expirations led to more deals in generics.
A. number of deals in
B. number of deal in
C. number of deals with
D. No Improvement

5. This is how the Bombay High Court responded to the state government's purported **moral stand which** dance bars were causing grave harm to society.
A. moral stand in B. moral stand at
C. moral stand that D. No Improvement

6. If you have a high credit limit, use **at least a** third of it.
A. atleast a B. at last a
C. utmost a D. No Improvement

7. Fitness experts will say that **first eating provides** fuel for a proper workout.
A. eating in the beginning provides
B. first eat provides
C. eating first provides
D. No Improvement

8. One study that examined the claim directly in 1995 found that a group of people did **burned much calories from fat on days** when they exercised on an empty stomach than on days when they had a small breakfast first.
A. burn more calories from fat on days
B. burn more calorie from fat on days

C. burnt more calories from fat on days
D. No Improvement

9. Carefree children spent their afternoons **to run about barefoot**, their clothes dusty, and telltale twigs of the neighbour's mango tree in their hair.
A. running barefoot in the sun
B. run about barefoot in the sun
C. running about barefoot in the sun
D. No Improvement

10. A year ago, a 13-year-old girl attempted suicide because her mother **refuses to pay his** mobile bills.
A. refuses to pay her
B. refused to pay her
C. refused to pay his
D. No Improvement

11. Discreet salience **is extremely important** to create that 'irresistible-yet-unattainable' image for brands that want to take India seriously
A. was extremely important
B. is mainly important
C. was important extremely
D. No Improvement

12. This, over a designer outfit that he wanted for a friend's party and **that his sensitive** parents refused him.
A. which his sensitive
B. which his insensitive
C. that his insensitive
D. No Improvement

13. Goa was full of non-Goa property hunters **rushing about buying up the place** like tomorrow was an expired lease.
A. rushing in buying up the place
B. rushed about buying up the place
C. rushing about to buy up the place
D. No Improvement

14. Property hunting is a **tired and hungry** making business.
A. is a tiresome and hungry
B. is a tiring and hungry
C. is a tiring and waste
D. No Improvement

15. Cultural differences aside, **till luxury need speaks** in a manner that befits.
A. luxury still needs to speak
B. luxury still need to speak
C. luxury till need to speak
D. No Improvement

16. Indian food—the culinary avatar of the subcontinent's social history presented on a platter—**is without doubt the best food** in the world.
A. is undoubtly the greatest food
B. is without doubt greatest food
C. is best food without doubt
D. No Improvement

17. It must retain the language of poetry. **It needed to create** stories, and not statements.
A. It needed creating
B. It needs creating
C. It needs to create
D. No Improvement

18. In 2005, Asia-Pacific has become the first region **to reach aggregate profiting** in biotech.
A. to reach aggregated profitability
B. to reach aggregate profitability
C. to reach aggregate of profit
D. No Improvement

19. India is deviating to embrace the West. If Western luxury brands deviate a little, **albeit selectively**, they will find rich Indian arms open far and wide.
A. though selectively
B. however selectively
C. albeit selectedly
D. No Improvement

20. China and India continued to attract attention and deals, motivated by the desire to increase access to these **largest and growing** drug markets and by the need to lower the costs of drug development.
A. larger and growing
B. large and growing
C. larger and grown
D. No Improvement

21. Luxury brands are **still above of the** clover curve here, with their elite (small) audiences.
A. still ahead of the
B. still in the
C. still far of the
D. No Improvement

22. Agencies **hence needed to be** sure of returns before investing, say ad men.
A. hence needs to be
B. so needs to be
C. hence need to be
D. No Improvement

23. India is still a nascent market and that's the spirit everyone's **looking at it**.
A. looking for it B. looking in it
C. looking with it D. No Improvement

24. Questioning the state's move to allow women to serve liquor but not dance in bars **of the ground that** dancing aroused physical lust.
A. on the grounds that
B. of the grounds that
C. over the grounds that
D. No Improvement

25. For England the positives from their crushing series lose come in the shape of James Anderson and Kevin Pietersen, **both of which** have made significant strides up the rankings.
A. both of which B. both of whom
C. both of who D. No Improvement

26. International campaigns can work well for luxury here, **but context cannot be** ignored.
A. so context cannot be
B. but context cannot
C. but context couldn't
D. No Improvement

27. For one, the Indian luxury context, **while evolved rapidly**, still has its own meaning, and its own implications.
A. while evolved rapid
B. which evolving rapidly
C. while evolving rapidly
D. No Improvement

28. But too much of availability can compromise a luxury brand or **made it lose** its lustre.
A. make her lose B. make him lose
C. make it lose D. No Improvement

29. Still, it's under-the-upper **layers themselves who** are aspiring for slivers of luxury.
A. layers themselves which
B. layer itself who
C. layers themself which
D. No Improvement

30. It is like saying Hindi movies, with skimpily dressed dancers, would **effect public** order.
A. effect your B. affect public
C. affected public D. No Improvement

31. The court held that a few women being involved in prostitution was no **justice to deny other** bar girls the right to livelihood.
A. justification to declare other
B. justification to deny other
C. justice to let other
D. No Improvement

32. All-rounder Irfan Pathan has also made some progress **over the** player rankings.
A. above the B. at the
C. up the D. No Improvement

33. Former PM V.P. Singh on Sunday **joined hands** with suspended SP Lok Sabha member Raj Babbar to float a new political outfit.
A. folded hands
B. walked hand in hand
C. shaked hands
D. No Improvement

34. Pakistan's former PMs Benazir Bhutto and Nawaz Sharif will meet in London on Monday **to ask** a strategy to return home from exile.
A. to chalk out B. to negotiate
C. to create D. No Improvement

35. It's a family potboiler, medical thriller and political drama **all in one**–except that it's all too real and all too grim.
A. all 3 in one
B. all coupled into one
C. all rolled into one
D. No Improvement

36. India's efforts to get international support for its civil nuclear energy programme got **a go ahead on** Sunday as Germany indicated it would not come in the way of the India-US nuclear deal.

A. a life in B. a boost on
C. a boost at D. No Improvement

37. Is it time for old bungalows to **bite the dust**?

A. go down B. get down
C. come down D. No Improvement

38. The bungalows was an outward manifestation of a certain **way in life**, and with that era gone.

A. way for life B. way of life
C. way at life D. No Improvement

39. The builder Mittals will reportedly **raise their money**-raking high-rise behind it.

A. highten their money
B. rise their money
C. raise there money
D. No Improvement

40. The impatient present has usually demolished **more of the** past before we wake up to the irretrievable loss.

A. much of B. much of their
C. much of the D. No Improvement

41. Preservation is a romantic notion; demolition **quiet** more practical reasons.

A. has many, B. had many,
C. have many, D. No Improvement

42. You must get back to your **charming self** and impress the audience with your social skills.

A. own self B. main self
C. own uniqueness D. No Improvement

43. Stay focused on your goals and don't **get disturbed by** non-materialistic possessions.

A. get involved by
B. get betrayed by
C. get distracted by
D. No Improvement

44. You may appear more optimistic than your detractors **may want it to be**.

A. want you to be
B. wish yourself to be
C. seek you be
D. No Improvement

45. There are a number of mineral springs in the Czech territory, which **has been used** for medicinal purposes since the early 15th century.

A. have been used B. had been used
C. has being used D. No Improvement

46. The picturesque mountains **offers** excellent bungee jumping spots.

A. shows B. provides
C. offer D. No Improvement

47. Begin your **meal with** traditional faves like potato soup, beef soup with liver dumplings or dill soup made from sour milk.

A. meals with B. meal in
C. meals of D. No Improvement

48. You can also **go to the** National Museum building and the famous Prague State Opera.

A. went to B. visit the
C. saw D. No Improvement

49. If they close the Gulf for a **length of time** to shipping, then certainly we could look at $150, probably higher.

A. larger amount of time
B. larger duration of time
C. larger amount of hours
D. No Improvement

50. **More of them** are owned by the state and even the privately-owned ones are open to the public.

A. Most of which B. Most of them
C. Most of all D. No Improvement

51. Constructed in the ninth century by the Prince Booivoj, the castle has transformed **oneself** from a wooden fortress surrounded by earthen bulwarks to the imposing form it has today.

A. himself B. herself
C. itself D. No Improvement

52. Apart from frequent art exhibitions, **their are also** permanent collections devoted to archaeology, anthropology, mineralogy, natural history and numismatics.

A. there is also B. there are also
C. their are also D. No Improvement

53. You can visit the Czech Museum of Fine Arts, **at a** permanent exhibition on Czech Kubism.
A. with a B. for a
C. in a D. No Improvement

54. Tensions **above** Iran come at a time of strong demand for energy.
A. under B. inside
C. over D. No Improvement

55. Because its shores line the narrow Straits of Hormuz, Iran **could quickly hit** both military and commercial shipping.
A. will quickly hit
B. shall quickly hit
C. will be quick hitting
D. No Improvement

56. US **can launch** strikes at uranium enrichment facilities in Iran.
A. might launch B. could launch
C. might launched D. No Improvement

57. Trust your instincts and **see** all hurdles.
A. get freedom from
B. visualize
C. overcome
D. No Improvement

58. You may lose the war, but with calm, poise and serenity you will win the big battle **that may be following**.
A. that may follows
B. that may follow
C. that might be following
D. No Improvement

59. **There is times** when your best efforts could prove fruitless because of wrong timing.
A. There are time
B. There are times
C. There is time
D. No Improvement

60. You'll be a little more romantic and may want to **go away** from the hustle-bustle around you.
A. get away B. have get away
C. got away D. No Improvement

61. All you want are a few more hugs of affection, which will not be too difficult **to come**.
A. to come by B. to came
C. to come in D. No Improvement

62. People **around you** could get too sensitive, but try to respect them for that perhaps it will help you during pay-back time.
A. by you B. about you
C. near you D. No Improvement

63. Success **is a made up of** good fortune and hard work.
A. is B. is a
C. is a blend of D. No Improvement

64. The flower style and placement can completely change **the feel of** a room.
A. the feeling of B. the feeling for
C. an feel of D. No Improvement

65. The material (of artificial flower), style of arrangement and location should **complementing each other**.
A. complement one another
B. complement each other
C. complement other
D. No Improvement

66. Houses with **more of** carvings in their interiors, can go for gerberas.
A. many B. lots of
C. lot of D. No Improvement

67. For an artistic look, have lots of cherry blossoms **put together** in a vase.
A. together
B. jumbled together
C. made together
D. No Improvement

68. If you **have heavy carving** furniture, go for an arrangement in a container with an antique touch.
A. have heavy carved
B. had heavy carved
C. had heavy carving
D. No Improvement

69. For a traditional party, such as Diwali or Holi, traditional marigold and jasmine are **a best option**.
A. the better option
B. the best option
C. the best options
D. No Improvement

70. Don't expose to direct sun or keep them **under fan and near an AC**.
A. under fan or near an AC
B. beside fan or near an AC
C. under fan or under an AC
D. No Improvement

71. Use of disprin and aspirin **help the** buds to bloom faster.
A. helped the B. helps in the
C. helps the D. No Improvement

72. If you prefer the lived-in comfy look, clear glass flower vases **make for** cheerful addition.
A. makes for B. make for a
C. makes for a D. No Improvement

73. Cut the stem of the flower every other day. This helps it to consume water and last for a **longer duration of time**.
A. longer span of time
B. longer period of time
C. larger period of time
D. No Improvement

74. The ability to trust others, and understand the needs of others, is **directly relates** to touching.
A. directly relating B. directly related
C. direct relation D. No Improvement

75. Touch and positive attitudes **has been proven** to go together.
A. have been proven
B. have been proved
C. have been prove
D. No Improvement

76. New Delhi **was watching the** political thriller unfold in the hilly kingdom with apparent nervousness.
A. was watching the
B. is watching the
C. was watching a
D. No Improvement

77. Anti-monarch agitators cheer **on top of a** bus in Kathmandu on Tuesday.
A. above a B. at the top of a
C. above the D. No Improvement

78. Indian Railway Catering and Tourism Corporation an autonomous body under the railways ministry, **has drawing up** a plan to open 2000 such stalls which would serve standard food.
A. has drawed up B. have drawn up
C. has drawn up D. No Improvement

79. The stalls are **to come** up at "A" and "B" grade station.
A. likely to be coming
B. likely to come
C. like to come
D. No Improvement

80. To avoid controversies, IRCTC also **plans to continue** samosa-chai stalls which currently dot stations.
A. plan to continue
B. plan's to continue
C. plan to continuing
D. No Improvement

81. Airbus has been quietly pitching the standing-room only option to Asian carriers, though **none had agreed** to it yet.
A. none have been agreed
B. none have being agreed
C. none have agreed
D. No Improvement

82. High fuel costs, for example, are **making it difficult for** carriers to turn a profit.
A. making difficult for
B. making difficulty for
C. making it as difficult as
D. No Improvement

83. The new seat technology alone, **when used in** add more places for passengers, can add millions in additional annual revenue.
A. used to B. when used to
C. when using to D. No Improvement

84. While you may never win the lottery, **able to** get cash for paper assets is a sure bet.
A. being able to
B. getting able to
C. in being able to
D. No Improvement

85. At Chattarpur Enclave, **the first thing** that hits you is a massive under construction illegal building where work has been stopped.
A. a first thing
B. one of the first thing
C. the first best thing
D. No Improvement

86. Multi-storeyed housing units would be constructed through public private partnership **at the land** occupied by slum-dwellers.
A. in the land B. on the land
C. over the land D. No Improvement

87. In view of the **few availability of** land, the ministry has decided to take up rehabilitation work on a self-sustaining basis.
A. little availability of
B. some availability of
C. scarce availability of
D. No Improvement

88. A new notification by the urban development ministry now **makes land available to school** only through auction.
A. makes land available to schools
B. making land available to schools
C. making land available to school
D. No Improvement

89. One of the first **lesson that a** young MNC manager learns is that ''God is in the details.''
A. lesson which a
B. lessons that a
C. lessons which a
D. No Improvement

90. Likewise, investors are more interested in crunching numbers than **they are for** fielding calls from potential sellers.
A. they are in
B. they are at
C. they are in favour of
D. No Improvement

91. With each passing day your memories **grow deep**, your loving nature will always be cherished.
A. grew deep
B. grew deeper
C. grow deeper
D. No Improvement

92. It may not beat winning the lottery, **but money** you can take to the bank.
A. but it's money
B. so it's money
C. but it's money that
D. No Improvement

93. Wisdom, Vision, Ideals & Thought **continue to guide** us every moment in our Journey ahead.
A. continue to guiding
B. continuously guide
C. continuing at guiding
D. No Improvement

94. Delhi government **are now blaming** DDA for stalling big infrastructure projects in the Capital.
A. is now putting blaming on
B. is now blaming
C. is now blaming the
D. No Improvement

95. Be happy with the status quo and **preserve it by** conciliating others.
A. preserve that by
B. it is preserved
C. preserving it by
D. No Improvement

96. Have graceful movements, liquid eyes and a gliding walk, **although** overweight.
A. though B. even if
C. even D. No Improvement

97. But people resent that most of the poverty funds **are lost for** corruption and administrative expenses.
A. are lost in B. are lost at
C. is lost in D. No Improvement

98. It is **very difficult** to store and save almost everything—money, possessions, energy words food, fat.

A. most difficult
B. very much difficult
C. highly difficult
D. No Improvement

99. Now Pause Live TV & watch **with your convenience** and also Record your favorite TV programme.

A. at your convenient
B. your convenience
C. at your convenience
D. No Improvement

100. To avoid **last hour rushing**, please immediately deposit VAT and file your Monthly and Quarterly DVAT return.

A. last rush
B. last minute rush
C. last minute rushing
D. No Improvement

ANSWERS

1	2	3	4	5	6	7	8	9	10
A	D	C	A	C	D	C	A	C	C
11	**12**	**13**	**14**	**15**	**16**	**17**	**18**	**19**	**20**
D	C	D	B	A	D	C	C	D	B
21	**22**	**23**	**24**	**25**	**26**	**27**	**28**	**29**	**30**
C	C	D	A	C	D	C	C	C	C
31	**32**	**33**	**34**	**35**	**36**	**37**	**38**	**39**	**40**
B	C	C	A	C	B	D	B	D	C
41	**42**	**43**	**44**	**45**	**46**	**47**	**48**	**49**	**50**
A	D	C	A	D	C	A	B	D	B
51	**52**	**53**	**54**	**55**	**56**	**57**	**58**	**59**	**60**
C	B	A	C	D	A	C	B	B	A
61	**62**	**63**	**64**	**65**	**66**	**67**	**68**	**69**	**70**
A	C	C	D	B	B	D	A	B	A
71	**72**	**73**	**74**	**75**	**76**	**77**	**78**	**79**	**80**
C	D	B	B	A	A	D	C	B	C
81	**82**	**83**	**84**	**85**	**86**	**87**	**88**	**89**	**90**
C	D	B	A	D	B	C	A	B	A
91	**92**	**93**	**94**	**95**	**96**	**97**	**98**	**99**	**100**
C	A	A	B	D	B	A	D	C	B

7. Sentence Error Corrections

Spotting errors forms a part of almost all the important examinations that have objective English test on their syllabus. Hence it is necessary that all candidates taking up these examinations have the knowledge and awareness of the basic rules of grammar and its usages. With a view to help in detecting the errors and avoiding them as well, a list of rules are being given here which may serve as practical tips.

Errors in Use of Articles

1. Use of 'An'

(*i*) 'An' is used before a word beginning with a vowel *e.g.*, an apple, an elephant, etc.

(*ii*) Before words beginning with silent 'h'; *e.g.*, an hour, an honest man, an honourable member, etc.

(*iii*) Before words that do not begin with a vowel but begin with vowel sound *e.g.*, 'm' has the sound of 'em'. Such consonants which begin with a vowel sound are—F, H, L, M, N, R, S, X. 'An' is used before abbreviations beginning with these letters.
e.g., An M.L.A., An N.C.C. Officer, An X-ray, An S.P., etc.

2. Use of 'A'

(*i*) Before a singular countable noun; *e.g.*, It is a statue of Nehru.

(*ii*) In the sense of one
e.g., He couldn't speak a word in his favour.
e.g., Twenty-four hours make a day.

(*iii*) With one
e.g., a one-man show
a one-rupee note.

(*iv*) With vowel letters that begin with consonant sound of 'yu'.
e.g., a university, a European language, a unique person, a unit, etc.

(*v*) Before a singular countable if it represents a class; *e.g.*, A student should respect his teacher.

(*vi*) With units and rate per:
e.g., He earns rupees two thousand a month.
Rice sells twenty rupees a kg.
I need a metre length of this cloth.

(*vii*) In exclamatory expressions before singular nouns.
e.g., Such a huge crowd!
What a strange sight!

(*viii*) Before two nouns seen as a single unit
e.g., I need a fork and knife.
Kindly lend me a cup and saucer.

(*ix*) Before an abstract noun when it is restricted by a phrase; *e.g.*, We are looking for someone with a good knowledge of computers.

(*x*) With certain expressions of quantity
e.g., a lot of, a couple, a dozen, etc.

(*xi*) To make a common noun of a proper noun
e.g., A Daniel come to judgement!
This man is a second Shakespeare

(*xii*) With a special meal to celebrate something or in someone's honour.
e.g., He called his colleagues to a dinner to celebrate his promotion.

(*xiii*) Before the word 'most' when it is used in the sense of very much or exceedingly; as *e.g.*, Tushar is a most intelligent boy. The earthquake in Gujarat is a most unfortunate event.

3. Use of 'the'

The Definite Article 'the' is used:

(*i*) When an already mentioned thing is spoken of: as the ball is in the field. I am unable to give the book you wanted to read.

(*ii*) When a singular Noun represent a whole class; the horse runs fast. The crocodile is found in water.

Note: *'The' is not used before 'man' or 'woman' used in a general sense to represent the human race.*

(*iii*) Before the names of rivers, mountains, oceans, islands, etc. *e.g.*, The Himalayas lie to the North of India.

(*iv*) With common nouns indicating what is unique *e.g.*, the Sun, the Moon, etc.

(*v*) Before well known books, magazines, newspapers, names of trains/ship building, etc.

(*vi*) Before Musical instruments

(*vii*) Before the inventions: *e.g.*, Bell invented the telephone. The computer is the greatest scientific invention.

(*viii*) Before Parts of body: *e.g.*, She was wounded in the head.

(*ix*) Before the names religious groups, political parties, empire, dynasty or historical event, club and foundations.

(*x*) With what is referred to is understood or unique in the context: *e.g.*, Would you pass the newspaper The postman is waiting at the door.

(*xi*) Before proper, material or abstract nouns when used in a particular sense: *e.g.*, The pollution in Delhi is increasing day by day. The climate of Bangalore is very pleasant.

(*xii*) Before a noun when they are defined by phrases or clauses; *e.g.*, The man acting on *the* stage is my brother. He has learned to operate the computer he had bought yesterday.

(*xiii*) With comparative adjectives when only two things/places/persons are compared; *e.g.*, He is *the* wiser of the two candidates. Prerna is *the* taller of the two girls.

(*xiv*) Before a noun to give emphasis of a superlative *e.g.*, Saurabh was declared *the* man of the match. This is *the* best book on current affairs.

(*xv*) With ordinals: *e.g.*, Our house is on *the* third floor.

(*xvi*) Before an adjective when the noun is understood *e.g.*, *The* poor should not be overlooked. We must take care of *the* disabled.

OMISSION OF ARTICLES *A/AN/THE*

Do not use article:

1. Before proper nouns: *e.g.*, Shimla is the capital of Himachal pradesh.
2. Before plural common nouns used in general sense: *e.g.*, Girls are talkative than boys.
3. Before abstract nouns used in general sense: *e.g.*, Honesty is appreciated by all.
4. Before any material: Milk is white. Vegetables are fresh.

Note: *'The' is used only in the case of specified material.*

e.g., The milk which is sold here is costly.

5. Before institutions, markets, religious places, other places like schools, hospitals, market, prison etc. Which when visited for its common purpose. *e.g.*, Patients visit hospitals. Children go to school

Note: *'The' is allowed with these in case of any particular purpose.*

e.g., The parents went to the school on Annual day etc.

6. Before the names of relations—father, mother, brother, cook, nurse, etc.
Cook has gone in search of another job.
7. Before the names of languages and subjects—English, Hindi, Maths, etc.
8. Before predicative nouns denoting positions that is normally held at one time by one person only.
e.g., He was chairman of Railway Board.

ERRORS IN USE OF NOUNS

1. *Some nouns which always take a singular verb:*
   (*a*) Scenery, news, advice, information, furniture. machinery, stationery, business, poetry, mischief, fuel, issue, repair, bedding.
   e.g., He gave me a lot of news of my friends.
   His advice is always good.
   He has given no information so far.
   (*b*) All subjects like Physics, English, Mathematics; Athletics, innings, gallows.
   e.g., Physics is a very interesting subject.
   The Indian team defeated the Sri Lankan by an innings.
   (*c*) Brick, bread, fruit, word as promise:
   e.g., Let me eat some bread.
   He is true to his word.
   (*d*) Words like dozen, score, hundred, thousand, million when preceded by a numeral.
   e.g., I bought two dozen bananas.
   (*e*) Expressions as a ten-rupee note, a three-hour journey, a two-mile walk, a five-man committee, a Five-year plan, etc.
2. *Nouns though singular in form but used only in plural form and always take a plural verb:*
Cattle, peasantry, artillery, people, clergy, police, company, gentry, vermin
e.g., The cattle are grazing in the ground
3. *Nouns which are plural in form and never take a singular verb:*
Trousers, goods, premises, thanks, tidings, stockings, spectacles, shorts, alms, remains, riches, measles, etc.
e.g., Household goods are kept in the garden for auction.
4. *Nouns used both as singular and plural in the same form:*
   (*i*) Deer, sheep, fish, apparatus, wages.
   e.g., The wages of sin is death.
   The wages of the teachers have been raised.
   A fish is in the aquarium.
   Fish are found of different variety.
   (*ii*) Collective nouns as public, jury, audience, team, comittee, government, congregation, etc.
   e.g., The team are looking confident.
   The team has come out victorious
   From the above examples, it is clear that when these collective nouns indicate a unit the verb is singular, otherwise the verb will be plural.
5. *Some nouns have one meaning in the singular and another in the plural.*
e.g., authority means command; and; authorities means persons in power.
6. *One of or any of is followed by plural words.*
e.g., I want one of the pens kept on the table.
Any of my classmates can come with me.
7. *Plural nouns are used with fractions.*
e.g., He took two and a half hours to complete the painting.
8. *Some confusing nouns:*

Incorrect form	***Correct usage***
Boarding	Boarding house
Family member	Members of the family
Maths teacher	The teacher of Maths
Cousin brother or sister	Cousin

9. *Pairs of nouns that must be used with caution:*
   (*a*) Cause—produces a result.
   Reason—explains or justifies a cause.
   (*b*) Men—Plural of man.
   People—used for persons.
   e.g., There are four men in the living room.
   The people of Kashmir are good looking.
   (*c*) Shade—a place sheltered from the sun.
   Shadow—the shade of a distinct form or object.
   (*d*) House—a building to live in
   Home—one's native place.
   (*e*) Cost—amount paid by the shopkeeper
   Price—amount paid by the customer.

10. *When two nouns express a single idea then they will take a singular verb.*
e.g., Bread and omelette *is* what I usually prefer for breakfast.
11. *When two subject nouns either mean the same thing or refer to the same person, then they will take a singular verb.*
e.g., The power and influence of the American President *is* much more than that of the Indian President.
12. *When a singular noun is used in the distributive sense then it will take a plural verb.*
e.g., The panel *are* divided on the Constitutional Review's issue.
13. *When a plural proper noun stands for a collective unit, then it will take a singular verb.*
e.g., The eastern states *is* the largest producer of tea in India.
14. *When a plural noun denotes a specific quantity taken as a whole, then it will take a singular verb.*
e.g., Five hundred rupees is not a small amount for the middle class people to spend on crackers.
15. *Each of two or more connecting nouns implying separate possessions must take the possessions must take the possessive sign; as .... Shelley's and Keats's poems, Ram's and Laxman's business, etc.*

ERRORS IN USE OF PRONOUNS

A pronoun must agree with its antecedent in person, number and gender. If this rule is not followed then one commits the error. In order to avoid this error one must keep the following points in mind:

1. The pronoun 'one' must be followed by 'one's'.
e.g., One must do one's duty to one's country.
One must finish one's work within the alloted time.
2. When one means one in number, the pronoun for it is third person singular pronoun.
e.g., One of them is ready to donate his blood.
3. Everyone or everybody must be followed by his.
e.g., Everyone should respect his elders.
4. Each, every, anyone, anybody must be followed by the singular pronoun of their gender.
e.g., Each of the boys in this class has finished his work.
5. Let is followed by pronoun in the objective case.
e.g., Let her do it.
Let him solve this sums.
6. 'But' and 'except' are followed by pronoun in the objective case.
e.g., Everyone attended the Annual function except him.
7. 'Such as' is followed by pronoun in the subjective case.
e.g., I never bother for such a person as he.
8. When first, second and third person singular pronouns are used together, they are placed in the order: you, he and I.
e.g., you, he and I are close friends.
In case of plural pronouns, the order is: we, you and they.
9. When two or more singular nouns are joined together by 'either–or'; 'neither–nor'; and 'or', the pronoun is singular.
e.g., Either Marcus or Martin will give *his* pen.
Neither Vineet nor Anand has brought his notebook.
10. When a singular and a plural noun are joined by 'or', 'nor', the pronoun must be plural.
e.g., Either the Manager or his assistants did not performed *their* duty.
11. Verbs like enjoy, avail, pride, resign, acquit, apply, assert, absent, are followed by reflexive pronouns.
e.g., He absented *himself* from the meeting.
She resigned *herself* to fate.
We enjoyed *ourselves* at the excursion.
12. 'Who' denotes the subject and 'whom' denotes object.
13. 'Whose' is used for living persons and which for non-living things.
14. 'Which' conveys additional information and 'that' explains a certain thing.
e.g., This is the book *which* I wanted to read.
I am studying those chapters *that* have been included in our new syllabus.
15. The relative pronoun 'that' is used in preference to 'which' and 'who' before 'all', 'any', 'only', 'same', man and animal, superlative degree, interrogative expression etc.

16. 'Each other' is used when there are two subjects or objects and 'one another' when there are more than two.
17. The complement of the verb 'to be' is expressed by a pronoun, it should be in Nominative case [I, We, He, She, They, Who].
e.g., It was he who saved him.
18. The Relative pronoun should be placed as near as possible to the antecedent.
e.g., I have read *Chaucer's Works* who was a great poet. [Incorrect sentence].
I have read *the works of Chaucer* who was a great poet. [Correct sentence]
19. When a pronoun stands for a collective noun, it must be in the singular number and in the neuter gender if the collective noun is viewed as a whole.
e.g., The Planning Committee gave its report.
20. If the collective noun conveys the idea of separate individuals comprising the whole, the pronoun standing for it must be plural.
e.g., The Planning Committee were divided in their opinion about levying the taxes on kerosene oil.

ERRORS IN SUBJECT–VERB AGREEMENT

1. Singular subject must have singular verb and plural subject must have plural verb.
2. Two singular subjects joined by 'or' or 'nor' will take a singular verb.
e.g., Neither a doctor nor a nurse is present in the clinic.
3. A singular subject and a plural subject joined by 'or' or 'nor' will take a singular or plural verb depending on which subject is nearer the verb. The violation of this rule leads to errors of proximity.
e.g., Neither Neetu nor her friends are coming here.
Neither her friend nor Neetu is coming here.
4. If the subject is singular and the predicate is plural, the verb must agree with its subject and not its predicate.
5. Indefinite pronouns such as someone, somebody, each, no body, anybody, anyone, everyone, everybody, one, no one, either, neither, etc. always take a singular verb.
6. Indefinite pronouns which indicate more than one like several, many, few, both, etc., always take a plural verb.
7. Title of the books require singular verbs.
e.g., 'Othello' is a good book.
'The Merchant of Venice, is a drama written by William Shakespeare.'
8. If two subjects are joined together by 'as well as' the verb will be in accordance to the first subject.
e.g., He as well as his juniors is playing cricket.
9. The subject 'Many a .....' is always followed by the singular verb.
e.g., Many a man was killed in the riot.
10. If two subjects are joined together by 'which' then the verb should be according to the subject.
11. The subject 'The number of ......' is always followed by a singular verb.
e.g., The number of boys participating in debate is eight.
12. If the subject begins with 'A number of ....', then the verb used should be plural.
e.g., A number of files are missing.
13. When adjectives such as much, less, little and more are used as nouns, they must have a singular verb.
e.g., More than hundred people have died in the train accident.
Much is said in his praise.

ERRORS IN THE USE OF TENSES

The changed forms of a verb that indicate time of the action, the continuance of action and the completeness of action are called tenses of the verb.

1. When the first verb in the sentence is in the past tense, then all the following verbs are also used in the past tense forms. *e.g.*,
He said that he might visit his sister soon.
He said that he had done his work.
2. But a past tense in the principal clause may or may not be followed by the past tense in the subordinate clause if the latter expresses universal

or habitual truth. *e.g.*, The doctor said that mosquitoes spread the disease of malaria.

The teacher said that the Pluto is the farthest planet.

3. Any tense may be used in the subordinate clause if it gives a comparison by using the word 'than': *e.g.,* He helped him in his work more than he helps his own children.
   Here the use of tense depends upon the sense required in the subordinte clause.
4. Any tense can be used when the subordinate clause is in a quotation:
   e.g., He said, "He will face the interview tomorrow". I said, "I am going to meet my friend today".
5. The present perfect tense [subject + has/have + verb.] cannot be used when an expression of past time is used.
   e.g., I finished my work yesterday.
6. In conditional sentences beginning with 'if', the subordinate clause is generally in present or past tense but not in future tense.
   e.g., If he had worked hard, he would have succeeded.
7. If two actions in a sentence are shown happening in the past, one after the other. The tense of the action happening first should be past perfect and that of the second should be past indefinite.
   e.g., The train had departed before he arrived the station.
8. Two actions in the past, one depending on the other, should have the sequence as follows:
   Past perfect + Future perfect
   Had + past participle + would + have + past participle
   e.g., If you had practised regularly, you would have come out successful.
   Had you worked hard, you would have succeeded in qualifying the entrance exam.
9. If in a sentence, two actions are indicated which are to take place in future, the sequence of tenses will be as follows:
   The principal clause in present indefinite; and the subordinate clause in future indefinite.
   e.g., If it rains, I shall not go to the movie.
10. When an action that has taken place in the past and still continues in the present, the perfect continuous tense form of the verb should be used.
    India has been independent for the last fifty-four years.
11. With the phrases 'as if' and 'as though', past tense and plural form of the verb should be used.
    e.g. She behaves as if she were a principal of this school.
12. Words like usually, generally, often, whenever, etc. are used in present indefinite tense.
    e.g., I usually go to library.
    I often go there.

USE OF INFINITIVE
[to + first form of the verb]

1. Verbs like 'will', 'can', 'do', 'must', 'let' are followed by infinitive without to;
   e.g., He must call him.
2. Verbs like 'would rather', 'would sooner', 'sooner than' 'rather than', 'had better' are followed by infinitive without to.
   e.g., I would go rather than wait for him.
3. Verb 'see' can be used with infinitive or without it.
   e.g., You must go to see that beautiful place. Go and see that beautiful place.
4. Verb 'need' and 'dare' except when they are conjugated with do, will or would, take infinitive without 'to'
   e.g., You need not say anything.
   She dare not do it.
5. Infinitive is not used with 'to' after verbs of sensation like to hear, to see, to watch, etc.
   e.g., I heard him come upstairs.'
6. The Infinitive is used after adjective expressing emotions like glad, delight, angry, astonished, surprised, disappointed, etc.
   e.g. I was disappointed to find him at my office.
7. An infinitive is represented by only 'to' after certain verbs like want, wish, like, hate, hope, try etc,
   e.g., You may not complete the work but I will have to.
   You may do or not but I wish to.

8. There are certain verbs which are followed by object + infinitive. These are—tell, invite, oblige, order, permit, compel, teach, instruct, advise, encourage, urge, warn, encourage, forbid, request, temind, show, how.
   e.g., He showed them how to use a microwave oven.
9. Avoid using split-infinitive:
   'The Managing Director decided to not sanction any leave this year' is incorrect.
   The correct form is :
   'The Managing Director decided not to sanction any leave this year'.

USE OF GERUND
[Verb + ing]

1. When an action is being considered in general sense, gerund is used as subject.
   e.g., Playing football is his favourite pastime.
   Throwing objects is a common habit in children.
2. Verb such as help, stop, detest, avoid, risk, deny, recollect, no good, no use, resent, delay, postpone, defer, enjoy, suggest, excuse, forgive pardon etc. are followed by the gerund.
   e.g., I enjoy eating sweets.
   You must stop finding faults in others.
3. A gerund is placed after a preposition:
   e.g., She is fond of music
4. Nouns, followed by a gerund are put in the possessive case.
   e.g., I dislike my child's watching T.V. all the time.
5. Adjective before gerund are put in the possessive case.
   e.g., I do not care your leaving the job.
6. 'With a view to' is always followed by a gerund and not an adjective.
   e.g., We go to theatre with a view to watching drama.

USE OF AUXILIARY VERBS
[helping verbs]

1. be, have do, can, may, must, need, will, shall, ought, dare, used are used with infinitives to indicate possibility, permission obligation, etc.
2. Auxiliaries like 'be', 'have', 'ought', 'used' are followed by an infinitive 'to'.
   e.g., He has to find some solution.
3. 'Need' and 'Dare' take infinitive without 'to' but when conjugated with 'do' they take infinitive 'to'.
   e.g., How dare you blame me.
   He did not dare to blame me.
4. 'Do' as an auxiliary is used in negative and interrogative of the present simple and past simple tenses of ordinary verbs.
   e.g., I do not appreciate him.
   Do you know about the accident?
5. 'Do' is used before an imperative to make the request more persuasive.
   e.g., Do join us.
6. 'Do' is used in tag questions and short answers.
   e.g., You know painting, do you?
7. 'Do' is not used in question which have 'who', 'what' or 'which' as their subject.
   e.g., Who said that ? What is it? Which place is that?
8. But if who, what or 'which' is the object of the sentence then 'do' is used.
   e.g., Which pen do you want?
   What did you see?
9. 'Should' and 'ought' have similar meanings, but 'ought' is followed by 'to' and it has a more objective force.
10. While 'may' is used to express permission, 'must' is used to give strong advice or orders.
    'Must' is followed by the infinitive without 'to'.
    e.g., I must finish this work today.

ERRORS IN USE OF ADJECTIVES

1. The adjectives ending in 'ior' like junior, superior, prior, posterior, inferior etc. take 'to' and not 'after' them. *e.g.*, He is senior to me.
2. Comparative degree is used in comparing two things or persons. *e.g.*, It is the better of the two movies.
3. Superlative degree is used in comparing more than two things or persons. *e.g.*, It is the worst of the three paintings.

4. The superlative adjective is always preceded by the definite article 'the'.

5. When comparative degree is used in superlative sense, it is followed by 'any other'.
Sachin is better than any other batsman.

6. Some adjectives like unique, ideal, perfect, chief, impossible, infinite, universal, extreme etc. are not compared.
e.g., 'Taj Mahal is the most unique monument' is incorrect.
This sentence should be as 'Taj Mahal is a unique monument'.

7. When two changes happen together, comparative degree is used in both.
e.g., *The longer* one lives, *the quieter* one becomes.

8. When two adjectives with varying degree of comparison are used, then they should be complete in themselves.
e.g., She is *as intelligent* as, if not intelligent than her friend.

9. Double comparatives and superlatives cannot be used
e.g., Most wiser, more brighter, etc.

10. When we compare two qualities in the same person or thing, the comparative ending ...... 'er' is not used. *e.g.*, 'You are wiser than old' is incorrect. It should be 'You are more wise than old'.

11. When two adjectives in superlative or comparative degree are used together, the one formed by adding more or most must follow the other adjective.
He is more intelligent and wise than his brother.... is incorrect.
The correct expression is ......
He is wiser and more intelligent than his brother.

12. Compound adjective formed by adding 'worth' is placed after the noun it qualifies.
e.g., This is a worth seeing sight ....is incorrect.
The correct expression is :
This is a *sight worth* seeing

13. When two or more comparatives are joined, they must be in the same degree.
e.g., He is one of the *wisest* and most experienced worker of this office.

14. When there are two objects of comparison, then to avoid repetition of noun, *'that'* is used for singular noun and 'those' for plural noun.
e.g., The climate of Dehradun is better than that of Delhi.

15. If comparison is made by using 'other', 'than' is used instead of 'but'.
e.g., He turned out to be no other than my close friend.

16. 'Likely', 'certain' and 'sure' are followed by 'to'.
e.g., He is sure to pass the exam.

17. Correct use of confusing adjectives:-

(a) Some, any.
'Some' is used in affirmative sentences, and 'any' in interrogative and negative sentences.
e.g., He has sent me some parcels. [Affirmative]
Has he sent me any parcels? [Interrogative]
He hasn't sent me any parcels. [Negative]

(b) Less, few
'Less' refers to quantity 'fewer' denotes number.
e.g., There is not less than a litre of oil in this bottle.
They have fewer books than I have.

(c) Other, another, the other
'Other' refers to person or things not already named.
e.g., The Principal has come, others are coming.
'another' refers to an additional one.
e.g., Give him another cup of tea.
'the other' is used when there are a pair, or only two.

(d) Last, Latest
'Last refers to the final one
'Latest' is last upto the present.
e.g., 'Z' is the last letter of the alphabet.
This is the latest edition of magazine.

(e) Each, Every
'Each' is used for one of two or more things.
e.g., Each of the two answers was incorrect.
'Every' is used for more than two things, taken as a group.
e.g., I have read every book of this publication.

(*f*) *Little, few, a little, a few*
'Little' and 'few' mean 'almost no' or 'hardly any'. But 'a little' means not much; at least some and 'a few' means not many.

ERRORS IN USE OF ADVERBS

While the adjective qualifies Nouns, the Adverb qualifies Verbs.

1. Many adverbs of 'Manner' like openly, slowly; and some adverbs of Degree like completely, entirely, nearly etc. are formed by adding 'ly' to the corresponding adjectives
2. Nine classes of Adverbs are
   (*a*) Adverbs of manner—slowly, swifty, openly.
   (*b*) Adverbs of time—daily, now.
   (*c*) Adverbs of frequency—rarely, once, twice
   (*d*) Adverbs of degree—almost, very
   (*e*) Adverbs of certainty or Affirmation or Negation—certainty, difinitely
   (*f*) Adverbs of place—there, down, up.
   (*g*) Adverbs of reason—hence, therefore
   (*h*) Adverbs of interrogation—why?, where?
   (*i*) Relative Adverbs—where? which?
3. Adverbs of manner, place and time are usually placed after the verb of object.
   e.g., He was driving slowly
   He went up to find his room on the *top* floor.
   He finished his work yesterday.
4. Adverbs of frequency and other adverbs are normally put between subject and verb. If there is more than one word in the verb, they are put after first word. *e.g.*, He often goes to Bombay.
5. The adverb 'enough' is placed after the adjective.
6. Adverb 'not' shouldn't be used with words having negative meaning.
   e.g., My friend forbade me to resign from my job.
7. An adverb should not be used before an infinitive
   e.g., He immediately did the work—is incorrect.
   The correct expression is—
   He did the work immediately.
8. The auxiliaries have 'to' and 'used to' come after the adverb.
   e.g., He never used to go to theatre.
9. Some peculiar adverbs
   (*a*) adverb of good is well.
   (*b*) 'Kindly' can be both-adjective and adverb.
   (*c*) 'Friendly', likely' and 'lonely' are adjectives. They take peculiar adverbial forms:
   e.g., Friendly—in a friendly manner.
   Likely—probably.
   Lonely—alone.
   (*d*) 'Hard' is both an adjective and an adverb.
   (*e*) Seldom is used only as adverb.
   (*f*) 'Ago' is used with Simple Past Tense.
   e.g., He left India ten years ago.
   'Since' is used with perfect tense.
   He left India ten years ago and has not returned since.
   (*g*) 'Only' and 'even' must be placed just before the words they modify.
   'Even' as an adverb invites comparison of what happened with what might have happened.
   e.g., Even a child can do it. [This implies that no doubt, adults can do it.]
   Only as an adverb means "and no one", and, 'and nothing'.
   e.g., Only he can solve my problem.
   He can only solve my problem.
   (*h*) 'Very' and 'Much':
   'very' does not modify verbs. It modifies adjectives and adverbs in the positive Degree and is used before Present Participles.
   e.g., This movie is very entertaining.
   She answers very politely.
   Much is used for modifying verbs and past participles. It modifies the adjectives and adverbs in their Comparative Degree forms.
   e.g., The great writer doesn't write much these days. [modifies verb].
   The old man is much better now. [modifies adverb]
   He did the work much more efficiently [modifies adjective].
   The Plan was much considered. [modifies past participle].
   (*i*) Still, Yet
   'Still' means even to this or that time; and it also indicates action which continues from the past into the present.
   e.g., He is still hoping for a job.
   The old man is working still.

Yet—means 'upto now'. It is generally used in negative and conditional sentences and is usually placed in the middle position.
e.g., Is he working yet in that office? [Has he left]
Is your relative here yet? [Have they arrived].

(*j*) Fairly, Rather–'Fair' is used for favourable comments and 'rather' for unfavourable comments.
e.g., He is fairly good in Mathematics.
He is rather poor in History.

ERRORS IN USE OF CONJUNCTIONS

1. 'Though' is followed by 'yet'.
e.g., Though he worked hard yet he failed.

2. 'Scarcely' or 'Hardly' is followed by 'when'
e.g., Scarcely had he entered the room, when the phone rang.

3. 'No sooner' is followed by 'than'.
e.g., No sooner than did the train enter the platform there was a commotion.

4. 'Not only' is followed by 'but also'.
e.g., Not only did he give his book, but also helped in doing her homework.

5. 'Lest' is negative and so should not be followed by 'not'; it is followed by should.
e.g., Revise again lest you should forget.

6. 'Else' is followed by 'would' or 'may'.
e.g., Give him food, else he may die.

7. 'Both' is complemented by 'and' not by 'as well as'.
e.g., Both Tushar and Tarini are good at games.

8. 'So' and 'as' together is used in negative sentences;
e.g., He is not so wise as his brother.

9. 'As' and 'as' together is used in affirmative sentences.
e.g., He is as wise as his brother.

10. 'Other' is followed by than.
e.g., The workers have no other demand than their bonus.

11. 'Reason' is followed by 'that' and not by 'because'.
e.g., The reason why he didn't go on picnic was that he was ill.

12. 'Unless', 'until', 'if not', 'so that' should not be followed by 'not.'
e.g., Work hard until you succeed.
Do not go unless I return.

13. Some co-ordinating conjunctions are used in pairs.
'both .... and'; 'either .... or'; 'not only ..... but also'.

14. 'If' is used in conditional sense; 'whether' is used in uncertainty.
e.g., If he comes, he will get a prize.
I don't know whether the report was genuine.

15. To express time 'until' or 'till' is used while to express how long 'as long as' is used.
He stayed in hostel until he was fifteen years old.
Struggle as long as you can.

16. 'Such' is followed by 'as' and 'that'.
e.g., We discussed about such subjects as the pollution.

17. 'Like' is followed by pronoun; 'as' is followed by a clause.
e.g., She writes like me.
She writes as I do.

18. 'Since', 'because', 'as' and 'for' .... all mean 'because', but there is a difference in their degree.
'Since' and 'because' are used for stronger cases and 'as' and 'for' for weak cases.
e.g., I respect him because he is my tutor.
I could not go to play as it is raining.

SOME MORE TIPS TO AVOID COMMON ERRORS

1. 'What to speak of' is incorrect; the correct expression is 'not to speak of'.

2. Avoid the use of 'lots', 'a whole lot' and 'a lot' in the sense of 'much' or great deal.
e.g., He hopes to save a lot of money. [incorrect].
He hopes to save a great deal of money.

3. 'Cent per cent' and 'word by word' are incorrect; the correct expressions are 'hundred per cent' and 'word for word'.

4. No sentence should begin with 'due to' because it modifies a noun and not a verb.

5. 'When' indicates a general sense and 'while' implies a time during the process of doing a work.

6. When two nouns are closely connected, apostrophe's will be written after second only.
e.g., Ayush and Shalu's mother is ill.
7. 'Supposing' and 'if' cannot be used together in the same sentence.
8. Avoid the use of 'had' with 'ought'.
e.g., You had not ought to punish him .... Incorrect.
You ought not to punish him. ... correct.
9. 'All of' is used in conversation, not in standard written English.
10. 'Hardly' refers to degree, while 'scarcely' refers to quantity.
e.g., I hardly see anything from here.
He has scarcely enough money to meet his both ends.

MULTIPLE CHOICE QUESTIONS

Directions (Qs. 1 to 200): *Read each sentence to find out whether there is any grammatical error in it. The error, if any, will be in one part of the sentence marked A, B or C. The letter of that part is the answer. If there is no error, the answer is 'D'. (Ignore the errors of punctuation, if any).*

1. (A) He managed to make sense of the book/ (B) even though it was the first time/(C) he read anything on the subject./(D) No error.
2. (A) A large scale exchange of nuclear weapons/(B) will produce unprecedented amounts of radiation/(C) that can penetrate into the biological tissue./(D) No error.
3. (A) No sooner did I open the door/(B) when the rain, heavy and stormy, rushed in/(C) making us shiver from head to foot./(D) No error.
4. (A) After opening the door/(B) we entered into the room/(C) next to the kitchen/(D) No error.
5. (A) Locke's treatises on government toleration and education/(B) show a mind fully awake in/(C) the possibilities of social reconstruction./(D) No error.
6. (A) There was very heavy rain last night,/(B) and the rivers have overflown their banks/(C) causing severe hardship to the people living by them./(D) No error.
7. (A) A leading textile manufacturer, one of the fastest growing in the industry,/(B) is looking for a marketing manager/(C) to look up the marketing network of the company./ (D) No error.
8. (A) Last month we celebrated/(B) the wedding of our sister for whom/(C) we have been looking for a suitable alliance for three years./(D) No error.
9. (A) The method suggested in the lecture/(B) enables a student to learn more quickly/(C) and to have remembered for a longer period of time./(D) No error.
10. (A) She is/(B) no longer popular as she has/ (C) a friends./(D) No error.
11. (A) He said that he/(B) will mind if/(C) I refused his offer./(D) No error.
12. (A) He ensured his bank manager/(B) that he would soon/(C) repay the loan./(D) No error.
13. (A) Both of you two/(C) can come with me/ (C) to the play tonight./(D) No error.
14. (A) Mr. Smith was accused for murder/(B) but the court found him not guilty/(C) and acquitted him./(D) No error.
15. (A) If I had known/(B) this yesterday/(C) I will have helped him./(D) No error.
16. (A) Not one of the hundreds/(B) of striking workers/(C) were allowed to go near the factory./(D) No error.
17. (A) The meeting adjourned abruptly/(B) by the Chairman after/(C) about three hours of deliberation./(D) No error.
18. (A) Having read a number of stories/(B) about space travel,/(C) his dream now is about to visit the moon./(D) No error.
19. (A) The news of the disturbance/(B) was broadcasted/(C) the same evening./(D) No error.
20. (A) Everyone visiting the house asked the young girl/(B) how could she kill the wolf/ (C) single handed and without a weapon./(D) No error.
21. (A) While walking slowly in the park/(B) on a quiet summer afternoon/(C) a mad dog suddenly attacked him from behind/(D) No error.

22. (A) Since the attachment of air-conditioned sleeping cars to all important trains,/(B) travelling became very pleasant,/(C) especially during the summer season./(D) No error.

23. (A) It is the newspaper/(B) that exposes us to the widest range/(C) of human experiences and behaviour./(D) No error.

24. (A) When the dentist came in/(B) my tooth was stopped aching/(C) out of fear that I might lose my tooth./(D) No error.

25. (A) Emphasis on equality of life ensures/(B) for the health and happiness/(C) of every individual./(D) No error.

26. (A) The students were/(B) awaiting for/(C) the arrival of the chief guest./(D) No error.

27. (A) You will come/(B) to my party tomorrow,/(c) isn't it?/(D) No error.

28. (A) All the four sons/(B) of the old man/(C) quarrelled between themselves./(D) No error.

29. (A) I have never seen/(B) so large animal/(C) before./(D) No error.

30. (A) If she will be promoted/(B) she will get/ (C) a higher salary./(D) No error.

31. (A) He accused/(B) one of his friends/(C) of stealing his watch./(D) No error.

32. (A) One of my favourite actor/(B) is acting/ (C) in this play also./(D) No error.

33. (A) I have read/(B) too many books/(C) by R.K. Narayan./(D) No error.

34. (A) He says that/(B) his car does/(C) eight kilometres in a litre/(D) No error.

35. (A) On the busy Ring Road/(B) we witnessed a collusion/(C) between a truck and an auto./ (D) No error.

36. (A) I have/(B) an appointment/(C) on the 9th September on five o'clock/(D) No error.

37. (A) Jayesh is getting/(B) fatter because he/ (C) does not take exercise at all/(D) No error.

38. (A) If you listen with/(B) the questions carefully/(C) you will be able to answer them easily/(D) No error.

39. (A) Had you not/(B) reached in time/(C) he would have lost all our belongings./(D) No error.

40. (A) Neeraj said/(B) that he would rather fail than copying/(C) in the examination/(D) No error.

41. (A) He is generally/(B) more hungry/(C) than she is./(D) No error.

42. (A) She walked in/(B) the room where the murder/(C) had taken place./(D) No error.

43. (A) Do the roses in your garden smell/(B) more sweetly/(C) than those in ours?(D) No error.

44. (A) He told to the story in detail/(B) and the children listened/(C) to it with great interest./ (D) No error.

45. (A) Having received your letter/(B) this morning, we are writing/(C) to thank you for the same./(D) No error.

46. (A) I fail to understand/(B) why he replied in negative/(C) when the proposal was in his favour./(D) No error.

47. (A) Though he stoutly persisted in denying his involvement in the case,/(B) the facts made it very clear/(C) that he had hand in the cruel murder of his wife./(D) No error.

48. (A) Please try to understand/(B) that the dispute on this issue is between my brother and myself,/(C) and concerns nobody else./ (D) No error.

49. (A) Regretfully, profits earned by your company/(B) fell by 20 per cent last year/(C) despite higher sales./(D) No error.

50. (A) In the interim period, various student groups, in small numbers,/(B) met me and informed that the notice for strike/(C) was issued without proper consultation./(D) No error.

51. (A) A team of three Indians, two Canadians and three Japanese/(B) was successful in climbing the highest mountain peak on/(C) its third attempt./(D) No error.

52. (A) He enquired me/(B) why I had not seen him the previous day/(C) as I had promised to do./(D) No error.

53. (A) I am sure that all my monthly expenses/ (B) would exceed the income/(C) If I do not economic/(D) No error.

54. (A) He explained the matter/(B) at great length/(C) but I was not the wiser/(D) No error.

55. (A) Salim and Antony are such good friends/ (B) that one won't go to the pictures/(C) without his coming too./(D) No error.

56. (A) He loved/(B) none but/(C) his neighbour's daughter./(D) No error.

57. (A) It does not matter how you do it;/(B) what I want is that/(C) you should finish the work within a month./(D) No error.

58. (A) Most of the members at the meeting felt/ (B) that the group appointed for investigating the case/(C) were not competent to do the job efficiently./(D) No error.

59. (A) Samir, who is a close friend of mine,/(B) told me that he was smelling/(C) the rice from a distance of fifty yards while coming to my house./(D) No error.

60. (A) She hardly knew how to do that problem,/(B) and so went to her teacher, and asked her,/(C) "How this problem is to be solved?"/(D) No error

61. (A) The course provide/(B) not only theoretical inputs/(C) but also practical training/(D) No error.

62. (A) Since we are friends/(B) there should be no secret/(C) between you and I./(D) No error.

63. (A) Shanghai is/(B) bigger than any city/(C) of the world/(D) No error.

64. (A) The person which was/(B) recommended for the position/(C) did not fulfil the prescribed qualifications./(D) No error.

65. (A) It is time/(B) we should accept all our people as equals/(C) and as partners in the task of building a strong and united nation./ (D) No error.

66. (A) Every motorist knows,/(B) road signs—whether symbols or colour codes—have an immediacy/(C) that neither the spoken nor the written word can match./(D) No error.

67. (A) I had hoped to have met him yesterday/ (B) to discuss the matter with him/(C) but he was not in his house, and so I could not meet him./(D) No error.

68. (A) He speaks/(B) not only Tamil/(C) but Telugu as well./(D) No error.

69. (A) Troy was taken by Greeks;/(B) this formed the basis of a story/(C) which has become famous./(D) No error.

70. (A) Our conception of/(B) what should a science of mental life be/(C) has changed considerably since James' time./(D) No error.

71. (A) In these days of inflation/(B) a ten rupee's note will not buy you/(C) even an ordinary meal./(D) No error.

72. (A) The retiring principal asked his old pupils/(B) to take the interest in the school/ (C) after he has retired./(D) No error.

73. (A) It is difficult/(B) for anyone/(C) to past time thus./(D) No error.

74. (A) When I get a cold/(B) it takes me weeks/ (C) to shake it off./(D) No error.

75. (A) You must/(B) remember me/(C) to post this letter./(D) No error.

76. (A) I am thinking of/(B) to go to Agra/(C) for my cousin's marriage./(D) No error.

77. (A) Had I/(B) known it earlier/(C) I would contact you./(D) No error.

78. (A) He was sure/(B) that he should/(C) win the Prize./(D) No error.

79. (A) He is wiring/(B) for the/(C) last four hours./(D) No error.

80. (A) He was in such hurry/(B) that he didn't/ (C) wait for me./(D) No error.

81. (A) Will you lend me/(B) little money/(C) to tide over this crisis./(D) No error.

82. (A)The President had hardly spoken/(B) a few words/(C) when the microphone stopped functioning./(D) No error.

83. (A) In an English paper/(B) examiners should give as much weightage to language/(C) as they give to contents./(D) No error.

84. (A) My father is going/(B) to the office/(C) five day week./(D) No error.

85. (A) The thief broke in the/(B) house at the/ (C) dead of night./(D) No error.

86. (A) The long-awaited moment at last came,/ (B) and we set out for the station,/(C) as merry a band of children as I have ever seen before or since./(D) No error.

87. (A) In a report issued by Indian Statistical Institute,/(B) the Iron and Steel Industry is investing more than any other/(C) Indian industry in fighting pollution./(D) No error.

88. (A) Block of Residential flats/(B) are coming up/(C) near our house./(D) No error.

89. (A) The test will not need/(B) more than one and half hour/(C) to finish./(D) No error.

90. (A) Will you be/(B) at Board meeting/(C) on next Wednesday?/(D) No error.

91. (A) If you will work hard,/(B) you will get goods grades/(C) in examinations./(D) No error.

92. (A) Do you know/(B) to play/(C) the guitar?/ (D) No error.

93. (A) At the station,/(B) I'll hire a coolie/(C) to carry my baggages/(D) No error.

94. (A) The geography teacher/(B) told the class that/(C) the earth was round./(D) No error.

95. (A) There is still/(B) little tea/(C) left in the cup./(D) No error.

96. (A) He has not been attending/(B) English classes/(C) since one month./(D) No error.

97. (A) He persisted/(B) to do it/(C) in spite of my advice/(D) No error.

98. (A) You can get/(B) all the information that you want/(C) in this book./(D) No error.

99. (A) I am hearing/(B) a lot about/(C) the problem of AIDS these days./(D) No error.

100. (A) It is easy to see that/(B) a lawyer's demeanour in court/(C) may be prejudicial against the interests of his client./(D) No error.

101. (A) If you lend him a book/(B) he will lend it to someone else/(C) and never you will get it back./(D) No error.

102. (A) What does Professor Dhavan/(B) spend so many hours/(C) in the laboratory for?/(D) No error.

103. (A) Sixty miles/(B) are/(C) a good distance./ (D) No error.

104. (A) The tall three girls/(B) had left/(C) the day before./(D) No error.

105. (A) After sunset/(B) every memeber of the team/(C) went to their houses./(D) No error.

106. (A) Each one of the boys/(B) have paid/(C) the tuition-fee./(D) No error.

107. (A) With little patience/(B) you will be able to/(C) cross this hurdle./(D) No error.

108. (A) He was in a hurry/(B) because he had an appointment/(C) with the company's director./(D) No error.

109. (A) Many health-conscious people/(B) prefer margarine/(C) than butter./(D) No error.

110. (A) Mr. Praful Patel/(B) is not attending his office/(C) for the last one month./(D) No error.

111. (A) The customer handed over/(B) a hundred-rupees note/(C) to the shopkeeper./ (D) No error.

112. (A) The reason Ram/(B) is absent from his duty/(C) is because he is unwell./(D) No error.

113. (A) If I were him,/(B) I would have taught/(C) those cheats a lesson./(D) No error.

114. (A) You must either tell me/(B) the whole story or, at least/(C) the first half of it/(D) No error.

115. (A) Twice twelve/(B) makes/(C) twenty-four/ (D) No error.

116. (A) It is necessary/(B) that everybody/(C) must have a house/(D) No error.

117. (A) The school is/(B) within hundred yards/ (C) from the church/(D) No error.

118. (A) It is true/(B) that God helps those/(C) who helps themselves./(D) No error.

119. She has never/(B) approve of him/(C) working as a clerk./(D) No error.

120. (A) My wife has got/(B) a new job/(C) a month ago./(D) No error.

121. (A) He is not to blame/(B) for what has happened/(C) for he is in no way connected with it./(D) No error.

122. (A) Whenever you go to a temple/(B) you must put off/(C) your shoes at the entrance./ (D) No error.

123. (A) I asked my servant/(B) to burn the lamp/ (C) as it was getting dark./(D) No error.

124. (A) The charges in this hospital/(B) are less than/(C) the hospital near my house./(D) No error.

125. (A) The company has put up an advertisement/(B) in newspapers/(C) all over the country./(D) No error.

126. (A) Will you please buy/(B) some jaggery for me/(C) if you go to the market?/(D) No error.

127. (A) After leaving his office/(B) he went directly/(C) to a restaurant./(D) No error.

128. (A) I am much pleased/(B) to know that/(C) you have topped the list./(D) No error.

129. (A) My papa is/(B) in bad mood/(C) today./(D) No error.

130. (A) My friend asked me/(B) if I can lend him my Parker pen/(C) for a few days./(D) No error.

131. (A) Rita is going/(B) for aerobics classes/(C) everyday in the morning./(D) No error.

132. (A) She is/(B) five years/(C) senior than me./(D) No error.

133. (A) We are four brothers and sisters living in this house/(B) but neither of us is/(C) satisfied with it./(D) No error.

134. (A) The Prime Minister has said that India would not have spent so much on defence/(B) if some of the neighbouring countries/(C) adopted the policy of restricting defence expenditure/(D) No error.

135. (A) That house/(B) is costing me/(C) ten thousand rupees/(D) No error.

136. (A) I wonder/(B) how am I/(C) to do it/(D) No error.

137. (A) Sheela has scored a first class/(B) in her final exams,/(C) isn't it?/(D) No error.

138. (A) A lot of travel delay is caused/(B) due to the inefficiency and lack of good management/(C) on behalf of the railways./(D) No error.

139. (A) The warden/(B) forbade the student/(C) from leaving the hostel./(D) No error.

140. (A) He will certainly help you/(B) if you will ask him/(C) in a pleasant manner./(D) No error.

141. (A) Two-thirds of the book/(B) were/(C) rubbish./(D) No error.

142. (A) The world/(B) comprises/(C) good and bad people./(D) No error.

143. (A) The conductor asked the passenger/(B) why hadn't he purchased a ticket/(C) in advance to board the bus./(D) No error.

144. (A) It is unfortunate that/(B) many youngsters get/(C) addicted to gamble./(D) No error.

145. (A) Can I lend/(B) your pencil/(C) for a minute, please?/(D) No error.

146. (A) The eminent speaker's speech/(B) was broadcasted over/(C) all the major radio-stations./(D) No error.

147. (A) The child/(B) picked up a burned paper/(C) from the street./(D) No error.

148. (A) The Sharmas/(B) are living in this colony/(C) for the last eight years./(D) No error.

149. (A) All the furnitures have been/(B) sent to the new house/(C) located in a village./(D) No error.

150. (A) The serial which appeared quite interesting initially/(B) turned out to be boring/(C) in its latter parts/(D) No error.

151. (A) A body of volunteers/(B) have been organised/(C) to spread the message of the saint./(D) No error.

152. (A) If I will have the time/(B) I shall try and make it/(C) to the zoo this afternoon./(D) No error.

153. (A) To facilitate exports and improve sales in the domestic market/(B) some of the improvised fabrics and garments fabricated out from them/(C) are displayed in the main pavilion./(D) No error.

154. (A) He gave them no money/(B) nor did help them/(C) in any way./(D) No error.

155. (A) Azharuddin is one of the finest batsmen/(B) that India have produced/(C) over the decades./(D) No error.

156. (A) An Indian ship/(B) laden with merchandise/(C) got drowned in the Pacific./(D) No error.

157. (A) Though senior in age,/(B) his father is junior than/(C) my father in service./(D) No error.

158. (A) If I am you/(B) I would have seen to it/(C) that I won the prize./(D) No error.

159. (A) His father died of cholera/(B) but his mother also,/(C) though very weak, is out of danger./(D) No error.

160. (A) He asked me/(B) why did I call/(C) him a rogue./(D) No error.

161. (A) I have got/(B) my M.Sc. degree/(C) in 1988./(D) No error.

162. (A) They/(B) enjoyed thoroughly/(C) at the party./(D) No error.

163. (A) After the humiliating exposure/(B) he hanged his head/(C) in shame./(D) No error.

164. (A) Kamala's fountain-pen/(B) is as expensive/(C) as Shyama./(D) No error.

165. (A) I shall certainly/(B) write you/(C) when I shall reach New Delhi./(D) No error.

166. (A) The criminal was/(B) caught, convicted the hung/(C) in a short period of time./(D) No error.

167. (A) You will get/(B) all the information/(C) if you read this booklet carefully./(D) No error.

168. (A) She sang/(B) very well/(C) isn't it?/(D) No error.

169. (A) He is working in/(B) a bank is New Delhi/(C) for the past several months./(D) No error.

170. (A) There is no question/(B) of my failing/(C) in the examination./(D) No error.

171. (A) No sooner did the sun rise/(B) when we took a hasty breakfast/(C) and resumed the journey./(D) No error.

172. (A) I suppose/(B) you have heard the latest news:/(C) John has married that girl./(D) No error.

173. (A) The presumption that the average investor does not understand/(B) or take interest in the affairs of the company/(C) is not correct./(D) No error.

174. (A) In spite of several reminder,/(B) he did not so far send/(C) any reply to my letters./(D) No error.

175. (A) Looking back, I find that among the many impressions of the people of India,/(B) absorbed while I lived among them,/(C) are their reverence for great men and women./(D) No error.

176. (A) He fell from a running train/(B) and would have died/(C) if the villagers did not get him admitted in the nearby hospital immediately./(D) No error.

177. (A) Even though the shirt is rather expensive/(B) but I wish to/(C) purchase it with my own money./(D) No error.

178. (A) The man told to her/(B) that he had not brought his dog/(C) out for a walk as he was afraid that it would rain./(D) No error.

179. (A) They left/(B) their luggages/(C) at the railway station./(D) No error.

180. (A) None of the students attending your class/(B) answered your questions/(C) did they?/(D) No error.

181. (A) The police broke upon the robbers/(B) when they were in the lonely place/(C) to divide their booty./(D) No error.

182. (A) It is the duty of every citizen to do his utmost/(B) to defend the hardly-won/(C) freedom of the country./(D) No error.

183. (A) When we consider all the factors, which are many,/(B) the number of school dropouts/(C) are quite disturbing./(D) No error.

184. (A) I could not convince them/(B) because they persisted to suggest/(C) that I was lying./(D) No error.

185. (A) If you are great at ideas but not very good at getting into/(B) the nitty gritty/(C) of things and implementing them, then you work on a team,/(D) that has someone who can implement. No error.

186. (A) Remember that you are part of/(B) the team and your success depends on the support/(C) you are able to give and get from your other team members./(D) No error.

187. (A) The ability to plan,/(B) organise and coordinate work is all fundamental/(C) to working within deadline./(D) No error.

188. (A) He is going everyday/(B) for a morning walk/(C) with his friends and neighbours/(D) No error.

189. (A) In management, as you rise higher,/(B) the problems you face become more and more unstructured and you can't just fall back on/(C) the tools you had been/(D) taught. No error.

190. (A) The whole thing moves/(B) around the concept of building a small dynamic/(C) organisation into a larger one./(D) No error.

191. (A) Arun's parents died when he was young and/(B) he looked after his aunt/(C) who had no children./(D) No error.

192. (A) He is/(B) too intelligent/(C) to make a mistake./(D) No error.

193. (A) If a man diligently seeks to come into the contact/(B) with the best that has been thought and said in this world/(C) he will become simple and unselfish./(D) No error.

194. (A) Another reason for pharmaceutical companies beefing up their/(B) OTC (Over the Counter) divisions is that prescription drugs with proven safety records which have been reached/(C) the end of the their patent protection period are/(D) allowed to be sold without a prescription. No error.

195. (A) Unless you stop to make noise at once/ (B) I will have no option but to/(C) bring the matter to the attention of the police./(D) No error.

196. (A) He couldn't but help/(B) shedding tears at the plight of the villagers/(C) rendered homeless by a devastating cyclone./(D) No error.

197. (A) Since it was his first election campaign, the candidate was confused;/(B) none could clearly understand/(C) either the principles he stood for or the benefits he promised./(D) No error.

198. (A) It is an established fact that the transcendental American poets and philosophers,/(B) who lived in the latter half of the nineteenth century,/(C) were more influenced by Indian philosophy, in particular by Upanishadic Philosophy./(D) No error.

199. (A) The crew were on board/(B) and they soon busied themselves/(C) in preparing to meet the storm./(D) No error.

200. (A) One of the members/(B) expressed doubt if/(C) the Minister was an athiest./(D) No error.

ANSWERS

1	2	3	4	5	6	7	8	9	10
C	C	B	B	B	B	C	C	C	C
11	12	13	14	15	16	17	18	19	20
B	A	A	A	C	C	A	C	B	B
21	22	23	24	25	26	27	28	29	30
A	B	D	B	B	B	C	C	B	A
31	32	33	34	35	36	37	38	39	40
D	A	B	C	B	C	B	A	C	B
41	42	43	44	45	46	47	48	49	50
D	A	B	D	D	A	C	B	A	C
51	52	53	54	55	56	57	58	59	60
D	B	C	B	C	D	B	C	D	A
61	62	63	64	65	66	67	68	69	70
A	C	B	A	B	D	A	C	A	B
71	72	73	74	75	76	77	78	79	80
B	B	C	A	B	B	C	B	A	A
81	82	83	84	85	86	87	88	89	90
B	D	D	C	A	C	C	A	B	C

91	92	93	94	95	96	97	98	99	100
C	B	C	D	B	C	B	B	A	D
101	**102**	**103**	**104**	**105**	**106**	**107**	**108**	**109**	**110**
C	A	B	A	C	B	A	D	C	B
111	**112**	**113**	**114**	**115**	**116**	**117**	**118**	**119**	**120**
B	A	A	D	B	C	B	C	B	A
121	**122**	**123**	**124**	**125**	**126**	**127**	**128**	**129**	**130**
A	B	B	C	A	D	D	A	B	B
131	**132**	**133**	**134**	**135**	**136**	**137**	**138**	**139**	**140**
C	C	B	A	B	B	C	C	D	B
141	**142**	**143**	**144**	**145**	**146**	**147**	**148**	**149**	**150**
B	B	C	C	A	B	D	B	A	C
151	**152**	**153**	**154**	**155**	**156**	**157**	**158**	**159**	**160**
B	A	B	B	B	C	B	A	B	B
161	**162**	**163**	**164**	**165**	**166**	**167**	**168**	**169**	**170**
A	B	B	C	C	C	A	C	A	B
171	**172**	**173**	**174**	**175**	**176**	**177**	**178**	**179**	**180**
B	A	D	B	A	C	B	A	B	C
181	**182**	**183**	**184**	**185**	**186**	**187**	**188**	**189**	**190**
A	B	C	B	C	A	C	A	B	C
191	**192**	**193**	**194**	**195**	**196**	**197**	**198**	**199**	**200**
B	D	A	B	A	A	D	C	C	B

8. Direct & Indirect Narration

Direct and Indirect Speech

The exact words spoken by the speaker are known as Direct Speech.

The words spoken by somebody and expressed by someone else with some modification are known as Indirect Speech.

(a) Ram says to me, "You do not help me."

(b) Ram tells me that I do not help him.

The sentence (*a*) shows the words spoken by Ram. So, it is a sentence of direct speech.

The sentence (*b*) shows the words spoken by Ram and expressed by someone else with certain modification. So, it is a sentence of Indirect Speech.

The following points should be noted while changing Direct speech into Indirect speech:

1. The verb outside the inverted commas is called the Reporting verb.

2. The verb or sentence inside the inverted commas is called the Reported Speech.

3. If the Reporting verb is in the Present or Future Tense, there is no change in the tense in the Reported Speech.

4. If the Reporting verb is in the Past tense, the tense in the Reported speech is changed.

5. The Reporting verb may be in any Tense, in it the pronouns are changed as under:

(*i*) First Person according to subject

(*ii*) Second person according to object

(*iii*) Third Person, No change.

6. If the Reporting verb is in the Past tense the adverb will change as under in the Indirect speech.

Direct	**Indirect**
now	then
here	there
after	before
today	that day
yesterday	the previous day
these	those
tomorrow	the next day
last week	the previous week
this	that

7. Adjectives/Determiners are changed as under:

Direct	**Indirect**
this	that
these	those

Rules for Change of Tense

Reporting Verb	**Reporting Speech**	**Change of Tense**
Present Tense	Any Tense	No change
Future Tense	Any Tense	No change
Past Tense	Present/Future Tense	Change into corresponding Past Tense
Past Tense	Past Indefinite Tense	Change into Past Perfect Tense
Past Tense	Past Continuous Tense	Change into Past Perfect Continuous Tense
Past Tense	Past Pefect/Perfect Continuous Tense	No change
Past Tense	Universal Truth	No change
Past Tense	Proverb	No change

Transformation Based on Special Rules

1. Rule Related to Interrogative Sentence

- If the answer of an interrogative sentence is possible in yes-no manner.

Illustration.

Dhoni said to Sachin, "Will you help me?"

Dhoni asked Sachin whether he would help him.

(**Note :** The answer of R.S. is possible in yes-no manner)

Rule of Transformation from Direct to Indirect speech

Step I : Change R.V. into ask.

Step II : In place of comma use 'if/whether'.

Step III : Change interrogative sentence into assertive sentence.

- If the answer of an interrogative sentence is not possible in yes-no manner.

Illustration:

Sachin said to Dhoni, "What do you want?"

Sachin asked Dhoni what he wanted.

(**Note :** Only in Step II, you have to avoid comma and inverted comma and rest will be same as mentioned above).

2. Rule related to Imperative Sentence

- Imperative sentence is a sentence which shows Order/Advice/Request

Illustration:

My teacher said to me, "Go there".

My teacher ordered me to go there.

Rule of Transformation from Direct to Indirect Speech

Step I : Change R.V. as per meaning/sense of R.S. into order/request/advise.

Step II : In place of comma, use 'to'.

Step III : Rest portion will be same.

3. Rule related to Optative Sentence

- Optative sentence is a sentence which expresses the feeling of bless/curse/pray/wish.

Illustration:

Mother said to me, "May you live long!"

Mother blessed me that I might live long.

Rule of Transformation from Direct to Indirect Speech

Step I : Change R.V. as per meaning/sense of R.S. into bless/curse/pray/wish.

Step II : In place of comma, use 'that'.

Step III : Change optative sentence into assertive sentence.

4. Rule related to Exclamatory Sentence

- Exclamatory sentence is a sentence which takes note of exclamatory (!) mark in that sentence showing inner feeling.

Illustration:

She said, "Alas! I am ruined".

She exclaimed with sorrow that she was ruined.

Rule of Transformation from Direct to Indirect Speech

Step I : Change R.V. as per meaning/sense of R.S. into exclaim/exclaims/exclaimed/will or shall exclaim + joy/sorrow/anger/surprise/applause/contempt.

Step II : Change comma into that.

Step III : Change note of exclamation (!) into full (.)

Step IV : Change exclamatory sentence into assertive sentence.

Universal, Historical truth, etc.

If the Reported speech expresses a Universal or Historical or Habitual truth, its Tense will not change.

1. The teacher said to the students, "The sun rises in the east."

   The teacher told the students that the sun rises in the east.

2. My father said to me, "The First Battle of Panipat was fought in 1526."

   My father told me that the First Battle of Panipat was fought in 1526.

MULTIPLE CHOICE QUESTIONS

Directions (Qs. 1 to 13): *Please tick the correct indirect speech for the following sentences:*

1. I said to him, "I shall help you."
A. I told him that I can help him.
B. I told him that I would help him.
C. I told him that I will help him.
D. I told him that I shall be helping him.

2. My Teacher said to me, "The earth revolves round the sun."
A. My teacher told me that the earth revolve round the sun.
B. My teacher told me that the earth revolve round the sun.
C. My teacher told me that the earth had been revolving round the sun.
D. My teacher told me that the earth has been revolving round the sun.

3. I said to my friend, "My father daily goes for a walk."
A. I told my friend that my father daily goes for a walk.
B. I told my friend that my father daily went for a walk.
C. I told my friend that my father has to go for a walk.
D. I told my friend that my father had gone for a walk.

4. He said to me, "May God bless you!"
A. He requested that God can bless me.
B. He prayed that God can bless me.
C. He prayed that God might bless me.
D. He prayed that God will bless me.

5. The patient said, "Thank you, doctor."
A. The patient thanked the doctor.
B. The patient requested the doctor with thanks.
C. The patient told the doctor thanks.
D. The patient suggested the doctor thanks.

6. Satish said, "No, I shall not talk to him."
A. Satish told that he should not talk to him.
B. Satish suggested that he would not have talked to him.
C. Satish exclaimed with sorrow that he would not talk with him.
D. Satish refused to talk to him.

7. The child said, "What a lovely place!"
A. The child exclaimed with sorrow that it was a lovely place.
B. The child thought that the place was lovely.
C. The child exclaimed with joy that the place was very lovely.
D. The child suggested that the place was lovely.

8. He said, "What a fool I have been!"
A. He told himself with a sorrow that he was a fool.
B. He confessed with regret that he had been a great fool.
C. He said himself a fool.
D. He suggested that he could be a fool.

9. He said, "Alas! I am ruined."
A. He told me that he had been ruined.
B. He exclaimed with joy that he had been ruined.
C. He exclaimed with sorrow that he was ruined.
D. He told me that he should not be ruined.

10. The accused said, "I am not guilty."
A. The accused exclaimed with sorrow that I am not guilty.
B. The accused exclaimed with joy that he was not guilty.
C. The accused stated that he was not guilty.
D. The accused told me that he has not been guilty.

11. My teacher said, "The earth is round".
A. My teacher said that the earth was round.
B. My teacher says that the earth is round.
C. My teacher said that the earth is round
D. My teacher ordered that the earth is round.

12. He said, ''What a place it is!''
A. He said that it was a very fine place.
B. He said that is a very fine place.
C. He said that the place is fine.
D. He exclaimed with joy/surprise that it was a very fine place.

13. Ria said, ''Shall I thread the needle?''
A. Ria asked if she should thread the needle.
B. Ria asked if she shall thread the needle.
C. Ria ordered if she should thread the needle.
D. Ria says that if she would thread the needle.

Directions (Qs. 14 to 33): *Pick out the correct alternative that completes the incomplete sentence which is changed into indirect narration.*

14. She said to me, "I shall see you as soon as I get time."
She told me:
A. that she will see me as soon as she will get time.
B. that she would see me as soon as she would get time.
C. she would see me whenever she got time.
D. that she would see me whenever she gets time.

15. My secretary said me, "Your plane will leave if you do not go at once."
My secretary told me that:
A. her plane would leave if she did not go at that time.
B. her plane would leave if I do not go at once.
C. my plane would leave if I do not go at that very time.
D. my plane will leave if I did not go at that time.

16. My mother said to me, "Don't quarrel among yourselves".
My mother:
A. forbade me to quarrel among ourselves.
B. asked me not to quarrel among ourselves.
C. asked me that not to quarrel among ourselves.
D. asked me to quarrel not among ourselves.

17. Her father said to her mother, "Excuse the daughter."
Her father:
A. requested her mother to excuse the daughter.
B. asked her mother to excuse the daughter.
C. asked her mother to have excused the daughter.
D. asked her mother to have been excused.

18. He said to his friend, "Wait here till father comes."
He requested his friend:
A. to wait here till father had come.
B. that to wait there till his friend came.
C. to wait there till father came.
D. to wait here until his friend came.

19. She said to her maid, "Run and catch the thief."
She ordered her maid:
A. ran and catch the thief.
B. that to run and to catch the theif.
C. ran and caught the thief.
D. to ran and catch the thief.

20. Anita said Sunita, "What are you doing?"
Anita asked Sunita:
A. what she will be doing?
B. that what she is doing?
C. that what she was doing?
D. what she was doing?

21. She said to me, "Are you meeting me today?"
She enquired of me:
A. whether I am meeting her that day.
B. whether I was meeting her today.
C. whether I was meeting her that day.
D. I was meeting her that day.

22. Nitish said to me, "When did you buy this pen?"
Nitish asked me:
A. when I was to buy that pen.
B. when I would buy that pen.
C. when I had bought that pen.
D. when I was buying that pen.

23. She said to me, "Are you going to market?"
She enquired of me:
A. I am going to market.
B. I was going to market.
C. if I was going to market.
D. if I had been going to the market.

24. Damini said, "Why did not you change your clothes?"
Damini asked me:
A. why I had not changed my clothes.
B. why I did not change my clothes.
C. why I would not change my clothes.
D. why I have not been changing my clothes.

25. Umesh asked me, "Have you read that novel?"
Umesh asked me:
A. if he was reading that novel.
B. if he had read that novel.
C. if I had read that novel.
D. if I was reading that novel.

26. She said to me, "I shall forgive you."
A. She told me that she will forgive me.
B. She told me that she was going to forgive me.
C. She told me that she will not forgive me.
D. She told me that she would forgive me.

27. I said to her, "It was very hot last night."
I told her:
A. that it had been very hot the previous night.
B. that it was very hot the previous night.
C. that it has been very hot the last night.
D. that it had been very hot this night.

28. She said to me, "I thank you for the help you have given."
She:
A. told me that she thanked me for the help I had given.
B. thanked me for the help I have given.
C. thanked to me for the help I have given.
D. thanked me for the help I had given.

29. Mohini said to me, "Trust in God."
Mohini advised me:
A. that I should trust in God.
B. should trust in God.
C. trusted in God.
D. to trust in God.

30. I said to him, "Let us go to school."
I told him:
A. we would go to school.
B. we shall go to school.
C. that we would go to school.
D. that we should go to school.

31. Rajni said, "May God bless you?"
Rajni:
A. exclaimed with wish that God might bless me.
B. expressed a wish that God might bless me.
C. asked God to bless me.
D. shouted with joy to bless me.

32. My mother said me, "Do not have so many friends."
My mother forbade me:
A. to have so many friends.
B. not to have so many friends.
C. to have been so many friends.
D. to possess so many friends.

33. Ram said, "Pay attention to me."
Ram asked:
A. pay attention to him.
B. paid attention to him.
C. having paid attention to him.
D. to pay attention to him.

Directions (Qs. 34 to 38): *Each of the following groups contains four sentences. Only one sentence in each group is correctly changed into indirect narration, and the rest are incorrect. Pick out that one sentence from each group.*

34. A. The mother told her son bring that book.
B. The mother asked her son bring that book.
C. The mother exclaimed her son to bring that book.
D. The mother asked her son to bring that book.

35. A. Padmini asked me to do not tell a lie.
B. Padmini asked me not to tell a lie.
C. Padmini told me to not tell a lie.
D. Padmini spoke me to tell a lie.

36. A. He asked which is your house.
B. He exclaimed which his house was.
C. He asked which his house was.
D. He asked which your house is.

37. A. She requested me to wind the clock.
B. She asked me wind the clock.
C. She exclaimed me to wind the clock.
D. She told me wind the clock.

38. A. The general said Bravo my men fight.
B. The general encouraged his men to fight.
C. The general told his men you fight.
D. The general shouted fight on my men.

Directions (Qs. 39 to 45): *Each of the following groups contains only one sentence incorrectly changed into indirect narration, and the rest are correct. Pick out that one sentence from each group.*

39. A. She asked me not to sing.
B. She advised me that I should not sing.
C. She spoke to me for not singing.
D. She requested me not to sing.

40. A. He replied he has not done this.
B. He replied he has not done that.
C. He replied that he had not done that.
D. He replied oh, I had not done that.

41. A. She asked if I could name the thief.
B. She asked why I could not name the thief.
C. She wanted to know if I could name the thief.
D. She asked name the thief.

42. A. He said we always tried to please you.
B. He told him that he had been quick.
C. He confessed that he had been smoking.
D. He informed her that they were waiting outside.

43. A. I ordered the servant to shut the door.
B. I exclaimed to brush her teeth.
C. I requested my friend to accompany me.
D. I told him that he should work hard.

44. A. I asked her to go away.
B. She asked her children to go to school.
C. He ordered the servant put off your shoes.
D. She told me to write fast.

45. A. He asked if I knew who was coming.
B. He asked whether I knew about his coming.
C. He told me if I knew that I was coming.
D. He wanted to know if I was coming.

Directions (Qs. 46 to 50): *A sentence correctly changed into indirect narration is followed by four sentencs in the direct narration. Pick out from the alternative one which, when changed into indirect narration will be the same as the indirect sentence preceding the alternatives.*

46. The driver asked the mechanic if he would repair his car.
A. "Repair the car," the driver ordered the mechanic.
B. "Please repair the car," the driver asked the mechanic.
C. "O, please repair the car," the driver asked the mechanic.
D. "Will you repair my car," the driver asked the mechanic.

47. She thanked me and asked me not to disturb her.
A. "Thank you. Do not disturb me," she said.
B. "Dear friend than you, do not disturb," she said.
C. "Disturb not, thank you," she said.
D. "Thank you, please ask not to disturb," she said.

48. In a tone of anger she asked her boy-friend why he had come.
A. "You fool, why have you come," she said.
B. "Oh, why have you come," said she.
C. "You damned, why have you come," she said.
D. "You, you, O you why have you come," she said.

49. Calling him a coward, the girl asked him to come out.
A. "Come out, you coward," said the girl.
B. "Come out," said the girl to the coward.
C. The girl said, "Alas coward come."
D. The girl said, "Come out".

50. He called her a naughty girl.
A. "Oh! naughty girl," said he.
B. "You naughty girl" said he.
C. He said, "naughty girl."
D. "Naughty," boy said to her.

ANSWERS

1	2	3	4	5	6	7	8	9	10
B	A	A	C	A	D	C	B	C	C
11	**12**	**13**	**14**	**15**	**16**	**17**	**18**	**19**	**20**
C	D	A	B	A	A	B	C	D	D
21	**22**	**23**	**24**	**25**	**26**	**27**	**28**	**29**	**30**
C	C	C	A	C	D	A	A	A	D
31	**32**	**33**	**34**	**35**	**36**	**37**	**38**	**39**	**40**
B	A	D	D	B	C	A	B	C	C
41	**42**	**43**	**44**	**45**	**46**	**47**	**48**	**49**	**50**
D	A	B	C	C	D	A	C	A	B

9. Active & Passive Voice

A sentence in active voice focuses on the person or thing doing the action. A sentence in passive voice focuses on the person or thing affected by the action. e.g.,

The idol was built. (Active voice)

Someone built the idol. (Passive voice)

Transformation of voice

- Voice and Tense are closely associated with each other.
- Tense plays an important role while transforming the voice.

On the basis of following points, voice can be transformed from active to passive voice.

THE PRESENT INDEFINITE TENSE

Active voice: Subject + V_1 + Object

Passive voice: Subject + is, am, are + V_3 + by + Object

1. **Active voice:** He sings sweet songs.
   Passive voice: Sweet songs are sung by him.
2. **Active voice:** She does not cause any hindrance in my work.
   Passive voice: No hindrance in my work is caused by her.
3. **Active voice:** Do they love their country?
   Passive voice: Is their country loved by them?

THE PRESENT CONTINUOUS TENSE

Active voice: Subject + is/am/are + V_1 + ing + Object.

Passive voice: Subject + is/am/are + being + V_3 + by + Object.

1. **Active voice:** She is cooking food.
   Passive voice: Food is being cooked by her.
2. **Active voice:** Rita is not knitting a sweater.
   Passive voice: A sweater is not being knitted by Rita.
3. **Active voice:** Is Meena baking a cake?
   Passive voice: Is a cake being baked by Meena?

THE PRESENT PERFECT TENSE

Active voice: Subject + has/have + V_3 + Object.

Passive voice: Subject + has/have + been + V_3 + by + Object.

1. **Active voice:** I have written an essay.
   Passive voice: An essay has been written by me.
2. **Active voice:** They have not whitewashed the fence.
   Passive voice: The fence has not been whitewashed by them.
3. **Active voice:** Have you cut the cake?
   Passive voice: Has the cake been cut by you?

THE PAST INDEFINITE TENSE

Active voice: Subject + V_2 + Object

Passive voice: Subject + was/were + V_3 + by + Object

1. **Active voice:** He composed a new song.
   Passive voice: A new song was composed by him.
2. **Active voice:** He did not operate the computer.

Passive voice: The computer was not operated by him.

3. **Active voice:** Did she catch a big fish?

   Passive voice: Was a big fish caught by her?

THE PAST CONTINUOUS TENSE

Active voice: Subject + was/were + V_1 + ing + Object

Passive voice: Subject + was/were + being + V_3 + by + Object

1. **Active voice:** The farmers were ploughing the fields.

   Passive voice: The fields were being ploughed by the farmers.

2. **Active voice:** He was not administering the new drug to the patient.

   Passive voice: The new drug was not being administered to the patient by him.

3. **Active voice:** Was she sewing a dress?

   Passive voice: Was a dress being sewn by her?

THE PAST PERFECT TENSE

Active voice: Subject + had + V_3 + Object.

Passive voice: Subject + had + been + V_3 + by + Object

1. **Active voice:** He had issued me an import licence.

   Passive voice: I had been issued an import licence.

2. **Active voice:** We had not visited the Taj.

   Passive voice: The Taj had not been visited by us.

3. **Active voice:** Who had taught you English?

   Passive voice: By whom had you been taught English?

THE FUTURE INDEFINITE TENSE

Active voice: Subject + will/shall + V_1 + Object.

Passive voice: Subject + will/shall + be + V_3 + by + Object.

1. **Active voice:** He will remove the dust from the shelf.

   Passive voice: The dust from the shelf will be removed by him.

2. **Active voice:** He will not open the main gate.

   Passive voice: The main gate will not be opened by him.

3. **Active voice:** Will you help us?

   Passive voice: Shall we be helped by you?

THE FUTURE PERFECT TENSE

Active voice: Subject + will/shall + have + V_3 + Object.

Passive voice: Subject + will/shall + have + been + V_3 + by + Object.

1. **Active voice:** They will have sold their house by then.

   Passive voice: Their house will have been sold by them by then.

2. **Active voice:** He will not have informed the police about it.

   Passive voice: The police will not have been informed about it by him.

3. **Active voice:** Will they have accepted the deal?

   Passive voice: Will the deal have been accepted by them?

IMPERATIVE SENTENCES

1. **Active voice:** Open the window.

   Passive voice: You are ordered to open the window.

   Or

   Let the window be opened.

2. **Active voice:** Please/kindly open the window.

Passive voice: You are requested to open the window.

3. **Active voice:** Never make a noise.

Passive voice: A noise should never be made.

INFINITIVES

1. **Active voice:** It is time to open the shop.

Passive voice: It is time for the shop to be opened.

2. **Active voice:** He begged the officer to forgive him.

Passive voice: He begged the officer to be forgiven.

3. **Active voice:** He has to break the door.

Passive voice: The door has to be broken by him.

PREPOSITIONAL VERB

1. **Active voice:** She laughed at the beggar.

Passive voice: The beggar was laughed at by her.

2. **Active voice:** He listened to the news.

Passive voice: The news was listened to by him.

3. **Active voice:** They called in the doctor.

Passive voice: The doctor was called in by them.

DOUBLE OBJECT

1. **Active voice:** He gave me a pen.

Passive voice: A pen was given to me by him.

Or

I was given a pen by him.

2. **Active voice:** She told us a story.

Passive voice: A story was told (to) us by her.

Or

We were told a story by her.

USE OF PREPOSITION OTHER THAN 'BY'

1. **Active voice:** The jug contains juice.

Passive voice: Juice is contained in the jug.

2. **Active voice:** The audience thronged the hall.

Passive voice: The hall was thronged with the audience.

3. **Active voice:** I know her.

Passive voice: She is known to me.

QUASI PASSIVE VERBS

1. **Active voice:** Quinine tastes bitter.

Passive voice: Quinine is bitter when tasted.

Or

Quinine is bitter when it is tasted.

2. **Active voice:** Sugar is sweet (to taste).

Passive voice: Sugar is sweet when tasted.

Or

Sugar is sweet when it is tasted.

IMPLIED SENTENCES

1. **Active voice:** The driver drove the bus.

Passive voice: The bus was driven.

2. **Active voice:** Someone read the news.

Passive voice: The news was read.

3. **Active voice:** They say work is worship.

Passive voice: It is said that work is worship.

MULTIPLE CHOICE QUESTIONS

Directions (Qs. 1 to 20): *In the following questions, a sentence has been given in Active/Passive Voice. Out of the four alternatives suggested, select the one that Best Expresses the same sentence in Passive/Active Voice.*

1. Circumstances will obligs me to go.
A. I will oblige the circumstances and go.
B. I shall be obliged to go by the circumstances.
C. Under the circumstances, I should go.
D. I shall be obliged by the circumstances to go.

2. We waste much time on trifles.
A. Much time was wasted on trifles.
B. Much time will be wasted on trifles.
C. Much time is wasted by us on trifles.
D. Much time is wasted on trifles.

3. Mohan gave the beggar an old shirt.
A. An old shirt was given to Mohan by the beggar.
B. An old shirt was given to the beggar by Mohan
C. The begger was gave an old shirt by Mohan.
D. An old shirt was gave to the beggar by Mohan.

4. They have made him a king.
A. A king has been made by him.
B. He was made a king by them.
C. They have been made kings by him.
D. He has been made a king by them.

5. Who taught you English?
A. By whom English was taught to you?
B. By whom you were taught English?
C. By whom was English taught to you?
D. By whom are you taught English?

6. Was he knocking at the door?
A. Was the door being knocked at by him?
B. Was the door being knocked by him?
C. Was the door knocked by him?
D. Was the door knocking at him?

7. What was Rani doing?
A. What was done by Rani?
B. What was Rani being done?
C. What was being done by Rani?
D. What was being doing Rani?

8. Why were you wasting your Time?
A. Why was your time being wasted?
B. Why was your time being wasted by you?
C. Why was your time wasted by you?
D. Why was your time wasted?

9. She has laid out a small garden.
A. A small garden has been laid by her.
B. A small garden has laid her.
C. A small garden being laid by her.
D. A small garden has been laid out by her.

10. She had already solved all the sums.
A. All the sums had already been solved by her.
B. All the sums have already been solved by her.
C. All the sums have been solved by her.
D. All the sums are solved by her.

11. He will have posted the letter.
A. The letter has been posted by him.
B. The letter will be posted by him.
C. The letter will have been posted by him.
D. The letter is posted by him.

12. They will have sold all the books by 4 P.M.
A. All the books will be sold by 4 P.M.
B. All the books will have been sold by 4 P.M.
C. All the books were being sold by 4 P.M.
D. All the books must be sold by 4 P.M.

13. Do you speak English?
A. Is English spoken by you?
B. Does English spoken by you?
C. Is English being spoken by you?
D. Does English being spoken by you?

14. Had they seen me before?
A. Had myself been seen by them before?
B. Had me being seen by them before?
C. Had I been seen by them before?
D. Had I being seen by them before?

15. May I take this pen?
A. May this pen will be taken by me?
B. May this pen shall be taken by me?
C. May this pen should be taken by me?
D. May this pen be taken by me?

16. Can we send it by air?
A. Can this be sent by air?
B. Can it be sent by air?
C. Can it go by air?
D. Can it be send by air?

17. Who wrote this book?
A. By whom was this book written?
B. By whom is this book written?
C. By whom was this book being written?
D. By whom is this book being written?

18. What did you buy?
A. What is bought by you?
B. What is being bought by you?
C. What was bought by you?
D. What was being bought by you?

19. Whom do you want?
A. Who is wanted by you?
B. Who is being wanted by you?
C. You are wanted by whom?
D. You are being wanted by whom?

20. When will you raise this question?
A. When this question will be raised by you?
B. When will this question be raised by you?
C. When this question is being raised by you?
D. When is this question being raised by you?

Directions (Qs. 21 to 35): *In each of the following questions, a sentence is given in active voice. Below it are given four alternatives suggesting the passive voice form of the above sentence. Choose the correct alternative.*

21. Who did this?
A. This was done by whom?
B. By whom was this done?
C. Who has done this?
D. By whom this was done?

22. One should keep ones promises.
A. Promises should be kept.
B. Ones promises should be kept by one.
C. Promises must be kept.
D. Ones promises one should keep.

23. Give the order.
A. Order given.
B. Order be given.
C. Let the order be given.
D. Order may be given by you.

24. You will have to do it.
A. It will be done by you.
B. It will have to be done by you.
C. It has to be done by you.
D. It would have to be done by you.

25. Keep to the left.
A. You are ordered to keep to the left.
B. You ought to keep to the left.
C. You are advised to keep to the left.
D. You must keep to the left.

26. They will arrange a party.
A. A party will have to be arranged by them.
B. A party they will have to arrange.
C. A party will be arranged by them.
D. A party by them will be arranged.

27. Someone has picked my pocket.
A. My pocket is picked.
B. My pocket has picked.
C. My pocket has been picked.
D. My pocket was picked.

28. He kept me waiting.
A. I kept waiting for him.
B. I kept waiting by him.
C. I was waiting for him.
D. I was kept waiting by him.

29. Why do you tell a lie?
A. Why is a lie told by you?
B. Why is told a lie by you?
C. Why is told by you a lie?
D. Why has a lie been told by you?

30. I have written a letter.
A. A letter is written by me.
B. A letter has been written by me.
C. A letter was written by me.
D. A letter had been written by me.

31. They will have helped you.
A. You will have helped by them.
B. You will have been helped by them.
C. You will be helped by them.
D. You will be helped by them.

32. Open the door.
A. Door may be opened.
B. Let the door be open.
C. Let the door be opened.
D. Door be opened.

33. I am reading a book.
A. A book is read by me.
B. A book is being read by me.
C. A book has been read by me.
D. A book in been read by me.

34. Why did your brother write such a letter?
A. Why your brother wrote such a letter?
B. Why was by brother written such a letter?
C. Why was such a letter written by your brother?
D. Why was written such a letter by your brother?

35. Did you run a great risk?
A. Was a great risk run by you?
B. Was run a great risk by you?
C. Was by you run a great risk?
D. Had you run a great risk?

Directions (Qs. 36 to 50): *In each of the following questions, a sentence is given in passive voice. Below it are given four alternatives suggesting the active voice form of the above sentence. Choose the correct alternative.*

36. He was made king.
A. He became king.
B. They made him king.
C. They had made him king.
D. He has been made king.

37. Good news is expected by us.
A. We are expecting good news.
B. We have been expecting good news.
C. We had expected good news.
D. We expect good news.

38. The child must be looked after.
A. The child you must look after.
B. You must look after the child.
C. You must look the child after.
D. You may look after the child.

39. What is wanted by you?
A. What you want?
B. What did you want?
C. What do you want?
D. What you do want?

40. Your father is known to me.
A. I am known to your father.
B. I know your father.
C. I have known your father.
D. I knew your father.

41. She may be told the story by you.
A. The story may be told by you to her.
B. You may tell the story to her.
C. You may tell her the story.
D. You may tell to her the story.

42. Duty ought to be done.
A. Let duty be done.
B. One ougth to do one's duty.
C. One should do his duty.
D. Do you duty.

43. Is English spoken by you?
A. Did you speak English?
B. Do you speak English?
C. Have you spoken English?
D. Do you know how to speak English?

44. Gold coins are contained in this box.
A. This box contains gold coins.
B. This box has contained gold coins.
C. This box is containing gold coins
D. This box has gold coins.

45. Character is revealed by manners.
A. Manners revealed character.
B. Manners reveal character.
C. Manners have revealed character.
D. Manners do reveal character.

46. The gate was opened by the peon.
A. The peon opened the gate.
B. The peon had opened the gate.
C. The peon has opened the gate.
D. The peon is open the gate.

47. He will be conquered by me.
A. I will conquer him.
B. I will conquer he.
C. I will have conquered him.
D. I will be conquered him.

48. He was praised by his teacher.
A. His teacher praise him.
B. His teacher praises him.
C. His teacher has praised him.
D. His teacher was praised him.

49. A song was sung by her.
A. She sings a song.
B. She sang a song.
C. She sung a song.
D. She has sung a song.

50. She will blamed.
A. You will blame her.
B. I will blame her.
C. Everybody will blame her.
D. She will blame her.

ANSWERS

1	**2**	**3**	**4**	**5**	**6**	**7**	**8**	**9**	**10**
D	C	B	D	C	A	C	B	D	A
11	**12**	**13**	**14**	**15**	**16**	**17**	**18**	**19**	**20**
C	B	A	C	D	B	A	C	A	B
21	**22**	**23**	**24**	**25**	**26**	**27**	**28**	**29**	**30**
B	A	C	B	C	C	C	D	A	B
31	**32**	**33**	**34**	**35**	**36**	**37**	**38**	**39**	**40**
B	C	B	C	A	B	D	B	C	B
41	**42**	**43**	**44**	**45**	**46**	**47**	**48**	**49**	**50**
C	B	B	A	B	A	A	B	B	C

10. Ordering of Words in a Sentence

Different words form a sentence but they convey their true meaning when arranged in proper order. Try and practise this skill in this exercise.

MULTIPLE CHOICE QUESTIONS

Directions (Qs. 1 to 50): *In each question below, there is a sentence of which some parts have been jumbled up. Re-arrange these parts which are labelled P, Q, R and S to produce the correct sentence. Choose the proper sequence.*

1. He has
P: while has in a reverie
Q: found the book
R: at the bus-stop
S: he lost
The proper sequence should be:
A. Q R S P B. P R Q S
C. Q S R P D. P Q S R

2. Then the women
P: lamenting their evil desire
Q: that had brought
R: wept loudly
S: this sorrow upon them
The proper sequence should be:
A. R P Q S B. R Q P S
C. P Q S R D. P R Q S

3. It is easy to excuse
P: but it is hard
Q: in a boy of fourteen
R: the mischief of early childhood
S: to tolerate even unavoidable faults
The proper sequence should be:
A. R P Q S B. Q R S P
C. Q R P S D. R P S Q

4. I don't remember
P: I saw a man dying in front of a hospital
Q: but when I left Lucknow in 1984
R: hit apparently by a fast moving car
S: the exact date
The proper sequence should be:
A. S Q R P B. S Q P R
C. Q R P S D. S P R Q

5. Since the beginning of history
P: have managed to catch
Q: the Eskimos and Red Indians
R: by a very difficult method
S: a few specimens of this acquatic mammal
The proper sequence should be:
A. Q P R S B. S Q P R
C. S Q R P D. Q P S R

6. I saw that
P: but seeing my host in this mood
Q: I deemed it proper to take leave
R: as I had frequently done before
S: it had been my intention to pass the night there
The proper sequence should be:
A. Q P S R B. Q R P S
C. S P Q R D. S R P Q

7. It was to be
P: before their school examination
Q: which was due to start
R: the last expedition
S: in a month's time

The proper sequence should be:
A. S R Q P B. R Q S P
C. R P Q S D. S P R Q

8. They felt safer
P: to watch the mountain
Q: of more than five miles
R: as they settled down
S: from a distance
The proper sequence should be:
A. R P S Q B. R S Q P
C. P Q S R D. P R S Q

9. If you need help
P: promptly and politely
Q: ask for attendants
R: to help our customers
S: who have instructions
The proper sequence should be:
A. S Q P R B. Q P S R
C. Q S R P D. S Q R P

10. He was so kind and generous that
P: he not only
Q: made others do so
R: but also
S: helped them himself
The proper sequence should be:
A. P S R Q B. S P Q R
C. P R S Q D. Q P R S

11. People
P: at his dispensary
Q: went to him
R: of all professions
S: for medicine and treatment
The proper sequence should be:
A. Q P R S B. R P Q S
C. R Q S P D. Q R P S

12. When it began to rain suddenly on the first of January
P: to celebrate the new year
Q: we ran for shelter
R: to the neighbouring house
S: where many people had gathered
The proper sequence should be:
A. Q R P S B. P S Q R
C. P R S Q D. Q R S P

13. The master
P: who was very loyal to him
Q: punished the servant
R: without giving any valid reason
S: when he left the work unfinished
The proper sequence should be:
A. R Q P S B. R Q S P
C. Q P S R D. Q R P S

14. The appearance
P: this dinosaurs were at their peak
Q: of the first mammals on the earth
R: at the time when
S: went almost unnoticed
The proper sequence should be:
A. S R P Q B. Q S R P
C. Q R P S D. R P Q S

15. It is easier
P: to venture into space
Q: for men
R: beneath their feet
S: than to explore
The proper sequence should be:
A. Q R P S B. Q P S R
C. P S R Q D. P Q S R

16. It is very easy
P: a great deal more than one realises
Q: may mean
R: that a phrase that one does not quite understand
S: to persuade oneself
The proper sequence should be:
A. R S Q P B. S P Q R
C. S R Q P D. R Q P S

17. The national unity of a free people
P: to make it impracticable
Q: for there to be an arbitrary administration
R: depends upon a sufficiently even balance of political power
S: against a revolutionary opposition that is irreconciably opposed to it.
The proper sequence should be:
A. Q R P S B. Q R S P
C. R P Q S D. R S P Q

18. He told us that
P: and enjoyed it immensely
Q: in a prose translation
R: he had read Milton
S: which he had borrowed from his teacher
The proper sequence should be:
A. R S Q P B. Q R P S
C. R Q S P D. R Q P S

19. This time
P: exactly what he had been told
Q: the young man did
R: beyond his dreams
S: and the plan succeeded
The proper sequence should be:
A. Q P R S B. Q P S R
C. P Q S R D. Q S R P

20. As a disease
P: and breaks up marriages
Q: accidents and suicides
R: alcoholism leads to
S: affecting all ages
The proper sequence should be:
A. S R P Q B. R P S Q
C. S R Q P D. R Q P S

21. This majestic mahogany table
P: belongs to an old prince
Q: which has one leg missing
R: who is no impoverished
S: but not without some pride
The proper sequence should be:
A. P Q S R B. Q R S P
C. P R S Q D. Q P R S

22. We have to
P: as we see it
Q: speak the truth
R: there is falsehood and darkness
S: even if all around us
The proper sequence should be:
A. R Q S P B. Q R P S
C. R S Q P D. Q P S R

23. He sat
P: through the Town Hall Park
Q: which flanked a path running
R: under the boughs
S: of a spreading tamarind tree
The proper sequence should be:
A. P Q S R B. R S Q P
C. R S P Q D. P R S Q

24. We went
P: along the railway line
Q: and had a right to
R: where other people were not allowed to go
S: but daddy belonged to the railway
The proper sequence should be:
A. R P Q S B. P R S Q
C. R S Q P D. P R Q S

25. In the darkness
P: the long, narrow beard
Q: was clearly visible with
R: the tall stooping figure of the doctor
S: and the aquiline nose
The proper sequence should be:
A. R Q P S B. P S Q R
C. R S Q P D. Q P R S

26. Little
P: that he had been let down
Q: stood by all these years
R: did he realise
S: by a colleague whom he had
The proper sequence should be:
A. R P S Q B. R S Q P
C. Q S R P D. Q S P R

27. There was
P: needed for it everyday life
Q: a time when each family
R: for itself most of the things it
S: actually produced
The proper sequence should be:
A. Q R S P B. R Q P S
C. R S P Q D. Q S R P

28. He thought that
P: he would be able to make at least three or four trips daily to the town and back
Q: if he could get Alagu's bullock
R: and thus swell his profits
S: at a very cheap price
The proper sequence should be:
A. Q P S R B. Q P R S
C. Q S P R D. P S Q R

29. Then
P: it struck me
Q: of course
R: suitable it was
S: how eminently
The proper sequence should be:
A. S P Q R B. Q S R P
C. P S R Q D. Q P S R

30. The grocer
P: did not listen to the protests of the customer
Q: who was in the habit of weighing less
R: whom he had cheated
S: with great audacity

The proper sequence should be:
A. P R S Q B. Q S P R
C. Q P R S D. P Q S R

31. Walking along the road
P: before their enchanted mates
Q: he saw
R: from the orchard to his residence
S: peacocks dancing
The proper sequence should be:
A. R P Q S B. Q S R P
C. Q S P R D. R Q S P

32. Though he dialled frequently
P: on telephone
Q: my brother could not contact me
R: and had left no information
S: as I had gone out of office
The proper sequence should be:
A. Q P R S B. S Q R P
C. Q P S R D. S P Q R

33. He said,
P: "here is the cat
Q: throughout the night
R: which had been playing havoc with things
S: that ate the rat"
The proper sequence should be:
A. P S Q R B. P S R Q
C. Q P R S D. Q R P S

34. By this time
P: at the railway station
Q: reported mass looting
R: reports of violence were flooding in
S: while police dispatches
The proper sequence should be:
A. R S P Q B. S P R Q
C. S Q R P D. R S Q P

35. It would
P: appear from his statement
Q: about the policy of the management
R: in dealing with the strike
S: that he was quite in the dark
The proper sequence should be:
A. R P S Q B. P S Q R
C. R Q P S D. P R Q S

36. It is not, therefore
P: that I pay a tribute
Q: to conductors as a class
R: with any feeling of unfriendliness
S: to a particular member of that class
The proper sequence should be:
A. P Q R S B. R Q P S
C. R S P Q D. P S R Q

37. The impact
P: is to be seen
Q: in the diverse changes in consumer habits
R: of technological and industrial development
S: in cities, towns and even in village conglomerates
The proper sequence should be:
A. P S Q R B. R P Q S
C. P Q R S D. R S P Q

38. During hibernation
P: they have lost a good deal of weight
Q: of course the animals consume
R: and when they awake again
S: the fats accumulated in the summer
The proper sequence should be:
A. R Q S P B. S Q P R
C. P Q R S D. Q S R P

39. P: We must read
Q: if we want to absorb the fruits of great literature
R: but with concentration
S: them not as we do cricket stories
The proper sequence should be:
A. Q P S R B. P S Q R
C. P R S Q D. P R Q S

40. Work is the one thing
P: and without it
Q: that is necessary
R: to keep the world going
S: we should all die
The proper sequence should be:
A. Q P S R B. R P Q S
C. S R P Q D. Q R P S

41. I read an advertisement that said
P: posh, airconditioned
Q: gentlemen of taste
R: are available for
S: fully furnished rooms
The proper sequence should be:
A. P Q R S B. P S R Q
C. P S Q R D. S R P Q

42. It has been established that
P: Einstein was
Q: although a great scientist
R: weak in arithmetic
S: right from his school days

The proper sequence should be:
A. S R P Q B. Q P R S
C. Q P S R D. R Q P S

43. I was
P: and stay for a few days in Delhi
Q: when my father told me
R: very excited
S: that I could go with him
The proper sequence should be:
A. P Q R S B. R Q S P
C. Q R S P D. S P Q R

44. All such students
P: get success
Q: who are honest and hardworking
R: and recognition
S: in very walk of life
The proper sequence should be:
A. S P R Q B. P R Q S
C. Q P R S D. P S R Q

45. He knew that
P: and then to save himself
Q: was to save all the lives
R: entrusted to his care
S: the duty of a captain
The proper sequence should be:
A. P Q R S B. S Q R P
C. S P R Q D. Q S R P

46. Women,
P: till the other day
Q: who were content being housewives
R: about spending their time cooking
S: now sound apologetic
The proper sequence should be:
A. P Q R S B. R S P Q
C. Q P S R D. R Q P S

47. Jawaharlal Nehru
P: under the Cabinet Mission Scheme
Q: was the first to articulate
R: long before such an assembly was set up
S: the idea of a Constituent Assembly
The proper sequence should be:
A. S R P Q B. R P Q S
C. P Q S R D. Q S R P

48. Of many artists
P: those who impressed me the most
Q: I was as a child
R: but those with unique personalities off stage
S: were not always the successful ones
The proper sequence should be:
A. S R Q P B. Q R S P
C. R S P Q D. Q P S R

49. India is
P: a cultural unity amidst diversity
Q: a geographical and economic unity
R: a bundle of contradictions
S: held together by strong but invisible threads
The proper sequence should be:
A. Q P R S B. P Q R S
C. R S P Q D. S Q P R

50. I enclose
P: and the postage
Q: a postal order
R: the price of the books
S: which will cover
The proper sequence should be:
A. R P S Q B. Q S P R
C. Q S R P D. Q P S R

ANSWERS

1	2	3	4	5	6	7	8	9	10
C	A	D	B	D	D	C	A	C	A
11	**12**	**13**	**14**	**15**	**16**	**17**	**18**	**19**	**20**
C	D	C	C	B	B	D	C	B	C
21	**22**	**23**	**24**	**25**	**26**	**27**	**28**	**29**	**30**
D	D	B	B	A	A	D	C	C	C
31	**32**	**33**	**34**	**35**	**36**	**37**	**38**	**39**	**40**
D	C	B	C	B	C	B	D	A	D
41	**42**	**43**	**44**	**45**	**46**	**47**	**48**	**49**	**50**
B	B	B	C	B	C	D	D	A	C

11. Ordering of Sentences

Words form a sentence and different sentences form a paragraph but without properly arranging sentences in it the true meaning of it will be spoiled. Try and practise this skill in this exercise.

MULTIPLE CHOICE QUESTIONS

Directions (Qs. 1 to 50): *In questions below, each passage consists of six sentences. The first and the sixth sentences are given in the beginning. The middle four sentences in each have been removed and jumbled up. These are labelled P, Q, R and S. Find out the proper order for the four sentences.*

1. S_1: Since the sixties there has been an increasing interest in human neurophysiology, which deals with the neural bases of mental activity and behaviour.

S_6: So far the journal has published a mixture of articles including reports and investigations.

P : It has format which is very similar to that of *Brain and Language,* a sister journal.

Q : Since then, a number of journals devoted entirely to this area of research have appeared.

R : Before the 1960's when this field was the concern of a small number of investigators, research articles were scattered in various neurological journals.

S : *Brain and Cognition* is one such journal.

The proper sequence should be:

A. R Q S P B. Q R S P
C. Q S P R D. R S P Q

2. S_1: She said on the phone that she would report for duty next day.

S_6: Eventually we reported to the police.

P : We waited for a few days, then we decided to go to her place.

Q : But she did not.

R : We found it locked.

S : Even after that we waited for her for quite a few days.

The proper sequence should be:

A. P R S Q B. Q P S R
C. Q P R S D. S Q P R

3. S_1: A force of attraction exists between everybody in the universe.

S_6: The greater the mass, the greater is the earth's force of attraction on it—we call this force of attraction gravity.

P : Normally it is very small but when one of the bodies is a planet, like the earth, the force is considerable.

Q : It has been investigated by many scientists including Galileo and Newton.

R : Everything on or near the surface of the earth is attracted by the mass of the earth.

S : This gravitational force depends on the mass of the bodies involved.

The proper sequence should be:

A. P R Q S B. P R S Q
C. Q S R P D. Q S P R

4. S_1: Metals are today being replaced by polymers in many applications.

S_6: Many Indian Institutes of Science and Technology run special programmes on polymer science.

P : Above all, they are cheaper and easier to process, making them a viable alternative to metals.

Q : Polymers are essentially long chains of hydrocarbon molecules.

R : Today polymers as strong as metals have been developed.

S : These have replaced the traditional chromium-plated metallic bumpers in cars.

The proper sequence should be:

A. Q R S P　　B. R S Q P
C. R Q S P　　D. Q R P S

5. S_1: Biological evolution has not fitted man to any specific environment.

S_6: That brilliant sequence of cultural peaks can most appropriately be termed the ascent of Man.

P : It is by no means a biological evolution, but it is a cultural one.

Q : His imagination, his reason, his emotional subtlety and toughness, make it possible for him not to accept the environment but to change it.

R : And that series of inventions by which man from age to age has reshaped his environment is a different kind of evolution.

S : Among the multitude of animals which scamper, fly, burrow and swim around us, he is the only one who is not locked into his environment.

The proper sequence should be:

A. Q P R S　　B. S R Q P
C. Q R S P　　D. S Q R P

6. S_1: Growing up means not only getting larger, but also using our senses and our brains to become more aware of the things around us.

S_6: In other words, we must develop and use our ability to reason, because the destruction or the preservation of the places in which we live depends on us.

P : Not only does he have a memory but he is able to think and reason.

Q : In this, man differs from all other animals.

R : Before we spray our roadside plants or turn sewage into our rivers, we should pause to think what the results of our actions are likely to be.

S : That is to say, he is able to plan what he is going to do in the light of his experience before he does it.

The proper sequence should be:

A. Q R S P　　B. S P Q R
C. S P R Q　　D. Q P S R

7. S_1: It is regrettable that there is widespread corruption in the country at all levels.

S_6: This is indeed a tragedy of great magnitude.

P : So there is hardly anything that the government can do about it now.

Q : And there are graft and other malpractices too.

R : The impression that corruption is a universal phenomenon persists and the people do not cooperate in checking this evil.

S : Recently several offenders were brought to book, but they were not given deterrent punishment.

The proper sequence should be:

A. Q S R P　　B. S Q R P
C. R S Q P　　D. P Q S R

8. S_1: Smoke oozed up between the planks.

S_6: Most people bore the shock bravely.

P : Passengers were told to be ready to quit the ship.

Q : The rising gale fanned the smouldering fire.

R : Everyone now knew there was a fire on board.

S : Flames broke out here and there.

The proper sequence should be:

A. S R Q P　　B. Q P S R
C. R S P Q　　D. Q S R P

9. S_1: It was a dark moonless night.

S_6: They all seemed to him to be poor and ordinary—mere childish words.

P : He turned over the pages, reading passages here and there.

Q : He heard them on the floor.

R : The poet took down his books of poems from his shelves.

S : Some of them contained his earliest writings which he had almost forgotten.

The proper sequence should be:

A. R P Q S B. R Q S P
C. R S P Q D. R P S Q

10. S_1: A noise started above their heads.

S_6: Nearly two hundred lives were lost on the fateful day.

P : But people did not take it seriously.

Q : That was to show everyone that there was something wrong.

R : It was a dangerous thing to do.

S : For, within minutes the ship began to sink.

The proper sequence should be:

A. P Q S R B. P R Q S
C. Q P R S D. Q P S R

11. S_1: The cooperative system of doing business is a good way of encouraging ordinary workers to work hard.

S_6: The main object is to maintain the interest of every member of the society and to ensure that the members participate actively in the projects of the society.

P : If the society is to be well run, it is necessary to prevent insincere officials being elected to the committee which is solely responsible for the running of the business.

Q : They get this from experienced and professional workers who are not only familiar with the cooperative system, but also with efficient methods of doing business.

R : To a large extent, many cooperative societies need advice and guidance.

S : The capital necessary to start a business venture is obtained by the workers' contributions.

The proper sequence should be:

A. S Q P R B. P Q S R
C. S R Q P D. P S R Q

12. S_1: American private lives may seem shallow.

S_6: This would not happen in China, he said.

P : Students would walk away with books they had not paid for.

Q : A Chinese journalist commented on a curious institution: the library.

R : Their public morality, however, impressed visitors.

S : But in general they returned them.

The proper sequence should be:

A. P S Q R B. Q P S R
C. R Q P S D. R P S Q

13. S_1: The *Bhagavadgita* recognises the nature of man and the needs of man.

S_6: A man who does not harmonise them, is not truly human.

P : All these three aspects constitute the nature of man.

Q : It shows how the human being is a rational one, an ethical one and a spiritual one.

R : More than all, it must be a spiritual experience.

S : Nothing can give him fulfilment unless it satisfies his reason, his ethical conscience.

The proper sequence should be:

A. P S R Q B. R S P Q
C. Q P S R D. P S Q R

14. S_1: I usually sleep quite well in the train, but this time I slept only a little.

S_6: It was shut all night, as usual.

P : Most people wanted it shut and I wanted it open.

Q : As usual, I got angry about the window.

R : The quarrel left me completely upset.

S : There were too many people and too much luggage all around.

The proper sequence should be:

A. R S Q P B. S Q P R
C. S Q R P D. R S P Q

15. S_1: For decades, American society has been called a melting pot.

S_6: In recent years, such differences—accentuated by the arrival of immigrants from Asia and other parts of the world in the United States—have become something to celebrate and to nurture.

P : Differences remained—in appearance, mannerisms, customs, speech, religion and more.

Q : The term has long been a cliche, and a half-truth.

R : But homogenisation was never achieved.

S : Yes, immigrants from diverse cultures and traditions did cast off vestiges of their native lands and become almost imperceptibly woven into the American fabric.

The proper sequence should be:

A. Q R S P B. S Q R P

C. S Q P R D. Q S R P

16. S_1: While talking to a group, one should feel self-confident and courageous.

S_6: Any man can develop his capacity if he has the desire to do so.

P : Nor is it a gift bestowed by Providence on only a few.

Q : One should also learn how to think calmly and clearly.

R : It is like the ability to play golf.

S : It is not as difficult as most men imagine.

The proper sequence should be:

A. S Q P R B. Q S P R

C. Q R S P D. R S Q P

17. S_1: In 1934, William Golding published a small volume of poems.

S_6: *But Lord of the Flies* which came out in 1954 was welcomed as "a most absorbing and instructive tale".

P : During the World War II (1939-45) he joined the Royal Navy and was present at the sinking of the *Bismarck.*

Q : He returned to teaching in 1945 and gave it up in 1962, and is now a full-time writer.

R : In 1939, he married and started teaching at Bishop Wordsworth's School in Salisbury

S : At first his novels were not accepted.

The proper sequence should be:

A. R P Q S B. R P S Q

C. S R P Q D. S Q P R

18. S_1: Our ancestors thought that anything which moved itself was alive.

S_6: Therefore some scientists think that life is just a very complicated mechanism.

P : The philosopher Descartes thought that both men and animals were machines.

Q : But a machine such as a motorcar or a steamship moves itself, and as soon as machines which moved themselves had been made, people asked, "Is man a machine?"

R : And before the days of machinery that was a good definition.

S : He also thought that the human machine was partly controlled by the soul action on a certain part of the brain, while animals had no souls

The proper sequence should be:

A. P R S Q B. R P Q S

C. P S Q R D. R Q P S

19. S_1: But how does a new word get into the dictionary?

S_6: He sorts them according to their grammatical function, and carefully writes a definition.

P : When a new dictionary is being edited, a lexicographer collects all the alphabetically arranged citation slips for a particular word.

Q : The dictionary makers notice it and make a note of it on a citation slip.

R : The moment a new word is coined, it usually enters the spoken language.

S : The word then passes from the realm of hearing to the realm of writing.

The proper sequence should be:

A. P Q R S B. P R S Q

C. R Q P S D. R S Q P

20. S_1: There is a touching story of Professor Hardy visiting Ramanujan as he lay desperately ill in hospital at Putney.

S_6: It is the lowest number that can be expressed in two different ways as the sum of two cubes."

P : 'No, Hardy, that is not a dull number in the very least.

Q : Hardy, who was a very shy man, could not find the words for his distress.

R : It was 1729.

S : The best he could do, as he got to the bedside was: "I say, Ramanujan, I thought the number of the taxi I came down in was a very dull number".

The proper sequence should be:

A. P R S Q B. Q S R P
C. Q S P R D. S Q R P

21. S_1: The heart is the pump of life.

S_6: All this was made possible by the invention of the heart-lung machine.

P : They have even succeeded in heart transplants.

Q : Nowadays surgeons are able to stop a patient's heart and carry out complicated operations.

R : A few years ago it was impossible to operate on a patient whose heart was not working properly.

S : If the heart stops we die in about five minutes.

The proper sequence should be:

A. S R Q P B. S P R Q
C. S Q P R D. S R P Q

22. S_1: On vacation in Tangier, Morocco, my friend and I sat down at a street cafe.

S_6: Finally a man walked over to me and whispered, "Hey buddy ..... this guy's your waiter and he wants your order."

P : At one point, he bent over with a big smile, showing me a single gold tooth and a dingy fez.

Q : Soon I felt the presence of someone standing alongside me.

R : But this one wouldn't budge.

S : We had been cautioned about beggars and were told to ignore them.

The proper sequence should be:

A. S Q R P B. S Q P R
C. Q S R P D. Q S P R

23. S_1: There is only one monkey we can thoroughly recommend as an indoor pet.

S_6: Finally, let me say that no other monkey has a better temper or more winning ways.

P : They quickly die from colds and coughs after the first winter fogs.

Q : It is the beautiful and intelligent Capuchin monkey.

R : The lively little Capuchins, however, may be left for years in an English house without the least danger to their health.

S : The Marmosets, it is true, are more beautiful than the Capuchins and just as pleasing, but they are too delicate for the English climate.

The proper sequence should be:

A. P Q R S B. Q R P S
C. Q S P R D. R P S Q

24. S_1: Hungry, with a population of about ten million, lies between Czechoslovakia to the north and Yugoslavia to the south.

S_6: The new industries derive mainly from agricultural production.

P : Here a great deal of grain is grown.

Q : In recent years, however, progress has been made also in the field of industrialisation.

R : Most of this country consists of an extremely fertile plain, through which the river Danube flows.

S : In addition to grain, the plain produces potatoes, sugar, wine and livestock.

The proper sequence should be:

A. Q R S P B. R P S Q
C. P R S Q D. R Q S P

25. S_1: Throughout history man has used energy from the sun.

S_6: This energy comes from inside atoms.

P : Today, when we burn wood or use electric current we are drawing on energy.

Q : However, we now have a new supply of energy.

R : All our ordinary life depends on the sun.

S : This has come from the sun.

The proper sequence should be:

A. S Q P R B. R Q P S

C. Q S R P D. P S R Q

26. S_1: In India marriages are usually arranged by parents.

S_6: She felt she was a modern girl and not a subject for bargaining

P : Sometimes girls and boys do not like the idea of arranged marriages.

Q : Most young people accept this state of affairs.

R : Shanta was like that.

S : They assume their parents can make good choices.

The proper sequence should be:

A. S P R Q B. P S R Q

C. Q S P R D. R Q P S

27. S_1: I had halted on the road.

S_6: I decided to watch him for a while and then go home.

P : As soon as I saw the elephant I knew I should not shoot him.

Q : It is a serious matter to shoot a working elephant.

R : I knew that his 'must' was already passing off.

S : The elephant was standing eighty yards from the road.

The proper sequence should be:

A. S P Q R B. P Q S R

C. R Q P S D. S R P Q

28. S_1: A man can be physically confined within stone walls.

S_6: No tyranny can intimidate a lover of liberty.

P : But his mind and spirit will still be free.

Q : Thus his freedom of action may be restricted.

R : His hopes and aspirations still remain with him.

S : Hence, he will be free spiritually if not physically.

The proper sequence should be:

A. P Q R S B. S R Q P

C. Q P R S D. Q P S R

29. S_1: The dictionary is the best friend for your task.

S_6: Soon you will realize that this is an exciting task

P : That may not be possible always.

Q : It is wise to look it up immediately.

R : Then it must be firmly written on the memory and traced at the first opportunity.

S : Never allow a strange word to pass unchallenged.

The proper sequence should be:

A. P Q R S B. S P Q R

C. Q R P S D. S Q P R

30. S_1: Far away in a little street there is a poor house.

S_6: His mother has nothing to give but water, so he is crying

P : Her face is thin and worn and her hands are coarse, pricked by a needle, for she is a seam-stress.

Q : One of the windows is open and through it I can see a poor woman.

R : He has a fever and a asking for oranges.

S : In a bed in a corner of the room her little boy is lying ill.

The proper sequence should be:

A. S R Q P B. P Q S R

C. Q P S R D. R S P Q

31. S_1: Calcutta unlike other cities, kept its trams.

S_6: The foundation stone was laid in 1972.

P : As a result, there is horrendous congestion.

Q : It was going to be the first in South Asia.

R : They run down the centre of the road.

S : To ease in the city decided to build an underground railway line.

The proper sequence should be:

A. P R S Q B. P S Q R

C. S Q R P D. R P S Q

32. S_1: We now know that oceans are very deep.

S_6: This reaches from India to the Antarctic.

P : For example, the Indian Ocean has a range called the Indian Ridge.

Q : Much of it is fairly flat.

R : However, there are great mountain ranges as well.

S : On average the bottom is two and a half to three and a half miles down.

The proper sequence should be:

A. S Q P R B. P Q S R

C. R S Q P D. Q P R S

33. S_1: As he passed beneath her he heard the swish of her wings.

S_6: The next moment he felt his wings spread outwards.

P : He was not falling head long now.

Q : Then monstrous terror seized him

R : But it only lasted a minute.

S : He could hear nothing.

The proper sequence should be:

A. P S Q R B. Q S P R

C. Q S R P D. P R Q S

34. S_1: When a satellite is launched, the rocket begins by going slowly upwards through the air.

S_6: Consequently, the rocket still does not become too hot.

P : However, the higher it goes, the less air it meets.

Q : As the rocket goes higher, it travels faster.

R : For the atmosphere becomes thinner.

S : As a result there is less friction.

The proper sequence should be:

A. Q P R S B. Q S P R

C. P Q R S D. P Q S R

35. S_1: Sunbirds are among the smallest of Indian birds.

S_6: Our common sunbirds are the purple sunbird, the glossy black species and purplerumped sunbird, the yellow and maroon species

P : Though they are functionally similar to the hummingbirds of the New World, they are totally unrelated.

Q : They do eat small insects too.

R : They are also some of the most brilliantly-coloured birds.

S : Sunbirds feed on nectar mostly and help in pollination.

The proper sequence should be:

A. S Q P R B. R P S Q

C. Q P R S D. P S R Q

36. S_1: Venice is a strange and beautiful city in the north of Italy.

S_6: This is because Venice has no streets.

P : There are about four hundred old stone bridges joining the island of Venice.

Q : In this city there are no motor cars, no horses and no buses.

R : These small islands are near one another.

S : It is not an island but a hundred and seventeen islands.

The proper sequence should be:

A. P Q R S B. P R Q S

C. S R P Q D. P Q S R

37. S_1: A ceiling on urban property.

S_6: Since their value would exceed the ceiling fixed by the Government.

P : No mill-owner could own factories or mills or plants.

Q : And mass circulation papers.

R : Would mean that.

S : No press magnate could own printing presses.

The proper sequence should be:

A. Q S R P B. R P S Q

C. S R P Q D. Q P S R

38. S_1: The weather-vane often tops a church spire, tower or high building.

S_6: The weather-vane can, however, give us some indication of the weather.

P : They are only wind-vanes.

Q : Neither alone can tell us what the weather will be.

R : They are designed to point to the direction from which the wind is coming.

S : Just as the barometer only tells us the pressure of the air, the weather-vane tells us the direction of the wind.

The proper sequence should be:

A. P Q R S B. P S R Q

C. P R S Q D. S P Q R

39. S_1: Most of the universities in the country are now facing financial crisis.

S_6: The Government should realise this before it is too late.

P : Cost benefit yardstick thus should not be applied in the case of the universities.

Q : The current state of affairs cannot be allowed to continue for long.

R : Universities cannot be equated with commercial enterprises.

S : Proper development of universities and colleges must be ensured

The proper sequence should be:

A. Q R P S B. Q S P R

C. Q R S P D. Q P R S

40. S_1: I keep on flapping my big ears all day.

S_6: Am I not a smart, intelligent elephant?

P : They also fear that I will flap them all away.

Q : But children wonder why I flap them so.

R : I flap them so to make sure they are safely there on either side of my head.

S : But I know what I am doing.

The proper sequence should be:

A. S R Q P B. Q P S R

C. Q P R S D. P S R Q

41. S_1: Some old people are oppressed by the fear of death

S_6: Gradually the river grows wider, the banks recede, the waters flow more quietly, and in the end, without any visible break, they become merged in the sea and painlessly lose their individual being.

P : An individual human existence should be like a river—small at first narrowly contained within its banks, and rushing passionately past boulders and over waterfalls.

Q : In the young there is a justification for this feeling

R : Young men who have reason to fear that they will be killed in battle may justifiably feel bitter in the thought that they have been cheated of the best thing that life has to offer.

S : but in the old man who has known human joys and sorrows, the fear of death is somewhat abject and ignoble, and the best way to overcome it is to make your interests gradually wider and more impersonal

The proper sequence should be:

A. R S Q P B. P Q S R

C. Q R S P D. Q P S R

42. S_1: Of the scholars who compose a university, some may be expected to devote an unbroken leisure to learning, their fellows having the advantage of their knowledge from their conversation, and the world perhaps from their writings.

S_6: There classes of persons, then, go to compose a university as we know it — the scholar, the scholar who is also a teacher, and those who come to be taught, the undergraduate

P : Others, however, will engage themselves to teach as well as to learn

Q : Those who come to be taught at a university have to provide evidence that they are not merely beginners; and not only do they have displayed before them the learning of their teachers, but they are offered a curriculum of study, to be followed by a test and the award of a degree

R : But here again, it is the special manner of the pedagogic enterprise which distinguishes a university

S : A place of learning without this could scarcely be called a university

The proper sequence should be:

A. S R P Q B. Q P S R

C. S P R Q D. R Q S P

43. S_1: A father, having offered to take the baby out in a perambulator, was tempted by the sunny morning to slip into a pub for a glass of beer.

S_6: She waited for him, anticipating the white face and quivering lips which would soon appear with the news that the baby had been stolen.

P : Indignant at her husband's behaviour, she decided to teach him a lesson.

Q : She wheeled away the pram.

R : A little later, his wife came by, where to her horror, she discovered her sleeping baby.

S : Leaving the pram outside, he disappeared inside the bar.

The proper sequence should be:

A. S R P Q B. R Q P S

C. S P Q R D. P Q S R

44. S_1: Urban problems differ from State to State and city to city.

S_6: There is no underground drainage system in most cities, and the narrow historical roads are already congested.

P : Most of the cities have neither water nor the required pipelines.

Q : The population in these cities has grown beyond the planners' imagination.

R : However, certain basic problems are common to all cities.

S : Only broad macro-planning was done for such cities, without envisaging the future growth, and this has failed to meet the requirements.

The proper sequence should be:

A. P Q S R B. Q P S R

C. R Q P S D. R S Q P

45. S_1: A gentleman who lived alone always had two plates placed on the table at dinner time.

S_6: In this way the cat showed her gratitude to her master.

P : One day just as he sat down to dine, the cat rushed into the room.

Q : One plate was for himself and the other was for his cat.

R : She dropped a mouse into her own plate and another into her master's plate.

S : He used to give the cat a piece of meat from his own plate.

The proper sequence should be:

A. Q S P R B. P S R Q

C. Q R S P D. R P Q S

46. S_1: I took cigarettes from my case.

S_6: Then he continued to draw on it.

P : But when the fit of coughing was over, he replaced it between his lips.

Q : I lit one of them and placed it between the lips.

R : Then with a feeble hand he removed the cigarette.

S : Slowly he took a pull at it and coughed violently.

The proper sequence should be:

A. P S Q R B. Q P S R

C. Q S R P D. S R P Q

47. S_1: Forecasting the weather has always been a difficult business.

S_6: He made his forecasts by watching flights of the birds or the way smoke rose from fire.

P : During a period of drought, streams and rivers dried up, the cattle died from thirst and the crops were ruined.

Q : Many different things affect the weather and we have to study them carefully to make an accurate forecast.

R : Ancient Egyptians had no need of this weather in the Nile valley hardly ever changes.

S : In early times, when there were no instruments, such as thermometer or the barometer, man looked for tell-tale signs in the sky.

The proper sequence should be:

A. P R Q S B. Q P R S

C. Q R P S D. S P Q R

48. S_1: The commonest form of forgetfulness, I suppose occurs in the matter of posting letters.

S_6: Weary of holding it in my hand, I then put it for safety into one of my pockets and forget all about it.

P : So common is it that I am always reluctant to trust a departing visitor to post an important letter.

Q : As for myself, anyone who asks me to post a letter is a poor judge of character.

R : Even if I carry the letter in my hand I am always past the first pillar-box before I remember that I ought to have posted it.

S : So little I rely on his memory that I put him on his oath before handing the letter to him.

The proper sequence should be:

A. P R Q S B. P S Q R
C. Q S P R D. R Q S P

49. S_1: Once upon a time there lived three young men in a certain town of Hindustan.

S_6: All of them set out in search of their foe called Death.

P : All the people of the neighbourhood were mortally afraid of them.

Q : They were so powerful that they could catch growling lions and tear them to pieces.

R : Someone told them that they would become immortal if they killed Death.

S : The young man believed themselves to be very good friends.

The proper sequence should be:

A. Q P R S B. S Q P R
C. R S Q P D. S R P Q

50. S_1: Duryodhana was a wicked prince.

S_6: This enraged Duryodhana so much that he began to think of removing Bhima from his way.

P : One day Bhima made Duryodhana fall from a tree from which Duryodhana was stealing fruits.

Q : He did not like that Pandavas should be loved and respected by the people of Hastinapur.

R : Duryodhana specially hated Bhima.

S : Among the Pandavas, Bhima was extraordinarily strong and powerful.

The proper sequence should be:

A. P S Q R B. Q P R S
C. Q S R P D. P S R Q

ANSWERS

1	2	3	4	5	6	7	8	9	10
A	C	D	A	C	D	A	A	D	C
11	**12**	**13**	**14**	**15**	**16**	**17**	**18**	**19**	**20**
A	B	B	B	B	B	A	C	A	B
21	**22**	**23**	**24**	**25**	**26**	**27**	**28**	**29**	**30**
A	C	B	B	D	C	B	A	D	C
31	**32**	**33**	**34**	**35**	**36**	**37**	**38**	**39**	**40**
D	A	C	A	A	C	B	D	A	B
41	**42**	**43**	**44**	**45**	**46**	**47**	**48**	**49**	**50**
C	B	A	D	A	C	B	B	B	C

12. COMPREHENSION

Comprehension is a very important part of General English paper. The questions on comprehension lay particular stress on understanding a given passage. You are required to read a passage and answer a few questions based on it. Various comprehension questions are set solely with the objectives named below:

1. To test your ability to detect the central idea or the focal point in the given passage.
2. To test your ability to understand and interpret the given passage.
3. To judge your capability to pick out the various arguments put forward by the writer for or against something.
4. To test your accuracy and richness of vocabulary.
5. To test your academic ability to understand the implied and the clearly and fully expressed ideas of the writer of the passage.
6. To test, occasionally, your power of appreciating critically the views contained in the given passage.

While answering comprehension questions, you must comply with the following important points:

1. First, read the whole passage attentively, carefully and quickly.
2. Read it for the second time, slowly but steadily.
3. Work out the probable meaning of new words, from the context in which they have been used.
4. Underline and look for transitional words and phrases as an aid to comprehension.
5. The process of elimination should be used while selecting the correct answer.
6. Your answers should be brief and to the point, where ever required.

MULTIPLE CHOICE QUESTIONS

Directions: *Read each of the following passages carefully and choose the best answer to each question out of the four alternatives and mark it in the Answer Sheet.*

PASSAGE–1

Laws of nature are not commands but statements of acts. The use of the word "law" in this context is rather unfortunate. It would be better to speak of uniformities of nature. This would do away with the elementary fallacy that a law implies a law-giver. If a piece of matter does not obey a law of nature it is not punished. On the contrary, we say that the law has been incorrectly started.

1. Laws of nature differ from man-made laws because

A. the former state facts of nature.
B. they must be obeyed.
C. they are natural.
D. unlike human laws, they are systematic.

2. If a piece of matter violates nature's law, it is not punished because

A. it is not binding to obey it.
B. there is no superior being to enforce the law of nature.
C. it cannot be punished.
D. it simply means that the facts have not been correctly stated by the law.

3. The author is not happy with the word 'law' because
   A. it connotes rigidity and harshness.
   B. it implies an agency which has made them.
   C. it does not convey the sense of nature's uniformity.
   D. it gives rise to false beliefs.
4. The laws of nature based on observation are
   A. conclusive about the nature of the universe.
   B. true and unfalsifiable
   C. figments of the observer's imagination.
   D. subject to change in the light of new facts.

PASSAGE–2

Male lions are rather reticent about expending their energy in hunting—more than three-quarters of kills are made by lionesses. Setting off at dusk on a hunt, the lionesses are in front, tensely scanning ahead, the cubs lag playfully behind and the males bring up the rear, walking slowly, their massive heads nodding with each step as if they were bored with the whole matter. But slothfulness may have survival value. With lionesses busy hunting, the males function as guards for the cubs, protecting them particularly from hyenas.

1. According to the passage, male lions generally do not go for hunting because
   A. they do not like it.
   B. they want lioness to get training.
   C. they wish to save their vigour for others things.
   D. they are very lazy.
2. Lionesses go for hunting
   A. all alone.
   B. with their male partners only.
   C. with their cubs and male partners.
   D. with their cubs only.
3. When lionesses go in search for their prey, they are very
   A. serious B. cautious
   C. playful D. sluggish
4. Male lions protect their cubs
   A. from the members of their own species.
   B. from hyenas only.
   C. from hyenas as much as from other enemies.
   D. more from hyenas than from other animals.

PASSAGE–3

At this stage of the civilisation, when many nations are brought into close and vital contact for good and evil, it is essential, as never before, that their gross ignorance of one another should be diminished, that they should begin to understand a little of one another's historical experience and resulting mentality. It is a fault of the English to expect the people of other countries to react as they do, to political and international situations. Our genuine goodwill and good intentions are often brought to nothing, because we expect other people to be like us. This would be corrected if we knew the history, not necessarily in detail but in broad outlines, of the social and political conditions which have given to each nation its present character.

1. According to the author, the 'mentality' of a nation is mainly a product of its
   A. history.
   B. international position.
   C. politics.
   D. present character.
2. Englishmen like others to react to political situations like
   A. us. B. themselves.
   C. others. D. each other.
3. The character of a nation is the result of its
   A. mentality.
   B. cultural heritage.
   C. gross ignorance.
   D. socio-political conditions.
4. The need for a greater understanding between nations
   A. was always there.
   B. is no longer there.
   C. is more today then ever before.
   D. will always be there.
5. According to the author, his countrymen should
   A. read the history of other nations.
   B. have a better understanding of other nations.
   C. not react to other nations.
   D. have vital contacts with other nations.

PASSAGE–4

What needs to be set right is our approach to work. It is a common sight in our country of employees reporting for duty on time and at the same time doing little work. If an assessment is made of the time they spent in gossiping, drinking tea, eating "pan" and smoking cigarettes, it will be shocking to know that the time devoted to actual work is negligible. The problem is the standard which the leadership in administration sets for the staff. Forget the ministers because they mix politics and administration. What do top bureaucrats do? What do the officials down below do? The administration set up remains weak mainly because the employees do not have the right example to follow and they are more concerned about being in the good books of the bosses than doing work.

1. According to the writer, the administration in India
A. is by and large effective.
B. is very strict and firm.
C. is affected by red tape.
D. is more or less ineffective.

2. The central idea of the passage could be best expressed by the following
A. The employees outlook towards work is justified.
B. The employees must change their outlook towards work.
C. The employees would never change their work culture.
D. The employer-employee relationship is far from healthy.

3. The employees in our country
A. are quite punctual but not duty conscious.
B. are not punctual, but somehow manage to complete their work.
C. are somewhat lazy but good-natured.
D. are not very highly qualified.

4. The leadership in administration
A. sets a fine example to the employees.
B. is of a reasonably high standard.
C. is composed of idealists.
D. is of a very poor standard.

5. The word 'assessment' means
A. enquiry B. report
C. evaluation D. summary

PASSAGE–5

Speech is a great blessing but it can also be a great curse, for while it helps us to make our intentions and desires known to our fellows, it can also, if we use it carelessly, make our attitude completely misunderstood. A slip of the tongue, the use of an unusual word, or of an ambiguous word, and so on, may create an enemy where we had hoped to win a friend. Again, different classes of people use different vocabularies, and the ordinary speech of an educated man may strike an uneducated listener as pompous. Unwittingly, we may use a word which bears a different meaning to our listener from what it does to men of our own class. Thus speech is not a gift to use lightly without thought, but one which demands careful handling. Only a fool will express himself alike to all kinds and conditions of men.

1. Speech can be a curse, because it can
A. hurt others.
B. lead to carelessness.
C. create misunderstanding.
D. reveal our intentions.

2. A 'slip of the tongue' means something said
A. wrongly by chance.
B. unintentionally.
C. without giving proper thought.
D. to hurt another person.

3. While talking to an uneducated person, we should use
A. ordinary speech.
B. his vocabulary.
C. simple words.
D. polite language.

4. If one used the same style of language with everyone, one would sound
A. flat B. boring
C. foolish D. democratic

5. The best way to win a friend is to avoid
A. irony in speech.
B. promposity in speech.
C. verbosity in speech.
D. ambiguity in speech.

PASSAGE–6

Mahatma Gandhi believed that industrialisation was no answer to the problems that plague the mass of India's poor and that villagers should be taught to be self-sufficient in food, weave their own cloth from cotton and eschew the glittering prizes that the twentieth century so temptingly offers. Such an idyllic and rural paradise did not appear to those who inherited the reins of political power.

1. Which one of the following best illustrates the relationship between the phrases:
(i) 'eschew the glittering prizes' and
(ii) 'idyllic and rural paradise'?
A. unless you do (i), you cannot have (ii)
B. (i) and (ii) are identical in meaning
C. first of all you must have (ii) in order to do (i)
D. the meaning of (i) is directly opposite to (ii)

2. Mahatma Gandhi's views opposed industrialisation of villages because
A. it would help the poor and not the rich.
B. it would take away the skill of the villagers.
C. it would affect the culture of the Indians.
D. it would undermine self-sufficiency and destroy the beauty of life of the villager.

3. The meaning of 'the glittering prizes that the twentieth century so temptingly offers' is
A. pursuit of a commercialised material culture.
B. replacement of rural by urban interests.
C. complete removal of poverty.
D. absence of violence and corruption.

4. Mahatma Gandhi's dream of 'an idyllic and rural paradise' was not shared by
A. those who did not believe in the industrialisation of the country.
B. those who called him the Father of the Nation.
C. those who inherited political power after independence.
D. those who believed that villages should be self-sufficient in food and cloth.

5. The basis of 'an idyllic and rural paradise' is
A. rapid industrialisation of villages.
B. self-sufficiency in food and clothes and simplicity of the lifestyle.
C. bringing to the villages the glittering prizes of the twentieth century.
D. supporting those holding powerful political positions.

PASSAGE–7

Organisations are institutions in which members compete for status and power. They compete for the resources of the organisation, for example, finance to expand their own departments, for career advancement and for power to control the activities of others. In pursuit of these aims, groups are formed and sectional interests emerge. As a result, policy decisions may serve the ends of the political and career systems rather than those of the concern. In this way, the goals of the organisation may be displaced in favour of sectional interests and individual ambition. These preoccupations sometimes prevent the emergence of organic systems. Many of the electronics firms in their study had recently created research and development departments employing highly qualified and well-paid scientists and technicians. Their high pay and expert knowledge were sometimes seen as a threat to the established order of rank, power and privilege. Many senior managers had little knowledge of the technicalities and possibilities of new developments and electronics. Some felt that close cooperation with the experts in an organic system would reveal their ignorance and show that their experience was now redundant.

1. The author makes out a case for
A. organic system.
B. research and development in organisations.
C. an understanding between senior and middle level executives.
D. a refresher course for senior managers.

2. The theme of the passage is
A. groupism in organizations.
B. individual ambitions in organizations.
C. frustration of senior managers.
D. emergence of sectional interests in organizations.

3. Policy decision in organization would involve
   A. cooperation at all levels in the organization.
   B. modernization of the organization.
   C. attracting highly qualified personnel.
   D. keeping in view the larger objectives of the organization.
4. "Organic system" as related to the organization implies its
   A. growth with the help of expert knowledge.
   B. growth with inputs from science and technology.
   C. steady all-round development.
   D. natural and unimpeded growth.
5. The author tends to see the senior managers as
   A. ignorant and incompetent.
   B. a little out of step with their work environment.
   C. jealous of their younger colleagues.
   D. robbed of their rank, power and privilege

PASSAGE–8

Corduroy is fast establishing itself as this year's fabric. While the ribbed cotton itself provides utilitarian tenacity, texture and warmth, it is the fabric's long-held associations that may provide a hint to its current revival as a fabric for all seasons.

It is corduroy's link with good breeding and country living that made it an essential ingredient in the gentleman's wardrobe along with Wellington boots and a decent wooly. It combines the comfortable nonsense appeal of cotton with the perfectly correct luxury finish of velvet. Corduroy has the ability to appear either supremely sophisticated or rough and ready.

1. Which one of the following best describes the passage?
   A. It tells us about the usefulness of corduroy.
   B. It talks about the virtues of corduroy.
   C. It persuades us to buy corduroy.
   D. It makes as understand the everlasting appeal of corduroy to the young.
2. According to the author, the special quality of corduroy is that
   A. it needs no ironing.
   B. it combines the virtues of both cotton and velvet.
   C. it contains the correct mixture of cotton and velvet.
   D. both the rich and that not-so-rich can afford to buy it.
3. According to the passage, corduroy is essential in a gentleman's wardrobe because
   A. it goes with Wellington boots.
   B. its current revival gives a taste of the latest fashion.
   C. it has its associations with good upbringing and a conservative lifestyle.
   D. it can be an idea alternative to woollen clothes.
4. When the writer refers to corduroy's 'utilitarian tenacity' he means that
   A. though expensive, it is economic in the long-run.
   B. it is useful because it is durable.
   C. it has remained fashionable over several years.
   D. it does not need frequent washing.
5. Corduroy is a fabric for all seasons because
   A. it can be worn not only in winter but also in summer.
   B. of its peculiar texture and warmth.
   C. it is made popular by catchy advertisements.
   D. gentlemen can wear it on both formal and informal occasions.

PASSAGE–9

The enjoyment of physical possession of things would seem to be one of the prerogatives of wealth which has been little impaired. Presumably nothing has happened to keep the man who can afford them from enjoying his Rembrandts and his home-grown orchids. But enjoyment of things has always been associated with the third prerogative of wealth which is the distinction it confers. In a world where nearly everyone was poor, this distinction was very great. It was the natural consequence of rarity. In England, it is widely agreed, the ducal families are not uniformly superior. There is a roughly normal incidence of intelligence and stupidity, good taste and bad taste, morality, immorality, homosexuality and incest. But very few people are dukes and duchesses, although the latter have become rather more frequent with the modern easing of the divorce laws. As a result, even though they may be intrinsically unexceptional, they are regarded with some awe. So it has long been with the rich. Were dukes numerous, their position would deteriorate. As the rich have become more numerous, they have inevitably become a debased currency.

1. Among the ducal families
A. there is a great deal of immorality.
B. there is a fairly even spread of virtues and vices.
C. there is a great deal of bad taste.
D. there is either great intelligence or great stupidity.

2. There are more duchesses now because
A. it is easier for dukes to divorce and remarry
B. dukes are more immoral than they used to be
C. their position has deteriorated
D. they are debased

3. The enjoyment of the physical possession of things
A. is one of the privileges of wealth which has not been changed
B. is one of the privileges of wealth which should be curtailed
C. has little to do with the prerogatives of wealth
D. is a prerogative of wealth which cannot be disputed

4. The distinction conferred by wealth
A. was unfair to the poor
B. was unlikely to spread throughout the world
C. was very great when there were many rich people
D. was very great when there were few rich people

5. Ducal families in England
A. are generally agreed to be fairly common
B. are generally agreed to be superior
C. are superior because they are rich
D. are generally agreed not to be always better than others.

PASSAGE–10

Nehru's was a many-sided personality. He enjoyed reading and writing books as much as he enjoyed fighting political and social evils or resisting tyranny. In him, the scientist and the humanist were held in perfect balance. While he kept looking at special problems from a scientific standpoint, he never forgot that we should nourish the total man. As a scientist, he refused to believe in a benevolent power interested in men's affairs, but, as a self-proclaimed non-believer, he loved affirming his faith in life and the beauty of nature. Children he adored. Unlike Wordsworth, he did not see them trailing clouds of glory from their recent sojourn in heaven. He saw them as blossoms of promise and renewal, the only hope for mankind.

1. A 'many-side personality' means
A. a complex personality
B. a secretive person
C. a person having varied interests
D. a capable person

2. Nehru enjoyed
A. reading and writing books
B. fighting political and social evils
C. resisting tyranny
D. doing all the above and much more

3. Nehru thought that childern.
A. were trailing clouds of glory.
B. held promise for a better future.
C. were like flowers to be loved and admired.
D. held no hope for mankind.

4. Which of the following statements reflects Nehru's point of view?
A. Humanism is more important than science
B. Science is supreme and humanism is subordinate to it
C. Science and humanism are equally important
D. There is no common ground between science and humanism

5. In this passage, 'a benevolent power interested in men's affairs' means
   A. a supernatural power or God
   B. beauty of nature
   C. the spirit of science
   D. the total man

PASSAGE–11

Until the end of his first year at school, Cyril retained many of the pleasures and pursuits he had brought with him from home, and he kept an old interest in butterflies and fossils. His grandmother had presented him with a fine birds' eggs cabinet, but he could never bring himself to risks in climbing trees. Once or twice he dissected dead birds from sheer determination to overcome his horror of the operation. Probably it was his envy of those physically unlike himself that brought on a phase during which he drew massive athletes with thick necks and square shoulders. Again he was pitying himself for what he could never be.

1. Until the end of the first year, Cyril retained his interest in
   A. bird's eggs
   B. butterflies and fossils
   C. dissecting birds
   D. drawing pictures of athletes
2. Cyril's early schooling was in some ways like home life because
   A. he had all his old friends with him
   B. the food and the climate were the same as at home
   C. he kept on doing what gave joy and recreation at home
   D. his family visited him often
3. Cyril did NOT want to climb trees because he
   A. loved to play on the ground
   B. was scared of falling down
   C. disliked trees
   D. thought it was childish
4. Cyril dissected dead birds to
   A. see if he would like to become a doctor
   B. please his grandmother
   C. satisfy his curiosity
   D. overcome the fear of the act
5. The reason why Cyril made drawings of athletes was that
   A. though he admired them, he lacked a fine physique himself
   B. he loved violent exercises
   C. athletics was a passion with him
   D. he had to complete an assignment

PASSAGE–12

The assault on the purity of the environment is the price that we pay for many of the benefits of modern technology. For the advantages of automotive transportation we pay a price in smog-induced diseases; for the powerful effects of new insecticides, we pay a price in dwindling wildlife and disturbances in the relation of living things and their surroundings; for nuclear power, we risk the biological hazards of radiation. By increasing agricultural production with fertilisers, we worsen water pollution.

The highly developed nations of the world are not only the immediate beneficiaries of the good that technology can do, they are also the first victims of the environmental diseases that technology breeds. In the past, the environmental effects which accompanied technolgical progress were restricted to a small place and relatively short time. The new hazards are neither local nor brief. Modern air pollution covers vast areas of the continents: Radioactive fallout from nuclear explosions is worldwide. Radioactive pollutants now on the Earth's surface will be found there for generations, and in the case of Carbon-14, for thousands of years.

1. The passage emphasises that modern technology
   A. is an unmixed blessing
   B. has caused serious hazards to life
   C. has produced powerful chemicals
   D. has benefited highly developed nations
2. According to the passage, the increasing use of fertilisers is responsible for
   A. abundance of food
   B. disturbance in the ecological system
   C. water pollution
   D. increase in diseases

3. The widespread use of insecticides has
   A. reduced the number of wild animals
   B. caused imbalance in the relation between living beings and their environment
   C. eliminated diseases by killing mosquitoes and flies
   D. caused biologcial hazards
4. Radioactive pollutants
   A. are limited in their effect
   B. will infest the atmosphere for thousands of years
   C. will be on the surface of the earth for a very long time
   D. will dissipate in a short span of time
5. The harmful effects of modern technology are
   A. widespread but short-lived
   B. widespread and long-lasting
   C. limited and long-lasting
   D. severe but short-lived

PASSAGE–13

There was a marked difference of quality between the personages who haunted the near bridge of brick and the personages who haunted the far one of stone. Those of lowest character preferred the former, adjoining the town; they did not mind the glare of the public eye. They had been of no account during their successes; and though they might feel dispirited, they had no sense of shame in their ruin. Instead of sighing at their adversaries they spat, and instead of saying the iron had entered into their souls they said they were down in their luck. The miserables who would pause on the remoter bridge were of a politer stamp-persons who did not know how to get rid of the weary time. The eyes of this species were mostly directed over the parapet upon the running water below. While one on the townward bridge did not mind who saw him so, and kept his back to the parapet to survey the passer-by, one on this never faced the road, never turned his head at coming foot-steps, but, sensitive on his own condition, watched the current whenever a stranger approached, as if some strange fish interested him, though every finned thing had been poached out of the river years before.

1. In this passage, the author is trying to
   A. explain the difference between the constructon of the two bridges.
   B. describe the way different sections of people like to dress.
   C. explain the variety of ways in which strangers can be treated.
   D. describe how people of different classes behaved when unhappy.
2. People belonging to the lower strata in their moments of distress
   A. remembered their days of glory.
   B. dressed shabbily to earn sympathy.
   C. visited the brick-made bridge
   D. felt ashamed of their failures.
3. The bridge of stone was frequented by
   A. all the sections of society
   B. those fond of fishing
   C. the sophisticated but luokless
   D. none of the above
4. The two bridges were known
   A. for their similar design.
   B. for being equidistant from town.
   C. for being haunted places.
   D. for attracting dejected people to them.
5. The attitude of the lowly and genteel towards strangers was
   A. virtually the same
   B. entirely different
   C. completely indifferent
   D. virulently hostile

PASSAGE–14

Nationalism, of course, is a curious phenomenon which at a certain stage in a country's history gives life, growth and unity but, at the same time, it has a tendency to limit one, because one thinks of one's country as something different from the rest of the world. One's perspective changes and one is continuously thinking of one's own struggles and virtues and failing to the exclusion of other thoughts. The result is that the same nationalism which is the symbol of growth for a people becomes a symbol of the cessation of that growth in the mind. Nationalism, when it becomes successful, sometimes goes on spreading in an aggressive way and becomes a danger internationally. Whatever line of thought you follow, you arrive at the conclusion that some kind of balance must be found. Otherwise something that was good can turn into evil. Culture, which is essentially good becomes not only static but aggressive and something that breeds conflict and hatred when looked at from a wrong point of view. How are you to find a balance, I don't know. Apart from the political and economic problems of the age, perhaps that is the greatest problem today because behind it there is a tremendous search for something which it cannot find. We turn to economic theories because they have an undoubted importance. It is folly to talk of culture or even of God when human beings starve and die. Before one can talk about anything else one must provide the normal essentials of life to human beings. That is where economics comes in. Human beings today are not in the mood to tolerate this suffering and starvation and inequality when they see that the burden is not equally shared. Others profit while they only bear the burden.

1. Aggressive nationalism
 A. breeds threat to international relations
 B. leads to stunted growth
 C. endangers national unity
 D. isolates a country

2. Suitable title for this passage can be
 A. Nationalism breeds unity
 B. Nationalism—a road to world unity
 C. Nationalism is not enough
 D. Nationalism and national problems

3. 'Others' in the last sentence refers to
 A. other people
 B. other nations
 C. other communities
 D. other neighbours

4. Negative national feeling can make a nation
 A. selfish B. self-centred
 C. indifferent D. dangerous

5. The greatest problem' in the middle of the passage refers to the question
 A. how to mitigate hardship to human beings
 B. how to contain the dangers of aggressive nationalism
 C. how to share the economic burden equally
 D. how to curb international hatred

PASSAGE–15

Detective stories tend to glorify crime. Murderers, gangsters and crooks of all kinds are described as tough, cunning and courageous individuals who know how to take care of themselves and how to get what they want. In James McCain's *The Postman Always Rings Twice*, for instance, the villain is a much more impressive character than his victim. He is casual, brave smart and successful with women. It is true that he finally gets caught. But he is punished for a crime that he did not commit, so that his conviction is hardly a triumph of justice. Besides, looking back over the exciting life of the criminal, the reader might conclude that it was worth the risk.

1. According to the passage given above, detective stories
 A. make interesting reading
 B. are hardly worth reading
 C. encourage readers to commit crimes
 D. tend to create wrong notions about crimes and punishment

2. Murderers, gangsters and crooks referred to in the passage given above
 A. always manage to get away
 B. are often glorified in detective stories
 C. are wiser than their victims
 D. know how to escape from law

3. According to the passage, the life of a criminal
 A. is exciting
 B. is hardly worth the risk
 C. is seldom presented in the right perspective
 D. ends in a triumph of justice

4. The passage mentions James McCain.
 A. as an author of a detective story
 B. as brave, smart and successful with women
 C. as tough cunning and courageous
 D. as being more impressive than others

5. According to this passage, a criminal in a detective story generally gets caught
   A. for the crimes he has committed
   B. because of his careless mistakes
   C. because the police is smarter than the criminals
   D. for the crimes he has not committed

PASSAGE–16

There is more than modicum of truth in the assertion that "a working knowledge of ancient history is necessary to the intelligent interpretation of current events". But the sage who uttered these words of wisdom might well have added something on the benefits of studying, particularly, the famous battles of history for the lessons they contain for those of us who lead or aspire to leadership. Such a study will reveal certain qualities and attributes which enabled the winners to win—and certain deficiencies which caused the losers to lose. And the student will see that the same pattern recurs consistently, again and again, throughout the centuries.

1. The expression "more than a modicum of truth" means
   A. some truth.
   B. much truth.
   C. more than a small amount of truth.
   D. nothing but truth.
2. In this context,"intelligent interpretation of current events" means
   A. rational explanation of events.
   B. appropriate understanding of events.
   C. intellectual outlook on events.
   D. skilful interpretation of events.
3. According to the writer, a study of the famous battles of history would
   A. be beneficial to wise men
   B. provide food to modern leaders for reflection.
   C. be more useful than a general knowledge of ancient history.
   D. help us understand the art of modern warfare.
4. A knowledge of history is necessary to interpret current problems because
   A. they have roots in the past.
   B. they can be contrasted with the past events.
   C. they may be repetitions of past events.
   D. only then they can be put in a proper context.
5. A person who aspires to lead could learn from the history of battles
   A. what led the previous leaders win a battle.
   B. what made them lose a battle.
   C. the qualities and deficiencies of commanders of these battles.
   D. the strategies that they have evolved in course of these battles.

PASSAGE–17

The casual horrors and the real disasters are thrown at newspaper readers without discrimination. In the contemporary arrangements for circulating the news, an important element, evaluation, is always weak and often wanting entirely. There is no point anywhere along the line where someone puts his foot down for certain and says, "This is important and That doesn't amount to a row of beans; deserves no one's attention, and should travel the wires no farther". The junk is dressed up to look as meaningful as the real news.

1. The writer of the above passage
   A. seems to be happy with the contemporary arrangements for circulating news
   B. is shocked by the casual stories about horrors and disasters reported in the newspapers
   C. wants better evaluation of news before publication
   D. wants to put his foot down on news stories
2. Newspapers lack a sense of discrimination because
   A. they do not separate the real news from mere sensationalism
   B. they have to accept whatever is received on the wires
   C. limited manpower makes serious evaluation impossible
   D. people don't see the difference between 'junk' and real' news

3. The passage implies that
   A. there has to be censorship on newspapers
   B. there is no point in having censorship
   C. newspapers always dress up junk to look meaningful
   D. one has to be strict in selecting news items
4. Evaluation of news would imply
   A. less dependence on modern systems of communication
   B. more careful analysis of each news story and its value
   C. separating beans from junk
   D. discriminating horrors from disasters
5. In the above passage, the phrase "amounts to a row of beans"means that the news
   A. is weak and often wanting entirely
   B. deserves no one's attention
   C. should travel the wires
   D. is junk dressed up as real news

PASSAGE–18

The world dismisses curiosity by calling it idle or mere idle curiosity—even though curious persons are seldom idle. Parents do their best to extinguish curiosity in their children becasue it makes life difficult to be faced everyday with a string of unanswerable questions about what makes fire hot or why grass grows. Children whose curiosity survives parental discipline are invited to join our university. With the university, they go on asking their questions and trying to find the answers. In the eyes of a scholar, that is what a university is for. Some of the questions which the scholars ask seem to the world to be scarcely worth asking, let alone answering. They asked questions too minute and specialised for you and me to understand without years of explanation. If the world inquires of one of them why he wants to know the answer to a particular question he may say especially if he is a scientist, that the answer will in some obscure way make possible a new machine or weapon or gadget. He talks that way because he knows that the world understands and respects utility.

But to you who are now part of the university, he will say that he wants to know the answer simply because he does not know it, the way the mountain climber wants to climb a mountain, simply because it is there. Similarly a historain asked by an outsider why he studies history may come out with the argument that he has learnt to repeat on such occasions, something about knowledge of the past making it possible to understand the present and mould the future. But if you really want to know why a historian studies the past, the answer is much simpler, something happened and he would like to know what. All this does not mean that the answers which scholars find to their questions have no consequences. They may have enormous consequences but these seldom form the reason for asking the question or pursuing the answers. It is true that scholars can be put to work answering questions for the sake of the consequences as thousands are working now, for example, in search of a cure for cancer. But this is not the primary function of the scholars. For the consequences are usually subordinate to the satisfaction of curiosity.

1. The common people consider some of the questions that the scholars ask unimportant
   A. as they are too lazy and idle
   B. as they are too modest
   C. as it's beyond their comprehension
   D. as it is considered a waste of time
2. A historian really studies the past
   A. to comprehend the present and to reconstruct the future
   B. to explain the present and plan the future
   C. to understand the present and make fortune
   D. to understand the present and mould the future
3. Children whose curiosity survives parental discipline means
   A. children retaining their curiosity in spite of being discouraged by their parents
   B. children pursuing their mental curiosity
   C. children's curiosity subdued due to parents' intervention
   D. children being disciplined by their parents

4. According to the passage, parents do their best to discourage curiosity in their childern
   A. because they have no time
   B. because they have no patience to answer them
   C. because they feel that their children ask stupid questions continuously
   D. because they are unable to answer all their questions
5. According to the passage, the children make life difficult for their parents
   A. by their ceaseless curiosity
   B. by unceasing bombardment of questions
   C. by asking irrelevant questions
   D. by posing profound questions

PASSAGE–19

He saw nothing, he had no knife or sharp instrument, the grating of the window was of iron and he had too often assured himself of its solidity. His furniture consisted of a bed, a chair, a table, a pail and a jug. The bed had iron clamps, but they were screwed to the wall and it would have requird a screwdriver to take them off.

Dantes had but one resource which was to break the jug and with one of the sharp fragments attack the wall. He let the jug fall on the floor and it broke in pieces. He concealed two or three of the sharpest fragments in his bed, leaving the rest on the floor. The breaking of the jug was too natural an accident to excite suspicion, and next morning the gaoler went grumblingly to fetch another, without giving himself the trouble to remove the fargments. Dantes heard joyfully the key grate in the lock as the guard departed.

1. Dantes probably broke the jug
   A. in the morning
   B. during the night
   C. after breakfast
   D. at exactly 3 p.m.
2. The guard left the fragments because he
   A. didn't notice them
   B. wished to punish Dantes
   C. was too lazy to bother
   D. wanted Dantes to clear up
3. Dantes heard the key grate in the lock when the
   A. cell door was shut
   B. cell door was opened
   C. storeroom was opened
   D. storeroom was shut
4. Dantes was in
   A. a hostel
   B. a dining room
   C. an army barracks
   D. a prison
5. Dantes was planning to
   A. carve his name
   B. make his escape
   C. tease the guard
   D. call for breakfast

PASSAGE–20

The greatest thing this age can be proud of is the birth of Man in the consciousness of men. In his drunken orgies of power and national pride man may flout and jeer at it. When organised national selfishness, racial antipathy and commercial self-seeking begin to display their ugly deformities in all their nakedness, then comes the time for man to know that his salvation is not in political organisations and extended trade relations, not in any mechanical re-arrangement of social system but in a deeper transformation of life, in the liberation of consciousness in love, in the realisation of God in man.

1. According to the author, "salvation" of human beings lies in the
   A. extended trade relations.
   B. spiritual transformation of life.
   C. orgy of national pride.
   D. wholehearted participation in political organisations.
2. In the phrase "the birth of Man in the consciousness of men", Man stands for
   A. power and arrogance
   B. egocentricity
   C. noble human qualities
   D. an idealistic notion of the human self
3. The author uses the expression 'ugly deformities' to show his indignation at

A. political organisations
B. the liberation of human consciousness
C. selfishness and materialism of the people
D. the drunken orgies of power

4. People jeer at the 'birth of Man' in the human consciousness when they
A. begin to think of themselves as God
B. become power-hungry
C. restructure the social system
D. become mentally deranged

5. In this passage, the phrase "God in man" implies
A. God having assumed the shape of man
B. neither fully godly nor fully human
C. man being transformed into God
D. the divine qualities in man

PASSAGE–21

Modern economics does not differentiate between renewable and non-renewable materials, as its method is to measure everything by means of a money price. Thus, taking various alternative fuels, like coal, oil, wood or water power: the only difference between them recognised by modern economics is relative cost per equivalent unit. The cheapest is automatically the one to be preferred, as to do otherwise would be irrational and 'uneconomic'. From a Buddhist point of view, of course this will not do, the essential difference between non-renewable fuels like coal and oil on the one hand and renewable fuels like wood and water-power on the other cannot be simply overlooked. Non-renewable goods must be used only if they are indispensable, and then only with the greatest care and the highest concern for conservation. To use them carelessly or extravagantly is an act of violence, and while complete non-violence may not be possible on this earth, it is nonetheless the duty of man to aim at the ideal of non-violence in all he does.

1. The Buddhist economist's attitude implies that fuels like coal and oil must be used only if
A. there is a plentiful supply
B. wood and water-power can be dispensed with
C. the relative cost of each is than that of wood and water
D. there is no alternative fuel available

2. According to the passage, Buddhist economists are not in favour of
A. measuring everything in terms of money
B. using non-renewable sources
C. economic development
D. applying non-violence to every sphere of life

3. In this passage the author is trying to
A. differentiate between renewable and non-renewable materials
B. show that the modern economist is concerned only with costs
C. underline the need for conserving natural resources
D. differentiate between two economic philosophies

4. Which of the following statements may be assumed to be false from the information in the passage?
1. The writer finds the attitude of modern economists towards natural resources to be uneconomic.
2. Buddhist economists are indifferent to the cost of fuels.
3. To use oil on non-essentials is contrary to the Buddhist economic philosophy.
4. To fell a tree is an act of violence not permitted by Buddhist economists.

Of the above statements
A. 1 and 2 are false
B. 1, 2 and 4 are false
C. 3 and 4 are false
D. All 1, 2, 3 and 4 are false

5. Fill in the blanks with the appropriate pair of phrases:
The passage suggests that while a modern economist, considers it uneconomic to use ..... form of fuel, a Buddhist economist considers it uneconomic to use ..... form a fuel
A. a cheap, a renewable
B. an irrational, an essential
C. an expensive, an unrenewable
D. a rational, an unessential

PASSAGE–22

Sometimes we went off the road and on a path through the pine forest. The floor of the forest was soft to walk on; the frost did not harden it as it did the road. But we did not mind the hardness of the road because we had nails in the soles and heels of our boots and the heel nails bit on the frozen ruts and with nailed boots it was good walking on the road and invigorating. It was lovely walking in the woods.

1. Sometimes we walked through the pine forest as
- A. the path was unaffected by the frost
- B. it was good walking with nails in the boots
- C. the walk was invigorating
- D. it was sheer joy to walk in the forest

2. The floor of the forest was soft because
- A. the frost did not harden it on account of trees
- B. the travellers were wearing boots
- C. the shoes had nails on their sole and heel
- D. they enjoyed walking in the woods

3. We did not mind the hardness of the road because
- A. we had nailed boots on
- B. it was good walking on the road
- C. the walk was refreshing
- D. the nails bit on the frozen roads

4. 'Frozen ruts' means
- A. very cold roads
- B. wheel marks in which frost had become hard
- C. the road covered with frost
- D. hard roads covered with snow

5. We found great joy on account of
- A. wearing nailed boots
- B. the good long walk on the road
- C. walking occasionally through the forest
- D. walking on frost with nailed boots on

PASSAGE–23

Many Sociologists have argued that there is a functional relationship between education and economic system. They point to the fact that mass formal education began in industrial society and is an established part of all industrial societies. They note that the expansion of the economies of industrial societies is accompanied by a corresponding expansion of their educational systems. They explain this correspondence in terms of the needs of industry for skilled and trained manpower, needs which are met by the educational system. Thus, the provision of mass elementary education in Britain in 1870 can be seen as a response to the needs of industry for a literate and numerate workforce at a time when industrial processes were becoming more complex and the demand for technical skills was steadily growing.

1. The Sociologists referred to in the passage say that the relationship between industry and elementary education was one
- A. based on mutual need.
- B. based entirely on the need of the industry.
- C. based entirely on economic need.
- D. based on some inexplicable historical forces.

2. The author argues that
- A. formal education can be traced to industrial society.
- B. industrial society is responsible for expansion of education at the mass level.
- C. industrial society gave rise to vocational education.
- D. industrial society changed the pattern of education.

3. By 'functional relationship' is meant
- A. a short-term relationship.
- B. practical and utilitarian relationship.
- C. temporary arrangement.
- D. close and unbreakable relationship.

4. The observations of the Sociologists are based on a study of
- A. the statistical data available in a historical context.
- B. economic system of the 19th century.
- C. the correlation between industry and education in a historical context.
- D. growth of industry in the 19th century.

5. The industry needs a literate workforce because
- A. its expansion needs sound learning

B. it relies heavily on expertise.
C. it promotes a competitive spirit.
D. its operations need intricate technical knowledge.

PASSAGE–24

The Indian Middle Class consists of so many strata that it defies categorisation under a single term class, which would imply a considerable degree of homogeneity. Yet two paradoxical features characterise its conduct fairly uniformly: extensive practice and intensive abhorrence of corruption.

In the several recent surveys of popular perceptions of corruption, politicians of course invariably and understandably top the list, closely followed by bureaucrats, policemen, lawyers, businessmen and others—the quintessential middle class. If teachers do not figure high on this priority list, it is not for lack of trying, but for lack of opportunities. Over the yeras, the sense of shock over acts of corruption in the middle class has witnessed a steady decline, as its ambitions for a better material life have soared but the resources for meeting such ambitions have not kept pace.

What is fascinating, however, is the intense yearning of this class for a clean corruptionless polity and society, a yearning that has again and again surfaced with any figure public or obscure, focusing on his mission of eradicating corruption. Even the repeated failure of this promise on virtually every man's part has not subjected it to the law of diminishing returns.

1. The Indian Middle Class is
   A. defiant B. mysterious
   C. homogeneous D. stratified
2. Teachers are not high on the list of corruption because they do not have
   A. courage B. opportunities
   C. support D. ambition
3. This yearning, over the years, has
   A. persisted B. soared
   C. declined D. disappeared
4. Who figure on top of the list of corruption?
   A. Businessmen B. Lawyers
   C. Politicians D. Policemen
5. The Indian Middle Class intensely yearns for
   A. better material resources
   B. extensive practice of corruption
   C. clean honest society
   D. law of increasing returns

PASSAGE–25

Piccadilly Circus was full of loneliness. It seethes and echoes with it. To live near it, looking down on it, is a discomforting experience. You can't feel the pulse of London there, though people expect to. To Londoners it is a maddening obstruction between one place and another, and few voluntarily linger there. The only locals are those who live off the lingerers; the lingerers are primarily sightseers, with a fair sprinkling of people hoping to draw attention to themselves—both typically from the provinces. They have come to see the heart of London and expect to see spectacle, glamour and vice.

1. The passage implies that
   A. some Londoners love to spend their time near Piccadilly Circus
   B. no Londoner wants to be in Piccadilly Circus
   C. Piccadilly Circus is a hazardous place
   D. Piccadilly Circus is a place of vice
2. Piccadilly Circus is
   A. the name of a circus company
   B. a lonely and resounding old building
   C. a centrally located area in London
   D. a huge heap of ruins
3. The lingerers found in Piccadilly Circus are mainly
   A. the citizens of London
   B. sightseers from provincial areas of Britain
   C. people who want to show off
   D. local idlers
4. For those who live near Piccadilly Circus, it is
   A. a very noisy place
   B. crowded with people
   C. an obstruction to traffic
   D. an awkward structure

5. According to this passage, people from outside London go to Piccadilly Circus because it is
   A. a historical place
   B. full of glamour
   C. full of exciting people
   D. the pulse of London

PASSAGE–26

Today perhaps your only association with the word 'polio' is the Sabin Oral Vaccine that protects children from the disease. Fifty-five years ago, this was not so. The dreaded disease, which mainly affects the brain and the spinal cord, causes stiffening and weakening of the muscles, crippling and paralysis—which is why I am in a wheelchair today. If somebody had predicted, when I was born, that this would happen to me, no one would have believed it. I was the seventh child in a family of four pairs of brothers and sisters, with a huge 23-year gap between the first and the last. I was told that, unlike the others, I was so fair and brown-haired that I looked more like a foreigner than a Dawood Bohri. I was also considered to be the healthiest of the brood.

1. In this passage, the narrator is a patient of
   A. heart disease
   B. polio
   C. paralysis
   D. nervous weakness
2. The narrator was the seventh child in a family of
   A. 8 children B. 16 childern
   C. 23 children D. 4 children
3. In his childhood, the narrator was
   A. a weakling
   B. very healthy
   C. tall and slim
   D. short and stout
4. In his childhood, the narrator looked "more like a foreigner than a Dawood Bohri". This was because he was
   A. a foreign child
   B. a very healthy boy
   C. tall and smart
   D. fair and brown-haired
5. In this passage, the word 'brood' refers to
   A. polio victims
   B. foreign children
   C. children in the family
   D. Indian children

PASSAGE–27

Soft-bodied animals like caterpillars often fall a prey to voracious hunters like birds or reptiles. Despite having no means to' actively' defend themselves, with weapons like claws or jaws, they have nevertheless, evolved other equally effective deterrents. A particular species of the caterpillar lives at an altitude of over 2,500 metres in the Himalayas. It uses prominent colours to inform would be predators of its inedibility. In the event that an inexperienced or adventurous bird did eat the caterpillar, it would probably vomit it out soon after, and subsequently desist from attacking similar species in the future. Though this would do the unfortunate victim no good, the species benefits. A rare example of the martyr among animals.

1. Caterpillars cannot defend themselves because they
   A. are passive animals.
   B. are lazy.
   C. cannot acquire weapons.
   D. have no claws or jaws
2. The Himalayan caterpillar uses prominent colours to
   A. warn the predator.
   B. attack the predator.
   C. reveal itself.
   D. defend itself.
3. The expression "others equally effective deterrents" means
   A. preventive weapons which have equal effect of others.
   B. mechanism which scares everyone equally well.
   C. preventive equipment which is as effective as something that has been already mentioned in the passage.
   D. deterrents that are as powerful as those the caterpillars have.

4. Experienced birds do not attack the Himalayan caterpillars because they are
   A. repulsive.
   B. very aggressive.
   C. inedible
   D. diseased.
5. In the context of this passage, a martyr is one who dies
   A. without putting up resistance.
   B. without any gain to oneself.
   C. while defending one's homeland.
   D. to save others.

PASSAGE–28

Mountaineering is now looked upon as the king of sports. But men have lived amongst the mountains since pre-historic times and in some parts of the world, as in the Andes and Himalayas, difficult mountain journeys have inevitably been part of their everyday life. However, some of the peaks were easily accessible from most of the cities of Europe. It is quite interesting that while modern mountaineers prefer difficult routes for the greater enjoyment of sport, the early climbers looked for the easiest ones, for the summit was the prize they all set their eyes on. Popular interest in mountaineering increased considerably after the ascent of the Alpine peak of Matterhorn in 1865 and Edward Whymper's dramatic account of the climb and fatal accident which occurred during the descent.

In the risky sport of mountaineering the element of competition between either individuals or teams is totally absent. Rather one can say that the competition is between the team and the peaks themselves. The individuals making up a party must climb together as a team, for they depend upon one another for their saftey. Mountaineering can be dangerous unless reasonable precautions are taken. However, the majority of fatal accidents happen to parties which are inexperienced or not properly equipped. Since many accidents are caused by bad weather, the safe climber is the man who knows when it is time to turn back, however tempting it may be to press on and try to reach the summit.

1. Mountaineers climb as a team because
   A. the height is too much for one individual
   B. the competition is between the team and the peak
   C. they have to rely on each other for safety
   D. there is no competition among them
2. Mountaineering is different from other sports because
   A. it is risky and dangerous
   B. it can be fatal
   C. it is most thrilling and exciting
   D. there is no competition between individuals
3. "...the summit was the prize they all set their eyes on. "In the context of the passage this means
   A. reaching the top was their exclusive concern
   B. they kept their eyes steadily on reaching the summit
   C. they cared for nothing but the prize of reaching the summit
   D. they chose a route from which they could see the summit clearly
4. People living in the Andes and the Himalayas made mountain journeys because
   A. it was a kind of sport
   B. they had to undertake them in their day-to-day life
   C. they lived in pre-historic times
   D. of the challenge offered by the difficult journey
5. "To press on" in the last sentence of the passage means
   A. to struggle in a forceful manner
   B. to force upon others
   C. to work fearlessly
   D. to continue in a determined manner

PASSAGE–29

The *Mahabharata* is a record of human beings with human weaknessess. The entire *Ramayana*, on the other hand, is in praise of an ideal man. Whatever was good in the world was embodied in Rama, and it was to present this ideal to the world that Valmiki wrote the *Ramayana*. As Rama is the ideal man so is Sita the ideal woman. In fact, the whole *Ramayana* is filled with idealized characters—the ideal brother, the ideal servant, ideal subjects, even ideal villains. It is not that the *Mahabharata* has no extraordinary characters. But even while depicting the extraordinary person, the post does not let us forget the ordinary in him.

The *Ramayana* is principally the story of one man, with the other characters serving as a background to set the hero in relief. Besides Ram stands Sita. She has parents as well as in-laws, but her parents' home is a home in name only. Of her relations with her in-laws we hear a little more, but in this context too the characters remain sketchy. Sita goes into the forest with Rama, returns, is later cast off during pregnancy by Rama, and is finally swallowed up by the earth, but we do not hear a single protest from her father or mother. It is as if Sita were an orphan. There is a description of the greatness of her father, Janak, but this greatness of his is of no help to Sita in her times of need.

1. The *Ramayana* and the *Mahabharata* contrast with each other
   A. in terms of extraordinary idealized characters in one and characters with both extraordinary qualities and ordinary human weaknesses in the other
   B. in terms of idealized characters in one and ordinary characters in the other
   C. with *Ramayana* having more idealized characters than the *Mahabharata*
   D. in terms of the sufferings of principal characters in one and the happiness of such characters in the other

2. The phrase 'swallowed up' here means
   A. eaten up   B. seized upon
   C. digested in   D. sucked in

3. The *Ramayana* is
   A. a record of great events in the life of Rama
   B. a story of the sufferings of Rama and Sita
   C. a story of idealized extraordinary characters
   D. a sketchy story of Rama and Sita

4. The writer says "it is as if Sita were an orphan", because
   A. Sita had lost her parents in childhood
   B. her real father was not Janaka
   C. her parents never came to her help in her hour of need
   D. her parents never protested against her ill-treatment by her in-laws

5. The characters in the *Ramayana* apart from Rama are so sketchy, because
   A. they are meant to serve as a background to Rama
   B. our whole interest is in the story of Rama and Sita
   C. Rama is an ideal character
   D. none of them has any quality to make him superior to Rama

PASSAGE–30

Several years ago my parents, my wife, my son and I ate at a restaurant. After a wonderful dinner, the waiter set the bill in the middle of the table. That's when it happened: my father did not reach for the bill.

Conversation continued. Finally it dawned on me. I was supposed to pay the bill. After hundreds of restaurant meals with my parents, after a lifetime of thinking of my father as the one with the money, it had all changed. I reached for the bill, and my view of myself suddenly altered. I was an adult.

Some people mark off their lives in years; I measure mine in small events—in rites of passage. I did not become a young man at a particular age, like 13, but rather when a boy strolled into the shop where I worked and called me "mister". The realisation hit me like a punch: I was suddenly a mister.

I never thought that I would fall asleep in front of the television set as my father did. Now it's what I do best. I never thought I would prefer to stay at home, but now I find myself forgoing parties. I used to think that people who watched birds were weird, but this summer I found myself watching them, and may be I'll get a book on the subject. I yearn for a religious conviction that I never thought I'd want, feel close to my ancestors long gone, and echo my father in arguments with my son. I still lose.

One day I became a father, and not too long after that I picked up the bill for my own father. I thought then it was a rite of passage for me. But one day, when I was a little order, I realised it was one for him too.

1. The passage tells us about the author's
A. growing into an adult
B. growing into an intellectual
C. growing into a rich man
D. growing into a talented artist

2. 'I was suddenly a mister' here means
A. The author felt that he had become an adult
B. the author was highly respected
C. The author was addressed as the owner of the shop
D. the author was now a responsible person

3. The author had begun to forgo parties because
A. he had begun to take interest in watching birds
B. he had become somewhat abnormal
C. he had become a party-hater
D. he had become self-centred

4. The realisation of adulthood for the first time dawned on the author
A. in a restaurant
B. in a shop
C. in a mutual conversation
D. on a playground

5. Some people mark off their lives in years, but the author measures his life in
A. deeds B. small events
C. noble thoughts D. great ideals

ANSWERS

Passage–1

1	2	3	4
A	B	A	D

Passage–2

1	2	3	4
C	C	B	D

Passage–3

1	2	3	4	5
A	B	D	C	B

Passage–4

1	2	3	4	5
D	B	A	D	C

Passage–5

1	2	3	4	5
C	C	B	C	D

Passage–6

1	2	3	4	5
D	B	C	A	B

Passage–7

1	2	3	4	5
A	D	C	B	A

Passage–8

1	2	3	4	5
B	D	C	B	A

Passage–9

1	2	3	4	5
B	A	A	D	D

Passage–10

1	2	3	4	5
C	D	B	C	A

Passage–11

1	2	3	4	5
B	C	B	D	A

Passage–12

1	2	3	4	5
B	C	B	C	B

Passage–13

1	2	3	4	5
D	C	C	D	B

Passage–14

1	2	3	4	5
D	C	A	B	B

Passage–15

1	2	3	4	5
D	B	C	A	D

Passage–16

1	2	3	4	5
C	A	B	C	C

Passage–17

1	2	3	4	5
C	A	C	B	B

Passage–18

1	2	3	4	5
C	D	A	D	A

Passage–19

1	2	3	4	5
B	C	D	D	B

Passage–20

1	2	3	4	5
B	D	C	B	D

Passage–21

1	2	3	4	5
D	B	D	B	C

Passage–22

1	2	3	4	5
A	A	A	C	D

Passage–23

1	2	3	4	5
B	A	B	D	D

Passage–24

1	2	3	4	5
C	B	A	C	C

Passage–25

1	2	3	4	5
C	C	B	C	B

Passage–26

1	2	3	4	5
B	A	B	D	C

Passage–27

1	2	3	4	5
D	A	B	C	D

Passage–28

1	2	3	4	5
C	B	A	B	D

Passage–29

1	2	3	4	5
A	D	C	C	A

Passage–30

1	2	3	4	5
A	A	A	A	B

13. Cloze Test

A cloze test is a procedure in which a person is asked to supply words that have been removed from a passage as a test of his ability to comprehend text. Practise it regularly to score well.

MULTIPLE CHOICE QUESTIONS

Directions: *In each of the following passages some numbered blank spaces are given. For each numbered blank space four answer choices are given. Pick out the one which is the most appropriate for that blank space, keeping the trend of the passage in mind.*

PASSAGE-1

Every action we perform ....(1).... a result. And, naturally, we lay claim ....(2).... the results or fruits ....(3).... from that action in the ....(4).... that it is we who perform the action. This is .....(5).... ignorance because ....(6).... is it the Lord who ....(7).... the result of any action, it is by His will ....(8).... that even the action is accomplished. The will of the Lord ....(9).... whether we cooperate with His will or strive ....(10).... . If God wills that an action takes place, he arranges for the ....(11).... for it to happen. It is ....(12).... experience that sometimes despite our best efforts we ....(13).... achieve the results we desire, and at other times the seemingly most ....(14).... situations mysteriously get ....(15).... . ....(16).... way man chooses to act, both the act and the outcome of the cost are dependent ....(17).... on the will of the Lord.

QUESTIONS

1. A. produce B. produces
C. causes D. undergoes

2. A. on B. at
C. to D. for

3. A. occuring B. obtaining
C. deriving D. falling

4. A. belief B. hope
C. fantasy D. folly

5. A. sheen B. keen
C. sheer D. sheathe

6. A. alone B. only that
C. not only D. for only

7. A. declares B. decides
C. ordains D. ornate

8. A. completely B. entirely
C. only D. alone

9. A. prevails always
B. prevails everywhere
C. is prevalent
D. always prevails

10. A. alone B. always
C. constantly D. independently

11. A. wherewithal B. whereabouts
C. whatsoever D. wherefore

12. A. usual B. general
C. universal D. common

13. A. does not B. may not
C. do not D. might not

14. A. intractable B. intangible
C. internecine D. intricate

15. A. subsided B. resolved
C. solved D. converted

16. A. Whatever B. All the
C. All those D. Whichever

17. A. mainly B. actually
C. entirely D. generally

PASSAGE-2

For centuries, women not only in India but all over the world ....(1).... treated as ....(2).... secondary position to men. ....(3).... human history men ....(4).... far greater power then women to name, classify, and order the worlds in which they both live. ....(5).... studies in various parts of the world point out to a wide ....(6).... in male and female roles ....(7).... cultures and demonstrate the possibility of change in these sex-determined roles. The 20th century in particular ....(8).... the cause of gender justice by internationalizing struggles for equality ....(9).... women and other oppressed people. Women's struggles against their ....(10).... were interwined in ....(11).... degrees with ideologies and movements based on the values of freedom, self-determination, equality, democracy and justice.

QUESTIONS

1. A. has been B. have been
C. had been D. were

2. A. occupying B. taking
C. possessing D. serving

3. A. All through B. Throughout
C. Since D. From

4. A. have B. had
C. have had D. enjoy

5. A. Sociological B. Anthropological
C. General D. Practical

6. A. concord B. repulsion
C. disagreement D. variation

7. A. among B. across
C. between D. of

8. A. developed B. envolved
C. promoted D. entertained

9. A. for B. to
C. among D. by

10. A. subsidiary B. subsequent
C. subservience D. subordination

11. A. various B. varying
C changing D. differing

PASSAGE-3

What is required today in our country is ....(1).... of a new political culture based on full respect for human liberty, on pluralism and on a better soical deal for all. The major ....(2).... facing us today is to carry out democratic transformation in all the ....(3)...., social, cultural, economic and political. The events of the 20th century ....(4).... one thing absolutely clear that human ....(5)...., everywhere, specially in countries whose political structures were ....(6).... to reflect the revolutionary aspirations of the people ....(7).... not only under stress and strain but are ....(8).... vast upheavals because of the ....(9).... of democracy. At the same time it has also to be understood that democracy cannot be ....(10).... into a static mould.

QUESTIONS

1. A. growing B. developing
C. creating D. creation

2. A. development B. crisis
C. challenge D. drawback

3. A. corners B. context
C. realm D. spheres

4. A. have made B. has made
C. had made D. made

5. A. travails B. traverse
C. trapse D. transverse

6. A. supposed B. meant
C. caused D. forced

7. A. were B. was
C. are D. have been

8. A. developing B. evolving
C. experiencing D. faced with

9. A. denial B. rebuff
C. rebuttal D. absence

10. A. shaped B. flex
C. frozen D. caused

PASSAGE-4

We are living in very exciting ....(1).... . The ....(2).... change is dizzying and the impact this progress is having on our present and — more importantly — on our future is difficult to ....(3).... in its ...(4).... . This is the age of ....(5).... micro processors, sophisticated software, new hardware technology and high bandwith, high-speed networks. The PC gave us a new way to work, play and ....(6).... . In fact, it brought ....(7).... our desktops computing power, which until a few years ....(8).... had only been available to corporates. With the ....(9).... of the internet, the PC ....(10).... us the most convenient and flexible way to head on to the Net.

QUESTIONS

1. A. periods B. days
C. phase D. times

2. A. phase B. pace
C. sphere D. drastic

3. A. guess B. forecast
C. comprehend D. approximate

4. A. whole B. entirety
C. fruition D. fullness

5. A. strong B. changing
C. powerful D. sonorous

6. A. convey B. communicate
C. entertain D. enjoy

7. A. onto B. to
C. on D. at

8. A. back B. earlier
C. behind D. before

9. A. addendum B. adherence
C. afoot D. advent

10. A. allowed B. privileged
C. brought D. offered

PASSAGE-5

The development of an area depends on the resources ....(1).... in the area, the needs and ....(2).... of the people living there and the technological skill ....(3).... by them. Humans play an important and decisive role in the ....(4).... of development of an area. We choose the ....(5).... of resources which could be developed to our ....(6).... . The natural ....(7).... available in an area ....(8).... value as a resource only when people find a use for them. There are ....(9).... where large potential resources are available, but they ....(10).... developed for economic reasons. Lack of capital for investments, roads and railway lines, and other ....(11).... facilities may stand in the way of resource development.

QUESTIONS

1. A. present B. prevalent
C. available D. exist

2. A. inspirations B. aspirations
C. ambitions D. curiosity

3. A. handled B. practised
C. availed D. possessed

4. A. system B. design
C. pattern D. style

5. A. class B. group
C. variety D. types

6. A. good B. advantage
C. approach D. favour

7. A. secrets B. phenomenon
C. products D. endowments

8. A. get B. acquire
C. possess D. takes

9. A. instances B. events
C. circumstances D. happenings

10. A. have not yet been
B. haven't been
C. are not yet
D. yet have not been

11. A. common B. general
C. infrastructural D. structural

PASSAGE-6

The Naxal problem in India is basically socio-economic in ....(1).... . The main reasons ....(2).... the Naxal movement in India are the ....(3).... of peasants and their weak social and economic position. ....(4).... of the peasants are landless labourers whose lands have been ....(5).... occupied by the landlords. Moreover, the landlords give ....(6).... wages to the peasants. Their ....(7).... suffering at the hands of the landlords thus encourage many peasants to take law ....(8).... their own hands. Due to their poor economic condition the peasants easily ....(9).... the trap of the naxal leaders who have their ....(10).... interests. Illeteracy, unemployment, police excessess, corruption and ....(11).... administration furthur ....(12).... this complex problem.

QUESTIONS

1. A. form B. shape
C. behaviour D. nature

2. A. for B. of
C. in D. behind

3. A. complaisance B. exploitation
C. domination D. excultation

4. A. Many B. Much
C. Most D. All

5. A. imperiously B. imperatively
C. forcefully D. forcibly

6. A. inproper B. small
C. inadequate D. insufficient

7. A. long B. brutal
C. pathetic D. great

8. A. in B. into
C. on D. by

9. A. fall into B. fall in
C. fell in D. fell into

10. A. selfish B. vested
C. vicious D. vindictive

11. A. failed B. improper
C. inefficient D. bureaucratic

12. A. heighten B. deepen
C. add D. worsen

PASSAGE-7

Visualisation is a strong ....(1).... to memory. Those persons who ......(2)..... a powerful memory cannot do so without taking the help of visualisation. Such persons have developed the skills to ....(3).... visualisation even in such ....(4).... tasks as remembering names and numbers. These persons have the names and numbers ....(5).... in their brain even after hearing those names and figues only once. On the other hand those who take the help of revising to memorise ....(6).... to forget it once they have ....(7).... the practice of revising ....(8).... the ones who have applied visualisation to memorise. Psychologists ....(9).... in visualisation a powerful tool for personality development. The more you visualise, the more you are ....(10).... your attitude and behaviour to the blue prints of your vision and ....(11).... more you are inching towards success.

QUESTIONS

1. A. way B. path
C. aid D. symptom

2. A. command B. master
C. rule D. enjoy

3. A. use B. apply
C. put D. place

4. A. trivial B. difficult
C. mundane D. unscrupulous

5. A. impress B. imprinted
C. impinge D. store

6. A. bent B. incline
C. prone d. tend

7. A. dropped B. left
C. gave up D. given up

8. A. unlike B. opposite
C. contrary D. not like

9. A. found B. have found
C. sees D. finds

10. A. shaping B. moulding
C. making D. attuning

11. A. actually B. factually
C. subsequently D. consequently

PASSAGE-8

No doubt various ....(1).... and Acts are there to eliminate the ....(2).... practice of child labour. But the ....(3).... is that, these are not being implemented in both letter and spirit, for which the ....(4).... of the problem remains as it was. Therefore a judicious, pragmatic, integrated and time-bound ....(5).... supplemented by ....(6).... follow-up action is essential to ....(7).... the problem that ....(8).... deep root in our Society. It is true that child labour cann't be ....(9)... with a magic wand. If we ....(10).... time-bound goals and follow, of course, with the ....(11).... assistance of ILO and UNICEF, it is possible to eliminate the problem of child labour. With strong political will power and people's backing nothing is ....(12).... . Rather ....(13).... the bud we should let it blossom and spread its fragrance all around. ....(14).... lies the progress and prosperity of the society.

QUESTIONS

1. A. means B. methods C. source D. provisions

2. A. unjust B. inhuman C. mal D. illegal

3. A. anxiety B. abrasion C. tragedy D. conclusion

4. A. magnitude B. depth C. gravity D. soaring

5. A. approach B. analysis C. survey D. scheme

6. A. continuous B. thorough C. throughout D. regular

7. A. outroot B. uproot C. downroot D. grassroot

8. A. have B. has C. had D. has taken

9. A. wipe out B. wipe off C. wipe up D. wiped

10. A. keep B. put C. put up D. set

11. A. ongoing B. continuing C. unending D. frequent

12. A. insurmountable B. intangible C. inscrutable D. incorrigible

13. A. killing B. hurting C. destroying D. nipping

14. A. Here B. There C. Therein D. Herein

PASSAGE-9

Though the government has tried to ....(1).... Naxalism with all its might, much more needs to be done to totally root out the ....(2).... of Naxalism. The roots of Naxalism ....(3).... economic backwardness and social exploitation of the peasants and the weaker classes. Thus, the best way to ....(4).... Naxalism is to bring the naxals ....(5).... the mainstream. ....(6).... policies and schemes should be implemented effectively ....(7).... the Naxals economically stable. They should be ....(8).... to participate in democratic processes. The government has to ....(9).... the social upliftment of the Naxals. Use of force in ....(10).... Naxalism will yield little success.

QUESTIONS

1. A. crush B. handle C. tackle D. suppress

2. A. menace B. whole C. gamut D. stems

3. A. lies in B. are in C. abound in D. exist in

4. A. crash B. crush C. break D. defy

5. A. in B. on C. into D. within

6. A. Current B. Latest C. Occuring D. Existing

7. A. so that B. so as to make C. such that D. to make

8. A. insisted B. brought C. encouraged D. forced

9. A. assure B. insure C. guarantee D. ensure

10. A. countering B. deflying
C. banishing D. desecrating

PASSAGE-10

Mankind's most ....(1).... treasure of thoughts is carefully preserved in the golden casket of books. The ....(2).... of books is as vast as the universe, for there is no corner of it which they have left ....(3).... . There is no ....(4).... of books on any topic, be it as simple as the composition of sodium nitrate or as ....(5).... as the mechanism of a spacecraft rocketing towards mars. The ....(6).... of books is not only most easily available but is enlightened, dependable and lifelong. In times of distress they make us stoically ....(7).... of the object that causes uneasiness and we learn to ....(8).... with the sting of adversity.

QUESTIONS

1. A. costly B. important
C. valuable D. vast

2. A. area B. scope
C. storage D. kingdom

3. A. unexplored B. unseen
C. untouched D. unapproached

4. A. lack B. dearth
C. shortage D. insufficiency

5. A. extriate B. intricate
C. intrinsic D. internecine

6. A. company B. assistance
C. friendship D. companionship

7. A. defiant B. defendant
C. defensible D. delusive

8. A. adapt B. adopt
C. exist D. co-exist

PASSAGE-11

The common ....(1).... deeply embedded in all holy scriptures is to know one's real self. This message serves as a warning as well as ....(2).... to humankind to rise above body-mind consciousness. Living in this world just for ....(3).... of carnal desires and thinking it to be-all of life is a great ....(4).... . It is very important to know that we will ....(5).... to suffer till we ....(6).... to identify ourselves with gross body and mind. Thus, ...(7).... of our true divine nature is of ....(8).... importance.

QUESTIONS

1. A. inscriptions B. belief
C. message D. notions

2. A. an exhortation
B. emendation
C. exegesis
D. entrenchment

3. A. satiation B. satiety
C. content D. sensuality

4. A. sin B. curse
C. fallacy D. farcial

5. A. go on B. continue
C. subject D. cause

6. A. end B. stop
C. cease D. leave

7. A. knowledge B. realisation
C. appreciation D. recognition

8. A. spiritual B. worldly
C. general D. paramount

PASSAGE-12

We are all ....(1).... of the communal riots in Godhra and its ....(2).... . There are many who believe that the events in the rest of Gujarat were a ....(3).... to Godhra. We can understand a common man's reaction on seeing a close relative or friend being ....(4).... . ....(5)..., on such occasions, may be .....(6).... as a natural emotional reaction. But people in authority cannot ....(7).... to make such a comment. The Government cannot allow anyone to take the law ....(8).... his hands and it is duty bound to maintain law and order. ....(9)...., we are not a vigilante society yet. The violence in Gujarat is an ....(10).... . It is the ....(11).... of undesirable elements that are fortunately not ....(12).... in number. The majority of our people will get over this ....(13).... so that India can continue its march towards becoming a just society and an internationally competitive and ....(14).... economy.

QUESTIONS

1. A. conscious B. knowing
C. aware D. sensitive

2. A. follows B. consequences
C. subsequence D. aftermath

3. A. reaction B. reply
C. response D. restitution

4. A. humiliated B. assaulted
C. affronted D. annihilated

5. A. Retrogression B. Revengeful
C. Retrocede D. Retaliation

6. A. understood B. understandable
C. pardonable D. thought

7. A. expect B. think
C dare D. afford

8. A. in B. on
C. into D. at

9. A. Since B. After all
C. Above all D. As

10. A. aberration B. abysmal
C. apotheosis D. aversion

11. A. cause B. built-up
C. planning D. creation

12. A. great B. much
C. large D. big

13. A. catharasis B. catastrophe
C. crisis D. castigation

14. A. self-developed B. self-realised
C. self-recognised D. self-reliant

PASSAGE-13

This book is ....(1).... of the disquiet that ....(2).... in the minds and hearts of the women of the region. The objective of this work is to ....(3).... attention to the tragedy of Kashmir. The fact that while ....(4).... of the secular and mixed tradition of Kashmir is all gone, its breathtaking beauty is ....(5).... by the harsh realities of the terror and brutality, the ....(6).... violence that people, especially the women, have to ....(7).... . The writer hopes that the book can ....(8).... a move towards peace and ....(9).... . It is a ....(10).... objective. This is a book which ....(11).... to be read for its honest ....(12).... to capture the voices, the images, the very spirit, sometimes crushed sometimes ....(13)..., of the women of the region called Kashmir.

QUESTIONS

1. A. an exploration B. chronicle
C. record D. an exploitation

2. A. stays B. lies
C. rages D. exist

3. A. focus B. draw
C. pull D. direct

4. A. most B. many
C. each D. much

5. A. belied B. removed
C. destructed D. influenced

6. A. prevailing B. growing
C. continuing D. regular

7. A. go through B. live through
C. succumb D. face

8. A. effect B. affect
C. influence D. invigorate

9. A. retreat B. transquility
C. negotiation D. reconciliation

10. A. superb B. fruitful
C. wise D. brave

11. A. meant B. supposed
C. needs D. deserves

12. A. endeavour B. effusion
C. endurance D. empathy

13. A. yielding B. indomitable
C. indiscernible D. ineffable

PASSAGE-14

....(1).... has been said during 2002 about a new global effort to ....(2).... sustainable development. ....(3).... were adopted and declarations were issued on a new ....(4).... between rich and poor countries that would ....(5).... the world to the Millennium Development Goals on poverty, health, education and gender .....(6).... . The global fight against hunger is in ....(7).... need of a much stronger ....(8).... If a ....(9).... in the spread of undernourishment is proving hard to ....(10)...., elimination of hunger must be a goal that keeps getting ....(11).... further and further ....(12).... the future. In the vast majority of developing countries there is a ....(13).... in the efforts to reduce malnutrition.

QUESTIONS

1. A. Lot B. Much C. Large D. More

2. A. accentuate B. accelerate C. adjurate D. actuate

3. A. Agreement B. Arrangement C. Plans D. Agendas

4. A. coalition B. friendship C. partnership D. combination

5. A. bring B. get C. take D. place

6. A. equality B. liberty C. prosperity D. partiality

7. A. absolute B. acute C. urgent D. substantial

8. A. thrust B. thump C. bolt D. thrash

9. A. minimisation B. diminish C. reduction D. reduce

10. A. bring B. bring about C. achieve D. attain

11. A. pulled B. pushed C. motion D. acuteness

12. A. towards B. to C. in D. into

13. A. sickness B. slackening C. inactiveness D. inception

PASSAGE-15

....(1).... people today remember the war that was fought after China invaded India in 1962. Not because the war was never really ....(2).... . Nor because it was ....(3).... almost before it began. The reason is ....(4).... that most of us were yet to be born. The main reason for the Chinese attack seems to ....(5).... to establish the ....(6).... order, expose our ....(7)...., put us in our place. The official reason, ...(8)...., was the territorial dispute, ...(9).... more than 100,000 square kilometres. ....(10).... speaking, India borders Tibet, not China. The McMohan Line ....(11).... the border with Tibet in what is now Arunachal Pradesh was the result of a 1914 treaty ....(12).... British India and Tibet. This was not ....(13).... to the Chinese the result was a .....(14)..... nose. The Chinese attack was ....(15).... fast and furious. ....(16).... brave soldiers ....(17).... down their lives, but India was simply unable to halt the ....(17).... . Panic quickly ....(18)....

QUESTIONS

1. A. A few B. Few C. Fewer D. A little

2. A. joined B. combined C. acted D. approved

3. A. finished B. ceased C. over D. stopped

4. A. simple B. simply C. common D. commonly

5. A. had been B. have C. had D. have been

6. A. pecking B. unavoiding C. powerful D. selfish

7. A. projections B. pretensions C. presumption D. pretending

8. A. more over B. probably C. perhaps D. however

9. A. effecting B. causing C. affecting D. influencing

10. A. Formally B. Informally C. Broadly D. Technically

11. A. relating B. dividing C. defining D. laying

12. A. among B. between C. of D. by

13. A. favourable B. favoured
C. acceptable D. accepting

14. A. angry B. bloody
C. honed D. blitz

15. A. quick B. prick
C. sudden D. unassuming

16. A. Some B. Few
C. Many D. A lot of

17. A. onrush B. onset
C. omnipotence D. omen

18. A. come in B. gone in
C. set in D. set out

PASSAGE-16

Man has always been ....(1).... with flying because it ....(2).... a sense of freedom, of romance and thrill-something too ....(3).... to resist. It is the task of the ....(4).... of the skies to safeguard Indian air-space from unwelcome ....(5)..... . The Indian Air Force ....(6).... a chequered and glorious history. From its ....(7).... days of single-engine aeroplanes like Tempests and Spitfires to the state of the art multi-engine, supersonic MIG and Sukhoi fighters, the Indian Air Force ....(8).... a long way. In addition to the already existing ....(9).... of aircraft and weapon systems, plans are ....(10).... to enhance its air defence power and ....(11).... capability through upgradation and ....(12).... .

QUESTIONS

1. A. fascinated B. moved
C. inspired D. fancied

2. A. generates B. cultivates
C. reaps D. evokes

3. A. envisaging B. impressing
C. enchanting D. laudable

4. A. sentiness B. sedulous
C. venturous D. fervid

5. A. emigrants B. intruders
C. foreigners D. tourists

6. A. had B. have
C. have had D. has had

7. A. early B. undeveloped
C. growing D. embryonic

8. A. had come B. has come
C. have come D. came

9. A. invention B. inventory
C. mechanism D. technique

10. A. progressive B. afresh
C. afoot D. affluent

11. A. combat B. increase
C. intensify D. ensure

12. A. acquisition
B. acknowledgement
C. acquiescence
D. accumulation

PASSAGE-17

Libraries were never ....(1).... the place to ....(2).... They never will be. But those who've visited libraries for the ....(3).... pleasure of it will testify to the feeling of ....(4).... on entering the labyrinth ....(5).... high with books. Suddenly, a ....(6).... spent reading seems the ideal. It's a similar experience to ....(7).... in a bookshop. The difference : in the second situation, despair ....(8).... you as your eyes zoom ....(9).... on the price; in the first there is the ....(10).... that all these books are yours for the asking. Today, ...(11)...., library use is almost ....(12).... necessity-based. The reading room is ....(13).... full with students poring ....(14).... their books..

QUESTIONS

1. A. realised B. seen
C. recognised D. considered

2. A. hung out B. hang out
C. hang out in D. hung out in

3. A. mere B. sheer
C. trivial D. trifle

4. A. exhilaration B. exhaustion
C. expedition D. extrapolation

5. A. going B. moving
C. pik D. towering

6. A. long time B. whole life
C. life time D. life long

7. A. browsing B. move about
C. move D. stroll

8. A. swamps B. swab
C. swoon D. swoop

9. A. at B. on
C. in D. upon

10. A. idea B. surity
C. certainty D. knowledge

11. A. although B. however
C. in fact D. moreover

12. A. wholly B. partially
C. outwardly D. purely

13. A. tight B. completely
C. over crowded D. cramped

14. A. into B. onto
C. over D. upon

PASSAGE-18

The ridge is on the ....(1).... of collapse. The stems of trees are being slaughtered without any ....(2).... or reason. The nearby residents cut plants just for cooking purpose ....(3).... realising that their ....(4).... act will spoil the environment. Though the forest department must have foreign guards in the area yet they ....(5).... seem to have the will and strength to take ....(6).... to stop the felling of trees. Everyday one can see wood and fresh cut stems which ....(7)... taken away by those living in the neighbourhood. It is not clear as to why they ....(8).... about the crime of felling of trees which is punishable ....(9).... the law.

QUESTIONS

1. A. verge B. limit
C. border D. boundary

2. A. sense B. rhyme
C. rhythm D. ultimatum

3. A. without B. scarcely
C. not D. hardly

4. A. foolish B. absurd
C. mean D. unmindful

5. A. does not B. do not
C. don't D. won't

6. A. part B. step
C. enthusiasm D. measures

7. A. has been B. have been
C. are D. had been

8. A. are not being told
B. are not told
C. have not been told
D. had not been told

9. A. by B. under
C. in D. in according

PASSAGE-19

The ....(1).... of a country does not depend on the abundance of its revenue but more ....(2).... by its citizens; its men of education, enlightenment and character. It is for the ....(3).... of higher learning to ....(4).... an academic environment of equity, justice and fair play where those ....(5).... in the ....(6).... task of nation building can ....(7).... their responsibilities in a spirit of sincerity, dedication and commitment. Higher education in India ....(8).... great strides after independence. The ideal of education is to ....(9).... for self-preservation but which also prepares us to recognise and ....(10).... the rights of others and to shoulder our ....(11).... as responsible citizens.

QUESTIONS

1. A. prospects B. fortune
C. protrusion D. gaiety

2. A. illustrated B. emancipated
C. defined D. apprehended

3. A. institute B. centre
C. college D. university

4. A. encourage B. embark
C. promote D. polish

5. A. employed B. recruited
C. held D. engaged

6. A. paramount B. ardous
C. lucrative D. laudable

7. A. dispense B. disburse
C. carry D. discharge

8. A. have taken B. had taken
C. has taken D. is taking

9. A. evoke B. prepare
C. encourage D. cultivate

10. A. concede B. preserve
C. coddle D. clung

11. A. obligations
B. obduracy
C. obsequiousness
D. portfolio

PASSAGE-20

A people's relation to their culture ....(1).... the same as the relation of a child to its mother's breast. There is ....(2).... any doubt that religious belief is part of the culture of a people. ....(3).... it is their religious faith which ....(4)... their lives in many ways, ...(5).... not only which god they worship and how, but also helping them ....(6).... an internal value system, making social living ....(7)...., and impacting the most important events in ordinary lives by ....(8).... the do's and don'ts and the rituals that ....(9).... birth, death and marriage. Whenever a religious conversion ....(10)...., indeed it must be painful, as painful as it is for a child being ....(11).... away from its mother's breast.

QUESTIONS

1. A. is B. has been
C. have been D. are

2. A. never B. hardly
C. improbably D. implicitly

3. A. Probably B. Perhaps
C. Incidently D. Often

4. A. protect B. shield
C. sustain D. defend

5. A. determining B. deciding
C. suggesting D. laying

6. A. create B. construct
C. invent D. develop

7. A. coherent B. co-existing
C. cohesive D. coerce

8. A. laying down B. putting up
C. determining D. formulating

9. A. circle B. cycle
C. encircle D. surround

10. A. takes place B. took place
C. had taken place D. has taken place

11. A. removed B. snatched
C. weaned D. took

PASSAGE-21

Observation is one of the key ....(1).... of modern corporate behaviour. Indeed it has long been the ....(2).... for humans and animals generally. It is essential for every corporate citizen to be able to taste the ....(3).... of what is happening around him all the time, not merely to survive but to ... (4).... . ....(5).... the corporate corridors to check which way the wind is blowing! Know when it is appropriate to get your ....(6).... in and when it is ....(7).... to maintain a low profile. To ....(8).... a career with the ease and ....(9).... of a winner, you need to be able to ....(10).... a disaster before it happens! You need to take an advantage before someone else ....(11).... . You need to be at the right place before someone else ....(12).... there. Observation or paying attention to what's happening around us is essential ....(13).... . We need to take the time to ....(14).... the habit of paying attention so that we can make our work ....(15).... and so that we can stand at ease! Career ....(16).... will be the happy outcome!

QUESTIONS

1. A. approach B. method
C. tactics D. means

2. A. rule B. norm
C. convention D. technique

3. A. presence B. essence
C. events D. problem

4. A. thrive B. throb
C. fare D. blow

5. A. Sniff B. Snuffle
C. Spin-off D. Splutter

6. A. shore B. oar
C. objective D. ogle

7. A. correct B. right
C. prudent D. prudish

8. A. carry B. initiate
C. continue D. conduct

9. A. caprice B. comfort
C. over-confidence D. aplomb

10. A. forecast B. apprehend
C. guess D. foretell

11. A. do B. does
C. takes D. gets

12. A. come B. comes
C. get D. gets

13. A. everytime B. alltime
C. everywhere D. forever

14. A. reap B. sow
C. cultivate D. grow

15. A. easy B. easier
C. easiest D. simple

16. A. advancement B. progression
C. achievement D. cultivation

PASSAGE-22

The ....(1).... Euphoria over the ....(2).... fall in the cost of domestic air travel has ....(3).... to a more realistic appraisal of what is on offer. The aggressive ....(4).... schemes offered since the beginning of July have certainly been good news for certain categories of passengers who probably value .....(5).... above anything else. For them, the heavily discounted fare ....(6).... enables them to afford air travel for the first time. In fact, the ....(7).... of the fare cut ....(8).... such that in specific instances air travel compares ....(9).... to the fares charged by the Railways for upper class travel. Obviously, it ....(10).... for a change in mindset to switch to air travel in ....(11).... to, say, rail transport in India. Economy and affordability will certainly be key ....(12).... but they must be made available ....(13).... a fairly long period. To put it differently, cheaper air travel or at least a ....(14).... fare structure ....(15).... institutionalised in the country.

QUESTIONS

1. A. embryonic B. early
C. ending D. initial

2. A. casual B. sudden
C. surprising D. dramatic

3. A. raised B. caused
C. given way D. gave way

4. A. lucrative B. lofty
C. laudable D. promotional

5. A. expenses B. affordability
C. comfort D. time

6. A. scheme B. structure
C. system D. circular

7. A. portion B. ratio
C. magnitude D. proportion

8. A. are B. is
C. has been D. have been

9. A. very slightly B. very favourably
C. specifially D. generally

10. A. causes B. calls
C. invites D. lures

11. A. choice B. favour
C. preference D. alternative

12. A. determinants B. detrimentals
C. performers D. issues

13. A. over B. for
C. to D. through

14. A. different B. distinctive
C. reducing D. differential

15. A. must be B. has to be
C. ought to be D. have to be

PASSAGE-23

We all know that good political understanding is ....(1).... a matter of getting history right, for we ....(2).... where we have come from in order to understand the present. ....(3)...., we can understand contemporary Indian politics only in the light of our freedom movement, which was to set the ....(4).... for contemporary Indian politics. ....(5)...., the main pillars of the constitution – democracy, secularism, social justice, and fundamental and minority rights — were forged ....(6).... sustained political mobilisation.

QUESTIONS

1. A. wholly B. largely
   C. particularly D. generally
2. A. do need to know B. must know from
   C. must know about D. must know
3. A. As such B. As per
   C. Accordingly D. After all
4. A. coarse B. course
   C. flow D. pattern
5. A. Above all B. After all
   C. In fact D. Since
6. A. throughout B. for
   C. in and through D. to

PASSAGE-24

"I need a break" is a common .....1..... among the ....(2).... middle and elite classes — under ....(3).... pressure to perform, to live up to their own artificial standards, to earn, and earn some more and ....(4).... some more. But in this vortex, time is at a ....(5)...., and the much needed break ....(6).... materialises because harried professionals are unable to stay away from work long enough ....(7).... from the city and breathe in some fresh air — metaphorically and literally. And weekends? They are ....(8).... lazing at home, ...(9).... on chores, or may be watching some mind numbing television programme. Because it would be hard to think of a place you ....(10).... escape to that was far enough from the city to be ....(11).... and yet close enough to ....(12).... as a weekend break.

QUESTIONS

1. A. restrain B. refrain
   C. remark D. saying
2. A. hurried B. harried
   C. worried D. busy
3. A. continuous B. consequent
   C. constant D. stable
4. A. even B. add
   C. farther D. then
5. A. premium B. minimum
   C. limitation D. restriction
6. A. never often B. often never
   C. although never D. sometimes do not
7. A. to stay away B. to escape
   C. to go away D. to get moved
8. A. there B. for
   C. those D. some
9. A. getting B. catching
   C. catching up D. catching down
10. A. can B. ever
    C. would D. could
11. A. refreshed B. refreshing
    C. resting D. rejoining
12. A. consider B. anticipate
    C. contemplate D. meditate

PASSAGE-25

Every monsoon I'm reminded of an incident that ....(1).... many years ago when I was a young man ....(2).... my first job in Mumbai. I was staying with my sister in those days. On one wet and windy night I ....(3).... with friends, and as it happens when you are in pleasant company, the ....(4).... . It was past ten when I finally bid goodby to my companions and moved towards my sister's house. It had rained the whole day, and it ....(5).... to drizzle again. The rain had ....(6).... people indoors earlier than usual and the dimly — lit street I was walking along was ....(7).... . I had heard that the road was ....(8).... . They said one could hear a woman calling for help on some nights. As I proceeded, I suddenly saw a figure walking ....(9).... me. A bandicoot chose to ....(10).... across my path, just then she seemed to have ....(11).... into thin air. Then I heard a faint ....(12).... for help. This frightened me and as such I turned and fled. The next morning I came to know from my sister that the bandicoot was no other but her friend who had mistakenly thought she was being ....(13).... . Out of fear she was looking behind and walking when she ....(14).... into a ditch. Now every monsoon, I'm reminded of my ....(15).... on that wet night.

QUESTIONS

1. A. happened B. occurred C. took place D. had taken place

2. A. in B. on C. working at D. working with

3. A. had been out B. went for outing C. had gone D. was out

4. A. time passes B. time runs C. time flies D. time files

5. A. has B. was C. began D. had begun

6. A. pushed B. sent C. send D. driven

7. A. calm B. peace C. lonely D. deserted

8. A. mysterious B. ghostly C. haunted D. devilish

9. A. before B. in front of C. a head D. near

10. A. scuttle B. scurry C. scuff D. scrouge

11. A. faded B. vanished C. vaporised D. melted

12. A. sound B. voice C. cry D. whisper

13. A. followed B. chased C. pursued D. caught

14. A. fall B. stumbled C. threw D. jumped

15. A. foolishness B. ignorance C. confusion D. cowardice

PASSAGE-26

In every country there are people who work day and night against the best interests of their countrymen, ...(1).... the laws of the land to which they belong, and follow such practices as are socially and morally ....(2).... . Anti-social elements are the greatest enemies of their country because they ....(3).... its stability by ....(4).... chaotic conditions from which they ....(5).... enormous monetary gains. These agents of lawlessness and enemies of the public weal trade in contraband goods, ...(6).... foodstuffs and products of industry underground, and create an artificial ....(7).... of all vital necessaries of life, causing ....(8).... and ....(9).... the normal life of the people. The activities of anti-social traders are so ....(10)...., so well-organised and so elusive that there is ....(11).... chance of their ....(12).... by the ordinary processes of law.

QUESTIONS

1. A. break B. violate C. avoid D. overlook

2. A. resprehensible B. deterrent C. disapproved D. repellent

3. A. imbalance B. affect C. undermine D. disturb

4. A. causing B. building C. releasing D. creating

5. A. make B. deduce C. infer D. derive

6. A. take B. keep C. drive D. put

7. A. shortage B. deficiency C. scarcity D. lacking

8. A. inflation B. deterioration C. deflation D. infringement

9. A. disturbing B. disrupting C. breaking D. rapturing

10. A. subtle B. despotic C. subterranean D. subterfuge

11. A. a few B. a little C. few D. little

12. A. detection B. detonation C. discovery D. revelation

PASSAGE-27

No society can ....(1).... itself to be civil if it ....(2).... its weak. Children are ....(3).... the weakest, who are not even aware of their rights. Even if they are, they can do ....(4).... little about it. The various ....(5).... against child abuse are thus mere words on paper for a boy or a girl who is .....(6).... at school and physically humiliated by a teacher. Educational institutions do, in this day and age, still ....(7).... to the ....(8).... forms of punishment that are also psychologically ....(9).... . Caning, boxing and slapping someone incapable of ....(10).... himself are nothing short of ....(11).... which reveals a medieval ....(12).... : the rod can be spared only at the cost of ....(13).... a child.

QUESTIONS

1. A. fancy B. hold
C. believe D. take

2. A. discards B. ignores
C. disapproves D. brutalises

3. A. definitely B. supposedly
C. perhaps D. sympathetically

4. A. hardly B. scarcely
C. precious D. good

5. A. procession B. agendas
C. banners D. compaigns

6. A. spanked B. punished
C. hurt D. punched

7. A. retort B. resort
C. confine D. manifest

8. A. ill B. meanest
C. unworthly D. unsuitable

9. A. demeanour B. demeaning
C. condemned D. discouraged

10. A. protecting B. shielding
C. retaliating D. defending

11. A. bravery B. valour
C. cowardice D. boldness

12. A. tempo B. temperament
C. mindset D. feelings

13. A. correcting B. spoiling
C. hurting D. torturing

PASSAGE-28

Most of India's educational institutions, ...(1).... by hiring people who are ....(2).... qualified to be teachers. They are ....(3).... an unhappy group, which is ill-paid and which commands ....(4).... respect. Sadly, it is these men and women who have the enormous duty of ...(5).... tomorrow's society, a responsibility that remains ...(6)... . Children are ....(7).... in this terrifying circle : they are ....(8).... into submission, their innocence is destroyed and their lives become ....(9).... joyless. What follows is still ....(10).... . A violent childhood ....(11).... a violent adulthood. A child who faces the ....(12).... of an adult grows up ....(13).... that violence is the answer to all problems. They become ....(14).... individuals and often their intellectual development ....(15).... in the absence of congenial peace.

QUESTIONS

1. A. get away B. manage
C. run D. go away

2. A. not really B. really not
C. virtually not D. not actually

3. A. commonly B. mainly
C. specifically D. usually

4. A. scant B. scanty
C. scarce D. rare

5. A. forming B. moulding
C. framing D. making

6. A. unsatisfied B. unprecedented
C. unfulfilled D. unrequited

7. A. taught B. caught
C. captured D. chained

8. A. battered B. split
C. squeezed D. shaped

9. A. universally B. utterly
C. wholly D. complete

10. A. unfavourable B. bad
C. not good D. worse

11. A. may lead to B. may grow to
C. may reach to D. would develop to

12. A. consequences B. wrath
C. grief D. wretch

13. A. thinking B. supposing
C. infering D. believing

14. A. complex B. complicated
C. rough D. sanguine

15. A. slows down B. moves slowly
C. hampers D. brakes

PASSAGE-29

Men ....(1).... the maker of their own destinies and they ....(2).... make the destiny of the society and the nation. Life is a great gift of God to men and man ....(3).... making constant efforts to live a ....(4).... life right from the stone age to the modern one. But it is man who ....(5).... to think out how to live well. The ....(6).... before mankind today is between self-preservation and self destruction. Science has given men all the powers that they need but the new millennium ....(7).... new Challenges. We are ....(8).... what nature has given us — forests are being cut down, slums are being ....(9)...., rivers are being polluted. Medical science has made great ....(10)....; but the population is growing in a geometrical ....(11).... . Our natural resources like coal and oil are being ....(12).... . Atomic energy is our only hope. The ....(13).... welcome of the New Millennium lies in our determination and hope for self-preservation ....(14).... self-destruction.

QUESTIONS

1. A. are B. have been
C. being D. had been

2. A. unitedly B. ultimately
C. conjointly D. co-exist to

3. A. have been B. are
C. has been D. have had been

4. A. congenial B. cordial
C. congregational D. congruent

5. A. have B. is
C. are D. has

6. A. optional B. choice
C. possibilities D. probabilities

7. A. presents B. places
C. offers D. puts forth

8. A. destroying B. ignoring
C. neglecting D. wasting

9. A. developed B. constructed
C. created D. manufactured

10. A. advancement B. advances
C. achievement D. inventions

11. A. dimension B. angle
C. index D. proportion

12. A. deported B. deplored
C. depleted D. disposed

13. A. actual B. real
C. warm D. innate

14. A. upon B. over
C. on D. above

PASSAGE-30

There is no longer the slightest scope for confusion about the nature of the ...(1)... economic crisis. Superficially, the ...(2)... in the economy appears as a severe ...(3)... between financial resources and physical output. The sharp rise in the prices of the ...(4)... of life and the stagnation of employment opportunities have ...(5)... the distribution of income in favour of the well off, especially the rich farmers, traders, industrialists, professionals and the upper ...(6)...of the salaried classes. On the other hand, even the best organised ...(7).. of the working class have suffered ...(8)... of their real earnings.

QUESTIONS

1. A. current B. latest
C. existing D. present

2. A. malaise B. malice
C. evils D. factors

3. A. inequity B. inequality
C. disequilibrium D. imbalance

4. A. usages B. requirement
C. essentials D. daily needs

5. A. disturbed B. destructed
C. violated D. distorted

6. A. echleons B. ecclesiastics
C. oppulent D. section

7. A. branches B. proportion
C. segment D. part

8. A. an erosion B. an earthquake
C. a scourge D. scorch

ANSWERS

Passage-1

1	2	3	4	5	6
B	C	B	A	C	C
7	8	9	10	11	12
C	D	D	D	A	D
13	14	15	16	17	
C	A	B	D	C	

Passage-2

1	2	3	4	5	6
B	A	B	C	B	D
7	8	9	10	11	
B	C	D	D	B	

Passage-3

1	2	3	4	5	6
D	C	D	A	A	B
7	8	9	10		
C	C	A	C		

Passage-4

1	2	3	4	5	6
D	B	C	B	C	B
7	8	9	10		
A	D	D	D		

Passage-5

1	2	3	4	5	6
C	B	D	C	D	B
7	8	9	10	11	
D	B	A	A	C	

Passage-6

1	2	3	4	5	6
D	A	B	C	D	C
7	8	9	10	11	12
A	B	A	B	C	D

Passage-7

1	2	3	4	5	6
C	A	B	C	B	D
7	8	9	10	11	
A	A	B	D	D	

Passage-8

1	2	3	4	5	6
D	B	C	A	A	D
7	8	9	10	11	12
B	D	B	D	B	A
13	14				
D	C				

Passage-9

1	2	3	4	5	6
C	A	A	B	C	D
7	8	9	10		
B	C	D	A		

Passage-10

1	2	3	4	5	6
C	D	A	B	B	D
7	8				
A	D				

Passage-11

1	2	3	4	5	6
C	A	A	C	B	C
7	8				
B	D				

Passage-12

1	2	3	4	5	6
C	D	A	B	D	B
7	8	9	10	11	12
D	C	B	A	D	C
13	14				
B	D				

Passage-13

1	2	3	4	5	6
A	C	B	A	A	C
7	8	9	10	11	12
B	B	D	D	C	A
13					
B					

Passage-14

1	2	3	4	5	6
B	B	D	C	C	D
7	8	9	10	11	12
C	A	C	B	B	D
13					
B					

Passage-15

1	2	3	4	5	6
B	A	C	B	A	A
7	8	9	10	11	12
B	D	C	A	C	B
13	14	15	16	17	18
C	B	C	C	A	C

Passage-16

1	2	3	4	5	6
A	D	C	A	B	D
7	**8**	**9**	**10**	**11**	**12**
D	B	B	C	A	A

Passage-17

1	2	3	4	5	6
D	C	B	A	D	C
7	**8**	**9**	**10**	**11**	**12**
A	A	C	D	B	D
13	**14**				
D	A				

Passage-18

1	2	3	4	5	6
A	B	D	D	B	D
7	**8**	**9**			
C	A	B			

Passage-19

1	2	3	4	5	6
A	C	B	C	D	B
7	**8**	**9**	**10**	**11**	
D	C	B	A	A	

Passage-20

1	2	3	4	5	6
A	B	D	C	B	B
7	**8**	**9**	**10**	**11**	
C	A	D	A	C	

Passage-21

1	2	3	4	5	6
C	B	B	A	A	B
7	**8**	**9**	**10**	**11**	**12**
C	A	D	D	B	D
13	**14**	**15**	**16**		
C	C	B	B		

Passage-22

1	2	3	4	5	6
D	D	C	D	B	B
7	**8**	**9**	**10**	**11**	**12**
C	C	B	B	C	A
13	**14**	**15**			
A	D	C			

Passage-23

1	2	3	4	5	6
B	A	C	B	B	C

Passage-24

1	2	3	4	5	6
B	B	C	D	A	B
7	**8**	**9**	**10**	**11**	**12**
A	B	C	D	B	C

Passage-25

1	2	3	4	5	6
B	C	A	A	D	D
7	**8**	**9**	**10**	**11**	**12**
D	C	C	B	B	C
13	**14**	**15**			
A	B	D			

Passage-26

1	2	3	4	5	6
B	A	C	D	D	C
7	**8**	**9**	**10**	**11**	**12**
C	A	B	A	D	A

Passage-27

1	2	3	4	5	6
A	D	C	C	D	A
7	**8**	**9**	**10**	**11**	**12**
B	B	B	D	C	C
13					
B					

Passage-28

1	2	3	4	5	6
A	B	D	A	B	C
7	**8**	**9**	**10**	**11**	**12**
B	A	B	D	A	B
13	**14**	**15**			
D	A	A			

Passage-29

1	2	3	4	5	6
B	C	C	A	D	B
7	**8**	**9**	**10**	**11**	**12**
C	A	C	B	D	C
13	**14**				
B	B				

Passage-30

1	2	3	4	5	6
A	A	D	C	D	A
7	**8**				
C	A				

General Intelligence

REASONING ABILITY

Chapter 1

TEST OF ANALOGY

Analogy implies finding corresponding words or pairs. In test of analogy a pair of words/figures with well difined relationship is given and a similar relationship is to be established between two others by selecting from the given answer.

Some examples are given below to make understand the test of analogy.

Example 1 :

Cow : Calf : : Lion : Cub

Ans. Here Calf is young one of Cow where as Cub is the young one of Lion.

Example 2 :

Doctor : Patient : : Lawyer : Client

Ans. Here Doctor is to attend the Patient and Lawyer is to attend the Client.

Example 3 :

Needle : Sew : : Knife : Cut

Ans. A Needle is used for Sewing hence Knife is used for Cutting.

Example 5 :

Lizard : Reptile : : Ostrich : Bird

Ans. Lizard belongs to the class of Reptile and Ostrich belongs to the class of Bird.

EXERCISE

1. Book : Read : : Pen : ?
A. Publisher B. Stationery
C. Ink D. Write

2. Bird : Cage : : Prisoner : ?
A. House B. Police Station
C. Jail D. Court

3. War : Death : : Smoke : ?
A. Burning B. Fire
C. Pollution D. Sky

4. Apple : Iron : : Grapes : ?
A. Vitamin A B. Vitamin B
C. Vitamin D D. Vitamin C

5. Blacksmith : Anvil : : Author : ?
A. Book B. Novel
C. Poem D. Pen

6. Rough : Smooth : : Depression : ?
A. Joy B. Happiness
C. Disease D. Mound

7. Sun : Shine : : Cloud : ?
A. Rain B. Dark
C. Burst D. Lightning

8. Bud : Flower : : Sapling : ?
A. Plant B. Garden
C. Water D. Soil

9. Gun : Shoot : : Knife : ?
A. Cut B. Stice
C. Run D. Cuts

10. Anger : Rage : : Quarrel : ?
A. Dispute B. Fight
C. War D. Murder

11. Attack : Defend : : Sink : ?
A. Float B. Swim
C. Boat D. Water

12. Oil : Sunflower : : Plant : ?
A. Twing B. Taste
C. Flower D. Seed

13. Gun : Bullet : : Chimney : ?
A. Smoke B. Roof
C. House D. Ground

14. Good : Bad : : Rough : ?
A. Plane B. Clean
C. Smooth D. Thick

15. Bank : River : : Coast : ?
A. Flood B. Waves
C. Sea D. Beach

16. Man : Machine : : Master : ?
A. Slave B. House

C. Manager D. Worker

17. Campa : Drink : : Medicine : ?
A. Take B. Swallow
C. Sip D. Taste

18. Sharp : Blunt : : Light : ?
A. Heavy B. Dark
C. Empty D. Night

19. Adder : Snake : : Crocodile : ?
A. Marsh B. Reptile
C. Ruminant D. Carnivore

20. Propellor : Aircraft : : Feathers : ?
A. Neck B. Bird
C. Tail D. Decoration

21. Head : Cap : : Finger : ?
A. Nail B. Blood
C. Skin D. Thumb

22. Leg : Foot : : Hand : ?
A. Arm B. Thigh
C. Wrist D. Elbow

23. Bunch : Key : : Bouquet : ?
A. Pack B. Gift
C. Flower D. Present

24. Army : Soldiers : : Galaxy : ?
A. Stars B. Meteor
C. Universe D. Planet

25. Water : Thirst : : Food : ?
A. Hunger B. Rice
C. Earn D. Distribute

26. Cup : Drink : : Plate : ?
A. Silver B. Dine
C. Fork D. Supper

27. Blood : Circulation : : Harmone : ?
A. Egestion B. Control
C. Digestion D. Coordination

28. Steel : Bokaro : : Hosiery : ?
A. Calcutta B. Mumbai
C. Kanpur D. Ludhiana

29. Bull : Draugut : : Cow : ?
A. Fodder B. Farm
C. Milk D. Livestock

30. Cobra : Snake : : Leopard : ?
A. Tiger B. Lion
C. Cat D. Zebra

31. Horse : Hay : : Cow : ?
A. Leaves B. Fodder
C. Milk D. Straw

32. Movie : Theatre : : Banquet : ?
A. Hotel B. Party
C. Feast D. Supper

33. Water : Ocean : : Snow : ?
A. Peaks B. Hail
C. Glacier D. Mountain

34. Poison : Socrates : : Crucification : ?
A. Jesus B. Christians
C. Aristotle D. Church

35. Tempest : Storm : : Slim : ?
A. Fat B. Plump
C. Slender D. Beautiful

36. Chopper : Meat : : Spanner : ?
A. Vegetables B. Cakes
C. Nuts D. Flash

37. Kilometre : Distance : : Poundal : ?
A. Density B. Acceleration
C. Force D. Momentum

38. Sparrow : Seed : : Silkworm : ?
A. Silic B. Maple
C. Mulberry D. Pine

39. Tobacco : Nerves : : Alcohol : ?
A. Liver B. Liquor
C. Head D. Intoxication

40. Arm : Forcep : : Leg : ?
A. Thigh B. Ankle
C. Toe D. Foot

41. Medicine : Disease : : Surgery : ?
A. Headache B. Tumour
C. Vomiting D. Pain

42. Abnormal : Normal : : Mad : ?
A. Good B. Sound
C. Sane D. Perfect

43. Die = Punch, Knife = ?
A. Cut B. Sharpen
C. Vegetable D. Murder

44. Cloud : Rain : : Snowstorm : ?
A. Hail B. Dew
C. Snow D. Fog

45. Beautiful : Ugly : : Brave : ?
A. Coward B. Timid
C. Strong D. Dummy

46. Labour = Wage, Clerk = ?
A. Remuneration B. Salary
C. Payment D. Money

47. Author : Book : : Poet : ?
 A. Novel B. Book
 C. Song D. Poem

48. Ascorbic Acid : Vitamin : : Glucose : ?
 A. Minerals B. Carbohydrates
 C. Vitamins D. Proteins

49. Life : Death : : Hope : ?
 A. Sad B. Despair
 C. Pain D. Cry

50. Cub : Tiger : : Fawn : ?
 A. Stag B. Monkey
 C. Ass D. Sheep

ANSWERS

1	2	3	4	5	6	7	8	9	10
D	C	C	D	D	D	A	A	A	C
11	12	13	14	15	16	17	18	19	20
A	D	A	C	C	A	A	B	B	B
21	22	23	24	25	26	27	28	29	30
A	C	C	A	A	B	D	D	C	C
31	32	33	34	35	36	37	38	39	40
B	A	C	A	C	C	C	C	A	A
41	42	43	44	45	46	47	48	49	50
B	C	A	C	A	B	D	B	B	A

EXPLANATORY ANSWERS

1. Book is used for Reading, Pen is used for Writing.
2. Birds are kept in Cage likewise Prisoners are kept in Jail.
3. Second is the Result of first.
4. We are getting Vitamin C from Grapes.
5. Anvil is used by Blacksmith, Pen is used by Author.
6. Second word is antonym of first.
7. The Sun gives Shine (Sunrays) whereas Clouds give Rains.
8. A Bud blooms into a Flower whereas a Sapling blooms into a Plant.
9. The usage of Knife is for Cutting.
10. The extreme of Anger is Rage and the extreme of Quarrel is War.
11. Second word is antonym of first.
12. First item is developed from the second one.
13. Second one is the outcome of the first one.
14. Second word is antonym of first.
15. Coast is the land beside the Sea.
16. Machine is made to work by a Man, Slave works under Master.
17. Medicine is always Taken.
18. The pairs comprise antonyms.
19. Crocodile is a Reptile.
20. A Propellor helps the Aircraft fly and Feathers help the Bird fly.
21. Nails cover the Fingers.
22. Wrist is attached to Hand.
23. The former in each pair belongs to the latter.
24. An Army comprises the Soldiers and a Galaxy comprises the Stars.
25. Water satisfies the Thirst of a person and Food satisfies the Hunger of a person.
26. Plates are kept of Dine.
27. Second is the function of first.
28. Ludhiana is famous for Hosiery.
29. Bull is a Draughter animal and Cow is Milk animal.
30. The second one denotes the family to which the first one belongs.
31. The second one is the food for the first one.
32. Second is the place where first is held.
33. Ocean is moving body of Water, Glacier is moving body of Snow.
34. First became the cause of death of the second.
35. First is of higher intensity.
36. First is the tool applied at the second.
37. Poundal is a unit of Force.

38. First feed at the second.

39. Alcohol affects the Liver.

40. The upper portion of Leg is Thigh.

41. Medicine is used to cure disease, Surgery is done to remove Tumour.

42. Second word is antonym of first.

43. We use a Die for Punching and we use a Knife for Cutting.

44. A Cloud gives Rains and a Snowstorm gives Snow.

45. Second word is antonym of first.

46. Clerks are given Salary.

47. Poet writes Poems.

48. Ascorbic Acid is a Vitamin and Glucose is a Carbohydrate.

49. The words in each pair are antonyms of each other.

50. First one is the young offspring of the second one.

Chapter 2

SERIES COMPLETION

In this chapter, some series of numbers or Alphabatical letters have been given. A particular pattern is followed and the student has to calculate his answer according to the pattern.

Example 1 : Which number will replace the question mark (?) :

2, 5, 9, 19, 37, ?

A. 45 B. 52

C. 69 D. 75

Ans. $2 \times 2 + 1 = 5$

$5 \times 2 - 1 = 9$

$9 \times 2 + 1 = 19$

So $37 \times 2 + 1 = 75$ Right Answer is D.

Example 2 : Find out the missing number :

0, 3, 8, ?, 24

A. 12 B. 14

C. 15 D. 11

Ans. $1^2 - 1$

$2^2 - 1$

$3^2 - 1$

So, $4^2 - 1 = 15$ Right Answer is C.

Example 3 : Which number would replace question mark (?) :

7, 12, 19, ?, 39

A. 29 B. 26

C. 28 D. 24

Ans. Given sequence follows this pattern :

$7 + 5 = 12$

$12 + 7 = 19$

$19 + 9 = 28$ Hence the Answer is C.

Example 4 : Find the odd man out:

3, 5, 7, 11, 13

A. 7 B. 11

C. 9 D. 13

Ans. Pattern is : 9 is the only number whose square-root is possible and here, 9 is the odd man out.

Example 5 : Find the odd man out:

3, 8, 15, 24, 34, 48, 63

A. 15 B. 24

C. 34 D. 48

E. 63

Ans. The, differences between the numbers are 5, 7, 9, 11 .... and so on. So, after 24, there should be (24 + 11), *i.e.*, 35. Hence the odd man is 34.

EXERCISE

Complete the Series:

1. 196, 16, 144, 36, 100, 64, ?

A. 36 B. 64

C. 80 D. 100

2. 8, 48, 12, ?, 18, 108

A. 52 B. 72

C. 78 D. 64

3. 1, 4, 27, 16, 125, ?

A. 36 B. 81

C. 144 D. 216

4. 1, 2, 5, 12, 27, 58, 121, ?

A. 246 B. 247

C. 248 D. 249

5. 3, 6, 5, 20, 7, 42, 9, ?

A. 54 B. 60

C. 66 D. 72

6. 2, 3, 8, 63, ?

A. 1038 B. 1998

C. 3008 D. 3968

7. 3, 15, 35, ?, 99, 143

A. 63 B. 69

C. 77 D. 81

8. 2, 5, 9, 19, 37, ?

A. 45 B. 52

C. 69 D. 75

9. 240, ? 120, 40, 10, 2

A. 240 B. 120

C. 40 D. 10

10. 4, 7, 3, 6, 2, 5, ?
A. 8 B. 1
C. 4 D. 3

11. 1, 5, 8, 10, 11, ?
A. 5 B. 7
C. 9 D. 11

12. ?, 6, 30, 120, 360, 720
A. 3 B. 2
C. 1 D. 0

13. 1, 3, 1, 9, 1, 81, 1, ?
A. 4 B. 1
C. 243 D. 6561

14. 10, 12, 11, 14, 16, 15, ?
A. 18, 20, 19 B. 18, 19, 20
C. 17, 19, 18 D. 21, 23, 24

15. 5, 24, 61, 122, 213, 340, ?
A. 27 B. 61
C. 122 D. 509

16. 7, 28, 63, 124, ?
A. 127 B. 214
C. 215 D. 227

17. 1, 24, 60, 120, ?
A. 210 B. 240
C. 260 D. 215

18. 3, 5, 7, 9, 11, 13, ?
A. 15 B. 17
C. 18 D. 14

19. 3, 9, 27, 81, ?
A. 324 B. 243
C. 210 D. 311

20. 2, 5, 9, ?, 20, 27
A. 14 B. 16
C. 18 D. 20

21. 0, 1, 4, 9, 16, ?
A. 24 B. 20
C. 25 D. 28

22. 30, 29, 27, 24, 20, ?
A. 16 B. 17
C. 15 D. 14

23. 2, 3, 4, 9, 16, 54, 96, ?
A. 486 B. 768
C. 560 D. 324

24. 3, 19, 41, 71, 109, ?
A. 155 B. 157
C. 153 D. 158

25. 2, 12, 36, 80, 150, ?
A. 252 B. 256
C. 216 D. 284

ANSWERS

1	2	3	4	5	6	7	8	9	10
B	B	A	C	D	D	A	D	A	B
11	**12**	**13**	**14**	**15**	**16**	**17**	**18**	**19**	**20**
D	C	D	A	D	C	A	A	B	A
21	**22**	**23**	**24**	**25**					
C	C	A	A	A					

EXPLANATORY ANSWERS

1. There are two series :
I : $14^2 - 12^2 - 10^2$ and so on.
II : $4^2 - 6^2 - 8^2$ and so on.

2. (8×6) (12×6) (18×6)

3. $1^3, 2^2, 3^3, 4^2, 5^3, 6^2$

4. $(121 \times 2 + 6)$

5. (3×2) (5×4) (7×6) (9×8)

6. $(2)^2 - 1 = 3; (3)^2 - 1 = 8; (8)^2 - 1 = 63, (63)^2 - 1 = 3968$

7. One series is 4, 3, 2, 1. Other (alternate) series is 7, 6, 5, 4.

8. $\times 2 + 1, \times 2 - 1$

9. (2×5) (10×4) (40×3) (120×2)

10. Our series is 4, 3, 2, 1. Other (alternate) series is 7, 6, 5, 4.

11. $(1 + 4)$ $(5 + 3)$ $(8 + 2)$ $(10 + 1)$ $(11 + 0)$

12. (1×6) (6×5) (30×4) (120×3) (360×2)

13. $1^2, 3^2, 9^2, 81^2$

14. (10 ... 12) (14 ... 16) ... (18 ...)

15. $(8^3 - 3)$

16. $(2^3 - 1)$ $(3^3 - 1)$ $(4^3 - 1)$ $(5^3 - 1)$ $(6^3 - 1)$

17. $(1^3 - 0)$ $(3^3 - 3)$ $(4^3 - 4)$ $(5^3 - 5)$ $(6^3 - 6)$

18. difference of 2.

19. (3×3) (9×3) (27×3) (81×3)

20. increasing difference 3, 4, 5, 6

21. 5^2

22. $(30 - 1)$ $(29 - 2)$ $(27 - 3)$ $(24 - 4)$ $(20 - 5)$

23. Alternate (3×3) (9×6) (54×9)

24. $(12^2 + 11)$

25. $1^3 + 1^2, 2^3 + 2^2, 3^3 + 3^2, 4^3 + 4^2, 5^3 + 5^2, 6^3 + 6^2$

Chapter 3

WRONG NUMBER OUT

In this type of test the candidates are asked to find out one figure which is not similar to any of the others. The given series are either in continuation or in a specific pattern or having some similarity but one of them is different. So we have to find out which number/alphabet is misfit and not following the rubs of the series or having the some properties as that of other, number/alphabet.

Find the Wrong Number:

1. 1, 3, 5, 7, 8, 11, 13
A. 3 B. 7
C. 9 D. 11

2. 3, 7, 11, 15, 17
A. 7 B. 11
C. 17 D. 15

3. 7, 26, 63, 124, 210
A. 26 B. 124
C. 210 D. 7

4. 24, 51, 33, 42, 72
A. 51 B. 42
C. 72 D. 33

5. 14, 6, 8, 16, 21
A. 6 B. 8
C. 16 D. 21

6. 24, 27, 31, 33, 36
A. 24 B. 27
C. 31 D. 33

7. 8, 13, 21, 32, 47, 63, 83
A. 13 B. 21
C. 32 D. 47

8. 3, 10, 27, 4, 16, 64, 5, 25, 125
A. 3 B. 4
C. 10 D. 27

9. 15, 16, 22, 29, 45, 70
A. 16 B. 22
C. 45 D. 70

10. 1, 3, 7, 15, 27, 63, 127
A. 7 B. 15
C. 27 D. 63

11. 11, 5, 20, 12, 40, 26, 74, 54
A. 5 B. 20
C. 40 D. 26

Replace the Wrong Number:

12. 1, 2, 11, 36, 84
A. 30 B. 28
C. 37 D. 85

13. 3, 8, 18, 38, 75
A. 78 B. 75
C. 65 D. 58

14. 2, 3, 5, 8, 13, 34
A. 21 B. 25
C. 29 D. 34

Complete the Alphabet Series:

15. A, Z, B, Y, C, X, ?
A. W B. U
C. V D. D

16. AC, CE, DF, EG, ?
A. GF B. GI
C. GK D. GE

17. AZ, BY, CX, ?
A. DW B. DU
C. DV D. DX

18. YEB : WFD : VGF : SHH : ?
A. QIJ B. QUL
C. TOL D. None of these

19. AD, EH, IL, ?, QT
A. LM B. MN
C. MP D. OM

20. JE, LH, OL, SQ, ?
A. WV B. WX
C. VW D. XW

21. DF, GJ, KM, NQ, RT, ?
A. UW B. YZ
C. XZ D. UX

22. CE, GI, KM, OQ, ?
A. TW B. TV
C. SU D. RT
E. UW

23. AZ, BY, CX, ?
A. EP B. GH
C. IJ D. DW

24. CAT, FDW, IGZ, ?
A. KJA B. KTC
C. LHO D. LJC

25. QPO, SRQ, UTS, WVU, ?
A. XVZ B. ZYA
C. YXW D. VWX
E. AZY

ANSWERS

1	2	3	4	5	6	7	8	9	10
C	D	D	C	D	C	D	C	B	C
11	**12**	**13**	**14**	**15**	**16**	**17**	**18**	**19**	**20**
C	D	A	A	D	B	A	A	C	D
21	**22**	**23**	**24**	**25**					
D	C	D	D	C					

EXPLANATORY ANSWERS

1. $\sqrt{9} = 3$
2. 15 has got a fraction 5 × 3.
3. 7 has got no fraction.
4. There are two series with a common difference of 9, *i.e.*, 24, 33, 42 and 51, 42, ... So, 72 is the odd number here.
5. 21 is not divisible by 2.
6. 31 does not have any fraction.
7. 47 is wrong and must be replaced by (32 + 14) = 46.
8. The correct sequence is $3, 3^2, 3^3 \ldots 4, 4^2, 4^3 \ldots$ 10 should be replaced by 9.
9. 22 is wrong and must be replaced by (16 + 4) 20.
The pattern is $1^2 + 2^2 + 3^3 \ldots$.
10. 27 is wrong must be replaced by $(15 + 2^4) = 31$.
11. The given sequence is a combination of two series (*i*), 11, 20, 40, 74; (*ii*) 5, 12, 26, 54.
40 is wrong and must be replaced by 38.
12. The correct sequence is
$1 + (1)^2 = 2, 2 + (3)^2 = 11, 11 + (5)^2 = 36$
So, $36 + (7)^2 = 85$. Hence 84 should be replaced with 85.
13. Wrong figure is 75. It must be replaced by 78
$(3\times2+2)(8\times2+2)(18\times2+2)(38\times2+2)$
14. Clearly each terms of the series is the sum of preceding terms.
So the term 21 is missing and 34 is a wrong entry.
15. The embedded series is A – B – C – D.
16. GI is correct choice as the series moves after shipping one alphabet.
17. A – B – C – D and W... X...Y...Z are the two series embedded in one another.
18. OIJ is the right sequence.
19. The first and second letters of each term are moved ahead by four alphabets.
20. The first letters of the first, second, third *etc.* terms are moved ahead by two, three and four alphabets, respectively
21. There is a gap of one letter between both the letters of first terms, a gap of two letters between both the letters of second terms .....
22. The letters of each terms are alternate and also the last letter of each term and the first letter of the next term and alternate.
23. The first letter if each term is moved by one alphabet forward and the second letter is moved one step backward .
24. All the letters of each term are moved by three alphabets forward .....
25. Each term in the series consists of three consecutive letters in reverse order. The first letter of each term and the last letter of the next term are two series.

Chapter 4

LETTER SERIES

In the letter series test, some sequence of alphabets have been given. Based on this sequence, we have to find out next combination of alphabets. Nowadays, two or more than two questions are being asked in this area. Topic itself is very simple and requires a little concentration. Some examples have been given so as to make our readers understand the basic concepts and applications.

Example : aab — aab — aab —

A. bba B. abb

C. bab D. aab

E. bbb

Ans. Proceed Step by Step

The sequence is aabb, aabb, aabb

Hence Right Answer is (E).

EXERCISE

1. a — ba — cbaac — aa — ba

A. c, c, b, b B. c, a, b, c

C. c, b, c, b D. b, b, c, c

2. ab — baabc — aabcb — abcb —

A. b, c, a, a B. c, b, a, a

C. a, b, c, a D. a, a, c, b

3. — ba — ababa — aba — ab

A. a, a, a, b B. a, a, a, a

C. a, b, a, b D. a, b, b, b

4. — aba — abaa — baa — ba

A. b, b, b, b B. a, b, b, b

C. a, a, a, a D. b, a, a, a

5. ac — baac — b — acbb —

A. b, a, a, b B. a, b, b, c

C. a, a, b, c D. b, b, a, a

6. a — bdb — c — ca — acbdb — cac — d

A. a, d, b, d, c, b B. c, d, a, d, a, b

C. a, b, a, d, d, c D. c, b, a, d, b, a

7. aa — aaa — aaaa — aaaa — b

A. b, a, a, a B. b, b, a, a

C. b, b, b, b D. b, b, b, a

8. aa — aabb — b — aa — aabb — bb

A. b, a, b, b, a B. b, b, b, a, a

C. b, a, b, b, a D. a, a, b, b, b

9. ababb — b — b — ab — bb

A. b, b, a, a B. b, b, a, b

C. a, a, b, a D. a, a, b, b

10. — bbaaba — ba —

A. b, b, a, a B. a, a, b, b

C. a, b, a, b D. b, a, b, a

11. — baabbaa — b — a

A. a, a, b B. a, b, a

C. b, a, b D. b, b, a

12. — — abbbab bb — b

A. b, b, a B. a, a, b

C. a, a, a D. b, b, b

13. b — bb — abbbab —

A. a, a, b B. b, b, b

C. a, b, a D. a, b, b

14. — baa — ba — aab —

A. b, a, b, a B. b, b, a, a

C. a, b, b, b D. b, b, a, b

15. — aabb — a — ab — b.

A. b, b, a, a B. a, b, a, b

C. b, a, b, a D. b, c, a, b

16. — aa — baa — ab — a

A. a, b, a, b B. b, b, a, a

C. a, b, b, b D. a, a, b, b

17. a — baa — aa — ab

A. b,b,b,b B. b,b,a,a

C. a, b, b, a D. a, a, a, a

18. — aa — a — baaa —

A. b,a,b,a B. b,b,a,a

C. b,b,a,b D. b,a,b,b

19. — a — b — aaab — aa

A. b,b,b,b B. a,a,a,b

C. b,a,a,b D. a,b,a,b

20. — b — baaabb — a —

A. a,b,b,a B. a,b,a,b

C. b,a,b,a D. b,a,a,b

21. — a — aabb — aab —

A. a,b,b,a B. a,a,a,b

C. b,a,a,b D. b,b,a,b

22. — baa — ab — aaa — aaa —

A. b,a,b,a B. a,b,a,b

C. a,a,b,b D. a,a,a,b

23. — b — baaa — bba —

A. a,b,b,b B. b,a,a,b

C. a,b,b,a D. b,a,b,a

24. — ba — baa — ab — a

A. b,a,a,b B. b,a,b,a

C. a,a,a,b D. a,b,b,b

25. baa — a — a — bab — aba

A. a,a,b,b B. a,b,b,a

C. b,b,a,a D. b,b,b,a

ANSWERS

1	2	3	4	5	6	7	8	9	10
B	B	D	C	D	D	D	A	C	D
11	**12**	**13**	**14**	**15**	**16**	**17**	**18**	**19**	**20**
D	A	D	C	B	A	C	D	D	A
21	**22**	**23**	**24**	**25**					
D	D	C	D	C					

EXPLANATORY ANSWERS

1. *acba, acba, acba, acba*
2. *abcba, abcba, abcba, abcba* . . . .
3. *ab, ab, ab, ab* . . . .
4. *aaba, aaba, aaba* . . . .
5. *acbba, acbba, acbba* . . . .
6. Series *acbdbbcacad* repeated two times.
7. *aab,— aaab, — aaaab, — aaaaab*
8. *aab, aab, babb, aab, aab, babb.*
9. Series *ababb* repeated three times.
10. Series *babbaa* repeated twice.
11. Series *bbaa* repeated three times.
12. Series *bbab* repeated three times.
13. Series *babb* repeated three times.
14. Series *abaabb* repeated twice.
15. Series *aaabbb* repeated twice.
16. Series *aaabba* repeated twice.
17. Series *aabaab* repeated twice.
18. Series *baaaab* repeated twice.
19. *aabbaa* repeated twice.
20. Series *abbaa* repeated twice.
21. Series *baaabb* repeated twice.
22. Series *abaaa* repeated twice.
23. Series *abbbaa* repeated twice.
24. Series *ababba* repeated twice.
25. Series *baaba* repeated three times.

Chapter 5

DIRECTION TEST

Direction Test is a test to judge the candidate's ability to understand and find out the four directions correctly and also, the distance covered while he is moving in different directions from a Starting point.

The following figure shows the four main Directions—*N* for North, *S* for South, *E* for East and *W* for West. There are four cardinal directions also — named as *NW, NE, SW* and *SE.*

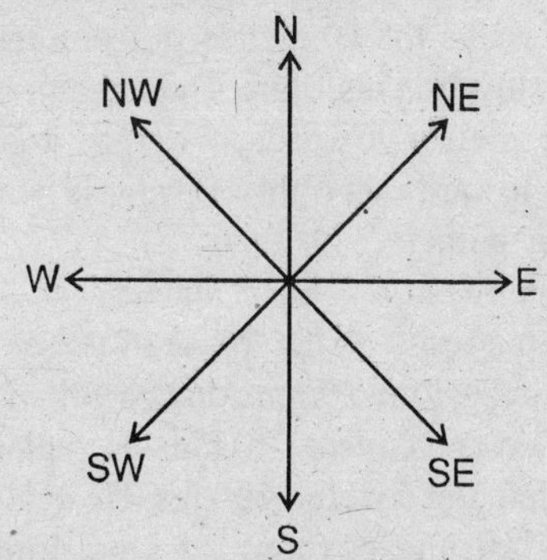

Example 1 : Mr. Mohan moves 10 km towards East then again moves 10 km left, again moves 10 km left. How much is the distance from starting point and in which direction he is now?

Ans.

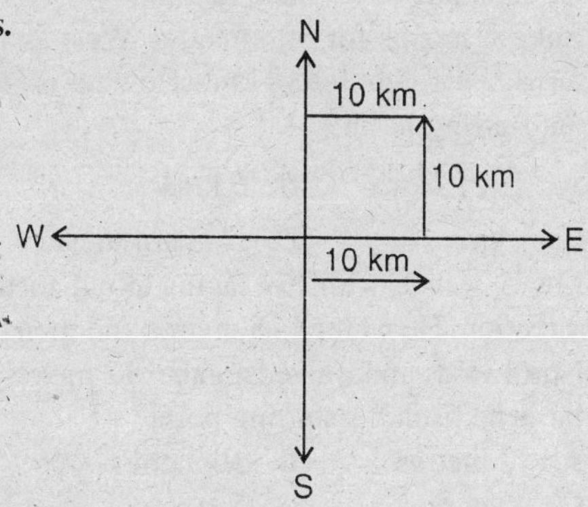

According to the figure Mr. Mohan is in North direction and is 10 km away from the starting point.

Example 2 : Mr. Ram left home and cycled 15 km to South thereafter he turned his left and cycled 20 km, again turned left and cycled 15 km and again turned left and cycled 20 km. Where is he at present?

Ans.

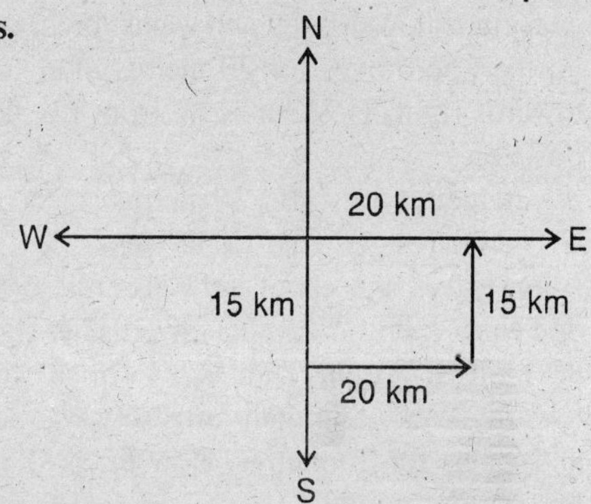

According to the figure Mr. Ram is at the starting point.

Example 3 : A boy is looking for his brother. He went 4 km towards East and then turned to his left and went as for as 3 km. He found his brother there. What is the distance from the starting point and the meeting point (where he meet his brother)?

Ans.

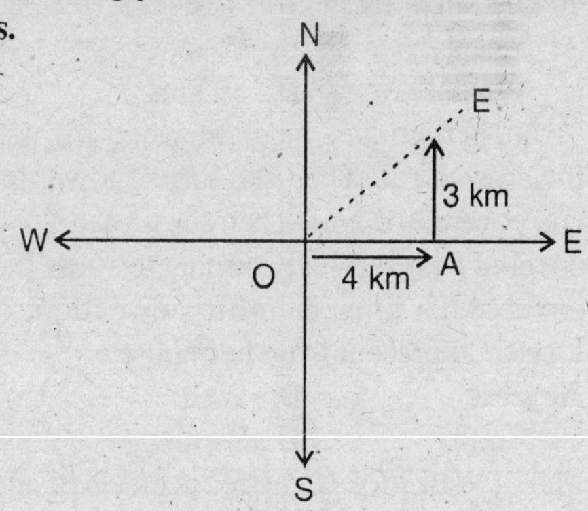

$$OE = \sqrt{OA^2 + AE^2}$$

$$= \sqrt{4^2 + 3^2}$$

$$= \sqrt{16 + 9}$$

$$= 5 \text{ km.}$$

EXERCISE

1. A man is facing North and turned to his right at an angle of 180°, again he turned right at an angle of 90°. In which direction is he now?
   A. East B. North
   C. West D. South
2. Suresh walks 20 metres towards North. He then turns towards left and walks for 40 metres. He again turns towards left and walks for 20 metres. Further, he moves for 20 metres after turning towards right. How far is he from his starting position?
   A. 20 metres B. 30 metres
   C. 60 metres D. 50 metres
3. A girl leaves her school and walks for 20 metres due North. Next she walks towards her right for 30 metres. Again, she walks for 40 metres towards West. She then turns towards her left and walks for 20 metres. How far is she from her starting point?
   A. 30 metres B. 20 metres
   C. 10 metres D. 15 metres
4. Mohan went for 15 kms towards the West from his office and then turned towards his left and walked for 20 kms. He then turned East and walked 25 kms and finally turning left covered 20 kms. How far he from office?
   A. 5 kms B. 10 kms
   C. 40 kms D. 80 kms
5. From her house, Neelam went for 15 kms towards North. Then she turned towards West and covered 10 kms. Then she turned South and covered 5 kms. Finally turning towards East she covered 10 kms. In which direction, is she located at present from her house?
   A. East B. West
   C. North D. South
6. Manoj Walks for 10 metres in due East and then for 10 metres towards his right. Then every time turning to his left he walks for 5, 15 and 15 metres, respectively. How far is he from his starting point?
   A. 5 metres B. 10 metres
   C. 20 metres D. 23 metres
7. Mr Lokesh moved for 20 kms towards North and turned back to South by distance of 40 kms. He turned towards his left and travelled for 20 kms. Again, he turned towards his left for 10 kms, again moved towards left for 20 kms. How far is he from his starting point.
   A. 10 kms B. 20 kms
   C. 30 kms D. 25 kms
8. Ram moves for 30 kms due East and then turns towards left and travels for 40 kms. How far is Ram from his starting point and in which direction?
   A. *NE* 50 kms B. *SE* 40 kms
   C. *NW* 30 kms D. *WS* 60 kms
9. Mr. *A* walks for 10 metres in front and for 10 metres towards his right. Then again, he walks for 10 metres towards his right and for 10 metres towards his right. How far is he from the starting point?
   A. 0 metre B. 5 metres
   C. 10 metres D. None of these
10. Rahul cycled for 20 kms due North and turned to his left and covered 20 kms. He again turned to his left and covered 60 kms. He again turned to his left and covered 20 kms. Finally, he moved for 40 kms towards his left. How far is he from his starting point?
    A. 0 km B. 5 kms
    C. 20 kms D. 40 kms
11. Rakesh moves for 30 kms due West and then, turns to his right for 10 kms. How far is he from his starting point?
    A. $10\sqrt{10}$ kms B. 5 kms
    C. 7 kms D. None of these
12. Mr. *A* stands with his facing point to the *SE* direction. He walked 15 metres and then turned Northwards and walked another 12 metres. How far is he from his starting point?
    A. 12 metres B. 10 metres
    C. 9 metres D. 5 metres
13. *K* went 10 m towards East and then, turned towards North and walked for another 15 m. Then, he turned towards West and covered 12 m and then, turned towards South and covered

15 m. How far is he from starting point?

A. 2 metres B. 5 metres
C. 6 metres D. 10 metres

14. Anil walked for 3 m. towards North and turned towards West and walked for 2 m. Then, he turned towards North and walked for 1 m and then, he turned towards East and walked for 5 m. How far is he from his starting point?

A. 1 metre B. 2 metres
C. 3 metres D. 5 metres

15. I went for 15 metres due North. Then, I turned towards South and coverd 5 metres and then, I turned towards East and covered 10 metres. In which direction, am I?

A. East B. West
C. North D. South

16. *A*, *B*, *C*, and *D* are playing cards. *B* is sitting in front of *D*. *A* is sitting to right of *D*, facing *C*. *D* is facing South. Which direction is being faced by *C*?

A. East B. West
C. North D. South

17. *A* and *B* start their journeys in opposite directions. *A* is facing North and walked for 10 kms whereas Mr. *B* walked for 20 kms. Mr. *A* turned to his right and walked for 15 kms. Again, he turned towards his left and covered 10 kms. Mr. *B* turned towards his left for 15 kms and again, towards his left for 20 kms. At what direction, are they meeting?

A. East B. South
C. North D. West

18. *A*, *B*, *C* and *D* are playing a game of Carrom. *A*,*C* and *B*,*D* are partners. *D* is to the right of *C* who is facing West. Then *B* is facing.

A. North B. East
C. South D. West

19. If *A* is to the South of *B* and *C* is to the East of *B*, in what diretion is *A* with respect to *C*?

A. *NE* B. *NW*
C. *SE* D. *SW*

20. Rakesh's School bus is facing North when he reaches his school. After starting from Rakesh's house, it turns towards right twice and then towards left, before reaching to school. What direction was the bus facing, when it left the bus stop in front of Rakesh's House?

A. North B. South
C. East D. West

21. Rinku starts his journey towards West and walked 10 kms then, he moves towards his left 20 kms and again moves towards left for 40 kms. Again, he moves towards left for 20 kms. How for is he from starting point?

A. 20 kms B. 30 kms
C. 40 kms D. 10 kms

22. Suresh left his office towards North and covered 15 kms. He turned towards his right and covered 10 kms. Again, he moved towards right and covered 30 kms. How far is he from his starting point?

A. $\sqrt{325}$ B. $\sqrt{275}$
C. $\sqrt{1015}$ D. $\sqrt{513}$

23. *A*, *B*, *C* and *D* are playing Carrom. *B* is sitting in front of *C* and is facing North. *A* is sitting to the left of *B*. Which direction is being faced by *D*?

A. East B. West
C. North D. South

24. Ashok moved towards East and covered 4 kms. He then moved towards South 3 kms. Again he moved his right and covered 7 kms. How far is he from his starting point?

A. $\sqrt{18}$ B. $\sqrt{27}$
C. $\sqrt{25}$ D. $\sqrt{35}$

25. Two friends, Ravi and Chavi, left together towards North and covered 10 kms. Ravi turned to his left for 15 kms and again, turned towards left and covered 10 kms. Again he turned towards left for 30 kms. Chavi turned to his right for 15 kms. Again he turned toward right for 10 kms. At which direction, are they meeting again and at what distance?

A. East 15 kms B. West 10 kms
C. North 10 kms D. South 20 kms

ANSWERS

1	2	3	4	5	6	7	8	9	10
C	C	C	C	C	A	A	A	A	A

11	12	13	14	15	16	17	18	19	20
A	C	A	D	A	B	A	A	D	D
21	**22**	**23**	**24**	**25**					
B	A	B	A	A					

EXPLANATORY ANSWERS

1.

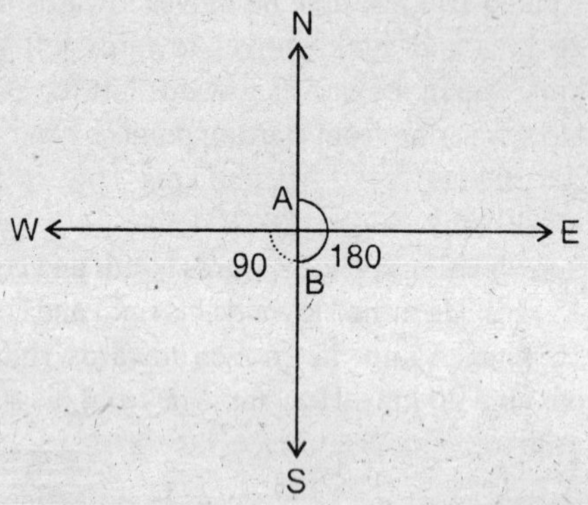

Man turns to his right at an angle of 180°, so he is at point *B* and again he moves towards his right at an angle of 90°, so he is at point *C*. His direction is West.

2.

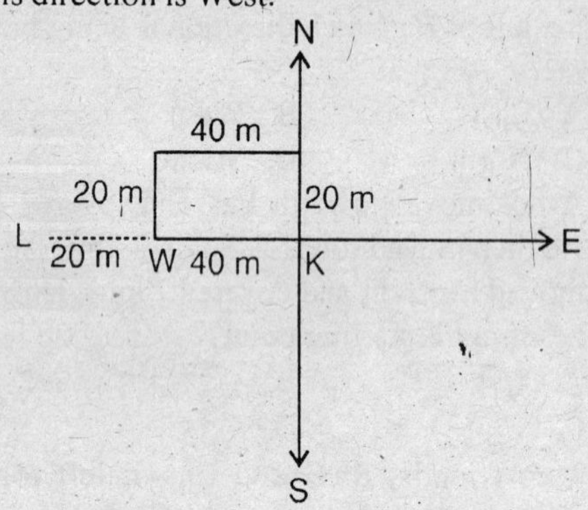

He is at point *L*, *i.e.*, 60 km from starting point.

3.

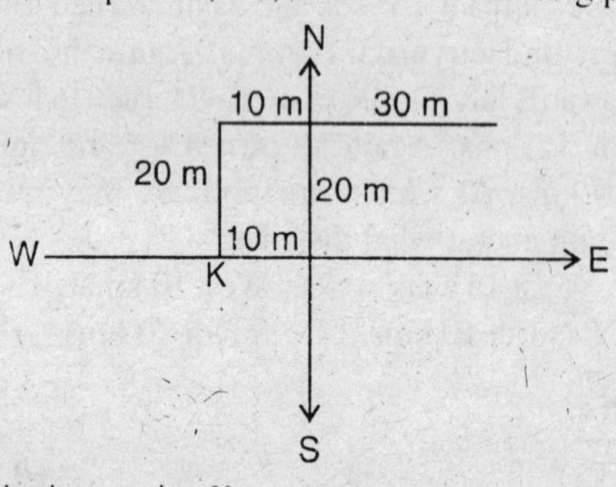

She is at point *K*.

4.

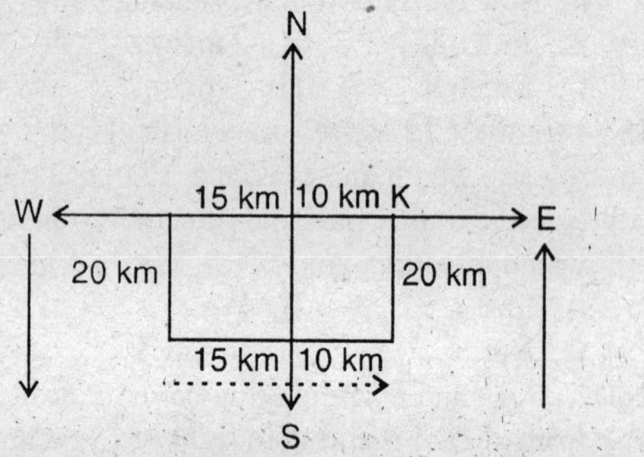

He is at point *K* 10 km from his starting point.

5.

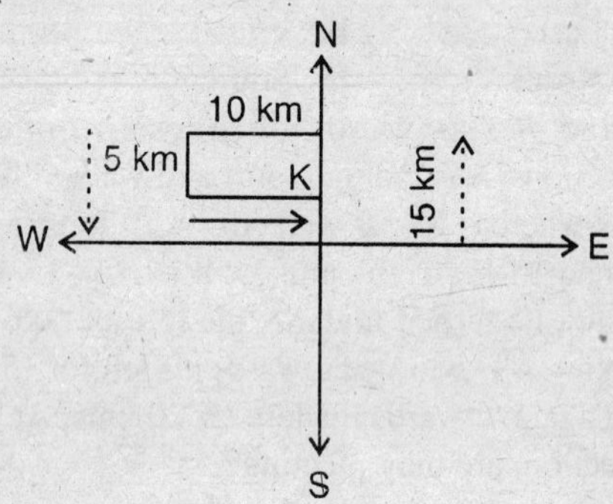

She is at point *K* which is in North.

6.

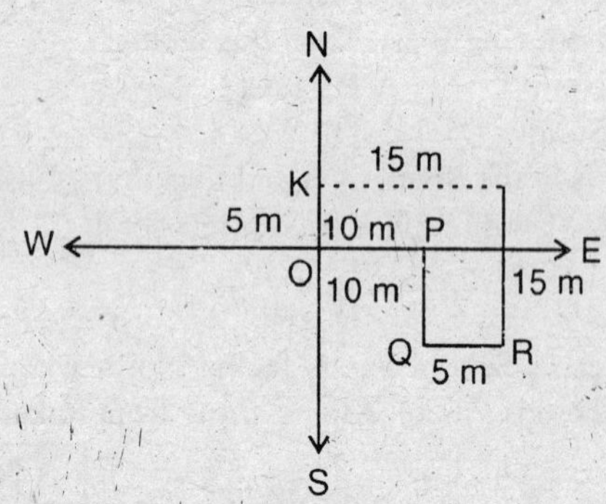

He is at point *K* 5 metres away.

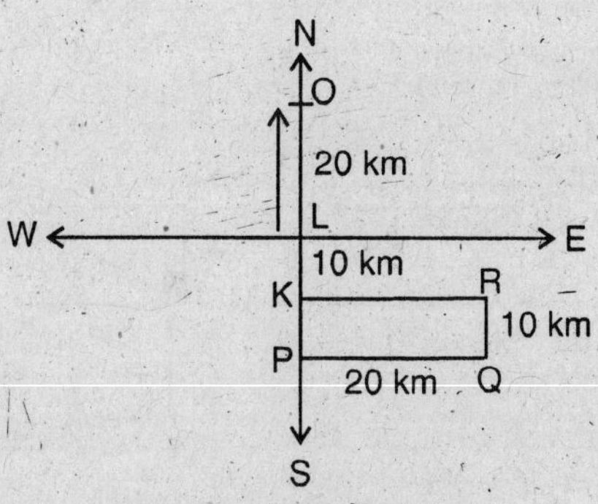

L to *O*, *O* to *P*, *P* to *Q*, *Q* to *R*, *R* to *K*.

8.

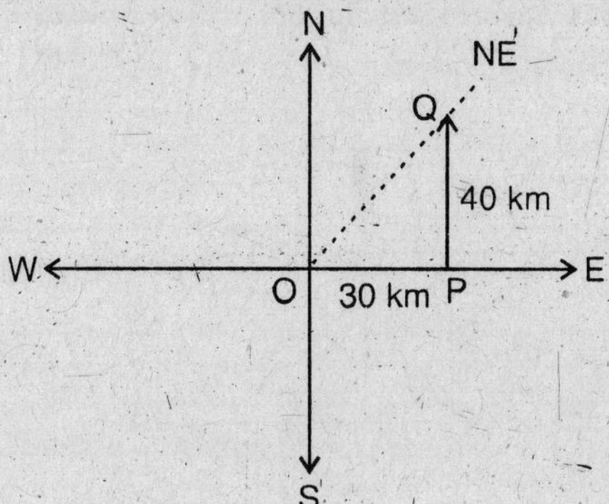

$\sqrt{30^2 + 40^2} = 50$ m.

9.

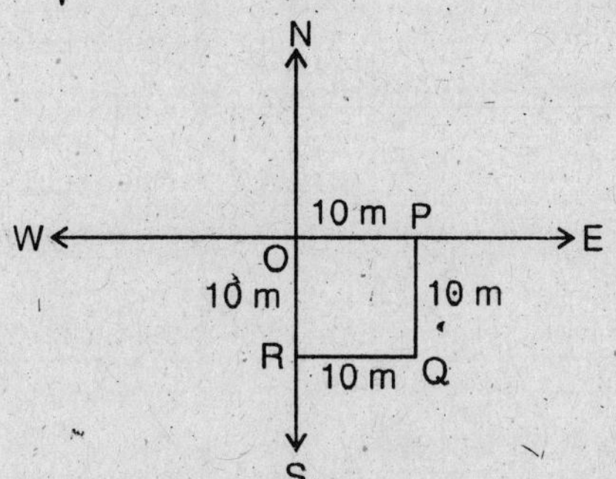

He is at his starting point.

10.

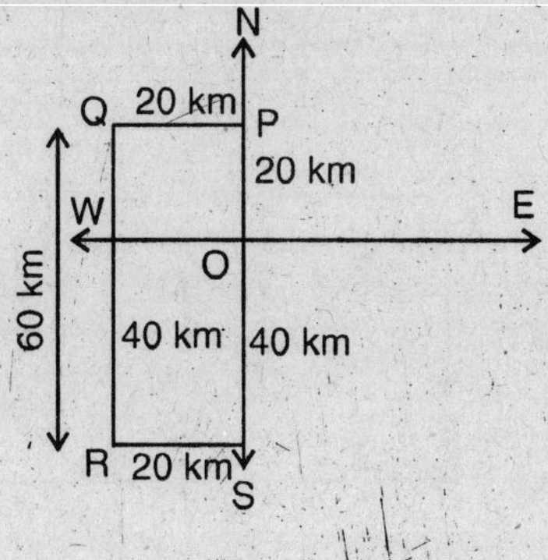

Rahul is at original point.
His journey is *OP*, *PQ*, *QR*, *RS*, *SO*.

11.

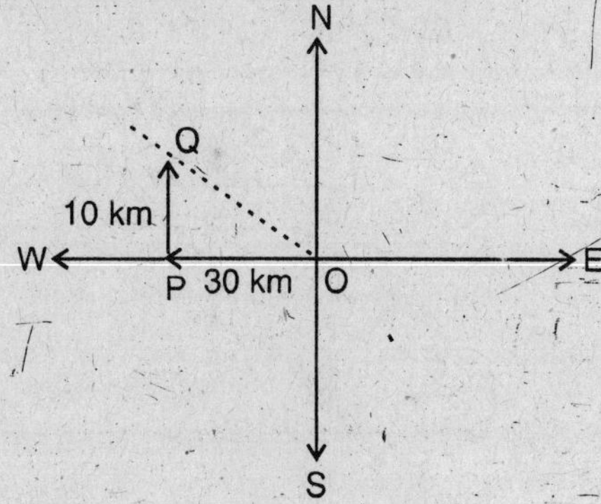

$\sqrt{30^2 + 10^2} = \sqrt{1000} = 10\sqrt{10}$

12.

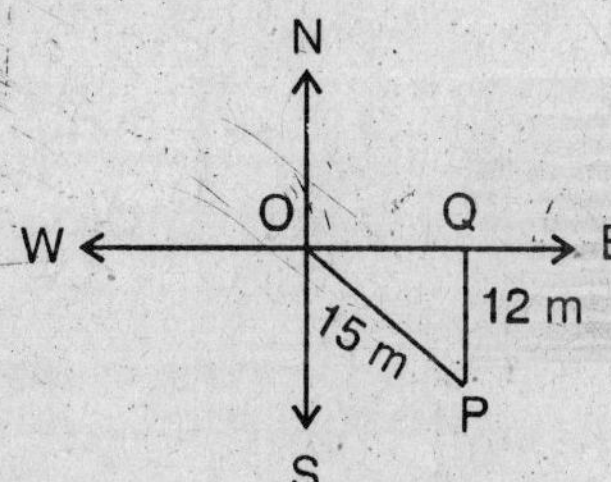

$B = \sqrt{H^2 - P^2} = \sqrt{15^2 - 12^2} = 9$ m.

13.

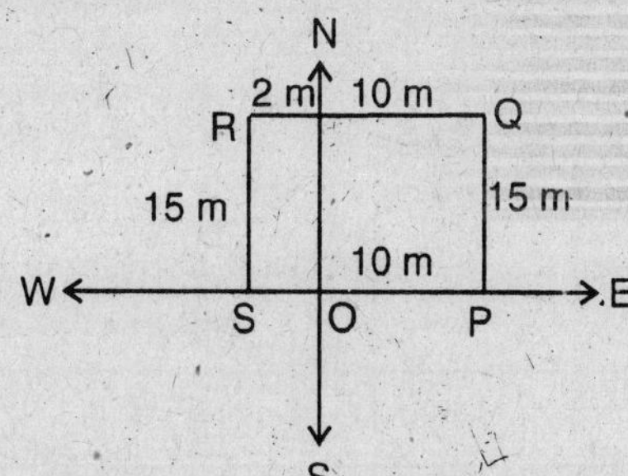

OP, *PQ*, *QR*, *RS*. He is at point *S*, 2 metres away from starting point.

14.

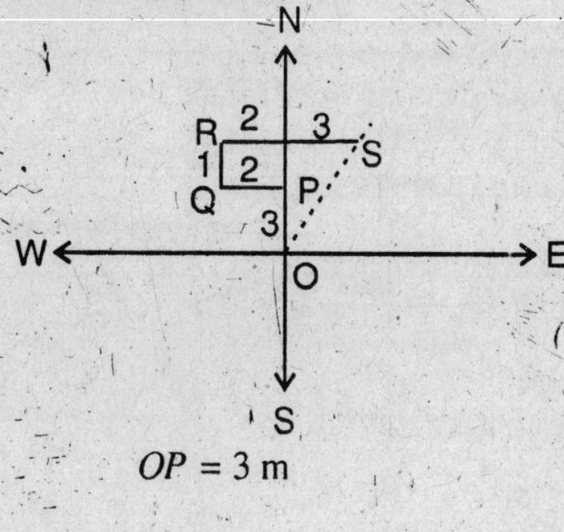

$OP = 3$ m

$PQ = 2$ m
$QR = 1$ m
$RS = 5$ m
$NS = 3$ m

$$OS = \sqrt{NO^2 + NS}$$
$$= \sqrt{4^2 + 3^2}$$
$$= \sqrt{25} = 5 \text{ m.}$$

15.

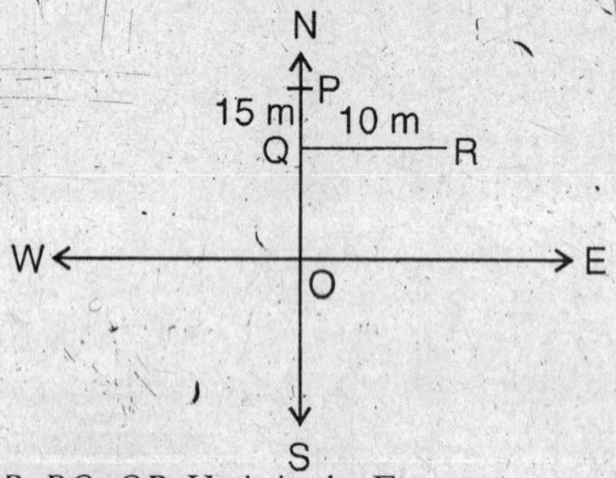

OP, PQ, QR. He is in the East.

16.

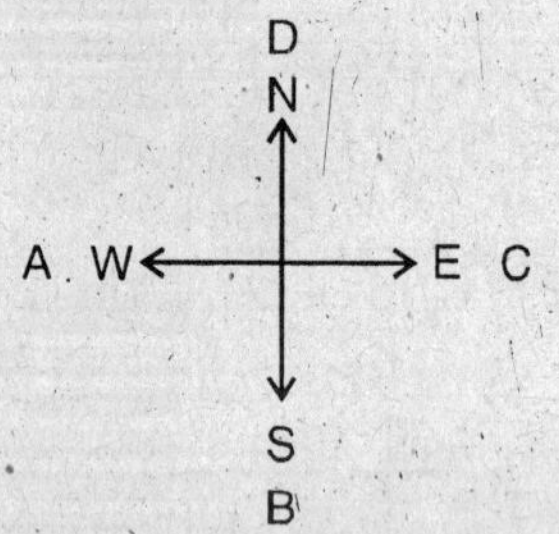

17.

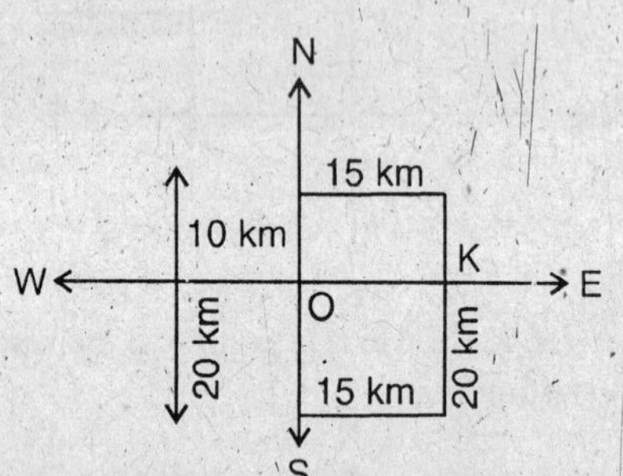

They are meeting at point *K*.

18.

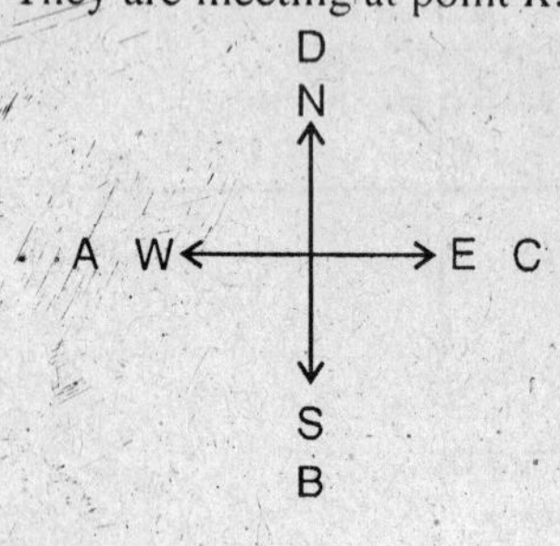

19. South-West.

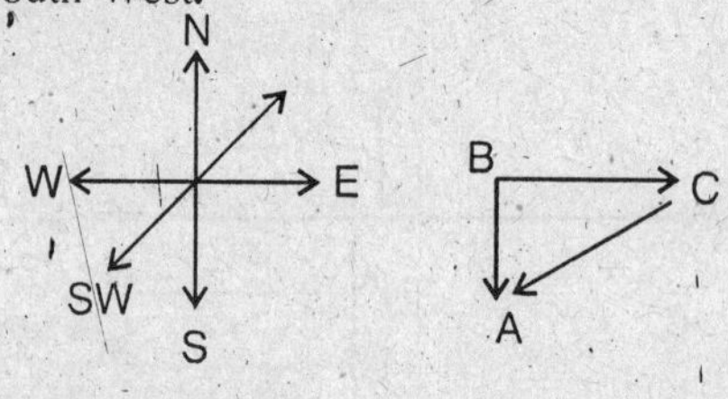

20.

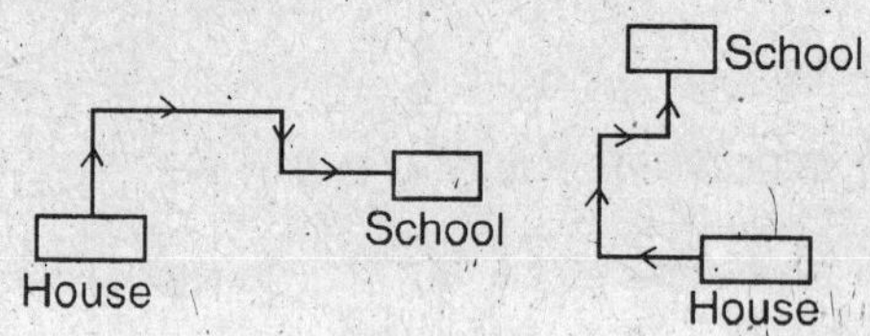

21.

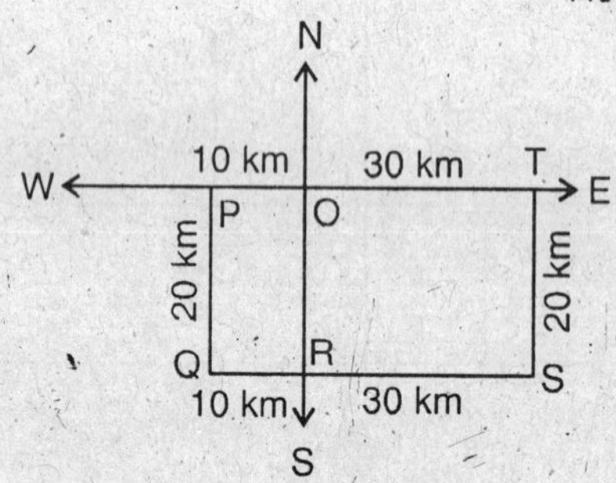

He is at point *T*, *i.e.*, 30 km.

22.

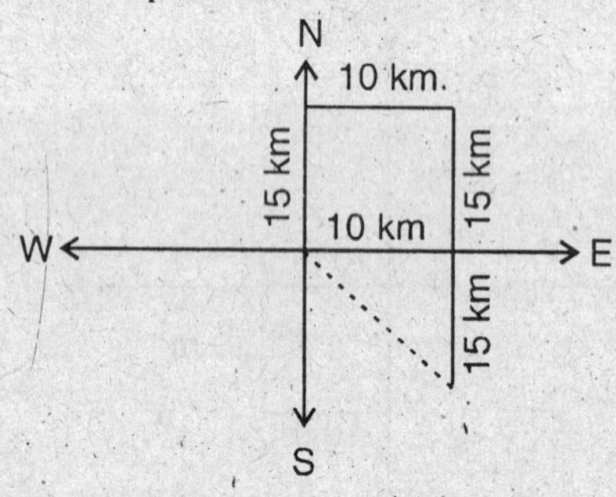

$$\sqrt{325} = \sqrt{10^2 + 15^2}$$

23.

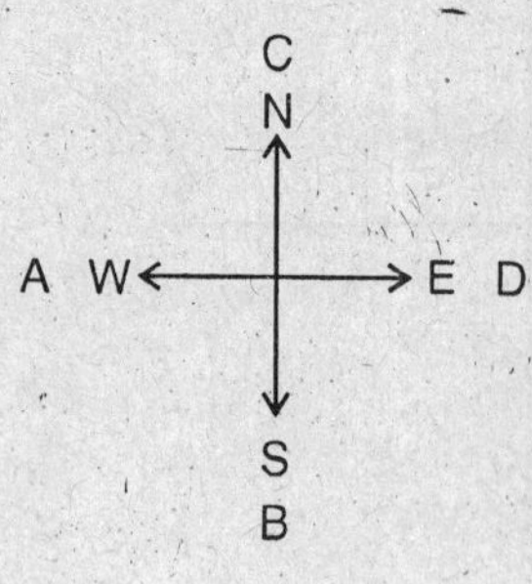

24.

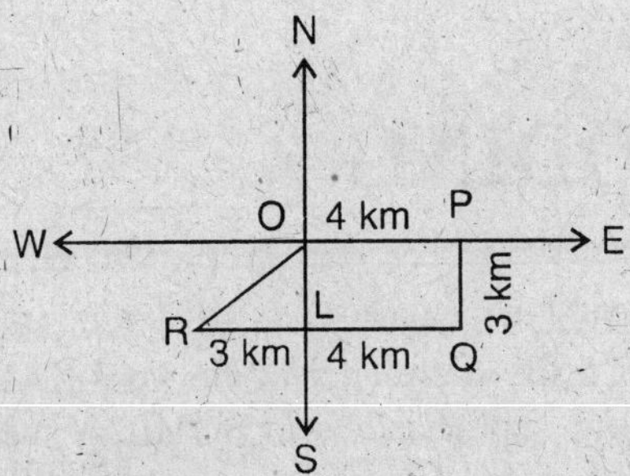

$OP = 4$
$PQ = 3$
$QR = 7$
$LR = 3$

$RO = \sqrt{3^2 + 3^2} = \sqrt{18}$

25.

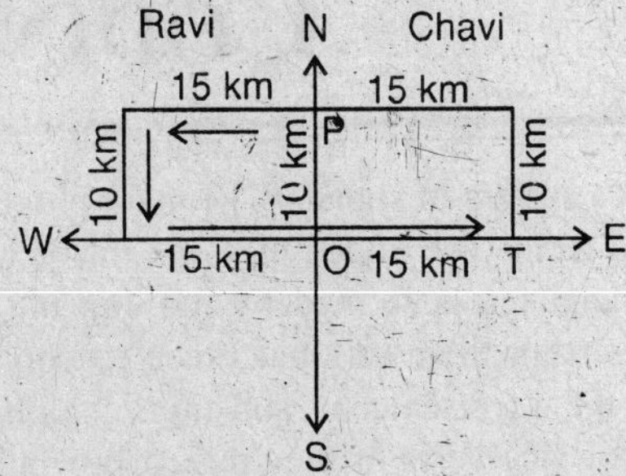

East 15 km At point T.

Chapter 6

CODING-DECODING

It is a system of signals. The main purpose is to send and recine the coded message information. In this, a language is fromed by moving the letters/numbers from their original place to some other place in the word/sentence, substituting alphabet for number or vice versa or they may follow any other set/defined pattern.

ALPHABETS

Example 1 : In a certain code, KANPUR has been coded as LBOQVS. How can Bombay be coded?

Ans. Clearly each letter in the word KANPUR is moved one step ahead so in BOMBAY the code word will be :

C P N C B Z.

Example 2 : According to a certain code, BHART is loded as AIZSS. How NEPAL be coded?

Ans. Clearly, in Each word, we are using the previous and next alphabet after the given alphabet. Hence, NEPAL will be Loded as MFOBK.

EXERCISE

1. In a certain code, KANPUR is written as RUPNAK. How could JAIPUR be coded?

A. IJAPRU B. RUPIAJ
C. PURIJA D. RIJAUP

2. In a certain code, MASTER is coded as NBTUFS. How could SERVANT be coded?

A. RBSUBOI B. TFSWBOU
C. PQRSTVI D. TFSWAOV

3. In a certain code MONKEY is written as XDJMNL. How could TIGER be written?

A. QDFHS B. SDFHS
C. UJHFS D. SHFDQ

4. In a certain code, BLOCK is written as AMNDL.How could STREET be written?

A. RUPDDU B. RUQFDU
C. RUQDFU D. RUQFUD

5. In a certain code CARROM is written as BZQQNL. How could HOUSE be coded?

A. IPVTF B. TFVPI
C. IPTVE D. IPTVF
E. GNTRD

6. In a certain code, LUCK is written as JSAI. How could MUST be coded?

A. KSQR B. KSRQ
C. SKRQ D. KRQS

7. In a certain code, CHAMPION is coded as HCMAIPNO. How could NEGATIVE be written in such a code?

A. ENAGITEV B. NEAGVEIT
C. MGAETVIE D. EGAITEVN

8. In a certain code DELHI is written as HIELD. How MADRAS is written?

A. ASDRMA B. ASRDAM
C. ADMASR D. MARDAS

9. In a certain code, MONDAY is written as OMDNYA. How could FRIDAY be written?

A. RFDIYA B. RFIDAY
C. RFAYID D. AYIDRF

10. GOOD has been coded as EMMB. How could BAD be coded?

A. ZYB B. YZB
C. ZBY D. BYZ

ANSWERS

1	2	3	4	5	6	7	8	9	10
B	B	A	B	E	A	A	A	A	A

EXPLANATORY ANSWERS

1. Reverse order of JAIPUR is RUPIAJ.
2. S E R V A N T
   T F S W B O U
   Followed by one alphabet ahead.
3. T I G E R
   Q D F H S
   One alphabet back from the last alphabet.
4. S T R E E T
   R U Q F D U
   One alphabet before and after.
5. H O U S E
   G N T R D
   One alphabet back.
6. L U C K · M U S T
   J S A I K S Q R
   Two alphabet back.
7. The letters of the word are reversed in order, taking two at a time to obtain the code.
8. D E L H I M A D R A S
   H I E L D A S D R M A
   Reverse order of each pair of alphabets.
9. M O N D A Y F R I D A Y
   O M D N Y A R F D I Y A
   Position of alphabets is interchanged in pairs.
10. G O O D B A D
    E M M B Z Y B
    Two alphabets back.

NUMBER CODING

Example 1 : In a certain code A has been coded as 1, B is 2, C is 3 and so on. How GHAI is coded.

Ans. A B C D E F G H I
1 2 3 4 5 6 7 8 9

Clearly the code for GHAI will be 7819.

Example 2 : If LEARN is coded as 45896 and TUB as 732. How is BURN coded?

Ans. Clearly the code for BURN will be 2396

L E A R N T U B
4 5 8 9 6 7 3 2

EXERCISE

1. If ROSE is coded as 6821, CHAIR is coded as 73456 and PREACH is coded as 961473, what will be the code for SEARCH?
   A. 246173 B. 214673
   C. 214763 D. 216473
2. If BAD is coded as 214, how is CAGE coded?
   A. 3175 B. 3167
   C. 3716 D. 3617
3. If DIG is coded as 497. How is BIG coded?
   A. 297 B. 479
   C. 792 D. None of these
4. If DIG = 20; BIG = 18, how would CID be written?
   A. 16 B. 18
   C. 21 D. 24
5. If D = 4; COVER = 63, how RING would be written?
   A. 78 B. 48
   C. 38 D. 42
6. If MADRAS is coded as 56, how would KANPUR be coded?
   A. 81 B. 71
   C. 91 D. 75

(Qs. 7 to 10) : The following is a certain code :

5 4 7 9 8 3 2
A P L N O C I

How are the following figures coded?

7. 98745
   A. NOPLA B. ONPLA
   C. NOLPA D. ONALP
8. 47382
   A. LPCOI B. PLCOI
   C. COILP D. OICLP
9. 5479832
   A. APLNOCI B. LNOCIAP
   C. PALNOCI D. APNLOCI
10. 2389745
    A. ICONAP B. ICONLPA
    C. IOCNAP D. ICOLNPA

11. If Black is called is Blue, Blue is called Yellow, Yellow is called Red, Red is called Sky Blue, what is the colour of Sky?

A. Yellow B. Red
C. Blue D. Black

12. If Banana is Apple, Apple is Grapes, Grapes is Mango, Mango is Nuts and Nuts is Guava, which of the following is a Yellow fruit?

A. Mango B. Guava
C. Apple D. Nuts
E. Grapes

13. If Head is Mouth, Mouth is Ear, Ear is Palm, Palm is Elbow, then, what is Ear?

A. Palm B. Ear
C. Head D. Mouth

14. If Rain is Water, Water is Road, Road is Cloud, Cloud is Sky, Sky is Sea, Sea is Path, where do Helicopters fly?

A. Road B. Sea
C. Cloud D. Water

ANSWERS

1	2	3	4	5	6	7	8	9	10
B	A	A	A	B	A	A	B	A	B
11	**12**	**13**	**14**						
B	D	A	B						

EXPLANATORY ANSWERS

1. R O S E CHAIR SEARCH
6 8 2 1 7 3 4 5 6 2 1 4 6 7 3

2. B A D C A G E
2 1 4 3 1 7 5

Code : A B C D E F G H I
1 2 3 4 5 6 7 8 9

3. D I G B I G
4 9 7 2 9 7

4. D I G
4 9 7 (4 + 9 + 7)
B I G (2 + 9 + 7)
C I D (3 + 9 + 4)

5. C O V E R = 63; D = 4
RING=18 + 9 + 14 + 7

6. (10 + 1 + 14 + 16 + 21 + 18)

7. NOLPA

8. PLCOI

9. APLNOCI

10. ICONLPA

11. Sky blue is Red. So Red is Right.

12. Because mango is called nuts.

13. Palm, because ear is known as Palms.

14. Because Helicopter fly in Sky which is known as Sea.

MIXED LETTER CODING

Example :

Lip	Sip	Tip
Flowers	are	Red.
Tip	Zip	Kip
Shirt	is	Red
Sip	Xip	Lip
They	are	Good

What is the code for Flowers, Red and Are?

Ans.

Flowers = Lip
Red = Tip
Are = Sip

Common between 1st and 2nd is Red and common code is Tip.

EXERCISE

1. Lee Pee See means Drink Mango Juice. See Tee Yee means Mangoes are Sour. Pee Nee Yee means Apples are Sweet. Which word denotes *are*?

A. Pee B. Lee
C. See D. Yee

2. Tip Tok Pok means Fast and Accurate. Tok Lok Sok means Dull and Wrong. Zok Tip Tok means Fast and Clever. What is the code for Fast?

A. Tip B. Tok
C. Pok D. Zok

3. In a certain code, 247 means Spread Red Carpet, 256 means Dust one Carpet and 236 means One Red Carpet. Which digit means Dust?

A. 2 B. 3
C. 5 D. 6

4. In a certain code, 123 means Grass is Green, 345 means Flower is Yellow, 567 means Wear Yellow Colour. What is the code for *Yellow*?

A. 3 B. 6
C. 7 D. 5

5. In a certain code, Sunil is written as RVMJK. How RAMESH is written?

A. QBLFRI B. FRILBQ
C. BLQIRF D. QBLRIF

6. If Good is written as 347, Bad is written as 743, Right is written as 52347, what will be the code for *Wrong*?

A. 74325 B. 47325
C. 74352 D. 74523

7. If

Right = a e i o u
Might = p e i o u
Sight = k e i o u
Night = l e i o u

What will be the code for R, M, S, N.

A. a p k l B. a p d c
C. l e i o D. a p l k

8. In a certain code, ROAD is written as URDG. How is SWAN written in that code?

A. VXDQ B. VZDQ
C. UXDQ D. VZCQ

9. In a certain code, LONDON is written as HPOEPO. Which of the following word is written as CVOHSZ?

A. MEXICO B. ISLAND
C. HOLAND D. HUNGRY

10. In a certain code CHAIR is written as EGCHT. How AUDIT is written?

A. CTFHV B. CSFHV
C. BTFHV D. CTEHV

11. In a certain code, PROSE is written as PPOQE. How LIGHT is to be written?

A. LIGFT B. LLGFE
C. JIEHR D. LGGHT
E. LGGFT

12. DELHI can be coded as CCIDD. How BOMBAY is written?

A. AMIWUR B. AMJXVS
C. MJXVSU D. AJIMJX

13. In a certain code, Sweet is written as 5467, Bitter is written as 7645 and Handsome is written as 1276. What will be code for Ugly?

A. 7621 B. 6721
C. 2761 D. 1276

14. In a certain code, RED is written as 27. How will BAD be written?

A. 8 B. 7
C. 9 D. 5

15. DEAD is written as 14. How BREAD will be written?

A. 30 B. 28
C. 31 D. 36

ANSWERS

1	2	3	4	5	6	7	8	9	10
D	A	C	D	A	A	A	B	D	A
11	12	13	14	15					
E	B	B	B	A					

EXPLANATORY ANSWERS

1. Yee is common code between second and third, are is also common between second and third sentence.
2. Tip is common between first and third terms whereas are is common in all the three. So Tok means are and Tip means fast.
3. 2 means Carpet. Six is meant for one. So, 5 means Dust.

4. Because 5 is common between second and third codes. Further, Yellow is common between them.
5. S U N I L RAMESH
   R V M J K QBLFRI
   One alphabet back and one alphabet ahead.
6. Bad is opposite to good, Wrong is opposite to Right. So, 74325 is the right code.
7. i g h t is common in all.
   So, RMSN = apkl
8. Two alphabets missing in between.
9. First alphabet has three alphabets in between with the shipping of one alphabet.
10. One word next and one word back.
11. First alternate is same and then two before.
12. One before two before....
13. Opposite to Handsome.
14. R E D = 27
    18 + 5 + 4 = 27
    B A D = 2 + 1 + 4 = 7.
15. B R E A D
    2 18 1 4
    2 + 18 + 5 + 1 + 4 = 30.

Chapter 8

LOGICAL VENN DIAGRAMS

TYPE I

This topic deals with questions, which analyse a candidate's ability to relate a certain group of items and represent them diagrammatically.

Example 1 : Teacher (A), Lawyer (B), Doctor (C).

Ans. Since all the three are of different categories. Therefore, the Venn diagram will be

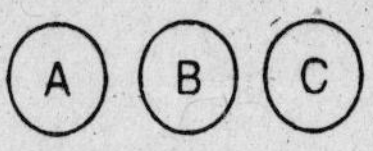

Example 2 : Kilometre (A), Metre (B), Centimetre (C).

Ans. One item belongs to the class of second and second belongs to the class of third. Therefore the diagram will be

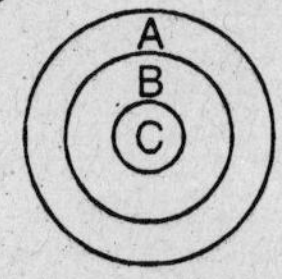

Example 3 : Chair (A), Table (B), Furniture (C).

Ans. Chair and table are separate but the parts of furniture. So, the diagram will be

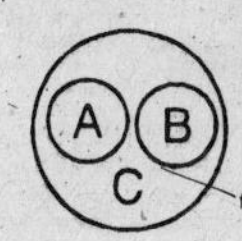

EXERCISE

(Qs. 1 to 6): *Which of the diagrams correctly represent the items mentioned in each question?*

1. Tiger, Deers, Animals.

A. 

B. 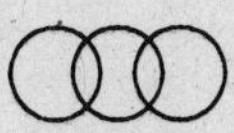

C. 

D. 

2. Clerks, Government Employees, Educated persons.

A. 

B. 

C. 

D. 

3. Doctor, Cats, Human beings.

A. 

B. 

C. 

D. 

4. Banana, Apple, Fruits.

A. 

B. 

C. 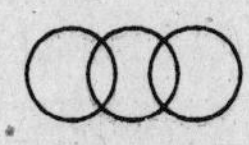

D. 

5. Fan, Cooler, Air Conditioner.

A. 

B. 

C. 

D. 

6. Brother, Male, Father.

A. 

B. 

C. 

D. 

Directions for questions 7 to 11: *From the following figures decide, which figure will represent the relationships mentioned in each question.*

A.  B. 

C.  D. 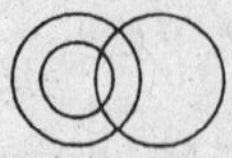

7. Women, Mother, Players.
8. Poet, Teacher, Men.
9. Crow, Sparrow, Birds.
10. Campa, Limca, Cold drinks.
11. Girls, Students, Atheletes.

Directions for questions 12 to 21: *Identify the right figure after correlating the terms given in each question.*

A.  B. 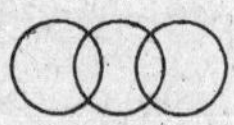

C.  D. 

E.  F. 

12. Haryana, Punjab, Rohtak.
13. Carrot, Radish, Vegetable.
14. Engineer, Doctor, People.
15. Hours, Minutes, Seconds.
16. Educated, Brother, Sister.
17. Pigeons, Birds, Parrot.
18. Diseases, Leprosy, T.B.
19. Animals, Men, Plants.
20. Biology, Zoology, Botany.
21. Science, Physics, Chemistry.

Directions for questions 22 to 30: *Identify the right figure for satisfying the set of items given in each question.*

A.  B. 

C.  D. 

E.  F. 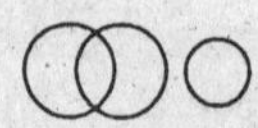

22. Yak, Tiger, Animal.
23. Tallmen, Shortmen, Indian.
24. Society, President, Sceretary.
25. Mother, Father, Brother.
26. Human beings, Doctor, Teacher.
27. Rich, Poor, Men.
28. Student, Boys, Girls.
29. Pen, Pencil, Stationery.
30. Engineer, Doctor, Educated.

TYPE II

Each Geometrical Figure respresents a certain class.

Example :

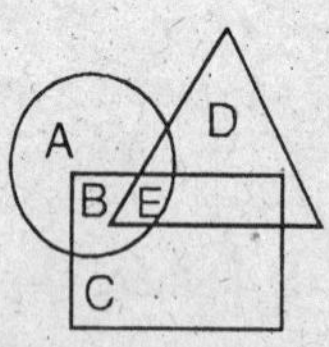

Circle represents Educated
Triangle represents Engineer
Square Represents Villagers.

On the basis of above diagram indicate the following:

1. Alphabet, which represents only the Educated.
2. Alphabet, which represents only Engineer.
3. Alphabet, which represents only Villager.
4. Alphabet, which represents all the three.
5. Alphabet, which represents Villager as well as Educated.

Solution :

1. *A* is the point which indicates only Educated.
2. *D* represents triangle which means only Engineer.
3. *C* which is covered by square represents only villagers.
4. *E* covers all the three figures so represent Educated as well as Engineers and Villagers.
5. *B* covers only circle and square therefore, it represents those who are Villagers as well as Educated.

Question 31 :

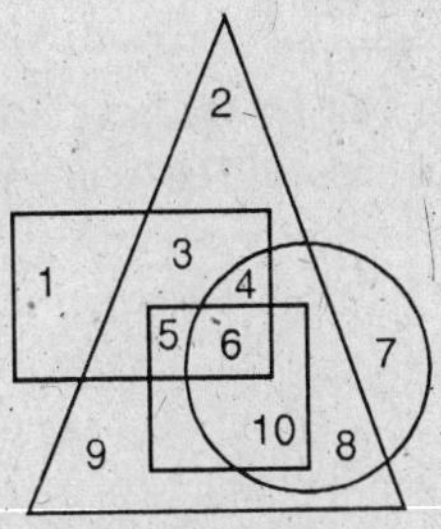

Directions for questions 31 to 36 : The questions are based on the above diagram.

1. Rectangle represents Doctors.
2. Triangle represents Villagers.
3. Square represents Graduates.
4. Circle represents Government Employees.

31. Which number indicates Doctor as well as Villagers?

A. 1 B. 2
C. 3 D. 6

32. Which number indicates only Doctors?

A. 1 B. 7
C. 8 D. 9

33. Which number indicates all the four categories?

A. 2 B. 4
C. 6 D. 8

34. Which number indicates Doctors, Government Employees and Villagers?

A. 4 B. 6
C. 8 D. 7

35. Which number indicates only Graduates?

A. 1 B. 2
C. 7 D. 6

36. Which number indicates Graduates, Doctors and Vi!!agers?

A. 5 B. 6
C. 7 D. 8

Directions for questions 37 to 40 : *Refer the following diagram, which indicates the following information in terms of numbers.*

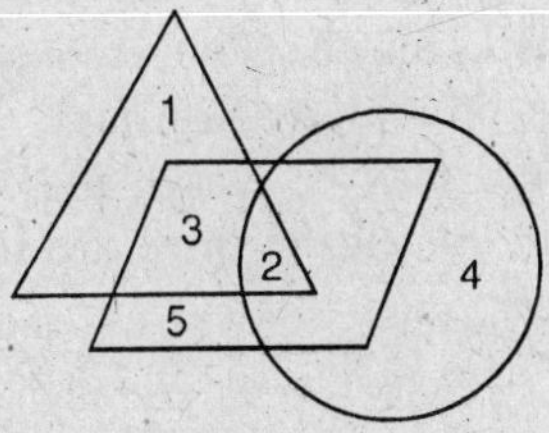

Rectangle represents Lady police. Circle represents Sub Inspector and Triangle represents Graduates.

37. Which number indicates Lady police Sub Inspector and Graduates?

A. 1 B. 2
C. 3 D. 4

38. Which number indicates Lady police and Graduates?

A. 2 B. 3
C. 5 D. 4

39. Which number indicates only Sub Inspector?

A. 5 B. 4
C. 2 D. 1

40. Which number indicates Lady police only?

A. 4 B. 5
C. 3 D. 2

ANSWERS

1	2	3	4	5	6	7	8	9	10
A	C	B	B	A	A	D	A	C	C
11	**12**	**13**	**14**	**15**	**16**	**17**	**18**	**19**	**20**
A	D	E	E	F	B	C	E	A	E
21	**22**	**23**	**24**	**25**	**26**	**27**	**28**	**29**	**30**
E	E	D	E	F	E	E	D	E	E
31	**32**	**33**	**34**	**35**	**36**	**37**	**38**	**39**	**40**
C	A	C	A	C	A	B	B	B	B

EXPLANATORY ANSWERS

1.

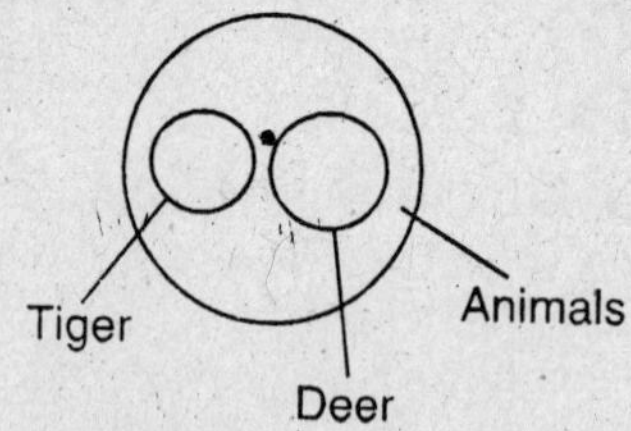

2. Some clerks may be Govt. employees and some may be educated. Similarly some Govt. employees may be clerks and some may be educated. So all the three are interrelated to each other.

3.

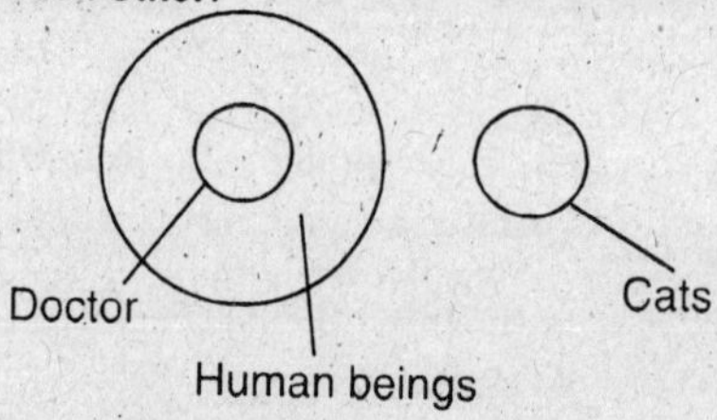

4.

5.

6. All the three are interrelated to some extent.

7. Some mothers and players are women.

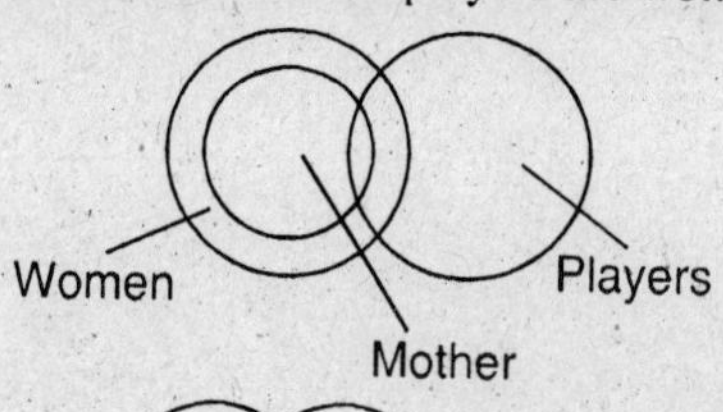

8.

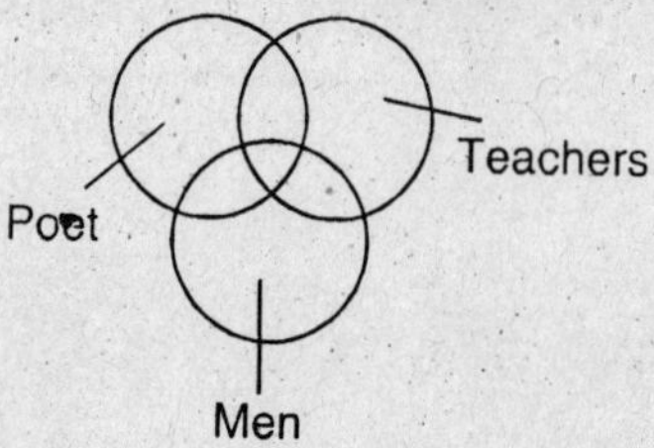

Some poet can be teachers and some teachers can be poet also. These are partly related to each other.

9.

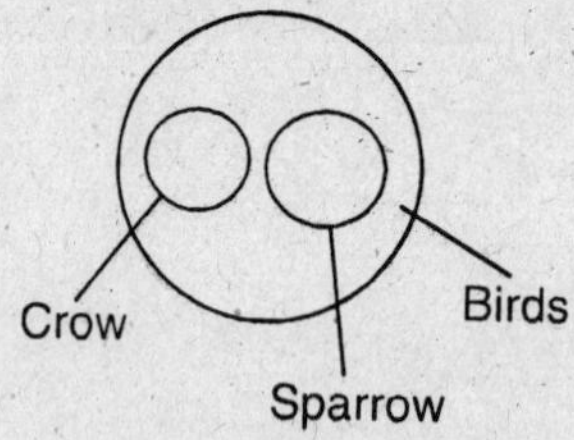

10.

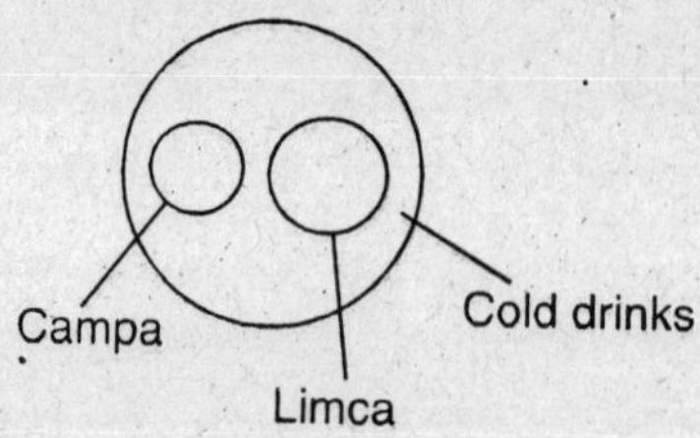

11.

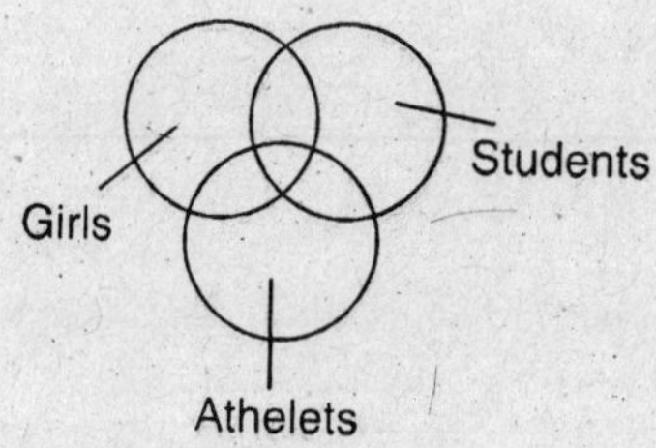

All the three are partly related to each other.

12.

13.

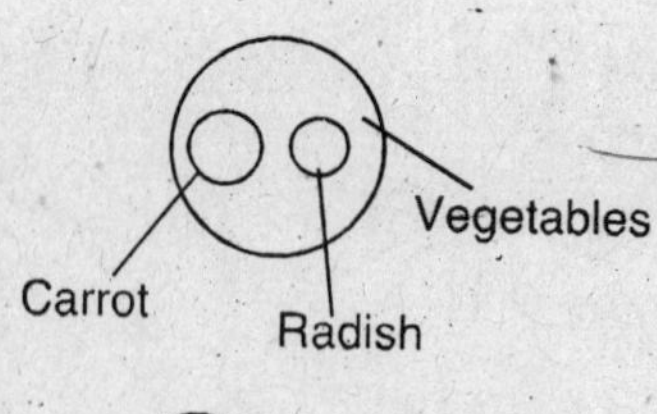

14.

15.

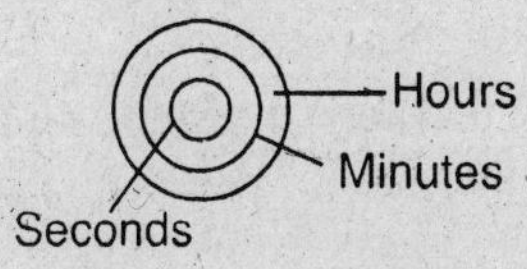

16.

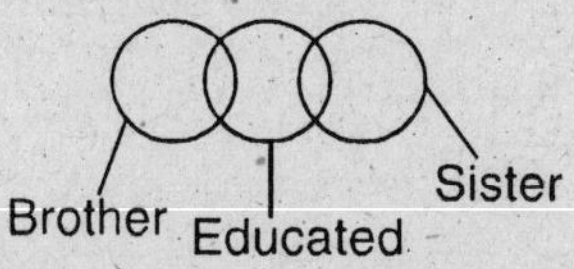

17.

18.

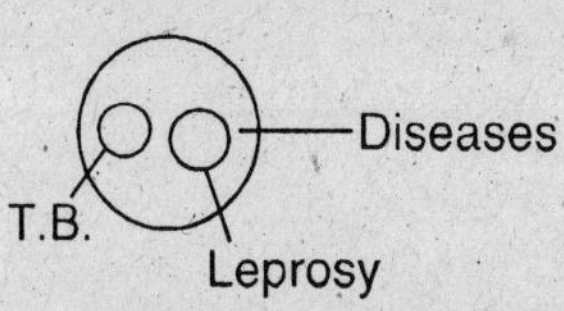

19.

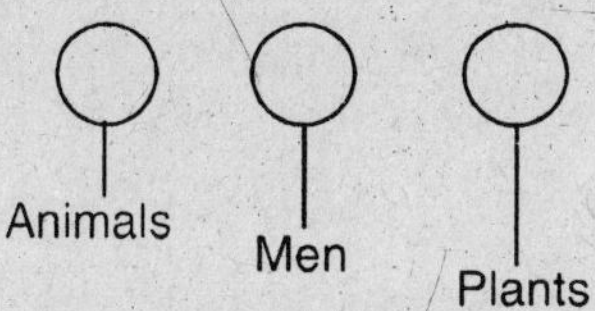

are the three altogether different.

20.

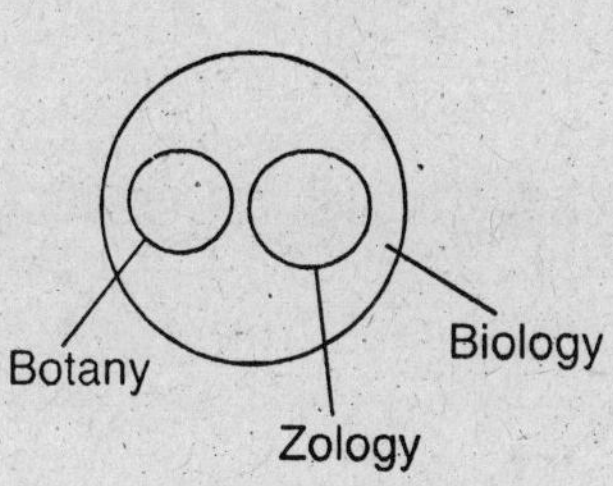

21.

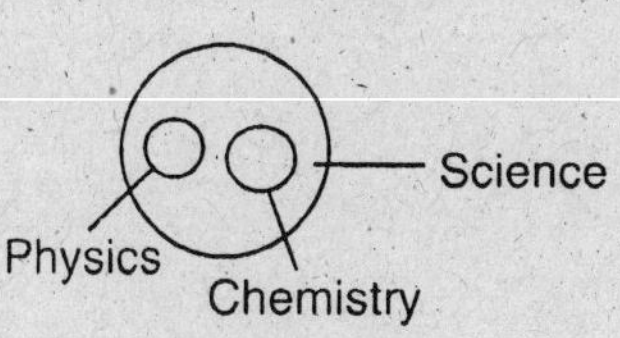

22.

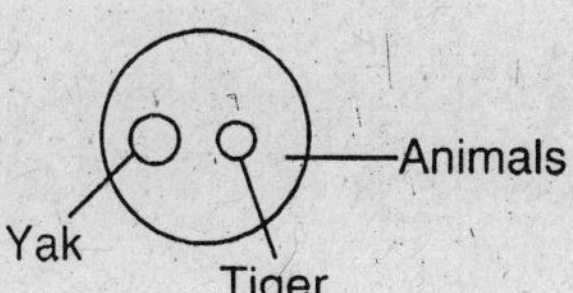

23.

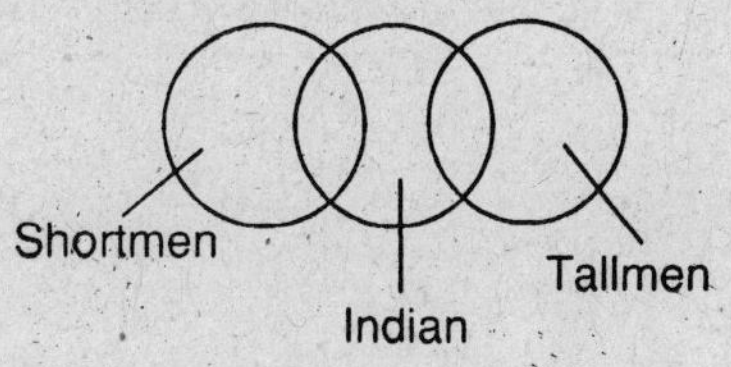

24.

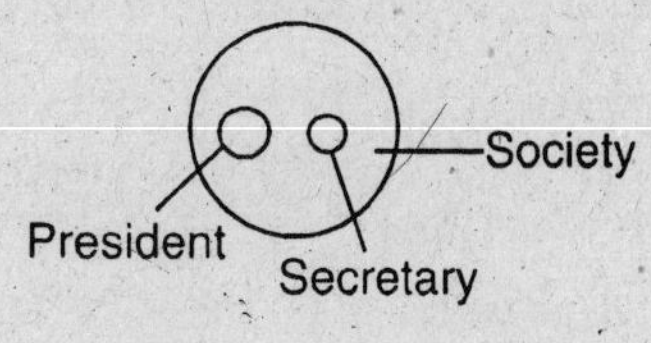

25.

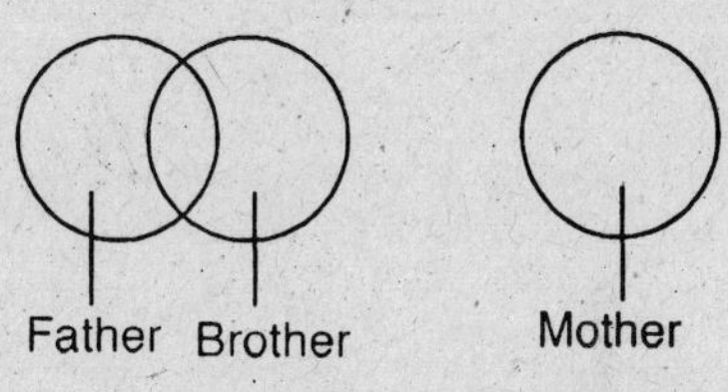

26.

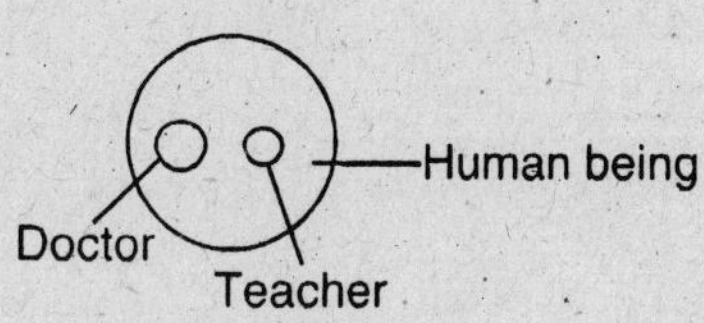

27.

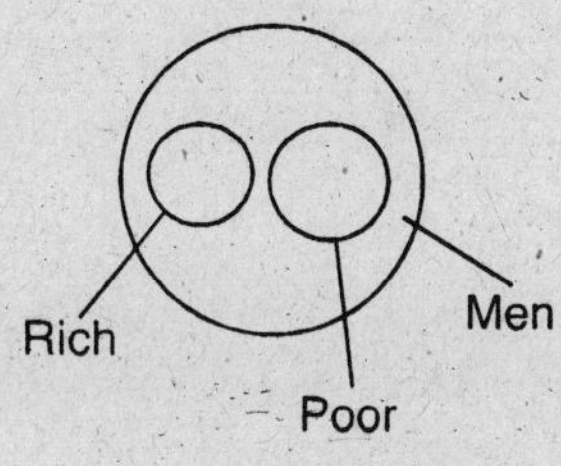

28.

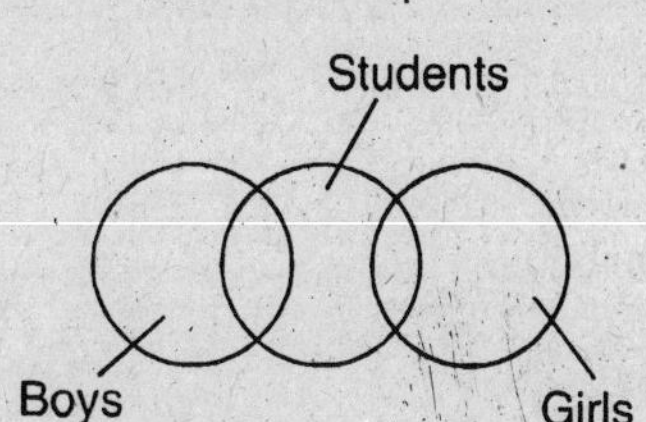

29.

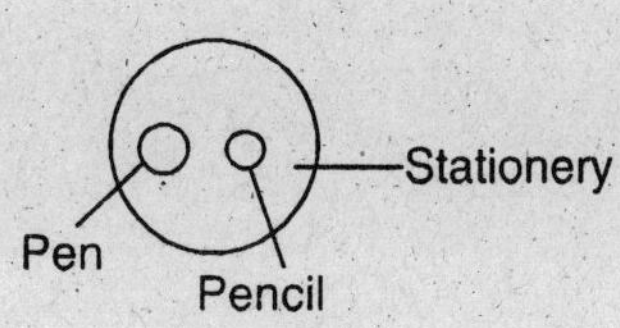

30.

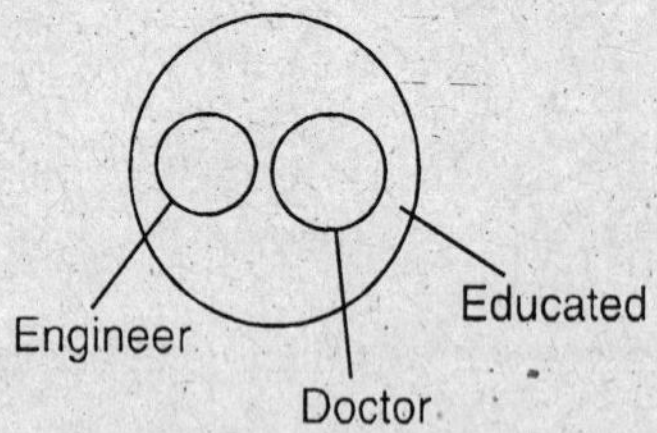

31. because No. 3 covers both □ and △.

32. because No. 1 covers only □.

33. No. 6 covers all category.

34. because No. 4 covers □ △ ○.

35. It covers only ○.

36. It covers □ △ □.

37. No. 2 covers all the three.

38. It covers △ ▱.

39. It covers only ○.

40. It covers only ▱.

Chapter 8

BLOOD RELATION

In this type of questions, the success of a student depends upon the knowledge of blood relations. Some of the important relationships have been listed as follows:

Father's *or* mother's Son	Brother.
Father's *or* mother's Daughter	Sister.
Father's *or* mother's Brother	Uncle.
Father's *or* mother's Sister	Aunt.
Father's *or* mother's Father	Grandfather.
Father's *or* mother's Mother	Grandmother.
Uncle's or Aunt's Son	Cousin.
Brother's Daughter	Niece.
Brother's Son	Nephew.
Daughter's Husband	Son-in-law.
Son's Wife	Daughter-in-law.
Husband's or wife's Brother	Brother-in-law.
Sister's Husband	Brother-in-law.

Example 1 : Pointing to a photograph, a lady said that his maternal uncle and my maternal uncle both are brothers. What is the relationship of that lady with the person in the photograph?

Ans : Clearly, it is the photograph of his son. Because the maternal uncle of his son is the brother of his mother.

Example 2 : Introducing a man to her husband, a lady said that he is the brother of the son of her grandfather. What is the relationship of the lady with that person?

A. Uncle B. Brother

C. Grandfather D. Daughter

Ans : Obviously, she is the daughter because the son of grandfather is the brother of her uncle.

Example 3 : Introducing a man, a woman said, "His wife is the only daughter of my father." How was that man related to that lady?

Ans : That lady is the wife of that man because only daughter of my father means she is saying about herself.

Example 4 : Introducing a lady, a man said, "She is the only daughter of the only son of his father." How is that man is related to that lady?

Ans : That man is the only son of his father and that lady is his only daughter. So, that man is the father of that lady.

Example 5 : Pointing towards a person in a photograph, Anshu said, "He is the only son of the father of my sister's brother." How is that person related to Anshu.

Ans : Sister's brother is Anshu's brother. But brother's father is her own father. So, the father's son is her brother.

EXERCISE

1. A lady pointed towards a photograph and said that his maternal uncle's sister is the mother of her son. How is the person in photograph related to that lady?

   A. Son B. Sister

   C. Daughter D. Uncle

2. A man said that Sita is the only daughter of his father-in-law. How is Sita related to that man?

   A. Wife B. Sister-in-law

   C. Daughter D. Sister

3. A man said to a woman, "Your only brother's son is my wife's brother." How is the woman, related to the man's wife?

   A. Mother B. Aunt

   C. Sister D. Can't explained

4. Introducing Sita, Ram said, "Her father is the only son of my father." How Ram is related to Sita?

   A. Father B. Brother

   C. Uncle D. Son

5. Introducing a woman, a man said, "Her only brother's son is my wife's brother." How is the

woman related to the man's wife?

A. Aunt B. Mother

C. Sister D. Can't explained

6. Pointing to a photograph a man said, "Her mother is the only daughter of my father-in-law. What is the relation of the photo with that man?

A. Daughter B. Wife

C. Daughter-in-law D. Can't explained

7. *X* is the mother of *A* and *B*. *D* is the wife of *A* and *C* is the husband of *B*. What is the relationship of *X* with *C*?

A. Mother-in-law B. Daughter-in-law

C. Aunt D. None of these

8. Both *A* and *B* are the children of *X*. Mr. *B* is *A*'s brother but *A* is not the brother of *B*. How is *A* related to *B*?

A. Cousin B. Sister

C. Brother D. Can't explained

9. *X* and *Y* both are the children of *Z*. If *Z* is the mother of *X* and *X* is the son of *Z* but *Y* is not the daughter of *Z*. How are *X* and *Y* related?

A. Both are brother B. *X* is sister of *Y*

C. *Y* is sister of *X* D. None of these

10. A lady pointed towards a photograph and said that she is the daughter of the son of my father. What is the relationship of that lady with that photograph?

A. Aunt and Niece B. Aunt and her daughter

C. Both are sisters D. None of these

11. A boy said to a woman, "Your mother is the wife of my father's elder son." How is that boy related to that woman?

A. Uncle B. Father

C. Brother D. None of these

12. Mrs. *X*, a dcotor, was operating a patient and told that the patient is the elder brother of the son of my grandfather. What is the patient to the doctor?

A. Father's elder brother

B. Maternal uncle

C. Uncle

D. None of these

***Directions for questions 13 to 15** : Read the information given below and answer the questions.*

1. $X - Y$ means *X* is the wife of *Y*
2. $X + Y$ means *X* is the daughter of *Y*
3. $X \times Y$ means *X* is the son of *Y*

then about

13. $A \times B - C$, which of the following is true?

A. C is the wife of *B*

B. *C* is the father of *A*

C. *A* is the daughter of *B*

D. *B* is the father of *A*

14. $X - Y \times T - S$, which of the following is not true?

A. *T* is the mother of *Y*

B. *S* is the husband of *T*

C. *Y* is the daughter of *T*

D. *X* is the wife of *Y*

15. Which statement is correct

A. $A - B$ means *A* is the brother of *B*

B. $A \times B$ means *A* is the son of *B*

C. $A + B$ means *B* is the daughter of *A*

***Directions for questions 16 to 21:** Questions are based on the following information :*

There are six members in the family *PQRSTU*. *Q* is the son of *R* but *R* is not the mother of *Q*. *P* and *R* are married couple. *T* is the brother of *R*. *S* is the daughter of *P* and *U* is the brother of *Q*.

16. How many male members are there in the family?

A. 1 B. 2

C. 3 D. 4

17. Who is the mother of *Q*?

A. *S* B. *U*

C. *T* D. *P*

18. How many children *P* have?

A. 1 B. 2

C. 3 D. 4

19. Who is the wife of *T*?

A. *P* B. *U*

C. *Q* D. None of these

20. Which of the following is a pair of females?

A. *PT* B. *QS*

C. *SU* D. *PS*

21. How is *T* related to *S*?

A. Father B. Brother

C. Uncle D. None of these

***Directions for questions 22 to 25** : Questions are based on the following information :*

$A + B$ means *A* is the son of *B*.

$A = B$ means *A* is the sister of *B*.

$A - B$ means A is the wife of B.
$A \times B$ means A is the brother of B.
$A \div B$ means A is the mother of B.

22. What we mean by $X + Z - Y$?
A. Y is the father of X
B. Y is the son of X
C. Y is the uncle of X
D. Y is the brother of X

23. What we mean by $X \times Z \div Y$?
A. X is the brother of Z
B. X is the father of Y
C. X is the uncle of Y
D. X is the nephew of Y

24. What we mean by $X = Z + Y$?
A. X is the aunt of Y
B. X is the daughter of Y
C. X is the niece of Y
D. X is the sister of Y

25. What we mean by $X = Z \div Y$?
A. X is the aunt of Y
B. X is the sister of Y
C. Y is the niece of X
D. Y is the daughter of X

ANSWERS

1	2	3	4	5	6	7	8	9	10
A	A	B	A	B	A	A	B	A	A
11	12	13	14	15	16	17	18	19	20
A	A	B	C	B	A	D	C	D	D
21	22	23	24	25					
C	A	C	B	A					

EXPLANATORY ANSWERS

1. Photo's maternal uncle's sister is the mother of her son. So the person in the photo is sister of the lady.

2. Father-in-law's only daughter is his wife.

3. The woman is man's wife father's sister.

4. Ram is Sita's father.

5. The woman is man's wife father's sister.

6. That photograph is of his daughter.

7. Mother-in-law.

8. Sister.

9. Both are brothers.

10. Aunt and niece.

11. Uncle.

12. Because the grandson is a doctor, and patient is elder brother of his father.

13. $A \times B - C$, means A is the son of B who is the wife of C which further means A is the son of C. The right answer is B.

14. $X - Y \times T - S$ means X is the wife of Y who is the son of T and who is the wife of S. This means X is the wife of the son of S (the father) *i.e.*, X is the daughter-in-law of S. So the right answer is C.

15. Obviously, B is the right answer.

(For Qs. 16 to 21) Q is the son of R. But R is not the mother of Q means R is the father of Q. P is married to R means P is the father of Q. U is the brother of Q means U is the son of P and R. S is the daughter of P means S is the daughter of P and R. So

16. P is the mother hence, she is female.
Q is the son hence male.
R is the father hence male.
S is the daughter hence female.
T is the brother hence male.
U is son hence male. So there are four males.

17. Clearly, P is the mother of Q. So D is the right answer.

18. P have 2 son and one daughter.

19. Cannot be determined.

20. Because females are the mother P and daughter S.

21. T is the uncle of S.

22. $X + Z - Y$ means X is the son of Z who is the wife of Y, *i.e.*, Y is the father X. So, the answer is A.

23. $X \times Z \div Y$ means X is the brother of Z who is the mother of Y, *i.e.*, X is the uncle of Y. So the answer is B.

24. $X = Z + Y$, means X is the sister of Z who is the son of Y, *i.e.*, X is the daughter of Y. So the answer is B.

25. $X = Z \div Y$ means X is the sister of Z who is the mother of Y, *i.e.*, X is the aunt of Y. The answer is A.

Chapter 9

CLASSIFICATION (ODD MAN OUT)

The very purpose of this test is to judge the candidate's ability of differentiation. There is a group of certain things in which one is different from the other and that is known as odd man out.

Example 1 : A. Green B. Red
C. Blue D. Pink
E. Yellow pale.

Ans. Clearly except Pink all are dark colour hence D is the odd man out.

Example 2 : A. Butter B. Oil
C. Petrol D. Ink
E. Curd F. Milk

Ans. Except milk all are processed things therefore milk is the odd man out.

Example 3 : A. Japan B. USA
C. China D. Korea
E. Delhi

Ans. Except Delhi all are the names of countries so Delhi is the odd man out.

EXERCISE

Find the odd one:

1. A. Potato B. Tomato
C. Lady finger D. Cucumber
E. Brinjal
2. A. Book B. Note Book
C. Pen D. Ink
E. Novel
3. A. Horse B. Tiger
C. Elephant D. Lion
E. Dog
4. A. River B. Lake
C. Sea D. Pool
E. Pond
5. A. Sun B. Moon
C. Star D. Mars
E. Universe
6. A. Pineapple B. Orange
C. Malta D. Banana
E. Lemon
7. A. Carpenter B. Tailor
C. Blacksmith D. Barber
E. Engineer
8. A. Hostel B. Inn
C. Hotel D. Club
E. Motel
9. A. Ear B. Heart
C. Lungs D. Kidney
E. Eye
10. A. Doe B. Drone
C. Bitch D. Mare
E. Sorceress
11. A. Baboon B. Gibbon
C. Chimpanzee D. Gorilla
E. Jaguar
12. A. Tiger B. Lion
C. Fox D. Leopard
E. Panther
13. A. Botany B. Zoology
C. Physics D. Chemistry
E. Mathematics
14. A. January B. March
C. July D. August
E. February
15. A. Beijing B. Delhi
C. Pakistan D. Washington
E. Tokyo
16. A. Water B. Air
C. Forest D. Hill
E. Garden
17. A. Hokey B. Football
C. Cricket D. Pollo
E. Table Tennis

18. A. Broker B. Salesman
C. Customer D. Hawker

Choose the odd number out:

19. A. 3 B. 5
C. 7 D. 9
E. 11

20. A. 12 – 4 B. 36 – 6
C. 96 – 12 D. 27 – 3
E. 33 – 9

21. A. 29 B. 38
C. 92 D. 74
E. 54

22. A. 23 – 29 B. 19 – 25
C. 13 – 17 D. 3 – 5

23. A. 4 B. 16
C. 49 D. 64
E. 100

24. A. 3 – 4 B. 4 – 7
C. 5 – 12 D. 20 – 21

Choose the odd letter group:

25. A. AC B. JL
C. PR D. TV
E. WX

26. A. AZ B. BY
C. CX D. DW
E. EU

27. A. VWY B. QRT
C. LMO D. JKL
E. DEG

28. A. Wine : Grapes B. Paper : Pulp
C. Shoes : Leather D. Rice : Crop

29. A. Lawyer : Court B. Writer : Book
C. Poet : Poem D. Chemist : Medicine
E. Car : Owner

30. A. Carrot B. Potato
C. Ladyfinger D. Cabbage

ANSWERS

1	2	3	4	5	6	7	8	9	10
A	E	E	C	E	D	D	D	B	B
11	12	13	14	15	16	17	18	19	20
E	C	E	E	C	E	E	C	D	E
21	22	23	24	25	26	27	28	29	30
E	B	C	D	E	E	D	D	E	A

EXPLANATORY ANSWERS

1. Potato is under ground vegetable except others. The right answer is A.
2. All, except Novel, are available at stationery shop.
3. All, except Dog, are wild animal.
4. All, except River, contain stagnant water.
5. All, except Universe, are the part of universe.
6. All, except Banana, are used in juice.
7. All, except Barber, need raw material to work.
8. All, except Club, are staying places.
9. All, except Heart, are in pairs.
10. All, except Drone, are females.
11. All, except Jaguar, are species of monkey.
12. All, except Fox, belong to the cat family.
13. All, except Mathematics, are Science subject.
14. All, except February, have 31days.
15. All, except Pakistan, are capital.
16. All, except Garden, are natural.
17. All are outdoor game.
18. All others earn from customers.
19. 9 is the square of 3.
20. First one is the multiple of second.
21. Except E all other have their sum 11.
22. All, except B, are the pairs of prime numbers.
23. Others are the squares of even numbers.
24. In all other pairs, the numbers are prime.
25. WX of alphabets is continuous pair.
26. They are not in sequence.
27. They are not in proper sequence as others.
28. In all others, second is used in the first one.
29. All others are related to each other for operation.
30. Carrot is used in salad.

Chapter 10

INSERTING THE MISSING NUMBER

In this type of questions a figure, a set of figures or a matrix is given having a certain character—following a certain pattern. The candidate is required to find out the missing number.

Example 1 :

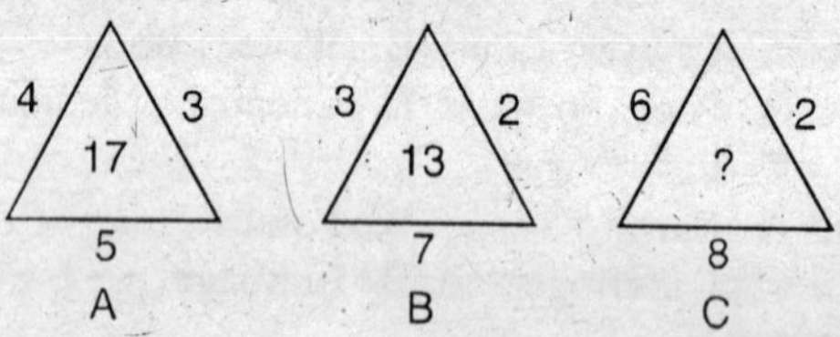

A. 16 B. 19
C. 20 D. None of these

Ans. Figure *A* $4 \times 3 + 5 = 17$

B $3 \times 2 + 7 = 13$

Like wise $6 \times 2 + 8 = 20$

So the right answer is C.

Example 2 :

?	8	12
6	4	8
5	6	7
4	2	3

A. 5 B. 6
C. 7 D. 8

Ans. In the second column, $6 + 4 - 2 = 8$

third column, $8 + 7 - 3 = 12$

Like wise $6 + 5 - 4 = 7$

So C is the right answer.

Example 3 :

A	D	H
F	I	M
?	N	R

A. K B. N
C. O D. P

Ans. The letter in the second and third rows are five steps ahead. So, the missing number is

K (F G H I J K)
1 2 3 4 5

Example 4 :

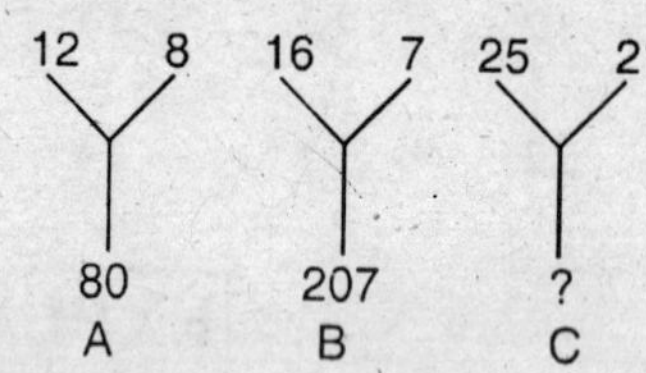

A. 184 B. 210
C. 241 D. 425

in figure

$A = 12^2 - 8^2 = 80$

$B = 16^2 - 7^2 = 207$

$C = 25^2 - 21^2 = 184$

So, A is the right answer.

EXERCISE

1.

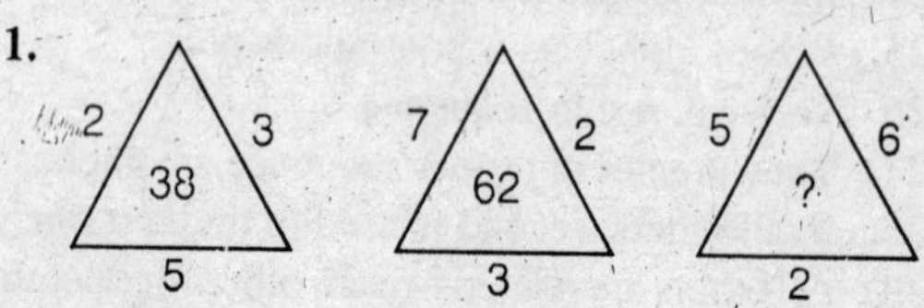

A. 65 B. 68
C. 70 D. 75

2.

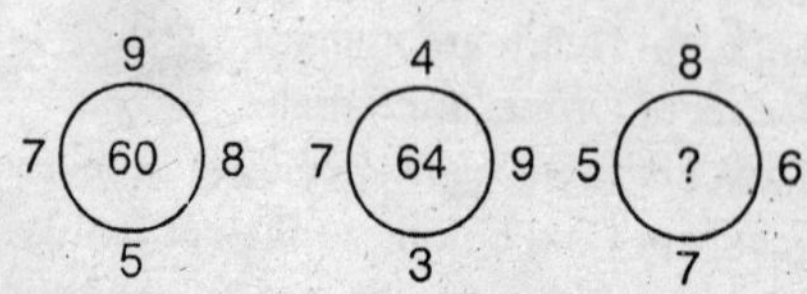

A. 35 B. 31
C. 30 D. None of these

3.

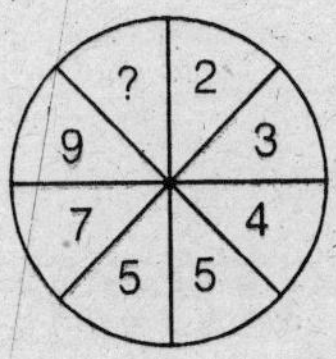

A. 10 B. 11
C. 12 D. 13

4.

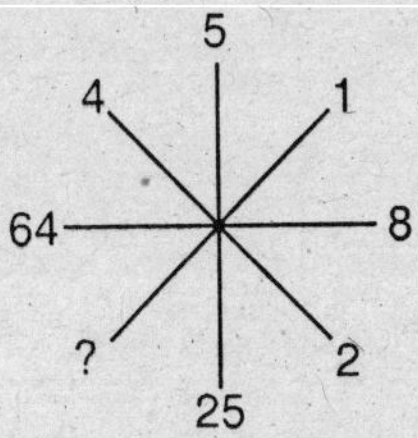

A. 1 B. 2
C. 3 D. 4

5.

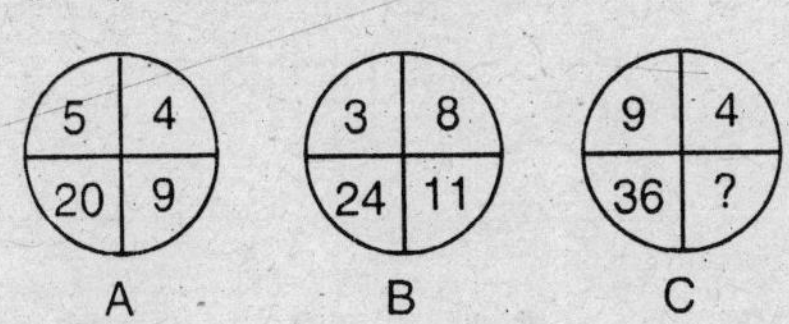

A. 15 B. 36
C. 13 D. None of these

6.

6	4	3	21
8	6	5	43
12	6	2	?

A. 72 B. 70
C. 74 D. 76

7.

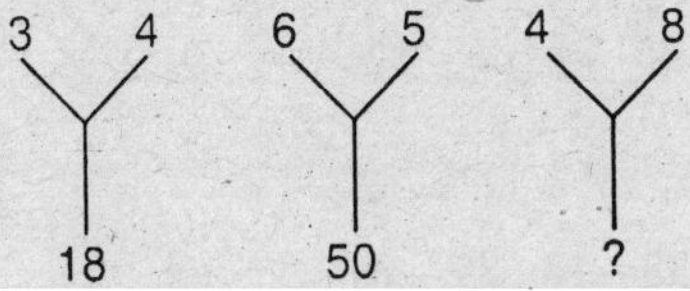

A. 68 B. 78
C. 80 D. 72

8.

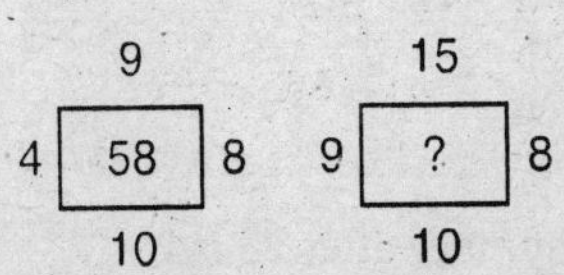

A. 117 B. 100
C. 78 D. 63

9.

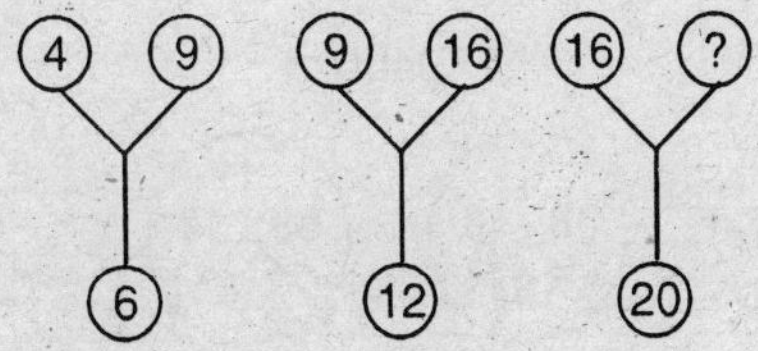

A. 60 B. 50
C. 25 D. 21

10.

6	11	25
8	6	16
12	5	?

A. 16 B. 25
C. 48 D. 59

11.

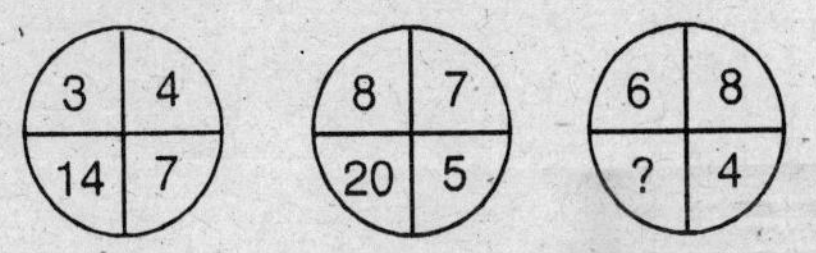

A. 18 B. 20
C. 21 D. 28

12.

963	2	844
464	?	903

A. 1 B. 2
C. 3 D. 4

13.

B	G	N
D	J	R
G	N	?

A. U B. V
C. W D. N

14.

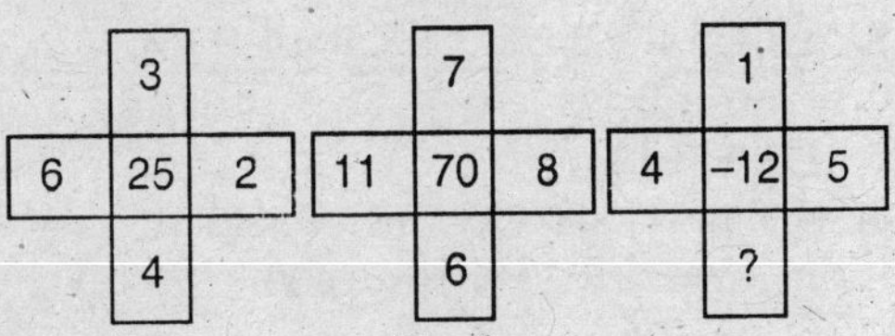

A. 10 B. 6
C. 2 D. 1

15.

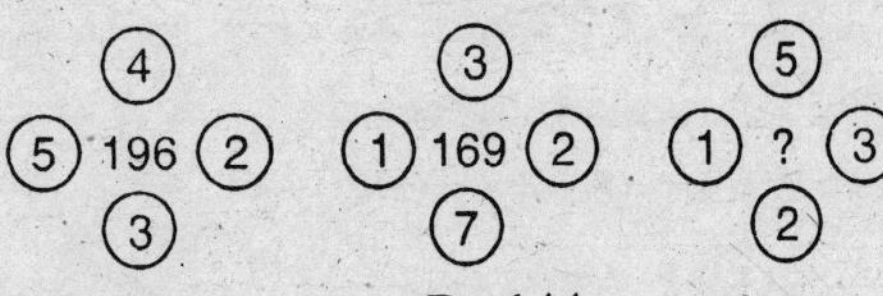

A. 121 B. 144

C. 169 D. 400

16.

A. 15 B. 13
C. 19 D. 17

17.

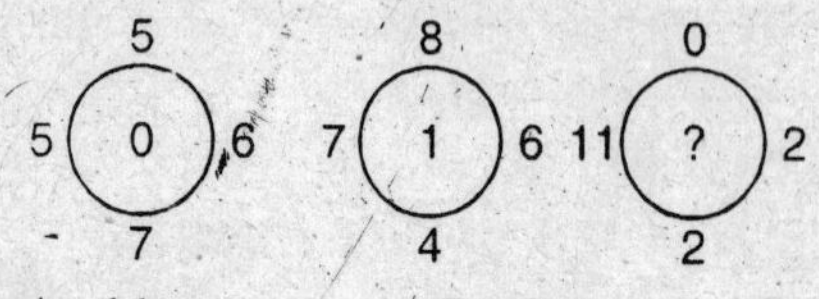

A. 11 B. 0
C. 2 D. 12

18.

3	4	5
3	7	12
3	?	22

A. 11
B. 10
C. 8
D. 9

19.

3	2	3	75
4	2	2	?

A. 75
B. 72
C. 70
D. None of these

20.

3	5	7
11	13	17
19	23	?

A. 29
B. 31
C. 33
D. None of these

ANSWERS

1	2	3	4	5	6	7	8	9	10
A	B	B	A	C	B	A	C	C	A
11	**12**	**13**	**14**	**15**	**16**	**17**	**18**	**19**	**20**
A	B	C	C	A	A	A	B	B	A

EXPLANATORY ANSWERS

1. $5^2 + 6^2 + 2^2 = 65$
2. $7 \times 8 + 9 - 5, 7 \times 9 + 4 - 3, 5 \times 6 + 8 - 7$
3. In second half no. is 5, 7, 9, 11
4. $1^2 = 1$
5. $5 \times 4, 5 + 4, 3 \times 8, 3 + 8, 9 \times 4, 9 + 4$
6. $12 \times 6 - 2$
7. $4^2 + 8^2 - 12$
8. $(9 \times 10 - 4 \times 8)\ (15 \times 10 - 9 \times 8)$
9. $16 \times x = 20 \times 20$ or $16x = 400$
   $\therefore \quad x = 25$
10. $11 \times 2 + \frac{6}{2}, 6 \times 2 + \frac{8}{2}, 5 \times 2 + \frac{12}{2}$
11. $(3 + 4 + 7)\ (8 + 7 + 5)\ (6 + 8 + 4)$
12. $(9 + 6 + 3) - (8 + 4 + 4) = 2$
    $(4 + 6 + 4) - (9 + 0 + 3) = 2$
13. Skipping of alphabets in first column is in the order 1–2; in second column 2–3; in third column 3–4.
14. $(1^2 + 4^2) - (5^2 + x^2) = - 12$
    $x^2 = 29 - 25 = 4 = 2$
15. $(1 + 5 + 3 + 2)^2 = 11^2 = 121$
16. $\frac{25 + 17}{7}, \frac{38 + 18}{7}, \frac{89 + 16}{7}$
17. $= (11 + 2 - 0 + 2) = 11$
18. 3 + 4 under 4 is 7.
    3 + 7 under 7 is 10.
19. $(3 + 3)^2 \times 2; (4 + 2)^2 \times 2$
20. The next prime number after 23 is 29.

Chapter 11

NUMBER, RANKING AND TIME SEQUENCE TEST

Number Test

Example : How many 8's are there in the following number series, which are followed or preceded by 2.

8 2 4 5 1 7 2 8 4 8 4 2 2 8 2 6 9 8 2 4 5 8 2 3 7 8 2 5 2 8

A. 5 B. 6

C. 7 D. 8

Ans. The number, which comes after, is said to follow and which comes before, is known as precedes. In the given series the total no of 8s is 7, which are followed or preceded by 2.

Ranking Test

Example 1 : Amit is ranked ninth from the top and thirty-eighth from the bottom in a class. How many students are there in the class.

A. 46 B. 45

C. 47 D. 48

Ans. The whole class consists of 8 students who have a rank higher than Amit and Rahul. 37 students who have a rank lower than that of Amit.

So, the total students = 8 + 1 + 37 = 46

Example 2 : In a row of students, Anshul is seventh from the left and Madhuri is twelth from the right. If they interchange their positions, Anshul becomes twenty-second from the left. How many students are there in the row?

A. 31 B. 32

C. 33 D. 34

Ans. Anshul's new position is twenty-second from left. But it is the same as Madhuri's earlier position, which is 12th from the right.

Thus the Row consists of (21 + 1 + 11) = 33 students.

Time Sequence Test

Example : Suresh remembers that his brother's birthday is after fifteenth but before eighteenth of February, whereas his sister, Komal, remembers that her brother's birthday is after 16th but before 19th February. On which day in February does Suresh's brother's birthday fall?

A. 16th B. 17th

C. 18th D. 19th

Ans. Clearly Suresh's brother's birthday is on the day common to both, *i.e.*, 17th of February.

EXERCISE

1. How many 6s are there in the following number series, which are preceded by 7 but not immediately followed by 9?

6 7 9 5 6 9 7 6 8 7 6 7 8 6 9 4 6 7 7 6 9 5 7 6 3

A. 3 B. 5

C. 4 D. 2

2. In the following list of numerals, how many 2s are followed by 1s but not preceded by 4?

4 2 1 2 1 4 2 1 1 2 4 4 4 1 2 2 1 2 1 4 4 2 1 4 2 1 2 1 2 4 1 4 2 1 2 4 1 4 6

A. 2 B. 5

C. 3 D. 4

3. How many 7s are there in the following series which are not immediately followed by 3 but immediately preceded by 8?

8 9 8 7 6 2 2 6 3 2 6 9 7 3 2 8 7 2 7 7 8 7 3 7 7 9 4

A. 10 B. 3

C. 2 D. 0

4. In the series
6 4 1 2 2 8 7 4 2 1 5 3 8 6 2 1 7 1 4 1 3 2 8 6
How many pairs of alternate numbers have a difference of 2?
A. one B. two
C. three D. four

5. How many odd numbers are there in the sequence which are immediately preceded and also immediately followed by even numbers?
5 1 4 7 3 9 8 5 7 2 6 2 1 5 8 6 3 8 5 2 2 4 3 4 9 6
A. 1 B. 2
C. 3 D. 4
E. More than Four

6. In a row of trees one tree is fifth from either end of row. How many trees are there in the row?
A. 8 B. 10
C. 9 D. 11

7. Ram ranks seventh from the top and twenty eighth from the bottom in a class. How many students are there in the class?
A. 34 B. 36
C. 37 D. 35

8. Ramesh ranks twelfth in a class of forty-six. What will be his rank from the last?
A. 35 B. 33
C. 34 D. 37

9. Ram is 7 rank ahead of Shyam in a class of 39. If Shyam's rank is 17th from the last, what is Ram's rank from the start?
A. 16th B. 14th
C. 15th D. 17th

10. Three persons *X*, *Y* and *Z* who are standing in a queue. There are five persons between *X* and *Y* and eight persons between *Y* and *Z*. If there are three persons ahead of *Z* and 21 persons behind *X*, what could be the minimum number of persons in the queue?
A. 41 B. 40
C. 28 D. 27

11. If the day before Yesterday was Thursday, when would Sunday fall?
A. Tomorrow
B. Today
C. Two days after today
D. None of the above

12. How many days will be there from 26th January, 1996 to 15th May, 1996 (both days included).
A. 111 B. 110
C. 112 D. 115

13. Sita remembers that her father's birthday was certainly after eighth of December but before 13th of December. Her sister Mohini remembers that their father's birthday was definitely after 9th but before 14th of December. On which date, did their father's birthday fall?
A. 10th
B. 11th
C. 12th
D. on any day in between 10, 11, 12

14. If it was Saturday on 17th December, 1982, what will be the day on 22nd December, 1984?
A. Monday B. Tuesday
C. Wednesday D. Sunday

15. If the seventh day of a month is three days earlier than Friday, what day will it be on 19th day of the month?
A. Sunday B. Monday
C. Wednesday D. Friday

ANSWERS

1	2	3	4	5	6	7	8	9	10
C	C	C	B	D	C	A	A	A	B
11	**12**	**13**	**14**	**15**					
A	A	D	D	A					

EXPLANATORY ANSWERS

1. 6 7 9 5 6 9 7 $\underline{6}$ 8 7 $\underline{6}$ 7 8 6 9 4 6 7 7 6 9 5 7 $\underline{6}$ 3

2. 4 2 1 $\underline{2}$ 1 4 2 1 1 2 4 4 4 1 2 $\underline{2}$ 1 $\underline{2}$ 1 4 4 2 1 4 2 1 $\underline{2}$ 1 2 4 1 4 2 1 2 4 1 4 6

3. 8 9 8 $\underline{7}$ 6 2 2 6 3 2 6 9 7 3 2 8 $\underline{7}$ 2 7 7 8 7 3 7 7 9 4

4. (6, 1) (4, 2) (1, 2) (2, 8) (2, 7) (8, 4) (7, 2) (4, 1) (2, 5) (1, 3) (5, 8) (3, 6) (8, 2) (6, 1) (2, 7) (1, 1)

(7, 4) (1, 1) (4, 3) (1, 2) (3, 8) (2, 6) pairs with a difference of 2 are.
(4, 2) (1, 3).

5. 5 1 4 7 3 9 8 5 7 2 6 2 1 5 8 6 3 8 5 2 2 4 3 4 9 6.
6. No. of trees in the row (4 + 1 + 4) = 9
7. Clearly, the number of Students is (6 + 11 + 27) = 34
8. Obviously, his rank is 35 the (46 – 11)
9. Shyam is 17th from the last and Ram is 24th (7 steps ahead), which means that Ram is 16th from the start.
10. There are 40 persons at least
...21... X ...5... Y ...8... Z ...3...
$(21 + 5 + 8 + 3 + X + Y + Z) = 40$ persons.
11. The day before yesterday was Thursday that means today is Saturday and tomorrow will be Sunday.
12. $6 + 29 + 31 + 30 + 15 = 111$
(1996 is a leap year Feb-29)
13. Common days of the sister are 10, 11, 12,
14. **Note :** (1) A year has 365 days.
(2) A year divisible by 4 is a leap year and February is of 29 days, and total days in a year would be 366.
(3) The last day of the year is the same as first day.
(4) If the year is a leap year, then the last day will be one ahead of the first day.
15. As mentioned the 7th day of the month is 3 days earlier than Friday, which is Tuesday. So 14th day is also Tuesday and thus 19th day is Sunday.

Chapter 12

MATHEMATICAL OPERATIONS

In this type of problems, some symbols are given for Addition, Substraction, Multiplication and Division and the problems are to be solved according to the symbols. These symbols are artificial. The candidate has to substitute the real sign and has to solve the question accordingly.

In the solving these type questions BODMAS Formula is used, *i.e.*, the sequence to be followed while solving a question is fixed and bourded by rules in which bracket is solved first and the subtraction performed in the last.

B = Bracket
O = Of
D = Division
M = Multiply
A = Addition
S = Subtraction

Example 1 : If + means ÷
– means ×
× means –
÷ means +

Find out the value of $16 \div 8 - 4 + 2 \times 4$?

A. 16 B. 28
C. 32 D. 44

Ans. Put proper signs in the given equation

$16 + 8 \times 4 \div 2 - 4 = 16 + 8 \times 2 - 4 = 28$

So the answer is B.

Example 2 : If *A* means plus, *B* means minus, *C* means division and *D* means multiplication, then $18A\ 12C\ 6D\ 2B5$ = ?

A. 17 B. 25
C. 27 D. 45

Ans. Using proper signs,

$18 + 12 \div 6 \times 2 - 5 = 18 + 2 \times 2 - 5$
$= 18 + 4 - 5 = 17$

Right answer is A.

ARITHMETICAL REASONING

Example 1 : In a Chess tournament each of six players will play every other player exactly once. How many matches will be played during the tournament?

A. 12 B. 15
C. 30 D. 36

Ans. Matches of the first player with other 5 players.

Matches of second player with 4 players and so on.

So, number of matches played during the tournament = 5 + 4 + 3 + 2 + 1 = 15

So, B is the right answer.

Example 2 : *A, B, C* and *D* play a game of cards. *A* says to *B*, "If I give you 8 cards, you will have as many as *C* has and I shall have 3 less than what *C* has." Also, "If I take 6 cards from *C*, I shall have twice as many as *D* has." If *B* and *D* together have 50 cards, how many cards are with *A*?

A. 40 B. 37
C. 27 D. 23

Ans.
$B + 8 = C$ ...(*i*)
$A - 8 = C - 3$ ...(*ii*)
$A + 6 = 2D$ ...(*iii*)
$B + D = 50$ ...(*iv*)

Putting $C = A - 5$ from (*ii*) into (*i*) we have

$B + 8 = A - 5$
or $A - B = 13$ ...(*v*)

Putting $D = 50 - B$ from (*iv*) into (*iii*) we have,

$A + 6 = 100 - 2B$
or $A + 2B = 94$ ...(*vi*)

Solving, (*v*) and (*vi*), we get, $B = 27$
$A = 40$

So, *A* has 40 cards.

Hence, answer is A.

Example 3: A worker may claim Rs. 15 for each km travelled by taxi and Rs. 5 for each km, for which he travells by car. If, in one week, he claimed Rs. 500 for travelling 80 kms, how many kms did he cover by taxi?

A. 40 B. 30
C. 20 D. 10

Ans. Let the distance covered by taxi be x km.
Distance covered by car = $(80 - x)$ km.

$$15x + 5(80 - x) = 500$$
$$15x + 400 - 5x = 500$$
$$10x = 100$$
$$x = 10$$

So, the correct answer is D.

EXERCISE

1. If X stands for addition, ÷ stands for subtraction, + stands for multiplication and – stands for division, then 20 × 8 ÷ 8 – 4 + 2= ?
A. 80 B. 25
C. 24 D. 5
2. If a means plus, b means minus, c means multiplication and d means division, then 18c 14a 6b 16 d 4 = ?
A. 63 B. 254
C. 288 D. 1208
3. If + means –, – means ×, × means ÷ and ÷ means +, then 15 × 3 ÷ 15 + 5 – 2 = ?
A. 15 B. 12
C. 10 D. 8
4. If x stands for add, y stands for subtract, z stands for divide and p stands for multiply, then what is the value of (7p3)y 6x5?
A. 5 B. 10
C. 15 D. 20
5. If + means ×, ÷ means –, × means ÷ and – means +, what will be the value of
4 + 11 ÷ 5 – 55 = ?
A. – 48.5 B. – 11
C. 79 D. 94

Arithmetical Reasoning

6. Ram is twice as old as Shyam. Three years ago, he was three times as old as Shyam. How old is Ram now?
A. 6 years B. 7 years
C. 8 years D. 12 years
7. The age of a mother is twice that of the elder daughter. Ten years hence the age of mother will be three times of the younger daughter. If the difference of the ages of two daughters is 15 years, the age of mother is
A. 50 years B. 55 years
C. 60 years D. 70 years
8. A group of 1200 persons comprises captains and soldiers and is travelling in a train. For every 15 soldiers, there is one captain. The number of captains in the group is
A. 85 B. 80
C. 75 D. 70
9. Ram cuts a cake into two halves and then, cuts one half into smaller pieces of equal size. Each of the small pieces is of twenty grams (in wieght). If he has seven pieces of the cake in all, what was the weight of the original cake?
A. 120 gms B. 140 gms
C. 240 gms D. 280 gms
10. A father is now three times as old as his son. Five years ago, he was four times as old as his son. The age of the son is
A. 12 years B. 15 years
C. 18 years D. 20 years

Directions for questions 11 to 15: Questions are based on the information given below :

Data of 450 students who took an examination in Social Sciences, Maths, and Science is given below:

Passed in all subjects	167
Failed in all subjects	60
Failed in Social Science	175
Failed in Mathematics	199
Failed in Science	191
Passed in Social Science only	62
Passed in Mathematics only	48
Passed in Science only	52

11. How many students failed in one subject only?
A. 152 B. 144

C. 61 D. 56

12. How many students failed in Social Science only?

A. 15 B. 21

C. 30 D. 42

13. How many students passed at least in one subject?

A. 450 B. 390

C. 304 D. 167

14. How many students failed in two subjects only?

A. 56 B. 61

C. 152 D. 162

15. How many students passed in Mathematics and in at least one more subject?

A. 210 B. 203

C. 170 D. 94

ANSWERS

1	2	3	4	5	6	7	8	9	10
C	B	C	D	D	D	A	C	C	B
11	**12**	**13**	**14**	**15**					
C	A	B	D	B					

EXPLANATORY ANSWERS

1. Using the correct symbols, we have
$20 + 8 - 8 \div 4 \times 2$
$= 20 + 8 - 2 \times 2 = 20 + 8 - 4 = 24$

2. Using the correct symbols, we have
$18 \times 14 + 6 - 16 \div 4$
$= 18 \times 14 + 6 - 4 = 252 + 6 - 4 = 254$

3. Using the correct symbols, we have
$15 \div 3 + 15 - 5 \times 2$
$= 5 + 15 - 5 \times 2 = 5 + 15 - 10 = 10$

4. Using the correct symbols, we have
$(7 \times 3) - 6 + 5 = 21 - 6 + 5 = 20$

5. Using the correct symbols, we have
$4 \times 11 - 5 + 55 = 44 - 5 + 55 = 94$

6. Let Shyam's present age is x years then Ram's present age is $= 2x$ years. Three years ago Shyam's age $= x - 3$ and Ram's age $= (2x - 3)$
So, $(2x - 3) = 3(x - 3)$
or $2x - 3 = 3x - 9$ or $x = 6$
Hence Ram's present age $= 2 \times 6 = 12$.

7. Let the age of elder daughter be $= x$
Then the age of younger daughter $= (x - 15)$
and age of mother $= 2x$
So, $2x + 10 = 3(x - 15 + 10)$
$2x + 10 = 3x - 15$ or $x = 25$
$\therefore$ Mother's age $2x = 25 \times 2 = 50$ yrs.

8. Out of every 16 persons there is one Captain
So, number of Captains is $= 1200/16 = 75$

9. The seven pieces consist of 6 smaller equal pieces and 1/2 cake piece.
Weight of each small piece = 20 gms.
So total weight of cake $= 2 \times (20 \times 6) = 240$ gms.

10. Let the age of son is $= x$
The father's age is $= 3x$
Five years ago father's age $= 3x - 5$
and son's age $= x - 5$
So, $3x - 5 = 4(x - 5)$ or $x = 15$.

11. Candidates failed in one subject only = (total number of candidates) – (candidates passed in all subject + candidates failed in all subjects + candidate passed in one subject only).
$= 450 - (167 + 60 + 62 + 48 + 52)$
$= 450 - 389 = 61$.

12. Candidates failed in Social Science only = (candidates failed in Social Science) – (candidates failed in all subjects + candidates passed in Science only + candidates passed in Maths only).
$= 175 - (60 + 52 + 48) = 175 - 160 = 15$

13. Candidates passed atleast in one subject = (candidates passed in one subject only) + (candidates passed in two subjects only) + (candidates passed in all subjects).
$= 162 + 61 + 167 = 390$

14. Candidates failed in two subjects only = candidates passed in one subject only.
$= 62 + 48 + 52 = 162$

15. Candidates failed in Science only
= Candidate failed in Science – (candidates pass in Social Science only + Candidates failed in all subjects + Candidates passed in Mathematics only) $= 191 - (62 + 60 + 40) = 21$
Candidates failed in Social Science = 15
$\therefore$ Candidates passed in Maths and atleast one more subjects $= (21 + 15 + 167) = 203$.

Chapter 13

ANALYTICAL REASONING

This topic has been introduced to assess or check the analytical knowledge of the candidate. The problems are related to the counting of geometrical figures in a given complete figure.

EXERCISE

1. How many Triangles are there in the figure below?

A. 5 B. 6
C. 8 D. 10

2. How many Parallelograms are there in the figure below?

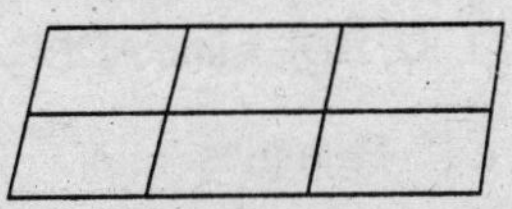

A. 15 B. 18
C. 16 D. 14

3. Count the number of Triangles in the following figure :

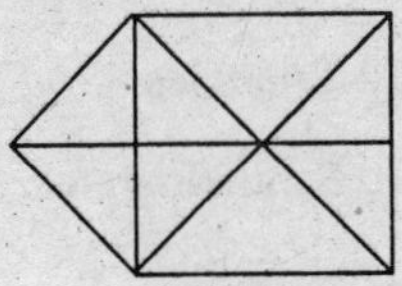

A. 18 B. 16
C. 15 D. 17

4. Find out the maximum no. of Squares.

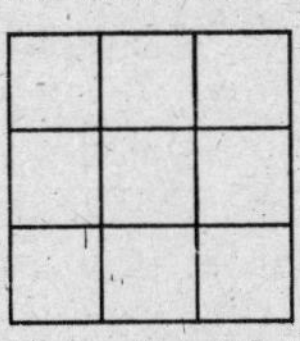

A. 10 B. 13
C. 9 D. 14

5. How many Triangles are there in the following figure?

A. 9 B. 10
C. 11 D. 12

6. Count the number of Triangles in the following figure?

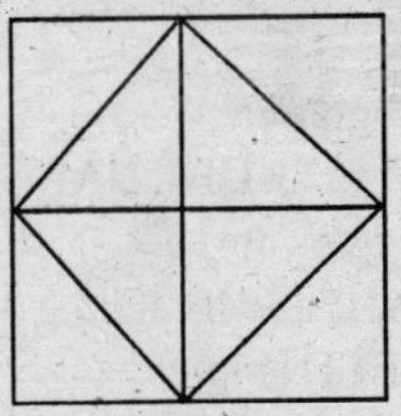

A. 12 B. 10
C. 8 D. 14

7. How many Parallelograms are there in the following figures?

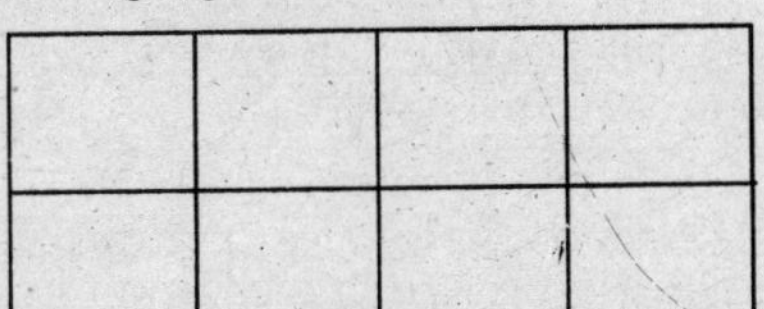

A. 30 B. 29
C. 20 D. 12

8. How many Triangles are there in the figure?

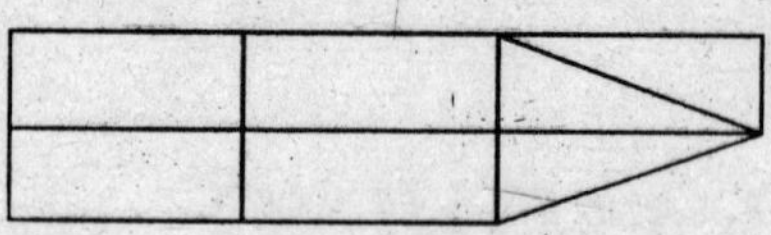

A. 2 B. 4
C. 3 D. 5

9. How many Triangles are there in the figure?

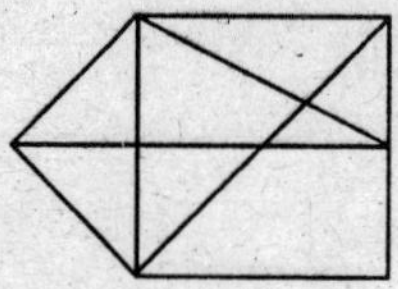

A. 15
B. 14
C. 13
D. 12

10. Count how many Circles are there in the figure?

A. 2
B. 4
C. 5
D. 7

ANSWERS

1	2	3	4	5	6	7	8	9	10
D	C	D	D	D	A	A	B	A	C

EXPLANATORY ANSWERS

1. There are 10 Triangles in the given figure.

Outer Triangles are
ABC, CDE, EFG, GHI, IJA
Other Triangles are
HBE, HDA, JFC, BIF, JGD
There are 10 Triangles.

2. There are sixteen Parallelograms

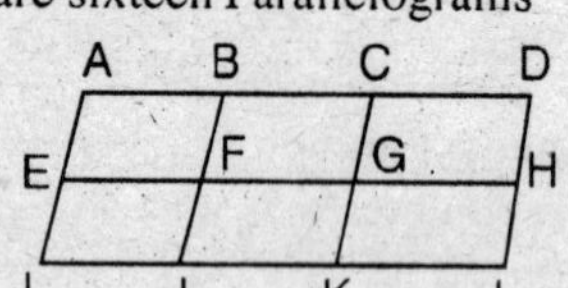

ABFE, BCGF, CDHG, EFJI, FGKJ, GHKL, ACGE, BDHF, EGKI, FHLJ, ABJI, BCKJ, CDLK, ACKI, BDLJ, and ADLI.

3. There are 17 Triangles.

Hence D is the right answer.

4. There are 4 Squares.

5. There are 12 Triangles.

6. There are 12 Triangles.

7. There are 30 Parallelograms.

8. There are 4 Triangles.

9. There are 15 Triangels.

10. There are 5 Circles.

Chapter 14

DICE AND CUBES

Problems of Dice and Cubes have become an important part of non-verbal reasoning. This test is meant to judge candidate's ability to solve the problems in a three-dimensional prespective. In this type of problems, you are given different positions of a Cube or Dice and you have to find out the right answer.

Example 1 : The following are the different positions of a Cube and you have to find out, which number will come on the face opposite to the face carrying 4?

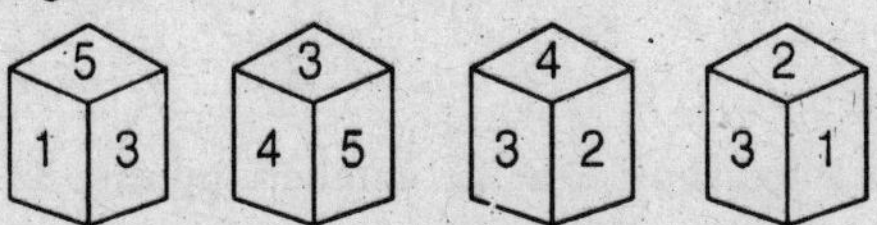

(i) *(ii)* *(iii)* *(iv)*

A. 1 B. 6
C. 5 D. 3

Ans. (1) 5 and 3 exist with 1.

(2) 5 and 3 exist with 4.

So 1 will be opposite to 4. Hence A is the right answer.

Example 2 :

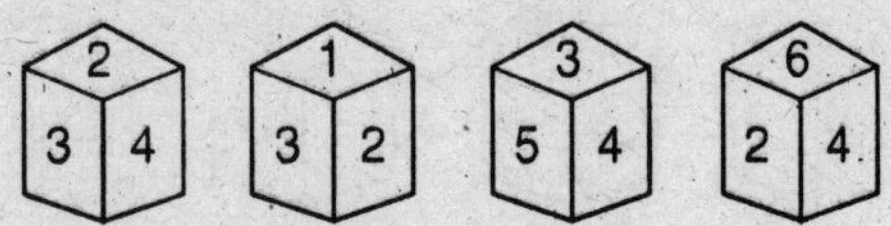

(i) *(ii)* *(iii)* *(iv)*

A dice is thrown four times and its four different positions are given below. Find the number on the fall opposite the few snowing?

A. 3 B. 4
C. 5 D. 6

Ans. In the problem figure, No. 2 appears in three dices 1, 2, 4 and also we can see that the number 2, 4 and 1 and 6 appears adjacent to 3. So none of these numbers can be present opposite 2. The only No. is 5 left. So the right answer is C.

EXERCISE

1.

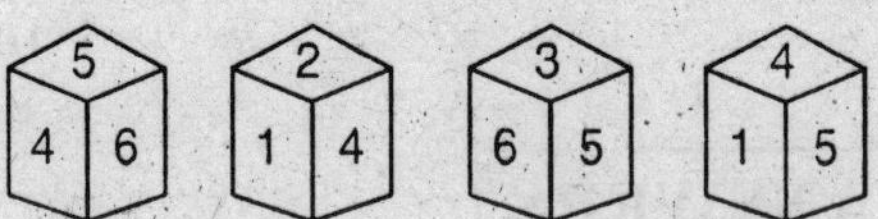

(i) *(ii)* *(iii)* *(iv)*

Which number is opposite 3?

A. 1 B. 2
C. 4 D. 6

2.

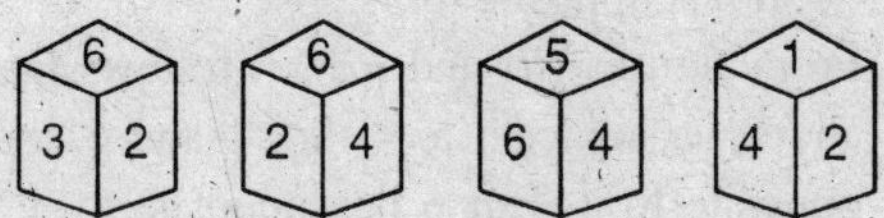

(i) *(ii)* *(iii)* *(iv)*

Which number is on the face opposite 6?

A. 1 B. 2
C. 3 D. 4

3.

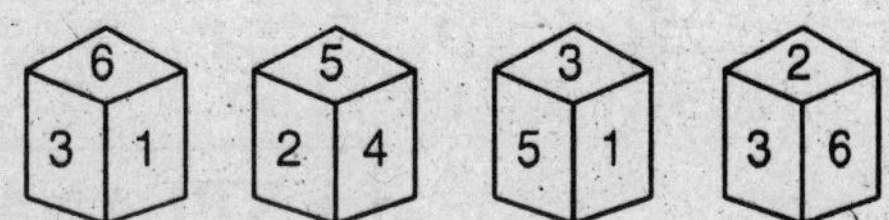

(i) *(ii)* *(iii)* *(iv)*

What number is opposite 3?

A. 2 B. 3
C. 4 D. 6

4.

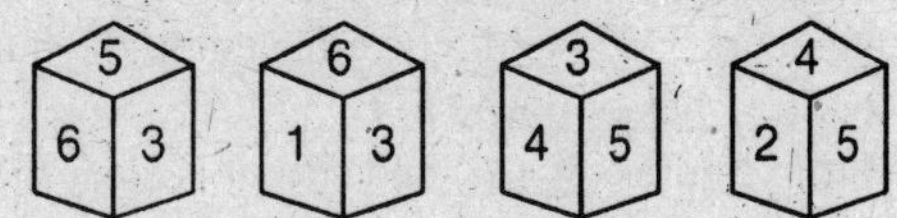

(i) *(ii)* *(iii)* *(iv)*

Which number is opposite 6?

A. 1 B. 2
C. 4 D. 5

5. 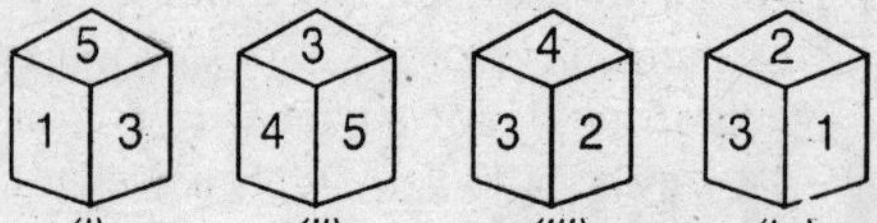

(i) (ii) (iii) (iv)

What number is opposite 4?

A. 1 B. 2

C. 5 D. 6

Directions : *Questions 6 to 8 are based on the following illustrations, which are four views of a cube.*

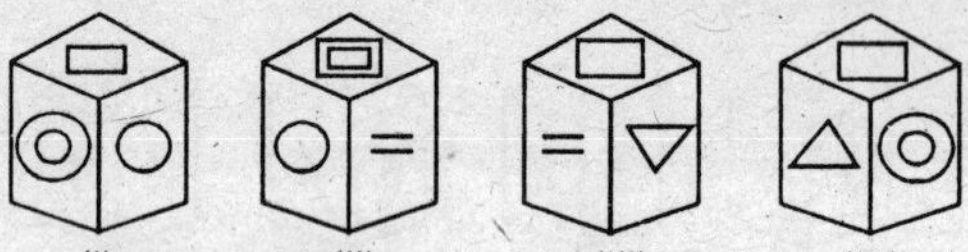

(i) (ii) (iii) (iv)

Study these illustrations carefully and attempt questions 6 to 8.

The symbol at the bottom of (*iv*) is

6. A. ○ B. ◎

C. △ D. ▣

7. The symbol opposite the face having the symbol = is

A. ○ B. △

C. ◎ D. ▭

8. The symbol opposite the face having triangle is

A. ○ B. ◎

C. = D. ▣

9. If the total number of dots on opposite faces of cubical block is always 7, find the figure which is correct.

A. 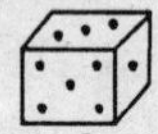 B. 

C.  D. 

10. 

(i) (ii) (iii)

What should be the number opposite 3?

A. 1

B. 6

C. 5

D. 4

ANSWERS

1	2	3	4	5	6	7	8	9	10
C	A	C	C	A	D	C	A	A	B

EXPLANATORY ANSWERS

1. From figure (*i*), (*iii*) and (*iv*), we find that the numbers adjacent to 4 are 5, 6, 1 and 2. So, 3 lies opposite to 4.
2. From figure (*i*), (*ii*) and (*iii*), it is clear that the numbers 3, 2, 4 and 5 lie adjacent to the number 6. So, 1 lies opposite to 6.
3. From figures (*i*), (*iii*) and (*iv*), it is clear that the numbers 6, 1, 5 and 2 lie adjacent to 3. So, 4 lies opposite to 3.
4. No. 1, 3 and 5 appear adjacent to 6 so 2 and 4 can appear opposite to 6. The numbers 1, 4, 5 and 6 appear adjacement to 3. So, they cannot appear opposite to 3. The only number is 3 with 2.
5. From figures (*i*), (*ii*) and (*iii*), it is clear that the number 1, 5, 4 and 2 lie adjacent to number 3. So, 6 lies opposite to 3.

   From figures (*ii*) and (*iii*), it follows that 3, 5 and 2 lie adjacent to 4. So, 1 and 6 could be opposite to 4. But 6 lies opposite to 3. So, 1 lies opposite to 4.
6. From figures (*i*), (*iii*) and (*iv*), we observe that the symbols ○, ○ = and Δ lie adjacent to ▭, so, ▭ lies oppoiste to ▭.
7. From figures (*ii*) and (*iii*), it is clear that the

symbol □, ○ □ and Δ lie adjacent to = sign. So, ○ lies oppoiste to =.

8. From figures (*iii*) and (*iv*), it follows that the symbol □, = and ○ lies adjacent to Δ. So, one of the symbols ○ or □ can lie opposite to Δ. But □ lies opposite to □. So, ○ lies opposite to Δ.

9. Since the sum of the number of dots on opposite faces of the block is always 7, we cannot get 1 dot adjacent to 6 dots, 2 dots adjacent to 5 dots or 3 dots adjacent to 4 dots. So, the figures *b, c* and *d* cannot be correct.

10. From the three given figures, it is clear that the numbers 1, 2, 5 and 4 appear adjacent to 3. So, none of these can appear opposite to 3. Therefore, 6 appears opposite to 3.

Chapter 15

MATRICES

In these type of questions a set of numbers or letters are given in a figure which is divided into different cells. Some logic is applied to form a pattern in rows or columns. One of the cells is left empty. The candidates are required to analyse the logic and from the given options select one which will complete the given incomplete matrix.

SOLVED EXAMPLES

1. Which one number can be placed at the sign (?) of interrogation?

15	6	5
13	3	9
8	2	?
20	7	13

(*a*) 1 (*b*) 4
(*c*) 6 (*d*) 7

Ans. (***a***): The pattern of logic is columnwise. The sum of numbers in first and second column equals the sum of numbers in third and fourth column, *i.e.*, 15 + 13 = 8 + 20, *i.e.*, 28 each. So, 5 + 9 = 14 and 14 − 13 = 1

∴ 1 completes the matrix.

2. Identify the set for the given word.

	0	1	2	3	4
0	A	B	C	D	K
1	D	K	A	C	E
2	C	E	D	K	A
3	K	A	C	E	D
4	E	D	K	A	C

	5	6	7	8	9
5	T	O	P	N	L
6	N	L	T	O	P
7	O	P	N	L	T
8	L	T	O	P	N
9	P	N	L	T	O

POND

(*a*) 76, 87, 65, 22 (*b*) 88, 99, 77, 33
(*c*) 57, 68, 89, 42 (*d*) 68, 99, 77, 33

Ans. (***a***): Here 'P' is represented by row 7 and column 6
'O' by row 8 and column 7
'N' by row 6 and column 5, and
'D' by row 2 and column 2.

EXERCISE

Directions (Qs. 1 and 2): *In each question given below which one number when placed at the sign of interrogation shall complete the number matrix.*

1.

7	4	5
8	7	6
3	3	?
29	19	31

(*a*) 4 (*b*) 3
(*c*) 6 (*d*) 5

2.

15	18	21
3	6	7
4	5	?
9	8	7

(*a*) 4 (*b*) 6
(*c*) 7 (*d*) 5

Directions (Qs. 3 to 5): *In each question given below which letters when placed at the sign of interrogation shall complete the matrix?*

3.

H	K	Q
C	N	O
E	J	?

(*a*) L (*b*) N
(*c*) P (*d*) M

4.

H	N	Z
W	E	M
L	T	?

(*a*) V (*b*) J
(*c*) A (*d*) F

5.

J	B	M
N	F	Q
R	J	?

(*a*) U (*b*) P
(*c*) S (*d*) X

Directions (Qs. 6 to 10): *In questions given below, a word is represented by only one set of numbers as given in any one of the alternatives. The sets of numbers given in the alternatives are represented by two classes of alphabets as in the 2 matrices given below. The columns and rows of matrix I are numbered from 0 to 4 and that of matrix II from 5 to 9. A letter from these matrices can be represented first by its row and next by column number. Identify the set for the word given in each question.*

6.

	0	1	2	3	4
0	E	A	T	S	H
1	A	H	T	A	S
2	E	H	A	S	T
3	H	E	A	T	S
4	S	H	T	A	E

	5	6	7	8	9
5	O	R	K	L	P
6	L	P	O	R	K
7	O	K	R	P	L
8	P	R	K	L	O
9	R	L	K	O	P

REAP

(*a*) 56, 00, 22, 59
(*b*) 68, 21, 22, 86
(*c*) 96, 00, 01, 99
(*d*) 86, 34, 24, 69

7.

	0	1	2	3	4
0	C	A	F	E	D
1	C	D	A	E	D
2	D	E	C	F	E
3	A	D	D	D	C
4	D	C	A	C	A

	5	6	7	8	9
5	T	R	R	S	M
6	S	T	M	R	S
7	R	S	P	T	P
8	P	S	T	R	T
9	P	M	P	M	S

FARM

(*a*) 02, 30, 85, 65
(*b*) 20, 31, 76, 68
(*c*) 23, 12, 68, 96
(*d*) 44, 43, 87, 57

8.

	0	1	2	3	4
0	C	H	H	N	N
1	I	N	C	B	B
2	N	E	C	H	I
3	I	C	N	E	I
4	B	B	E	C	I

	5	6	7	8	9
5	Y	P	S	P	K
6	K	T	S	R	R
7	K	Y	R	Y	Y
8	P	R	K	P	R
9	S	Y	S	T	S

PREY

(*a*) 82, 76, 34, 77
(*b*) 80, 70, 43, 12
(*c*) 94, 87, 43, 56
(*d*) 88, 77, 33, 79

9.

	0	1	2	3	4
0	D	K	A	E	C
1	C	D	K	A	E
2	K	C	E	A	D
3	K	C	D	E	A
4	E	D	A	K	C

	5	6	7	8	9
5	P	L	O	T	N
6	T	P	N	L	O
7	P	N	T	O	L
8	O	N	T	P	L
9	L	O	P	N	T

COLD

(*a*) 10, 85, 79, 24 (*b*) 31, 99, 77, 22
(*c*) 30, 66, 86, 43 (*d*) 44, 96, 95, 22

10.

	0	1	2	3	4
0	M	M	R	M	R
1	O	F	R	F	N
2	R	N	O	R	O
3	F	O	F	M	O
4	F	M	R	R	F

	5	6	7	8	9
5	T	G	J	T	G
6	P	J	G	G	U
7	U	T	P	T	J
8	U	T	T	J	P
9	G	U	G	T	P

TURF

(*a*) 57,86, 44, 11 (*b*) 86, 75, 20, 32
(*c*) 77, 68, 41, 44 (*d*) 89, 97, 12, 30

ANSWERS

1	2	3	4	5	6	7	8	9	10
(*d*)	(*a*)	(*d*)	(*a*)	(*a*)	(*a*)	(*c*)	(*d*)	(*a*)	(*b*)

EXPLANATORY ANSWERS

1. $(7 \times 3) + 8 = 29$
$(4 \times 3) + 7 = 19$
So, $(31 - 6) \div 5 = 25 \div 5$, *i.e.*, 5 in the third row completes the matrix.

2. $(15 \div 3) + 4 = 9$
$(18 \div 6) + 5 = 8$
So, $7 - (21 \div 7) = 7 - 3$, *i.e.*, 4 in the third row completes the matrix.

3. The matrix is based on position of alphabet.
Q (17) – H (8) + 2 = K (11)
O (15) – C (3) + 2 = N (14)
So, J (10) + E (5) – 2, *i.e.*, M (13) in the last column completes the series.

4. The letters in first row, second row and third row are formed by three, four and two straight lines respectively.

5. The letters in each column are moved four steps forward.

J → N → R (+4, +4)

B → F → J (+4, +4)

M → Q → U (+4, +4)

6. R is represented by row 5, column 6
E by row 0, column 0
A by row 2, column 2
P by row 5, column 9

7. F is represented by row 2, column 3
A by row 1, column 2
R by row 6, column 8
M by row 9, column 6

8. P is represented by row 8, column 8
R by row 7, column 7
E by row 3, column 3
Y by row 7, column 9

9. C is represented by row 1, column 0
O by row 8, column 5
L by row 7, column 9
D by row 2, column 4

10. T is represented by row 8, column 6
U by row 7, column 5
R by row 2, column 0
F by row 3, column 2

Chapter 16

STATEMENT & CONCLUSIONS

VALIDITY OF CONCLUSION

Syllogism is a logical argument in three propositions, two premises and a conclusion that follows necessarily from them. The conclusion is Valid or Invalid.

Example : All women are mothers.

All girls are women.

Inference : All girls are mothers.

If the two premises are drawn, the logical diagram will be :

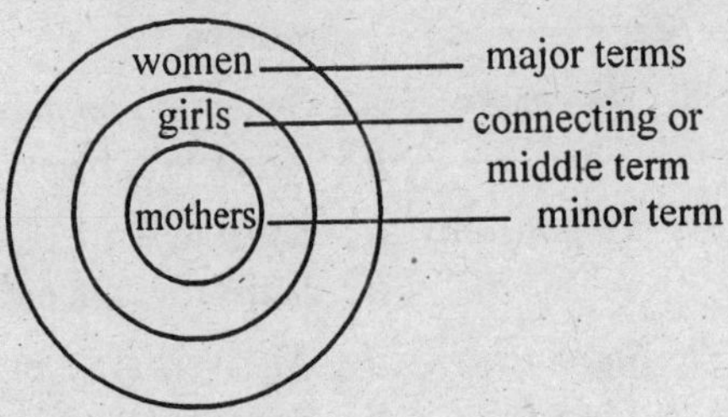

So, the given conclusion or inference is valid.

Such problems on syllogism can be solved mentally with a little bit of intelligence and common sense.

In this reasoning pattern the two premises are followed by two conclusions drawn from them. Five options *(a)*, *(b)*, *(c)*, *(d)* and *(e)* are given as answers. Based on the two statements the candidate has to select the right option as answer.

SOLVED EXAMPLES

In the questions below the answer is given as :

(a) if only conclusion I follows.

(b) if only conclusion II follows.

(c) if either I or II follows.

(d) if neither I nor II follows, and

(e) if both I and II follows.

1. *Statements* *I :* All officers are lazy.
II : Some men are officers.

Conclusions *I :* All lazy are men.
II : Some men are lazy.

Ans. *(b)*: When all officers are lazy and some men are officers then some men must be lazy. Therefore, conclusion II is correct.

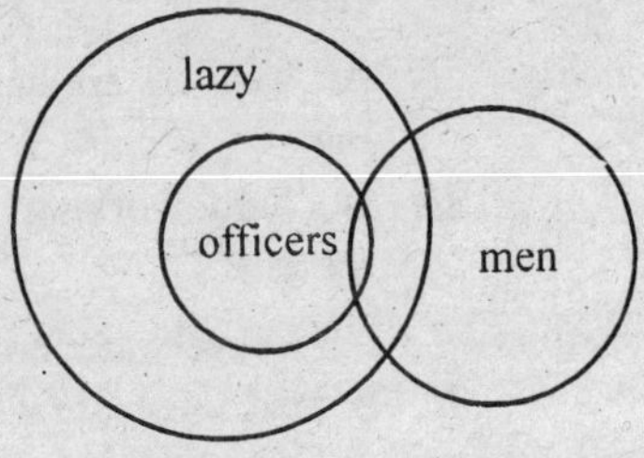

EXERCISE

Directions (Qs. 1 to 10): *In each question below are given two statements followed by two conclusions numbered I and II. You have to take the two given statements to be true even if they seem to be at variance from commonly known facts and then decide which of the given conclusions logically follows from the two given statements, disregarding commonly known facts. Read both the statements and—*

Give answer (a) if only conclusion I follows; give answer (b) if only conclusion II follows; give answer (c) if either I or II follows; give answer (d) if neither I nor II follows and give answer (e) if both I and II follows.

1. *Statements* I: All tomatoes are red.
   II: All grapes are tomatoes.
   Conclusions I: All grapes are red.
   II: Some tomatoes are grapes.
2. *Statements* I: All painters are smilling.
   II: Some authors are painters.
   Conclusions I: All smiling authors are painters.
   II: Some authors are smiling.
3. *Statements* I: All peons in this office are efficient.
   II: Ramu is not efficient.
   Conclusions I: Ramu is not peon in this office.
   II: Ramu should be more efficient.
4. *Statements* I: All weavers are hard working.
   II: No hard working men are foolish.
   Conclusions I: No weavers are foolish.
   II: Some foolish are weavers.
5. *Statements* I: All fishes are cars.
   II: All cars are vegetables.
   Conclusions I: Some vegetables are cars.
   II: Some vegetables are fishes.
6. *Statements* I: Some dogs are pups.
   II: All horses are pups.
   Conclusions I: Some dogs are horses.
   II: Some horses are dogs.
7. *Statements* I: All beautiful women are mothers.
   II: All mothers are understanding.
   Conclusions I: All beautiful women are understanding.
   II: All mothers are beautiful women.
8. *Statements* I: Some toys are tables.
   II: No table is black.
   Conclusions I: Some toys are black.
   II: Some toys are not black.
9. *Statements* I: All rivers are mountains.
   II: Some rivers are deserts.
   Conclusions I: Some mountains are deserts.
   II: Some deserts are not mountains.
10. *Statements* I: All men are horses.
    II: All horses are elephants.
    Conclusions I: All men are elephants.
    II: All elephants are men.

Directions (Qs. 11 and 12): *In the following statements, state if the inference drawn (the third statement) is valid or invalid.*

11. Some tables are chairs.
    Some stools are chairs.
    Some tables are stools.
12. No grapes are roses.
    All guards are grapes.
    All guards are roses.

ANSWERS

1	2	3	4	5	6	7	8	9	10
(*e*)	(*b*)	(*a*)	(*a*)	(*e*)	(*d*)	(*a*)	(*c*)	(*e*)	(*a*)

EXPLANATORY ANSWERS

1. When all tomatoes are red and all grapes are tomatoes, then all grapes are also red. When all grapes are tomatoes, then some tomatoes must be grapes. Therefore, both conclusions I and II are correct.

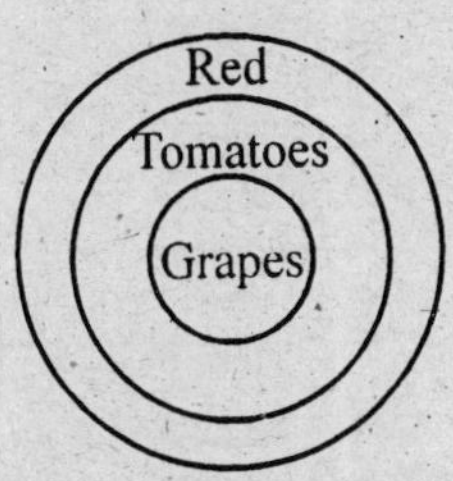

2. When all painters are smiling and some authors are painters, then some authors are smiling. Therefore, only conclusion II is correct.

3. When all the peons of the office are efficient, then Ramu cannot be a peon in this office. Therefore, only conclusion I is correct.

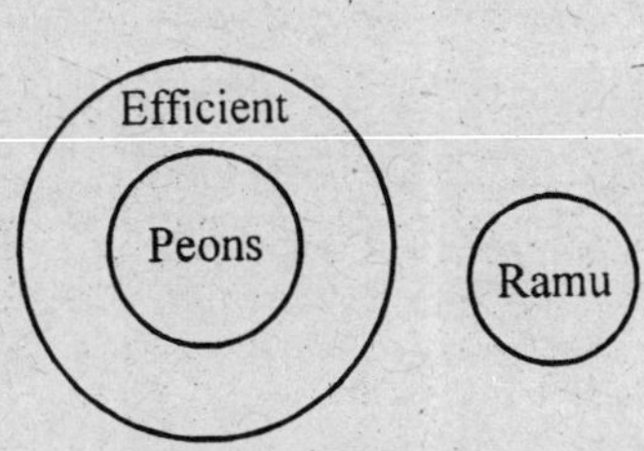

4. When all weavers are hardworking and no hardworking men are foolish, then no weavers are foolish. Therefore, only conclusion I is correct.

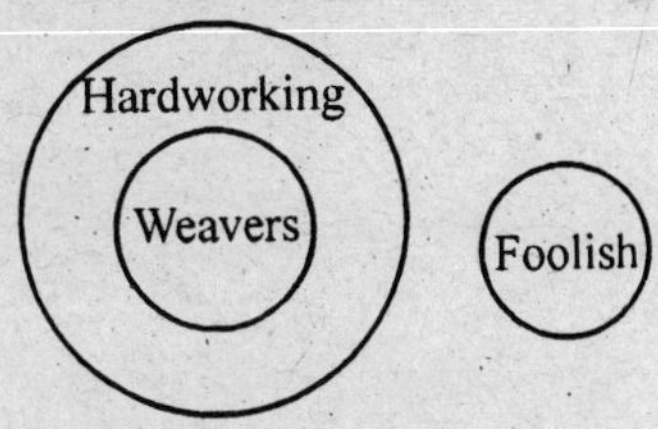

5. When all fishes are cars and all cars are vegetables, then all fishes will naturally be vegetables. This means that some vegetables are fishes. And when all cars are vegetables, then some vegetables will be cars naturally. Therefore, both the conclusions I and II are correct.

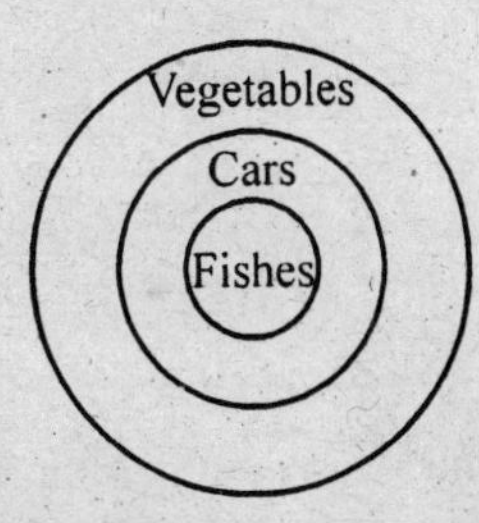

6. No relationship can be established between the two statements. Therefore, neither conclusion I nor conclusion II is correct.

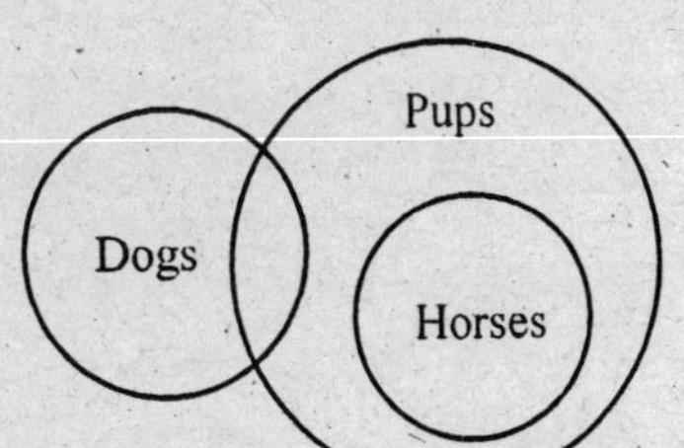

7. When all beautiful women are mothers and all mothers are understanding, then naturally all beautiful women are understanding. All mothers need not be beautiful women. Therefore, only conclusion I is correct.

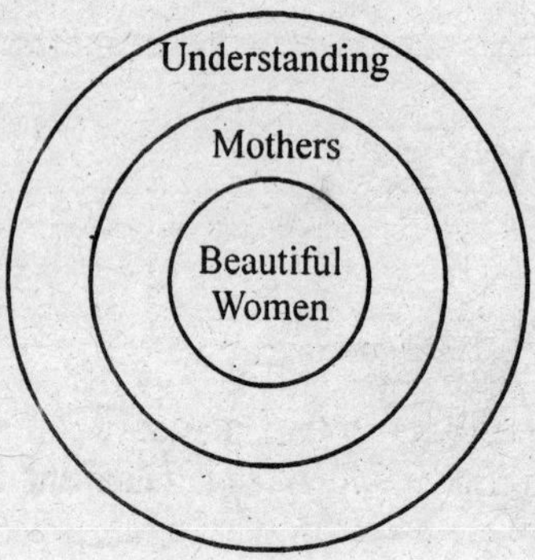

8. When some toys are tables and no table is black, then it is indicated that some toys can be black, as all toys are not tables. On the other hand, some toys may not be black. Therefore, there is a possibility that some toys may or may not be black. As such, either conclusion I or conclusion II can be correct.

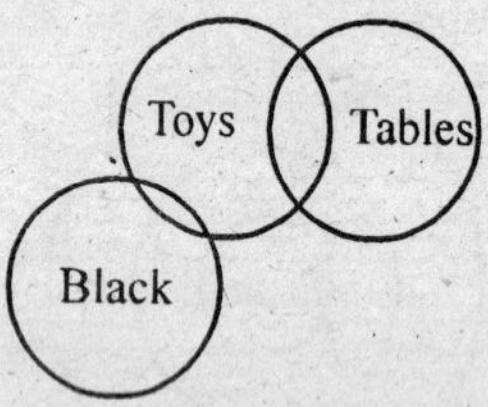

9. When all rivers are mountains and some rivers are deserts, then some deserts cannot be mountains and also, some mountains need not be deserts. Therefore, both conclusion I and conclusion II are correct.

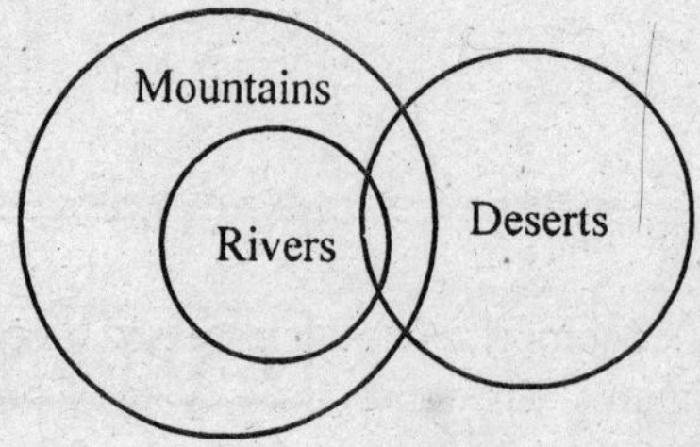

10. When all men are horses and all horses are elephants then, naturally all men are elephants, but all elephants need not be men. Therefore, only conclusion I is correct.

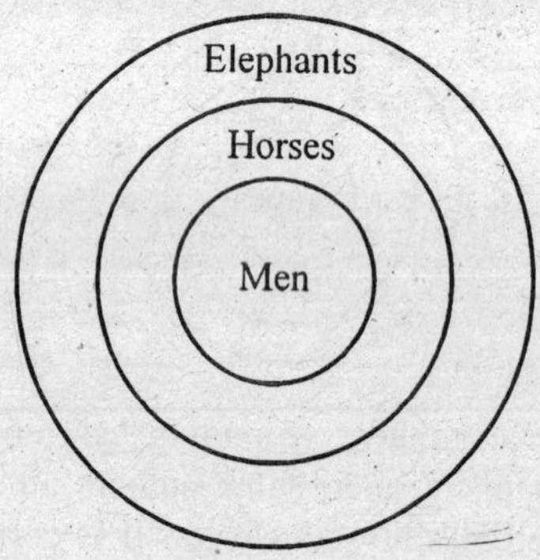

11. Invalid 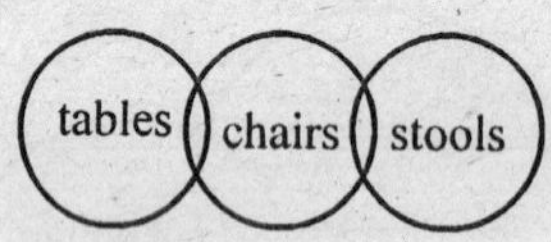

12. Invalid 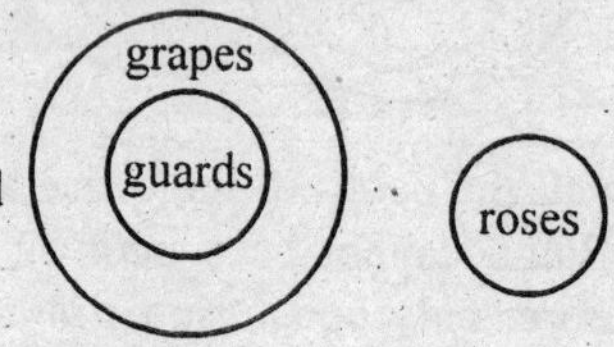

Chapter 17

SERIES

This chapter comprises problems based on continuation of figures. There are many types of problems but all of them are based on the same pattern. There is a particular sequence of figures. Candidate has to pick out the next figure from the Answer Figures.

Example-1 : Problem Figures:

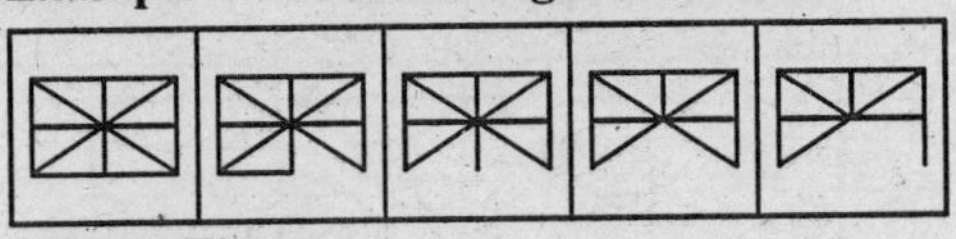

Answer Figures

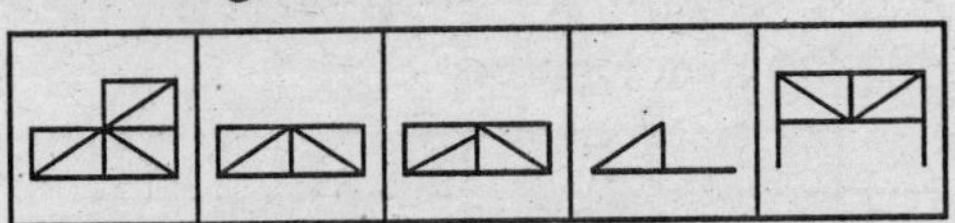

A B C D E

Answer E : Problem Figures consist of a rectangle divided into sections. At each step one of the lines is removed. First from the right, then left and then the centre. To continue this pattern, a right diagonal line is removed. In the answer figure a left diagonal line should be removed. Answer Figure 'E' continues the series.

Example-2 : Problem Figures:

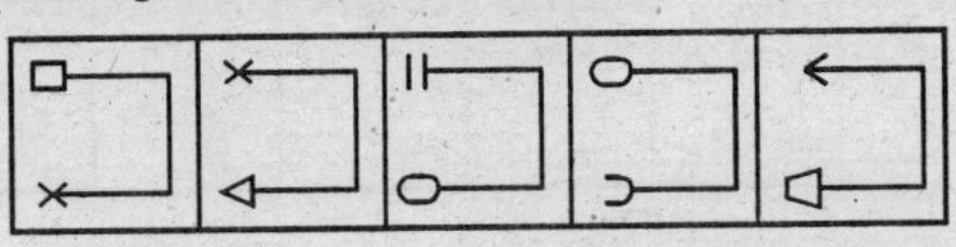

Answer Figures

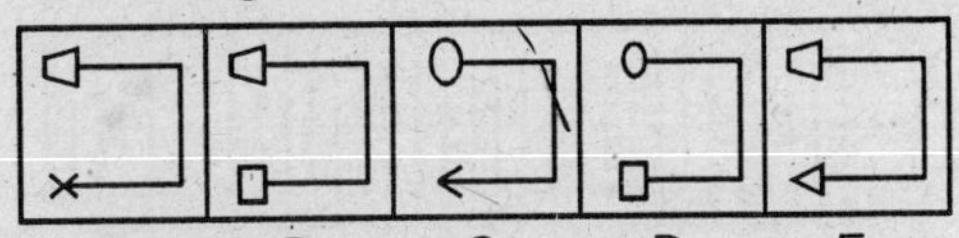

A B C D E

Answer B : Observe the series. Figure one corelates to figure two in the manner that the places of both the elements on the left are inter changed and then the element at the bottom is replaced by a new element. Similarly, Figure three corelates to figure four and answer figure 'B' corelates to figure five.

Example-3 : Problem Figures:

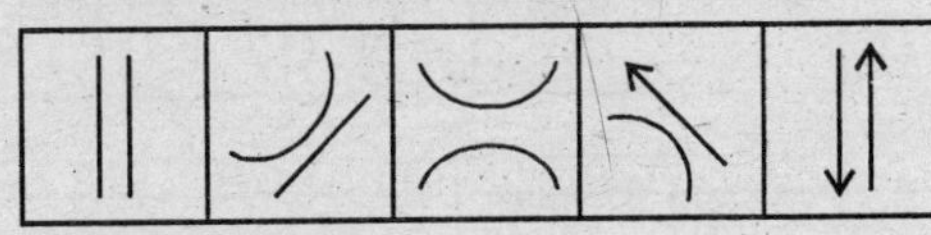

Answer Figures

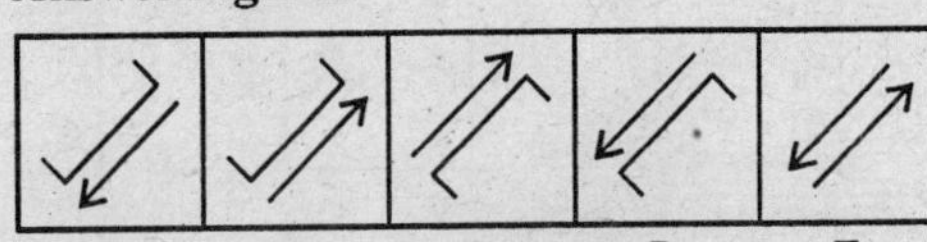

A B C D E

Answer B : The two elements are rotated 45° clockwise. Beginning from the top both the elements are changed one by one in a set pattern. Answer figure 'B' continues the series.

EXERCISE–I

1. Problem Figures

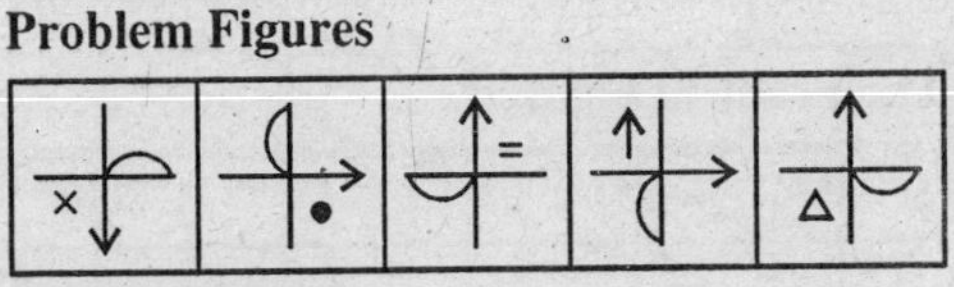

Answer Figures

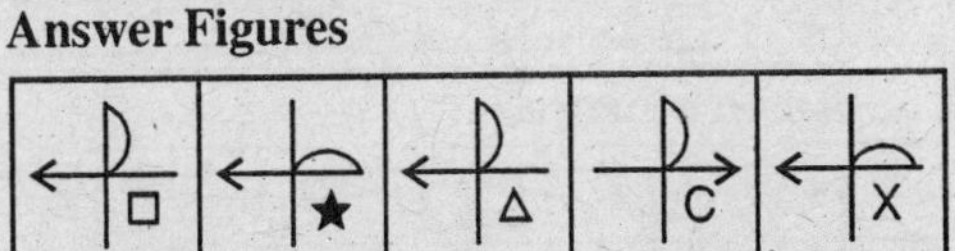

A B C D E

2. Problem Figures

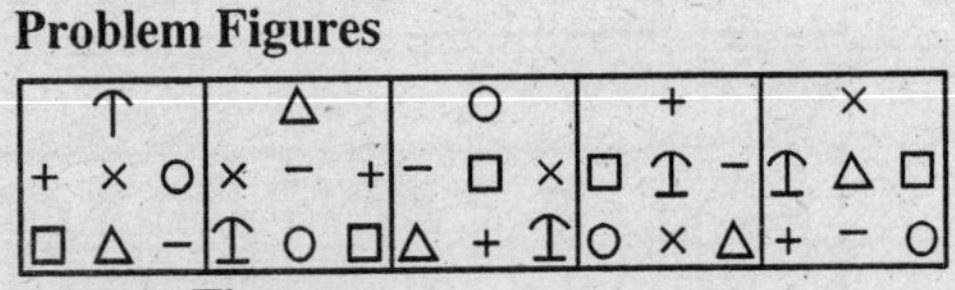

Answer Figures

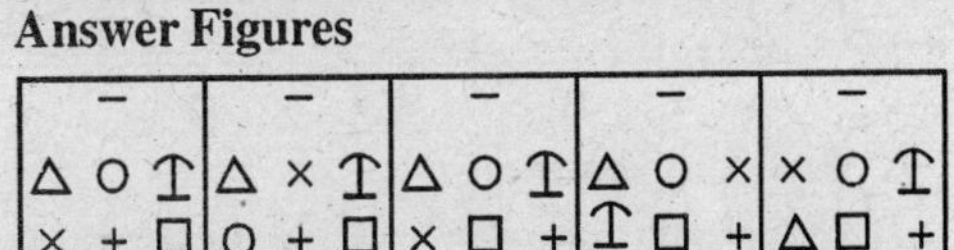

A B C D E

3. Problem Figures

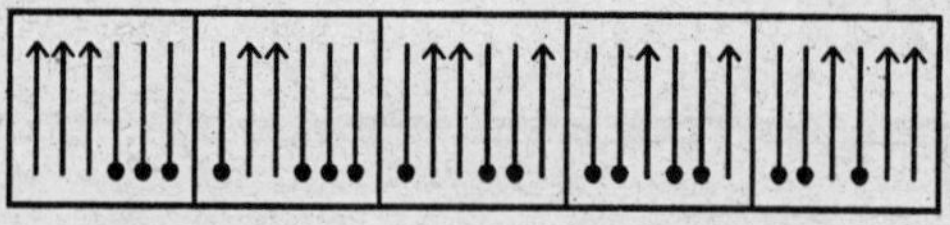

Answer Figures

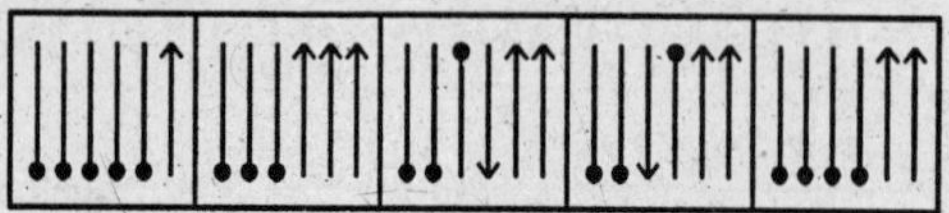

A B C D E

4. Problem Figures

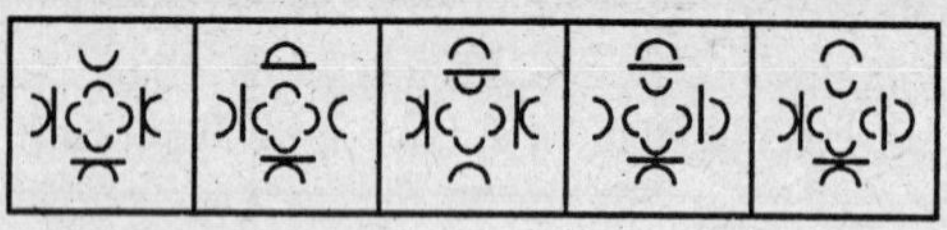

Answer Figures

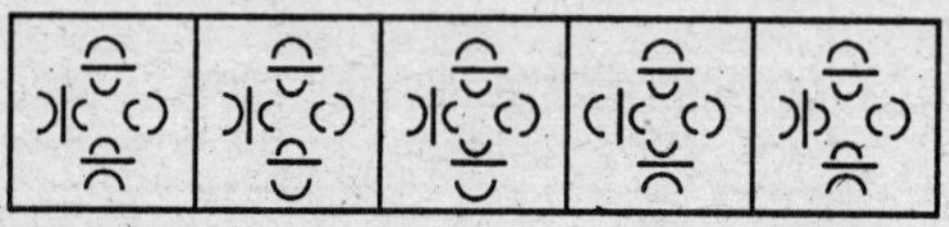

A B C D E

5. Problem Figures

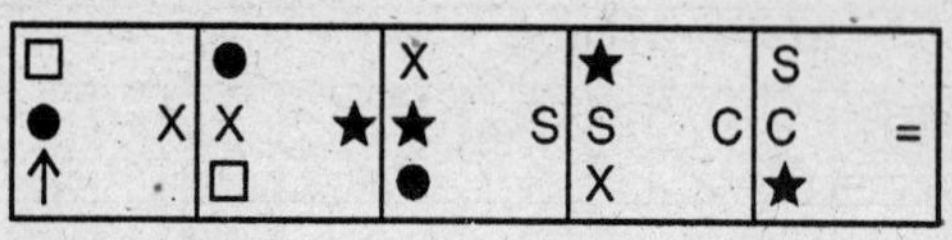

Answer Figures

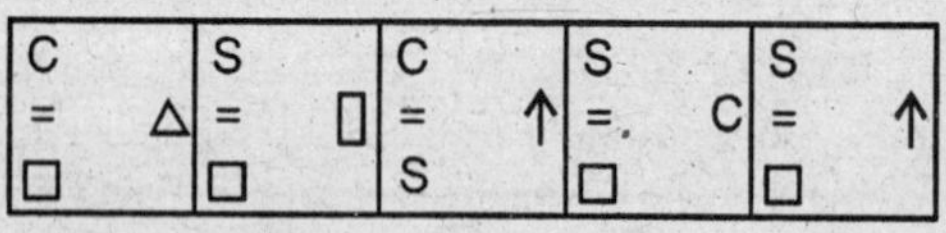

A B C D E

6. Problem Figures

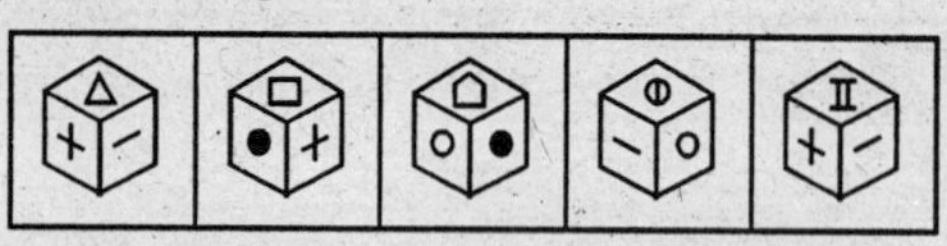

Answer Figures

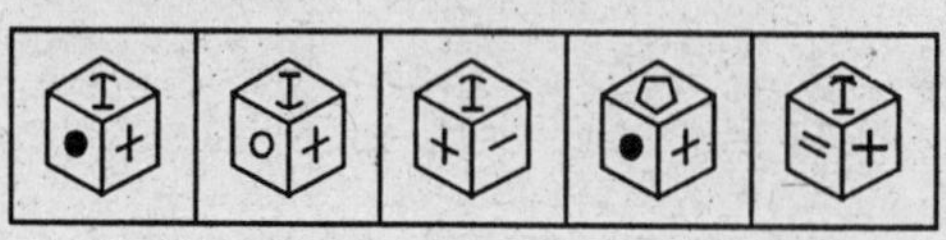

A B C D E

7. Problem Figures

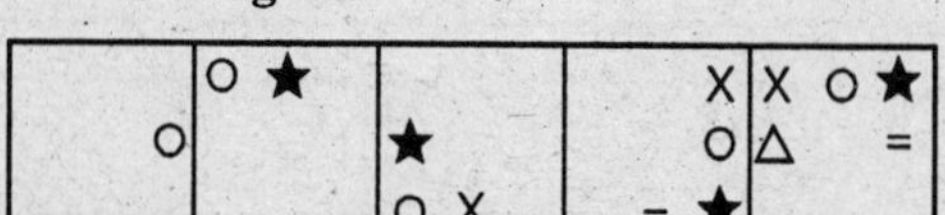

Answer Figures

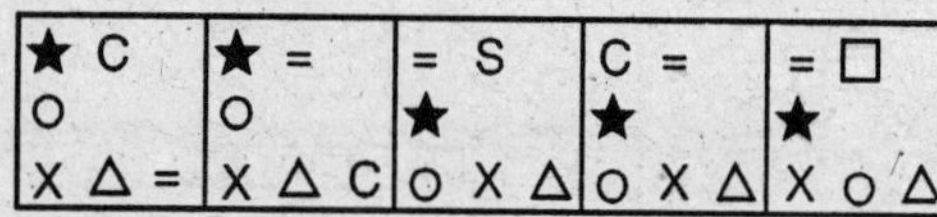

A B C D E

8. Problem Figures

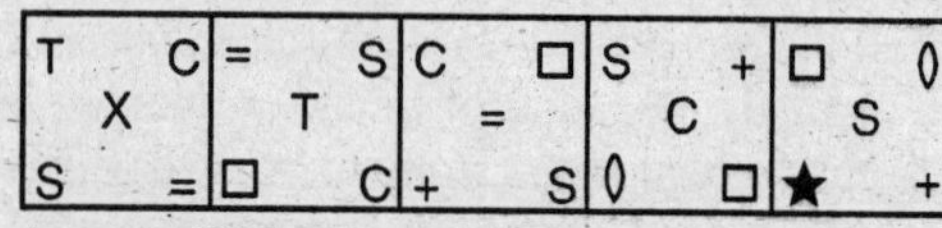

Answer Figures

A B C D E

9. Problem Figures

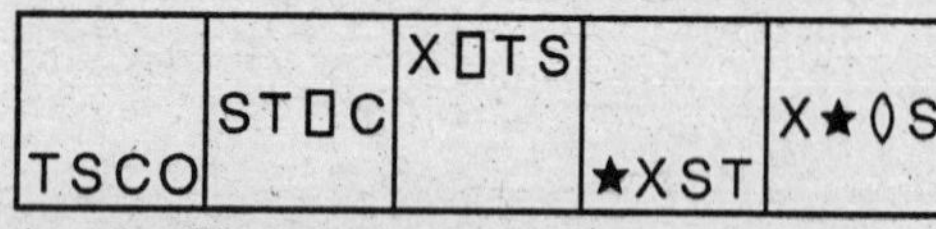

Answer Figures

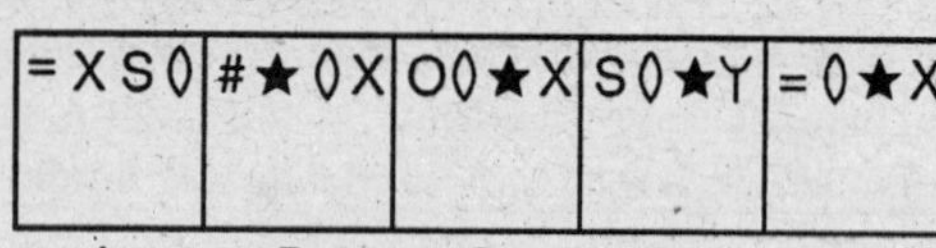

A B C D E

10. Problem Figures

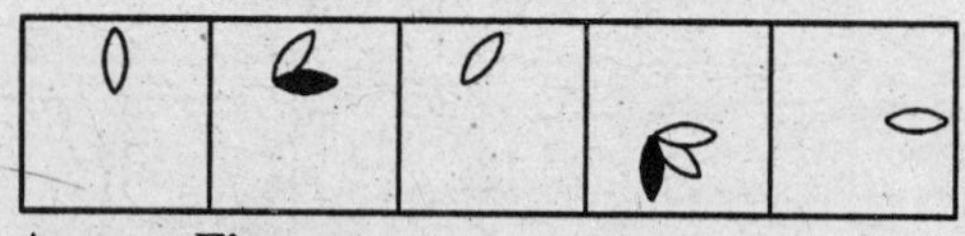

Answer Figures

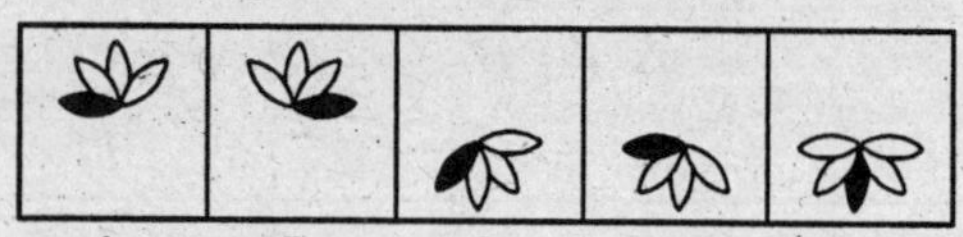

A B C D E

11. Problem Figures

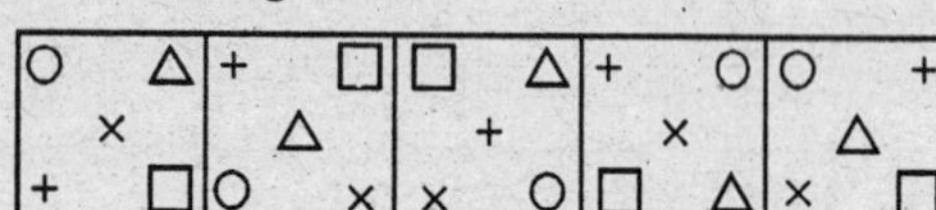

Answer Figures

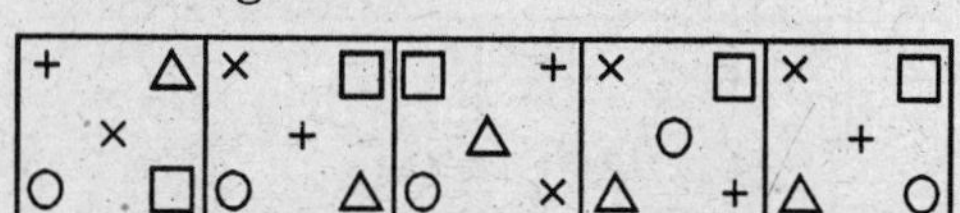

A B C D E

12. Problem Figures

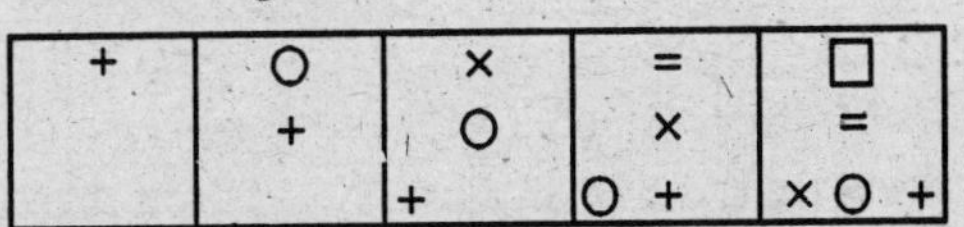

Answer Figures

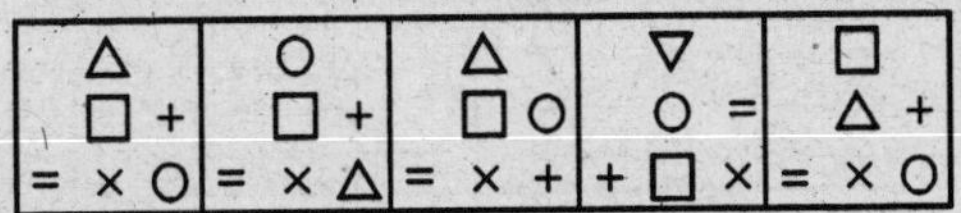

A B C D E

13. Problem Figures

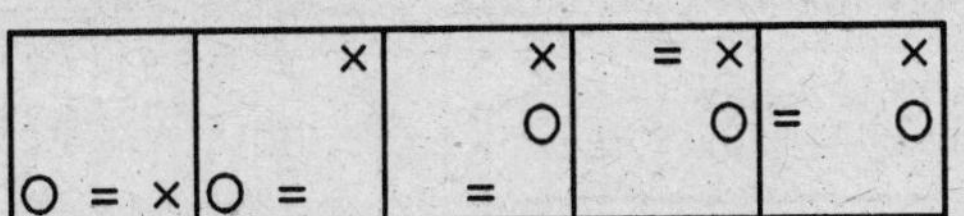

Answer Figures

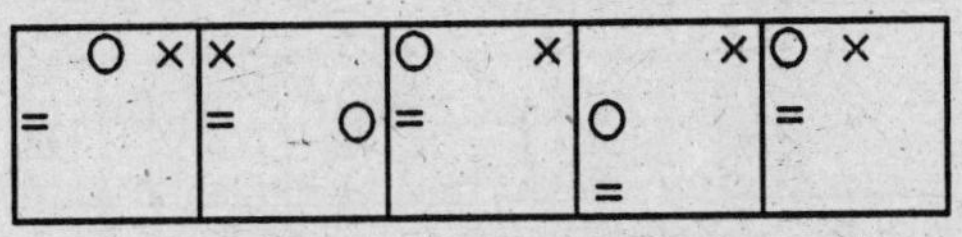

A B C D E

14. Problem Figures

Answer Figures

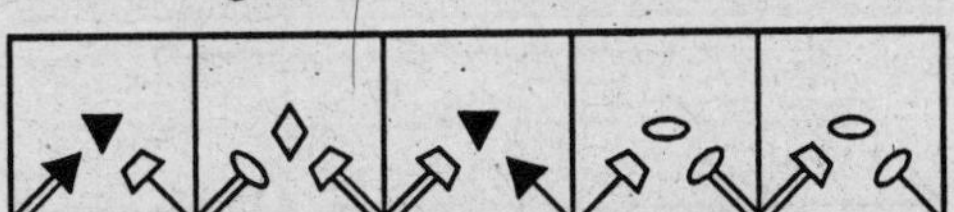

A B C D E

15. Problem Figures

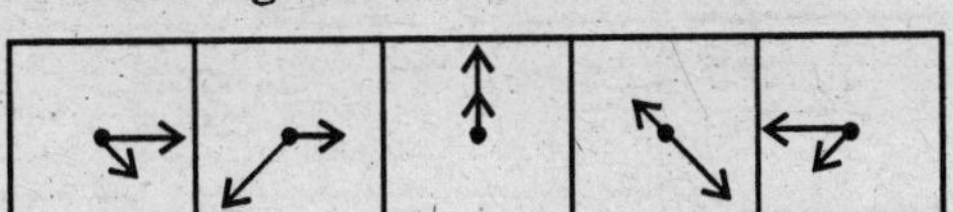

Answer Figures

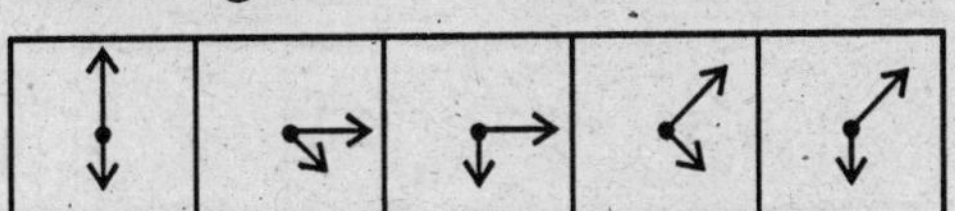

A B C D E

16. Problem Figures

Answer Figures

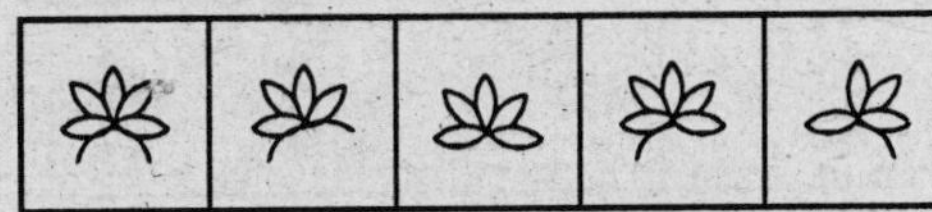

A B C D E

17. Problem Figures

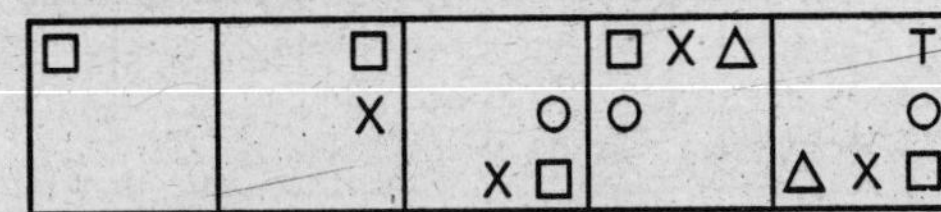

Answer Figures

A B C D E

18. Problem Figures

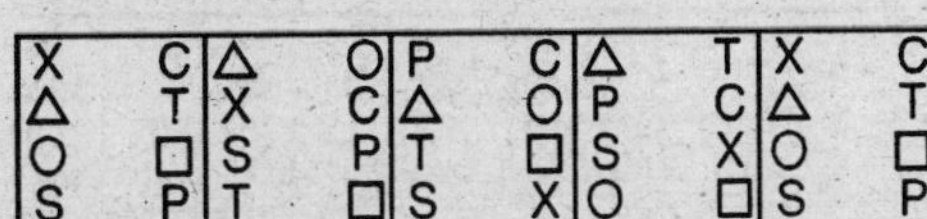

Answer Figures

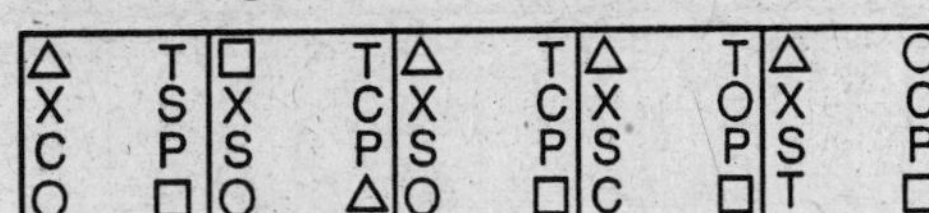

A B C D E

19. Problem Figures

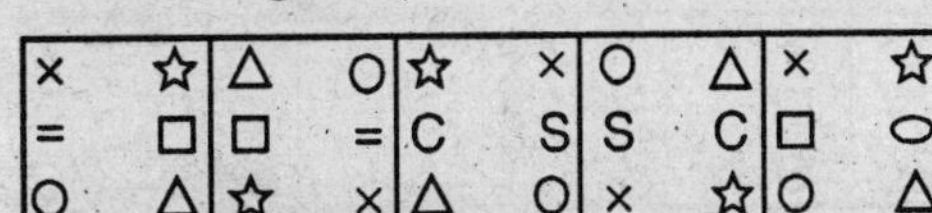

Answer Figures

A B C D E

20. Problem Figures

Answer Figures

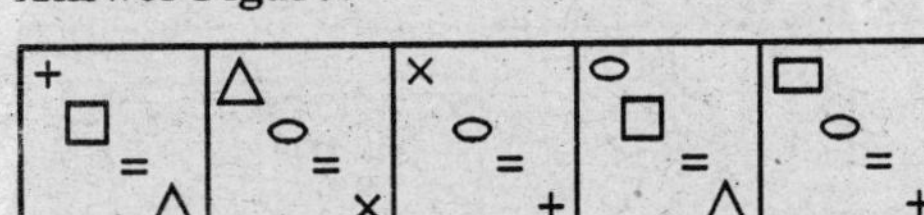

A B C D E

21. Problem Figures

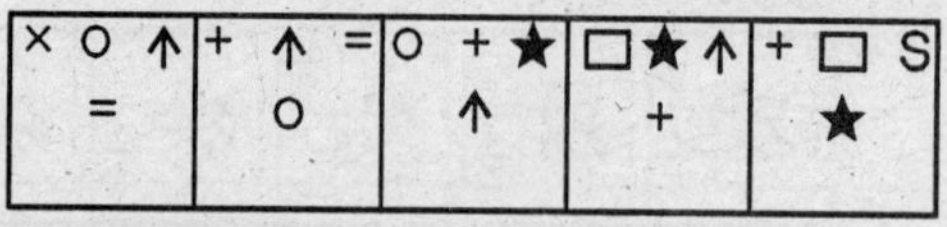

Answer Figures

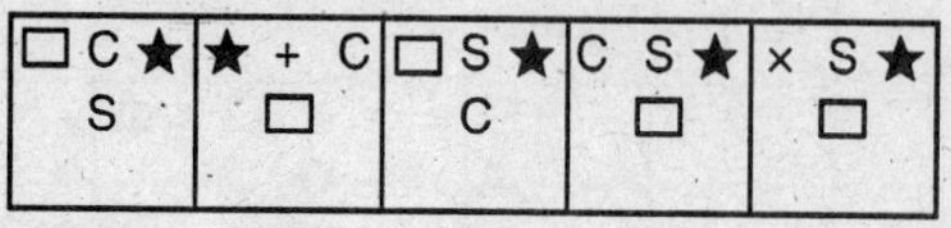

A B C D E

22. Problem Figures

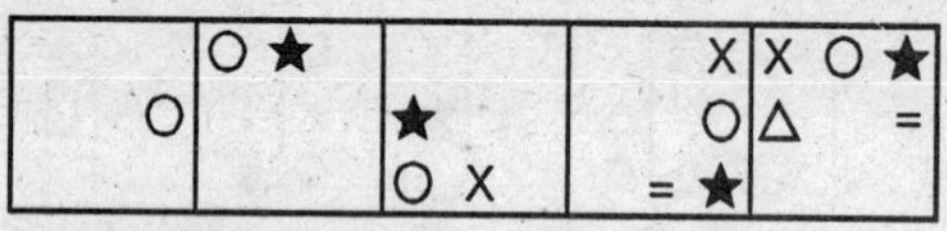

Answer Figures

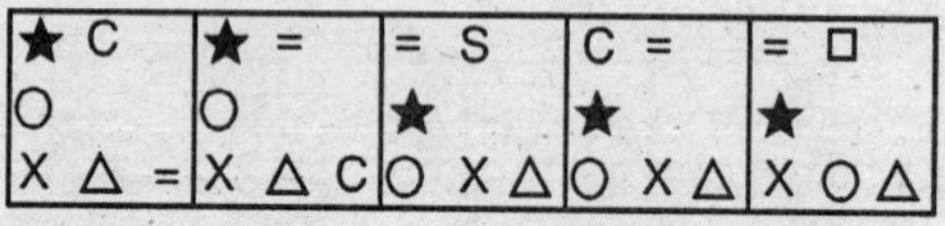

A B C D E

23. Problem Figures

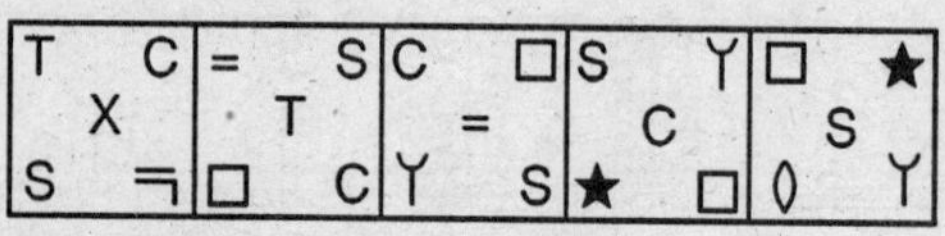

Answer Figures

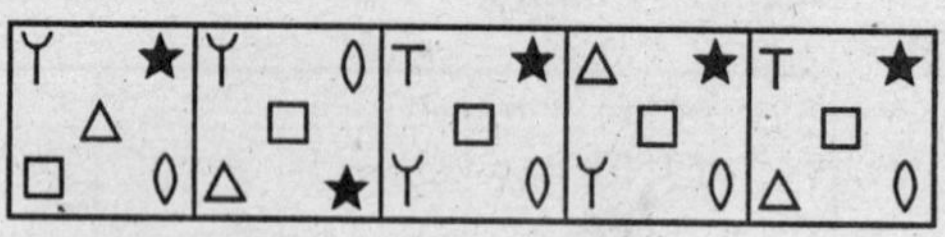

A B C D E

24. Problem Figures

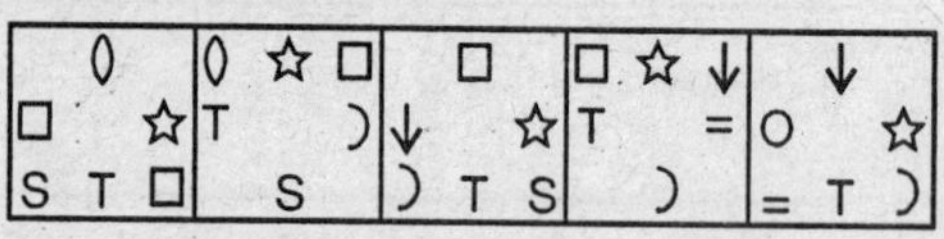

Answer Figures

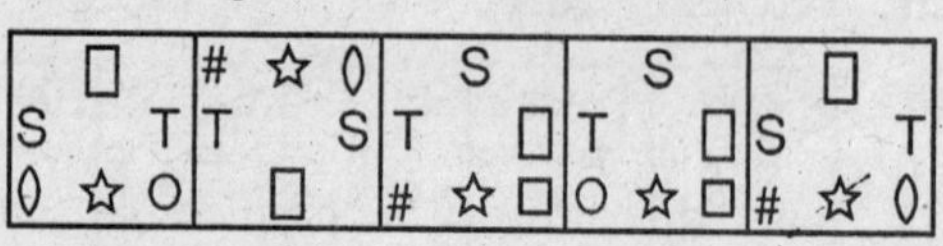

A B C D E

25. Problem Figures

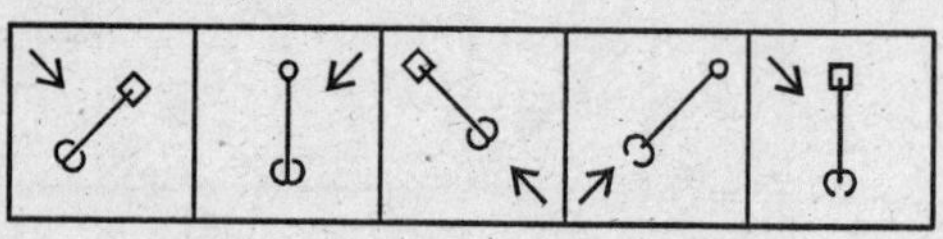

Answer Figures

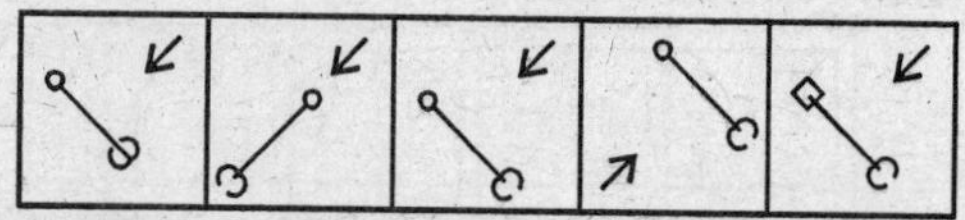

A B C D E

26. Problem Figures

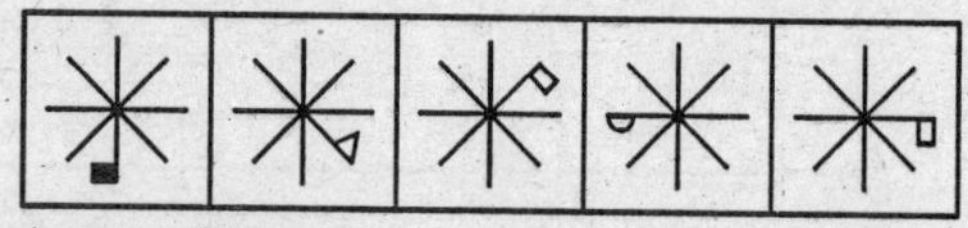

Answer Figures

A B C D E

27. Problem Figures

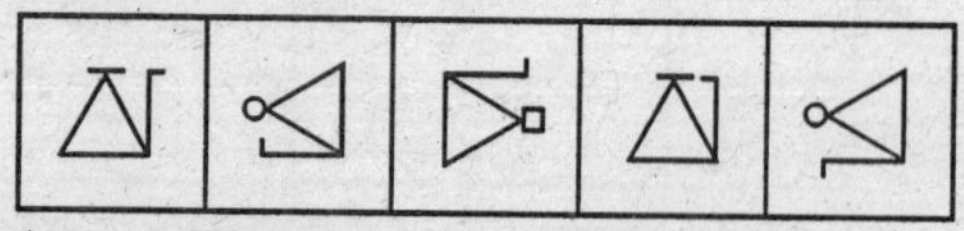

Answer Figures

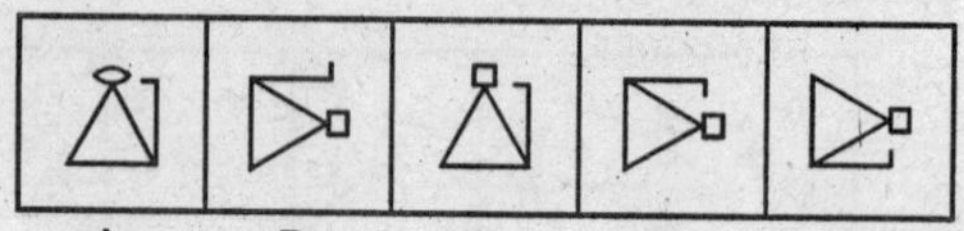

A B C D E

28. Problem Figures

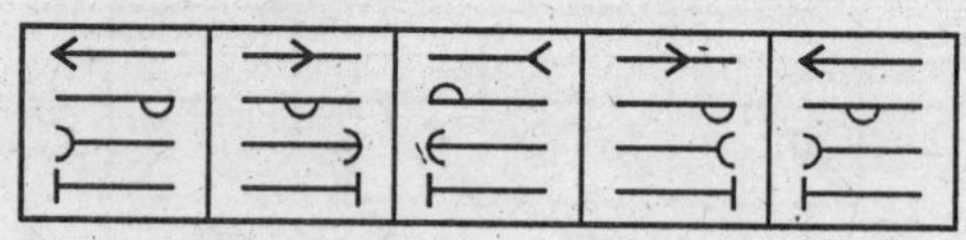

Answer Figures

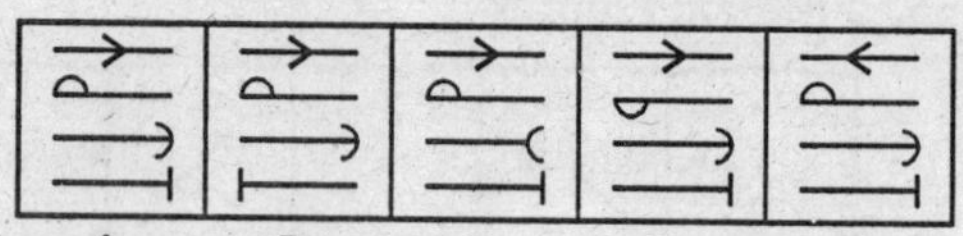

A B C D E

29. Problem Figures

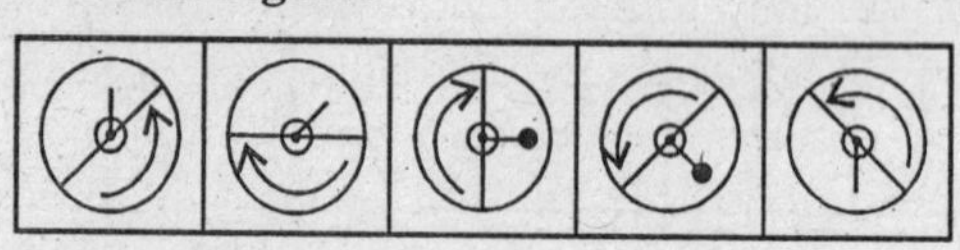

Answer Figures

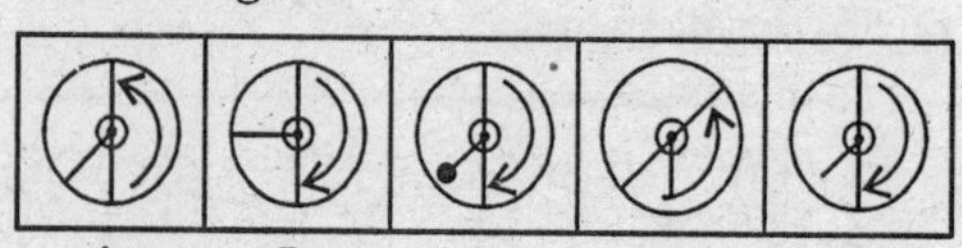

A B C D E

30. Problem Figures

Answer Figures

A B C D E

ANSWERS

1	2	3	4	5	6	7	8	9	10
A	C	E	C	B	E	C	C	E	D
11	12	13	14	15	16	17	18	19	20
B	A	C	B	E	D	A	E	A	E
21	22	23	24	25	26	27	28	29	30
D	C	B	B	C	C	D	A	E	B

EXPLANATORY ANSWERS

1. Observe the first three figures. The cross with its elements is rotated 90° anticlock-wise and each time the loose element is replaced by a new element. The process is repeated from figure four.
2. At each step, the single element on the top is moved to the bottom left position, the bottom left element is moved to the bottom right position, the bottom right element is moved to the centre, the centre element is moved to the left, the left element is moved to the right, the right element is moved to the bottom middle position, and the bottom middle element is moved to the top.
3. First, one arrow is replaced by a dot bar, then in the next step one dot bar is replaced by an arrow. The replacing pattern follows a set order.
4. The three line segments in the middle are moved on step clockwise. Clockwise, the arcs are turned by 180° one by one in a set order. First the top arc, then the one below it, followed clockwise by the right arc and the arc behind it and so on.
5. The element on the right is moved to the left, this middle element is moved up, the top element is moved to the bottom, the bottom element is moved to the right and is replaced by a new element.
6. The elements in the sections are moved one step anticlockwise. Only the element in the right section is left untouched while the other two elements are replaced by entirely new elements (none of the earlier elements are repeated).
7. The circle is moved one and a half steps and one step anticlockwise alternately. Each time a new element is added, first behind the circle and then ahead of it. Answer figure 'C' follows the series.
8. The bottom left element is moved to the diagonally opposite corner, the top right element is moved one step clockwise, the bottom right element is moved to the diagonally opposite corner, the top left element is moved to the centre, and the element in the centre which is replaced by a new element is moved to the bottom left position.
9. Note the first three figures. From figure one to figure two the positions of two left elements are interchanged, the positions of two right elements are interchanged and the second element from the right is replaced by a new element. From figure two to figure three the places of two middle elements are interchanged, the places of two corner elements are inter changed and the left most

element is replaced by a new element. At each step the elements are moved half way up. The process is repeated from figure four.

10. In figures one, three and five the petal is rotated 45° clockwise. In figures two and four the petals are rotated 90° anticlockwise and a new petal added on the right. Answer figure 'D' continues the pattern.

11. The places of the circle and one element anticlockwise are inter changed at each step while the places of other three elements are shifted anticlockwise.

12. The plus sign is the leading element. At each step a new element is added and all elements follow the plus sign.

13. From figure one to figure two, the leading element is moved one step anticlockwise. From figure two to figure three the trailing is moved one and a half steps anticlockwise. From figure three to figure four the left out element is moved two steps anticlockwise. The above process is repeated from figure five.

14. Observe the figures. Figure two corresponds to figure one and figure four to figure three. Of the two corner elements the left element is moved to the diagonally opposite corner and the element in the centre is replaced by a new element. Similarly, Answer Figure 'B' corresponds with figure five.

15. The smaller arrow is rotated 45° and 90° anticlockwise alternately and the larger arrow is rotated 135° clockwise at each step.

16. As the flower is rotated, first half new petal on the left is added and then half on the right is added. Similarly, first the left half petal is completed and then the half petal on the right is completed. Figure 'D' continues the series, half petal on the left is added.

17. The square is moved 1, 1, 2, 2 steps clockwise. One new element is added ahead of it and behind it in a set order. To get the answer figure the square should be moved 3 steps clockwise alongwith other elements.

18. From figure one to figure two the two top elements and two bottom elements are moved to the second and thirds rows respectively; the elements in the second and third rows are moved to the top and bottom rows respectively; and then the places of top right element and bottom left element are interchanged. From figure two to figure three the movement of elements in the rows is same as above except that in this the places of top left element and bottom right element are interchanged. The above process is repeated.

19. From figure one to figure two the position of four corner elements is interchanged diagonally and the places of two middle elements are interchanged. The same rule is applied to figures three and four; and figures five and six.

20. First the bottom right element is moved to the second position and the two elements shifted down diagonally while the top most element is replaced by a new element. Then, the top left element is moved to the third position and the two elements shifted up diagonally while the bottom right element is replaced by a new element. The above process is repeated.

21. First the top left element is replaced by a new element while the other three elements are rotated anticlockwise. Then the top right element is replaced by a new element while the other three elements are rotated clockwise. The above process is repeated.

22. The circle is moved one and a half steps and one step anticlockwise alternately. A new element is added first behind it and then ahead of it in alternate figures.

23. At each step the top left element is moved to the centre, the top right element is moved to bottom right position, the two bottom elements are moved to the diagonally opposite corners on the top, and the element in the centre is moved to the bottom left position and is replaced by a new element.

24. Alternate figures 1, 3 and 5 have one elements on the top and three at the bottom. Whereas in figures 2 and 4 there are three elements on the top and one at the bottom. Answer figure B continues the series.

25. Between figure one and figure four, figure two and figure five, the square is replaced by a circle and vice versa, the direction of the two curves at the base is changed, the arrow is rotated 90° anticlockwise and moved one step anticlockwise. Similarly, answer figure C coordinates with figure three.

26. The element is replaced by a new element each time and is moved anticlockwise in increasing numerical order. Also, it is alternately on the right and left side of the spike.

27. Observe that figure one and figure four are identical except that one line segment is turned to the opposite direction. The same holds for figure two and figure five. Answer figure D coordinates with figure three.

28. The arrowhead is moved to the right end of the line segment and back in a set pattern and its direction is reversed at each step. The semicircle is moved from right end to the left end of the line segment in a set pattern and is placed on the other side. The arc is moved from end to end of the line segment and its direction is reversed in alternate figures. The bottom element is same in alternate figures.

29. From figure one to figure two the diagonal with circle and dot bar are rotated 45° clockwise and the direction of the arrow is reversed. Same applies to figure three and figure four. Answer figure E coordinates with figure five.

30. One and two line segments from the top are alternately removed from the zig zag pattern on the left. On the right side when a dot is removed a line segment is added at the base and when a line segment is removed, a dot as added; this process is alternate.

EXERCISE–II

1. Problem Figures

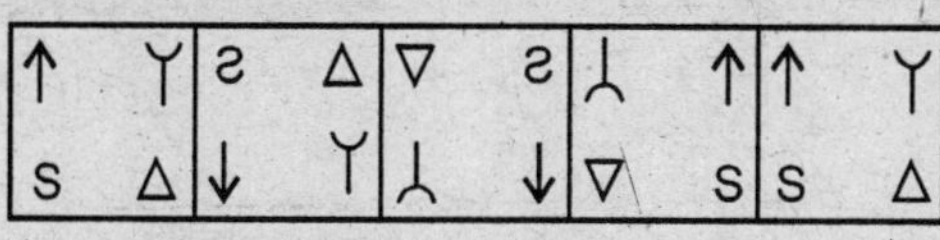

Answer Figures

A B C D E

2. Problem Figures

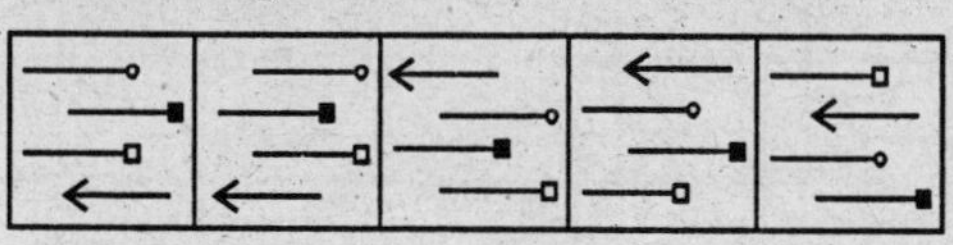

Answer Figures

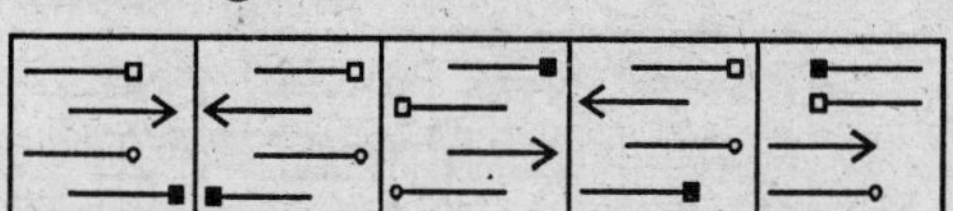

A B C D E

3. Problem Figures

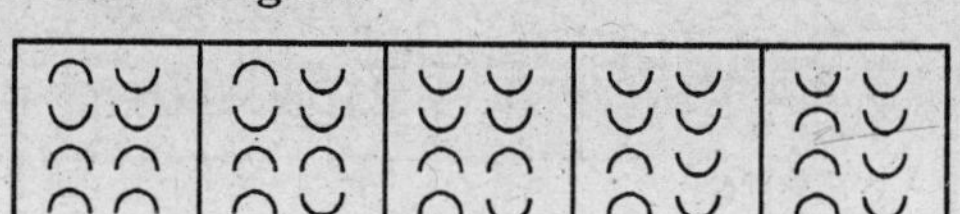

Answer Figures

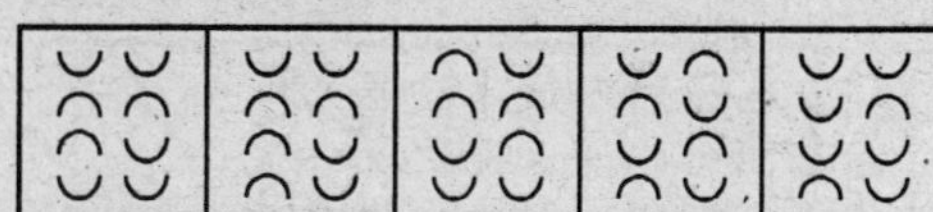

A B C D E

4. Problem Figures

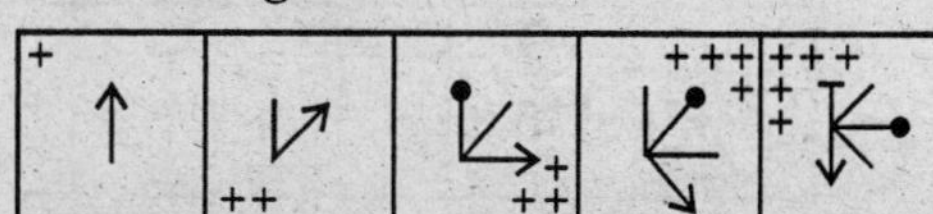

Answer Figures

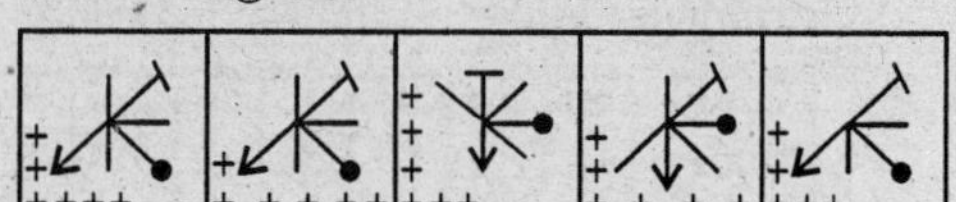

A B C D E

5. Problem Figures

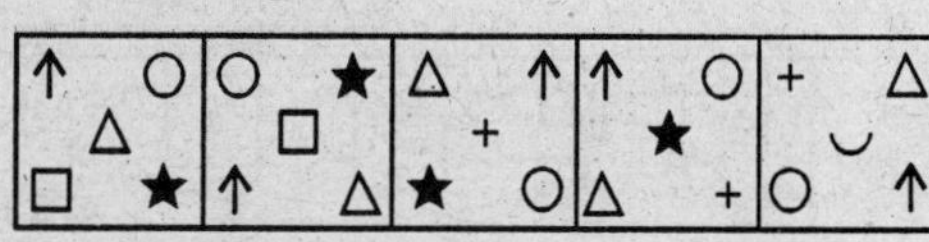

Answer Figures

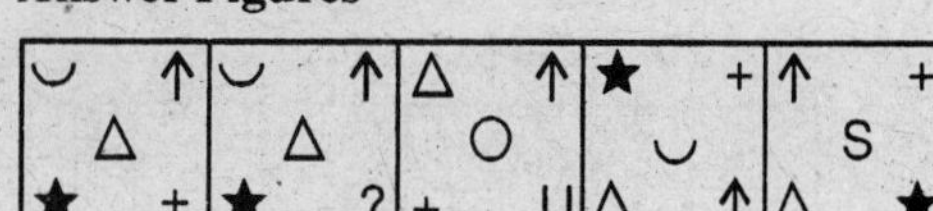

A B C D E

6. Problem Figures

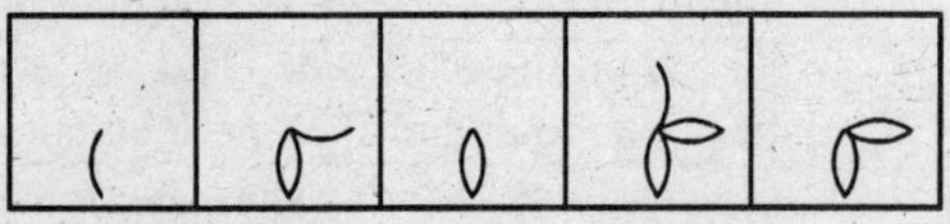

Answer Figures

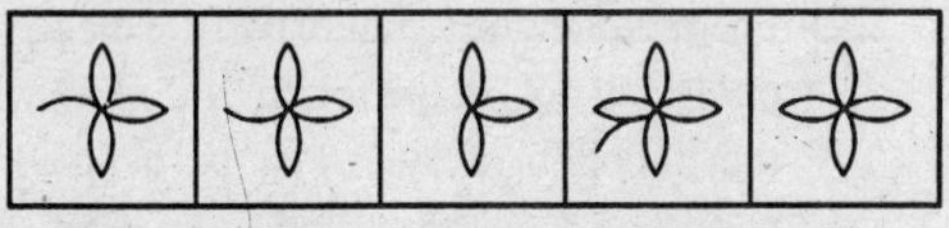

A B C D E

7. Problem Figures

Answer Figures

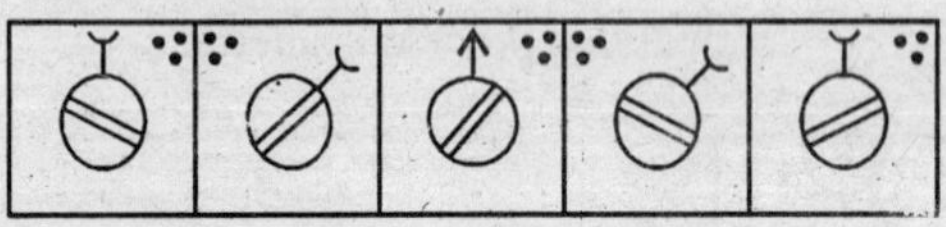

A B C D E

8. Problem Figures

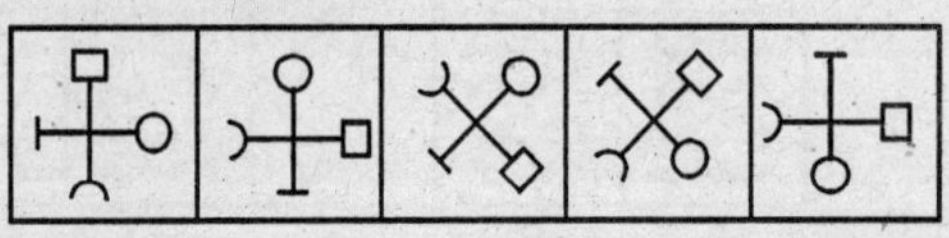

Answer Figures

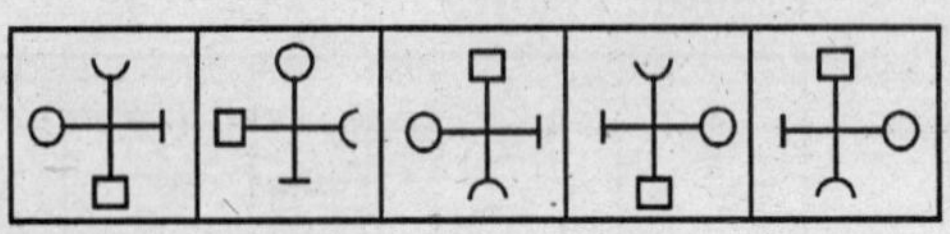

A B C D E

9. Problem Figures

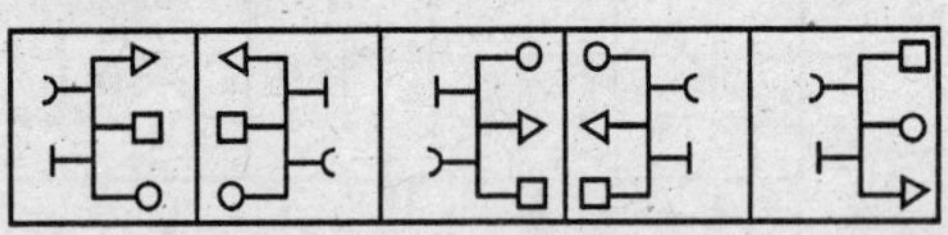

Answer Figures

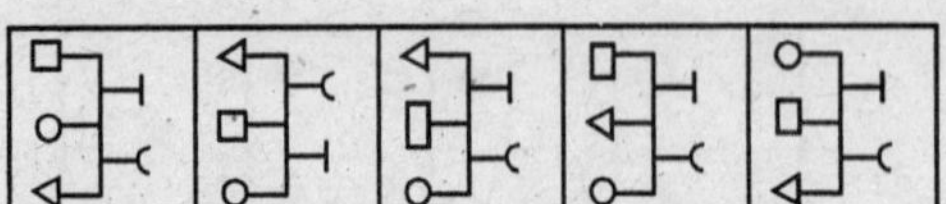

A B C D E

10. Problem Figures

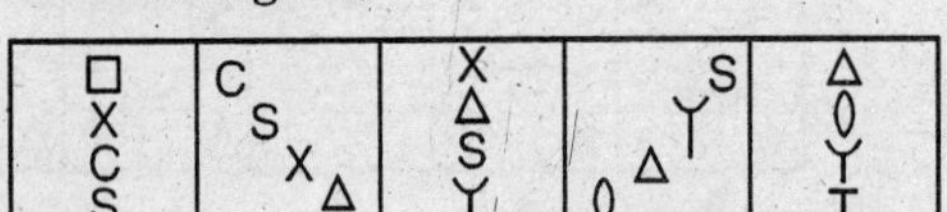

Answer Figures

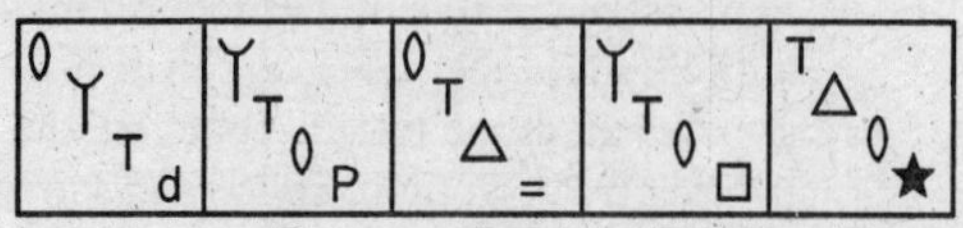

A B C D E

11. Problem Figures

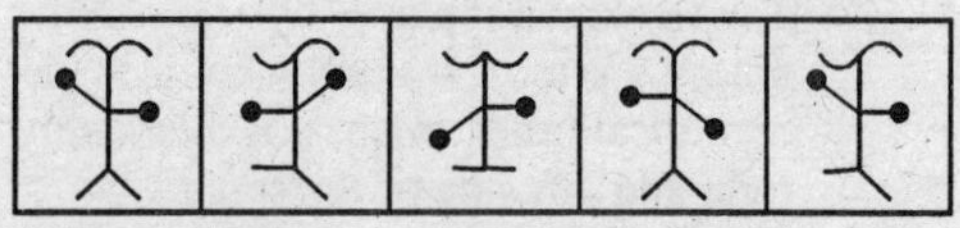

Answer Figures

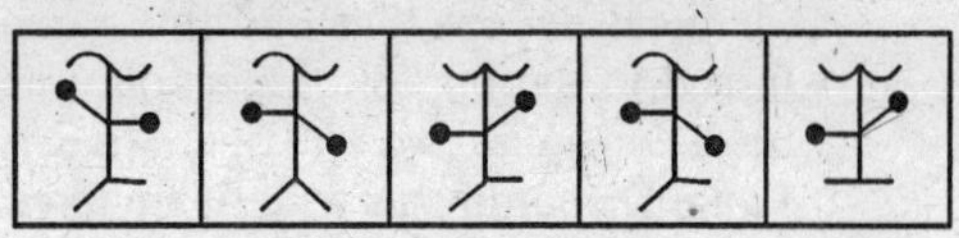

A B C D E

12. Problem Figures

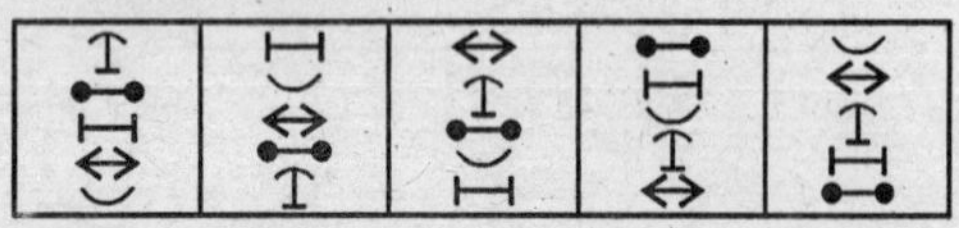

Answer Figures

A B C D E

13. Problem Figures

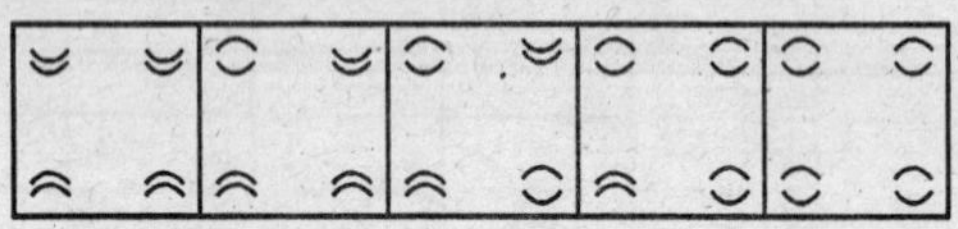

Answer Figures

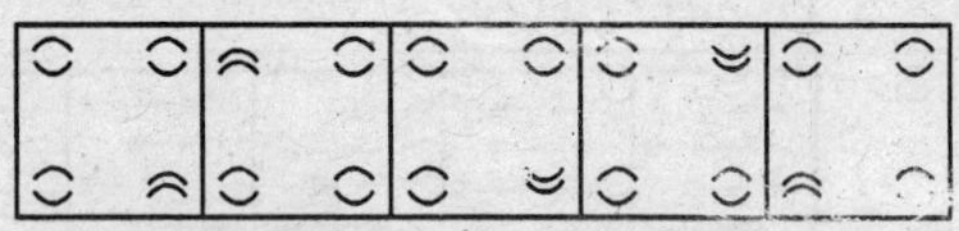

A B C D E

14. Problem Figures

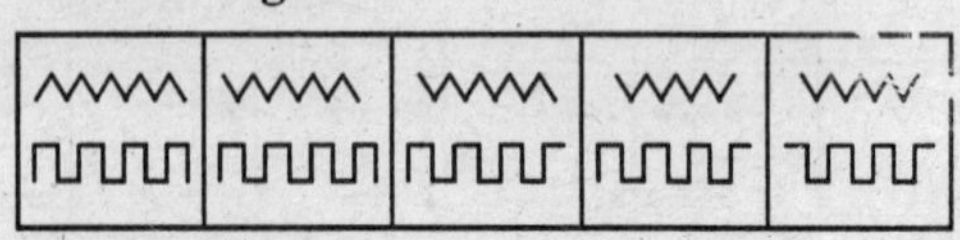

Answer Figures

A B C D E

15. **Problem Figures**

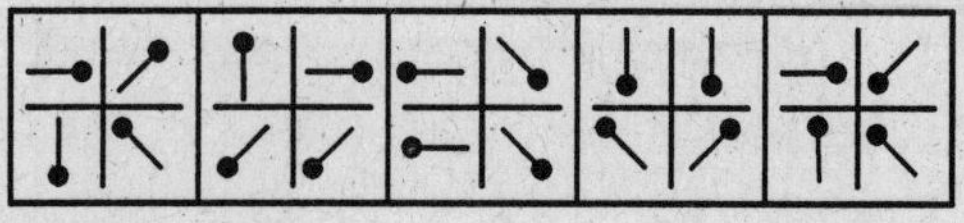

Answer Figures

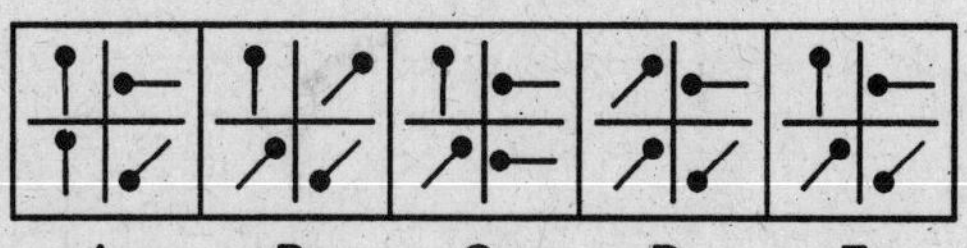

A B C D E

16. **Problem Figures**

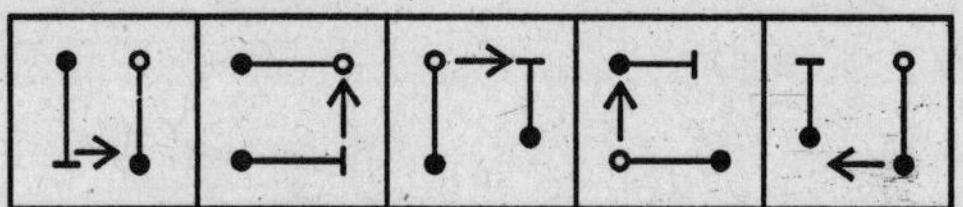

Answer Figures

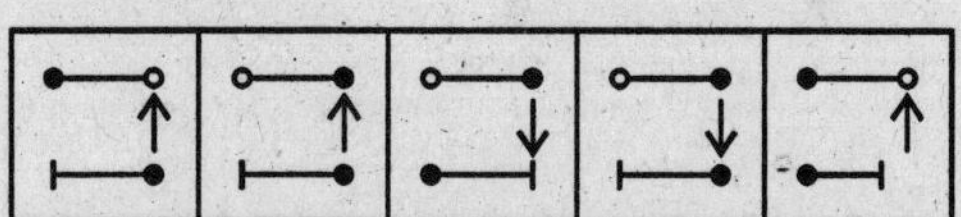

A B C D E

17. **Problem Figures**

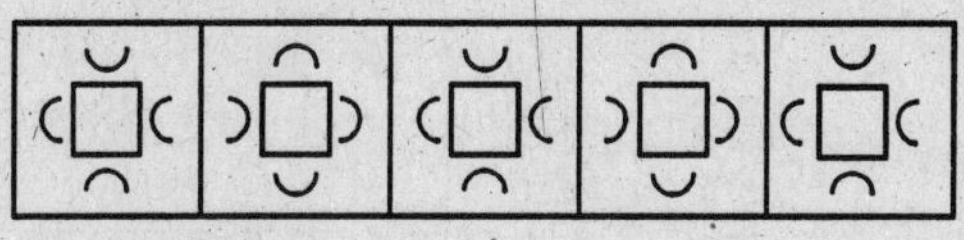

Answer Figures

A B C D E

18. **Problem Figures**

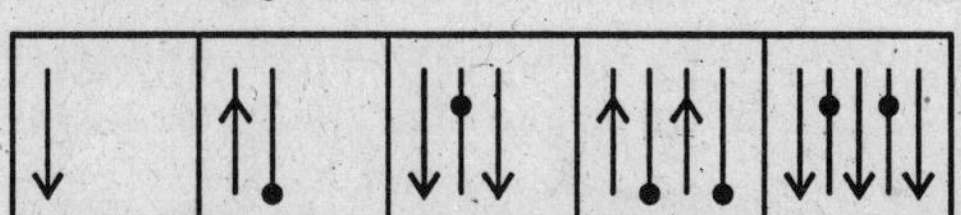

Answer Figures

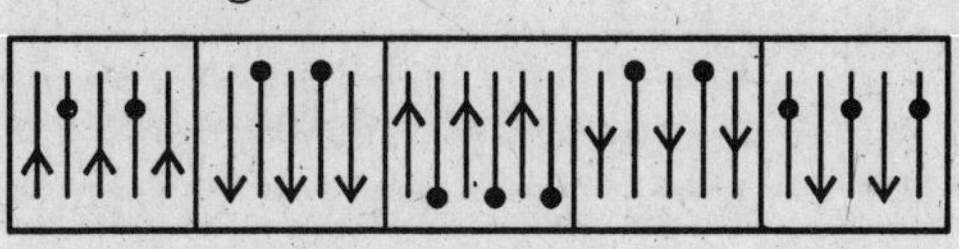

A B C D E

19. **Problem Figures**

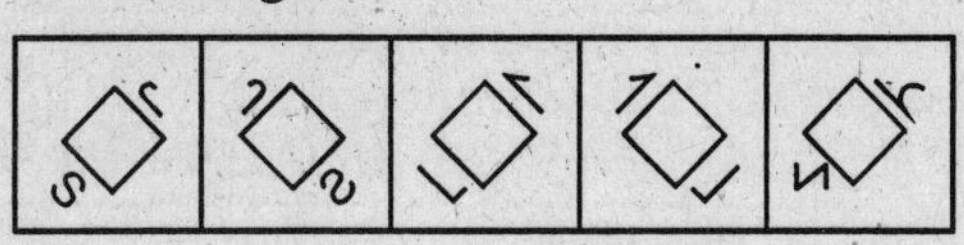

Answer Figures

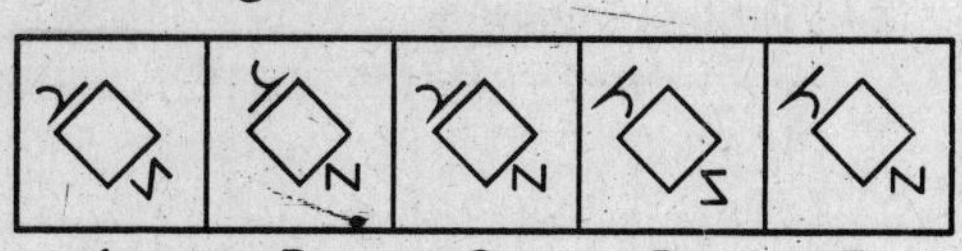

A B C D E

20. **Problem Figures**

Answer Figures

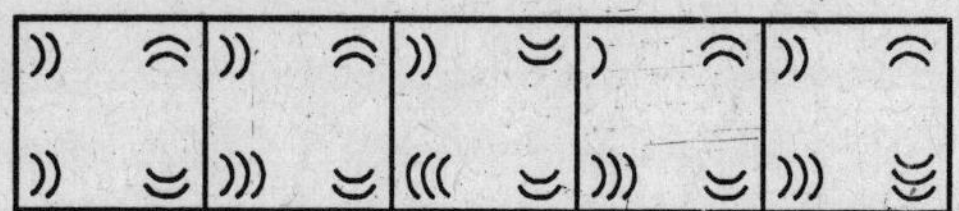

A B C D E

21. **Problem Figures**

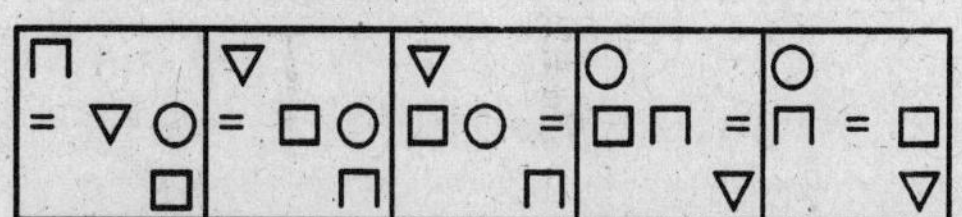

Answer Figures

A B C D E

22. **Problem Figures**

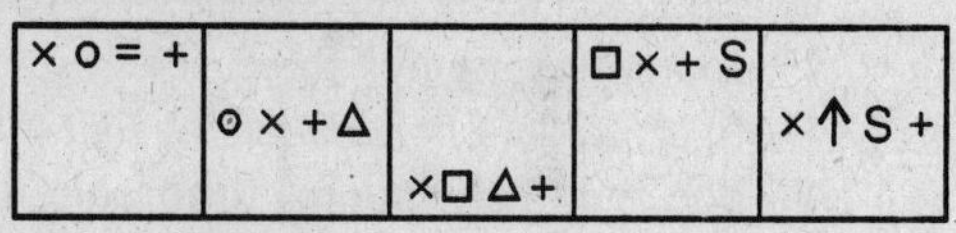

Answer Figures

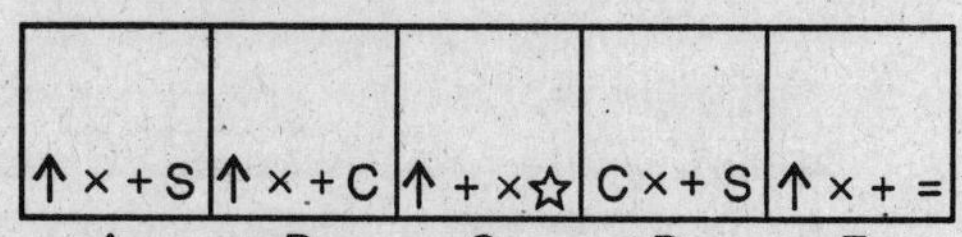

A B C D E

23. **Problem Figures**

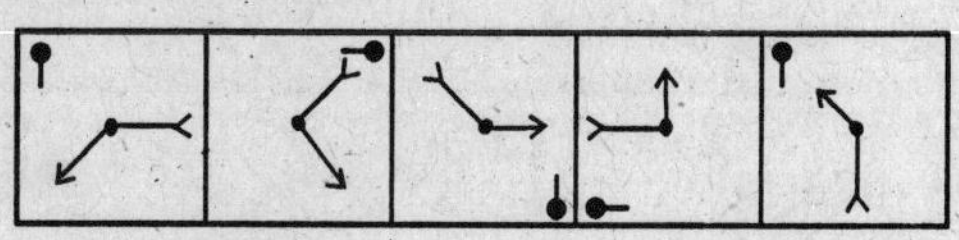

Answer Figures

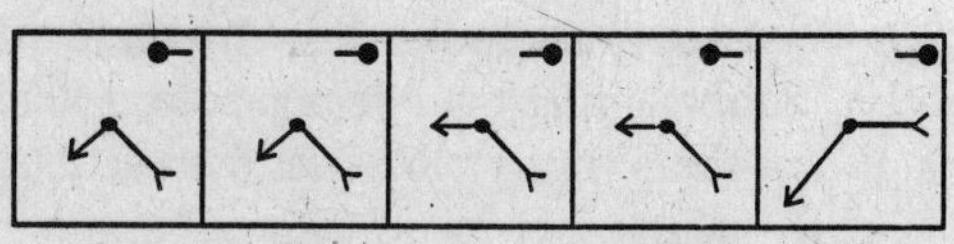

A B C D E

24. Problem Figures

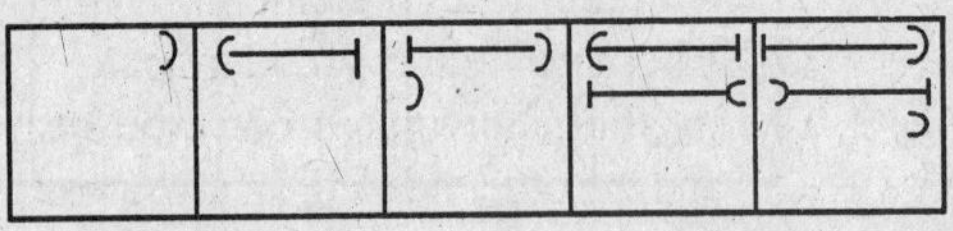

Answer Figures

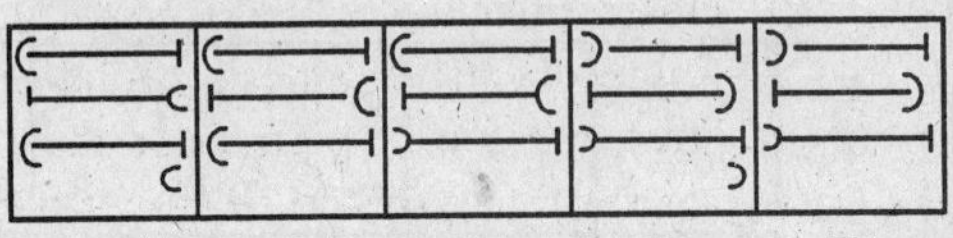

A B C D E

25. Problem Figures

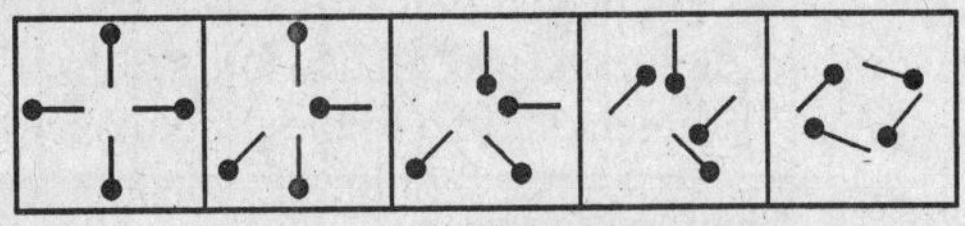

Answer Figures

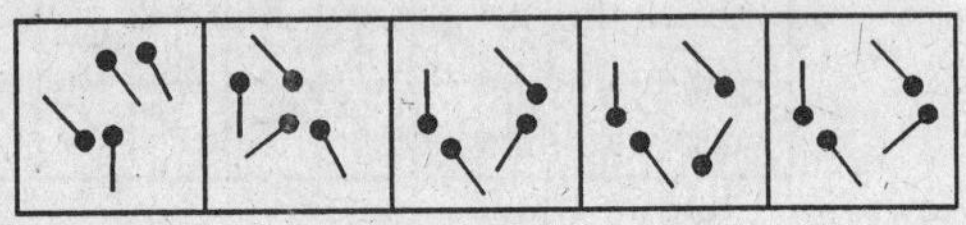

A B C D E

ANSWERS

1	2	3	4	5	6	7	8	9	10
C	D	B	A	C	E	E	D	A	B
11	**12**	**13**	**14**	**15**	**16**	**17**	**18**	**19**	**20**
E	E	B	A	E	B	E	C	C	B
21	**22**	**23**	**24**	**25**					
A	B	B	B	E					

EXPLANATORY ANSWERS

1. Observe that the series restarts from figure five. Answer figure should be identical to figure two.
2. Observe that figures one and two are identical and so are figures three and four. Answer figure should be identical to figure five.
3. The right column arcs from bottom to top, and the left column arcs from top to bottom are inverted one by one alternately in a set pattern.
4. In alternate figures the arrow is rotated 90° clockwise, one simple line segment and one line segment with busy end are added in a set pattern and the cross is moved to the diagonally opposite corner and one more sign on either side is added.
5. From figure one to figure two the elements on the top and bottom right are shifted one step anticlockwise while the places of remaining two elements are interchanged. From figure two to figure three the places of diagonally opposite elements are interchanged while the element in the centre is replaced by a new element. The above steps are repeated.
6. The parts of petal are added and removed anticlockwie in the manner plus two, minus one, plus three, minus one; and to continue the series four parts should be added.
7. Observe the series. Note that figure one corresponds with figure five in such a manner that the three dots in triangle form are inverted and moved to the diagonally opposite corner, and the arrow is moved to 90° clockwise position. Similarly, answer figure E coordinates with figure two.
8. The places of circle and square are interchanged and the places of the arc and line segment are interchanged. Then the cross is rotated 45° clockwise. The above two steps are repeated.
9. Figure two is the lateral inversion of figure one except that the places of two elements on one side are interchanged. The same applies to figures three and four. Answer figure A coordinates with figure five.

10. The four elements are oscillated from left to right in a set pattern. At each step the last two elements are placed on the top, the first element shifted to the third place (from top) and the last (bottom) element is replaced by an entirely new element.
11. Both the dot bars move like a pendulum in a set manner. From figure one to figure two the arc and line segment on the left of the vertical line are moved. From figure two to figure three the arc and line segment on the right of the vertical line are moved. From figure three to figure four both the arcs and the line segments are moved. This process is repeated.
12. At each step, beginning from the top, the first, second, third, fourth and fifth (last) elements are moved to the fifth (last), fourth, first, third and second positions respectively.
13. One by one, one of the two arcs are inverted in a set order top left, bottom right, top right and bottom left. To continue the series, the remaining arcs will be inverted in the same order.
14. From figure one to figure two one line segment on the left of the upper element is removed. From figure two to figure three one line segment on the right of the lower element is removed. From figure three to figure four one line segment on the right of the upper element is removed. From figure four to figure five one line segment on the left of the lower element is removed.
15. The dot bars on top left, top right, bottom left and bottom right are rotated 90° anticlockwise, 45° clockwise, 45° clock-wise and 90° anticlockwise respectively.
16. All the elements are moved anticlockwise and each time, the direction of one of the elements is reversed in a set order beginning with the leading element.
17. Alternate figures are identical.
18. In alternate figures one line bearing a dot and the other bearing an arrowhead are added in a set pattern.
19. Observe that figure two is the mirror image of figure one. The same is applied to figures three and four. To continue the series, the answer figure should be the mirror image of figure five.
20. The arc shapes are turned 90° anticlockwise at each step and two and one arcs are added alternately in anticlockwise manner.
21. From figure one to figure two the places of three elements placed diagonally are shifted one place upwards and the top element is placed at the bottom. From figure two to figure three the three elements on the horizontal are shifted one place to the left and the left most element is placed on the extreme right. The above steps are repeated.
22. All the elements are moved half way down two steps and then to the top. The positions of two element on the left are interchanged and the positions of two elements on the right are interchanged, while doing so, first the fourth element is replaced by a new element and then the second. The process is repeated.
23. In alternate figures the design in the centre is rotated by 135° anticlockwise. The element in the corner is moved clockwise and turned 90° clockwise at each step.
24. In alternate figures one 'T' bar and an arc are added in a set pattern.
25. Clockwise, from one figure to next, the direction of one element is changed and one element is turned 45° anticlockwise.

Chapter 18

CLASSIFICATION

Classification means arranging the given content in groups or classes having qualities of same kind. In classification type questions, the figures or items are sorted out in groups on the basis of their similarities in qualities in shapes, size, pattern, structure, genus, order, species, grade, style, constituents and other specifications, and thus the answer is found out.

Example-1

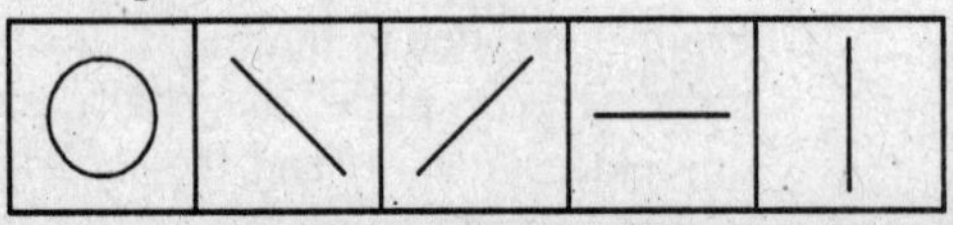

A B C D E

Answer A : A is a circle, whereas B, C, D and E are straight lines pointing to different directions. Note that the common characteristic in each of the four figures B, C, D and E is that they are straight lines. Thus, they belong to a class. As against these figures, A is a circle and does not belong to that class.

Therefore, the figure that does not belong to the class is A.

Example-2

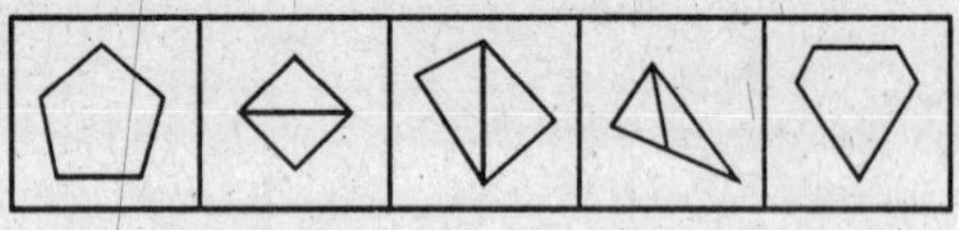

A B C D E

Answer D : Figures A, B, C and E are made of 5 straight lines, while D has only four straight lines. Thus A, B, C and E have a common characteristic (they have 5 straight lines each), but D does not have this characteristic. Therefore, D is different from the other four figures.

EXERCISE

1. 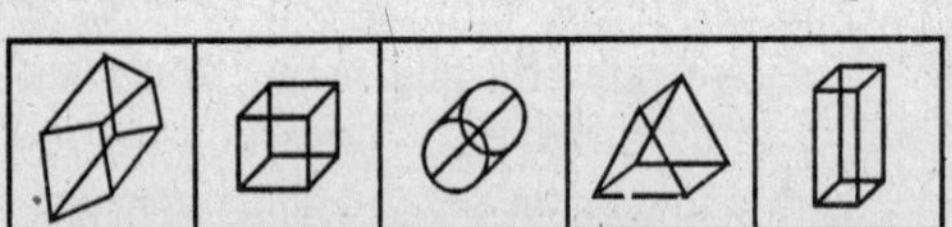

A B C D E

2. 

A B C D E

3. 

A B C D E

4. 

A B C D E

5. 

A B C D E

6. 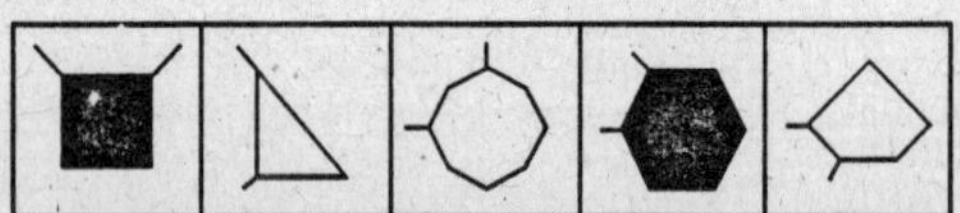

A B C D E

7. 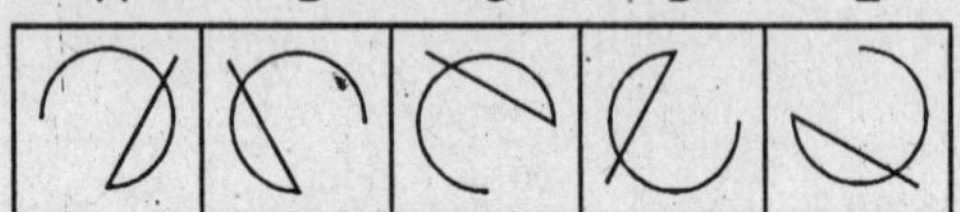

A B C D E

8. 

A B C D E

9. 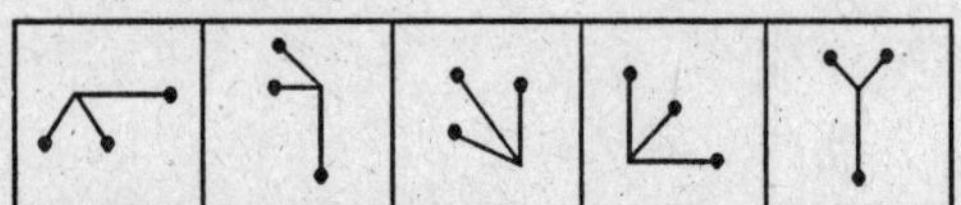

A B C D E

10. 

A B C D E

11. 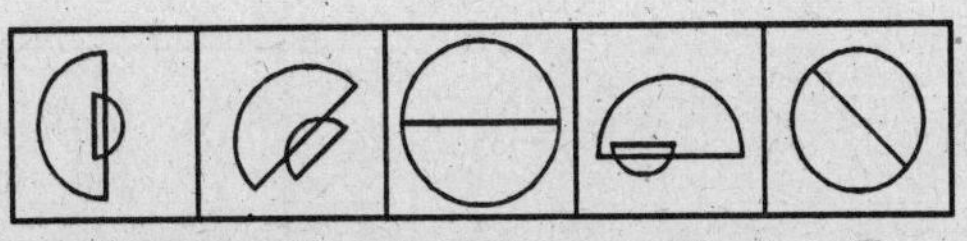

A B C D E

12. 

A B C D E

13. 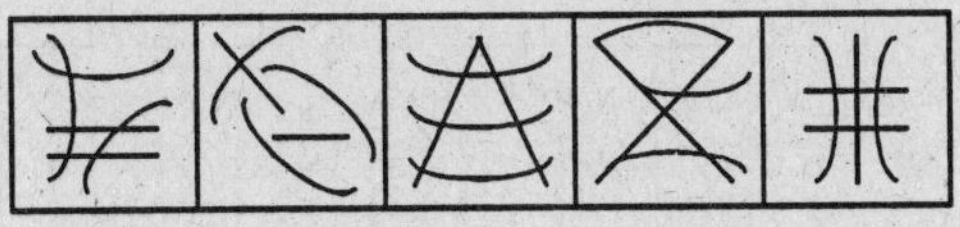

A B C D E

14. 

A B C D E

15. 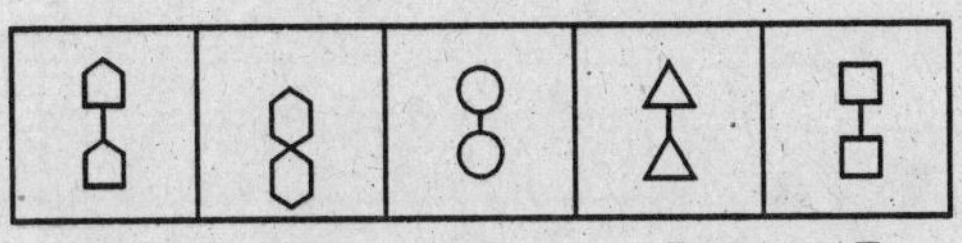

A B C D E

16. 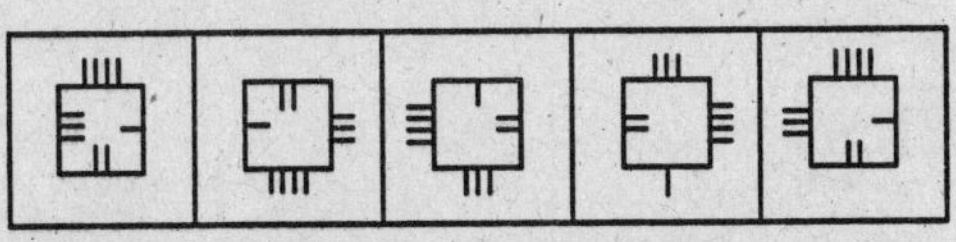

A B C D E

17. 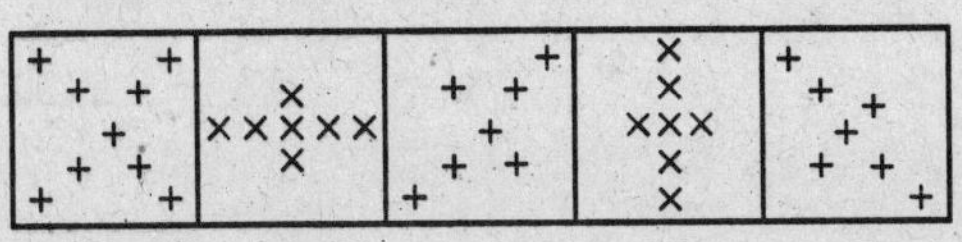

A B C D E

18. 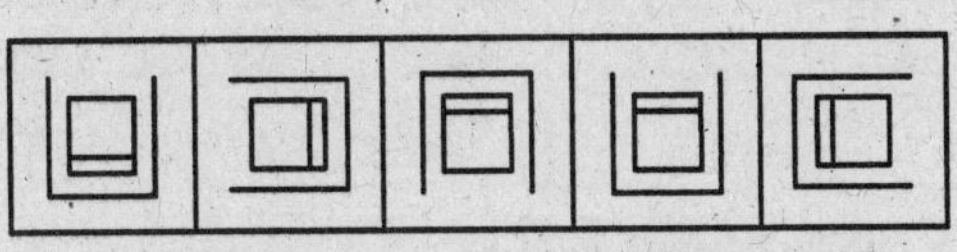

A B C D E

19. 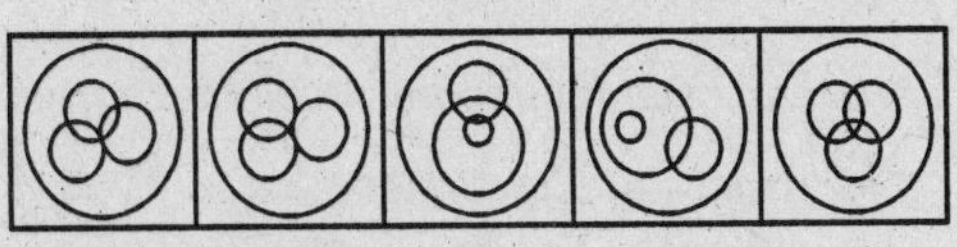

A B C D E

20. 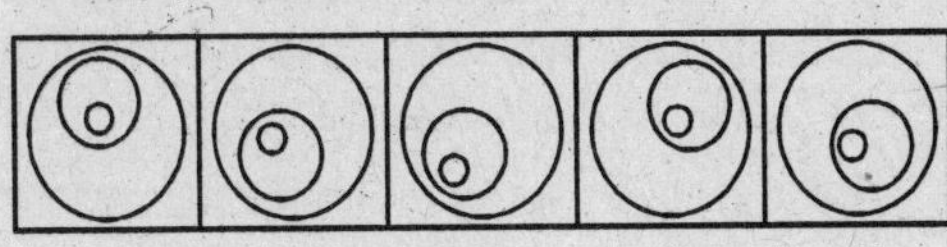

A B C D E

21. 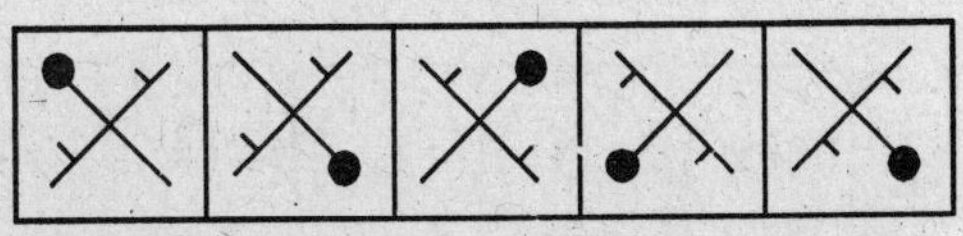

A B C D E

22. 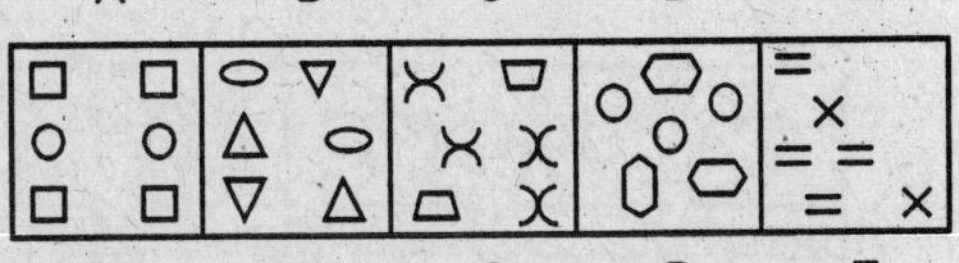

A B C D E

23. 

A B C D E

24. 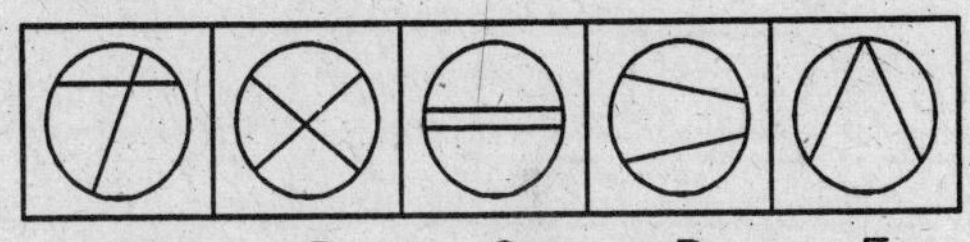

A B C D E

25. 

A B C D E

26. 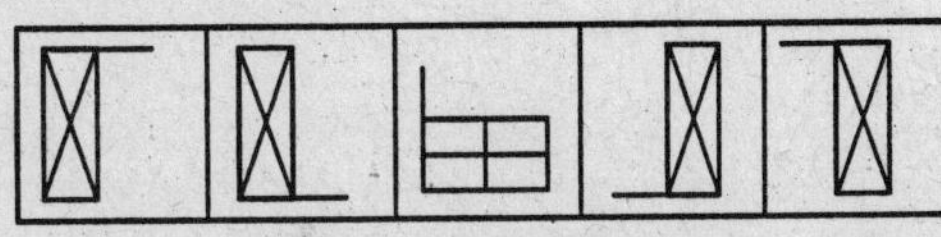

A B C D E

27. 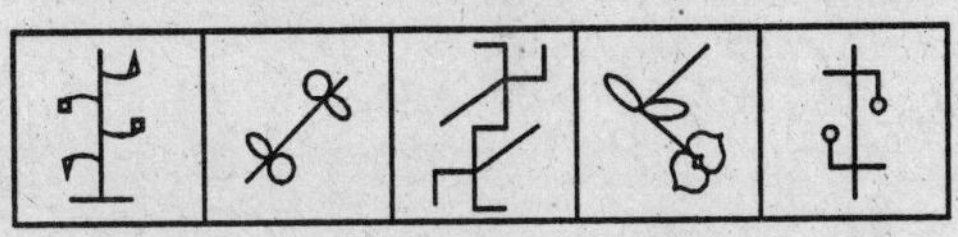

A B C D E

28. 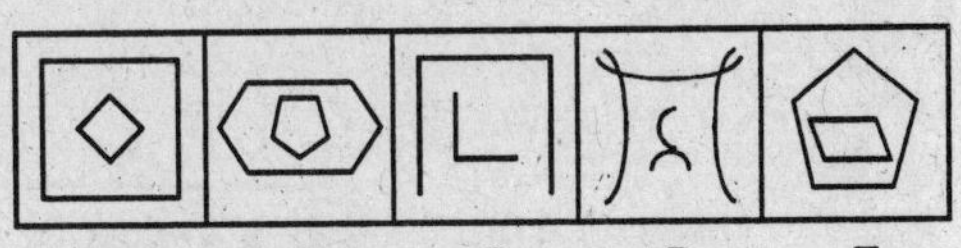

A B C D E

29. 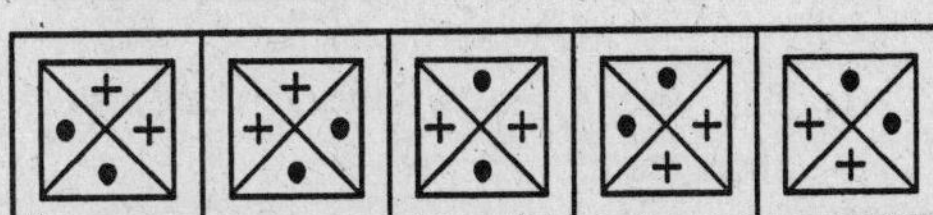

A B C D E

30. 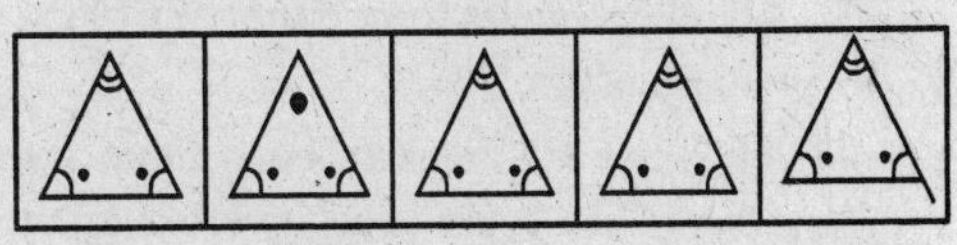

A B C D E

31. 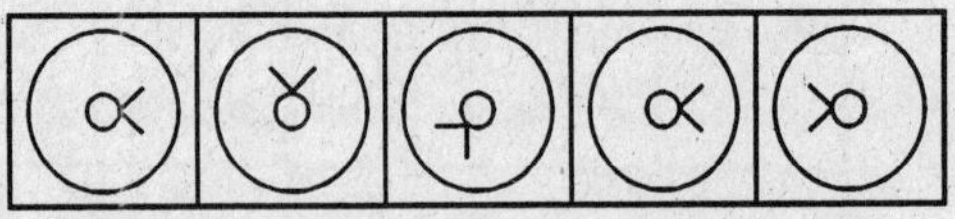

A B C D E

32. 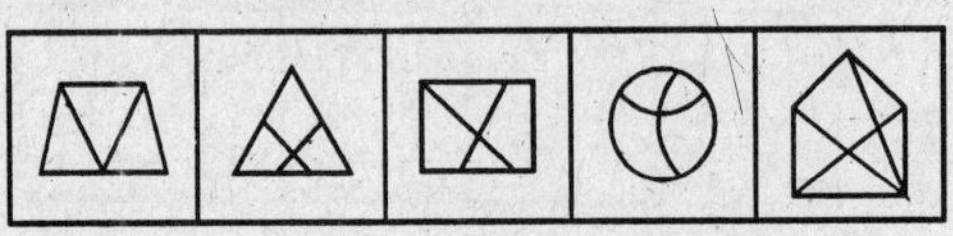

A B C D E

33. 

A B C D E

34. 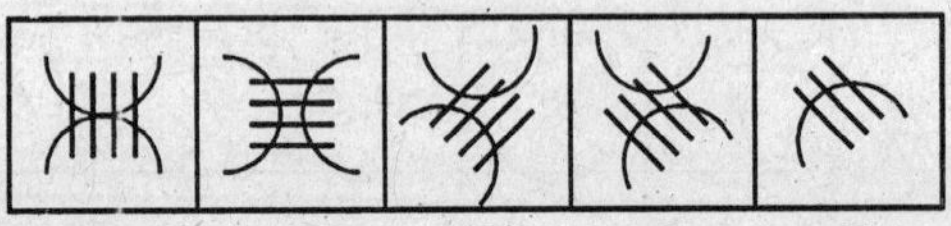

A B C D E

35. 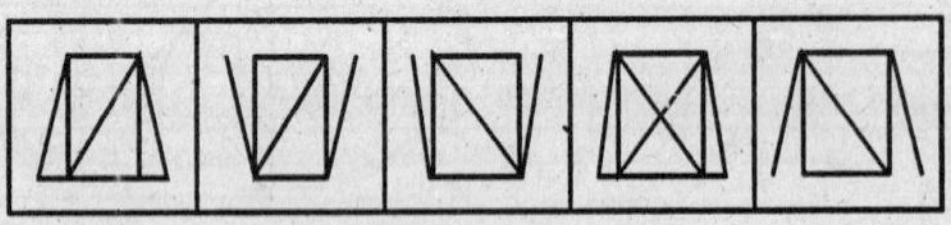

A B C D E

36. 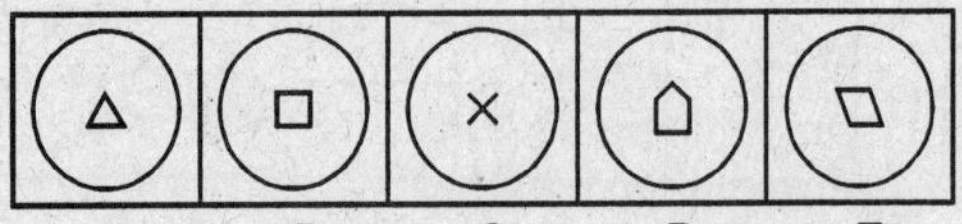

A B C D E

37. 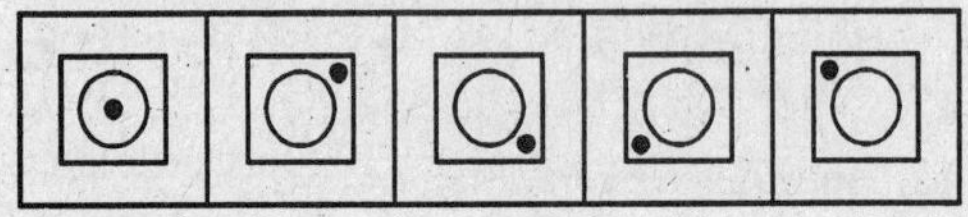

A B C D E

38. 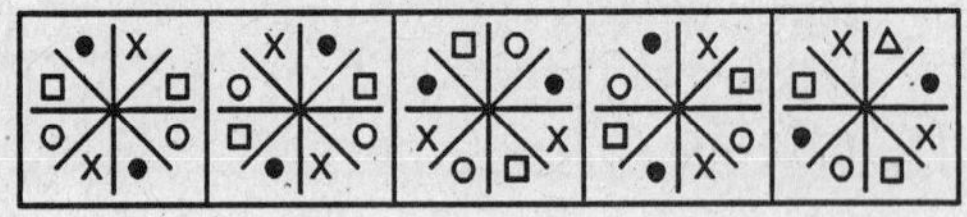

A B C D E

39. 

A B C D E

40. 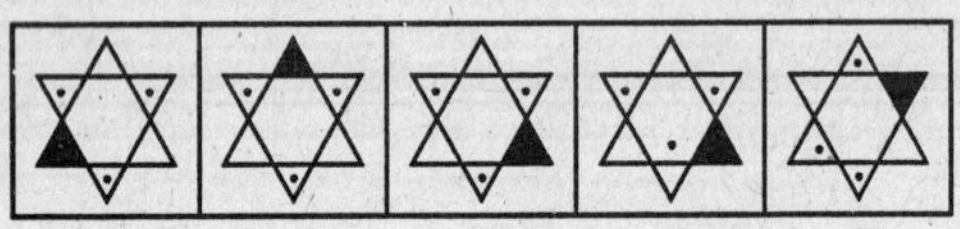

A B C D E

ANSWERS

1	2	3	4	5	6	7	8	9	10
D	E	E	C	B	C	B	C	D	D
11	**12**	**13**	**14**	**15**	**16**	**17**	**18**	**19**	**20**
D	A	E	B	B	A	A	D	E	C
21	**22**	**23**	**24**	**25**	**26**	**27**	**28**	**29**	**30**
B	D	C	C	D	C	D	A	C	B
31	**32**	**33**	**34**	**35**	**36**	**37**	**38**	**39**	**40**
E	D	B	E	D	C	A	E	A	D

EXPLANATORY ANSWERS

1. All other figures have at least two parallel surfaces.
2. Only this figure has been intersected twice.
3. All other figures have either one black or one white design.
4. All other figures can be rotated into each other. This figure is an inverted image of all other figures.
5. All other figures are made of six straight lines.
6. In all other figures the lines are extended from adjacent corners.
7. All other figures can be rotated into each other. In this figure the shape is inverted.
8. Only this figure does not include an acute angle.

9. Only in this figure the dots are in a straight line.
10. Only this figure does not contain a diamond shape in the middle.
11. All other figures contain two semi-circles. In this figure there is only one semi-circle, the other one is less than a semi-circle.
12. In other figures the small square is either in the middle or in the mid of the side of the square containing it. In this figure the small square is in the corner.
13. In all other figures there are two straight lines and three curved lines. In this figure it is opposite.
14. All other figures can be rotated into each other. In this figure the small lines are towards the smaller part of the reetangle.
15. In all other figures the two identical shapes are joined by a line segment.
16. In all other figures the three and four small lines protrude outside. In this figure three lines are inside the square.
17. Only this figure has nine crosses
18. All other figures can be rotated into each other. Only in this figure the smaller part of the contained square is towards the open side of the larger square.
19. Only in this figure all the circles are overlapping each other in equal proportions.
20. In all other figures the innermost cirle is in the centre.
21. All other figures can be rotated into each other. Only in this figure the black circle is not on the side same as of the two small line segments.
22. Only in this figure the two different elements are equal in number.
23. In all other figures the inner figure is not touching the outer figure.
24. Only in this figure the two lines inside the circle are parallel to each other.
25. All other figures are made of odd number of straight lines.
26. In all other figures the rectangle is divided into four parts by two diagonals.
27. In all other figures identical elements are diagonally placed on either side of the middle line.
28. In all other figures the number of lines making the larger or outer form is one more than the number of lines making the smaller or inner form.
29. In all other figures the identical elements are in adjacent sections. In this figure they are in opposite sections.
30. Only in this figure there is a dot, instead of lines, in the apex of the triangle.
31. In all other figures the 'V' shape attached to the inner circle is not touching the outer circle.
32. All other figures are made of straight lines.
33. In all other figures the number of lines making the inner figure is one less than the number of lines making the outer figure.
34. In all other figures the number of curved lines is half the number of straight lines.
35. All other figures are made of seven straight lines.
36. In all other figures the circle contains a closed figure in the centre.
37. In all other figures the dot is outside the circle.
38. Only in this figure there is a triangle instead of circle.
39. In all other figures the single arrow is pointing to the opposite direction of the two arrows.
40. Only in this figures one dot is not inside the triangle.

Chapter 19

THE WRONG FIGURE OUT

This type of questions begin with unnumbered figure, followed by five figures, which are numbered from A to E. Then again, unnumbered figure follows the extreme right. One and only one figure out of the figures given does not fit in the series. Therefore, the wrong figure has to be identified.

Example-1

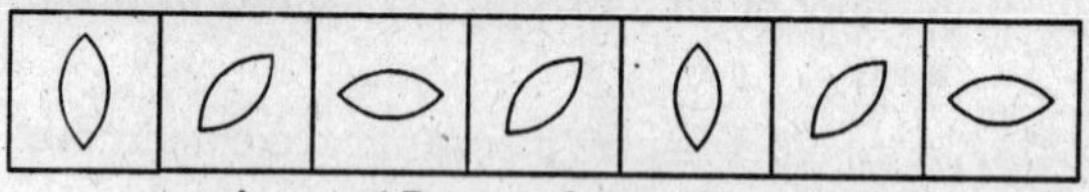

A B C D E

Answer C : Observe the pattern of the petal in each box. At each step it is moved 45° clockwise. In figure marked 'C' the petal is moved 45° anticlockwise and this movement does not fit into the order of the given series.

Example-2

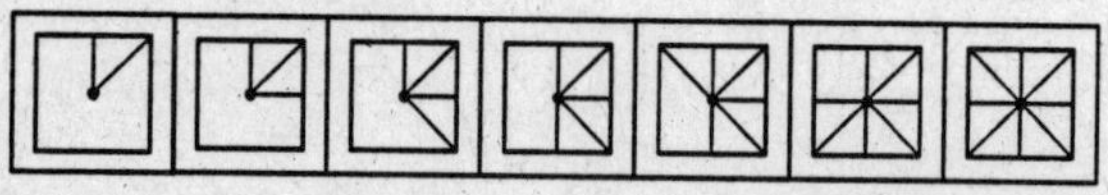

A B C D E

Answer D : Note that at each step one line segment is drawn from the centre of the square clockwise in a set pattern. In figure marked 'D' the diagonal line segment should have been touching the bottom left corner instead of the top left corner to fit into the series of the given figures.

EXERCISE

1.

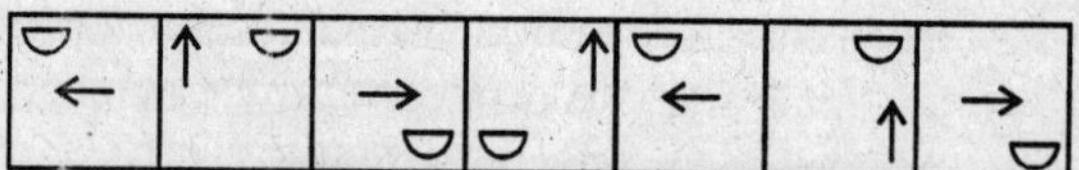

A B C D E

2.

A B C D E

3.

A B C D E

4.

A B C D E

5.

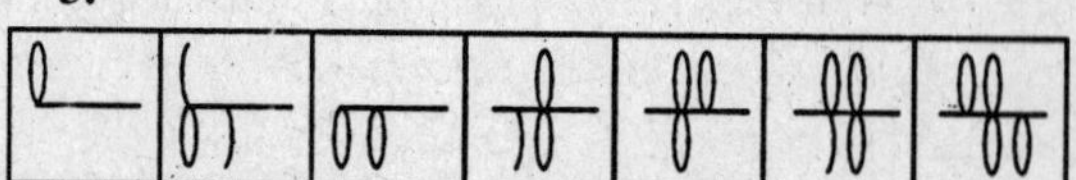

A B C D E

6.

A B C D E

7.

A B C D E

8.

A B C D E

9.

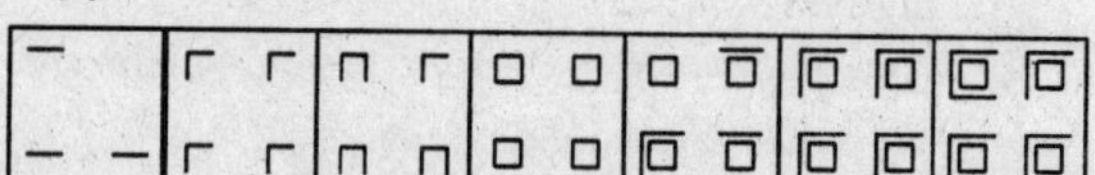

A B C D E

10.

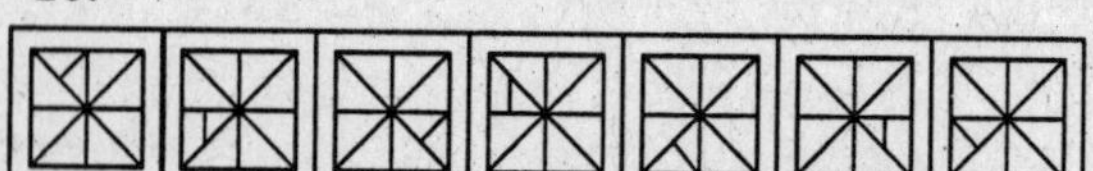

A B C D E

11.

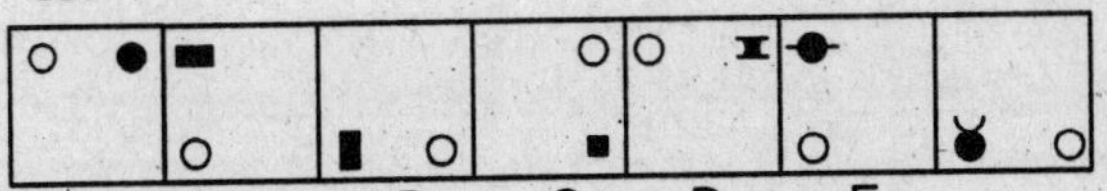

A B C D E

12.

A B C D E

13.

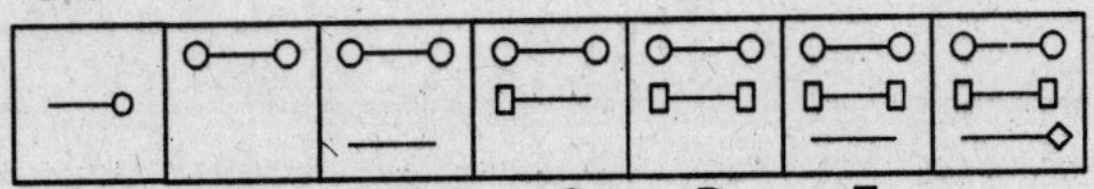

A B C D E

14.

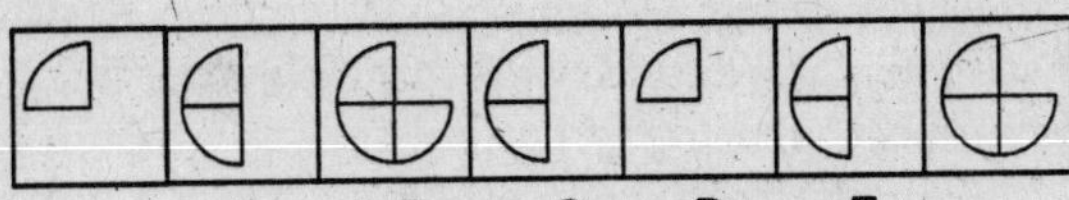

A B C D E

ANSWERS

1	2	3	4	5	6	7	8	9	10
D	C	C	D	A	A	D	B	C	E
11	12	13	14						
D	E	B	C						

EXPLANATORY ANSWERS

1. The semicircle is moved one step clockwise, and the arrow is moved 90° clockwise, placed in the centre and clockwise corners alternately.
2. The dot is moved 1, 2, 3, 4, 5, 6 steps in the series. In figure 'C' the dot should have been on the vertical line.
3. One and two small lines are added to the figure alternately to complete the human sketch. In option 'D' two lines are added instead of one.
4. First two lines are removed and then two lines are added. The process is repeated. In figure 'A' only one line is removed.
5. Each time half a petal is added to the figure irrespective of the side. In figure 'A' two half petals are added.
6. First a new figure is placed inside the large figure and in the next figure this new figure is enlarged. The process is repeated. In option 'D' the hexagon is tilted, which is wrong.
7. One dot and one circle are increased in alternate figures. Figure 'B' should have two circles and two dots.
8. The shade is moved 3 steps and 4 steps anticlockwise in alternate figures. After four steps one section clockwise is also shaded. The process is continued. In figure 'E' wrong sections are shaded.
9. Five and three lines are added in alternate figures to complete the squares. In figure 'D' four lines are added instead of three.
10. The slanting bar is moved three, two and one steps clockwise in alternate figures and the vertical bar is moved one and two steps clockwise in alternate figures. In figure E it is moved four steps clockwise instead of two.
11. The circle is moved one step anticlockwise and the other unit which is made new each time is moved behind the circle. In figure 'B' it is not changed.
12. The figure is rotated 45° and 90° clockwise in alternate figures and the arrows turned outward and inward alternately. In figure 'A' the rotation is done 90° clockwise instead of 45°.
13. The new element is added first on the right and then on the left of the line segment. In option 'C' it is added on the left side of the line segment.
14. One quarter section of the circle is added at each step and the series is repeated from figure D. In option 'C' one section of the circle is missing.

Chapter 20

ANALOGY

In this type of problems, some relationship is to be established among two figures and on the basis of this relationship, the answer is to be found out from the Answer Figures.

Example-1 : Problem Figures

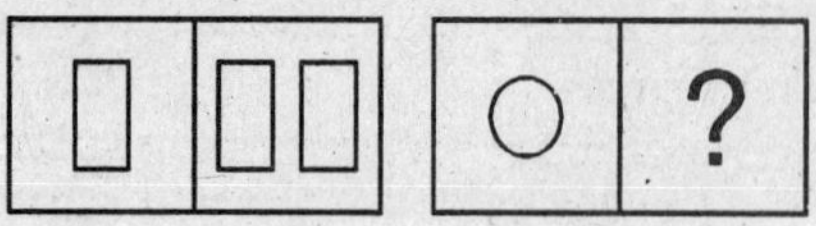

Answer Figures

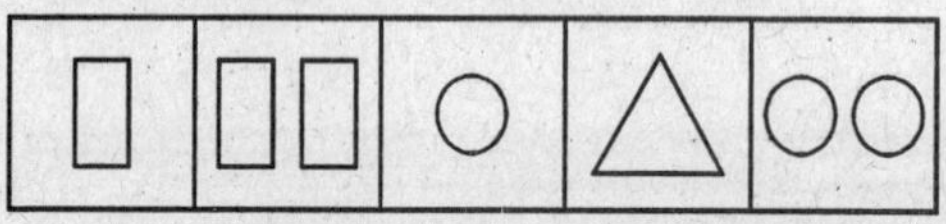

A B C D E

Answer E : Observe that the Problem Figures are in two parts. In the first part there are two figures, while in the second part there is one figure followed by a question mark (?). The figures in the first part show a particular relationship and the figures in the second part seek a solution on the basis of this relationship provided in the first part.

The two figures in the first part of the Problem Figures have one and two rectangles respectively. The, first figure has one rectangle whereas the second figure has two rectangles. It means that the relationship between them is—the second figure has double the number of rectangles the first figure has.

The relationship between the two figures in the second part of the Problem Figures must be similar to one that exists between the two figures of the first part of the Problem Figures. i.e. on the same analogy, when the first figure of the second part of Problem Figure has a circle, the second Part must have double the number of circles ie 2 circles.

Example-2 : Problem Figures

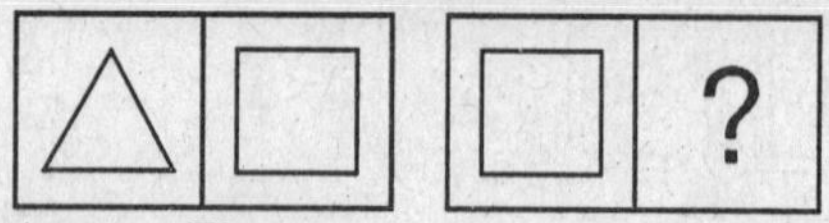

Answer Figures

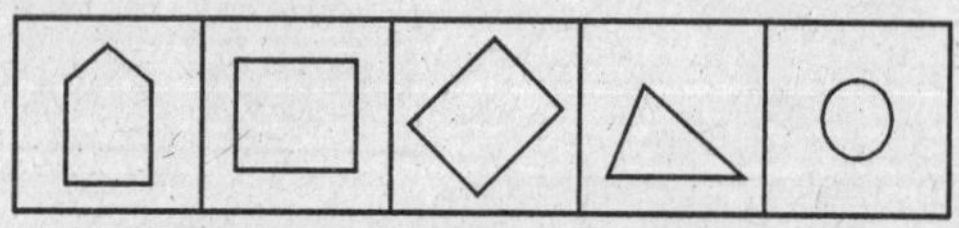

A B C D E

Answer A : Study the two figures in the first part of the Problem Figures. They are a triangle and a square. The first figure (a triangle) has three angles and three sides, while the second figure (a square) has four angles and four sides. The relationship between them is—the second figure has one angle and one side more than what the first figure has.

On this analogy the figure to suit in the space marked by ? should be one with 5 angles and 5 sides (one angle and one side more than what the first figure of the second part of the Problem Figures has).

EXERCISE

1. Problem Figures

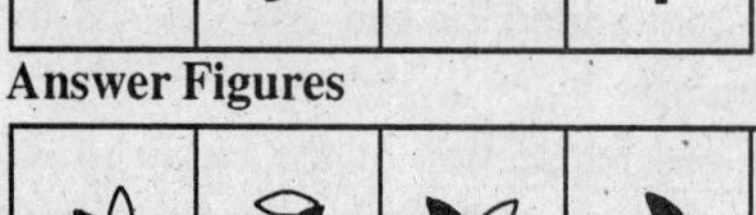

Answer Figures

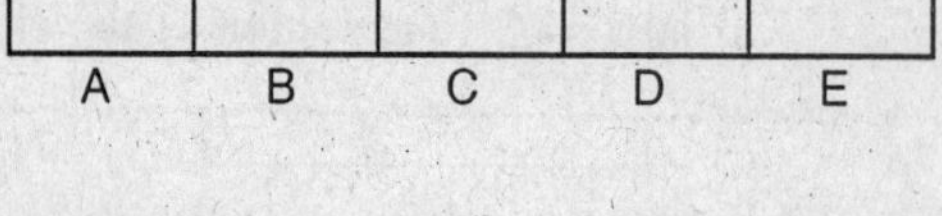

A B C D E

2. Problem Figures

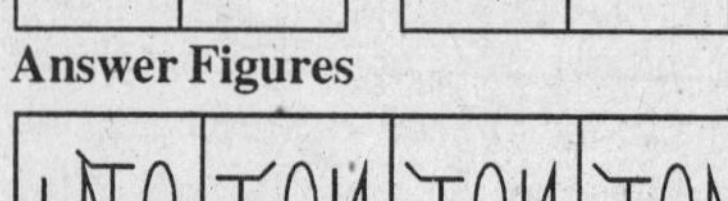

Answer Figures

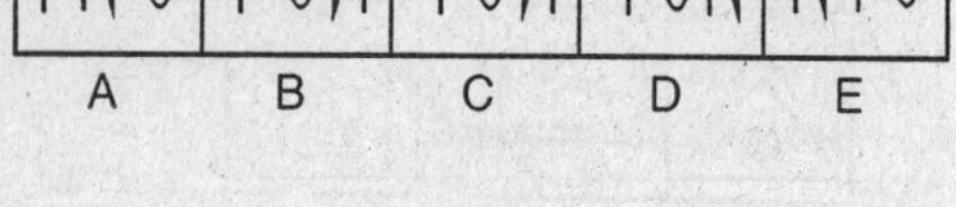

A B C D E

3. Problem Figures

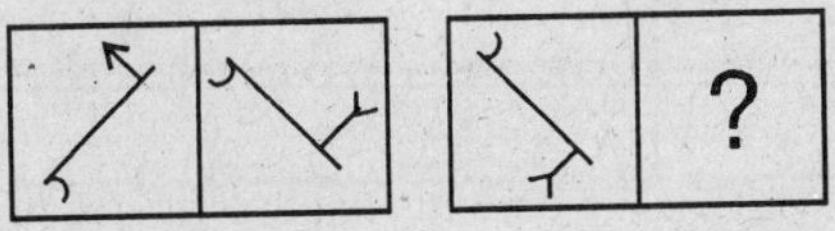

Answer Figures

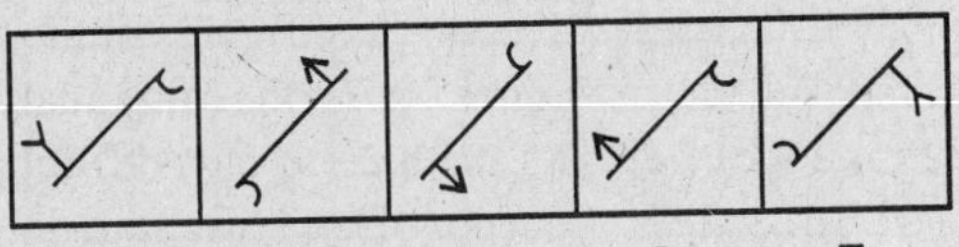

A B C D E

4. Problem Figures

Answer Figures

A B C D E

5. Problem Figures

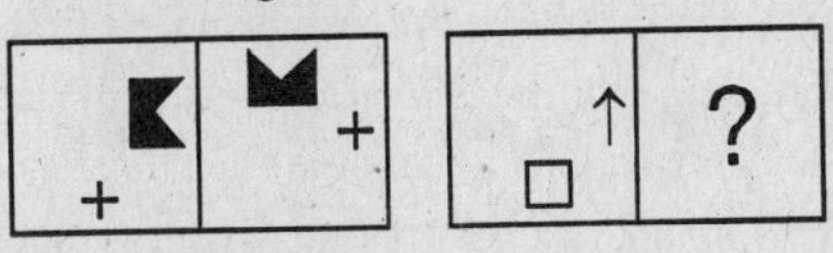

Answer Figures

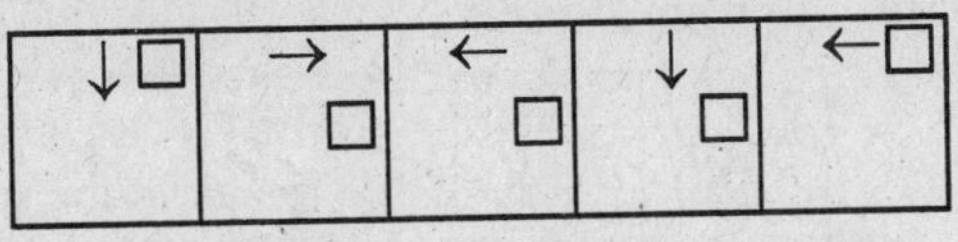

A B C D E

6. Problem Figures

Answer Figures

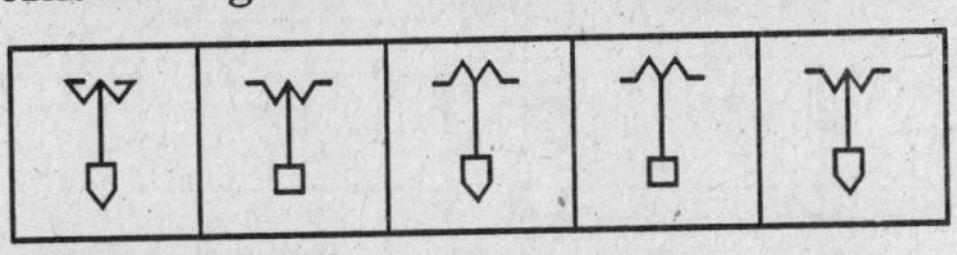

A B C D E

7. Problem Figures

Answer Figures

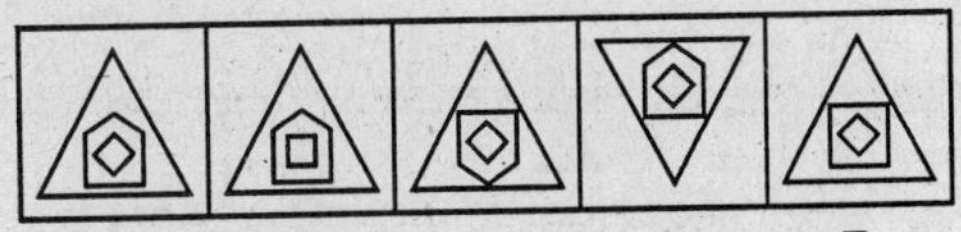

A B C D E

8. Problem Figures

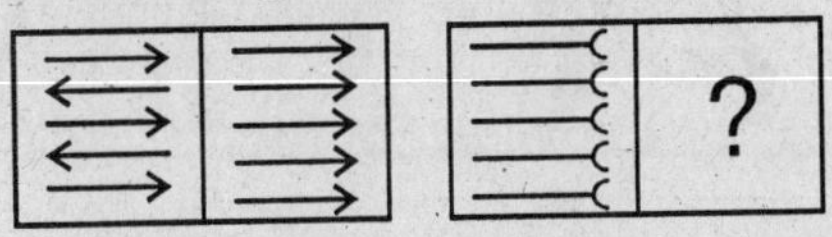

Answer Figures

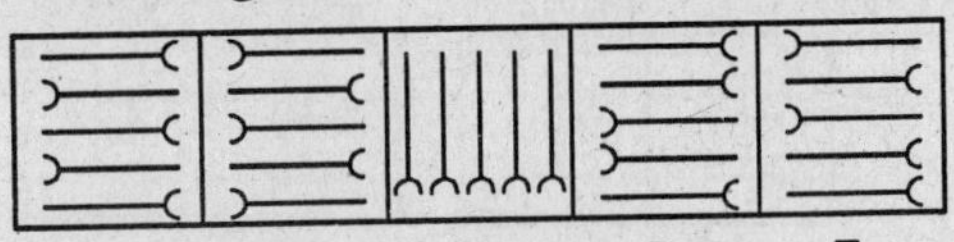

A B C D E

9. Problem Figures

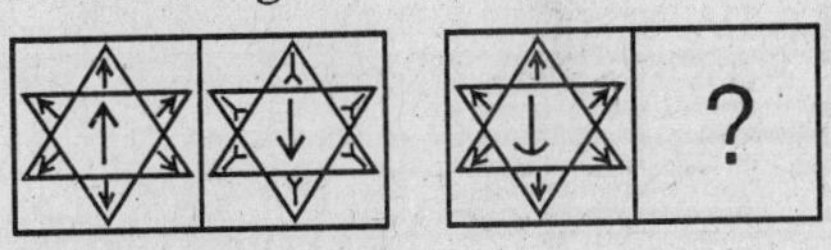

Answer Figures

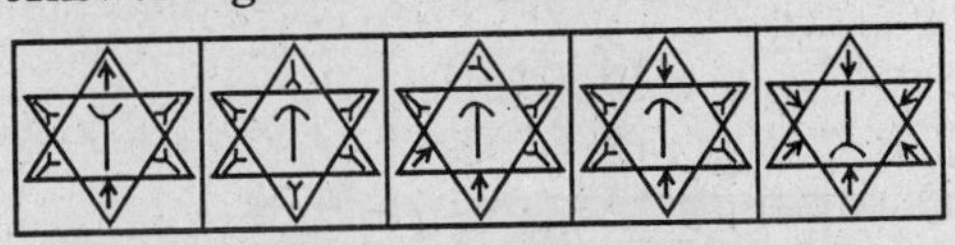

A B C D E

10. Problem Figures

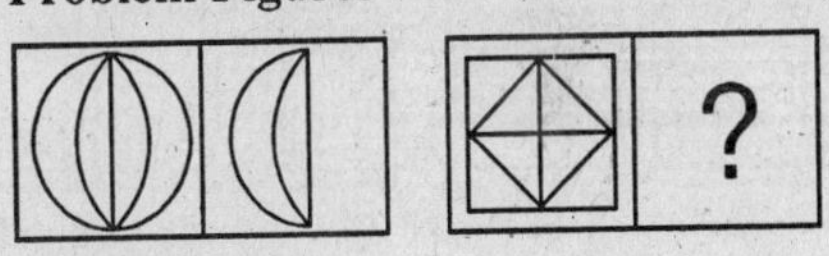

Answer Figures

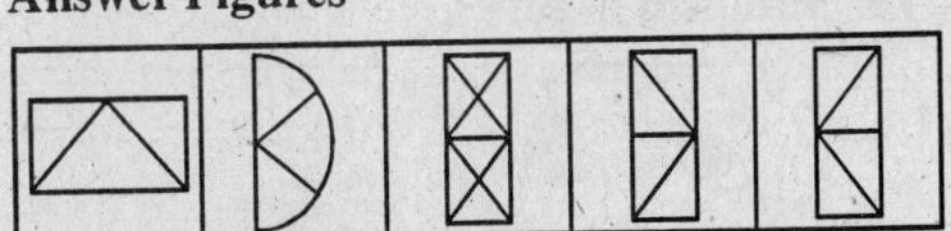

A B C D E

11. Problem Figures

Answer Figures

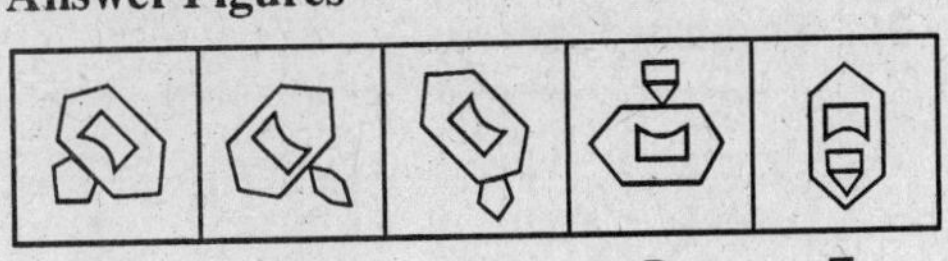

A B C D E

12. Problem Figures

Answer Figures

A B C D E

13. Problem Figures

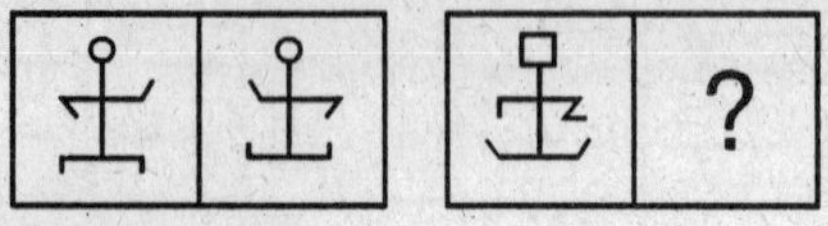

Answer Figures

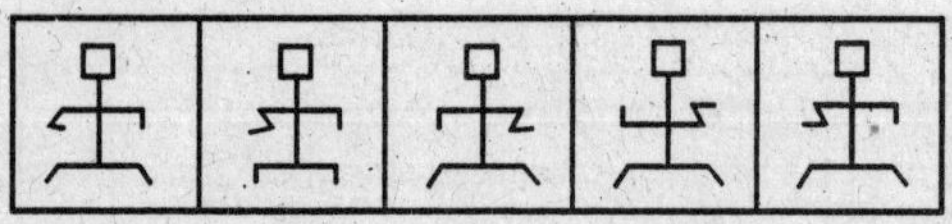

A B C D E

14. Problem Figures

Answer Figures

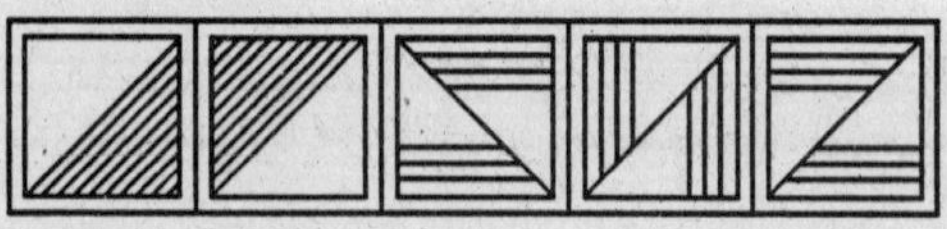

A B C D E

15. Problem Figures

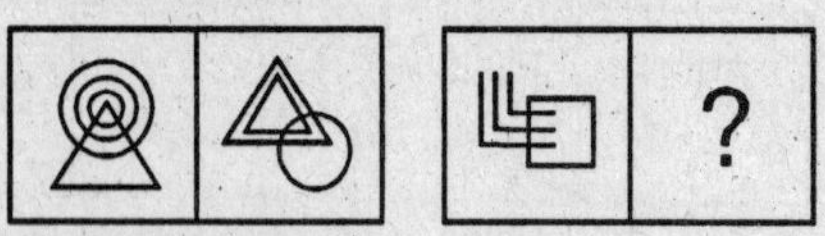

Answer Figures

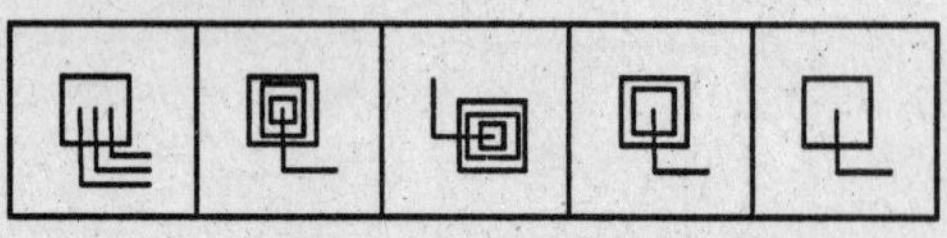

A B C D E

16. Problem Figures

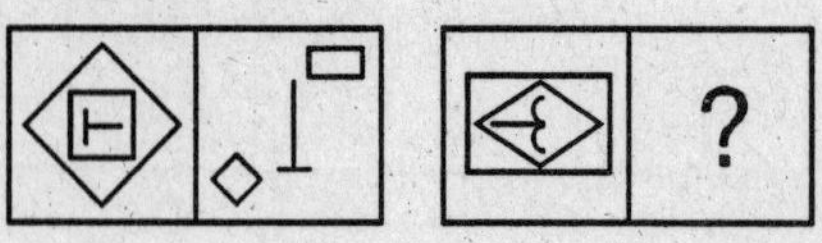

Answer Figures

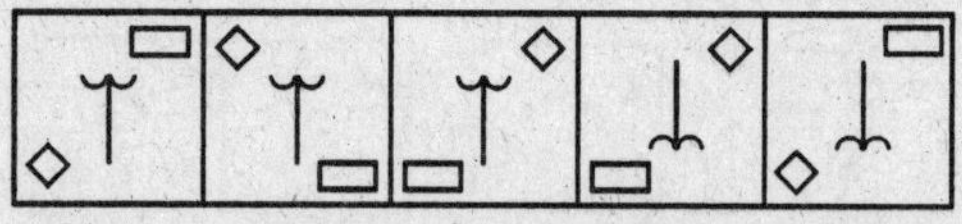

A B C D E

17. Problem Figures

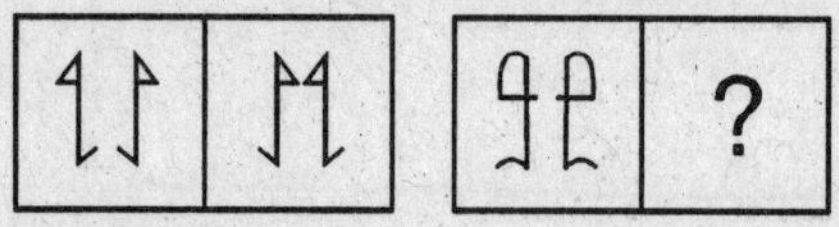

Answer Figures

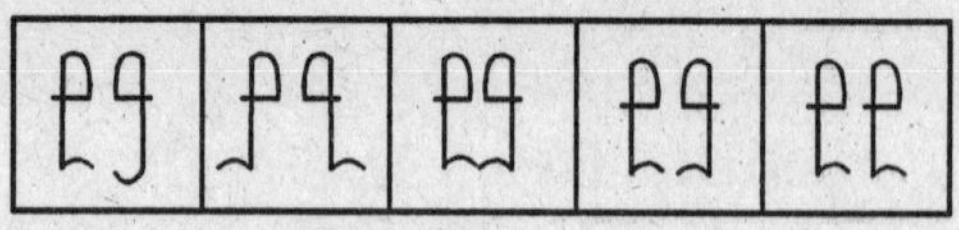

A B C D E

18. Problem Figures

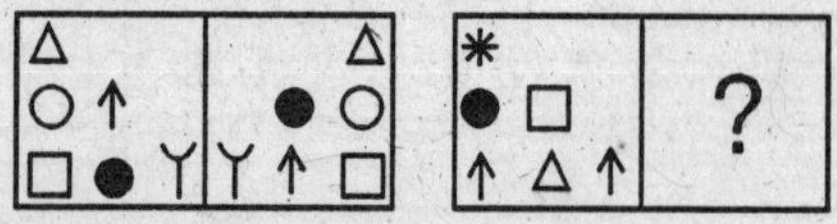

Answer Figures

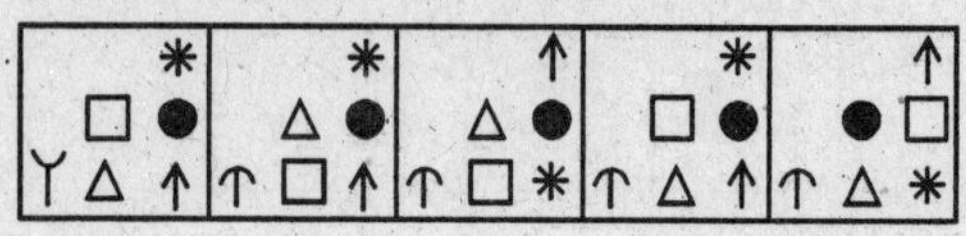

A B C D E

19. Problem Figures

Answer Figures

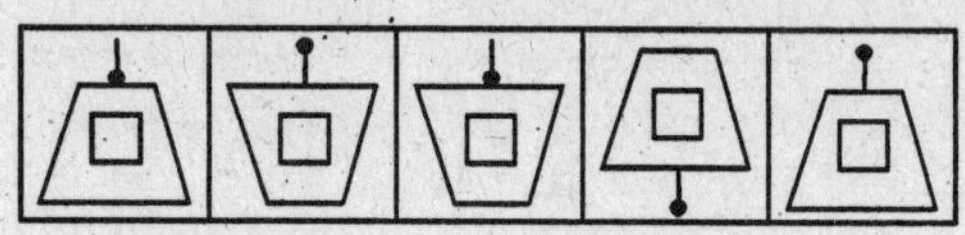

A B C D E

20. Problem Figures

Answer Figures

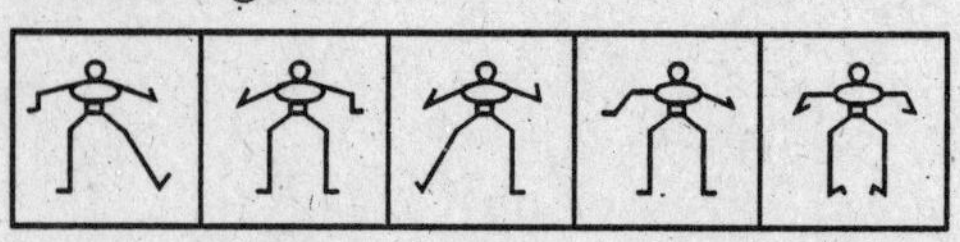

A B C D E

ANSWERS

1	2	3	4	5	6	7	8	9	10
A	C	D	D	C	E	A	A	B	E
11	12	13	14	15	16	17	18	19	20
C	B	D	D	D	C	D	B	E	B

EXPLANATORY ANSWERS

1. The petals in first figure are turned 135° anticlockwise to get the second figure.
2. The element on the extreme right is moved to the extreme left and the other two elements shifted to the right. The T with a bent is turned by 180° and N/N shape is laterally inverted.
3. The design is turned 90° clockwise and the lines making the arrowhead are turned in opposite direction.
4. The first number in each figure is the alphanumeric position (A = 1).
5. The element at the base is moved one step anticlockwise. The other element is turned 90° anticlockwise and moved one step anticlockwise.
6. The places of the elements on the top and at the bottom of the design are interchanged and then one of the elements is made new.
7. The innermost design in the first figure is enlarged and made the outermost design in the second figure. The new innermost design is turned by 90°.
8. Only the direction of the second element from the top and second element from the bottom is changed.
9. The element in the middle of the star is turned upside down. The elements inside the triangles of the star are turned upside down and the lines making the arrowhead are turned in opposite direction.
10. The right half portion of the first figure is removed to get the second figure.
11. The design in the bottom right is enlarged and turned 135° anticlockwise. The design in the middle is turned 135° anticlockwise and placed inside the enlarged design. The design in the top left is turned 135° anticlockwise and placed at the bottom.
12. The design is turned by 180° and then the right half of the top part and left-half of the bottom part are shaded.
13. The hands and legs of the figure are turned to the opposite side.
14. The dotted lines in first figure are completed in the second figure.
15. The design on the top is made single-lined the design at the bottom is double-lined and then the places of both the designs are interchanged.
16. The innermost design is turned 90° anti-clockwise, enlarged the placed in the centre, the outermost design is reduced and placed in the bottom left corner, and the third design is reduced and placed in the top right corner.
17. Both the elements in first figure are laterally inverted to get the second figure.
18. The three elements on the left are moved to the right side, the single element on the right is moved to the left side and the places of two elements in the middle are interchanged.
19. The two enclosed designs are laterally inverted. The design on the top is enlarged and the design at the bottom is placed above it. The large and outer design is reduced and placed inside the lower figure.
20. From first figure to the second figure the changes in the symmetrical human sketch are same on either side.

Chapter 21

IMAGES AND REFLECTIONS

Directions (Qs. 1 to 10): *In each question given below which one would be the mirror image of the given figure when the mirror is placed along the line shown in each figure.*

1. Problem Figure

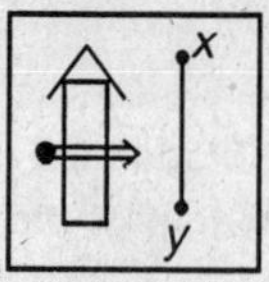

Answer Figures

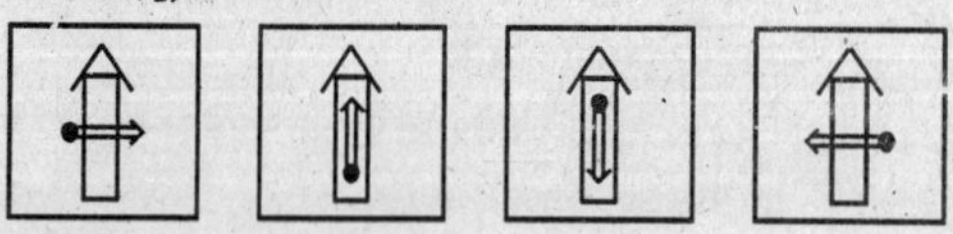

(*a*) (*b*) (*c*) (*d*)

2. Problem Figure

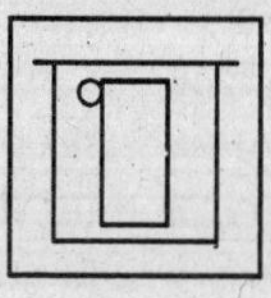

Answer Figures

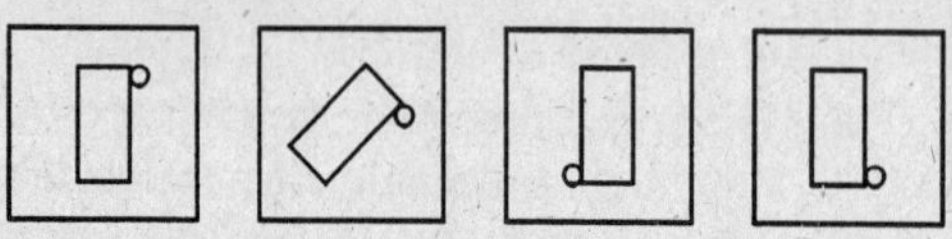

(*a*) (*b*) (*c*) (*d*)

3. Problem Figure

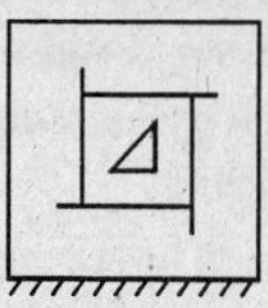

Answer Figures

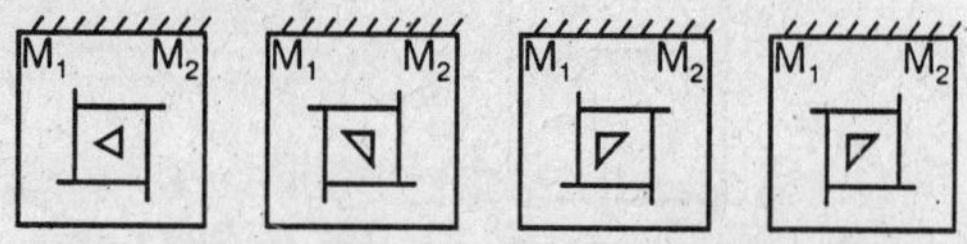

(*a*) (*b*) (*c*) (*d*)

4. Problem Figure

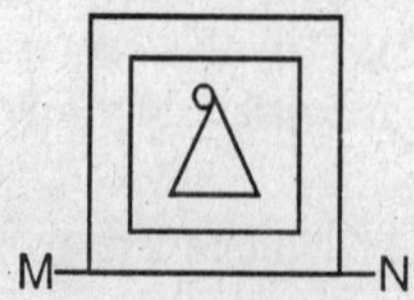

Answer Figures

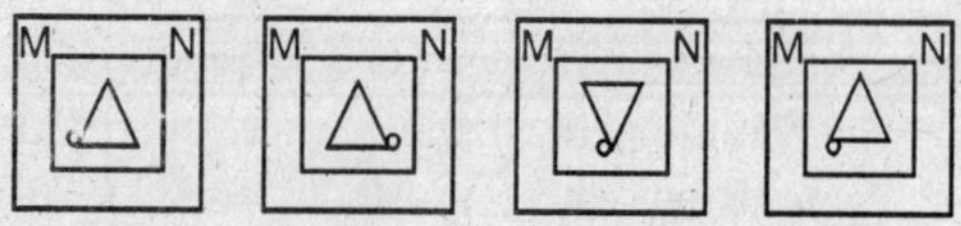

(*a*) (*b*) (*c*) (*d*)

5. Problem Figure

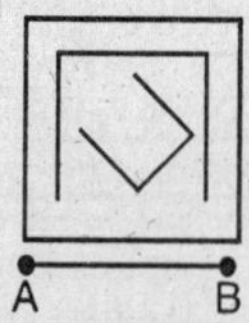

Answer Figures

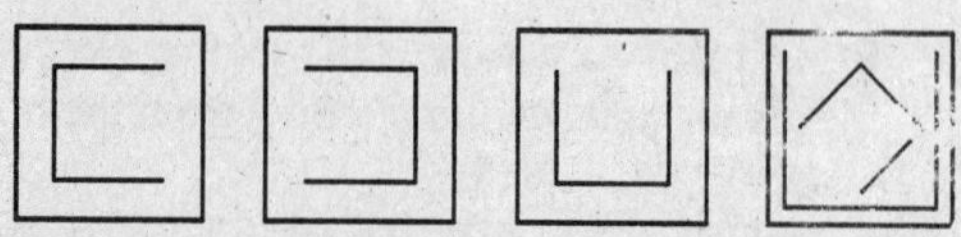

(*a*) (*b*) (*c*) (*d*)

6. Problem Figure

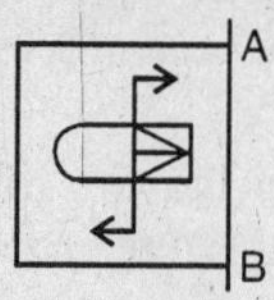

Answer Figures

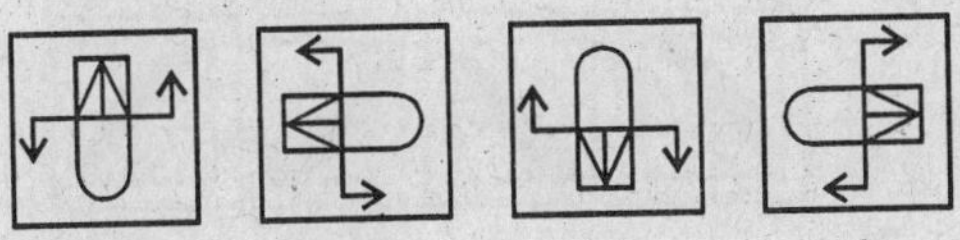

(a) (b) (c) (d)

7. Problem Figure

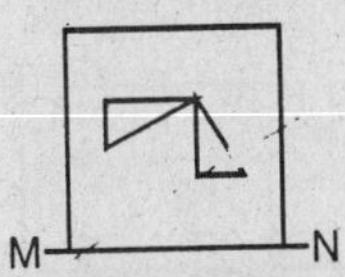

Answer Figures

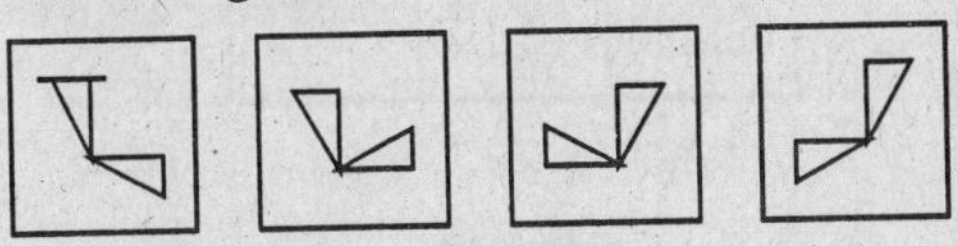

(a) (b) (c) (d)

8. Problem Figure

Answer Figures

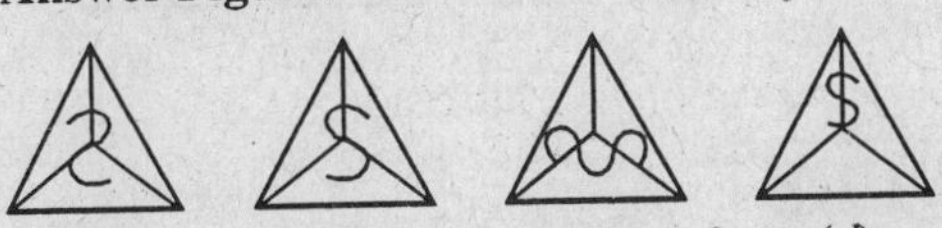

(a) (b) (c) (d)

9. Problem Figure

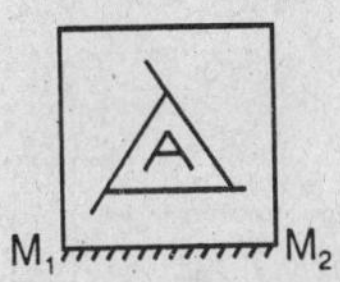

Answer Figures

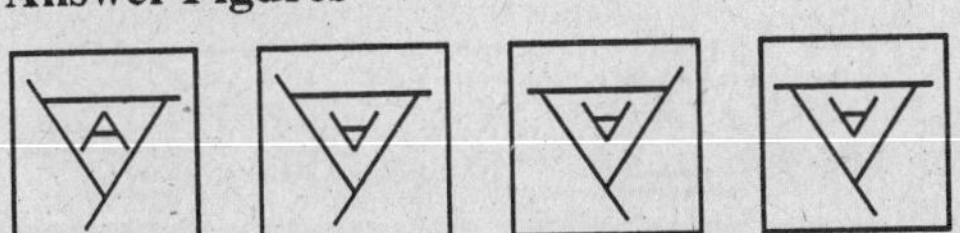

(a) (b) (c) (d)

10. Problem Figure

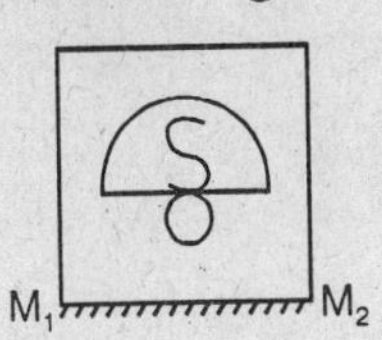

Answer Figures

(a) (b) (c) (d)

Directions (Qs. 11 to 20): *In each question, which one of the alter-native figures will complete the given figure pattern?*

11. Pattern 

Alternative figures

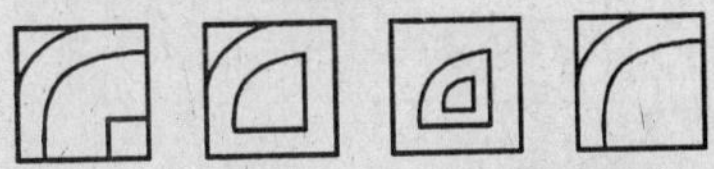

(a) (b) (c) (d)

12. Pattern 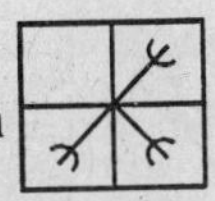

Alternative figures

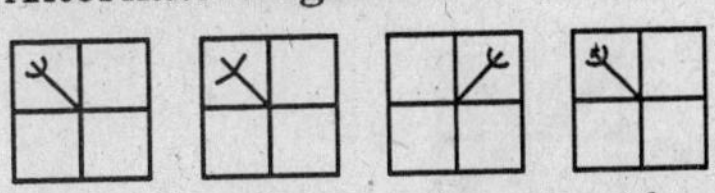

(a) (b) (c) (d)

13. Pattern 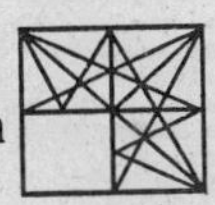

Alternative figures

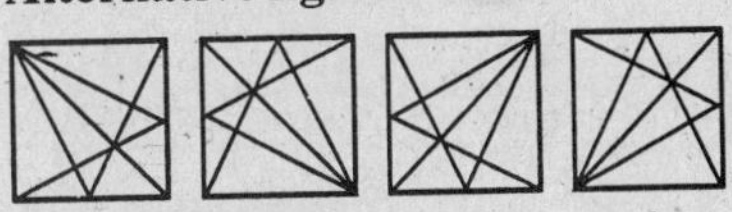

(a) (b) (c) (d)

14. Pattern 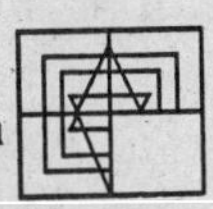

Alternative figures

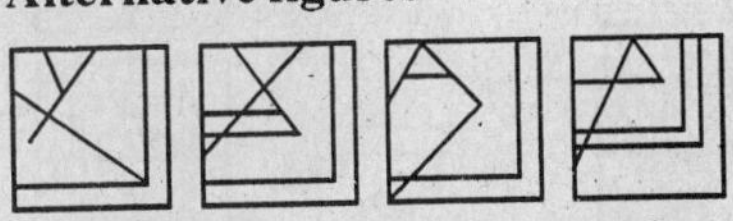

(a) (b) (c) (d)

15. Pattern 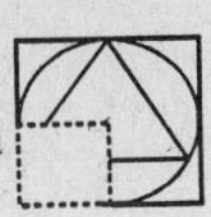

Alternative figures

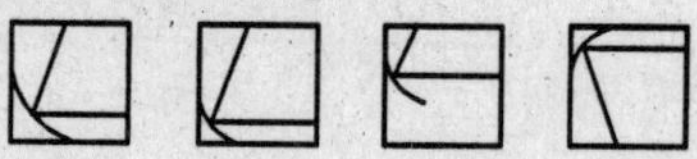

(*a*) (*b*) (*c*) (*d*)

16. Pattern 

Alternative figures

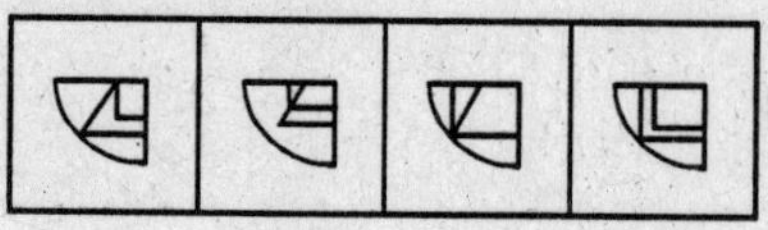

(*a*) (*b*) (*c*) (*d*)

17. Pattern 

Alternative figures

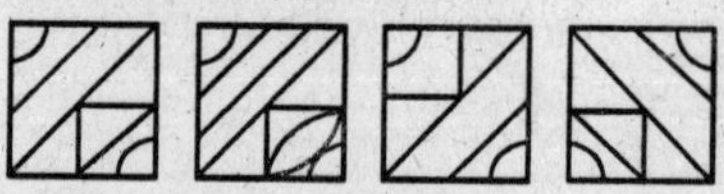

(*a*) (*b*) (*c*) (*d*)

18. Pattern 

Alternative figures

(*a*) (*b*) (*c*) (*d*)

19. Pattern 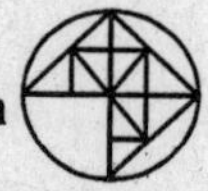

Alternative figures

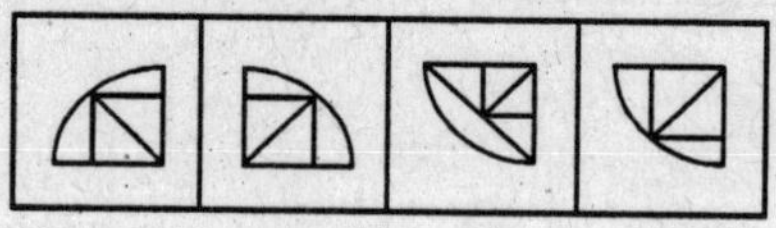

(*a*) (*b*) (*c*) (*d*)

20. Pattern 

Alternative figures

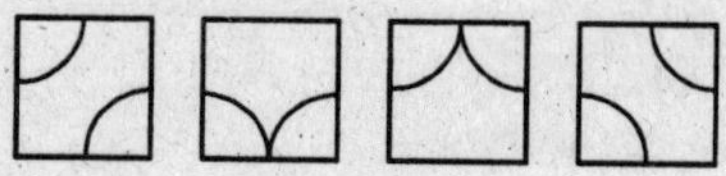

(*a*) (*b*) (*c*) (*d*)

ANSWERS

1	2	3	4	5	6	7	8	9	10
(*d*)	(*c*)	(*b*)	(*c*)	(*d*)	(*b*)	(*c*)	(*a*)	(*b*)	(*c*)
11	**12**	**13**	**14**	**15**	**16**	**17**	**18**	**19**	**20**
(*b*)	(*a*)	(*d*)	(*d*)	(*a*)	(*b*)	(*c*)	(*b*)	(*c*)	(*b*)

EXPLANATORY ANSWERS

11. 

12. 

13. 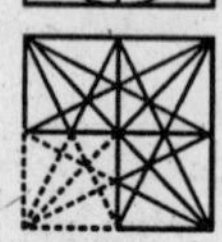

14. 

15. 

16. 

17. 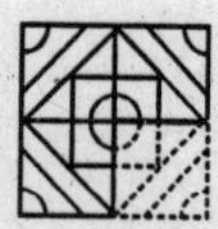

18. 

19. 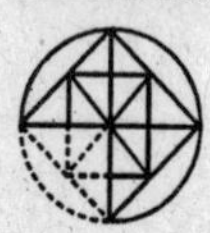

20. 

NUMERICAL AND DATA ANALYSIS

1. SIMPLIFICATION

BODMAS-RULE

This rule is very important for the arithmetical simplification. When vinculum, bracket, of, division, multiplication, addition, subtraction all or two or more than two operations are present in any question, then we can find out the result (answer) with the help of BODMAS - Rule. Details of BODMAS-Rule is given below :

Order	Abbreviated Letter Used in rule	Meaning	Notation
1.	V	Vinculum or Bar	——
2.	B	Brackets	[ ], { }, ( )
3.	O	Of	of
4.	D	Division	÷
5.	M	Multiplication	×
6.	A	Addition	+
7.	S	Subtraction	–

Note :

(*i*) Order of the letter which is used in BODMAS Rule is always fixed.

(*ii*) Absence of any operation or more than one operations does not changes the order of BODMAS.

(*iii*) 'of' means multiplication.

BRACKETS

When all brackets are present in a question, in that condition **ViCiCuSq-Rule** is applied. This ViCiCuSq-Rule stands for brackets and represents the order of calculation of brackets. Details are given below :

Order	Abbreviated Letter Used in rule	Meaning	Notation
1.	Vi	Vinculum	——
2.	Ci	Circular Bracket	( )
3.	Cu	Curly Bracket	{ }
4.	Sq	Square Bracket	[ ]

Note : This order of brackets (ViCiCuSq) is also fixed and not variable.

SOLVED EXAMPLES

Example 1: $\frac{3}{5}$ of $\frac{5}{7}$ of 357 = ?

A. 51 B. 153
C. 255 D. 159

Solution: $357 \times \frac{5}{7} \times \frac{3}{5} = 153$

Example 2: 125% of 860 + 75% of 480 = ?

A. 1415 B. 1385
C. 1435 D. 1365

Solution: $\frac{860 \times 125}{100} + \frac{480 \times 75}{100}$

$= 1075 + 360 = 1435$

Example 3: 1121.21 + 121.021 + 21.0021 = ?

A. 1263.2331
B. 1263.2121
C. 1163.2121
D. 1163.2331

Solution: 1121.21 + 121.021 + 21.0021
= 1263.2331

Example 4: $\left(\sqrt{5}-\sqrt{6}\right)^2 + \left(\sqrt{3}+\sqrt{10}\right)^2 = (?)^3 - 40$

A. 8 B. 4
C. 3 D. 6

Solution: Let ? = x

$\therefore \left(\sqrt{5}-\sqrt{6}\right)^2 + \left(\sqrt{3}+\sqrt{10}\right)^2 = (x)^3 - 40$

$\Rightarrow 5+6-2\sqrt{30}+3+10+2\sqrt{30} = x^3 - 40$

$\Rightarrow 24 = x^3 - 40$

$\Rightarrow x^3 = 40 + 24 = 64 = 4^3$

$\Rightarrow x = 4$

MULTIPLE CHOICE QUESTIONS

1. 68% of $\sqrt{2916} \times 25 = ? + 189$

A. 728 B. 718
C. 729 D. 739

2. $\sqrt{5^2 \times 41 \times 5 - 17^2 - 75} = ?$

A. 69 B. 61
C. 71 D. 79

3. 8.88 × 88.8 × 88 = ?

A. 68301.142 B. 79391.642
C. 65365.824 D. None of these

4. $\dfrac{9 \div 2 \times 27 \div 9}{18 \div 7.5 \times 5 \div 4} = ?$

A. 4.5 B. 5.7
C. 2.5 D. 6.8

5. $\sqrt{\sqrt{2500} + \sqrt{961}} = (?)^2$

A. 81 B. 3
C. 6561 D. 9

6. $64^{12} \div 4^{15} = 64^{?}$

A. 9 B. 3
C. 12 D. 7

7. $\sqrt{97344} = ?$

A. 302 B. 322
C. 292 D. None of these

8. 14% of 255 + ?% of 405 = 124.8

A. 22 B. 24
C. 18 D. 15

9. 19.25 × 16.4 × ? = 3472.7

A. 15 B. 17
C. 12 D. None of these

10. 83.04 – 66.46 – 11.71 = ?

A. 5.63 B. 2.92
C. 3.87 D. None of these

11. $\sqrt{529} \div 46 \times 7.4 + (8)^3 - 251 = ?$

A. 265.1 B. 246.1
C. 256.4 D. None of these

12. $(16 \times 4)^3 \div (4)^5 \times (2 \times 8)^2 = (4)^?$

A. 5 B. 6
C. 3 D. 8

13. 534.58 – 386.89 + 221.45 – 195.42 = ?

A. 162.65 B. 109.65
C. 173.72 D. None of these

14. $\sqrt{5625} \times \dfrac{3}{5} + (85)^2 = ?$

A. 7270 B. 7280
C. 7260 D. 7250

15. $(7)^3 \times (3)^3 \div (6)^2 = ?$

A. 12348 B. 85.75
C. 1543.5 D. 257.25

16. $\dfrac{17^{6.87}}{17^{4.23}} = 17^{(?)}$

A. 1.62 B. 2.64
C. 11.1 D. 29.06

17. $\sqrt{2401} \times \sqrt{3249} = ?$

A. 2793 B. 2842
C. 2679 D. 2891

18. (5967 – 2437 – 1910) ÷ ? = 27

A. 60 B. 50
C. 65 D. 45

19. $\sqrt[3]{12167} \times \sqrt{?} = 621$

A. 841 B. 27
C. 625 D. None of these

20. 4.5% of 800 ÷ 0.5% of 640 = ?

A. 11.75 B. 12
C. 112.05 D. 11.25

21. 383 ÷ 25 × 2.5 + 12 = ?

A. 50.30 B. 222.14
C. 68.30 D. 124.24

22. 5083 + 25% of ? + 289 = 6385.5

A. 4044 B. 4054
C. 4154 D. 4104

23. $0.2 \times 10^{-2} = ?$

A. 2 B. 0.02

C. 0.002 D. 0.0002

24. $15 - 10 + 5 \times 2 \div 5 = ?$

A. 70 B. 4

C. 5 D. None of these

25. 37% of 150 – 0.05% of 1000 = ?

A. 50 B. 55

C. 55.5 D. 55.55

26. $(15)^{98} \times (15)^{-95} = ?$

A. 3375 B. 225

C. 45 D. 75

27. $\sqrt[3]{?} = (36 \times 24) \div 9$

A. 884736 B. 804036

C. 854734 D. 814736

28. (43% of 2750) – (38% of 2990) = ?

A. 49.3 B. 44.7

C. 43.6 D. 46.3

29. $40 \times 2 \div 10 + 5 - 4 = ?$

A. 5 B. 8

C. 11 D. 9

30. $28 \times 104 \div (18 + 6) + 3 = ?$

A. $124\frac{1}{3}$ B. $104\frac{1}{3}$

C. $125\frac{1}{3}$ D. 128

31. $0.99 \times 14 \div 11 \div 0.7 = ?$

A. 2.9 B. 1.6

C. 1.8 D. 2.8

32. $8\frac{1}{3}+5\frac{1}{4}\times 13\frac{1}{5} \div 6\frac{3}{5} = ?$

A. $19\frac{1}{3}$ B. $18\frac{1}{2}$

C. $21\frac{1}{3}$ D. None of these

33. $\frac{14}{3}$ of $\frac{5}{8}$ of 72 = ?

A. 209 B. 217

C. 210 D. 199

34. $10 \times 10 \times 10 \div (20 \div 10 \times 10 - 10) + 6 = ?$

A. 108 B. 111

C. 106 D. 114

35. $\dfrac{\frac{1}{3}\times 20 \div 4}{\frac{1}{4}\times 25 \div 5} = ?$

A. $\frac{7}{3}$ B. $\frac{4}{3}$

C. $\frac{5}{3}$ D. $\frac{10}{3}$

36. $\dfrac{2.70\times 2.70+4.30\times 4.30+8.60\times 2.70}{2.70+4.30} = ?$

A. 6.8 B. 7.0

C. 7.6 D. 8.5

37. $1150 \div 50 \div 23 + 15 = ?$

A. 16 B. 20

C. 22 D. 18

38. $\dfrac{(0.08)^3+(0.011)^3}{(0.08)^2-0.08\times 0.011+(0.011)^2} = ?$

A. 0.087 B. 0.091

C. 0.077 D. 0.067

39. $22 \div \left[(28-13)\div\{(32-8)\div\left(5+\frac{1}{3}\right)\}\right] = ?$

A. 7.9 B. 6.8

C. 6.6 D. 5.7

40. $\dfrac{\left(20^2-10^2\right)\div 5\times 3+10}{\frac{1}{3}\text{ of } 27+10\div 2+1} = ?$

A. $10\frac{2}{3}$ B. $14\frac{1}{3}$

C. 15 D. $12\frac{2}{3}$

41. $11^2 - 6^2 \div 6 \times \frac{5}{2} = 2$ of $10 = ?$

A. 126 B. 108

C. 110 D. 125

42. $\frac{25}{3}-\frac{4}{7}$ of $\frac{7}{5}+\frac{11}{3}\div\frac{2}{3}-4$ = ?

A. $8\frac{1}{15}$ B. $9\frac{1}{30}$
C. $7\frac{1}{30}$ D. $9\frac{1}{5}$

43. 35 × 0.07 – 21 × 0.03 = ?

A. 2.75 B. 1.72
C. 1.82 D. 2.13

44. $60 \times [35 - \{25 - (18 - \overline{9-3}) \div 11\}]$ = ?

A. $566\frac{5}{7}$ B. $665\frac{5}{11}$
C. $665\frac{8}{11}$ D. $765\frac{5}{11}$

45. $\dfrac{140-44\times9\div3}{\frac{1}{2}\text{ of }18\div9+2}$ = ?

A. $2\frac{2}{3}$ B. $3\frac{1}{3}$
C. $4\frac{2}{3}$ D. $6\frac{4}{5}$

46. $4\frac{1}{3} \times 5\frac{1}{3} \div 6\frac{1}{3} \div \frac{1}{3} + 5\frac{1}{3} - 2\frac{1}{3}$ = ?

A. $14\frac{14}{19}$ B. $13\frac{19}{21}$
C. $13\frac{18}{19}$ D. $17\frac{8}{11}$

47. $1+\dfrac{1}{1+\dfrac{1}{1+\dfrac{1}{3}}}$ = ?

A. $1\frac{4}{7}$ B. $2\frac{4}{7}$
C. $3\frac{4}{7}$ D. $4\frac{4}{7}$

48. $3 - [9 + \{14 - (6 - \overline{3-21})\}]$ = ?

A. 0 B. 4
C. 18 D. 6

49. (8 ÷ 88) × 8888088 = ?

A. 8008008 B. 808088
C. 808080 D. 808008

50. 1260 ÷ 15 ÷ 7 = ?

A. 588 B. 122
C. 58 D. 12

51. 2 – [2 – {2 – 2(2 + 2)}] = ?

A. 6 B. – 6
C. 4 D. – 4

52. 100 × 10 – 100 + 2000 ÷ 100 = ?

A. 979 B. 920
C. 780 D. 29

53. 3640 ÷ 14 × 16 + 340 = ?

A. 3500 B. 4500
C. 3525 D. 4480

54. 25 – 5 [2 + 3 {2 – 2 (5 – 3) + 5} –10] ÷ 4 = ?

A. 5 B. 25
C. 23.25 D. 23.75

55. $(-5)\ (4)\ (2)\left(-\frac{1}{2}\right)\left(\frac{3}{4}\right)$ = ?

A. 15 B. –15
C. 30 D. –30

ANSWERS

1	2	3	4	5	6	7	8	9	10
C	A	D	A	B	D	D	A	D	D
11	**12**	**13**	**14**	**15**	**16**	**17**	**18**	**19**	**20**
D	D	D	A	D	B	A	A	D	D
21	**22**	**23**	**24**	**25**	**26**	**27**	**28**	**29**	**30**
A	B	C	D	B	A	A	D	D	A
31	**32**	**33**	**34**	**35**	**36**	**37**	**38**	**39**	**40**
C	D	C	C	B	B	A	B	C	D

41	42	43	44	45	46	47	48	49	50
A	B	C	B	A	C	A	B	D	D
51	**52**	**53**	**54**	**55**					
B	B	B	D	B					

SOME SELECTED EXPLANATORY ANSWERS

1. $\sqrt{2916} \times 68\% \times 25 = ? + 189$

$\Rightarrow 54 \times \frac{68}{100} \times 25 = ? + 189$

$\Rightarrow 918 = ? + 189$

$\Rightarrow ? = 918 - 189 = 729$

2. $? = \sqrt{25 \times 41 \times 5 - 17^2 - 75}$

$= \sqrt{5125 - 289 - 75}$

$= \sqrt{4761} = 69$

3. $8.88 \times 88.8 \times 88 = 69391.872$

4. $\frac{9 \div 2 \times 27 \div 9}{18 \div 7.5 \times 5 \div 4} = \frac{\frac{9}{2} \times \frac{27}{9}}{\frac{18}{7.5} \times \frac{5}{4}} = \frac{\frac{27}{2}}{3} = 4.5$

5. $\sqrt{\sqrt{2500 + 961}}$

$= \sqrt{\sqrt{50 + 31}} = \sqrt{9} = \sqrt{(3)^2} = 3.$

6. Let $(64)^x = 64^{12} \div 4^{15}$

$\Rightarrow \quad 4^{3x} = 4^{36-15} = 4^{21}$

$\therefore \quad 3x = 21 \quad \therefore x = 7$

7. $\sqrt{97344} = 312$

8. $\because$ 14% of 255 + ?% of 405 = 124.8

$\Rightarrow \quad 35.7 + 405 \times ? = 124.8$

$\Rightarrow \quad \frac{405 \times ?}{100} = 124.8 - 35.7 = 89.1$

$\therefore \quad ? = \frac{98.1 \times 100}{405} = \frac{891 \times 10}{405}$

$= \frac{891 \times 2}{81} = \frac{1782}{81} = 22.$

9. $\because \; 19.25 \times 16.4 \times ? = 3472.7$

$\therefore \quad ? = \frac{3472.7}{19.25 \times 16.4} = 11$

10. $83.04 - 66.46 - 11.71 = 4.87$

11. $\sqrt{529} \div 46 \times 7.4 + (8)^3 - 251$

$= \frac{23}{46} \times 7.4 + 512 - 251$

$= 3.7 + 512 - 251 = 264.7$

12. $(4)^? = (16 \times 4)^3 \div (4)^5 \times (2 \times 8)^2$

$(4)^? = \frac{(4)^9}{(4)^5} \times (4)^4 = (4)^{9+4-5}$

$\therefore \quad ? = 8.$

13. $534.58 - 386.89 + 221.45 - 195.42 = 172.72$

14. $\sqrt{5625} \times \frac{3}{5} + (85)^2 = 75 \times \frac{3}{5} + 7225 = 7270$

15. $343 \times 27 \div 36 = 257.25$

16. $17^{(?)} = \frac{17^{6.87}}{17^{4.23}} = 17^{6.87-4.23} = 17^{2.64}$

$\therefore \; ? = 2.64.$

17. $\sqrt{2401} \times \sqrt{3249} = 49 \times 57 = 2793.$

18. $(5967 - 2437 - 1910) \div ? = 27$

$\therefore \quad \frac{1620}{?} = 27$

$\therefore \quad ? = \frac{1620}{27} = 60$

19. $\because \; \sqrt[3]{12167} \times \sqrt{?} = 621$

$\Rightarrow \quad 23 \times \sqrt{?} = 621$

$\Rightarrow \quad \sqrt{?} = \frac{621}{23} = 27$

$\therefore \quad ? = (27)^2 = 729$

20. $\frac{4.5}{100}$ of 800 ÷ $\frac{0.5}{100}$ of 640

$= 36 \div 3.2 = 11.25$

21. 383 ÷ 25 × 2.5 + 12

$= \frac{383}{25} \times 2.5 + 12 = 50.30.$

22. फ $5083 + \frac{25}{100}$ of ? + 289 = 6385.5

$\Rightarrow$ 0.25 × ? = 6385.5 – 5083 – 289

$\therefore$? $= \frac{1013.5}{0.25} = 4054.$

23. $0.2 \times 10^{-2} = 0.2 \times \frac{1}{100} = 0.002$

24. 15 – 10 + 5 × 2 ÷ 5

$= 15 - 10 + \frac{5 \times 2}{5}$

$= 15 - 10 + 2$

$= 7$

25. 37% of 150 – 0.05% of 1000

$= \frac{37}{100}$ of 150 – $\frac{0.05}{100}$ of 1000

$= \frac{111}{2} - 0.5$

$= 55.5 - 0.5 = 55.$

26. $(15)^{98} \times (15)^{-95} = (15)^3 = 375$

27. $(36 \times 24) \div 9 = \sqrt[3]{?}$

$\Rightarrow 4 \times 24 = \sqrt[3]{?}$

$\therefore$? $= 96^3 = 884736$

28. (43% of 2750) – (38% of 2990)

$= 0.43 \times 2750 - 0.38 \times 2990 = 46.3$

29. $\because$ $40 \times 2 \div 10 + 5 - 4 = 40 \times \frac{2}{10} + 5 - 4$

$= 8 + 5 - 4 = 9$

30. $\because$ 28 × 104 ÷ (18 + 6) + 3

$= 28 \times 104 \div 24 + 3$

$= 28 \times \frac{104}{24} + 3 = 28 \times \frac{13}{3} + 3$

$= \frac{364}{3} + 3 = \frac{373}{3} = 124\frac{1}{3}$

31. $\because$ 0.99 × 14 ÷ 11 ÷ 0.7

$= 0.99 \times \frac{14}{11} \div 0.7 = \frac{0.99 \times 14}{11 \times 0.7} = 1.8$

32. $\because$ $8\frac{1}{3} + 5\frac{1}{4} \times 13\frac{1}{5} \div 6\frac{3}{5}$

$= \frac{25}{3} + \frac{21}{4} \times \frac{66}{5} \div \frac{33}{5} = \frac{25}{3} + \frac{21}{4} \times \frac{66}{5} \times \frac{5}{33}$

$= \frac{25}{3} + \frac{21}{2} = \frac{50 + 63}{6} = \frac{113}{6} = 18\frac{5}{6}$

33. $\because$ $\frac{14}{3}$ of $\frac{5}{8}$ of 72 $= \frac{14 \times 5 \times 72}{3 \times 8} = 210$

34. 10 × 10 × 10 ÷ (20 ÷ 10 × 10 – 10) + 6

$= 10 \times 10 \times 10 \div \left(\frac{20}{10} \times 10 - 10\right) + 6$

$= 10 \times 10 \times 10 \div (20 - 10) + 6$

$= 10 \times 10 \times 10 \div 10 + 6 = 10 \times 10 \times \frac{10}{10} + 6$

$= 10 \times 10 \times 1 + 6 = 100 + 6 = 106$

35. $\because$ $\frac{\frac{1}{3} \times 20 \div 4}{\frac{1}{4} \times 25 \div 5} = \frac{\frac{1}{3} \times 5}{\frac{1}{4} \times 5} = \frac{\frac{5}{3}}{\frac{5}{4}} = \frac{4}{3}$

36. $\frac{2.70 \times 2.70 + 4.30 \times 4.30 + 8.60 \times 2.70}{2.70 + 4.30}$

$= \frac{(2.70)^2 + (4.30)^2 + 2 \times 4.30 \times 2.70}{2.70 + 4.30}$

$= \frac{(2.70 + 4.30)^2}{2.70 + 4.30}$

$[\because a^2 + b^2 + 2ab = (a + b)^2]$

$= 2.70 + 4.30 = 7.00$

37. $1150 \div 50 \div 23 + 15 = \frac{1150}{50} \div 23 + 15$

$= 23 \div 23 + 15$

$= \frac{23}{23} + 15 = 1 + 15 = 16.$

38. $\dfrac{(0.08)^3+(0.011)^3}{(0.08)^2-0.08\times0.011+(0.011)^2}$

$\dfrac{(0.08+0.011)\left[(0.08)^2-0.08\times0.011+(0.011)^2\right]}{(0.08)^2-0.08\times0.011+(0.011)^2}$

$[\because a^3+b^3=(a+b)(a^2-ab+b^2)]$

$=0.08+0.011=0.091.$

39. $22\div\left[(28-13)\div\left\{(32-8)\div\left(5+\dfrac{1}{3}\right)\right\}\right]$

$=22\div\left[15\div\left\{24\div\dfrac{16}{3}\right\}\right]$

$=22\div\left[15\div\dfrac{24}{\frac{16}{3}}\right]=22\div\left[15\div\dfrac{9}{2}\right]$

$=22\div\dfrac{15}{\frac{9}{2}}=22\div\dfrac{10}{3}=\dfrac{22\times3}{10}=6.6$

40. $\dfrac{(20^2-10^2)\div5\times3+10}{\frac{1}{3}\text{ of }27+10\div2+1}$

$=\dfrac{(400-100)\div5\times3+10}{9+10\div2+1}=\dfrac{300\div5\times3+10}{9+5+1}$

$=\dfrac{60\times3+10}{15}=\dfrac{190}{15}=\dfrac{38}{3}=12\dfrac{2}{3}$

41. $11^2-6^2\div6\times\dfrac{5}{2}+2\text{ of }10$

$=11^2-6^2\div6\times\dfrac{5}{2}+20$

$=11^2-6\times\dfrac{5}{2}+20=11^2-15+20$

$=121+5=126.$

42. $\dfrac{25}{3}-\dfrac{4}{7}\text{of}\dfrac{7}{5}+\dfrac{11}{3}\div\dfrac{2}{3}-4$

$=\dfrac{25}{3}-\dfrac{4}{5}+\dfrac{11}{3}\div\dfrac{2}{3}-4=\dfrac{25}{3}-\dfrac{4}{5}+\dfrac{11}{2}-4$

$=\dfrac{83}{6}-\dfrac{24}{5}=\dfrac{415-144}{30}=\dfrac{271}{30}=9\dfrac{1}{30}$

43. $35\times0.07-21\times0.03=2.45-0.63=1.82$

44. $60\times[35-\{25-(18-\overline{9-3})\div11\}]$

$=60\times[35-\{25-(18-6)\div11\}$

$=60\times[35-\{25-12\div11\}]$

$=60\times\left[35-\left\{25-\dfrac{12}{11}\right\}\right]=60\times\left[35-\dfrac{263}{11}\right]$

$=60\times\dfrac{122}{11}=665\dfrac{5}{11}$

45. $\dfrac{140-44\times9\div3}{\frac{1}{2}\text{ of }18\div9+2}=\dfrac{140-44\times3}{9\div9+2}$

$=\dfrac{140-132}{1+2}=\dfrac{8}{3}=2\dfrac{2}{3}$

46. $4\dfrac{1}{3}\times5\dfrac{1}{3}\div6\dfrac{1}{3}\div\dfrac{1}{3}+5\dfrac{1}{3}-2\dfrac{1}{3}$

$=\dfrac{13}{3}\times\dfrac{16}{3}\div\dfrac{19}{3}\div\dfrac{1}{3}+\dfrac{16}{3}-\dfrac{7}{3}$

$=\dfrac{13}{3}\times\dfrac{16}{19}\div\dfrac{1}{3}+\dfrac{16}{3}-\dfrac{7}{3}$

$=\dfrac{13}{3}\times\dfrac{48}{19}+\dfrac{16}{3}-\dfrac{7}{3}=\dfrac{208}{19}+\dfrac{16}{3}-\dfrac{7}{3}$

$=10\dfrac{18}{19}+3=13\dfrac{18}{19}$

47. This type of questions is solved starting from the bottom.

$1+\dfrac{1}{1+\dfrac{1}{1+\dfrac{1}{3}}}=1+\dfrac{1}{1+\dfrac{1}{\frac{4}{3}}}$

$=1+\dfrac{1}{1+\dfrac{3}{4}}=1+\dfrac{1}{\frac{7}{4}}=1+\dfrac{4}{7}=\dfrac{11}{7}=1\dfrac{4}{7}$

48. $3-[9+\{14-(6-\overline{3-21})\}]$

$=3-[9+\{14-(6+18\}]$

$=3-[9+\{14-24\}]=3-[9-10]$

$=3+1=4.$

49. $(8\div88)\times888808=\dfrac{8}{88}\times8888088=808008$

50. $1260 \div 15 \div 7 = 1260 \times \frac{1}{15} \times \frac{1}{7} = 12$

51. $2 - [2 - \{2 - 2(2 + 2)\}]$
$= 2 - [2 - \{2 - 8\}] = 2 - [2 + 6]$
$= 2 - 8 = -6$

52. $100 \times 10 - 100 + 2000 \div 100$
$= 100 \times 10 - 100 + 20$
$= 1000 - 100 + 20 = 920$

53. $3640 \div 14 \times 6 + 340$

$= 3640 \times \frac{1}{14} \times 16 + 340 = 4160 + 340 = 4500$

54. $25 - 5\ [2 + 3\ \{2 - 2\ (5 - 3) + 5\} - 10] \div 4$
$= 25 - 5\ [2 + 3\ \{2 - 4 + 5\} - 10] \div 4$
$= 25 - 5\ [2 + 9 - 10] \div 4$

$= 25 - 5 \times 1 \times \frac{1}{4} = 25 - \frac{5}{4} = \frac{95}{4} = 23.75$

55. $(-5)\ (4)\ (2) \left(-\frac{1}{2}\right)\left(\frac{3}{4}\right)$

$= -5 \times 4 \times 2 \times -\frac{1}{2} \times \frac{3}{4} = 15$

2. L.C.M. & H.C.F.

LCM

Multiple : A number is said to be multiple of other when it is exactly divisible by the other.

Common multiple : A common multiple of two or more numbers is a number which is exactly divisible by each of them. For example, for 2 and 3, common multiples are 6, 12, 18, 24 and so on.

Explanation:

Consider the two numbers 2 and 3

Multiple of 2 are 2, 4, 6, 8, 10, 12, ...

Multiple of 3 are 3, 6, 9, 12, 15, ...

$\therefore$ Common multiples are 6, 12, 18, ...

Least Common Multiple (L.C.M.) : L.C.M. of two or more given numbers is the least number which is exactly divisible by each of them. For example,

6 is a common multiple of 2 and 3

12 is also common multiple of 2 and 3

18 is also common multiple of 2 and 3

But 6 is the least common multiple (L.C.M.) of 2 and 3.

Methods to find out L.C.M.

L.C.M. of two or more given numbers is determined by following two methods:

1. By prime factorization method

2. By division method

1. By prime factorization method : Resolve the given numbers into their prime factors and then find the product of the highest power of all the factors that occur in the given numbers. This product will be the L.C.M.

Example 1 : Find the L.C.M. of 40, 50, 60 and 80.

Sol :
$$40 = 2 \times 2 \times 2 \times 5 = 2^3 \times 5$$
$$50 = 2 \times 5 \times 5 = 2 \times 5^2$$
$$60 = 2 \times 2 \times 3 \times 5 = 2^2 \times 3 \times 5$$
$$80 = 2 \times 2 \times 2 \times 2 \times 5 = 2^4 \times 5$$

Here, the prime factors that occur in the given numbers are 2, 3 and 5 and their highest powers are respectively 2^4, 5^2 and 3.

Hence, the required L.C.M. $= 2^4 \times 3 \times 5^2$
$= 1200$.

2. By division method : This is the quicker method to find the prime factors and hence L.C.M.

For determining L.C.M. of the numbers 40, 50, 60 and 80, following process of division is adopted:

2	40, 50, 60, 80
2	20, 25, 30, 40
2	10, 25, 15, 20
5	5, 25, 15, 10
	1, 5, 3, 2

Now required L.C.M. $= 2 \times 2 \times 2 \times 5 \times 5 \times 3 \times 2 = 1200$

L.C.M. of decimal : First of all, we find out the L.C.M. of numbers without decimal and then, we see the number in which decimal is given in the minimum digit from right to left. We put the decimal in our result which is equal to that number of digits.

Example : Find the L.C.M. of 0.6, 9.6 and 0.36.

Sol : The given numbers are equivalent to 0.60, 9.60 and 0.36.

Now, we find out the L.C.M. of 60, 960 and 36, which is equal to 2880.

Hence, the required L.C.M. = 2880.

L.C.M. of fraction : The L.C.M. of two or more fractions is the least fraction or integer which is exactly divisible by each of them.

If $\frac{a}{b}, \frac{c}{d}, \frac{e}{f}$ be the proper fractions, then their L.C.M. is given by

$$\frac{\text{L.C.M. of numerators } a, c, e}{\text{H.C.F. of denominators } b, d, f}$$

An example : Find the L.C.M. of $\frac{1}{2}, \frac{3}{5}, \frac{4}{7}$ and $\frac{5}{12}$

Sol : $$\text{L.C.M.} = \frac{\text{L.C.M. of } 1, 3, 4, 5}{\text{H.C.F. of } 2, 5, 7, 12}$$

$$= \frac{60}{1} = 60$$

HCF

Factor : One number is said to be a factor of other when it divides the other exactly. Hence, 5 and 7 are factors of 35.

Common factor : A common factor of two or more numbers is a number that divides each of them exactly. Hence, 5 is a common factor of 15, 25, 35 and 55.

Highest Common Factor (H.C.F.) : H.C.F. of two or more numbers is the largest number by which each given number is divisible without leaving any remainder.

An example : It is required to find the H.C.F. of 6 and 8.

Factors of 6 are 1, 2, 3, 6 and

Factors of 8 are 1, 2, 4, 8.

The common factors are 1, 2, but highest of these is 2. Hence, 2 is the H.C.F.

Note : *The terms Highest Common Divisor (H.C.D.) and Greatest Common Measure (G.C.M.) are often used in the sense of Highest Common Factor (H.C.F.)*

We can find H.C.F. by two methods:

1. By prime factorization method :

An example : Find the H.C.F. of 144, 336 and 2016.

Sol : $144 = 2 \times 2 \times 2 \times 2 \times 3 \times 3 = 2^4 \times 3^2$

$336 = 2 \times 2 \times 2 \times 2 \times 3 \times 7$

$= 2^4 \times 3 \times 7$

$2016 = 2 \times 2 \times 2 \times 2 \times 2 \times 7 \times 3 \times 3$

$= 2^5 \times 7 \times 3^2$

$\therefore$ H.C.F. of given numbers $= 2^4 \times 3 = 48$.

2. By division method : Divide the greater number by the smaller number, divide the divisor by the remainder, divide the remainder by the next remainder, and so on until no remainder is left. The last divisor is the required H.C.F.

An example : Find the H.C.F. of 48, 168 and 324.

Sol :

```
48 ) 168 ( 3
     144
     ---
      24 ) 48 ( 2
           48
           --
           ××
```

Thus, the H.C.F. of 48 and 168 is 24.

Now, we find out the H.C.F. of 24 and 324

```
24 ) 324 (13
     24
     --
     84
     72
     --
     12 ) 24 ( 2
          24
          --
          ××
```

$\therefore$ Required H.C.F. = 12.

H.C.F. of Decimals : First of all find the H.C.F. of the given numbers ignoring decimals and then put decimal at maximum digits from right to left.

An example : Find the H.C.F. of 0.0012, 1.6 and 2.8.

Sol : First we find the H.C.F. of 12, 16 and 28, which comes to 4.

So, H.C.F. of 0.0012, 1.6 and 2.8 will be 0.0004.

H.C.F. of Fractions : If $\frac{a}{b}, \frac{c}{d}, \frac{e}{f}, \ldots$ be the proper fraction, their H.C.F. is equal to $\frac{\text{H.C.F. of numerators}}{\text{L.C.M. of denominators}}$

An example : Find the H.C.F. of $\frac{54}{9}, 3\frac{9}{17}$ and $\frac{36}{51}$

Sol : Here, $\frac{54}{9} = \frac{6}{1}$; $3\frac{9}{17} = \frac{60}{17}$ and $\frac{36}{51} = \frac{12}{17}$

Hence, the fractions are $\frac{6}{1}, \frac{60}{17}$ and $\frac{12}{17}$

$$\therefore \text{ H.C.F.} = \frac{\text{H.C.F. of } 6, 60, 12}{\text{L.C.M. of } 1, 17, 17} = \frac{6}{17}.$$

Relationship Between Two Numbers and Their L.C.M. and H.C.F.

Product of the H.C.F. and the L.C.M. of two numbers is equal to the product of the given numbers.

i.e., 1st number × 2nd number = H.C.F. × L.C.M.

MULTIPLE CHOICE QUESTIONS

1. The largest three-digit number, when divided by 6, 9 and 12 leaves 1 as remainder in each case, will be
A. 887 B. 987
C. 973 D. 730

2. Two numbers are in the ratio of 8 : 15. If their H.C.F. is 4, the numbers are
A. 32 and 60 B. 16 and 30
C. 80 and 150 D. 64 and 120

3. The largest number that will divide 226 and 272 leaving 1 and 2 as remainders respectively, is
A. 36 B. 45
C. 55 D. 59

4. Which of the following is the greatest common divisor of 1170 and 102?
A. 8 B. 4
C. 6 D. 3

5. A number, when 3 is added to it, becomes divisible by 36, 45 and 50. The smallest such number is
A. 987 B. 798
C. 986 D. 897

6. The least perfect square number which is completely divisible by 10, 20, 30 and 40 is
A. 4800 B. 3600
C. 4400 D. 2500

7. The product of two numbers is 2160 and their H.C.F. is 12. How many such pairs of numbers can be possibly formed?
A. 3 B. 1
C. 2 D. None

8. The greatest number that will divide 366, 513 and 324 leaving the same remainder in each case is
A. 21 B. 18
C. 27 D. 42

9. The sum of two numbers is 216 and their H.C.F. is 27. These numbers are
A. 60 and 90 B. 81 and 135
C. 64 and 128 D. 30 and 84

10. The L.C.M. of two numbers is 45 times their H.C.F. If the sum of the L.C.M. and the H.C.F. of these two numbers is 1150 and one of the numbers is 125, then the other number is
A. 256 B. 225
C. 250 D. 255

11. The H.C.F. and the L.C.M. of two numbers are 50 and 250 respectively. On dividing one of these numbers by 2, 50 is obtained as quotient. The numbers are
A. 100, 125 B. 80, 100
C. 125, 100 D. 200, 250

12. The largest three-digit number, which when successively divided by 6, 9 and 12, leaves 3 as remainder in each case, is
A. 575 B. 795
C. 975 D. 525

13. The greatest number that will divide 33, 64 and 80 leaving 3, 4 and 5 as remainders respectively, is
A. 10 B. 20
C. 15 D. 22

14. The H.C.F. of three numbers is 12. If the three numbers are in the ratio of 1 : 2 : 3, then the numbers are
A. 14, 28, 42 B. 12, 24, 36
C. 15, 30, 45 D. 24, 48, 72

15. The greatest four-digit number completely divisible by 2, 3, 4 and 5 is

A. 9960 B. 9690
C. 8990 D. 9980

16. Three bells ring respectively at an interval of 15 seconds, 20 seconds and 24 seconds. If they ring continuously for 12 minutes then how many times, during this period, will they ring together?
A. 2 times B. 6 times
C. 5 times D. 3 times

17. The smallest number, on being successively divided by 5, 6, 8, 9 and 12 leaves 1 as remainder in each case and is completely divisible by 13, will be
A. 4603 B. 6305
C. 4503 D. 3601

18. If in the process of finding H.C.F. of two numbers by continued division method, 49 is the last divisor and quotients obtained (from the beginning) are 17, 3 and 2 respectively, then the numbers are
A. 432 and 4929 B. 343 and 5829
C. 388 and 5830 D. 472 and 5930

19. A, B and C start running together in a particular direction from a particular point on a 12 kms long circular path. If the speeds of A, B and C are 3 kms/h, 7 kms/h and 13 kms/h respectively, then after how many hours will they meet together again?
A. 8 B. 6
C. 12 D. 10

20. Which of the following has most numbers of divisors?
A. 182 B. 176
C. 101 D. 99

ANSWERS

1	2	3	4	5	6	7	8	9	10
C	A	B	C	D	B	C	A	B	B
11	**12**	**13**	**14**	**15**	**16**	**17**	**18**	**19**	**20**
A	C	C	B	A	B	D	B	C	B

SOME SELECTED EXPLANATORY ANSWERS

1. L.C.M. of 6, 9 and 12

3	6, 9, 12
2	2, 3, 4
	1, 3, 2

$\therefore$ LCM $= 3 \times 2 \times 3 \times 2 = 36$.

$\because$ Largest 3-digit number = 999

36) 999 (27
72
279
252
× 27

$\therefore$ Largest 3-digit number which is exactly divisible by 6, 9 and 12

$= 999 - 27 = 972$

$\therefore$ The required number $= 972 + 1 = 973$

2. Let the numbers be $8x$ and $15x$

$$8x = 2 \times 2 \times 2 \times x$$
$$15x = 3 \times 5 \times x$$

$\therefore$ LCM of $8x$ and $15x = 2 \times 2 \times 2 \times x \times 3 \times 5 = 120x$

Now, 1st number × 2nd number = HCF × LCM

$\Rightarrow \quad 8x \times 15x = 4 \times 120x$

$\Rightarrow \quad 120x^2 = 4 \times 120x$

$\Rightarrow \quad x = 4$

$\therefore$ Numbers are $8 \times 4 = 32$ and $15 \times 4 = 60$

3. $226 - 1 = 225$ and $272 - 2 = 270$

Now, HCF of 225 and 270

225) 270 (1
225
45) 225 (5
225
×

$\therefore$ The required number is 45.

4. $1170 = 2 \times 5 \times 3 \times 3 \times 13$

$102 = 2 \times 3 \times 17$

$\therefore$ Greatest common divisor $= 2 \times 3 = 6$

5. It is clear from the given conditions of the problem that the smallest number will be 3 less than the LCM of 36, 45 and 50.

$\therefore$ LCM of 36, 45 and 50

$$\begin{array}{c|l} 3 & 36,\ 45,\ 50 \\ \hline 2 & 12,\ 15,\ 50 \\ \hline 3 & 6,\ 15,\ 25 \\ \hline 5 & 2,\ 5,\ 25 \\ \hline & 2,\ 1,\ 5 \end{array}$$

$\therefore$ LCM $= 3 \times 2 \times 3 \times 5 \times 2 \times 5 = 900$

$\therefore$ Required number $= 900 - 3 = 897$.

6. LCM of 10, 20, 30 and 40

$$\begin{array}{c|l} 2 & 10,\ 20,\ 30,\ 40 \\ \hline 5 & 5,\ 10,\ 15,\ 20 \\ \hline 2 & 1,\ 2,\ 3,\ 4 \\ \hline & 1,\ 1,\ 3,\ 2 \end{array}$$

$\therefore$ LCM $= 2 \times 2 \times 5 \times 3 \times 2$

But the number is a perfect square number

$\therefore$ Required number $= 2 \times 2 \times 5 \times 5 \times 3 \times 3 \times 2 \times 2 = 3600$.

7. Product of two numbers = their HCF $\times$ their LCM

$$2160 = 12 \times \text{LCM}$$

$$\therefore \quad \text{LCM} = \frac{2160}{12} = 180$$

Therefore such pairs of numbers in which product of numbers is 2160 and HCF is 12 will be only 2. *i.e.,* 12×180 and 36×60.

8. Difference between 366 and 513

$= 513 - 366 = 147$

and difference between 513 and 324

$= 513 - 324 = 189$

$\therefore$ HCF of 147 and 189

```
147 ) 189 ( 1
      147
      ×42 ) 147 ( 3
            126
            ×21 ) 42 ( 2
                  42
                   ×
```

$\therefore$ The required largest number is 21.

9. Let the numbers be x and y.

$\therefore x + y = 216 = 27 \times 8$

Since HCF of these two numbers is 27, hence, common factor of these two numbers is 27. Therefore these numbers will be of the form of 27×1, 27×2, 27×3, ... etc.

According to the condition of the problem sum of these numbers is 216.

$\therefore$ The numbers will be $27 \times 3 = 81$

and $27 \times 5 = 135$

10. LCM of the two numbers $= 45 \times$ HCF

and LCM + HCF = 1150

$\Rightarrow \quad 45 \times \text{HCF} + \text{HCF} = 1150$

$\Rightarrow \quad \text{HCF}(45 + 1) = 1150$

$$\Rightarrow \quad \text{HCF} = \frac{1150}{46} = 25$$

$\therefore \quad \text{LCM} = 45 \times 25 = 1125$

$\because$ 1st number $\times$ 2nd number = LCM $\times$ HCF

$\therefore$ $125 \times$ 2nd number $= 1125 \times 25$

$$\therefore \quad \text{2nd number} = \frac{1125 \times 25}{125} = 225.$$

11. According to the condition of the problem, 50 is obtained on dividing one of the numbers by 2

$\therefore$ One of the numbers $= 50 \times 2 = 100$

Now, 1st number $\times$ 2nd number = LCM $\times$ HCF

$\therefore \quad 100 \times$ 2nd number $= 250 \times 50$

$$\therefore \quad \text{2nd number} = \frac{250 \times 50}{100} = 125$$

Hence, numbers are 100 and 125.

12. LCM of 6, 9 and 12 = 36 and largest 3-digit number = 999

$\therefore$ HCF of 36 and 999

```
36 ) 999 ( 27
     72
     279
     252
      27
```

$\therefore$ Largest three-digit number completely divisible by 6, 9 and 12

$= 999 - 27 = 972$

Since 3 is left as remainder in each case,

$\therefore$ Required largest number of 3-digit

$= 972 + 3 = 975$.

13. $33 - 3 = 30$, $64 - 4 = 60$ and $80 - 5 = 75$

Now, HCF of 30, 60 and 75:

$$30 = 2 \times \underline{3 \times 5}$$
$$60 = 2 \times 2 \times \underline{3 \times 5}$$
$$75 = \underline{3 \times 5} \times 5$$

$\because$ Common factor $= 3 \times 5 = 15$

$\therefore$ Required largest number = 15.

14. Let the numbers be x, $2x$ and $3x$ respectively. Here, HCF of the three numbers is 12, therefore 12 is the largest common factor of these three numbers. Thus, it is clear that $x = 12$

$\therefore$ These numbers are 12, 24 and 36 respectively.

15. LCM of 2, 3, 4 and 5 = 60

Largest 4-digit number = 9999

Now, 60) 9999 (166
```
        60
       ----
       399
       360
      -----
     × 399
       360
      -----
        39
```

$\therefore$ Largest 4-digit number completely divisible by 2, 3, 4 and 5

$= 9999 - 39 = 9960$

$\therefore$ Required number = 9960

16. LCM of 15, 20 and 24

5	15, 20, 24
4	3, 4, 24
3	3, 1, 6
	1, 1, 2

LCM $= 5 \times 4 \times 3 \times 2 = 120$

$\because$ 12 minutes $= 12 \times 60 = 720$ seconds

$\therefore$ Number of times the bells will ring together during 12 minutes

$$= \frac{720}{120} = 6 \text{ times.}$$

17. LCM of 5, 6, 8, 9 and 12 = 360. Hence, the smallest number which when divided by 5, 6, 8, 9 and 12 leaves 1 as remainder in each case will be $360 + 1 = 361$. But 361 is not completely divisible by 13. Hence, on considering $360 \times 2 + 1$, $360 \times 3 + 1, \ldots, 360 \times n + 1$, we conclude that $360 \times 10 + 1 = 3601$ is the required number.

18. This question is based on finding HCF by continued division method. Now according to the condition of the problem,

Last divisor = 49

and Last quotient = 2

$\therefore$ dividend $= 49 \times 2 = 98$

Now, divisor = 98 and quotient = 3

and remainder = 49

$\therefore$ dividend $= 98 \times 3 + 49 = 343$

Now, divisor = 343

quotient = 17

and remainder = 98

$\therefore$ Dividend $= 343 \times 17 + 98 = 5829$

Therefore, these numbers are 343 and 5829.

19. A, B and C will take 4 hours, $\frac{12}{7}$ hours and $\frac{12}{13}$ hours respectively in completing one round on the circular path.

$\therefore$ LCM of $\frac{4}{1}, \frac{12}{7}$ and $\frac{12}{13}$

$$= \frac{\text{LCM of } 4, 12 \text{ and } 12}{\text{HCF of } 1, 7 \text{ and } 13}$$

$\because$ LCM of 4, 12 and 12 = 12 and HCF of 1, 7 and 13 = 1

$\therefore$ Required LCM $= \frac{12}{1} = 12$

Hence, they will meet together again after 12 hrs.

20.

Numbers		*Their divisors*
182	→	1, 2, 7, 13, 14, 26, 91 and 182
176	→	1, 2, 4, 8, 16, 22, 44, 88 and 176
101	→	1 and 101
99	→	1, 3, 9, 11, 33 and 99

Therefore, 176 has the most number of divisors.

3. RATIO & PROPORTION

Some Important Facts:

1. If a and b are two quantities, then
   (*a*) Duplicate ratio of $a : b = a^2 : b^2$
   (*b*) Sub-duplicate ratio of $a : b = \sqrt{a} : \sqrt{b}$
   (*c*) Triplicate ratio of $a : b = a^3 : b^3$
   (*d*) Sub-triplicate ratio $a : b = \sqrt[3]{a} : \sqrt[3]{b}$
   (*e*) Inverse or reciprocal ratio of $a : b = \frac{1}{a} : \frac{1}{b}$

2. If $a : b = c : d$, then
   (*a*) Third proportional (c) to 'a' and 'b' $= \frac{b^2}{a}$
   (*b*) Fourth proportional (d) $= \frac{bc}{a}$
   (*c*) Mean proportional between a and $b = \sqrt{ab}$
   (*d*) If $\frac{a}{b} = \frac{c}{d}$ then $\frac{a+b}{a-b} = \frac{c+d}{c-d}$
   (Componendo and dividendo)

3. (*a*) Comparision of ratios $(a : b) > (c : d) \Leftrightarrow \frac{a}{b} > \frac{c}{d}$
   (*b*) Compounded ratio of $(a : b), (c : d), (e : f) = \frac{ace}{bdf}$

4. If $A : B = x : y$ and $B : C = p : q$, then
   (*a*) $A : C = \frac{x \times p}{y \times q}$
   (*b*) $A : B : C = px : py : qy$

5. In what *ratio* the two kinds of tea must be mixed together one at ₹ x per kg and another at ₹ y per kg, so that the mixture may cost ₹ z per kg?

$$\text{Ratio} = \frac{z-y}{x-z}$$

6. A grey hound persues a hare as takes J_1 leaps for every J_2 leaps of the hare. If K_1 leaps of the hound are equal to K_2 leaps of the hare, then the Ratio of speeds of the hound and hare is

$$\frac{J_2 \times K_1}{J_1 \times K_2}$$

7. The incomes of two persons are in the ratio of $a : b$ and their expenditure are in the ratio of $x : y$. If the saving of each person is ₹ s, then income of each is ₹ $\frac{as(y-x)}{ay-bx}$ and ₹ $\frac{bs(y-x)}{ay-bx}$ respectively.

8. In a mixture of z litre, the ratio of milk and water is $x : y$. If another p litres of water is added to the mixture, the ratio of milk and water in the resulting mixture $= \frac{xz}{yz + p(x+y)}$

9. There are four members a, b, c and d, then formula for
   (*a*) What should be added to each of these numbers so that the remaining numbers may be proportional $= \frac{ad-bc}{(b+c)-(a+d)}$.
   (*b*) What should be subtracted from each of these numbers so that the remaining numbers may be proportional $= \frac{ad-bc}{(a+d)-(b+c)}$.

10. In a mixture the ratio of milk and water is $a : b$. If in this mixture another K litre of water is added, then the ratio of milk and water in the resulting mixture becomes $a : m$. Then the quantity of milk in the original mixture $= \frac{ak}{m-b}$ and quantity of water $= \frac{bk}{m-b}$.

SOLVED EXAMPLES

Example 1: The ratio between the three angles of a quadrilateral is 6 : 7 : 8 respectively. The value of the fourth angle of the quadrilateral is 108°. What is the difference between the largest and the smallest angles of the quadrilateral?

Solution: $6x + 7x + 8x = 360° - 108°$

$\Rightarrow \quad 21x = 252°$

$\Rightarrow \quad x = 12°$

$\therefore$ Required difference $= 108° - 6 \times 12°$

$= 108° - 72° = 36°.$

Example 2: Three-fifth of a number is equal to 70% of another number. What is the ratio between the first number and the second number respectively?

Solution: Let the numbers are x and y respectively.

$$\therefore \quad x \times \frac{3}{5} = y \times \frac{70}{100}$$

$$\Rightarrow \quad x \times \frac{3}{5} = y \times \frac{7}{10}$$

$$\Rightarrow \quad \frac{x}{y} = \frac{7}{10} \times \frac{5}{3} = 7 : 6.$$

Example 3: The respective ratio between the speeds of a car, a train and a bus is 5 : 9 : 4. The average speed of the car, the bus and the train is 72 km/hr together. What is the average speed of the car and the train together?

Solution: Let the speed of car, train and bus be $5x$, $9x$ and $4x$ km/hr respectively.

$\because \quad 5x + 9x + 4x = 72 \times 3$

$\therefore \quad x = 12$

$\therefore$ Average speed of car and train

$$= \frac{5x+9x}{2} = \frac{14 \times 12}{2} = 84 \text{ km/hr}$$

Example 4: The ratio between the present ages of Meena and Priya is 3 : 4 respectively. Ten years ago the ratio between their ages was 4 : 7 respectively. What will be Meena's age after 5 years?

Solution: Let the present age of Meena be $3x$ years

$\therefore$ The present age of Priya $= 4x$ years

$$\frac{3x-10}{4x-10} = \frac{4}{7}$$

$$21x - 70 = 16x - 40$$

$$x = \frac{70-40}{5} = 6$$

$\therefore$ Meena's age after 5 years $= 3 \times 6 + 5$

$= 23$ years.

MULTIPLE CHOICE QUESTIONS

1. An amount of rupees 4500 is to be distributed among Shrinath, Ramnath and Raghunath in the ratio of 3 : 7 : 5 respectively. If ₹ 500 is added to each of the share, the new ratio will become ......?

A. 7 : 10 : 13
B. 9 : 16 : 13
C. 2 : 4 : 3
D. 4 : 5 : 2

2. The total number of students studying in a school is 10396. The ratio of the total number of girls to the total number of boys studying in the school is 52 : 61 respectively. What is the total number of girls studying in the school?

A. 4874 B. 4784
C. 5216 D. 5612

3. In a box the numbers of one rupee, half rupee and quarter rupee are in the ratio 3 : 4 : 5 and the total value of the coins is ₹ 100. Find the number of each kind of coins respectively—

A. 48, 64, 80 B. 48, 60, 70
C. 55, 78, 90 D. 44, 68, 80

4. The ratio of the ages of two persons is 4 : 7 and the age of one of them is more than the other by 30 years. What is the sum of their ages in years?

A. 100 B. 110
C. 120 D. 130

5. The ratio of the amounts of A and B is 4 : 3 and the sum of their amount is ₹ 700. What amount in rupees should A give B to make the ratio 1 : 1?

A. 100 B. 200
C. 150 D. 50

6. The ratio of the volumes of water and glycerine in 240 c.c. glycerine mixed with water is 1 : 3. What additional volume of water should be mixed with it so that the ratio of the volumes of water and glycerine becomes 2 : 3?

A. 70 c.c. B. 80 c.c.
C. 60 c.c. D. 50 c.c.

7. If 15% of A is the same as 20% of B, then A : B is :

A. 9 : 11 B. 4 : 3
C. 3 : 4 D. 6 : 7

8. The fourth proportional to 1, 3 and the third proportional to 1 and 3 is :

A. 9 B. 81
C. 3 D. 27

9. The ratio of third proportional to 12 and 30 and the mean proportional to 9 and 25 is :

A. 5 : 1 B. 2 : 1
C. 9 : 14 D. 7 : 15

10. If $a + b : b + c : c + a = 6 : 7 : 8$ and $a + b + c = 14$ then the value of c is :

A. 14 B. 7
C. 8 D. 6

11. ₹ 120 are divided among P, Q, R such that P's share is ₹ 20 more than Q's and ₹ 20 less than R's share. What is Q's share?

A. ₹ 20 B. ₹ 15
C. ₹ 25 D. ₹ 10

12. If four numbers are in the ratio 5 : 7 : 11 : 13 be such that the sum of their cubes is 3996, find the average of four numbers.

A. 13 B. 11
C. 12 D. 9

13. If 2A = 3B = 4C then A : B : C is :

A. 2 : 3 : 4
B. 4 : 3 : 2
C. 6 : 4 : 3
D. 3 : 4 : 6

14. If $\frac{1}{5} : \frac{1}{x} = \frac{1}{x} : \frac{1}{1.25}$, then the value of x is :

A. 1.25 B. 1.5
C. 2.5 D. 2.25

15. A fraction bears the same ratio to $\frac{1}{27}$ as $\frac{3}{7}$ does to $\frac{5}{9}$. The fraction is :

A. $\frac{7}{45}$ B. $\frac{1}{35}$
C. $\frac{45}{7}$ D. $\frac{5}{21}$

16. The fourth proportional to 0.2, 0.12 and 0.3 is:

A. 0.13 B. 0.15
C. 0.18 D. 0.8

17. A bag contains 25 paise, 10 paise and 5 paise coins in the ratio 1 : 2 : 3. If their total value is ₹ 30, the number of 5 paise coins is :

A. 50 B. 100
C. 150 D. 200

18. In a class, the number of boys is more than the number of girls by 12% of the total strength. The ratio of boys to girls is :

A. 11 : 14 B. 14 : 11
C. 25 : 28 D. 28 : 25

19. A right cylinder and a right circular cone have the same radius and the same volume. The ratio of the height of the cylinder to that of the cone is :

A. 3 : 5 B. 2 : 5
C. 3 : 1 D. 1 : 3

20. The speeds of three cars are in the ratio 3 : 4 : 5. The ratio between times taken by them to travel the same distance is :

A. 3 : 4 : 5
B. 5 : 4 : 3
C. 12 : 15 : 20
D. 20 : 15 : 12

21. A and B are two alloys of gold and copper prepared by mixing metals in proportions 7 : 2 and 7 : 11 respectively. If equal quantities of the alloys are melted to form a third alloy C, the proportion of gold and copper in C will be :

A. 5 : 9 B. 5 : 7
C. 7 : 5 D. 9 : 5

22. If $a : b = c : d$, then $\frac{ma + nc}{mb + nd}$ is equal to :

A. $m : n$ B. $na : mb$
C. $a : b$ D. $md : nc$

23. Vijay got thrice as many marks in Maths as in English. The proportion of his marks in Maths and History is 4 : 3. If his total marks in Maths, English and History are 250, what are his marks in English?

A. 120 B. 90
C. 40 D. 80

24. A mixture contains milk and water in the ratio 5 : 1. On adding 5 litres of water, the ratio of milk and water becomes 5 : 2. The quantity of milk in the mixture is:

A. 16 litres B. 25 litres
C. 32.5 litres D. 22.75 litres

25. Two equal glasses are respectively $\frac{1}{3}$ and $\frac{1}{4}$ full of milk. They are then filled up with water and the contents mixed in a tumbler. The ratio of milk and water in the tumbler is:

A. 7 : 5 B. 7 : 17
C. 3 : 7 D. 11 : 23

26. The ratio between two numbers is 3 : 4 and their L.C.M. is 180. The first number is :

A. 15 B. 20
C. 45 D. 60

27. A man has some hens and cows. If the number of heads be 48 and number of feet equals 140, the number of hens will be :

A. 22 B. 23
C. 24 D. 26

28. The ratio between the ages of Kamal and Savita is 6 : 5 and the sum of their ages is 44 years. The ratio of their ages after 8 years will be :

A. 5 : 6 B. 7 : 8
C. 8 : 7 D. 14 : 13

29. One year ago the ratio between Laxmi's and Gopi's salary was 3 : 4. The ratios of their individual salaries between last year's and this year's salaries are 4 : 5 and 2 : 3 respectively. At present the total of their salary is ₹ 4160. The salary of Laxmi now, is :

A. ₹ 1040 B. ₹ 1600
C. ₹ 2560 D. ₹ 3120

30. If 15% of x = 20% of y, then $x : y$ is :

A. 3 : 4 B. 4 : 3
C. 17 : 16 D. 16 : 17

31. If $\frac{x}{5} = \frac{y}{8}$, then $(x + 5) : (y + 8)$ is equal to :

A. 3 : 5 B. 13 : 8
C. 8 : 5 D. 5 : 8

32. The salaries of A, B, C are in the ratio 2 : 3 : 5. If the increments of 15%, 10% and 20% are allowed respectively in their salaries, then what will be the new ratio of their salaries?

A. 3 : 3 : 10
B. 10 : 11 : 20
C. 23 : 33 : 60
D. Cannot be determined

33. A sum of ₹ 1300 is divided amongst P, Q, R and S such that $\frac{\text{P's share}}{\text{Q's share}} = \frac{\text{Q's share}}{\text{R's share}} = \frac{\text{R's share}}{\text{S's share}} = \frac{2}{3}$.

Then, P's share is :

A. ₹ 140 B. ₹ 160
C. ₹ 240 D. ₹ 320

34. The ratio of the number of boys and girls in a college is 7 : 8. If the percentage increase in the number of boys and girls be 20% and 10% respectively, what will be the new ratio?

A. 8 : 9

B. 17 : 18

C. 21 : 22

D. Cannot be determined

35. The third proportional to 0.36 and 0.48 is :

A. 0.64 B. 0.1728

C. 0.42 D. 0.94

36. An alloy is to contain copper and zinc in the ratio 9 : 4. The zinc required to be melted with 24 kg of copper is :

A. $10\frac{2}{3}$ kg B. $10\frac{1}{3}$ kg

C. $9\frac{2}{3}$ kg D. 9 kg

37. 15 litres of mixture contains 20% alcohol and the rest water. If 3 litres of water be mixed with it, the percentage of alcohol in the new mixture would be :

A. 15% B. $16\frac{2}{3}\%$

C. 17% D. $18\frac{1}{2}\%$

38. The sides of a triangle are in the ratio $\frac{1}{2}:\frac{1}{3}:\frac{1}{4}$ and its perimeter is 104 cm. The length of the longest side is :

A. 52 cm B. 48 cm

C. 32 cm D. 26 cm

39. x varies inversely as square of y. Given that $y = 2$ for $x = 1$. The value of x for $y = 6$ will be equal to :

A. 3 B. 9

C. $\frac{1}{3}$ D. $\frac{1}{9}$

40. Which of the following ratios is greatest?

A. 7 : 15 B. 15 : 23

C. 17 : 25 D. 21 : 29

ANSWERS

1	2	3	4	5	6	7	8	9	10
E	B	A	B	D	C	B	D	A	D
11	**12**	**13**	**14**	**15**	**16**	**17**	**18**	**19**	**20**
A	D	C	C	B	C	C	B	D	D
21	**22**	**23**	**24**	**25**	**26**	**27**	**28**	**29**	**30**
C	C	C	B	B	C	D	C	B	B
31	**32**	**33**	**34**	**35**	**36**	**37**	**38**	**39**	**40**
D	C	B	C	A	A	B	B	D	D

SOME SELECTED EXPLANATORY ANSWERS

2. From question,

The total number of students in the school = 10396

and ratio of number of girls : boys = 52 : 61

∴ The total number of girls in that school

$$= \frac{10396 \times 52}{(52+61)}$$

$$= \frac{10396 \times 52}{113} = 92 \times 52 = 4784.$$

3. $$3x + 4x \times \frac{1}{2} + 5x \times \frac{1}{4} = 100$$

$$12x + 8x + 5x = 400$$

$$x = 16$$

Number of 1 rupee = 48

Number of 1/2 rupee = 64

Number of quarter rupee = 5 × 16 = 80

4. ∵ $7x - 4x = 30,$

$x = 10$

$\therefore$ Sum of their ages = $(4 + 7) \times 10$

$= 11 \times 10 = 110$ years

5. $\because$ $4x + 3x = 700$

$\Rightarrow$ $x = 100$

400 300

Ⓐ Ⓑ

$\because$ $\dfrac{400 - x}{300 + x} = \dfrac{1}{1}$

$\Rightarrow$ $400 - x = 300 + x$

$\therefore$ $x = 50$

6. Quantity of water in 240 cc glycerine and water

$= \dfrac{1}{4} \times 240 \text{ cc} = 60 \text{ cc}$

Quantity of glycerine = $(240 - 60)$ cc

$= 180$ cc

$\because$ $\dfrac{60 + x}{180} = \dfrac{2}{3}$

$\Rightarrow$ $x = 60$ cc.

8. First we find the third proportional to 1 and 3. Let the third proportional to 1 and 3 is

$\Rightarrow$ $1 : 3 :: 3 : x$

$\Rightarrow$ $x = 3 \times 3$

$\Rightarrow$ $x = 9$

The fourth proportional to 1, 3 and the third proportional to 1 and 3

= The fourth proportional to 1, 3 and 9. Let the fourth proportional to 1, 3 and 9 is y, then $1 : 3 :: 9 : y$

$\Rightarrow$ $1 \times y = 3 \times 9$

$\Rightarrow$ $y = 27$

$\therefore$ Required answer is 27.

9. Let the third proportional to 12 and 30 be y, then $12 : 30 :: 30 : y$

$\Rightarrow$ $12y = 30 \times 30$

$y = \dfrac{30 \times 30}{12} = 75$

Mean proportional to 9 and 25

$= \sqrt{9 \times 25} = 3 \times 5 = 15$

$\therefore$ The required ratio is $75 : 15 = 5 : 1$

10. Given

$$\left.\begin{array}{l} a + b = 6x \\ b + c = 7x \text{ and } c + a = 8x \end{array}\right\} \quad ...(1)$$

and $a + b + c = 14$ ...(2)

adding equations in (1) we get

$2(a + b + c) = 21x$

using (2) we get

$2 \times 14 = 21x$

$\Rightarrow$ $x = \dfrac{2 \times 14}{21}$

$= \dfrac{2 \times 2}{3} = \dfrac{4}{3}$

$a + b = 6x = 6 \times \dfrac{4}{3} = 8.$

Using $a + b + c = 14$ and $a + b = 8$

We get $c = 6$.

11. Given P's share = Q's share + ₹ 20

P's share = R's share − ₹ 20

let Q's share be y.

then P's share = $y + 20$

$y + 20$ = R's share − ₹ 20

$\Rightarrow$ R's share = $y + 40$

P's share + Q's share + R's share = 120

$y + 20 + y + y + 40 = 120$

$3y + 60 = 120$

$3y = 120 - 60 = 60$

$y = 20$

$\therefore$ Q's share = y = ₹ 20.

12. Let the four numbers be $5x$, $7x$, $11x$ and $13x$.

Given $(5x)^3 + (7x)^3 + (11x)^3 + (13x)^3 = 3996.$

$125x^3 + 343x^3 + 1331x^3 + 2197 . x^3 = 3996$

$\Rightarrow$ $3996x^3 = 3996$

$\Rightarrow$ $x^3 = 1 \Rightarrow x = 1$

$\therefore$ The four numbers are 5, 7, 11 and 13.

Average of these four numbers

$= \dfrac{5 + 7 + 11 + 13}{4} = \dfrac{36}{4} = 9.$

13. Let $2A = 3B = 4C = x$.

Then, $A = \dfrac{x}{2}$, $B = \dfrac{x}{3}$ and $C = \dfrac{x}{4}$.

$\therefore$ A : B : C = $\frac{x}{2}:\frac{x}{3}:\frac{x}{4}$ = 6 : 4 : 3.

Hence, A : B : C = 6 : 4 : 3.

14. $$\frac{1}{x}\times\frac{1}{x} = \frac{1}{5}\times\frac{1}{1.25}$$

or, $$\frac{1}{x^2} = \frac{4}{25}$$

or, $$x^2 = \frac{25}{4}$$

$\therefore$ $$x = \frac{5}{2} = 2.5.$$

15. $x : \frac{1}{27} = \frac{3}{7}:\frac{5}{9} \Rightarrow \frac{5}{9}x = \frac{1}{27}\times\frac{3}{7}.$

$\therefore$ $\frac{5}{9}x = \frac{1}{63}$ or $x = \left(\frac{1}{63}\times\frac{9}{5}\right) = \frac{1}{35}.$

16. Let 0.2 : 0.12 :: 0.3 : x.
Then, $0.2x = 0.12 \times 0.3$ or

$$x = \frac{0.12\times 0.3}{0.2} = 0.18.$$

17. Ratio of their values = $\frac{1}{4}:\frac{2}{10}:\frac{3}{20}$

= 5 : 4 : 3.

$\therefore$ Value of 5-paise coins = ₹ $\left(30\times\frac{3}{12}\right)$

= ₹ 7.50.

$\therefore$ Number of 5-paise coins = $\frac{750}{5}$ = 150.

19. Let the heights of the cylinder and cone be h and H respectively. Then, $\pi r^2 h = \frac{1}{3}\pi r^2$ H or

$\frac{h}{H} = \frac{1}{3}.$

So, their heights are in the ratio 1 : 3.

20. Ratio of time taken = $\frac{1}{3}:\frac{1}{4}:\frac{1}{5}$ = 20 : 15 : 12.

21. Gold in C = $\left(\frac{7}{9}+\frac{7}{18}\right) = \frac{21}{18} = \frac{7}{6}.$

Copper in C = $\left(\frac{2}{9}+\frac{11}{18}\right) = \frac{15}{18} = \frac{5}{6}.$

$\therefore$ Gold : Copper = $\frac{7}{6}:\frac{5}{6}$ = 7 : 5.

22. Let $\frac{a}{b} = \frac{c}{d} = k$. Then, $a = bk$ and $c = dk$.

$\therefore$ $\frac{ma+nc}{mb+nd} = \frac{mbk+ndk}{mb+nd} = k\left(\frac{mb+nd}{mb+nd}\right)$

$= k = \frac{a}{b}.$

23. M = 3E and $\frac{M}{H} = \frac{4}{3}.$

$\therefore$ H = $\frac{3}{4}$M = $\frac{3}{4}\times$3E = $\frac{9}{4}$E.

Now, M + E + H = 250

$\Rightarrow$ 3E + E + $\frac{9}{4}$E = 250

$\therefore$ 25E = 1000 or E = 40.

24. Let quantity of milk and water be $5x$ and x litres.

Then, $\frac{5x}{x+5} = \frac{5}{2}$ or, $10x = 5x + 25$

or, $x = 5$.

$\therefore$ Quantity of milk = $5x$ = 25 litres.

26. Let the numbers be $3x$ and $4x$.
Then, their L.C.M. = $12x$.
$\therefore$ $12x = 180$ or $x = 15$.
Hence, the first number = 45.

27. Let the number of hens = x and number of cows = y.
Then, $x + y = 48$ and $2x + 4y = 140$.
Solving these equations, we get, $2y = 44$
or $y = 22$.
So, $x = (48 - 22) = 26$.
$\therefore$ Number of hens = 26.

28. Let their ages be $6x$ and $5x$ years.
$\therefore$ $6x + 5x = 44$ or, $x = 4$.

So, their present ages are 24 years and 20 years.

Ratio of their ages after 8 years = 32 : 28
= 8 : 7.

29. Let the salaries of Laxmi and Gopi one year before be x_1, y_1 respectively and now x_2, y_2 respectively. Then,

$$\frac{x_1}{y_1} = \frac{3}{4}, \frac{x_1}{x_2} = \frac{4}{5}, \frac{y_1}{y_2} = \frac{2}{3} \text{ and } x_2 + y_2 = 4160.$$

Solving these equations, we get $x_2 = 1600$.

30. 15% of x = 20% of y

$$\Rightarrow \frac{15x}{100} = \frac{20y}{100}$$

$$\Rightarrow \frac{x}{y} = \left(\frac{20}{100} \times \frac{100}{15}\right) = \frac{4}{3}$$

$$\Rightarrow x : y = 4 : 3.$$

31. Let $\frac{x}{5} = \frac{y}{8} = k$. Then, $x = 5k$ and $y = 8k$.

$$\therefore \frac{x+5}{y+8} = \frac{5k+5}{8k+8} = \frac{5(k+1)}{8(k+1)} = \frac{5}{8}$$

$$\Rightarrow (x + 5) : (y + 8) = 5 : 8.$$

32. Let A = $2k$, B = $3k$ and C = $5k$

$$\text{A's new salary} = \frac{115}{100} \text{ of } 2k$$

$$= \left(\frac{115}{100} \times 2k\right) = \frac{23}{10}k$$

$$\text{B's new salary} = \frac{110}{100} \text{ of } 3k$$

$$= \left(\frac{110}{100} \times 3k\right) = \frac{33}{10}k$$

$$\text{C's new salary} = \frac{120}{100} \text{ of } 5k$$

$$= \left(\frac{120}{100} \times 5k\right) = 6k.$$

$$\therefore \text{ New ratio} = \frac{23k}{10} : \frac{33k}{10} : 6k = 23 : 33 : 60.$$

34. Originally, let the number of boys and girls in the college be $7x$ and $8x$ respectively. Their increased number is (120% of $7x$) and (110% of $8x$)

i.e., $\left(\frac{120}{100} \times 7x\right)$ and $\left(\frac{110}{100} \times 8x\right)$

i.e. $\frac{42x}{5}$ and $\frac{44x}{5}$.

$$\therefore \text{ Required ratio} = \frac{42x}{5} : \frac{44x}{5} = 21 : 22.$$

35. Let the third proportional to 0.36 and 0.48 be x.

Then, 0.36 : 0.48 :: 0.48 : x

$$\Rightarrow x = \left(\frac{0.48 \times 0.48}{0.36}\right) = 0.64.$$

36. Let the required quantity of copper be x kg.

Then, 9 : 4 :: 24 : x $\Rightarrow$ $9x = 4 \times 24$

$$\Rightarrow x = \frac{4 \times 24}{9} = 10\frac{2}{3}.$$

Hence, the required quantity of copper is $10\frac{2}{3}$ kg.

37. Alcohol in 15 litres of mixture = 20% of 15 litres = $\left(\frac{20}{100} \times 15\right)$ litres = 3 litres.

Water in it = (15 – 3) litres = 12 litres.

New quantity of mixture = (15 + 3) litres = 18 litres.

Quantity of alcohol in it = 3 litres.

Percentage of alcohol in new mixture

$$= \left(\frac{3}{18} \times 100\right)\% = 16\frac{2}{3}\%.$$

38. Ratio of sides = $\frac{1}{2} : \frac{1}{3} : \frac{1}{4}$ = 6 : 4 : 3.

$$\text{Largest side} = \left(104 \times \frac{6}{13}\right) \text{cm} = 48 \text{ cm}.$$

39. Given $x = \frac{k}{y^2}$, where k is a constant.

Now, $y = 2$ and $x = 1$ gives $k = 4$.

$\therefore \; x = \frac{4}{y^2} \quad \Rightarrow \quad x = \frac{4}{6^2}$,

when $y = 6 \quad \Rightarrow \quad x = \frac{4}{36} = \frac{1}{9}$.

40. $\frac{7}{15} = 0.466$, $\frac{15}{23} = 0.652$,

$\frac{17}{25} = 0.68$ and $\frac{21}{29} = 0.724$.

Clearly, 0.724 is greatest and hence, 21 : 29 is greatest.

4. AGE AND AVERAGE

IMPORTANT FACTS

1. The present age of the father is x times the age of his son. T years hence, the father's age become y times the age of his son. Then the present ages of the father and his son are:

   Present age of the son $= \frac{(y-1)T}{x-y}$ years and

   age of the father $= \frac{(y-1)T \times x}{x-y}$ years.

2. T years ago, the father's age was x times that of his son and at present the father's age is y times the age of his son. Then their present ages are:

   Son's age $= \frac{T(x-1)}{x-y}$ years;

   Father's age $= \frac{T(x-1)}{x-y} \times y$ years.

3. Average Speed $= \frac{\text{Total travelled distance}}{\text{Total taken time}}$

4. If equal distances are travelled at the rate X and Y, then Average Speed $= \frac{2XY}{X+y}$

5. When a person leaves a group and another person joins the group in the place of person left, then

   I. In the case of increasing of average age, Age of the newcomer = Age of person left + no. of persons in the group X increase in average age.

   II. In the case of decreasing of average age, Age of the newcomer = Age of person left – no. of persons in the group X decrease in average age.

6. When a person joins a group without replacing any previous person from that group, then

   I. In the case of increasing of average age, Age of the newcomer = Previous of the age + no. of all persons (including newcomer) × increaser in average age.

   II. In the case of decreasing of average age, Age of the newcomer = Previous average age – no. of all persons (including new comer) × decrease in average age.

7. When a person leaves the group but nobody joins this group, then

   I. In the case of increasing of average age, Age of man left = Previous Average of the age – no. of present persons × decrease in the average age.

   II. In the case of decreasing of average age, Age of man left = Previous Average age + no. of present persons × increase in average age.

8. Average related to Natural Numbers

   I. Average of consecutive natural numbers till n $= \frac{(n+1)}{2}$

   II. Average of squares of numbers till n $= \frac{(n+1)(2n+1)}{6}$

   III. Average of cubes of consecutive natural numbers till $n = \frac{n(n+1)^2}{4}$

9. Average related to Even Numbers

   I. Average of n = consecutive even numbers $= n + 1$

II. Average of consecutive even number till $n = (n/2 + 1)$

III. Average of squares of n consecutive even numbers $= \frac{2(n+1)(2n+1)}{3}$

IV. Average of squares of consecutive even numbers till $n = \frac{(n+1)(2n+1)}{3}$

10. Average related to Odd Numbers

I. Average of n consecutive odd numbers $= n$

II. Average of consecutive odd numbers till $n = \frac{n(n+1)}{3}$

III. Average of squares of consecutive odd numbers till $n = \frac{n(n+1)}{3}$

SOLVED EXAMPLES

Example 1: Ankur's present age is 12 years more than Raman's age 5 years ago. Presently Raman is 24 years older than Raju's present age who is 12 years younger than Amit. If Amit's present age is 42 years, what is Ankur's age 3 years ago?

Solution: Amit's present age = 42 years

Raju's present age = 42 – 12 = 30 years

Raman's present age = 30 + 24 = 54 years

Ankur's present age = 54 – 5 + 12 = 61 years

∴ Ankur's age 3 years ago = 58 years

Example 2: Present ages of Leela and Shivani are in the ratio of 4 : 5 respectively. Three years hence this ratio becomes 5 : 6. What is the difference between their present ages?

Solution: Let Leela's and Shivani's present ages be $4x$ and $5x$ years respectively.

After 3 years,

$$\frac{4x+3}{5x+3} = \frac{5}{6}$$

$\Rightarrow$ $25x + 15 = 24x + 18$

$\Rightarrow$ $25x - 24x = 18 - 15 = 3$

$\therefore$ $x = 3$ = Required difference

Example 3: Radha's present age is three years less than twice her age 12 ages ago. Also the respective ratio between Raj's present age Radha's present age is 4 : 9. What will be Raj's age after 5 years?

Solution: Let the present age of Radha be x years. As per question,

$\because$ $x = (x - 12) \times 2 - 3$

$\Rightarrow$ $x = 2x - 27$

$\therefore$ $x = 27$

$\because$ Present age of Raj

$$= \frac{4}{9} \times 27 = 12 \text{ years}$$

∴ Raj's age after 5 years = 12 + 5 = 17 years

Example 4: If $12a + 12b = 45$, what is the average of a and b?

Solution: $\because$ $12a + 12b = 45$

$\Rightarrow$ $12(a + b) = 45$

$\therefore$ $\frac{a+b}{2} = \frac{45}{12 \times 2} = 1.875.$

Example 5: The sum of five numbers is 555. The average of first two numbers is 75 and the third number is 115. What is the average of last two numbers?

Solution: Average of last two numbers

$$= \frac{555 - 2 \times 75 - 115}{2}$$

$$= \frac{555 - 150 - 115}{2} = \frac{290}{2} = 145.$$

Example 6: The average marks of nine students in a group is 63. Three of them scored 78, 69 and 48 marks. What are the average marks of remaining six students?

Solution: The average marks of remaining 6 students

$$= \frac{9 \times 63 - (78 + 69 + 48)}{6}$$

$$= \frac{567 - 195}{6} = 62.$$

MULTIPLE CHOICE QUESTIONS

1. The sum of 8 consecutive odd numbers is 656. Also average of four consecutive even number is 87. What is the sum of the smallest odd number and second largest even number?
A. 165
B. 175
C. 163
D. Cannot be determined

2. The ages of Meena, Tina and Seema are in the ratio of 6 : 4 : 7 respectively. If the sum of their ages is 34 years, what is Seema's age?
A. 12 years
B. 10 years
C. 18 years
D. None of these

3. The average of 4 positive integers is 52.5. The highest integer is 76 and the lowest integer is 34. The difference between the remaining two integers is 4. Which of the following integers is higher of the remaining two integers?
A. 52
B. 54
C. 48
D. Cannot be determined

4. The present age of Deepa is 3 times the present age of his son. Five years hence the ratio of their ages will be 34 : 13 respectively. What is the present age of Deepa?
A. 63 years B. 68 years
C. 58 years D. 60 years

5. The average of 5 consecutive even numbers A, B, C, D and E is 66. What is the product of B and E?
A. 4352
B. 4340
C. 4620
D. None of these

6. The present age of father is 34 years more than that of his son. Twelve years ago father's age was 18 times the age of his son. What is the present age of the son in years?
A. 16 B. 14
C. 12 D. 18

7. A father is older than his first son by 30 years, the first son is older than the second son by 10 years.
If the sum of their ages by 95 years, find the age of father—
A. 65 years B. 55 years
C. 45 years D. 50 years

8. In 10 years, Alok will be twice as old as Babul was 10 years ago. If Alok is now 9 years older than Babul, the present age of Babul is :
A. 19 years B. 29 years
C. 39 years D. 49 years

9. The difference between the ages of two persons is 10 years. 15 years ago, the elder one was twice as old as the younger one. The present age of the elder person is :
A. 25 years B. 35 years
C. 45 years D. 55 years

10. Ratio of Anshu's age to Jolly's age is equal to 4 : 3. Anshu will be 26 years old after 6 years. How old is Jolly now?
A. 12 years B. 15 years
C. $19\frac{1}{2}$ years D. 21 years

11. The ratio between the ages of Asha and Bhushan at present is 2 : 3. Five years hence the ratio of their ages will be 3 : 4. What is the present age of Asha?
A. 10 years
B. 15 years
C. 25 years
D. data inadequate

12. Three years ago the average age of A and B was 18 years. With C joining them, the average becomes 22 years. How old is C now?
A. 24 years B. 27 years
C. 28 years D. 30 years

13. Ten years ago A was half of B in age. If the ratio of their present ages is 3 : 4, what will be the total of their present ages?

A. 8 years B. 20 years
C. 35 years D. 45 years

14. Out of three numbers, the first is twice the second and is half of the third. If the average of the three numbers is 56, the three numbers in order are :

A. 48, 96, 24 B. 48, 24, 96
C. 96, 24, 48 D. 96, 48, 24

15. The average of 50 numbers is 38. If two numbers, namely 45 and 55 are discarded, the average of the remaining numbers is :

A. 36.5 B. 37.0
C. 37.5 D. 37.52

16. The average temperature of the first three days is 27° C and that of the next three is 29° C. If the average of the whole week is 28.5° C, the temperature of the last day of the week is:

A. 10.5° C B. 21° C
C. 31.5° C D. 42° C

17. The average of an adult class is 40 years. 12 new students with an average age of 32 years join the class, thereby decreasing the average by 4 years. The original strength of the class was :

A. 10 B. 11
C. 12 D. 15

18. The average weight of 8 persons is increased by 2.5 kg when one of them whose weight is 56 kg is replaced by a new man. The weight of the new man is :

A. 66 kg B. 75 kg
C. 76 kg D. 86 kg

19. In a TV factory, an average of 60 TVs are produced per day for the first 25 days of the month. A few workers fell ill for the next five days, reducing the daily average for the month to 58 sets per day. The average production per day for the last 5 days is :

A. 45 B. 48
C. 52 D. 58

20. The average expenditure of a man for the first five months is ₹ 120 and for the next seven months it is ₹ 130. If he saves ₹ 290 in that years, his monthly average income is :

A. ₹ 140 B. ₹ 150
C. ₹ 160 D. ₹ 170

21. The average age of 24 students in a class is 10. If the teacher's age is included, the average increases by one. The age of the teacher is :

A. 25 years B. 30 years
C. 35 years D. 40 years

22. A batsman has a certain average runs for 11 innings. In the 12th inning he made a score of 90 runs and thereby decreased his average by 5. His average after 12th inning is :

A. 127 B. 145
C. 150 D. 217

23. The average weight of three men A, B and C is 84 kg. Another man D joins the group and the average now becomes 80 kg. If another man E, whose weight is 3 kg more than that of D, replaces A, then the average weight of B, C, D and E becomes 79 kg. The weight of A is :

A. 70 kg B. 72 kg
C. 75 kg D. 80 kg

24. A man whose bowling average is 12.4 takes 5 wickets for 26 runs and thereby decreases his average by 0.4. The number of wickets, taken by him, before his last match, is :

A. 85 B. 78
C. 72 D. 64

25. The present ages of three persons are in proportions 4 : 7 : 9. Eight years ago, the sum of their ages was 56. Find their present ages (in years).

A. 8, 20, 28
B. 16, 28, 36
C. 20, 35, 45
D. Cannot be determined

26. A is two years older than B who is twice as old as C. If the total of the ages of A, B and C be 27, then how old is B?

A. 7 B. 8
C. 9 D. 10

27. A person's present age is two-fifth of the age of his mother. After 8 years, he will be one-half of the age of his mother. How old is the mother at present?

A. 32 years B. 36 years
C. 40 years D. 48 years

28. Quasab is as much younger than Rahim as he is older than Tanveer. If the sum of the ages of Rahim and Tanveer is 50 years, what is definitely the difference between Rahim's and Quasab's age?

A. 1 year
B. 2 years
C. 25 years
D. Can not be determined

29. A father said to his son, "I was as old as you are at present at the time of your birth." If the father's age is 38 years now, the son's age five years back was :

A. 14 years B. 19 years
C. 33 years D. 38 years

30. Asha's father was 38 years of age when she was born while her mother was 36 years old when her brother four years younger to her was born. What is the difference between the ages of her parents?

A. 2 years B. 4 years
C. 6 years D. 8 years

31. A student was asked to find the arithmetic mean of the numbers 3, 11, 7, 9, 15, 13, 8, 19, 17, 21, 14 and x. He found the mean to be 12. What should be the number in place of x?

A. 3 B. 7
C. 17 D. 31

32. If a, b, c, d, e are five consecutive odd numbers, their average is :

A. $5(a + 4)$

B. $\frac{abcde}{5}$

C. $5(a + b + c + d + e)$

D. None of these

33. Of the four numbers, the first is twice the second, the second is one-third of the third and the third is 5 times the fourth. The average of the numbers is 24.75. The largest of these numbers is :

A. 9 B. 25
C. 30 D. 45

34. Of the three numbers, the average of the first and the second is greater than the average of the second and the third by 15. What is the difference between the first and the third of the three numbers?

A. 15 B. 45
C. 60 D. None of these

35. The average temperature of the town in the first four days of a month was 58 degrees. The average for the second, third, fourth and fifth days was 60 degrees. If the temperatures of the first and fifth days were in the ratio 7 : 8, then what is the temperature on the fifth day?

A. 64 degrees
B. 62 degrees
C. 56 degrees
D. 46 degrees

36. The captain of a cricket team of 11 members is 26 years old and the wicket keeper is 3 years older. If the ages of these two are excluded, the average age of the remaining players is one years less than the average age of the whole team. What is the average age of the team?

A. 23 years B. 24 years
C. 25 years D. 32 years

37. A cricketer has a certain average for 10 innings. In the eleventh inning, he scored 108 runs, thereby increasing his average by 6 runs. His new average is :

A. 48 runs B. 52 runs
C. 55 runs D. 60 runs

38. The average weight of 3 men A, B and C is 84 kg. Another man D joins the group and the average now becomes 80 kg. If another man E, whose weight is 3 kg more than that of D, replaces A, then the average weight B, C, D and E becomes 79 kg. The weight of A is :

A. 70 kg B. 72 kg
C. 75 kg D. 80 kg

39. The average age of husband, wife and their child 3 years ago was 27 years and that of wife and the child 5 years ago was 20 years. The present age of the husband is :

A. 35 years B. 40 years
C. 50 years D. 36 years

40. In an examination, a pupil's average marks were 63 per paper. If he had obtained 20 more marks for his Geography paper and 2 more marks for his History paper, his average per paper would have been 65. How many papers were there in the examination?

A. 8 B. 9
C. 10 D. 11

ANSWERS

1	2	3	4	5	6	7	8	9	10
C	D	A	A	D	B	B	C	B	B
11	**12**	**13**	**14**	**15**	**16**	**17**	**18**	**19**	**20**
A	A	C	B	C	C	C	C	B	B
21	**22**	**23**	**24**	**25**	**26**	**27**	**28**	**29**	**30**
C	B	C	A	B	D	C	D	A	C
31	**32**	**33**	**34**	**35**	**36**	**37**	**38**	**39**	**40**
B	D	D	D	A	A	A	C	B	D

SOME SELECTED EXPLANATORY ANSWERS

1. Let the smallest odd and smallest even numbers are x and y respectively. Then,

$\because\ x + (x + 2) + (x + 4) + (x + 6) + (x + 8) + (x + 10) + (x + 12) + (x + 14) = 656$

$\Rightarrow \quad 8x + 56 = 656$

$\therefore \quad x = \dfrac{656-56}{8} = 75$

$\because\ y + (y + 2) + (y + 4) + (y + 6) = 4 \times 87$

$\Rightarrow \quad 4y + 12 = 348$

$y = \dfrac{348-12}{4} = 84$

$\therefore$ Reqd. sum of the smallest odd number and second largest even number

$= x + (y + 4) = 75 + (84 + 4) = 163$

2. Seema's age $= \dfrac{7 \times 34}{(6+4+7)} = 14$ years.

3. Let the 4 positive integers, kept in descending order be a, b, c and d respectively. Then from question,

$\because \quad a + b + c + d = 4 \times 52.5 = 210$

$\Rightarrow 76 + (b + c) + 34 = 210$

$\Rightarrow \quad (b + c) = 100 \quad ...(i)$

Again from question,

$b - c = 4 \quad ...(ii)$

Solving (*i*) and (*ii*), we get

$b = 52$

and $c = 48$

Hence, higher integer $= b = 52$

4. Let the present age of Deepa's son $= x$ years.

Then from question,

Deepa's present age $= 3x$ years

$\because \quad \dfrac{3x+5}{x+5} = \dfrac{34}{13}$

$\Rightarrow \quad 39x + 65 = 34x + 170$

$\Rightarrow \quad 5x = 105$

$\therefore \quad x = 21$

Deepa's present age $= 3x = 3 \times 21 = 63$ years

5. From question,

$A + B + C + D + E = 66 \times 5 = 330$

Let the 1st even number A be n, then

$\because n + (n + 2) + (n + 4) + (n + 6) + (n + 8) = 330$

$\Rightarrow \quad 5n + 20 = 330$

$\Rightarrow \quad 5n = 310$

$\therefore \quad n = 62$

Thus the required product

$= B \times E = (n + 2) \times (n + 8)$

$= 64 \times 70 = 4480$

7. Age of 1st son $= x$

Father's age $= x + 30$

Age of 2nd son $= x - 10$

$\because x + (x + 30) + (x - 10) = 95$

$\Rightarrow \quad 3x + 20 = 95$

$\Rightarrow \quad 3x = 75$

$\therefore \quad x = 25$

$\therefore$ Father's age = (25 + 30) years = 55 years

8. Let the present ages of Babul and Alok be x years and $(x + 9)$ years respectively.

Then, $(x + 9 + 10) = 2(x - 10)$ or $x = 39$.

9. Let the present age of the elder person be x years.

Then, the present age of the other person $= (x - 10)$ years

$(x - 15) = 2(x - 10 - 15)$ or $x = 35$

$\therefore$ The present age of the elder person is 35 years.

10. Let Anshu's age $= 4x$ and Jolly's age $= 3x$ years.

$\therefore 4x + 6 = 26 \quad \Rightarrow \quad x = 5$

$\therefore$ Jolly's age $= 3x = 15$ years.

11. Let the ages of Asha and Bhushan be $2x$ and $3x$ years.

$$\frac{2x+5}{3x+5} = \frac{3}{4}$$

$\Rightarrow \quad 4(2x + 5) = 3(3x + 5)$

$\Rightarrow \quad x = 5.$

$\therefore$ Asha's present age $= 2x = 10$ years.

12. Sum of ages of A and B, 3 years ago

$= (18 \times 2)$

$= 36$ years.

Sum of ages of A, B and C $= (22 \times 3)$

$= 66$ years.

Sum of ages of A and B $= (36 + 6)$ years

$= 42$ years.

$\therefore$ C's age $= (66 - 42)$ years $= 24$ years.

14. Let second number $= x$. Then, first one $= 2x$ and third number $= 4x$.

$$\therefore \frac{x+2x+4x}{3} = 56 \Rightarrow 7x = 168 \text{ or } x = 24.$$

So, the numbers are 48, 24, 96.

15. Total of 50 numbers $= (50 \times 38) = 1900.$

Total of 48 numbers $= [1900 - (45 + 55)]$

$= 1800.$

$$\therefore \text{ Required average} = \frac{1800}{48} = \frac{225}{6} = 37.5.$$

16. $3 \times 27 + 3 \times 29 + x = 7 \times 28.5$

$\therefore \quad x = 31.5$

17. Let original strength $= x$. Then,

$40x + 12 \times 32 = (x + 12) \times 36$

or $40x + 384 = 36x + 432$ or $4x = 48$

or $\quad x = 12.$

18. Total increase $= (8 \times 2.5)$ kg $= 20$ kg.

Weight of new man $= (56 + 20)$ kg $= 76$ kg.

19. Production during these 5 days

$= (30 \times 58 - 25 \times 60) = 240.$

$$\therefore \text{ Average for 5 days} = \frac{240}{5} = 48.$$

20. Total income = ₹ 120 × 5 + 130 × 7 + 290)

= ₹ 1800.

Average monthly income = ₹ $\left(\frac{1800}{12}\right)$

= ₹ 150.

21. Age of the teacher $= (25 \times 11 - 24 \times 10)$ years

$= 35$ years.

22. $11x + 90 = (x - 5) \times 12$ or $x = 150.$

$\therefore$ Average after 12th inning $= (150 - 5)$

$= 145.$

23. $A + B + C = 3 \times 84 = 252$, $A + B + C + D$

$= (4 \times 80) = 320.$

$\therefore$ D = (320 – 252) = 68 and so E
= (68 + 3) = 71.
Now, B + C + D + E = (4 × 79) = 316
So, A = (320 – 245) = 75 kg.

24. Let the number of wickets taken before the last match = x.

Then, $\frac{12.4x+26}{x+5} = 12 \Rightarrow x = 85.$

25. Let their present ages be $4x$, $7x$ and $9x$ years respectively.
Then, $(4x - 8) + (7x - 8) + (9x - 8) = 56$
$\Rightarrow 20x = 80 \Rightarrow x = 4.$
$\therefore$ Their present ages are 16 years, 28 years and 36 years respectively.

26. Let C's age be x years.
Then, B's age = $2x$ years.
A's age = $(2x + 2)$ years.
$\therefore (2x + 2) + 2x + x = 27$
$\Rightarrow 5x = 25 \Rightarrow x = 5.$
Hence, B's age = $2x$ = 10 years.

27. Let the mother's present age be x years. Then,

the person's present age = $\left(\frac{2}{5}x\right)$ years.

$\therefore \left(\frac{2}{5}x+8\right) = \frac{1}{2}(x+8)$

$\Rightarrow 2(2x + 40) = 5(x + 8) \Rightarrow x = 40.$

28. Rahim – Quasab = Rahim – Tanveer
$\Rightarrow$ Quasab = Tanveer
Also, Rahim + Tanveer = 50
$\Rightarrow$ Rahim + Quasab = 50.
So, (Rahim – Quasab) cannot be determined.

29. Let the son's present age be x years.
Then, $(38 - x) = x$
$\Rightarrow 2x = 38$
$\Rightarrow x = 19.$
$\therefore$ Son's age 5 years back = (19 – 5) years
= 14 years.

30. Mother's age when Asha's brother was born
= 36 years.
Father's age when Asha's brother was born
= (38 + 4) years = 42 years.
$\therefore$ Required difference = (42 – 36) years
= 6 years.

31. Clearly, we have

$$\left(\frac{3+11+7+9+15+13+8+19+17+21+14+x}{12}\right) = 12$$

or, $137 + x = 144$
or, $x = 144 - 137 = 7.$

32. Clearly, $b = a + 2$, $c = a + 4$, $d = a + 6$ and $e = a + 8$.
$\therefore$ Average

$$= \frac{a+(a+2)+(a+4)+(a+6)+(a+8)}{5}$$

$$= \left(\frac{5a+20}{5}\right) = (a + 4).$$

34. Let the numbers be x, y and z.

Then, $\left(\frac{x+y}{2}\right)-\left(\frac{y+z}{2}\right) = 15$

or, $(x + y) - (y + z) = 30$
or, $x - z = 30.$

35. Sum of temperatures on 1st, 2nd, 3rd and 4th days
= (58 × 4) = 232 degrees ...(*i*)
Sum of temperatures on 2nd, 3rd, 4th and 5th days
= (60 × 4) = 240 degrees ...(*ii*)
Subtracting (*i*) from (*ii*), we get :
Temperature on 5th day – Temperature on 1st day = 8 degrees.
Let the temperatures on 1st and 5th days be $7x$ and $8x$ degrees respectively.
Then, $8x - 7x = 8$ or $x = 8$.
$\therefore$ Temperature on the 5th day = $8x$ = 64 degrees.

36. Let the average age of the whole team be x years.
$\therefore 11x - (26 + 29) = 9(x - 1)$
$\Rightarrow 11x - 9x = 46 \Rightarrow 2x = 46$
$\Rightarrow x = 23.$
So, average age of the team is 23 years.

37. Let average for 10 innings be x. Then,

$$\frac{10x + 108}{11} = x + 6$$

$\Rightarrow \quad 11x + 66 = 10x + 108$

$\Rightarrow \quad x = 42.$

$\therefore$ New average $= (x + 6) = 48$ runs.

39. Sum of the present ages of husband, wife and child $= (27 \times 3 + 3 \times 3)$ years $= 90$ years.

Sum of the present ages of wife and child $= (20 \times 2 + 5 \times 2)$ years $= 50$ years.

$\therefore$ Husband's present age $= (90 - 50)$ years $= 40$ years.

40. Let the number of papers be x.

Then, $63x + 20 + 2 = 65x$

or, $\quad 2x = 22$

or, $\quad x = 11.$

5. PERCENTAGE

IMPORTANT FACTS

To solve quickly the problems related to percentage, remember following rules:

Rule 1:

(*a*) Of the given two numbers if the first is $x\%$ more than the second, then the second will be $\left(\frac{100 \times x}{100 + x}\right)\%$ less than the first.

(*b*) Of the given two numbers if the first is $x\%$ less than the second, then the second will be $\left(\frac{100 \times x}{100 - x}\right)\%$ more than the first.

(*c*) If two numbers are respectively $x\%$ and $y\%$ more than a third number, then the first number will be $\left(\frac{100 + x}{100 + y} \times 100\right)\%$ of the second.

(*d*) If two numbers are respectively $x\%$ and $y\%$ less than a third number, then the first number will be $\left(\frac{100 - x}{100 - y} \times 100\right)\%$ of the second.

Rule 2 :

(*a*) If a number or quantity is increased by $x\%$ then in order to restore its original value it must be decreased by $\left[\frac{100 \times x}{100 + x}\right]\%$.

(*b*) If a number or quantity is decreased by $x\%$ then in order to restore its original value it must be increased by $\left[\frac{100 \times x}{100 - x}\right]\%$.

Rule 3 :

(*a*) If a number is successively increased by $x\%$ and $y\%$ then a single equivalent increase in that number will be $\left(x + y + \frac{xy}{100}\right)\%$

(*b*) If two successive discounts of $x\%$ and $y\%$ are allowed on a particular amount, then a single discount that is equivalent to the two successive discounts will be $\left(x + y - \frac{xy}{100}\right)\%$

(*c*) If a number is successively increased by $x\%$, $y\%$ and $z\%$, then a single equivalent increase in that number will be

$$\left[(x + y + z) + \left(\frac{xy + yz + zx}{100}\right) + \frac{(xyz)}{10000}\right]\%$$

(*d*) If three successive discounts of $x\%$, $y\%$ and $z\%$ are allowed on an amount, then a single discount that is equivalent to the three successive discounts will be

$$\left[x + y + z - \frac{(xy + yz + zx)}{100} + \frac{xyz}{10000}\right]\%$$

Rule 4 :

(*a*) If a number is increased by $x\%$ and thereafter reduced by $x\%$, then the number will be reduced by $\left(\frac{x^2}{100}\right)$ per cent.

(*b*) If a number is reduced by $x\%$ and thereafter increased by $x\%$ then the number will be reduced by $\left(\frac{x^2}{100}\right)$ per cent.

(*c*) If due to an increase of $x\%$ in the selling price of certain commodity the sell/consumption of the commodity decreases by $y\%$, then gross receipts on account of sale of that commodity will be increased or decreased by $\left(x-y-\frac{xy}{100}\right)\%$, where $x > y$ and will be decreased by $\left(y-x+\frac{xy}{100}\right)\%$, where $y > x$.

SOLVED EXAMPLES

Example 1: If the numerator of a fraction is increased by 200% and the denominator is increased by 400%. The resultant fraction is $1\frac{1}{20}$. What was the original fraction?

Solution: Let original fraction = $\frac{x}{y}$; then

$$\frac{x+2x}{y+4y} = \frac{21}{20}$$

$$\frac{3x}{5y} = \frac{21}{20}$$

$$\frac{x}{y} = \frac{21\times 5}{20\times 3} = \frac{7}{4} = 1\frac{3}{4}.$$

Example 2: In a class of 65 students and 4 teachers, each student got sweets that are 20% of the total number of students and each teacher got sweets that are 40% of the total number of students. How many sweets were there?

Solution: The share of each student = $\frac{20}{100}\times 65$ = 13 sweets

The share of each teacher = $\frac{40}{100}\times 65$ = 26 sweets

Total number of sweets = 65 × 13 + 4 × 26 = 845 + 104 = 949.

Example 3: Bovina spent ₹ 44,668/- on her air tickets, ₹ 56,732/- on buying gifts for the family members and the remaining 22% of the total amount had as cash with her. What was the total amount?

Solution: Let total amount = ₹ x ; then

$$\frac{78}{100}\times x = 44668 + 56732$$

$$\Rightarrow x = \frac{101400\times 100}{78} = ₹\ 1,30,00.$$

Example 4: Rubina decided to donate 16% of her monthly salary to an NGO. On the day of donation she changed her mind and donated ₹ 6,567/- which was 75% of what she had decided earlier. How much is Rubina's monthly salary?

Solution: Let her monthly salary be ₹ x ; then

$$\frac{16}{100}\times\frac{75}{100}\times x = 6567$$

$$\Rightarrow \frac{3}{25}x = 6567$$

$$\Rightarrow x = \frac{6567\times 25}{3} = ₹\ 54725$$

Thus, her monthly salary = ₹ 54725.

MULTIPLE CHOICE QUESTIONS

1. Mr. Rajesh spent 20% of his monthly income on grocery and household expenses. Out of the remaining he spent 25% on children's education 20% on transport and 15% on entertainment. He is left with an amount of ₹ 14,400 after incurring above expenses. What was his monthly income?

A. ₹ 45,000 B. ₹ 24,000
C. ₹ 36,000 D. ₹ 32,000

2. Number of students in a school in June every year increases by 10% from the previous year. If the school had 2,400 students in 2009, how many students did it have in June 2011?

A. 2,840 B. 2,880
C. 2,904 D. 2,920

3. On a test consisting of 150 questions, Reema answered 40% of the first 75 questions correctly. What per cent of the other 75 questions does she need to answer correctly for her grade on the entire exam to be 60%?
A. 80 B. 70
C. 40 D. 50

4. If the numerator of a fraction is increased by 200% and the denominator is increased by 300%. The resultant fraction is $\frac{9}{17}$. What was the original fraction?

A. $\frac{11}{17}$

B. $\frac{9}{11}$

C. $\frac{13}{17}$

D. None of these

5. One-sixth of a number is 53. What will 57% of that number be?
A. 181.26 B. 136.74
C. 197.16 D. 149.46

6. Mrs. Sudha Jain invests 14% of her monthly salary, *i.e.* ₹ 7,014 in Insurance Policies. Later she invests 21% of her monthly salary on Family Mediclaim Policies; also she invests another 6.5% of her salary on Mutual Funds. What is the total annual amount invested by Mrs. Sudha Jain?
A. ₹ 25,050 B. ₹ 50,100
C. ₹ 2,42,550 D. ₹ 2,49,498

7. A sum of ₹ 817 is divided among A, B and C such that 'A' receives 25% more than 'B' and 'B' receives 25% less than 'C'. What is the 'A's share in the amount?
A. ₹ 228 B. ₹ 247
C. ₹ 285 D. ₹ 304

8. Ms. Sujan invests 7% *i.e.* ₹ 2170 of her monthly salary in mutual funds. Later she invests 18% of her monthly salary in recurring deposits also, she invests 6% of her salary on NSC's. What is the total annual amount invested by Ms. Sujan?
A. ₹ 1,25,320 B. ₹ 1,13,520
C. ₹ 1,35,120 D. ₹ 1,15,320

9. What is the 30% of 40% of $\frac{2}{5}$th of 2500?
A. 500 B. 400
C. 360 D. 120

10. A sum of ₹ 731 is divided among A, B and C, such that 'A' receives 25% more than 'B' and 'B' receives 25% less than 'C'. What is C's share in the amount?
A. ₹ 172 B. ₹ 200
C. ₹ 262 D. None of these

11. Thirty five per cent of 740 is 34 more than a number. What is two-fifth of the number?
A. 45 B. 90
C. 180 D. 120

12. Ramu scored 456 marks in an exam and Shama got 54 per cent marks in the same exam which is 24 marks less than Ramu. If the minimum passing marks in the exam is 34 per cent, then how much more marks did Ramu score than the minimum passing marks?
A. 184 B. 196
C. 190 D. 180

13. Shreyas bought an article and sold for 125% of its cost price. What was the cost price of the article, if Shreyas sold it for ₹ 30,750?
A. ₹ 24,600 B. ₹ 25,640
C. ₹ 24,250 D. ₹ 23,200

14. When 20% of a number is added to another number the number increases by 50%. What is the respective ratio between the first and the second number?
A. 3 : 2
B. 2 : 3
C. 5 : 2
D. Cannot be determined

15. If a number is added to seven-ninth of thirty five per cent of 900, the value so obtained is 325. What is the number?

A. 60 B. 120
C. 90 D. None of these

16. The difference between 60% of a number and 20% of the same number is 316. What is 35% of that number?
A. 270.5 B. 285.5
C. 276.5 D. 275

17. In an examination it is required to get 36% of the aggregate marks to pass. A student gets 174 marks and is declared failed by 96 marks. What is the maximum aggregate marks a student can get?
A. 750
B. 650
C. 600
D. Cannot be determined

18. There is a rebate of 15%, if electric bills are paid in time. A man got a rebate of ₹ 54 by paying the bill in time. What was his electric bill in rupees?
A. 300 B. 350
C. 360 D. 380

19. A number is increased by 20% then again by 20%. By what per cent the original number is changed?
A. 40% B. 50%
C. 44% D. 36%

20. In an examination 62% of the examinees got plucked in Mathematics, 52% passed in English and 22% failed in both the subjects. If 108 is the number of examinees who passed in both the subjects then find out the total number of candidates—
A. 1200 B. 900
C. 800 D. 1000

21. Ramesh gets 10% more than Mohan. How much per cent will Mohan get less than Ramesh?
A. 10% B. 9%
C. $9\frac{1}{11}\%$ D. 11%

22. By what quantity the use of coal is to be reduced to keep one's family budget same when the price of coal is increased b 25%?
A. 25% B. 20%
C. 30% D. 15%

23. The percentage equivalent to the fraction 3/4 is :
A. 75% B. 25%
C. 60% D. 80%

24. If each side of a square be increased by 10%, what is the percentage increase of the area?
A. 21% B. 10%
C. 20% D. 100%

25. Suppose 35% of the males are married. Find the percentage of unmarried females in the total population, if $\frac{5}{7}$ part of the population in a village are males.
A. 21% B. 25%
C. $3\frac{4}{7}\%$ D. 28%

26. In an examination, 80% of the students failed in English, 85% in Maths and 75% in both English and Maths. If 40 students passed in both the subjects, the total number of students is
A. 200 B. 400
C. 600 D. 800

27. If the ratio of Rohan's expenditure on food and clothes be 3 : 2 and the prices register an increase of 20% on food and 25% on clothes of expenditure. By how much should his salary be increased in order that he may maintain the same level of consumption as before, his present salary being ₹ 1750?
A. ₹ 2135 B. ₹ 1200
C. ₹ 387 D. ₹ 385

28. A hockey team lost 20% of the total number of matches it played during a year If it won 70% of the matches played by the team and 40 matches were drawn. What was the total number of matches played by the team during the year.
A. 400 B. 200
C. 500 D. 300

29. A rise of 25% in the price of groundnuts compels a person to buy 1.5 kg of groundnuts less for ₹ 240, original price of groundnuts per kg. is :

A. ₹ 40 B. ₹ 100
C. ₹ 32 D. ₹ 140

30. In an election between two candidates A and B, A got 55% of the total valid votes. 20% of the votes were declared invalid. If the total votes were 7500, the number of valid votes polled in favour of the candidate B is :

A. 2700 B. 3300
C. 7500 D. 1500

31. The population of a city is 35000. On an increas of 6% in the number of men and an increase of 4% in the number of women, the population would become 36700. The number of men and women separately in thousand is:

A. 15, 16 B. 16, 17
C. 17, 18 D. 18, 17

32. After 30 kg of water were evaporated from a solution of salt and water which had 15% of salt, the remaining solution had 20% salt. The weight of the original solution is :

A. 30 kg B. 60 kg
C. 120 kg D. 600 kg

33. X's salary is half that of Y. If X got a 50% rise in his salary and Y got a 25% rise in his salary, then find the percentage increase in combined salaries of both.

A. 25% B. $16\frac{2}{3}\%$
C. 30% D. $33\frac{1}{3}\%$

34. In a particular school in a rural area, 80% of students with age below 14 years in the area are enrolled; of them, 75% come regularly to the school. If 270 students are regular, how many students are there in the area who are below 14 years?

A. 270 B. 370
C. 450 D. 550

35. A's weight is 25% that of B's and 40% that of C's. What percentage of C's weight is B's weight?

A. 80% B. 60%
C. 160% D. 90%

ANSWERS

1	2	3	4	5	6	7	8	9	10
A	C	A	D	A	D	C	D	D	D
11	**12**	**13**	**14**	**15**	**16**	**17**	**18**	**19**	**20**
B	A	A	C	D	C	A	C	C	B
21	**22**	**23**	**24**	**25**	**26**	**27**	**28**	**29**	**30**
C	B	A	A	C	B	D	A	C	A
31	**32**	**33**	**34**	**35**					
D	C	D	C	C					

SOME SELECTED EXPLANATORY ANSWERS

1. Let Rajesh's monthly income be ₹ 100.

∴ Expenditure on grocery and household expenses = ₹ 20.

Expenditure on education etc.

$= \frac{80 \times 60}{100}$ = ₹ 48

Saving = 100 – 20 – 48 = ₹ 32

Now,

when saving ₹ 32 then income = ₹ 100

when saving ₹ 14400 then income

$$= \frac{100}{32} \times 14400 = ₹\ 45000$$

2. Required number of students

$$= 2400\left(1+\frac{10}{100}\right)^2 \quad \left[P = P_0\left(1+\frac{R}{100}\right)^T\right]$$

$$= 2400 \times \frac{11}{10} \times \frac{11}{10} = 2904.$$

3. Required % $= \dfrac{150 \times \frac{60}{100} - 75 \times \frac{40}{100}}{75} \times 100\%$

$$= \frac{90-30}{75} \times 100\% = 80\%$$

4. Let the fraction be $\dfrac{x}{y}$

$\therefore \quad \dfrac{x+2x}{y+3y} = \dfrac{9}{17}$

$\Rightarrow \quad \dfrac{3x}{4y} = \dfrac{9}{17}$

$\therefore \quad \dfrac{x}{y} = \dfrac{9}{17} \times \dfrac{4}{3} = \dfrac{12}{17}$

5. Let the number be x

$\because \quad \dfrac{x}{6} = 53$

$\Rightarrow \quad x = 53 \times 6$

$\therefore \quad x \times \dfrac{57}{100} = \dfrac{53 \times 6 \times 57}{100} = 181.26$

6. Let the monthly salary be ₹ x

$\because \quad x \times \dfrac{14}{100} = 7014$

$\Rightarrow \quad x = \dfrac{7014 \times 100}{14} = ₹\ 50100$

$\therefore$ Total amount of annual investment

$$= \frac{(14+21+6.5)}{100} \times 50100 \times 12 = ₹\ 249498$$

8. Monthly salary of Ms. Sujan $= \dfrac{2170 \times 100}{7}$

= ₹ 31,000.

$\therefore$ Total money invested by her in a year

$$= 31000 \times \frac{(7+18+6)}{100} \times 12$$

= ₹ 9610 × 12

= ₹ 115320

9. $2500 \times \dfrac{30}{100} \times \dfrac{40}{100} \times \dfrac{2}{5} = 120.$

10. Let the share of C be ₹ x

$\therefore \quad$ Share of B $= \dfrac{75x}{100} = ₹\ 0.75x$

and share of A $= 0.75x \times \dfrac{125}{100} = ₹\ 0.9375x$

$\because \ 0.9375x + 0.75x + x = 731$

$\therefore \quad x = \dfrac{731}{2.6875} = ₹\ 272$

11. Number $= 740 \times \dfrac{35}{100} - 34 = 225$

$\therefore \ \dfrac{2}{5}$ of the number $= 225 \times \dfrac{2}{5} = 90.$

12. Let the maximum marks of the eximination be x. Then, from question—

$\because \quad 54\%$ of $x = 456 - 24 = 432$

$$x = \frac{432 \times 100}{54} = 800$$

$\Rightarrow$ Minimum passing marks $= \dfrac{34}{100} \times 800$

$= 272$

$\therefore$ Required difference = 456 − 272 = 184.

13. C.P. of the article $= \dfrac{30750 \times 100}{125} = ₹\ 24600.$

14. Let the two numbers be x and y respectively. Then,

$\because \quad \dfrac{20x}{100} + y = y + \dfrac{50y}{100}$

$$\Rightarrow \quad \frac{x}{5}+y = y+\frac{y}{2}$$

$$\Rightarrow \quad \frac{x}{5} = \frac{y}{2}$$

$$\Rightarrow \quad \frac{x}{y} = \frac{5}{2}$$

$\therefore \quad x : y = 5 : 2$

15. Let the number be x.

$$\because \quad 900\times\frac{35}{100}\times\frac{7}{9}+x = 325$$

$\therefore \quad x = 325 - 245 = 80$

16. Let the number be 'n', then from question,

$\because \quad (60\% - 20\%)$ of $n = 316$

$\Rightarrow \quad 40\%$ of $n = 316$

$$\Rightarrow \quad 35\% \text{ of } n = \frac{316}{40}\times 35$$

$$= 276.5$$

17. Let the maximum marks of the exam. paper = n.

Then from question,

$$n\times\frac{36}{100} = 174 + 96$$

$$\Rightarrow \quad n = \frac{270\times 100}{36}$$

$\therefore \quad n = 750$

18. 15% = ₹ 54

$$100\% = ₹\ \frac{54}{15}\times 100$$

= ₹ 360

19. Let the first number be 100.

After 20% increase, the number becomes = 120

After again 20% increase, the number becomes

$$= 120\times\frac{120}{100} = 144$$

$\therefore$ Original number is changed by (144 – 100)% = 44%

20. Failed in Mathematics = 62%

Failed in English = (100 – 52)% = 48%

Failed in both = 22%

Failed only in Maths = (62 – 22)% = 40%

Failed only in English = (48 – 22)% = 26%

$\therefore$ Total failed = (40 + 26 + 22)%

= 88%

$\therefore$ Passed in both = (100 – 88)% = 12%

12% = 108

$$100\% = \frac{108}{12}\times 100 = 900$$

21. Ramesh gets = 110,

Mohan = 100

$$\text{Required percentage} = \frac{10}{110}\times 100 = 9\frac{1}{11}\%.$$

22.
$$\text{Required percentage} = \frac{25}{(100+25)}\times 100$$

$$= \frac{25}{125}\times 100 = 20\%.$$

23.
$$\text{Required percentage} = \frac{3}{4}\times 100\% = 75\%.$$

24. Percentage increase in area

$$= \frac{(110)^2-(100)^2}{(100)^2}\times 100\%$$

$$= \frac{210\times 10}{100\times 100}\times 100\% = 21\%.$$

26. Let the total number of students be x. Number of student failed in one or both is given by

$n(A \cup B) = n(A) + n(B) - n(A \cap B)$

= 80% of x + 85% of x – 75% of x

$$= \frac{90x}{100} = \frac{9x}{10}$$

$$\text{passed in both} = \left(x-\frac{9x}{10}\right) = \frac{x}{10}$$

$$\text{From question, } \frac{x}{10} = 40$$

$\Rightarrow \quad x = 400$

27. Let expenditure on food and clothes be ₹ $3x$ and ₹ $2x$.

From question, $3x + 2x = 1750$

$$x = 350$$

$$\text{Food} = 3 \times 350 = 1050$$

$$\text{Clothes} = 2 \times 350 = 700$$

New expenditure = 120% of 1050 + 125% of 700

$$= \left(\frac{120}{100} \times 1050\right) + \left(\frac{125}{100} \times 700\right)$$

$$= ₹\ 2135$$

∴ Required increase = 2135 – 1750 = ₹ 385.

28. Let the total number of matches played be x.

From question, 20% of x + 70% of x + 40 = x

$$\Rightarrow \quad \frac{20x}{100} + \frac{70x}{100} + 40 = x$$

$$\Rightarrow \quad x = 400.$$

30. Total votes = 7500

Invalid votes = 20% of 7500 = $\frac{20}{100} \times 7500$

$= 1500$

∴ Valid votes = 7500 – 1500 = 6000

Valid votes polled in favour of the candidate A

$$= 55\% \text{ of } 6000 = \frac{55}{100} \times 6000 = 3300$$

∴ Valid votes polled in favour of the candidate B = 6000 – 3300 = 2700.

31. Increase in the population = 36760 – 35000 = 1760

Let the number of men in the population be x

∴ Increase in the men population = 6% of x

$$= \frac{6x}{100}$$

Population of women = 35000 – x

Increase in the women population

$$= 4\% \text{ of } (35000 - x) = \frac{4}{100}(35000 - x)$$

Now From question,

$$\frac{6x}{100} + \frac{4}{100}(35000 - x) = 1760$$

$$\Rightarrow \quad 6x + 4(35000 - x) = 176000$$

$$\Rightarrow \quad 2x = 176000 - (35000 \times 4)$$

$$\Rightarrow \quad 2x = 176000 - 140000$$

$$\Rightarrow \quad 2x = 36000;\ x = \frac{36000}{2} = 18000$$

∴ Numbere of men in the population of city = 18000 and Number of women in the population of city

$= 35000 - 18000 = 17000.$

32. Let the weight of the original solution be x kg.

The weight of salt at 15% = $\frac{15}{100} \times x$

$= \frac{15x}{100}$ kg.

Weight of the remaining solution when 30 kg of water from the solution is evaporated

$= (x - 30)$ kg.

∴ Percentage of salt in the remaining solution

$$= \frac{15x/100}{x-30} \times 100\% = \left(\frac{15x}{x-30}\right)\%$$

It is given that the remaining solution had 20% salt (Given)

$$\therefore \quad \frac{15x}{x-30} = 20$$

$$\Rightarrow \quad 15x = 20(x - 30)$$

$$\Rightarrow \quad 20x - 15x = 600$$

$$\therefore \quad 5x = 600;$$

$$x = 600 \div 5 = 120$$

Hence, the weight of the original solution is 120 kg.

33. Suppose the initial salary of Y = ₹ 100

Then, initial salary of X = $\frac{1}{2}$ × ₹ 100 = ₹ 50

Increase in Y's salary = 25% of ₹ 100 = ₹ 25

Increase in X's salary = 50% of ₹ 50

$$= ₹\left(50 \times \frac{50}{100}\right) = ₹\ 25$$

∴ Total increase = ₹ (25 + 25) = ₹ 50

$\therefore$ Percentage increase in combined salaries of both

$$= \frac{50}{(100+50)} \times 100$$

$$= \frac{50}{150} \times 100 = 33\frac{1}{3}\%.$$

34. Let total number of students with age below 14 years in the area be 100

Number of students enrolled = 80% of 100 = 80

Number of students who come regularly = 75% of 80

$$= 80 \times \frac{75}{100} = 60$$

If number of regualr students is 60, total number = 100

If number of regular students is 270, total number

$$= \frac{100}{60} \times 270 = 450.$$

6. PROFIT & LOSS

GENERAL FORMULAE

1. Gain % = $\left(\frac{\text{Gain}}{\text{C.P}} \times 100\right)$
2. Loss % = $\left(\frac{\text{Loss}}{\text{C.P}} \times 100\right)$
3. S.P = $\left(\frac{100 + \text{Gain }\%}{100}\right) \times \text{C.P}$
4. S.P = $\left(\frac{100 - \text{Loss }\%}{100}\right) \times \text{C.P}$
5. C.P = $\left(\frac{100}{100 + \text{Gain }\%}\right) \times \text{S.P}$
6. C.P = $\left(\frac{100}{100 - \text{Loss }\%}\right) \times \text{S.P}$

Formulae For Short Cut Solution

Type 1 :

Conditional Tricks

If cost price of X goods = Selling price of Y goods then,

I. Gain % = $\frac{X - Y}{Y} \times 100$ (In case of $X > Y$)

II. Loss % = $\frac{Y - X}{Y} \times 100$ (in case of $X < Y$)

Type 2 :

I. If X_1 and X_2 both are the rate of gain or both are the rate of loss, then, C.P. = $\left(\frac{100}{X_1 - X_2}\right) \times$ amount of difference between S.Ps.

II. If in X_1 and X_2 one is the rate of gain and another is the rate of loss, then C.P.= $\left(\frac{100}{X_1 + X_2}\right) \times$ amount of difference between S.Ps

Type 3 :

Miscellaneous Tricks

I. When a man buys two things on equal price and in those things one is sold on the profit of X % and another is sold on the loss of X %, then there is no loss or gain percent.

II. When a man sells two things at the same price each and in this process his loss on first thing is X % and gain on second thing is X % then in such type of questions, there is always a loss.

$$\text{Loss } \% = X \% \text{ of } X = \frac{X^2}{100} = \left(\frac{X}{10}\right)^2$$

III. Dishonest dealer and less weight

$$\text{Gain} = \frac{\text{Error}}{\text{True value} - \text{Error}} \times 100$$

Where, error = 100 gm – used weight of goods

IV. If A sells a thing to B at a gain of R_1 %, B sells it to C at a gain of R_2 % and C sells it to D at a gain of R_3 %

Then, cost price of D = Cost Price of $A\,(1 + R_1/100)\,(1 + R_2/100)\,(1 + R_3/100)$

V. If A sells a thing, to B at a loss of R %, B sells it to C at a loss of R % and C sells it to D at a loss of R % then, Cost price of D = Cost price of $A\,(1 - R_1/100)\,(1 - R_2/100)\,(1 - R_3/100)$

SOLVED EXAMPLES

Example 1: Suman purchased an item of ₹ 72,000 and sold it at a loss of 27 percent. With that amount she purchased another item and sold it at a gain of 30 percent. What is her overall profit/loss?

Solution: First S.P. = $\frac{72000 \times 73}{100}$ = ₹ 52560

Second S.P. = $\frac{52560 \times 130}{100}$ = ₹ 68328

Loss = 72000 – 68328 = ₹ 3672.

Example 2: Mr. Babulal purchased 100 pieces of an article at the rate of ₹ 480 per piece. He then listed the price so as to gain a profit of 25%. While selling the articles he offered a discount of 5%. What is the percentage of profit earned in the deal?

Solution: Profit per cent = $\left(x + y + \frac{xy}{100}\right)\%$

Here, $x = 25\%$, $y = -5\%$

$= \left(25 - 5 - \frac{25 \times 5}{100}\right)\% = 18.75\%.$

Example 3: The profit earned after selling an article for ₹ 625 is the same as loss incurred after selling the article for ₹ 435. What is the cost price of the article?

Solution: C.P. of the article = $\frac{625 + 435}{2}$ = ₹ 530.

Example 4: A man sold an item for ₹ 6,750 at a loss of 25%. What will be the selling price of same item if he sells it at a profit of 15%?

Solution: C.P. of the item = $\frac{6750 \times 100}{75}$ = ₹ 9000

∴ Required S.P. of the item = $\frac{9000 \times 115}{100}$
= ₹ 10350.

Example 5: A man sold a wristwatch for ₹ 2,400 at a loss of twenty-five per cent. At what rate should he have sold the wristwatch to earn a profit of twenty five per cent?

Solution: C.P. of the wristwatch = $\frac{100 \times 2400}{100 - 25}$
= ₹ 3200

∴ Required S.P. of the wristwatch

= $\frac{125 \times 3200}{100}$ = ₹ 4000.

MULTIPLE CHOICE QUESTIONS

1. What profit / loss per cent did Raveena earn if she purchased an item of ₹ 5,600 and sold it at three-fourth of its cost price?
A. Loss of 20 per cent
B. Gain of 25 per cent
C. Neither gain nor loss
D. Loss of 15 per cent

2. By what per cent must the cost price be raised in fixing the sale price in order that there may be a profit of 20% after allowing a commission of 10%?

A. 30% B. $33\frac{1}{3}\%$
C. 25% D. 40%

3. A sold a watch to B at a loss of 10%. B sold it to C at a gain of 10%. If A had sold at the same price which C paid for it, what would have been his gain or loss per cent?
A. 1% loss
B. 10% gain
C. 12% gain
D. 11% loss

4. A shopkeeper purchased two cycles at ₹ 1600 and sold the first at 10% profit and second one at 20% profit. If he could sell the first cycle at a profit of 20% and the second one at a profit of 10% then he could get ₹ 5 more. What will be the cost price of each in rupees?
A. 925, 675
B. 1000, 600
C. 825, 775
D. 900, 700

5. A person makes a profit of 25%, by selling an article for ₹ 35.50. By how much should he increase his selling price so as to make a profit of 40%?

A. ₹ 4.60 B. ₹ 4.26
C. ₹ 4 D. ₹ 3.90

6. A man bought a pen and sold it at a loss of 20%. If he had bought it for 30% less and sold it for ₹ 60 more, he would have made a profit of 50%. Find the C.P. of the article.

A. ₹ 200 B. ₹ 140
C. ₹ 240 D. ₹ 210

7. The cost price of 15 article is equal to S.P. of 10 articles. The gain percent is:

A. 50% B. 25%
C. $16\frac{2}{3}\%$ D. 100%

8. Raghav bought a radio with 20% discount on the labelled price. Had he bought it with 25% discount, he would have saved ₹ 500. At what price did he buy the radio?

A. ₹ 1000 B. ₹ 500
C. ₹ 5000 D. ₹ 10000

9. A man buys mangoes at ₹ 5 a dozen and an equal number at ₹ 4 a dozen. He sells them at ₹ 5.50 a dozen and makes a profit of ₹ 50. How many mangoes does he buy?

A. 30 dozens
B. 40 dozens
C. 50 dozens
D. 60 dozens

10. How many for a rupee must a shopkeeper sell to gain 25%, if he bought toys at 10 for a rupee?

A. 10 B. 9
C. 8 D. 6

11. Suppose the ratio of two investment be 3 : 2. What is the gain or loss on the two investments taken together if a man loses 20% on an investment but gains 25% on another investment.

A. 2.5% B. 0.2%
C. 2% D. 3%

12. A shopkeeper gives 12% additional discount after giving an initial discount of 20% on the labelled price of a T.V. If the sale price of the T.V. is ₹ 704. What is the labelled price of the T.V?

A. ₹ 844.80 B. ₹ 929.28
C. ₹ 1000 D. ₹ 900

13. By selling 12 oranges for a rupee, a man loses 10%. How many oranges for a rupee be sold to gain 20%?

A. 5 B. 4
C. 9 D. 12

14. A dishonest shopkeeper professes to sell pulses at his cost price but uses a false weight of 950 gm for each kilogram. His gain per cent is :

A. $5\frac{5}{19}\%$ B. 19%
C. $4\frac{5}{19}\%$ D. 95%

15. Sushil bought two boxes for ₹ 1300. He sold one box at a profit of 20% and the other box at a loss of 12%. If the selling price of both boxes is the same. Then the cost price of each box is :

A. ₹ 850, ₹ 650
B. ₹ 750, ₹ 750
C. ₹ 550, ₹ 750
D. ₹ 750, ₹ 650

16. A producer sells his articles to a wholesaler at 10% profit. The wholesaler sells it to a retailer at 20%. The retailer sells it to a customer at ₹ 41.25 making 25% profit. Then the cost of production is :

A. ₹ 52 B. ₹ 132
C. ₹ 110 D. ₹ 25

17. A bought two oxen for ₹ 1080. He sold one at a loss of 5% and the other at a gain of 7%. He neither gained nor lost in this transaction. C.P. of each is :

A. ₹ 630, ₹ 450
B. ₹ 680, ₹ 400
C. ₹ 600, ₹ 480
D. ₹ 540, ₹ 540

18. A businessman makes a profit of 20% in the first year. In the subsequent year, he had a loss of 25% on the capital which he had at the beginning of the second year. His overall gain or loss per cent in the capital is:
A. 120% B. 90%
C. 100% D. 10%

19. A co-operative society manufactures note books. It makes a profit of ₹ 9.00 when it sells 100 copies to a local shop. The local shop, in turn, makes a profit of ₹ 2 on selling 50 copies at 69 paisa per copy. How much did it cost the society to manufacture 100 note books?
A. ₹ 65 B. ₹ 55
C. ₹ 56 D. ₹ 32.50

20. A man marks his goods at a price that would give him 40% profit. He sells three-fourths of his goods at the marked price. For the remaining, he has to lower the marked price by 40%. His per cent profit on the entire transaction is:
A. 21% B. 84%
C. 52% D. 26%

21. By reducing the selling price of an article by ₹ 80 a gain of 5% turns into a loss of 5%. Then the original selling price of the article is:
A. ₹ 1050 B. ₹ 525
C. ₹ 510 D. ₹ 515

22. A man bought a horse and a carriage for ₹ 3000. He sold the horse at a gain of 20% and carriage at a loss of 10%, thereby gaining 2% on the whole. Then the cost of the horse is:
A. ₹ 3060 B. ₹ 1200
C. ₹ 2100 D. ₹ 3000

23. If 20% more would be gained by selling a price of cloth for ₹ 45.50 than by selling it for ₹ 39. What per cent would be gained by selling if for ₹ 42.25?
A. 32% B. 42%
C. 30% D. 35%

24. There would be 10% loss if rice is sold at ₹ 5.40 per kg. At what price per kg should it be sold to earn a profit of 20%?
A. ₹ 6 B. ₹ 6.48
C. ₹ 7.02 D. ₹ 7.20

25. A fruitseller buys lemons at 2 for a rupee and sells them at five for three rupees. His gain per cent is:
A. 10% B. 15%
C. 20% D. 25%

26. By selling 100 bananas, a fruitseller gains the selling price of 20 bananas. His gain per cent is :
A. 10% B. 15%
C. 20% D. 25%

27. A shopkeeper mixes two varieties of tea, one costing ₹ 35 per kg and another at ₹ 45 per kg in the ratio 3 : 2. If he sells the mixed variety at ₹ 41.60 per kg, his gain or loss per cent is :
A. $6\frac{2}{3}$% gain B. $6\frac{2}{3}$% loss
C. 4% gain D. 4% loss

28. A dishonest dealer professes to sell his goods at cost price. But he uses a false weight and thus gains $6\frac{18}{47}$%. For a kg, he uses a weight of :
A. 953 gms B. 940 gms
C. 960 gms D. 947 gms

29. By selling toffees at 20 for a rupee, a man loses 4%. To gain in 20%, for one rupee he must sell
A. 16 toffees B. 20 toffees
C. 25 toffees D. 24 toffees

30. A man sold two houses for ₹ 7.81 lakhs each. On one he gained 5% and on the other he lost 5%. What per cent is the effect of the sale on the whole?
A. 0.25% loss B. 0.25% gain
C. 25% loss D. 25% gain

31. By selling 45 oranges for ₹ 40, a man loses 20%. How many should he sell for ₹ 24 so as to gain 20% in the transaction?
A. 16 B. 18
C. 20 D. 22

32. A man gains 10% by selling an article for a certain price. If he sells it at double the price, the profit made is :

A. 20% B. 60%
C. 100% D. 120%

33. A man sells two horses for ₹ 4000 each, neither losing nor gaining in the deal. If he sold one horse at a gain of 25%, the other horse is sold at a loss of:

A. $16\frac{2}{3}\%$ B. $18\frac{2}{9}\%$
C. 25% D. 20%

34. Due to an increase of 30% in the price of eggs, 3 eggs less are available for ₹ 7.80. The present rate of eggs per dozen is :

A. ₹ 8.64 B. ₹ 8.88
C. ₹ 9.36 D. ₹ 9.25

35. The per cent profit when an article is sold for ₹ 78 is twice as when it is sold for ₹ 69. The C.P. of the article is :

A. ₹ 49 B. ₹ 51
C. ₹ 57 D. ₹ 60

36. 6% more is gained by selling a radio for ₹ 475 than by selling for ₹ 451. The C.P. of the radio is :

A. ₹ 400 B. ₹ 434
C. ₹ 446.50 D. ₹ 500

37. A tradesman by means of a false balance defrauds to the extent of 8% in buying goods and also defrauds to 8% in selling. His gain per cent is :

A. 15.48% B. 16%
C. 16.64% D. 20%

38. While selling a watch, a shopkeeper gives a discount of 5%. If he gives a discount of 7%, he earns ₹ 15 less as profit. The marked price of the watch is :

A. ₹ 697.50 B. ₹ 712.50
C. ₹ 787.50 D. ₹ 750.00

39. The marked price is 10% higher than the cost price. A discount of 10% is given on the marked price. In this kind of sale, the seller

A. bears no loss, no gain
B. gain 1%
C. loss 1%
D. gain 10%

40. The difference between a discount of 40% on ₹ 500 and two successive discounts of 36% and 4% on the same amount is :

A. 0 B. ₹ 2
C. ₹ 1.93 D. ₹ 7.20

ANSWERS

1	2	3	4	5	6	7	8	9	10
E	B	A	C	B	C	A	D	C	C
11	**12**	**13**	**14**	**15**	**16**	**17**	**18**	**19**	**20**
C	C	C	A	C	D	A	D	C	D
21	**22**	**23**	**24**	**25**	**26**	**27**	**28**	**29**	**30**
B	B	C	D	C	D	A	C	A	B
31	**32**	**33**	**34**	**35**	**36**	**37**	**38**	**39**	**40**
B	D	A	C	D	A	C	D	C	D

SOME SELECTED EXPLANATORY ANSWERS

1. S.P. of the item = $5600 \times \frac{3}{4}$ = ₹ 4200

$\therefore$ Loss % = $\frac{5600 - 4200}{5600} \times 100 = 25$

2. Let $x\%$ must the cost price be raised

$\therefore$ $$\text{S.P.} = (100 + x)$$

$\because$ $$(100+x)\frac{90}{100} = 120$$

$\Rightarrow$ $$3x = 100$$

$\therefore$ $$x = 33\frac{1}{3}\%.$$

3. Let A's C.P. = ₹ 100

$$\text{A's S.P.} = 100\times\frac{90}{100};$$

$$\text{B's S.P.} = 100\times\frac{90}{100}\times\frac{110}{100}$$

$$\text{C paid} = \text{B's S.P.} = 100\times\frac{90}{100}\times\frac{110}{100}$$

$$= 99$$

If A had sold at ₹ 99

Then, his loss = (100 – 99)% = 1%.

4. Let the C.P. of 1st cycle = ₹ x

and C.P. of 2nd cycle = ₹ $(1600 - x)$

Total S.P. in 1st case

$$= x\times\frac{110}{100}+(1600-x)\times\frac{120}{100}$$

$$= \frac{12\times1600 - x}{10}$$

Total S.P. in 2nd case

$$= x\times\frac{120}{100}+(1600-x)\times\frac{110}{100}$$

$$= \frac{11\times1600 + x}{10}$$

$\because$ $$\frac{11\times1600+x}{10}-\frac{12\times1600-x}{10} = 5$$

$\therefore$ $$x = \frac{1650}{2} = 825$$

C.P. of 1st cycle = 825

C.P. of 2nd cycle = 1600 – 825 = 775.

5. Let new S.P. be ₹ x

Then (100 + Gain%) : (1st S.P.)

= (100 + Gain%) : (2nd S.P.)

$$125 : 35.50 = 140 : x$$

$\Rightarrow$ $$x = \frac{35.50\times140}{125} = ₹\ 39.76$$

$\therefore$ Increased in S.P. = ₹ (39.76 – 35.50)

= ₹ 4.26.

6. Let original C.P. be ₹ x

$$\text{S.P.} = 80\%\text{ of } x = \frac{80x}{100} = \frac{4x}{5}$$

$$\text{New C.P.} = 70\%\text{ of } x = \frac{70x}{100} = \frac{7x}{10}$$

$$\text{New S.P.} = 150\%\text{ of } \frac{7x}{10} = \frac{21x}{20}$$

$\therefore$ $$\frac{21x}{20}-\frac{4x}{5} = 60$$

$\Rightarrow$ $$\frac{x}{4} = 60$$

$$x = 240$$

7. Let C.P. of each article be ₹ 1

Then C.P. of 10 article = ₹ 10

S.P. of 10 article = ₹ 15

$$\text{Gain }\% = \left(\frac{15-10}{10}\times100\right)\% = \left(\frac{5}{10}\times100\right)\%$$

$$= 50\%.$$

8. Let the labelled price be x

$\therefore$ $$\text{S.P.} = 80\%\text{ of } x = \frac{4x}{5}$$

$$\text{New S.P.} = 75\%\text{ of } x = \frac{3x}{4}$$

$\therefore$ $$\frac{4x}{5}-\frac{3x}{4} = 500$$

$\Rightarrow$ $$x = ₹\ 10000.$$

9. C.P of 2 dozens of mangoes = ₹ (5 + 4)

= ₹ 9

S.P. of 2 dozens of mangoes = ₹ 11

2 dozens of mangoes are bought at a profit of ₹ 2.

If profit is ₹ 50, mangoes bought $= \frac{2}{2}\times50$

= 50 dozens.

10. C.P of 10 toys = ₹ 1

Gain = 25%

S.P of 10 toys = $\frac{125}{100} \times 1$ = ₹ $\frac{5}{4}$

Thus S.P of 10 toys is ₹ $\frac{5}{4}$

∴ For ₹ 1, Number of toys = $10 \times \frac{4}{5} = 8$

So he must sell 8 toys for a rupee.

11. Let the investments are $3x$ and $2x$

Then total investment = $5x$

Receipt = (80% of $3x$ + 125% of $2x$)

= $(2.4x + 2.5x) = 4.9x$

∴ loss = $\left(\frac{0.1x}{5x} \times 100\right)\% = 2\%$

12. Let the labelled price of the T.V be ₹ x

Initial S.P = 80% of $x = \frac{80x}{100}$

New S.P = 88% of $\frac{80x}{100}$

$= \frac{88}{100} \times \frac{80x}{100} = \frac{704x}{1000}$

From question,

$\frac{704x}{1000} = 704$

$704x = 704 \times 1000$

⇒ $x = 1000$

∴ The labelled price of the T.V = ₹ 1000.

14. Let C.P. of 1 gm pulses be ₹ 1

∴ C.P. of 950 gm pulses = ₹ 950

S.P. of 950 gm = C.P. of 1 kg

= C.P. of 1000 gm = ₹ 1000

∴ Gain = ₹ (1000 – 950) = ₹ 50

∴ Gain % = $\frac{50}{950} \times 100 = 5\frac{5}{19}\%$.

17. From question,

∴ Loss on one = Gain on other

∴ 5% of the C.P. of one = 7% of the C.P. of the other

⇒ $\frac{\text{C.P. of 1st}}{\text{C.P. of 2nd}} = \frac{7\%}{5\%} = \frac{7}{5}$

or, C.P. of 1st : C.P. of 2nd = 7 : 5

Divide ₹ 1080 in the ratio of 7 : 5

∴ C.P. of the 1st = $\frac{7}{12} \times 1080$ = ₹ 630.

and C.P. of the 2nd = ₹ $\frac{5}{12} \times 1080$ = ₹ 450.

18. Let his capital at the beginning of first year be ₹ 100

Profit during first year = 20% of ₹ 100 = ₹ 20

∴ Capital at the beginning of the second year

= ₹ (100 + 20) = ₹ 120

Loss during second year = 25% of ₹ 120

= ₹$\left(120 \times \frac{25}{100}\right)$ = ₹ 30

∴ Capital at the end of second year

= ₹ (120 – 30) = ₹ 90

∴ Loss = ₹ (100 – 90) = ₹ 10

Overall Loss % on his capital = $\left(\frac{10}{100} \times 100\right)\%$

= 10%.

19. The local shop sells 50 copies @ 69 paisa per copy

= ₹ (50 × 0.69) = ₹ 34.50

His profit = ₹ 2

∴ The local shop purchases 50 copies for

= S.P. – Profit = ₹ (34.50 – 2) = ₹ 32.50

∴ The local shop purchases 100 copies for

= ₹$\left(\frac{32.50}{50} \times 100\right)$ = ₹ 65

∴ Co-operative society sells 100 copies for ₹ 65

Profit = ₹ 9

∴ Co-operative society manufactures 100 copies for

= ₹ (65 – 9) = ₹ 56.

23. Let C.P. of cloth be ₹ x. Then $x \times \frac{20}{100}$

$= ₹\ (45.50 - 39) = ₹\ 6.50$

$\Rightarrow \quad x = \frac{6.50 \times 100}{20} = ₹\ 32.50$

Gain = ₹ (42.25 – 32.50) = ₹ 9.75

$\therefore$ Gain% $= \frac{9.75}{32.50} \times 100 = 30\%$.

24. 90 : 5.40 :: 120 : x

$\therefore x = \frac{5.40 \times 120}{90} = 7.20.$

So, the rice must be sold at ₹ 7.20 per kg.

25. Suppose he buys 10 lemons.

C.P. $= ₹\left(\frac{10}{2}\right) = ₹\ 5$, S.P. $= ₹\left(\frac{3}{5} \times 10\right) = ₹\ 6.$

Gain% $= \left(\frac{1}{5} \times 100\right)\% = 20\%.$

26. Gain = (S.P. of 100 bananas) – (C.P. of 100 bananas)

(S.P. of 20) = (S.P. of 100) – (C.P. of 100)

₹ S.P. of 80 = C.P. of 100.

Let C.P. of each = ₹ 1.

C.P. of 80 = ₹ 80

S.P. of 80 = ₹ 100.

$\therefore$ Gain % $= \left(\frac{20}{80} \times 100\right)\% = 25\%$

27. Suppose he purchases 3 kg and 2 kg of tea of first and second kind respectively.

C.P. = ₹ (3 × 35 + 2 × 45) = ₹ 195.

S.P. = ₹ (5 × 41.60) = ₹ 208.

Gain % $= \left(\frac{13}{195} \times 100\right)\% = 6\frac{2}{3}\%.$

28. Let the error be x gms. Then,

$$\frac{x}{1000 - x} \times 100 = \frac{300}{47} \text{ or } \frac{x}{1000 - x} = \frac{3}{47}$$

$\therefore 47x = 3000 - 3x$ or $x = 60$.

So, he uses a weight = (1000 – 60) gm = 940 gm for a kg.

29. Suppose he sells 20 toffees.

Then, S.P. = ₹ 1 and Loss = 4%.

$\therefore$ C.P. $= \left(\frac{100}{96} \times 1\right) = ₹\frac{25}{24}$

Gain = 20%

$\therefore$ S.P. $= ₹\left(\frac{120}{100} \times \frac{25}{24}\right) = ₹\frac{5}{4}.$

For ₹ $\frac{5}{4}$, toffees sold $= \left(20 \times \frac{4}{5}\right) = 16.$

So, he must sell 16 toffees for a rupee.

30. Loss % $= \left(\frac{5}{10}\right)^2 = \frac{1}{4}\% = 0.25\%.$

31. S.P. of 1 orange $= ₹\left(\frac{40}{45}\right) = ₹\frac{8}{9}.$

80% of C.P. $= \frac{8}{9}$ or C.P. $= \left(\frac{8}{9} \times \frac{100}{80}\right) = ₹\frac{10}{9}.$

S.P. $= \left(120\% \text{ of } \frac{10}{9}\right) = ₹\frac{4}{3}.$

For ₹$\frac{4}{3}$, he sells 1 orange

For ₹ 24, he would sell $\left(\frac{3}{4} \times 24\right) = 18$ oranges.

32. Let C.P. = ₹ x.

First S.P. = 110% of $x = ₹\left(\frac{11}{10}x\right)$

Second S.P. $= \frac{22}{10}x$

New gain $= \left(\frac{22}{10}x - x\right) = \frac{12x}{10}.$

New gain % $= \left(\frac{12x}{10 \times x} \times 100\right)\% = 120\%.$

33. C.P. of two horses = ₹ 8000.

S.P. of one horse = ₹ 4000, gain = 25%.

$\therefore$ C.P. of this horse = ₹$\left(\frac{100}{125}\times 4000\right)$

= ₹ 3200.

C.P. of another horse = ₹ (8000 − 3200)

= ₹ 4800.

S.P. of this horse = ₹ 4000.

$\therefore$ Loss% = $\left(\frac{800}{4800}\times 100\right)\%$ = $16\frac{2}{3}\%$.

35. Let the C.P. be ₹ x.

Then, $\frac{2(69-x)}{100} = \frac{78-x}{100}$

or, $138 - 2x = 78 - x$

or, $x = 60$

$\therefore$ C.P. = ₹ 60.

36. Difference between two selling prices = ₹ 24

$\therefore$ 6% of C.P. = ₹ 24

Hence, C.P. = ₹$\left(\frac{24\times 100}{6}\right)$ = ₹400.

37. **Rule.** In such questions we adopt the rule :

Gain % = $\frac{(100+\text{common gain\%})^2}{100} - 100$

$= \left\{\frac{(108)^2}{100} - 100\right\}\%$ = 16.64%.

38. Let the marked price be ₹ x.

Then, (7% of x) − 15 = 5% of x

or, $\frac{7x}{100} - \frac{5x}{100} = 15$ or $x = 750$.

39. Let C.P. = ₹ 100.

Marked Price = ₹ 110.

S.P. = 90% of ₹ 110 = ₹ 99.

$\therefore$ Loss = 1%.

40. Price after 40% discount = 60% of ₹ 500

= ₹ 300.

Price after 36% discount = 64% of ₹ 500

= ₹ 320.

Price after next 4% discount = 96% of ₹ 320

= ₹ 307.20.

Difference in two prices = ₹ 307.20 − ₹ 300.00

= ₹ 7.20.

7. MIXTURE & ALLIGATION

Alligation deals with calculation of values or properties of a mixture. Alligation is the rule that enables us—

(1) to find the proportion in which the two or more ingredients at the given prices must be mixed to yield a mixture at the given price. This is termed as "Alligation Alternate".

(2) to calculate the average or mean value of a mixture when the prices of two or more ingredients which are to be mixed together and proportion in which they are to be mixed are given. This is termed as "Alligation Medial".

1. Rule of Alligation:

$$\frac{\text{A of Cheap mixture}}{\text{A of Dearer mixture}} = \frac{\text{CP of Dearer} - \text{Mean Price}}{\text{Mean Price} - \text{CP of Cheaper}}$$

Here cost price of unit quantity of the mixture is called the *Mean Price.*

The above rule may be represented schematically as under:

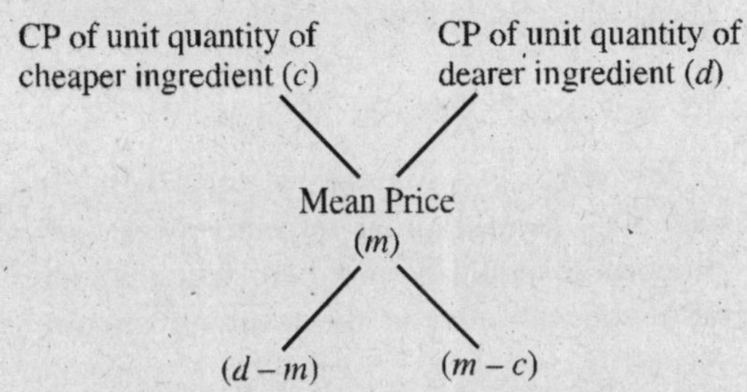

(Cheaper quantity) : (Dearer quantity) $= (d - m) : (m - c)$

This relationship is very helpful in solving problems on mixture involving percentage values, rates, prices, speeds etc.

2. m gm of sugar solution has x % sugar in it. To increase the sugar content in the solution to y %,

quantity of sugar need to be added $= \dfrac{m(y-x)}{100-y}$

3. A vessel contains x litres of liquid A. y litres are withdrawn and replaced by liquid B. Next y litres of the mixture is withdrawn and again replaced by liquid B.
This operation is repeated n times.

$$\frac{\text{Quantity of liquid A left after } n\text{th operation}}{\text{Whole quantity of liquid A initially present}}$$

$$= \left(\frac{x-y}{x}\right)^n \text{ or } \left(1-\frac{y}{x}\right)^n$$

SOLVED EXAMPLES

Example 1: Find the quantities of two types of wheat, one @ ₹ 6 per kg and the other @ ₹ 4 per kg. to get 20 kgs. of wheat mixture worth ₹ 4.5 per kg.

Solution:

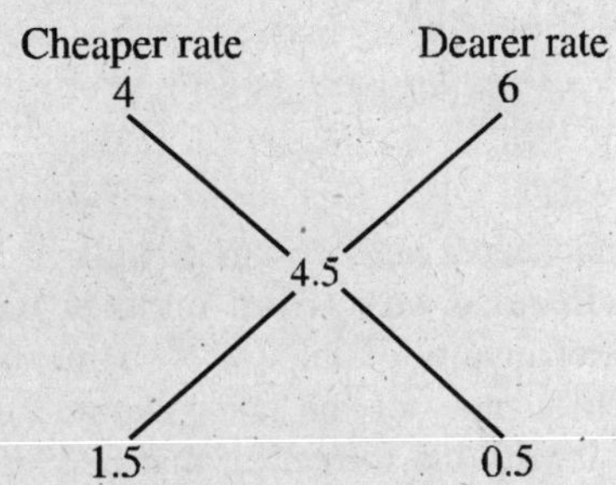

$$\frac{\text{Quantity of cheaper wheat}}{\text{Quantity of dearer wheat}} = \frac{1.5}{0.5} = \frac{3}{1}$$

Quantity of cheaper wheat

$$= \frac{3}{3+1} \times 20 = 15 \text{ kgs}$$

Quantity of dearer wheat

$$= \frac{1}{3+1} \times 20 = 5 \text{ kgs.}$$

Example 2: In what proportion water be mixed with pure milk in order to make a profit of 20% by selling it at cost price?

Solution: Let cost price of pure milk be Re. 1 per litre.

The SP of mixture = ₹ 1 per litre

Profit = 20%

So, CP of 1 litre of mixture

$$= ₹ \left(1 \times \frac{100}{120}\right) = ₹ \frac{5}{6}$$

We assume that CP of 1 litre of water is zero. Using the rule of alligation on 1 litre,

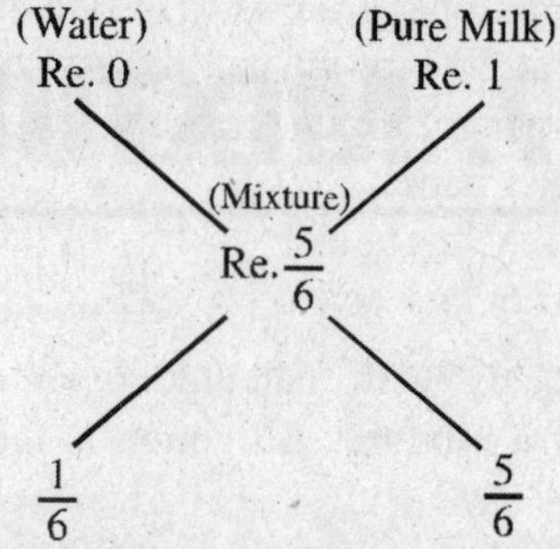

$$\frac{\text{Quantity of water}}{\text{Quantity of pure milk}} = \frac{\frac{1}{6}}{\frac{5}{6}} = \frac{1}{5}$$

or, Ratio of water to pure milk in the mixture = 1 : 5.

MULTIPLE CHOICE QUESTIONS

1. In what proportion must tea at ₹ 62 per kg be mixed with tea at ₹ 72 per kg in order to obtain the mixture worth ₹ 65 per kg?

A. 4 : 6 B. 7 : 3
C. 2 : 3 D. 4 : 7

2. Find the quantity of rice @ ₹ 10 per kg. which should be mixed with 25 kgs of rice @ ₹ 8 per kg, so that on selling the mixture @ ₹ 15 per kg there is 80% profit.

A. 6 kgs B. 7 kgs
C. 3 kgs D. 5 kgs

3. A shopkeeper buys 26 kgs of milk @ ₹ 16 per kg. He also buys from another source an inferior quality of milk @ ₹ 10 per kg. How much quantity of the latter should he buy to mix it with the former so that he can sell the mixture @ ₹ 14 per kg without making any loss?

A. 13 kgs B. 12 kgs
C. 14 kgs D. 16 kgs

4. Two vessels A and B contain milk and water in the ratio 7 : 5 and 17 : 7 respectively. In what ratio mixtures from two vessels should be mixed to get a new mixture containing milk and water in the ratio 5 : 3?

A. 1 : 2 B. 2 : 1
C. 2 : 3 D. 3 : 2

5. Two vessels A and B contain mixture of milk and water in the ratio 4 : 1 and 9 : 11 respectively. They are mixed in the ratio of 3 : 2. Find the ratio of milk : water in the resulting mixture.

A. 34 : 16 B. 33 : 17
C. 16 : 34 D. 17 : 33

6. A person has two solutions of sugar with 30% and 50% concentration respectively. In what proportion should he mix two solutions to get 45% concentration in the resulting mixture?

A. 1 : 3 B. 3 : 1
C. 2 : 3 D. 3 : 2

7. 6 litres of milk and water mixture has 75% milk in it. How much milk should be added to the mixture to make it 90% pure?

A. 8 litres B. 9 litres
C. 10 litres D. 12 litres

8. In what ratio must water be added to spirit to gain 25% by selling it at cost price?

A. 1 : 4 B. 4 : 1
C. 3 : 4 D. 4 : 3

9. A shopkeeper has 50 kgs of rice. He sells a part of it at 20% profit and the rest at 40% profit. If he gains 25% on the whole, find the quantity of each part.

A. 12.5 kgs and 37.5 kgs
B. 37.5 kgs and 12.5 kgs
C. 23.5 kgs and 21.5 kgs
D. 21.5 kgs and 23.5 kgs

10. A shopkeeper has 100 kgs of tea. He sells a part of it at 20% profit and the rest at 5% loss. If his overall profit is 10%, find the quantity for each part.

A. 20 kgs   B. 25 kgs
C. 30 kgs   D. 40 kgs

ANSWERS

1	2	3	4	5	6	7	8	9	10
B	D	A	B	B	A	B	A	A	D

SOME SELECTED EXPLANATORY ANSWERS

1.

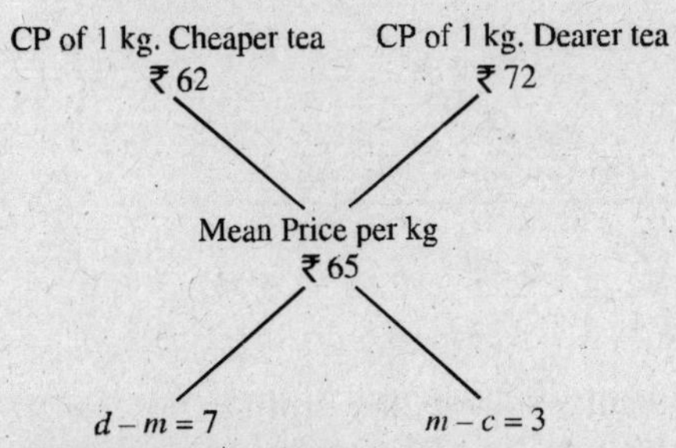

Using Alligation rule,

$$\frac{\text{Quantity of cheaper tea}}{\text{Quantity of dearer tea}} = \frac{d-m}{m-c} = \frac{7}{3}$$

Therefore, they must be mixed in the ratio of 7 : 3.

2. Cost price of the mixture $= 15 \times \frac{100}{180}$

$= ₹\ \frac{25}{3}$ per kg

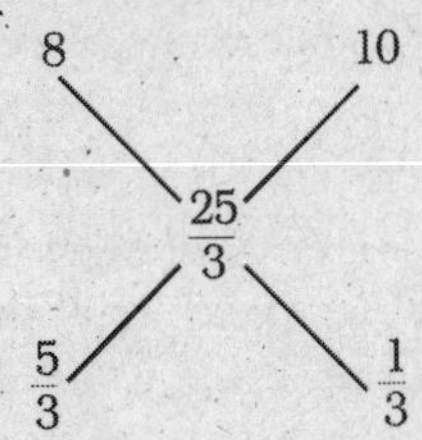

$$\frac{\text{Quantity of rice @ ₹ 8 per kg}}{\text{Quantity of rice @ ₹ 10 per kg}} = \frac{5/3}{1/3} = \frac{5}{1}$$

Quantity of rice @ ₹ 10 per kg $= 25 \times \frac{1}{5}$

= 5 kgs.

3.

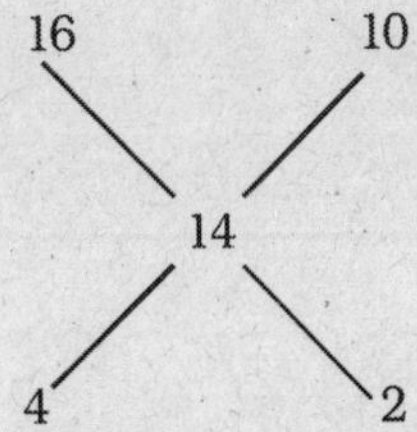

or 2 : 1

$$\frac{\text{Quantity of milk @₹ 10 per kg}}{\text{Quantity of milk @₹ 16 per kg}} = \frac{1}{2}$$

So, quantity of milk @ ₹ 10 per kg. $= \frac{26}{2}$

= 13 kgs.

4. First of all we write the fraction of milk present in three mixtures.

In A : $\frac{7}{12}$ In B : $\frac{17}{24}$

In combination of A and B : $\frac{5}{8}$

We now apply alligation rule on these fractions.

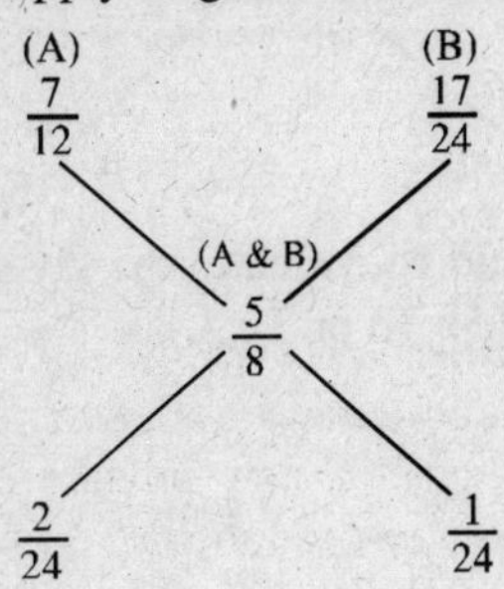

or, 2 : 1

So, Ratio of A : B = 2 : 1.

5. Fraction is

	Milk	*Water*
A :	$\frac{4}{5}$	$\frac{1}{5}$
B :	$\frac{9}{20}$	$\frac{11}{20}$

$(3A + 2B) = A \text{ and } B : \left(\frac{12}{5}+\frac{9}{10}\right) \left(\frac{3}{5}+\frac{11}{10}\right)$

$\frac{33}{10} \quad \frac{17}{10}$

So, Ratio of milk : water in the resulting mixture = 33 : 17.

6.

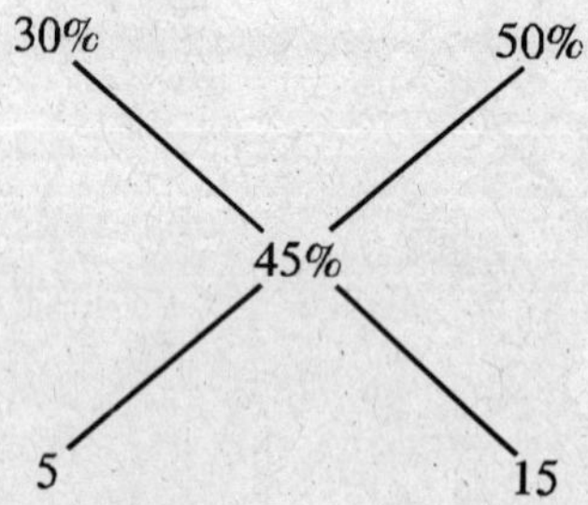

He should mix 30% and 50% in the ratio 5 : 15 or 1 : 3.

$\frac{30\% \text{ Solution}}{50\% \text{ Solution}} = \frac{1}{3}$

or 1 : 3

7. The given solution has 75% milk.
Milk to be added has 100% milk.

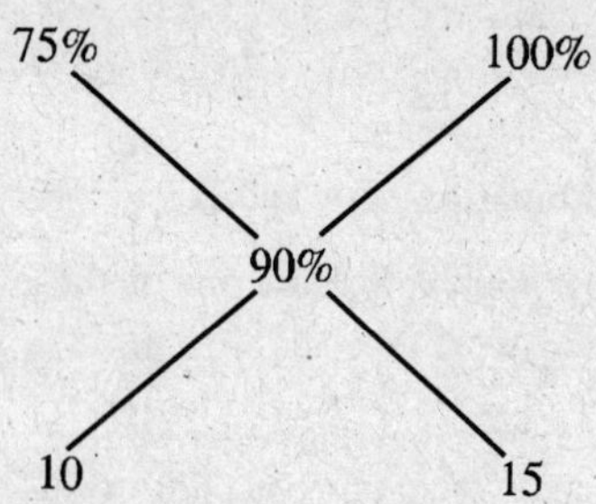

Milk should be added to the given mixture in the ratio 15 : 10 or 3 : 2.

∴ Quantity of milk to be added = $\frac{3}{2} \times 6$
= 9 litres.

8. Let cost price of spirit be Re. 1 per litre.
Then SP of mixture = Re. 1 per litre
Gain = 25%

So, CP of mixture $= 1 \times \frac{100}{125} = \text{Re. } \frac{4}{5}$

We assume that CP of water is zero.
Using alligation rule on cost price,
Water should be mixed to spirit in the ratio $\frac{1}{5} : \frac{4}{5}$ or 1 : 4.

9.

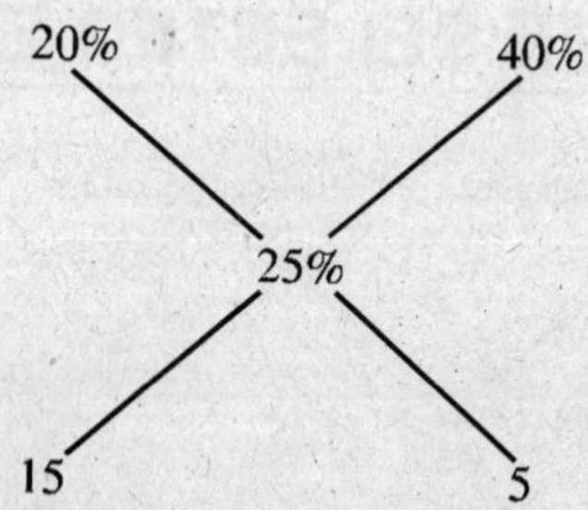

or 3 : 1

Quantity sold at 20% profit = $\frac{3}{3+1} \times 50$
= 37.5 kgs.

Quantity sold at 40% profit = (50 – 37.5)
= 12.5 kgs.

10.

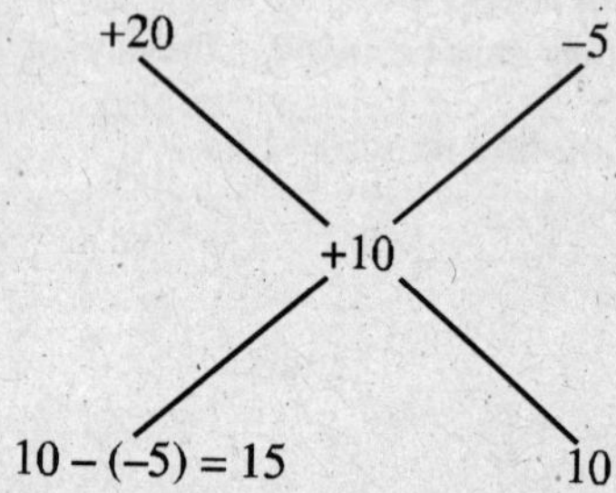

or 3 : 2

Quantity sold at 20% profit = $\frac{3}{3+2} \times 100$
= 60 kgs.

Quantity sold at 5% loss = (100 – 60)
= 40 kgs.

8. SIMPLE & COMPOUND INTERESTS

SIMPLE INTEREST

Interest is the money paid for the use of money borrowed, *i.e.*, extra money paid for using other's money is called *interest.*

The sum borrowed is called the principal. The sum of interest and principal is called the *Amount.*

If the interest on a certain sum borrowed for a certain period is reckoned uniformly, then it is called simple interest, denoted by S.I.

Thus, if A = Amount, P = Principal,
I = Interest, T = Time (in year),
R = Rate per cent per annum, then

(*a*) $I = \frac{P \times R \times T}{100}$ (*b*) $P = \frac{100 \times I}{R \times T}$

(*c*) $T = \frac{100 \times I}{P \times R}$ (*d*) $R = \frac{100 \times I}{P \times T}$

(*e*) $P = \frac{100A}{100 + RT}$ (*f*) $A = P + I.$

COMPOUND INTEREST

In business transaction if interest as it becomes due is not paid to the lender but is added on to the principal, the money is said to be lent at *compound interest* and the total sum owed after a given time is called the amount at compound interest for that time.

After a certain period, the difference between the amount and the original principal is called the compound Interest (C.I.).

Some Important Formulae :

Let Principal = P
Time = n years
Rate = r% p.a.

then, the amount,

(*a*) when interest is compounded annually:

then, Amount $= P\left(1 + \frac{r}{100}\right)^n$

(*b*) when interest is compounded half yearly:

then, Amount $= P\left(1 + \frac{r/2}{100}\right)^{2n}$

(*c*) when interest is compounded quarterly :

then, Amount $= P\left(1 + \frac{r/4}{100}\right)^{4n}$

(*d*) when time is fraction of a year, say $4\frac{1}{3}$ years,

then, Amount $= P\left(1 + \frac{r}{100}\right)^4 \times \left(1 + \frac{\frac{1}{3}r}{100}\right)$

(*e*) when rates are r_1%, r_2% and r_3% for Ist, IInd and IIIrd year respectively;
then, Amount =

$$P\left(1 + \frac{r_1}{100}\right)\left(1 + \frac{r_2}{100}\right)\left(1 + \frac{r_3}{100}\right)$$

SOLVED EXAMPLES

Example 1: A man gets a simple interest of ₹ 1,000 on a certain principal at the rate of 5% p.a. in 4 years. What compound interest will the man get on twice the principal in two years at the same rate?

Solution: $\because$ Principal $= \dfrac{1000 \times 100}{4 \times 5} =$ ₹ 5000

$$\therefore \text{ Required C.I.} = 1000\left[\left(1+\frac{5}{100}\right)^2 - 1\right]$$

$$= 1000\left[\frac{441-400}{400}\right]$$

$$= 1000 \times \frac{41}{400}$$

$= ₹$ 1025.

Example 2: The simple interest accrued on an amount of ₹ 25,000 at the end of four years is ₹ 8,000. What would be the compound interest accrued on the same amount at the same rate in the same period?

Solution: Rate $= \dfrac{8000 \times 100}{25000 \times 4}\% = 8\%$

$$\therefore \quad \text{C.I.} = 25000\left[\left(1+\frac{8}{100}\right)^4 - 1\right]$$

$$= 25000\left(\frac{27^4 - 25^4}{25^4}\right)$$

$$= 25000\left[\frac{531441 - 390625}{390625}\right]$$

$= ₹$ 9012.224

Example 3: The difference between the amount of compound interest and simple interest accrued on an amount of ₹ 26,000 at the end of 3 years is ₹ 2994.134. What is the rate of interest p.c.p.a.?

Solution: $\because \quad 2994.134 = \dfrac{26000r^2}{(100)^2}\left(\dfrac{r}{100}+3\right)$

$$= \frac{26r^2}{10}\left(\frac{r+300}{100}\right)$$

$$\Rightarrow \quad 2994134 = 26r^3 + 7800r^2$$

$$\Rightarrow \quad 115159 = r^3 + 300r^2$$

$$\therefore \quad r = 19$$

Example 4: What would be the compound interest accrued on an amount of ₹ 45,400/- at the end of two years at the rate of 15% p.a.?

Solution: $\quad \text{C.I.} = 45400\left[\left(1+\dfrac{15}{100}\right)^2 - 1\right]$

$$= 45400\left[\frac{23}{20} \times \frac{23}{20} - 1\right]$$

$$= 45400 \times \frac{129}{400}$$

$= \dfrac{29283}{2} = ₹$ 14641.5

MULTIPLE CHOICE QUESTIONS

1. Anshul borrowed some money at the rate of 4% p.a. for the first three years, at the rate of 8% p.a. for the next two years and at the rate of 9% p.a. for the period beyond 5 years. If he pays a total simple interest of ₹ 19,550 at the end of 7 years, how much money did he borrow?
   A. ₹ 39,500
   B. ₹ 42,500
   C. ₹ 41,900
   D. ₹ 43,000
2. The simple interest accrued on an amount at the end of five years @ 12.5% p.a. ₹ 1,575. What is the amount?
   A. ₹ 2,050 B. ₹ 2,550
   C. ₹ 2,250 D. ₹ 2,520
3. Siyaram invested equal sum of money in two schemes. Under scheme X, the compound interest rate was 10% p.a. and under scheme Y, the compound interest rate was 12% p.a. The interest after two years on the sum invested in Scheme X was ₹ 63. How much is the interest earned under Scheme Y after two years?
   A. ₹ 79.0272
   B. ₹ 70.56
   C. ₹ 76.32
   D. Cannot be determined

4. What would be the compound interest accrued on an amount of ₹ 15,000 at the rate of 15% at the end of three years?
A. ₹ 7813.125
B. ₹ 7762.50
C. ₹ 7762.125
D. ₹ 11235.09375

5. If the difference between the simple interest and compound interest earned on an amount @ 15% p.a. at the end of 3 years is ₹ 595.35, what is the amount?
A. ₹ 8,400
B. ₹ 9,200
C. ₹ 6,800
D. Cannot be determined

6. What will be the simple interest earned on an amount of ₹ 988 @ 18% p.a., at the end of 5 years?
A. ₹ 711.36
B. ₹ 898.2
C. ₹ 799.25
D. None of these

7. The simple interest accrued on a sum of certain principal is ₹ 1,200 in four years at the rate of 8% p.a. What would be the simple interest accrued on thrice of that principal at the rate of 6% p.a. in 3 years?
A. ₹ 2,025 B. ₹ 3,025
C. ₹ 2,250 D. ₹ 2,150

8. What amount of compound interest can be obtained on an amount of ₹ 18,000 at the rate of 10% p.a. at the end of three years?
A. ₹ 5,628 B. ₹ 5,400
C. ₹ 5,940 D. None of these

9. Shrivastava invests ₹ 14500 for 6 years at the certain rate of simple interest. After 6 years his invested sum becomes ₹ 21460. Find out the rate of interest per annum—
A. 4% p.a. B. 10% p.a.
C. 6% p.a. D. 8% p.a.

10. A sum of ₹ 12,500 amounts to ₹ 15,500 in 4 years at the rate of simple interest. What is the rate of interest?
A. 3% B. 4%
C. 5% D. 6%

11. A sum fetched a total simple interest of ₹ 4016. 25 at the rate of 9% p.a. in 5 years. What is the sum?
A. ₹ 4462.50 B. ₹ 8032.50
C. ₹ 8900 D. ₹ 8925

12. ₹ 800 becomes ₹ 956 in 3 years at a certain rate of simple interest. If the rate of interest is increased by 4%, what amount will ₹ 800 become in 3 years?
A. ₹ 1020.80
B. ₹ 1025
C. ₹ 1052
D. Data inadequate

13. A certain amount earns simple interest of ₹ 1750 after 7 years. Had the interest been 2% more, how much more interest would it have earned?
A. ₹ 35
B. ₹ 245
C. ₹ 350
D. Cannot be determined

14. Neelam borrowed some money at the rate of 6% p.a. for the first three years, 9% p.a. for the next five years and 13% p.a. for the period beyond eight years. If the total interest paid by him at the end of eleven years is ₹ 8160, how much money did he borrow?
A. ₹ 8000 B. ₹ 10,000
C. ₹ 12000 D. Data inadequate

15. The simple interest on a sum of money will be ₹ 600 after 10 years. If the principal is trebled after 5 years, what will be the total interest at the end of the tenth year?
A. ₹ 600 B. ₹ 900
C. ₹ 1200 D. ₹ 1500

16. Simple interest on a certain sum at a certain annual rate of interest is $\frac{1}{9}$ of the sum. If the numbers representing rate percent and time in years be equal, then the rate of interest is :
A. $3\frac{1}{3}\%$ B. 5%
C. $6\frac{2}{3}\%$ D. 10%

17. A borrowed some money from B at 12% p.a. S.I. for 3 years. He then added some more money to the borrowed sum and lent it to C for the same period at 14% p.a. rate of interest. If A gains ₹ 93.90 in the whole transaction, how much money did he add from his side?

A. ₹ 35 B. ₹ 55
C. ₹ 80 D. ₹ 105

18. A sum of ₹ 725 is lent in the beginning of a year at a certain rate of interest. After 8 months, a sum of ₹ 362.50 more is lent but at the rate twice the former. At the end of the year, ₹ 33.50 is earned as interest from both the loans. What was the original rate of interest?

A. 3.6%
B. 4.5%
C. 5%
D. None of these

19. The difference between the simple interest received from two different sources on ₹ 1500 for 3 years is ₹ 13.50. The difference between their rates of interest is :

A. 0.1% B. 0.2%
C. 0.3% D. 0.4%

20. Priya invested an amount of ₹ 12,000 at the rate of 10% p.a. simple interest and another amount at the rate of 20% p.a. simple interest. The total interest earned at the end of one year on the total amount invested became 14% p.a. Find the total amount invested.

A. ₹ 20,000 B. ₹ 22,000
C. ₹ 24,000 D. ₹ 25,000

21. If the rate increases by 2%, the simple interest received on a sum of money increases by ₹ 108. If the time period is increased by 2 years, the simple interest on the same sum increases by ₹ 180. The sum is :

A. ₹ 1800 B. ₹ 3600
C. ₹ 5400 D. Data inadequate

22. A sum of ₹ 2600 is lent out in two parts in such a way that the interest on one part at 10% for 5 years is equal to that on another at 9% for 6 years. The sum lent out at 10% is :

A. ₹ 1150 B. ₹ 1250
C. ₹ 1350 D. ₹ 1450

23. A sum of 1550 was lent partly at 5% and partly at 8% p.a. simple interest. The total interest received after 3 years was ₹ 300. The ratio of the money lent at 5% to that lent at 8% is :

A. 5 : 8 B. 8 : 5
C. 16 : 15 D. 31 : 6

24. Deepak invested certain amount in three different schemes A, B and C with the rate of interest 10% p.a., 12% p.a. and 15% p.a. respectively. If the total interest accrued in one years was ₹ 3200 and the amount invested in Scheme C was 150% of the amount invested in Scheme A and 240% of the amount invested in Scheme B, what was the amount invested in Scheme B?

A. ₹ 5000
B. ₹ 6500
C. ₹ 8000
D. Cannot be determined

25. Shyam invested ₹ 15,000 @ 10% per annum for one year. If the interest is compounded half-yearly, then the amount received by Shyam at the end of the year will be :

A. ₹ 16,500 B. ₹ 16,525.50
C. ₹ 16,537.50 D. ₹ 18,150

26. The difference between simple interest and compound interest on ₹ 1200 for one year at 10% per annum reckoned half-yearly is :

A. ₹ 2.50 B. ₹ 3
C. ₹ 3.75 D. ₹ 4

27. There is 60% increase in an amount in 6 years at simple interest. What will be the compound interest of ₹ 12,000 after 3 years at the same rate?

A. ₹ 2160 B. ₹ 3120
C. ₹ 3972 D. ₹ 6240

28. The difference between compound interest and simple interest on an amount of ₹ 15,000 for 2 years is ₹ 96. What is the rate of interest per annum?

A. 8
B. 10
C. 12
D. Cannot be determined

29. The difference between the simple interest on a certain sum at the rate of 10% per annum for 2 years and compound interest which is compounded every 6 months is ₹ 124.05. What is the principal sum?

A. ₹ 6000 B. ₹ 8000
C. ₹ 10,000 D. ₹ 12,000

30. Mr Dubey invested money in two schemes A and B offering compound interest @ 8% p.a. and 9% p.a. respectively. If the total amount of interest accrued through two schemes together in two years was ₹ 4818.30 and the total amount invested was ₹ 27,000, what was the amount invested in Scheme A?

A. ₹ 12,000
B. ₹ 13,500
C. ₹ 15,000
D. Cannot be determined

31. A sum of money becomes ₹ 13,380 after 3 years and ₹ 20,070 after 6 years on compound interest. The sum is :

A. ₹ 8800 B. ₹ 8890
C. ₹ 8920 D. ₹ 9040

32. A sum of ₹ 12,000 deposited at compound interest becomes double after 5 years. After 20 years, it will become :

A. ₹ 96,000 B. ₹ 1,20,000
C. ₹ 1,24,000 D. ₹ 1,92,000

33. The least number of complete years in which a sum of money put out at 20% compound interest will be more than doubled is :

A. 3 B. 4
C. 5 D. 6

34. What annual payment will discharge a debt of ₹ 1025 due in 2 years at the rate of 5% compound interest?

A. ₹ 550 B. ₹ 551.25
C. ₹ 560 D. ₹ 560.75

35. A sum of money is borrowed and paid back in two annual instalments of ₹ 882 each allowing 5% compound interest. The sum borrowed was:

A. ₹ 1620 B. ₹ 1640
C. ₹ 1680 D. ₹ 1700

ANSWERS

1	2	3	4	5	6	7	8	9	10
B	D	C	A	A	D	A	D	D	D
11	**12**	**13**	**14**	**15**	**16**	**17**	**18**	**19**	**20**
D	C	D	A	C	A	D	D	C	A
21	**22**	**23**	**24**	**25**	**26**	**27**	**28**	**29**	**30**
D	C	C	A	C	B	C	A	B	A
31	**32**	**33**	**34**	**35**					
C	D	B	B	B					

SOME SELECTED EXPLANATORY ANSWERS

2. Required amount $= ₹\dfrac{1575 \times 100}{12.5 \times 5} = ₹\ 2520.$

3. Suppose Sriram invested ₹ P in each scheme.

$$\because \quad 63 = P\left[\left(1+\frac{10}{100}\right)^2 - 1\right]$$

$$\Rightarrow \quad 63 = P\left(\frac{121}{100} - 1\right) = \frac{21P}{100}$$

$$\therefore \quad P = \frac{63 \times 100}{21} = ₹\ 300$$

Compound interest of 2 years under scheme Y

$$= 300\left[\left(1+\frac{12}{100}\right)^2 - 1\right]$$

$$= \frac{300 \times 159}{625} = ₹\ 76.32.$$

5. $\because$ Required Difference $= \dfrac{P \times r^2}{(100)^2}\left(\dfrac{r}{100}+3\right)$

$$\Rightarrow \quad 595.35 = \frac{P \times 15 \times 15}{100 \times 100}\left(\frac{15}{100}+3\right)$$

$$= \frac{225P}{10000} \times \frac{315}{100}$$

$$\therefore \quad P = \frac{595.35 \times 1000000}{225 \times 315} = ₹\ 8400$$

6. $S.I. = \dfrac{988 \times 18 \times 5}{100} = ₹\ 889.20$

7. Principal $= \dfrac{1200 \times 100}{4 \times 8} = ₹\ 3750$

$$\therefore \quad S.I. = \frac{3750 \times 3 \times 3 \times 6}{100} = ₹\ 2025$$

9. From question,

$$(21460 - 14500) = \frac{14500 \times r \times 6}{100}$$

$$\Rightarrow \quad \frac{6960}{145 \times 6} = r$$

$$\therefore \quad r = 8$$

Hence the rate of interest per annum = 8%.

10. S.I. = ₹ (15500 – 12500) = ₹ 3000.

$$\text{Rate} = \left(\frac{100 \times 3000}{12500 \times 4}\right)\% = 6\%.$$

11. Principal $= ₹\left(\dfrac{100 \times 4016.25}{9 \times 5}\right)$

$$= ₹\left(\frac{401625}{45}\right) = ₹\ 8925.$$

12. S.I. = ₹ (956 – 800) = ₹ 156.

$$\text{Rate} = \left(\frac{100 \times 156}{800 \times 3}\right)\% = 6\frac{1}{2}\%.$$

$$\text{New rate} = \left(6\frac{1}{2}+4\right)\% = 10\frac{1}{2}\%.$$

$$\text{New S.I.} = ₹\left(800 \times \frac{21}{2} \times \frac{3}{100}\right) = ₹\ 252.$$

$\therefore$ New amount = ₹ (800 + 252) = ₹ 1052.

13. We need to know the S.I., principal and time to find the rate. Since the principal is not given, so data is inadequate.

14. Let the sum be ₹ x. Then,

$$\left(\frac{x \times 6 \times 3}{100}\right)+\left(\frac{x \times 9 \times 5}{100}\right)+\left(\frac{x \times 13 \times 3}{100}\right) = 8160$$

$$\Rightarrow \quad 18x + 45x + 39x = (8160 \times 100)$$

$$\Rightarrow \quad 102x = 816000 \quad \Rightarrow \quad x = 8000.$$

15. Let the sum be ₹ x. Now, S.I. = ₹ 600, T = 10 years.

$$\text{Rate} = \left(\frac{100 \times 600}{x \times 10}\right)\% = \left(\frac{6000}{x}\right)\%.$$

$$\text{S.I. for first 5 years} = ₹\left(\frac{x \times 5 \times 6000}{x \times 100}\right) = ₹\ 300.$$

$$\text{S.I. for last 5 years} = ₹\left(3x \times 5 \times \frac{6000}{x \times 100}\right) = ₹\ 900.$$

$\therefore$ Total interest = ₹ 1200.

16. Let sum = x. Then, S.I. $= \dfrac{x}{9}$.

Let rate = R% and time = R years.

$$\therefore \quad \left(\frac{x \times R \times R}{100}\right) = \frac{x}{9} \quad \Rightarrow R^2 = \frac{100}{9}$$

$$\Rightarrow \quad R = \frac{10}{3} = 3\frac{1}{3}.$$

Hence, rate $= 3\frac{1}{3}\%$.

17. Let the money added be ₹ x Then,

$$\frac{(830+x) \times 14 \times 3}{100} - \frac{830 \times 12 \times 3}{100} = 93.90$$

$$\Rightarrow \quad 830 \times 42 + 42x - 830 \times 36 = 9390$$

$$\Rightarrow \quad 42x + 830 \times (42 - 36) = 9390$$

$\Rightarrow \quad 42x = 9390 - 4980 \Rightarrow x = \frac{4410}{42} = 105.$

$\therefore$ Money added = ₹ 105.

18. Let the original rate be R%. Then, new rate = (2R)%.

$\therefore \left(\frac{725 \times R \times 1}{100}\right) + \left(\frac{36250 \times 2R \times 1}{100 \times 3}\right) = 33.50$

$\Rightarrow (2175 + 725)\,R = 33.50 \times 100 \times 3 = 10050$

$\Rightarrow \; R = \frac{10050}{2900} = 3.46.$

$\therefore$ Original rate = 3.46%.

19. $\left(\frac{1500 \times R_1 \times 3}{100}\right) - \left(\frac{1500 \times R_2 \times 3}{100}\right) = 13.50$

$\Rightarrow \; 4500\,(R_1 - R_2) = 1350$

$\Rightarrow \; R_1 - R_2 = \frac{1350}{4500} = 0.3\%.$

20. Let the second amount be ₹ x. Then,

$\left(\frac{12000 \times 10 \times 1}{100}\right) + \left(\frac{x \times 20 \times 1}{100}\right)$

$= \left[\frac{(12000 + x) \times 14 \times 1}{100}\right]$

$\Rightarrow \; 120000 + 20x = 168000 + 14x$

$\Rightarrow \; 6x = 48000 \Rightarrow x = 8000.$

$\therefore$ Total investment = ₹ (12000 + 8000)
= ₹ 20000.

21. Let the sum be ₹ x, rate be R% p.a. and time be T years.

Then, $\left[\frac{x \times (R + 2) \times T}{100}\right] - \left(\frac{x \times R \times T}{100}\right) = 108$

$\Rightarrow \quad 2xT = 10800 \quad ...(i)$

And, $\left[\frac{x \times R \times (T + 2)}{100}\right] - \left(\frac{x \times R \times T}{100}\right) = 180$

$\Rightarrow \quad 2xR = 18000 \quad ...(ii)$

Clearly, from (*i*) and (*ii*), we cannot find the value of x.
So, the data is inadequate.

22. Let the sum lent at 10% be ₹ x and that lent at 9% be ₹ $(2600 - x)$. Then,

$\left(\frac{x \times 10 \times 5}{100}\right) = \frac{(2600 - x) \times 9 \times 6}{100}$

$\Rightarrow \; 50x = (2600 \times 54) - 54x$

$\Rightarrow \; x = \left(\frac{2600 \times 54}{104}\right) = 1350.$

$\therefore$ Sum lent at 10% = ₹ 1350.

23. Let the sum lent at 5% be ₹ x and that lent at 8% be ₹ $(1550 - x)$. Then,

$\left(\frac{x \times 5 \times 3}{100}\right) + \left[\frac{(1550 - x) \times 8 \times 3}{100}\right] = 300$

$\Rightarrow \; 15x - 24x + (1550 \times 24) = 30000$

$\Rightarrow \; 9x = 7200 \quad \Rightarrow \; x = 800.$

$\therefore$ Required ratio = 800 : 750 = 16 : 15.

24. Let x, y and z be the amounts invested in schemes A, B and C respectively. Then,

$\left(\frac{x \times 10 \times 1}{100}\right) + \left(\frac{y \times 12 \times 1}{100}\right) + \left(\frac{z \times 15 \times 1}{100}\right) = 3200$

$\Rightarrow \quad 10x + 12y + 15z = 320000 \quad ...(i)$

Now, $\quad z = 240\%$ of $y = \frac{12}{5}y \quad ...(ii)$

And, $\quad z = 150\%$ of $x = \frac{3}{2}x$

$\Rightarrow \; x = \frac{2}{3}z = \left(\frac{2}{3} \times \frac{12}{5}\right)y = \frac{8}{5}y \quad ...(iii)$

From (*i*), (*ii*) and (*iii*), we have :
$16y + 12y + 36y = 320000 \Rightarrow 64y = 320000$
$\Rightarrow \; y = 5000.$

$\therefore$ Sum invested in Scheme B = ₹ 5000.

25. P = ₹ 15000; R = 10% p.a. = 5% per half-year; T = 1 year = 2 half-years.

$\therefore$ Amount = ₹$\left[15000 \times \left(1 + \frac{5}{100}\right)^2\right]$

= ₹$\left(15000 \times \frac{21}{20} \times \frac{21}{20}\right)$

= ₹ 16537.50.

26. S.I. = ₹$\left(\frac{1200 \times 10 \times 1}{100}\right)$ = ₹ 120.

C.I. = ₹$\left[1200 \times \left(1 + \frac{5}{100}\right)^2 - 1200\right]$ = ₹ 123.

$\therefore$ Difference = ₹ (123 − 120) = ₹ 3.

27. Let P = ₹ 100. Then, S.I. = ₹ 60 and T = 6 years.

$\therefore \quad R = \frac{100 \times 60}{100 \times 6} = 10\%$ p.a.

Now, P = ₹ 12000, T = 3 years and R = 10% p.a.

$$\therefore \quad \text{C.I.} = ₹\left[12000 \times \left\{\left(1+\frac{10}{100}\right)^3 - 1\right\}\right]$$

$$= ₹\left(12000 \times \frac{331}{1000}\right) = ₹\ 3972.$$

28. $\left[15000 \times \left(1+\frac{R}{100}\right)^2 - 15000\right] - \left(\frac{15000 \times R \times 2}{100}\right) = 96$

$$\Rightarrow \quad 15000\left[\left(1+\frac{R}{100}\right)^2 - 1 - \frac{2R}{100}\right] = 96$$

$$\Rightarrow \quad 15000\left[\frac{(100-R)^2 - 10000 - 200R}{10000}\right] = 96$$

$$\Rightarrow \quad R^2 = \frac{96 \times 2}{3} = 64 \Rightarrow R = 8.$$

$\therefore$ Rate = 8%.

30. Let the investment in scheme A be ₹ x. Then, investment in scheme B = ₹ $(27000 - x)$

$$\therefore \left[x \times \left\{\left(1+\frac{8}{100}\right)^2 - 1\right\} + (27000-x)\left\{\left(1+\frac{9}{100}\right)^2 - 1\right\}\right] = 4818.30.$$

$$\Rightarrow \quad \left(x \times \frac{104}{625}\right) + \frac{1881(27000-x)}{10000} = \frac{481830}{100}$$

$\Rightarrow \quad 1664x + 1881\ (27000 - x) = 48183000$

$\Rightarrow \quad (1881x - 1664x) = (50787000 - 48183000)$

$\Rightarrow \quad 217x = 2604000$

$$\Rightarrow \quad x = \frac{2604000}{217} = 12000.$$

32. $12000 \times \left(1+\frac{R}{100}\right)^5 = 24000$

$$\Rightarrow \quad \left(1+\frac{R}{100}\right)^5 = 2$$

$$\therefore \quad \left[\left(1+\frac{R}{100}\right)^5\right]^4 = 2^4 = 16$$

$$\Rightarrow \quad \left(1+\frac{R}{100}\right)^{20} = 16$$

$$\Rightarrow \quad P\left(1+\frac{R}{100}\right)^{20} = 16P$$

$$\Rightarrow \quad 12000\left(1+\frac{R}{100}\right)^{20} = 16 \times 12000 = 192000.$$

33. $P\left(1+\frac{R}{100}\right)^n > 2P$ or $\left(\frac{6}{5}\right)^n > 2$

Now, $\left(\frac{6}{5} \times \frac{6}{5} \times \frac{6}{5} \times \frac{6}{5}\right) > 2$. So, n = 4 years.

34. Let each instalment be ₹ x. Then,

$$\frac{x}{\left(1+\frac{5}{100}\right)} + \frac{x}{\left(1+\frac{5}{100}\right)^2} = 1025$$

$$\Rightarrow \quad \frac{20x}{21} + \frac{400x}{441} = 1025$$

$\Rightarrow \quad 820x = 1025 \times 441$

$$\Rightarrow \quad x = \left(\frac{1025 \times 441}{820}\right) = 551.25.$$

So, value of each instalment = ₹ 551.25

35. Principal = (P.W. of ₹ 882 due 1 year hence) + (P.W. of ₹ 882 due 2 years hence)

$$= \left[\frac{882}{\left(1+\frac{5}{100}\right)} + \frac{882}{\left(1+\frac{5}{100}\right)^2}\right]$$

$$= \left(\frac{882 \times 20}{21} + \frac{882 \times 400}{441}\right) = ₹\ 1640.$$

9. TIME & WORK

IMPORTANT FACTS

1. If A can do a piece of work in n days, then work done by A in 1 day $= \frac{1}{n}$.
2. If work done by A in 1 day $= \frac{1}{n}$; then A can finish the whole work in n days.
3. If A is twice as good a workman as B then; Ratio of work done by A and B = 2 : 1
   Ratio of times taken by A and B to finish a work = 1 : 2.
4. If a pipe can fill a tank in x hours, then the part filled in 1 hour $= \frac{1}{x}$.
5. If a pipe can empty a tank in y hour, then the part of the tank emptied in 1 hour $= \frac{1}{y}$.
6. If two pipes can fill a tank in x and y hours respectively and both the pipes are opened simultaneously then, the part filled in 1 hour $= \frac{1}{x} + \frac{1}{y}$.
7. (*a*) A tap fills a cistern in x hours and the other can empty the cistern in y hours. If both the taps are opened simultaneously, then the net part of the tank filled in 1 hour $= \frac{1}{x} - \frac{1}{y}$; when $y > x$.

   (*b*) A tap can fill a tank in x hours and other can empty in y hours. If both the taps are opened simultaneously, then the net part of tank emptied in 1 hour $= \frac{1}{y} - \frac{1}{x}$; when $x > y$.

SOLVED EXAMPLES

Example 1: A and B together can complete a piece of work in 4 days. If A alone can complete the same piece of work in 5 days, in how many days will B alone complete it?

Solution: (A + B)'s 1 day's work $= \frac{1}{4}$

A's 1 day's work $= \frac{1}{5}$

$\therefore$ B's 1 day work $= \frac{1}{4} - \frac{1}{5} = \frac{5-4}{20} = \frac{1}{20}$

$\therefore$ B alone will complete the work 20 days.

Example 2: Four examiners can examine a certain number of answer papers in 10 days by working for 5 hours a day. For how many hours in a day would 2 examiners have to work in order to examine twice the number of answer papers in 20 days?

Solution:

No. of exam	Hrs. per day	No. of papers	Days
4 ↓	5 ↓	1 ↓	10 ↓
2	x	2	20

$$\left.\begin{array}{ccc} 2 & : & 4 \\ 1 & : & 2 \\ 20 & : & 10 \end{array}\right\} :: 5 : x$$

$$\therefore \quad x = \frac{4 \times 2 \times 10 \times 5}{2 \times 20} = 10 \text{ hrs./day}$$

Example 3: 6 women and 6 men together can complete a piece of work in 6 days. In how many days can 15 men alone complete the piece of work if 9 women alone can complete the work in 10 days?

Solution: $\because$ Work of 1 woman for 1 day

$$= \frac{1}{9\times10} = \frac{1}{90}$$

$\Rightarrow$ Work of 6 women for 6 days

$$= \frac{1}{90}\times6\times6 = \frac{2}{5}$$

$\Rightarrow$ Work of 6 men for 6 days

$$= 1-\frac{2}{5} = \frac{3}{5}$$

$\Rightarrow$ Work of 1 man for 1 day

$$= \frac{3}{5\times6\times6} = \frac{1}{60}$$

$\therefore$ Work of 15 men for 1 day

$$= \frac{1}{60}\times15 = \frac{1}{4}.$$

Hence, 15 men will complete the work in 4 days.

Example 4: Six boys or four men can complete a piece of work in 24 days. In how many days will 3 boys and 10 men together complete the same piece of work?

Solution: 4 men = 6 boys

$$\therefore \quad 10 \text{ men} = \frac{6}{4}\times10 = 15 \text{ boys}$$

$$\therefore \quad 10 \text{ men} + 3 \text{ boys} = 15 + 3 = 18 \text{ boys}$$

$$\therefore \text{Required number of days} = \frac{6\times24}{18} = 8.$$

MULTIPLE CHOICE QUESTIONS

1. 24 men can complete a piece of work in 16 days. The same work can be completed by 8 women in 72 days, whereas 24 children take 32 days to complete it. If 10 men, 15 women and 24 children work together, in how many days can the work be completed?

A. 18 B. 8
C. 22 D. 12

2. 18 Men alone can complete a piece of work in 24 days. 54 Women alone can complete the same piece of work in 12 days and 16 children alone can complete the same piece of work in 54 days. In how many days can 3 men, 9 women and 6 children together complete the piece of work?

A. 18
B. 36
C. 27
D. Cannot be determined

3. If 80 persons can finish a work within 16 days by working 6 hours a day then how many hours per day should 64 persons work to complete that very job within 15 days?

A. 7 hrs B. 8 hrs
C. 6 hrs D. 5 hrs

4. A and B can do a piece of work in 12 days. B and C in 15 days and C and A in 20 days. In how many days A, B and C together can do the work?

A. 8 days B. 12 days
C. 10 days D. 14 days

5. 5 labourers can make 5 mats in 5 hours. How many mats will 10 labourers make in 10 hours?

A. 10 B. 20
C. 30 D. 35

6. A can do $\frac{1}{2}$ of a work in 9 days while B can do $\frac{1}{3}$ of the same work in 6 days. How long would it take for A and B together to complete the work?

A. 18 B. 6
C. 12 D. 9

7. A can do a piece of work in 40 days. He works on it for 5 days and then B completes it in 21 days. How long will A and B together take to complete the work?

A. 20 days B. 15 days
C. 30 days D. 10 days

8. A, B and C can complete a work separately in 24, 36 and 48 days respectively. They started together but C left after 4 days of start and A left 3 days before the completion of work. In how many days will the work be completed?

A. 15 days B. 18 days
C. 10 days D. 12 days

9. A and B can do a piece of work in 12 days. B and C together can do it in 15 days. If A is twice as good a work man as C, find in what time B alone can do it?

A. 12 days B. 15 days
C. 20 days D. 24 days

10. If 4 men or 6 boys can finish a piece of work in 20 days, in how many days can 6 men and 11 boys finish it?

A. 20 days B. 12 days
C. 8 days D. 6 days

11. 5 men and 2 boys together in 1 hour do 4 times work as 1 man and 1 boy do in an hour. Determine the ratio of the specified times of works of a man and a boy.

A. 4 : 1 B. 1 : 4
C. 3 : 4 D. 2 : 1

12. 75 boys finish a work in 24 days. How many men will complete twice the work in 20 days while 2 men do in a day same work as 3 boys do in a day?

A. 50 B. 24
C. 60 D. 120

13. If 3 men and 4 boys together earn ₹ 264 in 8 days and 2 men and 3 boys together earn ₹ 184 in the same time, then in how many days will 6 men and 7 boys together earn ₹ 315?

A. 5 days B. 6 days
C. 9 days D. 10 days

14. Pipes A and B can fill a tank in 36 and 48 hours respectively. Both pipes are opened together to fill the tank. After some time pipe B is closed and the tank is full in 24 hours. For how much time was the pipe B opend?

A. 20 hrs. B. 16 hrs.
C. 48 hrs. D. 36 hrs.

15. A tank is normally filled in 9 hours. But because of a leak in its bottom it takes 3 hours more to fill. How much time will it take the leak to empty the full tank?

A. 12 hrs. B. 24 hrs.
C. 36 hrs. D. 48 hrs.

16. Three pipes A, B and C are connected to a tank. A and B can fill it in 20 and 30 minutes respectively, while C can empty it in 15 minutes. If A, B and C are kept open successively for 1 minute each, how soon will the tank be filled?

A. 176 min B. 167 min
C. 180 min D. 170 min

17. Two pipes A and B can separately fill a cistern in $7\frac{1}{2}$ minutes and 5 minutes respectively and a waste pipe C can carry off 14 litres per minute. If all the pipes are opened when the cistern is full, it is emptied in 1 hour. How many litres does it hold?

A. 40 litres B. 20 litres
C. 36 litres D. 30 litres

18. Two workers A and B are engaged to do a work. A working alone takes 8 hours more to complete the job than if both worked together. If B worked alone, he would need $4\frac{1}{2}$ hours more to complete the job than they both working together. What time would they take to do the work together?

A. 4 hours B. 5 hours
C. 6 hours D. 7 hours

19. Savita can do a piece of work in 20 days. Tripti is 25% more efficient than Savita. The number of days taken by Tripti to do the same piece of work is :

A. 15 B. 16
C. 18 D. 25

20. A machine P can print one lakh books in 8 hours, machine Q can print the same number of books in 10 hours while machine R can print them in 12 hours. All the machines are started at 9 a.m. while machine P is closed at

11 a.m. and the remaining two machines complete the work. Approximately at what time will the work be finished?

A. 11:30 a.m. B. 12 noon
C. 12:30 p.m. D. 1 p.m.

21. A and B can do a piece of work in 45 days and 40 days respectively. They began to do the work together but A leaves after some days and then B completed the remaining work in 23 days. The number of days after which A left the work was :

A. 6 B. 8
C. 9 D. 12

22. A, B and C are employed to do a piece of work for ₹ 529. A and B together are supposed to do $\frac{19}{23}$ of the work and B and C together $\frac{8}{23}$ of the work. What amount should A be paid?

A. ₹ 315 B. ₹ 345
C. ₹ 355 D. ₹ 375

23. A sum of money is sufficient to pay A's wages for 21 days and B's wages for 28 days. The same money is sufficient to pay the wages of both for :

A. 12 days B. $12\frac{1}{4}$ days
C. 14 days D. $24\frac{1}{2}$ days

24. 12 men complete a work in 9 days. After they have worked for 6 days, 6 more men join them. How many days will they take to complete the remaining work?

A. 2 days B. 3 days
C. 4 days D. 5 days

25. 10 men and 15 women together can complete a work in 6 days. It takes 100 days for one man alone to complete the same work. How many days will be required for one woman alone to complete the same work?

A. 90 B. 125
C. 145 D. 150

26. 12 men can complete a piece of work in 4 days. While 15 women can compete the same work in 4 days. 6 men start working on the job and after working for 2 days, all of them stopped working. How many women should be put on the job to complete the remaining work, if it is to be completed in 3 days?

A. 15 B. 18
C. 22 D. Data inadequate

27. 10 women can complete a work in 7 days and 10 children take 14 days to complete the work. How many days will 5 women and 10 children take to complete the work?

A. 3
B. 5
C. 7
D. Cannot be determined

28. Twenty-four men can complete a work in sixteen days. Thirty-two women can complete the same work in twenty-four days. Sixteen men and sixteen women started working and worked for twelve days. How many more men are to be added to complete the remaining work in 2 days?

A. 16 B. 24
C. 36 D. 48

29. A pump can fill a tank with water in 2 hours. Because of a leak, it took $2\frac{1}{3}$ hours to fill the tank. The leak can drain all the water of the tank in :

A. $4\frac{1}{3}$ hrs B. 7 hrs
C. 8 hrs D. 14 hrs

30. Two pipes A and B together can fill a cistern in 4 hours. Had they been opened separately, then B would have taken 6 hours more than A to fill the cistern. How much time will be taken by A to fill the cistern separately?

A. 1 hr B. 2 hrs
C. 6 hrs D. 8 hrs

31. A tank is filled in 5 hours by three pipes A, B and C. The pipe C is twice as fast as B and

B is twice as fast as A. How much time will pipe A alone take to fill the tank?

A. 20 hrs

B. 25 hrs

C. 35 hrs

D. Cannot be determined

32. Bucket P has thrice the capacity as bucket Q. It takes 60 turns for bucket P to fill the empty drum. How many turns it will take for both the buckets P and Q, having each turn together to fill the empty drum?

A. 30 B. 40

C. 45 D. 90

33. A large tanker can be filled by two pipes A and B in 60 and 40 minutes respectively. How many minutes will it take to fill the tanker from empty state if B is used for half the time and A and B fill it together for the other half?

A. 15 min B. 20 min

C. 27.5 min D. 30 min

34. A leak in the bottom of a tank can empty the full tank in 8 hours. An inlet pipe fills water at the rate of 6 litres a minute. When the tank is full, the inlet is opened and due to the leak, the tank is empty in 12 hours. How many litres does the cistern hold?

A. 7580 B. 7960

C. 8290 D. 8640

35. Two pipes can fill a tank in 20 and 24 minutes respectively and a waste pipe can empty 3 gallons per minute. All the three pipes working together can fill the tank in 15 minutes. The capacity of the tank is :

A. 60 gallons B. 100 gallons

C. 120 gallons D. 180 gallons

ANSWERS

1	2	3	4	5	6	7	8	9	10
D	B	B	C	B	D	B	A	C	D
11	**12**	**13**	**14**	**15**	**16**	**17**	**18**	**19**	**20**
D	D	A	B	C	B	A	C	B	D
21	**22**	**23**	**24**	**25**	**26**	**27**	**28**	**29**	**30**
C	B	A	A	E	A	C	B	D	C
31	**32**	**33**	**34**	**35**	**36**	**37**	**38**	**39**	**40**
C	C	D	D	C					

SOME SELECTED EXPLANATORY ANSWERS

1. In 16 days the work is completed by 24 men.

∴ In 1 day the work is completed by

$= 24 \times 16 = 384$ men.

Similarly in 1 day the work is completed by

$= 72 \times 8 = 576$ women

and in 1 day the work is completed by

$= 24 \times 32 = 768$ children

∵ 384 men = 768 children

∴ 10 men $= \frac{768 \times 10}{384} = 20$ children

and 576 women = 768 children

∴ 15 women $= \frac{768 \times 15}{576} = 20$ children

∴ $(20 + 20 + 24) = 64$ children

∵ 24 children complete the work in 32 days.

∴ 64 children complete the work in $= \frac{32 \times 24}{64}$

$= 12$ days.

2. Work done by 3 man + 9 women + 6 children in 1 day

$$= \frac{3\times1}{24\times18}+\frac{9\times1}{12\times54}+\frac{6\times1}{54\times16}$$

$$= \frac{1}{144}+\frac{1}{72}+\frac{1}{144} = \frac{1}{36}$$

$\because \frac{1}{36}$ work is done in 1 day.

$\therefore$ 1 work is done in $= \frac{1\times36}{1}$ = 36 days.

3. 80 persons can do the job in 16 days by working = 6 hrs daily

1 person can do the job in 16 days by working = 6 × 80 hrs daily

1 person can do the job in 1 day by working = 6 × 80 × 16 hrs daily

64 persons can do the job in 15 days by working

$$= \frac{6\times80\times16}{64\times15} \text{ hrs} = 8 \text{ hr.}$$

5. 5 labourers in 5 hrs. can make = 5 mats

1 labourer in 5 hrs. can make $= \frac{5}{5}$ mats

1 labourer in 1 hrs. can make $= \frac{5}{5\times5}$ mats

10 labourers in 10 hrs. can make

$$= \frac{5\times10\times10}{5\times5} = 20 \text{ mats.}$$

6. A's 9 day's work $= \frac{1}{2}$

$\therefore$ A's 1 day's work $= \frac{1}{2\times9} = \frac{1}{18}$

B's 6 day's work $= \frac{1}{3}$

$\therefore$ B's 1 day's work $= \frac{1}{3\times6} = \frac{1}{18}$

$\therefore$ (A + B)'s 1 day's work $= \frac{1}{18}+\frac{1}{18}$

$$= \frac{2}{18} = \frac{1}{9}$$

$\therefore$ A and B both together will complete the work in 9 days.

8. Let the work be completed in x days. Therefore, A worked for $x - 3$ days, B for x days and C for 4 days.

A's 1 day's work $= \frac{1}{24}$

B's 1 day's work $= \frac{1}{36}$

and, C's 1 day's work $= \frac{1}{48}$

$$\therefore (x-3)\times\frac{1}{24}+x\times\frac{1}{36}+4\times\frac{1}{48} = 1$$

$$\Rightarrow \frac{x-3}{24}+\frac{x}{36}+\frac{1}{12} = 1$$

$$\Rightarrow \frac{3x-9+2x+6}{72} = 1$$

$$\Rightarrow 5x - 3 = 72$$

$$\Rightarrow 5x = 75$$

$$\Rightarrow x = \frac{75}{5} = 15$$

Hence, the work was completed in 15 days.

11. Work of (5 men + 2 boys) = 4 (work of 1 man + 1 boy)

= Work of 4 men + 4 boys

$\Rightarrow$ Work of (5 men – 4 men)

= Work of (4 boys – 2 boys)

$\Rightarrow$ Work of 1 man = Work of 2 boys

$\therefore$ Required ratio = 2 : 1

12. Work of 3 boys = Work of 2 men

$\therefore$ Work of 1 boy = Work of $\frac{2}{3}$ man

$\therefore$ Work of 75 boys = Work of $\frac{2}{3}\times75$

= 50 men

$\because$ 1 work is completed in 24 days by 50 men

$\therefore$ 1 work is completed in 1 day by 50 × 24 men

$\therefore$ 2 works are completed in 20 days by

$$\frac{50\times24\times2}{20} = 120 \text{ men.}$$

13. Let men be denoted by m and boys by b.

$3m + 4b$ earn in 8 days = ₹ 264

$\therefore$ $3m + 4b$ earn in 1 day = $\frac{264}{8}$ = ₹ 33 ...(i)

And, $2m + 3b$ earn in 8 days= ₹ 184

$\therefore$ $2m + 3b$ earn in 1 day = $\frac{184}{8}$ = ₹ 23 ...(ii)

By (ii) × 3 – (i) × 2, we have

$$6m + 9b - 6m - 8b = 69 - 66$$

$$\Rightarrow \quad 1b = ₹\ 3$$

$$\therefore \quad 3m + 4b = 33$$

$$3m = 33 - 4 \times 3 = 21$$

$$1m = 7$$

$\therefore$ Wages for 1 day of 6 men and 7 boys

$$= 6 \times 7 + 7 \times 3$$

$$= 42 + 21 = ₹\ 63$$

$\because$ ₹ 63 are wages for 1 day

$\therefore$ ₹ 315 are wages for = $\frac{315}{63}$ = 5 days.

15. Without the leak, in 1 hour $\frac{1}{9}$ of the tank is filled.

$\therefore$ In extra 3 hrs, the pipe fills $\frac{3}{9}=\frac{1}{3}$ of the tank more.

In (9 + 3) = 12 hours, the leak empties this extra $\frac{1}{3}$ of the tank.

$\therefore$ The leak will empty the full tank in $12\times\frac{3}{1}$ = 36 hrs.

16. $\left(\frac{1}{20}+\frac{1}{30}-\frac{1}{15}\right) = \frac{1}{60}$ of the tank is filled in first 3 minutes

$$\frac{1}{20}+\frac{1}{30} = \frac{5}{60}$$

$$1-\frac{5}{60} = \frac{55}{60}$$

This $\frac{55}{60}$ part of the tank will be filled in $3 \times 55 = 165$ minutes.

The last $\frac{5}{60}$ part will be filled in 2 minutes, successively by A and B.

Total time = 165 + 2 = 167 minutes.

17. Cistern filled by (A + B) in 1 minute

$$= \left(\frac{2}{15}+\frac{1}{5}\right) = \frac{1}{3}$$

Net emptying work done by (A + B + C) in 1 minute = $\frac{1}{60}$

Work done by C in 1 minute = $\left(\frac{1}{60}+\frac{1}{3}\right)=\frac{7}{20}$

$\therefore$ C alone can empty the cistern in $\left(\frac{20}{7}\right)$ minutes

Water thrown out by C in 1 minute = 14 litres

Water thrown out by C in $\left(\frac{20}{7}\right)$ minutes =

$$\left(14\times\frac{20}{7}\right) = 40 \text{ litres}$$

$\therefore$ Capacity of the cistern = 40 litres.

18. Let A and B together take x hours to complete the work. Then,
A alone takes $(x + 8)$ hrs and B alone takes $\left(x+\frac{9}{2}\right)$ hrs to complete the work. Then,

$$\frac{1}{(x+8)}+\frac{1}{\left(x+\frac{9}{2}\right)} = \frac{1}{x}$$

$$\Rightarrow \quad \frac{1}{(x+8)}+\frac{2}{(2x+9)} = \frac{1}{x}$$

$$\Rightarrow \quad x(4x + 25) = (x + 8)(2x + 9)$$

$$\Rightarrow \quad 2x^2 = 72$$

$$\Rightarrow \quad x^2 = 36$$

$\Rightarrow \qquad x = 6.$

19. Ratio of times taken by Savita and Tripti

$= 125 : 100$
$= 5 : 4.$

Suppose Tripti takes x days to do the work.

$5 : 4 :: 20 : x \Rightarrow x = \left(\frac{4\times 20}{5}\right)$

$\Rightarrow x = 16$ days.

Hence, Tripti takes 16 days to complete the work.

21. (A + B)'s 1 day's work $= \left(\frac{1}{45}+\frac{1}{40}\right) = \frac{17}{360}.$

Work done by B in 23 days $= \left(\frac{1}{40}\times 23\right)$

$= \frac{23}{40}.$

Remaining work $= \left(1-\frac{23}{40}\right) = \frac{17}{40}.$

Now, $\frac{17}{360}$ work was done by (A + B) in 1 day.

$\frac{17}{40}$ work was done by (A + B) in

$\left(1\times\frac{360}{17}\times\frac{17}{40}\right) = 9$ days.

∴ A left after 9 days.

22. Work done by A $= \left(1-\frac{8}{23}\right) = \frac{15}{23}.$

∴ A : (B + C) $= \frac{15}{23}:\frac{8}{23} = 15 : 8.$

So, A's share = ₹$\left(\frac{15}{23}\times 529\right)$ = ₹ 345.

23. Let total money be ₹ x.

A's 1 day's wages = ₹$\frac{x}{21}$, B's 1 day's wages

= ₹$\frac{x}{28}$.

∴ (A + B)'s 1 day's wages

= ₹$\left(\frac{x}{21}+\frac{x}{28}\right)$ = ₹$\frac{x}{12}$.

∴ Money is sufficient to pay the wages of both for 12 days.

24. 1 man's 1 day's work $= \frac{1}{108}.$

12 men's 6 day's work $= \left(\frac{1}{9}\times 6\right) = \frac{2}{3}.$

Remaining work $= \left(1-\frac{2}{3}\right) = \frac{1}{3}.$

18 men's 1 day's work $= \left(\frac{1}{108}\times 18\right) = \frac{1}{6}.$

$\frac{1}{6}$ work is done by them in 1 day.

∴ $\frac{1}{3}$ work is done by them in $\left(6\times\frac{1}{3}\right) = 2$ days.

25. 1 man's 1 day's work $= \frac{1}{100}.$ (10 men + 15 women)'s 1 day's work $= \frac{1}{6}.$

15 women's 1 day's work $= \left(\frac{1}{6}-\frac{10}{100}\right) = \frac{1}{15}.$

1 woman's 1 day's work $= \frac{1}{225}.$

∴ 1 woman alone can complete the work in 225 days.

26. 1 man's 1 day's work $= \frac{1}{48}$; 1 woman's 1 day's work $= \frac{1}{60}.$

6 men's 2 day's work $= \left(\frac{6}{48}\times 2\right) = \frac{1}{4}.$

Remaining work $= \left(1-\frac{1}{4}\right) = \frac{3}{4}.$

Now, $\frac{1}{60}$ work is done in 1 day by 1 woman.

So, $\frac{3}{4}$ work will be done in 3 days by

$\left(60\times\frac{3}{4}\times\frac{1}{3}\right) = 15$ women.

27. 1 woman's 1 day's work $= \frac{1}{70}$; 1 child's 1 day's work $= \frac{1}{140}$.

(5 women + 10 children)'s 1 day's work

$$= \left(\frac{5}{70} + \frac{10}{140}\right) = \frac{1}{7}.$$

$\therefore$ 5 women and 10 children will complete the work in 7 days.

29. Tank emptied by the leak in 1 hour $= \left(\frac{1}{2} - \frac{3}{7}\right)$

$$= \frac{1}{14}.$$

$\therefore$ Leak will empty the tank in 14 hrs.

30. Let the cistern be filled by pipe A alone in x hours.

Then, pipe B will fill it in $(x + 6)$ hours.

$$\therefore \quad \frac{1}{x} + \frac{1}{(x+6)} = \frac{1}{4}$$

$$\Rightarrow \quad \frac{x+6+x}{x(x+6)} = \frac{1}{4}$$

$$\Rightarrow \quad x^2 - 2x - 24 = 0$$

$$\Rightarrow \quad (x - 6)(x + 4) = 0$$

$$\Rightarrow \quad x = 6.$$

32. Let capacity of P be x litres. Then, capacity of Q $= \frac{x}{3}$ litres.

Capacity of the drum = $60x$ litres.

Required number of turns $= \dfrac{60x}{\left(x + \frac{x}{3}\right)} = 45.$

33. Part filled by (A + B) in 1 minute

$$= \left(\frac{1}{60} + \frac{1}{40}\right) = \frac{1}{24}.$$

Suppose the tank is filled in x minutes.

$$\text{Then} \quad \frac{x}{2}\left(\frac{1}{24} + \frac{1}{40}\right) = 1$$

$$\Rightarrow \quad \frac{x}{2} \times \frac{1}{15} = 1$$

$$\Rightarrow \quad x = 30 \text{ min.}$$

35. Work done by the waste pipe in 1 minute

$$= \frac{1}{15} - \left(\frac{1}{20} + \frac{1}{24}\right) = \left(\frac{1}{15} - \frac{11}{120}\right) = -\frac{1}{40}.$$

[–ve sign means emptying]

$\therefore$ Volume of $\frac{1}{40}$ part = 3 gallons.

Volume of whole = (3 × 40) gallons
= 120 gallons.

10. TIME & DISTANCE

IMPORTANT FORMULAE

1. Speed = Distance ÷ Time
2. Distance = Time × Speed
3. Time = Distance ÷ Speed
4. x km/hr = $\left(x \times \frac{5}{18}\right)$ m/sec
5. x m/sec = $\left(x \times \frac{18}{5}\right)$ km/hr.
6. If the speed of a body is changed in the ratio $m : n$, then the ratio of the time taken changes in the ratio $n : m$.
7. When a man covers a certain distance with a speed of x km/h and another equal distance at the rate of y km/h, then for the whole journey, the average speed is given by

   Average speed = $\frac{2xy}{x+y}$ km/h.
8. The time taken by a train in passing a signal post or a telegraph pole or a man standing near a railway line = $\frac{\text{Length of the train}}{\text{Speed of the train}}$
9. The time taken by a train of length x passing a railway bridge or a platform or a tunnel or a train of length y at rest = $\frac{x+y}{\text{Speed}}$
10. (*a*) Time taken by faster train of length x and speed u to pass the slower train of length y and speed v in the same direction $= \frac{x+y}{u-v}$

    (*b*) Time taken by the trains in passing each other while moving in opposite direction $= \frac{x+y}{u+v}$
11. (*a*) Time taken by the train of length x and speed u to cross a man moving with speed v in same direction $= \frac{x}{u-v}$

    (*b*) Time taken by the train to cross a man moving in the opposite direction $= \frac{x}{u+v}$
12. If two trains start at the same time from two points A and B towards each other and after crossing, they take a and b hours in reaching B and A respectively. Then,

    A's speed : B's speed = $\left(\sqrt{b} : \sqrt{a}\right)$

SOLVED EXAMPLES

Example 1: Distance between two railway stations A and B is 1536 kms. A train covers a journey between A to B at the uniform speed of 60 km/hr and returns from B to A at the uniform speed of 40 km/hr. What is the average speed of the train during the whole journey?

Solution: Average speed of train $= \frac{2 \times 40 \times 60}{40+60}$

$= \frac{2 \times 40 \times 60}{100} = 48$ km/hr.

Example 2: A car covers the first 39 km of its journey in 45 minutes and covers the remaining 25 km in 35 minutes. What is the average speed of the car?

Solution: Total time $= \frac{45}{60} + \frac{35}{60} = \frac{4}{3}$ hrs.

and total distance = 39 + 25 = 64 km

$\therefore$ Average speed $= \frac{64 \times 3}{4} = 48$ km/hr.

Example 3: A train covered a distance of 1235 km in 19 hours. Also, the average speed of a car is four-fifth the average speed of the train. How much distance will the car cover in 22 hours?

Solution: Speed of the train $= \frac{1235}{19} = 65$ km/hr

$\therefore$ Speed of the car $= 65 \times \frac{4}{5} = 52$ km/hr

$\therefore$ Reqd. distance $= 52 \times 22 = 1144$ km.

Example 4: A 320 metre long train moving with an average speed of 120 km/hr crosses a platform in 24 seconds. A man crosses the same platform in 4 minutes. What is the speed of man in metre/second?

Solution: Let the length of the platform be x metre. Then,

$\because$ Speed of the train = 120 km/hr $= 120 \times \frac{5}{18}$

$= \frac{100}{3}$ m/sec.

From question,

$\because \quad 320\text{m} + x = \frac{100}{3} \times 24$

$\therefore \quad x = 800 - 320$

$= 480$ metre.

$\therefore$ Reqd. speed of man $= \frac{480 \text{ m}}{4 \times 60 \text{ sec}} = 2$ m/sec.

Example 5: A 260 metre long train crosses a platform thrice its length in 80 seconds. What is the speed of the train in km/hour?

Solution: Speed of the train

$= \frac{(260+780)}{80} \times \frac{18}{5}$ km/hr.

$= 46.8$ km/hr.

MULTIPLE CHOICE QUESTIONS

1. A boat while travelling upstream covers a distance of 18 km at the speed of 3 km/hr, whereas while travelling downstream it covers the same distance at a speed of 9 km/hr. What is the speed of the boat in still waters?
A. 3 km/hr
B. 5 km/hr
C. 7 km/hr
D. None of these

2. The speed of a car is 1.5 times the speed of a bus. If the car travels at the speed of 60 km/hr what will be the difference in the time taken by the bus and the time taken by the car to cover 720 km?
A. 5 hours B. 6 hours
C. 4 hours D. 8 hours

3. A car covers a distance of 540 km in 9 hours. Speed of a train is double the speed of the car. Two-third the speed of the train is equal to the speed of a bike. How much distance will the bike cover in 5 hours?
A. 450 km B. 360 km
C. 400 km D. 500 km

4. A train travels at a speed of 30 km per hour for 12 minutes and then for the next 8 minutes at a speed of 45 km per hour. What is the average speed for the journey?
A. 40 km/hr B. 36 km/hr
C. 43 km/hr D. 46 km/hr

5. The ratio of the speeds of two trains is 7 : 8. If the second train runs 400 km in 5 hrs., find the speed of the first train.
A. 60 km/hr B. 55 km/hr
C. 70 km/hr D. 75 km/hr

6. A train travels from Dehradun to Delhi at a speed of 40 km/hr and returns at 60 km/hr. Find the average speed for the entire journey—
A. 50 km/hr B. 45 km/hr
C. 48 km/hr D. 52 km/hr

7. A car runs at 60 km per hr. A man runs at one-third the speed of the car and reaches office from his house in 15 minutes. How far is his office from his house?
A. 20 km B. 10 km
C. 5 km D. 4 km

8. Two men A and B start walking simultaneously from P to Q, a distance of 21 kms, at the speeds of 3 km and 4 km an hour respectively. B reaches Q, returns immediately and meets A at R. Then the distance from P to R is :

A. 6 km B. 12 km
C. 18 km D. 24 km

9. A monkey climbing up a greased pole ascends 12 metres and slips down 5 metres in alternate minutes. If the pole is 63 metres high, how long will it take him to reach the top?

A. $12\frac{7}{16}$ B. $7\frac{12}{16}$
C. $16\frac{7}{12}$ D. $10\frac{7}{12}$

10. A carriage driving in a fog passed a man who was walking at the speed of 6 km/hr. in the same direction. He could see the carriage for 4 minutes and it was visible to him up to a distance of 200 metres. The speed of the carriage is :

A. 9 km/hr B. 4 km/hr
C. 6 km/hr D. 8 km/hr

11. A train met with an accident 3 hours after starting, which detains it for one hour, after which it proceeds at 75% of its original speed. It arrives at the destination 4 hours late. Had the accident taken place 150 km further along the railway line, the train would have arrived only $3\frac{1}{2}$ hours late. Find the length of the trip :

A. 1200 km B. 1000 km
C. 2100 km D. 1050 km

12. Two places A and B are 162 kms apart. A train leaves A for B and at the same time another train leaves B for A. The two trains meet at the end of 6 hours. If the train travelling from A to B travels 8 km per hr. faster than the other. Then the speed of the faster train is :

A. $9\frac{1}{2}$ km/h B. 27 km/hr
C. $17\frac{1}{2}$ km/hr D. 19 km/hr

13. A train takes 18 seconds to pass completely through a station 162 metres long and 15 seconds to pass completely through another station 120 metres long. The length of the train is :

A. 60 m B. 75 m
C. 90 m D. 100 m

14. A man covered a distance of 3990 km partly by air, partly by sea and remaining by land. The time spent in air, on sea and on land is in the ratio 1 : 16 : 2 and the ratio of average speeds is 20 : 1 : 3 respectively. If total average speed is 42 km per hr, Then the distance covered by sea is :

A. 1502 kms B. 2520 kms
C. 1520 kms D. 1500 kms

15. A man is walking at a speed of 10 km/hr. After every kilometre, he takes rest for 5 minutes. How much time will he take to cover a distance of 5 km?

A. 1 hr B. 50 min
C. 20 min D. 30 min

16. Walking $\frac{5}{6}$ of his usual speed, a man reaches the station 10 min late. His usual time to reach the station is :

A. 30 min B. 40 min
C. 50 min D. 60 min

17. A is four times as fast as B and B is six times as fast as C. A certain distance is covered by B in 28 minutes. Then the time taken by C to cover the same distance is :

A. 2 : 48 hrs B. 2 : 40 hrs
C. 2 : 28 hrs D. 3 hrs

18. It takes eight hours for a 600 km journey, if 120 km is done by train and the rest by car. It takes 20 minutes more, if 200 km is done by train and the rest by car. The ratio of the speed of the train to the speed of the car is :

A. 2 : 3 B. 6 : 9
C. 3 : 4 D. 4 : 3

19. A bus takes two hours less for a journey of 300 km if its speed is increased by 5 kmph from its normal speed. The normal speed is

A. 30 kmph B. 25 kmph
C. 35 kmph D. 50 kmph

20. A boy goes to school with a speed of 3 km/hr and returns to the village with a speed of 2 km/hr. If he takes 5 hours in all, the distance between the village and the school is :

A. 6 km B. 7 km
C. 8 km D. 9 km

21. Rahim covers a certain distance in 14 hrs 40 min. He covers one half of the distance by train at 60 km/hr and the rest half by road at 50 km/hr. The distance travelled by him is :

A. 960 km B. 720 km
C. 1000 km D. 800 km

22. Two men start together to walk to a certain destination, one at 3.75 km an hour and another at 3 km an hour. The former arrives half an hour before the latter. The distance is:

A. 9.5 km B. 8 km
C. 7.5 km D. 6 km

23. A thief steals a car at 1.30 p.m. and drives it at 40 km an hour. The theft is discovered at 2 p.m. and the owner sets off in another car at 50 km an hour. He will overtake the thief at:

A. 3.30 p.m. B. 4 p.m.
C. 4.30 p.m. D. 6 p.m.

24. A man travels 35 km partly at 4 km/hr and at 5 km/hr. If he covers former distance at 5 km/hr and later distance at 4 km/hr, he could cover 2 km more in the same time. The time taken to cover the whole distance at original rate is :

A. 9 hours B. 7 hours
C. $4\frac{1}{2}$ hours D. 8 hours

25. A certain distance is covered at a certain speed. If half of this distance is covered in double the time, the ratio of the two speeds is :

A. 4 : 1 B. 1 : 4
C. 2 : 1 D. 1 : 2

26. A person sees a train passing over 1 km long bridge. The length of the train is half that of bridge. If the train clears the bridge in 2 minutes, the speed of the train is :

A. 50 km/hr B. 45 km/hr
C. 60 km/hr D. 30 km/hr

27. Two trains are running on parallel lines in the same direction at a speed of 50 km and 30 km per hour respectively. The faster train crosses a man in slower train in 18 seconds. The length of the faster train is :

A. 170 metres B. 100 metres
C. 98 metres D. 85 metres

28. A train speeds past a pole in 15 seconds and speeds past a platform 100 metres long in 25 seconds. Its length in metres is :

A. 200 B. 150
C. 50 D. Data inadequate

29. A train overtakes two persons who are walking in the same direction in which the train is goning, at the rate of 2 kmph and 4 kmph and passes them completely in 9 and 10 seconds respectively. The length of the train is :

A. 72 metres B. 54 metres
C. 50 metres D. 45 metres

30. A boat travels upstream from B to A and downstream from A to B in 3 hours. If the speed of the boat in still water is 9 km/hr and the speed of the current is 3 km/hr, the distance between A and B is :

A. 4 km B. 6 km
C. 8 km D. 12 km

31. Speed of a boat in standing water is 6 km/hr and the speed of the stream is 1.5 km/hr. A man rows to a place at a distance of 22.5 km and comes back to the starting point. The total time taken by him, is :

A. 6 hrs 30 min. B. 8 hrs 24 min.
C. 8 hrs D. 4 hrs 12 min.

32. A man can row $9\frac{1}{3}$ km/hr in still water and he finds that it takes him thrice as much time to row up than as to row down the same distance in river. The speed of the current is :

A. $3\frac{1}{3}$ km/hr B. $3\frac{1}{9}$ km/hr

C. $1\frac{1}{4}$ km/hr D. $4\frac{2}{3}$ km/hr

33. Sound is said to travel in air at about 1100 feet per second. A man hears the axe striking the tree, $\frac{11}{5}$ seconds after he sees it strike the tree. How far is the man from the wood chopper?

A. 2197 ft B. 2420 ft
C. 2500 ft D. 2629 ft

34. Asha left for city A from city B at 5.20 a.m. She travelled at the speed of 80 km/hr for 2 hours 15 minutes. After that the speed was reduced to 60 km/hr. If the distance between two cities is 350 kms, at what time did Asha reach city A?

A. 9.20 a.m. B. 9.25 a.m.
C. 9.35 a.m. D. None of these

35. A motorist covers a distance of 39 km in 45 minutes by moving at a speed of x kmph for the first 15 minutes, then moving at double the speed for the next 20 minutes and then again moving at his original speed for the rest of the journey. Then, x is equal to :

A. 31.2 B. 36
C. 40 D. 52

36. A train when moves at an average speed of 40 kmph, reaches its destination on time. When its average speed becomes 35 kmph, then it reaches its destination 15 minutes late. Find the length of journey.

A. 30 km B. 40 km
C. 70 km D. 80 km

37. With a uniform speed a car covers the distance in 8 hours. Had the speed been increased by 4 km/hr, the same distance could have been covered in $7\frac{1}{2}$ hours. What is the distance covered?

A. 420 km
B. 480 km
C. 640 km
D. Cannot be determined

38. A 270 metres long train running at the speed of 120 kmph crosses another train running in opposite direction at the speed of 80 kmph in 9 seconds. What is the length of the other train?

A. 230 m B. 240 m
C. 260 m D. 320 m

39. Two trains running in opposite directions cross a man standing on the platform in 27 seconds and 17 seconds respecively and they cross each other in 23 seconds. The ratio of their speeds is :

A. 1 : 3 B. 3 : 2
C. 3 : 4 D. 2 : 3

40. A boat covers a certain distance downstream in 1 hour, while it comes back in $1\frac{1}{2}$ hours. If the speed of the stream be 3 kmph, what is the speed of the boat in still water?

A. 12 kmph B. 13 kmph
C. 14 kmph D. 15 kmph

ANSWERS

1	2	3	4	5	6	7	8	9	10
D	B	C	B	C	C	C	C	C	A
11	12	13	14	15	16	17	18	19	20
A	C	C	C	B	C	A	C	B	A
21	22	23	24	25	26	27	28	29	30
D	C	B	D	A	B	B	B	C	D
31	32	33	34	35	36	37	38	39	40
C	D	B	D	B	C	B	A	B	D

SOME SELECTED EXPLANATORY ANSWERS

1. Speed of boat in still water = $\frac{9+3}{2}$ = 6 km/hr.

2. Speed of bus = $60 \times \frac{1}{1.5}$ = 40 km/hr.

Hence, required difference = $\frac{720}{40} - \frac{720}{60}$
= 18 – 12 = 6 hrs.

3. Speed of the car = $\frac{540}{9}$ = 60 km/hr.

∴ Speed of train = 60 × 2 = 120 km/hr.

and speed of bike = $120 \times \frac{2}{3}$ = 80 km/hr.

∴ Reqd. distance = 80 × 5 = 400 km.

4. In 12 minutes, the train with 30 km per hour speed goes

$$= 30 \times \frac{5}{18} \times 60 \times 12 \text{ m}$$

$$= \frac{5 \times 5 \times 20 \times 12}{1000} \text{ km} = 6 \text{ km}$$

In 8 minutes, the train with 45 km per hr. speed goes

$$= 45 \times \frac{5}{18} \times 60 \times \frac{8}{1000} \text{ km} = 6 \text{ km}$$

Average speed = $\frac{12 \text{ km}}{20 \text{ min}} = \frac{12}{20} \times 60$ km/hr
= 36 km/hr.

5. $x : \frac{400}{5} = 7 : 8$

$\Rightarrow x \times \frac{5}{400} = \frac{7}{8}$ ∴ x = 70 km/hr.

6. Reqd. average speed = $\frac{2 \times 40 \times 60}{(40+60)}$

$$= \frac{2 \times 2400}{100} = 48 \text{ km/hr.}$$

8. Let A and B meet after time t hours.

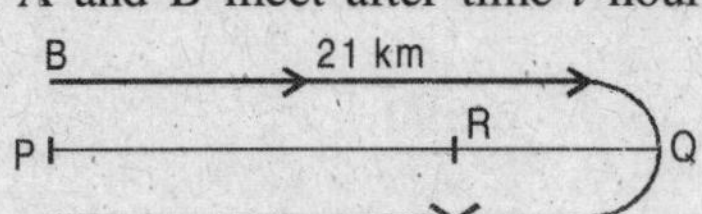

Distance covered by A in t hours = 3 t km.
Distance covered by B in t hours = 4 t km.
Total distance covered by A and B = $(3t + 4t)$ km
= 7 t km.

From the diagram we can see that the total distance covered by A and B is equal to twice the distance between P and Q.

∴ $7t = 2 \times 21$

$t = \frac{2 \times 21}{7}$

t = 6 hours

Distance (PR) = 6 × 3 = 18 kms.

9. From question,
In 2 minutes the net ascending of the monkey is 12 – 5 = 7 metres. So, to cover 63 metres to above process is repeated $\frac{63}{7}$ = 9 times.

Since on 9th time, it will climb to the top.

Hence, Time taken to cover 56 metres = $\frac{56 \times 2}{7}$
= 16 minutes

Remaining distance = 63 – 56 = 7 metres

Time taken to ascend 7 metres = $\frac{7}{12}$ minutes

∴ Total time taken = $16 + \frac{7}{12} = 16\frac{7}{12}$ minutes.

10. The distance covered by man in 4 minutes

$$= \frac{6 \times 1000 \times 4}{60} = 400 \text{ metres}$$

The distance coverd by carriage in 4 minutes = 200 + 400 = 600 metres

∴ Sepeed of carriage = $\frac{600}{4} \times \frac{60}{1000}$ km/hr.
= 9 km/hr.

12. Both trains meet after 6 hours.

∴ The relative speed of two trains = $\frac{162}{6}$
= 27 km/hr.

The speed of the slower train starting from B

$= \frac{27-8}{2} = \frac{19}{2} = 9\frac{1}{2}$ km/hr.

$\therefore$ The speed of the faster train $= 9\frac{1}{2} + 8$

$= 17\frac{1}{2}$ km/hr.

13. Let the length of the train = x metres

Then, in 18 sec. the train travels $(x + 162)$ metres ...(*i*)

and in 15 sec. the train travels $(x + 120)$ metres

$\therefore$ In $(18 - 15) = 3$ sec. the train travels $(x + 162) - (x + 120) = 42$ m

$\therefore$ In 1 sec the train travels $= \frac{42}{3} = 14$ metes ...(*ii*)

$\therefore$ In 18 sec. the train travels $= 14 \times 18$

$= 252$ metres ...(*iii*)

From equations (*i*) and (*iii*)

$\therefore \quad x + 162 = 252$

$\Rightarrow \quad x = 252 - 162 = 90$

$\therefore$ Length of the train = 90 metres.

14. Total distance travelled = 3990 km

Ratio of time spent = 1 : 16 : 2

$\therefore$ Ratio of time × speeds = 20 × 1 : 16 × 1 : 2 × 3

= 20 : 16 : 6

Sum of the ratios = 20 + 16 + 6

= 42

$\therefore$ Distance covered by sea $= \frac{3990}{42} \times 16$

= 1520 kms.

15. Total time = walking time + rest time

Walking time $= \frac{5}{10}$ hour $= \frac{1}{2}$ hour = 30 min

Rest time = 4 × 5 min = 20 min

$\therefore$ Required time taken = 30 min + 20 min

= 50 min.

17. Let the speed of C be x kmph

$\therefore$ B's speed = $6x$ kmph

and A's speed = $4 \times 6x$ kmph = $24x$ kmph

The distance covered by B in 28 minutes

$= 6x \times \frac{28}{60}$ km

$= \frac{28x}{10}$ km $= \frac{14x}{5}$ km

The time taken by C to cover the same distance

$= \frac{\frac{14x}{5}\text{ km}}{x \text{ kmph}} = \frac{14}{5}$ hrs

$= 2\frac{4}{5}$ hours = 2 hrs 48 minutes

19. Let s be the normal speed and t be the normal time taken by the bus

$\therefore \quad s \times t = 300 \quad$ ...(1)

new speed = $s + 5$

new time = $t - 2$

$\therefore \quad (s + 5)(t - 2) = 300$

$(s+5)\left(\frac{300}{s} - 2\right) = 300$ (from (1))

$(s + 5)(300 - 2s) = 300s$

$300s - 2s^2 + 1500 - 10s = 300s$

$\Rightarrow \quad 2s^2 + 10s - 1500 = 0$

$\Rightarrow \quad 2s^2 + 60s - 50s - 1500 = 0$

$\Rightarrow \quad 2s(s + 30) - 50(s + 30) = 0$

$\Rightarrow \quad (s + 30)(2s - 50) = 0$

$\therefore \quad s = 25$

$\therefore$ The normal speed of the bus is 25 kmph.

20. Let the required distance be x km. Then,

$\frac{x}{3} + \frac{x}{2} = 5$

$\Rightarrow \quad 2x + 3x = 30$

$\Rightarrow \quad x = 6.$

21. Let the total distance be x km. Then,

$\frac{x}{2} \times \frac{1}{60} + \frac{x}{2} \times \frac{1}{50} = \frac{44}{3}$

or $\quad \frac{x}{120} + \frac{x}{100} = \frac{44}{3}$

or $\quad 5x + 6x = 8800$

or $\quad x = 800.$

$\therefore$ Required distance = 800 km.

22. Let the distance be x km. Then,

$$\frac{x}{3} - \frac{x}{3.75} = \frac{1}{2}$$

or $$\frac{3.75x - 3x}{3 \times 3.75} = \frac{1}{2}$$

or $$1.5x = 3 \times 3.75$$

or $$x = \frac{3 \times 3.75}{1.5} = 7.5 \text{ km}$$

23. Distance covered by thief in (1/2) hour = 20 km. Now, 20 km is compensated by the owner at a relative speed of 10 km/hr in 2 hours. So, he overtakes the thief at 4 p.m.

24. Suppose the man covers first distance in x hrs and second distance in y hrs. Then,

$$4x + 5y = 35$$

and $$5x + 4y = 37.$$

Solving these equations, we get $x = 5$ and $y = 3$.

∴ Total time taken = (5 + 3) hrs = 8 hrs.

25. Let x km be covered in y hrs. Then,

1st speed = $\left(\frac{x}{y}\right)$ km/hr.

2nd speed = $\left(\frac{x}{2} \div 2y\right)$ km/hr = $\left(\frac{x}{4y}\right)$ km/hr.

∴ Ratio of speed = $\frac{x}{y} : \frac{x}{4y} = 1 : \frac{1}{4} = 4 : 1$.

26. Distance covered in $\frac{2}{60}$ hr = $\left(1 + \frac{1}{2}\right)$ km

$= \frac{3}{2}$ km.

Distance covered in 1 hr = $\left(\frac{3}{2} \times \frac{60}{2}\right)$ km = 45 km.

Hence, speed of the train = 45 km/hr.

27. Relative speed=(50 – 30) km/hr = 20 km/hr.

$= \left(20 \times \frac{5}{18}\right)$ m/sec = $\left(\frac{50}{9}\right)$ m/sec.

Let the length of faster train be x

Then, $x \times \frac{9}{50} = 18 \Rightarrow x = \frac{18 \times 50}{9} = 100$ m.

28. Let the length of the train be x metres and its speed be y metres/sec.

Then, $\frac{x}{y} = 15 \Rightarrow y = \frac{x}{15}$.

Now, $\frac{x + 100}{25} = \frac{x}{15} \Rightarrow x = 150$ m.

30. Speed in downstream = (9 + 3) km/hr = 12 km/hr.

Speed in upstream = (9 – 3) km/hr = 6 km/hr.

Let the distance AB = x km.

Then, $\frac{x}{6} + \frac{x}{12} = 3 \Rightarrow 2x + x = 36$

$\Rightarrow x = 12$.

∴ Distance AB = 12 km.

31. Speed in upstream = (6 – 1.5) km/hr = 4.5 km/hr.

Speed in downstream = (6 + 1.5) km/hr = 7.5 km/hr.

Total time taken = $\left(\frac{22.5}{4.5} + \frac{22.5}{7.5}\right)$ hrs. = 8 hrs.

32. Let speed in upstream = x km/hr

Then, speed in downstream = $3x$ km/hr

∴ Speed in still water = $\frac{1}{2}(x + 3x)$ km/hr

= $2x$ km/hr

Speed of the current = $\frac{1}{2}(3x - x)$ km/hr

= x km/hr

∴ $2x = \frac{28}{3}$ or $x = \frac{14}{3} = 4\frac{2}{3}$ km/hr.

33. Distance = $\left(1100 \times \frac{11}{5}\right)$ feet = 2420 feet.

34. Distance covered in 2 hrs 15 min

i.e., $2\frac{1}{4}$ hrs = $\left(80 \times \frac{9}{4}\right)$ km = 180 km.

Time taken to cover remaining distance

$$= \left(\frac{350-180}{60}\right) \text{hrs} = \frac{17}{6} \text{hrs}$$

$$= 2\frac{5}{6} \text{hrs} = 2 \text{ hrs } 50 \text{ min.}$$

Total time taken = (2 hrs 15 min + 2 hrs 50 min)

= 5 hrs 5 min.

So, Asha reached city A at 10.25 a.m.

35. $x \times \frac{15}{60} + 2x \times \frac{20}{60} + x \times \frac{10}{60} = 39$

$$\Rightarrow \quad \frac{x}{4} + \frac{2x}{3} + \frac{x}{6} = 39$$

$$\Rightarrow \quad 3x + 8x + 2x = 468$$

$$\Rightarrow \quad x = 36.$$

36. Difference between timings = 15 min = $\frac{1}{4}$ hr.

Let the length of journey be x km.

Then, $\frac{x}{35} - \frac{x}{40} = \frac{1}{4}$

$$\Rightarrow \quad 8x - 7x = 70$$

$$\Rightarrow \quad x = 70 \text{ km.}$$

37. Let the distance be x km. Then,

$$\frac{x}{7\frac{1}{2}} - \frac{x}{8} = 4 \Rightarrow \frac{2x}{15} - \frac{x}{8} = 4$$

$$\Rightarrow \quad x = 480 \text{ km.}$$

38. Relative speed = (120 + 80) km/hr

$$= \left(200 \times \frac{5}{18}\right) \text{m/sec} = \left(\frac{500}{9}\right) \text{m/sec.}$$

Let the length of the other train be x metres.

Then, $\frac{x+270}{9} = \frac{500}{9}$

$$\Rightarrow \quad x + 270 = 500$$

$$\Rightarrow \quad x = 230.$$

40. Let the speed of the boat in still water be x kmph. Then,

Speed in downstream = $(x + 3)$ kmph,

Speed in upstream = $(x - 3)$ kmph.

$$\therefore \quad (x + 3) \times 1 = (x - 3) \times \frac{3}{2}$$

$$\Rightarrow \quad 2x + 6 = 3x - 9$$

$$\Rightarrow \quad x = 15 \text{ kmph.}$$

11. MENSURATION

Triangle

1. Perimeter = 3 × side (Equilateral triangle)
2. Area $= \frac{1}{2} \times \text{base} \times \text{height}$, or

   Area $= \sqrt{s(s-a)(s-b)(s-c)}$

   where *a, b, c,* are the lengths of the sides of triangle and $s = \frac{a+b+c}{2}$

Right Angled Triangle : It is one whose one of the angles is right angle, *i.e.*, 90°.

1. $(\text{Hypotenuse})^2 = (\text{Perpendicular})^2 + (\text{Base})^2$
2. Area $= \frac{1}{2} \times \text{Base} \times \text{Perpendicular}$

Equilateral Triangle : All three sides are equal in length and all three angles are equal to 60°.

1. Area $= \frac{\sqrt{3}}{4} \times (\text{Side})^2$
2. Area $= \frac{(\text{Height})^2}{\sqrt{3}}$
3. Height $= \frac{\sqrt{3}}{2} \times \text{side}$
4. Perimeter = 3 × side

Isosceles Triangle : Two sides are equal in lengths.

1. Area $= \frac{b}{4}\sqrt{4a^2 - b^2}$

   where a = lengths of equal sides
   b = length of unequal side
2. In an isosceles right triangle,

   (a) Hypotenuse $= \sqrt{2} \times \text{congruent side (a)}$

   (b) Area $= \frac{1}{2} \times a^2$

   (c) Perimeter $= \sqrt{2} \times a(\sqrt{2}+1)$

Rectangle :

1. Area = length(l) × breadth(b)
2. Perimeter = $2(l + b)$
3. Diagonal $= \sqrt{l^2 + b^2}$

Square :

1. Area = $(\text{Side})^2$
2. Perimeter = 4 × side
3. Diagonal $= \text{side} \times \sqrt{2}$

Parallelogram: Area = Base × Height.

Trapezium : Area $= \frac{1}{2} \times \text{Height} \times$ (Sum of parallel sides). Here, height is the distance between the two parallel sides.

Rhombus :

1. Area $= \frac{1}{2} \times \text{Product of diagonals}$
2. Side $= \sqrt{\left(\frac{d_1}{2}\right)^2 + \left(\frac{d_2}{2}\right)^2}$, where d_1 and d_2 are diagonals
3. Perimeter = 4 × side

Quadrilateral : Area $= \frac{1}{2} \times \text{One diagonal} \times$ (Sum of perpendicular to it from the opposite vertices)

$$= \frac{1}{2} \times d \times (a+b)$$

Circle :

1. Diameter = 2 × Radius
2. Area $= \pi r^2 = \frac{\pi}{4} d^2$;

   where d = diameter $= \sqrt{\frac{4A}{\pi}}$
3. Circumference $= 2\pi r = \pi d$

4. Radius = $\frac{\text{Circumference}}{2\pi} = \frac{\sqrt{\text{Area}}}{\pi}$

5. Length of an Arc = $\frac{\theta}{360^\circ} \times 2\pi r$

6. Area of sector = $\frac{\theta}{360^\circ} \times \pi r^2 = \frac{1}{2} \times \text{Arc} \times r$

Polygon :

1. Interior angle + Exterior angle = 180°
2. Each interior angle = $\left(\frac{2n-4}{n}\right) \times 90^\circ$

   where n = number of sides
3. Sum of Exterior angles = 360°
4. Perimeter = Number of sides × Length of side.
5. For an equilateral triangle of side 'a'

   (*a*) radius of inscribed circle $= \frac{a}{2\sqrt{3}}$

   and side of the triangle = $2\sqrt{3}r$,

   (*b*) radius of circumcircle = $\frac{a}{\sqrt{3}}$
6. Area of regular polygon = $\frac{1}{2}$(No. of sides) (Radius of the inscribed circle)
7. Area of regular hexagon = $\frac{3\sqrt{3}}{2}(\text{side})^2$

   = 2.598 $(\text{side})^2$
8. Area of a regular octagon

   $= 2\left(\sqrt{2}+1\right)(\text{side})^2$ = 4.828 $(\text{side})^2$
9. Area of quadrilateral, A

   $= \sqrt{s(s-a)(s-b)(s-c)(s-d)}$

   where, $s = \frac{a+b+c+d}{2}$

VOLUME AND SURFACE AREA OF SOLIDS

Cuboid : A cuboid has six faces, each one a ractangle. It has 12 edges. For example, a rectangular brick.

Let Length = l, Breadth = b and Height = h, then,

1. Volume = (Length × Breadth × Height)
2. Whole Surface Area = $2(lb + bh + lh)$
3. Diagonal = $\sqrt{l^2+b^2+h^2}$
4. Area of 4 walls of a room = $2 \times h\,(l + b)$

Cube : In a cube, Length = Breadth = Height

1. Volume = $(l)^3$
2. Length = $\sqrt[3]{\text{Volume}}$
3. Whole Surface Area = $6\,l^2$
4. Diagonal = $l \times \sqrt{3}$
5. Lateral Surface Area = $4\,l^2$

Cylinder :

1. Volume = $\pi r^2 h$
2. Curved Surface Area = $2\pi rh$
3. Total Surface Area = $2\pi r(r + h)$

   where r = radius, h = height

Spherical Cell :

1. Volume = $\frac{4}{3}\pi\left(R^3 - r^3\right)$
2. Total Surface Area= $4\pi(R^2 - r^2)$

   where R = Outer radius

   r = Inner radius

Sphere :

1. Volume = $\frac{4}{3}\pi r^3$
2. Surface Area = $4\pi r^2$

Semi-sphere :

1. Volume = $\frac{2}{3}\pi r^3$
2. Curved surface area = $2\pi r^2$
3. Total surface area = $3\pi r^2$

Cone :

1. Slant height $(l) = \sqrt{r^2+h^2}$
2. Volume = $\frac{1}{3}\pi r^2 h$
3. Curved surface area = πrl
4. Total surface area = $\pi r\,(l + r)$
5. If the depth of the frustum of a cone be k and the radii of its ends are r_1 and r_2, then

   (*i*) Slant height of the frustum of a cone

   $= \sqrt{k^2 + (r_1 - r_2)^2}$

(*ii*) Curved surface of the frustum
$= \pi(r_1 + r_2)\, l.$

(*iii*) Volume $= \dfrac{\pi k}{3}\left(r_1^2 + r_1 r_2 + r_2^2\right)$

SOLVED EXAMPLES

Example 1: What is the longest rod that can be placed in a room which is 7 m long, 9 m broad and $\sqrt{39}$ m high?

Solution: Required length of rod

$= \sqrt{7^2 + 9^2 + (\sqrt{39})^2} = \sqrt{49+81+39}$

$= \sqrt{169} = 13$ m.

Example 2: The total area of a circle and a square is equal to 5450 sq. cm. The diameter of the circle is 70 cms. What is the sum of the circumference of the circle and the perimeter of the square?

Solution: Let side of the square = x cm

Also $\pi \times 35 \times 35 + x^2 = 5450$

$\Rightarrow \quad \dfrac{22}{7} \times 35 \times 35 + x^2 = 5450$

$\Rightarrow \quad x^2 = 5450 - 3850 = 1600$

$\therefore \quad x = 40$ cm

$\therefore$ Required sum $= \pi \times d + 4x$

$= \left(\dfrac{22}{7} \times 70 + 4 \times 40\right) = 380$ cm.

Example 3: Perimeter of a circle is equal to the prmimeter of a square whose area is 484 cm^2. What is the radius of the circle?

Solution: Side of a square $= \sqrt{\text{Area}} = \sqrt{484} = 22$ cm.

Perimeter of square $= 4 \times \text{side} = 4 \times 22 = 88$ cm.

$\therefore \quad 2\pi r = 88$

$\Rightarrow \quad 2 \times \dfrac{22}{7} \times r = 88$

$\Rightarrow \quad r = \dfrac{88 \times 7}{2 \times 22} = 14$ cm.

Example 4: The perimeter of a square is equal to twice the perimeter of a rectangle of length 8 cm and breadth 7 cm. What is the circumference of a semicircle whose diameter is equal to the side of the square? (Rounded off to the two decimal place)

Solution: $\because$ Perimeter of the square

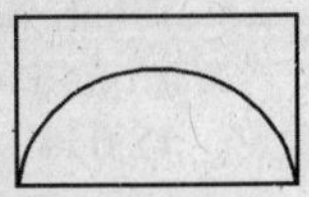

$= 2 \times$ Perimeter of rectangle

$= 2(8 + 7) \times 2 = 60$ cm

One side of the square = 15 cm

Radius of the semicircle (R) $= \dfrac{15}{2}$ cm

$\therefore$ Perimeter of the semicircle $= \pi R + 2R$

$= \dfrac{22}{7} \times \dfrac{15}{2} + 15 = 23.57 + 15$

$= 38.57$ cm

MULTIPLE CHOICE QUESTIONS

1. What is the area of a circle whose radius is equal to the side of a square whose perimeter is 112 metres?

A. 176 sq m B. 2504 sq m
C. 284 sq m D. None of these

2. The sum of the circumference of a circle and the perimeter of a rectangle is 132 cm. The area of the rectangle is 112 sq cm and breadth of the rectangle is 8 cms. What is the area of the circle?

A. 616 sq cm
B. 540 sq cm
C. 396 sq cm
D. Cannot be determined

3. The total area of a circle and a rectangle is equal to 1166 sq cm. The diameter of the circle is 28 cm. What is the sum of the circumference of the circle and the perimeter of the rectangle if the length of the rectangle is 25 cm?

A. 186 cm
B. 182 cm
C. 184 cm
D. Cannot be determined

4. What would be the cost of laying a carpet on a floor which has its length and breadth in the respective ratio of 32 : 21 and where its perimeter is 212 feet, if the cost per square foot of laying the carpet is ₹ 2.5?
A. ₹ 6,720
B. ₹ 5,420
C. ₹ 7,390
D. Cannot be determined

5. A triangle's perimeter is 25 cms. Which of the following may be true or is a possibility?
(*a*) The sides are 7 cms., 7 cms. and 11 cms.
(*b*) It is an equilateral triangle.
(*c*) The value of sides can be in integer only.
A. Only (*a*)
B. Only (*a*) and (*b*)
C. Only (*c*)
D. Only (*b*) and (*c*)

6. What will be the cost of building a fence around a circular field with area equal to 18,634 sq. metres; if the cost of building the fence per metre is ₹ 365?
A. ₹ 1,76,660 B. ₹ 68,01,410
C. ₹ 2,43,250 D. ₹ 56,60,220

7. The area of a square is 196 sq cms whose side is half the radius of a circle. The circumference of the circle is equal to breadth of a rectangle. If perimeter of the rectangle is 712 cm. What is the length of the rectangle?
A. 196 cm B. 186 cm
C. 180 cm D. 190 cm

8. The circumference of a circular plot is 484 metres. Find out the area of that circular plot—
A. 15246 m^2 B. 18634 m^2
C. 20328 m^2 D. 13552 m^2

9. A room measures 22 dm by 16 dm. I wish to buy a carpet for the floor leaving an uncarpeted margin 2 dm wide along each of the shorter sides of the room and a margin 0.5 dm wide along each of the longer sides of the room. If the price of the carpet is ₹ 500 per sq. metre, what is the cost of the whole carpet required?
A. ₹ 500 B. ₹ 2700
C. ₹ 2000 D. ₹ 1350

10. A paper is in the form of a rectangle ABCD where AB = 22 cm and BC = 14 cm. A semi-circular portion with segment BC as a diameter is cut off. Find the area of remaining paper.
A. 231 cm^2 B. 213 cm^2
C. 321 cm^2 D. 200 cm^2

11. How many plants can be put in a circular flower bed whose circumference is 880 dm allowing 35 dm^2 for each plant?
A. 880 B. 1760
C. 1000 D. 1500

12. An athletic track 14 m wide consists of two straight sections 120 m long joining semi-circular ends whose inner radius is 35 m. Calculate the area of the track :
A. 5670 m^2 B. 7065 m^2
C. 5607 m^2 D. 7056 m^2

13. A square park has each side of 100 m. At each corner of the park, there is a flower bed in the form of a quadrant of radius 14 m. Then the area of the remaining part of the park is :
A. 9384 m^2 B. 9834 m^2
C. 9000 m^2 D. 8900 m^2

14. The length of minute hand of a clock is 14 cm. Then the area swept by the minute hand in one minute is:
A. 10 m^2 B. 12.26 m^2
C. 20.26 m^2 D. 10.26 m^2

15. Find the area of ring between two concentric circles whose circumference are 77 cm and 55 cm.
A. 770 cm^2 B. 321 cm^2
C. 231 cm^2 D. 230 cm^2

16. A rectangle water reservoir is 10.8 metres long and 3.75 metres wide at base. Water flows into it at the rate of 18 m per sec. through the pipe having the cross section 7.5 cm × 4.5 cm. Then the height to which the water will rise in the reservoir in 30 minutes is :
A. 7.2 m B. 2.7 m
C. 3.7 m D. 7.3 m

17. A rectangular sheet of 44 cm × 18 cm is rolled along its length and a cylinder is formed. Then the volume of cylinder is :

A. 7227 cm^3 B. 7272 cm^3
C. 2727 cm^3 D. 2772 cm^3

18. How many metres of cloth 5 metre wide will be required to make a conical tent, the radius of whose base is 7 metre and height is 24 metre?
A. 100 m B. 110 m
C. 550 m D. 55 m

19. The surface area of a sphere whose volume is 4851 cubic metres is :
A. 1386 m^2 B. 1380 m^2
C. 1286 m^2 D. 3186 m^2

20. A hollow sphere of external and internal diameter 4 cm and 2 cm respectively, is melted into a cone of base diameter 8 cm. Then the height of the cone is :
A. 12 cm B. 14 cm
C. 20 cm D. 24 cm

21. The diamensions of a metallic rod are 19 cm × 4 cm × 2 cm and each side of a metallic cube is 4 cm. Both are melted and recast into a new cube. Find the length of edge of cube so formed.
A. 4 cm B. 5 cm
C. 6 cm D. 7 cm

22. An agricultural field is in the form of a rectangle of length 35 metres and width 15.4 metres. A pit 5.5 metres long, 4 metres wide and 2.5 metres deep is dug in the corner of the field and the earth taken out of the pit is spread uniformly over the remaining area of the field. The extent to which the level of the field has been raised is :
A. 16.6 cm B. 10.6 cm
C. 16.1 cm D. 6.10 cm

23. The side of a square exceeds the side of the another square by 4 cm and the sum of areas of two squares is 400 sq. cm. Find the dimensions of the square.
A. 8 cm, 12 cm
B. 10 cm, 14 cm
C. 12 cm, 16 cm
D. 14 cm, 18 cm

24. The cost of levelling a rectangular field at the rate of 85 paise per square metre is ₹ 624.75. Then the perimeter of the field if its sides are in the ratio of 5 : 3 is :
A. 35 m B. 21 m
C. 112 m D. 49 m

25. The diagonal of a rectangular field is 15 m and its area is 108 sq. m. What will be the total expenditure in fencing the field at the rate of ₹ 5 per metre?
A. ₹ 441 B. ₹ 420
C. ₹ 210 D. ₹ 120

26. The minute hand of a clock is 10 cm long. The area of the face of the clock described by the minute hand between 9 AM and 9.35 AM is :
A. 140 cm^2
B. 183.3 cm^2
C. 180 cm^2
D. 175.3 cm^2

27. The length of a rectangular plot is 60% more than its breadth. If the difference between the length and the breadth of that rectangle is 24 cm, what is the area of that rectangle?
A. 2400 sq. cm
B. 2480 sq. cm
C. 2560 sq. cm
D. Data inadequate

28. The area of a rectangle is 460 square metres. If the length is 15% more than the breadth, what is the breadth of the rectangular field?
A. 15 metres
B. 26 metres
C. 34.5 metres
D. None of these

29. The ratio between the length and the breadth of a rectangular field is 3 : 2. If only the length is increased by 5 metres, the new area of the field will be 2600 sq. metres. What is the breadth of the rectangular field?
A. 40 metres
B. 60 metres
C. 65 metres
D. Cannot be determined

30. If the length and breadth of a rectangular plot be increased by 50% and 20% respectively, then how many times will its area be increased?

A. $1\frac{1}{3}$ B. 2

C. $3\frac{2}{5}$ D. None of these

31. The length of a rectangle is decreased by *r*%, and the breadth is increased by (*r* + 5)%. Find *r*, if the area of the rectangle is unaltered.

A. 5 B. 8
C. 10 D. 20

32. The length and breadth of the floor of the room are 20 feet and 10 feet respectively. Square tiles of 2 feet length of different colours are to be laid on the floor. Black tiles are laid in the first row on all sides. If white tiles are laid in the one-third of the remaining and blue tiles in the rest, how many blue tiles will be there?

A. 16 B. 24
C. 32 D. 48

33. A park square in shape has a 3 metre wide road inside it running along its sides. The area occupied by the road is 1764 square metres. What is the perimeter along the outer edge of the road?

A. 576 metres
B. 600 metres
C. 640 metres
D. Data inadequate

34. What will be the length of the diagonal of that square plot whose area is equal to the area of a rectangular plot of length 45 metres and breadth 40 metres?

A. 42.5 metres
B. 60 metres
C. 75 metres
D. Data inadequate

35. The length of one pair of opposite sides of a square is increased by 5 cm on each side; the ratio of the length and the breadth of the newly formed rectangle becomes 3 : 2. What is the area of the original square?

A. 25 sq. cm B. 81 sq. cm
C. 100 sq. cm D. 225 sq. cm

36. What will be the ratio between the area of a rectangle and the area of a triangle with one of the sides of the rectangle as base and a vertex on the opposite side of the rectangle?

A. 1 : 2 B. 2 : 1
C. 3 : 1 D. Data inadequate

37. A cow is tethered in the middle of a field with a 14 feet long rope. If the cow grazes 100 sq. ft. per day, then approximately what time will be taken by the cow to graze the whole field?

A. 2 days B. 6 days
C. 18 days D. 24 days

38. A circular ground whose diameter is 35 metres, has a 1.4 m broad garden around it. What is the area of the garden in square metres?

A. 160.16 B. 176.16
C. 196.16 D. None of these

39. The cost of the paint is ₹ 36.50 per kg. If 1 kg of paint covers 16 square feet, how much will it cost to paint outside of a cube having 8 feet each side?

A. ₹ 692 B. ₹ 768
C. ₹ 876 D. ₹ 972

40. The capacity of a cylindrical tank is 246.4 litres. If the height is 4 metres, what is the diameter of the base?

A. 1.4 m B. 2.8 m
C. 14 m D. 28 m

ANSWERS

1	2	3	4	5	6	7	8	9	10
D	A	B	A	A	A	C	B	D	A
11	**12**	**13**	**14**	**15**	**16**	**17**	**18**	**19**	**20**
B	D	A	D	C	B	D	B	A	B

21	22	23	24	25	26	27	28	29	30
C	B	C	C	C	B	C	D	A	D
31	**32**	**33**	**34**	**35**	**36**	**37**	**38**	**39**	**40**
D	A	B	B	C	B	B	D	C	D

SOME SELECTED EXPLANATORY ANSWERS

1. $\because$ Radius of the circle $= \frac{112}{4} = 28$ m

$\therefore$ Area of the circle $= \frac{22}{7}\times 28\times 28 = 2464$ m^2.

2. Length of the rectangle $= \frac{112}{8} = 14$ cm.

$\therefore$ Perimeter of the rectangle $= 2(14 + 8)$
$= 44$ cm.

$\therefore$ Circumference of the circle $= 132 - 44$
$= 88$ cm.

$\therefore$ $r = \frac{88\times 7}{2\times 22} = 14$ cm

$\therefore$ Area of the circle

$= \frac{22}{7}\times 14\times 14 = 616$ sq cm.

3. From question—

$\because$ Diameter of the circle $= 28$ cm.

$\Rightarrow$ Area of the circle $= \frac{22}{7}\times(14)^2 = 616$ cm^2

$\therefore$ Area of the rectangle $= 1166 - 616$
$= 550$ cm^2

$\Rightarrow$ Breadth of the rectangle $= \frac{550}{25} = 22$ cm.

$\therefore$ Required sum $= 2\times\frac{22}{7}\times(14) + 2(25+22)$
$= 88 + 94 = 182$ cm.

4. Length of the floor $= \frac{212\times 32}{2\times(32+21)} = 64$ ft.

and breadth the floor $= \frac{64\times 21}{32} = 42$ ft.

$\therefore$ Area of the floor $= 64 \times 42 = 2688$ sq. ft.

$\therefore$ Reqd. cost $=$ ₹ $2688 \times 2.5 =$ ₹ 6720.

5. Only statement A may be true or possibility.

6. Area of the circular field $= 18634$ m^2

$\because$ $\pi r^2 = 18634$

$\Rightarrow$ $r^2 = 18634\times\frac{7}{22} = 5929$

$\Rightarrow$ $r = 77$ m

$\because$ Length of the fence $= 2\times\frac{22}{7}\times 77$
$= 484$ m

$\therefore$ Total cost $= 484 \times 365$
$=$ ₹ 176660.

7. One side of the square $= \sqrt{196} = 14$ cm

$\therefore$ Radius of the circle $= 28$ cm

$\therefore$ Circumference of the circle $= 2\times\frac{22}{7}\times 28$
$= 176$ cm

$\therefore$ Breadth of the rectangle $= 176$ cm

$\therefore$ Length of the rectangle $= \frac{712}{2} - 176$
$= 356 - 176$
$= 180$ cm.

8. Let r be the radius of the circular plot then from problem,

$\because$ The circumference of the circular plot $= 484$ m

$\Rightarrow$ $2\pi r = 484$

$r = 484\times\frac{7}{22}\times\frac{1}{2} = 77$ metres

$\therefore$ Area of the circular plot $= \pi r^2 = \frac{22}{7}\times(77)^2$
$= 18634$ m^2.

10. Area of the whole paper ABCD $= 22 \times 14$
$= 308$ cm^2

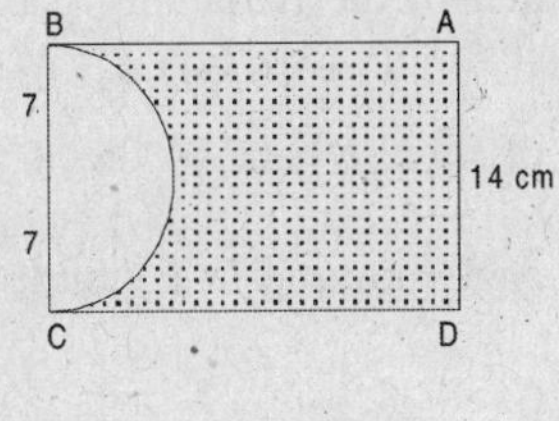

Radius of the semi-circle = $\frac{1}{2} \times 14 \text{ cm} = 7 \text{ cm}$

$\therefore$ Area of the semi-circle = $\frac{1}{2}\pi r^2$

$$= \frac{1}{2} \times \frac{22}{7} \times 7 \times 7$$

$$= 77 \text{ cm}^2$$

$\therefore$ Area of the remaining part of the paper

$$= 308 \text{ cm}^2 - 77 \text{ cm}^2 = 231 \text{ cm}^2.$$

11. Circumference of flower bed = 880 dm

$\Rightarrow \quad 2\pi r = 880$ dm

$\Rightarrow \quad r = \frac{880}{2\pi}$ dm $= \frac{880 \times 7}{2 \times 22} = 140$ dm

Area of flower bed = $\pi r^2 = \frac{22}{7} \times (140)^2$ dm^2

$\therefore$ Required number of plants

$$= \frac{\frac{22}{7} \times 140 \times 140}{35} \text{ dm}^2$$

$$= \frac{22}{7} \times \frac{140 \times 140}{35} = 1760.$$

13. Area of each quadrant = $\frac{\theta}{360} \times \pi r^2$

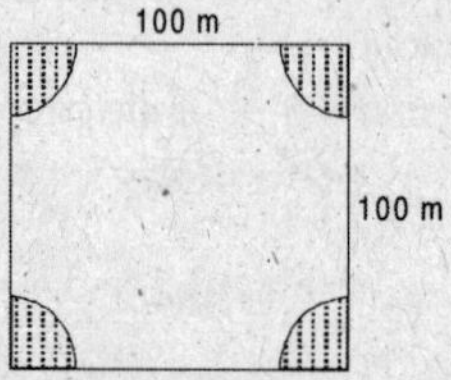

$$= \frac{90}{360} \times \frac{22}{7} \times 14 \times 14 \text{ m}^2 = 154 \text{ m}^2$$

$\therefore$ Area of 4 quadrants = 154×4 m^2 = 616 m^2

Area of park = $(100)^2$ = 10,000 m^2

Hence area of the remaining part of the park

$$= 10{,}000 - 616 = 9{,}384 \text{ m}^2.$$

14. Length of minute hand of clock = r = 14 cm

Central angle covered in 1 minute = $\frac{360}{60} = 6°$

$\therefore$ Area swept in one minute = Area of sector with central angle 6°

$$= \frac{\theta}{360} \times \pi r^2 = \frac{6}{360} \times \frac{22}{7} \times 14 \times 14$$

$$= \frac{154}{15} = 10.26 \text{ cm}^2.$$

15. Let R be the radius of outer circle and r the radius of inner circle.

Circumference of outer circle = 77 cm

$\therefore \quad 2\pi R = 77$

$$\Rightarrow R = \frac{77}{2\pi} = \frac{77 \times 7}{2 \times 22} = \frac{49}{4} \text{ cm}$$

Circumference of inner circle = 55 cm

$\therefore 2\pi r = 55 \Rightarrow r = \frac{55}{2\pi} = \frac{55 \times 7}{2 \times 22} = \frac{35}{4}$ cm

$\therefore$ Area of ring = $\pi(R^2 - r^2)$

$$= \frac{22}{7} \times \left(\frac{49}{4} + \frac{35}{4}\right)\left(\frac{49}{4} - \frac{35}{4}\right) = 231 \text{ cm}^2$$

16. Volume of water that flows in one second

$$= (18 \times 0.075 \times 0.045) \text{ m}^3$$

Volume of water that flows in 30 minutes

$$= 18 \times 0.075 \times 0.045 \times 30 \times 60$$

$$= 109.35 \text{ m}^3.$$

Area of the base of the reservoir = 10.8×3.75 m^2

$\therefore$ Height of water = $\frac{109.35}{10.8 \times 3.75} = 2.7$ metres.

17. Let r cm be the radius of the base and h cm be the height. Then, h = 18 cm.

Now, circumference of the base = Length of the Sheet

$\Rightarrow \quad$ Circumference = 44 cm

$\Rightarrow \quad 2\pi r = 44$

$\Rightarrow \quad 2 \times \frac{22}{7} \times r = 44$

$\Rightarrow \quad r = 7$ cm

Volume of the cylinder = $\pi r^2 h$ cm^3

$$= \frac{22}{7} \times (7)^2 \times 18 \text{ cm}^3$$

$$= 2772 \text{ cm}^3$$

18. Slant height, $l = \sqrt{r^2 + h^2}$

$$= \sqrt{7^2 + 24^2} = 25 \text{ metres}$$

Curved Surface area of cone = πrl

$$= \frac{22}{7}\times 7\times 25 = 550 \text{ m}^2$$

$\therefore$ Area of the cloth required = 550 m^2

$\therefore$ Length of the cloth = $\frac{550}{5}$ = 110 metres.

21. Volume of the metallic rod = 19 × 4 × 2 = 152 cu.cm.

Volume of the cube = 4^3 = 64 cu. cm.

Total volume of both after melting them = 152 + 64 = 216 cu.cm.

$\therefore$ Volume of new cube = 216 cu. cm.

$\Rightarrow$ Side = 6 cm.

23. Let S_1 and S_2 be the two squares. Let the side of the square S_1 be x cm. Then the side of the square $S_2 = (x + 4)$ cm.

$\therefore$ Area of square $S_1 = x^2$

and, Area of square $S_2 = (x + 4)^2$

$\therefore$ According to the question,

$$x^2 + (x + 4)^2 = 400$$

Solving the equation, weget

$$x = -16 \text{ and } 12$$

But x cannot be negative

$\therefore$ Side of the square S_1 = 12 cm

and that of square $S_2 = x + 4 = 12 + 4 = 16$ cm.

26. Angle described by minute hand in 60 minutes = 360°

Angle described by minute hand in 35 minutes

$$= \frac{360}{60}\times 35 = 210°$$

$\therefore$ The required area swept by the minute hand = Area of sector r = 10 cm

and, $\theta = 210°$

$$= \frac{22}{7}\times 10\times 10\times \frac{210}{360}$$

$= 183.3$ cm^2.

27. Let breadth = x cm. Then, length = $\left(\frac{160}{100}x\right)$ cm

$$= \frac{8}{5}x \text{ cm.}$$

So, $\frac{8}{5}x - x = 24 \Rightarrow \frac{3}{5}x = 24$

$$\Rightarrow x = \left(\frac{24\times 5}{3}\right) = 40.$$

$\therefore$ Length = 64 cm, Breadth = 40 cm.

Area = (64 × 40) cm^2 = 2560 cm^2.

28. Let breadth = x metres. Then, length

$$= \left(\frac{115x}{100}\right) \text{ metres.}$$

$$\therefore \quad x\times \frac{115x}{100} = 460$$

$$\Rightarrow x^2 = \left(\frac{460\times 100}{115}\right) = 400$$

$\Rightarrow x = 20.$

29. Let length = $(3x)$ metres and breadth = $(2x)$ metres.

Then, $(3x + 5) \times 2x = 2600$

$\Rightarrow 6x^2 + 10x - 2600 = 0$

$\Rightarrow 3x^2 + 5x - 1300 = 0$

$\Rightarrow (3x + 65)(x - 20) = 0$

$\Rightarrow x = 20.$

$\therefore$ Breadth = $2x$ = 40 m.

31. Let original length = x and original breadth = y. Then, original area = xy.

$$\text{New area} = \left[\frac{(100-r)}{100}\times x\right]\left[\frac{(105+r)}{100}\times y\right]$$

$$= \left[\left(\frac{10500-5r-r^2}{10000}\right)xy\right]$$

$$\therefore \left(\frac{10500-5r-r^2}{10000}\right)xy = xy$$

$\Rightarrow r^2 + 5r - 500 = 0$

$\Rightarrow (r + 25)(r - 20) = 0 \quad \Rightarrow r = 20.$

32. Area left after laying black tiles = [(20 – 4) × (10 – 4)] sq. ft = 96 sq. ft.

Area under white tiles = $\left(\frac{1}{3}\times 96\right)$ sq. ft

$= 32$ sq. ft

Area under blue tiles $= (96 - 32)$ sq. ft
$= 64$ sq. ft

Number of blue tiles $= \dfrac{64}{(2\times 2)} = 16.$

33. Let the length of the outer edge be x metres. Then, length of the inner edge $= (x - 6)$ m.

$\therefore \quad x^2 - (x - 6)^2 = 1764$

$\Rightarrow x^2 - (x^2 - 12x + 36) = 1764$

$\Rightarrow \quad 12x = 1800$

$\therefore \quad x = 150.$

$\therefore$ Required perimeter $= (4x)$ m
$= (4 \times 150)$ m
$= 600$ m.

34. Area $= (45 \times 40)$ m^2

$\Rightarrow \dfrac{1}{2} \times (\text{diagonal})^2 = 1800$

$\Rightarrow$ diagonal $= 60$ m.

35. Let original length of each side $= x$ cm.

Then, its area $= (x^2)$ cm^2.

Length of rectangle formed $= (x + 5)$ cm and its breadth $= x$ cm.

$\therefore \quad \dfrac{x+5}{x} = \dfrac{3}{2} \Rightarrow 2x + 10 = 3x \Rightarrow x = 10.$

$\therefore$ Original length of each side $= 10$ cm and its area $= 100$ cm^2.

36. Area of rectangle $= lb$ sq. units.

Area of the triangle $= \dfrac{1}{2} lb$ sq. units.

$\therefore$ Required ratio $= lb : \dfrac{1}{2} lb = 2 : 1.$

37. Area of the field grazed $= \left(\dfrac{22}{7}\times 14\times 14\right)$ sq. ft
$= 616$ sq. ft.

Number of days taken to graze the field $= \dfrac{616}{100}$ days $= 6$ days (approx.).

38. Radius of the ground $= 17.5$ m.

Radius of inner circle $= (17.5 - 1.4)$ m $= 16.1$ m.

Area of the garden $= \pi \times [(17.5)^2 - 16.1)^2]$ m^2

$= \left[\dfrac{22}{7}\times(17.5+16.1)(17.5-16.1)\right] m^2$

$= \left(\dfrac{22}{7}\times 33.6\times 1.4\right) m^2 = 147.84\ m^2.$

39. Surface area of the cube $= (6 \times 8^2)$ sq. ft
$= 384$ sq. ft.

Quantity of paint required $= \left(\dfrac{384}{16}\right)$ kg $= 24$ kg.

$\therefore$ Cost of painting $=$ ₹ $(36.50 \times 24) =$ ₹ 876.

12. PERMUTATION & COMBINATION

IMPORTANT RESULTS

(*i*) Number of permutations of n distinct things taken r at a time, $0 \le r \le n$
$= n(n-1)(n-2)\ldots(n-r+1)$
$= n!/(n-r)! = {}^nP_r$.
This is equivalent to filling r places by r objects taking from n distinct objects.

(*ii*) The number of permutations of n distinct objects taken all at a time $= n!$

(*iii*) The number of combinations of n objects taken r at a time, $0 \le r \le n$. $= {}^nC_r$

$$= \frac{n!}{(n-r)!.r!}.$$

(*iv*) The number of permutations of n dissimilar things taken r at a time when each thing can be repeated any number of times $= n^r$.

(*v*) The number of combinations of n distinct objects taken r at a time when any object may be repeated any number of times
$=$ coefficient of x^r in $(1 + x + x^2 + \ldots + x^r)^n$
$=$ coefficient of x^r in $(1-x)^n = {}^{n+r-1}C_r$.

(*vi*) Number of combinations of n distinct things taken r at a time when p particular things always occur $= {}^{(n-p)}C_{(r-p)}$.

(*vii*) The number of permutations of n distinct things taken r at a time when p particular things always occur $= {}^{(n-p)}C_{(r-p)}.r!$.

(*viii*) Number of combinations of n distinct things taken r at a time when p particular things never occur $= {}^{(n-p)}C_r$.

(*ix*) Number of permutations (arrangements) of n distinct things taken r at a time when p particular things never occur $= {}^{(n-p)}C_r.r!$.

(*x*) Number of permutations of n things, taken all at a time when p_1 are alike of one kind, p_2 are alike of second kind, ..., p_r of them are alike of the r-th kind $p_1 + p_2 + \ldots + p_r \le n$,
and remaining things are all different $= n!/\{p_1!p_2! \ldots p_r!\}$.

(*xi*) If $3n$ things are to be divided into three equal groups, then the number of ways

$$= \frac{(3n)!}{n!.n!.n!.3!}.$$

(*xii*) If $3n$ things are to be divided equally between 3 persons (*i.e.*, division of $3n$ things into 3 equal groups with permutation of groups) then the number of ways $= \dfrac{(3n)!}{(n!)^3}$.

(*xiii*) Greatest value of ${}^nC_r$
${}^nC_r$ is greatest when $r = n/2$ if n is even
$r = (n-1)/2$ or $(n+1)/2$ if n is odd.

(*xiv*) ${}^nC_r = {}^nC_{n-r}$.

(*xv*) ${}^nC_r + {}^nC_{r+1} = {}^{n+1}C_{r+1}$.

(*xvi*) ${}^nC_r = {}^nC_s \Rightarrow r = s$ or $r + s = n$.

(*xvii*) The number of circular permutations of n different things taken all at a time $= (n-1)!$

(*xviii*) The number of arrangements of n persons on a round table $= (n-1)!$.

(*xix*) The number of arrangements of n flowers to make a garland $= \dfrac{1}{2}(n-1)!$.

SOLVED EXAMPLES

Example 1: In how many different ways can the letters of the word 'PRIDE' be arranged ?

Solution: Required number of arrangements

$= {}^5P_5 = 5! = 120$

Example 2: In how many different ways can the letters of the word 'PRAISE' be arranged ?

Solution: Required number of ways

$= {}^6P_6 = 6! = 720$

Example 3: On a shelf there are 4 books on Economics, 3 books on Management and 4 books on Statistics. In how many different ways can the books be arranged so that the books on Economics are kept together ?

Solution: Required number of different ways

$= {}^8P_8 \times {}^4P_4 = \underline{|8} \times \underline{|4}$

$= 40320 \times 24 = 967680$

Example 4: In how many different ways can the letters of the word 'PRETTY' be arranged?

Solution: Required ways $= \frac{\underline{|6}}{\underline{|2}} = 360$

Example 5: In how many different ways can the letters of the word 'PEANUT' be arranged ?

Solution: Required ways $= {}^6P_6 = \underline{|6}$

$= 6 \times 5 \times 4 \times 3 \times 2 \times 1 = 720.$

MULTIPLE CHOICE QUESTIONS

1. How many seven digit numbers can be made from the number 3428651, using each digit only once ?

A. 49 B. 180
C. 5040 D. 2520

2. How many words can be formed from the letters of the word 'DIRECTOR' so that the vowels are always together?

A. 2106 B. 1206
C. 360 D. 2160

3. In how many ways a committee of 5 members can be selected from 6 men and 5 ladies, consisting of 3 men and 2 ladies?

A. 120 B. 220
C. 200 D. 320

4. In how many ways can the letters of the word 'APPLE' be arranged?

A. 720 B. 120
C. 60 D. 180

5. How many words can be formed by using all the letters of the word. 'ALLAHABAD'?

A. 3780 B. 1890
C. 7560 D. 2520

6. How many words can be formed from the letters of the word 'SIGNATURE' so that the vowels always come together?

A. 720 B. 1440
C. 2880 D. 17280

7. In how many different ways can the letters of the word 'BANKING' be arranged so that the vowels always come together?

A. 120 B. 240
C. 360 D. 720

8. In how many ways can a group of 5 men and 2 women be made out of a total of 7 men and 3 women?

A. 63 B. 90
C. 126 D. 45

9. In a group of 6 boys and 4 girls, four children are to be selected. In how many different ways can they be selected such that at least one boy should be there?

A. 159 B. 194
C. 205 D. 209

10. A box contains 2 white balls, 3 black balls and 4 red balls. In how many ways can 3 balls be drawn from the box, if at least one black ball is to be included in the draw?

A. 32 B. 48
C. 64 D. 96

11. In how many ways can a team of 3 boys and 3 girls be selected from 5 boys and 4 girls?
A. 14 B. 40
C. 18 D. 140

12. The number of ways of selecting 9 balls from 6 red, 5 white and 5 blue if each selection consists of 3 balls of each colour is :
A. 1200 B. 20000
C. 2200 D. 2000

13. In how many ways can we select 4 red balls and 3 blue balls from 8 red balls and 9 blue balls?
A. 8550 B. 5850
C. 5880 D. 8580

14. Find the number of diagonals of a decagon
A. 45 B. 35
C. 55 D. 25

15. In how many ways can a student choose a programme of 5 courses if 9 courses are available and 2 specific courses are compulsary for every student?
A. 53 B. 14
C. 35 D. 28

16. Seven different lecturers are to deliver lectures in seven periods of a class on a particular day. A, B and C are three of the lecturers. The number of ways in which a routine for the day can be made such that A delivers his lecuture before B, and B before C, is
A. 420 B. 120
C. 210 D. 840

17. The number of words that can be made by rearranging the letters of the word APURBA so that vowels and consonants alternate is
A. 18 B. 35
C. 36 D. 24

18. The number of ways in which the letters of the word ARTICLE can be rearranged so that the even places are always occupied by consonants is
A. 576 B. ${}^4C_3 \times (4!)$
C. 2(4!) D. 288

19. The number of ways in which a couple can sit around a table with 6 guests if the couple take consecutive seats is
A. 1440 B. 720
C. 5040 D. 2880

20. The number of ways in which 20 different pearls of two colours can be set alternately on a necklace, there being 10 pearls of each colour, is
A. $9! \times 10!$ B. $5(9!)^2$
C. $(9!)^2$ D. $(18!)^2$

21. There are 4 mangoes, 3 apples, 2 oranges and 1 each of 3 other varieties of fruits. The number of ways of selecting at least one fruit of each kind is
A. 10! B. 9!
C. 4! D. 5!

22. The number of ways in which 6 different balls can be put in two boxes of different sizes so that no box remains empty is
A. 62 B. 64
C. 36 D. 60

23. The number of arrangements of the letters of the word BHARAT taking 3 at a time is
A. 72 B. 120
C. 14 D. 48

24. Find the number of different permutations of the letters of the word BANANA.
A. 16 B. 60
C. 61 D. 36

25. A box contains two white balls, three black balls and four red balls. In how many ways can three balls be drawn from the box if at least one black ball is to be included in the draw?
A. 16 B. 32
C. 64 D. 128

26. All the letters of the word EAMCET are arranged in possible ways. The number of such arrangement in which not two vowels are adjacent to each other is:
A. 360 B. 144
C. 72 D. 54

27. The number of arrangements which can be made by using all the letters of the word LAUGH, if the vowels are adjacent, is:

A. 10 B. 24
C. 48 D. 120

28. There are 10 lamps in a hall. Each one of them can be switched on independently. The number of ways in which the hall can be illuminated is:

A. 10^2 B. 1023
C. 210 D. 10!

29. Everybody in a room shakes hands with everybody else. The total number of hand shakes is 66. The total number of persons in the room is:

A. 11 B. 12
C. 8 D. 14

30. 20 persons are invited for a party. The number of ways in which they and the host can be seated at a circular table, if two particular persons be seated on either side of the host, is equal to:

A. 18! . 2!
B. 18! . 3!
C. 19! . 2!
D. 19! . 3!

31. The number of ways in which 5 prizes be distributed among 4 boys, while each boy is capable of having any number of prizes is:

A. 6^4
B. 4^5
C. $4! \, . \, 2^4$
D. 6 . (4!)

32. In an examination there are three multiple choice questions and each question has 4 choices. Number of ways in which a student can fail to get all answers correct, is:

A. 11 B. 12
C. 27 D. 63

33. 7 men and 7 women are to sit round a table so that there is a man on either side of a woman. The number of seating arrangement is:

A. $(7!)^2$ B. $(6!)^2$
C. $6! \times 7!$ D. 7!

34. Three men have 4 coats, 5 waist coats and 6 caps. In how many ways can they wear them?

A. 178200
B. 172000
C. 172800
D. 1720800

35. To fill 12 vacancies there are 25 candidates of which 5 are from scheduled castes. If 3 of the vacancies are reserved for scheduled caste candidates while the rest are open to all, find the number of ways in which the selection can be made.

A. 4974200
B. 4947200
C. 4972400
D. 4927400

ANSWERS

1	2	3	4	5	6	7	8	9	10
C	D	C	C	C	D	D	A	D	C
11	**12**	**13**	**14**	**15**	**16**	**17**	**18**	**19**	**20**
B	D	C	B	C	D	C	A	A	B
21	**22**	**23**	**24**	**25**	**26**	**27**	**28**	**29**	**30**
C	A	A	B	C	C	C	B	B	A
31	**32**	**33**	**34**	**35**					
B	D	C	C	A					

SOME SELECTED EXPLANATORY ANSWERS

1. Required number of ways = $^7P_7 = \lfloor 7 = 5040$

2. In the given word, we treat the vowels IEO as one letter.
Thus, we have DRCTR (IEO).
This group has 6 letters of which R occurs 2 times and others are different.
Number of ways arranging these letters
$= \frac{6!}{2!} = 360.$
Now 3 vowels can be arranged among themselves in 3! = 6 ways.
∴ Required number of ways = (360 × 6) = 2160.

3. (3 men out of 6) and (2 ladies out of 5) are to be chosen.
∴ Required number of ways
$= (^6C_3 \times {}^5C_2)$
$= \left(\frac{6\times5\times4}{3\times2\times1}\times\frac{5\times4}{2\times1}\right) = 200.$

4. The word 'APPLE' contains 5 letters, 1A, 2P, 1L and 1E.
∴ Required number of ways
$= \frac{5!}{(1!)(2!)(1!)(1!)} = 60.$

5. The word 'ALLAHABAD' contains 9 letters, namely 4A, 2L, 1H, 1B and 1D.
∴ Required number of words
$= \frac{9!}{(4!)(2!)(1!)(1!)(1!)} = 7560.$

6. The word 'SIGNATURE' contains 9 different letters.
When the vowels IAUE are taken together, they can be supposed to form an entity, treated as one letter.
Then, the letters to be arranged are SGNTR (IAUE).
These 6 letters can be arranged in $^6P_6 = 6!$ = 720 ways.
The vowels in the group (IAUE) can be arranged amongst themselves in $^4P_4 = 4! = 24$ ways.
∴ Required number of words = (720 × 24) = 17280.

7. In the word 'BANKING', we treat the two vowels AI as one letter. Thus, we have BNKNG (AI).
This has 6 letters of which N occurs 2 times and the rest are different.
Number of ways of arranging these letters
$= \frac{6!}{(2!)(1!)(1!)(1!)(1!)} = 360.$
Now, 2 vowels AI can be arranged in 2! = 2 ways.
∴ Required number of ways = (360 × 2) = 720.

8. Required number of ways
$= (^7C_5 \times {}^3C_2)$
$= (^7C_2 \times {}^3C_1) = \left(\frac{7\times6}{2\times1}\times3\right) = 63.$

9. We may have (1 boy and 3 girls) or (2 boys and 2 girls) or (3 boys and 1 girl) or (4 boys).
∴ Required number of ways
$= (^6C_1 \times {}^4C_3) + (^6C_2 \times {}^4C_2) + (^6C_3 \times {}^4C_1) + (^6C_4)$
$= (^6C_1 \times {}^4C_1) + (^6C_2 \times {}^4C_2) + (^6C_3 \times {}^4C_1) + (^6C_2)$
$= (6\times4)+\left(\frac{6\times5}{2\times1}\times\frac{4\times3}{2\times1}\right)+\left(\frac{6\times5\times4}{3\times2\times1}\times4\right)+\left(\frac{6\times5}{2\times1}\right)$
= (24 + 90 + 80 + 15) = 209.

10. We may have (1 black and 2 non-black) or (2 black and 1 non-black) or (3 black)
∴ Required number of ways
$= (^3C_1 \times {}^6C_2) + (^3C_2 \times {}^6C_1) + (^3C_3)$
$= \left(3\times\frac{6\times5}{2\times1}\right)+\left(\frac{3\times2}{2\times1}\times6\right)+1 = (45+18+1)$
= 64.

13. 4 red balls from 8 red balls can be selected in $^8C_4$ ways

3 blue balls from 9 balls can be selected in $^9C_3$ ways

$\therefore$ Total number of selection = $^8C_4 \times {}^9C_3$

$$= \frac{8\times7\times6\times5}{1\times2\times3\times4}\times\frac{9\times8\times7}{1\times2\times3}$$

= 70 × 84 = 5880.

14. A decagon has 10 vertices

Join any two vertices in $^{10}C_2$ lines 10 lines will be sides.

$\therefore$ Number of diagonals = $^{10}C_2 - 10$

$$= \frac{10\times9}{1\times2}-10$$

= 45 – 10 = 35

16. As the order of A, B and C is not to change they are to be treated identical in arrangement.

So, the required Number of ways = $\frac{7!}{3!}$.

$$= \frac{7\times6\times5\times4\times3\times2\times1}{3\times2\times1} = 840.$$

18. The number of ways to fill the three even places by 4 consonants = $^4P_3$.

After filling the even places, remaining places can be filled in $^4P_4$ ways.

So, the required number of words

= $^4P_3 \times {}^4P_4$

= 4! × 4! = 24 × 24 = 576.

19. A couple and 6 guests can be arranged in (7 – 1)! ways. But the two people forming the couple can be arranged among themselves in 2! ways.

$\therefore$ The required number of ways = 6! × 2!

= 720 × 2 = 1440.

20. Ten pearls of one colour can be arranged in 1/2 (10 – 1)! ways. The number of arrangements of 10 pearls of the other colour in 10 places between the pearls of the first colour = 10!.

$\therefore$ The required number of ways = $\frac{1}{2}\times9!\times10!$

= 5 × 9! × 9! = $5(9!)^2$.

22. Each ball can be put in 2 ways (either in one box or the other).

$\therefore$ 6 balls can be put in 2 × 2 × ... to six times, i.e., 2^6 ways. But in two of the ways one box is empty. So, the required number of ways = $2^6 - 2$. = 62.

23.

Possibilities	*Selections*	*Arrangements*
One pair, one different	$^1C_1 \times {}^4C_1$	$^1C_1\times{}^4C_1\times\frac{3!}{2!}$ = 12
Three different	$^5C_3$	$^5C_3 \times 3!$ = 60

$\therefore$ The required number of ways = 72

24. BANANA

3A's, 2N's, B, i.e., 6 letters, 3 alike of one type and 2 of another type. Number of words taken all at a time is $\frac{6!}{3!\,2!}=\frac{6\times5\times4}{2}$ = 60.

25. The required number of ways

= $^3C_1 \times {}^6C_2 + {}^3C_2 \times {}^6C_1 + {}^3C_3$ = 64.

26. First we place 3 consonant in 3! ways and then at four places (2 between them and 2 on sides) 3 vowels in which one vowels is repeated can be placed in $^4P_3/2!$ ways.

Hence, required number = 3! $^4P_3/2!$ = 72.

27. Considering two vowels together as a letter, there are 4 letters in all which can be arranged in 4! ways while 2 vowels can also be arranged in 2! ways.

$\therefore$ Total number of arrangements = 4! . 2! = 48.

28. Each bulb has two choices, either switched on or off.

$\therefore$ Required number = $2^{10} - 1$ = 1023

(Since in one way, when all switches are off, the hall will not be illuminated.)

29. Let there be n persons in a room.

$\therefore$ Total no. of shakehands $= {}^nC_2 = 66$

$$\Rightarrow \quad \frac{1}{2}n(n-1) = 66$$

$$\Rightarrow \quad n^2 - n - 132 = 0$$

$$\Rightarrow \quad (n+11)(n-12) = 0$$

$$\Rightarrow \quad n = 12 \qquad (\because n \neq -11)$$

30. Host can sit on any seat. Two particular guests can sit on either sides of host in $2! = 2$ ways and remaining 18 guests in $(18)!$ ways.

Hence, total ways $= 2.(18)!$.

31. Since every prize can be given by any of the four boys, so number of ways $= 4 \times 4 \times 4 \times 4 \times 4 = 4^5$.

32. Each question can be answered in 4 ways and all questions can be answered correctly in only one way, so the required number of ways $= 4^3 - 1 = 63$.

33. First the seven women sit round the table in 6! ways and then seven men will sit in the spaces between every pair of two women in 7! ways.

$\therefore$ Required seating arrangements $= 6! \times 7!$.

34. ${}^4P_3 \times {}^5P_3 \times {}^6P_3 = 172800$.

35. $5C_3 \times {}^{22}C_9 = 4974200$.

13. PROBABILITY

1. **Random Experiment:** If the result of an experiment is not certain and is any one of the several possible outcomes, the experiment is called a trial or a random experiment.
2. **Sample Space:** The set of all possible outcome of an experiment is called the sample space provided no two or more of these outcomes can occur simultaneously and exactly one of these outcomes must occur whenever the experiment is conducted.
3. **Events:** The outcomes of an experiment, *i.e.*, sample points of the sample space are usually known as simple events and any subset of the sample space 'S' is called an event.

   Thus throwing of a dice is an experiment, S = {1, 2, 3, 4, 5, 6} is the sample space, {1}, ... {6} are simple events and {1, 2}, etc., are events. The empty set ϕ is also an event as $\phi \subset S$ and it is called an impossible event. The sample space S is also a subset of S and so it is also an event. S represents the sure event, *i.e.*, certainty.
4. **Equally Likely Events:** A set of events is said to be equally likely if taking into consideration all the relevant factors there is no reason to expect one of them in preference to others.

   For example, when a fair coin is tossed, the occurrence of a tail or a head are equally likely.
5. **Exhaustive Events:** A set of events is said to be exhaustive if the performance of the experiment always results in the occurrence of atleast one of them.

   For example, if we throw a dice, then the events A_1 = {1, 2}, A_2 = {2, 3, 3} are not exhaustive as we can get 5 as outcome of the experiment which is not the member of any of the events A_1 and A_2. If we consider the events E_1 = {1, 2, 3} and E_2 = {2, 4, 5, 6}, then the set E_1, E_2, is exhaustive.
6. **Mutually Exclusive Events:** A set of events is said to be mutually exclusive if they have no point in common, *i.e.*, happening of one of them eliminates the happening of any of the remaining events. Thus E_1, E_2, E_3, ... are mutually exclusive iff $E_i \cap E_j = \phi$ for $i \neq E_1$ and E_2 are mutually exclusive.
7. **Complement of An Events:** The complement of an event A, denoted by $\overline{A}$, A' or A^c, is the set of all sample points of the space other than the sample points in A.

   e.g., In the experiment of throwing a fair dice, S = {1, 2, 3, 4, 5, 6}. If A = {1, 3, 5, 6}, then $\overline{A}$ = {2, 4}

   Note that $A \cap \overline{A} = S$.
8. **Classical Definition of Probability:** If there are n exhaustive mutually exclusive and equally likely outcomes of an experiment and m of them are favourable to an event A, the probability of the happening of A is defined as the ratio m/n.

   Thus, denoting the probability of the happening of an event A by p, we have $p = m/n$.

   Clearly p is a positive number not greater than unity, so that $0 \leq p \leq 1$.

   Since the number of cases in which the event A will not happen is $n - m$, the probability q that the event will not happen is given by

   $$q = \frac{(n-m)}{n} = 1 - \frac{m}{n} = 1 - p. \therefore p + q = 1$$

If probability of happening of an event A is 1, then A is certain event and if probability of happening of an event A is 0, then A is impossible event.

9. Odds in Favour and Odds against an Event: As a result of an experiment if *a* of the outcomes are favourable to an event E and *b* of the outcomes are against it, then we say that odds are *a* to *b* in favour of E or odds are *b* to *a* against E.

Thus, odds in favour of an event E

$$= \frac{\text{number of favourable cases}}{\text{number of unfavourable cases}}.$$

Similarly, odds against an event E

$$= \frac{\text{number of unfavourable cases}}{\text{number of favourable cases}}.$$

If odds in favour of an event are $a : b$ then the probability of the occurrence of that event is $\frac{a}{a+b}$ and the probability of the non-occurrence of that event is $\frac{b}{(a+b)}$.

Addition Theorem:

(*a*) If 'A' and 'B' are any two events in a sample space S, then $P(A \cup B) = P(A) + P(B) - P(A \cap B)$.

(*b*) If 'A' and 'B' are mutually exclusive then $P(A \cap B) = 0$ so that $P(A \cup B) = P(A) + P(B)$.

(*c*) If A is any event in S, then $P(A') = 1 - P(A)$.

Total Probability Theorem:

The probability that one of several mutually exclusive events $A_1, A_2, ..., A_n$ will happen, is the sum of the probabilities of the separate events. In symbol,

$$P(A_1 + A_2 + ... + A_n) = P(A_1) + P(A_2) + ... + P(A_n).$$

Conditional Probability:

The probability of B under the assumption that A has occurred is called the conditional probability of B under the condition that the event A has taken place and is denoted by P(B/A). P(B/A) is read as "probability at the event B given A^B."

Conditional Probability Theorem:

If A and B are any two events in the sample space S, the conditional probability of B relative to A is given by $P(B/A) = \frac{P(B \cap A)}{P(A)} = \frac{n(B \cap A)}{n(A)}, A \neq \phi.$

Some Important Remarks about Coins, Dice and Playing Cards:

(*a*) **Coins:** A coin has a head side and a tail side. If an experiment consist of more than a coin, coins are considered to be distinct if not otherwise stated.

(*b*) **Dice:** A die (cubical) has six faces marked 1, 2, 3, 4, 5, 6. We may have tetrahedral (having four faces 1, 2, 3, 4) or pentagonal (having five faces 1, 2, 3, 4, 5) die. As in the case of dice, if we have more than one die, all dice are considered to be distinct if not otherwise stated.

(*c*) **Playing Cards:** A pack of playing cards usually contain 52 cards.

There are 4 suits (spade, heart, diamond and club) each having 13 cards. There are two colours — red (heart and diamond) and black (spade and club) each having 26 cards.

In thirteen cards of each suit, there are 3 face cards namely king, queen and jack, so there are in all 12 face cards (4 kings, 4 queens and 4 jacks).

Also there are 16 honours cards, 4 of each suit namely ace, king, queen and jack.

SOLVED EXAMPLES

Example 1: A bag contains 7 Red balls, 4 Green balls and 5 Yellow balls. What is the probability that 3 balls drawn at random are either Green or Yellow?

Solution: Total ways = $^{16}C_3 = \frac{\lfloor 16}{\lfloor 13 \lfloor 3} = 560$

Favourable ways = ${}^4C_3 \times {}^5C_3 = \frac{\lfloor 4}{\lfloor 3 \lfloor 1} \times \frac{\lfloor 5}{\lfloor 3 \lfloor 2}$

$= 4 \times 10 = 40.$

$\therefore$ Reqd. Probability $= \frac{40}{560} = \frac{1}{14}.$

Example 2: A basket contains three Red and four Green balls. If four balls are drawn at random from the basket, what is the probability that two are Red and two are Green?

Solution: Reqd. Probability $= \frac{{}^3C_2 \times {}^4C_2}{{}^7C_4} = \frac{3 \times 6}{35}$

$= \frac{18}{35}.$

Example 3: A box contains 8 Red, 16 Blue, 4 Yellow and 12 Black bolls. Two balls are picked up randomly. What is the chance that both are Red?

Solution: Total results $= {}^{40}C_2 = \frac{40 \times 39}{2} = 780$

and favourable results $= {}^8C_2 = \frac{\lfloor 8}{\lfloor 2 \lfloor 6} = \frac{8 \times 7}{2}$

$= 28.$

$\therefore$ Required probability $= \frac{28}{780} = \frac{7}{195}.$

Example 4: A bag contains 8 Red, 16 Blue, 12 Black and 4 Yellow marbles. One marbles is picked up randomly. What is the probability that it is not Blue?

Solution: Total results $= {}^{40}C_1 = 40$

Favourable results when it is Blue $= {}^{16}C_1 = 16.$

$\therefore$ Favourable results when it is not Blue

$= 40 - 16 = 24$

$\therefore$ Reqd. probability $= \frac{24}{40} = 0.6.$

MULTIPLE CHOICE QUESTIONS

Directions (Qs. 1 to 3) : *Study the information carefully to answer the questions that follow.*

A bucket contains 8 Red, 3 Blue and 5 Green marbles.

1. If 4 marbles are drawn at random, what is the probability that 2 are Red and 2 are Blue?

A. $\frac{11}{16}$ B. $\frac{3}{16}$

C. $\frac{11}{72}$ D. $\frac{3}{65}$

2. If 2 marbles are drawn at random, what is the probability that both are Green?

A. $\frac{1}{8}$

B. $\frac{5}{16}$

C. $\frac{2}{7}$

D. None of these

3. If 3 marbles are drawn at random, what is the probability that none is Red?

A. $\frac{3}{8}$ B. $\frac{1}{16}$

C. $\frac{1}{10}$ D. None of these

Directions (Qs. 4 to 5) : *Study the information and answer the questions that follow.*

A basket contains 3 Red balls, 5 Blue balls and 2 Green balls.

4. If three balls are drawn at random, what is the probability that none is Blue?

A. $\frac{1}{6}$ B. $\frac{1}{12}$

C. $\frac{1}{5}$ D. $\frac{3}{10}$

5. If four balls are drawn at random, what is the probability that at least one is Green?

A. $\frac{2}{3}$ B. $\frac{1}{2}$

C. $\frac{1}{3}$ D. $\frac{2}{5}$

6. If two balls are drawn at random, what is the probability that both are Red?

A. $\frac{1}{5}$ B. $\frac{3}{10}$

C. $\frac{3}{5}$ D. $\frac{1}{15}$

7. A dice is thrown once. Find the probability of getting a number greater than 3.

A. $\frac{2}{3}$ B. $\frac{1}{3}$

C. $\frac{1}{2}$ D. $\frac{3}{2}$

8. A bag contains 5 Red balls, 8 White balls, 4 Green balls and 7 Black balls. If one ball is drawn at random, find the probability that it is Black.

A. $\frac{7}{24}$ B. $\frac{5}{24}$

C. $\frac{5}{6}$ D. $\frac{1}{4}$

9. Find the probability that a number selected from the numbers 1 to 25 is not a prime number when each of the given number is equally to be selected.

A. $\frac{9}{25}$ B. $\frac{16}{25}$

C. $\frac{21}{25}$ D. $\frac{14}{25}$

10. A bag contains 3 Red balls and 5 Black balls. A ball is drawn at random from the bag. What is the probability that the ball drawn is not Red?

A. $\frac{3}{8}$ B. $\frac{5}{8}$

C. $\frac{1}{8}$ D. $\frac{7}{8}$

11. A die is thrown once. Find the probability of getting an odd number.

A. $\frac{1}{2}$ B. $\frac{3}{2}$

C. $\frac{2}{3}$ D. $\frac{1}{3}$

12. A letter is chosen at random from the word REED the probability of choosing an E is –

A. $\frac{3}{4}$ B. $\frac{1}{2}$

C. $\frac{1}{4}$ D. $\frac{2}{3}$

13. A card is drawn at random from a well-shuffled deck of playing cards. Find the probability that the card drawn is a card of spade or an ace.

A. $\frac{11}{13}$ B. $\frac{1}{26}$

C. $\frac{4}{13}$ D. $\frac{9}{13}$

14. If a letter is chosen at random from the word TRIANGLE.
What is the probability that it a vowel?

A. $\frac{3}{8}$ B. $\frac{5}{8}$

C. $\frac{1}{4}$ D. $\frac{3}{4}$

15. What is the chance that a leap year, selected at random, will contain 53 Sundays?

A. $\frac{52}{365}$ B. $\frac{52}{366}$

C. $\frac{2}{7}$ D. $\frac{5}{7}$

16. In a book of 300 pages, if a page is opened at random; find the probability that the sum of the digits in its number is 10.

A. $\frac{8}{15}$ B. $\frac{9}{15}$

C. $\frac{7}{75}$ D. $\frac{14}{15}$

17. A die is thrown once. Find the probability of getting an even number.

A. $\frac{1}{3}$ B. $\frac{1}{2}$

C. $\frac{1}{4}$ D. $\frac{1}{6}$

18. Two friends were born in the year 2000. What is the probability that they have the same birthday?

A. $\frac{1}{500}$ B. $\frac{1}{730}$

C. $\frac{1}{365}$ D. $\frac{1}{366}$

19. A number is chosen at random from among the first 30 natural numbers. The probability of the number chosen being prime is :

A. $\frac{1}{3}$ B. $\frac{3}{10}$

C. $\frac{1}{30}$ D. $\frac{11}{30}$

20. The probability that a number selected at random from the set of numbers {1, 2, 3, 4, ..., 100} is a cube is :

A. $\frac{1}{25}$ B. $\frac{2}{25}$

C. $\frac{3}{25}$ D. $\frac{4}{25}$

21. A single letter is selected at random from the word 'COLLEGE'. Find the probability of getting a vowel.

A. $\frac{3}{7}$ B. $\frac{4}{7}$

C. $\frac{5}{7}$ D. $\frac{2}{7}$

22. A box contains 5 Red balls, 4 Green balls and 7 White balls. A ball is drawn at random from the box. Find the probability that the ball drawn is neither Red nor White.

A. $\frac{2}{7}$ B. $\frac{3}{4}$

C. $\frac{1}{4}$ D. $\frac{1}{2}$

23. In a cricket match, a batsman hits boundary 8 times out of 40 balls he plays. Find the probability that he didn't hit boundary.

A. 0.8 B. 0.6

C. 0.5 D. 0.4

24. Two coins are tossed simultaneously. The probability of getting atmost one head is :

A. $\frac{1}{4}$ B. $\frac{3}{4}$

C. $\frac{1}{2}$ D. $\frac{1}{4}$

25. A bag contains 50 coins and each coin is marked from 51 to 100. One coin is picked at random. The probability that the number on the coin is not a prime number is :

A. $\frac{1}{5}$ B. $\frac{3}{5}$

C. $\frac{2}{5}$ D. $\frac{4}{5}$

26. In a football match, a player makes 4 goals from 10 penalty kicks. The probability of converting a penalty kick into a goal by the player, is :

A. $\frac{1}{4}$ B. $\frac{1}{6}$

C. $\frac{1}{3}$ D. $\frac{2}{5}$

27. Three unbiased coins are tossed. What is the probability of getting at least 2 heads?

A. $\frac{1}{4}$ B. $\frac{1}{2}$

C. $\frac{1}{3}$ D. $\frac{1}{8}$

28. In a simultaneous throw of two dice, what is the probability of getting a total of 7?

A. $\frac{1}{6}$ B. $\frac{1}{4}$

C. $\frac{2}{3}$ D. $\frac{3}{4}$

29. What is the probability of getting a sum 9 from two throws of a dice?

A. $\frac{1}{6}$ B. $\frac{1}{8}$

C. $\frac{1}{9}$ D. $\frac{1}{12}$

30. Tickets numbered 1 to 20 are mixed up and then a ticket is drawn at random. What is the probability that the ticket drawn bears a number which is a multiple of 3?

A. $\frac{3}{10}$ B. $\frac{3}{20}$

C. $\frac{2}{5}$ D. $\frac{1}{2}$

31. A card is drawn from a pack of 52 cards. The probability of getting a queen of club or a king of heart is :

A. $\frac{1}{13}$ B. $\frac{2}{13}$

C. $\frac{1}{26}$ D. $\frac{1}{52}$

32. Two cards are drawn together from a pack of 52 cards. The probability that one is a spade and one is a heart, is :

A. $\frac{3}{20}$ B. $\frac{29}{34}$

C. $\frac{47}{100}$ D. $\frac{13}{102}$

33. A bag contains 6 white and 4 red balls. Three balls are drawn at random. What is the probability that one ball is red and the other two are white?

A. $\frac{1}{2}$ B. $\frac{1}{12}$

C. $\frac{3}{10}$ D. $\frac{7}{12}$

34. A box contains 20 electric bulbs, out of which 4 are defective. Two bulbs are chosen at random from this box. The probability that at least one of these is defective, is :

A. $\frac{4}{19}$ B. $\frac{7}{19}$

C. $\frac{12}{19}$ D. $\frac{21}{95}$

35. Two dice are tossed. The probability that the total score is a prime number is :

A. $\frac{1}{6}$ B. $\frac{5}{12}$

C. $\frac{1}{2}$ D. $\frac{7}{9}$

ANSWERS

1	**2**	**3**	**4**	**5**	**6**	**7**	**8**	**9**	**10**
D	A	A	B	C	D	C	A	B	B
11	**12**	**13**	**14**	**15**	**16**	**17**	**18**	**19**	**20**
A	B	C	A	C	C	B	D	A	A
21	**22**	**23**	**24**	**25**	**26**	**27**	**28**	**29**	**30**
A	C	A	B	D	D	B	A	C	A
31	**32**	**33**	**34**	**35**					
C	D	A	B	B					

SOME SELECTED EXPLANATORY ANSWERS

1. Total number of ways = ${}^{16}C_4 = \frac{\lfloor 16}{\lfloor 12 \lfloor 4}$

$= 1820$

And favourable number of ways = ${}^{8}C_2 \times {}^{3}C_2$

$= \frac{\lfloor 8}{\lfloor 6 \lfloor 2} \times \frac{\lfloor 3}{\lfloor 1 \lfloor 2} = 84$

$\therefore$ Reqd. probability = $\frac{84}{1820} = \frac{3}{65}$.

2. Total number of ways = ${}^{16}C_2 = \frac{\lfloor 16}{\lfloor 14 \lfloor 2} = 120$

And favourable number of ways = ${}^{5}C_2$

$= \frac{\lfloor 5}{\lfloor 3 \lfloor 2} = 10$

$\therefore$ Reqd. probability = $\frac{10}{120} = \frac{1}{12}$.

3. Total number of ways = ${}^{16}C_3 = \frac{\lfloor 16}{\lfloor 13 \lfloor 3} = 560$

Total number of ways when all the marbles are Red

$= {}^{8}C_3 = \frac{\lfloor 8}{\lfloor 5 \lfloor 3} = 56$

$\therefore$ Probability when all the three are Red

$= \frac{56}{560} = \frac{1}{10}$

$\therefore$ And probability when none is Red = $1 - \frac{1}{10}$

$= \frac{9}{10}$.

4. Probability that none is blue

$= \frac{{}^{5}C_3}{{}^{10}C_3} = \frac{10}{120} = \frac{1}{12}$

5. Probability that none is green

$= \frac{{}^{8}C_4}{{}^{10}C_4} = \frac{70}{210} = \frac{1}{3}$

$\therefore$ Probability that at least one is green

$= 1 - \frac{1}{3} = \frac{2}{3}$

6. Probability that both are red

$= \frac{{}^{3}C_2}{{}^{10}C_2} = \frac{3}{45} = \frac{1}{15}$

7. Sample space S = {1, 2, 3, 4, 5, 6} ; $n(S) = 6$
Let A = "getting a number grater than 3" then

A = {4, 5, 6} ; $n(A) = 3$

$P(A) = \frac{n(A)}{n(S)} = \frac{3}{6} = \frac{1}{2}$.

9. We are given numbers from 1 to 25.
$n(S) = 25$.
Prime numbers from 1 to 25 are 2, 3, 5, 7, 11, 13, 17, 19, 23.
These are 9 prime numbers.
Let E denote the event 'Number drawn is not prime'.

$\therefore \quad n(E) = 25 - 9 = 16$

$p(E) = \frac{n(E)}{n(S)} = \frac{16}{25}$.

10. Total number of balls in the bag = 3 + 5 = 8
Let E denote the event 'ball drawn is red'.

$\therefore \quad n(E) = 3$ and $n(S) = 8$.

(*i*) $p(E) = \frac{n(E)}{n(S)} = \frac{3}{8}$

(*ii*) $p(\text{not red}) = p(\bar{E})$

$= 1 - p(E) = 1 - \frac{3}{8} = \frac{5}{8}$.

11. Sample S = {1, 2, 3, 4, 5, 6} ; $n(S) = 6$
Let F denote the event 'getting an odd number'.

F = {1, 3, 5} ; $n(S) = 3$

$\therefore \quad P(F) = \frac{n(F)}{n(S)} = \frac{3}{6} = \frac{1}{2}$.

12. The sample space is {R, E_1, E_2, D}
There are 2 ways to choose the letter E from the four letters

$\therefore \quad P(E) = \frac{2}{4} = \frac{1}{2}.$

13. There are 52 cards in a deck of 52 playing cards.
There are 13 spades and 4 aces in 52 playing cards. Out of 13 spades there is one ace.
∴ Favourable no ways for the card drawn to be spade or an ace = 13 spades + 3 aces = 16.

$\therefore$ P(a card of spade or an ace) $= \frac{16}{52} = \frac{4}{13}.$

14. Since there are 3 vowels out of a total of 8 letters, the probability of choosing a vowel is 3/8.

15. A Leap year has 366 days. In a leap year, here are 52 complete weeks (52 Sundays) and 2 days over these two days can be as follows. Sunday and Monday, Monday and Tuesday, Tuesday and Wednesday, Wednesday and Thursday, Thursday and Friday, Friday and Saturday, Saturday and Sunday.
Out of these 7 possibilities, only two (Saturday and Sunday; Sunday and Monday) are favourable for having 53 Sundays)

Required chance $= \frac{2}{7}.$

17. A die is thrown once. Its sample space is
$S = \{1, 2, 3, 4, 5, 6\}, n(S) = 6$
Let E : an even number, then $E = \{2, 4, 6\}$
Number of favourable cases $= n(E) = 3$

$\therefore \quad P(E) = \frac{n(E)}{n(S)} = \frac{3}{6} = \frac{1}{2}.$

18. Year 2000 is a leap year. There are 366 days in the year 2000. Total number of cases in which two friends can be born on the same day are 366.
Out of 366 days, number of favourable ways in which two friends have the same birthday = 1

$\therefore$ Required probability $= \frac{1}{366}.$

19. The prime numbers from first 30 natural numbers are 2, 3, 5, 7, 11, 13, 17, 19, 23, 29.
We find that there are 10 prime numbers from 1 to 30.
∴ Probability that the number chosen being prime is $= \frac{10}{30} = \frac{1}{3}.$

20. From the natural numbers 1 to 100 the four number 1, 8, 27 and 64 are cubes

$\therefore$ Required Probability $= \frac{4}{100} = \frac{1}{25}.$

23. Let A denote the event that the batsman did not hit a boundary.
We have, Total number of trials = 40
Number of trials in which the event A happened
$= 40 - 8 = 32$

$\therefore \quad P(A) = \frac{32}{40} = \frac{4}{5} = 0.8.$

27. Here S = {HH, HT, TH, TT}.
Let E = Event of getting at least one head = {HT, TH, HH}.

$\therefore \quad P(E) = \frac{n(E)}{n(S)} = \frac{4}{8} = \frac{1}{2}.$

28. We know that in a simultaneous throw of two dice, $n(S) = 6 \times 6 = 36$.
Let E = Event of getting a total of 7 = {(1, 6), (2, 5), (3, 4), (4, 3), (5, 2), (6, 1)}.

$\therefore \quad P(E) = \frac{n(E)}{n(S)} = \frac{6}{36} = \frac{1}{6}.$

29. In two throws of a die, $n(S) = (6 \times 6) = 36$.
Let E = Event of getting a sum 9 = {(3, 6), (4, 5), (5, 4), (6, 3)}.

$\therefore \quad P(E) = \frac{n(E)}{n(S)} = \frac{4}{36} = \frac{1}{9}.$

30. Here, S = {1, 2, 3, 4, ..., 19, 20}.
Let E = Event of getting a multiple of 3 = {3, 6, 9, 12, 15, 18}.

$\therefore \quad P(E) = \frac{n(E)}{n(S)} = \frac{6}{20} = \frac{3}{10}.$

31. Here $n(S) = 52$.
Let E = Event of getting a queen of club or a king of heart.
Then, $n(E) = 2$.

$$\therefore \quad P(E) = \frac{n(E)}{n(S)} = \frac{2}{52} = \frac{1}{26}.$$

32. Let S be the sample space. Then,

$$n(S) = {}^{52}C_2 = \frac{(52 \times 51)}{(2 \times 1)} = 1326.$$

Let E = Event of getting 1 spade and 1 heart.
$\therefore$ $n(E)$ = Number of ways of choosing 1 spade out of 13 and 1 heart out of 13

$$= ({}^{13}C_1 \times {}^{13}C_1) = (13 \times 13) = 169.$$

$$\therefore \quad P(E) = \frac{n(E)}{n(S)} = \frac{169}{1326} = \frac{13}{102}.$$

33. Let S be the sample space. Then,
$n(S)$ = Number of ways of drawing 3 balls out of 10

$$= {}^{10}C_3 = \frac{(10 \times 9 \times 8)}{(3 \times 2 \times 1)} = 120.$$

Let E = Event of drawing 1 red and 2 white balls
$\therefore$ $n(E)$ = Number of ways of drawing 1 red ball out of 4 and 2 white balls out of 6

$$= ({}^4C_1 \times {}^6C_2) = \left(4 \times \frac{6 \times 5}{2 \times 1}\right) = 60.$$

$$\therefore \quad P(E) = \frac{n(E)}{n(S)} = \frac{60}{120} = \frac{1}{2}.$$

34. P (None is defective)

$$= \frac{{}^{16}C_2}{{}^{20}C_2} = \left(\frac{16 \times 15}{2 \times 1} \times \frac{2 \times 1}{20 \times 19}\right) = \frac{12}{19}.$$

$$\text{P (at least one is defective)} = \left(1 - \frac{12}{19}\right) = \frac{7}{19}.$$

35. Clearly, $n(S) = (6 \times 6) = 36$.
Let E = Event that the sum is a prime number.
Then, E = {(1, 1), (1, 2), (1, 4), (1, 6), (2, 1), (2, 3), (2, 5), (3, 2), (3, 4), (4, 1), (4, 3), (5, 2), (5, 6), (6, 1), (6, 5)}

$\therefore \quad n(E) = 15$

$$\therefore \quad P(E) = \frac{n(E)}{n(S)} = \frac{15}{36} = \frac{5}{12}.$$

14. DATA ANALYSIS

TABLES

Tables are often used in reports, magazines and newspaper to present as set of numerical data. It is one of the easiest and most accurate ways of presenting data. One of the main purposes of tables is to make complicated information easier to understand. Hence, the advantage of presenting data in a table is that one can see the information at a glance. We present below an example of tabular presentation of annual expenditure of 5 families for last 4 years.

Annual Expenditure of 5 families (in ₹ Thousands)

Years → **Families ↓**	**2005**	**2006**	**2007**	**2008**
A	35	50	55	60
B	40	60	65	75
C	45	50	70	80
D	30	40	45	50
E	50	55	60	70

Essentials of a Tables:

(i) **Title:** Heading of the table
(ii) **Stub:** The section of the table containing row headings in called Stub.
(iii) **Column Captions** : The heading of each column is designated as column caption.
(iv) **Body**
(v) **Footnotes**
(vi) **Source**

Example 1. Directions: *Study the folloiwng table and answer the questions given below:*

Categories of students according to their enrolment in various courses in a vocational college.

Courses	*Categories (Faculty)*			
	Arts		*Science*	
	Boys	*Girls*	*Boys*	*Girls*
1. Business Management	45	25	65	25
2. Typewriting	186	23	32	20
3. Stenography	120	25	58	12
4. Typewriting and Stenography	100	12	5	3

1. If 60% boys and 70% girls pass in their respective courses, then total pass percentage is:
A. 58% B. 66% C. 54% D. 62%

2. The total number of students who have opted the course of Business Management and the course of Stenography exceeds the number of students studying in typewriting course by:
A. 44% B. 66% C. 33% D. 55%

3. In which of the following courses, percentage of girls is the highest?
A. Stenography B. Business Management
C. Typewriting D. Typewriting and Stenography

4. In the art faculty number of students who have opted the course of stenography is how much per cent of the total student in the faculty?
A. 27% B. 10% C. 18% D. 15%

5. Total number of boys studying in the college exceeds the total number of girls in the college by:
A. 321% B. 280% C. 308% D. 250%

Solution 1. $\because$ Total boys = 45 + 186 + 120 + 100 + 65 + 32 + 58 + 5 = 611

$\therefore$ Number of boys who pass in their respective courses = 60% of 611 = $611 \times \frac{60}{100} = 366.60$

Total number of girls = 25 + 23 + 25 + 12 + 25 + 20 + 12 + 3 = 145

Number of girls who pass in their respective courses = 70% of 145 = $\frac{145 \times 70}{100} = 101.50$

$$\therefore \text{Combined pass per cent} = \frac{(366.6 + 101.5) \times 100}{611 + 145} = \frac{46810}{756} = 61.92 \simeq 62\%$$

Solution 2. $\because$ Number of students in Business Management course = 160
Number of students in typewriting course = 261
Number of students in stenography corse = 215

$$\therefore \text{Required per cent} = \left(\frac{160 + 215 - 261}{261}\right) \times 100 \approx 44\%$$

Solution 3. Percentage of girls in Business Management course = $\frac{(25 + 25) \times 100}{160} = 31.25$

Percentage of girls in typewriting course = $\frac{(23 + 20) \times 100}{261} = 16.47$

Percentage of girls in stenography course = $\frac{(25 + 12) \times 100}{215} = 12.56$

And percentage of girls in typewriting and stenography course = $\frac{(12 + 3) \times 100}{120} = 12.50$

Hence, it is clear from the above that percentage of girls in Business Management course is the highest.

Solution 4. Required percentage = $\frac{(25 + 120) \times 100}{536} \times 100 \simeq 27$

Solution 5. Total number of boys = 45 + 65 + 186 + 32 + 120 + 58 + 100 + 5 = 611
Total number of girls = 25 + 23 + 25 + 12 + 25 + 20 + 12 + 3 = 145

$\therefore$ Required percentage = $\left(\frac{611-145}{145}\right)\times 100 \simeq 321\%$

Example 2. Directions: *Figures of biscuit exports from a country during various years are given in the following table. Study the table carefully and answer the questions that follows:*

VOLUME OF EXPORT OF BISCUITS FROM A COUNTRY

Year	*Quantity (in lakh tins)*	*Price (in crores ₹)*
2004	100	150
2005	75	150
2006	150	330
2007	160	400
2008	200	500

1. During which year per tin export price remained at lowest level?
A. 2007 B. 2006 C. 2005 D. 2004

2. During which years price per tin remained at the same level?
A. 2006 and 2008 B. 2006 and 2007 C. 2007 and 2008 D. 2006 and 2004

3. The export price of biscuit increased from 2004 to 2008 by how much per cent?
A. 100 B. $116\frac{2}{3}$ C. $233\frac{1}{3}$ D. 350

4. The difference between the number of biscuit tins exported in 2008 and that in 2007 is:
A. 40 B. 40,000 C. 4,00,000 D. 40,00,000

Solution 1. Export price per tin in 2004 = $\frac{₹\ 150 \text{ crores}}{₹\ 100 \text{ lakhs}}$ = ₹ 150

Export price per tin in 2005 = $\frac{₹\ 150 \text{ crores}}{₹\ 75 \text{ lakhs}}$ = ₹ 200

Export price per tin in 2006 = $\frac{₹\ 330 \text{ crores}}{₹\ 150 \text{ lakhs}}$ = ₹ 220

Export price per tin in 2007 = $\frac{₹\ 400 \text{ crores}}{₹\ 160 \text{ lakhs}}$ = ₹ 250

Export price per tin in 2008 = $\frac{₹\ 500 \text{ crores}}{₹\ 200 \text{ lakhs}}$ = ₹ 250

Hence, it is clear that per tin export price was at lowest level in 2004.

Solution 2. From the explanation given in the answer of Q.No. 1, it is clear that per tin export price was same in 2007 and 2008.

Solution 3. From the level of 2004 percentage increase in export price in 2008

$$= \left(\frac{500-150}{150}\right)\times 100 = 233\frac{1}{3}\%$$

Solution 4. Required difference = 200 – 160 = 40 lakh tins = 40,00,000 tins.

Example. 3. Directions: *Study the following table carefully and answer the questions given below:*

Number of Employees Working in Various departments of a Factory

Year	*Production Deptt.*	*Sale Deptt.*	*Procurement Deptt.*	*Administration & Accounts Deptt.*	*Research & Development Deptt.*
2003	150	25	50	45	75
2004	225	40	45	62	70
2005	450	65	30	90	73
2006	470	73	32	105	70
2007	500	80	35	132	74
2008	505	75	36	130	75

1. During which of the following years number of employees working in production deptt. of the factory was less than 50% of the total employees of the factory?
A. 2003 B. 2005 C. 2006 D. 2007

2. During which year the number of employees working in each department was more than those in the previous year and nearly equal to next year?
A. 2007 B. 2006 C. 2005 D. 2004

3. In which department of the factory number of employees remained nearly same during the years from 2003 to 2008?
A. Production
B. Sale
C. Research and Development
D. Administration and Accounts
E. Procurement

4. In which department of the factory number of employees are maximum from 2003 to 2008?
A. Production
B. Sale
C. Research and Development
D. Administration and Accounts
E. Sale and Procurement

5. During which year number of employees in the factory became nearly double the total number of employees working in the factory during 2003.
A. 2008 B. 2007 C. 2006 D. 2005

Solution 1. Number of total employees in 2003 = 150 + 25 + 50 + 45 + 70 = 345

$\therefore$ Percentage number of employees working in producton deptt. = $\frac{150\times 100}{345} = 43.48\%$

Number of total employees in 2004 = 225 + 40 + 45 + 62 + 70 = 442

$\therefore$ Percentage number of employees working in production deptt. = $\frac{225\times 100}{442} = 50.9\%$

Number of total employees in 2005 = 450 + 65 + 30 + 90 + 73 = 708

$\therefore$ Percentage number of employees working in proudction deptt. = $\frac{450 \times 100}{708} = 63.56\%$

Total number of employees in 2006 = 470 + 73 + 32 + 105 + 70 = 750

$\therefore$ Percentage number of employees working in production deptt. = $\frac{470 \times 100}{750} = 62.67\%$

Total number of employees in 2007 = 500 + 80 + 35 + 132 + 74 = 821

$\therefore$ Percentage number of employees working in production deptt. = $\frac{500 \times 100}{821} = 60.9\%$

Total number of employees in 2007 = 505 + 75 + 36 + 130 + 75 = 821

$\therefore$ Percentage number of employees working in production in deptt. = $\frac{505 \times 100}{821} = 61.51\%$

Hence, it is clear that percentage number of employees working in production deptt. was less than 50% in 2003.

Solution 2. It is clear from the table that it was the year 2007 when the number of employees working in each department was more than that in the previous year and nearly equal to next year.

Solution 3. According to the table in the research and development department number of employees remained nearly same during the year from 2003 to 2008.

Solution 4. Production.

Solution 5. Total number of employes in 2003 = 345
Total number of employees in 2005 = 708
Hence, it was the year 2005 when total number of employees in the factory became nearly double the total number of emplyees working in the factory during 2003.

Example. 4. *Study the table carefully to answer the questions that follow.*

Number of students studying in six different classes of six different schools.

Class → School ↓	**V**	**VI**	**VII**	**VIII**	**IX**	**X**
P	152	160	145	156	147	144
Q	148	166	150	155	157	143
R	161	152	140	145	143	165
S	159	142	149	140	142	168
T	147	144	158	163	154	150
U	150	160	162	160	161	140

1. What is the respective ratio of students studying in class IX of schools Q and R together to those studying in class VI of schools S and T together?

A. 143 : 150 B. 150 : 143 C. 127 : 181 D. 181 : 127

2. Number of students studying in class X from school P forms approximately what per cent of the total number of students studying in class X from all schools together?
A. 9 B. 12 C. 16 D. 24

3. Total number of students studying in school T from all classes together forms what per cent of total number of students studying in school S from all classes together?
A. 100.26 B. 101.78 C. 102.64 D. 103.52

4. The number of students studying in class VII from school U forms what per cent of the total number of students from all the classes together from that school?
A. 15.93 B. 16.14 C. 17.36 D. 18.28

5. Which class has the maximum number of students from all schools together?
A. V B. VI C. VII D. X

Solution 1. Number of students of class IX of schools Q and R = 157 + 143 = 300
Number of students of class VI of schools S and T = 142 + 144 = 286
Hence, required ratio = 300 : 286 = 150 : 143

Solution 2. Total number of students of class X from all schools
= 144 + 143 + 165 + 168 + 150 + 140 = 910

Required percentage = $\frac{144}{910} \times 100 = 15.82 \simeq 16\%$

Solution 3. Total number of students of school T from all classes
= 147 + 144 + 158 + 163 + 154 + 150 = 916
Total number of students of school S from all classes
= 159 + 142 + 149 + 140 + 142 + 168 = 900

Required percentage = $\frac{916}{900} \times 100 = 101.78\%$

Solution 4. Total number of students of school U from all the classes
= 150 + 160 + 162 + 160 + 161 + 140 = 933

Required percentage = $\frac{162}{933} \times 100 = 17.36\%$

Solution 5. Total number of students of class V from all the schools
= 152 + 148 + 161 + 159 + 147 + 150 = 917
Total number of students of class VI from all the schools
= 160 + 166 + 152 + 142 + 144 + 160 = 924
Total number of students of class VII from all the schools
= 145 + 150 + 140 + 149 + 158 + 162 = 904
Total number of students of class VIII from all the schools
= 156 + 155 + 145 + 140 + 163 + 160 = 919
Total number of students of class IX from all the schools
= 147 + 157 + 143 + 142 + 154 + 161 = 904
Total number of students of class X from all the schools
= 144 + 143 + 165 + 168 + 150 + 140 = 910
Hence, the class VI has maximum number of students.

BAR GRAPHS

Given quantity of a bar graph can be compared by the height or length. A bar graph can have either vertical or horizontal bars. You can compare different quantities or the same quantity at the different times. The bars may be placed adjacent to each other or may be separated from each other by spaces depending upon the problem.

For Example:

Registration of New Vehicles in Delhi (in thousands)

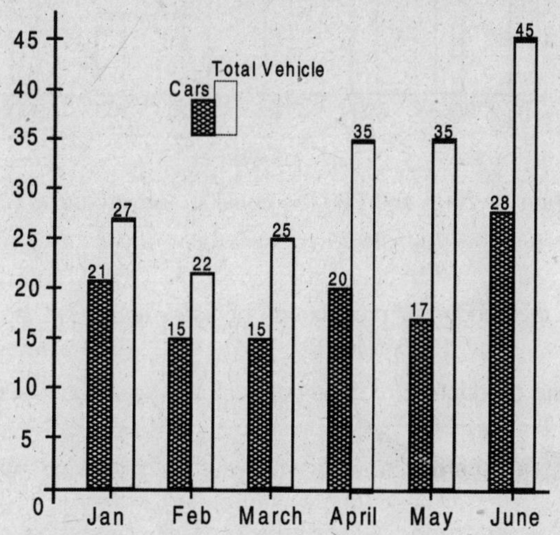

CUMULATIVE GRAPH

These are usually bar or line graphs where the height of the bar or line is divided up proportionally among various quantities presented in the graph. The representation of quantities may be done in terms of either percentage of the total or in absolute figures. These are also called sub-divided graphs. Thus, cumulative graph may be conveniently used for making comparisons.

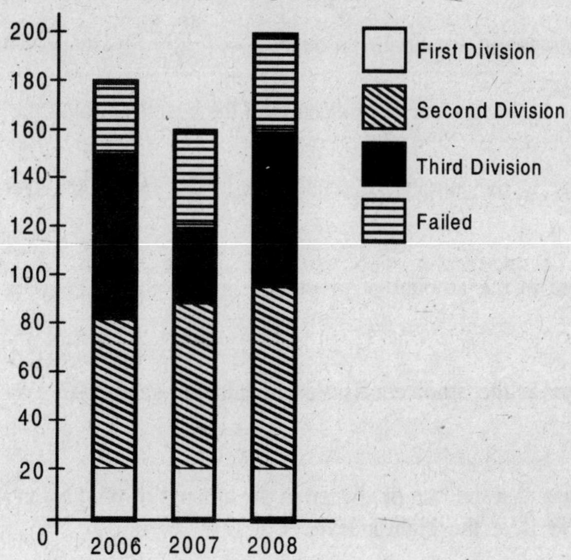

Example 1: Directions: *The following bar graph shows the production of food grains in India during certain year. Study the graph carefully and answer the questions given below:*

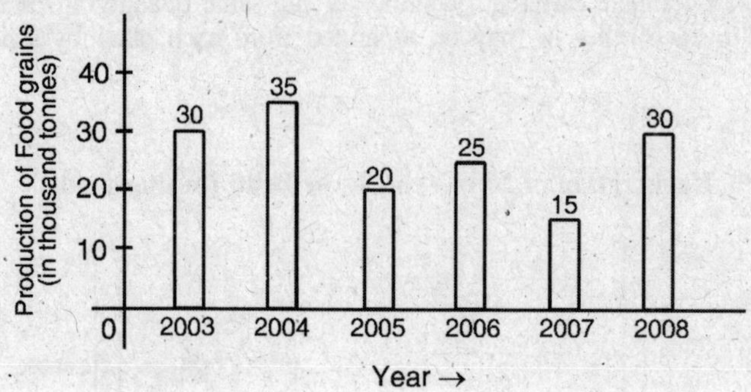

1. Total food grain production in 2005 and 2007 is equal to the production during which of the following years?

A. 2003 B. 2004 C. 2006 D. 2008

2. The difference between the foodgrain productions of 2004 and 2008 is:

A. 500 tonnes B. 1000 tonnes C. 5000 tonnes D. 10000 tonnes

3. Percentage increase in the production of foodgrains in the year 2008 over the year 2007 is:

A. 15% B. 30% C. 50% D. 100%

4. Rate of change in quantity of production in which of the following two consecutive years is at the minimum level?

A. 2003 and 2004 B. 2005 and 2006 C. 2007 and 2008 D. 2006 and 2007

Solution 1. Total production in 2005 and 2007 = 20 + 15 = 35 thousand tonnes. This total production is equal to the production in the year 2004.

Solution 2. Difference between the production of foodgrains during 2004 and 2008 = 35 − 30 = 5 thousand tonnes.

Solution 3. Percentage increase in foodgrain production = $\frac{30-15}{15} \times 100 = 100\%$

Solution 4. Rate of change in the amount of production in the year 2004 over the year 2003 = $\frac{35-30}{30} \times 100$

$= 16.67\%$

Rate of change in the amount of production in the year 2006 over the year 2005

$= \frac{(25-20)}{20} \times 100 = 25\%$

Rate of change in the amount of production in the year 2008 over the year 2007

$= \frac{(30-15)}{15} \times 100 = 100\%$

Rate of change in the amount of production in the year 2007 over the year 2006

$= \frac{(25-15)}{15} \times 100 = 66.67\%$

Hence, it is clear that the rate of change in the amount of production during the consecutive years 2007 and 2008 is at the highest level.

Example 2: Directions: *The bar graph as shown below gives information about the sale and profit details of a departmental store during the years from 2001–2008. Study the graph carefully and answer the questions asked here under.*

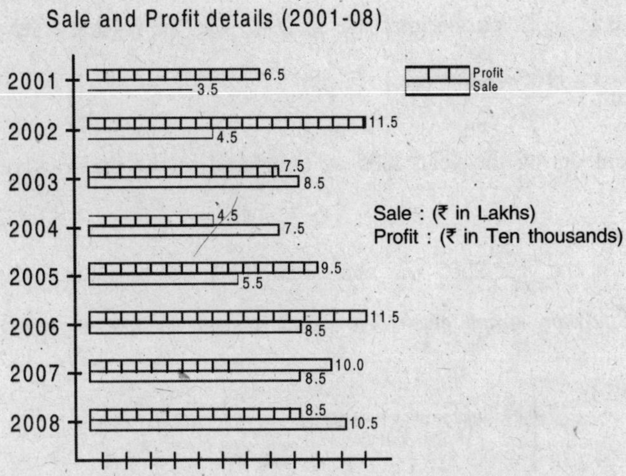

1. Mean of annual increase in sale from 2003 to 2008 (rupees in lakhs) is:
A. 0.1 B. 0.2 C. 0.3 D. 0.4

2. Annual mean profit of the store (rupees in ten thousands) is approximately:
A. 8.5 B. 8.6 C. 8.7 D. 9.0

3. During which of the following years percentage of profit earned by the store on the total sale was at the highest level?
A. 2001 B. 2002 C. 2003 D. 2005

4. Assuming the profit earned during the year 2001 as base (100), the profit made by the store during the year 2008 was:
A. 76 B. 105 C. 121 D. 131

5. During which year between 2001 to 2006 profit made by the store as compared to the previous year was more than 100%?
A. 2008 B. 2007 C. 2005 D. 2003

Solution 1. Mean of annual increase in sale from 2003 to 2008 $= \dfrac{10.5+8.5}{5} = 4$

Solution 2. Annual mean profit of the store (rupees in ten thousands)

$$= \frac{(6.5+11.5+7.5+4.5+9.5+11.5+10.0+8.5)}{8} = \frac{69.5}{8} = 8.7 \text{ (approx.)}$$

Solution 3. Percentage of profit on the total sale in 2001 $= \dfrac{6.5\times10000\times100}{3.5\times100000} = 18.57$

Percentage of profit on the total sale in 2002 $= \dfrac{11.5\times10000\times100}{4.5\times100000} = 25.56$

Percentage of profit on the total sale in 2003 = $\frac{7.5 \times 10000 \times 100}{8.5 \times 100000}$ = 8.82

And percentage of profit on the total sale in 2005 = $\frac{9.5 \times 10000 \times 100}{5.5 \times 100000}$ = 17.27

∴ Percentage of profit on the total sale in 2002 was the highest level.

Solution 4. Required profit = $\frac{100 \times 8.5}{6.5}$ = 131

Solution 5. Profit per cent during the year 2005 as compared to the previous year

$$= \frac{(9.5 - 4.5) \times 100}{4.5} = 111.11\%$$

Hence, profit in the year 2005 was more than 100% as compared to the previous year.

Example 3: Directions: *Study the graph given below and answer the questions asked there under.*

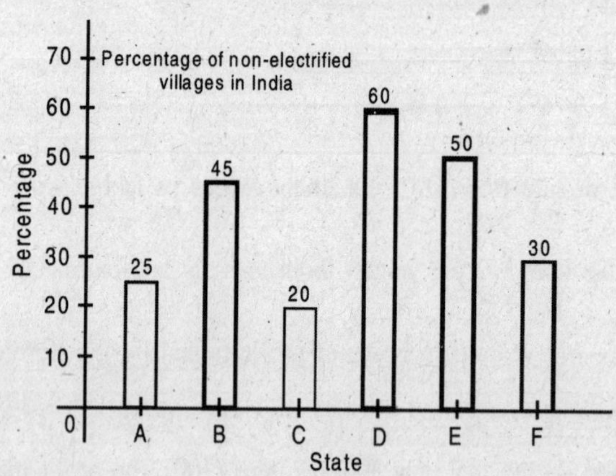

1. According to the table given below which state of India has the highest percentage of electrified villages?
A. A B. B C. C D. D E. E

2. If central govt. decides to extend financial assistance for prompt electrification and begins with the state having the least electrified villages, then in the order of preference which of the following states will be fourth?
A. C B. B C. A D. E E. F

3. How many states have at least 60% or more electrified villages?
A. Five B. Three C. Four D. Two E. One

4. In which of the following states percentage of electrified villages is double the percentage of electrified villages in state (D)?
A. C B. F C. A D. B E. E

5. What is the percentage of electrified villages in the state (A)?
A. 65% B. 25% C. 35% D. 75% E. None of these

Solution 1. In the state (C) percentage of non-electrified villages is the least. It means the percentage of electrified villages for the state (C) is the highest.

Solution 2. The order of preference of the least electrified villages is given as: D, E, B, F, A, C.

Solution 3. In A, C and F states, percentage of non-electrified villages are 25, 20 and 30 per cent respectively. Hence, percentages of electrified villages for these three states are 75, 80 and 70 per cent respectively.

Solution 4. Percentage of electrified villages in state D = 100 – 60 = 40
Percentage of electrified villages in state C = 100 – 20 = 80
Hence, the percentage of electrified villages in the state C is double the percentage of electrified villages in state D.

Solution 5. Percentage of electrified villages in the state A = 100 – 25 = 75%

Example 4: Directions: *The following bar chart shows the amount accrued from additional taxation by the government during certain successive years. Study the chart carefully and answer the questions that follow:*

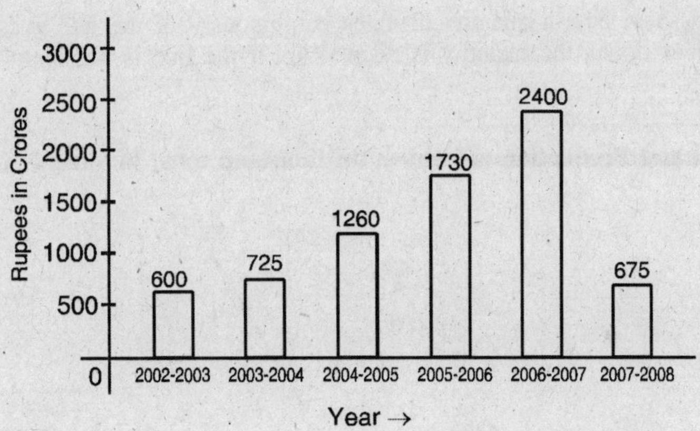

1. In between which of the following two successive financial years increase in taxation was at the highest level?
   A. 2002-2003 and 2003-04 B. 2005-06 and 2006-07
   C. 2006-07 and 2007-08 D. 2004-05 and 2005-06
2. Total increase in taxation was how much per cent between the years 2004-05 and 2005-06?
   A. 37.3% B. 35.4% C. 38.5% D. 36.6%
3. Percentage decrease in taxation in between the years 2006-07 and 2007-08 was:
   A. 71.8% B. 68.8% C. 72.6% D. 75%
4. Between the years 2005-06 and 2006-07 the taxation was increased by:
   A. ₹ 670 crores B. ₹ 650 crores C. ₹ 700 crores D. ₹ 715 crores
5. What is the average amount of taxation during all these years?
   A. ₹ 1233.7 crores B. ₹ 1433.5 crores C. ₹ 1231.7 crores D. ₹ 1400 crores

Solution 1. Between the financial years 2005-06 and 2006-07, maximum increase of ₹ 670 crores had been registered in taxation.

Solution 2. Percentage of total increase = $\dfrac{(1730-1260)}{1260}\times 100 = \dfrac{470\times 100}{1260} = 37.3\%$

Solution 3. Percentage of total decrease in taxation between the years 2006-07 and 2007-08

$$= \frac{(2400-675)}{2400}\times 100 = \frac{1725\times 100}{2400} = 71.8\%$$

Solution 4. Increase in taxation in between the financial years 2005-06 and 2006-07

= ₹ (2400 – 1730) = ₹ 670 crores

Solution 5. Average of the total taxation during the years = $\dfrac{600+725+1260+1730+2400+625}{6}$

$$= \frac{7390}{6} = ₹\ 1231.7 \text{ crores}$$

LINE GRAPHS

Line graphs are used to show how a quantity changes continuously. If the line goes up, the quantity is increasing; if the line goes down, the quantity is decreasing; if the line is horizontal, the quantity is not changing.

For Example:

Demand and Production of rubber (in thousand tons) in various years

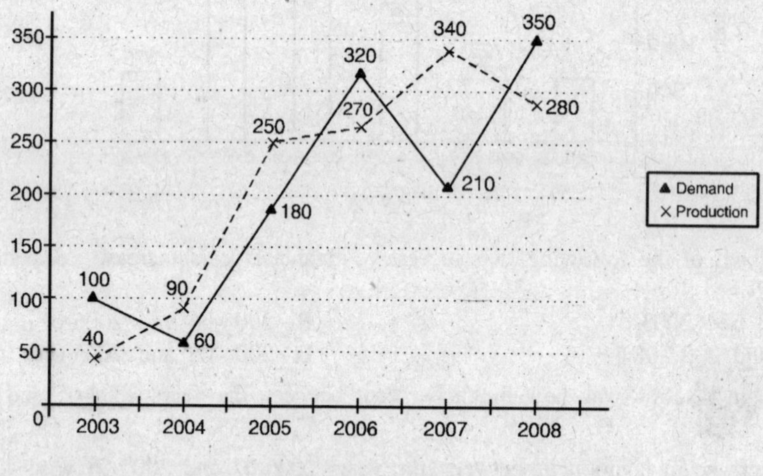

Example 1: Directions: *Study carefully the graph given below and answer the questions that follow:*

1. Price of a machine during 2005 was:

   A. ₹ $5\frac{1}{3}$ thousand B. ₹ 50 thousand C. ₹ 5103 D. ₹ 3 thousand

2. The percentage decrease in the production in 2007 over the previous year 2006 was:

   A. 5% B. 20% C. 25% D. 30%

3. The difference in revenue collection from the sale of machines during 2007 and 2008 was:
A. ₹ 10 lakhs B. ₹ 1 crore C. ₹ 4 crores D. ₹ 6 crores

4. Had the company sold its machines in 2008 at 25% inhanced price of 2007, what would have been the total selling price of machines produced during the year?
A. ₹ 35 crores B. ₹ 20 crores C. ₹ 12.5 crores D. ₹ 15.5 crores

5. Difference between the price of a machine in the year 2006 and that in the eyar 2007 was:
A. ₹ 1500 B. ₹ 2500 C. ₹ 1800 D. ₹ 3200

Solution 1. No. of machines produced during the year 2005 = 15000
And price of the machines = ₹ 8,0000000

∴ Price of 1 machine in 2005 = ₹ $\frac{80000000}{15000}$ = $5\frac{1}{3}$ thousand

Solution 2. Percentage decrease in production of machines during 2007 over the previous year 2006

$$= \frac{(25-20)\times 100}{25} = 20\%$$

Solution 3. Difference in revenue collected from sale of machines during 2007 and 2008
= 16 – 10 = ₹ 6 crores.

Solution 4. On enhancing price by 25% in 2008, total price of the machines produced during the years 2008

$$= \frac{10\times 125}{100} = ₹\ 12.5 \text{ crores}$$

Solution 5. Price of 1 machine in 2006 = $\frac{80000000}{25000}$ = ₹ 3200

Price of 1 machine in 2007 = $\frac{100000000}{20000}$ = ₹ 5000

∴ Required difference = ₹ (5000 – 3200) = ₹ 1800

Example 2: Directions: *Study the graph carefully to answer the questions that follow:*

Percentage Increase in profit of two companies over the years

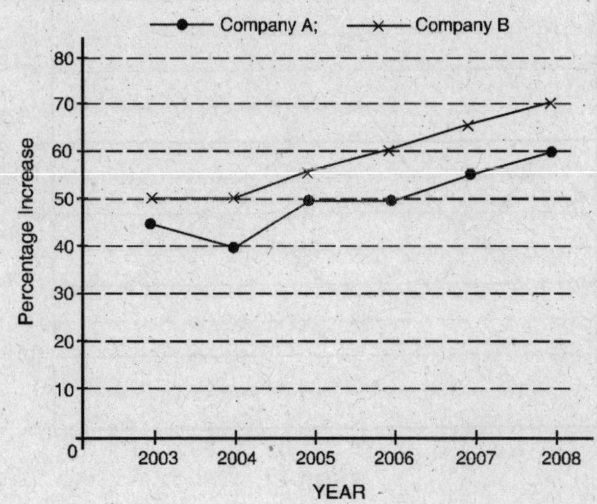

1. What is the per cent increase in profit of company A in the year 2007 from the previous year?
   A. 5 B. 10 C. 45 D. 60
2. What is the per cent increase in profit of company A in the year 2008 from the previous year?
   A. 7.64 B. 9.09 C. 8.12 D. 10.11
3. What is the per cent increase in profit of company A in the year 2005 from the previous year?
   A. 10 B. 15 C. 20 D. 25
4. If the profit of company B in the year 2003 was ₹ 6,79,995, what would its profit have been in the year 2002?
   A. ₹ 4,24,530 B. ₹ 4,53,330 C. ₹ 5,01,500 D. ₹ 5,53,330
5. Based on the graph, which of the following statements is True?
   A. Company B has made the highest profit in the year 2008
   B. Company A has made the lowest profit in the year 2004
   C. Company B has made more amount of the profit than company A over the years
   D. There is no increase in the profit of company B in the year 2005 from the previous year.

Solution 1. Required percentage = $\frac{55-50}{50}\times 100 = 10\%$

Solution 2. Required percentage = $\frac{60-55}{55}\times 100 = 9.09\%$

Solution 3. Required percentage = $\frac{50-40}{40}\times 100 = 25\%$

Solution 4. Required profit = $\frac{100}{150}\times 6{,}79{,}995 =$ ₹ 4,53,330

Solution 5. It is clear from the graph that company B has made the highest profit in the year 2008, i.e., 70%

Example 3: Directions: *Study the following graph carefully to answer these questions:*

Quantity of Various items sold and price per kg

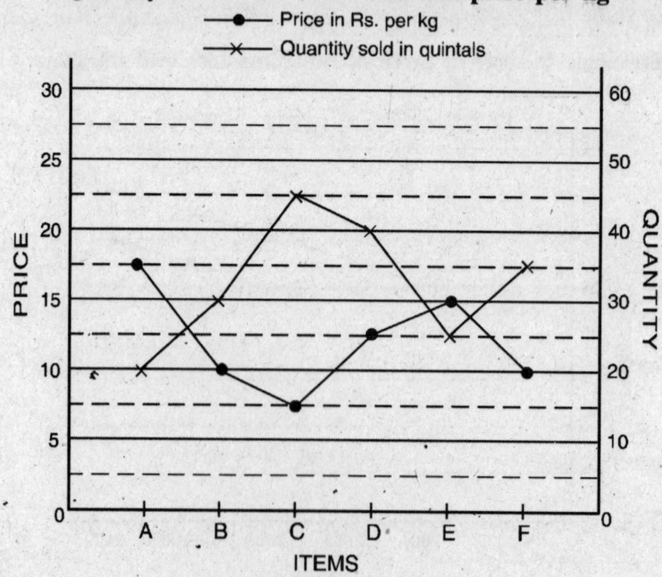

1. If the quantity sold of item D increased by 50% and the price reduced by 10%, what was the total value of the quantity sold for Item D?

A. ₹ 675 B. ₹ 6750

C. ₹ 67500 D. ₹ 67550

2. What is the ratio between the total values of quantity sold for items E and F respectively?

A. 3 : 2 B. 5 : 7

C. 7 : 5 D. 15 : 14

3. If the price as well as the quantity sold is increased by 20% for item A, what is the total value of quantity sold for item A?

A. ₹ 42000 B. ₹ 48500

C. ₹ 49000 D. ₹ 50400

4. What is the average price per kg. of items A, B and C?

A. ₹ 7.50 B. ₹ 9

C. ₹ 9.50 D. ₹ 11.67

5. Total value of quantity sold for item C is what per cent of the total value of the quantity sold for item E?

A. 85 B. 87.5

C. 90 D. 111

Solution 1. New quantity of item D = $\frac{150}{100} \times 40 = 60$ quintal

New price per kg of item D = $\frac{90}{100} \times 12.50 =$ ₹ 11.25

Since, total value = ₹ (60 × 100 × 11.25) = ₹ 67500

Solution 2. Required ratio = (25 × 100 × 15) : (35 × 100 × 10) = 15 : 14

Solution 3. New price of item A per kg = $\frac{120}{100} \times 17.50 =$ ₹ 21

New quantity of item A = $\frac{120}{100} \times 20 = 24$ quintal

Since, total value = ₹ (24 × 100 × 21) = ₹ 50400

Solution 4. Average price per kg of items A, B and C = $\frac{17.50 + 10 + 7.50}{3} =$ ₹ 11.67

Solution 5. Required percentage = $\frac{45 \times 100 \times 750}{25 \times 100 \times 15} \times 100 = 90\%$

Example 4: Directions: *Study the following graph carefully and answer the questions that follow:*

Percentage profit earned by two companies over the given years

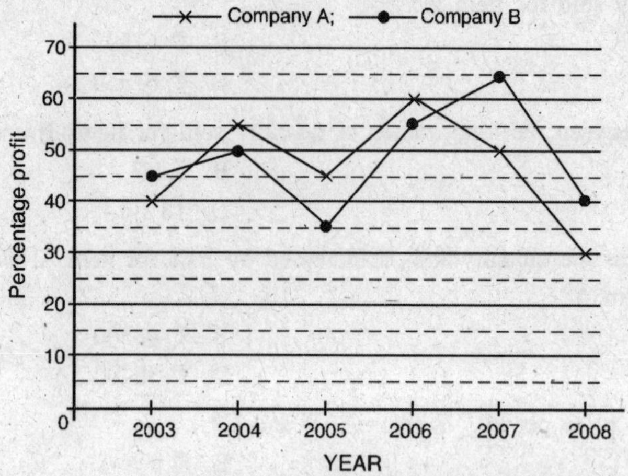

1. If the income of company A in 2005 was equal to its expenditue in 2007, what was the ratio between company's expenditure in the years 2005 and 2007 respectively?

A. 19 : 20 B. 20 : 19 C. 20 : 29 D. 29 : 20

2. If the total expenditure of the two companies in 2008 was ₹ 18 lakhs and expenditure of companies A and B in that year in the ratio of 4 : 5 respectively, then what was the income of company B in that year (in lakh ₹)?

A. 8 B. 10 C. 10.4 D. 14

3. If the total income of company A in all the years together was equal to the total expenditure of company B in all the years together, which was ₹ 265 lakhs, then what was the total percentage profit earned by Company A for all the years together?

A. 37 B. 45 C. 52 D. Cannot be determined

4. If the income of company B in 2006 was ₹ 18.6 lakhs and ratio of incomes of company A and B in 2006 was 2 : 3, what was the expenditure of company A in 2006 (in lakhs)?

A. 7.75 B. 9.75 C. 12 D. 12.4

5. If the income of company A in 2006 was equal to the total expenditure of company B in 2007, then what was the ratio of expenditure of company A in 2006 to the income of company B in 2007?

A. 10 : 13 B. 13 : 10 C. 25 : 66 D. 66 : 25

Solution 1. Let income of company A in 2005 = Expenditure of Company A in 2007 = ₹ x and also expenditure of company A in 2005 = ₹ x_1; then

For company A in 2005,

$$\frac{x - x_1}{x_1} \times 100 = 45 \qquad \Rightarrow 29x_1 = 20x \qquad \therefore\ x_1 = \frac{20x}{29}$$

Since, required ratio $= \frac{20x}{29} : x = 20 : 29$

Solution 2. In 2008, expenditure of company B = $\frac{5}{4+5} \times 18$ lakhs = ₹ 10 lakhs.

Let, income of company B in 2008 = ₹ x lakhs; then

$$\frac{x-10}{10} \times 100 = 40 \qquad \Rightarrow x - 10 = 4 \qquad \therefore x = ₹\ 14 \text{ lakhs}$$

Hence, income of company B in 2008 = ₹ 14 lakhs

Solution 3. Here, total income of company A in all the years together = ₹ 265 lakhs, while individual profit percentages for different years are given so the profit earned by company A for the years together can not be determined.

Solution 4. In 2006, income of company A = ₹ $\frac{18.6}{3} \times 2$ = ₹ 12.4 lakhs

Let in 2006, expenditure of company A = ₹ x lakhs, then

$$\frac{12.4 - x}{x} \times 100 = 60 \qquad \Rightarrow 8x = 62 \qquad \therefore x = \frac{62}{8} = ₹\ 7.75 \text{ lakhs}$$

Hence, expenditure of company A in 2006 = ₹ 7.75 lakhs

Solution 5. Let income of company A in 2006 = Expenditure of company B in 2007 = ₹ x lakhs also ₹ x_1 lakhs, and ₹ x_2 lakhs be the expenditure of company A in 2006 and income of company B in 2007 respectively; then

For company A in 2006,

$$\frac{x - x_1}{x_1} \times 100 = 60 \qquad \Rightarrow 8x_1 = 5x \qquad \therefore x_1 = ₹\ \frac{5x}{8} \text{ lakhs}$$

For company B in 2007,

$$\frac{x_2 - x}{x} \times 100 = 65 \qquad \Rightarrow 20x_2 = 33x \quad \therefore x_2 = ₹\ \frac{33x}{20} \text{ lakhs}$$

$$\text{Since, required ratio} = \frac{5x}{8} : \frac{33x}{20} = \frac{5x}{8} \times 40 : \frac{33x}{20} \times 40 = 25 : 66$$

PIE CHARTS

These are used to show the share of various sectors in the total. They usually show the percentage share of each sector in the whole (taken as 100%). In such representation the total quantity in question is distributed over a total angle of 360°. The area of each sector is proportional to the relative frequency of the class represented by the sector.

$$\text{Sector angle} = \frac{\text{Class frequency}}{\text{Total frequency}} \times 360°$$

For Example: ***Distribution of Expenditure of a family***

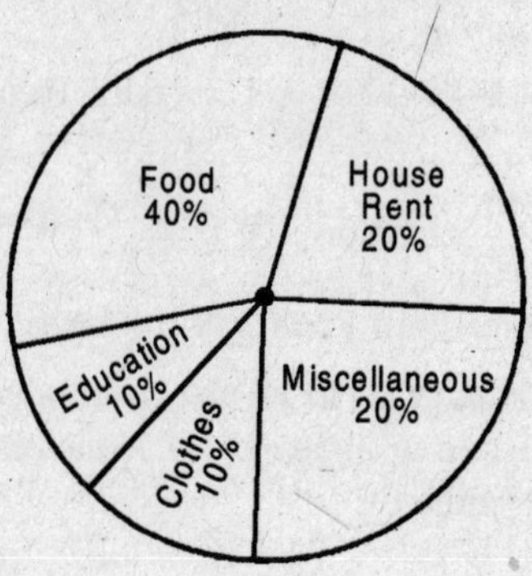

Example 1: Directions: *The pie-chart given below shows the household expenditure of a family on different items. Study the chart carefully and answer the questions that follows:*

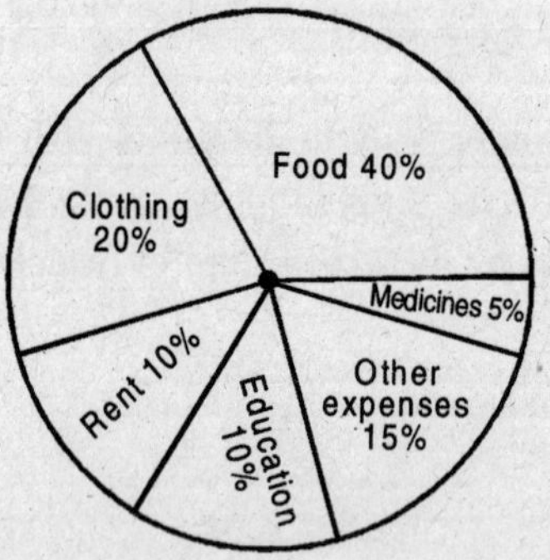

1. If the family's expenditure on education is ₹ 375 then the same amount is being expent by this family on which of the following items?
   A. Medicines B. Other expenses C. Rent D. Clothing
2. If the family expends ₹ 750 per month on food, what is the annual expenditure of this family on education?
   A. ₹ 2150 B. ₹ 1022.50 C. ₹ 2250 D. ₹ 1400
3. If total expenditure of this family is ₹ 4500, find the expenditure of the family on clothing?
   A. ₹ 800 B. ₹ 900 C. ₹ 840 D. ₹ 950
4. What is the angle subtended on the centre by the segment representing other expenses?
   A. 64° B. 54° C. 36° D. 15°
5. What is the ratio of total expenses on rent and clothing to the total expenses on medicines and other expenses of this family?
   A. 2 : 3 B. 3 : 4 C. 3 : 5 D. 3 : 2

Solution 1. Both segments representing education and rent respectively are each 10%. Hence, family's expenditure on these two items will be equal, *i.e.*, ₹ 375 will be expent on rent.

Solution 2. Here, 40% = ₹ 750

$$\Rightarrow 10\% = \frac{750}{40} \times 10 = ₹\ 187.50$$

∴ Annual expenditure of the family on education = 187.50 × 12 = ₹ 2250

Solution 3. Expenditure on clothing $= \frac{20}{100} \times 4500 =$ ₹ 900

Solution 4. Central angle for 15% $= \frac{15}{100} \times 360° = 54°$

Solution 5. Expenditure on rent and clothing = 10% + 20% = 30%
Expenditure on medicine and other expenses = 5% + 15% = 20%
∴ Ratio of the two = 30% : 20% = 3 : 2

Example 2: Directions: *The pie chart, drawn here, shows the spending of a country on various sports during a particular year. Study the graph carefully and answer the questions that follow:*

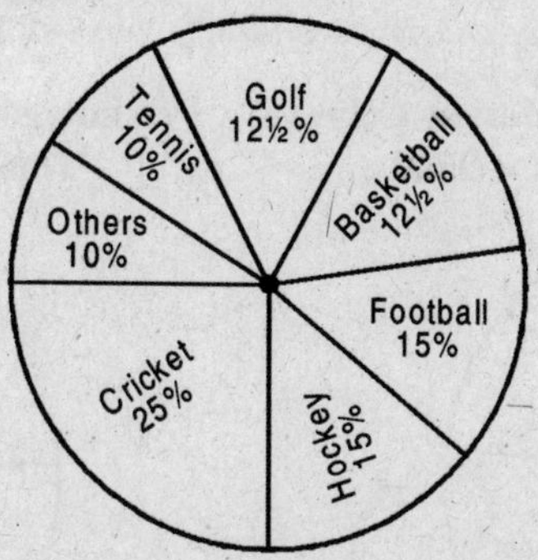

1. Graph shows that the most popular game of the country is:
   A. Football B. Hockey C. Cricket D. Tennis
2. Out of the following the country spent the same amount on:
   A. Hockey and Cricket B. Hockey and Football
   C. Hockey and Golf D. Tennis and Golf
3. The ratio of the total amount spent on football to that spent on hockey is:
   A. 2 : 1 B. 1 : 1 C. 1 : 2 D. 3 : 2
4. If the total amount spent on sports during the year was ₹ 1,20,00,000, how much was spent on basketball?
   A. ₹ 16,00,000 B. ₹ 18,00,000 C. ₹ 3,00,000 D. ₹ 15,00,000
5. If the total amount spent on sports during the year was ₹ 30,00,000, the amount spent on cricket and hockey together was:
   A. ₹ 18,00,000 B. ₹ 12,00,000
   C. ₹ 15,00,000 D. ₹ 20,00,000

Solution 1. According to the graph, expenditure on cricket is the maximum. Therefore cricket is the most popular game.

Solution 2. According to the graph, equal amount has been spent on Hockey and Football.

Solution 3. Expenditure on the game of Football = 15% of total amount spent
Expenditure on the game of Hockey = 15% of total amount spent.
Therefore, the ratio of the expenditure on the two games = 1 : 1

Solution 4. 100% = ₹ 1,20,00,000
∴ Expenditure on the game of Basketball = 12½% of 1,20,00,000

$$= \frac{25 \times 1{,}20{,}00{,}000}{100} = ₹\ 15{,}00{,}000$$

Solution 5. 100% = ₹ 30,00,000
∴ Expenditure on the games of Cricket and Hockey = 25% + 15% = 40%
∴ Total expenditure on the games of Cricket and Hockey = 20% of 30,00,000

$$= \frac{40 \times 30{,}00{,}000}{100} = ₹\ 12{,}00{,}000.$$

Example 3: Directions: *Study the pie-charts carefully to answer the questions that follow.*

Percentage of Students in Six different Colleges
Total number of Students = 3500

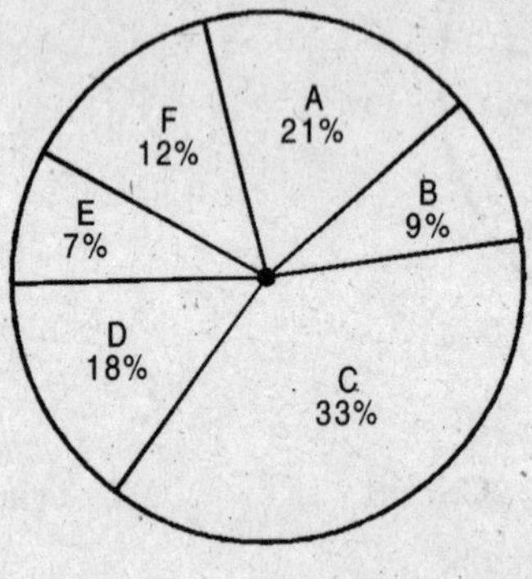

Percentage of Girls in each of the Colleges
Total number of Girls = 1800

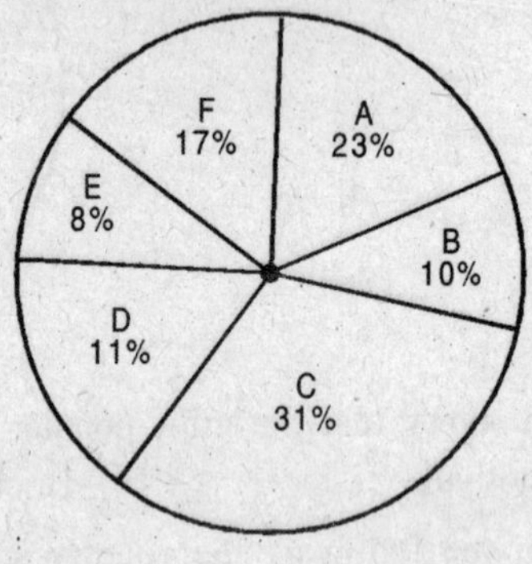

1. What is the number of girls in college D?
   A. 176 B. 188 C. 192 D. 198
2. The number of boys from College A form what per cent of total number of students from that college?
   A. 22.83 B. 38.41 C. 43.67 D. 56.29
3. Which college has the maximum number of boys?
   A. A B. B C. C D. D
4. Which college has lowest number of girls?
   A. B B. D C. E D. F
5. What is the total number of boys from Colleges E and F together?
   A. 215 B. 251 C. 283 D. 310

Solution 1. Number of girls in College D = $\frac{11}{100} \times 1800 = 198$

Solution 2. Number of students from College A = $\frac{21}{100} \times 3500 = 735$

Number of girls from College A = $\frac{23}{100} \times 1800 = 414$

Since, number of boys from college A = 725 – 414 = 321

Required percentage = $\frac{321}{735} \times 100 = \frac{2140}{49} = 43.67\%$

Solution 3. Number of boys in college A = $\frac{21}{100} \times 3500 - \frac{23}{100} \times 1800 = 735 - 414 = 321$

Number of boys in college B = $\frac{9}{100} \times 3500 - \frac{10}{100} \times 1800 = 315 - 180 = 135$

Number of boys in college C = $\frac{33}{100} \times 3500 - \frac{31}{100} \times 1800 = 1155 - 558 = 597$

Number of boys in college D = $\frac{18}{100} \times 3500 - \frac{11}{100} \times 1800 = 630 - 198 = 432$

Hence, number of boys in college C has maximum.

Solution 4. It is clear from the pie-chart that percentage of girls in college E is minimum, hence, college E has lowest number of girls.

Solution 5. Number of boys from college E = $\frac{7}{100} \times 3500 - \frac{8}{100} \times 1800 = 245 - 144 = 101$

Number of boys from college F = $\frac{12}{100} \times 3500 - \frac{17}{100} \times 1800 = 420 - 306 = 114$

Hence, their total = 101 + 114 = 215

Example 4: Directions: *Study the following pie-diagrams carefully to answer these questions.*

Number of students studying in different faculties in the years 2008 and 2009 from State X

Year-2008
Total students = 35000

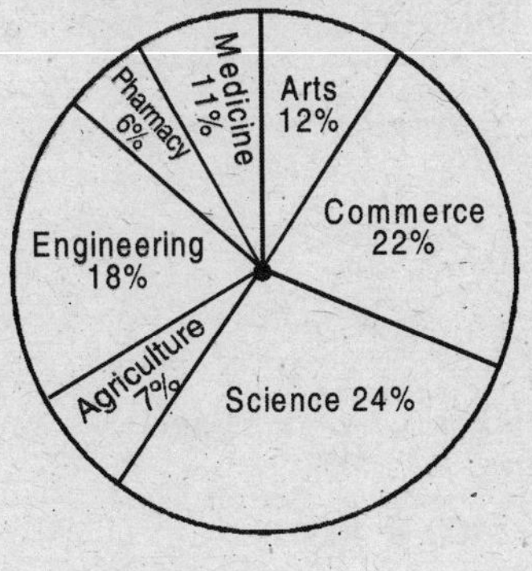

Year-2009
Total students = 40000

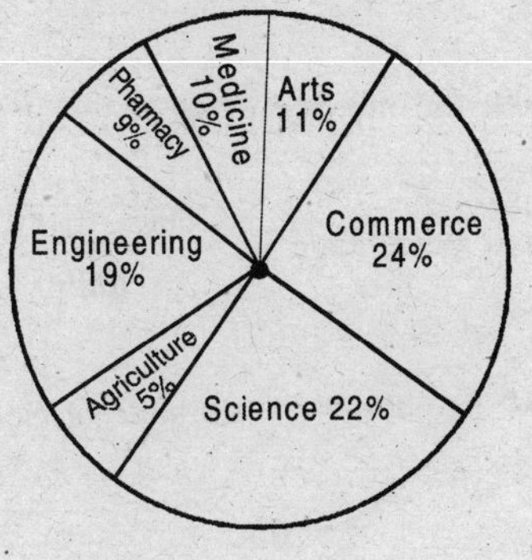

1. In which faculty there was decrease in the number of students from 2008 to 2009?
A. Arts B. Agriculture C. Pharmacy D. None of these

2. What was the approximate percentage increase in the number of students of Engineering from year 2008 to 2009?
A. 15 B. 17 C. 20 D. 25

3. In which of the following faculties the percentage increase in the number of students was minimum from 2008 to 2009?
A. Science B. Commerce C. Arts D. Medicine

4. What is the ratio between the number of students studying Pharmacy in the years 2008 and 2009 respectively?
A. 4 : 3 B. 5 : 7 C. 7 : 12 D. 8 : 13

5. In the year 2008, the number of students studying Arts and Commerce together is what per cent of the number of students studying these subjects together in 2009?
A. 76 B. 79 C. 82 D. 85

Solution 1. In 2008, number of students in Arts $= \frac{12}{100} \times 35000 = 4200$

In 2009, number of students in Arts $= \frac{11}{100} \times 40000 = 4400$

In 2008, number of students in Agriculture $= \frac{7}{100} \times 35000 = 2450$

In 2009, number of students in Agriculture $= \frac{5}{100} \times 40000 = 2000$

In 2008, number of students in Pharmacy $= \frac{6}{100} \times 35000 = 2100$

In 2009, number of students in Pharmacy $= \frac{9}{100} \times 40000 = 3600$

Hence, in Agriculture there was decrease in the number of students from 2008 to 2009.

Solution 2. In 2008, the number of students in Engineering $= \frac{18}{100} \times 35000 = 6300$

In 2009, the number of students in Engineering $= \frac{19}{100} \times 40000 = 7600$

Required percentage $= \frac{7600 - 6300}{6300} \times 100 = \frac{1300}{63} = 20.6 \approx 20\%$

Solution 3. Increase in number of students of Science $= \frac{22}{100} \times 40000 - \frac{24}{100} \times 35000$

$= 8800 - 8400 = 400$

Hence, Increase percentage = $\frac{400}{8400} \times 100 = 4\frac{16}{21}\%$

Increase in number of students of Commerce = $\frac{24}{100} \times 40000 - \frac{22}{100} \times 35000$

$= 9600 - 7700 = 1900$

Hence, their increase percentage = $\frac{1900}{7700} \times 100 = 24\frac{52}{77}\%$

Increase in number of students of Arts = $\frac{11}{100} \times 40000 - \frac{12}{100} \times 35000 = 4400 - 4200 = 200$

Hence, their increase percentage = $\frac{200}{4200} \times 100 = 4\frac{16}{21}\%$

Increase in number of students of Medicine = $\frac{10}{100} \times 40000 - \frac{11}{100} \times 35000 = 4000 - 3850 = 150$

Hence, their increase percentage = $\frac{150}{3850} \times 100 = 3\frac{69}{77}\%$

So, in Medicine the percentage increase in the number of students was minimum from 2008 to 2009.

Solution 4. In 2008, the number of students studying Pharmacy = $\frac{6}{100} \times 35000 = 2100$

In 2009, the number of students studying Pharmacy = $\frac{9}{100} \times 40000 = 3600$

Hence, their ratio = 2100 : 3600 = 7 : 12

Solution 5. In 2008, the number of students studying Arts and Commerce together

$= \frac{(12+22)}{100} \times 35000 = 34 \times 350 = 11900$

In 2009, the number of students studying Arts and Commerce together

$= \frac{(11+24)}{100} \times 40000 = 35 \times 400 = 14000$

Hence, required percentage = $\frac{11900}{14000} \times 100 = 85\%$

Example 5: *Study the following Graph carefully and answer the questions given below:*

Percentage of students in various courses (A, B, C, D, E, F) and Percentage of girls out of these. Total students = 1200 (800 girls + 400 boys)

Percentage in Various Courses

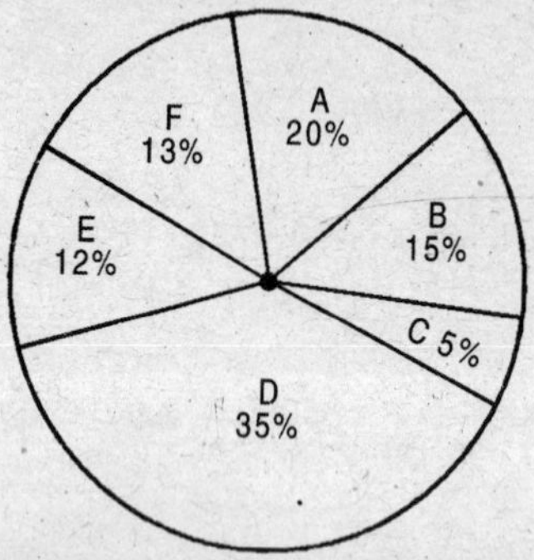

(Total girls = 800)
Percentage of Girls in Various courses

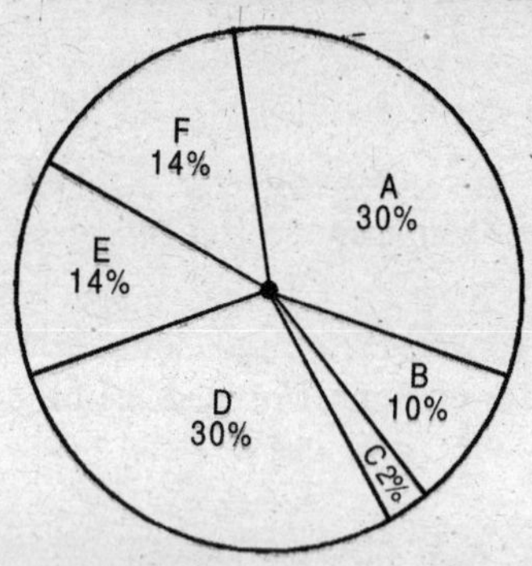

1. For which course is the number of boys the minimum?

(a) A *(b)* C *(c)* E *(d)* F

2. For course D what is the respective ratio of boys and girls?

(a) 3 : 4 *(b)* 3 : 5 *(c)* 4 : 5 *(d)* 5 : 6

Solution 1. Number of boys in course 'A' = $\frac{20}{100}\times1200-\frac{30}{100}\times800 = 240 - 240 = 0$

Number of boys in course 'C' = $\frac{5}{100}\times1200-\frac{2}{100}\times800 = 60 - 16 = 44$

Number of boys in course 'E' = $\frac{12}{100}\times1200-\frac{14}{100}\times800 = 144 - 112 = 32$

Number of boys in course 'F' = $\frac{13}{100}\times1200-\frac{14}{100}\times800 = 156 - 112 = 44$

Hence, in course 'A' number of boys is minimum *i.e.*, zero.

Solution 2. For course D,

Number of boys = $\frac{35}{100}\times1200-\frac{30}{100}\times800 = 420 - 240 = 180$

Number of girls = $\frac{30}{100}\times800 = 240$

Since, required ratio = 180 : 240 = 3 : 4

GENERAL KNOWLEDGE

INDIAN HISTORY

ANCIENT INDIA

INDUS VALLEY CIVILISATION (2500-1750 BC)

- The earliest excavations in the Indus valley were done at Harappa in the West Punjab and Mohenjodaro in Sindh. Both places are now in Pakistan.

Important Sites

- The most important sites are Kot Diji in Sindh, Kalibangan in Rajasthan, Ropar in the Punjab, Banawali in Haryana, Lothal, Surkotada and Dhaulavira, all the three in Gujarat.
- Mohenjodaro is the largest of all the Indus cities and it is estimated to have spread over an area of 200 hectares.

Indus Valley Civilisation : An Objective Study

Major Sites	Excavators	Year	River	Location	Important Findings
1. Harappa	D.R. Sahni	1921	Ravi	West Punjab (Pakistan)	Granaries, Virgin Goddess, Cemetery, Stone symbol of Lingam and Yoni
2. Mohenjodaro	R.D. Banerjee	1922	Indus	Sindh (Pakistan)	Great Bath, Great Granary, Assem bly Hall, Proto-Shiva, Brick Kilns, Mesopotamian seals
3. Chanhudaro	N.G. Mazumdar	1931	Indus	Sindh (Pakistan)	Bronze toy cart, Ink-pot, Lipstick, City without a citadel
4. Kalibangan	B.B. Lal & B.K. Thapar	1953	Ghaggar	Ganganagar (Rajasthan)	Decorated bricks, ploughed field surface, Firealtars
5. Lothal	S.R. Rao	1957	Bhogwa	Ahmedabad (Gujarat)	Dockyard, Rice husk, Fire altars, Double burial
6. Banawali	R.S. Bist	1973	Ghaggar	Hissar (Haryana)	Toy plough, Gridiron pattern of Town planning.
7. Dholavira	R.S. Bist	1990	Luni	Kutchh (Gujarat)	A Large well & a bath, A stadium
8. Surkotada	J. Joshi	1964	—	Gujarat	Bones of Horse, Pot burials

Salient Features of the Harappan Culture

- The Harappan Civilization was primarily Urban.
- Mohenjodaro and Harappa were the planned cities.
- The large-scale use of burnt bricks in almost all kinds of constructions are the important characteristics of the Harappan culture.
- Another remarkable feature was the underground drainage system connecting all houses to the street drains which were covered by stone slabs or bricks.
- The most important public place of Mohenjodaro is the Great Bath measuring 39 feet length, 23 feet breadth and 8 feet depth.

- Agriculture was the most important occupation. In the fertile soils, farmers cultivated two crops a year. They were the first who had grown paddy.
- Wheat and barley were the main crops grown besides sesame, mustard and cotton.
- Animals like sheep, goats and buffalo were domesticated. The use of horse is not yet firmly established.
- Bronze and copper vessels are the outstanding examples of the Harappan metal craft.
- A large number of seals numbering more than 2000 have been discovered.

Social Life

- Jewelleries such as bangles, bracelets, fillets, girdles, anklets, ear-rings and finger rings were worn by women. These ornaments were made of gold, silver, copper, bronze and semi precious stones.
- Fishing was a regular occupation while hunting and bull fighting were other pastimes.
- Manufacture of terracotta (burnt clay) was a major industry of the people.
- Figures of animals such as sacred bull and dove were discovered. The figures of Mother Goddesses were used for religious purposes.
- Most of the inscriptions were engraved on seals. It is interesting to note that the Indus script has not yet been deciphered.
- The Pipal tree was used as a religious symbol.
- The origin of the '*Swastika*' symbol can be traced to the Harrapan Civilization.
- The chief male deity was Pasupati, (proto-Siva) represented in seals as sitting in a yogic posture with three faces and two horns.

THE VEDIC PERIOD

RIG VEDIC AGE (1500 - 1000 B.C.)

- The Early Vedic period is known from the *Rig Veda*.
- The *Rig Veda* refers to Saptasindhu or the land of seven rivers. This includes the five rivers of the Punjab, namely, Jhelum, Chenab, Ravi, Beas and Sutlej along with the Indus and Saraswati.
- Historians view that the Aryans came from Central Asia. They entered India through the Khyber pass between 2000 B.C. and 1500 B.C. They first settled in seven places in the Punjab region which they called Sapta Sindhu. Slowly, they moved towards the Gangetic Valley.
- The Aryan Civilisation was a rural civilisation.

Vedic Literature

- The word 'Veda' is derived from the root 'vid', which means to know and signifies 'superior knowledge'.
- The Vedic literature consists of the four Vedas – Rig, Yajur, Sama and Atharva.
- The *Rig Veda* is the earliest of the four Vedas divided into 10 mandalas and it consists of 1028 hymns. The hymns were sung by *Hotri* in praise of various gods.
- The *Yajur Veda* consists of various details of rules to be observed at the time of sacrifice. Its hymns were recited by *Adharvayus*.
- The *Sama Veda* is set to tune for the purpose of chanting during sacrifice. It is called the book of chants and the origins of Indian music are traced in it. Its hymns were recited by *Udgatri*.
- The *Atharva Veda* contains details of rituals.
- Besides the Vedas, there are other sacred works like the Brahmanas, the Aranyakas, the Upanishads, and the epics Ramayana and Mahabharata.

Political Organisation

- During this period, the kingdom was tribal in character. Each tribe formed a separate kingdom.
- The basic unit of political organisation was *kula* or family.
- The highest political unit was called *jana* or tribe.
- There were several tribal kingdoms during the Rig Vedic period such as Bharatas, Matsyas, Yadus and Purus. The head of the kingdom was called as *rajan* or king.
- There were two popular bodies called the *Sabha* and *Samiti*. The former seems to have been a

council of elders and the latter, a general assembly of the entire people.

Social Life

- Family was the basis of the society.
- The head of the family was known as *grihapathi*.

Economic Condition

- The Rig Vedic Aryans were pastoral people and their main occupation was cattle rearing. Their wealth was estimated in terms of their cattle.
- Carpentry was another important profession.

RELIGION

- The important Rig Vedic gods were Prithvi (Earth), Agni (Fire), Vayu (Wind), Varuna (Rain) and Indra (Thunder).
- Indra was the most popular among them during the early Vedic period.
- There were also female gods like Aditi and Ushas. There were no temples and no idol worship during the early Vedic period.

Rigvedic Rivers

River	Name in Rigveda
Indus	Sindhu
Jhelum	Vitasta
Chenab	Asikni
Ravi	Parushini
Beas	Vipasa
Sutlej	Sutudri
Gomati	Gomal
Saraswati	Sarasvati
Ghaggar	Prishadavati

LATER VEDIC PERIOD (1000–600 B.C.)

- This age is also called as the Epic Age because the two great epics the Ramayana and Mahabharata were written during this period.
- The Sama, Yajur, Atharva Vedas, Brahmanas, Aranyakas, Upanishads and the two epics are the sources of information for this period.

Political Organisation

- Larger kingdoms were formed during the later Vedic period.
- The king performed various rituals and sacrifices to strengthen his position. They include Rajasuya (consecration ceremony), Asvamedha (horse sacrifice) and Vajpeya (chariot race).
- Kingship became hereditary.
- Kings assumed titles like Ekrat, Samrat and Sarvabhauma.

Economic Condition

- Iron was used extensively in this period and this enabled the people to clear forests and to bring more land under cultivation. Agriculture became the chief occupation.
- Taxes like Bali, Sulk and Bhaga were collected from the people.
- Wealth was calculated in terms of cows.

Social Life

- The four divisions of society (Brahmins, Kshatriyas, Vaisyas and Sudras) or the Varna system was thoroughly established during the Later Vedic period.
- The Ashrama system was formed to attain 4 purusharthas. They were *Dharma*, *Artha*, *Kama* and *Moksha*.

Religion

- Gods of the Early Vedic period like Indra and Agni lost their importance. Prajapathi (the creator), Vishnu (the protector) and Rudra (the destroyer) became prominent during the Later Vedic period.

JAINISM AND BUDDHISM

JAINISM

- Jainism originated in the 6th century B.C. It rejected Vedic religion and avoided its rituals.
- Founded by Rishabha Deva. Rishabha Deva was succeeded by 23 Thirthankaras (prophets). Mahavira was the 24th Thirthankara.

Vardhamana Mahavira (540-468 B.C.)

- Vardhamana was born in a village called Kundagrama near Vaishali in Bihar.
- His father was *Siddhartha*. He was the head of a famous Kshatriya clan.

- His mother was *Trisala*. She was a princess of the Lichchhavi clan. She was the sister of the ruler of Vaishali.
- Vardhamana was married to *Yasoda,* a princess. They had a daughter.
- At the age of 30, he left his home and family. He became an ascetic (monk). He wandered from place-to-place in search of truth for 12 years.
- In the 13th year of his penance, he attained the highest spiritual knowledge called Kevalya or Jnana. Thereafter, he was called Mahavira and Jina. His followers were called Jains and his religion Jainism.
- He died at the age of 72 in 468 B.C. at a place called Pavapuri near modern Rajgir in Bihar.

Teachings of Jainism

- The three principles of Jainism, also known as Triratnas (three gems), are:
  1. right faith.
  2. right knowledge.
  3. right conduct.
- Mahavira preached his disciples to follow the five principles. They are:
  1. Ahimsa—not to injure any living beings
  2. Satya—to speak the truth
  3. Asteya—not to steal
  4. Tyag—not to own property
  5. Brahmacharia—to lead a virtuous life.

Spread of Jainism

- Mahavira preached his religion in Prakrit language which was the language of the masses.
- Chandragupta Maurya, Kharavela of Kalinga and the royal dynasties of south India such as the Gangas, the Kadambas, the Chalukyas and the Rashtrakutas patronised Jainism.
- Jainism was divided into two sects after Vallabhi Council, namely *Svetambaras* (wearing white dresses) under Sthulbhadra and *Digambaras* (naked) under Bhadrabahu.
- The first Jain Council was convened at Pataliputra by Sthulabahu, the leader of the *Digambaras*, in the beginning of the 3rd century B.C.
- The second Jain Council was held at Vallabhi in 5th century A.D. The final compilation of Jain literature called *Twelve Angas* was completed in this council.

BUDDHISM

Gautama Buddha (563-483 B.C.)

- Buddha's original name was *Siddhartha*.
- Siddhartha was born in the Lumbini Garden near Kapilavastu in Nepal. His father was Suddhodana. He was a Sakya chief of Kapilavastu. His mother, Mayadevi, died when Siddhartha was only seven days old. He was brought up by his step mother Mahaprajapati Gauthami.
- At the age of sixteen Siddhartha, married Yasodhara and gave birth to a son, Rahul.
- The sight of an old man, a diseased man, a corpse and an ascetic turned him away from worldly life. He left home at the age of twenty-nine in search of Truth.
- He wandered for seven years and at last, he sat under a bodhi tree at Bodh Gaya in Bihar and did intense penance, after which he got Enlightenment (Nirvana) at the age of thirty-five. Since then, he became known as the Buddha or 'the Enlightened One'.
- Buddha delivered his first sermon at Sarnath near Banaras (now Varanasi).
- He died at the age of 80 in 483 B.C. at Kushinagar in Uttar Pradesh.

Teachings of Buddha

- The Four Noble Truths of Buddha are:
  1. The world is full of suffering.
  2. The cause of suffering is desire.
  3. If desires are get rid off, suffering can be removed.
  4. This can be done by following the Eightfold Path.
- The Eightfold Path consists of:
  1. Right Thought.
  2. Right Belief.
  3. Right Speech.

4. Right Action.
5. Right Living.
6. Right Efforts.
7. Right Knowledge.
8. Right Meditation.

Buddhist Literature

- In Pali language.
- Buddhist scriptures in Pali are commonly referred to as *Tripitakas, i.e.*, 'Three Baskets'.
- ***Vinaya Pitaka:*** Rules of discipline in Buddhist monasteries.
- ***Sutta Pitaka:*** Largest, contains collection of Buddha's sermons.
- ***Abidhamma Pitaka:*** Explanation of the philosophical principles of the Buddhist religion.

Main Buddhist Councils

Buddhist Council	Time	Place	Chairman	Patron
First	483 BC	Rajagriha	Mahakashyapa	Ajatasatru
Second	383 BC	Vaishali	Sabakamuni	Kalashoka
Third	250 BC	Patliputra	Moggaliputta Tissa	Ashoka
Fourth	AD 72	Kundalvana	Vasumitra, Ashwaghosa	Kanishka

The Mahajanapadas

Mahajanapadas	Capital
1. Kashi	Varanasi
2. Kosala	Shravasti
3. Anga	Champanagri
4. Magadh	Girivraj or Rajgriha
5. Vajji	Vaishali
6. Malla	Kushinagar and Pavapuri
7. Chedi	Shuktimati
8. Vatsa	Kaushambi
9. Kuru	Hastinapur, Indraprastha and Isukara
10. Panchal	Ahichhatra and Kampilya
11. Matsya	Viratnagar
12. Surasen	Mathura
13. Asmaka	Paudanya
14. Avanti	Ujjaini
15. Gandhara	Taxila
16. Kamboj	Rajpur (Hatak)

DYNASTIES OF ANCIENT INDIA

HARYANKA DYNASTY

- Bimbisara was the founder of Haryanka Dynasty.
- He was a contemporary of both Vardhamana Mahavira and Gautama Buddha.
- During his rule, Darius I, the Achaemenian emperor, conquered the Indus Valley area.
- Ajatasatru imprisoned his father Bimbisara.
- The first Buddhist Council was convened by Ajatasatru at Rajgir.
- The immediate successor of Ajatasatru was Udayin.
- Udayin laid the foundation of the new capital at Pataliputra situated at the confluence of the two rivers, the Ganges and the Sone.
- Shishunaga was the founder of Shishunaga dynasty.
- After Shishunaga, the mighty empire began to collapse. His successor was Kakavarman or Kalasoka. During his reign, the second Buddhist Council was held at Vaishali.
- Kalasoka was killed by the founder of the Nanda dynasty.

NANDAS

- The fame of Magadha scaled new heights under the Nanda dynasty.
- Mahapadmananda was the founder of Nanda rule in Magadha.
- The last Nanda ruler was Dhana Nanda. Alexander invaded India during his rule.

MAURYAN EMPIRE

CHANDRAGUPTA MAURYA (322–298 B.C.)

- Chandragupta Maurya was the founder of the Mauryan Empire. He overthrew Nanda dynasty with the help of Chanakya.
- Chandragupta defeated Seleukos Nikator, the Greek general of Alexander, in a battle in 305 B.C.
- Seleukos sent Megasthenes as Greek Ambassador to the Court of Chandragupta. Megasthenes wrote *Indica*.
- Chandragupta was a follower of Jainism.
- He came to Sravana Belgola, near Mysore with a Jain monk called Bhadrabahu. The hill in which he lived until his death is called Chandragiri.
- Chanakya served as prime minister during the reigns of Chandragupta and Bindusara.

BINDUSARA (298–273 B.C.)

- Chandragupta Maurya was succeeded by his son Bindusara.
- Bindusara was called by the Greeks as "*Amitraghatha*" meaning, slayer of enemies.

ASHOKA (273–232 B.C.)

- Ashoka was the most famous ruler of the Mauryan dynasty.
- The most important event of Ashoka's reign was his victorious war with Kalinga in 261 B.C.
- Ashoka convened the Third Buddhist Council at Pataliputra around 250 B.C. in order to strengthen the *Sangha*. It was presided over by Moggaliputta Tissa.
- Ashoka's edicts and inscriptions were deciphered by James Prinsep in 1837.
- The last Mauryan king, Brahadratha was killed by his minister Pushyamitra Sunga. It put an end to the Mauryan Empire.

SUNGAS

- The founder of the Sunga dynasty was *Pushyamitra Sunga*, who was the commander-in-chief under the Mauryas.
- He ascended the throne of Magadha in 185 B.C.
- Pushyamitra was a staunch follower of Brahmanism. He performed two asvamedha sacrifices.
- After the death of Pushyamitra, his son Agnimitra became the ruler.
- Agnimitra was a great conqueror. He was also the hero of the play *Malavikagnimitram* written by Kalidasa.

KANVA

- The last Sunga ruler was Devabhuti, who was murdered by his minister Vasudeva Kanva, the founder of the *Kanva dynasty*.
- The Kanva dynasty ruled for 45 years. After the fall of the Kanvas, the history of Magadha was a blank until the establishment of the Gupta dynasty.

SATAVAHANAS

- The founder of the Satavahana dynasty was Simuka.
- The greatest ruler of the Satavahana dynasty was *Gautamiputra Satakarni*.
- The greatest port of the Satavahanas was Kalyani on the west Deccan. Gandakasela and Ganjam on the east coast were the other important seaports.
- The fine painting at Amaravathi and Nagarjunakonda caves belong to this period.

SANGAM AGE (300 B.C. TO A.D. 300)

- The Sangam Age constitutes an important chapter in the history of South India.
- According to Tamil legends, there existed three Sangams (Academy of Tamil poets) in ancient Tamil Nadu popularly called Muchchangam. These Sangams flourished under the royal patronage of the Pandyas.
- *The first Sangam*, held at then Madurai, chaired by Agastya.
- *The second Sangam* was held at Kapadapuram, chaired by Tolkappiyar.
- *The third Sangam* at Madurai was founded by Mudathirumaran.

Political History

- The Tamil country was ruled by three dynasties namely the Chera, Chola and Pandyas during the Sangam Age.

CHERAS

- The Cheras ruled over parts of modern Kerala. Their capital was Vanji and their important seaports were Tondi and Musiris.
- The greatest Chera King was *Senguttuvan*.

CHOLAS

- The Chola kingdom of the Sangam period extended from modern Tiruchi district to southern Andhra Pradesh.
- Their capital was first located at Uraiyur and then shifted to Puhar. Kaveripattinam served as their port.

GUPTA PERIOD

- The Gupta period is considered as the *Golden Age* in the history of India because this period witnessed all round developments in Religion, Literature, Science, Art and Architecture.

CHANDRAGUPTA I (320-334 A.D.)

- In the beginning of the 4th Century A.D., Sri Gupta established a small Kingdom at Pataliputra. He is considered as the founder of the Gupta dynasty.
- The first notable ruler of the Gupta dynasty was Chandragupta I. He assumed the title *Maharajadhiraja*. The Meherauli Iron Pillar inscription mentions his extensive conquests.
- Chandragupta I is considered to be the founder of the Gupta era which starts with his accession in A.D. 320.

SAMUDRAGUPTA (335-380 A.D.)

- Samudragupta was the greatest of the rulers of the Gupta dynasty. The Allahabad Pillar inscription provides a detailed account of his reign.
- Because of his military achievements, Samudragupta was hailed as '*Indian Napoleon*'.

CHANDRAGUPTA II (380-414 A.D.)

- Samudragupta was succeeded by his son Chandragupta II Vikramaditya.
- The greatest of the military achievements of Chandragupta II was his war against the Saka *satraps* of western India.
- The famous Chinese pilgrim, Fahien visited India (A.D. 399 - A.D. 414) during the reign of Chandragupta II.

SUCCESSORS OF CHANDRAGUPTA II

- Kumaragupta (415-455) was the son and successor of Chandragupta II. His reign was marked by general peace and prosperity.
- Kumaragupta was the founder of the Nalanda University.
- Kumaragupta was followed by *Skandagupta* who ruled from A.D. 456 to A.D. 468.
- After Skandagupta's death, many of his successors like Purugupta, Narasimhagupta, Buddhagupta and Baladitya could not save the Gupta empire from the Huns. Ultimately, the Gupta power totally disappeared due to the Hun invasions and later by the rise of Yasodharman in Malwa.

PUSHYABHUTI DYNASTY (600 - 647 A.D.)

- The greatest king was *Harshavardhana*, son of Prabhakar Vardhana of Thaneshwar. He shifted the capital to *Kannauj*.
- *Hieun Tsang* visited during his reign.
- He established a large monastery at Nalanda. Banabhata adorned his court, wrote Harshacharita and Kadambari. Harsha himself wrote three plays–Priyadarshika, Ratnawali and Nagananda.

PALLAVAS

- The Pallavas established their kingdom in Tondaimandalam by Simhavishnu with its capital at Kanchipuram.
- Other great Pallava rulers were Mahendravarman I, Narasimhavarman I, and Narasimhavarman II.
- The *Kailasanatha temple* at Kanchipuram is the greatest architectural masterpiece of the Pallava art.

CHALUKYAS (543-755 A.D.)

- Pulakesin I was the founder of the Chalukya dynasty. He established a small kingdom with Vatapi or Badami as its capital.
- The structural temples of the Chalukyas exist at Aihole, Badami and Pattadakal (Virupaksha temple). Cave temple architecture was also famous under the Chalukyas. Their cave temples are found in Ajanta, Ellora and Nasik.

RASHTRAKUTAS (755-975 A.D.)

- The art and architecture of the Rashtrakutas were found at Ellora and Elephanta.

CHOLAS

- Cholas became prominent in the ninth century and established an empire comprising the major portion of South India. Their capital was Tanjore.
- The founder of the Chola kingdom was Vijayalaya.
- Rajaraja Chola built the famous Brihadeeswara temple at Tanjore.
- *Dancing Figure of Shiva* (Nataraja) belong to Chola period.

MEDIEVAL INDIA

ARAB CONQUEST OF SIND

- In 712 A.D., Muhammad bin Quasim invaded Sind. Quasim defeated Dahir, the ruler of Sind and killed him in a well-contested battle.

Mahmud of Ghazni

- In 1024, Mahmud marched from Multan across Rajaputana, defeated the Solanki King Bhimadeva I, plundered Anhilwada and sacked the famous temple of Somanatha. This was his last campaign in India. Mahmud died in 1030 A.D.
- Mahmud patronized art and literature. *Firdausi* was the poet-laureate in the court of Mahmud.

Muhammad Ghori

- Prithviraj Chauhan defeated Ghori in the first battle of Tarain near Delhi in 1191 A.D.
- In the Second Battle of Tarain in 1192, Muhammad Ghori thoroughly routed the army of Prithiviraj, who was captured and killed.
- After his brilliant victory over Prithvraj at Tarain, Muhammad Ghori returned to Ghazni leaving behind his favourite general Qutb-ud-din Aibak to make further conquests in India.

SULTANATE PERIOD

SLAVE DYNASTY (1206-1290)

- The Slave dynasty was also called Mamluk dynasty. Mamluk was the Quranic term for slave.

Qutb-ud-din Aibak

- Qutb-ud-din Aibak was a slave of Muhammad Ghori, who made him the Governor of his Indian possessions.
- After the death of Ghori in 1206, Aibak declared his independence. He assumed the title Sultan and made Lahore his capital.
- Muslim writers call Aibak Lakh Baksh or giver of lakhs because he gave liberal donations to them.
- He built the famous Quwat-Ul-Islam mosque at Delhi. He began the construction of the famous Qutb Minar at Delhi but did not live long to complete it. It was later completed by Iltutmish.

Iltutmish (1210-1236 A.D.)

- Iltutmish belonged to the Ilbari tribe and hence his dynasty was named as Ilbari dynasty.
- He shifted his capital from Lahore to Delhi.
- He organised the *Iqta system* and introduced reforms in civil administration and army.

Raziya (1236-1240 A.D.)

- She appointed an Abyssinian slave Yakuth as Master of the Royal Horses.
- In 1240, Altunia, the governor of Bhatinda revolted against her. She went in personally to

suppress the revolt but Altunia killed Yakuth and took Raziya prisoner.

- Bahram Shah, son of Iltutmish killed her.

Balban (1266-1286 A.D.)

- Balban introduced rigorous court discipline and new customs such as prostration and kissing the Sultan's feet to prove his superiority over the nobles.
- He also introduced the Persian festival of *Nauroz* to impress the nobles and people with his wealth and power.
- He established a separate military department - *diwan-i-arz* – and reorganized the army.

KHILJI DYNASTY (1290-1320 A.D.)

- The founder of the Khilji dynasty was Jalaluddin Khilji.
- Ala-ud-din Khilji was the greatest ruler of the Khilji Dynasty.
- He was the first Muslim ruler to extend his empire right upto Rameshwaram in the South.
- The Sultan had built a new city called Siri near Delhi.
- Amir Khusrau the great Persian poet, patronised by Balban, continued to live in Ala-ud-din Khilji's court also.
- He introduced the system of *dagh* (branding of horses) and prepared *huliya* (descriptive list of soldiers).
- Ala-ud-din Khilji maintained a large permanent standing army and paid them in cash from the royal treasury.

TUGHLAQ DYNASTY

- Ghiyas-ud-din Tughlaq was the founder of the Tughlaq dynasty.
- To have the capital at the centre of the empire and safe from the Mongol raids, Tughlaq chose Devagiri as his new capital in A.D. 1327. The Sultan renamed the new capital Daulatabad.
- In 1329-30, Muhammad-bin-Tughlaq introduced a token currency.
- Firoz Shah Tughlaq became Sultan after the death of Muhammad-bin-Tughlaq in A.D. 1351.
- He was the first Sultan to impose irrigation tax.
- He had built new towns of Firozabad, Jaunpur, Hissar and Firozpur.
- Timur—Mongol leader of Central Asia, ordered general massacre in Delhi (AD 1398) at the time of Nasiruddin Mahmud (later Tughlaq king).

SAYYID DYNASTY

- Before his departure from India, Timur appointed Khizr Khan as governor of Multan. He captured Delhi and founded the Sayyid dynasty in 1414.
- Mubarak Shah, Mohammed Shah and Alam Shah were some of the other important noteworthy rulers of Sayyid Dynasty.

LODHI DYNASTY

- The Lodhis were Afghans.
- Bahlol Lodhi was the first Afghan ruler while his predecessors were all Turks. He died in 1489 and was succeeded by his son, Sikandar Lodhi.
- In 1504, Sikandar Lodhi founded the city of Agra and transferred his capital from Delhi to Agra.
- Babar marched against Delhi and defeated and killed Ibrahim Lodhi in the first battle of Panipat (1526).

BAHMANI AND VIJAYANAGAR KINGDOMS

- The break up of the Delhi Sultanate provided an opportunity for the rise of a number of kingdoms in the Deccan.
- After the decline of the Tughlaqs, there arose two important kingdoms in the Deccan. They were the Bahmani and Vijayanagar kingdoms.

VIJAYANAGAR EMPIRE

- The Vijayanagar Kingdom was set up in A.D. 1336. Its aim was to check the spread of Muslim power and protect Hindu Dharma in South India.
- Four dynasties – Sangama, Saluva, Tuluva and Aravidu – ruled Vijayanagar from A.D. 1336 to 1672.

- Vijayanagar was founded in 1336 by Harihara and Bukka of the Sangama dynasty.
- The Moroccan traveller, Ibn Batuta, Venetian traveller Nicolo de Conti, Persian traveller Abdur Razzak and the Portuguese traveller Domingo Paes were among them who left valuable accounts on the socio-economic conditions of the Vijayanagar Empire.
- The Hampi ruins and other monuments of Vijayanagar provide information on the cultural contributions of the Vijayanagar rulers.

KRISHNA DEVA RAYA (1509-1530)

- The Tuluva dynasty was founded by Vira Narasimha.
- The greatest of the Vijayanagar rulers, Krishna Deva Raya belonged to the Tuluva dynasty.
- Krishna Deva Raya himself authored a Telugu work, *Amukthamalyadha* and Sanskrit works, *Jambavati Kalyanam* and *Ushaparinayam.*
- He built the famous *Vittalaswamy* and *Hazara Ramaswamy* temples at Vijayanagar.
- Krishna Deva Raya renovated Virupaksha temple in A.D. 1510.
- After his death the enemies of Vijayanagar joined together and defeated the Vijayanagar ruler in the battle of Talaikota.

BAHMANI KINGDOM

- The founder of the Bahmani kingdom was Alauddin Bahman Shah also known as Hasan Gangu in 1347. Its capital was Gulbarga.
- Ahmad Wali Shah shifted the capital from Gulbarga to Bidar.
- *Gol Gumbaj* was built by *Muhammad Adil Shah*; it is famous for the so called '*Whispering Gallery*'.
- *Quli Qutub Shah* built the famous *Golcunda Fort.*

MUGHAL EMPIRE (1526-1707 AD)

BABAR (1526-1530 AD)

- Babar was the founder of the Mughal Empire in India.
- On 21st April, 1526 the first Battle of Panipat took place between Babar and Ibrahim Lodhi, who was killed in the battle.
- Babar was the first one to use guns or artillery in a battle on the Indian soil.
- Babar defeated Rana Sanga of Mewar in the battle of Kanwah in A.D. 1527.
- Babar was a soldier-scholar and wrote his own autobiography called Babar Nama in Turkish language.

HUMAYUN (1530-1556 AD)

- Sher Shah defeated Humayun at Chausa in A.D. 1539 and again at Kannauj in A.D. 1540.
- After losing his kingdom, Humayun became an exile for the next fifteen years.
- In 1555, Humayun defeated the Afghans and recovered the Mughal throne. After six months, he died in 1556 due to his fall from the staircase of his library.
- *Gulbadan Begum*, Humayun's half-sister wrote *Humayun-nama.*

SHER SHAH SURI

- The founder of the Sur dynasty was Sher Shah, whose original name was Farid.
- Sher Shah became the ruler of Delhi in 1540.
- Sher Shah organized a brilliant administrative system. The central government consisted of several departments.
- He built a new city on the banks of the river Yamuna near Delhi. Now the old fort called Purana Quila and its mosque is alone surviving.
- He built a Mausoleum at Sasaram, which is considered as one of the master pieces of Indian architecture.

AKBAR (1556-1605 AD)

- When Akbar ascended the throne in A.D. 1556 he was only 14 years old. His guardian Bairam Khan served him as a faithful minister and tutor.
- Bairam Khan, along with Akbar met Hemu in the second Battle of Panipat in 1556. Hemu was initially successful, but lost his consciousness after an arrow hit him. Akbar killed him.

- Battle of Haldighati, was fought between Rana Pratap of Mewar and Mughal army led by Man Singh. Some hisorian say that this battle was indecisive but some say that Rana Pratap was defeated.
- Akbar abolished the pilgrim tax and in 1562, he abolished Jaziya.
- Akbar evolved a new faith called Din-i-Illahi or Divine Faith.

JAHANGIR (1605-1627 AD)

- When Akbar died, Prince Salim succeeded with the title Jahangir (Conqueror of World) in 1605.
- Jahangir's eldest son, Khusrau, rebelled against him. He was arrested and put into prison. *Guru Arjun Dev, the fifth Sikh Guru* was executed by Jahangir.
- In 1611, Jahangir married Mehrunnisa who was known as Nurjahan (Light of World).
- Jahangir died in A.D. 1627.

SHAHJAHAN (1628-1658 AD)

- The reign of Shahjahan is generally considered as the *Golden Age* of the Mughal period.
- Shahjahan is called as the *Prince of Builders*. He had built the Jama Masjid and Red Fort in Delhi and Taj Mahal in Agra.
- Fine arts like painting, music and literature reached high level of development during Shahjahan's time.

AURANGAZEB (1658-1707 AD)

- Aurangazeb was the last great Mughal ruler. He ascended the throne after killing his three brothers Dara, Shuja and Murad in a fratricidal war.
- Aurangazeb defeated Sikandar Shah of Bijapur and annexed his kingdom.
- Aurangazeb was against the Sikhs and he executed the ninth Sikh Guru Tegh Bahadur.
- He was called *Darvesh* or a *Zinda Pir*. He forbade *Sati*. Conquered Bijapur (AD 1686) and Golconda (AD 1687) and reimposed Jaziya and Pilgrim tax in AD 1679.
- He built *Biwi ka Makbara* on the tomb of his queen *Rabaud-Durani* at Aurangabad; *Moti Masjid* within Red Fort, Delhi; and the Jami or Badshahi Mosque at Lahore.
- Aurangazeb died in A.D. 1707.

LATER MUGHALS / FALL OF THE MUGHALS

Bahadur Shah (1707-1712)

- Assumed the title of *Shah Alam I.*

Jahandar Shah (1712-1713)

- First puppet Mughal emperor. He abolished *jaziya*.

Farrukhsiyar (1713-1719)

Mohammad Shah (1719-1748)

- Nadir Shah (*of Iran*) defeated him in the Battle of Karnal (1739) and took away *Peacock throne* and *Kohinoor diamond.*

Ahmad Shah (1748-1754)

Alamgir II (1754-1759),

Shah Alam II (1759-1806)

Akbar II (1806-1837)

- He gave Ram Mohan Roy the title '*Raja*'. He sent Raja Ram Mohan Roy to London to seek a raise in his allowance.

Bahadur Shah II (1837-1857)

- He was confined by the British to the Red Fort. During the revolt of 1857, he was proclaimed the Emperor by the rebels. He was deported to Rangoon after that.

Literature of Mughal Period

Author	Work
Babar	Tuzuk-i-Babari
Abul Fazal	Ain-i-Akbari, Akbarnamah
Jahangir	Tuzuk-i-Jahangiri
Hamid	Padshahnama
Darashikoh	Majm-ul-Bahrain
Mirza Md Qasim	Alamgirnama

THE MARATHAS

SHIVAJI (1627-1680 AD)

- Shivaji was born at Shivner in 1627. His father was Shahji Bhonsle and mother Jija Bai.

- His religious teacher was Samarth Ramdas and guardian was Dadaji Kondadev.
- In 1674, Shivaji crowned himself at Raigarh and assumed the title Chatrapathi.
- *Ashtapradhan* (eight ministers) helped in administration. These were Peshwas, Sar-i-Naubat (Military), Mazumdar or Amatya (Accounts); Waqenavis (Intelligence); Surnavis (Correspondence); *Dabir* or *Sumanta* (Ceremonies); *Nyayadhish* (Justice); and *Panditrao* (Charity).
- Successors of Shivaji were Shambhaji, Rajaram and *Shahu* (fought at Battle of Khed in AD 1708).

THE PESHWAS

- Balaji Vishwanath was the first Peshwa. He began his career as a small revenue official and became Peshwa in 1713.
- Baji Rao I was the eldest son of Balaji Vishwanath. He was considered as the "greatest exponent of guerilla tactics after Shivaji".
- It was during reign of Balaji Baji Rao (Nanasaheb) when the Marathas lost the Third Battle of Panipat.
- Baji Rao II (last Peshwa) was the first Maratha to have fled from the British attacks instead of fighting with them. Baji Rao II surrendered to Sir John Malcom.

THE SIKH

- Guru Nanak Dev was the founder of Sikhism, the religion that draws its elements from both Hinduism and Islam.
- Name of the ten Sikh Gurus and their works are given below:

1. **Guru Nanak Dev (1469-1539AD):** The founder of Sikhism.
2. **Guru Angad Dev (1504-1552AD):** Developed Gurmukhi.
3. **Guru Amar Das (1479-1574AD):** Struggled against Sati system and Purdah system.
4. **Guru Ram Das (1534-1581AD):** Founded Amritsar, the holy city of Sikhism.
5. **Guru Arjun Dev (1563-1606AD):** He built the *Swarn Mandir* (Golden Temple).
6. **Guru Hargobind (1595-1644 AD):** Established Akal Takht.
7. **Guru Har Rai (1630-1661 AD)**
8. **Guru Har Krishan (1656-1664 AD)**
9. **Guru Tegh Bahadur (1621-1675 AD)**
10. **Guru Gobind Singh (1666-1708 AD):** Founded the Khalsa and Sikh baptism, composed many poems, and nominated the Sikh sacred text as the final and enduring Guru.

MODERN INDIA

THE ADVENT OF THE EUROPEANS

THE PORTUGUESE

- Vasco-da-Gama, a Portuguese explorer, sailed through the route of Cape of Good Hope and reached near Calicut on 20th May 1498 A.D. during the reign of King Zamorin (Hindu King of Calicut).
- Vasco-da-Gama founded a factory at Cannanore on his second visit to India in 1501. In due course, Calicut, Cochin and Cannanore became the Portuguese trading centres.
- Francisco Almeida came to India in 1505. He was the first Governor of Portuguese possessions in India.
- The real founder of Portuguese power in India was *Alfonso de Albuquerque*. He captured Goa from the rulers of Bijapur in 1510. It was made their headquarters.

THE DUTCH

- The United East India Company of the Netherlands founded a factory at Masulipatnam in 1605. They built their first fort on the main land of India at Pulicut in 1609, near Madras (Chennai). They captured Nagapattinam from the Portuguese.
- They made Agra, Surat, Masulipatnam and Chinsura in Bengal as their trading centres.

THE DANES

- The Danish East India Company was established in 1616 in Denmark.
- They came to South India and founded a factory at Tranquebar (Tharangambadi) in 1620. They also made settlements at Serampore near Calcutta (Kolkata).

THE ENGLISH

- The English East India Company was formed in 1599 under a charter granted by Queen Elizabeth in 1600.
- The East India Company sent Sir William Hawkins to the court of the Mughal Emperor Jahangir in 1609 to obtain permission to erect a factory at Surat.
- In 1615, Sir Thomas Roe, another British merchant, came to Jahangir's court. He stayed for three years and succeeded in getting permission to set up their trading centres at Agra, Surat, Ahmedabad and Broach.
- In 1690, the British got permission from Aurangazeb to build a factory on the site of Calcutta. In 1696 a fort was built at that place. It was called Fort William.

THE FRENCH

- The French East India Company was established in 1664 under the inspiring and energetic leadership of Colbert, the economic adviser of the French King Louis XIV.
- In 1667, the first French factory was established at Surat by Francis Caron who was nominated as Director-General.
- French were defeated by English in the *Battle of Wandiwash* (1760).

EAST INDIA COMPANY

- After the Battle of Plassey in 1757 and the Battle of Buxar in 1764, the East India Company became a political power.
- India was under the East India Company's rule till 1858 when it came under the direct administration of the British Crown.
- Robert Clive was the first Governor of Fort William under the Company's rule.

GOVERNOR-GENERALS OF BENGAL

Warren Hastings (1772-85 AD)

- In 1772, the Company appointed Warren Hastings as the Governor of Fort William.
- The Dual System introduced by Robert Clive was abolished by Warren Hastings.
- Warren Hastings was known for his expansionist policy. His administration witnessed the Rohilla War, the First Anglo-Maratha War and the Second Anglo-Mysore War.
- Pitt's India Act (1784) was passed.

Lord Cornwallis (1786-93 AD)

- Cornwallis inaugurated the policy of making appointments mainly on the basis of merit thereby laying the foundation of the Indian Civil Service.
- Lord Cornwallis introduced Permanent Revenue Settlement.
- Tipu Sultan signed the Treaty of Srirangapatnam in 1792 with the British.

Sir John Shore (1793-98 AD)

- Played an important role in the introduction of Permanent Settlement.
- *Battle of Kharda* between the Nizams and the Marathas (1795).

Wellesley (1798-1805)

- Wellesley came to India with a determination to launch a forward policy that he adopted to achieve his object is known as the 'Subsidiary Alliance'.
- The Fourth Anglo-Mysore War started in 1799. The war was short and decisive. Tipu fought till his capital Srirangapatnam was captured and he himself was shot dead.
- Peshwa Baji Rao II signed the *Treaty* of *Bassein* with the British in 1802. It was a subsidiary treaty and the Peshwa was recognized as the head of the Maratha kingdom.
- The Treaty of Deogaon(1803) was signed between Bhonsle and Wellesley.

Lord Minto (1807-1813)

- Lord Minto concluded the Treaty of Amritsar with Ranjit Singh of Punjab in 1809.
- The Charter Act of 1813 was passed during this period.

Lord Hastings (1813-1823)

- Anglo Nepal War (1814-1816) and Treaty of Sugauli (1816).
- Third Maratha War (1817-18), dissolution of Maratha confederacy and creation of Bombay Presidency.
- He encouraged the freedom of the Press and abolished the censorship introduced in 1799.

GOVERNOR-GENERALS OF INDIA

Lord William Bentinck (1828-1835)

- Charter Act of 1833 was passed and he was made the first Governor-General of India. Before him, the designation was Governor-General of Bengal.
- The social reforms of William Bentinck made his name immortal in the history of British India. These include the abolition of *Sati*, the suppression of Thugs and the prevention of female infanticide.
- The Government Resolution in 1835 made English the official and literary language of India.

Lord Metcalfe (1835-36 AD)

- Known as liberator of press in India.

Lord Auckland (1836-42 AD)

- First Afghan War (1838-42), a disaster for the English.

Lord Ellenborough (1842-44 AD)

- Brought an end to Afghan war. War with Gwalior (1843), *Annexation of Sind* by Charles Napier (1843).

Lord Hardinge (1844-48 AD)

- First Anglo-Sikh War (1845-46) and Treaty of Lahore (1846). Gave preference to English educated persons in employment.

Lord Dalhousie (1848-1856)

- The Doctrine of Lapse was applied by Dalhousie.
- The first railway line connecting Bombay with Thane was opened in 1853.

VICEROYS OF INDIA

Lord Canning (1856-62 AD)

- Lord Canning became the first Viceroy of India in 1858.
- Revolt of 1857, Mutiny took place. Indian Penal Code 1860 was passed.

Lord Elgin (1862 AD)

- Wahabi Movement.

Lord John Lawrence (1864-69 AD)

- Established the *High Courts* at Calcutta, Bombay and Madras in 1865.
- Telegraphic communication was opened with Europe. Created the Indian Forest Department.

Lord Northbrooke (1872-76 AD)

- Kuka Rebellion in Punjab, Famine in Bihar.

Lord Lytton (1876-80)

- In 1878, the Vernacular Press Act was passed. This Act empowered a Magistrate to secure an undertaking from the editor, publisher and printer of a vernacular newspaper that nothing would be published against the English Government. This Act crushed the freedom of the Indian press.
- In 1878, the Arms Act was passed. This Act prevented the Indians to keep arms without appropriate license.
- Lord Lytton also held a Darbar at Delhi in 1877 in which Queen Victoria was declared as the Empress of India. This extravagant Darbar cost millions of ruppes.
- In 1878, the Statutory Civil Service was established exclusively for Indians.

Lord Ripon (1880-84 AD)

- Lord Ripon repealed the Vernacular Press Act and earned much popularity among Indians.

- Ripon appointed a Commission in 1882 under the chairmanship of Sir William Hunter.
- The Commission came to be known as the Hunter Commission. The Commission recommended for the expansion and improvement of the elementary education of the masses.
- Ripon was founder of local self-government in modern India.

Lord Dufferin (1884-88 AD)

- *Third Burmese War* (1885-86 AD). Establishment of the Indian National Congress in 1885.

Lord Lansdowne (1888-94 AD)

- Factory Act of 1891 granted weekly holiday and stipulated working hours for women and children.

Lord Elgin II (1894-99 AD)

- Southern uprisings of 1899. Great famine of 1896-1897 and Lyall Commission on famine was established.

Lord Curzon (1899-1905 AD)

- Curzon instituted in 1902, a Universities Commission to go into the entire question of university education in the country.
- On the basis of the findings and recommendations of the Commission, Curzon brought in the Indian Universities Act of 1904, which brought all the universities in India under the control of the government.

Lord Minto (1905-10 AD)

- Swadeshi Movement (1905-08); foundation of Muslim League (1906); Surat Session and split in the Congress (1907). Morley-Minto Reforms (1909).

Lord Hardinge (1910-16 AD)

- Capital shifted from Calcutta to Delhi (1911); Delhi Durbar; Partition of Bengal was cancelled. The Hindu Mahasabha was founded in 1915 by Pandit Madan Mohan Malaviya.

Lord Chelmsford (1916-21 AD)

- Gandhi returned to India (1915) and founded the Sabarmati Ashram (1916), Champaran Satyagraha, Satyagraha at Ahmedabad (1981), Kheda Satyagraha (1918).
- Rowlatt Act (March, 1919) and the Jallianwala Bagh Massacre (13th April, 1919).
- Khilafat Committee was formed and Khilafat Movement started (1919-20).
- Non-Cooperation Movement started (1920-22).

Lord Reading (1921-26)

- Moplah Rebellion (1921) took place. *Kakori Train* Robbery on 1st August, 1925. *Communal Riots* of 1923-25 in Multan, Amritsar, Delhi etc.

Lord Irwin (1926-31 AD)

- Lahore Session of Congress and *Poorna Swaraj* Declaration (1929).
- Simon Commission visited India in 1927.
- Dandi March (12th March, 1930). Civil Disobedience Movement (1930).
- First Round Table Conference was held in England in 1930. Gandhi-Irwin Pact.

Lord Willingdon (1931-36 AD)

- *Second Round Table Conference* in London in 1931 and *third* in 1932.

Lord Linlithgow (1936-43 AD)

- Congress Ministries resignation celebrated as '*Deliverance Day*' by the Muslim League (1939), the Lahore Resolution (23rd March, 1940) of the Muslim League demanding separate state for the Muslims. (It was at this session that Jinnah propounded his Two-Nation Theory). Outbreak of World War II in 1939. Cripps Mission in 1942. Quit India Movement (8th August, 1942).

Lord Wavell (1943-47 AD)

- Cabinet Mission Plan (16th May, 1946).
- First meeting of the Constituent Assembly was held on 9th December, 1946.
- Arranged the Shimla Conference on 25th June, 1945 with Indian National Congress and Muslim League but failed.

Lord Mountbatten (March to Aug, 1947)

- Last viceroy of British India and the first Governor-General of free India.
- Partition of India decided by the 3rd June Plan or Mountbatten Plan.

NATIONAL MOVEMENT (1885-1947)

INDIAN NATIONAL CONGRESS (1885)

- Allan Octavian Hume, a retired civil servant in the British Government took the initiative to form an all-India organization. Thus, the Indian National Congress was founded and its first session was held at Bombay in 1885. W.C. Banerjee was its first president. It was attended by 72 delegates from all over India.
- The second session was held in Calcutta in 1886 and the third in Madras in 1887.
- Between 1885 and 1905, the Congress leaders were moderates. The Moderates had faith in the British justice and goodwill. They were called moderates because they adopted peaceful and constitutional means to achieve their demands.
- In 1905, Gopal Krishna Gokhale founded the Servants of India Society to train Indians to dedicate their lives to the cause of the country.

Partition of Bengal (1905)

- By Lord Curzon on 16th October, 1905 through a royal proclamation, reducing the old province of Bengal in size by creating East Bengal and Assam out of the rest of Bengal.
- The partition of Bengal in 1905 provided a spark for the rise of extremism in the Indian National Movement.
- Curzon's real motives behind this partition were:
  - ❐ To break the growing strength of Bengali nationalism since Bengal was the base of Indian nationalism.
  - ❐ To divide the Hindus and Muslims in Bengal.
  - ❐ To show the enormous power of the British Government in doing whatever it liked.

Swadeshi Movement (1905)

- The Swadeshi Movement involved programmes like the boycott of government service, courts, schools and colleges and of foreign goods. It was both a political and economic movement.
- Lal, Bal, Pal and Aurobindo Ghosh played an important role.

Muslim League (1906)

- In December 1906, Muslim delegates from all over India met at Dacca for the Muslim Educational Conference.
- Taking advantage of this occasion, Nawab Salimullah of Dacca proposed the setting up of an organisation to look after the Muslim interests. The proposal was accepted.
- The All-India Muslim League was finally set up on December 30, 1906.

Minto Morley Reforms (1909)

- Minto, the Viceroy and Morley, the Secretary of State for India jointly proposed reforms to the Indian Councils. An Act, called the Indian Councils Act or the Minto-Morley Reforms Act was passed in 1909.
- A separate communal electorate was introduced for the Muslims.

The Lucknow Pact (1916)

- During the 1916 Congress session at Lucknow two major events occurred. The divided Congress became united. An understanding for joint action against the British was reached between the Congress and the Muslim League and it was called the Lucknow Pact.
- The signing of the Lucknow Pact by the Congress and the Muslim League in 1916 marked an important step in the Hindu-Muslim unity.

The Home Rule Movement (1916)

- Two Home Rule Leagues were established, one by B.G. Tilak at Poona in April 1916 and the other by Mrs. Annie Besant at Madras in September 1916.
- While Tilak's Movement concentrated on

Maharashtra, Annie Besant's Movement covered the rest of the country.

August Declaration

- On 20 August, 1917, Montague, the Secretary of State in England, promised the gradual development of self-governing institutions in India.
- This August Declaration led to the end of the Home Rule Movement.

Rowlatt Act (1919)

- In 1917, a committee was set up under the presidentship of Sir Sydney Rowlatt to look into the militant Nationalist activities. On the basis of its report the Rowlatt Act was passed in March 1919 by the Central Legislative Council. As per this Act, any person could be arrested on the basis of suspicion. No appeal or petition could be filed against such arrests.
- This Act was called the Black Act and it was widely opposed. An all-India hartal was organized on 6 April, 1919.

Jallianwala Bagh Massacre (13 April, 1919)

- On 13th April, the Baisakhi day (harvest festival), a public meeting was organized at the Jallianwala Bagh (garden). Gen. Dyer marched in and without any warning opened fire on the crowd. The firing continued for about 10 to 15 minutes and it stopped only after the ammunition exhausted.
- According to official report 379 people were killed and 1137 wounded in the incident. There was a nationwide protest against this massacre and Rabindranath Tagore renounced his knighthood as a protest.

Khilafat Movement (1920)

- The chief cause of the Khilafat Movement was the defeat of Turkey in the First World War.
- The Muslims in India were upset over the British attitude against Turkey and launched the Khilafat Movement.
- Ali brothers, *Mohd Ali* and *Shaukat Ali* started this movement. It was jointly led by the Khilafat leaders and the Congress.

Non-Co-operation Movement (1920-22)

- Mahatma Gandhi announced his plan to begin Non-Cooperation with the government as a sequel to the Rowlatt Act, Jallianwala Bagh massacre and the Khilafat Movement. It was approved by the Indian National Congress at the Nagpur session in December, 1920.
- The Congress observed the Non-Co-operation movement in 1920. The main aim of this movement was to attain Swaraj through non-violent and peaceful means.
- The whole movement was abruptly called off on 11th February, 1922 by Gandhi following the Chauri-Chaura incident in the Gorakhpur district of U.P. Many top leaders of the country were stunned at this sudden suspension of the Non-Co-operation Movement.
- On 5th February an angry mob set fire to the police station at *Chauri-Chaura* and twenty two police men were burnt to death.

Swaraj Party

- Leaders like Motilal Nehru and Chittranjan Das formed a separate group within the Congress known as the Swaraj Party on 1 January, 1923.
- The Swarajists wanted to contest the council elections and wreck the government from within.

Simon Commission (1927)

- The Act of 1919 included a provision for its review after a lapse of ten years. However, the review commission under the chairmanship of Sir John Simon was appointed by the British Government two years earlier of its schedule in 1927.
- Indian leaders opposed the commission, as there were no Indians in it, they cried *Simon Go Back*.
- The government used brutal repression and at Lahore, *Lala Lajpat Rai* was severely beaten in lathi-charge.

Nehru Report (1928)

- The Secretary of State, Lord Birkenhead, challenged the Indians to produce a Constitution that would be acceptable to all. The challenge was accepted by the Congress, which convened an all party meeting on 28 February, 1928.

- A committee consisting of eight was constituted to draw up a blueprint for the future Constitution of India. It was headed by Motilal Nehru. The Report published by this Committee came to be known as the Nehru Report.

Lahore Session (1929)

- On Dec. 19, 1929, under the Presidentship of J.L. Nehru, the INC, as its Lahore session, declared Poorna Swaraj (Complete Independence) as its ultimate goal.
- On Dec. 31, 1929, the newly adopted tricolour flag was unfurled and Jan. 26, 1930 was fixed as the First Independence Day, which was to be celebrated every year.

Dandi March (1930)

- On 12th March, 1930, Gandhi began his famous March to Dandi with his chosen 79 followers to break the salt laws. He reached the coast of Dandi on 5 April, 1930 after marching a distance of 200 miles and on 6 April formally launched the Civil Disobedience Movement by breaking the salt laws.

Civil Disobedience Movement

- Countrywide mass participation by women.
- The Garhwal soldiers refused to fire on the people at Peshawar.

Round Table Conference

- The first Round Table Conference was held in November 1930 at London and it was boycotted by the Congress.
- On 8th March, 1931 the Gandhi-Irwin Pact was signed. As per this pact, Mahatma Gandhi agreed to suspend the Civil-Disobedience Movement and participate in the Second-Round Table Conference.
- In September 1931, the Second Round Table Conference was held at London. Mahatma Gandhi participated in the Conference but returned to India disappointed.
- In January 1932, the Civil-Disobedience Movement was resumed.

Poona Pact (1932)

- The idea of separate electorate for the depressed classes was abandoned, but seats reserved for them in the provincial legislature were increased.
- Thus, Poona Pact agreed upon a joint electorate for upper and lower castes.

Demand for Pakistan

- *Chaudhary Rehmat Ali* gave the term *Pakistan* in 1933.
- In March 1940, the Muslim League demanded the creation of Pakistan.

Cripps Mission (1942)

- The British Government in its effort to secure Indian co-operation in the Second World War sent Sir Stafford Cripps to India on 23 March, 1942. This is known as Cripps Mission.
- The main recommendations of Cripps was the promise of Dominion Status to India.
- Congress rejected it. Gandhi called Cripp's proposals as a "Post-dated Cheque".

Quit India Movement (1942-1944)

- The All India Congress Committee met at Bombay on 8th August, 1942 and passed the famous Quit India Resolution. On the same day, Gandhi gave his call of 'do or die'.
- On 8th and 9th August, 1942, the government arrested all the prominent leaders of the Congress. Mahatma Gandhi was kept in prison at Poona. Pandit Jawaharlal Nehru, Abul Kalam Azad, and other leaders were imprisoned in the Ahamednagar Fort.
- Quit India Movement was the final attempt for country's freedom.

Indian National Army (INA)

- On July 2, 1943, Subhash Chandra Bose reached Singapore and gave the rousing war cry of *'Dilli Chalo'*. He was made the President of Indian Independence League and soon became the supreme commander of the Indian National Army. He gave the country the slogan of *Jai Hind.*

- INA had three fighting brigades named after Gandhi, Azad and Nehru. Rani of Jhansi Brigade was an exclusive women force. INA headquarters were at Rangoon and Singapore.

Cabinet Mission (1946)

- The Cabinet Mission put forward a plan for solution of the constitutional problem. A proposal was envisaged for setting up an Interim Government, which would remain in office till a new government was elected on the basis of the new Constitution framed by the Constituent Assembly.
- Elections were held in July 1946 for the formation of a Constituent Assembly.
- Muslim league observed the *Direct Action Day* on 16 August, 1946.
- An Interim Government was formed under the leadership of Jawaharlal Nehru on 2 September, 1946.

Mountbatten Plan (1947)

- On 20 February 1947, Prime Minister Atlee announced in the House of Commons the definite intention of the British Government to transfer power to responsible Indian hands by a date not later than June 1948.
- Lord Mountbatten armed with vast powers became India's Viceroy on 24 March, 1947. The partition of India and the creation of Pakistan appeared inevitable to him.
- After extensive consultation Lord Mountbatten put forth the plan of partition of India on 3 June, 1947. The Congress and the Muslim League ultimately approved the Mountbatten Plan.

Indian Independence Act, 1947

- The salient features of this Act was the partition of the country into India and Pakistan would come into effect from 15 August, 1947.
- On 15th August, 1947 India, and on the 14th August Pakistan came into existence as two independent states.
- Lord Mountbatten was made the first Governor General of Independent India, whereas Mohammad Ali Jinnah became the first Governor General of Pakistan.
- C. Rajagopalachari became the first and last Indian Governor-General of India. When India became a Republic on 26 January, 1950 Dr. Rajendra Prasad became the first President of our country.

Socio-Religious Movements and Organisation

Name of the Organisation	*Founder*	*Year*	*Place*
Atmiya Sabha	Ram Mohan Roy	1815	Calcutta
Brahmo Samaj	Ram Mohan Roy	1828	Calcutta
Dharma Sabha	Radhakanta Dev	1829	Calcutta
Tattvabodhini Sabha	Debendranath Tagore	1839	Calcutta
Nirankaris	Dayal Das, Darbara Singh, Rattan Chand etc.	1840	Punjab
Manav Dharma Sabha	Durgaram Manchharam	1844	Surat
Paramhansa Mandli	Dadoba Pandurung	1849	Bombay
Namdharis	Ram Singh	1857	Punjab
Radha Swami Satsang	Tulsi Ram	1861	Agra
Brahmo Samaj of India	Keshab Chandra Sen	1866	Calcutta
Dar-ul-Ulum	Maulana Hussain Ahmed	1866	Deoband
Prarthna Samaj	Atmaram Pandurung	1867	Bombay
Arya Samaj	Swami Dayanand Saraswati	1875	Bombay
Theosophical Society	Madam H.P. Blavatsky and Col. H.S. Olcott	1875	New York (USA)
Sadharan Brahmo Samaj	Anand Mohan Bose	1878	Calcutta

Deccan Education Society	G.G. Agarkar	1884	Pune (Poona)
Muhammadan Educational Conference	Syed Ahmad Khan	1886	Aligarh
Indian National Conference	M.G. Ranade	1887	Bombay
Deva Samaj	Shivnarayan Agnihotri	1887	Lahore
Nadwah-ul-Ulama	Maulana Shibli Numani	1894	Lucknow
Ramakrishna Mission	Swami Vivekananda	1897	Belur
Servents of Indian Society	Gopal Krishna Gokhale	1905	Bombay
Poona Seva Sadan	Mrs. Ramabai Ranade and G.K. Devadhar	1909	Pune (Poona)
Social Service League	N.M. Joshi	1911	Bombay
Seva Samiti	H.N. Kunzru	1914	Allahabad

Newspapers and Journals

- *Bengal Gazette* (1780) (India's first newspaper)—James Augustus Hikky
- *Kesari*—B.G. Tilak
- *Maratha*—B.G. Tilak
- *Sudharak*—G.K. Gokhale
- *Amrit Bazar Patrika*—Shishir Kumar Ghosh and Motilal Ghosh
- *Yugantar*—Bhupendranath Datta and Birender Kumar Ghosh
- *Bombay Chronicle*—Firoze Shah Mehta
- *New India (Daily)*—Annie Besant

Books and Authors

- *Causes of the Indian Mutiny*—Sir Syed Ahmed Khan
- *Ghulam Giri*—Jyotiba Phule
- *Anandmath*—Bankim Chand Chatterjee
- *Satyarth Prakash*—Swami Dayanand
- *Unhappy India*—Lala Lajpat Rai
- *India Divided*—Dr. Rajendra Prasad
- *The Discovery of India*—J.L. Nehru
- *Neel Darpan*—Dinbandhu Mitra
- *Hind Swaraj*—M.K. Gandhi
- *What Congress and Gandhi have done to the untouchables*—Dr. B.R. Ambedkar

Important Sayings

- *'Back to Vedas'*—Dayanand Saraswati
- *'Dilli Chalo!'*—Subhash Chandra Bose's battle cry of *Azad Hind Fauj*
- *'Do or Die'*—Mahatma Gandhi (while launching Quit India movement in 1942)
- *'Give me blood and I will give you freedom'*—Subhash Chandra Bose (in his address to soldiers of *Azad Hind Fauj)*
- *'My ultimate aim is to wipe every tear from every eye'*—Jawaharlal Nehru
- *'Swaraj is my birthright and I will have it'*—Bal Gangadhar Tilak
- *'Inqualab Zindabad'*—Bhagat Singh
- *'Jai Jawan, Jai Kisan'*—Lal Bahadur Shastri
- *'Sarfaroshi ki tamanna Ab Hamare Dil mein Hai'*—Ram Prasad Bismill
- *'Saare Jahan Se Achcha, Hindustan Hamara'*—Dr. Mohammed Iqbal
- *'Hindi, Hindu, Hindustan'*—Bhartendu Harishchandra
- *'Vande Mataram'*—Bankim Chandra Chatterjee

❒❒❒

GEOGRAPHY

WORLD GEOGRAPHY

THE UNIVERSE

- Existing matter and energy are together known as **Universe.**

GALAXY

- A galaxy is a huge system of billions of stars and clouds of dust and gases.
- Our solar system is a part of *Milky Way* galaxy.
- There are millions of galaxies that make the Universe.

STARS

- Stars account for 98 per cent of the matter in a galaxy. The stars nearest to the earth are *Proxima Centauri, Alpha Centauri, Barnard's Star, Sirius* and so on. Of these, *Sirius* is the brightest.

LIGHT YEAR

- Light year is the distance travelled by light in one year at a speed of 2,99,792.5 km. per second.

SOLAR SYSTEM

- The Sun, eight planets, satellites and some other celestial bodies known as asteroids and meteoroids form the solar system.

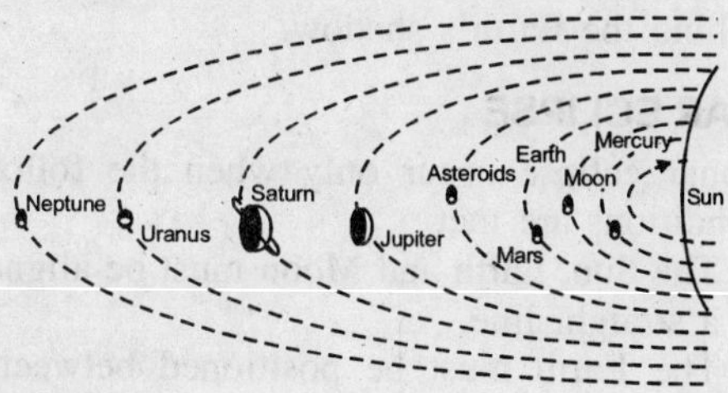

SUN

- The Sun is in the centre of the solar system.
- The Sun is a mixture of gases. It consists of 92% hydrogen, 7.8% helium and 0.2% other gases.
- The Sun is about 150 million km away from the earth.
- The sun is an ultimate source of energy for life on Earth.
- Sunlight takes 8 min 16.6 sec to reach earth.

Facts about Sun

Diameter	—1.392 × 10^6 km
Volume	—1.304 × 106 times the volume of earth
Temperature	—6000°C at surface and 15 million degree C at the centre
Relative density	—1.4
Gravitational Pull	—28 times the gravitational pull of the earth

Facts about Planets

Closest to Sun	*Mercury*
Farthest from Sun	*Neptune*
Heaviest	*Jupiter*
Hottest	*Venus*
Inner	*Mercury, Venus, Earth, Mars*
Largest	*Jupiter*
Smallest	*Mercury*
Moons, None	*Mercury, Venus*
Moon; Largest	*Ganymede (Jupiter), larger than Mercury*
Nearest to Earth	*Venus*
Orbits; Order	*Mercury (closest to Sun), Venus, Earth, Mars, Jupiter, Saturn, Uranus, Neptune.*
Rings/largest number	*Saturn*
Spin; Backwards	*Venus (East to West)*

COMETS

- It has a head and a tail. Its tail originates only when it gets closer to the sun. The tail can be 20-30 million km long. It always point away from the sun because of the force exerted by solar wind and radiation on the cometory material.

THE EARTH

- The earth is the third nearest planet to the Sun.
- From the outer space, the earth appears blue because its two-thirds surface is covered by water. It is, therefore, called a blue planet.
- It is the densest of all planets.
- Rotation is the movement of the earth on its axis. Due to this rotation, day and night occur.
- The earth takes about 23 hours 56 minutes and 4 seconds to complete one rotation around its axis.
- Earth takes 365¼ days (one year) to revolve around the sun.

THE EARTH: FACTS AND FIGURES

- *Mass of Earth*—5.972 × 10^{21} tonnes
- *Density of Earth*—5.517 times that of water
- *Volume of Earth*—1.083 × 10^{11} cubic km
- *Equatorial circumference*—4.007 × 104 km
- *Polar Diameter*—12,714 km
- *Equatorial Diameter*—12756 km
- *Polar or Meridional circumference*—4.0 × 10^4 km
- *Estimated Age*—At least 4600 million years
- *Land Surface*—148,951,000 sq km
- *Water Surface*—361,150,000 sq km (71 per cent of total area)
- *Highest Point of the land surface*—Mt. Everest (8,848 metres)
- *Lowest point of the land surface*—Shores of the Dead Sea (396 metres below the sea level)
- *Greatest Ocean depth*—Mariana Trench, East of Philippines (11,033 metres below the sea level)

THE MOON

- Earth has only one satellite, that is, the moon.
- Its diameter is only one-quarter that of the earth. It is about 3,84,400 km away from us.
- The moon moves around the earth in about 27 days. It takes exactly the same time to complete one spin. As a result, only one side of the moon (only 59% of its surface) is visible to us on the earth.
- Moonlight takes 1.3 sec. to reach earth.

LATITUDE

- Imaginary lines drawn parallel to the equator. Measured as an angle whose apex is at the centre of the earth.
- The equator represents 0° latitude, while the North Pole is 90°N and the South Pole 90°S.
- 23½°N represents Tropic of Cancer while 23½°S represents Tropic of Capricorn.

LONGITUDE

- It is the angular distance measured from the centre of the earth. On the globe the lines of longitude are drawn as a series of semicircles that extend from the North Pole to the South Pole through the equator. They are also called meridians.
- The distance between any two meridians is not equal. At the equator, 1 degree = 111 km. At 30°N or S, it is 96.5 km. It goes on decreasing this way until it is zero at the poles.

INTERNATIONAL DATE LINE

- It is the 180° meridian running over the Pacific Ocean, deviating at Aleutian Islands, Fiji, Samoa and Gilbert Islands.
- Travellers crossing the Date Line from west to east repeat a day and travellers crossing it from east to west lose a day.

INDIAN STANDARD TIME (IST)

- Indian Standard Time is calculated on the basis of 82.5°E longitude which passes through Uttar Pradesh, Madhya Pradesh, Odisha, Chattisgarh and Andhra Pradesh.

ECLIPSES

- Sun is the only source of light for both the Earth and Moon. Eclipses occur when the light thus received is either blocked by the earth or by the Moon.
- Eclipses occur when either the Earth moves behind the Moon's shadow or the Moon moves behind the Earth's shadow.

LUNAR ECLIPSE

- Lunar eclipse occur only when the following conditions are met.
  1. The Sun, Earth and Moon must be aligned in a straight line.
  2. The Earth must be positioned between the Sun and the Moon.
  3. The Moon must be in its full phase (Full Moon).

SOLAR ECLIPSE

- Solar eclipses occur only when the following conditions are met.
  1. The Sun, Earth and Moon must be aligned in a straight line.

2. The Moon must be positioned between the Sun and the Earth.
3. Must be a New Moon day.

ROCKS

- Rocks are composed of many minerals such as silica, aluminium, iron and magnesium. The nature of the rock is determined by the presence of its minerals.
- Rocks can be classified into three types:
  1. ***Igneous rocks*** are formed by magma that reaches the earth's surface along deep cracks and at volcanic vents. e.g., Mica, Granite etc.
  2. ***Sedimentary rocks*** are formed by the accumulation and cementation of mud, silt, or sand derived from weathered igneous rock fragments. e.g., Gravel, Peat, Gypsum etc.
  3. ***Metamorphic rocks*** are igneous or sedimentary rocks that have been altered by heat and/or pressure, either because they have been buried and folded deep in the crust, or because they have come into contact with molten igneous rock, e.g., Gneiss, Marble, Quartzite etc.

VOLCANOES

Sudden eruption of hot magma (molten rock), gases, ash and other material from inside the Earth to its surface.

- ***Active*** which erupts frequently, e.g., Mauna Loa (Hawaii), Etna (Sicily), Vesuvius (Italy), Stromboli (Mediterranean Sea).
- ***Dormant*** Not erupted for quite sometime, e.g., Fujiyama (Japan), Krakatoa (Indonesia), Barren Island (Andamans).
- ***Extinct*** Not erupted for several centuries, e.g., Arthur's Seat, Edinburgh, Scotland.

EARTHQUAKES

- Earthquakes are a form of wave energy that is transferred through bedrock. It is transmitted from the point of the earthquake focus, as spherical seismic waves. They travel in all directions outward.
- The intensity of earthquake waves is recorded by *Seismograph.*

LANDFORMS

- There are three major landforms: mountains, plateaus and plains.

MOUNTAINS

- A mountain can be defined as an area of land that rises abruptly from the surrounding region.
- There are three types of mountains- *Fold Mountains, Block Mountains* and the ***Volcanic Mountains***.
- Himalayas, Alps, Andes, Rockies, Atlas, etc are examples of Fold Mountains.
- The Aravali range in India is one of the oldest **fold mountain** systems in the world.
- The Rhine valley and the Vosges mountain in Europe are examples of such mountain systems.
- Volcanic mountains are formed due to volcanic activity.
- Mt. Kilimanjaro in Africa and Mt. Fujiyama in Japan are examples of such mountains.

Major Mountain Ranges of the World

Range	Location	Highest Peak (m)	Length (km)
Andes	South America	6,960	7,200
Himalayas-Karakoram-Hindukush	South Central Asia	8,848	4,800
Rockies	North America	4,401	4,800
Great Dividing Range	East Australia	2,228	3,600
Western Ghat	Western India	2,637	1,610
Caucasus	Europe	5,642	1,200
Alaska	USA	6,194	1,130
Alps	Europe	4,808	1,050
Apennines	Europe	2,912	—
Ural	Asia	1,895	—
Atlas	North West Africa	—	1,930

PLATEAUS

- A plateau is an elevated flat land. It is a flat-topped table land standing above the surrounding area.

Principal Mountain Peaks of the World

Mountains	Height in Metres
1. Mount Everest	8,848
2. K-2 (Godwin Austen)	8,611
3. Kanchenjunga	8,597
4. Lhotse	8,511
5. Makalu I	8,481
6. Dhaulagiri I	8,167
7. Mansalu I	8,156
8. Chollyo	8,153
9. Nanga Parbat	8,124
10. Annapurna I	8,091
11. Gasherbrum I	8,068
12. Broad Peak I	8,047
13. Gasherbrum II	8,034
14. Shisha Pangma (Gosainthan)	8,014
15. Gasherbrum III	7,952

PLAINS

- A relatively low-lying and flat land surface with least difference between its highest and lowest points is called a Plain.

OCEANS

- Oceans of the world is classified into four groups: the Pacific, the Atlantic, the Arctic and the Indian.
- The Pacific is the largest ocean, being twice the size of the Atlantic. It covers about a third of the Earth's surface, and contains more than half the water on the planet.

Oceans of the World

Names	Area (Sq. Km.)	Greatest Depth
Pacific	166,240000	Mariana Trench
Atlantic	86,560000	Puerto Rico Trench
Indian	73430000	Java Trench
Arctic	13230000	—

Major Rivers of the World

River	Origin	Falls in	Length (Km.)
Nile	Victoria lake	Mediterranean Sea	6,650
Amazon	Andes (Peru)	Atlantic Ocean	6,428
Yangtze	Tibetan Kiang Plateau	China Sea	6,300
Mississippi Missouri	Itaska lake (USA)	Gulf of Mexico (USA)	6,275
Yenisei	Tannu-Ola Mts.	Arctic Ocean	5,539
Hoang Ho	Kunlun Mts.	Gulf of Chibli	5,464
Ob	Altai Mts., Russia	Gulf of Ob	5,410
Congo	Lualaba & Luapula rivers	Atlantic Ocean	4,700
Amur	Northeast China	Sea of Okhotsk	4,444
Lena	Baikal Mts	Laptev Sea	4,400
Mekong	Tibetan Highlands	South China Sea	4,350
Mackenzie	Great Slave Lake	Beaufort Sea	4,241
Niger	Guinea	Gulf of Guinea	4,200

Major Gulfs of the World

Names	Area (Sq. Km.)	Names	Areas (Sq. Km.)
Gulf of Mexico	15,44,000	Gulf of St. Lawrence	2,37,000
Gulf of Hudson	12,33,000	Gulf of California	1,62,000
Arabian Gulf	2,38,000	English Channel	89,900

Important Straits of the World

Straits	Water Bodies joined	Area
Bab-al-Mandeb	Red Sea & Arabian Sea	Arabia & Africa
Bering	Arctic Ocean & Bering Sea	Alaska & Asia
Bosphorus	Black Sea & Marmara Sea	Turkey
Dover	North Sea & Atlantic Ocean	England & Europe
Florida	Gulf of Mexico & Atlantic Ocean	Florida & Bahamas Islands
Gibralter	Mediterranean Sea & Atlantic Ocean	Spain & Africa
Malacca	Java Sea & Bay of Bengal	India & Indonesia
Palk	Bay of Bengal & Indian Ocean	India & Sri Lanka
Magellan	South Pacific & South Atlantic Ocean	Chile
Sunda	Java Sea & Indian Ocean	Indonesia

Important Lakes of the World

Lake	Location	Area (Sq. Km.)
Caspian	Russia and CIS	371000
Superior	Canada and USA	82414
Victoria	Tanzania (Africa)	69485
Huron	Canada and USA	59596
Michigan	USA	58016
Tanganyika	Africa	32892
Baikal	Russia (CIS)	31502
Great Bear	Canada	31080
Malawi	Malawi (Tanzania)	30044
Great Slave	Canada	28438

Highest Waterfalls of the World

Name(s) (Foreign)	Location
Angel (Salto Angel)	Canaima Nat'l Park, Venezuela
Tugela	Natal Nat'l Park, South Africa
Utigord (Utigordsfoss)	Norway
Monge (Mongefoss)	Marstein, Norway
Gocta Cataracts	Chachapoyas, Peru
Mutarazi (Mtarazi)	Nyanga Nat'l Park, Zimbabwe
Yosemite	Yosemite Nat'l Park, California, U.S.
Espelands (Espelandsfoss)	Hardanger Fjord, Norway
Lower Mar Valley (Ostra Mardolafoss)	Eikesdal, Norway
Tyssestrengene	Odda, Norway

Important Cities on River Banks (World)

City	Country	River
Adelaide	Australia	Torrens
Amsterdam	Netherlands	Amsel
Alexandria	Egypt	Nile
Ankara	Turkey	Kazil
Bangkok	Thailand	Chao Praya
Basra	Iraq	Eupharates and Tigris
Baghdad	Iraq	Tigris
Berlin	Germany	Spree
Bonn	Germany	Rhine
Budapest	Hungary	Danube
Bristol	UK	Avon
Buenos Aires	Argentina	Laplata
Chittagong	Bangladesh	Majyani
Canton	China	Si-Kiang
Cairo	Egypt	Nile
Chung King	China	Yang-tse-kiang
Cologne	Germany	Rhine
Dandzing	Germany	Vistula
Dresden	Germany	Elbe
Dublin	Ireland	Liffy
Hamburg	Germany	Elbe
Kabul	Afghanistan	Kabul
Karachi	Pakistan	Indus
Khortoum	Sudan	Confluence of Blue & White Nile
Lahore	Pakistan	Ravi
Leningrad	Russia	Neva

City	Country	River
Lisbon	Portugal	Tagus
Liverpool	England	Messey
London	England	Thames
Moscow	Russia	Moskva
Montreal	Canada	St. Lawrence
Nanking	China	Yang-tse-kiang
New Orleans	U.S.A.	Mississipi
New York	U.S.A.	Hudson
Ottawa	Canada	Ottawa
Paris	France	Seine
Philadelphia	U.S.A	Delaware
Perth	Australia	Swan
Prague	Czech Republic	Vitava
Quebec	Canada	St. Lawrence
Rome	Italy	Tiber
Rotterdam	The Netherlands	New Moss
Stalingrad	Russia	Volga
Shanghai	China	Yang-tse-kiang
Sidney	Australia	Darling
Saint Louis	U.S.A	Mississippi
Tokyo	Japan	Arakava
Vienna	Austria	Danube
Warsaw	Poland	Vistula
Washington D.C.	U.S.A.	Potomac
Yangoon	Myanmar	Irawaddy

World's Geographical Surnames

City of Sky-scrapers—New York
City of Seven Hills—Rome
City of Dreaming Spires—Oxford
City of Golden Gate—San Francisco
City of Magnificent Buildings—Washington D.C.
City of Eternal Springs—Quito (S. America)
China's Sorrow—Hwang Ho
Cockpit of Europe—Belgium
Dark Continent—Africa
Emerald Isle—Ireland
Eternal City—Rome
Empire City—New York
Forbidden City—Lhasa (Tibet)
Garden City—Chicago
Gate of Tears—Strait of Bab-el-Mandeb
Gift of the Nile—Egypt
Granite City—Aberdeen (Scotland)
Hermit Kingdom—Korea
Herring Pond—Atlantic Ocean
Holy Land—Jerusalem
Island Continent—Australia
Islands of Cloves—Zanzibar
Isle of Pearls—Bahrein (Persian Gulf)
Key to the Mediterranean—Gibralter
Land of Cakes—Scotland
Land of Golden Fleece—Australia
Land of Maple Leaf—Canada
Land of Morning Calm—Korea
Land of Midnight Sun—Norway
Land of the Thousand Lakes—Finland
Land of the Thunderbolt—Bhutan
Land of White Elephant—Thailand
Land of Thousand Elephants—Laos
Land of Rising Sun—Japan
Loneliest Island—Tristan De Gunha (Mid-Atlantic)
Manchester of Japan—Osaka
Pillars of Hercules—Strait of Gibraltar
Pearl of the Antilles—Cuba
Playground of Europe—Switzerland
Quaker City—Philadelphia
Queen of the Adriatic—Venice
Roof of the World—The Pamirs, Central Asia
Sugar bowl of the world—Cuba
Venice of the North—Stockholm
Windy City—Chicago
Whiteman's grave—Guinea Coast of Africa
Yellow River—Huang Ho (China)
Sickman of Europe—Turkiye

Important Boundaries

Durand Line	Pakistan & Afghanistan
MacMohan Line	India & China
Radcliff Line	India & Pakistan
Maginot Line	France & Germany
Oder Niesse Line	Germany & Poland
Hindenberg Line	Poland & Germany (at the time of First World War)
38th Parallel	North & South Korea
49th Parallel	USA & Canada

Continents: Some Facts

Continent	Biggest Counrty	Highest Peak	Longest River
Asia	China	Mt. Everest (8848 m)	Yangtze Kiang
Africa	Algeria	Mt. Kilimanjaro (5895 m)	Nile
North America	Canada	Mt. Mckinley (6194 m)	Mississippi Missouri
South America	Brazil	Mt. Acancagua (6960 m)	Amazon
Europe	Russia	Mt. Elbrus (5642 m)	Ob
Australia	Australia	Mt. Coscuisco (2228 m)	Darling
Antarctica	—	Vinson Massif (5140 m)	—

INDIAN GEOGRAPHY

AREA AND LOCATION

- India is in the southern parts of the Asian continent. In the west of India lies the Arabian Peninsula while in the east lies the Indo-China Peninsula.
- India extends between 8°4' N and 37°6' N latitudes and between 68°7' E and 97°2' E longitudes.
- India, has a total geographic area of 32,87,263 sq. km. This is only 2.42 % of the total geographic area of the world but holds 17 per cent of the world's population.
- The 23½°N, which is the Tropic of Cancer, runs across the country.
- India has a length of 3214 km from north to south and 2933 km from east to west. It has a land frontier of 15200 km.
- The total length of the coastline of the mainland, Lakshadweep Islands and Andaman and Nicobar Islands is 7,516.6 km.
- India ranks seventh among the countries of the world, in terms of the geographical extent.
- India is bordered on three sides by water and on one by land, it is also a peninsula.
- India shares its common border with Afghanistan and Pakistan in the north-west, China and Bhutan in the north, and Bangladesh in the east. In the south, Sri Lanka is separated from India by a strait, known as the Palk Strait.
- 82°30' E longitude is considered as the Indian Standard Meridian. The local time of this longitude is taken as the Indian Standard Time (IST). This is 5½ hours ahead of the Greenwich Mean Time.

THE INDIAN STATES ON INTERNATIONAL BOUNDARIES ARE:

- ***Bordering Pakistan:*** Jammu and Kashmir, Punjab, Rajasthan, Gujarat.
- ***Bordering China:*** Ladakh, Himachal Pradesh, Uttarakhand, Sikkim, Arunachal Pradesh.
- ***Bordering Nepal:*** Bihar, Uttarakhand, UP, Sikkim, West Bengal.
- ***Bordering Bangladesh:*** West Bengal, Mizoram, Meghalaya, Tripura, Assam.
- ***Bordering Bhutan:*** West Bengal, Sikkim, Arunachal Pradesh, Assam.
- ***Bordering Myanmar:*** Arunachal Pradesh, Nagaland, Manipur, Mizoram.
- ***Bordering Afghanistan:*** Jammu and Kashmir (Pakistan-occupied area).

Important Passes

Jammu and Kashmir	Burzi-La
Himachal Pradesh	Bara La, Cha-La, Shipki-La
Uttarakhand	Niti-La, Lipu-Lekh-La
Sikkim	Jelep-La, Nathu-La
Arunachal Pradesh	Bomdi-La
Ladakh	Joji-La

Heighest Mountain Peaks of India

Peaks	Elevation• (in mts.)
Godwin Austin (K2)	8611*
Kanchenjunga	8598
Nanga Parvat	8126
Gasherbrum	8068*
Broad Peak	8047*
Dastegil	7885*
Masherbrum (East)	7821
Nanda Devi	7817
Masherbrum (West)	7806*
Rakoposhi	7788*
Kamet	7756
Saser Kangdi	7672

• *Above mean sea level in metres.*

* *Situated in Pak occupied Kashmir (PoK).*

Towns at River Banks

Town	River
Agra	Yamuna
Prayagraj	Confluence of the Ganges and the Yamuna
Ayodhya	Saryu
Badrinath	The Ganges
Kolkata	Hooghly
Cuttuck	Mahanadi
Delhi	Yamuna
Dibrugarh	Brahmaputra
Ferozepur	Satluj
Guwahati	Brahmaputra
Hardwar	The Ganges
Hyderabad	Musi
Jabalpur	Narmada
Kanpur	The Ganges
Kota	Chambal
Kurnool	Tungbhadra
Lucknow	Gomti
Ludhiana	Sutlej
Nasik	Godavari
Pandharpur	Bhima
Patna	The Ganges
Sambalpur	Mahanadi
Srinagar	Jhelum
Srirangapattam	Cauveri
Surat	Tapti
Varanasi	The Ganges
Vijaywada	Krishna

Important Waterfalls of India

Waterfall	Hgt (Mt.)	River	State
Kunchikal	455	Varahi	Karnataka
Dudhsagar	310	Mandvi	Goa
Jog/Gersoppa	260	Sharavati	Karnataka
Rakim Kund	168	Gaighat	Bihar
Chachai	127	Bihad	Madhya Pradesh
Kevti	98	Mahanadi	Madhya Pradesh
Sivasamudram	90	Cauveri	Karnataka

Important Lakes of India

Name of lake	State/UT
Pulicat Lake	Tamil Nadu & Andhra Pradesh Border
Sambhar Lake	Rajasthan
Tso Moriri Lake	Jammu & Kashmir
Vembanad Lake	Kerala
Wular & Dal Lakes	Jammu and Kashmir
Chilka Lake	Odisha
Kolleru Lake	Andhra Pradesh
Loktak Lake	Manipur
Lonar Lake	Maharashtra
Pangong Lake	Ladakh

Rivers of India

Name	Originates From	Falls Into
Yamuna	Yamunotri	Ganga
Chambal	Singar Chouri Peak, Vindhyan escarpment	Yamuna
Ghaghara	Matsatung Glacier	Ganga

Name	Originates From	Falls Into
Kosi	Near Gosain Dham Peak	Ganga
Sabarmati	Aravalis	Gulf of Khambat
Krishna	Western Ghats	Bay of Bengal
Godavari	Nasik district in Maharashtra	Bay of Bengal
Caveri	Brahmagir Range of Western Ghats	Bay of Bengal
Tungabharda	Western Ghats	Krishna
Ganges	Combines Sources	Bay of Bengal
Sutlej	Mansarovar Rakas lakes	Chenab
Indus	Near Mansarovar Lake	Arabian Sea
Ravi	Kullu Hills near Rohtang Pass	Chenab
Beas	Near Rohtang Pass	Sutlej
Jhelum	Verinag in Kashmir	Chenab
Son	Amarkantak	Ganga
Brahmaputra	Near Mansarovar Lake	Bay of Bengal
Narmada	Amarkantak	Gulf of Khambat
Tapti	Betul District in Madhya Pradesh	Gulf of Khambat
Mahanadi	Raipur District in Chhattisgarh	Bay of Bengal
Luni	Aravallis	Rann of Kuchchh
Ghaggar	Himalayas	Near Fatehabad
Betwa	Vindhyanchal	Yamuna

Geographical Surnames

Bengal's Sorrow	Damodar River
City of Palaces	Kolkata
Gateway of India	Mumbai
Pink City	Jaipur
Paris of India	Jaipur
Manchester of India	Ahmedabad
Kashmir of South	Kerala
Son of Sea	Lakshadweep
Queen of Mountains	Mussourie
Iron City	Jamshedpur
Hollywood of India	Mumbai
Scotland of East	Meghalaya
City of Nababs	Lucknow
City of Temples & Ghats	Varanasi
Land of Five Rivers	Punjab
City of Golden Temple	Amritsar
Garden of India	Bangaluru
Spice Garden of India	Kerala
City of Lakes	Srinagar
Twin City	Hyderabad-Secunderabad
City of Seven Islands	Mumbai
Diamond Harbour	Kolkata
Switzerland of India	Kashmir
Rice Bowl	Chhattisgarh
Fruit Bowl	Himachal Pradesh
Ganga of South	Cauvery
Pitsburg of India	Jamshedpur
City of Bridges	Srinagar
Residence of God	Prayagraj
A Cross-road (Quadrivial) of National Highways	Kanpur
Heart of India	Delhi
Black River	Sharda
City of Festivals	Madurai
Queen of Deccan	Pune
Sorrow of Bihar	Kosi River

Some Major Irrigational and Multipurpose Projects

S.No.	Name of Project	Related State	River
1.	Bargi Project	Madhya Pradesh	Bargi
2.	Beas	Joint Venture of Haryana, Punjab and Rajasthan	Beas
3.	Bhadra	Karnakata	Bhadra
4.	Bhakra Nangal	Haryana, Punjab and Rajasthan	Sutluj
5.	Bhima I	Maharashtra	Pawana
6.	Bhima II	Maharashtra	Krishna
7.	Chambal	Joint Project of M.P. and Rajasthan	Chambal
8.	Damodar Valley Project	West Bengal and Bihar	Damodar
9.	Dulhasti Power Project	Jammu and Kashmir	Chenab
10.	Farakka	West Bengal	Hooghly
11.	Gandak	Bihar and U.P.	Gandak
12.	Ghataprabha	Karnataka	Ghataprabha
13.	Hasdeo Bango Project	Madhya Pradesh, Chhattisgarh	Hasdeo
14.	Hirakud	Odisha	Mahanadi
15.	Jayakwadi	Maharashtra	Godavari
16.	Kakrapara	Gujarat	Tapti
17.	Kangsbati	West Bengal	Kangsbati and Kumari
18.	Karjan	Gujarat	Karjan
19.	Kosi	Bihar	Kosi
20.	Koyana	Maharashtra	Koyana
21.	Krishna Project	Maharashtra	Krishna
22.	Kukadi	Maharashtra	Kukadi
23.	Left Bank Ghagra Canal	Uttar Pradesh	Ghagra
24.	Madhya Ganga Canal	Uttar Pradesh	Ganga
25.	Mahanadi Delta Scheme	Odisha	(The irrigation scheme will utilise releases from Hirakund Reservoir)
26.	Mahi	Gujarat	Mahi
27.	Malaprabha	Karnataka	Malaprabha
28.	Mayurakshi	West Bengal	Mayurakshi
29.	Nagarjunasagar	Andhra Pradesh	Krishna
30.	Panam	Gujarat	Panam
31.	Parambikulam Aliyar	Tamil Nadu and Kerala	Perimbikulam
32.	Pochampad	Andhra Pradesh	Godavari
33.	Pong Dam	Punjab	Beas
34.	Ramganga	Uttarakhand	Ramganga
35.	Ranjit Sagar Dam (Thein Dam)	Punjab	Ravi
36.	Rihand	Uttar Pradesh	Rihand
37.	Sabarmati	Gujarat	Sabarmati

S.No.	Name of Project	Related State	River
38.	Sharda Sahayak	U.P.	Ghagra
39.	Sone High Level Canal	Bihar	Sone
40.	Tawa	Madhya Pradesh	Tawa
41.	Tehri Dam	Uttarakhand	Bhagirathi
42.	Tungabhadra	Andhra Pradesh and Karnataka	Tungabhadra
43.	Ukai	Gujarat	Tapti
44.	Upper Krishna	Karnataka	Krishna
45.	Upper Penganga	Maharashtra	Penganga
46.	Uri Power Project	Jammu and Kashmir	Jhelum

Major Indian Crops

Crops	Temp(°c)	Water(cm)	States where Produced
Wheat	15°-25°	60-90	Uttar Pradesh, Madhya Pradesh, Punjab, Haryana
Rice	24°-26°	80-200	West Bengal, Telangana, Uttar Pradesh, Punjab, Andhra Pradesh, Bihar
Maize	18°-21°	50-60	Karnataka, Bihar, Madhya Pradesh, Maharashtra, Uttar Pradesh
Jowar	20°-35°	40-60	Maharashtra, Madhya Pradesh, Karnataka
Soyabean	25°-27°	50-120	Madhya Pradesh, Maharashtra, Rajasthan
Cotton	20°-30°	80-150	Gujarat, Maharashtra, Telangana, Karnataka, Madhya Pradesh
Tobacco	20°-25°	75-80	Andhra Pradesh, Madhya Pradesh, Gujarat, Karnataka, Maharashtra, Uttar Pradesh
Tea	24°-30°	100-200	Assam, West Bengal, Kerala, Tamil Nadu, Uttar Pradesh
Ground Nut	15°-25°	60-130	Gujarat, Rajasthan, Maharashtra
Pulses	20°-35°	40-60	Madhya Pradesh, Maharashtra, Rajasthan

Mineral Wealth at a Glance (Metallic Minerals)

Mineral	Chief Producers
Bauxite	Odisha, Gujarat, Jharkhand
Chromite	Odisha, Andhra Pradesh
Coal	Chhattisgarh, Jharkhand, Odisha
Copper	Rajasthan, Madhya Pradesh, Jharkhand
Diaspore	Uttar Pradesh, Madhya Pradesh
Gold	Karnataka, Andhra Pradesh
Iron	Odisha, Karnataka, Goa
Lead	Rajasthan, Andhra Pradesh, Madhya Pradesh
Lignite	Tamil Nadu, Jammu & Kashmir
Manganese	Madhya Pradesh, Odisha, Karnataka
Natural Gas	Gujarat, Assam
Petroleum	Maharashtra, Karnataka, Gujarat, Assam, Andhra Pradesh
Silver	Rajasthan, Jharkhand, Gujarat
Tungsten	Rajasthan
Zinc	Rajasthan, Maharashtra

Zones and Headquarters of Indian Railways

S.No.	Zone	Headquarters
1.	Central	Mumbai
2.	Eastern	Kolkata
3.	Northern	New Delhi
4.	North-Eastern	Gorakhpur
5.	North-East Frontier	Maligaon, Guwahati
6.	Southern	Chennai
7.	South-Central	Secunderabad
8.	South-Eastern	Kolkata
9.	Western	Mumbai
10.	East Coast	Bhubaneswar
11.	East Central	Hajipur
12.	North Central	Prayagraj
13.	North Western	Jaipur
14.	South Western	Hubballi (Hubli)
15.	West Central	Jabalpur
16.	South East Central	Bilaspur
17.	Metro Railway	Kolkata
18.	South Coast Railway	Vishakhapatnam (Proposed)

Major National Highways

NH	Connects
NH 44	Srinagar to Kanyakumari
NH 27	Porbandar to Silchar
NH 48	Delhi to Chennai
NH 52	Sangrur to Ankola
NH 30	Sitarganj to Ibrahimpatnam
NH 6	Jorabat to Seling
NH 53	Hazira to Paradip
NH 16	East Coast (West Bengal) to Chennai
NH 66	Panvel to Kanyakumari
NH 19	Delhi to Kolkata

Major Ports of Country

1. Syama Prasad Mookerjee (Kolkata)
2. Mumbai
3. J.L. Nehru Port (Nhava Sheva)
4. V.O. Chidambarnar (Tuticorin)
5. Chennai
6. Mormugao
7. New Mangalore
8. Paradeep
9. Deendayal (Kandla)
10. Vishakhapatnam
11. Cochin
12. Kamarajar (Ennore).

Major International Airports in India

International Airports	City
Indira Gandhi International Airport	Delhi
Anna International Airport	Chennai
Sri Guru Ram Das Jee International Airport	Amritsar
Rajiv Gandhi International Airport	Hyderabad
Calicut International Airport	Kozhikode
Chhatrapati Shivaji International Airport	Mumbai
Kempegowda International Airport	Bengaluru
Dabolim International Airport in Vasco di Gama City	Goa
Netaji Subash Chandra Bose International Airport	Kolkata
Trivendrum International Airport	Thiruvananthapuram
Lokpriya Gopinath Bordoloi International Airport	Guwahati
Sardar Vallabhbhai Patel International Airport	Ahmedabad

❑❑❑

INDIAN POLITY

INDIAN CONSTITUTION

- Demand for a Constituent Assembly composed of the people of India officially asserted by the Congress for the first time in 1935.
- The election for Indian Constitution Assembly held in 1946 according to the *Cabinet Mission Plan.*
- The first session of the Assembly was held in New Delhi on December 9, 1946. *Sachidanand Sinha* was elected provisional chairman of the session.
- On December 11, 1946, Dr. Rajendra Prasad was elected as the Permanent Chairman of the Constituent Assembly.
- The Constitution was framed by the Constituent Assembly of India, set-up in December 1946, in accordance with the Cabinet Mission Plan, under the Chairmanship of Sachidanand Sinha, initially.
- The total membership of Constituent Assembly after partition was 299, among them 70 were representatives from the Indian states and others from British India.
- The Chairman of the Drafting Committee was **Dr. BR Ambedkar**, also called the Father of the Constitution.
- The Constituent Assembly took 2 years, 11 months and 18 days to complete the Constitution.
- The Constitution, adopted on 8th November, 1949, contained 395 Articles and Schedules.
- The Constitution was delayed till 26th January because, in 1929, on this day Indian National Congress demanded Poorna Swaraj in Lahore Session under JL Nehru.
- Indian Constitution is a comprehensive document and it is the lengthiest written Constitution in the World.

THE PREAMBLE

- ***The Preamble of the Constitution:*** "We the people of India, having solemnly resolved to Constitute India into a Sovereign, Socialist, Secular Democratic Republic and to secure to all its citizen:

  Justice, Social, economic and political;

  Liberty of thought, expression, belief, faith and worship;

  Equality of status and of opportunity; and to promote among them all;

  Fraternity assuring the dignity of the individual and the unity and integrity of the nation;

  In our Constituent Assembly, this twenty-sixth day of November, 1949, do hereby adopt, enact and give to ourselves this constitution."

Foreign Sources of Indian Constitution

Foreign Sources	*Subject*
Britain	Parliamentary system, collective responsibilities of Cabinet
America	Fundamental right, Independent Judiciary, Judicial review
Canada	Division of powers
Ireland	Directive principles
Germany	Emergency provisions
Russia	Fundamental duties
Australia	Concurrent list

IMPORTANT ARTICLES

PART - I

UNION AND ITS TERRITORIES (ARTICLE 1 - 4)

- The Constitution says, "India, that is Bharat, shall be a Union of States".

- Parliament has the power to create any State, reduce it, change the name of boundaries of any State.

PART - II

CITIZENSHIP (ARTICLE 5 - 11)

- The Constitution provides for a single Citizenship.
- ***Indian Citizenship can be acquire:***
  1. by birth
  2. by descent
  3. by registration
  4. by naturalisation
  5. by incorporation of territory
- ***Indian Citizenship can be lost by:***
  1. renunciation;
  2. termination — it takes place if a citizen of India voluntary acquires the citizenship of another country; and
  3. deprivation — if the Government terminates the citizenship.

PART - III

FUNDAMENTAL RIGHTS (ARTICLE 12 - 35)

- Following fundamental rights are enjoyed by every Indian citizen, irrespective of caste, colour, creed and sex:
  1. ***Right to Equality:*** No special privileges, no distinction on grounds of religion, caste, creed and sex.
  2. ***Right to Freedom:*** The right to freedom of expression and speech, the right to choose one's own profession, the right to reside in any part of the Indian Union.
  3. ***Right to Freedom to Religion:*** Except when it is in the interest of public order, morality, health or other conditions, everybody has the right to profess, practice and propagate his religion freely.
  4. ***Cultural and Educational Rights:*** The Constitution provides that every community can run its own institutions to preserve its own culture and language.
  5. ***Right against Exploitation:*** Traffic in human beings and forced labour and the employment of children under 14 years in factories or mines, are punishable offences.
  6. ***Rights to Constitutional Remedies:*** When a citizen finds that any of his fundamental rights has been encroached upon, he can move the Supreme Court, which has been empowered to safeguard the fundamental rights of a citizen (Article 32).

PART - IV

DIRECTIVE PRINCIPLES OF STATE POLICY (ARTICLE 36 - 51)

- Directive principles are not enforceable through courts. Main aim of Directive principles is to provide social and economic base of a genuine democracy.

Some Important Directive Principles:

- Provisions for adequate means of livelihood for all citizens (Art. 39).
- Right to work (Art. 41).
- Right to human condition of work and maternity relief (Art. 42).
- Right to a living wage and condition of work ensuring decent standard of life of worker (Art. 43).
- Common Civil Code (Art. 44).
- Prohibit consumption of liquor (Art. 47).
- Prevent slaughter of useful cattle (Art. 48).
- Organise Panchayati Raj (Art. 40).
- Separate the judiciary from the executive (Art. 50).
- Protect and maintain places of historic monuments (Art. 49).
- International peace (Art. 51).

PART - IV A

FUNDAMENTAL DUTIES (ARTICLE 51A)

- The fundamental duties for the Indian citizens have been incorporated in the Constitution through the Constitution (42nd) Amendment Act, 1976. These duties are:
  1. to abide by the Constitution and respect its ideals and institutions, the National Flag and the National Anthem;

2. to cherish and follow the noble deeds which inspired our national struggle for freedom;
3. to uphold and protect the sovereignty, unity and integrity of India;
4. to defend the country and render national service when called upon to do so;
5. to promote harmony and the spirit of common brotherhood amongst all the people transcending religious, regional or sectional diversities and to renounce practices derogatory to the dignity of women;
6. to value and preserve the rich heritage of our composite culture;
7. to protect and improve natural environment including forests, lakes, rivers and wildlife, and to have compassion for living creatures;
8. to develop the scientific temper, humanism and the spirit of inquiry and reform;
9. to safeguard public property and to abjure violence;
10. to strive towards excellence in all spheres of individual and collective activity so that the nation constantly rises to higher levels of endeavour and achievement.
11. who is parent or guardian to provide opportunities for education to his child or, as the case may be, ward between age of six and fourteen years.

PART - V

UNION (ARTICLE 52 - 151)

THE PRESIDENT

- The President is the Constitutional head of the Republic of India. He is more or less the titular head of the executive.
- He is the constitutional head but not the real executive. The real power is vested in the hands of the Council of Ministers.
- President is the first citizen of India.
- ***Qualifications:*** (i) Indian citizen, (ii) age not less than 35 years, (iii) should have qualification for election to Lok Sabha, (iv) should not hold any office of profit, (v) should not be a Member of Parliament or State Legislature.
- ***Election:*** Indirectly elected through Electoral College consisting of elected members of both the Houses of the Parliament and elected members of the Legislative Assemblies of the States.
- According to the 70th Amendment Act, 1992, the expression 'States' include the National Capital Territory of Delhi and the Union Territory of Puducherry. Members of the Legislative Councils have no right to vote in the Presidential election.
- ***Powers:*** He makes appointments to all the constitutional posts.
- He can address either House of Parliament and dissolve Lok Sabha.
- All Bills passed by Parliament must receive his assent to become an Act.
- He issues ordinances when Parliament is not in session. No Money Bill can be introduced in Lok Sabha without his recommendation.
- He appoints 12 members of special repute in the Rajya Sabha.
- He has the power of *Pardon* to a criminal in special cases.
- The President holds the office for a period of five years. He is eligible for re-election.
- He is also entitled to rent free official residence called Rashtrapati Bhawan.

VICE-PRESIDENT

- *Article 63* of the Constitution stipulates a Vice-President for India.
- The Vice-President acts as the ex-officio Chairman of the Council of States (Rajya Sabha).
- He is elected by an electoral college consisting of the members of both Houses of Parliament in accordance with the system of proportional represen-tation by means of the single trans-ferable vote. He must be a citizen of India, not less than 35 years of age, and should be eligible for election as a member of the Council of States.

- Disputes in connection with election of a president or a vice-president are to be a dealt with in accordance with Article-71. Such disputes shall be decided by the Supreme Court.

Council of Ministers

- The Constitution of India provides for a parliament system of government under which the President is only Constitutional ruler and the real power is exercised by the Council of Ministers, headed by the Prime Minister.
- Council of Ministers is composed of all Union Ministers—the Prime Minister, Cabinet Ministers and Ministers of State.
- The Council of Ministers is Collectively responsible to the Lok Sabha.
- The Prime Minister is a link between the President and the Council of Ministers.

Prime Minister

- The Prime Minister is the leader of the majority party in the Parliament.
- He is appointed by the President. Other Ministers are appointed by the president on his advice.
- The Prime Minister is the head of the Government and the head of the Council of Ministers.
- Jawaharlal Nehru was the first Prime Minister and the longest serving so far.

Union Legislature

- The Legislature of the Union, which is called 'Parliament' consists of the President and the two Houses of Parliament known as the Council of states (Rajya Sabha) and the House of the People (Lok Sabha).

RAJYA SABHA

- The Rajya Sabha is the Upper House of the Parliament and it is constituted of representatives from the States or the Constituent units of the Indian Union.
- It is a permanent body, one third of its members retiring after every two years.
- Its maximum strength is 250. Out of these, twelve members are nominated by the President from well-known personalities in the realm of Science, Art, Literature and Social Service. Rest of 238 representatives of the States and Union Territories are elected.
- Currently, the strength of the Rajya Sabha is 245.

LOK SABHA

- The Lok Sabha whose life is five years, is the Lower House of Parliament and comprises of members directly elected by the people.
- The House of the people (Lok Sabha) at present consists of 543 members directly elected from the states and Union Territories. (By the 104th amendment of the constitution the reservation for two members of Anglo Indian Community nominated by President have been abolished).
- The House of the People shall continue for five years (unless sooner dissolved) from the date of its meeting and no longer and the expiry of the said period of 5 years shall operate as dissolution of the House.

Parliamentary Committees

- There are several Parliamentary Committees to assist the Parliament in its deliberations.
- These are appointed or elected by the respective Houses of Lok Sabha and Rajya Sabha on a motion made or are nominated by their presiding officers.
- Among the Standing Committees, three are financial Committees:
  - (*i*) Public Account Committee;
  - (*ii*) Estimate Committee;
  - (*iii*) Public undertaking Committee.

Speaker of Lok Sabha

- Speaker is elected by the Lok Sabha from among its members.
- The Speaker will have the final power to maintain order within the House of the People and to interpret its rules of procedure.
- A Deputy-Speaker is also elected to officiate in absence of the Speaker.
- *G.V. Mavlankar* was the first Speaker of the Lok Sabha (1952-1956).

Supreme Court

- The Constitution provides for the Supreme Court, which consists of Chief Justice and 33 judges. They are appointed by the President of India.

QUALIFICATION AND TENURE

- Eligibility conditions for a judge of the Supreme Court are that he must be : (i) a citizen of India; (ii) a judge of a high court for a minimum period of 5 years; or (iii) an advocate of a high court for at least ten years or a distinguished jurist.
- Judges hold office till the age of 65.
- They can resign earlier or can be removed by the President on the recommendation of the two Houses of the Parliament by 2/3rd majority of the members present and voting.

Powers

- *Original jurisdiction:* Cases involving Government of India and the states or cases involving the enforcement of Fundamental Rights fall under original jurisdiction.
- *Appellate Jurisdiction:* In cases which are brought to it in the form of appeals against the judgement of the lower courts—It hears appeals in civil and criminal cases.
- *Advisory functions:* the Supreme Court advises the President on the constitutionality of a particular legal matter. However, its advice is not binding on the President.

Other Powers:

1. it is a court of record and can punish for contempt of itself;
2. it can make rules for regulating the practice and procedure of courts with the approval of the President; and
3. it can recommend to the President the removal of chairman and members of the UPSC. Supreme Court enjoys the power of judicial review (right of the court which declares as unconstitutional, the laws passed by the legislature and orders issued by executive) though it is not specifically mentioned in the Constitution.

- The first Chief Justice of India was H.J. Kania (1950-51).

COMPTROLLER AND AUDITOR GENERAL (CAG) (ARTICLE 148-151)

- The Comptroller and Auditor General of India is guardian of the public purse.
- It is his duty to see that not a *paisa* is spent out of consolidated fund of India or of a state without the authority of the appropriate legislature.
- He is appointed by President of India.
- A person with long administrative experience and knowledge of accounts is appointed.
- Holds office for 6 yrs or till 65 yrs of age.
- The President can remove him only on the recommendation of the 2 houses of Parliament (as in case of judge of Supreme Court).
- The CAG submits its reports to the President (in case of accounts relating to the Union Government) or to the State Governors (for State Government Accounts).
- The first CAG of India was *V Narahari Rao* (1948-1954).
- The CAG is not eligible for further office under the Union or State Governments. The expenses of the office of the CAG is charged to the Consolidated Fund of India.

ATTORNEY GENERAL OF INDIA

- The Attorney General of India is the first law officer of the Government of India.
- Though he is not a member of cabinet he has the right to speak in the House of Parliament, but he has no right to vote.
- The Attorney General of India shall be appointed by the President and shall hold office during his pleasure.
- His duty shall be to give advice on such legal matter from time-to-time as may be referred to him by the President.
- To be appointed as Attorney General, a candidate must be qualified to be appointed as a Judge of the Supreme Court.
- The Attorney General can participate in proceedings of the Parliament without the Right to Vote (Article 88).
- The first Attorney General of Independent India was MC Setalvad (1950-1963).

PART - VI

THE STATES (ARTICLE 152 - 237)

THE GOVERNOR

- The Governor is appointed by the President and holds office during the pleasure of the President.
- Apart from the power to appoint the council of ministers, if the governor finds that the government of state cannot be carried on in accordance with the provisions of the constitution (Art. 356), he may send his report to the President who may assume to himself the functions of the government of the state. (This is popularly known as 'President's Rule').
- Article 161 gives the Governor the power to grant pardons, reprieves, remission of punishment to persons convicted under the state law.
- Article 171 states that the States where Legislative Councils exists, the Governor can nominate some members from amongst those distinguished in literature, science, arts, cooperative movement and social service.

STATES LEGISLATURE (ARTICLE 168 - 212)

- The state legislature consists of Governor and legislative assembly.
- In some state like *Bihar, Maharashtra, Andhra Pradesh, Karnataka, Uttar Pradesh and Telangana* have a legislative council.
- The membership of the council should not be more than *one-third* of the legislative assembly but not less than 40.
- The legislative assembly of each state shall be composed of members chosen by direct election on the basis of adult suffrage and the number of members shall not be more than 500 or less than 60.
- The assembly of Sikkim, Goa, Puducherry and Mizoram have less than 60 members.

HIGH COURTS (ARTICLE 214-232)

- The High Court stands at the apex of the State Judiciary.
- As per the Constitution, there shall be a High Court in each State. But there may be a common High Court for two or more States and Union Territory, if it is provided by a law of the Parliament. For example, the Chennai High Court has its Jurisdiction over the State of Tamil Nadu and the Union Territory of Puducherry.
- The State Government has no control over it.
- There are 25 High Courts in India.
- The Calcutta High Court, established in 1862, is the oldest High Court in India.

THE PANCHAYATS (ARTICLE 243-243 O)

- Panchayati Raj was introduced in India with a view to associate the people with administration at grass-root level.
- It is a three-tier system as recommended by Balwant Rai Mehta Committee.
- Introduced by the 73rd Amendment Act, 1992 which envisaged a three tier system of local governance.

These are:

1. Gram Panchayat at the village level
2. Panchayat Samiti at the block level
3. Zila Parishad at the district level.

Jurisdiction and Seat of High Courts

Name	Year	Territorial Jurisdiction	Seat
Allahabad	1866	Uttar Pradesh	Prayagraj (Bench at Lucknow)
Bombay	1862	Maharashtra, Goa, Dadar and Nagar Haveli and Daman and Diu	Mumbai (Benches at Nagpur, Panaji and Sambhaji Nagar)
Calcutta	1862	West Bengal and Andaman & Nicobar	Kolkata (Circuit Benches at Sri Vijaya Puram and Jalpaiguri)
Chhattisgarh	2000	Chhattisgarh	Bilaspur

Name	Year	Territorial Jurisdiction	Seat
Delhi	1966	Delhi	Delhi
Gauhati	1948	Assam, Nagaland, Mizoram and Arunachal Pradesh	Guwahati (Benches at Kohima, Aizawl and Itanagar)
Gujarat	1960	Gujarat	Ahmedabad
Himachal Pradesh	1971	Himachal Pradesh	Shimla
Jammu & Kashmir and Ladakh	1928	Jammu & Kashmir, Ladakh	Srinagar and Jammu
Jharkhand	2000	Jharkhand	Ranchi
Karnataka	1884	Karnataka	Bengaluru (Circuit Benches at Dharwar and Gulbarga)
Kerala	1958	Keralam & Lakshadweep	Kochi (Ernakulam)
Madhya Pradesh	1956	Madhya Pradesh	Jabalpur (Benches at Gwalior and Indore)
Madras	1862	Tamil Nadu & Puducherry	Chennai (Bench at Madurai)
Orissa	1948	Odisha	Cuttack
Patna	1916	Bihar	Patna
Punjab and Haryana	1966	Punjab, Haryana and Chandigarh	Chandigarh
Rajasthan	1949	Rajasthan	Jodhpur (Bench at Jaipur)
Sikkim	1975	Sikkim	Gangtok
Uttarakhand	2000	Uttarakhand	Nainital
Tripura	2013	Tripura	Agartala
Meghalaya	2013	Meghalaya	Shillong
Manipur	2013	Manipur	Imphal
Telangana	2019	Telangana	Hyderabad
Andhra Pradesh	2019	Andhra Pradesh	Amravati

THE MUNICIPALITIES (ARTICLE 243 P-243 ZG)

- Big cities have municipal corporations headed by the elected Mayor.
- For small towns there are elected boards or councils, in turn, elect their Presidents.
- Introduced by the 74th Amendment Act, 1993 which envisages three types of urban local bodies, namely, municipality (nagar palika), city council (nagar panchayat).
- Municipal governance in India was first introduced in Madras in 1688.

PART - XIII

(ARTICLE 301 - 307)

- In this part from Article 301-307 trade, commerce and intercourse within the territory of India are given.

PART - XIV

(ARTICLE 308 - 323)

- In this part services under the union and the states are given.
- ***Article 312:*** *All India Services* and ***Article 315:*** Public Service Commissions for the Union and for the States.
- The first Public Service Commission was set up in 1926, on the recommendations of the Lee Commission.

UNION PUBLIC SERVICE COMMISSION (UPSC)

- This Commission is responsible for:
  1. recruitment to all civil services and posts, under the Union Government by written examinations, interviews and promotions, and
  2. advising the Government on all matters relating to methods of recruitment, principles to be followed in making promotions and transfers. Its Chairman is appointed by the President.

STAFF SELECTION COMMISSION (SSC)

- The Union Government has constituted a Staff Selection Commission for recruitment to non-technical Class III posts in the central government and in subordinate offices.

- The Administrative Reforms Commission had recommended the setting up of such a Commission.
- The Commission has also been entrusted with the responsibility of making recruitment to Group 'B' services like Assistants' and Stenographers Grade 'C'.
- The Commission has a chairman and two members.

ELECTIONS (ARTICLE 324-329)

- The Constitution provides for an independent election commission to ensure free and fair election to the Parliament, the State legislature and the offices of President and Vice-President.
- Consists of Chief Election Commissioner +2 Election Commissioners. They all enjoy equal powers.
- The Chief Election Commissioner and other Election Commissioners are appointed by the President.
- Election Commissioners are appointed for a term of 5 yrs.
- They are not eligible for re-appointment. Also, they cannot hold any office of profit after their retirement.
- The Election Commission was established on 25th January, 1950 under Article 324 of the Constitution.
- The first Chief Election Commissioner was *Sukumar Sen.*

Functions

- Preparation of electoral rolls and keeping voters list updated.
- Recognition of various political parties and allotment of election symbols.

NITI AAYOG

- The Indian government has replaced Planing Commission with a new institution named **NITI Aayog (National Institution for Transforming India).**
- The Niti Aayog will comprise the following:
  1. Prime Minister of India as the Chairperson.
  2. Governing Council comprising the Chief Ministers of all the States and Lt. Governors of Territories.
  3. Regional Councils will be formed to address specific issues and contingencies impacting more than one state or a region. These will be formed for a specified tenure. The Regional Councils will be convened by the Prime Minister and will comprise of the Chief Ministers of States and Lt. Governors of Territories in the region. These will be chaired by the Chairperson of the NITI Aayog or his nominee.
  4. Experts, specialists and practitioners with relevant domain knowledge as special invitees nominated by the Prime Minister.
- The full-time organizational framework will comprise of, in addition to the Prime Minister as the Chairperson:
  1. Vice-Chairperson : To be appointed by the Prime Minister.
  2. Members : Full-time. : 3
  3. Part-time members : Maximum of 2 from leading universities research organizations and other relevant institutions in an ex-officio capacity. Part time members will be on a rotational basis.
  4. Ex Officio members : Maximum of 4 members of the Council of Ministers to be nominated by the Prime Minister.
  5. Chief Executive Officer : To be appointed by the Prime Minister for a fixed tenure, in the rank of Secretary to the Government of India.
  6. Secretariat as deemed necessary.

FINANCE COMMISSION

- The constitution of the Finance Commission is laid down in Art. 280.
- The chairman must be a person having experience in public affairs; and the other four members also having wide experience in financial matters.

- It consists of Chairman and 4 other members.
- It shall be the duty of the Finance Commission to advice the President on matters such as the distribution between the Union and States of the net proceeds of taxes that is required to be shared.
- The Finance Commission is not a permanent body. It is dissolved after it has submitted its recommendations.

Important Amendments to the Constitution

First Amendment, 1951	:	Added Ninth Schedule.
Twenty-second Amendment, 1969	:	Formation of Meghalaya within the state of Assam was facilitated.
Twenty-sixth Amendment, 1971	:	The privy and privileges of the former rulers of Indian States were abolished.
Thirty-first Amendment, 1973	:	The upper limit of representation of states was raised from 500 to 525. The upper limit for representation of the UTs was reduced from 25 to 20.
Thirty-sixth Amendment, 1975	:	Sikkim was made a full-fledged state of Indian Union and it was included in the First Schedule.
Thirty-eight Amendment, 1975	:	This act led to the amendment of Article 123, Article 213 and Article 352 which stated that the satisfaction of President or of Governor contained in these Articles would be called in question in any court of law.
Forty-second Amendment, 1976	:	This amendment was done in accordance with the recommendations of Swaran Singh Committee and included a number of amendments.
Forty-third Amendment, 1977	:	It provided for the restoration of the Jurisdiction of the Supreme Court and High Courts, curtailed by the enactment of the Constitution (Forty-Second Amendment) Act, 1976.
Forty-fourth Amendment, 1978	:	The right to property was deleted as Fundamental Right and was made a legal right.
Fifty-third Amendment, 1986	:	The Act grants statehood to the Union Territory of Mizoram, thus making it the 23rd State of the Indian Unions.
Fifty-sixth Amendment, 1987	:	The UT of Goa converted into Goa state through this amendment whereas Daman and Diu were organised under a new UT.
Seventy-third Amendment, 1992	:	It is concerning Panchayati Raj.
Seventy-fourth Amendment, 1992	:	It is regarding Municipal Boards and Corporations.
Eighty-ninth Amendment, 2003	:	It provides for constitution of a separate National Commission for Scheduled Tribes. (Earlier, there was a combined National Commission for both SC/STs).
Ninety-first Amendment, 2003	:	It is regarding restricting the total number of Ministers including Prime Minister/Chief Minister in Lok Sabha and State Legislatures to 15% of the total number of the Union or State Legislatures.
Ninety-sixth Amendment, 2011	:	Amendment of 8th Schedule, it replaces 'Orissa' with 'Odisha'.
Ninety-eight Amendment, 2013	:	(Insert Article 371 J) To empower the Governor of Karnataka to take steps to develop Hydrabad Karnataka Region.

Ninety-ninth Amendment, 2014	:	This Act led to the insertion of new Articles 124A, 124B and 124C after Article 124 of the Constitution.
One hundredth and first Amendment, 2016	:	The act amends the Constitution to introduce "The Goods and Services Tax (GST)."
One hundredth and Third Amendment, 2019	:	The Act providing 10 per cent reservation in government jobs and educational institutions to Economically Weaker Sections (EWS) of General Category, came into effect on January 14, 2019.
One hundredth and Fourth Amendment, 2019	:	This Act ceased the reservation of seats for Anglo-Indians in the Lok Sabha and Legislative assemblies and extended reservations for SCs and STs for up to ten years.
One hundredth and Fifth Amendment, 2021	:	This Act restores the power of State Governments to identify and specify Socially and Economically Backward Classes (SEBCs)
One hundredth and Sixth Amendment, 2023	:	This Act provides 33% reservation for women in Lok Sabha and State Legislative Assemblies.

NATIONAL SYMBOLS

STATE EMBLEM

- State Emblem of India is an adaptation from the Sarnath Lion Capital of Ashoka. It was adopted by the Government of India on January 26, 1950. In the adapted form, only three lions are visible, the fourth being hidden from the view.
- The wheel (Dharma Chakra) appears in relief in the centre of the abacus with a bull on the right and a horse on the left. The bell-shaped lotus has been omitted. The words ''Satyameva Jayate'' meaning ''Truth alone triumphs'' are inscribed below the Emblem in Devanagari script.

NATIONAL FLAG

- The National Flag of India is a horizontal tricolour of deep saffron (Kesari), white and dark green in equal proportion.
- In the centre of the white band there is a wheel in navy blue colour. It has 24 spokes.
- The ratio of the length and the breadth of the flag is 3 : 2. Its design was adopted by the Constituent Assembly of India on July 22, 1947.

NATIONAL ANTHEM

- Rabindranath Tagore's song 'Jana-gana-mana' was adopted by the Constituent Assembly as the National Anthem of India on January 24, 1950.

Jana-gana-mana-adhinayaka jaya he,
Bharata-bhagya-vidhata
Punjab-Sindh-Gujarat-Maratha-
Dravida-Utkala-Banga
Vindhya-Himachala-Yamuna-Ganga
Uchhala-jaladhi-taranga.
Tava subha name jage,
Tava subha asisa mange,
Gahe tava jaya gatha,
Jana-gana-mangala-dayak,
jaya he Bharata bhagya vidhata,
Jaya he, jaya he, jaya he,
Jaya jaya jaya, jaya he.

NATIONAL SONG

- Bankim Chandra Chatterji's 'Vande Mataram' which was a source of inspiration to the people in their struggle for freedom, has been adopted as National Song. It has an equal status with the National Anthem.

Vande Mataram
Sujalam, suphalam, malayaja-shitalam,
Shasya shyamalam, Mataram
Shubhrajyotsna, pulkita yaminim,
Phulla kusumita drumadalashobhinim,
Subhasinim sumadhura—bhashinim,
Sukhadam, Varadam, Mataram.

- **National Bird and Animal of India:** Peacock and Tiger.
- **National Aquatic Animal:** Dolphin
- **National Flower:** Lotus
- **National Calendar:** It was adopted on March 22, 1957. It has 365 days in the year and the first month of the year is Chaitra.

❑ ❑ ❑

GENERAL SCIENCE

PHYSICS

PHYSICAL QUANTITIES

- Physical quantities may be divided in two classes: 1. Scalar Quantities 2. Vector Quantities
- A scalar quantity is one which has only magnitude.
- A vector quantity has both magnitude and direction.
- Force, Velocity, Momentum, Acceleration are examples of vector quantities.
- Mass, length, time, volume, speed, energy, work are examples of scalar quantities.

UNITS

- All measurements in physics require standard units.
- In 1960, the General Conference of Weights and Measures recommended that a metric system of measurements called the International System of Units, abbreviated as SI units, be used.

Some Important Units

S.No.	Units	Quantity
1.	Metre	Length
2.	Kilogram	Mass
3.	Second	Time
4.	Ampere	Electric Current
5.	Candela	Luminous Intensity
6.	Newton	Force
7.	Joule	Workdone
8.	Watt	Power
9.	Coulomb	Electric Charge
10.	Volt	Potential Difference
11.	Ohm	Electrical Resistance
12.	Farad	Capacitance
13.	Henry	Inductance
14.	Lumen	Luminous Flux

- Very small distances are measured in micro-meters or (microns) (μm), angstroms (Å), nanometers (nm) and femtometres (fm).

MOTION

- When a body changes its position with respect to something else as time goes on, we say the body is in motion.
- There are two types of motion—translational (linear) and rotational (spin).
- The motion of a car on a road is translational whereas the motion of a top, spinning on its axis is rotational.

SPEED

- It is a scalar form of velocity and is defined as the distance travelled in one second.
- Speed = $\dfrac{\text{distance travelled}}{\text{time required}}$
- SI unit of speed is m/s.

VELOCITY

- The distance covered by an object in a specified direction in unit time interval is called velocity.
- The SI unit of velocity is m/s.
- Velocity is a vector quantity.

ACCELERATION

- The velocity of a body changes due to change in its speed or direction or both. The rate of change of the velocity of a body is called its acceleration.
- Acceleration = $\dfrac{\text{change in velocity}}{\text{time taken}}$

FORCE AND MOTION

GRAVITATIONAL FORCE

- It is the force of attraction between two masses.
- It is gravitational force that holds the moon in its orbit round the earth and the earth in its orbit round the sun.
- *Newton's Law of Universal Gravitation* states that every particle in the universe attracts every other particle with a force that is directly proportional to the product of their masses and inversely proportional to the square of the distance between them.
- The value of G is 6.67×10^{-11} SI units.

CENTRIPETAL FORCE

- The force acting towards the centre on a particle executing uniform circular motion is called centripetal force and is given by

$$F = \frac{mv^2}{r}$$

where, m = Mass of the object

v = Speed

r = Radius of the Circular Path

- In case of the moon, gravitational force between the earth and the moon acts as the centripetal force.
- Centripetal force always acts on the particle performing circular motion.

CENTRIFUGAL FORCE

- The pseudo force that balances the centripetal force in uniform circular motion is called centrifugal force.
- Centrifugal force is directed away from the centre along the radius.
- The centrifugal force is zero exactly at the poles and maximum at the equator.

WEIGHT

- The weight of a body is the force with which the earth attracts the body towards its centre.
- The mass of a body is a constant quantity whereas its weight varies slightly from place-to-place on the earth.
- The weight of a body is maximum at the poles and minimum at the equator. This variation in weight is due to:
  1. the shape of the earth.
  2. the rotation of the earth about its axis.
- The weight of an object is less at high elevations than at sea level.
- At the centre of the earth, the weight of a body would be zero.
- On the surface of the moon the value of the acceleration due to gravity is nearly one-sixth of that on earth and, therefore, an object on the moon would weigh only one-sixth its weight on the earth. The mass of an object on the moon would be the same as on earth.
- The weight of a body would be more if the earth stopped rotating. Conversely, if the speed of rotation were higher, the weight would be less.
- A person weighs more in a lift, which is accelerating upward.
- An astronaut feels weightless in a spaceship because he is not pushing against anything.

FRICTION

- Friction is the force which opposes the relative motion of two surfaces in contact.
- It is friction between the ground and the soles of our shoes that makes walking possible and it is lack of friction that makes our feet slip on highly polished surfaces.
- Friction in machines wastes energy and also causes wear and tear. This friction is reduced by using (1) lubricants, and (2) ball bearings.

NEWTON'S LAWS OF MOTION

First Law

- Every object continues in its state of rest or of uniform motion in a straight line if no net force acts upon it. It is also known as *law of inertia.*
- **Examples:** 1. An unwary passenger in a fast-moving bus falls forward when it stops suddenly. This happens because the feet of the passenger come to rest suddenly whereas his upper part of body continues to be in motion. 2. A person

getting down from a moving bus has to run some distance, in the direction of the bus, before stopping. If he does not run he is bound to fall because his feet come to rest whereas his body continues to be in motion.

Momentum

- The momentum of a body is defined as the product of its mass and velocity.

Second Law

- This law states that "the rate of change of momentum of a body is proportional to the applied force and takes place in the direction of the force."
- If we express force (F) in Newtons, mass (m) in kilograms and acceleration (a) in metres per second squared, we can write the second law as; $F = ma$.
- In travelling the same distance, a car consumes more fuel on a crowded road than on a free road. This happens because the car has to stop and start quite often on a crowded road. The repeated acceleration requires a force (second law), which ultimately comes from the fuel. On a free road the car runs at almost uniform speed requiring fewer accelerations and hence less fuel consumption.

Third Law

- This law states that "to every action there is an equal and opposite reaction."
- When a bullet is fired from a gun, equal and opposite forces are exerted on the bullet and the gun.
- The engine in a jet aeroplane works on the same principle as a rocket but there is a difference in the method of obtaining the high velocity as jet.

IMPULSE

- If a force acts on a body for a very short time, then the product of force and time is called the impulse.

Impulse= Change in momentum
= Force × Time

Application of Impulse

1. A cricket player draws his hand back while catching.
2. A person jumping on hard cement floor receives more injuries than a person jumping on muddy or sandy floor.

WORK, POWER AND ENERGY

WORK

- Whenever a force acting on a body displaces it, work is said to be done.

Work = Force × Distance moved in the direction of force.

- Work is a scalar quantity and its SI unit is Joule (J).

POWER

- Power is defined as the rate of doing work.

$$\text{Power} = \frac{\text{Work done}}{\text{Time taken}}$$

- The SI unit of power is Watt (W) and is also measured in horse power.

1 HP = 746 W

ENERGY

- Energy is defined as the capacity to do work.

Kinetic Energy

- The energy possessed by an object due to its motion is called kinetic energy and is described by the expression

$KE = \frac{1}{2}mv^2$; where, m = mass of the object
v = speed

Potential Energy

- Potential energy is the energy possessed by the body by virtue of its position, configuration or any condition of stress or strain.
- There are many examples of potential energy. A stone held at some height above the ground has potential energy. Water in an elevated reservoir possesses potential energy.

Transformation of Energy

S.No.	Equipment	Transformation
1.	Dynamo	Mechanical energy into electrical energy
2.	Microphone	Sound energy into electrical energy
3.	Loud Speaker	Electrical energy into sound energy
4.	Electric Bulb	Electrical energy into light and heat energy
5.	Battery	Chemical energy into electrical energy
6.	Electrical Motor	Electrical energy into mechanical energy

CENTRE OF GRAVITY

- The centre of gravity of a body is the point where the whole weight of the body can be considered to act.
- Racing cars are build low and with wide wheel bases to reduce the risk of overturning at sharp bends.
- While crossing a river in a boat, passengers are not allowed to stand. This keeps the CG of the system (boat and passengers) low and ensures stability.

ARTIFICIAL SATELLITES

- In the case of a satellite, the centripetal force is provided by the gravitational pull of the earth.
- If the speed of a satellite is more than 11.2 km/s or 25,000 miles/hour, the satellite would escape the earth entirely and would never come back. This is called escape velocity.
- The existence of gaseous atmosphere on the earth is due to the high value of its escape velocity.

Geostationary Satellites

- Geostationary satellites are stationary with respect to an observer on the earth. Their time period is 24-hour. There height above the surface of earth is 36,000 km. They are always in equatorial plane and their orbits are circular. They are also called parking orbits.

DENSITY AND RELATIVE DENSITY

DENSITY

- The mass per unit volume of a substance is called its density.

$$\text{Density} = \frac{\text{Mass}}{\text{Volume}}$$

- The SI unit of density is kilogram per metre cubed (kg/m^3).
- The relative density of a substance is the ratio of the density of the substance to the density of water.
- Relative density has no unit.

PRESSURE

- Pressure is defined as force acting per unit area.

$$\text{Pressure} = \frac{\text{Force}}{\text{Area}}$$

- The SI unit of pressure is newton per metre squared or pascal.
- Broad wooden sleepers are placed below the rails to reduce the pressure exerted by the weight of a train.
- The pressure of water increases with depth, therefore bottom of a dam is made much thicken than the top.
- The pressure exerted on an enclosed liquid at one place is transmitted equally throughout the liquid. This is called Pascal's Principle.
- Hydraulic presses, hydraulic brakes, hydraulic door closers, etc. are applications of the Pascal's Principle.
- At high attitudes where atmosphere pressure is less nose bleeding may occur due to the greater pressure of blood.
- In an aircraft flying at high altitude, normal atmospheric pressure is maintained by the use of air pumps. If this were not done, the crew and passengers would experience difficulty in breathing and consequently face dangers.
- Atmospheric pressure is measured with an instrument called the *Barometer*.

ARCHIMEDE'S PRINCIPLE

- This principle states that when a body is wholly or partially immersed in a fluid, it experiences an upthrust (upward force) equal to the weight of the fluid displaced.
- An iron nail sinks in water whereas a ship made of iron and steel floats. This is due to the fact that a ship is hollow and contains air and, therefore, its density is less than that of water.
- The density of sea water is more than that of river water, due to this a ship sinks less in sea water. It is for this reason that a ship rises a little when it enters a sea from a river.
- It is because of the higher density of sea water that it is easier to swim in the sea.
- A balloon filled with a light gas, such as hydrogen, rises because the average density of the balloon and the gas is less than that of air. The balloon cannot rise indefinitely because the density of the air decreases with increasing altitude. At a certain height, where the density of air is equal to the average density of the balloon, it ceases to rise and drifts sideways with the wind.
- When an ice block floats in water the water level will remain the same when all the ice melts into water.
- A *hydrometer* is an instrument used for measuring the relative density of liquids.
- A special type of a hydrometer called *Lactometer* is used for testing milk by measuring its density.

SURFACE TENSION

- Surface tension is that property of liquids owing to which they tend to acquire minimum surface area.
- Surface tension is caused by molecular attractions.
- When a paint brush is dipped in water all its hair spread out but when it is taken out it is covered with a thin film of water which contracts due to surface tension and pulls the hair together.
- Liquid drops, such as raindrops, oildrops, drops of molten metals, dewdrops etc. are all spherical because their surface tend to contract in order to have minimum surface area. For a given volume, a sphere has the minimum surface area.
- Soaps and detergents lower the surface tension of water. This increases the wetting power of water or its ability to detach dirt particles from clothes and untensils.
- The force of attraction between unlike molecules is called **adhesion** and that between like molecules **cohesion.**
- The melted wax of a candle is drawn up into the wick by capillary action. Oil rises up a lamp wick for the same reason.
- If one end of a sugar cube is dipped into tea, the entire cube is quickly wet on account of capillary action.

VISCOSITY

- The force which opposes the relative motion between different layers of liquid or gases is called viscous force.
- Viscosity is the property of liquids and gases both.

BERNOULLI'S THEOREM

- According to Bernoulli's theorem, in case of streamline flow of incompressible and non-viscous fluid (ideal fluid) through a tube, total energy (sum of pressure energy, potential energy and kinetic energy) per unit volume of fluid is same at all points.

  1. When a bowler spins a ball, it changes its direction (swings) in the air due to unequal pressure acting on it.

HEAT

- Heat is that form of energy which flows from one body to other body due to difference in temperature between the bodies. The amount of heat contained in a body depends upon the mass of the body.

TEMPERATURE

- The temperature of a body is the quantity that tells how hot or cold it is with respect to some standard body.

MEASUREMENT OF TEMPERATURE

- Temperature is measured by a thermometer.
- A thermometer may be graduated in following scales—
  1. The upper and lower points of centigrade scale are 100°C and 0°C.
  2. The upper and lower points of Fahrenheit scale are 212°F and 32°F.
  3. The upper and lower points of Reaumur scale are 80°R and 0°R.
  4. The upper and lower points of Kelvin scale are 373K and 273K.
  5. The upper and lower points of Rankine scale are 672° Ra and 460° Ra.
- At –40 degrees both celsius and Fahrenheit scales will show identical readings.
- Water cannot be used in a thermometer becaues it freezes at 0°C and also because of its irregular expansion.

THERMAL EXPANSION

- Solids, liquids and gases generally expand when heated and contract when cooled.
- Gaps have to be left in railway tracks to make allowance for expansion, otherwise the rails will buckle. Allowance is made for the expansion of long steel bridges. One end of such bridge is fixed while the other rests on rollers.
- Telephone wires sag more in summer than in winter due to thermal expansion.

EXPANSION OF WATER

- Water has its minimum volume and maximum density at 4°C.

TRANSMISSION OF HEAT

- There are three ways of heat transmission: 1. Conduction; 2. Convection; 3. Radiation.

Conduction

- In this process, heat is transferred from one place to other place by the successive vibration of the particles of the medium without bodily movement of the particles of the medium.
- Conduction takes place mainly in solids.
- Air is a very bad conductor of heat. The good insulating properties of wool, cotton, etc. are mainly due to the air spaces they contain.

Convection

- In this process, heat is transferred by the actual movement of particles of the medium from one place to other place.
- In liquids and gases heat is transmitted by convection.

Radiation

- In this mode of heat transmission heat is transferred from one place to another without effecting the intervening medium.

HEAT CAPACITY

- The heat capacity of a body is defined as the heat required to raise the temperature of the body by 1K. Its SI unit is J/K.

SPECIFIC HEAT CAPACITY

- The specific heat capacity of a substance is the heat required to raise the temperature of a unit mass of the substance by 1K.
- Its SI unit is J/kg K.
- It is because of its high specific heat capacity that water is used as a cooling liquid in car engine.

LATENT HEAT

- It is defined as the amount of heat absorbed or given out by a body during the change of state.
- Each gram of ice that melts absorbs 336 J of heat.

EVAPORATION

- Water can change into the vapour state either by boiling or by evaporation at lower temperatures.
- When sweat evaporates from the skin it draws much heat from the body and produces a cooling sensation.
- In summer, water is stored in pitchers for cooling. Water oozes out of the pores of the pitchers and cools on evaporation.

- The rate of evaporation increases with increase in temperature.

REFRIGERATOR

- In a refrigerator, cooling is produced by the evaporation of a volatile liquid, freon, inside a copper coil (evaporator), which surrounds the freezer.
- The cooling unit (freezer) in a refrigerator is fitted near the top to cool the whole of the interior.

RELATIVE HUMIDITY

- Relative humidity is defined as the ratio of the mass of water vapour in a given volume of air to the mass required for saturating the same volume of air at the same temperature.
- Relative humidity is measured with an instrument called the hygrometer.

PRESSURE COOKER

- The boiling point of a liquid depends on external pressure.
- When the atmospheric pressure is 76 cm of mercury, water boils at 100°C. But when the pressure is increased, the boiling point of water is raised.
- In a pressure cooker, water boils at temperatures higher than 100°C due to increased pressure. The increased boiling temperature allows water to hold more heat which cooks food faster.
- At higher altitudes, atmospheric pressure is reduced. This lowers the boiling point of water and food takes much longer to cook.

WAVE MOTION

- Wave motion may be defined as the transfer of energy without the net transfer of matter.
- If the particles of the medium vibrate perpendicular to the direction of propagation of wave, the wave is called transverse wave.
- Light waves are transverse waves.
- If the particles of the medium vibrate in the direction of propagation of wave, the wave is called longitudinal wave.
- Sound waves are longitudinal waves.

ELECTROMAGNETIC WAVE

- Electromagnetic waves include an enormous range of frequencies—from radio waves with frequencies less than 10^5 Hz to gamma rays having frequencies greater than 10^{20} Hz.
- All electromagnetic wave have the same speed (3×10^8 m/s) in vacuum. The relation $v = n\lambda$ holds good for all electromagnetic waves.

RADIO AND TELEVISION TRANSMISSION

- Radio waves sent out by radio stations are reflected by the ionosphere and can be received anywhere on the earth.
- At night the radio reception improves because the layers of the ionosphere are not exposed to sunlight and are more settled.
- Radar (Radio detection and ranging) employs high frequency radio waves for detecting objects like ships and aeroplanes.
- In microwave oven, when the waves fall on the food, these are absorbed by water, fats, sugars and certain other molecules whose consequent vibrations produce heat. Since heating occurs inside the food, without warming the surrounding air, the cooking time is greatly reduced.
- In microwave oven, food cannot be cooked in metal vessels because the metal blocks out the microwaves.

LIGHT

- Light is a form of energy which is propagated as electromagnetic waves.
- Light is a transverse wave.
- Speed of light in vacuum is 3×10^8 m/s.
- Light takes 8 minute 16.6 second to reach from sun to earth.

REFLECTION

- When light is incident upon a surface, part of it is reflected. But certain surfaces like mirrors and polished metals reflect almost all the light incident upon them.
- The law of reflection states that the angle of incidence is equal to the angle of reflection.

- To see full image in a plane mirror, a person requires a mirror of at least half of his height.

INCLINED MIRROR (NO. OF IMAGES)

- When an object is placed between two inclined mirrors, several images of the object are formed.

CURVED MIRRORS

- There are two types of curved spherical mirrors—1. Concave Mirror, 2. Convex Mirror.
- Concave mirror can concentrate the sun's radiation falling on it at one point, it can be used as a burning glass.
- Concave mirrors are also used in solar cookers.
- Large concave mirrors are used in reflecting telescopes for observing and photographing distant stars and other heavenly bodies.
- Concave mirror is also used as a shaving or make-up mirror.
- Small concave mirrors are used by dentists for examining teeth.
- Concave parabolic mirrors are used in searchlight and headlamps of cars.
- Convex mirrors are also used as rear view mirrors in vehicles.

REFRACTION

- When a ray of light passes from one medium to other it suffers a change in direction at the boundary of separation of two media. This phenomenon is called refraction.
- When a ray passes from one medium to another optically denser medium, e.g., from air to water or glass, it bends towards the normal. Conversely, a ray passing from water or glass into air is bent away from the normal.
- Rivers appear shallow, coin in a beaker filled with water appears raised, due to refraction.
- Another effect of refraction is the apparent upward bending of the immersed portion of a stick when dipped in water.
- It is due to refraction, produced by the earth's atmosphere, that the sun is visible for several minutes after it has set below the horizon. Thus, atmospheric refraction tends to lengthen the day.
- When the sun (or moon) is near the horizon, it appears elliptical, i.e., with the vertical diameter less than the horizontal diameter. This happens because rays from the lower edge of the sun are bent more than those from the upper edge (Atmospheric Refraction).
- One of the most interesting effects of atmospheric refraction and Mirage is a combined effect of atmospheric refraction and total internal reflection.

DISPERSION

- White light consists of seven colours—violet, indigo, blue, green, yellow, orange and red. These colours are called the spectrum of the white light.
- Violet has the minimum wavelength (or maximum frequency) and red the maximum wavelength (or minimum frequency).
- Due to different speeds, the colours are refracted through different angles and therefore, when a narrow beam of white light passes through a glass prism, it is split up into its constituent colours. This separation of light into colours is called dispersion.

COLOUR OF OBJECTS

- We see objects because of the light they reflect.
- When a rose is viewed in white light, its petals appear red and the leaves appear green, because the petals reflect the red part of the white light and leaves reflect the green part. The remaining colours are absorbed. When the same rose is viewed in green light, the petals will appear black and the leaves green. In blue or yellow light both the petals and leaves will appear black.
- Red, blue and green are primary colours.

LENSES

- There are mainly two types of lenses:

  1. Convex or Converging Lens

  2. Concave or Diverging Lens
- Converging or convex lens is used as a magnifying glass.
- Power of a lens is its capacity to deviate a ray.

Power of a lens is measured as the reciprocal of the focal length.

$$P = \frac{1}{f}$$

- SI unit of power of lens is dioptre (D).
- The power of a converging lens is positive and that of a diverging lens is negative.
- For all positions of the object, the images formed by diverging (concave) lens are virtual, erect and diminished.

EYE

- The light entering the eye is focused by the eye-lens to form an image on the retina.
- In front of the eye, lens is the coloured part of eye, called the iris, which automatically adjusts the size of the pupil to the intensity of light falling on it.
- In bright light the iris automatically shuts tighter, reducing the amount of light entering the pupil. This protects the retina from getting damaged.
- When a person enters a dark room after being in bright light, he is not able to see clearly for a while because the iris is unable to dilate the pupil immediately.
- Least distance of distinct vision is 25 cm.

DEFECTS OF VISION

- A person suffering from long sight (hypermetropia) can clearly see objects at infinity but cannot see near objects clearly. This defect is caused by the eyeball being too short and can be corrected by wearing converging lenses.
- In the case of a person suffering from short sight (myopia), the eye ball is too long and distant objects are focused in front of the retina. This defect can be corrected by wearing diverging lenses.
- ***Astigmatism:*** Curvature of cornea becomes irregular and image is not clear. Cylindrical lens is used.

SCATTERING OF LIGHT

- When light falls on atoms and molecules, it is scattered in all directions.
- Scattering of light is maximum for violet colour and minimum for red colour.
- Blue colour of sky is due to scattering of light.
- In the evening, the sun is lower in the sky and its light has to traverse a longer path through the atmosphere to reach an observer. Thus, at sunset, blue, green and other colours having been scattered only red and some orange light reach us and the sun appears a deep orange-red.
- In outerspace, *i.e.,* beyond the atmosphere, there is nothing to scatter the sunlight and therefore the sky appears dark and stars are visible even in the presence of the sun.

INTERFERENCE OF LIGHT

- The superposition of two (or more) waves of the same kind that pass the same point in space at the same time is called interference.
- Beautiful colours seen in soap bubbles and oil films on water are produced due to the interference of white light reflected by these surfaces.
- LASER (Light Amplification by Stimulated Emission of Radiation) is an optical device which produces an intense beam of coherent monochromatic light.
- Examples of Interference of Light: Holography, Laser.

DIFFRACTION OF LIGHT

- When a beam of light passes through a narrow slit or an aperture, it spreads out to a certain extent into the region of geometrical shadow. This is an example of diffraction, *i.e.,* of the failure of light to travel in a straight line.

SOUND

- Sound waves are longitudinal and cannot travel in vacuum. The transmission of sound requires a medium : air, liquid or solid.
- The longitudinal mechanical waves which lie in the frequency range 20 Hz to 20,000 Hz are called audible or sound waves. These waves are sensitive to human ear.

- The longitudinal mechanical waves having frequencies less than 20 Hz are called Infrasonic. These waves are produced by sources of bigger size such as earthquakes, volcanic eruptions, ocean waves etc.
- The longitudinal waves having frequencies greater than 20,000 Hz are called ultrasonic waves. Human ear cannot detect these waves. But some animals such as cats, dogs, bats can detect these waves.

PITCH

- The pitch (shrillness of a sound) depends on its frequency.
- A sound of higher frequency has a higher pitch.
- The pitch of a woman's voice is higher than that of a man.

LOUDNESS

- The relative loudness of a sound is measured in decibels (db).
- All stringed instruments, such as the violin, sitar, guitar, etc. have sound boxes attached to increase the loudness.

SPEED OF SOUND

- The presence of water vapour in the air increases the speed of sound.
- Sound travels faster through warm air than through cold air. The speed of sound is higher on a hot day than on a cold day.
- Thunder is heard much after the flash of lightning is seen because of the wide difference in the speeds of light and sound.

REFLECTION OF SOUND

- When a sound wave is reflected by a distant obstacle, such as a wall or a cliff, an echo is heard.
- To hear echo, the minimum distance between the observer and reflector should be 17 m.
- Exploration of underwater gas and oil is done by detecting the echoes of shock waves produced by explosions on the water surface.
- Bats emit ultrasonic waves of frequencies up to 80,000 Hz and use the reflection of these waves (echoes) to determine the presence and distance of objects on their way and from them respectively.

DOPPLER EFFECT

- The Doppler effect is the change in frequency of a wave (sound or light) due to the motion of the source or observer.
- It is due to the Doppler effect that the whistle of a train appears shriller when it approaches a listener than when it moves away from him.

ELECTRICITY

- Electricity produced by friction between two dissimilar objects is known as static electricity. Depending on the nature of the objects, one acquires a positive charge and the other an equal negative charge. For example, if a glass rod is rubbed with silk, the rod acquires positive charge and the silk an equal negative charge.
- *Lightning* is a gigantic electric discharge occurring between two charged clouds or between a charged cloud and the earth.

CONDUCTOR

- Conductors are those materials which allow electricity (charge) to pass through themselves.
- Metals conduct electricity because they have a large number of conduction or free electrons.

INSULATORS

- Insulators are those materials which do not allow electricity to flow through themselves. Insulators have no free electrons.

SUPER CONDUCTORS

- The resistance of metals to flow of electricity reduces with decreasing temperature. At temperatures near absolute zero, metals have almost zero resistance and became super conductors.

SEMI-CONDUCTORS

- Certain materials, such as silicon and germanium have electrical resistivity intermediate between those of conductors and insulators. These materials are termed as semi-conductors.

- Semi-conductors are good insulators in their pure crystalline form but their conductivity increases when small amounts of impurities are added to them.

ELECTRIC CURRENT

- Electric current is simply the flow of electric charge. In solid conductors the flow of electrons and in fluids the flow of ions as well as electrons constitute the current.
- SI units of electric current is Ampere (A).

ELECTRICAL RESISTANCE

- When electric current flows through a conductor, e.g., a metallic wire, it offers some obstruction to the current. This obstruction offered by the wire is called its electrical resistance.
- SI unit of Resistance is ohm.

OHM'S LAW

- If physical conditions like temperature, intensity of light etc. remains unchanged then electric current flowing through a conductor is directly proportional to the potential difference across its ends.

ELECTRIC MOTOR

- In an electric motor, electrical energy is converted into mechanical energy.
- Electric fans, mixers, washing machines, etc. work on electric motors.

INVERTER

- An inverter is a device which converts DC to AC. The inverters used in homes and offices are specially designed to:
  1. Convert DC from a battery to AC, and
  2. Charge the battery.

FUSE

- Electric fuse is a protective device used in series with an electric appliance to save it from being damaged due to high current.
- A fuse is a short piece of wire made of a tin-lead alloy, which has a low melting point.
- Fuses are always connected in the live wire in series.

COST OF ELECTRICITY

- The consumption of electrical energy in a house is measured in the unit kWh.
- Kilowatt hour is equal to the energy consumed in the circuit at the rate of 1 kilowatt for 1 hour.

MAGNETISM

- A magnet attracts and holds pieces of iron but does not attract pieces of copper.
- Iron, cobalt, nickel and certain alloys are strongly magnetic whereas copper, wood, glass, etc. are non-magnetic.
- Our earth behaves as a powerful magnet whose south pole is near the geographical north pole and whose north pole is near the geographical south pole.

ATOMIC & NUCLEAR PHYSICS

- Atom consists of three fundamental particles electron, proton and neutron. All the protons and neutrons are present in the central core of atom called nucleus. Electrons revolve around the nucleus.
- The total number of protons in the nucleus is called atomic number (Z).
- The total number of proton and neutrons in the nucleus is called mass number (A).
- Ernest Rutherford, discovered nucleus by the scattering of α-particles from gold foil.

RADIOACTIVITY

- Henry Bacquerel (1896) observed that a photographic plate blackened, when placed near double sulphate of potassium and uranium. He further observed that uranium emitted special kind of rays. They were called Becqueral rays.
- Pierre and Marie Curie observed that the radiation from pitchblende was four times stronger than uranium. In 1898, they finally discovered two new substances—Polonium and Radium. These newly discovered substances were called radioactive substances and this property of these substances was named radioactivity.
- No radioactive substance emits both α and β particles simultaneously.

X-RAYS

- X-rays are electromagnetic radiations having wavelength from a fraction of an Angestrom to about 100Å. They were discovered by Rontgen during his studies on the electrical discharge phenomena in gases—he found that an unknown radiation was produced when electrons collided with the walls of the tubes.

ATOMIC ENERGY

- India today ranks sixth in the atomic energy programmes. It has developed the required know-how and expertise to manufacture nuclear weapons, but it believes in the peaceful uses of atomic power. The Atomic Energy Commission was set-up in the country in 1948 under the Chairmanship of Dr. H. J. Bhabha.
- ***Bhabha Atomic Research Centre (BARC):*** The Bhabha Atomic Research Centre at Trombay near Mumbai (Maharashtra) has four research reactors: (*i*) APSARA—It is the first atomic reactor in Asia; (*ii*) CIRUS—It is a joint Indo-Canadian project; (*iii*) PURNIMA II—a zero energy fast reactor, and (*iv*) DHRUVA—a high power completely indigenous nuclear research reactor with most advanced laboratories in the world. Another fast breeder reactor KAMINI at Kalpakkam has been constructed. Today India is the seventh country in the world and the first developing nation to have mastered the fast breeder reactor technology.
- **Nuclear Power:** Under Nuclear Power Corporation of India Limited (NPCIL) there are seven nuclear power stations in operation in six States: (*i*) Tarapur—Maharashtra, (*ii*) Rawatbhata—Rajasthan, (*iii*) Kalpakkam—Tamil Nadu, (*iv*) Narora—U.P., (*v*) Kakrapara—Gujarat, (*vi*) Kaiga—Karnataka and (*vii*) Kudankulam—Tamil Nadu.
- **Heavy Water:** Heavy water is one of the essential input for Pressurised Heavy Water Reactors (PHWRs) used both as a coolant and moderator. The first heavy water plant was set-up in 1962 in Nangal. Subsequently 7 more plants have been set-up at (*i*) Baroda, (*ii*) Tuticorin, (*iii*) Kota, (*iv*) Talcher, (*v*) Thal, (*vi*) Hazira and (*vii*) Manuguru.
- **Research and Development Centres:** Four research centres namely (*i*) Bhabha Atomic Research Centre, Trombay (Maharashtra), (*ii*) Indira Gandhi Centre for Atomic Research, Kalpakkam (Tamil Nadu), (*iii*) Centre for Advanced Technology, Indore (Madhya Pradesh), (*iv*) Variable Energy Cyclotron Centre at Kolkata (West Bengal) are focal points of research and development work in nuclear energy and related discipline.
- **India's Nuclear Explosions:** On May 18, 1974 India conducted her first underground nuclear explosion at Pokhran (Rajasthan) in the Thar desert, 20 km. away from Jaisalmer, at a depth of more than 100 metres. The successful explosion made India the sixth nuclear nation in the world.
- India conducted 5 nuclear explosion tests at Pokhran in two phases on May 11 and May 13, 1998 and became a nuclear power state.

IMPORTANT INVENTIONS

Name of Invention	*Inventor*	*Nationality*	*Year*
Aeroplane	Orville & Wilbur Wright	U.S.A.	1903
Ball-Point Pen	John J. Loud	U.S.A.	1888
Barometer	Evangelista Torricelli	Italy	1644
Bicycle	Kirkpatrick Macmillan	Britain	1839-40
Bifocal Lens	Benjamin Franklin	U.S.A.	1780
Car (Petrol)	Karl Benz	Germany	1888
Celluloid	Alexander Parkes	Britain	1861
Cinema	Nicolas & Jean Lumiere	France	1895

Name of Invention	Inventor	Nationality	Year
Clock (mechanical)	I-Hsing & Liang Ling-Tsan	China	1725
Diesel Engine	Rudolf Diesel	Germany	1895
Dynamo	Hypolite Pixii	France	1832
Electric Lamp	Thomas Alva Edison	U.S.A.	1879
Electric Motor (DC)	Zenobe Gramme	Belgium	1873
Electric Motor (AC)	Nikola Tesla	U.S.A.	1888
Electro-magnet	William Sturgeon	Britain	1824
Electronic Computer	Dr. Alan M. Turing	Britain	1943
Film (moving outlines)	Louis Prince	France	1885
Film (musical sound)	Dr. Le de Forest	U.S.A.	1923
Fountain Pen	Lewis E. Waterman	U.S.A.	1884
Gramophone	Thomas Alva Edison	U.S.A.	1878
Helicopter	Etienne Oehmichen	France	1924
Jet Engine	Sir Frank Whittle	Britain	1937
Laser	Charles H. Townes	U.S.A.	1960
Lift (Mechanical)	Elisha G. Otis	U.S.A.	1852
Locomotive	Richard Trevithick	Britain	1804
Machine Gun	James Puckle	Britain	1718
Microphone	Alexander Graham Bell	U.S.A.	1876
Microscope	Z. Janssen	Netherlands	1590
Motor Cycle	G. Daimler	Germany	1885
Photography (on film)	John Carbutt	U.S.A.	1888
Printing Press	Johann Gutenberg	Germany	c.1455
Razor (safety)	King C. Gillette	U.S.A.	1895
Refrigerator	James Harrison & Alexander Catlin	U.S.A.	1850
Safety Pin	Walter Hunt	U.S.A.	1849
Sewing machine	Barthelemy Thimmonnier	France	1829
Ship (steam)	J.C. Perier	France	1775
Ship (turbine)	Hon. Sir C. Parsons	Britain	1894
Skyscraper	W. Le Baron Jenny	U.S.A.	1882
Slide Rule	William Oughtred	Britain	1621
Steam Engine (condenser)	James Watt	Britain	1765
Steel Production	Henry Bessemer	Britain	1855
Steel (stainless)	Harry Brearley	Britain	1913
Submarine	David Bushnell	U.S.A.	1776
Tank	Sir Ernest Swinton	Britain	1914
Telegraph	M. Lammond	France	1787
Telegraph Code	Samuel F.B. Morse	U.S.A.	1837
Telephone (perfected)	Alexander Graham Bell	U.S.A.	1876
Television (mechanical)	John Logie Baird	Britain	1926
Television (electronic)	P.T. Farnsworth	U.S.A.	1927
Thermometer	Galileo Galilei	Italy	1593
Transformer	Michael Faraday	Britain	1831
Transistor	Bardeen, Shockley & Brattain	U.S.A.	1948
Washing Machine (elec.)	Hurley Machine Co.	U.S.A.	1907
Zip-Fastener	W.L. Judson	U.S.A.	1891

Important Discoveries

Discovery	*Discoverer*	*Nationality*	*Year*
Aluminium	Hans Christian Oerstedt	Denmark	1827
Atomic number	Henry Moseley	England	1913
Atomic structure of matter	John Dalton	England	1803
Chlorine	C.W. Scheele	Sweden	1774
Electromagnetic induction	Michael Faraday	England	1831
Electromagnetic waves	Heinrich Hertz	Germany	1886
Electromagnetism	Hans Christian Oersted	Denmark	1920
Electron	Sir Joseph Thomson	England	1897
General theory of relativity	Albert Einstein	Switzerland	1915
Hydrogen	Henry Cavendish	England	1766
Law of electric conduction	Georg Ohm	Germany	1827
Law of electromagnetism	Andre Ampere	France	1826
Law of falling bodies	Galileo	Italy	1590
Laws of gravitation & motion	Isaac Newton	England	1687
Laws of planetary motion	Johannes Kepler	Germany	1609-10
Magnesium	Sir Humphry Davy	England	1808
Neptune (Planet)	Johann Galle	Germany	1846
Neutron	James Chadwick	England	1932
Nickel	Axel Cronstedt	Sweden	1751
Nitrogen	Daniel Rutherford	England	1772
Oxygen	Joseph Priestly, C.W. Scheele	England, Sweden	1772
Ozone	Christian Schonbein	Germany	1839
Pluto	Clyde Tombaugh	U.S.A	1930
Plutonium	G.T. Seaborg	U.S.A	1940
Proton	Ernest Rutherford	England	1919
Quantum Theory	Max Planck	Germany	1900
Radioactivity	Antoine Bacquerel	France	1896
Radium	Pierre & Marie Curie	France	1898
Silicon	Jons Berzelius	Sweden	1824
Special theory of relativity	Albert Einstein	Switzerland	1905
Sun as centre of solar system	Copernicus	Poland	1543
Uranium	Martin Klaproth	Germany	1789
Uranus (Planet)	William Herschel	England	1781
X-rays	Wilhelm Roentgen	Germany	1895

Scientific Instruments

Name of Instrument	Used for
Altimeter	measuring altitude
Ammeter	measuring strength of an electric current
Anemometer	measuring the velocity of wind
Audiometer	measuring level of hearing
Barometer	measuring atmospheric pressure
Callipers	measuring the internal and external diameters of tubes
Calorimeter	measuring quantity of heat
Compass	finding out direction
Dynamo	converting mechanical energy into electrical energy
Galvanometer	detecting and determining the strength of small electric currents
Hydrometer	measuring specific gravity of a liquid
Hygrometer	measuring the humidity in the atmosphere
Lactometer	measuring the purity of milk
Manometer	measuring the gaseous pressure
Micrometer	measuring minute distances, angles, etc.
Microscope	seeing magnified view of very small objects
Photometer	measuring intensity of light from distant stars
Pyrometer	measuring high temperatures
Radar	detecting and finding the presence and location of moving objects like aircraft, missile, etc.
Radiometer	measuring the emission of radiant energy
Rain Gauge	measuring the amount of rainfall
Seismograph	measuring and recording the intensity and origin of earthquake shocks
Sextant	measuring altitude and angular distances between two objects or heavenly bodies
Spectrometer	measuring the refractive indices
Spherometer	measuring the curvature of spherical objects/surface
Sphygmomanometer	measuring blood pressure
Stethoscope	ascertaining the condition of heart and lungs by listening to their function
Stroboscope	viewing objects that are moving rapidly with a periodic motion as if they were at rest
Tachometer	measuring the rate of revolution or angular speed of a revolving shaft
Telescope	viewing magnified images of distant objects
Thermocouple	measuring the temperature inside furnaces and jet engines
Thermometer	measuring human body temperature
Thermostat	regulating constant temperature
Ultrasonoscope	measuring utrasonic sounds
Viscometer	measuring the viscosity of a fluid
Voltmeter	measuring potential difference between two points.

CHEMISTRY

ELEMENTS

- An element may be defined as a substance which is made by same type of atoms and it can neither be broken into, nor built from two or more simpler substances by any known physical or chemical methods, e.g., copper, silver, hydrogen, carbon, oxygen, nitrogen, gold, iron etc.

COMPOUNDS

- A compound may be defined as a substance which contains two or more elements combined in some fixed proportion by weight and which can be decomposed into two or more elements by any suitable method.
- The properties of a compound are entirely different from those of the elements from which it is made.
- Some common examples of compounds are water, sugar, salt, aspirin, chloroform, alcohol and ether.

MIXTURES

- A material containing two or more elements or compounds in any proportion is a mixture.
- The components of a mixture can be separated by physical means like filtration, sublimation and distillation.

ATOMIC STRUCTURE

ATOM

- Atom is the smallest part of the element that takes part in a chemical reaction. Atom of an element can not be changed into that of another element by a chemical or physical means. It does not exist in free state.

MOLECULE

- A molecule is the smallest part of an element or compound that is capable of existing independently.

ATOMIC WEIGHT (OR ATOMIC MASS)

- The atomic mass of an element is the number of times its atom is heavier than 1/12th of the mass of carbon (C^{12}) atom.
- The unit used to measure atomic mass is called atomic mass unit, *i.e.,* amu.

ELECTRON

- The electron is a fundamental particle of an atom which carries a unit negative charge. It was discovered by J.J. Thomson in 1897.

PROTON

- It is a fundamental particle of an atom carrying a unit positive charge. It was discovered by Rutherford and Goldstein in 1886.

NEUTRON

- It is a fundamental particle of an atom carrying no charge. It was discovered by Chadwick in 1932.

ISOTOPES

- The atoms of the same element having different mass numbers are called isotopes.

ISOBARS

- Elements having the same atomic mass but differ in atomic number are called isobars.

ISOTONES

- Elements having the same number of neutrons are called isotones.

OXIDATION AND REDUCTION

- Oxidation is a process in which a substance adds on oxygen or loses hydrogen. In modern terms, oxidation is the process in which a substance loses electrons.
- Reduction is a process in which a substance adds on hydrogen or loses oxygen. In modern terms, reduction is the process in which a substance gains electrons.
- Oxidation and reduction always occur simultaneously. If one substance is oxidised, another is reduced. The reaction in which this oxidation-reduction process occurs is called a redox reaction.

- Oxidising agents are substances which bring about the oxidation of other substances, e.g., Potassium Permanganate, Potassium Dichromate, Nitric Acid, Hydrogen Peroxide, etc.
- Reducing agents are substances which bring about the reduction of other substances, e.g., hydrogen sulphide, hydrogen, carbon, sulphur dioxide, etc.

ACIDS, BASES AND SALTS

ACID

- An acid is any compound that can react with a base to form a salt, the hydrogen of the acid being replaced by positive metallic ion. According to modern theory, an acid is a compound which yields hydrogen ions (protons) to a base in a chemical reaction. In a water solution, an acid tastes sour, turns blue litmus red and produces free hydrogen ions.

Acid	Sources
Citric Acid	Lemons or Oranges (Citrus Fruits)
Lactic acid	Sour milk
Tartaric acid	Grapes
Acetic acid	Vinegar
Maleic acid	Apples
Oxalic acid	Tomato
Formic acid	Red ants

BASES

- Such compounds which gives salt and water with acid known as bases. Bitter in taste, turns red litmus paper into blue, contains replaceable hydroxyl group.
- Some important bases are sodium hydroxide, potassium hydroxide, sodium carbonate and ammonium hydroxide.
- All alkalies are bases but all bases are not alkalies because all bases are not soluble in water.

SALTS

- Salts are ionic compounds containing a positive ion (cation) and a negative ion (anion).
- When an acid reacts with a base, a salt and water are formed. This reaction is called neutralization since the acid and base neutralize each other's effect.

ELECTROLYSIS

- The process of decomposition of an electrolyte by the passage of an electric current through its molten state or its aqueous solution is called electrolysis.
- Device through which electric current is passed known as electrodes.

METALLURGY

- Metals occur in nature, in the native (in free state) as well as in the combined state.
- Naturally occurring materials containing metals are called minerals.
- A mineral from which a given metal is obtained economically is called an ore.
- The process of extraction of a metal in a pure state on a large scale from its ore by Physical and Chemical means is called metallurgy.
- The rocky and siliceous matter that associated with the ore is known as gangue.
- Substance that is added to ore to remove the gangue is known as flux.
- The process of removal of gangue from the ore is known as concentration.
- Calcination is the heating of the ore in the absence of air. This method is employed for obtaining the metal oxides from carbonates and hydroxides.
- Roasting is the heating of the ore in the presence of air. On roasting, part of the ore is oxidised to form an oxide. This oxide is then reduced to the metal.
- The industrial reduction process for obtaining metal from the treated ore is called smelting.

AMALGUM

- An alloy in which one of the component metals is mercury is known as amalgum.

IRON AND STEEL

- Iron is extracted from its ores by the blast furnace process.

- Iron obtained from blast furnace is called pig iron or cast iron containing about 5% carbon.
- Pure iron is called wrought iron which does not contain carbon more than 0.2%, or any other impurities or constituents.
- Steel contains 0.25% – 2% carbon and varying amounts of other elements.

CARBON AND ITS COMPOUNDS

ALLOTROPY

- Such substances which having the same chemical properties, but differ in physical properties, known as allotropes and this property is called allotropy.

DIAMOND

- Diamond is the purest form of carbon.
- It is non-conductor of heat and electricity.
- It is the hardest natural substance.
- It burns in air at 900°C and gives out CO_2.

GRAPHITE (BLACK LEAD)

- It is good conductor of heat and electricity.
- Graphite is used in making lead pencils.
- Graphite is also used as electrodes, lubricant, moderators, electrotyping and carbon arc.

AMORPHOUS FORMS OF CARBON

1. Wood Charcoal – Obtained from wood
2. Sugar Charcoal – Obtained from cane sugar
3. Bone or Animal Charcoal – Obtained from animal bones
4. Coke Charcoal – Obtained from coal

CARBON MONOXIDE (CO)

- Carbon monoxide is an active poison and is very dangerous as it is a colourless and odourless gas and can not, therefore, be easily detected.
- The extremely poisonous nature of carbon monoxide is a result of its combining with the haemoglobin of the blood to form carboxyhaemoglobin, which is not decompassed by any of the processes in the body.

HYDROCARBONS

- Compounds of carbon and hydrogen are called hydrocarbon.
- A natural source of hydrocarbon is petroleum obtained from sedimentary rocks.
- Compounds having the same molecular formula but differ in properties due to different structural formula known as isomers and this property is called isomerism.

SATURATED HYDROCARBONS (ALKANES)

- Containing single covalent bonds only.
- Such compounds are, in general, called alkanes for instance, Methane, Ethane, Propane, Butane.

UNSATURATED HYDROCARBONS

- Containing multiple bonds.
- Compounds with double bonds are called alkenes, e.g. ethylene, propyene etc. and triple bond containing compounds are called alkynes, e.g. acetylene, propyne etc.
- Benzene is an unsaturated cyclic hydrocarbon with the structure.
- Compounds derived from benzene are called aromatic compounds.

FUELS

Solid Fuels

- These contain carbon and, during combustion, form mainly carbon dioxide and carbon monoxide with a large amount of heat.
- Examples of solid fuels are wood, coal, coke and paraffin wax.

Liquid Fuels

- These are basically mixtures of several hydrocarbons. During combustion, they form carbon dioxide and water.
- Liquid fuels are obtained as different fractions during the distillation of petroleum.
- Examples of liquid fuels are kerosene oil, petrol, diesel oil and alcohol.

Gaseous Fuels

- Gaseous fuels do not leave ash on burning and have high content of heat.
- The main gaseous fuels are liquefied petroleum gas (LPG, mainly a mixture of propane and

butane and used in homes for cooking, water gas ($CO + H_2$), producer gas ($CO + N_2$), coal gas (mixture of hydrogen, methane, ethylene, carbon monoxide, nitrogen, oxygen and carbon dioxide) and natural gas (mixture of methane, ethane, propane and butane with traces of higher hydrocarbons obtained from oil well, above petroleum).

PETROLEUM AND NATURAL GAS

- Natural gas contains about 80% methane and 10% ethane, the remaining 10% being a mixture of higher gaseous hydrocarbons.
- Compressed Natural Gas (CNG) is natural gas filled in cylinders under high pressure.
- The quality of petrol for use in car engines is denoted by their anti-knock properties.
- To increase octane number, tetra ethyl lead (TEL) is added to petrol.

HEAVY WATER

- Chemically heavy water is deuterium oxide.
- Heavy water is used in nuclear reactors as a moderator because it slows the fast moving neutrons.

Hard and Soft Water

- Water which produces lather with soap solution readily is called soft water.
- Water which does not produce lather with soap solution readily is called hard water.
- The hardness of water is due to presence of the bicarbonates, chlorides and sulphates of calcium and magnesium.
- Temporary hardness of water is due to the presence of bicarbonates of calcium and magnesium.
- Permanent hardness of water is due to presence of sulphates, chlorides, nitrates of calcium and magnesium.

GLASS

- Ordinary glass is solid mixture of silica, sodium silicate and calcium silicate.
- Soft glass is a soda-lime silicate glass. It melts at low temperature. It is used in manufacturing of bottles, test tubes etc.
- Hard glass is potash lime silicate and melts at high temperature in comparison to soft glass and is used in manufacturing of flask etc.
- Flint glass is a lead potash silicate and is used in manufacturing of prism, lens and optical instruments.
- Pyrex glass is a mixture of sodium aluminium borosilicates. It is used in manufacturing of high quality equipments in laboratory because it does not melt at very high temperature.
- Safety glass is prepared by placing a layer of transparent plastic glass between two layers of glass by means of a suitable adhesive. It is used in making wind screen of automobiles, aeroplanes, trains etc.

CEMENT

- The approximate composition of Portland cement is:
  1. Calcium Oxide → 62%
  2. Silica → 22%
  3. Alumina → 7.5%
  4. Magnesia → 2.5%
  5. Ferric Oxide → 2.5%
- A small amount of gypsum is added to slow down the setting of cement.
- Cement containing excess amount of lime cracks during setting while cement containing less amount of lime is weak in strength.
- Cement containing no iron is white but hard to burn.

POLYMERS AND PLASTICS

- A polymer is a large molecule, built up from many hundreds of thousands of small unit called monomeric units or monomers.
- The process of formation of polymers from monomers is called polymerization.
- Plastics are cross-linked polymers and very tough.
- Some examples of plastics are — Celluloid, Bakelite and Vinyl Plastics.

RUBBER

- Natural and Synthetic rubbers are examples of polymers.
- Natural rubber is isomer of isoprene.

- When the natural rubber is heated along with sulphur called vulcanisation. The resulting rubber is elastic, hard and strong.
- Synthetic rubbers are made by polymerisation of chloroprene, styrene and butadiene mixtures and isobutylene.

SOAPS

- The soaps are sodium salts of higher fatty acids. They are useful only in soft water as they form an insoluble precipitate in hard water. This precipitate consists of salts of calcium and magnesium of higher fatty acids. No lather or emulsion is formed and washing is not possible.

Some Importants Alloys

Alloys	Composition
Brass	Cu, Zn
Bronze	Cu, Sn
Gun metal	Cu, Sn, Zn
Bel metal	Cu, Sn
German silver	Cu, Zn, Ni
Dutch metal	Cu, Zn
Aluminium	Al, Cu
Nichrome	Ni, Fe, Cr, Mn
Chromium steel	Cr, C, Fe

Chemical Formulae, Commercial Name of Chemical Compounds

Commercial Name	Chemical Compounds	Chemical formulae
Common salt	Sodium chloride	$NaCl$
Baking soda	Sodium bicarbonate	$NaHCO_3$
Washing soda	Sodium carbonate	$Na_2CO_3 . 10H_2O$
Caustic soda	Sodium hydroxide	$NaOH$
Chilli salt peter	Sodium nitrate	$NaNO_3$
Soda ash	Sodium carbonate	Na_2CO_3
Hypo	Sodium thiosulphate	$Na_2S_2O_3 . 5H_2O$

BIOLOGY

BRANCHES OF BIOLOGY

(*a*) **Anthropology:** Deals with the scientific study of man and the mankind.

(*b*) **Agronomy:** Deals with the management of farms and science of crop production.

(*c*) **Apiculture:** Deals with the process of bee keeping for commercial purposes.

(*d*) **Entomology:** Deals with the structure, habits and classification of insects.

(*e*) **Eugenics:** Deals with improving the human race.

(*f*) **Pathology:** Deals with the nature of disease, their causes, symptoms, effects, their cure and control.

(*g*) **Physiotherapy:** Deals with the treatment of diseases, body weakness or defects with the help of massage and exercise etc.

(*h*) **Sericulture:** Deals with the production of raw silk from silkworm.

(*i*) **Pharmacology:** Deals with the knowledge and manufacture of drugs.

(*j*) **Occupational therapy:** Deals with treating the physically handicapped or injured persons through exercise etc.

(*k*) **Psychology:** Deals with the study of human mind, its behaviour and mental qualities.

(*l*) **DNA finger printing:** Technique to help identify a person on the basis of genes.

ANIMALS/PLANTS

- The organisms that closely resemble one another

are placed in one group, the groups which have similarities are combined together into larger groups, and these into still larger ones. The most inclusive category is kingdom. Other major categories, in descending order are: phylum, class, order, family, genus, and species. Man belongs to Animal kingdom, chordata division or phylum, Mammalia class, Primates order, Hominidae family, Homo genus and Sapiens species.

CELL THEORY

- Cell is the basic unit of structure of all living organisms. According to the cell theory, all organism are composed of cells and cell products and growth and development results from the division and differentiation of cells.
- Cells membrane surrounds all living cells.
- Nucleus is the most important cell organelle which controls and coordinates all cell activities and also concerned with the transmission of heredity characters.
- Mitochondria, ribosomes, lysosomes and dictyosomes are present in plant and animal cells.
- Only plant cells have cell wall, chloroplast and vacuole.
- Viruses constitute a difficulty since in many ways they are intermediate between living and dead matter.
- The cell is said to be made up of a substance called Protoplasm which has two main constituents cytoplasm and nucleus, and is bounded by a cell membrane on outside.
- Cells take up the raw materials for metabolism through the cell membrane from extracellular fluid surrounding them.
- Cytoplasm inside is responsible for maintaining the internal distribution of organelles and also for free cell movements.
- Mitochondria inside provides energy for reactions inside the cell. Ribosomes are responsible for the synthesis of proteins.
- The Endoplasmic Reticulum helps in addition of other sugar units to proteins and their transportation to other parts of the cell.

FOOD

- It is a nutritive substance taken by an organism for growth, work, repair and maintaining life processes. It provides energy to do work and maintain body heat, provides materials for the growth of the body, makes necessary materials for reproduction and provides materials for the repair of damaged cells and tissues of our body.
- **Carbohydrates:** For a normal person, 400 to 500 gms of carbohydrates are required daily but for sportspersons, growing children and nursing mothers, it is on higher side.
- **Proteins:** They are complex organic compounds made up of carbon, hydrogen, oxygen and nitrogen. The building blocks of Protein are Amino acids and there are large number of amino acids.
- Proteins are essential for the growth of children and teenagers, and for maintenance and making good the wear and tear of the body tissues in adults.
- An adult needs about 1 gm of protein per kg of body weight.
- **Fats:** They are esters of long chain fatty acids and an alcohol called glycerol. Fats also contain atoms of carbon, hydrogen and oxygen.
- The main function of fats in the body is to provide a steady source of energy and for this purpose, they are deposited within the body.
- One gm of fat gives 37 kilojoules of energy which is more than double of that given by carbohydrates.
- Fats, the richest source of energy to our body, can be stored in the body for subsequent use. Fats, soluble in organic solvents and insoluble in water, also supply fat-soluble vitamins to our body.
- **Minerals:** Some of the important minerals needed by our body are — iron, iodine, calcium, phosphorus, sodium, potassium, zinc, copper, magnesium, chloride, fluoride and sulphur.
- We get most of the minerals in combined form from plant sources. Deficiency of these minerals causes many diseases.
- **Energy Requirements:** The energy requirement of a body varies according to age, sex, lifestyle, occupation, climate and special situations like pregnancy and lactation.

Age	Energy requirements
5 years	6000 kJ per day
11 years	9000 kJ per day
18 years	11000 kJ per day
Adult (normal work)	9600 kJ per day
Adult (heavy work)	12000 kJ per day
Adult (very heavy work)	16000 kJ per day

- **Vitamins:** They act as catalysts in certain chemical reactions of metabolism in our body.
- They don't provide energy to our body nor form body tissues.
- More than 15 types of vitamins are known and only 2 vitamins — D and K can be formed in our body.

Vitamin	Necessity	Source
Vitamin A	For maintaining healthy eyesight, normal skin and hair	Cod liver oil, fish, eggs, milk, carrot, leafy vegetables.
Vitamin B_1	For growth, carbohydrate metabolism, functioning of heart, nerves and muscles.	Milk, soya-food, meat, whole cereals, green vegetables.
Vitamin C	For keeping teeth, gums and joints healthy, for increasing resistance of body to infection	Citrus fruits, guava, tomatoes.
Vitamin D	For normal growth of bones and teeth	Milk, eggs, butter, cod liver oil, sun light.
Vitamin E	For normal reproduction, functioning of muscles and protection of liver	Green leafy vegetables, milk, butter, tomato.
Vitamin K	For normal clotting of blood and normal functioning of liver	Green leafy vegetables, soyabean, tomato.

- **Roughage:** Though it does not provide any energy to the body, yet keeps the digestive system in order, by helping in retaining water in the body and preserving constitution.
- The main source of roughage are salads, cabbage, corn cob, porridge, vegetables and fruits with stems.

DISEASES

COMMUNICABLE DISEASES

- They are the diseases which can be transmitted from reservoirs of infection or infected person to the healthy but susceptible persons.
- The disease causing agent or the pathogen can be transmitted directly or indirectly.

DEFICIENCY DISEASES

- These occur due to deficiency of some nutrients in the diet or some hormone due to hypo activity or damage to endocrine glands.

Diet Deficiency	Disease
Protein	Kwashiorkor
Protein-energy malnutrition	Marasmus
Vitamin A	Night-blindness, Xerophthalmia
Vitamin B_1	Beri-Beri
Vitamin B_2	Cheilosis
Vitamin B_5	Pellagra
Vitamin C	Scurvy
Vitamin D	Rickets (in children), (in adult) Osteomalacia
Vitamin K	Hypothrombinemia
Iron	Anaemia
Iodine	Goitre
Fluoride	Dental caries
Calcium and phosphorus	Affects formation of bones and teeth

Hormone Deficiency	Disease
Insulin	Diabetes
Thyroxine	Cretinism (child), Goitre
STH	Dwarfism, Gigantism

ALLERGIC DISEASE

- In these diseases, body becomes hypersensitive to some foreign agents, allergens, which cause inflammation when come in contact with the body or enter inside the body.

- Foreign agents can be dust, pollens, certain-foods, serum, certain drugs or fabrics.
- The unfavourable response of the body to allergens is called allergic reaction. Asthma and hay fever are allergic diseases.

BACTERIAL DISEASES

- Bacteria are minute organisms which are known to cause a number of diseases:

Disease	Incubation period	Spread through
Tuberculosis	2-10 weeks	Air-borne,droplet infection
Diptheria	2-6 days	Air-borne droplet infection
Cholera	6 hours to 2-3 days	Contaminated food and water. House flies are the vectors
Leprosy	Upto 5 years	Prolonged and intimate contact
Whopping cough	7-14 days	Droplet infection
Tetanus	3-21 days	Entry of cysts through any wound made by sharp object, dog bite or fall on the road
Typhoid	1-3 weeks	Directed and Contact
Plague	2-6 days	Rats and bed-bugs transmit the germs
Pneumonia	1-3 days	Air-borne

VIRAL DISEASES

Disease	Incubation period	Spread through
Chicken-pox	12-20 days	Direct contact with infected persons or infected objects
Smallpox	12 days	Droplet infection
Poliomyalitis	7-14 days	Direct and oral
Measles	10 days	Droplet infection
Mumps	12-26 days	Droplet infection
Rabies	1-3 months	Bite of rabied animal like dogs, monkeys, cats
Influenza	24-28 hours	Air-borne

DISEASES CAUSED BY PROTOZOA

- Amoebiasis (Amoebic dysentery), Malaria, Kala-azar, Trypanosomiasis and Giardiasis are main diseases caused by Protozoans.
- Malaria is a parasitic infection.

SYSTEM OF HUMAN BODY

DIGESTIVE SYSTEM

- The digestive system consists of alimentary canal and digestive glands. Alimentary canal is about 8-10 meters long tube of varying diameter. Food is taken in through mouth.
- The tongue helps in ingestion, chewing, tasting and swallowing of food and mixing of food and saliva.
- Salivary glands secret saliva which helps in digestion of starch. Gastric glands present in the mucosa of the stomach, provide acidic medium for the food digestion.
- Liver, the largest sized, reddish brown gland of body, secrets bile. Liver is present in the right upper part of the abdomen. The bile secreted by the liver is stored in gall bladder. It helps in the emulsification and digestion of fats.
- Pancreas is the second largest gland in human body and secretes pancreatic juices. Intestine also secret juices.

RESPIRATORY SYSTEM

- Oxygen is needed for the oxidation and expelling of carbon dioxide is necessary to avoid its-accumulation. This process of exchange of gases between the environment and the body, is called respiration.
- In some unicellular organisms like aerobic bacteria, amoeba, hydra, etc. there is direct exchange of gases between the carbon dioxide of the body and oxygen of water.
- There is no blood for transport of gases. However, in larger and complex form of animals, specialised respiratory organs are developed.
- Amphibians respire through skin, fishes through gills and mammals, birds and reptiles through lungs.
- A normal adult inspires or expires about 500 ml of gas with each breath and about 72 breathes per minutes.

CIRCULATORY SYSTEM

- Main components of the circulatory system are heart, blood vessels and blood.

- Heart is a thick, muscular, contractile and automatic pumping organ. In birds and mammals, heart is divided into four chambers.
- Arteries are thick walled blood vessels which always carry the blood away from the heart to various body parts.
- Veins are thin walled blood vessels which always carry the blood from various parts generally to the heart.
- In an adult healthy person, the normal rate of heart beat at rest is about 70-72 times per minute.

BLOOD

- It is red, opaque, somewhat sticky and viscous fluid in the body of animals.
- It is slightly alkaline (pH = 7.4), heavier than water (sp gr = 1.05) and five times more viscous than distilled water.
- Blood forms 6 to 10% of the body weight.
- An adult, on average, has about 6.8 litres of blood.
- Blood contains plasma and blood corpuscles with the former occupying 55-60% of the volume.
- Plasma transports food components, metabolic wastes and hormones; keeps constant level of pH of blood, maintains body temperature and helps in blood clotting.
- Erythrocytes or red blood corpuscles (RBCs), leukocytes or white blood corpuscles (WBCs) and blood platelets are other parts of the blood.
- Due to the presence of iron containing pigment haemoglobin, RBCs are red in colour. The RBCs are crucial for ex-change of oxygen and carbon dioxide. WBCs are nucleated and non-pigmented cells. They are larger in size than RBCs but far less in number (1 : 600).
- WBCs play an important role in immune system of the body. Blood platelets cause the coagulation of blood and clot formation to prevent excessive bleeding.
- Human blood is divided into four main Groups—A, B, AB and O.
- The plasma of Group A blood contains an anti-B factor and vice-versa, so that people of Groups A and B cannot accept each other's blood.
- Group AB contains neither anti-A nor anti-B factor and people with this group can receive transfusions from both but can give to neither.
- Group O contains both anti-A and anti-B and can receive blood only from Group O but can donate blood to all Groups. Group O is called universal donor because they can donate to all the Groups.
- Group AB is called universal acceptor because they can accept blood from all Groups.

SKELETON SYSTEM

- The frame or the hard structure of the human body is composed from the bones and the organs of making such frame are called skeleton system.

Bones

- Bone is the hardest tissue of the body and form the largest section of the body weight.
- Bones contain organic as well as inorganic matters. With advancing age, the inorganic matter's share increases, causing the bones to become more brittle.
- Long bones such as humerus and femur are hollow while small bones are solid.

EXCRETORY SYSTEM

- In men, excretory system is formed of one pair of kidneys, one pair of ureters, a urinary bladder and a urethra. Kidney is about 10 cm long, bean shaped, dark-red and slightly flattened structure.
- Sweet glands, oil glands, lungs and liver also act as additional excretory organ.
- In case of kidney failure, a man can treated by hemodialysis or transplantation of a kidney from a donor's body.

NERVOUS SYSTEM

- The system which controls and coordinates the body functions, retains memory and receives and sends signals, is called the nervous system.
- The nervous system comprises brain, spinal cord, nerves and nerve fibres.
- Human brain weighs about 1200 to 1400 gm. Main parts of the brain are cerebrum, cerebellum and medulla oblongata.

- Cerebrum controls voluntary function and is site of intelligence, will power, emotions, etc.
- Cerebellum controls involuntary functions like heart beat, respiration, etc.
- Spinal cord is about 45 cm long and about 35 gm in weight. It conducts impulses to and from the brain and controls reflex actions of the body.
- Various cranial (arising from ending into brain) and spinal nerves (arising from spinal cord) control smell, vision, movements of body parts, taste and hearing.

REPRODUCTION SYSTEM

- In this type of reproduction, there is formation and fusion of sex cells, called gametes.
- Organism develops from the zygote through embryo formation.
- It generally involves two parents — male and female.
- The offsprings are different from the parent as variations appear due to new combinations of genes. So, it plays an important role in evolution.
- All higher plants and animals reproduce sexually.

CHROMOSOMES

- Plants and animals have fixed number of chromosomes per cell.
- Genes are located on chromosomes and are responsible for transfer of characteristics from one cell to the next either in the same organism or from parents to offspring.
- Man has 23 pairs of chromosomes, of which one pair is sex chromosomes.
- Males child inherits X chromosomes from the female parent and Y from the male parent.
- Female child receives a X chromosome each from either of its parents.
- Mendel was the first scientist to explain transmission of units from reproductive cells of the parents to the off-springs.

CLONING

- It is the process of producing genetically identical copies of a biological material, starting from a single cell. The original genes are transplanted and thus one can produce organisms of known and desirable characteristics.

GENETIC ENGINEERING

- It is the method of artificial synthesis of new genes and their subsequent transplantation or methods of correcting the defective genes.
- It has helped in producing plants and animals with specific characters.
- So, crippling hereditary diseases can also be cured like hemophilia etc.

DNA FINGERPRINTING

- It consists of examining repetitive DNA in the genome for variations in the length of restriction fragments.
- Every individual has his own pattern, so that fingerprinting can match blood to a particular person, and patterns are inherited from parent to child, allowing the method to identify relationships between individuals.

IN-VITRO FERTILIZATION

- When a sperm and an egg are made to fertilize outside a living body (usually a test tube), it is called in-vitro fertilization.
- This process has been used to impregnate several females who could not do so through natural means.

Diseases and the Parts of Body they Affect

AIDS—Immune system of body	*Gout*—Joints of bone
Arthritis—Inflammation of joints	*Jaundice*—Liver
Asthma—Lungs	*Meningitis*—Brain or spinal cord
Cataract—Eyes	*Pleurisy*—Pleura (inflammation of)
Conjunctivitis—Eyes	*Polio*—motor neurons
Diabetes—Pancreas	*Pneumonia*—Lungs
Diphtheria—Throat	*Pyorrhoea*—Sockets of teeth
Glaucoma—Eyes	*Tuberculosis*—Lungs
Eczema—Skin	*Typhoid*—Intestine
Goitre—Front of the neck (due to enlargement of thyroid gland)	*Malaria*—Spleen
	Leukaemia—Blood
	Rickets—Bones

SPACE RESEARCH

First in Space

✶ First creator of rules regarding space research	Isaac Newton
✶ First artificial satellite launched in space	Sputnik-1 (1957)
✶ First living being sent in space	Louika (a dog)
✶ Firstever manned spacecraft	Vostok-I
✶ First man in space	Yuri Gagarin U.S.S.R. (1961)
✶ First woman in space	Valentina Tereshkova U.S.S.R. (June 1963)
✶ First man who moved in space out of the spacecraft	Alexi Livonov U.S.S.R. (June 1965)
✶ First person to land on moon	Neil Armstrong, America (21st July, 1969)
✶ First fourwheeled carriage without human being on moon	Leunokhev-I U.S.S.R. (1970)
✶ First space lab in orbit	Skylab (America, 1973)
✶ First space shuttle	Columbia (America, 1981)
✶ First Indian (man) in space	Squadron leader—Rakesh Sharma (13th April, 1984)
✶ First Indian (Woman) in space	Kalpana Chawla (19th Nov., 1997)
✶ First American woman in space	Sailyride (1983)
✶ First spacecraft on Mars	Pathfinder (6 July, 1997)
✶ First woman who lead spacecraft	Allin Collis (America)
✶ First spacecraft without man	Shenzoo, China (20th Nov. 1999)

Indian Space Programme : At a Glance

Satellite	*Date*	*Type*	*Launch Vehicle*	*Result*
Aryabhatta	19-04-75	Scientific	Cosmos	successful
Bhaskara I	07-06-79	Geosurvey	Cosmos	successful
Rohini	10-08-79	Geosurvey	S.L.V.3	unsuccessful
Rohini D-1	18-07-80	Geosurvey	S.L.V.3	successful
Rohini	31-05-81	Scientific	S.L.V.3	successful
Apple	19-06-81	Communication	Ariane	successful
Bhaskara II	20-11-81	Geosurvey	Cosonos	successful
INSAT-1A	10-04-82	Multipurpose	Delta	unsuccessful
Rohini	17-04-83	Scientific	S.L.V.3	successful
INSAT-1B	30-08-83	Multipurpose	Space Shuttle	successful
SROSS I	24-03-87	Technical	ASLV-D1	unsuccessful
IRS-1A	17-03-88	Remote sensing	Vostok	successful
SROSS II	17-07-88	Technical	ASLV-D2	unsuccessful
INSAT-1C	21-07-88	Multipurpose	Ariane-4	unsuccessful
INSAT-1D	12-06-90	Multipurpose	Delta	successful
IRS-1B	29-08-91	Remote sensing	Vostok	successful
INSAT-2A	10-07-92	Multipurpose	Ariane	successful
INSAT-1D	12-06-90	Multipurpose	Delta	successful
IRS-1B	29-08-91	Remote sensing	Vostok	successful
INSAT-2A	10-07-92	Multipurpose	Ariane	successful
IRS-ID	29-09-97	Remote sensing	PSLV	successful
INSAT-3B	22-03-2000	Multipurpose	Ariane	successful

Satellite	Date	Type	Launch Vehicle	Result
G-SAT-1	18-04-2001	Multipurpose	GSLV-D	successful
INSAT-3E	28-09-2003	Communication	Ariane-5	successful
Cartosat-1 & hamsat	05-05-2005	Maping and Communication	PSLV-C6	successful
Chandrayaan-I	22-10-2008	Maping and Scientific	PSLV-C11	successful
CARTOSAT-2B	12-07-2010	Communication	PSLV-C15	successful
GSAT-12	15-07-2011	Communication	PSLV-C17	successful
RISAT-1	26-04-2012	Remote Sensing	PSLV-C19	successful
GSAT-7	30-08-2013	Defence	Ariane-5	successful
MOM	5-11-2013	Mapping	PSLV-C25	successful
IRNSS-1B	04-04-2014	Mapping and Scientific	PSLV-C24	successful
GSAT-16	07-12-2014	Communication	Ariane-5	successful
IRNSS-1D	28-03-2015	Mapping and Scientific	PSLV-C27	successful
IRNSS-1E	20-01-2016	Mapping and Scientific	PSLV-C31	successful
Cartosat-2 & others	22-06-2016	Mapping and Scientific	PSLV-C34	successful
Scatsat-1 & others	26-09-2016	Multipurpose	PSLV-C35	successful
RESOURCESAT-2A	07-12-2016	Remote Sensing	PSLV-C36	successful
CARTOSAT-2 & 103 others	15-02-2017	Multipurpose	PSLV-C37	successful
GSAT-17	29-06-2017	Earth observation Satellite	Ariane-5 ECA	successful
Cartosat-2F & others	12-01-2018	Multipurpose	PSLV-C40	successful
GSAT-6A	29-03-2018	Communication	GSLV-F08	successful
GSAT-7A	19-12-2018	Military Satellite	GSLV-MK-II-F11	successful
Cartosat-3	27-11-2019	Earth Imagine Satellite	PSLV-C47	successful
GSAT-30	17-01-2020	Communication	Ariane-5	successful
EOS-01	07-11-2020	Earth Observation	PSLV-C49	successful
CMS-01/GSAT-12R	17-12-2020	Communication	PSLV-XLC50	successful
Amejonia and 19 others	28-02-2021	Communication	PSLV-C51	successful
EOS-04	14-02-2022	Earth Observation	PSLV-C52	successful
GSAT-24"	23-06-2022	Communication	Ariane-5	successful
DS-E0 and others	30-06-2022	Mapping	PSLV-C53	successful
Oceansat-3 and 8 others	26-11-2022	Earth observation Satellite	PSLV-C54	successful
EOS-07	10-02-2023	Earth observation Satellite	SSLV-02	successful
TeLEOS-2 and LUMILITE-4	22-04-2023	Communication	PSLV-C55	successful
Chandrayaan-3	14-07-2023	Lunar observation	LVM-3	successful
DS-SAR and 6 others	30-07-2023	Earth observation	PSLV-C56	successful
Aditya-L1	02-09-2023	Solar Mission	PSLV-C57	successful
XPoSat	01-01-2024	Earth observation	PSLV-C58	successful
INSAT-3DS	17-02-2024	Meteorological	GSLV-F14	successful
EOS-08	16-08-2024	Earth observation	SSLV-D3	successful
Proba-3	05-12-2024	Earth Observation	PSLV-C59	successful
NVS-02	29-01-2025	Navigation	GSLV-F15	successful
NISAR	30-07-2025	Earth Observation	GSLV-F16	successful
CMS-03	02-11-2025	Communication	LVM3-M5	successful
BlueBird Block-2	24-12-2025	Communication	LVM3-M6	successful

COMPUTER

- The computer is the system of that electronic device through which various informations are processed on the basis of a definite set of instructions called program and mathematical (numerical) and non-mathematical both types of informations are processed.
- The first mechanical computer was composed or fabricated by Blaise Pascal in 1642 and it is called Pascalene.
- But in 1833, Charles Babbage first time conceived an automatic calculator or computer.
- Charles Babbage is called the father of modern computer.
- Herman made an electronic tabulating machine based on punch cards which operates automatically.
- In 1937, first mechanical computer Mark-I was fabricated by Howard Akeen.
- The most outstanding contribution in the development of modern computer goes to John Wan Newmaan who brought the 2nd revolution in the area of computer in 1951.
- He discovered EDVAC (Electronic Discrete Variable Automatic Computer) and utilised the stored program and the binary number system in the computer.

FUNCTIONS OF COMPUTER

- 1. Collection and composition (input) of datas;
  2. Storage of datas.
  3. Processing of datas.
  4. Retrieval or output of the proccessed informations and datas.

UNITS OF COMPUTER

1. Input unit.
2. Central processing unit–CPU.
3. External Memory unit.
4. Output unit.

- The CPU of the computer is called brain of the computer and sometimes CPU is also called Micro Processor of the computer.
- The data is entered through the input unit in the computer and through the central processing unit with the help of External Memory Unit datas are arranged and processed.
- Ultimately by the output unit these datas or informations are issued or released.

PARTS OF COMPUTER

- **Monitor :** The monitor of the computer is like a television in which the picture appears in the form of doted points on the screen and these are called pixels.
- **Hard Disc and Floppy Disc :** The Hard Disc is the permanent disc in the computers while the Floppy Disc is the disc utilised when datas or informations are to be transferred from one computer to another.
- **Mouse :** The mouse of the computer is like the remote control of TV through which computer is directly regulated or controlled without utilising the key-board.
- **Printer :** The printer is a device which prints any documents or processed informations of the computer.

SOME HIGH LEVEL LANGUAGES

1. **FORTRAN :** This language was developed for solving the mathematical formulae very quickly and conveniently.
2. **COBOL :** This language was developed for the commerical purposes. For the processing of this language a group of sentences is selected called paragraph and all paragraphs composed are called a section, while all sections composed are called a division.
3. **BASIC :** In basic a definite part of the prescribed instruction is only inserted in the computer.
4. **ALGOL :** This was basically fabricated and designed for the complex algebraic calculations.
5. **PASCAL :** It is an amplified and modified form of ALGOL.

6. **COMAL :** This computer language is used for the students of secondary level.
7. **LOGO :** This language is used for children and kids for drawing Graphic line diagrams.
8. **PROLOG :** This language is developed in 1973 in France and is used for Artificial Intelligence which is capable and equivalent to the logical program.
9. **FORTH :** This language was invented by Charles Mure which is frequently used in all types of the works in the computer.

COMPUTER VIRUS

- The computer virus is an electronic code which is used to abolish or erradicate the inclusive informations or programs of the computer.
- Some important computer viruses are Micheleanjalo, Dork Avangor, kilo, filip, Macmug, Scores, Casecade, Jeruslem, Date crime, Coloumbs crime, Internet virus, Pachcom, Pach EXE, COM-EXE, Marizuana, C-brain, bloody, Chenge Mungu and Desi etc.

COMPUTER NETWORKING

- There are two types of networkings which are usually occur—Local Area Networking (LAN) and Wide Area Networking (WAN).

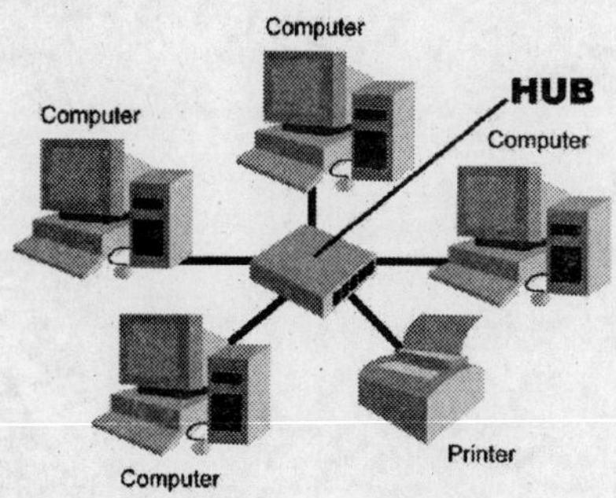

- By LAN all the computers of the same buildings are connected like the computers of university premises, computers of offices etc.
- By WAN all the comptuers of a large area are connected like the computers of all the offices of a city or town etc.
- In India a very large computer network namely INDONET has been installing through which all the main towns and cities has to be interlinked.

COMPUTER TERMINOLOGY

- **Bit :** The bit is a unit of measurement of the electronic data. One bit is either 0 or 1 but not both. On composing 8 bits, 1 byte is formed.
- **Bug :** The Bug is the error in the computer program or system and its eradication is called Debug.
- **Byte :** Total eight bits compose a byte. Thus 8 bits = 1 byte.
- **CD-ROM :** A CD like of music CD in which data can be stored substantially called CD-ROM. In a CD with comparison to floppy extremely more datas can be stored but one problem in it is that one time recorded data can not be deleted or modified.
- **Chip :** It is a thin slice on which by a special mechanism a circuit is designed which is normally made from Silicon.
- **Memory System :** The place where computer data and program are temporarily kept is called Memory system. Usually memory is implied from RAM.
- **Modem :** The device which converts digital signals into analogue signals and vice-versa is called Modem.
- **RAM :** It is Random Access Memory (a place) where datas to be processed are kept temporarily and it is unstable memory.
- **ROM :** It is Read Only Memory and it is stable or Non-valatile memory which doesn't ended after power off.
- **Scanner :** It is a device through which graphic image is transformed to digital image and the scanners are of usually two types one desktop and another hand operating.

PROGRAMING

- Computers perform phenomenal feats of calculation, but they do not do so in a complicated way.

- They actually carry out very simple operations, such as addition and subtraction.
- They achieve their fantastic computing power by carrying out these operations at incredible speed.
- The programme, or set of instructions for operating the computer, is therefore written as a sequence of very simple steps.

Several computer languages have been developed for different applications, including BASIC, COBOL, FORTRAN and PASCAL. Writing programmes is very skilled and time-consuming work.

- But for most typical computer applications ready-written programmes are available, called "packages".

❐ ❐ ❐

GENERAL KNOWLEDGE

FIRST IN THE WORLD

✶ First Chinese visitor to India	*Fahien*
✶ First foreign invader of India	*Alexander, the Great (Greek)*
✶ First person to climb Mt. Everest	*Tenzing Norgay (India) and Edmund Hillary (New Zealand) (1953)*
✶ First atom bomb dropped at	*Hiroshima (Japan)*
✶ First man in the space	*Yuri Gagarin (former USSR)*
✶ First woman in the space	*Valentina Tereshkova (former USSR)*
✶ First person to walk in the space	*Alexei Leonov (former USSR)*
✶ First person to land on the moon	*Neil Armstrong (USA)*
✶ First and the only woman to have climbed Mt. Everest twice	*Santosh Yadav (Indian; May, 1992; May, 1993)*
✶ First person on Mt. Everest without oxygen	*Phu Dorjee (Indian; May 9, 1984)*
✶ First person to climb Mt. Everest twice	*Nawang Gombu*
✶ First President of the USA	*George Washington*
✶ First woman Prime Minister	*Sirimavo Bandaranaike (Sri Lanka)*
✶ First person to swim across English Channel	*Mathew Webb*
✶ First woman to swim across English Channel	*Gertrude Caroline Ederle*
✶ First woman to climb Mt. Everest	*Junko Tábei (Japan)*
✶ First woman to climb Mt. Everest alone and without oxygen supplies	*Alison Hargreaves (Britain: May 13, 1995)*
✶ First Aeroplane to fly around the world without refuelling	*Voyager (Dec. 1986)*
✶ First test-tube Baby	*Louise Brown (UK; 1978)*
✶ First all-talking Film	*Jaz Singer (1927)*
✶ First Secretary-General of the UN	*Trygve Lie (Norway: 1946-53)*
✶ First woman President of the UN General Assembly	*Vijayalakshmi Pandit (India: 1953)*
✶ First woman to reach North Pole	*Ann Bancroft (1986)*
✶ First person to reach North Pole	*Robert Peary*
✶ First person to reach South Pole	*Amundsen (1911)*
✶ First woman to command Spacecraft in Space	*Ellin Collins*

SUPERLATIVES (WORLD)
(The Largest, Biggest, Smallest, Longest, Highest)

Airport	*Largest*	King Fahd International Airport, Dammam (Saudi Arabia)
Animal,	*Tallest*	Giraffe (Average height 6.09 m)
	Largest and Heaviest	Blue Whale (190 tonnes)
	Longest recorded	Boot lace Worm (55 m)
	Fastest	Cheetah (Approximately 100 km/hr)
Bay,	*With max. shore line*	Hudson Bay (Canada: 12268 km)
	With maximum area	Bay of Bengal (India: 217 million hc)
Building,	*Tallest*	Burj Khalifa (Dubai, 818 meter)
Canal,	*Big ship (longest)*	Suez Canal (160 km)
	Busiest	Kiel Canal (North Sea)
Canyon/Gorge,	*Deepest*	Hells Canyon, Snake River (Idaho : 7900 ft)
	Largest	Grand Canyon (Colarado River; USA; 446 km)
Church,	*Largest*	Basilica of St. Peter (Vatican City Rome– Area 23000 sq.m.)
City,	*Largest in Area*	Jiuquan Gansu, China (Area 1,67,996 Sq km)
Continent,	*biggest*	Asia (30,928,605 km^2)
	Smallest	Australia Mainland (Area 8,426,635 km^2)
Country,	*Largest in Population* (2021)	China (over 138.5 crore)
	Largest in Area	Russia (17,075,000 sq. km)
	With largest electorate	India (over 90 crores)
	Smallest independent	State of Vatican City (109 acre)
Delta,	*Largest*	Sundarban's Ganga-Brahmaputra delta (1,05,000 sq. km)
Desert,	*Largest*	Sahara (N. Africa; maximum length 5,150 km EW; maximum width 3,200 km NS)
Dome,	*Largest*	Singapore National Stadium (310 m)
Epic,	*Longest*	Mahabharata
Fish,	*Largest fresh water*	Plabeuk (China, Laos and Thailand)
	Most abundant	Bristle mouth
	Most venomous	Stone Fish (Indo-Pacific Waters)
Film,	*Most Oscars*	Ben Hur (11 Oscars–1959); Titanic (11 Oscars–1998); The Lord of Rings : The Return of the King (11 Oscars—2003).
Fountain,	*Tallest*	King Fahd's Fountain (Jeddah, Saudi Arabia)
Fruit,	*Most nutritive*	Avocado (Vitamins A, C, E and Proteins; Central and South America)
	Least nutritive	Cucumber

Gulf,	*Largest*	Gulf of Mexico (1,544,000 sq. km)
Island,	*Biggest*	Greenland (2,175,000 sq km)
Lake,	*Largest*	Caspian Sea (Azerbaijan, Russia, Iran border: 37.18 lakh km^2)
	Deepest	Baikal (Siberia)
	Largest (fresh water)	Superior Lake (USA–Canada border: 82,350 km^2)
Library,	*Biggest*	United States Library of Congress (Washington D.C. founded in 1800, contains 101 million items)
	Biggest non-statutory	New York Public Library
Mountain,	*Highest peak*	Mt. Everest (8848 m; Nepal)
	Highest range	Himalayas, Asia (upto 4200 m)
	Greatest mountain range	Himalaya-Karakoram (96 out of 109 peaks over 7315 m are here)
Museum,	*Largest*	American Museum of Natural History, New York
Ocean,	*Largest and Deepest*	The Pacific (Area: 166,240,000 km^2; Depth: 10,924 m)
Peninsula,	*Largest*	Arabia (3.25 million sq. km)
Places,	*Rainiest (annual mean)*	Mowsyrnam near Cherapunji (Meghalaya; India; 11873 mm)
Planet,	*Biggest*	Jupiter (equatorial diameter 142984 km)
	Brightest, hottest and nearest to Earth	Venus
	Nearest to Sun	Mercury
Plateau,	*Highest*	Tibetan Plateau (Central Asia: 4900 m)
Platform,	*Longest (rail)*	Shree Siddharoodha Swamiji Railway Station Hubballi, Karnataka, India (1507 m. long)
Railway Line,	*Longest*	Trans-Siberian Railway (Moscow-Nakhodka: 9438 km)
Railway Station,	*Largest*	Grand Central Terminal (New York City; 19 hc)
Religion,	*Oldest*	Hinduism
Religion,	*Largest*	Christianity
Rivers,	*Longest*	(i) Nile (6650 km) (ii) Amazon (6437 km)
Road,	*Longest*	Pan American Highway (from Alaska-Brasila: 24140 km)
Star,	*Brightest*	Sirius A (also called Dog Star)
Swimming	*Longest*	English Channel
Telescope,	*Largest (radio)*	Five Hundred meter Apertune Spherical Telescope (FAST), China.
Temple,	*Largest*	Angkor Wat (Cambodia: 402 acres)
Tunnel,	*Longest (railway)*	Gotthard Base Rail Tunnel (Switzerland; 57.1 km)
	Largest (road)	Laerdal, Norway (24.51 km)

Volcano	*Greatest concentration in*	Indonesia
	Highest (extinct)	Cerro Aconcagua (6960 m; Andes)
	Highest (dormant)	Volcan Llullaillaco (6723 m; Argentina-Chile)
	Highest (active)	Ojos del Salado (Chile-Argentina)
Waterfall,	*Highest*	Salto-Angel (in Venezuela on a branch of river Carrao, depth 807 m.)
	Largest	Khone Falls (Laos; width 10.8 km)

CAPITAL & CURRENCIES

Country	Capital	Currency
✶ Afghanistan	Kabul	Afghani
✶ Albania	Tirana	Lek
✶ Algeria	Algiers	Dinar
✶ Angola	Luanda	New Kwanza
✶ Argentina	Buenos Aires	Peso
✶ Armenia	Yeravan	Dram
✶ Australia	Canberra	Dollar
✶ Austria	Vienna	Euro
✶ Azerbaijan	Baku	Manat
✶ Bahrain	Manama	Dinar
✶ Bangladesh	Dhaka	Taka
✶ Barbados	Bridgetown	Dollar
✶ Belarus	Minsk	Ruble
✶ Belgium	Brussels	Euro
✶ Benin	Porto Novo	Franc CFA
✶ Bhutan	Thimphu	Ngultrum
✶ Bolivia	La paz	Boliviano
✶ Botswana	Gaborone	Pula
✶ Brazil	Brasilia	Real (BRL)
✶ Bosnia Herzegovina	Sarajevo	Convertible Marka
✶ Bulgaria	Sofia	Euro
✶ Cambodia	Phnom-Penh	Riel
✶ Canada	Ottawa	Dollar
✶ Chile	Santiago	Peso
✶ China	Beijing	Yuan
✶ Colombia	Bogota	Peso
✶ Congo Republic	Brazzaville	Franc CFA
✶ Croatia	Zagreb	Euro
✶ Cuba	Havana	Peso
✶ Cyprus	Nicosia	Euro
✶ Czech Republic	Prague	Koruna
✶ Denmark	Copenhagen	Krone
✶ Ecuador	Quito	Dollar
✶ Egypt	Cairo	Pound
✶ Estonia	Tallinn	Euro
✶ Ethiopia	Addis Ababa	Birr
✶ Fiji	Suva	Dollar
✶ Finland	Helsinki	Euro
✶ France	Paris	Euro
✶ Georgia	Tbilisi	Lari
✶ Germany	Berlin	Euro
✶ Ghana	Accra	Cedi
✶ Greece	Athens	Euro
✶ Guatemala	Guatemala City	Quetzal

Country	Capital	Currency
* Guyana	George Town	Dollar
* Hungary	Budapest	Forint
* Iceland	Reykjavik	Krona
* India	New Delhi	Rupee
* Indonesia	Jakarta	Rupiah
* Iran	Teheran	Rial
* Iraq	Baghdad	Dinar
* Ireland	Dublin	Euro
* Israel	Jerusalem	Shekel
* Italy	Rome	Euro
* Jamaica	Kingston	Dollar
* Japan	Tokyo	Yen
* Jordan	Amman	Dinar
* Kazakhstan	Astana	Tenge
* Kenya	Nairobi	Shilling
* Korea (S)	Seoul	Won
* Korea (N)	Pyongyang	Won
* Kyrgyzstan	Bishkek	Som
* Kuwait	Kuwait City	Dinar
* Laos	Vientiane	Kip
* Latvia	Riga	Euro
* Lebanon	Beirut	Pound
* Liberia	Monrovia	Dollar
* Libya	Tripoli	Dinar
* Lithuania	Vilnius	Euro
* Luxembourg	Luxembourg	Euro
* Macedonia	Skopje	Dinar
* Malawi	Lilongwe	Kwacha
* Malaysia	Kuala Lumpur	Ringgit
* Maldives	Male	Rufiyaa
* Mali	Bamako	Franc
* Mauritius	Port Louis	Rupee

Country	Capital	Currency
* Mexico	Mexico City	Peso
* Moldavia	Chisinau	Leu
* Mongolia	Ulan Bator	Tugrik
* Morocco	Rabat	Dirham
* Mozambique	Maputo	Metical
* Myanmar	Nay Pyi Taw	Kyat
* Namibia	Windhoek	Dollar
* Nepal	Kathmandu	Rupee
* Netherlands	Amsterdam	Euro
* New Zealand	Wellington	Dollar
* Nigeria	Abuja	Naira
* Norway	Oslo	Krone
* Oman	Muscat	Rial
* Pakistan	Islamabad	Rupee
* Panama	Panama City	Balboa
* Peru	Lima	New Sole
* Philippines	Manila	Peso
* Poland	Warsaw	Zloty
* Portugal	Lisbon	Euro
* Qatar	Doha	Riyal
* Romania	Bucharest	Leu
* Russia	Moscow	Ruble
* Saudi Arabia	Riyadh	Rial
* Senegal	Dakar	Franc
* Slovakia	Bratislava	Euro
* Spain	Madrid	Euro
* Sri Lanka	Colombo	Rupee
* Sudan	Khartoum	Dinar
* Suriname	Paramaribo	Guilder
* Sweden	Stockholm	Krona
* Switzerland	Berne	Swiss Francs
* Syria	Damascus	Pound

Country	Capital	Currency
✶ South Africa	Capetown (Legislative) Pretoria *(Administrative)*	Rand
✶ Tajikistan	Dushanbe	Somani
✶ Taiwan	Taipei	Dollar
✶ Tanzania	Dodoma	Shilling
✶ Thailand	Bangkok	Baht
✶ Tunisia	Tunis	Dinar
✶ Turkiye	Ankara	Lira
✶ Turkmenistan	Ashgabat	Manat
✶ Uganda	Kampala	Shilling
✶ Ukraine	Kiev	Hryvna
✶ United Arab Emirates	Abu Dhabi	Dirham
✶ U.K.	London	Pound Sterling
✶ U.S.A.	Washington	Dollar
✶ Uruguay	Montevideo	Peso
✶ Uzbekistan	Tashkent	Som
✶ Venezuela	Caracas	Bolivar
✶ Vietnam	Hanoi	Dong
✶ Yemen	Sana'a	Rial
✶ Zimbabwe	Harare	Dollar
✶ Congo (Democratic Republic)	Kinshasa	Franc CDF
✶ Zambia	Lusaka	Kwacha

GEOGRAPHICAL EXPLORATIONS/DISCOVERIES

Place	Explorer/Discoverer	Nationality	Year
America	Christopher Columbus	Italy	1492
Hawaii Islands (Sandwich Islands)	Captain James Cook	England	1778
Newfoundland	John Cabot	England	1497
New Zealand	Abel Janszoon Tasman	Holland	1642
North Pole	Robert Peary	USA	1909
Sea Route to India (via Cape of Good Hope)	Vasco da Gama	Portugal	1498
South Pole	Roald Amundsen	Norway	1911

NATIONAL MONUMENTS OF SOME FAMOUS COUNTRIES

Monument	Country	Monument	Country
Great Wall of China	China	Pyramid (Giza)	Egypt
Taj Mahal (Agra)	India	Kinder Disk	Denmark
Emperial Palace (Tokyo)	Japan	Leaning Tower of Pisa	Italy
Opera House (Sydney)	Australia	Statue of Liberty (New York)	USA
Eiffel Tower (Paris)	France	Kremlin (Moscow)	Russia

INTELLIGENCE AGENCIES OF SOME PROMINENT COUNTRIES

Country	Intelligence Agency
* India	*Research & Analysis Wing (RAW), Intelligence Bureau (I.B.), Central Bureau of Investigation (C.B.I.)*
* Pakistan	*Inter Service Intelligence (I.S.I.)*
* U.S.A.	*Central Intelligence Agency (CIA), Federal Bureau of Investigation (FBI)*
* Britain	*Military Intelligence (M.I.)-5 and 6, Special Branch, Ultra, Joint Intelligence Organisation*
* Israel	*Mosad*
* Egypt	*Mukhabarat*
* Japan	*Nicho*
* Russia	*K.G.B. (Komitel Gosudarstvennoy Bezopasnosty) (Committee for State Security)*
* Canada	*Security Intelligence Service (SIS)*
* S. Africa	*Bureau of State Security (BSS)*
* Iran	*Sabak*
* Iraq	*Al-Mukhabarat*
* Australia	*Australian Security and Intelligence Organisation (ASIO)*
* France	*S.D.E.C.E.*
* Spain	*C.E.S.I.D.*

MAJOR LANGUAGES OF THE WORLD AND THEIR SPEAKERS

Listing the languages spoken by approximately 1% of humankind (those spoken by more than 60,000,000 people), this table enumerates speakers of each tongue as a primary language.

Language	Speakers (millions)
* Chinese	1,322
* Spanish	471
* English	369
* Arabic	349
* Hindi	342
* Portuguese	232
* Bengali	228
* Russian	153
* Japanese	126
* Lahnda	99
* Punjabi (Western)	93
* Javanese	84
* Marathi	83
* Telugu	82
* Turkish	82
* Malay	81
* French	79
* Korean	77
* Tamil	77
* German	76
* Vietnamese	76
* Urdu	69
* Italian	64
* Persian	65

Source : The World Almanac 2022

IMPORTANT NEWS AGENCIES OF THE WORLD

Agency	Country
PTI, UNI, UNIVARTA	India
Antara	Indonesia
Tanjug	Serbia
Associated Press (AP)	America
Reuters, NAFEN	United Kingdom
Angence France Press (AFP)	France
TASS	Russia

NAME OF PARLIAMENTS OF SOME COUNTRIES

Country	Name of Parliament	Country	Name of Parliament
Afghanistan	Shora	Norway	Storting
Argentina	National Congress	Poland	Sejm
Australia	Federal Parliament	Russia	Federal Assembly (Council of the Federation and State Duma
Austria	National Assembly	South Africa	National Assembly and Senate
Bangladesh	Jatiya Sansad	Spain	Cortes Generales
India	Lok Sabha and Rajya Sabha	Sweden	Riksdag
Bhutan	Tshogdu (National Assembly)	Switzerland	Federal Assembly (Nationalrat and Standerat)
Britain	House of Commons and House of Lords	North Korea	Supreme People's Assembly
Canada	House of Commons and Senate	South Korea	National Assembly
China	National People Congress	U.S.A.	Congress (Senate and House of Representatives)
Denmark	Folketing	Ethiopia	Federal Council and House of Representatives
Iran	Majlis (Islamic Consultative Assembly)	Iceland	Alpingi
Israel	Knesset	Bulgaria	National Assembly
Japan	Diet	Cuba	National Assembly of People's Power
Myanmar	Pyithu Hluttaw (People's Assembly)		
Nepal	Rashtriya Panchayat		
The Netherlands	States-General		

LARGEST AND SMALLEST COUNTRIES (Top 5)

Largest Country (Area-wise)	Largest Country (Population-wise, 2021)	Smallest Country (Area-wise)	Smallest Country (Population-wise, 2021)
Russia	China	Vatican City	Vatican City
Canada	India	Monaco	Nauru
China	USA	Nauru	Tuvalu
United States	Indonesia	Tuvalu	Palau
Brazil	Brazil	San Marino	San Marino

MAJOR RELIGIONS OF THE WORLD

Religion	Member	Percentage	Religion	Member	Percentage
Christianity	2.5 billion	32.2%	Buddhism	545 million	6.9%
Islam	1.9 billion	24.7%	Sikhism	27 million	0.27%
Hinduism	1.0 billion	13.5%	Jews	14 million	0.14%

NATIONAL EMBLEMS OF IMPORTANT COUNTRIES

Country	National Emblem	Country	National Emblem
America	Golden Rod	Australia	Kangaroo
Ireland	Shamrock	Italy	White Lily
Israel	Candelabrum	Iran	Rose
Canada	White Lily	Great Britain	Rose
Chile	Candor and Huemul	Germany	Corn Flower
Japan	Chrysanthemum	Zimbabwe	Zimbabwe Bird
Denmark	Beach	Turkiye	Crescent and Star
The Netherlands	Lion	New Zealand	Kiwi, Fern Southern Cross
Norway	Lion	Nepal	Kukri
Pakistan	Crescent	Poland	Eagle
France	Lily	Belgium	Lion
Bangladesh	Water Lily	Mongolia	The Soyombo
Russia	Double headed eagle	Lebanon	Cedar Tree
Sudan	Secretary Bird	Syria	Eagle
India	Lioned Capital		

FIRST IN INDIA

✶ The first Indian to get the Nobel Prize for Literature	*Rabindra Nath Tagore*
✶ The first Indian to get the Nobel Prize for Physics	*C.V. Raman*
✶ The first Indian to get the Nobel Prize for Peace	*Mother Teresa*
✶ The first Indian to get the Nobel Prize for Economics	*Amartya Sen*
✶ The first Indian to get Special Oscar award (1992)	*Satyajit Ray*
✶ The first and the last Indian Governor-General of free India	*C. Rajagopalachari*
✶ The first woman to become the Governor of a State	*Smt. Sarojini Naidu*
✶ The first Indian Commenders-in-Chief	*General K.M. Cariappa*
✶ The first ever woman to become the Chief Minister of a State	*Smt. Sucheta Kripalani*
✶ The first Indian woman President of UN General Assembly	*Smt. Vijaylakshmi Pandit*
✶ The first Indian to become the President of International Court of Justice	*Dr. Nagendra Singh*
✶ The first Indian woman to swim across the English Channel	*Ms. Aarti Saha*
✶ The first Indian girl to become Miss Universe	*Miss Sushmita Sen*
✶ The first Indian girl to become Miss World	*Rita Faria*
✶ The first Indian to swim across the English Channel	*Mihir Sen*
✶ The first Field Marshal	*S.H.F.J. Manekshaw*
✶ The first Indian recipient of Victoria Cross	*Khudadad Khan*
✶ The first Indian to conquer Mt. Everest	*Sherpa Tenzing (May 29, 1953)*
✶ The first Indian Cosmonaut (man)	*Rakesh Sharma (April 3, 1984)*

✱ The first Indian Cosmonaut (woman)	*Kalpana Chawla (Nov. 19, 1997)*
✱ The first woman to climb Mt. Everest	*Miss Bachendri Pal (May 23, 1984)*
✱ The first ICS	*Satyendranath Tagore*
✱ The first to address the UN General Assembly in Hindi	*Atal Bihari Vajpayee*
✱ The first Newspaper	*Bengal Gazette (Jan 27, 1780)*
✱ The first Postage Stamp issued	*In 1852*
✱ The first Telegraph line laid	*In 1851 (Kolkata-Diamond Harbour)*
✱ The first Railways run	*April 16, 1853 (Mumbai-Thane)*
✱ The first Electric Train run	*1925 (Mumbai-Kurla)*
✱ The first Atomic Power Station	*Tarapore (Maharashtra)*
✱ The first passenger-cum-cargo ship made in India	*Harshavardhan*
✱ The first Satellite	*Aryabhatta (1975)*
✱ The first President of the Indian National Congress	*W.C. Banerjee*
✱ The first President of Indian Republic	*Dr. Rajendra Prasad*
✱ The first woman judge of the Supreme Court	*Ms Fatima Bibi*
✱ The first to climb Everest without oxygen	*Phu Dorjee (1987)*
✱ The first film (movie)	*Raja Harishchandra*
✱ The first film (talkie)	*Alam Ara*
✱ The first Metro Railway	*Kolkata Metro Railway*
✱ The first Test-tube baby, scientifically documented	*Born on August 6, 1986 at K.E.M. Hospital, Bombay*
✱ The first TV Centre	*At Delhi*
✱ The first Indian to get an Oscar	*Bhanu Athaiya*
✱ The first woman pilot in IAF	*Ms Harita Kaur Deol*
✱ The first woman to get Olympic Medal	*Karnam Malleswari*
✱ The first woman Foreign Secretary	*Chokila Iyer*

SUPERLATIVES (INDIA)

Highest, Biggest, Largest and Longest in India

✱ Award for Gallantry, highest	*Param Vir Chakra*
✱ Award, highest civilian	*Bharat Ratna*
✱ Bank, with largest number of branches	*State Bank of India*
✱ Road Bridge, Longest	*Bhupen Hazarika Bridge, Assam (9.15 km)*
✱ Road and Rail Bridge, Longest	*Bogibeel Bridge, Brahmaputra River, Assam*
✱ Cattle Fair, Largest	*Sonepur (Bihar)*
✱ City, Most Populous	*Mumbai metropolis*
✱ Corridor, Longest	*Rameshwaram Temple corridor (4,000 ft.)*
✱ Desert, Largest	*Thar (Rajasthan)*
✱ Dam, Longest	*Hirakud Dam (Odisha)*
✱ Delta, Largest	*Sunderban's Delta*

∗ Dome, Largest	*Gol Gumbaj (Bijapur)*
∗ Dam, Highest	*Tehri Dam (260 m)*
∗ Gateway, Highest	*Buland Darwaja at Fatehpur Sikri (176 ft.)*
∗ Fresh Water Lake, Largest	*Wular Lake (Kashmir)*
∗ Literacy, Highest	*Kerala (94%)*
∗ Museum, Largest	*Indian Museum (Kolkata)*
∗ Mosque, Biggest	*Jama Masjid (Delhi)*
∗ Peak, Highest**	*K-2 (Pak-Occupied Kashmir)*
∗ Railway Platform, Longest	*Shree Siddharoodha Swamiji Railway Station Hubballi, Karnataka (1507 m. long)*
∗ Railway Bridge, longest	*Vembanad Bridge, Kerala (4.6 km)*
∗ River, Longest***	*The Ganges (2525 Km)*
∗ Rainfall, Highest (annual mean)	*Mowsynram near Cherrapunji (1178 cm)*
∗ Road Longest	*NH-44 (3,745 km)*
∗ State, with maximum forest cover	*Madhya Pradesh*
∗ State, with maximum density of population	*Bihar*
∗ Telescope, Largest in Asia	*Vainu Bappu Telescope (at Kavalur: Chennai) 2.34m*
∗ Tunnel, Longest (Road)	*Dr. Shyama Prasad Mukherjee Tunnel (9.28 kms, J & K)*
∗ Tunnel, Longest (Railway)	*T-50 Tunnel, Khari-Sumber section (12.77 kms) Jammu & Kashmir.*
∗ Tallest Minaret	*Qutub Minar (Delhi 72.5 m.)*
∗ Waterfall, Highest	*Kunchikal Waterfall (Karnataka: 455 m.)*
∗ Zoo, Largest	*Arignar Anna Zoological Park, Chennai, Tamil Nadu*

** *Highest peak in the world is Mount Everest, which is in Nepal. K-2 is the second highest peak in the world. It is 8,611 metres high.*
*** *Indus and Brahmaputra (each 2900 km). Both of them, however, cover a long distance outside India.*

TABLE OF PRECEDENCE

1. President
2. Vice-President
3. Prime Minister
4. Governors of States within their respective states
5. Former Presidents

5A. Deputy Prime Minister

6. Chief Justice of India, Speaker of Lok Sabha
7. Cabinet Ministers of the Union, Chief Ministers of States within their respective States
   Deputy Chairman NITI Aayog, former Prime Ministers
   Leaders of opposition in Rajya Sabha and Lok Sabha

7A. Holders of the Bharat Ratna Decoration

8. Ambassadors Extraordinary and Plenipotentiary and High Commissioners of Commonwealth Countries accredited to India, Chief Ministers of States outside their respective States
9. Judges of the Supreme Court
10. Deputy Chairman Rajya Sabha, Deputy Chief Minister of States, Deputy Speaker Lok Sabha, Members of the NITI Aayog, Minister of State of the Union and Other Minister in the Ministry of Defence.

BOOKS AND AUTHORS

FOREIGN

Book	Author
* As You Like It	*William Shakespeare*
* A Tale of Two Cities	*Charles Dickens*
* Ben Hur	*Lewis Wallace*
* Das Kapital	*Karl Marx*
* David Copperfield	*Charles Dickens*
* Hamlet	*William Shakespeare*
* Iliad	*Homer*
* Inferno	*A. Dante*
* In Memoriam	*Lord Tennyson*
* Ivanhoe	*Walter Scott*
* Julius Caesar	*William Shakespeare*
* Lady Chatterley's Lover	*D.H. Lawrence*
* Lajja	*Taslima Nasreen*
* Les Miserable	*Victor Hugo*
* Leviathan	*Thomas Hobbes*
* Lolita	*V. Nobokov*
* Lycidas	*John Milton*
* Mein Kampf	*Adolf Hitler*
* Moor's Last Sigh	*Salman Rushdie*
* Mother	*Maxim Gorky*
* Mother India	*Katherine Mayo*
* Nana	*Emile Zola*
* Odyssey	*Homer*
* Origin of Species	*Charles Darwin*
* Othello	*William Shakespeare*
* Paradise Lost	*John Milton*
* Paradise Regained	*John Milton*
* Path to Power	*Margaret Thatcher*
* Pickwick Papers	*Charles Dickens*
* Razor's Edge	*Somerset Maugham*
* Republic	*Plato*
* The Tempest	*William Shakespeare*
* Time Machine	*H.G. Wells*
* Tom Sawyer	*Mark Twain*
* Treasure Island	*R.L. Stevenson*
* Twelfth Night	*William Shakespeare*
* Unto This Last	*John Ruskin*
* Utopia	*Thomas More*
* Wealth of Nations	*Adam Smith*
* Wonder that was India	*A.L. Basham*

INDIAN

Book	Author
* Ain-i-Akbari	*Abul Fazal*
* Anand Math	*Bankim Chandra Chatterjee*
* Arthashastra	*Kautilya*
* A Suitable Boy	*Vikram Seth*
* Bhagwat Gita	*Ved Vyas*
* Chidambara	*Sumitranandan Pant*
* Devdas	*Sarat Chandra Chatterjee*
* Discovery of India	*Jawaharlal Nehru*
* Ganadevata	*Tarashankar Bandopadhyaya*
* Geet Govind	*Jaya Dev*
* Geetanjali	*R. N. Tagore*
* Glimpses of World History	*Jawaharlal Nehru*
* Godaan	*Prem Chand*
* Gul-e-Nagma	*Firaq Gorakhpuri*
* Harsh Charita	*Bana Bhatta*
* India Divided	*Dr. Rajendra Prasad*
* Justice of Peace ke Aansu	Janardan Prasad Singh
* The Judgement	*Kuldip Nayyar*
* Kadambari	*Bana Bhatta*
* Kagaz Te Kanwas	*Amrita Pritam*
* Kamayani	*Jai Shankar Prasad*
* Kitni Nawon Mein Kitni Bar	*S. H. Vatsyayan*
* Kumar Sambhav	*Kalidas*
* Mahabharata	*Ved Vyas*
* Malgudi Days	*R.K. Narayan*
* Meghdoot	*Kalidas*
* Mritunjaya	*B.K. Bhattacharya*
* Mudrarakshasa	*Vishakhadatta*
* Prison Diary	*Jaya Prakash Narayan*
* Raghuvansha	*Kalidas*
* Rajtarangini	*Kalhana*
* Ramayana	*Balmiki*
* Ramcharit Manas	*Tulsidas*
* Rukh Te Rishi	*Harbhajan Singh*
* Satyarth Prakash	*Swami Dayanand*
* Sur Sagar	*Surdas*
* The Guide	*R.K. Narayan*

IMPORTANT DATES AND DAYS OF THE YEAR

∗ JANUARY

5-11 Road Safety Week
12 National Youth Day
15 Army Day
15-21 Pin Code Week
23 National Day of Patriotism
26 Republic Day
30 Martyr's Day

∗ FEBRUARY

1-14 Oil Conservation Fortnight
14 Valentine's Day

∗ MARCH

4 National Safety Day
8 International Women's Day
15 Consumers' Day
16 Immunisation Day
21 World Forest Day
22 World Day for Water
24 World Meteorological Day
1-7 Preservation of Blindness Week

∗ APRIL

7 World Health Day
7-13 Handloom Week
14-20 Fire Service Week
18 World Heritage Day
22 World Earth Day

∗ MAY

1 May Day
5 National Labour Day
8 World Red Cross Day
11 National Technology Day
15 International Day of the Family
17 World Telecommunication Day
24 Commonwealth Day
31 World No-Tobacco Day

∗ JUNE

5 World Environment Day
21 World Yoga Day
26 International Day against Drug Abuse and Illicit Trafficking

∗ JULY

11 World Population Day

∗ AUGUST

1-7 World Breast feeding Week
10 Sanskrit Divas
15 Independence Day
20 Sadbhavana Divas

∗ SEPTEMBER

1-7 National Nutrition Week
5 Teachers' Day
8 International Literary Day
14 Hindi Diwas
23 World Deaf Day
27 World Tourism Day

∗ OCTOBER

2 Gandhi Jayanti
International Day of Non Violence
Anti-Leprosy Day
4 World Animal Day
6 World Habitat Day *(Ist Monday)*
8 Indian Air Force Day
14 World Standard Day
15 International Day of Rural Women
16 World Food Day
24 United Nations Day
27 Infantry Day
28 World Thrift Day
31 Anti-Terrorism Day

∗ NOVEMBER

2 All Saints Day
14 Children's Day
15-21 National Cooperative Week
19-25 Quami Ekta Week
20 Child Rights Day
26 Constitution Day

∗ DECEMBER

1 World AIDS Day
3 World Day for the Disabled
4 Naval Day
7 Flag Day
8 SMRC Day
10 Human Rights Day
14 National Energy Conservation Day

INDIAN DEFENCE

- The Supreme Command of the Armed Forces is vested in the hands of the President of the Country.
- The responsibility for national defence, however, rests with the Cabinet. All important questions having a bearing on defence are decided by the Cabinet Committee on Political Affairs, which is presided over by the Prime Minister.
- The Defence Minister is responsible to Parliament for all matters concerning the Defence Services.
- All the administrative and operational control of Armed Forces are exercised by the Ministry of Defence. The three services—Army, Navy and Air Force function through their respective service head-quarters headed by the chief of Staff. The post of Chief of Defence Staff (CDS) was created in 2019.

Indian Army Commands

Command	***HQ Location***
Eastern Command	Kolkata
Western Command	Chandigarh
Northern Command	Udhampur
Southern Command	Pune
Central Command	Lucknow
Training Command	Shimla
South-Western Command	Jaipur

Indian Air Force Commands

Command	***HQ Location***
Western Air Command	New Delhi
Sout-Western Air Command	Gandhinagar
Central Air Command	Allahabad
Eastern Air Command	Shillong
Southern Air Command	Thiruvananthapuram
Training Command	Bengaluru

Indian Navy Commands

Command	***HQ Location***
Eastern Naval Command	Vishakhapatnam
Western Naval Command	Mumbai
Southern Naval Command	Cochin

Commissioned Ranks in Defence Services

Army	***Navy***	***Air Force***
General	Admiral	Air Chief Marshal
Lieutenant-General	Vice-Admiral	Air Marshal
Major-General	Rear-Admiral	Air Vice-Marshal
Brigadier	Commodor	Air Commodor
Colonel	Captain	Group Captain
Lieutenant-Colonel	Commander	Wing Commander
Major	Lt.Commander	Squadron Leader
Captain	Lieutenant	Flight Lieutenant
Lieutenant	Sub-Lieutenant	Flying Officer

Internal Security Organisations of India

S. No.	***Name of Organisation***	***Year of Creation***	***Headquarters***
1.	Assam Rifles (A.R.)	1835	Shillong
2.	Central Reserve Police Force (CRPF)	1939	New Delhi
3.	Territorial Army	1948	In different States
4.	Indo-Tibetan Border Police	1962	New Delhi
5.	Home Guard	1962	In different States

S. No.	Name of Organisation	Year of Creation	Headquarters
6.	Coast Guard	1978	New Delhi
7.	Border Security Force (B.S.F.)	1965	New Delhi
8.	Central Industrial Security Force (CISF)	1969	New Delhi
9.	National Security Guard	1984	New Delhi
10.	Police	—	In different States

Army Institutes

1.	Sainik Schools upto +2 Level	33 places in India
2.	Rashtriya Indian Military College (prepare for entrance to N.D.A.)	Dehradun
3.	National Defence Academy (three services)	Khadakwasla, Pune
4.	Indian Military Academy (Army)	Dehradun
5.	Officers Training Academy (3 services) Short Courses	Chennai
6.	National Defence College	New Delhi
7.	The College of Combat	Mhow
8.	The College of Military Engineering	Kirkee
9.	Military College of Telecommunication Engineering	Mhow
10.	The Armoured Corps Centre and School	Ahmed Nagar
11.	The School Artillery	Deolali
12.	The Infantry School	Mhow and Belgaum
13.	College of Material Management	Jabalpur

Air Force Institutions

✶ Air Force Academy	Hyderabad	✶ Helicopter Training School	Hakimpet
✶ Flying Instructors School	Tambaram, Chennai	✶ The College of Air Warfare	Secunderabad
✶ Air Force Administrative College	Coimbatore	✶ Air Force Technical College	Jalahalli

UNITED NATIONS (UN)

- The United Nations (UN) is an association of states which have pledged themselves to maintain international peace and security and cooperate in solving international political, economic, social cultural and humanitarian problems towards achieving this end.
- Trygve Lie of Norway (1946-52) was the first Secretary-General of the UN.
- ***Origin:*** UN Charter was signed by 50 members on June 26, 1945. Poland signed the charter later to become one of the original 51 member-states. It officially came into existence on October 24, 1945.
- ***UN Charter:*** The Charter is the Constitution of the UN and contains its aims and objectives and rules and regulations for its functioning.
- ***Aims and Objectives:*** They are security, welfare and human rights.
- ***Headquarters:*** New York.
- ***Flag:*** The flag is light blue in colour, and emblazoned in white, in its centre is the UN symbol—a polar map of world embraced by twin olive branches open at the top.
- ***Official Languages:*** The official languages of the UN are: English, French, Chinese, Russian, Arabic and Spanish. However, working languages are English and French only.

- ***Present Membership:*** At present 193 countries are members of the UN. South Sudan is the latest entrant to this world organisation.
- ***Main Organs of the UN:*** There are six main organs:
  1. General Assembly
  2. Security Council
  3. Economic and Social Council
  4. Trusteeship Council
  5. International Court of Justice, and
  6. Secretariat.

1. *General Assembly:* It consists of representative of all members of the UN. Each member country has only one vote. It meets once a year and passes UN Budget. It is the main place for discussions and policy making in the UN.
2. *Security Council:* It is the Executive body of the UN and is mainly responsible for maintaining international peace and security. It has 15 members, 5 of which (USA, UK, France, Russia and China) are permanent members. The 10 non-permanent members are elected by General Assembly for two-year term and are not eligible for immediate re-election.
3. *Economic and Social Council:* It has 54 members elected by General Assembly.
4. *Trusteeship Council:* It looks after interest of the people in areas not yet independent and leads them towards self-government.
5. *International Court of Justice:* It has 15 judges, no two of whom may be nationals of the same state. They are elected by General Assembly and Security Council for a term of 9 years. The Court elects its President and Vice-President for a 3-year term.
6. *Secretariat:* It is the Secretariat of the UN and is headed by the Secretary General.

Some Important UN Agencies

UN Agencies	Headquarters	Year of Establishment
∗ United Nations (U.N.)	New York	1945
∗ International Monetary Fund (I.M.F.)	Washington D.C.	1945
∗ World Health Organisation (W.H.O.)	Geneva	1948
∗ Food & Agricultural Organisation (FAO)	Rome	1945
∗ International Labour Organisation (ILO)	Geneva	1919
∗ UNESCO	Paris	1946
∗ Universal Postal Union (UPU)	Berne	1874
∗ UNIDO	Vienna	1966
∗ International Atomic Energy Agency (IAEA)	Vienna	1957
∗ United Nations Development Programme (UNDP)	New York	1965
∗ UNICEF	New York	1946
∗ International Maritime Organisation (IMO)	London	1958
∗ World Meteorological Organisation (WMO)	Geneva	1950
∗ International Telecommunication Union (ITU)	Geneva	1865
∗ World Trade Organisation (WTO)	Geneva	1995
∗ International Development Association (IDA)	Washington D.C.	1960
∗ World Intellectual Property Organisation (WIPO)	Geneva	1967

Famous International Organisations

International Organisations	Headquarters	Year of Establishment
* International Court of Justice	The Hague	1946
* International Civil Aviation Organisation (ICAO)	Montreal	1947
* International Finance Corporation (IFC)	Washington D.C	1956
* Arab League	Cairo	1945
* Commonwealth of Nations	London	1949
* International Bank for Reconstruction and Development (IBRD)	Washington D.C.	1945
* Organisation of Islamic Cooperation (OIC)	Jeddah (Saudi Arabia)	1969
* Red Cross	Geneva	1863
* Interpol	Lyons	1923
* Asian Development Bank (ADB)	Manila	1966
* North Atlantic Treaty Organisation (NATO)	Brussels	1949
* Association of South East Asian Nations (ASEAN)	Jakarta	1967
* South Asian Association for Regional Cooperation (SAARC)	Kathmandu	1985
* Asia-Pacific Economic Cooperation (APEC)	Singapore	1989
* Organisation for Economic Cooperation and Development (OECD)	Paris	1961
* Organisation of Petroleum Exporting Countries (OPEC)	Vienna	1960
* Commonwealth of Independent States (CIS)	Minsk	1991
* International Olympic Committee (IOC)	Lausanne (Switzerland)	1894
* European Union (EU)	Brussels	Changed form of EEC Established in 1958
* Amnesty International (AI)	London	1961
* Shanghai Cooperation Organisation (SCO)	Beijing	2001
* BRICS Development Bank	Shanghai	2014

AWARDS AND HONOURS

NATIONAL AWARDS

BHARAT RATANA

- Bharat Ratna is India's highest Civilian Award. It was first awarded in 1954.
- The actual award is designed in the shape of a *peepal* leaf with Bharat Ratna inscribed in Devanagri script in the Sun Figure.
- This is India's highest civilian award. It is given for exceptional work on art, literature, science and recognition of public service of the highest order.
- The emblem, the Sun and the rim are of platinum.
- The inscriptions are in burnished bronze.
- Government servants are not eligible for it.

.EPUBLIC DAY AWARDS

Padma Awards

They fall in line after the Bharat Ratna. They are also discontinued in 1977 along with the Bharat Ratna and award was started again in 1980.

There are three Padma Awards:

- ***Padma Vibhushan:*** This award is given for exceptional and distinguished service in any field, including service rendered by Govt. servants.
- ***Padma Bhushan:*** This award is given for distinguished service of a high order in any field, including service rendered by Govt. servants.
- ***Padma Shri:*** This award is given for distinguished service in any field, including service rendered by Government servants.

Gallantry Awards

- ***Param Vir Chakra:*** The highest award for bravery or some daring and pre-eminent act of valour or self-sacrifice in the presence of the enemy, whether on land, at sea or in the air.
- ***Mahavir Chakra:*** It is the second highest decoration and is awarded for acts of conspicuous gallantry in the presence of the enemy, whether on land, at sea or in the air.
- ***Vir Chakra:*** It is the third in order of awards given for acts of gallantry in the presence of enemy, whether on land, at sea or in the air.
- ***Ashok Chakra:*** This medal is awarded for the most conspicuous bravery or some daring or pre-eminent act of valour or self-sacrifice on land, at sea or in the air but not in the presence of enemy.
- ***Vishishta Sewa Medal:*** It is awarded to personnel of all the three Services in class I, II and III in recognition of distinguished service of the "most exceptional" and "exceptional" and a "high" order respectively. Prefixes Parma and Ati are added before first two categories of medals respectively.
- ***Jeewan Raksha Padak:*** Awarded for meritorious acts or a series of acts of a human nature displayed in saving life from drowning, fire and rescue operations in mines etc.

OTHER NATIONAL AWARDS

SAHITYA AKADEMI AWARDS

- These prizes are awarded annually to the authors of the most outstanding books of literary merit published in each of the 22 languages which are specified in the Eighth Schedule of the Constitution.
- There are also two awards for Rajasthani and English. The award, in form of a casket containing an inscribed copper plate and a cheque of ₹ 1 lakh is given to the author or his/her heir.

DADA SAHEB PHALKE AWARD

- The award carries a cash prize of ₹ 15 lakh, a Shawl and Swarna Kamal.
- Mrs Devika Rani Roerich was the first person to receive Dadasaheb Phalke Award in 1969.

BHARATIYA JNANPITH AWARD

- Instituted in 22nd May, 1961, carries a cash prize of ₹ 21 lakh, a citation and a bronze replica of Vagdevi (Saraswati).
- Instituted by a literary organisation in India.

SARASWATI SAMMAN

- Given for outstanding literary works, value ₹ 15 lakh.

VYAS SAMMAN

- This is awarded by KK Birla Foundation for outstanding Hindi Literary work by an Indian citizen that was published in the past decade. This carries a cash prize of ₹ 4.0 lakh.

BHARTENDU HARISHCHANDRA AWARDS

- The Bhartendu Harishchandra Awards were instituted in 1983, by the Ministry of Information and Broadcasting for original Hindi writing on any subject in mass communications like journalism, publication, advertising, broadcasting films, etc.

KALIDAS SAMMAN

- Instituted by the Madhya Pradesh Government, the award is of the value of ₹ 2 lakh.

KABIR SAMMAN

- The award is conferred annually on a person of literature of very high order on the basis of his or her superb creativity and consistent commitment to the most recent and latest trends of literary creation in any of the Indian languages. The award carries ₹ 3 lakh and a letter of citation.

INTERNATIONAL AWARDS

NOBEL PRIZES

- These Prizes were instituted in 1901 by a Swedish scientist, Dr. Alfred Nobel; the discoverer of Dynamite.
- Six prizes are awarded annually for (i) Chemistry, (ii) Physics, (iii) Medicine, (iv) Literature, (v) Peace and (vi) Economics —started since 1969.
- **Indians Honoured with Nobel Prize:** So far, following Indians have been honoured with these prizes. Their names are (i) Rabindra Nath Tagore for Literature, for his book 'Gitanjali', in 1913, (ii) Dr. C.V. Raman for Physics in 1930, for his discovery of 'Raman Effect', (iii) Mother Teresa for Peace in 1979, (iv) Prof. Amartya Sen in 1998 for Economics and (v) Kailash Satyarthi for Peace in 2014.

  In addition, four non-resident Indians have also been awarded the Nobel Prize. They are: (i) Hargobind Khurana for Medicine in 1968, (ii) Subramanian Chandrasekhar for Physics in 1983, (iii) Venkatraman Ramkrishnan for Chemistry in 2009, (iv) Abhijit Vinayak Banerjee for Economics in 2019.

GANDHI PEACE PRIZE

- The government instituted this ₹ 1 crore prize on the lines of the Nobel Peace Prize in 1995.
- It is the highest Civilian International award by the Govt. of India.

RAMON MAGSAYSAY AWARD

- The Ramon Magsaysay Award, named after a Philippines President, who died in an air crash in 1957, is given annually to Asian nationals or institutions who have made worthy contributions to public service, community leadership, journalism, literature and the creative arts and international understanding. It carries a gold medal, a certificate and US$ 50,000. It is awarded on August 31, every year. The Ramon Magsaysay Award is Asia's highest honor and is widely regarded as the region's equivalent of the Nobel Prize. It celebrates the memory and leadership example of the third Philippline president after whom the award is named, and is given every year to individuals or organizations in Asia who manifest the same selfless service and transformative influence that ruled the life of the late and beloved Filipino leader.

INDIRA GANDHI PRIZE FOR PEACE, DISARMAMENT AND DEVELOPMENT

- The award was instituted in the memory of Mrs. Indira Gandhi to foster creative cooperation among nations of the world.

MISS WORLD

- This competition was established in 1951 by the 'Miss World Incorporation'. The Winner of this competition gets cash as prize and she is selected on her physical and intellectual genius.

MISS UNIVERSE

- This competition was established in year 1952 by 'Miss Universe Incorporation'. The winner of this competition gets cash as prize. The most beautiful girl is selected in this competition on the basis of her beauty and multifarious genius.

Highest Honours of Some Countries

Country	*Highest Honour*
India	Bharat Ratna
Pakistan	Nishan-e-Pakistan
Kuwait	Mubarak-Al-kabir Medal
Saudi Arabia	Shah Abdul Aziz Medal
Argentina	The Order of Sona Martin
Nicaragua	Augusto-Caesar Sandino Order
Vietnam	The Order of the Golden Star
Hungary	The Order of Banner
Britain	Member of British Empire, Victoria Cross
Japan	Order of Moulovenice Sun
Denmark	Order of Diana Brog
France	Legend of Honour
America	Presidential Medal of Freedom
Germany	Pore Lee Merit Iron Cross
The Netherlands	Netherlands Lion

SPORTS

OLYMPICS

- First of all these games were held by the Greeks in 776 B.C. on Mount Olympus in honour of the Greek God Zeus. In this way, the history of Olympic Games is about twenty eight hundred years old. These games continued to be held every four years until 394 A.D. when these games were stopped by a royal order of the emperor of Rome.
- The modern Olympic Games which started in Athens in 1896, are the result of the devotion and dedication of a French educator Baron Pierre de Coubertin and the first Olympic meet in the modern series was held in 1896 in Athens, the Capital of Greece. Since then, they are being held every four years except for breaks during world wars.
- The Olympic flag is white in colour with five coloured rings, each ring symbolic of a continent. Summer as well as Winter Olympics are held in the same year.
- The official Olympic Motto is *Citius, Altius, Swifter, Higher, Stronger*. The Head Office of International Olympic Committee (IOC) is at Lausanne (Switzerland).

COMMONWEALTH GAMES

- The Commonwealth Games are held every four years, in the year in which Asian Games are held. All the Commonwealth Countries (former colonies of Britain) can take part in it.
- The first Commonwealth Games were held in 1930 at Hamilton (Canada). There are currently 54 members of the Commonwealth of Nations, and 71 teams participated in the games.

ASIAN GAMES

- After the Second World War, most of the Asian Countries gained independence. On the lines of Olympic Games, Asian Games were planned every four years. India hosted the first Asian Games in 1951.

WORLD CUP CRICKET

- The first Cricket World Cup was organised in England in 1975. A separate women's Cricket World Cup has been held every 4 years since 1973.

HOCKEY WORLD CUP

- The first Hockey World Cup was organised in Barcelona (Spain) in 1971. Women's Hockey World Cup has been held since 1974.

FOOTBALL WORLD CUP

- The Football World Cup is organised by FIFA (Federation of International Football Association). The World Cup is called 'Jules Rimet Cup' named after the name of FIFA President Jules Rimet. The first Football World Cup was organised in Uruguay in 1930.
- In 1942 and 1946, the Football World Cup was not played due to World War II.

SPORTS TERMS

* ***Badminton:*** Mixed doubles; Deuce; Drop; Smash; Let; Foot work; Setting.
* ***Base Ball:*** Pitcher; Put out, Strike; Home; Bunt.
* ***Billiards:*** Cue; Jigger; Pot; Break; In Baulk; In Off; Cannons.
* ***Boxing:*** Upper cut; Round; Punch; Bout; Knock down; Hitting below the belt; Ring.
* ***Bridge:*** Finesse; Dummy; Revoke; Grand Slam; Little Slam; No Trump; Rubber.
* ***Chess:*** Bishop, Gambit; Checkmate; Stalemate.
* ***Cricket:*** L.B.W. (leg before wicket); Creases, Popping-creases; Stumped; Bye; Leg-Bye; Googly; Hattrick; Maiden over; Drive; Bowling; Duck; Follow-on; No ball; Leg Break; Silly point; Cover point; Hit-wicket; Late-cut; Slip; Off-spinner; In-swing.
* ***Football:*** Off Side; Block; Drop-kick; Penalty-kick (or goal kick); Corner-kick; Free-kick; Dribble; Thrown-in; Foul.
* ***Golf:*** Boggy; Foursome; Stymic; Tee; Put; Hole; Niblic; Caddie; Links; The green; Bunker.
* ***Hockey:*** Carried; Short Corner; Bully; Sticks; Off side; Roll in; Striking Circle; Under-cutting; Dribble.
* ***Horse racing:*** Jockey; Punter.
* ***Polo:*** Bunker; Chukker; Mallet.
* ***Tennis:*** Back hand drive; Volley; Smash; Half-volley; Deuce; Service; Let; Grand Slam.

ALL THE HEROES

Sportsman	Game
Anand Amritraj	Tennis
Arati Saha	Swimming
Ashok Malik	Golf
Althea Gibson	Tennis
Ashe Arthur	Tennis
Mohd. Azharuddin	Cricket
A.K. Ghosh	Chess
Anju Dua	Gymnastics
Balbir Singh	Hockey
Bannerji, P.K.	Football
Bedi, B.S.	Cricket
Bapu Nadkarni	Cricket
Benaud, Richie	Cricket
Ben Johnson	Athletics
Bobby Fischer	Chess
Boris Becker	Tennis
Bharat Ram	Golf
Chetan Baboor	Table Tennis
Borde, Chandu	Cricket
Budding, Ingo	Tennis
Bungert, Williams	Tennis
Chandrashekhar	Cricket
Chandgi Ram	Wrestling
Charanjit Singh	Hockey
Carl Lewis	Athletics
Chuni Goswami	Football
Clandius	Hockey
Clive Loyd	Cricket
Connoly	Tennis
Chris Evert	Tennis
Dhyan Chand	Hockey
Dara Singh	Wrestling
Dinesh Khanna	Badminton
Diwan, G.	Table Tennis
Dolly Zazir	Swimming
Durrani, Salim	Cricket
Das, Susan	Tennis
Don Bradman	Cricket
Emerson, Roy	Tennis
Erlend Kops	Badminton
Elena Shushunova	Gymnastics
Flash Gordon	Wrestling
Florence Griffith Joyner	Athletics
Gurang Mehta	Chess
Goolagong, Even	Tennis
Ghose, A.L.	Golf
Hamida Bano	Wrestling
Haneef	Cricket
Harbans Singh	Wrestling
Harnek Singh	Hockey
Hasan Sardar	Hockey
Hazare, V.	Cricket
Henry Cotton	Golf
Hutton, Len	Cricket
Imran Khan	Cricket
Ivan Lendle	Tennis
Jaideep Mukherjee	Tennis
Jasjit Singh	Tennis
Jarnail Singh	Football
Jayant Vohra	Table Tennis
kapil Dev	Cricket
Maradona	Football
Martina Navratilova	Tennis
Mike Tyson	Boxing
Mohammed Ali Clay	Boxing
Mohammed Shahid	Hockey
Narendra Hirwani	Cricket
Nawab Pataudi	Cricket
Rod Lever	Tennis
RS Gentle	Hockey
Sachin Tendulkar	Cricket
Seth, T. N.	Badminton
Shirley Fry	Tennis
Shonny Liston	Boxing
Shiny Abraham	Athletics
Steffi Graf	Tennis
Sunil Gavaskar	Cricket
Udham Singh	Hockey
Umrigar, Poly	Cricket
Urmila Thapar	Tennis
Usha P.T.	Athletics
Vijay Amrithraj	Tennis
Vivian Richard	Cricket
Wasim Akram	Cricket
Wilson Jones	Billiards
Woong Pong	Badminton
Worrel, Frank	Cricket
Zafar Iqbal	Hockey

IMPORTANT CUPS & TROPHIES

International

- ✶ *American Cup* : Yacht Racing
- ✶ *Ashes* : Cricket
- ✶ *Davis Cup* : Lawn Tennis
- ✶ *Derby* : Horse Race
- ✶ *Grand National* : Horse Streple Chase Race
- ✶ *Jules Rimet Trophy* : World Soccer Cup
- ✶ *King's Cup* : Air Races
- ✶ *Merdeka Cup* : Football
- ✶ *Swaythling Cup* : Table Tennis (Men)
- ✶ *Ryder Cup* : Golf
- ✶ *Thomas Cup* : Badminton
- ✶ *U. Thant Cup* : Tennis
- ✶ *Walker Cup* : Golf
- ✶ *Wightman Cup* : Lawn Tennis
- ✶ *Rothman's Trophy* : Cricket
- ✶ *European Champions Cup* : Football
- ✶ *Edgbaston Cup* : Lawn Tennis
- ✶ *Grand Prix* : Lawn Tennis

National

- ✶ *Agha Khan Cup* : Hockey
- ✶ *Beighton Cup* : Hockey
- ✶ *Bombay Gold Cup* : Hockey
- ✶ *C.K. Naydu Trophy* : Cricket
- ✶ *Deodhar Trophy* : Cricket
- ✶ *Duleep Trophy* : Cricket
- ✶ *Durand Cup* : Football
- ✶ *Dhyan Chand Trophy* : Hockey
- ✶ *Dr. B.C. Roy Trophy* : Football (Junior)
- ✶ *Ezra Cup* : Polo
- ✶ *Guru Nanak Cup* : Hockey
- ✶ *Holkar Trophy* : Bridge
- ✶ *Irani Trophy* : Cricket
- ✶ *Murugappa Gold Cup* : Hockey
- ✶ *Nehru Trophy* : Hockey
- ✶ *Nixan Gold Cup* : Football
- ✶ *Rani Jhansi Trophy* : Cricket
- ✶ *Ranji Trophy* : Cricket
- ✶ *Rangaswami Cup* : Hockey
- ✶ *Ramanujan Trophy* : Table Tennis
- ✶ *Rene Frank Trophy* : Hockey
- ✶ *Rohinton Baria Trophy* : Cricket
- ✶ *Rovers Cup* : Football
- ✶ *Santosh Trophy* : Football
- ✶ *Subroto Cup* : Football

Stadiums & Places Associated with Sports

Name of Stadium	*Sports*	*Place*
Arun Jaitley Stadium	Cricket	Delhi
Jawaharlal Nehru Stadium	Athletics	Delhi
Shivajee Stadium	Hockey	Delhi
Ambedkar Stadium	Football	Delhi
Brabourne Stadium	Cricket	Mumbai
Wankhede Stadium	Cricket	Mumbai
National Stadium	Hockey etc.	Mumbai
Eden Garden	Cricket	Kolkata
Green Park Stadium	Cricket	Kanpur
Keenan Stadium	Cricket	Jamshedpur
Barabati Stadium	Cricket	Cuttack
Lords, Oval, Leeds	Cricket	Britain
Hedingle Manchester	Cricket	Britain
Black Heath	Rugby Football	London
Henley	Boat race	England
Wembley Stadium	Football	London
Narendra Modi Stadium	Cricket	Ahmedabad
White City	Dog-race	England
Aintree	Horse-race	England
Tentbridge	Cricket	England
Patnee Martlake	Boat-race	England
Tibankham	Rugby Football	England
Sandy Lodge	Golf	Scotland
Brooklyn	Baseball	New York
Melbourne	Cricket	Australia

Name of Playing Compound of Different Games

Name of Compound	Related Sports
Court	Lawn Tennis, Badminton, Netball, Hand ball, Volleyball, Squash, Kho-Kho, Kabaddi
Diamond	Baseball
Ring	Boxing, Skating, Wrestling, Circus, Riding display
Course	Golf
Board	Table Tennis
Pool	Swimming
Mat	Judo, Karate II
Arena	Horse Riding
Vellodrum	Cycling
Field	Polo, Football, Hockey
Track	Athletics
Pitch	Cricket, Rugby
Rink	Ice Hockey

❑ ❑ ❑

Multiple Choice Questions

1. Match List-I with List-II and select the correct answer from the codes given below the lists:

List-I

(*a*) Napoleon Bonaparte
(*b*) Jean Jacques Rousseau
(*c*) Croce
(*d*) Madame Roland

List-II

1. 'A history is contemporary history'
2. 'Liberty what crimes are committed in thy name'
3. 'Man is born free but everywhere he is in chains.'
4. 'I am the Child of Revolution'

Codes :

	(*a*)	(*b*)	(*c*)	(*d*)
A.	1	2	3	4
B.	4	3	1	2
C.	3	4	2	1
D.	3	4	1	2

2. Abraham Lincon was elected the President of United States in:
A. 1862 B. 1860
C. 1875 D. 1855

3. Who was known as the 'Prince of Humanists'?
A. Francisco Petrarch B. Dante
C. Boccacio D. Erasmus

4. D-Day is the day when:
A. Germany declared war on Britain
B. US dropped the atom bomb on Hiroshima.
C. Allied Troops landed in Normandy
D. Germany surrendered to the allies

5. Whose teachings inspired the French Revolution?
A. Locke
B. Rousseau
C. Hegel
D. Plato

6. At a time when empires in Europe were crumbling before the might of Napoleon which one of the following Governor-Generals kept the British flag flying high in India?
A. Warren Hastings B. Lord Cornwallis
C. Lord Wellesley D. Lord Hastings

7. Which one of the following statements regarding Fascism in Italy is *not* true?
A. The Fascists came to power as a result of popular uprising
B. In 1926, all political parties except Mussolini's party were banned
C. The Fascists suppressed the Socialist movement
D. The Fascists were hostile to the Communists

8. The fall of Czar Nicholas-II is known as:
A. Bloody Sunday
B. Bolshevik Revolution
C. February Revolution
D. October Revolution

9. Industrial Revolution took place first in:
A. France B. Germany
C. United Kingdom D. Japan

10. The British Prime Minister at the outbreak of World War II was :
A. Churchill B. Baldwin
C. Attlee D. Chemberlain

11. The 'Great Depression' (1929) economic crisis was met by adopting the policy of
A. Stimulus B. Marshall Plan
C. New Deal D. Open Door

12. The slogan "No taxation without representation" was raised during the:
A. American War of Independence
B. Russian Revolution
C. French Revolution
D. Indian Freedom struggle

13. In the nineteenth century the people of Europe started moving from the villages to the cities due to the impact of :

A. Epidemics
B. War
C. Industrialisation
D. Population explosion in villages

14. The important cause of the Civil War in America was:

A. Abolition of slavery
B. Quest for freedom
C. Industrialisation
D. Rebellion by the native Americans

15. Industrial Revolution could not have come about without:

A. Merchant capitalism
B. The Enclosure Movement
C. The services of the proletariat class
D. An agricultural revolution

16. Consider the following statements :
The French Revolution came about mainly due to the :

1. Extreme poverty of the people
2. Impact of the works of great writers
3. Cruelty of the rulers
4. Impact of impulsive reaction

Which of the above statements are correct?

A. 1, 2 and 4 B. 2 and 3
C. 1, 3 and 4 D. 1, 2, 3 and 4

17. Asia's oldest and largest Buddhist monastery is situated in :

A. Tawang (Arunachal Pardesh)
B. Lhasa (Tibet)
C. Trincomallee (Sri Lanka)
D. Ulan Bator (Mongolia)

18. Who was the main architect of the Russian Revolution?

A. Karl Marx B. Lenin
C. Stalin D. Tolstoy

19. V.I. Lenin is associated with :

A. Russian Revolution of 1917
B. Chinese Revolution of 1949
C. German Revolution
D. French Revolution of 1789

20. Which one of the following statements is *not* correct?

A. Voltaire believed in Natural Religion
B. Rousseau wrote *Social Contract*
C. Montesquieu authored *The Spirit of Laws*
D. Necker believed in 'General Will'

21. 6th April, 1930 is well known in the history of India because this date is associated with..........

A. Dandi March by Mahatma Gandhi
B. Quit India Movement
C. Partition of Bengal
D. Partition of India

22. Which ruler enforced the system of 'Price Control' in India?

A. Mohammad Tughlak
B. Razia Begum
C. Alauddin Khilji
D. Sher Shah Suri

23. The concept of 'Din-e-Elahi' was founded by which king?

A. Dara Shikoh B. Akbar
C. Sher Shah Suri D. Shahjahan

24. Who are supposed to be the earliest inhabitants of India? Where did they come from?

A. Aryans from Central Asia
B. Dravidians from Mediterranean
C. Negroids from Africa
D. Bhils and the Santhals from West Asia

25. The one chief characteristic of temple architecture of the Gupta Age was :

A. Absence of dome
B. Huge size
C. Beautiful carvings
D. absence of a covered courtyard for the gathering of worshippers

26. The Rigveda consists of :

A. 1000 hymns B. 2028 hymns
C. 1028 hymns D. 1038 hymns

27. The central point in Ashoka's dharma was :

A. royalty to kings
B. peace and non-violence
C. respect to elders
D. religious tolerance

28. The social evil which was conspicuously absent during ancient India was :
A. *Sati*-System B. *Devadasi*-System
C. Polygamy D. *Purdah*-System

29. Which, among the following, can be accepted as a novelty introduced by Mughal emperors to their buildings?
A. Domes B. Minarets
C. Arches D. Attached gardens

30. The first ruler of India who defeated Muhammud of Ghur was :
A. Mularaja II of Gujarat
B. Prithviraja Chauhan of Delhi
C. Jayachand of Kannauj
D. Parmaldeva of Bundelkhand

31. What important event happened in India in 1911?
A. Bengal was partitioned
B. Non-Cooperation movement was launched
C. India's capital was shifted from Calcutta to Delhi
D. Mahatma Gandhi presided over the Congress session

32. The first phase of the Congress Party (1885-1905) was characterized by its efforts to secure:
A. limited independence
B. complete freedom
C. Indianization of services
D. constitutional reforms

33. The Muslim League demanded a separate homeland for the Indian Muslims openly for the first time at its annual session held in Lahore in the year :
A. 1931 A.D. B. 1936 A.D.
C. 1940 A.D. D. 1941 A.D.

34. Under whose governorship did the East India Company secure the Diwani Rights in Bengal, Bihar and Odisha from Emperor Shah Alam?
A. Lord Cornwallis
B. Lord William Bentinck
C. Lord Clive
D. Lord Wellesley

35. The Simon Commission was generally boycotted by the Indian political parties. What was the reason for this general non-cooperation?
A. the Commission aimed at dividing the people
B. it was an 'all white' Commission
C. it came after the Jallianwala Bagh carnage
D. it was an eye wash

36. Aligarh Muslim University was founded by :
A. Dr. Saifuddin Kitchlu
B. Mohammad Ali Jinnah
C. Sir Syed Ahmed Khan
D. Maulana Mohammad Ali

37. Ibn Batutah was an African traveller visiting India during the time of :
A. Alivardi Khan
B. Ala-ud-din Khalji
C. Iltutmish
D. Mohammad-bin-Tughlaq

38. The battle of Wandiawash was fought in :
A. 1726 B. 1760
C. 1818 D. 1857

39. The abolition of *Sati* by government regulation was at the time of :
A. Warren Hastings B. Lord Wellesley
C. Lord Bentinck D. Lord Ahmerst

40. Pick out the wrong combination :
A. Dilwara Temple : Mt. Abu
B. Pashupati Temple : Kathmandu
C. Padmanabh Temple : Bangalore
D. Minakshi Temple : Madurai

41. Match the following:
(*a*) Chanhudaro (*b*) Kalibangan
(*c*) Lothal (*d*) Surkotada
1. Alleged discovery of the skeleton of horse.
2. Bead making.
3. Traces of a dock and ship on seal.
4. Evidence of ploughing the fields.
The Correct code is :

	(*a*)	(*b*)	(*c*)	(*d*)
A.	2	4	3	1
B.	2	1	3	4
C.	1	2	3	4
D.	2	1	4	3

42. Match the Harappan settlements with the banks of rivers on which they were located :

(*a*) Harappa		1. Ravi
(*b*) Mohenjodaro		2. Indus
(*c*) Ropar		3. Sutlej
(*d*) Kalibangan		4. Ghaggar
(*e*) Lothal		5. Bhogava

Codes :

	(*a*)	(*b*)	(*c*)	(*d*)	(*e*)
A.	1	2	3	4	5
B.	1	2	3	5	4
C.	2	1	3	5	4
D.	2	1	4	3	5

43. The Goddess 'Kannagi' whose many temples were erected during the 'Sangam Age' was the goddess of :

A. Chastity B. Love
C. Prowess D. Wisdom

44. The Jain goal of life is to attain deliverance from the fetters of mudane existence, the way to which lies through three jewels. Which one of the following was not included among the 'three jewels' of Jainism?

A. Right faith B. Right action
C. Right knowledge D. Right conduct

45. The most striking feature of the Ashokan pillar is polish. Name the Ashokan pillar which is considered to be the most graceful of all Ashokan pillars.

A. Sarnath
B. Rampurva
C. Laurya-Nandangarh
D. Rummindei

46. Which are the correct statements?

1. The land grants, started in Satavahana period, paved the way for feudal developments in India.
2. Silk and spices were the Chief Indian export articles of Indo-Roman trade.
3. The Guptas issued the largest number of gold coins in ancient India.
4. The first memorial of a 'SATI' dated 510 A.D. is found at Eran in Madhya Pradesh.

A. 1 and 2 B. 1, 3, and 4
C. 1 and 4 D. 1, 2, 3 and 4

47. Who among the following patronised the 'Gandhara' (Indo-Greek style) School of Art?

A. Ashoka, the Great
B. Harsha Vardhana
C. Kanishka
D. Chandragupta Vikramaditya

48. The Sultanate of Delhi had five ruling dynasties. The dynasty having longest and shortest period were :

A. Ilbari and Khalji
B. Tughlaq and Khalji
C. Tughlaq and Sayyid
D. Ilbari and Lodis

49. Which one of the following events took place at the last during reign of Muhammad-bin-Tughlaq?

A. Introduction of token currency
B. Increase of land-revenue in Doab
C. Transfer of Capital from Delhi to Devagiri.
D. Conquest of Khurasan and Iraq

50. The most learned medieval Muslim ruler who was well versed in various branches of learning including astronomy, mathematics and medicine was :

A. Jalaluddin Khilji
B. Sikander Lodi
C. Ghiyasuddin Tughlaq
D. Muhammad-bin-Tughlaq

51. The 'Sufis' had 12 silsilas. They propounded the idea of Union with God through:

A. Love B. Rituals
C. Fasts D. Prayers

52. Match the following:

(*a*) Peshwa	1. Foreign affairs
(*b*) Panditrao	2. Audit and accounts
(*c*) Amatya	3. Providing grants to scholars
(*d*) Sumant	4. General supervision
	5. Military affairs

Select the correct code :

	(*a*)	(*b*)	(*c*)	(*d*)
A.	2	3	4	5
B.	4	1	2	3
C.	4	3	2	1
D.	3	1	4	2

53. The Regulating Act of 1773 can be regarded as the first measure to :
A. assert the right of British Parliament to legislate for India
B. separate the legislature from the executive
C. separate the judiciary from the executive
D. centralise law-making

54. What was the exact constitutional status of the Indian Republic on 26th January, 1950?
A. A Democratic Republic
B. A Sovereign, Democratic Republic
C. A Sovereign, Secular, Democratic Republic
D. A Sovereign, Socialist, Secular, Democratic Republic

55. When the British obtained the grant of Diwani of Bengal, Bihar and Odisha they acquired the right to :
A. maintain law and order in these territories
B. administer civil justice and collect revenue in these territories
C. collect revenue and establish revenue administration in these territories
D. militarily defend these territories

56. Which of the following were responsible for the growth of nationalism in India during the British rule?
1. Economic exploitation of India.
2. Impact of western education.
3. Role of the Press.
Select the correct answer using the codes given below :
Codes:
A. 1, 2 and 3 B. 1 and 2
C. 2 and 3 D. 1 and 3

57. Which one of the following nationalist leaders has been described as being radical in politics but conservative on social issues?
A. G.K. Gokhale
B. B.G. Tilak
C. Lala Lajpat Rai
D. Madan Mohan Malviya

58. Provincial Autonomy in British India was envisaged by the :
A. Act of 1909 B. Act of 1919
C. Act of 1935 D. Act of 1947

59. Dyarchy means :
A. double government
B. a government in which the centre is very powerful
C. a government based on division of power between centre and provinces
D. None of the above

60. The Indian National Congress observed 'Independence Day' for the first time on 26th January in :
A. 1920 B. 1925
C. 1930 D. 1947

61. ....is situated near the banks of Sabarmati River
A. Bhavnagar B. Aurangabad
C. Ahmedabad D. Rajkot

62. Sericulture is:
A. science of the various kinds of serum
B. artificial rearing of fish
C. art of silkworm breeding
D. study of various cultures of a community

63. The most abundant constituents of earth's crust are:
A. Igneous rocks
B. Sedimentary rocks
C. Metamorphic rocks
D. Granite

64. Indian Standard Time is based on:
A. 80°E longitude B. 82½°E longitude
C. 110°E longitude D. 25°E longitude

65. Tides in the oceans are caused by :
A. Gravitational pull of the moon on the earth's surface including sea water
B. Gravitational pull of the sun on the earth's surface only and not on the sea water
C. Gravitational pull of the moon and the sun on the earth's surface including the sea water
D. None of these

66. Nagarjunasagar Project is situated on the river:
A. Tungabhadra
B. Cauvery
C. Krishna
D. Godavari

67. The difference between the Indian Standard Time and the Greenwich Mean Time is:
A. – 3½ hours B. + 3½ hours
C. – 5½ hours D. + 5½ hours

68. Which of the following dams is not on Narmada river?
A. Indira-Sagar Project
B. Maheshwar Hydel Power Project
C. Jobat Project
D. Koyna Power Project

69. Which of the following statements is **not true** about the availability of water on the earth, the crisis for which is going to increase in the years to come?
A. About 97.5 per cent of the total volume of water available on the earth is salty
B. 80 per cent of the water available to us for use comes in bursts as monsoons
C. About 2.5 per cent of the total water available on the earth is polluted water and cannot be used for human activities
D. Possibility is that some big glaciers will melt in the coming ten-fifteen years and sea level will rise by 3-4 metres all over the earth

70. Which of the following is **not** a cash crop?
A. Jute B. Paddy
C. Cashewnut D. Sugarcane

71. Through which States does Cauvery River flow?
A. Gujarat, M.P., Tamil Nadu
B. Karnataka, Kerala, Tamil Nadu
C. Karnataka, Kerala, Andhra Pradesh
D. M.P., Maharashtra, Tamil Nadu

72. Indian Standard Time is the local time of 82½°E which passes through :
A. Guntur B. Delhi
C. Allahabad D. Kolkata

73. The 17th parallel defines the boundary between:
A. North and South Korea
B. USA and Canada
C. North and South Vietnam
D. China and Russia

74. During the period of south-west monsoon, Tamil Nadu remains dry because:
A. the winds do not reach this area
B. there are no mountains in this area
C. it lies in the rain shadow area
D. the temperature is too high to let the winds cool down

75. Which country does top in producing cocoa?
A. Cote d'Ivoire B. Brazil
C. Ghana D. Nigeria

76. The biggest reserves of thorium are in :
A. India B. China
C. The Soviet Union D. U.S.A.

77. The Girnar Hills are situated in which of the following states?
A. Gujarat B. Karnataka
C. Madhya Pradesh D. Maharashtra

78. During December 22nd the sun is vertically over:
A. Tropic of Cancer
B. Tropic of Capricorn
C. The Equator
D. None of the above

79. Photosphere is described as the :
A. Lower layer of atmosphere
B. Visible surface of the sun from which radiation emanates
C. Wavelength of solar spectrum
D. None of the above

80. Broadly, there are three layers of the earth of the crust, the mantle and the core. The crust forms what percentage of the volume of the earth?
A. 0.5% B. 2.5%
C. 7.5% D. 12.5%

81. The grassland of Argentina is known as :
A. Pampas B. Campos
C. Savanna D. None of the above

82. Different seasons are formed because :
A. Sun is moving around the earth
B. of revolution of the earth around the Sun on its orbit
C. of rotation of the earth around its axis
D. All of the above

83. Eskers and Drumlins are features formed by:
A. underground water
B. running water
C. the action of wind
D. glacial action

84. Match List-I and List-II and select the correct answer using the codes given below the Lists :

List-I (*Rivers*)	List-II (*Towns*)
(*a*) Ghaghara	1. Lucknow
(*b*) Brahmaputra	2. Hoshangabad
(*c*) Narmada	3. Ahmedabad
(*d*) Sabarmati	4. Guwahati
	5. Ayodhya

	(*a*)	(*b*)	(*c*)	(*d*)
A.	4	5	1	2
B.	5	4	2	3
C.	5	4	3	1
D.	3	5	2	1

85. Which of the statements as regards the consequences of the movement of the earth is not correct?
A. Revolution of the earth is the cause of the change of seasons.
B. Rotation of the earth is the cause of days and nights.
C. Rotation of the earth causes variation in the duration of days and nights.
D. Rotation of the earth effects the movement of winds and ocean currents.

86. The world is divided into :
A. 12 time zones
B. 20 time zones
C. 24 time zones
D. 36 time zones

87. The 'Kiel' canal links the :
A. Pacific and Atlantic Oceans
B. Mediterranean Sea and Red Sea
C. Mediterranean Sea and Black Sea
D. North Sea and Baltic Sea

88. Match the following :

List-I	List-II
(*a*) Himadri	1. Outer Himalayas
(*b*) Shivalik	2. Inner Himalayas
(*c*) Himanchal	3. Middle Himalayas
(*d*) Sahyadri	4. Western Ghats

Codes:

	(*a*)	(*b*)	(*c*)	(*d*)
A.	1	2	3	4
B.	4	2	3	1
C.	2	1	3	4
D.	1	2	3	4

89. The term 'Regur' refers to:
A. Laterite soils
B. Black Cotton soils
C. Red Soils
D. Deltaic Alluvial Soils

90. Location of sugar industry in India is shifting from north to south because of:
A. cheap labour
B. expanding regional market
C. cheap and abundant supply of power
D. high yield and high sugar content in sugarcane

91. Consider the following statements :
1. Ozone is found mostly in the Stratosphere.
2. Ozone layer lies 55-75 km above the surface of the earth.
3. Ozone absorbs ultraviolet radiation from the Sun.
4. Ozone layer has no significance for life on the earth.

Which of the above statements are correct?
A. 1 and 3
B. 2 and 4
C. 2 and 3
D. 1 and 4

92. Match List-I with List-II and select the correct answer using the codes given below the Lists :

List-I (*Crops*)	List-II (*Producer*)
(*a*) Banana	1. Brazil
(*b*) Cocoa	2. Cote d'Ivoire
(*c*) Coffee	3. India
(*d*) Tea	4. China

Codes :

	(*a*)	(*b*)	(*c*)	(*d*)
A.	2	3	1	4
B.	3	2	1	4
C.	3	2	4	1
D.	2	3	4	1

93. Darjeeling and Dharamsala would be the right places to visit if one wanted to get a clear view respectively of :
A. Kanchanjunga and Dhauladhar ranges
B. Nandadevi and Dhauladhar ranges
C. Kanchanjunga and Nandadevi ranges
D. Nandadevi and Nanga Parvat

94. Atmosphere exists because:
A. The Gravitational force of the Earth
B. Revolution of the Earth
C. Rotation of the Earth
D. Weight of the gases of atmosphere

95. Victoria lake is located in the continent:
A. Africa
B. Asia
C. North America
D. South America

96. The famous Lagoon Lake of India is :
A. Dal Lake B. Chilka Lake
C. Pulicat Lake D. Mansarover

97. Where are most of the earth's active volcanoes concentrated?
A. Indian Ocean B. Pacific Ocean
C. Aral Sea D. Atlantic Ocean

98. Through which of the following states does the river Chambal flow?
A. U.P., M.P., Rajasthan
B. M.P., Gujarat, U.P.
C. Rajasthan, M.P., Bihar
D. Gujarat, M.P., U.P.

99. Which country is called the sugar bowl of the world?
A. Cuba B. India
C. Argentina D. USA

100. The area covered by forest in India as per ISFR-2023 is:
A. 46% B. 33%
C. 21.76% D. 25.50%

101. A closed economy is the one which :
A. does not permit emigration or immigration
B. permits emigration but no immigration
C. engages in no foreign trade
D. engages in no foreign and domestic trade or transit

102. In a developed economy the major share of employment originates in the :
A. primary sector B. tertiary sector
C. secondary sector D. any of the above

103. The Economic and Social Commission for Asia and Pacific (ESCAP) is located at :
A. Bangkok B. Kuala Lumpur
C. Manila D. Singapore

104. Commercial vehicles are not produced by which of the following companies in India?
A. TELCO B. Ashok Leyland
C. DCM Daewoo D. Birla Yamaha

105. In India, the Public Sector is most dominant in:
A. transport
B. steel production
C. commercial banking
D. organised term-lending financial institutions

106. The main argument advanced in favour of small scale and cottage industries in India is that:
A. cost of production is low
B. they require small capital investment
C. they advance the goal of equitable distribution of wealth
D. they generate a large volume of employment

107. The most serious economic problems of India are:
A. Poverty and unemployment
B. Stagnation, not poverty
C. Unemployment, not poverty
D. Underdevelopment, not poverty

108. Which of the following is not one of the three central problems of an economy?
A. What to produce
B. How to produce
C. When to produce
D. For whom to produce

109. Gender Responsive Budgeting has been adopted in India in the year:
A. 2017 B. 2004
C. 2014 D. 2005

110. In which of the following industries in India are the maximum number of workers employed?
A. Sugar B. Jute
C. Textiles D. Iron and Steel

111. Terrace Cultivation is practiced mostly:
A. in urban areas
B. on slopes of mountains
C. on tops of hills
D. in undulating tracts

112. Which of the following is a Selective Credit Control method?
A. Bank Rate
B. RBI directives
C. Cash Reserve Ratio
D. Open market operations

113. Which of the following taxes is not shared by the Central Government with the States?
A. Union excise duties
B. Customs duty
C. Income tax
D. Estate duty

114. ICICI is the name of a:
A. Financial Institution
B. Chemical Industry
C. Cotton Industry
D. Chamber of Commerce and Industry

115. Structural Unemployment arises due to
A. Deflationary conditions
B. Heavy industry bias
C. Shortage of raw material
D. Inadequate productive capacity

116. Which of the following is the largest single source of the government's earning from tax revenue?
A. Excise duties
B. Customs duties
C. Corporation tax
D. Income tax

117. The largest public sector bank in India is:
A. Central Bank of India
B. Punjab National Bank
C. State Bank of India
D. Indian Overseas Bank

118. Which of the following statements best explains the term contraband goods?
A. Goods produced only for exports
B. Goods produced in joint sector only
C. Goods for the trading of which licence is not required
D. Goods that are forbidden, from export, import or even possession, by law

119. Price in the market is fixed by:
A. Stock exchange rates
B. The demand and supply ruling in the market at a particular time
C. The Finance Minister
D. None of the above

120. Devaluation of currency helps to promote:
A. National Income
B. Savings
C. Imports at lower cost
D. Exports

121. Balanced economic growth can be achieved only if:
A. All the sectors of economy grow at the same rate
B. Population growth is arrested
C. All the inter dependent sectors grow in harmony
D. Basic and heavy industries are assigned highest priority

122. Which one of the following contributes most to the National Income in India?
A. Service Sector
B. Industrial Sector
C. Foreign Trade Sector
D. Agricultural Sector

123. IMF is the result of:
A. Brettonwood conference
B. Rome conference
C. Geneva conference
D. Hawana conference

124. Index 'Residex' is associated with:
A. Share Prices
B. Land Prices
C. Mutual Funds Prices
D. None of the above

125. The term 'devaluation' means:
A. Reducing the value of a currency in terms of another currency
B. Increasing the value of a currency
C. Revising the value of a currency
D. None of the above

126. Per capita net availability of pulses has shown a tendency of:
A. Increase over time
B. Decrease over time
C. Constant over time
D. First increase then decrease

127. National Income is the same as:
A. Net national product at market price
B. Net domestic product at market price
C. Net national product at factor cost
D. Net domestic product at factor cost

128. Which one of the following is not an example of indirect tax?
A. Sales tax B. Excise duty
C. Customs duty D. Expenditure tax

129. The major aim of devaluation is to:
A. encourage imports
B. encourage exports
C. encourage both exports and imports
D. discourage both exports and imports

130. Structural unemployment arises due to:
A. deflationary conditions
B. heavy industry bias
C. shortage of raw materials
D. inadequate productive capacity

131. When was the Family Planning Programme officially started in India?
A. 1950 B. 1952
C. 1956 D. 1962

132. When was the Reserve Bank of India nationalised?
A. 1947 B. 1949
C. 1950 D. 1951

133. Which of the following is *not* a feature of the Indian economy?
A. High rate of population growth
B. Disguised unemployment
C. Lowest rate of adult literacy
D. High rate of exports

134. The 'Relative Deprivation' approach for measuring poverty has been adopted by:
A. developing countries
B. developed countries
C. under-developed countries
D. None of the above

135. One of the main factors that led to rapid expansion of Indian exports is:
A. Imposition of import duties
B. Liberalisation of the economy
C. Recession in other countries
D. Diversification of exports

136. Sustainable economic development means an increase in the rate of growth of real:
A. total and per capita product
B. total and per capita product and level of literacy rate
C. total and per capita product and life expectancy at birth
D. total and per capita product, taking into account the cost of degradation of the quality of environment in this process

137. Functional unemployment occurs when:
A. unemployed have no qualification for job
B. people frequently change their job
C. people were thrown out from job due to recession
D. None of these

138. Which among the following does **not** have a 'free trade zone'?
A. Kandla B. Mumbai
C. Visakhapatnam D. Thiruvanantpuram

139. Sun Belt of USA is important for which one of the following industries?
A. Cotton textile
B. Petrochemicals
C. Hi-tech electronics
D. Food Processing

140. Commercial banking system in India is
A. unit banking B. branch banking
C. mixed banking D. None of the above

141. Who gives recognition to political parties in India?
A. Parliament

B. President
C. Supreme Court
D. Election Commission

142. The Quorum of the Legislative Council is :
A. one-fourth of its total membership
B. one-third of its membership
C. one-tenth of its membership
D. 25

143. The Indian Constitution is:
A. federal
B. unitary
C. a happy mixture of the federal and unitary
D. federal in normal times and unitary in times of emergency

144. Universal adult franchise implies a right to vote to all:
A. adult residents of the State
B. adult male citizens of the State
C. residents of the State
D. adult citizens of the State

145. When a resolution prefering a charge against the President has been passed by a specified majority in the House, it is sent to the other House for investigation. If, as a result of such an investigation, a resolution is passed through a specified majority by the other House, declaring that the charge has been sustained, the President shall leave his office. The specified special majority must not be less than :
A. two-third of the members present and voting
B. one-third of the members present and voting
C. three-fourth of the members present and voting and two-third of the total membership
D. two-third of the total membership

146. Which one of the following judicial powers of the President of India has been *wrongly* listed?
A. he appoints the Chief Justice and other judges of the Supreme Court
B. he can remove the judges of the Supreme Court on grounds of misconduct
C. he can consult the Supreme Court on any question of law or fact which is of public importance
D. he can grant pardon, reprieves and respites to persons punished under Union Law

147. The Vice-president of India can be removed from his office before the expiry of his term if :
A. the Rajya Sabha passes a resolution by a majority of its members and the Lok Sabha agrees with the resolution
B. if the Supreme Court of India recommends his removal
C. the President so desires
D. None of the above

148. 'Sengol', installed in the new Parliament building of India, was seen as a symbol of the path of service, duty and nation in which Empire of the past?
A. Gupta Empire B. Shunga Empire
C. Pandyan Empire D. Chola Empire

149. Which of the following statements is constitutionally not true about the passing of the Union Budgets and Finance Bill in India?
1. Under the law, Finance Bill should be adopted by both the Houses of the Parliament within 45 days of its introduction.
2. If the Finance Bill is not adopted within specified period, the government loses its authority to levy the taxes proposed in the budgets.
3. In the absence of full budget, a vote-on-account gives the power to the government to spend.
4. Government cannot raise revenues without a proper approval of the Finance Bill

A. Only 2 B. Only 3
C. Only 4 D. Only 1, 2 and 3

150. Normally, on whose advice the President's Rule is imposed in a State?
A. Chief Minister
B. Legislative Assembly
C. Governor
D. Chief Justice of High Court

151. Which Article of the Indian Constitution deals with Amendment procedure?
A. Article 368 B. Article 358
C. Article 367 D. All of these

152. Government is the agency through which the will of :
A. the state is expressed
B. the people is expressed
C. the head of the state is expressed
D. the majority is expressed

153. In a unitary system of government :
A. The centre is all powerful
B. The centre is weaker than the states
C. The centre and states stand at par
D. The states and centre are supreme in their respective spheres

154. In Cabinet System of Government the real executive authority rests with :
A. The Council of Ministers
B. The Prime Minister
C. The Constitution
D. The Parliament

155. The Head of the State under a parliamentary government:
A. is an elected representative
B. is a hereditary person
C. is a nominated person
D. may be any one of the above

156. In the event of a ministerial proposal being defeated on the floor of the legislature, under the parliamentary system :
A. the government waits for a general no-confidence motion
B. the minister concerned is taken to task by the Prime Minister
C. the minister is forced to resign
D. the whole Council of Ministers resign

157. The "due process of law" is an essential characteristic of the judicial system of:
A. UK B. France
C. USA D. India

158. Under the Constitution it is :
A. obligatory for the President to accept the advice of the Council of Ministers but is not obliged to follow it
B. obligatory for the President to accept the advice of the Council of Ministers
C. not obligatory for the President to seek or accept the advice of the Council of Ministers
D. obligatory for the President to seek the advice of the Council of Ministers if his own party is in power

159. Which one of the following statements is correct?
A. the Presiding Officer of Rajya Sabha is elected every year
B. the Presiding Officer of Rajya Sabha is elected for a term of two years at a time
C. the Presiding Officer of Rajya Sabha is elected for a term of six years
D. the Vice-President of India is the ex-officio Presiding Officer of Rajya Sabha

160. The introduction of "no confidence" motion in the Lok Sabha requires the support of at least:
A. 50 members B. 70 members
C. 60 members D. 80 members

161. The High Court comes under :
A. State List B. Union List
C. Concurrent List D. None of the above

162. Which one of the following has been wrongly listed as a Fundamental Duty of the Indian citizens?
A. to develop scientific temper, humanism and spirit of inquiry and reform
B. to work for raising the prestige of the country in the international sphere
C. to protect and improve the natural environment
D. to strive towards excellence in all spheres of individual and collective activity

163. Which one of the following is not a Fundamental Duty as outlined in Article 51A of the Constitution?
A. to abide by the Constitution and respect its ideals
B. to defend the country and render national service when called upon to do so

C. to work for the moral upliftment of the weaker sections of society
D. to preserve the rich heritage

164. The main characteristics of the Directive Principles of State Policy given in the Indian Constitution are :
A. not enforceable by any court
B. fundamental in the governance of the country
C. 'Like instruments, instructions, political manifesto and a code of moral precepts which have to guide governors of the country'
D. no law can be passed, which is opposed to these principles

165. Of the following which are true?
A. In a State, the Legislative Council is dominant with regard to non-financial bills and the Legislative Assembly with regard to financial (money) bills
B. Vidhan Parishad can virtually block legisla-tion even if the same is passed by the Vidhan Sabha
C. In case of a tie between the two Houses, the Governor is duty-bound to call a joint session of the two Houses to have the issue settled on a majority verdict
D. If a Bill is twice approved by the Vidhan Sabha, it becomes law even if rejected by the Vidhan Parishad

166. Which one of the following types of emergency can be declared by the President?
A. Emergency due to threat of war and external aggresion
B. Emergency due to break-down of constitu-tional machinery in a State
C. Financial emergency on account of threat to the financial credit of India
D. all the three emergencies

167. The chairman of which of the following parliamentary committees is invariably from the members of ruling party?
A. Committee on public undertakings
B. Public accounts committee
C. Estimates committee
D. Committee on delegated legislation

168. Which of the following is not a formally prescribed device available to the members of parliament?
A. Question hour
B. Zero hour
C. Half-an-hour discussion
D. Short duration discussion

169. Which of the following is not a tool of executive control over public administration?
A. Power of appointment and removal
B. Line agencies
C. Appeal to public opinion
D. Civil services code

170. If the Speaker of the State Legislative Assembly decides to resign, he should submit his resignation to the:
A. Judges of the High Court
B. Deputy Speaker
C. Chief Minister
D. Finance Minister

171. The Constitution of India provides for the nomination of two members of Lok Sabha by the President to represent:
A. the Parsis
B. men of eminence
C. the business community
D. the Anglo-Indian community

172. India is a Federal State because of:
A. dual judiciary
B. dual citizenship prevalent here
C. share of power between the Centre and the States
D. rigid Constitution

173. Residuary Subjects are those subjects which are:
A. contained in the State list
B. contained in the Union list
C. contained in the Concurrent list
D. not covered by any of the three lists

174. Which of the following writs can be issued, by the Supreme Court, to enforce Fundamental Rights?
A. Writ of Habeas Corpus
B. Writ of Mandamus
C. Writ of Quo Warranto
D. All of these

175. When the offices of both the President and the Vice-President of India are vacant, who will discharge their functions?
A. Prime Minister
B. Home Minister
C. Chief Justice of India
D. The Speaker

176. The Supreme Court tenders advice to the President of India on a matter of law or fact:
A. on its own
B. only when such advice is sought
C. only if the matter relates to some basic issue
D. only if the issue poses a threat to the unity and integrity of the country

177. Six months shall **not** intervene between two sessions of the Indian Parliament because :
A. it is the customary practice
B. it is the British convention followed in India
C. it is an obligation under the Constitution of India
D. None of the above

178. The States of the Indian Union can be recognised or their boundaries altered by:
A. the Union Parliament by a simple majority in the ordinary process of legislation
B. two-thirds majority of both the Houses of Parliament
C. two-thirds majority of both the Houses of Parliament and the consent of the legislatures of concerned States
D. an executive order of the Union government with the consent of the concerned State governments

179. The Basic Feature theory of the Constitution of India was propounded by the Supreme Court in the case of :
A. Minerva Mills Vs. Union of India
B. Golaknath Vs. State of Punjab
C. Maneka Gandhi Vs. Union of India
D. Keshavananda Vs. State of Kerala

180. Which one of the following writs is issued by a court in case of illegal detention of a person?
A. Habeas corpus B. Mandamus
C. Certiorari D. Quo-warranto

181. Name the instrument with the help of which a sailor in a submarine can see the objects on the surface of the sea.
A. Telescope B. Periscope
C. Gycroscope D. Stereoscope

182. 'HEMOPHILLIA' is the disease of ....
A. liver B. blood
C. brain D. bones

183. Vitamin A is abundantly found in ....
A. Brinjal B. Tomato
C. Carrot D. Cabbage

184. .... is not soluble in water.
A. Vitamin A B. Vitamin B
C. Vitamin C D. None of these

185. The blood vessels with the smallest diameter are called ....
A. capillaries B. arterioles
C. ventles D. lymphatics

186. Out of the following .... has the greatest elasticity.
A. steel B. rubber
C. aluminium D. annealed copper

187. Cooking gas is a mixture of which of the following two gases?
A. Carbon Dioxide and Oxygen
B. Butane and Propane
C. Carbon Monoxide and Carbon Dioxide
D. Methane and Ethylene

188. The substance most commonly used as a food preservative is:
A. sodium carbonate B. tartaric acid
C. acetic acid D. benzoic acid

189. Normally, the substances that fight against diseases in human systems are known as:
A. dioxyribonucleic acids
B. carbohydrates
C. enzymes
D. antibodies

190. The SI unit of temperature is ....
A. Kelvin B. Celsius
C. Fahrenheit D. None of the above

191. One of the common fungal diseases of man is :
A. plague B. ringworm
C. cholera D. typhoid

192. A clear sky is blue because:
A. red light is scattered more than blue
B. ultraviolet light has been absorbed
C. blue light is scattered more than red
D. blue light has been absorbed

193. Jenner introduced the method of making people immune to :
A. small pox B. rabies
C. cholera D. polio

194. The largest cell in the human body is :
A. Nerve cell B. Live cell
C. Muscle cell D. Kidney cell

195. What is the device that steps up or steps down the voltage?
A. Dynamo B. Conductor
C. Inductor D. Transformer

196. The protein deficiency disease is known as :
A. Kwashiorker B. Cirrhosis
C. Eczema D. Clycoses

197. Iron deficiency causes :
A. rickets B. anaemia
C. cirrhosis D. goitre

198. Blood group of an individual is controlled by :
A. Haemoglobin B. Shape of RBC
C. Shape of WBC D. Genes

199. In a normal man the amount of blood pumped out by the heart per minute is about :
A. 1 litre B. 3 litres
C. 4 litres D. 5 litres

200. Red/green colour blindness in man is known as :
A. Protanopia
B. Deutetanopia
C. Both A and B above
D. Marfan's syndrome

201. The blue colour of the water in the sea is due to :
A. Reflection of the blue light by the impurities in sea water
B. Reflection of the blue sky by sea water and scattering of blue light by water molecules
C. Absorption of other colours by water molecules
D. None of the above

202. The image formed on the retina of the eye is:
A. upright and real
B. larger than the object
C. small and inverted
D. enlarged and real

203. Unit of loudness of sound is:
A. bel B. decibel
C. phon D. none of these

204. Oil rises up the wick in a lamp :
A. because oil is volatile
B. due to the capillary action phenomenon
C. due to the surface tension phenomenon
D. because oil is very light

205. The 'stones' formed in human kidney consist mostly of :
A. calcium oxalate
B. sodium acetate
C. magnesium sulphate
D. calcium

206. We hear the sound later, while the light is seen earlier:
A. because light's speed is more than that of sound
B. because lights travel in a straight direction while sound in a zigzag direction
C. because sound's frequency is lower than light
D. All of the above

207. Which part of an eye is transplanted?
A. Cornea
B. Retina
C. Iris
D. Sciera

208. The Universal donor group of blood is:
A. O B. A
C. B D. AB

209. The green colour of the leaf is due to :
A. Presence of Chloroplast
B. Presence of Chromium
C. Presence of Nicoplast
D. Presence of excess of oxygen

210. Voice of a child is more shrill than that of an elderly person because:
A. the pitch of the child's voice is higher than that of the person
B. the pitch is lower
C. the child is more energetic
D. None of the above

211. Camel uses its hump for :
A. storing water
B. storing fat
C. for balancing the body
D. temperature regulation

212. A man standing in a free falling lift releases a ball from his hand. The ball would be :
A. moving down
B. moving up
C. stationary
D. moving up and down

213. To change the quality of sound produced by an instrument we need to vary the:
A. pitch
B. loudness
C. amplitude
D. number of overtonnes

214. The disease caused by Asbestos is:
A. Emphysema B. Paralysis
C. Diarrhoea D. Dysentery

215. Sweetness of a sound depends upon its
A. wavelength
B. frequency
C. amplitude
D. periodicity and regularity

216. Bats can fly in the dark because :
A. they have a better vision in the dark
B. the pupils of their eyes are very big
C. they are guided by ultrasonic waves produced by them
D. any bird can do so

217. Blood is formed in the human adult by the :
A. heart B. spleen
C. kidney D. bone marrow

218. Pencil 'lead' is made up of:
A. graphite B. charcoal
C. lead oxide D. lampblack

219. The deficiency of which one of the following vitamins leads to bleeding of gums and loosening of teeth?
A. Vitamin D B. Vitamin C
C. Vitamin B D. Vitamin A

220. How much blood does a normal person have in his body?
A. 8 litres B. 4 to 5 litres
C. 10 litres D. 2 litres

221. Match List-I with List-II and select the correct answer using the codes given below the Lists :

List-I	**List-II**
(*a*) Visakhadatta	1. Mrichhakatika
(*b*) Shudraka	2. Ritusamhara
(*c*) Kalidasa	3. Kamasutra
(*d*) Vatsyayana	4. Devichandraguptam

Codes :

	(*a*)	(*b*)	(*c*)	(*d*)
A.	1	4	2	3
B.	4	1	3	2
C.	1	4	3	2
D.	4	1	2	3

222. In which one of the following langauges is the *Dalit* writing more conspicuous?
A. Punjabi B. Assamese
C. Marathi D. Odiya

223. The first writer to use Urdu as the medium of poetic expression was:
A. Amir Khusrau
B. Mirza Ghalib
C. Bahadur Shah Zafar
D. Faiz

224. The religious text of the Zoroastrians is named as:
A. Torah B. The Analects
C. Tripatika D. Zend Avesta

225. Name the music duo which composed music for Raj Kapoor's film 'Bobby'?
A. Laxmikant Pyarelal B. Shankar Jaikishen
C. Kalyanji Anandji D. Nadeem Shravan

226. Raja Harishchandra, an early Indian film, was produced by :
A. D.G. Phalke B. Ashok Kumar
C. Ardeshir Irani D. None of the above

227. All films are certified by .... before they are publicly exhibited.
A. Films Division
B. National Film Development Corporation (NFDC)
C. Directorate of Advertising and Visual Publicity (DAVP)
D. Central Board of Film Certificate (CBFC)

228. Who among the following was the director of the film 'Taal'?
A. Gulzar B. Shekhar Kapoor
C. Satish Shah D. Subhash Ghai

229. Who amongst the following actresses has played the leading role in the film Elizabeth?
A. Gwyneth Paltrow B. Cate Blanchett
C. Simi Garewal D. Kim Basinger

230. The film 'Train to Pakistan' is based on the novel of the same name, written by:
A. Bhishma Sahani
B. Khushwant Singh
C. Amrita Pritam
D. Khwaja Ahmed Abbas

231. Which of the following is a folk dance form of Jharkhand?
A. Pali B. Jhumar
C. Nati D. Chhau

232. The first feature film (talkie) to be produced in India was:
A. Hatimtai B. Alam Ara
C. Pundalik D. Raja Harishchandra

233. Who directed the film "Bombay"?
A. Shyam Benegal B. Meera Nair
C. Shekhar Kapoor D. Mani Ratnam

234. Late Iftekhar Ahmad was famous in which of the following fields?
A. Acting B. Singing
C. Music D. Literature

235. Who among the following is the director of the film 'Kaho Na Pyar Hai'?
A. Subhash Ghai
B. Shekhar Kapoor
C. Ramesh Sippy
D. Rakesh Roshan

236. The character played by Jim Carrey in the movie *Man on Moon* is based on:
A. Andy Kaufman B. Edwin Aldrin
C. John Glenn D. Neil Armstrong

237. A popular Hindi film-based on the famous Sanskrit play *Mrichhakatika*, was titled:
A. Meghadoot B. Amrapali
C. Utsav D. Shakuntala

238. Who composed the song 'Zara Yad Karo Kurbani'?
A. Javed Akhtar
B. Pradeep
C. Nusrat Fateh Ali Khan
D. Raghupati Sahay 'Firaq'

239. Who was the producer of the serial 'Mahabharat'?
A. Shyam Benegal B. B.R. Chopra
C. Ramanand Sagar D. Mani Ratnam

240. Which of the following is a folk dance of Rajasthan?
A. Garba B. Dandya
C. Jhumar D. Kathak

241. 'The Colonel' is the nickname of which Indian Test Cricketer?
A. Colonel C.K. Naidu
B. Rahul Dravid
C. Mohinder Amarnath
D. Dilip Vengsarkar

242. The term 'Grandmaster' is used in which of these games?
A. Judo B. Chess
C. Bridge D. Karate

243. The term "Derby" is related with which of the following?
A. Polo B. Swimming
C. Racing D. Horse Racing

244. With which game is Geet Sethi associated?
A. Basketball B. Chess
C. Snooker D. Tennis

245. Beighton Cup is related with which of the following?
A. Hockey B. Polo
C. Cricket D. Soccer

246. Match List-I with List-II and select the correct answer using the codes given below the Lists :

List-I	List-II
(*a*) Basketball	1. Lob
(*b*) Bridge	2. Revoke
(*c*) Golf	3. Pivot
(*d*) Tennis	4. Bunker

Codes :

	(*a*)	(*b*)	(*c*)	(*d*)
A.	2	3	1	4
B.	2	3	4	1
C.	3	2	1	4
D.	3	2	4	1

247. The head office of the International Cricket Council (ICC) is situated in :

A. Zimbabwe B. Australia
C. South Africa D. UAE

248. Match the following :

List-I	List-II
(*a*) Deodhar Trophy	1. Volleyball
(*b*) Durand Cup	2. Football
(*c*) Davis Cup	3. Cricket
	4. Tennis

Codes:

	(*a*)	(*b*)	(*c*)
A.	3	2	4
B.	3	1	4
C.	2	3	1
D.	1	2	4

249. Which of the following is called 'Grand Slam'?

A. Winning the highest number of medals in the Olympic games
B. Winning the men's singles title in Wimbledon Championship
C. Winning the Wimbledon Singles title successively for two years
D. Winning all the four championships Australian, French, Wimblendon and US

250. With which game is the term 'butterfly stroke' associated?

A. Swimming B. Cricket
C. Gliding D. Skiing

251. Who is the first Indian to win the 'International Grand Master' title in Chess?

A. Anupama Abhayankar
B. Bhagyashree Sathe Thipsay
C. Vishwanathan Anand
D. D.V. Prasad

252. The XXII Commonwealth Games were held in 2022 in:

A. Kuala Lumpur B. Bangkok
C. Victoria D. Birmingham

253. The term 'Tee' is associated with which of the following sports?

A. Golf B. Table Tennis
C. Polo D. Judo

254. The famous woman Tennis player who was stabbed during a match, is

A. Steffi Graf B. Monica Seles
C. Mary Pierce D. Martina Navratilova

255. The term 'Baseline' is related to which of the following?

A. Golf B. Hockey
C. Badminton D. Polo

256. In which Indian State did the game of Polo originate?

A. Manipur B. Rajasthan
C. Gujarat D. West Bengal

257. Narendra Modi Stadium is located at:

A. Hyderabad B. Chennai
C. Ahmedabad D. Prayagraj

258. Rafael Nadal is the well-known player associated with:

A. Hockey B. Cricket
C. Tennis D. Chess

259. Neeraj Chopra is the well-known player associated with :

A. Javelin Throw B. Golf
C. Table Tennis D. Chess

260. Eden Garden, a famous Cricket stadium, is located in :

A. Kanpur B. Kolkata
C. Jamshedpur D. Pune

261. Maharaja Ranjit Singh Trophy is associated with :

A. Golf B. Hockey
C. Soccer D. Tennis

262. Harmanpreet Kaur is a distinguished player in which of the following games?
A. Swimming B. Weightlifting
C. Cricket D. Archery

263. Cricket was an Olympic event at which of the following Olympics?
A. London, 1908 B. Amsterdam, 1928
C. Paris, 1900 D. Melbourne, 1956

264. WISPA competitions are associated with :
A. Squash B. Yatching
C. Boxing D. Billiards

265. Ryder Cup is the famous trophy of :
A. Golf B. Chess
C. Boxing D. Polo

266. Davis Cup is associated with the sport of :
A. Cricket B. Football
C. Tennis D. Hockey

267. 'Volley', 'Chop' and 'Drive Spine' are the term associated with :
A. Lawn Tennis B. Badminton
C. Table Tennis D. Golf

268. Lal Bahadur Shastri Stadium is located at :
A. Hyderabad B. Chennai
C. Ahmedabad D. Varanasi

269. The first winner of Major Dhyan Chand Khel Ratna Award was :
A. Geet Sethi
B. Sachin Tendulkar
C. Viswanathan Anand
D. Karnam Malleswari

270. The winner of 2026 ICC Men's T-20 Cricket World Cup is:
A. India B. Sri Lanka
C. New Zealand D. England

271. The first team event introduced in 1900 at Paris Olympics was :
A. Hockey B. Football
C. Cricket D. Baseball

272. Which of the following international tennis tournaments is held on grass court?
A. US Open B. French Open
C. Wimbledon D. Australian Open

273. Which cricketer is nicknamed as the pied piper of Punjab?
A. Yuvraj Singh
B. Harbhajan Singh
C. Mohinder Amarnath
D. Navjot Singh Sidhu

274. 'Merdeka Cup' is associated with ....
A. Golf B. Football
C. Squash D. Hockey

275. The first time athletes marched into the stadium behind their nation's flag in Olympics:
A. at St. Louis 1904 B. at London 1908
C. at Antwerp 1920 D. at Paris 1924

276. The "Dronacharya Award" is associated with:
A. Eminent Surgeons B. Famous Sports Person
C. Sport Coaches D. Expert Engineers

277. Which cricketer is nicknamed as 'Jumbo'?
A. Venkatesh Prasad B. Anil Kumble
C. Glenn McGrath D. Shane Warne

278. The first time the Olympic Games were organised by a private company at:
A. Montreal, 1976 B. Los Angeles, 1984
C. Atlanta, 1996 D. Rome, 1960

279. In which Asian Games Cricket was played first?
A. Guangzhou, 2010 B. Doha, 2006
C. Busan, 2002 D. Seoul, 1986

280. The term 'Penalty cick' is used in :
A. Hockey B. Football
C. Baseball D. Golf

281. Which of the following countries is not a member of North Atlantic Treaty Organisation (NATO)?
A. Norway B. United Germany
C. Portugal D. Australia

282. Khmer Rouge is a dictatorial party of :
A. Cambodia B. Indonesia
C. Malaysia D. Thailand

283. Which country is not a member of SAARC
A. Russia B. Bangladesh
C. Nepal D. Pakistan

284. The headquarters of WTO is located at :
A. Geneva B. Paris
C. The Hague D. Washington

285. The main function of the World Trade Organisation (WTO) is:
A. enforcing of Uruguay Round Agreements
B. facilitating multi-lateral trade relations of member countries and reviewing trade policies
C. administering trade dispute settlement procedures
D. None of the above

286. The Secretary-General of the UNO is appointed by the:
A. General Assembly
B. Security Council
C. Trusteeship Council
D. World Bank

287. The United Nations officially came into existence in 1945 on :
A. November 24 B. October 14
C. October 24 D. November 14

288. Which one of the following is true of the International Court of Justice?
A. The Judges of the Court are appointed according to the discretion of the Secretary General
B. No two Judges may belong to the same country
C. The Court consists of 20 Judges
D. The statute of the International Court of Justice is not an integral part of the UN Charter

289. Which of the following was not among the six founding countries of the European Community?
A. Belgium B. France
C. Germany D. UK

290. The smallest country in South America is:
A. Ecuador B. Guyana
C. Surinam D. Uruguay

291. In which year "Human Rights Resolution" was adopted by the U.N.?
A. 1945 B. 1946
C. 1947 D. 1948

292. Where is the headquarters of INTERPOL located?
A. Berlin B. California
C. Lyons D. Montreal

293. Parliament of which of the following countries is known as Great People's Khural?
A. Malaysia B. Mongolia
C. Thailand D. Indonesia

294. Numbers of major organs of United Nations are:
A. 3 B. 4
C. 5 D. 6

295. When is the UN Day celebrated?
A. October 24 B. January 24
C. June 24 D. September 24

296. Which one of the following organ of United Nations is known as the 'Policeman of the World'?
A. Security Council
B. International Court of Justice
C. The Secretariat
D. General Assembly

297. The members of the NAFTA include:
A. USA, Canada and Mexico
B. USA, Canada, Mexico and UK
C. USA, UK, Russia and Mexico
D. USA, Canada and Brazil

298. The sits of International Court of Justice is located at :
A. Vienna B. Paris
C. Hague D. New York

299. Which of the following is known as the Constitution of the UN?
A. UN Charter
B. UN Assembly
C. UN Security Council
D. UN Secretariat

300. The Headquarters of the Amnesty International is located at :
A. New York
B. London
C. Geneva
D. Addis-Ababa

301. Who is the author of the book 'PRISON DIARY'?
A. Bal Gangadhar Tilak
B. Rajendra Prasad
C. Jai Prakash Narayan
D. Jawahar Lal Nehru

302. Who is the author of 'Satanic Verses'?
A. Lewis Carrol B. Salman Rushdie
C. Parry Mason D. Mulk Raj Anand

303. Who wrote 'Gitanjali'?
A. Kalidas
B. Gopal Das 'Neeraj'
C. Rabindra Nath Tagore
D. Jawahar Lal Nehru

304. Who, among the following, scholars flourishing during the Gupta Age, was the author of *Dasakumara-Charita?*
A. Asanga B. Dignaga
C. Dandina D. Bhattin

305. The author of *Gitagovinda* was:
A. Halayudha B. Jayadeva
C. Kalhana D. Jona-raja

306. "Ingenious Pain" is a book/novel written by:
A. Andrew Miller B. Santa Monica
C. Ben Johnson D. Bill Gates

307. Who amongst the following is the author of the famous book "An Equal Music"?
A. Salman Rushdie B. Shasthivrata
C. Vikram Seth D. Kamla Markandeya

308. The famous Moorti Devi Award is given for excellence in which of the following fields?
A. Medicine
B. Science & Technology
C. Social Service
D. Literature

309. Who has written "Devdas"?
A. Tarasankar Bandyopadhyay
B. Bankim Chandra Chattopadhyay
C. Rabindranath Tagore
D. Sarat Chandra Chattopadhyay

310. "Ain-i-Akbari" is written by:
A. Ṭodar Mal B. Abul Fazal
C. Sheikh Saadi D. Mirza Ghalib

311. "Alice in Wonderland" is written by :
A. Lewis Carrol B. Chester Bowles
C. Charles Dickens D. Jonathan Swift

312. "Mrichchhakatikam" is written by :
A. Vishakhadatta B. Vatsyayana
C. Sudraka D. Bana Bhatt

313. "My Experiments with Truth" is written by :
A. Jawaharlal Nehru
B. M.K. Gandhi
C. Abul Kalam Azad
D. Rajendra Prasad

314. Who wrote the book "India Wins Freedom"?
A. Maulana Abul Kalam Azad
B. Mahatma Gandhi
C. Sir Mohammad Iqbal
D. Abdul Gaffar Khan

315. Match List-I with List-II and select the correct answer using the codes given below the Lists :

List-I	List-II
(*a*) *Emma*	1. Graham Greene
(*b*) *Mother India*	2. E.M. Forster
(*c*) *Human Factor*	3. Jane Austen
(*d*) *Passage to India*	4. Katherine Mayo

Codes :

	(*a*)	(*b*)	(*c*)	(*d*)
A.	2	1	4	3
B.	3	4	1	2
C.	3	1	2	4
D.	4	2	1	3

316. 'Poverty and Un British Rule in India' is written by:
A. R.C. Dutt B. J.L. Nehru
C. D.B. Naoroji D. S.N. Sen

317. Name the author of the book *A Passage to England.*
A. E.M. Forster
B. Nirad C. Choudhuri
C. Vikram Seth
D. Eric Segal

318. The author of the book 'The Struggle in My Life' is:
A. Mandela B. J.L. Nehru
C. Tilak D. Gokhale

319. Which one among the following State capitals is closest to the Equator?
A. Panaji
B. Bhubaneswar
C. Hyderabad
D. Mumbai

320. Which of the following books is not written by Salman Rushdie?
A. The Satanic Verses
B. Shame
C. Naked Face
D. Midnight's Children

321. The different schools of modern socialism derive their strength primarily from the writings of ....?
A. Joseph Stalin B. Leo Tolstoy
C. Mao Tse-tung D. Karl Marx

322. Baba Amte was famous as a ....
A. Painter B. Singer
C. Politician D. Social Worker

323. Central Government says that .... was received well by citizens as 'imandari ka utsav'.
A. Demonetization
B. Goods and Services Tax
C. E-NAM
D. All of the above

324. Mr. Yehudi Menuhin, was a famous:
A. Sitarist B. Cartoonist
C. Journalist D. Violinist

325. Sundarlal Bahuguna, a famous environmentalist, was associated with :
A. Chipko Movement
B. Narmada Bachao Andolan
C. Satyagraha Movement
D. Anti-corruption Movement

326. Mother Teressa's native place was :
A. Albania B. France
C. Greece D. Italy

327. The live polio vaccine which can be taken by mouth was developed by :
A. Albert Sabin B. Edward Jenner
C. Jonas Salk D. Selman Waksman

328. Which of the following language is used for webpage development?
A. FORTRAN
B. C or C++
C. BASIC
D. HTML

329. The "Last Supper" is a famous renaissance painting. It was a masterpiece of :
A. Michael Angelo B. Leonardo da Vinci
C. Titian D. Raphael

330. Dhyanchand is associated with which sports?
A. Badminton B. Hockey
C. Tennis D. Football

331. 'Man is born free, yet every where he is in chains'. This was said by:
A. Voltaire B. John Stuart Mill
C. Rousseau D. Karl Marx

332. Who among the following was a prominent social reformer?
A. Baba Gurmukh Singh
B. Raja Mahendra Pratap
C. Bipin Chandra Pal
D. Jotiba Govind Phule

333. Whose real name was Gadadhar Chhattopadhyaya?
A. Swami Vivekanand
B. Ram Krishna Paramhansa
C. Dayanand Saraswai
D. Raja Ram Mohan Rai

334. Who was known as "Man of Destiny"?
A. Napoleon B. Nehru
C. Hitler D. Mussolini

335. Who discovered that mosquito served as a carrier of malaria?
A. Jonas Salk B. Ronald Ross
C. Louis Pasteur D. Robert Koch

336. Who was the first woman Governor of an Indian State?
A. Sushila Nayar B. Sucheta Kripalani
C. Sarojini Naidu D. Sulochana Modi

337. Who among the following founded the Bhartiya Jana Sangh?
A. Deen Dayal Upadhyaya

B. Veer Savarkar
C. Dr. Ram Manohar Lohia
D. Dr. Shyama Prasad Mukherjee

338. Who among the following President of India held his office for two successive terms?
A. V.V. Giri
B. Dr. Rajendra Prasad
C. Dr. S. Radhakrishnan
D. None of these

339. Ustad Amjad Ali Khan is an exponent of:
A. Flute B. Sitar
C. Sarod D. Tabla

340. Who is the first non-Indian to receive the Bharat Ratna?
A. Martin Luther King
B. Zubin Mehta
C. Mother Teressa
D. Khan Abdul Ghaffar Khan

ANSWERS

1 B	**2** C	**3** D	**4** C	**5** B	**6** C	**7** A	**8** C	**9** C	**10** D
11 C	**12** A	**13** C	**14** A	**15** A	**16** D	**17** A	**18** B	**19** A	**20** D
21 A	**22** C	**23** B	**24** C	**25** D	**26** C	**27** B	**28** D	**29** D	**30** B
31 C	**32** D	**33** C	**34** C	**35** B	**36** C	**37** D	**38** B	**39** C	**40** C
41 A	**42** A	**43** A	**44** B	**45** C	**46** D	**47** C	**48** B	**49** B	**50** D
51 A	**52** C	**53** A	**54** B	**55** B	**56** A	**57** B	**58** C	**59** A	**60** C
61 C	**62** C	**63** B	**64** B	**65** C	**66** C	**67** D	**68** D	**69** D	**70** B
71 B	**72** C	**73** C	**74** C	**75** A	**76** A	**77** A	**78** B	**79** B	**80** A
81 A	**82** B	**83** D	**84** B	**85** C	**86** C	**87** D	**88** C	**89** B	**90** D
91 A	**92** B	**93** A	**94** A	**95** A	**96** B	**97** B	**98** A	**99** A	**100** C
101 C	**102** B	**103** A	**104** D	**105** D	**106** D	**107** A	**108** C	**109** D	**110** C
111 B	**112** B	**113** B	**114** A	**115** D	**116** C	**117** C	**118** D	**119** B	**120** D
121 C	**122** A	**123** A	**124** B	**125** A	**126** D	**127** C	**128** D	**129** B	**130** D
131 B	**132** B	**133** D	**134** A	**135** B	**136** D	**137** B	**138** D	**139** D	**140** C
141 D	**142** C	**143** D	**144** D	**145** D	**146** B	**147** A	**148** D	**149** C	**150** C

151	152	153	154	155	156	157	158	159	160
A	B	A	A	A	D	C	B	D	A
161	162	163	164	165	166	167	168	169	170
B	B	C	B	D	D	C	B	B	B
171	172	173	174	175	176	177	178	179	180
D	C	D	D	C	B	C	A	D	A
181	182	183	184	185	186	187	188	189	190
B	B	C	A	A	A	B	D	D	A
191	192	193	194	195	196	197	198	199	200
B	C	A	A	D	A	B	D	D	A
201	202	203	204	205	206	207	208	209	210
B	B	B	B	A	A	A	A	A	A
211	212	213	214	215	216	217	218	219	220
B	A	A	A	D	C	D	A	B	B
221	222	223	224	225	226	227	228	229	230
D	C	A	D	A	A	D	D	B	B
231	232	233	234	235	236	237	238	239	240
D	B	D	A	D	D	C	B	B	C
241	242	243	244	245	246	247	248	249	250
D	B	D	C	A	D	D	A	D	A
251	252	253	254	255	256	257	258	259	260
C	D	A	B	C	A	C	C	A	B
261	262	263	264	265	266	267	268	269	270
B	C	C	A	A	C	C	A	C	A
271	272	273	274	275	276	277	278	279	280
B	C	A	B	A	C	B	B	A	B
281	282	283	284	285	286	287	288	289	290
D	A	A	A	B	A	C	B	D	C
291	292	293	294	295	296	297	298	299	300
D	C	B	D	A	A	A	C	A	B
301	302	303	304	305	306	307	308	309	310
C	B	C	C	B	A	C	D	D	B
311	312	313	314	315	316	317	318	319	320
A	C	B	A	B	C	B	A	A	C
321	322	323	324	325	326	327	328	329	330
D	D	A	D	A	A	C	D	B	B
331	332	333	334	335	336	337	338	339	340
C	D	B	A	B	C	D	B	C	D

❑❑❑